REAL ESTATE
Development

PRINCIPLES
AND
PROCESS

Third Edition

Mike E. Miles

Gayle Berens

Marc A. Weiss

**Urban Land
Institute**

About ULI–the Urban Land Institute

ULI–the Urban Land Institute is a nonprofit education and research institute that is supported and directed by its members. Its mission is to provide responsible leadership in the use of land in order to enhance the total environment.

ULI sponsors education programs and forums to encourage an open international exchange of ideas and sharing of experiences; initiates research that anticipates emerging land use trends and issues and proposes creative solutions based on that research; provides advisory services; and publishes a wide variety of materials to disseminate information on land use and development. Established in 1936, the Institute today has more than 15,000 members and associates from more than 50 countries representing the entire spectrum of the land use and development disciplines.

Richard M. Rosan
President

Recommended bibliographic listing:
Miles, Mike E., Gayle Berens, and Marc A. Weiss. *Real Estate Development: Principles and Process.* Third Edition. Washington, D.C.: ULI–the Urban Land Institute, 2000.

ULI Catalog Number: R34
International Standard Book Number: 0-87420-825-4
Library of Congress Catalog Card Number: 99-69308

Copyright 2000 by ULI–the Urban Land Institute
1025 Thomas Jefferson Street, N.W.
Suite 500 West
Washington, D.C. 20007-5201

Second Printing, 2000
Third Printing, 2001
Fourth Printing, 2002
Fifth Printing, 2003

Cover photo: J.A. Kraulis/Masterfile

ULI Project Staff

Rachelle L. Levitt
Senior Vice President, Policy and Practice
Publisher

Gayle Berens
Vice President, Real Estate Development Practice
Project Director

Nancy H. Stewart
Director, Book Program
Managing Editor

Barbara M. Fishel/Editech
Manuscript Editor

Helene Y. Redmond
HYR Graphics
Layout and Design

Betsy VanBuskirk
Art Director
Cover Design

Diann Stanley-Austin
Associate Director of Publishing Operations

Kim Rusch
Graphic Artist

Karrie Underwood
Word Processor

Dedication

This book is dedicated to the memory of Jim Graaskamp—
dynamic, insightful, slightly opinionated,
and one helluva guy.

About the Authors

Mike E. Miles, PhD, for five years was portfolio manager for the Fidelity Real Estate Asset Manager, a series of institutional investment vehicles that combine public securities with direct real estate ownership. Before joining Fidelity, Miles was executive vice president of the Prudential Realty Group and managing director of Prudential Real Estate Investors.

Miles previously held full-time academic positions at the University of North Carolina–Chapel Hill (where he held an endowed chair), the University of Wisconsin–Madison, and the University of Hawaii–Manoa. Before entering academia, Miles was vice president–finance for Alpert Investment Corporation, a real estate development firm.

Over his career, Miles has written several textbooks and monographs on real estate economics, as well as more than 50 journal articles. Miles is past president of both the National Council of Real Estate Investment Fiduciaries and the American Real Estate and Urban Economics Association. He has served as the editor of Institutional Investor's *Real Estate Finance* since 1994. In 1997, Miles received the Robert Toiga award for leadership in real estate portfolio management from Institutional Real Estate and in 1999 received the Graaskamp Award for contributions to real estate research from the Pension Real Estate Association.

Miles holds a BS from Washington and Lee University, an MBA from Stanford University, and a PhD from the University of Texas at Austin.

Gayle Berens is the vice president of real estate development practice for ULI–the Urban Land Institute. As vice president, Berens is responsible for directing the publications and education programs related to the practice of real estate and land development—from commercial to residential to parks. In addition, she directs and develops university-related programs for ULI, including the academic fellows program. Berens is the coauthor of several books, including *Urban Parks and Open Space,* published with the Trust for Public Land, and all three editions of *Real Estate Development: Principles and Process.* She is currently working on a new book on forming international partnerships for development. During her tenure with ULI, Berens has organized multiple symposia and mayors' forums dealing with city revitalization, and for six years, she directed ULI's Real Estate School. She earned an undergraduate degree from the University of Wisconsin at Green Bay and a graduate degree from Georgetown University.

Marc A. Weiss, PhD, is a senior fellow at the Center for National Policy, a public policy scholar at the Woodrow Wilson International Center for Scholars, and president of Metropolitan Investment Strategies in Washington, D.C. He recently served as special assistant to the Secretary of the U.S. Department of Housing and Urban Development, senior adviser to the director of the District of Columbia Department of Housing and Community Development, coordinator of strategic economic development planning for Washington, D.C., and author of the economic growth strategy for Baltimore, Maryland. Weiss is the author of *The Rise of the Community Builders,* and is currently coauthoring a book with former HUD Secretary Henry Cisneros on the future of American cities and metropolitan regions. Previously he was an associate professor of real estate development, urban planning, and historic preservation, and director of the Real Estate Development Research Center at Columbia University. He has taught at the Massachusetts Institute of Technology, the University of Illinois at Chicago, and the University of California at Los Angeles. Weiss has served as a fellow of the Urban Land Institute and the Lincoln Institute of Land Policy and as deputy director of the California Commission on Industrial Innovation.

Weiss has a BA with honors in political science from Stanford University and a PhD in city and regional planning from the University of California at Berkeley.

Contributors

The authors would like to thank many people for their contributions to this third edition of *Real Estate Development: Principles and Process*.

Contributing Authors (Third Edition)

Deborah L. Brett
President
Deborah L. Brett and Associates
Plainsboro, New Jersey

Mark J. Eppli, PhD
Associate Professor of Finance and Real Estate
Department of Finance
The George Washington University
Washington, D.C.

Kenneth M. Lusht, PhD
Chair, Department of Insurance and Real Estate
Smeal College of Business Administration
Pennsylvania State University
University Park, Pennsylvania

Douglas R. Porter
President
The Growth Management Institute
Chevy Chase, Maryland

Lynne B. Sagalyn, PhD
Earle W. Kazis and Benjamin Schore Director
MBA Real Estate Program
Professor, Finance and Economics
Graduate School of Business
Columbia University
New York, New York

Mary Boehling Schwartz
Survey Statistician
Financial and Market Characteristics Branch
Housing and Household Economic Statistics Division
U.S. Census Bureau
Suitland, Maryland

Ronald L. Silverman and associates
Attorneys-at-law
Cox, Castle & Nicholson LLP
Los Angeles, California

Additional Contributors

Chris Carney
Director of Asset Management
Fidelity Real Estate Group
Boston, Massachusetts

Edward F. Cassidy
Director
AEW Capital Management, LP
Boston, Massachusetts

Richard L. Haney, Jr., PhD
Professor, Real Estate and Finance
College of Business
Texas A&M University
College Station, Texas

Austin Jaffe, PhD
Philip H. Sieg Professor of Business Administration
Smeal College of Business Administration
Pennsylvania State University
University Park, Pennsylvania

Scott Muldavin
President
Muldavin Company
San Rafael, California

Grant Ian Thrall, PhD
Professor
Department of Geography
University of Florida
Gainesville, Florida

William Wcbb
Consultant
William N. Webb & Associates
Amelia Island, Florida

Mark Zandi
Chief Economist
RFA
West Chester, Pennsylvania

Preface

The impetus for writing the third edition of this textbook on the real estate development process has not changed since the first edition was published in 1991: real estate development continues to have an enormous effect on our society, and no other single textbook is designed to give future decision makers a complete look at the complex decision-making process involved in real estate development.

Development affects everyone as it shapes the built environment. Development produces shelter, one of the three needs fundamental to every human being's survival. As such, it constitutes a significant portion of gross private domestic investment, which represents our nation's investment in the future. In 1994, ULI found that the total value of real estate in the United States was around $21 trillion, and it continues to climb. More important, development today determines in many respects how we will live in the future.

The inherently interdisciplinary nature of the real estate development process and its entrepreneurial nature give development a special status and create a decision-making environment best suited to a well-rounded, disciplined, thick-skinned person. Though many activities related to development now take place under the corporate or institutional umbrella, the activities themselves still bear a distinctive entrepreneurial stamp.

Real estate development is also unusually dynamic, with rapid changes occurring in the links among construction, technological advances, regulation, marketing, finance, property management, and so on. The dynamic nature of the process contributes a factor of extra excitement and makes development the most challenging component of the real estate industry.

This textbook captures an understanding of the development process delineated with an eight-stage model of real estate development, first elaborated by coauthor Mike Miles in his PhD dissertation. The interrelated activities that collectively constitute the process are the academic/technical portion of development. With such knowledge of the overall process firmly in hand, the reader can then proceed to perform the additional detailed studies of particular product types and local markets necessary for successful development.

The book is divided into eight parts. *Part I, Introduction,* lays out a general framework of the development process in eight interactive stages, describing the primary players in the development process and the magnitude of dollars, land, and labor involved in contemporary development. In this edition, we have updated all the demographic information and added a section on the effects of evolutionary changes in the development process.

Part II, Finance, introduces the financial tools necessary for the decision-making period of the development process. Part II was revised almost entirely for this edition. Chapter 4 focuses on the institutional setting of real estate finance, illustrating how the U.S. system and most other market economies function, and covering the capital flow to real estate as well as equity and debt markets. Chapter 5 examines the logic behind real estate financing decisions, focusing on financing decisions as capital structure decisions, particularly the best combination of debt and equity to achieve the investor's goals. Chapter 6 concludes Part II by presenting information about what lenders and other investors are doing in today's market. Appendix A briefly describes the distinction between level one and level two of real estate ventures, and Appendix B provides some tools for calculating discounted cash flow and how the logic of discounted cash flow can help all participants in the process make better decisions about development.

Successfully anticipating the future and generating the numbers needed for the discounted cash flow analysis are best achieved by first studying the past. Thus, *Part III, The History of Real Estate Development in the United States,* thoroughly reviews the evolution of development in this country from colonial days to the present. This historic picture is clearly one of a dynamic relationship between public and private players. The players' exact roles have changed over time, but it has always been and always will be true that the public sector is a partner in the development process.

With the historical evolution clearly stated, the book moves on to the process of generating ideas for specific development projects. *Part IV, Ideas,* discusses the sources of ideas and how those ideas are refined as the developer starts to move through the initial two stages of the development process. The part emphasizes the role of market research as a decision-making tool.

Part V, Planning and Analysis: The Public Roles, deals with the public perspective of development. Chapter 13 focuses on the public's role in zoning, land use policy, impact fees, and financing of infrastructure and how the decisions made in the public sector affect private developers. Chapter 14 discusses public/private partnerships and a more proactive role for public sector players. And Chapter 15, which has been substantially rewritten and updated, looks at affordable housing, always an important political issue as our generally affluent society continues to leave certain people behind. Beyond its direct relevance, this chapter serves as food for thought. Future developers will be faced with new and increasingly difficult social issues as they change the structure of the urban terrain. Throughout the book, we emphasize the public sector as a partner in the development process. Part V explains in greater detail the kind of roles the public sector plays.

Part VI, Planning and Analysis: The Market Perspective, moves from a public to a private perspective. The chapters in this part deal with the feasibility studies and market analyses that facilitate decision making and with structuring the development team. The developer, as team leader, is responsible for seeing that all participants collectively are suited to the task and that the enterprise is worthwhile. Chapter 16, extensively revised, defines and outlines a holistic version of the feasibility study. Chapter 17, also extensively revised and updated, looks at market analysis and the role of properly collected and validated data. All new Chap-

ter 18 helps the analyst appreciate the data and looks at various data sources and forecasting models and how to understand their results. Chapter 18 is supplemented by an appendix that looks at demographics from a new perspective.

Part VII, Making It Happen, deals with everything from contract negotiations to construction to the formal opening. Thus, it reviews the legal aspects of putting the team together as well as the critically important management of the construction phase of development. Chapter 19 includes a considerable section on the environmental issues facing developers, particularly hazardous waste, wetlands, and air and water pollution, and how they affect financing, contracting, and managing the development process.

Part VIII, Making It Work, looks at the concerns that continue once the building is completed. Developments should never occur without planning for the project's operation. Thus, Chapter 21 explores the real estate management triad (property, asset, and portfolio managers). Chapter 22's emphasis is on marketing, sales, and leasing—work that continues once the development is completed. Finally, Chapter 23 deals with the future, reviewing what has passed and how development decision makers combine an analysis of today's market conditions with consideration of possible future market conditions to establish prospective cash flows. Developers must anticipate many different aspects of the future. By rigorously studying existing trends, developers can predict reactions and interactions with the expectation of developing what the public will perceive to be better buildings.

To integrate the many areas covered in the textbook, we include two case studies, both of which are woven throughout the text and integrated into the eight-stage model that forms the core of the text. The first case study, which appeared in earlier editions, covers the development of two phases of the Europa Center office buildings in Chapel Hill, North Carolina. The first phase of Europa Center was completed in the late 1980s, and that story is told through the developer's eyes—from finding the site to opening the project. The second phase was completed in the early 1990s under new ownership.

An all new case study of Museum Towers in Cambridge, Massachusetts, looks at the development of twin multifamily towers in a pioneering location on land that was purchased a decade before the project was actually started. This case study takes the reader through the process in a tough development environment from the perspective of an experienced, slightly maverick developer.

Insofar as it was possible, all the information in the textbook has been updated. The figures have been updated, and the profiles, feature boxes, and photos are new or updated. All bibliographies have been supplemented and revised.

This text is intended for university students in schools of business, planning, architecture, engineering, and law. It is also a useful beginning point for individuals shifting careers, either into development or between roles in development. While the text certainly does not guarantee success and/or financial reward, it does introduce readers to a process that is both enjoyable and rewarding. Once smitten with the development process, few people want to return to less challenging pursuits.

Note that we have chosen to use "he" throughout the text when referring to a developer, simply to enhance readability. The use of the pronoun does not reflect any bias on our or ULI's part. Although the number of men in development outweighs the number of women, the number of women involved in development is growing steadily, and women are entering the field in many capacities.

Many people had a hand in producing the third edition of this textbook, including academics from several different fields, practitioners from across the country, and numerous members of ULI's staff. Among the ULI staff, the authors would like to thank Michael Baker, André Bald, Lori Hatcher, Oliver Jerschow, Rachelle Levitt, Dave Mulvihill, Adrienne Schmitz, Mary Boehling Schwartz, Diann Stanley-Austin, Karrie Underwood, Betsy VanBuskirk, and especially Barbara Fishel, Helene Redmond, and Nancy Stewart for their remarkable patience. Beyond ULI, other people who deserve a special thanks for their contributions are listed elsewhere.

We are particularly indebted to our coauthors from the first and second editions—Richard Haney, Emil Malizia, and Ginger Travis—whose contributions were invaluable. In addition, we offer a special thanks to developers Whit Morrow and Dean Stratouly, who allowed us to look at the development process through their eyes.

Mike E. Miles, Gayle Berens, and Marc A. Weiss
December 1999

Contents

61 Part II. Finance

63 Chapter 4. Real Estate Finance: The Institutional Setting

81 Chapter 5. Financial Theory: The Logic behind Real Estate Financing Decisions

93 Chapter 6. Innovations in Real Estate Finance

103 Part II. Bibliography

You cannot study real estate development principles and process without looking at both the people who are involved in the process and the people who are the ultimate users of the product. While this book focuses on the role of the developer, many people affect and are affected by real estate development. Individuals ultimately provide financing for a project. Individuals make up the public sector that allows a development to be built. People in many allied professions produce the buildings that are used by people of many different backgrounds and income levels.

Therefore, anyone who is thinking about going into real estate development must be certain to understand who helps a development come to fruition and how they do it. Most important, developers must understand the users and their needs. Without users, buildings—no matter how aesthetically pleasing or how functional—lose value and crumble. People create real estate value.

Part I looks at the people who make a development possible—the developer, those who make up our society and are therefore potential users, and the many players who work with the developer.

Part I
Introduction

Chapter 1

Introduction to the Real Estate Development Process

Real estate development is the continual reconfiguration of the built environment to meet society's needs. Roads, sewer systems, houses, office buildings, and urban entertainment centers do not just happen. Someone must motivate and manage the creation, maintenance, and eventual re-creation of the spaces in which we live, work, and play.

The need for development is constant, because population, technology, and taste never stop changing. New generations and revolving immigrant groups, coupled with the technological evolution/revolution, drive economic changes in consumer tastes and individual preferences.

Whether consumer, new citizen, or real estate professional, all of us inhabit the built environment; therefore, we should all understand the development process. The development process creates the houses we live in, the publicly assisted apartment project in our town, the 25-story office tower downtown, the warehouse that stored the paper this book was printed on, and the convenient (but to some tastes terribly unattractive) fast-food restaurant on the commercial strip.

Both public and private participants in real estate development share compelling reasons for understanding the development process. The goals of private sector participants are to minimize risk while maximizing personal and/or institutional objectives—usually profit (wealth maximization) but often nonmonetary objectives as well. Few business ventures are as heavily leveraged as traditional real estate development projects, magnifying the risk of ruin but also increasing the potential for high returns to equity. Large fortunes have been and continue to be made and lost in real estate development.

The public sector's goal is to promote sound development, ensuring that construction is attractive and safe and that new developments are conveniently located to help the city or town function well and to enhance the economy. Sound development means balancing the public's need for both constructed space and economic growth against the public responsibility to provide services and improve the quality of life without harming the environment.

The public and private sectors are involved as partners in every real estate development project. A key tenet of this book is that all participants enjoy a higher probability of achieving their goals and objectives if they understand how the development process works, who the other players are, and how their objectives are interwoven.

This book was written for people who need to understand real estate development from the perspectives of both the public and private sectors. Its aim is to be useful to present and future developers, city planners, legislators, regulators, corporate real estate officers, land planners, lawyers specializing in real estate or municipal law, architects, engineers, building contractors, lenders, marketing analysts, and leasing agents/brokers. Readers are assumed to have already acquired the fundamentals of real estate and/or city planning. This book summarizes but does not repeat in great detail basic information about real estate law and finance, urban economics, and land planning and design. While the focus of our book is the individual entrepreneurial developer, it is important to note that developers can also be financial institutions, corporations, universities, medical centers, private investors, cities, municipalities, and others. The process laid out in this book remains essentially the same—no matter who the developer is. Market decisions still have to be made, the pro formas still need integrity, designers have to be consulted, and so on. The process might be layered by various institutional procedures and committees and boards of trustees, but the product is achieved by going through the same steps. In fact, many institutions and cities are hiring entrepreneurial developers on a fee basis to manage a project's development within the larger organizational framework.

Throughout, the book includes profiles of developers and the diverse set of professionals who work with developers. Their career paths are always interesting and often surprising. Their perspectives on development are especially valuable because these individuals have lived the process we are describing. Development decision making has become more difficult as the world has grown more complex, and developers' and professionals' insights help frame the development process in human terms.

In addition to the various profiles, the book focuses on two developers and two projects. The first developer is Whit Morrow of Fraser Morrow Daniels, whose project is the Europa Center. That project, a 95,000-square-foot Class A office building, was undergoing development while the first edition of this book was in preparation. Mostly through Morrow's own words, readers can follow his idea for an office project from conception through planning, permitting, financing, and construction to completion, leasing, and ongoing management. In the second edition, we learned how the building functioned over time and about the need for additional related development. In this third edition, we continue to follow the life of Europa Center in a changing development and economic environment. This edition also introduces a new project, this one a residential tower developed in Cambridge, Massachusetts, by Dean Stratouly of Congress Group Ventures. Museum Towers is a timely story of a development in a pioneering location. Both projects tell stories of unexpected complications and their resolution through the words of the developers.

To begin the discussion of the development process, this chapter lays out the functions of the development process and its many players:

- The definition of real estate development;
- The eight-stage model of real estate development;
- The characterization of developers and their reputations;
- The development team;
- The public/private partnership;
- Market and feasibility studies; and
- Design.

The next two chapters complete the introduction by defining the playing field—the spatial economics of the contemporary population—and then defining the roles of the various participants in the process. Chapter 2 describes the raw materials of the development process —demographics—while Chapter 3 adds detail and contemporary color to the process and the players.

Part II then covers the financial mechanics that support development decision making. Finance is not the goal, however; rather, the goal is the logic that allows the developer to bring together several participants (each with its own set of objectives) in a coordinated effort that will ultimately make a profit. The foundation established in the first two parts is complemented by the long-term historical perspective provided in Part III. The book then proceeds through the eight-stage model to look in detail at decision making in the real estate development process.

Defining Real Estate Development

Development is an idea that comes to fruition when consumers—tenants or owner-occupants—acquire and use the bricks and mortar (space) put in place by the development team. Land, labor, capital, management, and entrepreneurship are needed to transform an idea into reality. Value is created by providing usable space over time with associated services. It is these three things—space, time, and services—in association that are needed so consumers can enjoy the intended benefits of the built space. While the definition of real estate development remains simple, the activity continues to grow more and more complex. The product of the development process—a new or a redeveloped project—is a result of the coordinated efforts of many allied professionals. Developments do not happen without financial backing and often require multiple agreements to be negotiated by multiple financial players. Only then can physical construction or reconstruction be started, involving the myriad of design professionals, construction workers, engineers, and so on. Before, after, and during the process, the developer works with public sector officials on approvals, zoning changes, exactions, building codes, infrastructure, and so on. Increasingly, community groups in many cities demand to be key players in the development process, and the time needed to work with them has to be factored into the development equation. And, finally, selling or renting the space to users at the intended (or higher) price is the act that proves the entire project was justified. This consumation requires the expertise of marketing professionals, graphic artists, salespeople, lawyers, and others. The developer must ensure that all these elements—and many more to be identified later in this book—are completed on schedule, are properly executed, and are reasonably within budget.

Today, development requires more knowledge than ever before about prospective markets and marketing, patterns of urban growth, legal requirements, local regulations, public policy, conveyances and contracts, elements of building design, site development, construction techniques, environmental issues, infrastructure, financing, risk control, and time management.

Ever-increasing capacities and complexities along each of these dimensions have resulted in increased specialization. As more affiliated professionals work with developers, the size of the development team has expanded and the roles of some professionals have changed. Although greater complexity has generated the need for better-educated developers (educated both in book knowledge and hard knocks), it has not changed the steps they usually follow in the development process (or the personality traits that most developers share).

The Eight-Stage Model of Real Estate Development

Developers follow a sequence of steps from the moment they first conceive a project to the time they complete the physical construction of that project and begin ongoing asset management. Although various observers of the development process may delineate the sequence of steps slightly differently, the essence of the steps does not vary significantly. At a minimum, development requires the following elements: coming up with the idea, refining it, testing its feasibility, negotiating contracts, making a formal commitment, constructing the project, completing and opening it, and, finally, managing the new project. At almost all stages, the developer must have an exit strategy either not to go through with the project or to sell it upon completion. This text seeks to capture that essence in the eight-stage model depicted in Figure 1-1. Succeeding chapters detail the activities that collectively make up the eight-stage model of the development process.

Before proceeding further with the model, a few points about development must be emphasized. First, the development process is hardly straightforward or linear. A flow chart similar to that shown in Figure 1-1 can freeze the discrete steps and guide an understanding of development, but no chart can capture the constant repositioning that occurs in the developer's mind or the nearly constant renegotiation between the developer and the other participants in the process. And don't forget that redevelopment of existing projects requires many of the same steps as development. Moreover, in very large projects, individual development components can be "nested" within a larger development plan. For example, during the development of a community like the Kentlands, in suburban Washington, D.C., individual components of the community may be in different stages while the overall development plan is in stage six—construction.

Second, development is an art. It is creative, often extremely complex, partly logical, and partly intuitive. Studying the components of real estate development can help all players make the most of their chances for success; developers themselves can learn from studying the process. What cannot be taught are two ingredients essential to the success of the real estate developer/ entrepreneur: creativity and drive. At times, a smart developer will choose to move in a different order. Still, by using the model, the developer knows the full cost of such deviation and can weigh the cost against the motivation for deviation.

Third, at every stage, developers should consider all the remaining stages of the development process. In other words, developers should make current decisions fully aware of the implications of these decisions not just for the immediate next step but for the life of the project. By doing so, they ensure that the development plan and its physical implementation come closest to the optimum for the duration of the entire development process and, equally important, for the project's long expected life. Thus, the development process requires interaction among the different functions (construction, finance, management, marketing, and government relations) that interact in each of the eight stages as well as over time.

It is a huge mistake to underrate the importance of asset management and property management after the project is built or to overlook provision for them during design and construction. For example, operating "smart" buildings requires technical competence beyond the general management skills typical of most property managers. In addition, asset managers need to remarket space continually and to upgrade or remodel buildings periodically to keep the space competitive in an evolving market. Institutional investors and corporate owners are also keenly aware of the periodic need for and cost of major remodeling to prolong the economic life of buildings. Careful planning during stages one through seven should enable developers to find ways to minimize the frequency and cost of retrofitting buildings. Whether or not developers manage

Figure 1-1

The Eight-Stage Model of Real Estate Development

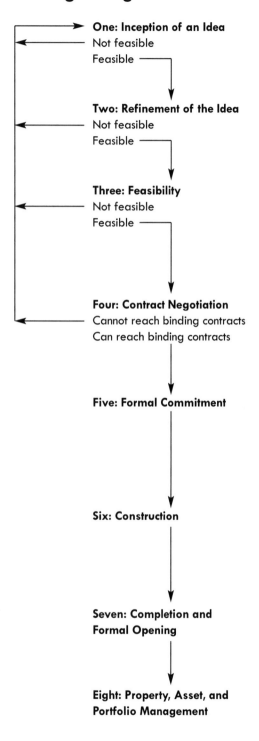

One: Inception of an Idea
Not feasible
Feasible

Developer with extensive background knowledge and a great deal of current market data looks for needs to fill, sees possibilities, has a dozen ideas, does quick feasibility tests in his head.

Two: Refinement of the Idea
Not feasible
Feasible

Developer finds a specific site for the idea; looks for physical feasibility; talks with prospective tenants, owners, lenders, partners, professionals; settles on a tentative design; options the land if the idea looks good.

Three: Feasibility
Not feasible
Feasible

Developer conducts or commissions formal market study to estimate market absorption and capture rates, conducts or commissions feasibility study comparing estimated value of project with cost, processes plans through government agencies. Demonstrates legal, physical, and financial feasibility for all participants.

Four: Contract Negotiation
Cannot reach binding contracts
Can reach binding contracts

Developer decides on final design based on what market study says users want and will pay for. Contracts are negotiated. Developer gets loan commitment in writing, decides on general contractor, determines general rent or sales requirements, obtains permits from local government.

Five: Formal Commitment

Contracts, often contingent on each other, are signed. Developer may have all contracts signed at once: joint venture agreement, construction loan agreement and permanent loan commitment, construction contract, exercise of land purchase option, purchase of insurance, and prelease agreements.

Six: Construction

Developer switches to formal accounting system, seeking to keep all costs within budget. Developer approves changes suggested by marketing professionals and development team, resolves construction disputes, signs checks, keeps work on schedule, brings in operating staff as needed.

Seven: Completion and Formal Opening

Developer brings in full-time operating staff, increases advertising. City approves occupancy, utilities are connected, tenants move in. Construction loan is paid off, and permanent loan is closed.

Eight: Property, Asset, and Portfolio Management

Owner (either developer or new owner) oversees property management (including re-leasing), reconfiguring, remodeling, and remarketing space as necessary to extend economic life and enhance performance of asset; corporate management of fixed assets and considerations regarding investors' portfolios come into play.

the property for the long term, they are responsible for considerations involving asset management during the first seven stages. Given that developers' actions largely determine future operating costs and that the expected magnitude of such costs represents a significant part of project value (i.e., what it will sell for), today's developers focus sharply on making building operations cost-efficient.

Fourth, it is imperative to remember that the development process is inherently interdisciplinary and dynamic. It is not a game won by exhibiting exceptional depth in one particular area, say, electrical design. Rather, it is a complex process that demands attention to all the different aspects of creating the built environment —political, economic, physical, legal, sociological, and so on. Good management of the interactions among various disciplines—with special attention to the areas that are most crucial to the specific project—is essential to successful development. Further, the components of this interdisciplinary world are experiencing an accelerating rate of change, and all the interfaces among the disciplines are constantly in flux.

Finally, U.S. real estate development is global in perspective. Financing is increasingly provided by international sources, tenants are served globally, and international building firms offer the full gamut of construction services. Most important, immigration is changing the consuming public, which, in turn, changes what people desire in the built environment. As different ethnic groups settle in U.S. cities, the configuration of cities and the needs of citizens shift. Developers must be prepared to respond to these changes.

Characterizing Developers

Developers are like movie producers in that they assemble the needed talents to accomplish their objectives and then assume responsibility for managing individuals to make sure that development potential is realized. They are proactive; they make things happen. As we will see in later chapters, a great deal of uncertainty is associated with the development process, just as with the introduction of any new product. Unlike most new products introduced (e.g., a new brand of toothpaste), real estate development involves long-term commitments (buildings last for decades). Thus, the cost of making a mistake is extraordinarily high. Just how much of the related risk the developer assumes personally is an important issue that commands significant attention throughout the book. Regardless of which risk control devices the developer finds appropriate for a particular project, the devel-

oper ultimately is responsible for managing all aspects of that project. Obviously, successful developers must be able to handle (and thrive under) intense pressure and uncertainty.

It is an error to assume that all developers are alike. Some, for example, develop only one type of property such as single-family houses; others develop anything commercial or industrial. Some developers carve out a niche in one city and refuse opportunities outside it; others work regionally, nationally, or internationally. Some developers run extremely lean organizations, hiring outside expertise for every function from design to leasing; others maintain needed expertise in house; and some work within the structure of a real estate investment trust (REIT). In between are many gradations. As in most professions, developers range from those who put reputation above profit to those who fail to respect even the letter of the law. Likewise, in ego and visibility, developers vary enormously. Some name buildings for themselves; others cherish anonymity.

One company featured in this book's case studies, Fraser Morrow Daniels, was founded to develop real estate in the Carolinas. Its focus is geographic; its products are office, residential, and hotel space.

Europa Center

The Development Company

Name
Fraser Morrow Daniels & Company (four partners)

Founded
1985 in affiliation with other ventures by Charles E. Fraser

Purpose
To develop real estate in the Carolinas, initially in the Research Triangle (Raleigh, Durham, Chapel Hill) of North Carolina

Projects Underway or Completed from 1985 to 1994
Park Forty Plaza—Class A office building, 125,000 square feet, Research Triangle Park, completed, approximate cost $12 million. Savings and loan association attempted to sell to private investor, but the Resolution Trust Corporation (RTC) stepped in and negated the sale. Ultimately sold to another investor.

Spring Hill—Residential community on 65 acres in Research Triangle Park, 25 single-family houses and 100 condominiums completed out of 600 housing units projected.

Ultimately taken over by lender after falling victim to oversupplied apartment market.

Rosemary Square—In-town hotel in Chapel Hill projected for 188 suites/rooms, 22,000 square feet of commercial space, and 516 parking spaces. Estimated cost $30 million. Designed, but marketing delayed by litigation until September 1987 in North Carolina Supreme Court. Project absorbed over $2 million, and in 1989 company decided not to build project. Site subsequently developed as public parking facility, with public open space on the top level.

Europa Center—Class A office building, 95,000 square feet in Phase I, 100,000 square feet in Phase II, Chapel Hill.

continued on page 13

Our second project, Museum Towers, was developed by a company that started with a historic property it converted from industrial to office space. Since its inception, the company has developed office, retail, multifamily, and light industrial projects.

▌▌▌ Museum Towers

The Development Company

Name
Congress Group Ventures (two partners)

Founded
1980

Purpose
Originally established to rehabilitate a historic property in downtown Boston; moved into development of commercial space, condominiums, and apartments.

Sample of Projects Underway or Completed from 1980 to 1999

Russia Wharf
Boston
Historic rehab

One Memorial Drive
Cambridge, Massachusetts
Office building

28 State Street
Boston
Office building redevelopment

Wayland Business Center
Wayland, Massachusetts
Office building redevelopment

continued on page 14

Private developers/entrepreneurs must balance an extraordinary number of requirements for completing a project against the needs of diverse providers and consumers of the product. As Figure 1-2 shows, developers first need the blessing of local government and neighbors around the site. Often, to obtain public approval, developers are required to redesign the project (politics). Therefore, appropriate flexibility is one of a developer's most crucial traits. Second, developers need to be able to find tenants or buyers who will pay for space delivered at the right price (marketing). Third, developers lead an internal team of specialists who depend on a given developer for their livelihood and recruit external players whose business is contracting with developers (construction supervision and process management). Fourth, developers demonstrate the project's feasibility to the capital markets and pay interest or assign equity positions in return for funding (finance). In every one of these areas as well as in interactions between areas, developers practice some form of risk management, initiating and managing a complex web of relationships from day one through the completion of the development process.

This book refers many times to the "development team" that designs and builds the developer's idea. It is worth noting that probably only 1 percent (perhaps fewer) of the people in real estate development are developers/entrepreneurs. The other 99 percent include a wide range of professionals, support staff, and building tradespeople who are indispensable players. Clearly, challenging work abounds in real estate development for all participants, not just for the developer. Still, understanding the decisions facing the developer is critical to all participants.

The developer's job description includes shifting roles as creator, promoter, negotiator, manager, leader, risk manager, and investor, adding up to a much more complex vision of an entrepreneur than a person who merely buys low to sell high. Developers are more akin to entrepreneurial innovators (the Bill Gateses of the world)—people who realize an idea in the marketplace —than to pure traders skilled primarily at arbitrage.

Figure 1-2

The Developer's Many Roles

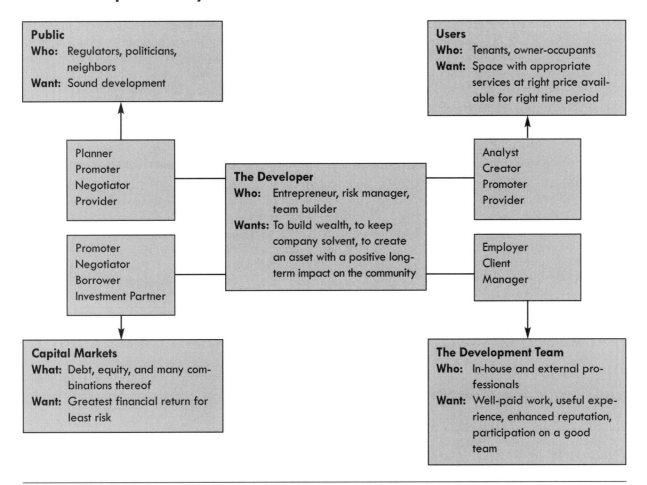

Balancing roles is part of the developer's art, something that can be described but not taught. Equally important and equally unteachable is the drive that makes developers persevere to the desired end despite problems and obstacles. Developers tend to be single-minded. This quality, perhaps more than the profit motive, accounts for the negative public image of some developers. Yet the same single-mindedness can lead to the design and construction of innovative projects. Without drive, no development would occur. As noted in later chapters, the potential roadblocks are numerous.

Sometimes, though, the tenacity that drives developers to produce a successful project can lead to disastrous results. The savings and loan debacle of the 1980s was in part the result of developers' desire to develop because they liked to do deals and because money was available. Many buildings were erected without enough thought given to proper market studies or design con-

siderations or basic need, leaving an inventory of unneeded buildings around the country that should never have been erected in the first place (see Chapter 9 for more details). Presumably all facets of the industry (particularly the regulators of financial institutions) are wiser now and will not repeat this expensive mistake any time soon. We hope this book will contribute to a healthier, more thoughtful way of doing business.

Developers' Reputations

Deserved or not, developers are not always held in high esteem by the general public. Without even knowing the individual or firm, people are often wary at the mention of a developer's involvement in a project in their locality. Given the impact that their work has on a community, it is not surprising that developers offend some people. Their product, which is so clearly manifested in the built environment, is there for everyone to see and criticize. And often their public persona is as much a part of a project as the product itself, making developers an easy target to blame for everything from increased traffic to crime.

Developers are also subject to attack because they engineer change in communities that is sometimes hard to accept, especially for long-time residents. Yet they provide a service as a community builder. They facilitate the production of shelter for living and working. They make possible new play areas, recreation areas, health care facilities. Ideally, they do so within the rules established by the public sector—planners, government staff, and elected officials.

As in any profession, some developers are models of ethical behavior and make innovative and attractive contributions to the built environment, and some developers exhibit low morals and appear on the front page of newspapers under indictment for shoddy construction and bribery.

Communities will always grow and change, with or without developers. With a good developer, however, growth and renewal can be managed and made to have a positive effect on a community.

The Development Team

If developers consistently play one role throughout the development process, it is that of a leader who can coordinate people and help realize a particular vision. Developers almost never work in isolation. To design, finance, build, lease or sell, and manage their dream, developers must engage the services of many other experts—public and private—some of them professionals and others entrepreneurs themselves.

Developers vary in the technical expertise they bring to the team. Earlier in their careers they might have been architects, lawyers, contractors, brokers, land planners, or lenders; almost all started elsewhere. Consequently, developers must hire the expertise they lack—whether they keep their experts on the payroll or contract for outside assistance. Developers must be able to find the right people, keep them motivated and on schedule, and ensure that their work is acceptable —or the project may not be successfully completed.

Often developers, like any team leader, motivate players with incentives other than money—with pride in the project, with the hope of future work, and with fear of the consequences of nonperformance. Knowing when and with whom to use different incentives is part of leading the development team.

With each new project, developers must shape and sell an idea to secure commitments from others. Thus, they are first and foremost promoters. Developers then spend a considerable part of their time managing other people when design and construction start. They have both the plan and the responsibility for making it happen; they are quarterback, coach, and team owner rolled into one. (See Chapter 3 for a more detailed discussion of the roles of other players.)

The Public Sector Is Always a Partner

Private sector real estate developers have a public sector partner in every deal—no exceptions—whether or not they choose to recognize that partner. Government—federal, state, and local—permeates the U.S. system of capitalism under which private developers operate. Real estate development itself is a highly regulated process. Taxes, labor law, property law, public infrastructure, financial market operations, zoning, building permits, and impact fees all issue from legislation, regulations, and public policy. In some cases, the public sector participates directly in the development process as a private developer's equity partner working toward the achievement of a public goal, such as downtown redevelopment. This participation is frequently the case with international development projects where the government's role is often greater than it is in the United States. Chapter 14 provides an in-depth discussion of public/private partnerships in which the public sector is a formal, risk-bearing partner in a development project. Although more and more local governments are initiating development projects, the public sector more often is engaged in a less formal partnership. Nonetheless, if developers do not work hand in hand with local governments, giving them the same amount of respect and attention they would give a private sector partner, delays and problems may occur.

Developers should also not overlook the people in the neighborhood who will be directly affected by the project. Time is money in real estate development, and overlooking or antagonizing public partners often costs a developer time, which translates into more interest payments and other costs. More important, the public sector can permanently delay a developer and can even change the rules in the middle of the game. Changing the plan and/or design midstream is usually quite expensive. In fact, changes forced by the public sector can make a project infeasible. And when it happens at a later stage in the development process,

The public/private partnership involving North General Hospital, Sparrow Construction, and the New York City Housing Development Corporation resulted in east Harlem's first for-sale middle-income residential construction in years. North General Hospital initiated the 135-unit inner-city infill project to help improve the community surrounding the site of its new facility.

developers often face almost insurmountable difficulties because of the costs already incurred. For these reasons, it pays for private developers to treat the public sector as a partner from the outset. The partnership is like a marriage: it can take many forms, but if it fails, it is psychologically and financially painful.

Market and Feasibility Studies

Textbooks on marketing and market research seldom cover real estate in great detail. Likewise, when real estate textbooks discuss market research, they typically fail to draw connections to the broader principles of marketing. Developers, planners, public officials, lenders, and investors can use fundamental concepts of mar-

keting to make better-informed decisions about real property. Only after studying marketing can business students develop a better understanding of the application of basic marketing tools to the real estate development process. Marketing fundamentals are also helpful to students of law, planning, or design who previously studied their particular sector of real estate development but now want to understand more about how ideas are judged and tested to see which actually become projects.

One important trend in development today is developers' increasing use of market research to make decisions at several stages in the development process, particularly to convince lenders to lend them money. Lenders remember the huge oversupplies of certain types of space in many large markets—for example,

Class A office space in downtown San Diego and Dallas during the early 1990s. Developers can no longer rely on instinct or optimism to decide what to build or to assure prospective lenders that the project will capture market share from competitors. A rigorous market study early in the process stimulates development ideas, improves initial concepts, and serves as a device to control risk.

Beyond convincing lenders and investors, market research is useful in development planning. Residential developers, for example, can use a market study of a projected design for a specific site to answer several questions. What is the anticipated employment growth rate in the market area? What is the anticipated household growth rate in the market area? What is the best configuration and size of housing units for the proposed residential subdivision? How many units will the market absorb, at what price, and over what period of time? What percent of that demand will the project capture and why? How should units be marketed to the targeted consumers? The market study's bottom line reveals how much operating income or revenue over what period of time the developer can expect a particular project to generate, given market conditions and expected competition. Parallel questions are appropriate for other types of development.

Equally important, the developer can use a market study to determine what project types will gain the support of public participants. In a sense, development creates "public goods" by placing long-lived products on the land, and everyone must live (at least visually) with the products for many years. The underlying research into the market area should include both regulatory requirements and the attitudes of neighbors and other "publics." Not only does market research guide the project's size and design; it also indicates ways for the developer to win public approval and/or gain various entitlements.

Furthermore, market studies are versatile in that they can accomplish other objectives. They can, as noted, be used to help obtain financing. After a project is financed, a market study can also be used as a marketing guide for the sales or leasing staff. To be salable, a project needs an identity in consumers' minds; the market study should provide a competitive analysis and identify a market niche that permits the proper targeting of advertising and promotion.

A feasibility study completes the rest of the equation in ever-simplified language (which is refined in Chapter 16). The project is feasible if its estimated value exceeds estimated costs. Value is a function of projected cash flow and a market-derived capitalization or discount rate (defined in Chapter 5).

Local real estate markets respond to neighborhood, regional, national, and international trends, be they development of interstate highways, amendments to the U.S. tax code, the collapse of oil prices, or fluctuations in the value of the dollar in world markets. A thorough market study looks beyond the primary market area to wider trends affecting local supply and demand. Ultimately, the project's revenues reflect these trends. Furthermore, savvy developers look for fresh design and marketing ideas outside local markets. Thus, developers must understand their local markets as well as recognize and respond to broader trends (the latter task may be easier said than done, as explained in this text's concluding chapter).

Information, of course, carries a cost. The more data an analyst gathers and the more time the analyst spends manipulating the data, the higher the price tag on the study. In all risk control techniques, the developer must weigh the cost in relation to the magnitude of the risk. In market studies, cost depends on the level of detail, who performs the analysis, and how much rigor a developer wants (or is forced by lenders or regulators) to pay for.

The future is not a straight-line extrapolation of the past. Although the market analyst scrupulously examines past performance and is exacting in determining current market conditions, the future is what matters most to real estate developers. Developers look for indications of the kind of space that will satisfy society's needs over a project's long expected life. The future is not just the one year or five years that it takes to develop a project; it is the entire useful life of the project, which may be 30, 50, 100, or 200 years. No one can fully anticipate the future, yet the developer's challenge is to be at least a few steps ahead.

Design Can Never Be An Afterthought

Good design has never been more important than it is today. Taking a cookie-cutter design off the shelf and applying it to an available site is not often the winning strategy in saturated markets or in markets where space needs are changing. Serious attention to the market—which means to the people who will use the project—can show developers and their architects and planners how to capture market share from competitors or how to build for a new niche.

Design has emerged as a versatile method of establishing contact with and discriminating between specific market segments. Buildings convey images that send direct messages, and architects who want to contribute successfully to development teams have had to become proficient in creating the appropriate design message. At the same time, it is important to remember that for some uses and certain tenants, the appropriate image is pure functionality—that is, the most functional bay sizes and core elements, covered with a skin whose operating costs are low.

Proficiency in design is hard won, for the right image is frequently elusive. Each player in the development process brings to the process some expectation of how the completed project will look and function. For example, hoping to maintain their town's character, public sector players bring images of desired interactions with surrounding areas. Different members of the development team might have visions of the project that range from minimalist to cosmetically dazzling. In the final analysis, the developer/entrepreneur charges the architect (and other design professionals) with solving the design problem and resolving the diversity of pictures into a single, coherent image. Still, the ultimate responsibility for good design rests with the developer.

The design of Europa Center was intended to bring big-city, Class A office space to a small but sophisticated town that offered nothing precisely comparable. Not by coincidence was the project located next door to the town's first luxury hotel.

⁙ Europa Center

A Summary of the Project

Location
Chapel Hill, North Carolina (population 35,000 in 1987, 38,700 in 1994), home of the University of North Carolina; 12 miles from Durham (population 100,000 in 1987, 136,611 in 1994), home of Duke University; ten miles from Research Triangle Park; 28 miles from Raleigh, the state capital and home of North Carolina State University; 18 miles from Raleigh-Durham Airport, site of an American Airlines hub.

Land
7.3 acres, zoned for office and industrial use, fronting U.S. 15-501 (four lanes, the main route to Durham, and, two miles farther east, a heavily developed commercial strip), Europa Drive (site of Hotel Europa), and Legion Road.

Land Cost
$2.1 million, $1 million allocated to Phase I, remainder to Phase II.

Buildings
Phase I—Five-story, 95,000-square-foot Class A office, poured-in-place reinforced concrete structure with glass curtain wall. Atrium lobby, marble, granite, and fabric panel finishes. Adjoining three-level parking deck.

Phase II—Adjoining five-story, 100,000-square-foot Class A office, poured-in-place reinforced concrete structure with glass curtain wall. Extended parking deck to increase spaces from 278 to 650.

Project Cost
Phase I—As of January 1987, projected at $9.3 million. Revised June 1987 to $10.5 million (construction close to budget, about $250,000 in construction changes, the remainder to fund slow leasing).

Phase II—Total construction cost about $11.3 million, including doubling of parking and three-story atrium connecting two phases. Completed 1991.

Initial Chronology
Land purchased—November 1985
Site preparation began—April 1986
Phase I building construction began—Summer 1986
Building certificate of occupancy issued—November 1987

Joint Venture Shares—Phase I
50 percent—Centennial Group buys land for $2.1 million.

35 percent—Fraser Morrow Daniels contributes up to $100,000 worth of research, planning, negotiating, and staffing, which is only partially reimbursed by joint venture.

15 percent—Centennial Group (a joint venture partner during construction) guarantees $1 million if needed to fund protracted leasing. This amount becomes additional equity in 1987 when Centennial is acquired by the construction lender and the entire financing is renegotiated to handle the slow leasing period.

continued on page 37

The Europa Center project was developed in a relatively small city, at the time not known as a hot spot for development, and its developers entered the market rather naively. In contrast, the Museum Towers project was developed in Cambridge, Massachusetts, home of MIT and Harvard University and across the Charles River from Boston. In the 1980s, the area was a developers' paradise—but everything crumbled in the early 1990s.

⦀ Museum Towers

A Summary of the Project

Location
Eight and Ten Museum Way (formerly 15 Monsignor O'Brien Highway), Cambridge, Massachusetts

Museum Towers at North Point was built in what many would consider a pioneering location. Located in east Cambridge, generally east of the Charlestown Avenue Bridge, Museum Towers is in the eastern section of the North Point development district, a 70-acre development zone master planned to provide a mix of commercial and residential development, upgraded infrastructure, and an extensive park network. The eastern portion was the last large parcel of undeveloped waterfront property in Cambridge.

North Point is adjacent to the highly successful Kendall Square and east Cambridge (Lechmere Canal) development areas, which have become vibrant centers of commercial development and professional job growth.

The eastern section of North Point is located across from the Museum of Science and bordered to the west by Monsignor O'Brien Highway, to the north by the Gilmore Bridge, to the east by I-93, and to the south by the Charles River, directly across from the west end area of downtown Boston. The site had been used for industrial purposes and was known as "the lost half-mile of the Charles River." For decades, it had been the wrong end of Cambridge.

Land
Original site 4.11 acres, three parcels of land. The site is bounded to the north by a 40-foot-wide private access way (Main Road) and beyond that by a parcel of land owned by the Massachusetts Water Resources Authority. Industrial Way, owned by the Massachusetts Bay Transportation Authority, borders the site to the east. To the east of Industrial Way is the site of North Point Park, which is owned by the Metropolitan District Commission. This parcel is clearly separated from all other nearby development by roadways, although these uses are very visible from the site and are clearly "industrial" except for the Museum of Science.

Land Cost
$13 million

Buildings
Two 24-story apartment buildings joined at the base by a low-rise area of apartments, support space, a central lobby, a health club, and a 490-vehicle parking garage.

Project Cost
$78 million

Initial Chronology
Land purchased—October 1987
Site preparation began—Fall 1995
Building construction began—Early 1997
Building certificate of occupancy issued—1998

continued on page 38

Configuring the built environment to create specific images has a long and instructive history. Early merchandisers knew that building a massive single structure sent a message of abundance that a profusion of small branch outlets could never achieve. In a similar vein, books of house plans containing Greek revival designs sold particularly well at the beginning of the 20th century. It was not the floorplans or the efficient space that was popular; rather, the strong identification with the image of an earlier democracy attracted homebuilders. Today, most travelers can readily identify the quality and cost of a motor hotel simply by the image projected by the building. Creating a formal image that becomes a vital, interactive component in a project's success is neither accidental nor mysterious. It results from careful consideration of design criteria during all eight stages of the real estate development process—not just exterior design but also all the functional aspects of interior design that are critical to tenants' efficient use of constructed space. (Later chapters deal with integrating both exterior and interior design criteria during the eight-stage development process.)

Finally, the implications of successful design go far beyond creating an effective structure. Architects, like the other players in the development process, are bound by ethical obligations. They understand space and urban design far better than laypersons. If architects do not see it as their responsibility to innovate and advance the state of the art, then society will not live up to its potential, at least not as related to improving the built environment. Architects must convince developers, who must make it happen.

Summary

As we move forward with the introductory framework in Chapters 2 and 3, it is important to keep the following concepts in mind:

1. Everyone is in some way connected to the development process. Consequently, the developer should see the public sector as a partner.
2. The developer ultimately is responsible for creating space over time with associated services that meet society's needs.
3. Because the development period decision-making environment is so complex and interactive, a model is useful so that future ramifications of current decisions can be more easily evaluated.
4. Development is an art that requires drive and creativity coupled with "appropriate" flexibility and risk management.
5. Development of the built environment is a long-term activity that justifies considerable planning. Provision for ongoing operating management should be a critical element of such planning.

Terms

Many of the following terms are introduced in this chapter and explained later in greater detail:

- Asset management
- Built environment
- Capital markets
- Corporate owners
- Development team
- Entrepreneur
- Equity
- Feasibility studies
- Infrastructure
- Institutional investors
- Interdisciplinary
- Leverage
- Market studies
- Niche
- Operating costs
- Private sector
- Public sector
- Real estate development
- Risk control
- RTC
- Value

Review Questions

1.1 Define real estate development.

1.2 Why does every real estate development project involve both the public and private sectors?

1.3 What is the role of the developer in the development process?

1.4 What are the eight stages of development as delineated in this textbook?

1.5 What are the advantages of using such a model? What are the pitfalls?

1.6 Why is real estate development inherently an interdisciplinary process?

1.7 Why and how do developers use market research?

1.8 Discuss the importance of good design in development.

1.9 What is Europa Center and who was its developer?

1.10 Describe the Museum Towers project.

Chapter 2

The Raw Material: Land and Demographics in the United States

The preceding chapter summarized the activities that constitute the development process. This chapter describes the spatial and population setting in which real estate development takes place. This is the playing field on which a dynamic game is constantly unfolding. Chapter 3 completes the introductory framework by reviewing the functions and motivations of its primary participants in the development process. Collectively, these three chapters provide the foundation for understanding how society's needs are met by the real estate development community.

Searching for future opportunities requires a continued "fresh look" at basic demographic and economic indicators as well as how they are expected to change. Understanding the recent past and the present tells us where we have been, while careful analysis of census projections can tell us much about the future users of real estate. Furthermore, by using demographic data, we can examine national, regional, and local markets, zeroing in on a particular site and its potential marketability.

This chapter offers a two-part overview of trends in U.S. demographics and landownership.

- Where we are—the demographic and economic underpinnings of real estate ownership and development in the United States today.
- Where we are heading—a brief discussion of how the future will differ from the past and how the built environment will need to change to accommodate demographic shifts.

The authors are indebted to Deborah L. Brett, Deborah L. Brett and Associates, Plainsboro, New Jersey, for her extensive revisions to this chapter.

Land, Wealth, and Population in The United States

Is Land Scarce?

The United States contains 3,536,278 square miles of land and supports a population of just over 270 million people. Physically, both Canada and China are slightly larger than the United States. Brazil is slightly smaller.

In contrast to a country such as the Netherlands (where overall land use is intensive), the United States can boast of extensive and relatively unused deserts, mountains, dry plains, tundra, and swamps. Developed land takes up only 5 percent or 92 million acres of the total land area of the United States.[1] The present land-to-people ratio in the United States is about 8.5 acres per person (75 persons per square mile), which may seem inconceivable to someone living in New York City but may sound crowded to a Montana rancher.

In addition to vast rural areas, huge land reserves exist even in the urbanized metropolitan areas of the United States. These reserves result from leapfrog suburban development,[2] abandoned or dying central-city neighborhoods, and relatively low-density development patterns in new urban areas. In recent years, however, the high cost of road, water, and sewer infrastructure (and decreasing federal funds for extending services) has constrained leapfrog development. Consequently, demand for developable land—that is, properly zoned land with the necessary infrastructure in place—has driven up land costs sharply in some areas, thereby producing higher-density commercial and residential land uses. At the same time, metropolitan areas continue to expand outward geographically as

Figure 2-1

Landownership in the United States

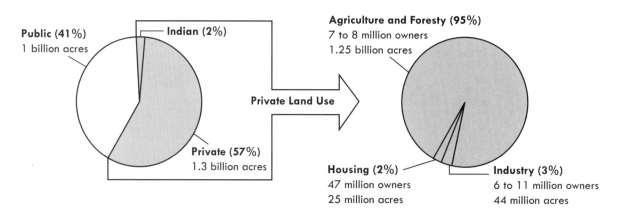

Public (41%)
1 billion acres

Indian (2%)

Private (57%)
1.3 billion acres

Private Land Use

Agriculture and Foresty (95%)
7 to 8 million owners
1.25 billion acres

Housing (2%)
47 million owners
25 million acres

Industry (3%)
6 to 11 million owners
44 million acres

Source: Charles H. Wurtzebach and Mike E. Miles, *Modern Real Estate,* 5th ed. (New York: John Wiley & Sons, 1994), p. 6.

the effect of population growth exceeds the impact of increased density. In 1960, metropolitan areas housed 63 percent of the U.S. population on 9 percent of the country's land area. By 1996, 80 percent of the nation's population lived in metropolitan areas and occupied 20 percent of the land.[3]

Americans' love of space is exemplified by recent trends in homebuilding. Despite experiments with smaller houses in the early 1980s, U.S. citizens continue to demand more interior living space. The median, new single-family house grew from 1,385 square feet in 1970 to 1,595 square feet in 1980 and reached 2,000 square feet in 1998. A significant corollary to less land/more house is the steadily increasing proportion of new houses with two or more stories: 17 percent in 1970, 31 percent in 1980, and 49 percent in 1997.[4] The perception that more living space with less land (but still some land around the house) is better than no land seems to explain Americans' tenacious demand for single-family detached housing and thus for relatively low-density, owner-occupied residential development.

Who Owns the Land and How Is It Used?

With 662 million acres (about 29 percent of the nation's 2.3 billion acres), the federal government is the largest single landowner in the United States; in fact, Uncle Sam owns 60 percent or more of five states: Alaska, Nevada, Utah, Idaho, and Oregon.[5] State and local governments collectively own another 8 percent of the nation's land, leaving private landowners and Native Americans on trust lands to share the remaining 59 percent of the pie (see Figure 2-1). As urbanization pushes

the boundaries of metropolitan areas outward, farm acreage is declining. At its peak in 1954, more than 1.2 billion acres was under cultivation. By 1998, only 954 million acres was still being farmed—a 4 percent drop from just a decade earlier.[6] Moreover, individually owned farms are gradually being replaced by a smaller number of larger, corporate-owned agricultural holdings. The family farm certainly has not disappeared, but globalization of food production, processing, and marketing is changing farm ownership and operations.

Although forest product companies and railroads still control extremely large land holdings, real estate in the United States is widely owned by individual citizens, a legacy of the 17th through early 20th centuries. The first European immigrants arrived in the New World hungry to own land. Later waves of immigrants in search of land pushed westward, buying land cheaply or staking claims under liberal government programs (see Chapter 8 for more on such programs). For social and political reasons (and not merely because of the huge land mass), people of little wealth but healthy ambition could acquire land inexpensively and easily.

Throughout U.S. history, governments at all levels have actively promoted private ownership of land and homes.[7] During the 20th century in particular, a variety of programs and policies advanced homeownership: the Federal Housing Administration's mortgage insurance program and the Veterans Administration's mortgage guarantee program (which revolutionized home mortgage lending in the 1940s and 1950s); the federally facilitated secondary mortgage market for home loans; tax legislation benefiting both homeowners and private investors in commercial and industrial real estate; and, most important, provision of the infrastructure needed to support private land- and homeownership.

Today, nearly two-thirds of all U.S. householders own their homes. Ownership of commercial and industrial properties rests in the hands of users (such as corporations and retail chains), institutional investors (insurance companies and pension funds), financial concerns (banks), real estate investment trusts, real estate development companies, and private individuals or partnerships. The relative ease of acquiring property that U.S. citizens take for granted strongly attracts foreign investors to U.S. real estate. In many other developed nations, real estate markets are much smaller, and laws dramatically restrict foreign investment.

Foreign Ownership of Real Estate In the United States

American property attracts foreign investment for several reasons: the country's perceived political stability, the sheer size of the market, the economy's persistent growth, and the foreign trade deficit. During the 1980s, U.S. trading partners with surplus dollars invested heavily in American commercial real estate. As of mid-1988, nearly two-thirds of the Class A office space in downtown Los Angeles, for example, was owned by foreign investors. In Chicago, foreign investors owned 20 percent of downtown office space, in Washington, D.C., 23 percent, and in downtown Manhattan 21 percent.[8] Aggressive Japanese buying, particularly the purchase of large office buildings in big cities, attracted considerable media attention. The inflow of Japanese capital was not a surprise. During the 1980s, the Japanese enjoyed a huge trade surplus with the United States;

accordingly, investment in U.S. stocks, bonds, and real estate gave the Japanese an outlet for their dollars. Furthermore, Japan's own real estate market was small and rates of return were minuscule by comparison. Although Japanese interests spent $77.3 billion on U.S. properties during the 1980s, their holdings lost as much as half their value from 1986 to 1993, with the steepest declines occurring in hotel and resort properties. In the mid- and late 1990s, Japanese investors sold off or restructured most of their holdings. By the late 1990s, ethnic Chinese companies (and families) were pursuing new deals far more actively than other Asians.

Foreign landownership and investment in agricultural land were of concern to federal and state elected officials in the 1970s. In 1978, Congress directed the U.S. Department of Agriculture to conduct an annual inventory of foreign-owned farmland, and considerable public discussion of the dangers of foreign ownership ensued. Although some states eventually enacted restrictions, the federal government did not, and the U.S. market for all types of real estate remains open to foreign investors.

Just how much land do foreign investors own? At the end of 1995, they held only 1 percent of U.S. farm and forest land (15 million acres). About half the foreign holdings are forest lands,[9] with much of it controlled by Canadian paper companies.

Although offshore interests continue to purchase highly visible office, hotel, and resort properties, their overall influence on U.S. property markets should not be a source of political concern. Real estate accounts for less than 6 percent of foreign investment in American industry, and it attracted only 1.7 percent of offshore capital invested in this country in 1998 (see Figure 2-2).

Figure 2-2

Foreign Direct Investment in U.S. Real Estate

(Billions of Dollars)

	Capital Inflows		Direct Investment Position[a]	
	1997	1998	1997	1998
Real Estate	$4.675	$3.284	$40.060	$44.436
All Industries	105.448	188.960	643.207	811.756
Real Estate Share	4.4%	1.7%	5.7%	5.5%

^aOn the basis of historical cost.

Source: Bureau of Economic Analysis, *Foreign Direct Investment in the United States,* September 15, 1999 (www.bea.doc/gov/bea/di/fdius-98.html).

U.S. Developers Look for Offshore Opportunities

By 1989, with many U.S. markets substantially overbuilt, some large American developers began looking for opportunities overseas, especially in Europe. London was soon overbuilt (thanks in part to development attitudes exported by U.S. and Canadian developers and U.S. investment bankers). Germany and France looked ripe for new development because both countries were still relying on 1950s-era office properties that were clearly substandard in a contemporary high-tech office environment. Despite initial enthusiasm within the U.S. real estate community, the economic slowdown caused by the merging of the former East and West Germany delayed action on many projects. Others did not lease as readily as anticipated.

The former Communist bloc nations also became a focus of developers' interest in housing and retail space, offices, and industrial facilities. U.S. developers learned, however, that the slow shift to a market economy meant long delays in moving projects forward; old regulatory and bureaucratic constraints were likewise slow to change. Although U.S. developers possess many of the skills needed to exploit European market opportunities, most have chosen to undertake joint ventures with politically sophisticated in-country organizations, thereby ensuring that they forge effective development teams.

In the early 1990s, interest shifted from Europe to Mexico. Our southern neighbor's consumer base (about 100 million people) and its proximity to the United States awakened real estate interests to Mexico's enormous economic potential. Ratification of the North American Free Trade Agreement (NAFTA) created development opportunities linked to increased trade with Mexico. Retail chains were in the vanguard of expansion into Mexico, with Wal-Mart, Price Club (now Costco), JCPenney, Dillard's, and Blockbuster eager to serve the Mexican market.

Nevertheless, investors remained concerned about Mexico's relative poverty, inadequate infrastructure, and sociopolitical tensions. U.S. corporations with Mexican operations have built their own stores and factories rather than rely on speculative multitenant buildings and inexperienced local management companies.

Further economic reforms and greater stability are still needed to make the Mexican market attractive to conservative U.S. lenders. As the market matures, U.S. companies will move from U.S./Mexican border cities (where *maquiladora* manufacturing and distribution operations are well established) to the interior of Mexico, where most of the population lives. Opportunities for U.S. developers to build retail centers,

warehouses, and factories will expand. Astute entrepreneurs will use Mexico as a gateway for expanding into other Central and South American countries.[10]

By the mid-1990s, the Asian Pacific region was attracting attention from U.S. and European real estate investors. With more and more multinational corporations building manufacturing facilities (taking advantage of Asia's lower production costs), demand for office space, warehouses, hotels, resorts, and other commercial properties accelerated. Enthusiastic construction far exceeded demand, however. And then currency problems and banking instability raised concerns. Moreover, operating in Asia is complicated by the dominance of family-controlled (and tightly held) real estate companies, as well as myriad government regulations and cultural norms not familiar to American developers. Local equity partners and advisers/consultants are vital to success.[11] With the significant repricing of Asian real estate as the result of domestic economic recessions and currency devaluation, America's more aggressive investors began pushing into Asian real estate with a new vigor in the late 1990s.

Real Estate, the Gross Domestic Product, Wealth, and Employment

It should come as no surprise that, given their central importance to the U.S. economy, real estate devel-

---

Figure 2-3

Private Fixed Investment in Land Improvements: 1998

(Billions of Dollars)

Nonresidential Structures

Nonresidential Buildings	$184.1
Utilities	34.7
Mining	21.3
Other Structures	6.8
Subtotal	$246.9

Residential

Single-Family	$187.3
Multifamily	24.4
Other Structures	149.4
Subtotal	$361.1

Total	**$608.0**

Source: Bureau of Economic Analysis, *Survey of Current Business,* April 1998.

Figure 2-4

Capital Sources: Total U.S. Commercial Real Estate

($4.01 Trillion as of June 30, 1999)

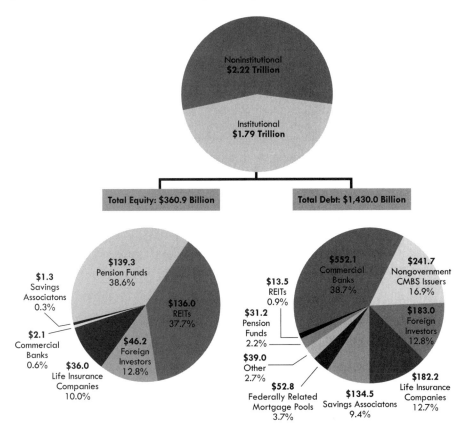

Source: Lend Lease Investment Research.

opment, construction, and investment are highly promoted and highly regulated by government at all levels. The U.S. gross domestic product (GDP) was $8.5 trillion in 1998—nearly $32,000 per person. Of this total, individuals consumed about 68 percent, the government purchased another 17 percent, and the private sector invested 15 percent. Real estate is the largest component of gross private domestic investment in the GDP. Forty-eight percent of 1998's domestic private investment ($608 billion) was in real property assets, and nearly 60 percent of that amount was for housing (see Figure 2-3).[12]

As just one example of the importance of housing investment, owners of existing residential property (all types) spent $119 billion in 1998 for improvements, repairs, additions, and alterations.[13] Owner-occupants accounted for $80 billion of the total invested in improvements. (These figures do not include governments' investment in real property.)

For individuals, real estate is an extremely important component of wealth. Besides providing shelter and psychic benefits such as pride and security, property investments constitute more than one-fourth of total personal net worth.[14]

Another way of looking at the importance of real estate to the national economy is to consider the investment value of its components. Commercial real estate is publicly traded in the form of shares in REITs, but the market capitalization of equity REITs is still small in comparison with corporate real estate holdings, private partnerships, and mortgages on commercial properties (see Figure 2-4). In turn, the total value of owner-occupied housing (debt and equity) is far greater than that of commercial real estate.

The importance of the real estate industry in the United States is also reflected in national employment figures. In 1998, the U.S economy provided 125.8 million nonfarm jobs, of which 1.5 million were in real estate businesses and another 6 million in construction, which is clearly part of the real estate development industry.[15] Overall, nearly 6 percent of the nation's employment is attributable to real estate development, management, and sales, suggesting why the industry is important to the nation's economic health.

It would be a mistake to note the magnitude of employment in the real estate industry without also recognizing its cyclical nature. Real estate–oriented employment shrinks and swells in parallel with construction starts, which, in turn, tend to move broadly up and down with interest rates and the balance between supply and demand. The employment figures for construction workers in Figure 2-5 show how many workers enter and leave construction in response to opportunity. Between 1989 and 1992, the number of construction workers dropped by 679,000. Workers in the real estate sector—in sales, finance, and management —have also felt the impact of cyclical fluctuations. Downsizing at real estate firms was a fact of life from 1990 through 1992 as commercial development activity shrank and residential sales slowed as a consequence of the real estate depression of the early 1990s. During six years of recovery and expansion (1992 to 1998), real estate businesses added 181,000 jobs.

Population Growth in the United States

Population growth alone does not ensure a strong, steadily growing economy. In many emerging nations, annual population growth rates of 2.5 to 3.5 percent are common, but economic prosperity is elusive. Growth in population and labor force can be powerful engines in expanding economies, however. Real estate development opportunities materialize when people with purchasing power increase in number. Construction can be triggered in stable communities as older, worn-out properties are redeveloped with new uses. In general, though, development opportunities expand with population growth.

National and regional populations grow in two ways: more people are born than die and more people migrate in than leave. In the earliest days of our country, immigration was the key source of population growth. This trend continued through the early part of the 20th century, but then immigration dropped to a trickle during the 1940s and 1950s. For the last four decades, both the number of newcomers and their share of population growth rose dramatically once again. As seen in Figure 2-6, legal immigration peaked during the first decade of the 20th century; however, projections suggest that the first decade of the 21st century may surpass this historic high. Between 1994 and 1996, the number of new legal residents averaged 814,000 per year. Illegal aliens add another 275,000 annually, for a total of 1.1 million newcomers.[16] Yet the immigration rate (the number of legal newcomers per 1,000 residents) is still less than half that seen at the turn of the last century. Figure 2-7 shows that net immigration has accounted for about one-third of the population growth in the United States since 1980.

Immigration is an important factor in the continued growth of border states such as California and Texas. Newcomers also help in maintaining the population of central cities of New York, Chicago, Los Angeles, Miami, and the like. Although new Americans can strain local government resources, they are an important source of demand for housing, stores, and service businesses. Immigration presents opportunities for entrepreneurs who see new needs and ways to satisfy them. Catering to ethnic tastes and consumer preferences can enhance market penetration, a strategy adopted not only by neighborhood retailers but also by such mass market chains as JCPenney. Gradually, as immigrants move into the economic mainstream, they support the real estate market as buyers of both new and existing housing. Homeownership rates for naturalized citizens are about the same as for native-born Americans.[17]

In the United States today, the rate of population growth (natural increase plus immigration) is extraordinarily low (less than 1 percent per year) and is expected to decrease even further. Nevertheless, the sheer number of new Americans is significant. The Census

---

Figure 2-5

Construction Workers Employed: 1977 to 1998

Year	Millions of Workers	Year	Millions of Workers
1977	3.85	1988	5.10
1978	4.23	1989	5.17
1979	4.46	1990	5.12
1980	4.35	1991	4.65
1981	4.19	1992	4.49
1982	3.90	1993	4.67
1983	3.95	1994	4.99
1984	4.38	1995	5.16
1985	4.67	1996	5.40
1986	4.82	1997	5.63
1987	4.97	1998	5.98

Source: **U.S. Department of Labor, Bureau of Labor Statistics.**

Figure 2-6

Legal Immigration to the United States

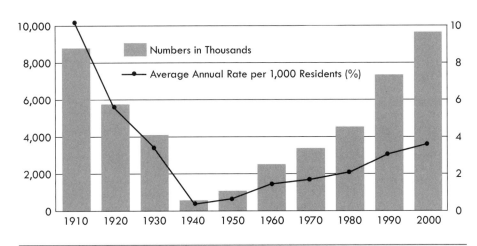

Figure 2-7

Immigration's Share of Population Growth by Decade

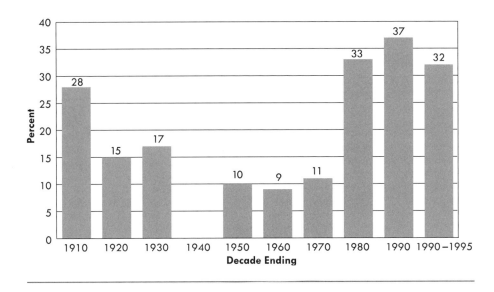

Bureau's middle-series projections suggest that the U.S. population will reach 297 million by 2010 and 394 million by 2050—28 million and 125 million, respectively, above the early 1998 figure.[18]

In the marketer's language of product life cycles, the U.S. population as a whole could be said to be in its mature phase. Figure 2-8 demonstrates how the United States grew from 3.9 million people at the time of the first census in 1790 to 270 million in 1998.

National Demographic Trends

Even though the total number of people living in the United States is growing only modestly, the characteristics of the population are changing dramatically. In determining opportunities for real estate development, the nature and composition of the population are as important as its total size. Understanding how the future will differ from the past is critical in project-

Figure 2-8

Population Growth in the United States: 1790 to 1998

Census	Number of People	Increase over Previous Decade (Percent)
1790	3,929,214	–
1800	5,308,483	35.1
1810	7,239,881	36.4
1820	9,638,453	33.1
1830	12,866,020	33.5
1840	17,069,453	32.7
1850	23,191,876	35.9
1860	31,443,321	35.6
1870	39,818,449	26.6
1880	50,155,783	26.0
1890	62,947,714	25.5
1900	75,994,575	20.7
1910	91,972,266	21.0
1920	105,710,620	14.9
1930	122,775,046	16.1
1940	131,669,275	7.2
1950	151,325,798	14.9
1960	179,323,175	18.5
1970	203,302,031	13.4
1980	226,545,805	11.4
1990	248,709,873	9.8
1998	270,298,524	–

Sources: **U.S. Department of Commerce, Census Bureau,** *Statistical Abstract of the United States,* **1997, Table 1, p. 8; and Population Estimates Program release, June 4, 1999.**

ing demand. A look at demographic trends tells us not only how many more people will reside in the United States 20 years from now but also their ages, household composition, educational attainment, and ethnicity. Looking beyond the totals helps predict and segment consumers' needs and desires more accurately.

Demographers used to talk about the population pyramid, with large numbers of children on the bottom and relatively few old people at the top. In 1970, the nation's median age was 28. By 1995, it was over 34, and by 2010, it will be more than 37.[19] Thus, the population profile for 2010 will be closer to a cube than to a pyramid (see Figure 2-9). Age cohorts younger than the baby boom generation will be increasingly equal in size. By 2010, the boomers—who constituted 35 per-

cent of the population in 1970—will account for only 25 percent of the nation's total.[20]

Most of America's short-term population growth will occur in the older age groups. One reason is the large bulge of post–World War II babies who are now middle aged. Another is the increase in life expectancy. Stated another way, the total population of all ages increased by only 22 percent from 1970 to 1990. Yet the number of people aged 65 to 74 increased by 45 percent, and the number aged 75 and older grew by 73 percent.[21]

As demonstrated by the 2025 demographic profile in Figure 2-9, no single generation will be large enough to dominate the public policy–making process, and each group will be equally important as real estate consumers. Politicians and retailers will have to please all age groups in a way that has not been true historically. If the distribution of population by age is overlaid with variations in income, race/ethnicity, and household characteristics, the large number of discrete target markets becomes clear. Regrettably, the real estate industry has been slow to properly segment overall demand and thus address this growing diversity.

For retailing, an aging population means higher disposable income, better-educated and more savvy consumers, and more money spent on discretionary purchases than on necessities. In the late 1980s, developers believed that an affluent, aging population also translated into strong demand for upscale active retirement communities. In practice, however, senior citizens did not readily accept either age-restricted living or its higher prices. The result was slow product absorption. Obviously, demographic numbers alone were insufficient to gauge demand: focus groups were needed to evaluate consumers' desires as well. A decade later, retirement housing is enjoying greater market acceptance. The need for assisted-living facilities catering to an increasingly frail population is evident. Real estate investment trusts specializing in assisted-living facilities and nursing homes are gaining the confidence of investors.

In the near term, the U.S. population will become more ethnically and racially diverse—partly because of differences in the age composition and birthrates of the existing minority population, but also because of increases in immigration that are expected to continue beyond the 1990s. Non-Hispanic whites constituted 76 percent of the population in 1990 but will represent only 68 percent by 2010. Hispanics (9 percent of the total in 1990) will be the fastest-growing minority in absolute numbers, reaching nearly 14 percent by 2010.[22] It is important to recognize that immigrants are not simply Asian or Hispanic or European; rather, Thais and Japanese are very different, as are Puerto

Figure 2-9

From Population Pyramid to Cube

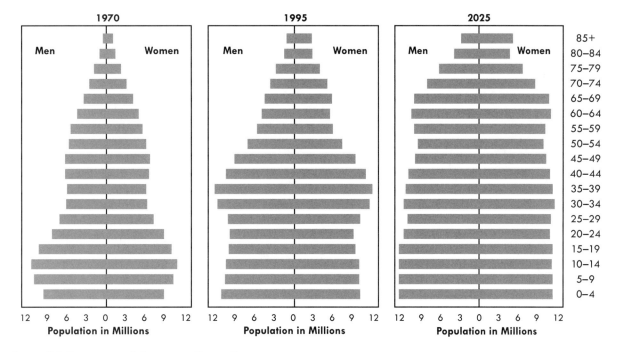

Source: U.S. Department of Commerce, Census Bureau.

Ricans and Peruvians, and Irish and Italians, and within each cultural group many socioeconomic variations further segment the populations. Real estate entrepreneurs have to become sensitive to the different cultural and economic norms that are reflected in shopping and housing choices.

Similarly, households are not homogeneous, and neither are their housing preferences. Demand no longer exists for the mass market suburban tract house that sold phenomenally well between 1950 and 1970. Instead, niche marketing will be the key to successful development into the 21st century. One-fourth of all households consist of a single person, and their numbers are rising rapidly. Growth in single-person households is fueled by adults who never marry, the still high divorce rate, and an increase in the number of older widows and widowers. Homeownership is increasingly attractive to singles, and their numerical growth will help offset a decline in future demand from family households.

Traditional "married couple with kids" families have declined sharply—from 40.3 percent of all households in 1970 to 25.8 percent in 1998. Fewer than 37 percent of *all* households include a child under 18, as shown in Figure 2-10. A growing share of families with children—more than 29 percent—has only one parent

(or another adult relative) at home, up from 11 percent in 1970.[23]

To gauge demand, homebuilders focus on aggregate growth in the number of households nationwide and in their trade areas. During the 1970s and 1980s, demand for homes and apartments was fueled by household formations that exceeded the rate of population growth. The reason is that average household size has fallen steadily, from 3.14 persons in 1970 to 2.76 persons in 1980 to 2.65 persons by 1996.[24] Americans are having fewer children as overall affluence rises, and more people are living alone. Average household size continues to fall, but at a slower rate than in the past. Consequently, aggregate demand for shelter will not grow at the same pace as in the past.

Residential and retail developers closely monitor household income characteristics and are alert to how age, race, and household composition affect both affordability and taste. As demonstrated by Figure 2-11, income can vary dramatically by age. Earning power is greatest in the 45–54 age bracket, followed by 35- to 44-year-olds and then by people aged 55 to 64. Over the next ten years, "middle-aged" population growth will be high and will generate demand for discretionary goods and services as well as for move-up housing.

Figure 2-10

Changing Composition of American Households

Household Type	Percent of All Households	
	1970	1998
Family Households	81.2	69.1
Married Couple	70.5	53.0
With Children under 18	40.3	25.8
Other Family	10.6	16.2
With Children under 18	5.0	10.7
Nonfamily Households	18.8	30.9
Living Alone	17.1	25.7
Not Living Alone	1.7	5.2

Source: **U.S. Department of Commerce, Census Bureau,** *House-hold and Family Characteristics, March 1998,* **Current Population Reports, P20-515.**

Figure 2-11

1998 Median Household Income By Age of Householder

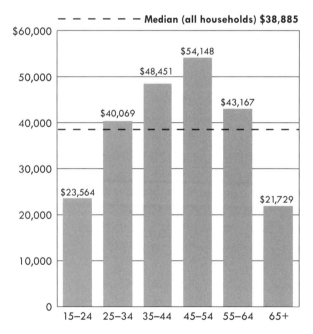

- - - - - Median (all households) $38,885

$54,148
$48,451
$43,167
$40,069
$23,564
$21,729

15–24 25–34 35–44 45–54 55–64 65+

Source: **U.S. Department of Commerce, Census Bureau,** *Money Income in the United States, 1998,* **Current Population Reports, P60-206.**

Household income data vary dramatically by place of residence (metropolitan versus nonmetropolitan areas, central cities versus suburbs), by household type, and by race. For example, median household income in 1998 was $40,634 in the Northeast but only $35,797 in the South. For Asians, it was $46,637, for whites $40,912, and for African Americans only $25,351. Suburbanites in large metropolitan areas (over 1 million population) had a median household income of $49,940, but nonmetropolitan households earned only $32,022.[25]

Census income data underestimate household purchasing power because many households fail to report all their earnings. In fact, a growing underground or "off-the-books" economy operates beyond the realm of traditional reporting practices. The magnitude of underground economic activity varies among markets, and unreported activities take many forms (second jobs paid in cash, street vending, agricultural barter, tutoring, home improvement work, domestic services)—all legal activities that produce cash that eventually makes it into the hands of retailers, landlords, and homebuilders.[26] No reliable methods exist to estimate the extent of unreported income in an individual market, but it is an important element in consumer demand in inner cities, blue- and pink-collar suburbs, and rural areas.

In addition, market analysts who focus only on current earnings are missing part of the wealth picture—household assets that will be inherited by today's younger households. In 1995, U.S. families had a median net worth of $56,400 held in investment vehicles ranging from equity in owner-occupied homes to interest-bearing accounts, stocks, bonds, and retirement plans. Net worth is highest for households aged 55 to 64, whose 1995 median net worth was $110,800.[27] Many young households, which may not be earning much right now, will enjoy greater affluence upon inheriting family assets.

Employment Growth

Whereas demand for housing and retail space is primarily a function of population and household growth and composition, demand for other commercial property development—office buildings, factories, research and development facilities, warehouses—is more closely tied to changes in the labor force and employment. The office construction boom of the 1970s and 1980s was fueled, in part, by a dramatic shift in the U.S. economy from production of goods to delivery of services and the concomitant growth of white-collar occupations. Manufacturing jobs dropped as a share of total employment, but the service sector—a diverse mix of jobs heavily concentrated in business services and

Figure 2-12

Private Sector Office Employment: Share of Total Nonfarm Jobs

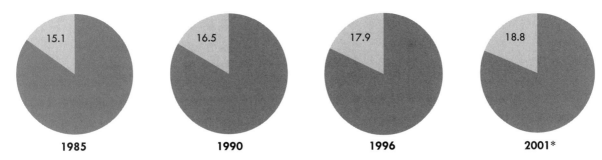

| 1985 | 1990 | 1996 | 2001* |

*Projected.
Source: Regional Financial Associates, July 1997.

health care—grew dramatically. Women entered the labor force in increasing numbers, and new technology created opportunities for both professional and clerical services and knowledge workers. Typical anchor tenants of new office buildings were expanding law, accounting, and investment firms, as well as corporations and banks seeking to enhance their images.

By 1989, aggressive expansion ended. The lending excesses of the 1980s led to failures in the savings and loan (S&L) industry and to bank mergers, which reduced the need for office space. More important, real estate lending came to a screeching halt. Growth in the labor force had been slowing for some time, but then employers cut back. Total wage and salary employment dropped by more than 1 million jobs between 1990 and 1991, and showed only a slight increase in 1992.

By 1993, the economic recovery was in full swing. Nonfarm jobs increased by more than 13.6 million between 1992 and 1997, and a significant share of the new employment was in industries that use office space—business services, communications, finance, and the professions. Occupancy of existing office buildings quickly improved, and by 1997 new construction was once again underway.

As Figure 2-12 shows, the share of private sector jobs found in office-prone industries will continue to grow. The Bureau of Labor Statistics predicts that more than 11 million new jobs will be created in the service sector between 1996 and 2006, for an annual growth rate of nearly 3 percent (see Figure 2-13). By 2006, the service sector will account for one-third of all nonfarm wage and salary jobs, up from 28 percent a decade earlier. Although employment in finance, insurance, and real estate (FIRE) will grow just 1 percent per year to 2006 (752,000 new jobs by 2006), the FIRE

sector's share of total employment will remain largely unchanged.[28] Computer- and data processing–related businesses, nonbank financial companies, management consultants and public relations firms, legal services, personnel agencies, and health practitioners' offices will continue to experience above-average growth.

Despite the strength of the service sector, demand for new office space in the 1990s has not matched that of the previous two decades. Much of the growth in service sector jobs is found at health care providers (home health care agencies or nursing homes) that do not require much multitenant office space. In banking, insurance, and government, a focus on consolidation, improvement in productivity, and cost containment means further job cutbacks and vacated office space.

Employment growth is just one of several determinants of demand for commercial and industrial real estate. The need for state-of-the-art warehouse space results primarily from new technology and changing methods of operation. Retail employment has grown along with shopping center square footage, but demand for new store space weakened in the 1990s.

Regional and Metropolitan Shifts

Opportunity for landownership drew early immigrants to the colonies and later led pioneers westward across the country. Early in the 20th century, migrants from rural areas sought and found better-paying jobs in northern cities. Southern African Americans, for example, moved north in large numbers to Chicago, Philadelphia, New York City, Detroit, and Washington, D.C. Post-1960s migration patterns, by contrast, reflect the movement of jobs to lower-wage areas and the migration of residents to warmer climates. Migration data—and the

Figure 2-13

Employment by Major Industry: 1986, 1996, and Projected to 2006

(Thousands)

	1986	1996	2006	Percent of Total 1986	Percent of Total 2006
Nonfarm Wage and Salary Employment	98,727	118,731	136,318	100.0	100.0
Mining	778	574	443	0.8	0.3
Construction	4,810	5,400	5,900	4.9	4.3
Manufacturing	18,951	18,457	18,108	19.2	13.3
Transportation, Communications, and Utilities	5,247	6,260	7,111	5.3	5.2
Wholesale Trade	5,751	6,483	7,228	5.8	5.3
Retail Trade	17,878	21,625	23,875	18.1	17.5
Finance, Insurance, and Real Estate	6,275	6,899	7,651	6.4	5.6
Services	22,346	33,586	44,852	22.6	32.9
Government	16,693	19,447	21,150	16.9	15.5

Source: James C. Franklin, "Industry Output and Employment," *Monthly Labor Review,* November 1997, p. 40.

factors that explain population movement—help in identifying opportunities for real estate development.

The U.S. population continues to shift from older metropolitan areas of the Northeast and Midwest toward the Sunbelt, the mountain states, and the Pacific Northwest (see Figure 2-14). Between 1990 and 1998, Nevada was the nation's fastest-growing state; its population increased by more than 45 percent. During the same period, Connecticut, Rhode Island, North Dakota, and the District of Columbia registered net population declines (see Figure 2-15). Because of California's prolonged recession in the early to mid-1990s, its population growth rate slowed dramatically. The Golden

State grew 9.7 percent between 1990 and 1998, solely because of international immigration and natural increase (more births than deaths). By contrast, the state grew 25.7 percent during the 1980s. California's net domestic migration (movement into the state from elsewhere in the United States) was strongly negative during most of the 1990s. More Americans left California than moved in, a reversal of earlier trends.[29]

Population expands fastest where jobs grow (and stagnates or declines in ailing economies). New England's economic boom of the 1980s turned into a recession in the early 1990s. States heavily dependent on income from a single industry—petroleum in the case of Texas, Oklahoma, Colorado, and Louisiana— were severely depressed during the mid-1980s. Texas and Colorado, however, aggressively courted nonenergy businesses and recovered in the early 1990s. Property markets in metropolitan areas with diverse economies are better able to withstand cyclical fluctuations than are regions dependent on one or two key industries or employers.

Population shifts have political ramifications that ultimately influence real estate interests. As people move from the Northeast and Midwest to the South and West or from central cities to suburbs, congressional districts are reapportioned accordingly. In 1990, states such as New York and Illinois lost seats in the U.S. House of Representatives, while Florida, California, and other expanding states increased their political clout. For public officials at the local level, growth is a

Figure 2-14

Population of the United States By Region

	Percent Share			
	1970	1980	1990	1998
Northeast	24.1	21.7	20.4	19.1
Midwest	27.8	26.0	24.0	23.3
South	30.9	33.3	34.4	35.3
West	17.1	19.1	21.2	22.3

Source: U.S. Census Bureau.

Figure 2-15

Percentage Change in State Populations: 1990 to 1998

Total U.S. Change = 8.7 percent

Under 3 Percent	3–5 Percent	5–10 Percent	10–15 Percent	Over 15 Percent
Connecticut (−0.4)	Iowa	Alabama	Alaska	Arizona
District of Columbia (−13.8)	Louisiana	Arkansas	Delaware	Colorado
Maine	New Jersey	California	Montana	Florida
Massachusetts	Ohio	Hawaii	New Mexico	Georgia
New York	Vermont	Illinois	North Carolina	Idaho
North Dakota (−0.1)		Indiana	Tennessee	Nevada
Pennsylvania		Kansas		Oregon
Rhode Island (−1.5)		Kentucky		Texas
West Virginia		Maryland		Utah
		Michigan		Washington
		Minnesota		
		Mississippi		
		Missouri		
		Nebraska		
		New Hampshire		
		Oklahoma		
		South Carolina		
		South Dakota		
		Virginia		
		Wisconsin		
		Wyoming		

Source: **U.S. Census Bureau, "State Population Estimates and Demographic Components of Population Change," ST-98-2, December 31, 1998.**

source of civic pride and means an expanding tax base, but it also triggers the need for costly public services and infrastructure. Rapid growth without adequate school, road, water, or sewer capacity often engenders no-growth attitudes among longer-term residents.

Population figures for metropolitan statistical areas (MSAs) and consolidated metropolitan statistical areas (CMSAs) underscore the Sunbelt/Frostbelt dichotomy. Figure 2-16 shows regional disparities, while Figure 2-17 highlights population losses in many older central cities, often because of suburban flight. For example, population in Atlanta's central city declined by 7.3 percent from 1980 to 1990, even though population in the metropolitan area grew by 32.5 percent. Not all central cities recorded losses during the 1990s. New York City and Chicago, both magnets for immigrants, maintained their populations. Many Sunbelt cities can grow because they are able to annex adjacent unincorporated land—an opportunity not available to most Northeast or Midwest cities ringed by incorporated suburbs.

The real estate industry, like any other producer of goods and services, profits by satisfying buyers' needs and wants. The developers, builders, and salespeople who pioneer new products and techniques spot trends early and assume that they can profit accordingly. Looking at broad demographic data is useful, not only for the big picture of trends in the United States and its regions, but also to stimulate obvious questions. Is the same trend affecting my local market? Will it continue in the future? What opportunities does it present?

Predicting the Future

For real estate players in all markets, understanding the present and past is the necessary first step in projecting future opportunities. Extrapolation is not simple, however. Life has a way of confounding the forecasters who lay down a straightedge and draw a line through two points in the past to project the future. Many changes are unforeseen. The surprising net mi-

Figure 2-16

Population Change in Selected CMSAs and MSAs: 1980 to 1996

CMSAs/MSAs	Population in 1996 (Thousands)	Rank	Percent Change 1980–1990	Percent Change 1990–1996
Northeast/Midwest				
New York-Northern NJ-Long Island, NY-NJ-CT-PA CMSA	19,938	1	+3.4	‖2.0
Chicago-Gary-Kenosha, IL-IN-WI CMSA	8,600	3	+1.5	+4.4
Philadelphia-Wilmington-Trenton, PA-NJ-DE-MD CMSA	5,973	6	+4.3	+1.4
Boston-Worcester-Lawrence, MA-NH-ME-CT CMSA	5,563	7	+6.5	+2.0
Detroit-Ann Arbor-Flint, MI CMSA	5,284	8	−2.0	+1.9
Cleveland-Akron-Lorain, OH CMSA	2,913	14	−2.7	+1.9
Minneapolis-St. Paul, MN-WI MSA	2,765	15	+15.5	+8.9
South/West				
Los Angeles-Riverside-Orange County, CA CMSA	15,495	2	+26.4	+6.6
Washington-Baltimore, DC-MD-VA-WV CMSA	7,165	4	+16.2	+6.5
San Francisco-Oakland-San Jose, CA CMSA	6,605	5	+16.4	+5.7
Dallas-Ft. Worth, TX CMSA	4,575	9	+32.5	+13.3
Houston-Galveston-Brazoria, TX CMSA	4,253	10	+19.6	+14.0
Atlanta, GA MSA	3,541	11	+32.5	+19.7
Miami-Ft. Lauderdale, FL CMSA	3,514	12	+20.8	+10.1
Seattle-Tacoma-Bremerton, WA CMSA	3,321	13	+23.3	+11.8

Source: **U.S. Census Bureau.**

gration from metropolitan to nonmetropolitan areas in the 1970s did not continue during the 1980s but regained momentum in the 1990s. (Between 1990 and 1996, the population of nonmetropolitan counties grew at an annual pace double that of the 1980s, and fewer rural counties lost population. Rural growth, however, is focused in counties that attract retirees or visitors. Three-fourths of rural counties that depend on farming show more people moving out than moving in.)[30]

Few people foresaw the 1980s' decline in oil prices that crippled cities such as Houston; even fewer people predicted the end of the Cold War, which has resulted in a dramatic downsizing of the military and related defense industries. Moreover, not all property cycles operate in unison. In 1998, office demand remained strong and vacancies were low. In contrast, finding tenants for empty store space was difficult, and values suffered as occupancy rates fell. The lesson for real estate practitioners is to stay well informed without becoming complacent. Participants in the industry should assume that the unforeseen is always just around the corner—and be ready to confront it.

The Shape of Our Cities

Cities exist because they create possibilities and opportunities. One of the original possibilities was trade. As people moved to cities and no longer grew their own food, they imported food from the countryside. In return, they "exported" manufactured goods or services such as warehousing, banking, or medical care; some cities also evolved into government administrative centers or "military towns." Early cities tended to locate at "economic transport points: at seaports, on navigable lakes and rivers, or at junctions of overland trade routes."[31] Obviously, some transport points (or breaks in transportation) have been determined by such natural features as deepwater ports. But other U.S. transport points grew up in the 19th century after the construction of canals and railroads; points along those transportation corridors immediately gained a cost advantage over other routes served only by horse and wagon. As a result, transportation hubs attracted industry and often evolved into manufacturing cities. In fact, Heilbrun asserts that railroads "proved to be the

Figure 2-17
Population Change in Central Cities

	1990 Total (Thousands)	1998 Total (Thousands)	1998 Rank	Percent Change 1980–1990	Percent Change 1990–1998
Northeast/Midwest					
New York City	7,323	7,420	1	3.5	1.3
Chicago	2,784	2,802	3	–7.4	0.7
Philadelphia	1,586	1,436	5	– 6.1	–9.4
Detroit	1,028	970	10	–14.6	–5.6
Boston	574	555	20	2.0	–3.3
Cleveland	506	496	28	–11.9	–1.9
South/West					
Los Angeles	3,486	3,598	2	17.4	3.2
Houston	1,654	1,787	4	2.2	8.0
San Diego	1,111	1,221	6	26.8	9.9
Phoenix	988	1,198	7	24.6	21.3
Dallas	1,008	1,076	9	11.3	6.8
San Francisco	724	746	12	6.6	3.0
Washington, D.C.	607	523	23	–4.9	–13.8
Seattle	516	537	22	4.5	4.0
Atlanta	394	404	39	–7.3	2.5
Miami	359	369	44	3.4	2.8

Source: U.S. Department of Commerce, Census Bureau, *Estimates of the Population of Cities with Populations of 100,000 and Greater*, SU 98-1, June 1999.

most powerful agglomerative invention of all time"[32] that is, railroads more than anything else made cities grow. (Remember that Atlanta was originally called Terminus.) Since the 1960s, airports have played an increasingly important role in stimulating economic development.

Intercity transportation also dictated the shape and density of U.S. cities. The classic old city was mononuclear: its one extremely dense center featured a business district, tightly surrounded by residential and manufacturing neighborhoods. Density was high because people and goods moved by "hoof and foot." Before the 1870s, workers could not live beyond the walking distance of jobs. Between 1853 and 1900, horse-drawn and then electric streetcars radically transformed housing patterns. Like spokes of a wheel, streetcar lines radiated out from the mononuclear city center, carrying workers to and from houses in outlying city neighborhoods or new suburbs. But people still worked downtown; commerce and manufacturing had to remain centralized because horses and wagons

still moved freight for short hauls. (The cost of transporting freight was higher than the cost of transporting people.) The peak in center-city development, according to Heilbrun, occurred between 1900 and 1920.

The next radical change in urban development was brought about by widespread use of the automobile after 1920. The newer cities of the South and West grew up relying on automobiles rather than urban mass transit, and because people with rising incomes also purchased more space around them wherever they could, the population density of younger cities is far lower than that of older cities, as indicated by the numbers in Figure 2-18. In the early part of the 20th century, the price of cars declined nearly as fast as computers did in the 1990s. The Model T cost two-thirds less 15 years after its introduction, which meant more people could afford this new means of transportation. The shape of our cities responded accordingly.

Both efficient manufacturing assembly and short-haul truck transport of freight dictated the construction of single-story plants that consumed far more land than

Figure 2-18

Population Density in Major U.S. Cities: 1990

	Population per Square Mile
Old Cities	
New York City	23,707
San Francisco	15,503
Chicago	12,254
Boston	11,860
New Cities	
San Diego	3,429
Denver	3,053
Atlanta	2,989
San Antonio	2,808

Source: **U.S. Department of Commerce, Census Bureau,** *Statistical Abstract of the United States, 1997,* **Table 46, pp. 45–47.**

multistory loft buildings. Consequently, manufacturing began moving to cheaper land away from the center city. In new outlying locations, manufacturing firms could lower production costs but still remain accessible to customers and suppliers. Eventually, retail trade followed the customers to the suburbs, to the extent that retailing in many urban areas is limited almost exclusively to suburban malls and strip centers at the expense of the downtown. And in many medium-sized U.S. cities, more office space now exists in outlying areas than in the central business district (CBD).

Growth of suburban activity centers has changed commuting patterns. Regional transportation planning no longer focuses primarily on the trip from the suburbs to downtown. Instead, circumferential highways and suburban arterials must accommodate the increasing proportion of workers who live in one suburb and work and shop in others.

Suburb-to-suburb commuting was one of the most significant changes in U.S. cities in the late 20th century. The advent of expressways changed patterns of travel and housing and altered the idea of "best location." No longer are the premier sites always in the CBD. Instead, highly accessible freeway interchanges have become some of the most desirable locations for commercial development. Despite the growth of suburban business nodes, the automobile has not killed the center city. Visually, the structure of cities since the advent of the automobile still resembles a hub with spokes, but now the spokes are connected by more lateral lines and often by one or more perimeter rings.

Beginning in the 1980s, changing communication technology reduced the need for businesses to locate close to one another. Rapid, interactive electronic communication—via corporate networks, pagers, cell phones, E-mail, the Internet, and even videoconferencing—is making face-to-face contact with clients and customers less important for many businesses. In an increasingly competitive labor market, firms need to be located where they can attract skilled workers. And more Americans are opting to work closer to home if possible or seeking more flexibility in their schedules by working at home some of the time or working four long days and having three days off.

In the future, technological changes and workers' emerging lifestyle choices could alter locational preferences for service businesses in much the same way that the automobile and the interstate highway system influenced the location of manufacturing jobs. Yet some business functions seem destined to remain concentrated in central business districts. For example, banking, law, finance, advertising, broadcasting, publishing, entertainment, and the corporate headquarters of certain large companies continue to require face-to-face contact in the daily conduct of business. For firms in these businesses, success depends on speed and creative interaction.

The growth of suburbia and the exodus of manufacturing firms and retail stores from central cities has meant fewer job opportunities for lower-income households. People living in working-class urban neighborhoods used to be able to find jobs near home without incurring the expense of owning and operating a car. But today, finding ways to move blue-collar workers from city neighborhoods to suburban factories is a major challenge for employers. The cost of urban land and the scarcity of assembled clean sites have pushed many manufacturers to the outer reaches of metropolitan areas and to small towns, leaving behind empty buildings with little apparent potential for manufacturing use. Aggressive economic development programs structured around a variety of incentives such as tax abatements and skills training programs have attempted to attract and retain employers in the nation's inner cities. For developers and planners alike, central cities with large pockets of decay present both a challenge and an opportunity for revitalization.

Summary

Throughout, this book stresses that real estate practitioners who best anticipate the future will reap the greatest rewards. Prudent players do not take the built world for granted. Technology, consumer preferences, government policy, demographics, sources of capital, and economic underpinnings all evolve—at times slowly and at other times rapidly in response to crisis.

Since 1973, the economic setting of the real estate industry has become much more volatile than in earlier decades. In the early 1980s, real estate markets in the "oil patch" experienced the deepest recession since the Great Depression (in some places even worse than the early 1930s). In 1986, a federal tax change sharply curtailed the real estate syndication business and drastically reduced apartment construction. In the late 1980s, huge investments of institutional capital led to dramatically overbuilt commercial real estate markets in many cities. Very successful development companies and professional real estate investors saw their fortunes reverse during the early 1990s when property markets crashed. Not only small players—the carpenter turned contractor and the part-time real estate agent turned investor—but also large companies became casualties.

Understanding the scope of the built environment, the institutions that support it, and their history cannot guarantee that observers will survive recessions or reap big profits in boom times. But a sense of perspective can put a developer or owner one step ahead of the competition and is a basic requirement for working with (or competing against) the best. All the participants in the development process need to understand the raw material that constitutes the playing field and how it is likely to change over time.

Terms

- Baby boomers
- Demographics
- Downsizing
- Gross domestic product (GDP)
- Infrastructure
- Leapfrog development
- *Maquiladora*
- Metropolitan statistical area (MSA)
- North American Free Trade Agreement (NAFTA)
- Population density
- Population pyramid
- Purchasing power
- Service sector
- Single-person households
- Underground economy

Review Questions

2.1 Why is ownership of real estate more attractive in the United States than in many other countries?

2.2 Why have U.S. developers been looking outside the country for development opportunities?

2.3 Why is real estate so important to the U.S. economy?

2.4 Describe the anticipated changes in the composition of the U.S. populace.

2.5 How does immigration affect demand for real estate?

2.6 How does employment growth influence the demand for commercial space?

2.7 Why is it important for real estate players to stay well informed about trends?

Notes

1. U.S. Department of Commerce, Census Bureau, *Statistical Abstract of the United States, 1997* (Washington, D.C.: U.S. Government Printing Office, 1997), Table 370, p. 229.

2. See Chapter 7 for a discussion of leapfrog development, which skips over undeveloped but expensive land in the existing city for less expensive land in the hinterland.

3. *Statistical Abstract, 1997,* Table 40, p. 39; U.S. Census Bureau, *Estimates of the Population of Metropolitan Areas,* MA-96-7, released December 1997.

4. U.S. Department of Commerce, *Characteristics of New Housing, 1997,* (Washington, D.C.: U.S. Government Printing Office, 1998), Table 14, p. 32.

5. *Statistical Abstract, 1997,* Table 369, p. 228.

6. U.S. Department of Agriculture, National Agricultural Statistics Service, "Farms and Land in Farms," February 26, 1999.

7. Government has continuously promoted private ownership, but government regulation of real estate development has been increasing for reasons explained subsequently and in Chapters 7 and 8.

8. Lawrence S. Bacow and Sean A. Burns, *Foreign Investments in U.S. Real Estate: Status, Trends, and Outlook, 1988* (Chicago: National Association of Realtors® and MIT Center for Real Estate Development, 1988).

9. U.S. Department of Agriculture, *Foreign Ownership of U.S. Farmland, 1995* (Washington, D.C.: U.S. Government Printing Office, 1995), p. 23. The United Kingdom is the largest foreign owner of U.S. farmland, with nearly 1.8 million acres. Canada owns more than 1.5 million. The state with the largest amount of foreign-owned farm or forest acreage is Maine, where 16 percent of the state's privately owned agricultural land is in foreign hands.

10. Adele Hayutin, "Economic Growth and Development in Mexico: Implications for Real Estate," in *ULI on the Future* (Washington, D.C.: ULI–the Urban Land Institute, 1994), pp. 50–61.

11. Ken Stearns, "Investing in Asian Pacific Real Estate," *Urban Land,* Asia Supplement, May 1997, pp. 10–13.

12. U.S. Department of Commerce, Bureau of Economic Analysis, *Survey of Current Business,* April 1999.

13. U.S. Department of Commerce, Census Bureau, *Expenditures for Residential Upkeep and Improvements.* Series C-50, 4th Quarter 1998, Table 2.

14. Recent growth in the value of stock portfolios has eclipsed that of owner-occupied homes. In 1997, real estate constituted 27 percent of household assets; in 1990, its share was 33 percent. Stocks as a percentage of household wealth grew from 12 percent to 28 percent during the same period. See Edward Wyatt, "Share of Wealth in Stock Holdings Hits 50-Year High," *New York Times,* February 11, 1998.

15. U.S. Department of Labor, Bureau of Labor Statistics data series.

16. The Immigration and Naturalization Service estimates that about 5 million undocumented immigrants resided in the United States in October 1996; the number of undocumented aliens was said to be growing by 275,000 per year. About 40 percent of the undocumented population lives in California. More than 40 percent of illegal residents are persons who entered the U.S. legally on a temporary basis but failed to depart.

17. U.S. Census Bureau, "Immigration Bolsters U.S. Housing Market," *Census Brief* CENBR/97-4, December 1997. See also Robert P. Prybolsky, "Housing the Immigration Wave," *Mortgage Banking,* October 1997, pp. 14–22.

18. U.S. Census Bureau, *Population Projections of the United States by Age, Sex, Race, and Hispanic Origin, 1995 to 2050,* Current Population Reports P25-1130 (Washington, D.C.: U.S. Government Printing Office, 1996), Table C, p. 5.

19. Ibid., Table M, p. 7.

20. Ibid., Table 2, p. 72.

21. U.S. Department of Commerce, Census Bureau, *U.S. Census of Population, 1970* and *1990.*

22. *Population Projections of the United States,* Table J, p. 13. Asians will continue to have the fastest growth rate, but in absolute numbers of persons, Hispanics will account for a larger segment of the population.

23. U.S. Census Bureau, *Household and Family Characteristics, March 1998,* Current Population Reports P20-515, October 1998.

24. Ibid.

25. U.S. Department of Commerce, Census Bureau, *Money Income in the United States, 1998,* Current Population Reports P60-206, September 1999, Tables A and 1.

26. M. Leanne Lachman and Deborah L. Brett, "Retail Trends: Consumers, Goods, and Real Estate," *Commentary* (New York: Schroder Real Estate Associates, June 1994), pp. 11–12.

27. "Family Finances in the U.S.: Recent Evidence from the Survey of Consumer Finances," *Federal Reserve Bulletin,* January 1997, p. 6.

28. James C. Franklin, "Industry Output and Employment," *Monthly Labor Review,* November 1997, Table 1, p. 40.

29. U.S. Census Bureau, "State Population Estimates and Demographic Components of Population Change," ST-98-2, released December 31, 1998.

30. U.S. Department of Agriculture, *Agricultural Fact Book, 1997* (Washington, D.C.: U.S. Government Printing Office, 1997), p. 52.

31. James Heilbrun, *Urban Economics and Public Policy,* 3d ed. (New York: St. Martin's Press, 1987), pp. 8–11. This section draws heavily on Heilbrun's lucid explanation of the evolution of U.S. cities. See especially Chapters 2 through 4.

32. Ibid.

Chapter 3
Developers and Their Partners

To appreciate fully the role of developers in molding the nation's raw material into the built environment, it is necessary to understand the function and motivation of all the major participants in the development process. Although this chapter deals with all the individual participants, the full complement of players should be seen as a team. Only then can the developer's roles be completely understood. Developers ultimately are responsible for the created space and how it will function over the life of a project. Because many different skills are needed to develop the kind of space society needs and wants, developers themselves usually do not provide all the expertise; rather, they select, motivate, and manage the team needed to get a job done.

By assuming ultimate responsibility, developers must make sure that team members meet development objectives and command the skills to do their part of the job. Development is a dynamic art that occurs over a considerable period of time—usually one to several years. During that time, the many changes likely to be made to the original development plan may require new skills and different players. The longer the development takes, the more likely it is that the participants or individuals and companies will change along the way. Companies may lose key employees, or the original lending institution may be subsumed by a merger.

Because pressures tend to become intense during the middle stages of the development process, initial contracts alone are often not enough to ensure that all team members will perform as agreed. There is no time to stop the program for a year to engage in a lawsuit—at least not without incurring great financial pain. Successful developers recognize that the ultimate responsibility for a project's success in the context of an intense, dynamic process requires the ability to anticipate and respond to change. Throughout the process, developers not only continue to verify that the project itself is feasible, but also check to see that the composition of the development team still makes sense for each participant, given changing situations. As you consider the roles of the various participants, try to keep this challenging management task in mind so that you can see how exciting (and sometimes frightening) the development process can be.

This chapter looks at the roles of the major players in the development process, among them:

- Private sector developer;
- Public sector developer;
- Architect;
- Engineer;
- Land planner;
- Landscape architect;
- Contractors;
- Environmental consultant;
- Transportation consultant;
- Appraiser;
- Attorneys and accountants;
- Real estate brokers/leasing agents;
- Financial players;
- Property manager;
- Market researcher;
- Marketing and public relations consultant;
- Regulators; and
- Final users.

 text rotated: Anice Hochlander

Rockville Center, including Courthouse Center public park, was one of the first projects completed by the developers to demonstrate their commitment to improving the downtown of Rockville, Maryland. The mixed-use public/private project was planned to revitalize the downtown by replacing a functionally obsolete mall with office, retail, and residential space.

After this detailed description of the various members of the development team, the chapter and the entire introduction conclude with a discussion of new trends in development. The eight-stage model first described in Chapter 1 is time honored. Still, within this model major evolutionary changes are occurring. After seeing how each team member fits into the model, we conclude by looking at these evolutionary changes to the development process.

Private Sector Developer

Like most good businesspeople, developers seek the maximum possible return with a minimum commitment of time and money. In development, the return consists of several components:

- The development fee, which is the stated direct compensation for developing the project;

- Profits on any sale to long-term investors (i.e., sale price less all costs needed to produce a fully functioning project);
- Possibly a long-term equity position (for which the developer may or may not contribute cash), in which case the developer's goals are similar to those of passive investors (discussed later);
- Personal and professional satisfaction in advancing a new concept or improving the urban environment; and
- Enhanced reputation, which creates future opportunities for development.

A developer's commitment of time is usually the length of the development period, which is increasing in most jurisdictions. If developers choose to retain ownership of a completed project, however, their commitment extends until the project is sold. Although the equity interests discussed later also wish to minimize the time of their involvement, they are not involved primarily in selling their time as are developers. Other professionals on the development team are either paid by the hour or participate in only a portion of the development process; therefore, they are less sensitive to the overall length of the development period.

Private developers may also profit through the ownership of entities that sell services to the development: insurance agencies, mortgage banking firms, leasing companies, management companies, or even general contracting firms. To the extent that these arrangements are made at arm's length and represent clearly understood agreements, developers are simply compensated for performing additional functions. On the other hand, if compensation for activities in which developers have an interest is above standard, any excess should be considered an addition to the development fee.

Private developers' financial exposure arises in two different ways. First, developers spend time and money before gaining assurance that a project will be built (i.e., before stage five, formal commitment). Naturally, developers seek to minimize such expenditures. Second, in addition to their own equity position (both contributed capital and debt for which developers are personally liable), developers might guarantee investors or lenders or both a certain project cost or a certain initial occupancy level. As primary risk bearers,[1] developers' financial exposure (beginning at stage six of the process) depends on the amount of their direct financial commitment plus the magnitude of any guarantees they make and the likelihood of the guarantees being called on.

Many developers are now receiving a new type of compensation as fee developers. A client such as a retailer, health care provider, or public sector agency hires a developer to see a project through from beginning to completion. Such developers are usually hired for a fee, like a consultant, with a bonus paid at the end for successful completion and timely delivery of the product. In these cases, developers assume no personal financial risk. Nonetheless, while the fees are not small, they do not match what developers might earn when they operate as traditional developers and assume considerably more risk.

Developers' personal qualities are a vital element in the development process. Chapter 1 referred to the drive and creativity that characterize developers. To be effective, though, developers must also possess clarity of vision. They must be focused dreamers with the ability to convince others that they can make their dreams a reality.

In addition, developers must be annoyingly persistent but not inflexible. If they are not flexible, their projects will remain unbuilt. Even the best developers encounter obstacles along the eight-stage road and must retain some flexibility and willingness to be consensus builders. Working with regulators and community groups forces successful developers to be flexible enough to alter their original plans to accommodate at least some of the concerns voiced by neighborhood residents who will be directly affected by a proposed development. Developers increasingly face design review boards that require alterations in the appearance of a building. Only by adopting a flexible stance will developers secure all needed approvals and commitments. Of course, too much compromise can result in an unfocused project or financial failure. Today's developers have arrived at their life's work from fairly diverse starting points, as indicated by the profiles of different developers featured throughout this book. Some people know when they graduate from college or business school that they want to become a developer and immediately begin working for a development company in one capacity or another, learning as much as they can before striking out on their own. For others, their family landholdings prompt them to enter the development business. In other cases, developers get started simply because they have invested in real estate. As their interest in real estate development grows, they start to participate directly in the process.

Some people, including Whit Morrow, just know early in life that they want to develop real estate. The accompanying segment of the Europa Center case study describes Morrow's decision to pursue a career in real estate development and his surprise at the complexity of the process.

⠿ Europa Center

The Developer, Whit Morrow, Speaks For Himself

I want you to hear about real estate development from someone who is up to his eyeballs in alligators right now in the marketplace. You should know how we started, how we got to where we are now, and how we're going to get out of it and make a profit at some point.

I grew up in Albemarle, North Carolina, a small town with about 10,000 people. My grandfather owned one-third of the office buildings in town, so I was vaguely aware of real estate at a young age. When I was older, I had a job making change in the old hardware store building. They had pneumatic tubes that went from the cash registers back to the central office where they kept all the money, and that was where I sat making change. That was the extent of my exposure to business before college, when I was trying to decide what I was going to do. When I headed off to college (Davidson College, 40 miles away, near Charlotte), I didn't even know what an architect was.

At Davidson College, the subject that fascinated me most was the readings we had on utopias—ideal communities. Davidson College had about 1,000 students and sat in the middle of the countryside, the most pristine *Walden II* setting you've ever seen. One of the books I read was *Walden II*, of course, about how B.F. Skinner made the ideal community, designing everything the way it ought to be, with all the people fitting into his community. So I decided during my college days that I wanted to go out there like Alexander the Great and build cities. Or be an industrialist and build Hershey, Pennsylvania. I thought that was the greatest thing you could possibly do.

Coming out of college with my BA degree, I was a little naive, and my advisers said I should go to business school. For me, going to Harvard Business School was like being drafted into the Marines. The first day or two of class when I talked about why I was there and what I wanted to do, they burst my bubble. So you want to go out and build cities, huh? Do you know what a REIT is? Do you know what a second mortgage is? I wasn't exposed to any of those things, even in college. I was totally shocked by all the intricate details that go into building a house or an office building or a street. But I survived Harvard Business School, and after learning the details, I thought I knew a lot more and got a job with the Sea Pines Company, the development company that was responsible for Hilton Head Island.

continued on page 198

Dean Stratouly didn't start out being a developer. He became an engineer because he didn't know what else to do and eventually discovered that he liked to take risks and liked to make big deals. Becoming a real estate developer was a natural fit.

▌▌▌ Museum Towers

The Developer, Dean Stratouly, Speaks For Himself

I was a Navy brat, so while I was born in Boston, I grew up in a whole series of places ranging from Boston to San Diego, Hawaii to Connecticut. All in all, it was a fairly unstable childhood, but being able to deal with such instability is an important characteristic of a developer.

I went to a Catholic boys' school in Connecticut during the time of the Vietnam War. Coming from a family with a military service background, my father wanted me to go either to the Naval Academy—his first choice—or to West Point—which would have been marginally acceptable—or possibly the Air Force Academy. The boys' school administrators thought I should go to a Catholic college, one of the five schools that everybody went to—Notre Dame, Holy Cross, Boston College, Villanova, or Georgetown. But they were all-boys' schools and I wanted to be around blond cheerleaders. So I applied to the University of Southern California as an anthropology major.

My father went berserk. As a compromise, I ended up going to Worcester Polytechnic, which was an engineering school. There was no rhyme or reason for my going there except that I was good at math and science and reasonable at English and it seemed the path of least resistance. The idea was to get a job when I got out. No more. No less.

When I graduated, I went to work in the nuclear power plant business and ended up with the company that had developed Three Mile Island. I was with them until 1980 and made a nice salary selling nuclear power plants.

It was actually very good training for being a developer, because the power plant projects were very large with complicated engineering and construction processes, difficult union issues, and multilayered financing. Everything you did had to be reviewed by various groups, so I had to learn to make presentations. Like real estate development, it had the elements of social controversy, economic risk, and long-term design and planning processes.

After about five or six years when I traveled nonstop, Three Mile Island erupted and the company was bought by another group. There were all sorts of changes occurring and I decided to move on. I was living in Chicago at the time and wanted to move to either the East Coast or the West Coast. I called a friend in San Francisco who was leaving for Tokyo for several weeks, and he offered me his apartment. After that I went to visit a girl in Boston that I was dating, and I ended up marrying her and staying in Boston.

continued on page 98

Public Sector Developer

Public sector developers must be distinguished from private sector developers. Increasingly, the public sector engages in real estate development in pursuit of community housing and economic development goals. A new breed of professional is emerging who could be referred to as a "public entrepreneur."

The term "public entrepreneur" is reserved for those public development professionals who plan, design, and financially structure the large-scale projects of such importance to the community that the government not only shares in their cost but also may assume much of the risk. Unlike private developers, public entrepreneurs are usually salaried employees. For three reasons, their compensation is generally higher than that of other planning professionals. First, they have developed a particular set of technical and analytical skills that are in scarce supply in the public sector. Second, they have the personality to make things happen in the public sector. Third, they are highly valuable to their cities. Properly structured transactions help make projects happen at minimum cost to the city while stimulating additional private investment at less public cost.

Significant public/private ventures are being developed throughout the United States and are not limited to large projects such as the $200 million renovation of Navy Pier in Chicago. The city of Chicago sold the Navy Pier for $10.00 to the Metropolitan Pier and Exposition Authority, an independent municipal corporation, and the state provided a $150 million "Build Illinois" grant for redevelopment, about half of which was spent on upgrading infrastructure and stabilizing the pier. The pier is now the site of a mixed-use project that combines commercial and public uses, entertainment (an IMAX® theater, a children's musuem, parks, and a carousel, among other attractions), recreation, and meeting facilities.

The public sector works with developers in many ways. In Portland, Oregon, the Tri-Metropolitan Transit Organization (Tri-Met) teamed up with the Gresham

Development Company to build Gresham Central—a 90-unit multifamily apartment community adjacent to the Gresham Central MAX light-rail station. Tri-Met donated a 0.58-acre right-of-way to the developer that was turned into a pedestrian promenade connecting the apartments and the MAX station. Tri-Met consolidated and realigned a myriad of utility easements on the parcel, maximizing the buildable area and allowing the developer to increase the residential densities. Tri-Met also arranged for the Portland Development Commission to apply for Congestion Mobility Air Quality funds from the Federal Transit Administration, to be used for constructing the pedestrian promenade and storm sewer system. The project would not have been financially feasible for the developer without Tri-Met's assistance. In return, the developer agreed to orient the project to the MAX station, build at higher than normal suburban densities (33 units per acre), create a design that blended with the surrounding residential community, and reduce the amount of parking. The final product is a thoughtfully designed transit-oriented development with a pedestrian-friendly atmosphere that encourages the use of Tri-Met's transit investments and is consistent with its development goals for the station area.

Architect

Architects are central to the development process from the perspective of aesthetics, physical safety, and political and market risk, yet the role of the architect in a project is not always fully understood or appreciated. The naive view of an architect is someone who simply draws the developer's or his own ideas and then produces a set of specifications used for obtaining construction bids and guiding the construction process. In fact, architects offer a menu of services to developers and, like other players, may work as outside professionals or as in-house, salaried members of the development team (although it is more and more unusual for developers to retain an architect on staff).

With development becoming increasingly complicated in most states, architects are becoming involved in the development process much earlier than in the past. In particular, they can be instrumental in securing planning and zoning approvals, working with community groups to understand their needs and preferences for proposed projects, and performing related site studies. Moreover, it may be that architects have a more favorable public image (whether or not earned) than developers and thus may be effective in dealing with the public and public sector agencies. In addition, architects can help guide a developer in selecting a site for a specified use or develop alternative concepts for a site and head the land use team to bring a concept to fruition.

Beyond assistance in basic planning and community relations, an architectural firm can provide the developer with the following basic services: predesign services (schematics) and final design, design development, preparation of construction contract documents, assistance in the bidding or negotiation process, administration of the agreements between the developer and the builder or contractor, and overall project administration and management services.[2] The schematic design is a diagram that relates the space to the building's functions and is then transformed into at least a preliminary idea of what the building will look like. The final design is a refined rendering of the building's facade as well as a preliminary delineation of at least the major components of the interior space.

During the design development phase, more players are brought in to refine the interior space and structural components. In addition, exact space allocations must be made for the HVAC (heating, ventilation, and air conditioning) system, elevators, interior stairwells, plumbing, column size, and so on. As these refinements are incorporated into the architect's renderings, the building begins to assume its final shape. The schematic phase and the design development phase require many iterations, with the developer heavily involved along the way.

The next phase of the architect's involvement is often assembling the construction package, including the package that is sent to contractors to solicit bids. The package includes the rules for bidding, standard forms for detailing the components of the bid, detailed specifications for identifying all components of the bid, and detailed working drawings. The architect, along with the developer, then usually reviews the bids and selects the best-qualified (or the lowest-cost qualified) contractor for the job.

Architects may continue monitoring the project during construction, but the degree of supervision varies as a result of time constraints (the need to be on site at particular times). Architects are also important in closing the loan as the project moves from construction to permanent financing. They must attest to compliance with plans and specifications and bear legal liability for the plans and specifications for some number of years (the term varies with the state). Architects are licensed under health and safety laws and must pass an examination administered by the National Council of Architectural Registration Boards (NCARB), which has promulgated standards and criteria adopted by licensing boards as their standard for admission to licensing examinations. The registration process takes about eight or nine years—five to six years of study at a university and three years as a paid intern in an architectural or related practice.

An architect can be paid in several ways. Many developers hire architects initially on an hourly basis and continue that way until the project is better defined and the scope of services clear. When the developer and architect establish that they will continue working together, they often negotiate a contract whereby an architect's fee is a percentage of the construction cost. Typically, the fee ranges from 3 percent to 7 percent, although it can be as little as 2 percent and as much as 10 percent. One disadvantage of the fee approach may be that the architect has less incentive to operate cost-efficiently on behalf of the owner. More important, some projects might be complicated to design but easy to build or vice versa. Further, what constitutes construction costs must be carefully delineated.

An architect can also be compensated under the terms of a fixed-price or stipulated-sum contract, which outlines the services expected of the architect. The stipulated sum generally includes the architect's direct personnel expenses, other direct expenses (such as salaries and benefits), other direct expenses chargeable to the project (such as consultant services), indirect expenses or overhead, and profit. If, at the request of the developer, the architect performs any additional duties, he bills the developer for additional compensation. A design/build firm would typically be paid in this way. An architect is (unless otherwise specified) entitled to reimbursement for such expenses as telephone calls, travel, photocopying, and so on. An architectural firm can also be hired for a stipulated sum per unit that is based on the number of square feet or apartment units.

For certain projects, developers should not underestimate the need to make full use of an experienced architect. What works in New York may not work in Dallas, and a good architect understands that. An architect may also increase the functional efficiency of a building. For service providers such as hotels and health care facilities, efficiency is critical, and architects can enhance or undermine the work environment for employees. On the other hand, it may not be cost-efficient or necessary to use a world-class architect to design a duplex on a simple site in a town where the developer has already built 100 similar homes.

The level of community involvement typically associated with any development has increased so much that developers need to stand ready to consider altering their ideas—conceptually and visually—if it means getting something built. In the case of some design features, the developer can compromise with the review board; in the case of other items, compromise may be inappropriate. The architect can help explain and differentiate between design features. A good architect can be a great asset to a developer in the midst of a strenuous approval process. Therefore, it is essential that the developer and the architect feel comfortable working together, that they understand each other's positions and concepts, and that they communicate with each other throughout every step of the development process.

Developers should investigate candidate architects as thoroughly as possible. They should look at finished buildings (not just unbuilt plans), talk to clients of the candidate architects, ask around, and interview prospective architects thoroughly to ascertain their level of understanding of the different services they will provide.

An architect is a key player in the development process and ultimately is responsible for much of the mark a developer leaves on society. A building stands in a city or town for a long time. People walk past it, drive past it, use it, and love it or hate it for years. Many cities are known and distinguished by their architecture, which often provides the charm that draws visitors. Developers have to think about how their buildings fit with what already exists and how people will see and use their buildings ten, 20, 30, or 100 years into the future.

Engineer

Several different kinds of engineers play important roles in the development process. Specifically, engineers are critical to physical safety, and their failure to deliver a safe product can have life-threatening consequences. Structural engineers usually work with the architect, particularly during the initial design phase, to ensure that plans are structurally sound and that mechanical systems will adequately serve the project. Structural engineers can assist in identifying cost-saving measures that simultaneously satisfy structural design and construction requirements. They are also responsible for producing drawings for the construction contractor that explain the structural system in detail, especially connections and the sizing of the structural elements. Mechanical engineers usually design necessary HVAC, plumbing, life safety, and other mechanical systems. Electrical engineers design electrical power and communications systems.

In more complex developments, engineers might also function as construction managers, supplementing the architect in supervising construction. Architects

For the Jin Mao building in Shanghai, China, engineers designed a foundation using a network of 429 213-foot-long below-grade steel piles—the longest ever used for a land-based building—to overcome the clay soil's poor bearing capacity. The 88-story, 1,380-foot mixed-use tower is the fourth tallest in the world. It has its own electrical, telephone, and water and sewage treatment systems.

most often subcontract with engineers with whom they regularly work, and the success of the design phase depends on a good working relationship between the architect and engineers. Typically, as head of the design team, the architect is responsible for managing the engineers. Often, they are included in the architect's budget.

Like architects, engineers bear legal liability for their plans and specifications for some number of years. The duration of liability corresponds to the nature of the undertaking and the time for recognizing defects. Shoddy construction and poor design both can cost dollars and lives, although shoddy construction usually manifests itself sooner than poor design. It is not surprising, then, that engineers are licensed under health and safety laws.

Civil engineers may be contracted with for their expertise in land development, particularly for the design and construction of such infrastructure as streets, and water, sewer, gas, electricity, telephone, cable, and storm drainage systems. They must ensure that all civil systems meet the health, safety, and welfare requirements of the state.

Soils engineers or geotechnical engineers are responsible for determining the soil's bearing capacity, the required depth of footings, various types of loads, the level of the groundwater table, the presence of any toxic materials, and related items. A geotechnical investigation is especially important when development is proposed for a new site. Soils engineers can help transform a site with poor soil into a developable site by advising the construction engineer on the use of fill and soil replacement. Most geotechnical engineers

perform a range of tests, including soil borings, seismic tests, percolation tests, and compaction tests. Engineers are particularly important in assessing whether the past uses of a site have included hazardous materials.

Environmental engineers may also be needed for a proposed development, particularly if an existing structure on the site—whether scheduled for renovation or demolition—contains any asbestos or other hazardous substances.

Engineers should be licensed by the state and should be members of a professional engineering society—for example, the National Society of Professional Engineers (NSPE), the American Society of Mechanical Engineers (ASME), or the American Society of Heating, Refrigerating, and Air-conditioning Engineers (ASHRAE).

Land Planner

For the land development phase of a project and for larger building projects, a land planner is often needed to help develop the master plan, which locates objects and uses on the site according to their physical properties and the uses that will bring the highest value.

A land planner works closely with the developer to determine the suitability of the site for the proposed development and makes alternative recommendations if necessary, working with input from engineers, marketing consultants, architects, and other team members. The land planner works with the developer to emphasize the important elements of the site, from natural features to programmed or marketing themes that the developer wishes to stress. A part of the land

Profile **Barbara Faga**

Chair of the Board, EDAW
Atlanta, Georgia

Barbara Faga is chair of the board for EDAW, an international consultancy firm with 21 offices worldwide offering expertise in a wide range of disciplines, including landscape design, urban design, environmental planning, and site engineering. Based in Atlanta, Faga directly oversees a staff of more than 70 and is responsible for the firm's activities in the Southeast. Her staff was responsible for the design of one of the firm's best-known projects, Centennial Olympic Park in Atlanta. The 21-acre urban park was adapted for festival use during the Olympics and has since become the centerpiece of Atlanta's downtown renaissance.

A native of Michigan, Faga earned her degree in landscape architecture from Michigan State University. Afterward, she studied city planning at Georgia Tech University in Atlanta. Upon leaving school, Faga joined an architectural firm in Atlanta and spent the next nine months working on grading for an airport in Cincinnati, where she quickly realized what she *didn't* want to do. Trying to find what she did want to do, Faga moved through a succession of jobs in several cities, including Chicago, Philadelphia, and Washington, D.C. Faga changed jobs eight times in ten years, an experience of which she says, "I don't recommend it for everyone, but it worked for me." Though tiresome, her experience exposed her to several management styles and piqued her interest in management. Faga was certain she didn't want to work "where slamming doors and yelling were a means of communication."

Her last job before joining EDAW was as an architect for the city of Alexandria, Virginia, an experience Faga says she enjoyed because "working for a city means you get to be the client and the administrator." Still looking for an opportunity to put into practice the management lessons she had learned, she joined EDAW in 1979. Faga was eager to join EDAW because of the scale of projects the firm undertook and because of its reputation.

Ironically, Faga began her career at EDAW drafting grading plans for projects. In 1981, she moved to Atlanta when the firm opened a regional office there and began to be involved in marketing projects for the firm. This particular aspect of the firm appealed to Faga because of the control it engendered: "You could market the types of projects you want to work on." After a succession of jobs, Faga finally arrived at a company whose management style matched her own.

A Firm without Walls

One of the most positive aspects of working for EDAW, according to Faga, is its emphasis on teamwork. With 21 offices and more than 500 employees worldwide, the firm can draw on an international pool of talent to address clients' individual needs. Project teams are assembled based on areas of expertise and interest rather than geographic location. This style of management provides clients with the best resources the company has to offer. It also gives EDAW employees the opportunity to work on the types of projects they're interested in, a practice that "brings better work from people."

The emphasis on pooling talent and on communication between and within offices is one way EDAW has earned the title "a firm without walls." The company's operations are very decentralized, with most decisions made locally. The company has about one principal for every 15 to 20 employees, who is responsible for assembling project teams. Operating in this way requires a great deal of trust and very small egos. Says Faga, "When a project starts, the egos go away. Each person knows what he or she is bringing to the project."

Communication and Learning

Good communication is the cornerstone of good management, says Faga. "Management doesn't work when you don't share everything." At some firms, managers feel a need to keep information to themselves, but, according to Faga, "this only creates a destructive environment. You never want to be the only person to know what's going on." Faga believes that facilitating good communication requires taking time with employees and clients to let them see what is going on. Communication also means listening, which is a trait that Faga believes has helped her in her career. "I want to listen to what people are really saying. I want to read everything, see everything, talk to everyone. By constantly knowing more, you can continually push the envelope and not become stale."

This communication and emphasis on learning extends through all levels of management at EDAW. A management group comprising personnel from each of the company's eight regions meets quarterly to review current issues and project trends. To ensure the broadest participation and exploration of issues, the makeup of the group is periodically changed. It's part of a culture of "continuous learning," resulting in a well-managed business and fresh, innovative

Strategically located between the Georgia World Congress Center/Georgia Dome complex and the downtown district, Centennial Olympic Park now serves as Atlanta's new central open space.

solutions to clients' always changing problems. "We don't want to repeat projects; we want to improve on them. If projects aren't always getting better," says Faga, "then we've missed the mark."

One of the best things EDAW does, according to Faga, is its sponsorship of an annual summer student project. For nearly two decades, EDAW has assembled students from around the world to work together for two weeks on a major project. Personnel from all levels of the company participate in the project, and outside speakers are brought in as well. Faga was the principal in charge of such a project in Miami Beach. The team was responsible for designing a plan for greenways for the city that includes beachfront, industrial, neighborhood, and parkland areas. At the conclusion of the project, the students worked in the various EDAW offices as interns for six weeks. The summer student program is another way that fresh ideas are injected into the planning process, and it serves as a wonderful recruiting tool (several current members of the firm participated in the program).

Global Learning

EDAW's participation in international projects offers another means of continuous learning for Faga. "I've learned a lot from projects in Europe, Australia, and Asia.

Clients there can often have a quite different perspective from American clients," says Faga, particularly in areas such as sustainability.

One such project is Diagonal Mar, a mixed-use project located along the Mediterranean coast in Barcelona, Spain. The project will complete the beachfront regeneration of the city, which began in 1989 with planning for the Summer Olympics in 1992. EDAW worked closely with Robert A.M. Stern Architects and Barcelona architect Enric Miralles on the site design for an 840,000-square-foot (78,000-m^2) retail center, a residential condominium complex, and the primary focus of the development, a 26-acre public park. The park, on a former brownfields site, will feature active and passive recreation, two lakes on different levels with a waterfall cascading between them, fountains, playgrounds, and several landscaped viewing mounds. A network of pathways will traverse the park, including a bridge passing over the waterfall. Sustainability was an important aspect of the project, according to Faga, right down to the details of what plants to use. The park will incorporate native plants to minimize the need for irrigation and pesticides. Half of the shoreline as well as a regional detention pond are to be edged with aquatic vegetation to aid water quality and to serve as a natural habitat for indigenous species. Grasses, plants, and trees known for their ability to withstand salt breezes will be planted near the water, while deciduous and evergreen trees will be planted farther back.

The Future

Faga believes that environmental issues such as sustainability will become an increasingly important component of projects in the United States and abroad. Clients, and particularly the public sector, are becoming more sophisticated and critical about design issues. Faga welcomes these changes. "Clients are very smart. We learn from them. They push us and we push them."

She also sees projects becoming increasingly complex, particularly as more brownfields are rehabilitated and readied for use. Faga believes EDAW is well positioned to meet these challenges, adding, "If there is a great location out there, there will always be a solution to make it work. We just need to listen." ■

planning process is testing the site capacity for the amount and type of uses envisioned by the developer.

The land planner deals with the site's limitations and possibilities. On the one hand, natural, environmental, and legislative limitations define acceptable uses and densities of development on the site. On the other, developers have certain expectations for the creation of a viable development on the site. Balancing the constraints with the potential is key to the challenges the land planner faces.

The master plan prepared by the land planner takes into consideration the potential natural amenities of the site (such as trees, water features, and rolling hills) and the potential constraints (floodplains, wetlands, and steep inclines, for example). The planner is usually responsible for determining traffic patterns and overall circulation, allocating open space, locating on-site uses and amenities, and so on. In bringing together the various issues related to site development, the land planner must also consider the impacts of all land planning decisions on cost and schedule.

Often the land planner works with the developer to create "themes" for the overall site development. An emphasis on creating a special sense of place, often enhanced by the architecture and landscape design, guides the land planner in determining the highest and best use for areas within the site. This vision of the developer and land planner sets the framework for the placement of buildings, infrastructure within the site, site features (such as foundations, special entries, or focal points within the site, landscape amenities, and private and shared public spaces), and other amenities.

Some of the land planner's expertise and contribution to the development can overlap with those of the landscape architect, which are identified below. Land planners are often housed in landscape architecture offices, or landscape architects are found in land planning firms, so it is not always possible to draw a clear line between their responsibilities on the development team.

The main professional society for land planners is the American Planning Association (APA), which has no licensing requirements but offers its members certification through the American Institute of Certified Planners (AICP).

Landscape Architect

Landscape architects bring to a development team a specialized set of skills that were often overlooked but now play a greater role in the planning process. Land-scape architects are responsible both for site planning in the context of the existing environment and for creating a sense of place by enhancing the natural environment to complement the built environment.

In today's development market, most communities and potential buyers or tenants are very concerned with the elements of the landscape that help define the character of "their" development. In seeking to create a distinctive image for their projects, developers often rely on the landscape design as much as they do the architecture to help define the special nature or theme of the project, especially in residential and mixed-use development projects, where the landscape design can help unite and define areas for the various uses.

Landscape architects produce the master plans for all landscaping and hard surfaces. They create the landscape environment through selection and siting of plant materials, landscape forms, and strategic use of light and shade as defined by the designed, yet natural environment. They design roadways, walkways, outdoor lighting, outdoor seating, water features, railings, signs, grates, retaining walls, bus shelters, picnic shelters, outdoor waiting areas, outdoor play areas, and bicycle and walking trails. Landscape design can often be used to create a sense of place, allowing tenants and residents to feel a sense of privacy within small site areas, and landscape forms can be used to soften the overall development. Architecture can create boundaries necessary to define different use areas within a tightly packed site, and landscape design can humanize those boundaries, maintaining them but making them softer and more in scale with the people who use the site. Landscape architects work with developers to create not just specific development sites but also transitions between adjacent land uses. Moreover, the demands on a site's appearance have never been greater.[3] Developers are spending more money than ever on the living environment surrounding their static products. In recent years, the quality of our environment has become a major concern, and, as a result, people are more aware of the quality of their "natural" surroundings.

Above all, it is important to realize that landscape architects help create places that capture the imagination of the public. Examples include New York City's Central Park, immediately recognizable by its bridges and landscape, or entire communities such as Straw Hill in Manchester, New Hampshire, whose charming rural New England character is achieved in large part through its plantings, open space, and overall site design.

Landscape architects develop entire greenways and park systems that help define and humanize large urban areas, such as Olmsted's "Emerald Necklace" in and around Boston (see the Museum Towers case study for more discussion about the parkland that the developer donated to the city).

Landscape architects can also provide consulting services for wastewater management, wetlands mitigation, the preservation of wildlife habitats, ecosystem management, xeriscaping and irrigation, sustainable site design, and land reclamation. In addition, landscape architects can contribute to a development's bottom line by extrapolating site amenities from what could be environmental problem areas. As the general public becomes more concerned with sustainable environments, the landscape architect is called upon to implement plans that use local vegetation and require less maintenance, irrigation, and control. Some enlightened developers and their clients understand that a "wilder" landscape can also provide a haven for beneficial birds and insects, and the landscape architect is therefore challenged to develop plans that accommodate the architecture of the planned project and are sustainable and sustaining. Sustainable site design helps ensure the long-term health of a project by keeping down the cost of landscape maintenance and making it financially feasible for owners or managers to maintain landscape features in good condition. Potential users will be turned off by dead or dying plants.

Increasingly, landscape architects are drawn into the environmental debate as developers face more stringent environmental rules and stronger public opposition to development. Accordingly, developers must rely on the expertise of land stewards to help them manage the delicate environment—both natural and political.

The American Society of Landscape Architects (ASLA) is a national professional society representing the landscape architecture profession in the United States. Forty-five states license landscape architects.

Contractors

Contractors are builders and managers of builders who turn ideas on paper into enduring physical forms: houses, apartment buildings, warehouses, stores, offices, public buildings. Our highly specialized society often takes for granted constructed space and its providers, yet without builders, each of us would face a simple choice: build our shelter ourselves or do without.

A general contractor (GC) typically executes a contract with the developer to build the project according to the plans and specifications developed by the architect and engineer (or sometimes according to the plans drawn up by the would-be homeowner who orders a

Trovare, a 168-unit condominium complex in Newport Coast, California, uses clusters of Italian cypress, unmanicured lawns, and untrimmed trees to give a more natural appearance and provide the atmosphere of a Mediterranean community.

house built) for a fixed price within a set time frame. General contractors then divide the contract among different subcontractors to perform different tasks: excavation, pouring and finishing concrete, rough carpentry, installation of mechanical, electrical, and plumbing systems, finish carpentry, and so on. General contractors schedule subcontractors' work and monitor quality to ensure that subcontractors' performance satisfies the general contractor's obligations to the developer. Typically, the GC's contract is executed with the developer, and subcontractors' contracts are executed with the general contractor, who pays the subcontractors as their work is completed. Many variations of these contractual arrangements are possible and appropriate in certain situations.

General contractors are often chosen through a selective bidding process in which the developer asks a number of contracting firms to submit proposals or general statements of qualifications that include descriptions of past projects, references from clients and lenders, résumés of key employees, and, possibly, verification that the company is bondable.

In the open bidding process, a developer sends out a notice requesting bids and statements of qualifications. Because the bidding process is very time consuming for contractors, many are reluctant to participate in open bids unless they think they have a good chance of being selected; thus, this process does not always attract an adequate number of responses.

Besides the obvious motivation of money, both general contractors and subcontractors work for a variety of nonpecuniary reasons: to gain experience, to enhance their reputations, to be their own boss, and to perform physical work they enjoy. The contractor submitting the lowest bid is not always the best choice; the best player for the development team may have other critical attributes, such as the necessary experience or unqualified reliability. The lower carrying costs implied in a shorter construction period can compensate for a higher construction bid. In some cases, developers experienced in building serve as their own general contractors and enter directly into contracts with subcontractors.

Many developers of large-scale projects hire a different kind of contractor—a construction manager (CM). A CM is brought into the development process early to perform a variety of services, both before and during construction. During the design phase, CMs advise the developer and the design team on cost-effective ways to execute the various elements of the design. The developer's agreement with a CM may be for preconstruction consulting only, or it might extend into the construction period. In the latter case, the CM is obligated to complete a project by a certain date and for a guaranteed maximum price. The CM retains all the subcontractors and assumes the risk associated with cost overruns and delays.

Associated Builders and Contractors (ABC) and Associated General Contractors (AGC) are just two of several trade associations for contractors.

Environmental Consultant

Environmental consultants perform environmental site reviews that in some states are critical considerations in a developer's decision to build. As environmental regulations grow more complex, developers need help in navigating the regulatory maze and deciding whether a site's environmental issues are too complicated and costly to make land purchase or development worthwhile.

If, for example, a developer thinks a site might contain wetlands, he can engage an environmental consultant to perform an assessment, delineate any wetlands, and confirm the jurisdiction (federal or state) under which the wetlands are regulated. Similarly, an environmental site review can determine the presence of hazardous materials and indicate the cost and feasibility of removal. An environmental review may even extend to testing for toxic wastes or, if that is not possible, to researching previous uses to determine the likely presence of toxic materials.

Environmental consultants can help developers identify the regulatory approvals needed for a proposed project or the types of permits required as a condition of approval. In addition, environmental consultants can help ascertain whether a developer can expect to get approvals for a proposed project that is expected to adversely affect the environment or, if approvals can be obtained, whether the project will make the developer liable for significant future litigation. Environmental consultants can also prepare environmental impact statements (EISs) or reports (EIRs) often required by zoning. They can provide advice on stormwater management, wildlife management, urban forestry, solid waste disposal—in short, all the environmental matters that communities increasingly regulate.

Transportation Consultant

As with environmental consultants, the role of transportation consultants is expanding. Few issues generate as much controversy during the approval process as traffic and transportation. Transportation consultants can provide needed expertise and assess important issues, such as how many cars and trucks will enter and leave the site at various times of the day, what the capacity is of existing roads, highways, and intersections, and how the existing streets will accommodate new levels of traffic. Moreover, strict enforcement of the Clean Air Act and provisions for reducing travel by employees have increased the need for greater compliance by employers and made additional demands on transportation consultants. The federal Clean Air Act Amendments of 1990 instituted traffic control measures as a strategy for reducing air pollution emissions from cars, trucks, and buses, and the federal government has been much more assertive in enforcing pollution control measures. Communities have adopted such traffic control measures as high-occupancy vehicle (HOV) lanes, ride-sharing programs, expanded public transportation programs, and expanded pedestrian and bicycle facilities. The federal government withheld billions of dollars of federal transportation aid from the city of Atlanta in 1998 because of chronic air pollution. In response, the governor of Georgia created the Georgia Regional Transportation Authority, which has broad powers to approve or veto most road and other transportation projects, as well as to build and operate mass-transit systems in 13 metropolitan counties that are at odds with federal air pollution standards. It also will have a say over large developments, such as shopping centers or large subdivisions, that could affect traffic and water and air quality beyond city or county borders. Thus, developers will need to work with transportation consultants to assess potential problems and levels of traffic.

Transportation consultants have wide experience in several specialties, including parking, traffic, and other transportation-related issues, and developers often call upon them to put together plans to meet the requirements of local jurisdictions. For example, if a jurisdiction has set a cap on the number of parking spaces that can be built for a development, a transportation consultant can help the developer establish certain programs to accommodate office tenants, which include a ride-sharing program, parking incentives for car pools, fare incentives for mass transit, and shuttle bus service between the project and transit facilities.

Most cities require traffic impact studies for developments over a certain size (most often those that are expected to generate at least 100 peak-hour peak-direction trips). Communities now actively assess whether or not the potential increase in traffic is worth the jobs that may be created. Transportation consultants can conduct traffic impact studies to investigate such issues. In addition, they can explain the impact of proposed government exactions and possibly find better ways to satisfy public objectives.

Parking consultants provide an array of parking-related services, from planning circulation for parking garages to designing access to developing shared parking plans for mixed-use projects. (Shared parking is the use of parking spaces to serve two or more individual land uses without conflict or encroachment.) With parking often an expensive part of a development project, parking consultants can help evaluate the cost-effectiveness of surface parking versus a parking structure. They can also assess the location of ingress and egress points as well as the cost of parking. For tenants, few issues are as important as how much parking is available and how close it is to the building. A parking consultant may be a transportation consultant with expertise in parking or a specialist who deals with no other transportation issues.

In choosing any kind of transportation consultant, developers must first be careful to clearly define the project and then select a consultant with knowledge of the required specialty. A transportation consultant could be paid according to several arrangements: a lump-sum fee, costs plus a fixed fee, salary costs times a multiplier, time and materials, or a percentage of construction costs.

Appraiser

Appraisers can be part of every stage of the development process—before, during, and after project completion. Appraisers are, of course, primarily responsible for valuation of a project. That is, they estimate the market value of property and typically prepare a formal document called an appraisal. Appraisals may be necessary when a developer transfers ownership, seeks financing and credit, resolves tax matters, and establishes just compensation in condemnation proceedings.

Appraisers can also evaluate a project as input to market studies, marketability studies, and feasibility studies. For example, before a development is initiated, appraisers can analyze the market for a particular project type and help a developer assess a potential project's marketability. Appraisers can also provide counseling, which covers a broad range of services from investment analysis to testifying in lawsuits.

As with any professional who works with a developer, the appraiser must be selected with extreme care. The savings and loan debacle of the 1980s was blamed in part on appraisers' inflated valuation of properties. Since then, federal law has mandated that appraisers working on projects for federally insured institutions be licensed or certified by the state, thereby ensuring tighter state control over appraisers.

The Appraisal Qualifications Board of the Appraisal Foundation has established four recommended levels of education and experience for appraisers: 1) *licensed real property appraisers* can value complex residential projects (of one to four units) worth less than $250,000 and noncomplex residential projects (of one to four units) with a transaction value of less than $1 million; 2) *certified residential real property appraisers* can value any residental project of one to four units without regard to value or complexity; 3) *certified general appraisers* can value any residential or commercial property of any size; and 4) *appraiser trainees* must work under the direct supervision of a licensed or certified appraiser. The required levels of education and experience vary accordingly.

The national Appraisal Institute also awards several designations: 1) MAI—experienced in valuation and evaluation of all types of property and permitted to advise clients on real estate investment decisions; 2) SRPA—experienced in the valuation of all types of property; 3) SREA—experienced in real estate valuation and analysis and permitted to advise clients on investment decisions; and 4) SRA and RM—residential appraisal.

Attorneys and Accountants

Because of complex legal interactions between buyers and sellers, lenders and borrowers, contractors and subcontractors, and users, lawyers and accountants are important players in the development process. In addition, attorneys sometimes serve as the developer's chief liaison with regulators. Zoning attorneys who know a particular zoning jurisdiction very well can take the lead in obtaining approvals for the project.

The great development lawyer is usually not the great litigator. Given the intense time pressure of the development process, the great development attorney is the one who anticipates problems and then structures legal documentation to minimize the necessity of resolving differences in court.

The great development accountant now comes in two forms. The developer still needs to have bills paid accurately, and, as we will see in stage six, paying construction invoices is not a simple task. Further, new investment participants in the process have extensive reporting requirements. Real estate investment trusts must please the Securities and Exchange Commission (SEC), while pension funds must report "unrelated business income tax" as required by the Department of Labor. The growing complexity of such rules increases the need for a group of skilled accountants and lawyers.

Real Estate Brokers/ Leasing Agents

Real estate brokers and leasing agents are hired to act in the name of the developer in leasing and selling space to prospective tenants or buyers. Their function, particularly in leasing large industrial and commercial spaces, is to carry out one of the most complex financial negotiations in the development process. Leasing agents must balance all the various users' individual needs against the developer's financial model. Clearly, leasing requires more than quoting a number of square feet at a price per square foot. Leasing involves setting the long-term price per square foot

and specifying who bears the various operating costs. In the process, it requires delineation of the user's special needs, such as extra electrical, heating, ventilation, or air-conditioning capacity.

Brokers and leasing agents are the key implementers of the marketing plan. They canvass prospects; show the product's features, functions, and benefits; negotiate the transaction; and provide the critical feedback to the developer for use in modifying the project. Developers must decide early in the development process whether leasing is to be carried out by in-house staff or outside professionals. They must find the right agent for the job and structure the agent's compensation to align the agent's motivations with the developer's objectives.

Financial Players

Joint Venture Partners

Any individual or institution that provides the developer with equity funding during the development period in return for a share of development profits can be called a joint venture partner. (The term "joint venture partner" is not a precise legal term.) The joint venture partner's equity contribution often bridges a portion of the gap between the project's cost and the debt financing available for construction. The remainder of the gap, if any, must be filled by the developer's equity.

Joint venture partners attempt to achieve the maximum possible share of returns from development based on the minimum possible financial exposure. The joint venture partner "helps" the developer provide the equity needed to cover the difference between cost and debt financing. The risk to joint venture partners is a function of the size of their contribution in the case of no personal liability or of the size of their contribution plus the amount of debt in the case of personal liability. In either case, partners are usually concerned with the size of their obligations (especially if the project fails) as well as the developer's talent and financial strength, which reduce project risk.

Construction Lenders

Construction lenders (frequently commercial banks) are responsible for financing during project construction and for seeing that the developer completes the project within budget and according to plans and specifications. Construction lenders' primary concern is not the project's long-term economic viability so long as a permanent loan commitment (the takeout commit-

A cohousing community is a small-scale neighborhood that seeks to balance residents' desire for personal privacy with their desire to live in a tightly knit community. The residents of Nyland —a 42-unit cohousing community in Lafayette, Colorado—were very active in the development process and helped design, plan, and manage the project with the guidance of an experienced developer.

ment) is secured. With such a commitment in hand, construction lenders are assured of repayment when the project is completed, assuming the work has been performed according to plan. Under the terms of the construction loan, construction lenders generally certify the degree of completion before each payment or draw, i.e., amounts the developer "draws" from the loan commitment to pay periodic project expenses.

Construction lenders face the risk that construction costs will exceed the amount of the construction loan that they have agreed to provide, requiring the developer to cover the difference. If the developer is unable or unwilling to cover the difference, construction lenders usually have the option of foreclosing on the property or extending the size of the construction loan beyond the size of the takeout. Such an extension creates the possibility of a long-term loan position, something banks try to avoid as their sources of funds are primarily short term in nature. Construction lenders weigh the risk of these undesirable outcomes against the expected return (in interest and loan origination fees) to be earned by lending the funds.

Permanent Lenders

Like construction lenders, permanent lenders seek to originate safe loans generating the maximum possible return. Because permanent lenders, unlike construction lenders, have no takeout commitment, the market value of the completed project is much more critical in that it serves as the primary collateral for the loan.

The project's value is a function of the expected cash flow, investors' required rates of return, and the project's expected economic life.

In addition to charging interest on the permanent loan, long-term lenders may receive a form of "contingent" interest. Sometimes referred to as "income" or "equity" kickers, contingent interest allows the lender to participate in the project's overall success. Income kickers, for example, may stipulate that the lender will receive a portion of gross income above some minimum, perhaps 15 percent of gross rent in excess of the first year's estimated gross rental receipts. In the case of equity kickers, the lender may also participate in a portion of the capital gains received upon sale of the project.

Like other players on the development team, lenders may also have nonpecuniary motives for participating in a project. Some lenders have an interest in serving particular social needs (for example, the development of low-income housing), while others are more attracted to innovative design and construction. Almost everyone enjoys an affiliation with a winner, and lenders are no exception. Successful developers bring to their team a lender whose nonpecuniary interests and preferences for risk and return fit the proposed development.

Long-Term Equity Investors

Long-term equity investors may or may not be involved during the construction period. They might either contract to purchase the completed property before construction begins (basing the price on pre-construction estimates of value) or invest after the project is completed. In the first case, the contract is usually signed before the point of commitment—the time immediately preceding the beginning of construction. Whatever the time of sale, the price is often not payable until completion; therefore, the funds are not available to the developer. A purchase commitment before construction may, however, substitute for or supplement the permanent loan commitment as a takeout for the construction lender.

Long-term equity investors are often passive investors during the development period and do not share development risks. On completion of the project, investors want the maximum possible operating returns (sometimes guaranteed by the developer for an initial period of one or more years) for the least possible price. These returns normally are lower than those accruing to investors who participated during the development period, because the latter assume more risk; that is, they bear the uncertainties of construction (and, possibly, of leasing).

Although early commitments for equity have become more difficult to obtain (because of changes in tax laws), developers' incentive for preselling long-term equity interests remains intact. The sale enables developers to avoid or minimize the market risks associated with changing estimates of value during the development period.

Property Manager

Property managers are typically thought to be needed when the development is close to opening and then during the project's life as an active facility. Smart developers recruit property managers for participation during the design stage, particularly if they are building a management-intensive project such as a hotel, housing project for seniors, or health care facility. The ongoing success of these projects depends largely on how well they are managed, and poor design may impede good management.

One of the biggest decisions regarding property management is whether to provide in-house management services or to contract with an outside property management firm. This decision is often based on several factors, such as the location of the project, the size of the development firm, the availability of trained in-house personnel, and the desire of the developer to be involved in the project's day-to-day operation. Compensation is typically a percentage of effective gross revenue receipts—often 3 to 5 percent—but can

also be a fixed amount. Commissions for leasing are usually separate from the management agreement.

Market Researcher

A major part of the upfront work that affects the go/no go development decision is a market study. Market researchers can tell a developer whether or not sufficient demand exists for the proposed project, who the competition is, whom the product might appeal to, how quickly it will lease or sell, and so on. In general, the developer uses the market researcher's work to determine the revenue assumptions for the economic analysis of the proposed project. (See Chapters 17 and 18 for a more extensive look at market studies.)

A market consultant's fee is usually determined by the scope of the work. The consultant who prepares an extensive market report is most often compensated on a lump-sum basis as determined by a contract. If a quick, preliminary report is required, the developer may pay the consultant on an hourly basis.

Marketing and Public Relations Consultant

Without the right kind of project promotion, even the best project can flounder. Accordingly, the development team often needs marketing and public relations personnel to help design a marketing strategy for the product.

Marketing and public relations may begin long before ground is broken and continue through the building of the project and after project completion. Many times buildings cannot be started until they are 50 to 75 percent preleased or presold. An appropriate marketing strategy will help a broker make that happen. Good public relations in the form of news releases, newsletters, neighborhood parties, and mailings can generate positive attitudes toward a project before it is even started or can help defuse opposition.

Once developers know what they want from the public relations firm, they should generate a short list of candidate firms based on referrals or colleagues' recommendations. The market consultant should be familiar with the local market and the type of project the developer proposes. Prospective firms are probably listed in local business journals. In addition, the firm's principals and employees may be members of the Public Relations Society of America and the American Marketing Association.

Payment can take the form of a fixed fee or an hourly rate for a short-term project. For large projects, however, many developers find it useful to establish a long-term relationship with a firm by keeping the firm on retainer and relying on the firm to provide marketing and media relations during all phases of the project.

Regulators

Public regulation of the development process should theoretically produce a fair and efficient system for allocating land uses and spur high-quality development. Developers must comply with local zoning requirements and subdivision regulations and must often obtain approvals locally for site plans and special use permits—all before development can begin. Once a project is underway, another host of regulations and regulators come into play to ensure safe construction in the name of public welfare. Additional regulators abound at the regional, state, and national levels. Their functions range from environmental and consumer protection to oversight of financial intermediaries, mortgage instruments, and lending practices.

In practice, the various rules and regulations often conflict. Rather than producing more harmonious, well-designed projects, such policies sometimes generate mundane projects that manage to meet all codes and other regulations but lack inspiration. (See Chapter 13 for more detailed information on the public sector as regulator.)

If society's needs are to be met through the private sector's development process, rule makers and regulators must learn how to protect the public interest without erecting roadblocks to well-designed, creative projects that respond to market needs. The development process has become so complex and costly that the only way to enhance the quality of the finished product is for the developer to view and treat the public sector as an active participant on the development team.

Final Users

A description of participants in the development process would be incomplete without mentioning the final users of the space: the direct consumers of the finished product. Developers anticipate users' needs when articulating the original project concept. The market study further elaborates on the idea and guides developers in developing products that fit their intended market(s). Ultimately, the final users determine the success of the project by accepting or rejecting the finished product as it is delivered to the marketplace.

Users often contract for space before construction begins (preleasing). By working with the developer's marketing representative, final users may interact with the developer's financial and construction representatives during construction of the project. In this way, they can make sure that the finished product meets their needs and, in so doing, become active participants in the development process.

Evolutionary Changes in the Development Process

Developers are ultimately the responsible parties when it comes to managing the creation of our built environment. They tend to be driven, innovative people who work with an extensive team of professionals to complete a complex and dynamic process. This process is best described by the eight-stage model laid out in Chapter 1. The model shows the time-honored relationships that continue to be fundamental in real estate decision making today. This process, along with an understanding of the history, current situation, and projected trends in demographics and land use, makes up the essential framework needed to consider 1) whether or not a development is feasible, 2) how best to create a development, and 3) how to manage the job.

The evolutionary changes that are occurring require adjustments and additions to the basic eight-stage model.

Availability of Data

Good developers have always relied on a great deal of background information gleaned over a lifetime of conversation, observation, and reading—newsletters, newspapers, academic journals, and the like. Data are fundamental to sophisticated players in the marketplace and will not make money for a developer. Assimilation of such historical and current public information, however, can help developers avoid large losses.

Throughout the discussion of the eight-stage model, we will refer to a host of traditional information sources. What is new is the extent and delivery capacity of the information available today. Technology now allows vast databases to be easily accessible to the development community via the Internet. As we flesh out the eight-stage model in the remaining chapters, we will refer to companies such as Regional Financial Associates (RFA) and its "data buffet," which allows real-time access to historic, current, and projected demographic data for MSAs and counties; the SNL securities firm that provides real-time information on the financial condition of publicly traded real estate companies; and Co-Star, which provides a sophisticated online commercial property equivalent of a residential multiple listing service where brokers, investors, or owners can know not just which buildings have a vacancy, but also the exact vacancy in every building in an area as large as New York City, with all asking rent terms and pictures of both the interior and exterior space.

We have truly seen a revolution in the availability of information. As quarterback for the process, the developer needs to use this information in establishing and refining the idea for development.

Global Influence

The world has been shrinking for some time. Business schools went from teaching international finance to a global perspective on all functional disciplines years ago. Real estate has always had international investors, and some of them, such as the Japanese in the late 1980s, had a tremendous impact on pricing of certain property types.

The difference today is the extent of the globalization of not just real estate finance, but also real estate marketing. Investors now move in and out of U.S. real estate with great rapidity. The Japanese invested in the late 1980s and began selling out in the middle 1990s. The ethnic Chinese were major investors in the early 1990s but disinvested with the "Asian flu" that passed through the Pacific Rim in the late 1990s.

In addition to more countries moving more rapidly through the real estate finance arena, we also see more international mergers and thus more demand for different types of space coming from outside the United States. When Daimler Benz acquired Chrysler, a cultural change occurred that will affect the kind of space as well as the amount of space needed. Certainly U.S. cities like Miami have reflected a distinctive cultural background for some time. We believe that smaller cities will also be subject to global influences and experience significant shifts in demand.

A Much Longer Venture Capital Period

As we move through detailed discussions of stages one, two, and three of the development process, we will review the traditional financing cycle, which moves from land acquisition financing to land development financing to construction financing to permanent financing. This sequence still holds, but the time required to move from the early stages to the closing of the construction financing has lengthened. Why? Because building sites are more complex in infill locations, negotiations are more difficult with ever more participants in the development process, and a host of other reasons. Why does it matter? Because the cost of funds is considerably higher in the early stages of the development process. A lender lending money for hard construction has relatively high-quality collateral. A lender or investor putting up the capital necessary for planning and political work over a period of many years before construction can start does not have good collateral. In fact, this kind of financing is much like the financing that a venture capital company would extend to a new small business. If the business fails, there's not much to liquidate and sell. The longer time period before construction means a longer venture capital period and thus a longer need for expensive financing. This issue significantly affects how relationships among the development team are structured throughout the first five stages of the development process.

A More Important "Level Two" Perspective

James Graaskamp's definition of a project's feasibility, written in the early 1970s, is still the best definition available: "A real estate project is 'feasible' when the real estate analyst determines that there is a reasonable likelihood of satisfying explicit objectives when a selected course of action is tested for fit to a context of specific constraints and limited resources."[4] It has always been important to understand not just the feasibility of the project, but also the feasibility of participating in the project for all members of the development team, particularly the developer himself.

What changes with the increasing complexity of the process and the longer venture capital period is the importance of focusing on feasibility for the individual members of the team ("level two"). Because timing of the project has been extended, everyone has to worry about personally going broke before the project is successful. As we will see throughout the text, it is the developer's responsibility to consider the viability of the venture, not just of the project itself, but also for each member of the development team.

Wall Street (and Related Avenues)

During the 1990s, securitization became much more important in real estate investment. As will be explained in Part II, very few publicly traded real estate companies existed before 1990. In fact, the market value of all REITs was less than $10 billion. As of 1998, more than $500 billion of securitized real estate (combining all the publicly traded equity and the new publicly traded debt) existed. Alternatively stated, from 10 to 15 percent of the aggregate value of all commercial real estate in the United States has now been securitized.

This change has two immediate impacts on the development environment. First, it creates a new level of reporting and thus greater availability of information. The SEC requires public companies to report their financial status, and Wall Street analysts provide considerable commentary on these public companies. More important, the investment banker mentality has hit real estate development. Morgan Stanley, Goldman Sachs, Merrill Lynch, and all the top investors now are involved in real estate investment and, more particularly for our purposes, in investment in real estate during the development process. Wall Street moves to a different beat from commercial banks, insurance companies, and wealthy families that have traditionally dominated the development process. Today's developer must contend with a faster and often harder world.

Increased Pressure for the Public Sector

A primary theme of this text is that the public sector is always a partner in the development process. As covered in Part III, the evolution of community planning, environmental safeguards, hazardous waste cleanup, and so on has produced a more complex environment in which the public sector has ever greater influence.

Today capitalism is almost a religion. Part of this new fervor involves a demand for less government and more efficient government, creating a relatively unstable environment for the public partner. Government at all levels is under tremendous pressure to perform better and often with fewer resources, and must deal more rapidly with a more complex environment. Your public sector partner was always unstable and is now insecure as well—not particularly good for real estate development, as will be seen in subsequent chapters.

A New Set of Risks and Management Challenges

Real estate development has always had a significant operating dimension. Good development always involved provision for operating the completed structure. As one moves from consideration of warehouse development to hotel development, the importance of operations increases dramatically.

Now, all types of development incur new sets of demands from tenants for more functional space. The new global order, the new competition that has come with the global ascent of capitalism, and the new information technology have tenants demanding more and more. It always took a great deal of effort to run a regional mall, but today the larger mall companies, such as the Simon Property Group, go so far as to establish national marketing tie-ins (Pepsi is the cola of choice at Simon malls). They also tie retail developments very closely with entertainment and the management of state-of-the-art arcades, movie theaters, and athletic enterprises—all of which means that developers must be closer and closer to the specialized operations of a particular set of prospective tenants. As we will see, it can be quite dangerous to build truly unique space. If the tenant leaves, the next highest and best use may be at a considerably lower rent. Nevertheless, failure to provide what the tenant needs dooms a development from the start.

Summary

This chapter has briefly described some of the players in the development process and some changes they face. Given that each development has different characteristics, developers must choose their consultants and coworkers with full knowledge of what is required for a proposed development. The importance of engaging reliable consultants cannot be overstated. With so many aspects of a project, the developer alone cannot attend to all details and therefore must be able to trust participants on the development team.

Partners should be chosen with a clear appreciation of both the time-honored fundamentals described in Chapter 1 and the evolutionary changes described in this chapter.

With the foundation established in this section, we will next review the financial logic supporting development decision making in Part II and then recount a detailed history of development in the United States in Part III. After these two parts expand the foundation, we will begin to cover each stage of the development process in detail.

Terms

- Appraiser
- Bearing capacity
- Development fee
- Ecosystem management

- Environmental consultant
- Environmental engineer
- General contractor
- Geotechnical engineer
- HVAC system
- Liability
- Structural engineer
- Subcontractor
- Sustainable site design
- Traffic impact study
- Transportation consultant
- Valuation
- Xeriscaping

Review Questions

3.1 What are the most common forms of compensation for developers?

3.2 What are some of the ways in which a public sector developer operates?

3.3 Describe the architect's role in the development process.

3.4 Why are contractors critical to a developer?

3.5 Describe the expanded role of a landscape architect.

3.6 Why do developers need environmental and transportation consultants more often now than 20 years ago?

3.7 Why are appraisers involved before, during, and at project completion?

3.8 Describe the various types of financial players and when they are involved in the development process.

3.9 Do you agree with the authors' evolutionary changes to the development process? Do you think other societal changes affect how developers get their projects completed?

Notes

1. It is certainly possible for investing lenders and/or city officials to err in underwriting and thus find themselves in the role of primary risk bearers, but that is not usually their intent in traditional situations. In more complex developments, risks may be shared in many creative ways, as shown in later chapters.

2. American Institute of Architects, *You and Your Architect* (Washington, D.C.: Author, 1995).

3. See Lloyd W. Bookout et al., *Value by Design: Landscape, Site Planning, and Amenities* (Washington, D.C.: ULI–the Urban Land Institute, 1994), for more information.

4. James A. Graaskamp, "A Rational Approach to Feasibility Analysis," *Appraisal Journal,* October 1972, p. 515. The late James Graaskamp, former chair and professor, Department of Real Estate and Urban Land Economics at the University of Wisconsin–Madison, was a noted author, teacher, and mentor. See Chapter 16 and the profile of Graaskamp in Chapter 21.

Part I
Bibliography

Basic Real Estate and Planning Books

Adler, Jerry. *High Rise*. New York: Harper Collins, 1993.

Alenick, Jerome, ed. *Real Estate Development Manual*. Boston: Warren, Gorham & Lamont, 1990.

American Institute of Architects. *You and Your Architect*. Washington, D.C.: Author, 1995.

Bacow, Lawrence S., and Sean A. Burns. *Foreign Investments in U.S. Real Estate: Status, Trends, and Outlook, 1988*. Chicago: National Association of Realtors® and MIT Center for Real Estate Development, 1988.

Barnett, Jonathan. *An Introduction to Urban Design*. New York: Harper & Row, 1982.

Beatley, Timothy, and Kristy Manning. *The Ecology of Place: Planning for Environment, Economy, and Community*. Washington, D.C.: Island Press, 1997.

Beyard, Michael D., and W. Paul O'Mara. *Shopping Center Development Handbook*. 3d ed. Washington, D.C.: ULI–the Urban Land Institute, 1999.

Beyard, Michael D., et al. *Developing Urban Entertainment Centers*. Washington, D.C.: ULI–the Urban Land Institute, 1998.

Bjork, Gordon C. *Life, Liberty, and Property*. Lexington, Mass.: Lexington Books, 1980.

Bookout, Lloyd W., Jr., et al. *Residential Development Handbook*. 2d ed. Washington, D.C.: ULI–the Urban Land Institute, 1990.

——. *Value by Design: Landscape, Site Planning, and Amenities*. Washington, D.C.: ULI–the Urban Land Institute, 1994.

Catanese, Anthony, and James C. Snyder. *Urban Planning*. 2d ed. New York: McGraw-Hill, 1988.

Colley, Barbara C. *Practical Manual of Land Development*. 3d ed. New York: McGraw-Hill, 1999.

Corgel, John B., and Halbert C. Smith. *Real Estate Perspectives: An Introduction to Real Estate*. 2d ed. Homewood, Ill.: Irwin, 1991.

Cullingworth, J.B. *Planning in the USA: Policies, Issues, and Processes*. New York: Routledge, 1997.

Dasso, Jerome, James D. Shilling, and Alfred A. Ring. *Real Estate Principles and Practices*. 12th ed. Englewood Cliffs, N.J.: Prentice-Hall, 1995.

De Chiara, Joseph, and Lee E. Koppelman. *Time-Saver Standards for Site Planning*. New York: McGraw-Hill, 1984.

DeGrove, John M. *The New Frontier for Land Policy: Planning and Growth Management in the States*. Cambridge, Mass.: Lincoln Institute of Land Policy, 1992.

de Neufville, Judith I., ed. *The Land Use Policy Debate in the United States*. New York: Plenum Press, 1981.

Downs, Anthony. *New Visions for Metropolitan America*. Washington, D.C.: Brookings Institution, 1994.

Ewing, Reid. *Best Development Practices: Doing the Right Thing and Making Money at the Same Time*. Chicago: American Planning Association, 1996.

Frantz, Douglas. *From the Ground Up: The Business of Building in the Age of Money*. Berkeley: Univ. of California Press, 1993.

Friedman, Jack P., and Jack C. Harris. *Dictionary of Real Estate Terms*. 4th ed. Hauppauge, N.Y.: Barron's Educational Series, 1997.

Gause, Jo Allen, et al. *Industrial Property Development Handbook.* 2d ed. Washington, D.C.: ULI–the Urban Land Institute, forthcoming 2000.

———. *Office Development Handbook.* 2d ed. Washington, D.C.: ULI–the Urban Land Institute, 1998.

Geschwender, Arlyne. *Real Estate Principles and Practices.* 6th ed. Upper Saddle River, N.J.: Gorsuch/Prentice-Hall, 1999.

Gordon, Paul A. *Seniors' Housing and Care Facilities: Development, Business, and Operations.* Vol. 1 & 2. 3d ed. Washington, D.C.: ULI–the Urban Land Institute, 1998.

Graaskamp, James A. *Fundamentals of Real Estate Development.* Washington, D.C.: ULI–the Urban Land Institute, 1981.

Greer, Gaylon E., and Michael D. Farrell. *Contemporary Real Estate: Theory and Practice.* Chicago: Dryden Press, 1983.

Harwood, Bruce, and Charles J. Jacobus. *Real Estate: An Introduction to the Profession.* 6th ed. Englewood Cliffs, N.J.: Prentice-Hall, 1992.

Healey, Patsey, and Rupert Nabarro. *Land and Property Development in a Changing Context.* Brookfield, Vt.: Ashgate Publishing Co., 1990.

Hecht, Bennett L. *A Guide to Real Estate Development for Nonprofit Organizations.* New York: Wiley, 1994.

Heilbrun, James. *Urban Economics and Public Policy.* 3d ed. New York: St. Martin's Press, 1987.

Jacobus, Charles J., and Bruce Harwood. *Real Estate Principles.* 8th ed. Upper Saddle River, N.J.: Gorsuch/Prentice-Hall, 1999.

———. *Real Estate Law.* 2d ed. Upper Saddle River, N.J.: Gorsuch/Prentice-Hall, 1997.

Jarchow, Stephen P., ed. *Graaskamp on Real Estate.* Washington, D.C.: ULI–the Urban Land Institute, 1991.

Jeer, Sanjay. *Online Resources for Planners.* Washington, D.C.: American Planning Association, 1997.

Johnson, David E. *Residential Land Development Practices: A Textbook on Developing Land into Finished Lots.* New York: ASCE Press, 1997.

Johnson, William C. *Urban Planning and Politics.* 2d ed. Chicago: American Planning Association, 1997.

Kaiser, Edward J., David R. Godschalk, and F. Stuart Chapin, Jr. *Urban Land Use Planning.* 4th ed. Champaign: Univ. of Illinois Press, 1994.

Katz, Peter. *The New Urbanism: Towards an Architecture of Community.* New York: McGraw-Hill, 1994.

Levy, John M. *Contemporary Urban Planning.* 4th ed. Upper Saddle River, N.J.: Gorsuch/Prentice-Hall, 1997.

Long, Deborah H. *Doing the Right Thing: A Real Estate Practitioners Guide to Ethical Decision Making.* 2d ed. Upper Saddle River, N.J.: Gorsuch/Prentice-Hall, 1998.

Lynch, Kevin. *Good City Form.* Cambridge, Mass.: MIT Press, 1984.

Lynch, Kevin, and Gary Hack. *Site Planning.* 3d ed. Cambridge, Mass.: MIT Press, 1984.

McHarg, Ian. *Design with Nature.* New York: Wiley, 1991.

McMahan, John. *Property Development.* 2d ed. New York: McGraw-Hill, 1989.

O'Mara, W. Paul, et al. *Developing Power Centers.* Washington, D.C.: ULI–the Urban Land Institute, 1996.

Peiser, Richard B., with Dean Schwanke. *Professional Real Estate Development: The ULI Guide to the Business.* Washington, D.C.: ULI–the Urban Land Institute, 1992.

Petersen, David C. *Sports, Convention, and Entertainment Facilities.* Washington, D.C.: ULI–the Urban Land Institute, 1996.

PFK Consulting. *Hotel Development.* Washington, D.C.: ULI–the Urban Land Institute, 1996.

Rocky Mountain Institute. *Green Development: Integrating Ecology and Real Estate.* New York: Wiley, 1998.

Saft, Stuart. *Real Estate Development Strategies for Changing Markets.* New York: Wiley, 1990.

Sandercock, Leonie. *Towards Cosmopolis: Planning for Multicultural Cities.* Chichester, N.Y.: Wiley, 1998.

Schmitz, Adrienne, and Lloyd W. Bookout. *Trends and Innovations in Master-Planned Communities.* Washington, D.C.: ULI–the Urban Land Institute, 1998.

Schwanke, Dean, et al. *Mixed-Use Development Handbook.* Washington, D.C.: ULI–the Urban Land Institute, 1987.

———. *Resort Development Handbook.* Washington, D.C.: ULI–the Urban Land Institute, 1997.

Shenkel, William M. *Modern Real Estate Principles.* 3d ed. Homewood, Ill.: Irwin, 1984.

Shirvani, Hamid. *The Urban Design Process.* New York: Van Nostrand Reinhold, 1985.

Simons, Robert A. *Turning Brownfields into Greenbacks: Developing and Financing Environmentally Contaminated Urban Real Estate.* Washington, D.C.: ULI–the Urban Land Institute, 1998.

Smith, Halbert C., Carl J. Tschappat, and Ronald L. Racster. *Real Estate and Urban Development.* 3d ed. Homewood, Ill.: Irwin, 1987.

So, Frank S., et al., eds. *The Practice of Local Government Planning.* 2d ed. Washington, D.C.: International City Management Association, 1988.

Southworth, Michael, and Eran Ben-Joseph. *Streets and the Shaping of Towns and Cities.* New York: McGraw-Hill, 1997.

Stein, Jay M. *Classic Readings in Real Estate Development.* Washington, D.C.: ULI–the Urban Land Institute, 1995.

——. *Classic Readings in Urban Planning.* New York: McGraw-Hill, 1995.

Suchman, Diane R. *Developing Timeshare and Vacation-Ownership Properties.* Washington, D.C.: ULI–the Urban Land Institute, 1999.

Suchman, Diane R., and Margaret B. Sowell. *Developing Infill Housing in Inner-City Neighborhoods: Opportunities and Strategies.* Washington, D.C.: ULI–the Urban Land Institute, 1997.

Unger, Maurice A., and George R. Karvel. *Real Estate: Principles and Practices.* 9th ed. Cincinnati: South-Western Publishing Co., 1990.

White, John R., ed. *The Office Building: From Concept to Investment Reality.* Chicago: Counselors of Real Estate, 1993.

White, John R., and Kevin D. Gray, eds. *Shopping Centers and Other Retail Properties.* New York: Wiley, 1996.

Whyte, William H. *City: Rediscovering the Center.* New York: Anchor/Doubleday, 1990.

Wofford, Larry E., and Terrence M. Clauretie. *Real Estate.* 3d ed. New York: Wiley, 1992.

Wolf, Peter M. *Land in America.* New York: Pantheon Books, 1981.

Wurtzebach, Charles H., and Mike E. Miles. *Modern Real Estate.* 5th ed. New York: Wiley, 1994.

Zuckerman, Howard A. *Real Estate Development Workbook.* Englewood Cliffs, N.J.: Prentice-Hall, 1991.

More specialized publications are available from textbook publishers and from the following sources:

American Institute of Architects
1735 New York Avenue, N.W.
Washington, DC 20006
(202) 626-7300
www.aiaonline.com

American Society of Landscape Architects
636 I Street, N.W.
Washington, DC 20001-3736
(888) 999-2752
www.asla.org

Appraisal Institute
875 North Michigan Avenue, Suite 2400
Chicago, IL 60611
(312) 335-4100
www.appraisalinstitute.org

Building Owners and Managers Association
International
1201 New York Avenue, N.W., Suite 300
Washington, DC 20005
(202) 408-2662
www.boma.org

Commercial-Investment Real Estate Council
Realtor's® National Marketing Institute
430 North Michigan Avenue, Suite 600
Chicago, IL 60611
(312) 321-4460
www.realtors.com

International Council of Shopping Centers
665 Fifth Avenue
New York, NY 10022
(212) 421-8181
www.icsc.org

Mortgage Bankers Association of America
1125 15th Street, N.W.
Washington, DC 20005
(202) 861-6500
www.mbaa.org

National Association of Home Builders
1201 15th Street, N.W.
Washington, DC 20005
(202) 822-0200
www.nahb.com

National Association of Industrial and Office Properties
2201 Cooperative Way, Third Floor
Herndon, VA 20171
(800) 666-6780
www.naiop.org

National Association of Realtors®
430 North Michigan Avenue
Chicago, IL 60611
(312) 329-8200
www.realtors.com

National Council of Real Estate Investment
   Fiduciaries
Two Prudential Plaza
180 North Stetson Avenue, Suite 2515
Chicago, IL 60601
(312) 819-5890
www.ncreif.com

Realtors® National Marketing Institute
430 North Michigan Avenue, Suite 500
Chicago, IL 60611
(312) 670-3780
www.realtors.com

Society of Industrial and Office Realtors®
National Association of Realtors®
700 11th Street, N.W., Suite 510
Washington, DC 20001-4511
(202) 737-1150
www.sior.com

ULI–the Urban Land Institute
1025 Thomas Jefferson Street, N.W.,
   Suite 500 West
Washington, DC 20007-5201
(202) 624-7000; (800) 321-5011
www.uli.org

Demographic Information

CACI Marketing Systems. *The Sourcebook of County Demographics.* 12th ed. Arlington, Va.: Author, 1999.

——. *The Sourcebook of Demographics and Buying Power for Every ZIP Code in the U.S.A.* Arlington, Va.: Author, 1990.

——. *The Sourcebook of ZIP Code Demographics.* 14th ed. Arlington, Va.: Author, 1999.

Campbell, Paul R. *Population Projections for States: By Age, Sex, Race, and Hispanic Origin, 1995 to 2025.* Current Population Reports PPL-47. Washington, D.C.: U.S. Census Bureau, 1996.

Casper, Lynne M., and Ken Bryson. *Household and Family Characteristics, March 1998.* U.S. Census Bureau PPL-101. Washington, D.C.: U.S. Government Printing Office, 1998.

Crispell, Diane, ed. *Insider's Guide to Demographic Know-How: Everything You Need to Know about How to Find, Analyze, and Use Information about Your Customer.* 3d ed. Ithaca, N.Y.: American Demographics, 1993.

Day, Jennifer Cheeseman. *Population Projections of the United States: By Age, Sex, Race, and Hispanic Origin, 1995 to 2050.* Current Population Reports P25-1130. Washington, D.C.: U.S. Census Bureau, 1996.

Eller, T.J., and Wallace Fraser. *Asset Ownership of Households, 1993.* Current Population Reports P70-47. Washington, D.C.: U.S. Census Bureau, 1995.

Long, Kim. *The American Forecaster Almanac, 1999.* 16th ed. Denver, Colo.: American Forecaster, 1999.

Myers, Dowell. *Analysis with Local Census Data: Portraits of Change.* San Diego: Academic Press, 1992.

Russell, Cheryl. *Americans and Their Homes: Demographics of Homeownership.* Ithaca, N.Y.: New Strategist Publications, 1998.

U.S. Bureau of Labor Statistics. *Monthly Labor Review.* Washington, D.C.: U.S. Government Printing Office. Published monthly.

U.S. Census Bureau. *Demographic Components of Population Change.* ST97-2. Washington, D.C.: U.S. Dept. of Commerce, 1998.

——. *Money Income in the United States, 1997.* With separate data on valuation of noncash benefits. Current Population Reports P60-200. Washington, D.C.: U.S. Dept. of Commerce, 1998.

——. *1990 Census of Population and Housing.* Washington, D.C.: U.S. Dept. of Commerce, 1993.

——. *Statistical Abstract of the United States.* Washington, D.C.: U.S. Dept. of Commerce. Published annually.

Waldrop, Judith. *The Seasons of Business: The Marketer's Guide to Consumer Behavior.* Ithaca, N.Y.: American Demographics, 1992.

Weinstein, Art. *Market Segmentation: Using Demographics, Psychographics, and Other Niche Marketing Techniques.* Chicago: Probus Publishing, 1993.

The following organizations collect large amounts of economic and demographic data and publish a variety of reports and studies, many of which are available on the World Wide Web (often at no charge):

U.S. Department of Commerce, Census Bureau
Customer Service Center
Washington, DC 20233
(301) 457-4100
www.census.gov

U.S. Department of Commerce, Bureau of
    Economic Analysis
Customer Service
BE-53
Washington, DC 20230
(202) 606-9900
www.bea.doc.gov

U.S. Department of Labor, Bureau of Labor Statistics
Division of Information Services
Two Massachusetts Avenue, NE, Room 2860
Washington, DC 20212
(202) 606-5886
www.bls.gov

The underlying concepts of finance are so important to the logic that governs development that we have devoted three chapters to financial issues alone. Developers and all the players on the team need to understand the whole picture—and finance is a critical part of that picture. Many great ideas are floating around that remain ideas simply because financing could not be secured.

Our discussion of finance starts with the institutional setting of real estate finance. Then we move on to financial theory and the logic behind real estate financing decisions. We close with a discussion of innovations in the field.

Although this part of the book is dedicated to finance, issues related to finance appear throughout as it is impossible to talk about any aspect of development without considering the financial angle as well. Financing is a means to an end for a developer, and rules and procedures change frequently. It's part of your responsibility as a development professional to keep abreast of trends in finance. This book provides you with the basics needed to understand evolving changes.

Part II
Finance

Chapter 4

Real Estate Finance: The Institutional Setting

Real estate finance plays a critical role in the development process. For real estate investors and developers, the link between real estate and the financial markets is an essential one. The evolution of real estate as an asset class within the global financial system has been well summarized.[1] From what amounted to a nearly separate market in the mid-1960s, real estate has been integrated into global financial markets in many ways:

- New securities based on real estate cash flows now trade in the same markets (for example, the New York Stock Exchange) as corporations like General Electric and Microsoft.
- A huge new volume of online data is available for both real estate and non–real estate decision makers.
- Numerous new research publications cover "the financial markets," including real estate.
- A complex new set of performance indices allows the application of traditional financial techniques to real estate decision making.

Further evidence of real estate's growing role in financial markets has been provided by other scholars, using a set of interconnected graphs that show the impact of financial markets on rents and the feedback of changes in rent to financial markets.[2] The relationship between real estate and the financial market is seen in the estimates of wealth developed at Fidelity

Management and Research (see Figure 4-1). These estimates show that real estate now contributes more than 40 percent to our stock of public and private wealth. The value of commercial real estate totals nearly $5 billion in the aggregate.

This part explores the institutional setting of real estate finance, the logic of the financing decision, and some recent innovations in financing. This chapter discusses:

- An intuitive model of the "market system of finance," illustrating how the U.S. system and most other market economies function;
- Primary and secondary loan markets;
- Current capital flows to real estate;
- Real estate equity and debt markets; and
- The financing cycle.

Chapter 5 examines the logic behind real estate financing decisions. Conventional wisdom holds that financing refers only to debt claims, with equity positions defined as ownership interests. The view adopted in this text is that the financing decision is a *capital structure decision;* in other words, deciding how the enterprise will be financed requires a decision as to what combination of debt and equity is best to achieve the investor's goals. As such, the financing decision is more than just calculating the payment on a loan. How much debt and equity are to be used is also a critical decision. The effect of financing on equity "or residual" cash flows is explained. The chapter concludes with an explanation of how debt financing is a prior claim on net operating income affecting both the actual return to equity and the riskiness of that return.

The primary authors of this chapter, Kenneth Lusht, PhD, professor, Pennsylvania State University, and Mike E. Miles, PhD, are grateful to Richard L. Haney, PhD, professor, Texas A&M University, for his early contributions to this chapter.

Figure 4-1

Components of U.S. Public and Private Markets[a]

	Value (Billions of Dollars)	Share of Domestic Universe (Percent)
Public Sector		
Publicly Traded Equities (including REITs and commercial real estate owned by corporations)[b]	$11,600	31
U.S. Government Obligations (Treasury and agency)	5,100	13
Corporate Bonds, State and Municipal Bonds, Mortgage-Backed Securities, Other Short-Term Investments[c]	8,900	23
Total Public Sector	$25,600	67
Private Sector		
Private Commercial Real Estate Equity (excluding corporate real estate, securitized real estate, REITs and commercial mortgage–backed securities, and the value of commercial real estate securing mortgages)	$1,800	5
Unsecuritized Commercial Mortgages	1,000	3
Owner-Occupied Residential	5,500	14
Unsecuritized Residential Mortgages	2,600	7
Venture Finance, Oil and Gas Reserves, Agricultural Land, Timberland	1,500	4
Total Private Sector	$12,400	33
Total Public and Private Sector Domestic Universe	$38,000	100

[a] Adding securitized real estate (included in public equities and private mortgage-backed securities), corporate-owned commercial real estate, private real estate equity, and commercial mortgages results in a total of about $5 billion for the commercial real estate universe. Estimates developed by updating Mike Miles and Nancy Tolleson, "A Revised Look at How Real Estate Compares with Other Major Components of the Domestic Investment Universe," *Real Estate Finance*, **Spring 1997, pp. 11–20.**
[b] Estimates from Wilshire 5000, June 1999.
[c] Estimates from Federal Reserve, May 1999.

Chapter 6 concludes this part by presenting information about what lenders and other investors are doing in today's market. The final section looks at the financing of Museum Towers from the perspective of the material presented in Chapters 4, 5, and 6.

An Intuitive Model of the Overall Financial System

It was once a widely held view that real estate markets were virtually separate from financial markets. Indeed, the players tended to use different terms and instruments for the same activities, depending on whether they were working in corporate finance or real estate offices. Although important differences remain between real estate transactions and those in other markets, real estate projects today are viewed as an important part of the financial system. Further, as one looks beyond the United States, it is clear that market forces reinforce the global view that real estate development is subject to the discipline of the financial market. While the relationship between real estate and financial markets is closest in the United States, the trend of globalization has required other countries to take notice of the growing importance of financial markets for real estate.

Reviewing the Basics: Savings And Investment

As you may recall from your first course in economics, the total tangible investment made by the global economy in any period must equal the total savings during that same period. In other words, as a group, we can

Figure 4-2

Capital Markets in the U.S. Financial System

Savers	Capital Market Players	Investors
Individuals	Commercial banks	Government
Businesses	Bank trust departments	Businesses
Life insurance companies	S&Ls	Individuals
Pension funds	Mutual savings banks	
	Credit unions	
	Life insurance companies	
	Real estate investment trusts	
	Mortgage bankers	
	Investment bankers	
	Venture capitalists	
	Investment managers	
	Syndicators	
	Government[a]	

[a]Facilitator, regulator, and occasionally lender.

invest only what we do not immediately consume. The amount saved is defined as total production less private consumption (food, clothing, and shelter) and government purchases of goods and services, that is,

$$Savings = Production - Private\ Consumption - Government\ Purchases = Investment.$$

The *Savings = Investment* equation works for the economy as a whole. For individuals, however, savings may or may not equal investment. An individual can save more in a given period than he wants to invest in tangible assets or, by borrowing, can invest more in tangible assets than he has saved. The financial system allows those choices by first *aggregating* all savings and then *allocating* those savings to individuals for investments. The intermediaries between the savers and the investors are the *capital markets*—markets for financial investments with terms longer than one year—where a variety of players perform the aggregation and the allocation functions (see Figure 4-2).

These functions are critically important, for only if we collectively save can we collectively invest. Furthermore, only if we as a nation invest in the most productive assets can we have the greatest economic opportunities tomorrow. If we do not invest in the most productive assets (those most likely to provide cost-efficient satisfaction of consumers' desires), the pie will be smaller tomorrow than it might have been, and, as a group, we will be worse off.

Allocating Savings to Investors

Within the capital markets, priorities for allocating funds are determined on the basis of a pricing structure driven by expected risks and returns. Expected returns at any given time are determined by the supply of, and demand for, funds within certain categories. These categories are usually classified according to the risks assumed by the lender and the length, or maturity, of the loan (investment). For example, short-term (30-day) loans to creditworthy corporations are a lower risk than long-term (30-year) mortgage loans on beach property.

Given that a significant percentage of lenders seek low-risk investments, it is not surprising that the U.S. government tends to have the first claim on our savings. Most government expenditures are financed by tax revenues. For the federal and some state governments, however, tax revenues have until very recently been insufficient to cover total government expenditures. One result is our federal debt, which must be financed by borrowing from savings. Because the U.S. government is the lowest-risk borrower (money is worthless if our government folds), it gets whatever it needs from the savings pool first. After the government is financed, competition for the remaining savings is considerable. Potential borrowers argue that they are in the low-risk category in an effort to obtain the funds they need at a rate as low as possible.

Major corporations tend to be next in line. From this perspective, the chief financial officer of General

Electric is really a purchasing agent standing between the corporation and the capital markets. The challenge is to borrow the money GE needs for growth and modernization at the lowest possible cost. Finally, after the government and major corporations have successfully claimed their shares of the savings pie, what remains is available for individuals to borrow and invest.

Primary and Secondary Loan Markets

Together, capital market intermediaries manage an enormous pool of savings, a large percentage of which is invested in the form of loans. In this endeavor, each intermediary tries to make loans that are compatible with the kinds of capital they raise. For example, institutions with short-term liabilities dominating their portfolio (such as the demand deposits of commercial banks) tend to prefer short-term real estate loans, notably construction loans. Conversely, institutions with long-term liabilities (such as life insurance companies) tend to prefer longer-term loans. For both, the idea is to match the maturities of their assets (loans) with their liabilities (deposits).

Loans are originated (created) in many ways and in various places, which together are known as the *primary financial market*. A business that raises capital by selling newly issued securities to the general public is raising capital in the primary market, as is the U.S. government when it sells a new issue of Treasury bonds. An S&L is also raising capital in the primary market when it agrees to finance the purchase of a home with a first mortgage loan. In all these instances, new debt is being created.

Once debt has been created, units of debt, represented by bonds, deeds of trust, notes and mortgages, and so on, may be traded in the *secondary financial markets*. The major secondary markets (for both common stocks and bonds) include the New York Stock and Bond Exchanges, the National Association of Security Dealers/American Stock and Bond Exchanges, and regional exchanges. Short-term debt instruments —such as U.S. Treasury bills and commercial paper issued by large corporations—are traded in the *money market,* which is a conceptual, rather than a geographic, designation.

Before World War II, only a limited secondary market existed for real estate mortgages. In recent years, however, a very active secondary mortgage market has developed. It has broadened the capital pool for financing real estate, making it possible for many new types

of savers and financial intermediaries to invest in real estate (lend money). The secondary mortgage market also facilitates interregional credit flows, which contribute to a more efficient national market. Finally, many traditional real estate lenders are able to make more real estate loans because of the liquidity provided by the secondary mortgage market. Selling loans replenishes lenders with funds, which they use to make more new loans. Thus, the secondary mortgage market expands the supply of funds to the primary mortgage market.

Current Capital Flows To Real Estate

Many sources of information are available about current capital flows to real estate. The most basic is the Federal Reserve's *Flow of Funds Accounts,* reported quarterly. Building on this base and using estimates from additional sources, Scott Muldavin (formerly of the Roulac Group) produced periodic estimates of real estate capital market flows for the *Pension Real Estate Quarterly* and the *Real Estate Capital Markets Report.* Examples of these estimates are shown in Figures 4-3 and 4-4. As the figures show, monitoring real estate capital flows involves tracking 15 distinct providers, which are segmented into four groups: private debt, public debt, private equity, and public equity.

The data in Figures 4-3 and 4-4 come from various sources. For banks, mortgage companies, S&Ls, and mutual savings banks, the primary source is the Department of Housing and Urban Development's (HUD's) *Survey of Mortgage Lending Activity.* This quarterly survey has been available for more than ten years; it comprehensively tracks private lending originations and holdings by financial institutions. Information lags by nearly six months, however, and to stay fully current, it is necessary to review the numerous, though more anecdotal, sources available on commercial mortgage debt.[3]

Data for pension fund debt and equity flows come from Institutional Real Estate, Inc., which conducts detailed quarterly surveys of aggregate real estate holdings and real estate investment activity. Information about commercial mortgage securities comes primarily from *Commercial Mortgage Alert,* while information about mortgage and equity REITs is provided by the National Association of Real Estate Investment Trusts. Information about public and private real estate limited partnerships is provided by Robert A. Stanger and Company. Foreign investment figures come from the Department of Commerce, Bureau of Economic

Figure 4-3

Annual Real Estate Capital Flows, 1993 to 1998

(Millions of Dollars)

	1993	1994	1995	1996	1997	1998[a]
Private Debt						
Life Insurance Companies	$45,793	($20,905)	$10,322	($13,274)	($2,401)	($3,615)
Banks and Mortgage Companies	8,100	7,989	25,513	24,642	36,679	23,455
S&Ls and Mutual Savings Banks	(27,793)	(10,728)	(5,338)	(144)	(9,493)	(1,866)
Pension Funds	(6,672)	1,173	2,490	(81)	(3,111)	1,687
Subtotal Private Debt	$19,428	($22,471)	$32,987	$11,143	$21,674	$19,660
Public Debt						
Government Credit Agencies	($6,934)	($6,634)	($3,895)	$56	($1,476)	($1,453)
Commercial Mortgage Securities	15,608	17,536	14,880	25,529	38,079	69,493
Mortgage REITs	1,380	(826)	892	1,383	2,592	142
Public Real Estate Limited Partnerships	(224)	(271)	(337)	(376)	(382)	(356)
Subtotal Public Debt	$9,831	$9,805	$11,540	$26,592	$38,813	$67,827
Total Debt	$29,259	($12,666)	$44,527	$37,735	$60,487	$87,487
Private Equity						
Pension Funds	$2,703	$4,694	$9,961	$14,617	$16,545	$4,210
Foreign Investors	(1,306)	(220)	172	(101)	56	727
Private Financial Institutions	(16,877)	(11,655)	(5,760)	(3,323)	(4,105)	(2,789)
Life Insurance Companies	3,250	745	(653)	(788)	(1,043)	(806)
Private Investors (larger properties)	1,680	(3,160)	6,835	7,520	13,803	12,781
Subtotal Private Equity	($10,550)	($9,596)	$10,555	$17,925	$25,258	$14,123
Public Equity						
REITs (equity and hybrid)	$14,557	$13,515	$12,343	$29,852	$49,165	$1,624
Public Real Estate Limited Partnerships	(3,773)	(3,261)	(3,203)	(3,109)	(2,823)	(2,629)
Subtotal Public Equity	$10,784	$10,254	$9,140	$26,743	$46,342	($1,005)
Total Equity	$234	$658	$19,695	$44,668	$71,598	$13,118
Total Capital	$29,493	($12,008)	$64,222	$82,403	$132,085	$100,605

[a]**Estimated based on third quarter data.**
Source: The Roulac Group, Inc.

Analysis. Private equity for private financial institutions and life insurance companies is calculated based on statistics from the FDIC's (Federal Deposit Insurance Corporation's) *Historical Statistics on Banking,* reports from the Federal Reserve, and data from the American Council of Life Insurance's *Fact Book.*

Capital flows for private investors are developed from a proprietary methodology involving a combination of sources, including CCIM/Landauer, Institutional Real Estate, the Federal Reserve System's *Balance Sheet of the U.S. Economy,* the FDIC, and others.

These sources, which provide most of the information in Figures 4-3 and 4-4, are supplemented by selected other sources and internal surveys and expertise that are used to estimate quarterly flows (in the few circumstances where good quarterly data are not available), estimate prepayment rates on mortgages backing commercial mortgage–backed securities (CMBSs), and make other minor adjustments and refinements.

The data in Figures 4-3 and 4-4 form a particularly good set of information to evaluate trends over time,

Figure 4-4

Quarterly Capital Flows, 1996 to 1998

(Millions of Dollars)

	3Q/96	4Q/96	1Q/97	2Q/97	3Q/97	4Q/97	1Q/98	2Q/98
Private Debt								
Life Insurance Companies	$6,349	($2,773)	($4,517)	$1,307	$6,314	($5,505)	($904)	($904)
Banks and Mortgage Companies	5,165	8,827	5,398	11,857	11,788	7,636	5,864	5,864
S&Ls and Mutual Savings Banks	1,607	163	(5,810)	(873)	(1,153)	(1,657)	(466)	(466)
Pension Funds	(900)	983	(3,812)	1,367	(869)	203	433	681
Subtotal Private Debt	$12,221	$7,200	($8,741)	$13,658	$16,080	$677	$4,926	$5,174
Public Debt								
Government Credit Agencies	$1,071	$167	($3,652)	($527)	($453)	$3,156	($363)	($363)
Commercial Mortgage Securities	2,242	12,512	4,920	8,342	8,046	16,771	17,651	21,760
Mortgage REITs	96	732	82	1,304	436	770	318	1,630
Public Real Estate Limited Partnerships	(94)	(94)	(95)	(96)	(95)	(95)	(89)	(89)
Subtotal Public Debt	$3,315	$13,317	$1,255	$9,023	$7,934	$20,601	$17,517	$22,938
Total Debt	$15,536	$20,517	($7,486)	$22,681	$24,014	$21,278	$22,443	$28,112
Private Equity								
Pension Funds	($149)	$8,365	$10,392	$2,823	$620	$2,709	($1,843)	$3,935
Foreign Investors	(616)	700	(85)	(147)	91	197	220	217
Private Financial Institutions	(831)	(831)	(1,026)	(1,026)	(1,026)	(1,026)	(697)	(1,070)
Life Insurance Companies	(197)	(197)	(261)	(261)	(261)	(261)	(202)	(202)
Private Investors (larger properties)	1,880	1,880	3,451	3,451	3,451	3,451	4,793	4,793
Subtotal Private Equity	$87	$9,917	$12,471	$4,840	$2,875	$5,070	$2,271	$7,674
Public Equity								
REITs (equity and hybrid)	$5,683	$17,639	$5,583	$9,992	$22,607	$10,983	$19,389	($1,943)
Public Real Estate Limited Partnerships	(777)	(777)	(756)	(756)	(656)	(656)	(655)	(655)
Subtotal Public Equity	$4,906	$16,862	$4,827	$9,236	$21,951	$10,327	$18,734	($2,598)
Total Equity	$4,993	$26,779	$17,298	$14,076	$24,827	$15,397	$21,005	$5,076
Total Capital	$20,529	$47,296	$9,812	$36,757	$48,841	$36,675	$43,448	$33,188

Source: **The Roulac Group, Inc.**

allowing short-term phenomena like the dramatic decline of the REIT market during the middle of 1998 and the collapse of the CMBS market in August 1998 to be put into a longer-term, historical perspective. Thus, while the upheavals in the real estate capital markets in 1998 hurt many participants, the capital flows projected for all of 1998 of near $100 billion were almost exactly equal to the inflation-adjusted average annual capital flows during the last 18 years. And although many market participants were concerned about overbuilding at the start of 1998, by late August there was talk of another "credit" crunch. Investment

decisions based solely on either of these emotional waves would not have been smart. Careful and thoughtful monitoring of historical trends can provide developers with an improved ability to predict the price and availability of capital and helps keep current activities in proper perspective. The result is a more strategic approach to decision making.

A final caveat when interpreting information about real estate capital flows: Figures 4-3 and 4-4 show only *current* capital flows, not aggregate market size or capital activity. Aggregate market size is total holdings at a given time. "Capital flows" refers to the change in aggregate holdings over a given time frame. Capital activity is the total origination or investment activity of a capital source before consideration of dispositions, writedowns, loan payoffs, or loan refinancing. These distinctions are important to developers, because even though capital flows may be low or even negative at a particular time, it does not mean no capital is available.

A Closer Look at Real Estate Equity and Debt Markets

In the past, most real estate capital was raised in private markets. Developers obtained loans from banks, mortgage companies, or life insurance companies, and sold equity interests in their projects through commercial brokers. This model still predominates in today's marketplace, but the trend is toward raising relatively more capital in the public markets, where both debt and equity funds can be generated through securitization. This section first discusses the characteristics of alternative ownership (equity) forms, and then the institutions involved in alternative forms of debt financing.

Forms of Ownership for Real Estate Equity Markets

Real estate ventures are owned either by an individual (person or firm) or some type of group structure. Figure 4-5 summarizes the features of various ownership forms, the most important of which are discussed in detail.[4]

S Corporation and Limited Partnership

Developers often form a *closely held corporation* (more formally known as an S corporation) devoted solely to a particular project. The S corporation form of organization limits the developer's personal liability to the capital he has contributed to the corporation. This so-called shell corporation, which typically is wholly owned by the developer or his firm, invests most of its assets in a single project. The developer then forms a *limited partnership,* which requires a general partner who bears unlimited liability and one or more limited partners whose liability is limited to their capital contributions. The shell corporation serves as the general partner, and equity funds for the venture are raised by selling limited partnership interests. This basic limited partnership framework can be adjusted in many ways to fit the particular environments in which the development firm operates.

In addition to the limited liability of the limited partnership, another attractive attribute is income tax–related. If a parcel of real estate is owned by an ordinary corporation (a C corporation, which is often a shell corporation with the parcel as its only income-generating asset), the corporate entity must pay taxes on any income the corporation earns. When that income is distributed to the corporation's stockholders, they must pay income taxes on the dividend income —known as "double taxation." Moreover, the nature of the income passed on to the shareholders as dividends is immaterial, because the recipient also receives capital gains as dividend income, and thus it is taxed at the higher tax rates for ordinary income. In contrast, a limited partnership is not subject to double taxation, and the distinction between ordinary income and capital gains is retained. To qualify for these attractive features, a limited partner must limit its management activity, truly becoming a passive investor and allowing the general partner to make all management decisions.

Limited partnership interests can be sold through various methods. In some cases, the developer uses personal contacts to sell the interests to high-net-worth acquaintances. In other cases, he uses a local real estate broker to solicit a small number of investors interested in a given opportunity for investment. Another technique that was more common before 1986 (when changes in U.S. income tax laws disallowed the practice of offsetting real estate losses—which frequently were paper losses only—against investors' non–real estate income, thus reducing their income taxes) was organizing a real estate *syndication,* which relied on a specialist to raise risk capital. In a public syndication, the syndicator, which could have been a securities firm that also sold stocks and bonds, would employ a sales force to solicit investors. In some cases, the syndicator would purchase the general partner's interest, thus freeing the developer's capital for investment in another development opportunity.

Limited Liability Company

A newer form of ownership is the *limited liability company.* This entity is attractive because it combines the advantages of an S corporation with the partnership form of business organization. Most important, it provides limited liability to its investors, known as members, while simultaneously providing flexibility in the allocation of income, deductions, gains, and losses. For example, compared with an S corporation, the limited liability company offers competitive advantages in the form of 1) no limitations on the number or kind of investors, 2) no limitations on the classes of investors,

Figure 4-5

Features of Selected Ownership Forms

Ownership Form	Ease of Formation	Ability to Raise Funds	Management	Personal Liability	Income Tax Treatment[a]	Transfer of Ownership	Dissolution
Individual	Simple and inexpensive	Limited	Flexible, independent, may lack expertise	Unlimited	Single[b]	Simple and inexpensive	Excellent
Tenancy in Common	Simple and inexpensive	Limited but superior to individual ownership	Depends on owners, may be cumbersome	Unlimited	Single	Potentially difficult	Potentially difficult
General Partnership	Moderately easy	Limited but superior to individual ownership	Generally by designated partner(s)	Unlimited	Single	Poor	Fairly simple
Limited Partnership	Moderately difficult and expensive	Limited but superior to general partnership	Good, by general partners or agents	Limited for limited partner; unlimited for general partner	Single	Poor for general partner; fair for limited partner	May be time-consuming and tie up invested capital
Ordinary Corporation (C Corporation)	Complex and expensive	No problem if closely held; if public, depends on investment	Continuous and centralized	Limited	Double	Superior	Simple process but needs shareholders' approval
S Corporation	Complex and expensive	Limited, un-suited for income property	Determined by relative share of ownership	Limited	Single	Impeded by ceiling on number of shareholders	Simple but needs shareholders' approval
Real Estate Investment Trust	Complex and expensive	Good	Centralized, by advisory group	Limited	Modified single	Superior[c]	Complex

[a]Losses may be passive and thus have no effect on an individual's taxes.

[b]Taxes at only one level, including for partnerships not ruled to be publicly traded partnerships, which results in tax treatment as a corporation.

[c]The ability of any legal entity to transfer shares of ownership readily depends on the presence of a market mechanism (such as a securities exchange) and on the quality of the investment itself.

Source: James H. Boykin and Richard L. Haney, Jr., *Financing Real Estate*, 2d ed. (Englewood Cliffs, N.J.: Prentice-Hall, 1993), p. 288.

3) the ability to include a share of nonrecourse debt in a member's basis, thereby increasing deductible losses, and 4) no restrictions on special allocations of income, gain, loss, deductions, or tax credits. When compared with a partnership, the limited liability company's most evident advantages are the limited liability of its members and the limited partners' retention of rights to participate in management. On the negative side, the decentralized management structure of the limited liability company means that each member has the ability to bind the company in a contract.

Joint Venture

The methods for raising equity capital discussed earlier are often combined in a *joint venture,* which is not a form of ownership per se. A developer and an institutional capital source such as a pension fund or a life insurance company agree to work together on the development and ownership of a specific project. Although a joint venture may take any desired form of ownership, it is most commonly organized as a general or limited partnership, followed by the limited liability company. The key is that the institution provides most if not all of the capital, while the developer contributes his development expertise. The parties then share in the operating cash flows, tax benefits, and property appreciation according to the formula they negotiate at the outset of the venture. Some institutional partners are reluctant to share ownership benefits with developers, preferring instead to hire developers on a fee-for-services basis and retain 100 percent of the ownership once the development process is complete. Although this arrangement neatly solves the developer's problem of raising both equity and debt capital, it requires the developer to dramatically alter his style of operation.

C Corporation

One way for a developer to diminish the likelihood of shifting from equity player to hired player (as in some joint ventures) is to become a *public corporation* (more formally known as a publicly traded C corporation). C corporation ownership provides access to the financial markets. It can raise new equity capital from the stock market and more readily raise borrowed corporate capital through both publicly and privately placed issues. Along with the benefits of raising capital more easily for a publicly traded corporation, however, come the burdens of public ownership, stockholders' demands for increasing earnings and more information about operations than most developers are comfortable providing, and the submission of onerous reports to regulators and shareholders.

Real Estate Investment Trust

Another alternative for the developer is the REIT, commonly pronounced "reet." Equity REITs are an important source of equity capital for developers who want to retain both an ownership interest and management control of a project. Shares of a REIT trade like a C corporation, but no income tax is levied on the entity as long as the REIT adheres to certain rules for ownership and distribution of income. The essential requirements are that most of the REIT's assets be real estate and that 95 percent of the taxable income be distributed annually to shareholders.

An alternative to retaining ownership is for a developer to sell the completed and leased product to an existing REIT. This arrangement is similar to the "fee-for-services developer" common in joint ventures, except that because the developer takes the initial risk of development and sale, the opportunity exists for larger profits.

Converting to a REIT has become popular among large developers. Although it is an expensive procedure and shares the disadvantages of publicly owned corporations, REITs can more readily tap the capital markets for funds (even when their privately owned competitors are unable to obtain financing), they allow the developers to maintain ownership and control over their projects, and they compensate management with stock options that are otherwise unavailable or illiquid. In fact, over the long run, liquidity may be the REIT's most important advantage.[5] Chapter 6 deals with the implications of the recent rapid growth of REITs.

Major Institutional Players in Real Estate Debt Markets

Like the overall financial market, real estate debt markets may be divided into (short-term) money markets and (long-term) capital markets. Money markets generally offer construction (or interim) loans even if the loan term exceeds one year, because their pricing is typically based on a short-term interest rate index. Capital markets offer most permanent mortgages. Because many of the factors that influence the two markets differ, they are discussed separately below.[6] The two types of markets share some common principles.

- Each institution tries to get the maximum return for the least risk. Lenders' revenues come from 1) the stated interest rate, 2) front-end fees in the form of a percentage of the loan, called "points," 3) the provision of related services such as mortgage life insurance, and 4) any "other business" that comes to the institution because it made a particular loan.
- Institutions prefer loans that fit their liability structure, that is, loans whose maturities are similar to their source of funds. Savers are the institution's source of funds, and different institutions cater to different groups of savers.
- The institution's contact with and knowledge of the different segments of real estate markets (by type of property and location) affect the types of loans the institution makes. Each institution's lending policy is a function of the segment of the industry

it understands. Some lenders avoid making certain types of loans because they lack experience. Others have a commitment to certain types of projects, such as downtown revitalization.

We look first at the institutions involved in construction and permanent lending, then at the sequence of their lending activities.

Construction Loans

Loans used to finance the developer's construction of on-site improvements are called *construction (or interim) loans.* They are generally variable–interest rate loans made by *commercial banks,* which specialize in short-term loans to businesses, including real estate developers. Banks invest depositors' funds in loans—typically commercial and industrial loans or consumer loans—or money market instruments. Banks choose to keep the maturity of their assets short term to match the short-term nature of their deposit liabilities. The short-term nature of bank assets means both their cost of funds and their return on investments are tied to money market interest rates. Therefore, it is important for developers to assess the prospect for changes in money market interest rates to adequately anticipate the cost of construction funds.

Money market interest rates fluctuate for two major reasons: 1) changes in businesses' supply of and demand for short-term funds, and 2) the Federal Reserve's policies. Changes in the supply of and demand for funds are primarily the result of the business cycle. When the need for bank financing diminishes during economic slowdowns, rates fall. Conversely, when the economy is expanding rapidly, businesses seek more bank financing, and the increased demand puts upward pressure on interest rates.

During the term of a loan, the interest rate changes based on an agreed-upon money market index. The most common index is the *prime interest rate,* which is the rate banks charge their most creditworthy medium-sized customers. Because most developments involve somewhat higher risk, the rate paid is above prime. Competition keeps the prime rate more or less in line with other money market rates. It may lag as market rates fall, but it generally moves coincidentally with increases in money market rates.

The other widely used money market index is the LIBOR, the London Interbank Offered Rate. It is usually the interest rate on three- or six-month Eurodeposits, although other terms and LIBOR quotes are available. The LIBOR market is highly competitive, and the LIBOR changes frequently as the supply of and demand for Eurodollars fluctuate. Compared with the prime rate, the LIBOR is much more reflective of daily changes in the financial markets, especially the global marketplace.[7]

The second determinant of money market interest rates is the actions of the Federal Reserve system. The Fed, as it is more commonly known, is responsible for formulating and implementing the nation's *monetary policy.* This policy is concerned with using a variety of tools to control the availability of loanable funds to achieve reasonable price stability, a stable dollar, and full employment. The Fed uses four important tools: 1) changing the reserves that banks must hold against their deposits, 2) changing margin requirements—the proportion of the price that purchasers of securities must pay for with nonborrowed funds, 3) changing the rates banks must pay (discount rates) to borrow from a Federal Reserve bank, and 4) buying and selling government securities (open-market operations), the most important tool available to the Fed.[8]

Fed open-market operations affect market interest rates by changing the supply of money in the banking system. When the Fed buys securities, it puts upward pressure on their prices. The higher the price an investor must pay for a fixed-rate instrument, the lower the return—or yield—to that investor. Thus, the Fed's purchases of securities cause yields to decrease. Fed purchases also inject money into the economy when the Fed pays for those securities, thereby tending to increase the money supply. Conversely, the Fed's sales of securities drive their prices down. With lower prices on fixed-rate instruments, investors receive a higher yield on their investment, thus boosting interest rates. Moreover, money is withdrawn from the banking system when investors pay for their purchases, resulting in a decrease in the money supply. As the effects of the Fed's activities are felt first on bank reserves, the Fed's funds rate (the interest rate on overnight loans of excess reserves from one commercial bank to another) is the interest rate most analysts look to when trying to divine changes in Federal Reserve policy.

In summary, construction loan interest rates are most often variable-rate loans, with changes in rates tied to an index such as the prime rate or LIBOR. These money market rates respond to shifts in the supply of and demand for savings, shifts that typically occur gradually as a result of changes in the business cycle in the United States and abroad. The Fed also affects money market rates as it attempts to control the availability of loanable funds through purchases and sales of securities on the open market. Changes in the Fed's activities are most frequently gauged by looking for changes in the Fed's funds rate.

Permanent Loans

Loans used to finance the long-term ownership or use of a parcel of real estate are referred to as *permanent loans*. Various institutions make permanent loans, including life insurance companies, commercial banks, S&Ls, savings banks, and pension funds.[9] Indirect permanent loans are available through real estate mortgage investment conduits.

Life Insurance Companies. Life insurance companies, which underwrite permanent loans based on the stream of income produced by the properties, are a primary income-property lender. Life insurance companies sell life insurance policies and various guaranteed annuity products, then invest the premiums and other funds they receive to pay the financial obligations associated with those products. Based on actuarial analysis, the timing of the need for the funds is typically long term and relatively easy to predict. Consequently, life insurance companies find that longer-term mortgage assets closely match their longer-term liabilities. Life insurance companies sometimes operate through branch offices, at other times use the services of local loan correspondents called mortgage bankers, and occasionally use a mortgage broker to locate lending opportunities.

Whether life insurance companies will increase or decrease their activity in permanent mortgage lending will depend on the relative strength of some offsetting factors. First, downward pressure on permanent lending comes first from the overbuilding of the 1980s,[10] which resulted in life insurance companies' suffering substantial problems in the form of foreclosed and nonperforming real assets. As a result, stockholder-owned life insurance companies have been pressured by investors to make fewer real estate loans until their balance sheets regain their former strength. The same is true for stockholder and mutually owned life insurance companies. Second, because they frequently borrow funds, life insurance companies need debt-rating agencies such as Fitch's, Moody's, Standard & Poor's, and Duff and Phelps, which also are averse to real estate and mortgage loans in the insurance companies' asset portfolios. Such agencies rate their debt lower (which means borrowing becomes more costly) when such assets are present. Third, the National Association of Insurance Commissioners has developed a model *risk-based capital adequacy law* for state governments to consider. Many have adopted it, and most of the remaining states are expected to do likewise. The model law requires insurance companies to hold additional capital if their portfolios consist of riskier assets, such as common stocks and real estate equity.[11]

Although new regulations and the problem loans of the 1980s pressured life insurance companies to reduce the proportion of their assets held in mortgage loans and real estate equities, mortgage yields remain attractive compared with the expected returns in the stock and bond markets. These yields are necessary to market their variable life insurance product to prospective policyholders.

On balance, risk-based capital requirements are likely to dominate the attraction of favorable yields, meaning life insurance companies will continue with their conservative loan underwriting practices and generally avoid real estate equities. In sum, life insurance companies will remain a significant source of permanent loans for the development community, especially as the real estate market completes its recovery and the life insurers' balance sheets improve.

Commercial Banks. Commercial banks, the second largest permanent lender for income-property mortgage loans, also specialize in short-term loans to businesses. As befits their short-term liabilities, their permanent loans (known as *miniperm* loans) are generally shorter term than life insurance companies' permanent loans. In fact, many of the miniperms were first granted because the banks had made open-ended construction loans, i.e., loans made without the benefit of a "takeout commitment" by a permanent lender to provide financing once construction was complete. When banks then found that their borrowers could not obtain permanent financing when the construction loan was due to be repaid, they made the best of an unanticipated situation by converting the construction loans into three- to five-year variable-rate loans with the interest rate tied to their prime rate. Given the steep yield curve,[12] borrowers were able to make the payments on these loans while the banks earned a satisfactory yield. Because the yield on miniperm loans is higher than that on most bank lending and investment alternatives, many banks continue to offer miniperm mortgages.

Thrift Institutions. Savings and loan associations and savings banks are known as *thrift institutions* because of their origins as financial institutions that provided thrifty individuals with a place to safeguard their savings. Historically, these savings were largely held in passbook and other short-term accounts, which the thrift institutions invested primarily in longer-term loans for single-family houses. This mismatch of assets and liabilities was at the root of the S&L crisis of the 1980s and 1990s. During the latter half of the 1970s and the first half of the 1980s, interest rates rose to historically high levels, with short-term rates higher than long-term rates (an inverted yield curve). This phenomenon caused the thrift institutions to suffer intense earnings pressures, as they had to pay their short-term depositors higher rates than their portfolios of fixed-rate long-term mortgage loans, some of which were originated during the 1950s, were earning. Many institutions became insolvent. Others, however, actively sought out permanent loans on income-producing properties because those loans provided higher interest rates and greater fees than the loans for single-family homes they typically originated.

Unfortunately, many thrift institutions ventured into loans for income properties they did not fully understand. And in the context of deteriorating real estate markets during the latter half of the 1980s and the early 1990s, the thrift institutions quickly realized that they had made some poor lending decisions. Moreover, some of the owners of thrift institutions took large dividends from their failing institutions and engaged in other self-dealing. Because the federal government insured savers' deposits, it bore the brunt of thrift institution owners' and managers' mismanagement. Several individuals were convicted of crimes, and even some U.S. senators were tainted by their earlier support of those convicted. (Appendix A at the end of this book discusses these events in greater detail.)

In 1989, Congress responded to the crisis by passing the Financial Institutions Reform, Recovery, and Enhancement Act (FIRREA), which dramatically changed the mortgage finance landscape. A new federal agency, the Resolution Trust Corporation (RTC), was established to dispose of the assets of the failed institutions. The government's previous thrift institution regulator and deposit insurer were disbanded and their duties handed to other agencies. Thrift institutions were required to hold additional capital and were largely restricted to their residential mortgage lending roots. As a result of these regulatory changes, S&Ls in the future will be much less active as real estate development lenders.

Pension Funds. Similar to life insurance companies, the liabilities of public and private *pension funds* are well suited to the longer-term nature of real estate equities and mortgage loans. Historically, however, their investments were limited primarily to the stock and bond markets. This situation changed in the 1980s when pension funds hired real estate advisers to help them select real estate and mortgage loan investments, concentrating on high-quality equities. They discovered a downside in the early 1990s, when they sought to sell some of these real estate–related investments and were frustrated at the slow pace of liquidation resulting from the commingled funds into which their investment monies had been placed.[13] In Chapter 6, we will learn that pension funds have invested heavily in "real estate opportunity funds" and,

in the process, have provided considerable capital for development.

Indirect Permanent Lending: Real Estate Mortgage Investment Conduits. Indirect yet relatively liquid investments in real estate debt instruments are available through commercial *real estate mortgage investment conduits* (REMICs). REMICs pool and sell commercial real estate mortgages in the financial markets. Commercial REMICs are modeled after residential REMICs (which became popular soon after enabling legislation was passed in the Tax Reform Act of 1986), with the difference being that they are backed by mortgage loans on income-producing properties. First issued in 1992 by the Resolution Trust Corporation, commercial REMICs grew dramatically during the 1990s.

Commercial REMICs depend on a mortgage banking company or a mortgage conduit to make a loan on either an existing income-producing property or a real estate developer's proposed or recently completed commercial project.[14] The loan originator then sells the loan to a securities dealer, who packages it and other commercial loans into a REMIC. The commercial REMIC is then sold to a pension fund, life insurance company, thrift institution, or commercial bank. The addition of the REMIC vehicle and involvement of the securities dealer broadens the market for commercial mortgages, but it also adds an extra layer of expense. Some believe that many commercial REMICs have lower-quality properties as collateral. The higher-quality properties tend to go to those who are willing to spend the extra time needed to appreciate the nuances of individual loans. The extra time is easier to justify on larger loans, which still tend to go to the life insurance companies (and increasingly Wall Street) that have traditionally made loans on commercial properties.

Commercial REMICs may take the form of a mortgage pass-through security in which the periodic debt service payments, less the servicing fee, are passed directly to the investor, or it may be a derivative security in which the cash flows derived from the underlying mortgages' cash flows are redirected to one investor category or another. For example, some investors may prefer their cash flows sooner than other investors, and the REMIC might have short-term, medium-term, and long-term *tranches* (mortgage-secured debt interests) to accommodate these investors. Some tranches may be interest only, in which case the investor receives only the mortgage interest, while others may be principal only. Some tranches may carry a variable interest rate, while others may have a fixed interest rate, all paid from the same package of commercial mortgages. Finally, some tranches may be rated higher than others because the tranche has a priority in the receipt of the project's income or the income flow is guaranteed by a third party. If a tranche carries an investment-grade rating (AAA, AA, A, or BBB), it is an eligible investment for most institutions. Noninvestment-grade tranches are most likely to be purchased by high-yield mutual funds or other more aggressive investor/developers.

The securities dealer adds value not only by finding investors interested in the REMICs but also by designing the different tranches to ensure the greatest appeal to investors. Commercial REMICs seek to attract investors by offering liquid debt investments at satisfactory yields and, at the same time, provide developers with an opportunity to obtain permanent financing for their development projects. (Chapter 6 includes more information about the commercial mortgage–backed securities market.)

What Determines the Interest Rates On a Permanent Mortgage?

The Risk-Free Rate. With the exception of many miniperm loans that carry a variable interest rate tied to a money market rate index, permanent mortgages have maturities that exceed one year and carry a fixed interest rate that must be competitive with other capital market rates to attract the necessary funds to the real estate markets. Capital markets operate efficiently in pricing perceived risks. Thus, interest on permanent loans reflects the risk-free rate plus various risk premiums. The base rate, or *risk-free interest rate,* is the rate of return on short-term debt obligations backed by the U.S. Treasury. Because the federal government is considered stable, an investor in U.S. Treasury securities is not rewarded with a risk premium—thus the term "risk-free rate." The risk-free interest rate has two return components—a real return and an inflation premium. The real return is the nominal return (the "contract rate") minus the inflation rate. Thus, the real rate of return is what the purchaser "really" receives after the loss in purchasing power attributable to the lost power of money, usually measured by the GDP deflator. Historically, real returns on Treasury bills have ranged from 1 percent to 4 percent.

Risk Premiums. For investors to consider the purchase of an individual commercial real estate mortgage or commercial REMIC, they must consider the riskiness of commercial mortgages and add a risk premium to the risk-free rate. The first premium that must be added relates to opportunity costs. Because capital market rates have maturities longer than one year, lenders demand that borrowers pay a *term* or maturity risk premium for funds. The longer the term

of the loan, the greater the premium, as lenders must forgo other investment opportunities during that period. Lenders also want to make sure they retain the purchasing power of the money they lend, so they seek compensation for *unexpected inflation.* Recall that expected inflation is already included in the risk-free rate. The premium for inflation risk is very important, because inflation can change so quickly and because mortgage loans are relatively long term. A business risk premium must also be added, that is, compensation for possible *default* (a credit risk premium). During the late 1980s and early 1990s, when overbuilt and rapidly deteriorating real estate markets were the cause of great concern among lenders, real estate loans carried large default risk premiums. As construction levels dropped dramatically and real estate markets improved, the business (default) risk premium declined.

A major risk in residential markets is *prepayment* or *callability risk.* Yield maintenance clauses or outright bans on prepayments have made prepayment risk a much more manageable form of risk for commercial borrowers.[15] Finally, *marketability risk* remains a major risk category for today's commercial loans, though that risk is declining as the secondary market for income-property loans expands.

The Financing Cycle

We conclude our overview of real estate finance by classifying real estate loans according to the time the loan is made, in a sequence that begins with the acquisition of raw land and ends with a fully developed property ready for use or sale. The object of the discussion is threefold:

- To demonstrate the importance of financing at every stage of the real estate development process;
- To indicate how different sources of financing are appropriate at different stages in the real estate development process; and
- To illustrate how loans at each stage are tailored, in their terms and interest rates, to reflect the lender's risks at each stage.

Land Acquisition

The feature that most distinguishes financing land acquisition is the absence of institutional lenders. Because lenders are concerned about the ability to service the debt, they generally consider risk to be in inverse proportion to the cash flow from the property. Raw land generates no income and as a matter of legal restrictions or internal policy, land loans are frequently avoided altogether or limited to a small percentage of most institutions' portfolios.

A common source of financing for land acquisitions is a *purchase money mortgage*—a loan taken back by the seller of the land. As the buyer develops the land, new financing is obtained and the seller is paid off.

Land Development

Land development is the process of preparing raw land for the construction of improvements. It includes grading land where necessary, obtaining rezoning if required, and installing utilities, sewers, streets, and sidewalks. Although developed land creates no more income than does raw land, it is nevertheless one step closer to its ultimate use. Still, it is quite difficult to finance land development, because "seller financing" has no parallel in land acquisition. Most land development loans represent a first lien on the property and are short term. The interest charged is usually tied to the commercial banks' prime lending rate (1 to 4 points above the prime rate).

Development loans are disbursed in draws (or stages) as development progresses. The lender allows release of specified tracts (lots) from the overall mortgage as development proceeds, and individual lots are sold to builders. When tracts or lots are sold and released, the borrower must make a payment to the lender in exchange for the release. The release price is generally 10 to 20 percent greater than the proportional principal and interest associated with the released tract, thus ensuring that the lender will receive more repayment of the early sale of the choice lots and deferring the developer's profit until the development has been nearly sold out.

Construction

Real estate construction finance is a specialized process in which commercial banks play a dominant role. Construction loans are used to pay for materials, labor, overhead, and related costs. The real estate is the primary collateral for the loan, with the developer sometimes required to post additional collateral, such as other real estate, securities, or possibly third-party guarantees.

Construction loans usually run from six months to two years and, similar to land development loans, are disbursed in stages (or draws) as construction proceeds. For example, 20 percent of the loan might be drawn down when the foundation is laid, the next 20 percent when the framing is completed, and so forth. In this way, the construction lender is assured that construc-tion funds are being used for the intended purpose, and in the event of a default, the value of the property will (the lender hopes) have been increased in an amount equal to disbursements on the construction loan. Typically, the borrower (developer) pays an initial loan fee plus interest on the funds actually drawn down.

The source of repayment of the construction loan is often the permanent loan. The construction lender, being a short-term lender, however, is often unwilling to contemplate the possibility that no permanent financing may be available when the construction is complete. To protect themselves, construction lenders sometimes require developers to obtain a *permanent loan commitment* as a condition of obtaining a construction loan. The commitment is an agreement by another lender (such as an S&L or a life insurance company) to make the permanent loan, provided the building is constructed in accordance with approved plans and specifications. This permanent loan commitment is often called a "takeout commitment" because it is the means whereby the construction lender will be taken out of the transaction when construction is completed.

In addition to the contract rate of interest, permanent loan commitments may include an equity participation by the lender and a fixed rate of interest. Participations allow the lenders to increase their yield by sharing in the project's operating income (income participation) or capital gain (equity participation).

Permanent Financing

The final stage in the real estate cycle begins when the property is put to use by the owner or by the tenants who have leased space. It is at this point that the long-term (permanent) loan is funded. Assuming a permanent loan commitment has been obtained, the developer need only provide the permanent lender with evidence of satisfactory completion, and the loan is disbursed. Most or all of the loan is used to pay off the construction lender.

Sometimes the permanent loan commitment requires not only that the improvements be completed, but also that a minimum level of rentals be achieved before the full amount of the permanent loan is funded. For example, a requirement for rental achievement might provide that, on completion of the improvements, 70 percent of the permanent loan will be disbursed, with the balance of the permanent loan to be disbursed once 80 percent of the building is rented at or above a certain rent. A loan containing this type of clause is called a *floor-to-ceiling loan,* because it is disbursed in two stages. The purpose of the clause is to assure the lender that sufficient income is forthcoming to service the loan before the entire amount is disbursed.

Suppose now that the construction lender has insisted on a permanent (takeout) loan commitment equal to the full amount of the construction loan. If the best the developer can do is obtain a floor-to-ceiling loan, with the ceiling equal to the construction financing, a gap will exist if only the floor amount of the permanent loan is funded at the completion of construction.

To close this gap, the developer may obtain an additional loan commitment to provide *gap financing*. With a gap commitment, another lender agrees to provide a permanent second mortgage in the event that the full amount of the permanent first mortgage is not advanced when construction is completed. As with most second mortgages, such an agreement will be more costly in terms of both interest and origination fees.

Over the life of the project, the permanent loan may be repaid in a number of ways, mostly *amortization, refinancing,* and *prepayment*.

Amortization

The loan may be gradually amortized (paid off) during its term, eventually being paid in its entirety at maturity. At that point, the owner's equity interest will equal the full market value of the property (full amount of mortgage plus equity value, if any).

Refinancing

Before the original mortgage matures, the owner may 1) renegotiate its terms with the original lender, 2) increase the loan amount, or 3) pay off the existing mortgage and obtain a new mortgage. These variations of *loan refinancing* occur for one of three reasons: 1) to increase the property's potential for sale by making the financing more attractive to a buyer, 2) to generate tax-free cash for the owner by increasing the existing debt, or 3) to decrease the existing debt so as to reduce the monthly debt service and increase cash flow to the owner.

Prepayment

Often the owner of a property will sell it before the existing mortgage has been paid off. In such an event, the lender may call the loan,[16] or the new owner may wish to pay off the existing mortgage and arrange new financing. The clause in the mortgage that permits early payoff is the prepayment clause.[17]

Summary

The financial markets are a broad aggregation of financial instruments, lenders, and investors using financial instruments to match those who need funds with those who have surplus funds. Real estate and real estate–related investments are major players in the financial markets. Equity may be raised in either the private or public markets in a variety of ownership structures, including a corporation, limited partnership, limited liability company, and REIT. Debt financing is both short term (construction loans) using money market instruments, and long term (permanent mortgage loans) using capital market instruments.

In the debt markets, the Fed has the greatest influence on short-term interest rates. Longer-term capital market rates change largely in response to shifts in expected inflation and various risk factors. An examination of several different lending institutions, including the traditional ones such as commercial banks and life insurance companies, underscores the pressures —from regulators, the raters of their debt, and the financial markets—under which these lenders operate. Pension funds maintain the potential to be a huge force in the real estate debt and equity markets. Traditional lenders like commercial banks and life insurance companies will continue to be large providers of debt capital in the future, just as the traditional sources of equity capital will continue to provide most equity funds. Nevertheless, investment bankers will significantly expand the role of the secondary mortgage markets for commercial loans through REMICs and of the public equity markets for real estate ownership shares through REITs.

Terms

- C corporation
- Capital markets—public and private
- Commercial bank
- Construction (or interim) loan
- Default or credit risk
- Fed funds
- Financial Institutions Reform, Recovery, and Enhancement Act (FIRREA)
- Floor-to-ceiling loan
- Gap loan
- Inflation risk
- Joint venture
- Land development
- LIBOR
- Life insurance company
- Limited liability company

- Limited partnership
- Marketability risk
- Miniperm
- Monetary policy
- Money markets
- Mortgage banker
- Mortgage broker
- Mortgage loan
- Open-market operations
- Pension fund
- Permanent loan
- Permanent loan commitment
- Prepayment
- Prime rate
- Purchase money mortgage
- Real estate investment trust (REIT)
- Refinancing
- REMIC
- Resolution Trust Corporation (RTC)
- Risk-free interest rate
- S corporation
- Securitization
- Syndication
- Takeout commitment
- Temporary financing
- Term or maturity risk premium
- Thrift institution
- Tranche

Review Questions

4.1 Explain the difference between money markets and capital markets.

4.2 How have funds for real estate been raised in the past? How are they raised now? Explain the reasons for changes.

4.3 Discuss the relationship between aggregate savings and aggregate investment in the economy.

4.4 Explain how financial markets allow individuals to "violate" the savings equals investment ratio.

4.5 The U.S. government tends to have the first claim on our savings. Why?

4.6 Differentiate between primary and secondary financial markets.

4.7 What are two main reasons for the fluctuation of money market rates?

4.8 Explain open-market operations and how they affect interest rates and the money supply.

4.9 Describe how risk-based capital adequacy regulations have affected lending by commercial banks and life insurance companies.

4.10 How did government intervention affect thrift institutions?

4.11 Describe REMIC and REIT structures.

Notes

1. See David J. Hartzell, Presidential Address delivered at the American Real Estate and Urban Economics Association meeting, New York, New York, January 4, 1999.

2. This literature starts with Jeff Fisher at Indiana University and extends through recent work by David Ling at the University of Florida.

3. For example, the Urban Land Institute's *Land Use Digest* summarizes key market trends for developers, including changes in the capital markets. The national accounting firms and several large commercial brokerage companies publish real estate newsletters. Investment banking firms publish digests of many of the other newsletters but emphasize conditions in the public debt and equity markets, because they concentrate on real estate's expanding role in these markets. Other sources of information include "The Ground Floor," a column in *Barron's* weekly newspaper, as well as quarterly publications such as *Real Estate Capital Markets Report, Real Estate Finance Journal, Real Estate Finance, Secondary Mortgage Markets,* and *Real Estate Review.*

4. See William Brueggeman and Jeffrey Fisher, *Real Estate Finance and Investments,* 10th ed. (Homewood, Ill.: Irwin, 1996), Chap. 12, for a detailed discussion of different organizational entities available to real estate developers.

5. Several major developers have converted to the REIT form of organization. Using a form of REIT called an UPREIT (umbrella partnership REIT) to minimize the tax consequences of conversion, Alfred Taubman's Michigan-based Taubman Co., Melvin Simon's Indianapolis-based Simon Property Group, and Oliver Carr's Washington, D.C.–based Carr Realty are development organizations that have adopted REIT status.

6. See Terrence Clauretie and G. Stacy Sirmans, *Real Estate Finance,* 3d ed. (Upper Saddle River, N.J.: Prentice-Hall, 1999), Chap. 17, "Sources of Funds for Commercial Real Estate Properties," for more detailed information about the real estate debt markets.

7. The prevailing prime interest rate, LIBOR, and several other money market rates are reported daily in the *Wall Street*

Journal. Look in the "Credit Markets" portion of the third section ("Money & Investing") under "Money Rates" for a list of current rates.

8. For further information about the Fed and the way it conducts monetary policy, see S. Kerry Cooper and Donald R. Fraser, *The Financial Marketplace,* 4th ed. (Reading, Mass.: Addison-Wesley Publishing Co., 1993); and Peter S. Rose, *Money and Capital Markets: The Financial System in an Increasingly Global Economy,* 5th ed. (Burr Ridge, Ill.: Richard D. Irwin, 1994).

9. See Clauretie and Sirmans, *Real Estate Finance,* 3d ed., Chap. 7, "Sources of Funds."

10. An excellent overview of the problems is contained in J. Thomas Black and William E. Hauser, "Moderating Cyclical Overbuilding in Commercial Real Estate," in *ULI on the Future* (Washington, D.C.: ULI–the Urban Land Institute, 1993).

11. A readable analysis of this complex issue is offered in Claude J. Zinngrabe, Jr., "Real Estate Investment by Insurance Companies," *Urban Land,* March 1994, pp. 12–14 +.

12. A yield curve is the relationship between the yield on an instrument and the number of years until it matures or comes due. Most commonly, the yield curve refers to U.S. Treasury instruments. It is published daily in the "Credit Markets" portion of the third section ("Money & Investing") of the *Wall Street Journal.* Yield curves are normally upward sloping, with higher yields on later-maturing instruments, but they may be flat or even downward sloping, as they were during much of the high-inflation 1970s.

13. See Dan McCaddrey and Peter McNally, "U.S. Pension Fund Investments in Real Estate: Current and Future Investment Strategy," *Real Estate Finance,* Winter 1997, pp. 46–58; and Terrence Ahern, Youguo Liang, and F.C. Neil Myer, "Leverage in a Pension Fund Real Estate Program," *Real Estate Finance,* Summer 1998, pp. 55–62.

14. The difference between a *mortgage banking firm* and a *mortgage conduit* is that the former services the loan for the institution that provides the mortgage funds, while the latter simply originates a loan in the funding institution's name, collecting an origination fee (as does the mortgage banker) but allowing the mortgage investor to arrange for the servicing by either performing it itself or contracting with another firm to do it. (The *loan servicer* collects the periodic payments when they are due, makes sure the real estate serving as collateral for the loan is maintained in good repair, checks to see that property taxes and fire and extended theft insurance premiums are paid on time, attempts to get the borrower to make any late payments, and—if necessary—forecloses on the loan if the borrower is unable or unwilling to cure any defaults. The lender pays compensation for servicing the loan out of the borrower's interest payment, typically computed as a small percentage of the outstanding loan balance.) Moreover, mortgage banking firms may also act as mortgage brokers in some instances and not service the loans they originate.

15. Commercial mortgage investors sometimes mistakenly attribute default risk to the category of callability risk. When a commercial mortgage defaults, the servicer sells the property, and the mortgage investors receive a large portion or perhaps all of their money back as proceeds from the foreclosure sale. This risk is default risk, although it may appear to be callability risk, because the funds are returned to the lender earlier than expected.

16. In residential mortgages, such a "call provision on sale" for lenders is common. It is less common in commercial mortgages.

17. In some cases, this early payoff must be accompanied by a payment of penalty interest.

Chapter 5

Financial Theory: The Logic behind Real Estate Financing Decisions

Chapter 4 described the financial marketplace in which the real estate developer competes for construction and permanent loans. This chapter focuses on the financial analysis tools available to lenders, investors, and developers.

Lenders and equity investors who provide funding expect rates of return commensurate with the risks taken. The first part of this chapter discusses the source of those returns, which is principally the property's net operating income. It then moves to a discussion of the costs and benefits of debt financing from the viewpoint of the equity investor; the last part of the chapter goes through the mechanics of the analytic tools that help lenders and equity investors make their investment decisions. The most important of these tools is the discounted cash flow model, which combines all relevant assumptions into a single estimate of value and thus determines whether a proposed development is worth more than it will cost to construct and whether its value provides sufficient collateral for a loan. Clearly, knowing how to satisfy lenders and equity investors is

critical to the developer, who is ultimately responsible for financing the project.

This chapter discusses:

- The productivity of property;
- Financing from the equity perspective;
- Financing from the lender's perspective and estimating the property's value;
- Ability to service the debt;
- A case study, 4455 Jefferson Avenue; and
- Leverage effects.

The Productivity of Property: The Starting Point

Net operating income (NOI) measures the property's productivity and is the source of the returns to lenders and equity investors. A basic statement of NOI looks like this (a detailed statement accompanies the case study in this chapter):

Potential Gross Income
−Vacancy Allowance
Effective Gross Income
−Operating Expenses
Net Operating Income.

Notice that NOI is a number not easily manipulated by the owner or manager, as rents, vacancies, and operating expenses are disciplined by the market. The development's features, functions, and benefits determine how the project's rent will compare with other projects

The primary authors of this chapter are Kenneth Lusht, PhD, professor, Pennsylvania State University, and Mike E. Miles, PhD. The authors are grateful to Richard L. Haney, PhD, professor, Texas A&M University, for his early contributions to this chapter; Mark J. Eppli, PhD, professor, George Washington University, for permission to use excerpts from Chapter 3 of the *Office Development Handbook* (Washington, D.C.: ULI– the Urban Land Institute, 1998); and Charles H. Wurtzebach and Susanne Etheridge Cannon for permission to use excerpts from *Modern Real Estate,* 5th ed. (New York: John Wiley & Sons, 1994).

in the market, but the market is the constraining factor. Gross rent is constrained by the competing properties in the market, and a significant increase in rents will bring increased vacancies. Operating expenses, too, will be forced to hover at or near market rates to maintain a competitive maintenance program so as not to lose tenants. Because calculations of NOI are based on market assumptions, NOI is a "same-for-all" number that measures the amount of income expected to be available to be divided between the debt and equity investors. How that income will be divided depends on the financing decisions made during the development process.

Making the Financing Decision: The Equity Perspective

For the past several decades, loan-to-value (LTV) ratios have clustered at 60 to 90 percent. Because this clustering is too concentrated to have occurred by chance, it indicates that benefits can accrue to owners through the use of debt financing. At the same time, most investors do not use 100 percent debt financing, which suggests that certain costs must eventually offset the benefits of debt, thus creating an optimal loan-to-value range.

The Benefits of Using Debt Financing

A basic benefit of debt is that it can be used to leverage the return to equity upward. This "positive" leverage, focusing on a single year's performance, occurs when the cost of debt financing (the *loan constant*) is lower than the overall return generated by the property (NOI divided by cost). In such situations, the percentage return to the equity investor is greater using debt than it is with no debt. Moreover, certain tax benefits may also be associated with the use of debt. Interest payments are typically tax deductible, and debt increases the tax basis beyond the equity investment, thus enhancing the tax shelter generated from depreciation. The use of debt financing also reduces the minimum investment necessary in any given project. Because investors have limited resources, a reduced minimum investment in one project allows them to spread their wealth over several investments, that is, to diversify. Diversification reduces portfolio risk, and lower risk means higher value.

Finally, by combining various debt and equity structures, the decision maker can create risk-return opportunities to fit investors' specific needs. This flexibility to tailor the investment to suit the client (investor) is an additional benefit of debt financing.

The Costs of Using Debt Financing

This discussion about the benefits of debt financing may suggest a free lunch for the borrower: it appears positive leverage creates higher returns and, through diversification, potentially lower risk. But that is only part of the story. The reality is that the basic relationship between risk and return is not suspended in the case of using debt. When equity investors borrow in an attempt to chase higher returns, they assume the cost of greater variability in those returns—higher risk. And, at the extreme, if the project's income drops below the level of debt service, the investor may face default and foreclosure.

In addition to creating more risk, borrowing also entails various direct costs. The financial institutions that aggregate savers' funds and then allocate them to equity investors charge fees for their service, and the charges are generally paid by the borrower. Further, as the LTV ratio increases, the lender's exposure increases. In response, lenders raise the interest rate. Finally, the paperwork required in mortgage lending and the lender's time (as a financial intermediary) must be compensated. Combining increased risk, the cost of potential foreclosure, and all the costs of using a financial middleman, it is not surprising that the incremental costs of debt eventually outweigh the incremental benefits. Just before that point, the optimal LTV ratio is reached. As we noted, evidence over an extended time suggests that that optimal point is between 60 percent and 90 percent debt.

Making the Financing Decision: The Lender's Perspective

In practice, of course, loan-to-value ratios are not solely the result of owners' decisions. Prospective lenders must also be convinced that an existing property or a new development will support the level of debt requested by the equity investor.

Lenders use two basic criteria for making their decisions about lending: 1) the adequacy of the property's value as collateral for the loan, and 2) the ability of the property's income stream to service the loan.

Estimating Property (Collateral) Value

Two approaches typically are used to estimate property value: 1) discounted cash flow (DCF) models, and 2) capitalization rates. The following discussion begins with the time-value-of-money concept that is central to DCF modeling.

Estimating Value Using the DCF Model

When comparing alternatives for investment, investors are motivated by two preferences:

- *More is better than less;* and
- *Sooner is better than later, or a dollar received today is more valuable than a dollar received in the future.*

These commonplace notions seem so simple as to be self-evident, yet they lie at the heart of the time-value-of-money concept that leads to the DCF method of analysis by lenders and investors.[1] Both statements refer to project income or cash flows and suggest that both the magnitude and timing of those cash flows are important. When comparing alternative investments that carry comparable risk and require an equal capital investment, investors prefer the alternative that will produce the most total income from operations and resale; hence, more is better than less. And among alternatives for investment with comparable risk and equal total income, investors prefer the option that will produce income more quickly; hence, sooner is better than later.

Three major concepts drive the notion that a dollar received today is more valuable than a dollar received in the future: 1) opportunity cost, 2) inflation, and 3) risk.

Opportunity Cost. A dollar in hand today provides more choices; it can be used for consumption or can be invested. If the dollar is not to be received for one year, the interest that could have been earned must be forgone. The forgone interest represents the opportunity cost associated with receiving a dollar in the future rather than today. Consequently, today's value, or the present value, of the dollar to be received in one year should be reduced by the cost of the lost opportunity.

Inflation. Inflation reduces the value of the dollar. When price levels rise, more dollars are required to purchase the same quantity and quality of goods and services than previously. When a dollar is to be received in the future, its present value is reduced if inflation occurs before the investor receives that dollar. Conversely, if money is borrowed today, dollars used for future repayments will have less value than the dollars borrowed should inflation occur in the interim.

Risk. If a dollar is due in the future, the possibility always exists that more or less than a dollar will be received or that inflation has been incorrectly estimated. Business risk and the risk of unexpected inflation diminish the present value of the future dollar.

The Consideration of Time-Value in the DCF Model

The fundamental idea that sooner is better than later is applied in DCF models by *discounting* future income at a rate that reflects the opportunity costs, inflation,

and risks accompanying the passage of time.[2] The word *discounting* describes exactly what occurs: the value of future income is discounted (reduced) to estimate its present value. (Appendix B at the end of this book contains a detailed discussion of the mechanics of the discounting process.) The following example is a simple application of the method.

Suppose an investment is expected to produce the income stream and the sale proceeds (reversion) at the end of the holding period shown below, and that a discount rate of 10 percent is considered appropriate. That is, a rate of 10 percent is considered reasonable to compensate the investor for the costs and risks associated with the passing of time.

Year	Income	Reversion
1	$110,000	
2	111,000	
3	112,000	
4	115,000	
5	125,000	$1,000,000

With application of the DCF model, the present value of the property is estimated as follows:

$$V = \left(\$110,000 \times \frac{1}{(1+.10)^1} \right) + \left(\$111,000 \times \frac{1}{(1+.10)^2} \right) +$$
$$\left(\$112,000 \times \frac{1}{(1+.10)^3} \right) + \left(\$115,000 \times \frac{1}{(1+.10)^4} \right) +$$
$$\left(\$1,125,000 \times \frac{1}{(1+.10)^5} \right) = \$1,052,960.$$

The estimated value of $1,052,960 is driven by the expected return of 10 percent. An investor who pays the estimated value and then receives the forecasted stream of income plus the reversion will make exactly a 10 percent annual return.

Calculating the discount factors

$$\frac{1}{(1+.10)^1}, \frac{1}{(1+.10)^2}, \ldots \frac{1}{(1+.10)^5}$$

yields 0.909, 0.826 . . . 0.621. The present value of $1.00 received *one* year from today, given the discount rate of 10 percent, is $.91, or $1.00 (.909). Similarly, a dollar received *two* years from today is worth only $.83, or $1.00 (.826).

Estimating Value Using Capitalization Rates

The second commonly used method to estimate the value of property (collateral) is to capitalize expected first year NOI by a *capitalization rate* extracted from sales of comparable properties. That is,

$$V = \frac{NOI}{R}$$

where
V is the value of the property and
R is the capitalization rate.

Suppose we have identified two properties similar to the property we valued above using the DCF model and that the following information is available:

Comparable Sale	Sale Price	NOI
1	$1,400,000	$145,000
2	$1,350,000	$150,000.

Thus, the capitalization rate on the first sale was $145,000 ÷ $1,400,000 = .104 and on the second sale was $150,000 ÷ $1,350,000 = .111.

Because the two sales are equally similar to the subject, data from the two sales suggest an average market capitalization rate of about .1075. Applying this rate to the first year's NOI of our example property yields

$$V = \frac{\$110,000}{.1075}$$

$$= \$1,023,256,$$

which can be compared with the estimate of value using DCF analysis of $1,052,960. In this case, the values estimated using the two models are very close, but in practice, that will not always be the case. When the estimates of value diverge, investors often rely more heavily on the results of the DCF analysis for two main reasons. First, DCF models force the analyst to think explicitly about future income and property value. Thus, the DCF model not only produces "the number," but also provides information about the income and sale price assumptions that produced the number.[3] Second, the use of cap rates assumes the properties from which the rates were extracted are very similar to the property being valued. Given the heterogeneity of most income properties, that assumption is often wrong. Although the projections used in the DCF analysis are only estimates —that is, they may not come true—the additional details and rigor usually make the DCF analysis slightly preferable. In practice, most people do both and start negotiations with whichever one works better for them.

Converting the Estimate of Value to a Loan Amount: Applying the Loan-to-Value Ratio

After estimating a property's value, the maximum loan amount is determined by applying the loan-to-value

ratio, which is the percentage of value the lender is willing to loan. Assume that the available loan-to-value ratio for our example is 70 percent; then a loan of about .70 × $1,050,000, or $735,000, is indicated. A 70 percent loan means a 30 percent value "cushion" exists before the property's value falls below the amount of the loan and puts the lender's principal at risk.

Ability to Service the Debt

Property value is not the only criterion for making loans. Equally, if not more, important is the ability of the property's income stream to service the debt. And just as the LTV ratio provides a collateral cushion, lenders demand an ability-to-service cushion. That cushion is measured by the debt service coverage ratio (DSCR), which is NOI divided by debt service:

$$DSCR = \frac{NOI}{Debt\ Service.}$$

To illustrate the use of the DSCR, we again use the example of the property we have valued at about $1,050,000.[4]

Suppose lenders require about a 20 percent cushion between NOI and debt service, that is, a DSCR of 1.20. Given the first year's expected NOI of $110,000 and the DSCR of 1.20, the *maximum* debt service the property can support is $91,667:

$$DS = \frac{NOI}{DSCR}$$

$$= \frac{\$110,000}{1.2}$$

$$= \$91,667.$$

This amount, $91,667, is now used to calculate a maximum loan amount. For any interest rate and term, an amount of debt service must be repaid each period to pay the lender's interest and fully amortize the loan. That amount of debt service divided by the original loan produces a percentage called the *mortgage constant* (MC):

$$MC = \frac{DS}{Loan.}$$

The mortgage constant is simply the percentage of the original loan that must be repaid each period. The mathematics of calculating the mortgage constant is presented in Appendix B.

We now have two key measures: the maximum debt service the property can support, based on the

DSCR, and the mortgage constant, based on the interest rate and term. Lenders use these two measures to calculate a maximum loan amount.

Assume for our example property that the mortgage constant is 12 percent. (That is, for the stated interest rate X and loan term Y, a payment of 12 percent of principal each year will pay off the loan in year Y with X percent interest on the unpaid balance.) Given the maximum debt service the property will support ($91,667), the justified loan amount is:

$$\text{Debt} = \frac{\text{NOI}}{\text{MC}}$$

$$= \frac{\$91,667}{.12}$$

$$= \$763,892.$$

Which criterion is constraining: collateral value or ability to service? Our analysis suggests that a $735,000 loan is justified based on a 70 percent loan-to-value ratio applied to property value, and that a $763,000 loan is justified based on ability to service. In practice, lenders tend toward the lower, more conservative amount, in this case $735,000.

4455 Jefferson Avenue: A Case Study

We now apply the ability-to-service and collateral value criteria to a more complete and realistic example. Figures 5-1 and 5-2 list the project data and assumptions and the pro forma income statement for 4455 Jefferson Avenue, a proposed build-to-suit office building with a net rentable area of 162,500 square feet.

Potential gross rent is based on a rental rate of $21.00 per square foot. The tenant's lease is a modified gross lease agreement in which no expenses are passed through to the tenant in the first year of the lease agreement, so zero expense pass-throughs are included in the income statement. Parking income is estimated at $125,000. These three income sources add up to a potential gross income of $3,537,500 a year for the project. A 7 percent vacancy factor produces effective gross income of $3,289,875.

Total expenses for 4455 Jefferson are made up of operating expenses, real estate taxes, and cash reserves for replacement. Typical operating expenses for an office building include payroll, insurance, cleaning services, utilities, maintenance and repair, and management fees. Operating expenses should be carefully projected during the design phase of development. The Building Owners and Managers Association's annual *Experience*

Figure 5-1

4455 Jefferson Avenue: Project Data and Assumptions

4455 Jefferson Avenue is a proposed build-to-suit office building with a net rentable area of 162,500 square feet. Before construction, a lease agreement was signed with one tenant to occupy the entire building. The lender's market and financial analyses have led to the following assumptions about the project's financial performance.

Income and Expenses

Rent	$21.00 per square foot
Rent Escalations	2% per year
Parking Income	$125,000
Vacancy Loss	7% of potential gross income
Operating Expenses	$735,000
Real Estate Taxes	$398,000
Cash Reserves	2% of potential gross income[a]

Lease

Type	Modified gross lease
Term	15 years

Permanent Loan

Interest Rate	9.5%
Term	10 years
Amortization Period	30 years
Amount	To be determined

[a]Potential gross income equals potential gross rent plus expense pass-throughs plus parking fees.

Exchange Report provides useful information on operating expenses and income based on a survey of U.S. office buildings. Experienced property managers and appraisers are another good source of information for projecting operating expense projections.

Line (i) in 4455 Jefferson's income and expense statement (Figure 5-2) indicates reserves for replacement, which is a contingency account that is used to pay for the replacement of major capital items such as HVAC systems, elevators, and roofs. As a new building, 4455 Jefferson needs to set aside only a relatively small amount of cash for replacements, essentially just enough to cover breakdowns beyond normal maintenance. In older buildings, the analyst should plan for specific expenditures for replacement of capital items expected to be replaced over the term of the analysis, usually ten years.

Figure 5-2

4455 Jefferson Avenue: First-Year NOI

Income

(a) Potential Gross Rent	$3,412,500
(b) Expense Pass-Throughs	0
(c) Parking Income	125,000
(d) Potential Gross Income	$3,537,500
(e) Vacancy Credit/Loss (7%)	(247,625)
(f) Effective Gross Income	$3,289,875

Expenses

(g) Operating Expenses	$735,000
(h) Real Estate Taxes	398,000
(i) Cash Reserves for Replacements	70,750
(j) Total Expenses	$1,203,750
(k) Net Operating Income	$2,086,125

Figure 5-3

4455 Jefferson Avenue: Calculation of Maximum Loan Amount

Potential Gross Income	$3,537,500
− Vacancy Credit/Loss	247,625
Effective Gross Income	$3,289,875
− Operating Expenses	735,000
− Real Estate Taxes	398,000
− Cash Reserves for Replacements	70,750
Net Operating Income	$2,086,125
÷ Debt Service Coverage Ratio	1.20
Cash Available for Debt Service	$1,738,438
÷ Mortgage Constant	10.09%
Maximum Loan Amount	$17,229,316
	say $17,200,000

The building's total annual expenses are expected to be $1,203,750. Subtracting this sum from the effective gross income produces an expected NOI of $2,086,125. Two categories of expenses—tenant improvements and leasing costs—are not included in the calculation of NOI for several reasons. First, these costs generally are not considered an expense for tax purposes but are depreciated over the life of the lease or the life of the building. Depreciation is not a cash expense, so these costs are excluded from NOI. Second, these costs are quite irregular. They vary from year to year, depending on the square footage of expiring leases, and if they were included, the NOI would fluctuate wildly from period to period. Third, the development budget usually includes funds to cover the initial leasing of the building.

Estimating the loan amount for 4455 Jefferson Avenue involves applying the ability-to-service criterion and the collateral value criterion.

Applying the Ability-to-Service Criterion

Now that first-year net operating income has been estimated for 4455 Jefferson, the lender can calculate a maximum loan amount based on the NOI, the mortgage constant, and the required DSCR (see Figure 5-3). With first-year NOI of $2,086,125 and an assumed DSCR of 1.20, 4455 Jefferson Avenue can support an annual debt service of $1,738,438. Dividing this debt service by the mortgage constant of 10.09 percent (the installment needed to amortize a dollar at 9.5 percent interest for 30 years on a monthly basis) yields a maximum loan amount of approximately $17,200,000.

The importance of the lender's required debt service coverage ratio in the determination of maximum loans cannot be overstated. Whether the loan is securitized through CMBSs or held as a whole loan by a commercial bank or insurance company, the debt service coverage ratio is a critical ratio that lenders use to assess whether or not they want to make a loan. Figure 5-4 illustrates how dramatically the amount of the loan on 4455 Jefferson would vary with changes in the DSCR and the mortgage constant.

Applying the Collateral Value Criterion

Cap Rate Approach

A number of real estate brokerage, appraisal, and consulting firms publish quarterly compilations of capitalization rates by property type and market area. Typically, cap rates for office developments in 4455 Jefferson's market range from 7 percent to 13 percent (see Figure 5-5), with most well-leased properties in good locations selling at cap rates of 7 to 9.5 percent. The low-risk profile of 4455 Jefferson Avenue justifies a low 8.75 percent cap rate. Capitalizing first-year NOI of $2,086,125 at .0875 produces an estimated value of $23,841,400.

DCF Approach

The DCF analysis for 4455 Jefferson is shown in Figure 5-6. Although a ten-year holding period is antici-

Figure 5-4

4455 Jefferson Avenue: Maximum Loan Amount Sensitivity Analysis

Mortgage Constant	Debt Service Coverage Ratio[a]		
	1.15	1.25	1.35
8.0%	$22,675,000	$20,861,000	$19,316,000
10.0%	$18,140,000	$16,689,000	$15,453,000
12.0%	$15,117,000	$13,907,000	$12,877,000

[a]Maximum loan amounts based on a net operating income of $2,086,125.

pated, 11th-year NOI is calculated to permit a determination of the property's reversion value. The reversion amount is simply the property's market value after ten years. That future market value will be based on the first-year NOI of the next owner, which is our Year 11.

Capitalizing Year 11 NOI ($2,761,000) by an estimated cap rate of 9.25 percent[5] yields a property reversion of $29,850,000. A 12 percent discount rate[6] applied to the income and the reversion sale price produces estimated present value of $22,422,000. This estimate is slightly lower than the $23,841,400 that was estimated as the project's value using the cap rate approach. Again, when estimates of value diverge, lenders tend toward the lower, more conservative number.

Applying an 80 percent loan-to-value ratio to the lower estimate of $22,422,000 produces a loan amount of $17,937,600 (.80 × $22,422,000). Recall that the maximum loan calculated based on the ability-to-service criteria was $17,200,000. How does the lender reconcile the two possible amounts? Recall that the ability-to-service and collateral value criteria assess two very different risks. The loan-to-value ratio applied to property value addresses the preservation of the loan principal. It provides a value cushion before the principal balance of the loan is at risk. The ability-to-service criterion addresses the ability of the income generated by the project to support the debt service. Because the two criteria address such different risks, you have probably already guessed which loan amount will be available—almost certainly the lower of the two.

For 4455 Jefferson Avenue, this amount is $17,200,000, based on ability to service the debt. The lender would welcome a loan request from a developer of less than $17,200,000 and would probably reject a request for an amount significantly in excess of $17,200,000.

Leverage Effects . . . Again

Earlier, we discussed the benefits and costs of the use of debt financing (leverage) in general terms. We identified a key trade: the potential to leverage expected equity returns upward versus the increased risk that accompanies this strategy. Now that we have worked through a detailed case study—4455 Jefferson Avenue—we return

Figure 5-5

Average Capitalization Rates for CBD and Suburban Office Properties: 1989 to 1997[a]

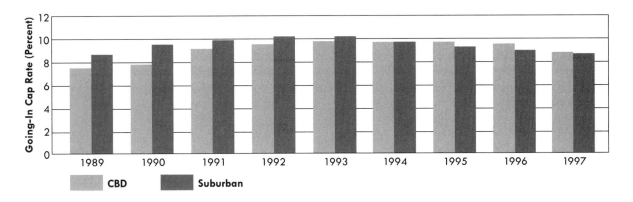

[a]All capitalization rates are fourth-quarter averages, except for 1997, which is the third-quarter average.

Source: Real Estate Research Corporation.

Figure 5-6

4455 Jefferson Avenue: Permanent Lender's Discounted Cash Flow Analysis (Thousands of Dollars)

	Year 1	Year 2	Year 3	Year 4	Year 5	Year 6	Year 7	Year 8	Year 9	Year 10	Year 11
Revenue											
(a) Gross Rent	$3,413	$3,481	$3,550	$3,621	$3,694	$3,768	$3,843	$3,920	$3,998	$4,078	$4,159
(b) Expense Pass-Throughs	0	46	93	143	194	248	304	362	422	486	552
(c) Parking Income	125	129	134	139	143	148	154	159	164	170	176
(d) Potential Gross Income	3,538	3,656	3,777	3,902	4,031	4,164	4,301	4,441	4,586	4,734	4,888
(e) Vacancy Credit/Loss	248	256	264	273	282	291	301	311	321	331	342
(f) Effective Gross Income	$3,290	$3,400	$3,513	$3,629	$3,749	$3,872	$4,000	$4,130	$4,264	$4,403	$4,546
Expenses											
(g) Operating Expenses	$735	$761	$788	$815	$843	$873	$904	$935	$968	$1,002	$1,037
(h) Real Estate Taxes	398	418	439	461	484	508	533	560	588	617	648
(i) Cash Reserves for Replacements	71	73	76	78	81	84	87	90	93	96	100
j) Total Expenses	$1,204	$1,252	$1,302	$1,354	$1,408	$1,465	$1,524	$1,585	$1,649	$1,716	$1,785
(k) Net Operating Income	$2,086	$2,148	$2,211	$2,275	$2,341	$2,408	$2,476	$2,545	$2,616	$2,688	$2,761
(l) Tenant Improvements	0	0	0	0	0	0	0	0	0	0	0
(m) Leasing Commissions	0	0	0	0	0	0	0	0	0	0	0
Return Analysis											
(n) Property Cash Flow	$2,086	$2,148	$2,211	$2,275	$2,341	$2,408	$2,476	$2,545	$2,616	$2,688	$2,761
(o) Reversion Sale Price	N/A	N/A	N/A	N/A	N/A	N/A	N/A	N/A	N/A	29,850	N/A
(p) Selling Cost	N/A	N/A	N/A	N/A	N/A	N/A	N/A	N/A	N/A	896	N/A
(q) Cash Flow	$2,086	$2,148	$2,211	$2,275	$2,341	$2,408	$2,476	$2,545	$2,616	$31,642	$2,761

(r) **Present Value of Cash Flow (at 12 percent discount rate): $22,422**

Assumptions: **Rent grows at 2 percent per year, operating expenses grow at 3.5 percent per year, the vacancy rate is 7 percent, real estate taxes grow at 5 percent per year, sales commissions equal 3 percent, reversion cap rate is 9.25 percent.**

to the tradeoff in risks and returns, using 4455 Jefferson as a point of reference.

Assume that 4455 Jefferson can be built for $19,000,000 (a later chapter details cost estimation; for now, the concern is financial analysis). Given the maximum loan amount of $17,200,000, the equity requirement is $1,800,000 ($19,000,000 cost minus $17,200,000 debt). With this background, we can analyze the impact of leverage on risk and return to 4455 Jefferson's owners. This analysis requires a comparison of two key measures of return: 1) the rate of return on total capital (ROR) and 2) the rate of return on equity (ROE).

Rate of Return on Total Capital

The ROR measures the overall return to the property, calculated as follows:

$$ROR = \frac{NOI}{Cost.}$$

You should recognize that ROR is similar to the overall capitalization rate we used to estimate property value. Both use NOI as the measure of monetary benefits. The difference is that the overall capitalization rate is the ratio of NOI to property *value,* while the ROR is the ratio of NOI to property *cost.*

The Year 1 ROR for 4455 Jefferson Avenue is

$$\text{ROR} = \frac{\$2,086,000}{\$19,000,000} = 10.98 \text{ percent.}$$

Rate of Return on Equity

While the ROR measures the return to the property, the ROE measures the return to the equity position. The ROE is the ratio of before-tax cash flow to the equity investment.[7]

$$\text{ROE} = \frac{\text{BTCF}}{\text{Equity Investment}}$$

Because the ROE is based on before-tax cash flow and the (cash) equity invested, it is often referred to as the cash-on-cash return.

For 4455 Jefferson Avenue, the ROE is calculated as follows:

Loan Amount × Mortgage Constant = Loan Payment

$17,200,000 × 10.09 (see Figure 5-3) = $1,735,480

NOI – Loan Payment = Before-Tax Cash Flow

$2,086,125 – $1,735,480 = $350,645

$$\text{ROE} = \frac{\$350,645}{\$1,800,000} = 19.48 \text{ percent.}$$

Positive and Negative Leverage

Notice that the expected ROE (19.48 percent) is significantly higher than the expected ROR (10.98 percent). Notice also that with 100 percent equity (no debt), ROR = ROE. Thus, for 4455 Jefferson Avenue, the use of debt has leveraged the expected ROE from 10.98 percent to 19.48 percent. Why? The answer is found by comparing the unleveraged return (ROR) with the cost of debt. The cost of debt in the Year 1 analysis is the mortgage constant. The general rule is that if MC is less than ROR, leverage is positive and works for the equity investor by increasing the expected return on equity. If MC is higher than ROR, however, leverage is negative and works against the equity investor by decreasing the expected return on equity. Put simply, if an investor pays less for borrowed funds than can be earned on the same funds when invested (MC < ROR), ROE will be leveraged upward, and vice versa.

For 4455 Jefferson, ROR is approximately 11 percent, and MC is 10.09 percent. Thus, leverage is positive, and as calculated earlier, the 80 percent loan increases the expected ROE from 10.98 percent to 19.48 percent.

Now suppose the financing associated with a particular project suggests negative leverage (ROR < MC). What can the investor do? The answer is "not very much." He can attempt to reduce MC by negotiating a lower interest rate or longer term, or attempt to increase ROR by raising rents, or reduce operating expenses, or pay less for the project. Generally, the terms of the financing are determined by the market, so little can be done to change MC. As for ROR, both rents and operating expenses are driven by the market, leaving the offering price as the only variable under the investor's control.

Leverage and the Variability of Returns

When an equity investor chases higher returns using leverage, it is at the cost of accepting higher risk. The logic is straightforward. Recall that debt has first claim on a property's NOI. If by contract a constant amount of the operating income (the debt service) must be paid to the lender, the impact of any variation in the overall operating cash flows will be felt entirely by the residual (equity) holder. This magnified effect is illustrated in Figure 5-7.

First assume the 80 percent loan. Assume also that a considerable supply of new office space opens in town and that many of the tenants at 4455 Jefferson are induced to leave at the end of their leases. Outcome 1 in Figure 5-7 assumes tenants renew their leases at the old rents (producing about $1,900,000 in NOI), whereas Outcome 2 assumes lower rents and NOI that reaches only $1,700,000. In both cases, the annual debt service is $1,735,480 and is not affected by the level of NOI. When NOI is $1,900,000, the ROE is 9.5 percent. But when NOI falls to $1,700,000, as in Outcome 2, ROE becomes negative and fails to cover the debt service.

This example demonstrates that even if positive leverage is *expected*, pro forma NOI is not always attained and ROE may fall drastically. Note in Figure 5-7 that if we assume an unleveraged situation and NOI falls to $1,700,000, the ROE would still decline but not as significantly (from 10 percent to 8.9 percent, compared with 9.5 percent to minus 2 percent in the leveraged situation). In sum, debt financing may increase the expected return to the equity investor, but only at the cost of exposing the investor to greater financial risk.

Level One and Level Two

Appendix A delineates the distinction between level one and level two of the real estate venture. The developer must be sure that the project works for all members of the development team, and financing is

Figure 5-7

4455 Jefferson: The Impact of Leverage

	Outcome 1	Outcome 2
I. Leveraged Return		
NOI	$1,900,000	$1,700,000
Annual Debt Service ($17,200,000 at 10.09%)	$1,735,480	$1,735,480
Before-Tax Cash Flow	$164,520	($35,480)
Equity Investment ($19,000,000 – $17,200,000)	$1,800,000	$1,800,000
Percentage ROE	9.5%	(2.0%)
II. Unleveraged Return		
NOI	$1,900,000	$1,700,000
Total Capital Invested	$19,000,000	$19,000,000
Percentage ROR	10%	8.9%

a major factor distinguishing level one from level two project feasibility. In subsequent chapters, we will return to this consideration and add an after-tax perspective. Any use of debt financing means that a disproportionate share of the project's depreciable basis goes to the equity holder, creating a significant level two benefit, as depreciation is a noncash expense that is tax deductible.

Summary

The financing decision can have an enormous impact on investment risks and expected returns. Historically, loan-to-value ratios have clustered around 60 to 90 percent, suggesting that a ratio in that range is optimal in terms of its costs and benefits to owners and lenders.

Two criteria dominate the financing decision, especially from the perspective of the lender. First, the property's value must provide adequate collateral to cover the loan, with a cushion of value shown in the loan-to-value ratio. Second, regardless of the adequacy of the collateral, the property must have an expected income stream adequate to service the loan, with the cushion of income measured by the debt service coverage ratio.

Collateral value is typically estimated in two ways: 1) by capitalizing first-year NOI with capitalization rates extracted from comparable sales, and 2) by discounting expected income and reversion using a discount rate that reflects the various risks and costs associated with real estate investment. The ability to service the debt is measured by the debt service coverage ratio, which produces the maximum amount for debt service. This maximum is then capitalized by the

mortgage constant, producing a maximum loan amount. When the loan amounts calculated by the collateral value and ability-to-service criteria differ, lenders tend to base their loans on the more conservative (lower) of the two.

The use of debt affects both expected risk and returns for the equity position. *Positive leverage* occurs when the cost of debt is lower than the overall return to the property; thus, leverage increases expected equity returns. *Negative leverage* occurs when the cost of debt exceeds the overall return to the property; thus, leverage reduces expected equity returns. The use of leverage to raise expected returns carries with it financial risk. Leverage increases cash flow variability, and should NOI become insufficient to service the debt, default and possibly foreclosure may result.

Terms

- Capitalization
- Capitalization rate (cap rate)
- Compound interest
- Debt service
- Debt service coverage ratio (DSCR)
- Discount rate
- Discounted cash flow (DCF) analysis
- Loan-to-value (LTV) ratio
- Mortgage constant
- Negative leverage
- Net operating income (NOI)
- Operating expenses

- Opportunity cost
- Positive leverage
- Present value
- Pro forma cash flow statement
- Time-value-of-money concept

Review Questions

5.1 What are an investor's two main concerns?

5.2 Discuss the basic benefits and costs of debt financing from the perspective of the equity investor.

5.3 What are the two basic criteria lenders use when evaluating a loan?

5.4 Explain how a lender calculates a maximum loan amount based on ability to service the loan.

5.5 What is the format for the statement of NOI?

5.6 Discuss and compare two methods of estimating collateral value.

5.7 What is the present value of an income stream of $1,000 per year for five years, $750 per year for the following three years, and $2,000 in the last year, plus a reversion of $18,000? Use a 10 percent discount rate. Relate your estimate of value to the discount rate.

Notes

1. Comprehensive discussions of time-value-of-money concepts and mechanics are found in Kenneth Lusht, *Real Estate Valuation: Principles and Applications* (Homewood, Ill.: Irwin, 1997), Chaps. 16 and 17; and William B. Brueggeman and Jeffrey D. Fisher, *Real Estate Finance and Investments,* 10th ed. (Homewood, Ill.: Irwin, 1996), Chap. 4, "The Interest Factor in Financing."

2. See C.F. Sirmans, "Research on Discounted Cash Flow Models," *Real Estate Finance,* Winter 1997, pp. 93–95, for a review of research on DCF models.

3. A more sophisticated, probabilistic approach to DCF modeling is developed in Wayne Nygard and Christophe Razaire, "Probability-Based DCF: An Alternative to Point-Value Estimates," *Appraisal Journal,* January 1999, pp. 68–74.

4. The use of the DSCR in lenders' decisions is put in historical perspective in Lusht, *Real Estate Valuation*, Chap. 15 (appendix).

5. Note that the "exit" capitalization rate is higher than the origination capitalization rate (in this case 9.25 percent versus 8.75 percent), because the ten-year-old property is less attractive as a result of higher capital requirements and less-than-ideal features, functions, and benefits.

6. The discount rate is composed of a real return, an inflation premium, and a risk premium. As previously defined in practice, investors think about "building up" a discount rate from these three components. They also look at returns on similar investments to determine an "appropriate" discount rate.

7. In Chapter 16 (and the two case studies, Europa Center and Museum Towers), this calculation will be extended to an after-tax ROE. For a more comprehensive treatment of financial leverage, investment risk, and return, see Brueggeman and Fisher, *Real Estate Finance and Investments,* and for a discussion of the effects of capital structure on risk, return, and value, see Lusht, *Real Estate Valuation,* Chap. 23.

Chapter 6

Innovations in Real Estate Finance

This chapter completes the section on real estate finance. Chapters 4 and 5 covered the foundations of real estate finance—the institutional setting, theory, and related analytic techniques. This chapter builds on that foundation with a discussion of recent innovations in the financial markets. The focus is on describing how those innovations (and evolutions) affect developers' financing their projects.

Although the underlying logic has not changed, the rules have evolved and new players have joined the game. Consequently, the traditional techniques are now often used in new and different ways. Underlying these changes are some basic principles:

- Real estate is no longer a separate market but has become an integrated part of global financial markets.
- Valuation is a function of the future income stream and the risk associated with that stream. Expected income is based largely on conditions in the local market. Properties operate in an economic environment characterized by an accelerating rate of change, so future income can seldom be known with certainty. (Details on risk analysis arc provided in Chapter 16.)
- Staying current is essential. If your competition finances its project more advantageously than you finance yours, it may provide them a sufficient edge

to overcome your better idea on a better location with better management. The bibliography at the end of this part is a beginning in the effort to stay current, but the literature continues to grow, particularly in electronic form.

- When thinking about real estate finance, never forget that the game involves two levels. Feasibility is critical at the project level, but it is also important for all the players on the development team and all the providers of capital. This distinction between level one (property) and level two (players) is carried throughout this book, but it is nowhere more important than in finance.

In a single chapter we will be able to cover only the tip of the iceberg. We will address how the major innovations affect development finance but not all of the legal details, because by the time you read this material, more innovations will have occurred and the field evolved further. This chapter will get you close to what is happening in the marketplace and will give you the foundation to understand the latest changes.

The first half of the chapter discusses:

- Opportunity funds;
- Real estate investment trusts;
- Commercial mortgage–backed securities;
- The evolution of traditional commercial real estate investors and lenders; and
- Changes in single-family residential lending.

With that background, the second half of the chapter continues the case study of Museum Towers, with a look at its financing.

The primary authors of this chapter are Kenneth Lusht, PhD, professor, Pennsylvania State University, and Mike E. Miles, PhD. The authors would like to thank Richard L. Haney, PhD, professor, Texas A&M University, for his early contributions to this chapter.

Opportunity Funds

The savings and loan crisis of the 1980s is now a distant memory, but it spawned important changes that continue to affect contemporary real estate finance. To handle the huge volume of nonperforming loans and bankrupt institutions, the federal government created the Resolution Trust Corporation. The RTC struggled for many years with the magnitude and complexity of the crisis but made only limited progress. In the end, the RTC turned to the private sector for a solution. A great deal of real estate had to change hands; both financial ownership and physical operation needed to reside with new players to begin the healing process. The "correction" was painful, but it was eventually accomplished. Given that the Japanese are still struggling with a similar problem, resolution of the S&L crisis must be seen as a success for the government, despite its high cost and significant inequities.

When the RTC turned to the private sector, it did not turn to the traditional real estate lenders. Instead, it looked to the other major players in the global capital markets, particularly those able to move quickly and handle a significant amount of risk. Wall Street firms, some private equity firms, and even hedge funds became involved. These high-risk, high-return players created what are now known as opportunity real estate funds. They used some of their own capital plus a great deal of capital raised from other investors (remember the aggregation and then allocation function of the capital markets) to buy nonperforming loans, often for ten to 50 cents on the dollar. They then found independent contractors to operate the distressed properties.

Morgan Stanley, Goldman Sachs, and Merrill Lynch were Wall Street leaders in setting up opportunity funds. On the private capital side, the Colony Capital Fund evolved from the Bass Brothers. From the hedge funds, the Westbrook Real Estate Fund evolved out of Julian Robertson's Tiger Fund. A veritable who's who of American capital markets participated in the solution of the S&L problem and, in doing so, created a major new participant—opportunity funds—in real estate capital markets.

The investment professionals running the opportunity funds are well compensated. A typical fund may earn a fee equal to 20 percent of all income generated by the fund so long as the returns exceed a minimum hurdle rate, usually around 10 percent. Thus, if a firm were to invest $50 million of its own money and then raise $450 million from pension funds and other investors for a $500 million fund, it could expect roughly the following compensation. If the fund earned, say,

25 percent on the $500 million of total capital, it would earn $125 million a year. The investment management firm would receive 20 percent of this amount, or $25 million, in fees, which would be in addition to receiving its pro rata share of fund income after fees— 10 percent ($50 million of $500 million)—like all the other investors. This fee schedule is far higher than real estate investment managers have traditionally received, but it is justified on the basis that 25 percent is a far higher return than pension funds and other institutional investors have historically received from commercial real estate.

It is important to understand that these fees are paid to manage the fund, not to lease or manage the property. Those functions are performed by operating professionals hired by the opportunity funds.

Historically, high-return opportunity funds have been possible not only because the loans (and in some cases the equity directly) were obtained at a fraction of their original cost, but also because in the early years the real estate cycle was on an upswing. The savings and loan crisis had slowed development, and job growth had for some time been exceeding growth in the inventory of space. Consequently, a combination of buying right and being at the right point in the cycle allowed for a very profitable situation. Figure 6-1 shows the real estate cycle from 1972 through 1998.[1] This simple ratio of the rolling three-year change in jobs to the same rolling change in real estate stock (relative to the average of this ratio over the past years) provides a straightforward indication of where rents are headed. When the index is at 1.0, the expectation is rental growth equal to inflation. Above 1.0, the expectation is for rents to grow faster than inflation, and vice versa. As you can see from Figure 6-1, the early 1990s were the "best of times" for rent growth, which played a large part in explaining the original success of the opportunity funds. It also played a large part in explaining the dramatic growth of real estate investment trusts.

After many years of 20+ percent returns for investors, opportunity funds continue to have success raising new capital. In 1998, these funds raised over $10 billion, which, when leveraged at 3 to 1, produces nearly $40 billion of real estate investment. With most of the 1980s' problems now solved and the real estate cycle moving to a different phase, however, it becomes harder for the opportunity funds to find the same kinds of investments. In response, in 1998 several of the funds moved a good portion of their activity to Europe. In 1999, they moved an even larger part to Asia. Still, their legacy in this country is tremendously important to real estate developers. They have money, they will take risks, and they can move rapidly—which

Figure 6-1

Space Market Index

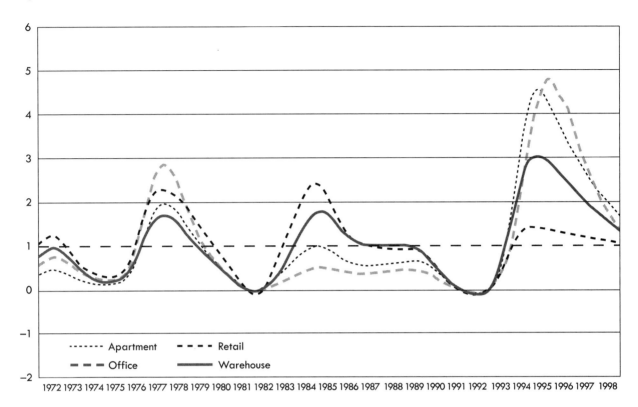

means that good ideas can be financed. They must be *very* good ideas, however, because opportunity funds still seek exceptional returns.

Real Estate Investment Trusts

Real estate investment trusts were created (through changes in the tax code) to allow small investors to participate in benefits of commercial real estate that were previously available only to wealthy individuals and large institutions. After a slow start in the 1960s, REITs enjoyed rapid growth in the early 1970s. Although some of these REITs were "equity REITs" that owned properties directly, a larger number were "mortgage REITs," which made loans secured by real estate. In the early 1970s, the mortgage REITs expanded rapidly, often through relaxed underwriting standards. The combination of relaxed lending standards and a severe recession created a financial crisis in the mid-1970s. In fact, the collapse of the REITs in the mid-1970s was similar to the collapse of S&Ls in the 1980s: a combination of unsound

decision making and an overall economic downturn led to a financial crisis.

Many of the equity REITs survived this period but were not particularly important to real estate finance until the early 1990s. The total capitalization (the number of publicly traded shares of REITs times the price of each share) was less than $10 billion in 1990. It was not long, however, before investment bankers saw an opportunity in real estate (refer to the space market index in Figure 6-1 and note the attractive position in the cycle at the time) and thought that these tax-favored vehicles (recall that REITs avoid entity-level taxes) were the way to enjoy the benefits of the upswing. Beginning with the KIMCO offering in late 1992, an explosion occurred of new REIT equity offerings by companies that had previously been private.

Working in the same environment as the opportunity funds, REITs were able to buy properties cheaply with funds provided by individual investors through the stock market. REITs became attractive growth stocks, because at a time when individual investors were looking for an 8 percent current return (dividend yield), real estate assets were providing a 10 percent return. Like the opportunity funds, the REITs rode the real estate recovery. They found they could increase earnings simply by selling shares and investing the proceeds in property. Although this strategy worked well during the cyclical upswing, it eventually became more difficult to obtain properties at prices low enough to generate 10 percent current return.

By the start of 1998, the cycle had moved on and growth in rents had slowed dramatically. Further, with the demand pressure from both themselves and the opportunity funds, real estate prices increased and yields declined. At that point, Wall Street took another look and concluded that REITs were not really a growth story. A well-leased building may be a solid value, but it is hard to make it grow as fast as Microsoft, Intel, or Amazon.com.

After a poor year in 1998, when stock prices of most REITs declined, they repositioned to look more like value companies. As shown in Figure 6-2, by the end of 1998, REIT equity capitalization stood at about $140 billion. Adding in debt and the joint venture interest, the REITs controlled (as of year-end 1998) well over $200 billion in property, or more than 5 percent of the commercial real estate universe. In the future, REITs will be likely buyers of properties revitalized by the opportunity funds, and, in the longer term, they are a likely

replacement for tax-oriented limited partnerships (big owners in the 1970s) and life insurance companies (big owners in the 1980s) as the primary holders of real estate equity.

Commercial Mortgage–Backed Securities

Yet another financing innovation traceable to the S&L debacle is the commercial mortgage–backed security.[2] The innovation was to securitize portfolios of real estate loans and sell them through the capital markets to individual and institutional investors. In this way, investors can buy a share in a pool of loans just as they can buy an interest in a REIT.

As was the case for opportunity funds and REITs, investment bankers saw an opportunity to make money by creating a new investment, in this case, through the securitization of real estate loans. They pushed Congress to provide the necessary legislation that would allow them to pool loans and sell investors various risk classes in the pool. The legislation was necessary to avoid any tax consequence of securitization.

An investment banker might, for example, put together 300 commercial loans, then divide the pool into risk classes, known as "tranches." As the loans are paid off, the lowest-risk tranche is paid first, with any losses going to the highest-risk tranche. In typical securitizations, 60 percent or more of the pool qualifies for a AAA rating by the credit-rating agencies,[3] because nearly 40 percent of the total pool of loans has to go bad before any loss would be experienced by this lowest-risk tranche. The AAA securities are sold at a very low spread to Treasuries (anywhere from 70 to 130 basis points, or 0.7 percent to 1.3 percent). Although the highest-risk tranches (referred to as "below investment grade," that is, BB, B, and unrated) sell at much higher spreads, the overall cost is heavily weighted by the 60+ percent in the AAA or low-cost category. Investment bankers are able to find situations in which the total payments from borrowers exceed the total of investors' requirements, that is, the summation of all tranche payments. The difference, of course, provides a profit.[4]

Opportunities for investment bankers come in two ways. First, they can help existing real estate lenders, S&Ls, commercial banks, and life insurance companies liquefy a portion of their portfolios by securitizing that pool of loans. Second, they can originate new loans strictly for the purpose of securitizing them. This process is known as the *conduit process,* and the loans are

---

Figure 6-2

REIT Market Capitalization

Year (As of December 31)	Value (Billions of Dollars)[a]
1988	$11.4
1989	$11.7
1990	$8.7
1991	$13.0
1992	$15.7
1993	$32.2
1994	$44.3
1995	$57.5
1996	$88.8
1997	$140.5
1998	$138.3
1999[b]	$142.0

[a]Reflects equity, not implied market capitalization, for all REITs.
[b]As of June.
Source: **NAREIT.**

called *conduit loans*. The investment bankers set up their own loan originators, and, as soon as a significant volume of loans is produced, the pool is securitized. This situation is much like traditional residential lending where local mortgage bankers originate loans and then sell the pool to life insurance companies.

The importance of conduits to the real estate developer is that they provide competition to the traditional long-term real estate lenders, particularly the life insurance companies. As we will see in the Museum Towers case at the end of this chapter, that competition drives down the cost of financing to real estate developers. Interestingly, some market segmentation occurs, with larger, higher-quality loans going to the life insurance companies (where they hold them for their own portfolios) and with higher-risk loans being securitized and sold to investors. As shown in Figure 6-3, the volume of CMBSs has grown even more rapidly than that of REITs. CMBS loans outstanding went from close to zero in 1988 to more than $207 billion at the end of 1998.

Traditional Commercial Real Estate Investors and Lenders

Historically, life insurance companies have been the major providers of long-term real estate credit. Through superior underwriting, life insurance companies avoided the extreme problems experienced by mortgage REITs in the 1970s and S&Ls in the 1980s. In the late 1980s and early 1990s, however, life insurance companies began to reevaluate their investment strategies in response to changes in regulations and their business markets. The most important regulatory change involved *risk-based capital*. The reserves that life insurance companies are required to hold were categorized by risk, and equity real estate was placed in a high reserve category. At the same time, the life insurance business was changing to more variable life insurance and less of the traditional whole life insurance, resulting in a need for more liquidity. These two events resulted in certain strategic decisions by senior management at the companies. The most basic was that most life insurance companies no longer intend to hold significant amounts of equity commercial real estate. Although most of them continue to be significant real estate lenders, an increasing number do this lending through the CMBS market. When needed, liquidity is provided by selling a pool of loans. In fact, some life insurance companies originate loans for the securitization process, in effect taking on the investment bankers at a portion of the investment banking/CMBS game.

Figure 6-3

CMBS Loans Outstanding

Year (As of December 31)	Value (Billions of Dollars)
1988	$5.4
1989	$9.8
1990	$14.8
1991	$21.5
1992	$33.4
1993	$47.5
1994	$63.1
1995	$75.4
1996	$98.3
1997	$132.8
1998	$207.4
1999[a]	$225.0

[a]**As of June.**
Source: Morgan Stanley, *Commercial Mortgage Alert*.

It also appears that the life insurance companies want to hold larger loans (which provide economies of scale in origination costs) and higher-quality loans for their own portfolios. They compete quite successfully with the conduit originators for this segment of the market, because they can tailor individual loans to the situation and borrower. Unlike the standardization necessary to securitize loans, when a loan will be held in an institution's portfolio, the institution has more flexibility in structuring timing of payments, increases in loans as buildings are leased, and so forth, to meet the borrower's needs. (This consideration is important in the Museum Towers case study.)

The market for short-term real estate credit is also changing. Commercial banks continue to be the major providers, but they have become much larger through consolidation and now look more like financial supermarkets. Rather than simply providing construction loans, large commercial banks now arrange almost any type of real estate financing. And, like investment bankers, they now look for fees for their services. In the 1960s and 1970s, developers worked in their local areas and commercial banks were smaller. In that world, relationships were tighter. As the banks have become national and global and many developers at least regional, the ties have weakened. Still, the relationship is much more personal than is the case with conduit lending. The story told by Tom Wolfe in *A Man in Full*[5] is essential reading for any aspiring real estate developer. The "workout confrontation" between PlannersBanc and Charlie Croker is as close to reality as fiction can get.

Changes in Single-Family Residential Lending

Led by the government, securitization came much earlier to single-family lending. The government provided the initial stimulus for the standardization of underwriting loans that is necessary for securitization. With its long history, finance of single-family dwellings has a rich menu of options for investors, loan originators, and borrowers.

Today, commercial banks operating as financial supermarkets can handle loans for individual homeowners from start to finish. But they have plenty of competition from small real estate brokerage boutiques, which provide even more aggressive service and tend to have lower operating costs. These small firms originate loans for commercial banks, life insurance companies, and other institutions. As an example of their personalized, aggressive services, many of the smaller loan originators call prospective borrowers to advise them of the best time to refinance in response to changes in the interest rate.

The securitization of single-family loans has been a tremendous help to developers. Before securitization, long-term single-family loans were largely the province of S&Ls. When interest rates went up and S&Ls could no longer compete for savers' accounts (as a result of Regulation Q, which set an absolute ceiling on the interest rate they could pay), S&Ls ran short of cash and were unable to make new loans. This *disintermediation* —the removal of funds from the S&L intermediary— crippled the operations of subdivision developers and homebuilders. This situation became a chronic problem in the 1960s and 1970s, when interest rates were routinely raised to cool the economy. When rates increased, disintermediation occurred, borrowers could not get loans, and developers therefore could not sell homes. Although an effective way to slow the economy, it was also a rather painful one. Today, through the securitization of all forms of residential lending, financing is available regardless of the interest rate. Although it remains harder for individuals to afford homes when interest rates are high, at least the credit is available.

Larger residential developers typically work with lenders to facilitate their customers' borrowing. The process may involve *buydowns* by the developer; that is, the developer pays certain of the financing costs so that buyers/borrowers can obtain what are nominally below-market interest rate loans. Though the developer must include the cost of the buydown somewhere in the price of the house, it is a way to tailor the product to fit the particular target population.

▌▌▌ Museum Towers

How Recent Innovations Can Affect the Financing of a Development

Museum Towers was built in what many would consider a pioneering location. Located on the river in east Cambridge, on a formerly industrial site, the area was known as "the lost half-mile of the Charles River." This apparently marginal piece of land was purchased for $13 million in 1987. The original site included three parcels on 4.11 acres. In 1996, the developer/owner, Congress Group Ventures, sold 50,000 square feet, and, as part of its development deal, gave away an acre to the state for a park and several thousand square feet to the city for roads, ending up with a 2.07-acre site.

The Museum Towers project consists of two 24-story towers with 435 rental apartment units and a gross building area of 619,500 square feet. The towers are joined by a central lobby and a 490-space parking garage. In total, the project contains four studio apartments, 181 one-bedroom units (40 in the low-rise portion of the towers), and 250 two-bedroom units. Most of the one-bedroom units have only one bathroom; the two-bedroom units have two full bathrooms. The base building is mostly cast-in-place concrete with precast concrete exterior panels. The floors are poured concrete. The windows are aluminum frame with a combination of awning windows, fixed windows, and sliding doors. The exterior doors are a combination of metal and glass in metal frames. The towers, part of the 40-acre North Point Park, feature great views of downtown Boston.

The Congress Group's pro forma showed that, when the project stabilizes, it is expected to generate annual net operating income of $8,874,391, a very attractive 11.6 percent return on investment. Like all developments, however, this return is only *expected*. Despite the attractiveness of the concept and the site and the very tight residential market in Cambridge, potential long-term lenders were understandably not willing to equate this expected NOI with an existing reality, i.e., "in-place NOI." On the plus side, the quality of the location, the idea, and the development group convinced a lender—Fleet Bank—to provide a first lien miniperm, a construction loan that extends beyond completion of the construction for a year or two so that the developer can demonstrate stabilized operations. After stabilization, a larger first lien can typically be obtained based on calculation of a maximum loan (see Chapter 5). The developer's problem is how to get to "stabilized" NOI and thus in a position to maximize the permanent loan. Although the financing process involves a series of negotiations that vary from development to development, some common strategies are involved. Three that were important in the process followed by Congress Group Ventures in financing Museum Towers are often critical for development financing: 1) leverage as inexpensively as possible; 2) get the cheap money and always have an exit strategy; and 3) consider alternative sources for high-risk dollars.

Strategy One: Leverage as Inexpensively as Possible

Congress Group Ventures wanted to maximize the eventual permanent loan because doing so would provide the cheapest overall financing (debt equity). Use of the miniperm provided by Fleet Bank allowed a slightly longer period in which to stabilize NOI before negotiating for permanent financing.

Nevertheless, the decision to go with the miniperm was not an easy one for the Congress Group. Long-term interest rates were relatively low in 1996, as pressure from the CMBS conduits had forced the traditional long-term lenders to reduce their spreads. Further, interest rates on short-term construction loans were lower than they had been for many years. Thus, a potentially attractive alternative to the miniperm was to negotiate for a longer-term loan immediately. But because the pro forma was, in fact, only a pro forma and not current operating income, it was not possible to obtain a first lien commitment of the size the Congress Group felt the project warranted. Consequently, the Congress Group went for the miniperm.

Because Museum Towers was a large, high-quality, highly visible project, the Congress Group approached a prominent local lender that could benefit from the association. Fleet Bank agreed to make a first lien miniperm of $55 million. The initial term was for three years with an upfront fee of 0.75 percent and a variable interest rate. To fix the rate, the Congress Group then conducted an interest rate swap, with the result a variable rate to Fleet Bank and a fixed rate (8 percent) to the Congress Group. The miniperm included a two-year extension option for an additional payment of 0.375 percent and an interest rate for the extension period of LIBOR plus 175 basis points. Thus, the miniperm provided the Congress Group with three years to build the project and the option for another two years to stabilize NOI to maximize the permanent loan.

In negotiating the terms, the Congress Group had to consider not just the cheapest rate for the money but also how all the "loan terms" affected other important parts of its strategy.

Strategy Two: Have an Exit Strategy

Although this project is the kind a developer might want to own over the long term, the Congress Group was smart enough to know that no individual developer is bigger than the cycle. It is always possible that the economy will hit another period like the middle 1980s, when so many new projects were developed that even the best products began to suffer. Today's informed developers have learned the hard lesson: they must always consider the eventual sale.

It looked as though a REIT would be a logical long-term holder of this property. Because REITs like to show growth in earnings, they typically do not develop the majority of their properties. Rather, they often prefer to buy properties after they have been developed and stabilized by entrepreneurial developers. If, at the end of the three-year miniperm, a REIT were a viable option, the Congress Group would sell; if not, it would pay the additional 0.375 percent fee, extend the loan for two years, and wait.

Another option with the miniperm is to sell to another investor. Here, the CMBS market is important. With the conduit loans pressuring traditional lenders, the Congress Group anticipated that attractive financing would be available should an entrepreneurial, possibly European, investor be the eventual buyer (as opposed to a REIT). The Congress Group was actively involved with a few larger European institutions (Boston being a favored American city in Europe) as well as a number of apartment REITs. One particular apartment REIT, Smith Residential, specialized in high-rise inner-city projects in the Northeast. The Congress Group cultivated a particularly close relationship with it.

Strategy Three: Consider Alternative Sources For High-Risk Dollars

No discussion of financing would be complete without considering the high-risk capital. If the developer cannot or does not want to put up all the required equity, then a partner may be needed. This approach can involve very complex relationships, and this topic will be revisited many times throughout this text. In the case of Museum Towers, the overall project cost of $78 million would be initially financed with the $55 million miniperm from Fleet Bank. The Congress Group did not want to put all the remaining $23 million into the project, however. In fact, it preferred to pull out some of the $13 million it had already invested. A logical place to look was the opportunity funds.

Although earlier in this chapter we concluded the discussion of opportunity funds by noting that any good idea is financeable, it may cost a great deal to attain such financing. The group of opportunity funds, however, includes some segmentation. Museum Towers was not a highly speculative project, given the housing market in Cambridge. Consequently, the Congress Group looked for a lower-risk opportunity fund (sometimes called "value-added funds"). The Congress Group found such an opportunity fund, also located in Boston, that it hoped would appreciate the tightness of the Cambridge market. Working with the Fidelity Real Estate Group, the Congress Group arranged a *participating secured second mortgage*. The site and improvements were the basic collateral along with certain pledges of equity interest in the project from the developer. These notes were subject to Fleet's first lien and had a similar term.

Face Amount—$16,500,000

Term—Five years

Base Interest Rate—15%

Additional Interest—50% of net operating cash flow and net capital appreciation during the term of the notes until Fidelity has earned a 20% internal rate of return; thereafter, Fidelity's participation drops from 50% to 30%

This debt structure allowed the Congress Group to pull $6,500,000 out of the project ($78,000,000 total cost − $55,000,000 first lien − $16,500,000 second lien = $6,500,000) while retaining control and the majority of the upside. The leverage from Fleet's financing produced expected equity returns of just over 25 percent. By bringing in Fidelity and further positive leverage, the expected equity return to the Congress Group was raised to over 40 percent. The expected return to the slightly lower-risk Fidelity portion was 21.5 percent and to the much lower-risk Fleet portion about 9 percent. These differences in expected returns reflect each entity's different risk position.

continued on page 200

Summary

The fundamentals of risk and return for debt and equity real estate investment have changed very little over the last two decades. What has changed dramatically is the institutional and regulatory environment in which investors operate, leading to important innovations in the financial markets. As a result, real estate finance in 2000 looks very different from what it did in 1980.

The S&L crisis of the 1980s led to the formation of opportunity funds that specialize in identifying problem properties and purchasing them at substantial discounts. Professional management, combined with being on the right side of the real estate cycle, produced very high returns over an extended period. As the cycle flattened in the late 1990s, opportunities in the United States became harder to find, and opportunity funds began to look to Europe and Asia for investments.

REITs have also grown rapidly, fueled by changes in the tax laws during the mid-1980s, the growth in mutual funds (which can access real estate only in "securitized" form), and the same market conditions that attracted the opportunity funds. As the market became more competitive in the late 1990s, many REITs evolved from "growth" to "value" companies, and they are likely to be major providers of real estate equity in the future.

Commercial mortgage–backed securities are another important innovation. Securitization offers an opportunity to invest in a pool of debt, just as REITs offer an opportunity to invest in a pool of equity. Legislation that allowed the formation of different risk categories (or tranches) has added to the investment appeal of CMBSs.

Traditional lenders such as life insurance companies and commercial bankers remain active, but their lending policies and competitive environments have changed. Life insurance companies are less attracted to equity real estate because of legislation that made real estate a more costly asset to hold in terms of reserve requirements and basic changes in life insurance markets. Today, many life insurance companies are active in the CMBS market. Commercial banks have expanded their lending activities from mainly construction loans to a full range of real estate loans.

The now mature market for securitized residential loans has stabilized credit for single-family homes by reducing the impact of changes in interest rates on lenders' liquidity and hence on the availability of credit for borrowers.

Terms

- Commercial mortgage–backed securities (CMBSs)
- Conduit loan
- Miniperm loan
- Opportunity fund
- Real estate investment trust (REIT)
- Regulation Q
- Resolution Trust Corporation (RTC)
- Risk-based capital requirements
- Securitization
- Tranche

Review Questions

6.1 Why are opportunity funds increasing their investments abroad?

6.2 REITs did not become major players until the early 1990s, when their market capitalization exploded. Discuss the reasons for their growth.

6.3 Wall Street no longer views REITs as primarily growth stocks. What, then, is their future?

6.4 Comment on the statement that CMBSs are to debt markets as REITs are to equity markets.

6.5 What are investment tranches?

6.6 Commercial banks, though they now offer more products to the real estate debt market, have more competition from smaller lenders and brokers. How are the small lenders able to compete?

6.7 The financing of Museum Towers involved three common strategies developers use. Discuss those strategies.

Notes

1. For a detailed explanation of this index, see Mike E. Miles et al., *Real Estate Finance,* Winter 1998, pp. 39–45. The index is published quarterly in *Institutional Real Estate Newsletter.*

2. See John Harding and C.F. Sirmans, "Commercial Mortgage–Backed Securities: An Introduction for the Professional Investor," *Real Estate Finance,* Summer 1997, pp. 43–52.

3. Moody's, S&P, and Duff and Phelps are the major credit-rating agencies.

4. A good review article on securitization and its impact on performance is David Geltner, "Securitization and Real Estate Performance Measurement," *Real Estate Finance,* Summer 1998, pp. 23–36.

5. Tom Wolfe, *A Man in Full* (New York: Farrar, Straus, Giroux, 1998). In early 1999, this "fictional account" of an Atlanta developer was number one on the best-seller lists.

Part II

Bibliography

Ahern, Terrance, Youguo Liang, and F.C. Neil Myer. "Leverage in a Pension Fund Real Estate Program." *Real Estate Finance* 15:2 (Summer 1998): 55–62.

Appraisal Institute. *The Appraisal of Real Estate.* 11th ed. Chicago: Author, 1996.

Axler, Michael M. "Valuing Development Projects." *Real Estate Finance Journal* 9:3 (Winter 1994): 17–22.

Bamberger, David C. "Developer's Disease Can Be Hazardous to Your Health." *Real Estate Issues* 17:1 (Spring/Summer 1992): 37–38.

Benjamin, John D., and H. Kent Baker. "Establishing an Active Secondary Market for Commercial Mortgages." *Real Estate Finance Journal* 10:1 (Summer 1994): 67–72.

Benjamin, John, Cris de la Torre, and Jim Musumeci. "Rationales for Real Estate Leasing versus Owning." *Journal of Real Estate Research* 15:3 (1998): 223–38.

Bertman, Richard J., and Dan Pinck. "Transforming Obsolescent Office Buildings: It's Not a Shell Game." *Real Estate Finance* 9:1 (Spring 1992): 95–98.

Black, J. Thomas, and William E. Hauser. "Moderating Cyclical Overbuilding in Commercial Real Estate." In *ULI on the Future.* Washington, D.C.: ULI–the Urban Land Institute, 1993.

Blew, J. Miller. "Third-Party Financing of Tenant Improvements." *Urban Land* 51:7 (July 1992): 9.

Boykin, James H., and Richard L. Haney, Jr. *Financing Real Estate.* 2d ed. Englewood Cliffs, N.J.: Prentice-Hall, 1993.

Brody, Michael J., and David S. Raab. "A Primer on Real Estate Investment Trusts and Umbrella Partnership Real Estate Investment Trusts." *Real Estate Finance Journal* 9:3 (Winter 1994): 35–40.

Bruce, Brian R., ed. *Real Estate Portfolio Management.* Chicago: Probus Publishing, 1991.

Brueggeman, William B., and Jeffrey D. Fisher. *Real Estate Finance and Investments.* 10th ed. Homewood, Ill.: Irwin, 1996.

Clauretie, Terrence M., and Stacey Sirmans. *The Theory and Practice of Real Estate Finance.* 3rd ed. Fort Worth, Tex.: Dryden Press, 1999.

Cooper, S. Kerry, and Donald R. Fraser. *The Financial Marketplace.* 4th ed. Reading, Mass.: Addison-Wesley, 1993.

Davis, Russell T. "Is the Multifamily Mortgage Market Unstable?" *Real Estate Finance Journal* 9:4 (Spring 1994): 80–86.

Diamond, Larry, and Carl Kane. "Converting Commercial Real Estate into Marketable Securities." *Urban Land* 51:12 (December 1992): 14–16.

Eichholtz, Piet. "Real Estate Securities and Common Stocks: A First International Look." *Real Estate Finance* 14:1 (Spring 1997): 70–74.

Fabozzi, Frank J., ed. *Pension Fund Investment Management.* Chicago: Probus Publishing, 1990.

Fiedler, Lawrence E., and Nina M. Weissenburger. "Will Neighborhood Shopping Centers Be Extinct by the Twenty-First Century?" *Real Estate Review* 24:2 (Summer 1994): 45–50.

Fraser, Lyn M. *Understanding Financial Statements.* 4th ed. Englewood Cliffs, N.J.: Prentice-Hall, 1995.

Geltner, David. "Capital Markets and Real Estate Fundamentals." *Real Estate Finance* 14:2 (Summer 1997): 77–87.

———. "Securitization and Real Estate Performance Measurement." *Real Estate Finance* 15:2 (Summer 1998): 23–36.

Gordon, Jacques. "The Real Estate Capital Markets Matrix: A Paradigm Approach." *Real Estate Finance* 11:3 (Fall 1994): 7–15.

Gorlow, Robert M., David M. Parr, and Louis W. Taylor. "The Securitization of Institutional Real Estate Investments." *Real Estate Review* 23:1 (Spring 1993): 22–28.

Greenberg, Alan. "Back to Basics: Negotiating Financing in the 1990s." *Real Estate Finance Journal* 7:3 (Winter 1992): 33–37.

Greer, Gaylon E. *Investment Analysis for Real Estate Decisions.* 4th ed. Chicago: Dearborn Financial, 1997.

Harding, John P., and C.F. Sirmans. "Commercial Mortgage–Backed Securities: An Introduction for Professional Investors." *Real Estate Finance* 14:1 (Summer 1997): 43–52.

Hauser, William E. "A Securitization Primer for Property Owners and Developers." *Urban Land* 53:6 (June 1994): 27–30.

Hudson-Wilson, Susan, and Charles H. Wurtzebach. *Managing Real Estate Portfolios.* Burr Ridge, Ill.: Irwin, 1994.

Kesler, Henry S. "Construction Lending Risks and Returns." *Mortgage Banking* 49:4 (January 1989): 62–70.

Lederman, Jess, ed. *The Handbook of Mortgage Banking.* Rev. ed. Chicago: Probus Publishing, 1993.

Liu, Crocker, David Hartzell, and Martin Hoesli. "International Evidence on Real Estate Securities as an Inflation Hedge." *Real Estate Economics* 25:2 (Summer 1997): 193–222.

Lusht, Kenneth. *Real Estate Valuation: Principles and Applications.* Homewood, Ill.: Irwin, 1997.

Lynford, Jeffrey H. "The Transformation of Multifamily Housing Ownership in the United States." *Real Estate Finance* 10:4 (Winter 1994): 38–45.

McCaddrey, Daniel, and Peter McNally. "U.S. Pension Fund Investments in Real Estate: Current and Future Investment Strategy." *Real Estate Finance* 13:4 (Winter 1997): 46–58.

McCoy, Bowen H. "The Creative Destruction of Real Estate Capital Markets." *Urban Land* 53:6 (June 1994): 19–22.

Mailer, Richard C. "Lease Economics: Follow the Money." *Real Estate Finance Journal* 6:4 (Spring 1991): 72–78.

Miles, Mike E., and Nancy Tolleson, "A Revised Look at How Real Estate Compares with Other Major Components of the Domestic Investment Universe." *Real Estate Finance* (Spring 1997).

Muldavin, Scott. "Fish or Cut Back?" *Real Estate Finance* 15:1 (Spring 1998): 79–63.

———. "Mortgage Lender Opportunity and Peril." *Real Estate Finance* 14 (Spring 1997): 5–10.

———. "The Old and the New Dominate Real Estate Finance Today." *Real Estate Finance* 14:4 (Winter 1998): 85–91.

Norris, Daniel M., and Mark Nelson. "Real Estate Loan Underwriting Factors in the Insurance Industry." *Real Estate Finance* 9:3 (Fall 1992): 79–86.

Nygard, Wayne, and Christopher Razaire. "Probability-Based DCF: An Alternative to Point-Value Estimates." *Appraisal Journal* (January 1999): 68–74.

Olasov, Brian. "Commercial Mortgage Securitization: Capital Markets Fill a Void." *Real Estate Review* 24:2 (Summer 1994): 18–24.

Parsons, John F.C. "Real Estate Investor Relations." *Urban Land* 52:11 (November 1993): 33–36.

Phyrr, Stephen A., James R. Cooper, Larry E. Wofford, Steven D. Kapplin, and Paul D. Lapides. *Real Estate Investment.* 2d ed. New York: Wiley, 1989.

Pollack, Bruce. "Commercial Real Estate Loan Underwriting Revisited." *Real Estate Finance Journal* 7:3 (Winter 1992): 63–68.

Rago, George J., and William J. Kimball. "Appraising Proposed Income-Producing Property for Construction Lending." *Appraisal Journal* 57:4 (October 1989): 537–43.

Rose, Peter S. *Money and Capital Markets: The Financial System in an Increasingly Global Economy.* 5th ed. Burr Ridge, Ill.: Irwin, 1994.

Rosenzweig, Patricia P. "Design/Build for the 1990s." *Real Estate Finance Journal* 8:1 (Summer 1992): 59–62.

Ross, Stan, and Richard Klein. "Real Estate Investment Trusts for the 1990s." *Real Estate Finance Journal* 10:1 (Summer 1994): 37–44.

———. "REITs as a Source of Capital: Considerations for Sponsors." *Real Estate Finance* 9:2 (Summer 1992): 13–18.

Rudisill, Cathy M. "Commercial Leases: Landlord, Tenant, and Lender Concerns." *Real Estate Finance Journal* 9:2 (Fall 1993): 31–34.

———. "Negotiating Loan Commitment Letters." *Real Estate Finance Journal* 8:2 (Fall 1992): 47–51.

Saft, Stuart M. "Borrowers' Defenses to Mortgage Fore-closures." *Real Estate Finance Journal* 7:2 (Fall 1991): 5–13.

Schulman, Stuart, and Phillip Kurpiewski. "Financing for Small- to Medium-Size Project Developers." *Real Estate Finance Journal* 5:3 (Winter 1990): 16–20.

Simondi, Michael P. "Wall Street: The New Take-Out Lender." *Real Estate Review* 24:3 (Fall 1994): 5–7.

Sirmans, C.F. "Research on Discounted Cash Flow Models." *Real Estate Finance* 13:4 (Winter 1997): 93–95.

Stein, Joshua. "Mortgage Loan Structures for the 1990s." *Real Estate Review* 24:1 (Spring 1994): 15–20.

Tebow, Brad. "In Defense of DCF Analysis." *Real Estate Review* 24:3 (Fall 1994): 43–49.

Vogel, John H., Jr. "Why the New Conventional Wisdom about REITs Is Wrong." *Real Estate Finance* 14:2 (Summer 1997): 7–12.

Williams, Joseph. "Redevelopment of Red Assets." *Real Estate Economics* 25:3 (Fall 1997): 387–408.

Willison, Daniel L. "Toward a More Reliable Cash Flow Analysis." *Appraisal Journal* (January 1999): 75–82.

Winzer, Ingo. "Cutting Back." *Mortgage Banking* 54:1 (October 1993): 28–33.

Wurtzebach, Charles H., and Mike E. Miles, with Susanne Ethridge Cannon. *Modern Real Estate.* 5th ed. New York: Wiley, 1994.

Yeskey, Dennis P. "Insurance Companies Churn Their Investments for the '90s." *Real Estate Financing* 10:4 (Winter 1994): 24–29.

Zell, Sam, and Peter Linneman. "The World According to Zell." *Urban Land* 53:9 (September 1994): 25–29.

Ziering, Barry, Youguo Liang, and Will McIntosh. "REIT Correlations with Capital Market Indexes: Separating Signal from Noise." *Real Estate Finance* 15:4 (Winter 1989): 61–67.

Zinngrabe, Claude J., Jr. "Real Estate Investment by Insurance Companies." *Urban Land* 53:3 (March 1994): 12–14.

One of the best ways to anticipate the future is to understand the past. Thus, Part III thoroughly reviews the evolution of development in this country from colonial days to the present. This historic picture is clearly one of a dynamic relationship between public and private players. Part III sets forth a full backdrop for the eight-stage model that follows.

The role and degree of involvement of the public sector might have changed over time, but it has always been and always will be true that the public sector is an active partner in private development. Students of real estate development should not underestimate the place of the real estate market in the economic life of the nation. Ownership of land and buildings is a fundamental right that Americans cherish and is more widespread in the United States than in any other country.

As you read through this section, keep in mind the adage that "history repeats itself." This adage is particularly true when you look at the boom and bust nature of the development business.

Part III
The History of Real Estate Development In the United States

Chapter 7

The Colonial Period to the Late 1800s

R eal estate has been a part of the American tradition for a long time. To paraphrase Calvin Coolidge, the business of the United States is real estate. The ownership of land and buildings in the United States is more widespread than in any other country; millions of people own, buy, and sell real property. Mass participation in the real estate market has been a fundamental characteristic of the economic life of this country since its origins.

The settlers and colonists who migrated here from many parts of the world came in search of greater freedom and prosperity—and owning land was essential to attaining both goals. Throughout the 18th and 19th centuries, Americans fought for greater legal rights and opportunities to become property owners. They battled for changes in the laws and administration of colonial governments, and later, after the successful war for independence, they lobbied the federal government and state and local governments for basic reforms to establish and protect private property rights, thereby making it easier and safer to obtain and develop land.

No institution or practice was left untouched by this sweeping movement: legislatures and the courts established and enforced new laws and definitions of the rights inherent in property and contracts, land was physically surveyed and real estate market mechanisms organized to facilitate sales, a vast array of subsidies was granted to prospective settlers to enable them to afford to own land, and enormous public investments in improved transportation and infrastructure helped make the land accessible and productive. All these actions

were designed to increase property values for the new private owners, and in many cases they succeeded.

The story of how these changes came about and how modern attitudes toward land evolved begins in this chapter and continues through Chapters 8 and 9. Specifically, Chapter 7 covers the history of real estate development from the colonial period to the late 1800s by examining:

- Real estate as an American tradition;
- Land subdivision and residential development; and
- The role of railroads and railroad barons in real estate development.

Real Estate as an American Tradition

The extensive privatization of U.S. land is a remarkable story, if only because the nation's settlers initially held land in a highly centralized pattern of ownership and control. During the colonial period, most land was in the hands of the various governors by authority of the English crown and other sovereign powers; beginning in the 17th century, it was purchased or violently appropriated from the Native American tribes that inhabited the continent when the European settlers first arrived.

In the early 1600s, settlers were brought to this country to farm land owned by the Virginia Company; they were paid for their labors in both money and shares of stock. The early settlers quickly rebelled against this practice, however, and insisted on ownership of the land they were farming. In 1616, the Virginia colonial governor acquiesced, granting free and clear title to a

This chapter was written and updated by Marc A. Weiss, PhD, Public Policy Scholar, Woodrow Wilson Center, Washington, D.C.

minimum of 100 acres for each farmer—an action that set an important precedent for patterns of settlement in the country.

Colonial governors had many different methods of distributing the ownership of land. Outright grants were given for farming the land; settling the frontier; serving in the military, in a religious order, or as an educator; and demonstrating political connections. Large parcels of land were sold to investors, speculators, land developers, and settlement ventures. In Massachusetts and other New England colonies, governors granted and sold land to groups for establishing towns.

Once independence was achieved and the colonies formed the United States, the federal and state governments together still owned the overwhelming share of all land. Much more land was added to the public domain during the next century through the Louisiana Purchase, the annexation of Texas, the war with Mexico, the purchase of Alaska, and several treaties with Spain and Great Britain. Much time and effort were expended dispensing this land from public to private ownership. Of the total current U.S. land area of 2.3 billion acres, only 20 percent of it was never in the public domain. The federal government disposed of more than 1 billion acres through land sales and land grants to veterans, homesteaders, railroads, and state governments. The states, in turn, sold or granted much of their public lands to private individuals and companies.

At first, public land was put into private ownership mainly through sales of large numbers of acres to individual investors. The sales occurred as a result of negotiated deals, public auctions, and fixed prices per acre set by Congress. This approach reached its peak in 1836, when the federal government sold 20 million acres, most of it for $1.25 an acre. The problem with this technique was that many prospective frontier settlers could not afford to pay even the minimum government price to purchase federal land, let alone the often much higher prices asked by private speculators who bought public land wholesale and attempted to resell it retail. The huge numbers of land-hungry pioneers were also voters, however, and they rebelled in the mid-19th century as their forebears had done two centuries earlier in Virginia.

Fee Simple Real Estate Transactions

In 1862, Congress responded to this political "Free Soil Movement" by passing the Homestead Act, enabling settlers who did not already own sufficient land to be granted title to 160 acres for each adult in the family simply by living on and improving the "homestead" for a period of five years. No cash payments were required, thereby opening up ownership to a wide segment of the population that had previously been excluded. Unfortunately, the system was subject to a great deal of fraud and abuse, allowing large landowners and wealthy investors to obtain substantial public acreage at bargain prices.

Despite the abuses, the Homestead Act was extremely popular and was followed in the 1870s by additional federal laws granting free 20- and 40-acre parcels to settlers engaging in mining and tree cultivation. In all, the government gave away nearly 300 million acres of public land to private owners through the various homesteading programs—almost as much land as through cash sales.

The creation of the fee simple system of complete property rights through private ownership, including the ability of one private party to convey those rights to another through sale, lease, or trade, generated a vibrant real estate market that attracted substantial amounts of investment capital. In the early years, the money moving into and out of real property was extremely volatile and subject to wide fluctuations in amounts and prices. By the late 18th century, land speculation had already become a main preoccupation of U.S. citizens. Legendary fortunes were made and lost as the steady influx of immigrants entered the new nation. Rapidly rising prices frequently led to a mania for land gambling. Many people, including Charles Dickens's character Martin Chuzzlewit, got caught up in the excitement and the greed and were swindled in the process; countless others were eventually disappointed when the inevitable financial panic led to a drastic drop in prices. Every time new territory was opened for settlement and land was subdivided for sale, the speculative boom/bust cycles repeated themselves. Many colorful books and articles have recounted tales of glory and grief in American "land bubbles" both before and after they burst.[1]

"Land-jobbing" or "town-jobbing" by obtaining land and selling it through promotional schemes to speculators and settlers was one of the principal means of accumulating wealth in the early days of the United States, and all the major business and government leaders—from Benjamin Franklin to George Washington—engaged in it. Indeed, the father of our country was a professional land surveyor in addition to being a planter, general, and president. An energetic entrepreneur in the real estate business, Washington was heavily involved in one of the country's first big development deals—the establishment of the District of Columbia as the nation's capital.

Developing the District of Columbia

The selection of the site for and development of the District of Columbia as the Federal City was based on President Washington's plan for encouraging private

Advertisement for the public auction of lots in Washington, D.C., in 1792, where the lowest acceptable bid was $3.00.

land sales and trading. In fact, speculative real estate activity in the nation's capital was so overheated before it crashed that the Duke de La Rochefoucauld, a visiting French dignitary, wrote in 1797:

In America, where more than in any other country in the world, a desire for wealth is the prevailing passion, there are few schemes [that] are not made the means of extensive speculations; and that of erecting the Federal City presented irresistible temptations, which were not in fact neglected. . . . The building of a house for the President and a place for the sittings of Congress excited, in the purchasers of lots, the hope of a new influx of speculations. The public papers were filled with exaggerated praises of the new city; in a word, with all the artifices [that] trading people in every part of the world are accustomed to employ in the disposal of their wares, and [that] are perfectly known, and amply practiced in this new world.[2]

Both the federal and state governments used land sales as a primary method of raising revenues to pay for public improvements. Washington, D.C., was to be developed on this basis, with President Washington and future Presidents Thomas Jefferson and James Madison among the private bidders for the purchase of subdivided urban lots at the initial public auction in 1791. Only 35 lots were sold at that time, leading to additional promotional efforts that culminated in the wholesale purchase on credit of 7,235 lots by a syndicate headed by Robert Morris, a Philadelphia merchant, well-known Revolutionary War financier, and major real estate investor in Pennsylvania and New York. Morris

and his partners, James Greenleaf and John Nicholson, promised to bring needed capital for land development and building construction into the Federal City, starting with the "Morristown" project, 20 two-story brick houses near the capitol. George Washington also built several for-sale rowhouses in the same area.

In 1791, President Washington commissioned Major Pierre Charles L'Enfant to design a long-term plan for development of the entire Federal City, including the layout of the street system and the public buildings. Though little of L'Enfant's scheme was immediately adopted, much of his grand conception was eventually realized over the next two centuries. In the 1790s, the federal government tried to stimulate new investment and economic and population growth by requiring all those who purchased lots to construct permanent, good-quality, two-story brick or stone buildings, with minimum and maximum prescribed heights to ensure uniformity in the appearance of the streetscape.

Unfortunately, Robert Morris's syndicate defaulted on its payments for the Washington lots and failed to complete construction of Morristown, and all three principals were sent to debtors' prison. Land prices fell precipitously, and the federal district remained for decades what Charles Dickens called "the City of Magnificent Intentions."[3] Nevertheless, the city named for George Washington eventually proved him right—that extensive public and private investment, good planning, quality development and construction, desirable location, a sound economic and employment base, and a growing population would ultimately produce a healthy real estate market with rising long-term values.

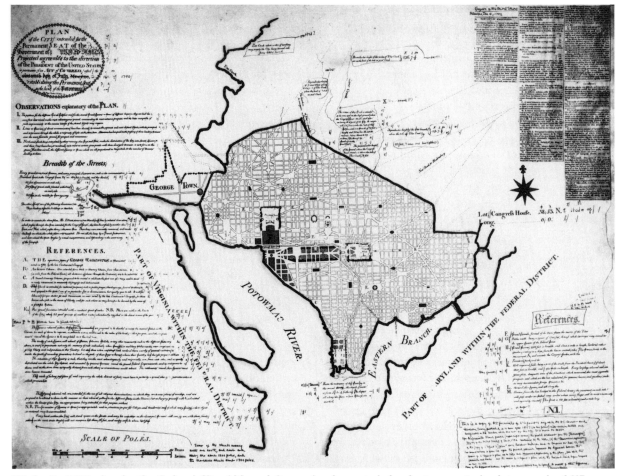

L'Enfant's 1792 plan for the Federal City. Although it was implemented slowly, two centuries later much of L'Enfant's original plan for a majestic city to rival any of the great European capitals is now complete.

Ground Leases

Ground leases formed the basis for the wealth of many early Americans. Under the terms of a long-term ground lease, the landlord received rental payments for the use of land. Renters could occupy the land themselves, lease it out for ground rent, sell their interest in the lease, or improve the property and then collect a building rent. Without surrendering the role of owner, landlords delegated control of the distribution, development, and use of land to the land tenants.[4]

The fact that this practice was common in 18th century England was incentive enough for George Washington. By 1773, Washington had gained ownership of 20,000 acres on the Ohio and Great Kanawha Rivers. On July 15, 1773, he advertised for settlers in *The Maryland Journal and Baltimore Advertiser.* He indicated that he would divide the land "into any sized tenements that may be desired, and lease them upon moderate terms, allowing a reasonable number of years rent free, pro-

vided, within the space of two years from the next October, three acres for every 50 contained in each lot . . . shall be cleared, fenced and tilled."[5]

New York's most noteworthy landlord was Trinity Church. Starting with a crown grant of 32 acres from Queen Anne in 1705, the vestrymen of the church accumulated approximately 1,000 city lots by the end of the 18th century. Before 1770, the church leased lots at a single rate: £2 annual ground rent for the first seven years, £3 a year for the second seven years, and £4 annually for the remainder of the 21-year term. The vestrymen calculated graduated increases to cover the doubling of land values, which they expected after 21 years.

Trinity's common leases ran for 21 years and anticipated occupancy. Such a term was long enough to allow tenants to benefit from any buildings they constructed on the lot. In contrast, longer leases, especially those running from 63 to 99 years (with rent increases at intervals of 21 or 33 years), projected a property interest that extended beyond the lifetime of the tenant. Under these longer leases, the tenant, who paid a fixed ground rent, retained any increases in the rent-generating value of property.[6]

Even today, several of New York's important buildings sit on land leased from Trinity Church and from such families as Goelet, Rhinelander, and Astor, all of which were active in the 18th century real estate market.

The Holland Land Company

While the story of the promotion of U.S. land and town sales is punctuated by a get-rich-quick hype and a string of broken promises and dreams, it is also the story of the fundamentals of real estate development as an entire continent's rural and urban land was brought into productive economic use. One example is the Holland Land Company, which bought 3.3 million acres of land in western New York State from Robert Morris in 1792. Morris had purchased the vast property on credit, hoping that rising prices would yield huge profits through quick turnover.

The Holland Land Company, a group of Dutch financiers and wealthy investors, acquired the immense territory with the intention of subdividing it into large parcels and rapidly dispensing the tracts wholesale to major investors. A serious downturn in property markets brought on by the financial panic that ensued after the collapse of Robert Morris's syndicate in Washington, D.C., however, led the Holland Land Company to reassess its strategy. Out of necessity, the principals decided to engage in long-term, value-added investment and development. Land would be sold retail to new settlers who could be induced to migrate to the region on the promise of infrastructure and services that would make both farmland and town sites physically accessible and economically viable locations for commerce, industry, and permanent residence.

In 1797, the Holland Land Company hired Joseph Ellicott, an experienced Pennsylvania land surveyor, to serve as chief land agent and to direct company operations in upstate New York. For the next two decades, Ellicott implemented a comprehensive long-term plan for the development of the territory and the retail sale of land. Included in the company's holdings was the city of Buffalo, which Ellicott laid out at the western boundary of the territory along Lake Erie.

Ellicott's long-term development strategy included the construction of hundreds of miles of roads through the wooded wilderness and the building of towns at strategic points along newly developed transportation routes. The company located land offices in the towns, and Ellicott engaged in a wide variety of promotional activities to stimulate population growth and settlement in both the towns and the hinterland. In addition to building long-distance roads, the Holland Land Company assisted in the construction of sawmills, gristmills, distilleries, and potash refineries to stimulate regional economic activity that would enhance demand for land sales and leasing. Further, when a town center was first platted and opened for development, the company frequently subsidized the pioneering private owners of general stores, inns, taverns, grain mills, ironworks, smithies, and other providers of essential goods and services. The company also donated land for schools, churches, and public squares.

Joseph Ellicott successfully sold a great deal of land and, within a decade, had brought more than 200,000 new settlers to the Holland Land Company's vast territory, prompting the president of Yale College to write in 1810, "It is questionable whether mankind had ever seen so large a tract changed so suddenly from a wilderness into a well-inhabited and well-cultivated country."[7] Unfortunately, most of the settlers who had bought land on credit with little or no downpayment found themselves unable to meet the credit terms to complete their purchases. Thus, they became essentially tenants of the Holland Land Company, and, in 1820, the company attempted to bail out of the situation by reselling all its land to the state of New York. The legislature refused to buy it, and the company was forced to squeeze more cash from the settlers or repossess their holdings.

Neither approach proved economically or politically worthwhile, and, in 1830, the company helped organize the New York Life Insurance and Trust Company, which began to refinance Holland Land's creditors by converting the unpaid sales contracts into first mortgage loans. In 1836, a powerful local businessman and politician named William H. Seward arranged for Wall Street and European investors to purchase the loans, a popular act that helped elect Seward governor of New York in 1838. As Seward put it, "In less than 18 months, 4,000 persons whom I found occupying lands, chiefly under expired and legally enforceable contracts of sale, and excited and embarrassed alike by the oppression and uncertainty of ever obtaining titles, became freeholders."[8]

In 1835, the Holland Land Company had sold its property to a New York investment syndicate for $1 million, leaving continuation of the massive enterprise for large-scale land development to a new group of real estate entrepreneurs. Fortunately for the Dutch owners of Holland Land, they managed to sell their holdings before the major economic depression of 1837. But the enduring heritage of Holland Land's nearly four decades in the land development business was not the record of financial deals; rather, it was Joseph Ellicott's national role model as an early American "community builder."

John Jacob Astor

An alternative model to either short-term speculators or long-term land developers of for-sale properties is the "Astor method," based on the real estate career of John Jacob Astor, one of the country's richest and best-known businessmen in the first half of the 19th century. Astor, who had started as a fur trader in the Pacific Northwest, owned a tremendous amount of real estate, including several land parcels and buildings in Manhattan, that he began accumulating in 1810. His philosophy of real estate was to purchase land at low prices and wait patiently for the market to change and for urban growth to drive values exponentially higher. While waiting for these long-term increases, he collected substantial rental income from his extensive commercial and residential real estate holdings.

Astor was always eager to buy properties when he could get a bargain, and he rarely sold except when he needed money to purchase more real estate or, occasionally, when values skyrocketed. Astor once sold a lot near Wall Street for $8,000 to a man who was convinced that he had outwitted Astor. The buyer said, "Why, Mr. Astor, in a few years this property will be worth $12,000." "No doubt," said Astor, "but with your $8,000 I will buy 80 lots north of Canal Street. By the time your lot is worth $12,000, my 80 lots will be worth $80,000." Needless to say, he was correct.

During the crash of 1837, Astor acquired several lots and buildings at "distress sale" prices and foreclosed on hundreds of properties on which he held or obtained the mortgages. He seldom invested in any significant improvements, preferring to lease properties and earn profits primarily from rental income. Often, Astor settled for a 5 percent return on the current value of land and left the risk of construction and property management to others. By 1840, Astor was the country's wealthiest man, with an annual income of over $1.25 million from ground rent alone and an estate worth more than $20 million largely attributable to the tremendous growth in the value of his urban real estate assets. Shortly before his death in 1848, he declared, "Could I begin life again, knowing what I now know, and had money to invest, I would buy every foot of land on the island of Manhattan."[9]

Capital Improvement Projects

Just as the Holland Land Company discovered it had to invest in infrastructure to enhance the value of its real estate assets, the federal, state, and local governments undertook wide-ranging development of roads, canals, ports, and a host of other facilities to enable them to turn public lands into private holdings and, most important, to promote population and employment growth. "Boosterism" and public investment went hand in hand. Often capital improvement projects were financed either by issuing bonds to be repaid from user fees such as bridge, highway, and canal tolls or by combining rail and transit fares with revenues from the sale or lease of nearby land that had increased in value because of new infrastructure. For over 200 years, private developers have used this same model when installing major improvements. In addition, private utility, transit, railroad, and other companies have frequently relied on these methods, sometimes with public powers of land acquisition or even outright grants of public land. In other cases, taxpayers voted to sell bonds for improvements to be repaid through increased property taxes. Voters anticipated that future population growth would increase the tax base and property values so that both the public treasury and private landowners who purchased local real estate would benefit by "boosting" the area with expensive new government-financed construction.

The public sector's role was crucial in facilitating successful development and widespread ownership. Forms of intervention ranged from the ubiquitous rectangular survey that opened up the West, to regulations such as building codes, the legal protection of property transactions, and land use controls that have enhanced the physical environment, public safety, and property values. Further, the role of financing has been essential to the success of real estate ventures, as the saga of the Holland Land Company demonstrates. In addition, as noted in earlier chapters, the federal and state governments, through controls on currency, regulatory oversight of publicly chartered financial institutions, and macroeconomic policies, have played a major role in encouraging and monitoring the apparatus of money and credit that has enabled U.S. real estate development to thrive and grow.

Land Subdivision and Residential Development

Although the disposition of public lands involved millions of acres sold or granted by the federal and state governments and resold by private investors and developers, the nature of land subdivision fell into two different categories: larger acreage for farming or other essentially rural uses, and smaller lots for towns and urban uses. As cities grew in the 19th century, more and more land was subdivided into building lots within existing urban areas and in the open countryside to establish new cities. Many of the rural enterprises never succeeded, leaving ghost towns in their wake, but some did emerge from modest beginnings. Chicago, for example, grew in a brief seven decades from a tiny hamlet inhabited by a few hundred pioneers in the 1830s to the fifth largest city in the world by 1900. The biggest single use of land in these metropolitan communities was allocated to house the steadily growing population. Land and, in some cases, buildings were continually carved up to provide dwelling units for new residents.

Given the abundance of cheap land, inexpensive construction materials, and a constant stream of innovations in transportation technology that made residential dispersion possible, an enormous amount of urban housing in the United States consisted of single-family detached dwellings. In the older and more crowded cities of the early 19th century, attached rowhouses (typically constructed in block groups by speculative builders) and multifamily dwellings converted from spacious mansions accommodated a high-density population that walked to work in areas where available space was limited. Later in the century, a number of other dwelling types made their debut, including luxury apartment buildings, squalid tenements, and two-to four-family structures whose modest-income owners often lived in one of the units and, in some cases, constructed the building themselves.

Unlike most other countries, the U.S. urban real estate market allowed for mass participation. Vacant building lots were frequently sold on credit with only small down-payments required, making it possible for a wide range of potential purchasers to enter the market. Millions of people bought lots, including families that wanted to build their own houses, entrepreneurial builders who wanted to construct dwellings for sale or rent, and investors who wanted to turn over land for a fast profit or hold it for long-term gain. Many subdivisions had only the most rudimentary improvements, such as unpaved streets, and lacked basic amenities like sanitary and storm sewers, a supply of fresh water, or curbs and sidewalks. In higher-income communities, developers sometimes installed key improvements in advance of sales and added those costs to lot prices. A more common approach was for infrastructure and amenities to be built after the initial sale of land, paid for by individual lot owners through special tax assessments. To reduce the costs of property ownership for people of limited means, subdivisions intended to house the working classes generally did without many amenities. Often these subdivisions even lacked basic features

Sears, Roebuck and Co. had a booming do-it-yourself homebuilding business in the early part of the 20th century. On the cover of this catalog of houses from 1929, Sears advertises itself as the world's largest building material dealer, a different Sears from the one we know today.

such as sewers and paved streets. As with building and housing codes, society's minimum acceptable standards for neighborhood development are much higher today than a century ago.

In the 19th century, most urban subdivisions, whether already built up and inhabited or new and vacant, lacked any significant land use controls. Mixtures of lot sizes and shapes and of building densities, heights, forms, occupancies, and uses were typical and could be limited only through actions by private owners. Deed restrictions in the form of private contracts were the one regulatory device available to developers and property owners, but they were difficult to establish and enforce and were used mostly in a small number of new, high-income residential neighborhoods. By the 1920s, the extensive use of private deed restrictions and the introduction of public controls through zoning and subdivision regulations brought new elements of stability and order to residential real estate development.

Not only was it possible for the first time for millions of people to become urban property owners, but many were also actively engaged in the real estate business. Selling one's own or someone else's property as an agent was a completely unregulated activity in the 19th century and occupied the time and energy of a substantial segment of the population, especially during boom times. Regrettably, some vendors indulged in unethical, fraudulent, fly-by-night practices that at times lent sales agents, developers, and landlords an unsavory image and later led to calls for reform by angry private citizens, concerned industry leaders, and progressive public officials.

In addition to ownership, sales, and property management, building construction was a widespread endeavor. Most contractors and subcontractors, particularly in the residential field, were small-scale operators, often shuttling back and forth between the roles of contractor and laborer. Nearly all houses were built under contract to the owner-users, many of whom constructed their dwellings with the help of family and friends. Stock architectural plans were readily available; only a small percentage of houses, mainly for the wealthy, were truly custom-designed by professional architects. By the early 20th century, the Sears catalog was selling many different models of prefabricated houses that came in pieces along with a manual explaining how to assemble them, much like today's Swedish furniture. Contract work was the principal mode, but many large and small builders also constructed houses as speculative investments, though the norm was generally just one or two and seldom more than five such houses per year. Merchant homebuilding, as this method came to be known, did not begin to dominate the housing industry until the 1950s. The standard approach for even sophisticated real estate developers was primarily to sell finished building lots, not completed houses.

Advances in Transportation and the Rise Of Suburban Development: Llewellyn Park, New Jersey, and Riverside, Illinois

The ability to plan and develop large-scale urban, primarily residential neighborhoods and communities depended on new advances in transportation technology that enabled residents to reach their places of employment without being confined to the tight boundaries, high densities, and mixed uses of the "walking city." By the early 19th century, the population of cities began to spread out and to differentiate uses by location. Commuter ferry service by steamship across rivers and other bodies of water served as one means of circulation.

Ground transportation started with both the omnibus—a horse-drawn urban stagecoach—for short in-city trips and the steam railroad for longer, inter- and intracity travel. Later, horse-drawn passenger cars running on rail rights-of-way, cable cars, electric streetcars or "trolley" cars, elevated and subway rail transit, electric rail, and, finally, the gasoline-powered automobile all helped turn the landscape into its present vast, low-density suburban world of houses, highways, industrial and office parks, shopping malls, and parking lots.

The first generation of major residential land developers was spawned by the coming of long-distance railroads in the 1840s and 1850s. Their developments were essentially elite, upper-middle-class suburbs in pastoral settings located on railroad lines connected to large central cities. Two of the earliest and best known of these suburbs are Llewellyn Park, New Jersey, and Riverside, Illinois.

Llewellyn Haskell, a successful New York merchant, together with eight partners, purchased 400 acres of land near West Orange, New Jersey, in the 1850s. The location was only 13 miles from Manhattan and directly on a railroad line into the city. Haskell was attracted by the natural beauty of the site, with its hills, streams, woods, and views of a mountain to the north and New York City to the east. His goal was to create a model community for "the wants of citizens doing business in New York, and yet wishing accessible, retired, and healthful homes in the country."[10] To further this goal, Haskell hired as his chief planner Alexander Jackson Davis, a well-known architect of luxurious and romantic country estates and author of *Rural Residences,* one of the bibles of stylish residential architecture.

Haskell and Davis worked together to make the most of the site's parklike environment. Missing was the familiar gridiron pattern of straight streets meeting at right angles; instead, roads and lanes curved with the natural contours of the land. The use of curvilinear streets later became a standard feature of suburban residential land development, but, in 1856, it was a bold innovation for a new real estate venture. The developer and his architect-planner also created "the Ramble," a 50-acre natural park that followed a stream at the side of the mountain. The Ramble was left in its natural state except for the addition of some curving pedestrian paths. Haskell organized a property owners' association to hold title to and maintain this common area, establishing another important precedent for new community projects—open space and recreation facilities dedicated by the developer.

Haskell also wrote restrictions into the deeds prohibiting industrial and commercial uses of the land, requiring large minimum lots (three acres), and barring fences on people's property. These and other rules were all designed to preserve Llewellyn Park as a quiet and green paradise for wealthy residents, who entered the exclusive private community through a security gatehouse. Haskell and Davis both moved there, the lots sold at high prices, and the partners earned an excellent return on their investment. The suburb's attractiveness as an elite enclave was so well conceived and executed that, more than a century later, the community remains as Haskell originally envisioned it.

Riverside is more familiar to many urbanists because it was planned by the famous American landscape architects Frederick Law Olmsted and Calvert Vaux, the designers of New York City's Central Park. Emery Childs and a group of investors acquired 1,600 acres of undeveloped land on the Des Plaines River and formed the Riverside Improvement Company in 1868 to build a new suburban community combining "the beauties and healthy properties of a park with the conveniences and improvements of the city."[11] The site was located nine miles west of downtown Chicago on the Burlington Railroad line, and Olmsted and Vaux were impressed by its attractive natural features, calling it "the only available ground near Chicago [that] does not present disadvantages of an almost hopeless character."[12]

Olmsted and Vaux planned a central 160-acre park along the river and several smaller parks and recreation areas. The streets were laid out in a naturalistic curvilinear pattern, and several other innovations in high-quality community planning and design were included in the development of this commuter suburb. Deed restrictions provided for an impressive array of controls, requiring everything from mandatory 30-foot setbacks, minimum home construction costs, and design review for houses, to prescribed rules for maintaining private lawns. Olmsted and Vaux also proposed a limited-access parkway from Riverside to downtown Chicago, an unrealized idea in 1868 that was a half century ahead of its time for American suburban development.

The Riverside Improvement Company hired William LeBaron Jenney, Chicago's leading architect, to review the house plans of those who purchased lots and to design the Riverside Hotel (built in 1870) overlooking the river. Jenney also built his own house in the new community and helped set a tone for the kind of style the developers and landscape planners desired.

Unfortunately, Emery Childs's and the Riverside Improvement Company's luck was not as good as that of Llewellyn Haskell and his partners. The costly im-

Downtown Philadelphia, 1897, where streets are clogged with horse–drawn carriages, trolley cars, and pedestrians.

provements installed to develop Riverside were not supported by vigorous land sales in the first few years. Many people still considered Riverside too far away from the city. Market demand, access to capital, and lot prices all fell dramatically after the 1871 Chicago fire, and the company went bankrupt during the national depression of 1873. By the 1880s, however, sales of lots and construction of houses in Riverside increased significantly. Despite the early disappointments, Riverside, which today is a historic district, was eventually built as a middle-class suburb according to Childs's vision, Olmsted and Vaux's plan, and Jenney's design. It served as an important early model for many later suburban developments from Roland Park in Baltimore to the Country Club District of Kansas City.

While the elite suburbs located along commuter railroad lines represented the earliest examples of large-scale residential subdivisions, further advances in transportation technology later in the 19th century enabled people of more modest means to move to suburban-style neighborhoods and to travel by electric transit to their jobs. "Streetcar suburbs" began to appear on the outskirts of growing cities. Often these new subdivisions, which today are urban neighborhoods, started as unincorporated areas that were later annexed to the nearby central city.

The development of subdivisions during this period was tied to the availability of mass transit. Sometimes the private transportation company was also the land subdivider, with the enormous profits on land sales helping to pay for an initially money-losing transit operation that used cheap promotional fares to encourage people to buy lots and build houses in a sparsely settled community. Real estate entrepreneurs of this type ranged from Boston's Henry M. Whitney, the leading subdivider of Brookline, Massachusetts, to F.M. "Borax" Smith, the largest land developer in Oakland, California. Developers who did not own transit companies usually had to pay subsidies to induce a transportation firm to extend its operations to outlying locations. The subsidies were an essential business cost for the developer, because without transit service, there would be no market for the subdivided land.

Samuel E. Gross

Most subdividers were small-scale real estate dealers, though some, especially the transit and utility companies and other large landowners, often sold a high volume of building lots. Rarely did any subdivision developer build more than a handful of houses, usually just enough to help define the character of the community and create an established, lived-in image. One exception to this general pattern was Samuel E. Gross, a flamboyant residential subdivider who built thousands of houses in the Chicago area in the 1880s and 1890s, mainly inexpensive and affordable houses for skilled blue-collar and white-collar workers earning modest incomes.

Samuel Gross had gone bankrupt in the Chicago real estate business during the 1873 panic, but, after working as a lawyer and a playwright, he reentered the real estate market in 1880. By 1892, he had sold 40,000 lots and built and sold 7,000 houses in the Chicago metropolitan area. Many of his subdivisions were in the nearly 20 new suburbs he developed. The best known is Brookfield, originally called Grossdale, located adjacent to Riverside.

This popular developer engaged in extensive and dramatic advertising campaigns, emphasizing the requirements of his easy-payment financing plan: a 10 percent downpayment, low monthly installments, and generous refinancing for delinquent borrowers. Where he built houses, he charged a single price for the house and lot. In addition, he always made sure that a major transit line ran through his subdivisions, sometimes by working in partnership with Charles T. Yerkes, Chicago's "traction king."

Gross also included major utilities and infrastructure in his developments and added special quality touches to the residential environment. Houses ranged from a modest four-room cottage that sold for $1,000 ($100 down and $10 a month) to larger and more expensive houses, such as a nine-room model that sold for $5,000. Most of the houses were built from orders and downpayments taken from customers, though Gross also maintained a small inventory available for immediate sale. He built from stock plans but provided touches to individualize the design and trumpeted this fact in his advertising.

Gross was aided in the production of inexpensive houses by the development of the balloon-frame method of construction in Chicago during the 1830s and 1840s. This technique, which used light wooden two-by-fours hammered together with machine-made nails rather than heavy timbers and elaborate joints, saved a tremendous amount of construction time, labor, and materials. By the time Gross entered the real estate business, the balloon-frame house had revolutionized homebuilding in the United States and, together with cheap land, made homeownership much more affordable in the United States than in Europe.

Samuel Gross's somewhat bigger houses and more extensive amenities were reserved for middle-income subdivisions such as Grossdale. The marketing of his explicitly working-class subdivisions, however, stressed

This photo, taken by Jacob Riis in 1888, depicts the living conditions in some of New York City's slums.

a small house and a modest environment designed to keep down the cost of the lots. Nonetheless, even in the most moderate-cost subdivisions, Gross always planted a considerable number of trees. His basic real estate development and marketing activities, involving small, inexpensive houses and lots sold on easy credit, were so well received that the Workingman's Party nominated Gross for mayor of Chicago in 1889. He declined the honor, but two years later the city's *Real Estate and Building Journal* crowned Samuel Eberly Gross "the Napoleon of homebuilders."[13]

The Growth of Inner-City Slums

While new housing was being built for the upper class, the middle class, and the more skilled working class, unskilled, low-income workers were still crowded into inner-city neighborhoods called "slums." Close to factories and warehouses that were the major sources of

employment for people who still walked to work, slums claimed the worst housing, the greatest overcrowding, and the highest rates of disease. In 1890, journalist and social reformer Jacob Riis attempted to arouse the nation's conscience with his photographically documented book *How the Other Half Lives,*[14] and, four years later, Carroll Wright, the U.S. Commissioner of Labor, systematically documented the deplorable conditions in his study of the slums of Baltimore, Philadelphia, New York City, and Chicago.[15]

Even though the individuals and families living in the slums had low incomes, landlords often packed so many rent-paying customers into a building and spent so little money on maintenance that slum properties could be highly profitable. Not only were older structures constantly converted to house greater numbers of cash-poor immigrants flocking to the central cities in search of economic opportunity, but new tenements and other forms of high-density residences were also frequently built. Many of even the newest structures lacked such basic necessities as indoor plumbing and windows that brought light and air into all rooms. Lot coverage was extremely high, with little open space around buildings and no place for people to congregate and recreate other than the streets and alleys, both of which were frequently covered with mud and littered with garbage.

In cities from New York to San Francisco, housing reform movements during the late 19th and early 20th centuries began to organize for stricter laws to regulate the minimum quality and standard features of new residential construction and existing housing. Unfortunately, these movements frequently met with stiff resistance from elements of the real estate industry. Where the movements did succeed, they often encountered the fundamental problem that many of the slum tenants could not afford to pay the higher rents necessary to finance the major physical improvements needed.

One strategy to reduce rents was to encourage philanthropic capitalists to build housing for workers under limited-profit financial arrangements. These efforts were intended as both physical models of better construction and design, and economic and social models to stimulate more extensive investment. Some real estate development firms, such as Alfred T. White's City and Suburban Homes Company of New York, became involved in these activities. Most of the leaders in this movement came from business and professional fields not directly related to the real estate industry. All together, however, these efforts did not produce enough housing to make even a dent in the immediate problem, though over the long run they had important symbolic value in helping to raise minimum standards and educating developers about better methods of planning and building low-cost housing.

Yet another approach, led by middle-class professional social workers, was to form settlement houses in slum neighborhoods. Settlement houses provided public health and education services to local residents to help them improve their living conditions and enhance their opportunities. Social workers in settlement houses also assisted members of the community in organizing labor unions and agitating for economic, political, and social reforms from business and government. Often the same people who contributed to the work of settlement houses were also involved in various attempts to regulate slum housing publicly and to promote the private, limited-dividend construction of new low-rent dwellings. The problem of housing the poor has a long history in this country and is marked by many serious initiatives that have not yet achieved long-term success (see Chapter 15).

The Role of Railroads and Railroad Barons in Real Estate Development

The coming of the railroad in the mid-19th century profoundly affected life in the United States. Railroads quickly became the prime mover of people and goods around the nation, into and out of cities and towns. In the 18th and early 19th centuries, water-based transportation routes had made some land accessible, permitting many towns to develop mainly because of their location near navigable bodies of water. In the first half of the 19th century, canals expanded the number of accessible sites for land development. But canals were nothing compared with the railroads. Tracks could be laid almost anywhere, and the volume of land potentially available for development thus expanded tremendously. At times, this expansion led to feverish speculation; no investor could predict with certainty which sites with access to rail transport would be in demand and at what price.

As railroads became the principal mode of long-distance passenger and freight transportation, areas depended on access to rail service for growth and, in many cases, even for survival. In the early years, some municipalities even organized their own short-haul rail corporations; later, many towns went deeply into debt paying huge subsidies to private railroad firms for providing service to their communities. Once regular rail service was established, local citizens bought land and marketed it to newcomers. Clearly, railroads and real estate development were twin forces for change in many growing areas.

The giant railroad corporations, the country's first truly big businesses, were intimately involved in real estate activity. The interstate long-distance rail carriers obtained their franchises and capitalization through the federal government's grant of not only rights-of-way but also of millions of acres of land along their proposed routes. Between 1850 and 1871, the federal government granted 130 million acres of public land to railroad companies. The rail carriers received about half of the land within six to 40 miles of the rights-of-way, with the government retaining the other half. The land was divided by sections into 640-acre parcels, and the railroads were granted every other section. Public officials argued that once the railroad was built, the government could sell its remaining sections for at least twice as much as it could have otherwise, though it did not always work out that way in practice. After the tracks were laid, the railroads and the government went into competition with each other over subdividing and selling their alternate sections.

Railroads entered the real estate promotion business in an enormous way. In addition to selling land, many railroad companies held onto their vast acreage, mortgaging it to bankers and bond buyers to obtain capital. Indeed, when some politicians and citizens tried to force the railroads to sell their publicly granted land, the companies responded that the assets were tied up as collateral and that they could not sell the land without the permission of their lenders—an argument upheld by the U.S. Supreme Court.[16] Over the years, railroads have retained ownership of immense quantities of rural and urban land. They have sold it, leased it, and developed it. It has been used for agriculture, forestry, mining, and recreation, and for commercial, industrial, and residential developments. In many cities today, railroads are still the biggest private landowners, and some have formed real estate development divisions to earn a greater return on their assets. Santa Fe–Southern Pacific's Mission Bay, a large mixed-use real estate development project near downtown San Francisco, is one such example.

The Effect of Railroads on Industrial Development

The railroads completely reshaped the industrial landscape of cities. Originally, in the preindustrial era of older cities, everyone was packed together within walking distance of the center, and artisan workshops were frequently inside or next to people's homes. Later, as cities expanded and manufacturing grew in importance, much manufacturing located in separate multistory "loft" buildings with high ceilings and open floor space. With the increasing demand for industrial space, supplying it became an important branch of the real estate business. Nonetheless, small manufacturers still needed to be concentrated near the center of the city to take advantage of water port facilities—the lifeblood of the transportation system. With the advent of the railroads, however, manufacturing and warehousing could spread out to many possible sites along the rail lines, and rail spurs and feeder lines were built to connect local shippers to the main, long-haul trunk lines.

By the latter part of the 19th century, large factories and factory complexes with workers' housing were built on new sites, owing to the railroads' cooperation in bringing in raw materials and shipping out finished products. In addition to the construction of entire factory towns for large manufacturers such as the new steel mill cities of Gary, Indiana, and Birmingham, Alabama, decentralized industrial parks began to appear on the outskirts of large cities and in nearby suburban locations. Unlike the giant factories, these parks were primarily

The growth of railroad construction brought with it a frenzy of land speculation like that along this line connecting Houston and New Orleans, circa 1880.

speculative real estate ventures. In some cases, the early parks were partially owned and financed by the railroad firms to promote more intensive use of their developed land and transportation services.

By the early 20th century, Chicago real estate developers had established both the Central Manufacturing District and the Clearing Industrial District. Each was located on the southwest side, far from the downtown area. Many manufacturing and warehouse firms relocated to the new districts to take advantage of cheaper rents, larger one-story floor spaces, easy access for cars and trucks to load and unload shipments, proximity to mass transit for workers, and, most important, excellent connections to railroad sidings. These industrial parks were professionally managed and offered low-rise and low-density buildings, newly developed and well-maintained grounds, clean sites, and, compared with the older loft neighborhoods and downtown railyards, more attractive landscaping. Although this type of industrial development did not become prominent in the United States until the 1950s, the earliest models were established in the 1910s and 1920s.

Railroad Barons as Real Estate Developers

Two railroad barons played a crucial role in shaping the patterns of real estate development and urbanization for entire regions: Henry M. Flagler on Florida's east coast and Henry E. Huntington in southern California.

Henry M. Flagler and the Growth of Southern Florida

Henry M. Flagler was one of John D. Rockefeller's original partners in the petroleum business; he became extremely wealthy through the growth of the Standard Oil Company. By the early 1880s, Florida was experiencing one of its periodic land booms. St. Augustine, where Flagler vacationed in 1885, was considered a favorable location because of its healthful climate. Flagler became captivated by the town and decided to develop it into a premier resort city for the upper classes, creating a southern version of Newport, Rhode Island. Flagler hired two young New York architects, John Carrère and Thomas Hastings, to design the massive and luxurious Spanish-style Hotel Ponce de Leon, named for

The lobby of the luxurious 500-room Breakers hotel, built by Henry M. Flagler in 1896 in West Palm Beach.

the man who had searched in St. Augustine for the fountain of youth. The Hotel Ponce de Leon opened in 1888 and proved so successful that, by the following year, Flagler built the Alcazar, a large entertainment center that included mid-priced hotel rooms. He also purchased a new, small luxury hotel called Casa Monica, which he renamed the Cordova. In addition, he built 14 expensive cottages for winter guests. The Alcazar contained ballrooms, theaters, swimming pools, and an array of other facilities, including Roman, Russian, and Turkish baths.

In the process of arranging for goods to be shipped to St. Augustine and marketing his hotels to the northeastern states, Flagler discovered that transportation to the site was a problem. To alleviate that problem, he began to acquire and reorganize local railroad lines. Eventually, he consolidated the lines and created the East Coast Lines, laying tracks southward along the coast toward Daytona Beach and thereby acquiring thousands of acres of public land grants from the state for his railroad-building activities. When Flagler's rail lines reached the Lake Worth area, he created the new resort community of West Palm Beach, starting with the Royal Poinciana, which, with 1,500 rooms, was the world's largest hotel when it opened in 1894. Two years later, he built Breakers, a 500-room hotel. West Palm Beach soon eclipsed St. Augustine. The elite from New York, Philadelphia, and Chicago traveled on Flagler's trains to this winter pleasure palace, and, by 1900, it had truly become the "Newport of the South."

During 1894 and 1895, Florida suffered from a series of winter freezes, and Flagler decided to extend his rail lines farther south, where the winter weather was even warmer. He settled on Dade County and negotiated thousands of acres in land grants from private landowners in exchange for promising to bring rail service to a little town called Ft. Dallas on the Miami River and Biscayne Bay. When the railroad reached the site in 1896, the town was incorporated as Miami, and Flagler built a huge hotel there, the Royal Palm, which opened in 1897. He also built a rail terminal, an electric plant, a sewage system, waterworks, docks and wharves, and, after dredging the Miami River, a harbor for ocean vessels. In addition, he laid out miles of streets; donated land for a civic center, public buildings, schools, parks, and churches; and started a newspaper called the *Miami Metropolis* at a time when the city had only a few hundred year-round residents. By 1910, rapidly growing Miami was already the state's fifth largest city, with a population of 11,000 and hotel accommodations for 100,000. Flagler took advantage of his extensive holdings to subdivide a tremendous amount of land for highly profitable sales and to develop additional hotels and other properties.

Besides the various railroad land grants, Flagler had acquired several large landowning companies in Florida—including a former canal promoter—and consolidated them all into his Florida East Coast Canal and Transportation Company, which also became the holding company for his railroad lines. Flagler made enormous profits by the timely linking of his land sales and development activities to the provision of rail service. In 1897, he added shipping to his transportation and development plans, founding the Florida East Coast Steamship Company to offer improved access from Miami to Havana, Nassau, and Key West, again building hotels and other projects and selling land in Nassau and Key West. His final project was extending the railroad to Key West, a major engineering achievement. Henry Flagler rode the inaugural train 225 miles over land and sea from his home in West Palm Beach to Key West for the grand opening in 1912. When he died a year later, the hotel, railroad, and land baron left an enduring legacy on the form and pattern of development and growth in the Sunshine State.

Henry E. Huntington and Southern California's First Boom

At the same time Henry Flagler was building the Hotel Ponce de Leon on the Atlantic Coast, southern California was in the midst of a wildly speculative land boom brought on by the arrival of transcontinental railroad service. Los Angeles was a small pueblo community of fewer than 6,000 inhabitants when it first began negotiating in the early 1870s for the Southern Pacific to extend its railroad lines to the town. The Angelenos offered free land, an ownership share in their local railroad, $600,000 in cash borrowed through municipal bonds, and other subsidies to the Southern Pacific before its chief executive Collis P. Huntington finally agreed to expand to Los Angeles during the 1880s.

The Atchison, Topeka, and Santa Fe Railroad was also building a new line over the mountains to terminate in Los Angeles, and, by 1887, the Santa Fe and the Southern Pacific were fighting a rate war to establish dominance in the market for coast-to-coast travel to southern California. At one point, they cut fares so low that passengers could ride all the way from Kansas City to Los Angeles for one dollar. The rate war brought in vast numbers of tourists, and the new rail connections to the East and Midwest set off a subdivision boom that lasted for one frenzied year and then quickly crashed. In Los Angeles County, 1,350 new subdivision maps were recorded in 1887, compared with ten in 1880 and 70 in 1890. In 1887, real estate transactions in the city of Los Angeles topped $100 million; only New York City and Chicago had more that year. Prices for acreage and for subdivision lots rose ten to 20 times higher within the year, only to drop back down again by 1888.

In all, the 60 new cities and towns covering 80,000 acres that were laid out and marketed in 1887 and 1888 contained enough land to house several million people at low densities. Yet, by 1889, fewer than 3,500 people were living in those communities. Though Los Angeles itself grew to a population of 50,000 by 1890, other boom towns quickly became ghost towns. One such town was Border City on the Mojave Desert, platted by Simon Homberg on land bought from the federal government. With great fanfare, he sold lots that cost him about ten cents each to East Coast investors for $250 each; when the buyers found out the true nature of their nearly worthless purchase, the market dried up like desert air.

The land speculation boom and bust in 1887 and 1888 left the Los Angeles real estate market in a somewhat weakened condition during the 1890s, and the national depression of 1893 added to local difficulties. Nonetheless, the long-term prospects for Los Angeles's growth turned out to be promising. Even during the 1890s, the population doubled in size, and, by 1901, the city was poised for a major revival of real estate activity. The most important figure in this revival was Henry E. Huntington, vice president of the Southern Pacific Railroad and nephew of its president, Collis Huntington.

When Collis Huntington died in 1900, Henry inherited an enormous fortune. He did not succeed in gaining control of the Southern Pacific, however, and left his position to embark on an entirely new venture in urban development based on interurban railroads. Huntington moved from San Francisco to Los Angeles and incorporated the Pacific Electric Railway in 1901. Earlier he had acquired the Los Angeles Railway, a downtown-oriented commuter service. The Pacific Electric, on the other hand, reached far out into the suburbs and to sparsely settled and mostly undeveloped areas of the vast metropolis.

Huntington laid out a transportation network over southern California that stretched from the San Fernando and San Gabriel Valleys of Los Angeles County all the way to Newport Beach on the Pacific Coast in central Orange County. By 1910, his various railway companies together covered more than 1,300 miles, making Huntington the owner of the largest private interurban transit system in the world. Many southern California communities owed their rapid growth in the first two decades of the 20th century to Huntington's rail service. By 1920, the population of Los Angeles City reached 576,000, and Los Angeles County was home to nearly 1 million people. The landscape of the metropolitan region was so strongly shaped by Huntington's rail network that many of today's freeways follow the old Pacific Electric rights-of-way.

The normal practice for streetcar extensions before Huntington's rise called for landowners to pay the transit company for capital costs in anticipation of the appreciation in property values once service was instituted. Huntington did not bother to pursue such an incremental strategy. He had his own capital and easy access to lenders and investors. Besides, he was his own biggest landowner along most of the suburban transit routes. The Huntington Land and Improvement Company and several other of his entities bought, subdivided, and sold real estate wherever the Pacific Electric's "big red cars" rolled along their tracks. Huntington brought rail service to areas he considered ripe for land development, even when the existing ridership was minimal. In many cases, those areas did grow rapidly once they became accessible through electric rail transportation. Depending on the target market, Huntington developed a wide variety of residential subdivisions, with lots of different sizes and prices and different deed restrictions, landscaping, street plans, and utilities.

In subdividing and selling land, Henry Huntington often worked closely with William May Garland, one of Los Angeles's leading real estate brokers and developers. Huntington was also a partner in the powerful syndicate headed by the owners of the *Los Angeles Times.* The syndicate made an estimated $100 million profit on the purchase of 108,000 acres of arid land in the San Fernando Valley and the subsequent subdivision and reselling of that same newly irrigated land after the completion of the 238-mile Owens Valley Aqueduct, which was paid for by the taxpayers of Los Angeles (and immortalized in the motion picture *Chinatown).*

Huntington's real estate developments ranged from exclusive upper-class areas in Pasadena and San Marino, where his own house was located (which is now the Huntington Museum and Library), to middle-class communities such as South Pasadena, Huntington Beach, and Redondo Beach, to working-class suburbs such as Alhambra, where Henry Huntington developed industrial land and even established his own large factory to promote industrialization and the availability of new homesites. Huntington Beach and Redondo Beach had oil wells, and, though residential development was the primary focus of Huntington's subdivisions, many of his projects also included commercial development, particularly retail stores and hotels; some even included industrial land uses such as power stations.

Another element of Huntington's ambitious metropolitan real estate development strategy was to move into the utilities business as a way of providing necessary services to enhance the value of the land he was

Downtown Los Angeles lined with streetcars and automobiles in the midst of a southern California real estate boom fueled by extensive rail service to outlying areas.

selling and to take advantage of his ownership of considerable land acreage and the transit system. Given that the Los Angeles Railway and the Pacific Electric were major users of electricity, Huntington established the Pacific Light and Power Company to provide hydroelectric and steam power both to his transit operations and to the areas that he was developing. By 1913, Pacific Light and Power was supplying 20 percent of the metropolitan region's electricity and natural gas as well as all the power for Huntington's streetcars. Having acquired so much rural land to obtain a source of water to generate power, Huntington also organized the San Gabriel Valley Water Company to supply fresh water to San Marino, Alhambra, and the greater Pasadena area.

The interrelationship of transportation, infrastructure, utilities, and real estate development that Henry Huntington exemplified on such a grand scale is aptly illustrated by a local joke from 1914. A mother was taking her daughter on a trolley ride to the beach. The daughter asked, "Whose streetcar are we riding in?" Her mother replied, "Mr. Huntington's." Passing a park, the girl asked, "What place is that?" "Huntington Park," responded her mother. "Where are we going, mother?" "To Huntington Beach" was the answer. Finally arriving at the sea, the child ventured one more query: "Mother, does Mr. Huntington own the ocean or does it still belong to God?"[17]

Summary

This chapter reveals how real estate in the 1800s began to contribute significantly to the country's overall economic growth. The railroads' twofold involvement in real estate—as transporters and as land developers and owners—strongly promoted new development.

Once the federal and state governments began privatizing the public lands, real estate became the great American pastime. At the same time that large tracts of land were exchanging hands and undergoing subdivision and development, the public sector was becoming more involved in financing those activities. It was also looking to the real estate industry for new sources of public revenue. Thus, the period saw the creation of large private fortunes made hand in hand with government support.

The next chapter explores the industry's continuing evolution from the late 1800s through World War II.

Terms

- Capital improvement project
- Deed restrictions
- Fee simple
- Ground lease
- Homesteaders
- Land development
- Slums
- Subdivision
- Syndicate

Review Questions

7.1 How was public land put into private ownership?

7.2 Describe the fee simple system of private ownership.

7.3 What was the Holland Land Company noted for?

7.4 What effect did private deed restrictions and public controls have on real estate in the 19th century?

7.5 Who was Llewellyn Haskell?

7.6 What is the balloon-frame method of construction, and what effect did it have on residential development?

7.7 Describe the evolution of slums.

7.8 Discuss the role of the railroads in land development.

Notes

1. See, for example, A.M. Sakolski, *The Great American Land Bubble: The Amazing Story of Land-Grabbing, Speculations, and Booms from Colonial Days to the Present Time* (New York: Harper, 1932); Glenn S. Dumke, *The Boom of the Eighties in Southern California* (San Marino, Calif.: Huntington Library, 1944); and Homer B. Vanderblue, "The Florida Land Boom," *Journal of Land and Public Utility Economics,* May 1927, pp. 113–31, and August 1927, pp. 252–69.

2. Sakolski, *The Great American Land Bubble,* pp. 147, 164.

3. Larry Van Dyne, "The Making of Washington," *Washingtonian,* November 1987, p. 172.

4. Elizabeth Blackmar, *Manhattan For Rent, 1785–1850* (Ithaca, N.Y.: Cornell Univ. Press, 1989), p. 36.

5. Sakolski, *The Great American Land Bubble,* p. 9.

6. Blackmar, *Manhattan For Rent,* pp. 31–32.

7. Sakolski, *The Great American Land Bubble,* p. 82.

8. Ibid., pp. 84–85.

9. Eugene Rachlis and John E. Marqusee, *The Land Lords* (New York: Random House, 1963), p. 3.

10. Kenneth T. Jackson, *Crabgrass Frontier: The Suburbanization of the United States* (New York: Oxford Univ. Press, 1985), p. 77.

11. Ann Durkin Keating, *Building Chicago: Suburban Developers and the Creation of a Divided Metropolis* (Columbus: Ohio State Univ. Press, 1988), p. 73.

12. Jackson, *Crabgrass Frontier,* p. 80.

13. Keating, *Building Chicago,* p. 76. See also Gwendolyn Wright, *Moralism and the Model Home: Domestic Architecture and Cultural Conflict in Chicago, 1873–1913* (Chicago: Univ. of Chicago Press, 1980).

14. Jacob Riis, *How the Other Half Lives: Studies among the Tenements of New York* (New York: Scribner's, 1890).

15. Carroll D. Wright, *The Slums of Baltimore, Chicago, New York, and Philadelphia.* Seventh Special Report of the Commissioner of Labor (Washington, D.C.: U.S. Government Printing Office, 1894).

16. *Platt v. Union Pacific R.R. Co.,* 9 U.S. 48 (October 1878).

17. William B. Friedricks, "A Metropolitan Entrepreneur Par Excellence: Henry E. Huntington and the Growth of Southern California, 1889–1927," *Business History Review,* Summer 1889, p. 354.

Chapter 8

The Late 1800s to World War II

In the latter half of the 19th century, a massive wave of industrialization took place in the United States, much of it concentrated in cities. Urban areas became magnets for an immense population migration from rural areas at home and abroad, of people looking to start their own businesses or to work in the factories, stores, and offices of the expanding metropolis. Adna F. Weber's landmark 1899 study, *The Growth of Cities in the Nineteenth Century,* fully documents this rapid urbanization, which he called "the most remarkable social phenomenon."[1] As cities gained population, they also spread out over a great deal of additional territory, with technological and organizational improvements by the public and private sectors in transportation, utilities, infrastructure, and urban services encouraging the mass movement of industry and residences away from the crowded city center. All but the richest and the poorest moved to outlying neighborhoods in search of newer and better housing and, in many cases, homeownership on cheaper land. Factories and warehouses moved along with the workers to industrial districts where space costs were lower, facilities were more modern, and it was easier to ship goods.

This chapter looks at the changing growth of cities and the increasing involvement of government and regulators in real estate development. It was a volatile era, encompassing two world wars and the Great Depression. The chapter covers several topics:

- Central business districts and commercial development;
- The beginning of the public sector's modern role;
- The real estate boom of the 1920s;
- Finance; and
- The Great Depression and World War II.

Central Business Districts and Commercial Development

What was left behind in the city center as people began moving farther and farther out of the city? High-volume, high-value activities that represented both the new concentration of wealth and power and the rise of the new administrative and consumer-oriented society. The central business district or "downtown" was the region's focal point for the largest banks, insurance companies, corporate headquarters, newspaper publishers, government functions, professional offices, general and specialty retailing and wholesaling, hotels, cultural activities, and much more. The main railroad and streetcar lines all terminated in and radiated out from downtown, bringing in and taking home most of the metropolitan population every day to work, shop, obtain services, and be educated and entertained.

As land values rose in the central core, many industrial and residential land uses were outbid, forced out, torn down, and replaced by an incredible commercial building boom. In downtown Pittsburgh, for example, more than 400 new buildings were completed in just a five-year period in the late 1880s and early 1890s, and nearly as many were completed over the next decade.

This chapter was written and updated by Marc A. Weiss, PhD, Public Policy Scholar, Woodrow Wilson Center, Washington, D.C.

Pittsburgh's downtown experienced remarkable growth in the late 1800s. Liberty Avenue, circa 1910, was one of the main streets leading to the convergence of the Allegheny and Monongahela Rivers.

The Growth of the Skyscraper

No symbol of the prosperous new corporate-commercial city and its growing downtown was more potent than the tall building or "skyscraper." Most skyscrapers were office buildings that replaced church spires as the highest points of reference—though perhaps not reverence—for the entire urban community and its rural hinterland.

By the 1880s, the invention of a workable electric elevator made it possible for buildings to rise above the previous six stories that represented the limit of how many flights of stairs people were willing to walk on a daily basis. Indoor plumbing, electric lighting, and other inventions made building interiors livable and functional, while the advent of structural steel frame construction enabled builders to transcend the constraints on physical height imposed by traditional masonry construction. Instead of thick, heavy load-bearing walls

that could support only so much weight and volume, the new steel skeletons with light masonry curtain walls and plate-glass windows allowed buildings to soar hundreds of feet in height in the 1880s and eventually to top 1,000 feet half a century later.

Life insurance companies erected many of the earliest and most prominent office buildings. The largest of these firms had substantial long-term capital to invest in real estate, needed their own headquarters, and desired to communicate visually their financial strength to millions of current and prospective policyholders. In New York City in the late 19th century, Manhattan Life, Mutual Life, Equitable, Prudential, Metropolitan, and others competed to build the tallest and most impressive structure. A similar battle took place among major metropolitan newspaper publishers, who desired the symbol of a distinctive office tower as a marketing device to boost circulation, advertising revenue, and prestige. Again in New York City, the Tribune and

Evening Post Buildings took the early lead but were soon eclipsed in 1892 by publisher Joseph Pulitzer's New York World Building, which, at 309 feet, was the first structure in the city taller than the steeple of Trinity Church. Not to be outdone, the *New York Times* fought back a decade later with the 362-foot Times Tower.

Two years later, the Singer Sewing Machine Company, a manufacturing corporation whose consumer products were distributed globally, stunned both the insurance and newspaper businesses by announcing plans to construct a new headquarters building more than 600 feet tall. The Singer Building on Broadway in lower Manhattan, designed by the distinguished architect Ernest Flagg, was, when completed in 1908, twice as high as nearly all of New York's and the world's other skyscrapers—and 40 feet taller than the Washington Monument in the nation's capital. The *New York Times* called a 34-story building under construction at the same time "a comparative dwarf alongside the Singer Tower"; ten years earlier this "dwarf" would have been the world's tallest building.[2]

Singer, however, was rapidly overshadowed by the Metropolitan Life Tower, which, when completed in 1909, was nearly 100 feet taller. Some city residents became so alarmed by the perceived negative impact of the new towers on urban overcrowding, sunlight, and safety that they lobbied municipal authorities to impose limitations on building height. By the 1890s, Boston and Chicago passed such restrictions, to be followed by Washington, D.C., Los Angeles, and several other cities. In most cases, the maximum permitted building height ranged between 100 and 200 feet. But by the 1920s, many of these regulations had been lifted or modified to allow continued vertical expansion.

Even though corporations put their names on skyscrapers for advertising value and usually also owned their headquarters buildings, they definitely did not occupy all of the office space. A great deal of it was leased to a variety of business and professional tenants. Not surprisingly, the new downtowns spawned a specialized real estate industry in architecture, construction, brokerage, and property management. The demand for office space was sufficiently strong that real estate developers and investors also put up purely speculative buildings to compete with the large company headquarters structures. In New York City, Singer's neighbors included the Trinity Building and the United States Realty Building, both built speculatively without an anchor or "name" tenant. A more famous example is the attractive and unusual triangle-shaped Flatiron Building on Fifth Avenue and Broadway, designed by the well-known Chicago architect Daniel Burnham and completed in 1903. The Flatiron Building was

occupied primarily by wholesalers and many other small firms.

The most important early commercial office building developers were the Brooks brothers from Boston. Peter and Shepherd Brooks were Boston property investors who in 1873 acquired the seven-story Portland Block, Chicago's first office building equipped with a passenger elevator. From this initial investment, the Brooks family developed many of the key structures that pioneered the world-famous Chicago school of architecture, noted for the design and construction of large commercial buildings during the late 19th century. The Portland Block, completed in 1872, was designed by William Le Baron Jenney, who later served as architect for the Home Insurance Building, considered by many to be the first modern skyscraper because of its pioneering use of steel frame construction. The Portland, also the first building in which every office enjoyed direct sunlight, paid off handsomely for the Brooks brothers and was completely occupied from the 1870s until its demolition in 1933. Peter and Shepherd Brooks hired Owen Aldis, an attorney, to manage the Portland

Once New York City's most famous skyscraper, the Flatiron Building (originally known as the Fuller Building), at the intersection of Fifth Avenue and Broadway, was designed by Daniel H. Burnham and completed in 1903. The facade is rusticated limestone, with French Renaissance details.

Block and serve as their real estate agent in Chicago. By the turn of the century, Aldis was managing 20 percent of the office space in downtown Chicago. He and his nephew Graham Aldis became national leaders in commercial building investment and management.

In 1881, Peter and Shepherd Brooks decided the downtown Chicago real estate market was robust enough to support construction of the city's first ten-story building, the Montauk Block. Peter Brooks wrote Owen Aldis that "an office building erected to suit modern notions, thoroughly equipped with modern appliances, would fill up with modern tenants, leaving the old and unremodeled houses to the conservative fogy."[3] He wanted a building whose modern construction techniques, attractive and simple design, and quality materials, methods, and maintenance would project a businesslike image of efficiency and strength: "The building throughout is to be for use and not for ornament. Its beauty will be in its all-adaptation to its use."[4] The architectural partners Daniel Burnham and John Wellborn Root designed the Montauk Block plus two other Brooks-Aldis office buildings of the 1880s, the Rookery and the Monadnock Block. The Brooks brothers and Owen Aldis teamed up to develop two other major Chicago office structures in the 1890s, the Pontiac Building and the Marquette Building, both designed by another famous architectural firm, Holabird and Roche.

Peter and Shepherd Brooks's and Owen Aldis's guidelines for the design of their numerous buildings included "height sufficient to warrant the use of elevators, as much light as possible, easy maintenance, high percentage of rentable space, and ornament sufficient to avoid absolute plainness."[5] Aldis also wrote rules for building management when the Marquette was completed in 1894, with the basic thrusts of the eight points being that building first-class space and providing first-class services are the best investments. It certainly turned out that way for Peter and Shepherd Brooks, who earned a substantial return on their investment in developing and owning Chicago office buildings. Owen Aldis also did extremely well financially from his investments and fee income. The buildings developed by Brooks-Aldis were fully rented when they opened in the 1880s and 1890s, and, though the Montauk was demolished in 1902, the others maintained high occupancy rates all the way through the mid-1960s. Interestingly, Aldis's leasing strategy was to "arrange [a] typical layout for intensive use." He went on to note:

> A large number of small tenants is more desirable than large space for large tenants because: a) a higher rate per square foot can be added for small tenants; b) they do not move in a body and leave the building with a large vacant space when hard times hit; c) they do not swamp your elevators by coming and going by the clock.[6]

The Growth of Downtown Hotels, Apartment Buildings, and Department Stores

High-rise office buildings were among the most distinctive new features of the rapidly growing urban downtowns, and they were soon joined by other prominent new structures and land uses. Large hotels, many of them also rising many stories, were an increasingly vital feature of downtowns, attracting business customers and the rapidly expanding tourist trade to meetings, social functions, entertainment, and, most important, the thousands of new guest rooms. Henry Flagler's thriving Florida hotel operations, though winter resorts, also anchored the downtowns of several growing cities, particularly Miami. In New York City, the heirs and descendants of John Jacob Astor built the luxurious Waldorf-Astoria Hotel in the 1890s on the site of their parents' mansions. Elsewhere, Potter Palmer in Chicago, Henry Huntington in southern California, and other developers built similar "grand hotels."

Another emerging urban innovation of the late 19th century, related to the residential hotel, was the apartment house. As land values rose in the central area, it became increasingly uneconomical to build or maintain single-family detached houses or attached townhouses other than as mansions for the wealthiest people. Spacious apartments, complete with the latest physical amenities and a wide assortment of extra services, provided an attractive alternative for many upper- and middle-class urbanites desiring to live close to the business and entertainment world of downtown. Some of the buildings with the most services and facilities, including dining rooms, were even called apartment hotels. This vertical lifestyle had already become popular in Paris by the mid-19th century, and, when first transplanted to the United States, the apartments were often referred to as "French flats."

The original American prototype for the French flat was the fashionable Stuyvesant Apartments in Manhattan, developed by rich socialite Rutherford Stuyvesant in 1869. Richard Morris Hunt, the first U.S. architect to be trained at the Ecole des Beaux Arts in Paris, designed the Stuyvesant. By 1900, apartment buildings accounted for an increasingly important use of land in New York City, Chicago, Boston, San Francisco, Washington, D.C., and a few other cities. Luxury apartments and working-class tenements were located in separate neighborhoods close to downtown, and middle-class multifamily dwellings were built farther out along the many avenues and boulevards traversed by streetcar lines.

The other major innovative urban land use was massive, multistory facilities for retail trade, originally called dry goods or general stores and, by the late 19th century, department stores. These massive structures, often designed as "pleasure palaces" with ornate exteriors and lavish interiors, catered especially to women shoppers. The stores employed service-oriented sales personnel and offered special events and promotions. The first major department store was Alexander T. Stewart's elaborate dry goods center, the Marble Palace, which opened in 1846 on Broadway and Chambers Street in New York City. Later in the century, larger and more spectacular department stores covering entire city blocks and serving as major downtown institutions flourished in many cities, including Filene's in Boston, Rich's in Atlanta, Marshall Field's in Chicago, The Emporium in San Francisco, Dayton's in Minneapolis, Hudson's in Detroit, Robinson's in Los Angeles, and several others. In every case, these stores acted as magnets for the real estate market. When Marshall Field's changed locations in Chicago from Lake Street to State Street in 1867, its new site became the prime "100 percent corner" almost immediately.

One of the greatest of all the department store ventures was Wanamaker's in Philadelphia. John Wanamaker and his partner Nathan Brown opened Oak Hall, their original men's and boys' clothing store, on the ground floor of a six-story building on Sixth and Market Streets in downtown Philadelphia in 1861. Their business philosophy, which Wanamaker elaborated throughout his long retailing career, called for selling quality merchandise at one everyday low price and guaranteeing money-back returns on all goods. Wanamaker emphasized a democratic, egalitarian ethic with his slogan "no favoritism."[7] Every customer was to be treated with equal respect, to be charged the same low prices, and to be served properly. In the early years, Wanamaker's made only cash sales, refunded only cash, and paid its workers daily in cash.

By the 1870s, Oak Hall proved so successful that John Wanamaker purchased an abandoned rail depot from the Pennsylvania Railroad and built the world's largest department store, a huge two-acre dry goods emporium at Thirteenth and Market Streets. Perhaps foreshadowing today's successful retail centers in former train stations, such as Union Station in Washington, D.C., Wanamaker dubbed his store "the Grand Depot." The new store opened in 1876 in the midst of the centennial celebration of the Declaration of Independence, which brought 10 million visitors to Philadelphia

The Waldorf-Astoria Hotel, built in the late 1890s by the descendants of John Jacob Astor in Second Empire style.

over a six-month period for a major exhibition in Fairmount Park. And one of the big tourist attractions was Wanamaker's Grand Depot. A year later, Wanamaker was already expanding, building an addition on Chestnut Street that connected through a stylish arcade to the main store. The Chestnut Street store, with its own separate and ornate entrance, was designed to specialize in "ladies' goods," which eventually became an even bigger business for Wanamaker's than its already brisk trade in men's and children's clothing, hats, and shoes. Linens, appliances, housewares, furniture, pianos, and everything else imaginable were eventu-

The grand atrium of Wanamaker's downtown Philadelphia store in 1911. This neoclassic, 13-story building was a block long.

ally added to various departments in the acres of retail space. Sales reached nearly 100,000 items on a single day in December 1896, breaking all previous records.

For many years, John Wanamaker's at Thirteenth and Market, with its distinctive clock tower, was known around the world as one of Philadelphia's central landmarks. In 1908, the Chestnut Street store was demolished and replaced by a much larger, block-long structure, complete with its own subway station. In 1896, Wanamaker acquired Alexander T. Stewart's flagship store, built in 1862 at Tenth and Broadway in Manhattan as an "uptown" branch of the Marble Palace, and reopened it as Wanamaker's New York City store. After a decade of growing sales, Wanamaker constructed a huge 16-story structure next to the old A.T. Stewart's Building, creating again one of the world's largest shopping complexes, with three separate stores: The Woman's Store, The Man's Store, and the Wanamaker Galleries of Furnishing and Decoration. (The last included "The House Palatial and Summer Garden," which brought in 70,000 shoppers on opening day.) By the

time John Wanamaker died in 1922, Wanamaker's, like other major department stores, was beginning to build suburban stores at prime locations near commuter train stations. Despite the subsequent urban decentralization, the role of Wanamaker and other central city department store owners in creating the modern commercial downtown is an enduring legacy.

The Beginning of the Public Sector's Modern Role

As cities grew larger and more complex in the late 19th and early 20th centuries, governments became increasingly involved in providing municipal services, promoting the development of public infrastructure, and regulating private real estate development. The advent of industrialization reinforced the urban trend away from the "walking city" and toward a growing separation of work and residence so that commuting, traffic congestion, and transportation technology all became more important public concerns. As greater numbers of people migrated to cities, issues ranging from overcrowding to pollution to public health and safety to the need for light, air, and adequate recreation all became subjects of heated debate. Concern over these issues led to various proposed solutions, to new forms of public intervention in private markets, and to the rise of urban and metropolitan planning.

Industry and trade brought rising prosperity to the cities, though many citizens disliked the unpleasant side effects such as filth and noise. In response and to celebrate their new wealth and power and the success of U.S. democracy, municipalities launched "City Beautiful" campaigns to construct attractive and often monumental public buildings—city halls, libraries, museums, and schools. Another element of this movement was the establishment of public parks, both large "pleasure gardens" and smaller neighborhood parks and playgrounds. New York City established its massive Central Park during the 1850s, and the principal designer, landscape architect Frederick Law Olmsted, then spent the next four decades designing parks and parkways in many cities across the country, including San Francisco's Golden Gate Park, Brooklyn's Prospect Park, and park systems for Boston, Chicago, and Buffalo.

Along with civic centers and parks came parkways —wide streets that coursed through parks or other natural settings—and boulevards—tree-lined thoroughfares bordered by buildings and other urban scenery. Although these roads initially were intended for leisurely promenading in carriages or automobiles, many of them later turned into principal transportation arteries overflowing with traffic. Given that 30 to 40 percent of the land in a typical city was used for streets and highways, the constant need to expand and upgrade the roadways preoccupied local governments. Further, local governments assumed responsibility for franchising, regulating, financing, building, maintaining, planning, and coordinating the movement of people and goods around and through urban areas. Structures such as docks, port facilities, bridges, and tunnels for cities on water; railroad lines and railway terminals for every city; and streetcars, subways, mechanized transit lines, and trucking all came under the purview of the public sector. These new areas of activity added to the already expanding demands for the public provision of infrastructure and utilities, such as water and sewer systems, and to the burgeoning growth of essential services, from police protection to street cleaning.

A good example of this expansion of government led by private initiative is the 1909 Plan of Chicago sponsored by the Commercial Club, a powerful downtown business group, and authored by a group of businessmen and professionals led by architect Daniel Burnham. The purposes of the plan were to establish the central area firmly as a modern corporate and commercial downtown, to reclaim the lakefront for recreational use and the development of luxury housing, and to encourage suburban growth by constructing radial highways emanating from downtown Chicago and designating regional forest preserves to maintain suburban open space. Nearly $300 million in public funds was spent during the first two decades of the 20th century to implement the plan, supplemented by a great deal of private investment and massive promotional campaigns by the Commercial Club and the Chicago Plan Commission.[8] The plan had wide-ranging effects:

- Downtown rail lines were covered over and air rights developed for parks, office buildings, and consolidated passenger terminals.
- The wholesale produce market was relocated to accommodate construction of the bilevel boulevard-style Wacker Drive along the Chicago River.
- Building the Michigan Avenue Bridge opened up the Magic Mile retail and office district and the Gold Coast residential neighborhood on the near north side.
- Other new bridges built over the Chicago River improved access to downtown.
- Chicago's "frontyard" was redeveloped and filled in with attractive new lakefront parks such as Grant Park and Burnham Park, museums, cultural institutions, the Navy Pier, and expanded and improved existing lakefront parks.

- Several major streets were widened and new thoroughfares developed.
- Suburban regional parks were created.

Public works proved to be a strong stimulus for private commercial and residential development, and Chicago citizens who voted for the many bond issues were pleased with the results.

One problem of urban living was the threat of fire from so many wooden buildings so close together. Major portions of Boston, Baltimore, Chicago, and San Francisco had been destroyed by conflagrations in the late 19th and early 20th centuries, and smaller fires were a common occurrence in cities everywhere. To safeguard the dense urban environment, cities not only organized fire departments but also increasingly promulgated building codes to improve the safety of urban structures. By the late 19th century, some municipalities prescribed fire-protective limits in the center city, requiring all new buildings to be constructed of brick. In addition to focusing on fireproof materials, building codes regulated building materials and methods of construction to increase the safety and longevity of structures. Because building codes regulated only general construction, many cities also developed specialized housing codes to require minimum standards of habitability for new and existing dwelling units.

Also in the latter part of the 19th century, cities began to limit to certain areas within the city those hazardous but necessary business and industrial activities that might cause fires or expose people to disease, harm, or noxious odors. Selective prohibition of these uses by geographic location was an early form of land use zoning. The first local government to initiate a broad zoning law was Los Angeles, which in 1908 divided the entire city into residential and industrial districts. Many cities, including Los Angeles, also imposed limitations on building height, with Boston and Washington, D.C., establishing differential height districts to allow taller buildings in the downtown than in the rest of the city. By 1916, New York City combined height and use restrictions with regulations on lot coverage and building bulk to create "comprehensive zoning." A series of U.S. Supreme Court decisions between 1909 and 1926 validated this new form of public limitation on private property rights, and, by the end of the 1920s, most large cities and many smaller towns and suburban villages (more than 1,000 in all) had enacted zoning ordinances and established planning agencies to implement the new regulations (see Chapter 13 for more detailed information about zoning practices).

Why did property owners agree to abridge their rights and exchange laissez-faire laws for stricter government supervision? In some cases they did not agree, and a great deal of protest and controversy ensued. But overall, the private sector—not just community groups but also many real estate entrepreneurs—strongly favored the growing number of public laws and codes regulating urban development and land use. They supported zoning restrictions to stabilize real estate markets, increase property values, and encourage new investment because they understood that the restrictions enabled them to build or buy property with less risk of unfavorable change on the adjoining lots and the surrounding neighborhoods. They welcomed subdivision controls for introducing a level of coordination that enabled both private developers and local governments to plan, finance, and construct more efficiently the new infrastructure and amenities that were essential to the success of real estate development projects.

Even before the introduction of zoning and other types of government controls, real estate owners and developers had created their own system of private restrictions that were written into property deeds as contractual obligations. Deed restrictions—a private form of land use regulation that evolved in the 19th century

—established the precedents and models later used in promulgating public sector development controls. Several state and local governments supported the application of these privately negotiated restrictions on property owners by publicly enforcing them in civil courts. More direct and extensive public intervention came in the 20th century after leaders of the real estate industry recognized that greater powers and flexibility for local governments were needed to regulate urban property and land uses more broadly and extensively than private efforts had been able to accomplish.

The Roaring Twenties

After a relatively dry spell in the period immediately before, during, and after World War I, the construction of downtown office space burgeoned in the 1920s, in structures of all shapes, sizes, and heights. Near the end of the decade, the Thompson-Starrett Company of New York, one of the world's largest private construction firms that specialized in skyscrapers, surveyed the country's 173 largest cities and found nearly 5,000 buildings ten stories or higher, many of them built during the 1920s. This list included hotels, department stores, manufacturing lofts, civic centers, and other private and public structures, but private office buildings predominated.[9]

While New York City accounted for more than three-fifths of the total for the entire country, many other cities had significant and growing numbers of skyscrapers. New York, Chicago, Los Angeles, Philadelphia, Detroit, and Boston all had more than 100 buildings taller than ten stories. St. Louis, Pittsburgh, Kansas City, San Francisco, Cleveland, Seattle, Baltimore, Minneapolis, Tulsa, Dallas, and Houston each had at least 30 buildings ten stories or higher. The growth in the height and bulk of these structures was made possible by new building technology but was fueled also by the increasing economic productivity and urban wealth of the 1920s and the tremendous expansion of cities both outward and upward. By the late 1920s, financing was flowing freely from institutional lenders, equity syndicators, and mortgage bond houses, further encouraging the construction of speculative office space. New organizations and methods of equity financing through the sale of stock—under the aegis of such firms as the Fred F. French Investing Company or Harry Black's United States Realty—and debt financing— through the likes of the S.W. Straus mortgage bond company—fed the rapid private development of highrise commercial and residential buildings.

Of the buildings listed in the 1929 census of skyscrapers, 377 were more than 20 stories high, with 188

Built in 1900, the 15-story Continental Building in downtown Baltimore, a classic early skyscraper in the Chicago style.

in New York City, including what was then the world's tallest: the 55-story, 792-foot-high Woolworth Building constructed in 1913 by the Thompson-Starrett Company. This neogothic "cathedral of commerce" was the corporate headquarters of the F.W. Woolworth Company, and its owner, Frank Woolworth, had paid $13 million in cash to build a monument to his empire of retail stores. The building had no mortgage, and though it advertised the Woolworth name, most of the office space was leased to other firms.

By the late 1920s, office buildings were going up so fast and American business tenants, investors, and real estate developers were all in such a confident mood that several new structures, including the 77-story, 1,030-foot-high, art deco Chrysler Building, far surpassed the Woolworth Building in height and prominence. The building that was to become the world's tallest for more than four decades, the Empire State Building, was not a corporate headquarters like some of the other giant skyscrapers but rather a purely speculative office building built quickly in what many considered a poor location (see Figure 8-1).

The Rise of Urban Apartment Buildings

One of the most notable trends of the 1920s was the tremendous increase in the construction of apartment buildings. Outside of New York City and a handful of other major cities, earlier waves of urbanization in the United States had been based on a relatively low-density pattern of small, detached single-family houses, attached rowhouses, or duplexes. Some cities, including Boston, had triple deckers, and in many cities, large older houses were subdivided into multiple apartments. This pattern began to change dramatically during the 1920s. Real estate investors, developers, lenders, and contractors all became active participants in the production of new apartment buildings. The apartments were built primarily as rental units, though in a few cities, some of the buildings were sold to occupants for cooperative ownership. The new structures, built mainly with brick or stucco exteriors, ranged from fashionable luxury residences with doormen and other services to more modest housing and from individual six-unit buildings to high rises and large complexes equipped with schools, parks, and community centers.

Perhaps the largest private rental housing development of the decade was the 2,125-unit, moderate-income Sunnyside apartment complex in New York City, with rents subsidized through a ten-year property tax abatement provided by the municipal government. The Metropolitan Life Insurance Company developed the apartments in 1922 to help ease New York's severe housing shortage. As an experiment in direct ownership and management of rental housing, Sunnyside proved economically successful and induced the insurance firm to build many larger apartment projects across the country during the 1930s and 1940s.

Living in Parisian-style apartments suddenly became more fashionable for many middle- and upper-income people. For families across the income spectrum, apartments offered a cost-effective form of housing. Rents were relatively high because of the lack of supply resulting from the low level of new residential construction during and immediately after World War I. With the growth in postwar housing demand, apartments became a good investment. The volume of apartments increased steadily throughout the decade, remaining at a high level of new construction starts through 1928. Starts of single-family housing, by contrast, peaked in 1925 and dropped sharply thereafter. Nearly 40 percent of all the dwelling units built during the 1920s were multi-family units. Further, the annual percentage of total residential construction devoted to multifamily dwellings rose from approximately 25 percent in 1921 to more than half of all residential building permits issued in 1928. In every region of the United States and in all urban areas, the absolute number and relative percentage of apartments expanded significantly.

New single-family houses also were built in record numbers during the 1920s. The peak year, 1925, established an all-time high for starts of new housing that remained unsurpassed until 1950. The level of U.S. nonfarm homeownership escalated by more than 5 percentage points from 1920 to 1930. Urban decentralization and suburbanization spread in all directions across the metropolitan landscape, the number of private automobiles increased by the millions, disposable income and savings among the middle class rose substantially, and land subdividers carved up an astonishing amount of acreage at the periphery of cities into building lots for sale. Massive land speculation and wild price escalation ensued in many rapidly growing areas of the country, helping to induce an unfortunate degree of mismanagement and fraud. In Florida alone, enough lots were subdivided, many of them in swampland or literally under water, to house the entire population of the United States.

At the height of the boom, new suburban subdivisions came onto the market daily along the country's "crabgrass frontier." Although most of the subdivisions were only modestly improved with basic infrastructure and amenities, a small but significant group of community builders was increasingly developing large-scale, well-planned, fully improved subdivisions complete with extensive landscaping, parks and parkways, and shopping centers. This pattern of development, with

Figure 8-1

The Story of the Empire State Building

The site of the Empire State Building was attractive to its investors because a very large parcel of land, 197 feet by 425 feet, was available. The old Waldorf-Astoria Hotel, which sat on that parcel, was slated to be demolished when the new hotel on Park Avenue was completed. After developer Floyd Brown, who had bought the site in 1928, defaulted on his mortgage payments, the property was sold to the Empire State Company, and the hotel was demolished just a few weeks before the stock market crashed in October 1929. Despite the crash, the Empire State Company, partially owned by the du Pont family and headed by former New York Governor Al Smith, decided to move forward with the project in the face of what it incorrectly perceived to be a brief economic downturn. The company invested a total of $45 million to acquire the site, demolish the hotel, and design and construct the world's tallest building, all in less than 18 months! The actual construction, managed by the general contracting firm of Starrett Brothers and Eken, took less than a year. At the peak of activity, 3,500 construction workers were adding one story a day. By the official opening on May 1, 1931, the building stood 1,250 feet tall, with 85 floors of offices and the equivalent of another 17 floors devoted to the magnificent mooring mast and observation decks.

When completed, the Empire State Building's skeleton consumed 57,000 tons of steel. The finished building contained 51 miles of pipe, 17 million feet of telephone cables, and seven miles of elevator shaft.

One reason for the speed of construction was that in those days commercial leases in New York expired on April 30, and if the Empire State Building were not ready for occupancy on May 1, the company would have to wait an entire year to attract tenants—a costly delay. The rationale for building it so tall was that the syndicate had paid

The completed Empire State Building in 1931—the symbol of New York for nearly 70 years. The facade is of limestone, granite, aluminum, and nickel, with a hint of art deco ornamentation.

roots in the 19th century, became more common and expanded in both the scale of operations and degree of capital investment during the 1920s. The most eloquent exponent of this trend was Jesse Clyde Nichols of Kansas City, Missouri, developer of the world-famous Country Club District and a founder of the Urban Land Institute (see profile).

The Spread of the Garden City

Part of what inspired J.C. Nichols to build his ideal of a stable, family-oriented, and beautifully landscaped community was his exposure to the European Garden City movement during his college years. In 1898, Sir Ebenezer Howard published the first edition of his international classic, *Garden Cities of Tomorrow,* and the following year founded the International Garden City Association in London.[10] By 1904, Letchworth, the first of the English garden cities, was under construction. The Garden City movement was a response to the rapid growth and overcrowding of the grimy, unsanitary, and crime-ridden industrial cities of the West. Howard envisioned balanced, self-contained, and modestly sized communities, each with an adequate economic base record high prices for a location at 34th Street and Fifth Avenue that was less than ideal for a quality office skyscraper: the principal office districts were at 23rd Street near Madison Square, 42nd Street near Grand Central Station, and downtown around Wall Street. The Empire State Building stood alone in the middle of a low-rise section of hotels, department stores, shops, and loft buildings, relatively far from the Grand Central and Pennsylvania Railroad Stations and several blocks from the nearest subway lines. The extreme height and distinctiveness of the building were designed to serve as an advertising beacon to attract office tenants.

Similarly, key architectural features were intended to maximize the net revenue that could be generated by the rentable space. For example, the building is less bulky than was permitted under the zoning laws. By designing almost the entire building as a setback tower over a wide, five-story base, the developers increased the rents per square foot by offering offices that were quieter and had more natural light. By building shallow floors with window access for every office, the developers also eliminated the disadvantage of their location relative to other tall buildings, offering prospective tenants panoramic and unobstructed views. In this design, constructing less space per floor made each square foot more valuable. Similarly, rather than building a simple flat rectangular structure that would have produced four corner offices on each floor, the Empire State Building was recessed in the north and south towers so that the extra angles of the structure would yield eight to 12 corner offices per floor, adding significantly to the potential rent.

The physical achievement of the Empire State Building obscures the fact that, like today's projects, it too had to meet legal and financial requirements for feasibility. John

Jacob Raskob, one of five partners in the development, asked his architect, William Lamb, "Bill, how high can you make it so it won't fall down?" The real question was, how high and still profitable? The answer depended on a stipulation in New York City's 1916 zoning ordinance that above the 30th floor, a building could occupy no more per floor than one-fourth of the total area on its lot. With two acres of ground, the Empire State tower could cover half an acre. Lamb determined that 36 million cubic feet would be a profitable size; he then began playing with alternatives. The 16th iteration (Plan K) was it: an 86-story tower. His client Raskob declared, "It needs a hat," and in a creative burst suggested a mooring mast for a dirigible. The 200-foot mast, intended to be an international arrival point for lighter-than-air craft, extended the building's total height to 1,250 feet. Because of high winds, the mast never worked as intended, but it was eventually used for observation. During the Great Depression, income from the observation platform offset large office vacancies and kept the Empire State Building in business.

Unfortunately, all the developer's sophisticated planning and marketing strategies designed to cope with the basic circumstances of no preleased tenants, a poor location, and a terrible office market during the Great Depression were in the short run to little avail. The building stood mostly vacant throughout the 1930s and was widely nicknamed "The Empty State Building." With the return of full employment and prosperity in the 1940s, however, the building filled up and has proved successful. Rather than being a symbol of a corporate, government, educational, medical, or cultural institution, the Empire State Building stands after nearly 70 years as a symbol of commercial real estate development. ■

---

of manufacturing employment near workers' housing; democratically self-governing institutions with public ownership of land and community facilities; physically well-planned surroundings with plenty of greenery, open space, and easy transport; and linkages to a regional system of small cities separated by a permanent greenbelt of agricultural land.

The philosophy of the Garden City movement comprised four elements: environmental reform, social reform, town planning, and regional planning. Many development efforts, including J.C. Nichols's Country Club District, were motivated primarily by interests

in environmental reform and town planning, with far less stress placed on the other two elements.

Radburn

The most ambitious attempt to give full expression to Ebenezer Howard's ideas in the United States was with the City Housing Corporation (CHC) of New York, headed by Alexander Bing. Bing, who along with his brother Leo was a successful developer of luxury apartment buildings in Manhattan, became more public-spirited during his service as a housing consultant to the federal government during World War I. After the

Profile **J.C. Nichols and the Development of the Country Club District in Kansas City, Missouri**

Jesse Clyde Nichols returned home to Kansas and entered the real estate business upon graduating from Harvard University in 1903. He started as a small, speculative home-builder, building and selling single-family houses on vacant lots in a partially improved subdivision. Two years later, he acquired a ten-acre subdivision just south of the city limits of Kansas City, Missouri, and began planning his vision: the long-term development of a large and high-quality urban community. By 1908, with capital from a group of wealthy investors, he had gained control of more than 1,000 acres on Kansas City's south side, calling it the Country Club District to emphasize its proximity to the Kansas City Country Club. Eventually, those 1,000 acres would contain 6,000 houses, 160 apartment buildings, and 35,000 residents.

By the 1920s, J.C. Nichols had already established the Country Club District as one of the most attractive and expensive communities in the region. The J.C. Nichols Company employed the well-known landscape architect George Kessler, who had previously designed a "City Beautiful" plan for Kansas City that included an elaborate park and parkway system, to do the initial planning and landscaping of the Country Club District. Later, S. Herbert Hare became the Country Club District's chief landscape designer. Nichols worked with the city government to extend and build two of the new parkways, the Ward and the Mill Creek, through the Country Club District, giving the community excellent transportation connections to the downtown and a vital community amenity. Ward Parkway became among the most fashionable addresses in Kansas City.

Nichols relied extensively on long-term deed restrictions to control the design, cost, and use of all private property in the district. For years, he advertised the Country Club District as "the one thousand acres restricted." Nichols invested heavily in a wide range of community facilities from landscaped parks to public art and in an ambitious program of community activities from pageants and regattas to flower shows. In addition, he was one of the first developers to establish a mandatory homeowners' association that collected fees to help legally enforce, revise, and renew deed restrictions, finance and maintain community facilities and activities, and establish an active, participatory community identity.

J.C. Nichols engaged in practices that were unusual for real estate developers in his day, and he was generally ahead of his time. Nichols regularly installed first-rate infrastructure in advance of development, adding its costs to the prices of the lots for sale. He also engaged architects to design model homes and built many houses both on a speculative basis and under contract with lot purchasers. Finally, Nichols saw the potential for developing and owning retail centers as a profitable enterprise and as a strategy for building community atmosphere, and over the years he developed and owned many neighborhood shopping centers. His flagship was a regional retail and office complex in the heart of the district called Country Club Plaza, developed beginning in 1922 and generally recognized as America's first suburban shopping center. Designed with a unified Moorish-Spanish architectural theme and controlled by centralized management, the plaza provided both on- and off-street parking, was well located for public transit, and drew a walk-in trade from residents of apartment buildings and workers in office buildings that Nichols developed nearby. Even today, both the district and the plaza are the "in" places to live and shop in Kansas City.

---

armistice, he was determined to embark on a path of social reform. Linking up with a group of visionaries called the Regional Planning Association of America headed by critic Lewis Mumford and architects and planners such as Clarence Stein, Henry Wright, and Catherine Bauer, Alexander Bing attracted sufficient investment capital to establish the City Housing Corporation with the intention of building a garden city in the United States. After developing one successful preliminary project called Sunnyside Gardens in New York City, the CHC bought a large parcel of land in Fair Lawn, New Jersey, within commuting range of Manhattan, and, in 1928, began developing Radburn, "a town for the motor age."

Planned and designed primarily by Clarence Stein and Henry Wright, Radburn incorporated many innovative features, such as the separation of vehicular and pedestrian traffic through the use of bridges, underpasses, and footpaths. Another major innovation was the use of extra large "superblocks" with interior parks and culs-de-sac to create common open green space, keep automobile through-traffic away from houses, and economize significantly on the typical costs of land and infrastructure development. Radburn also modeled new ways of establishing an unincorporated self-governing community through strict, comprehensive deed restrictions and an active and well-funded homeowners' association. While Radburn received global publicity

J.C. Nichols's Country Club District promised "spacious grounds for permanently protected homes, surrounded with ample space for air and sunshine."

The restrictive covenants unfortunately discriminated against racial, ethnic, and religious minorities, as was standard on most deed restrictions before the U.S. Supreme Court ruled such provisions legally unenforceable in 1948. And the district in general catered primarily to upper-income people, though beginning in the 1930s and 1940s, Nichols shifted some of the newer subdivisions to smaller houses and lots for a middle-income clientele. Yet for cre-

ative and successful real estate entrepreneurship over half a century, Nichols's achievement stands out. He provided leadership to the real estate community as an officer of the National Association of Realtors®, to the urban planning community as a founding member of the American Planning Association, and to large-scale developers in particular as the first chair of the Urban Land Institute's Community Builders Council. ■

and many of its planning ideas were widely imitated, it ran into the economic crisis of the 1930s, and only a small portion of the original design was actually built. The CHC encountered serious cash flow problems and was eventually forced into bankruptcy. Yet the development of Radburn remains one of this country's best-known and most-admired experiments in for-profit, speculative community building by a private real estate developer.

Shaker Heights

Shaker Heights is a model suburban community near Cleveland, Ohio, where the Van Sweringen brothers developed the financial skills that enabled them to

take over a major railroad and an important section of downtown Cleveland—with almost none of their own money. Oris P. and Mantis J. Van Sweringen were minor land developers in the Cleveland area in 1900 when they first approached the Buffalo syndicate that owned the property formerly occupied by a Shaker religious community. For more than ten years, the Buffalo group had been attempting to sell the property, which was valued at $240,000. The Vans, as they became known to Clevelanders, eventually convinced the Buffalo syndicate to give them a free 30-day option on a small section of the property. The option agreement contained a further option for an additional section twice the size of the first for a period twice as long as the first period. If they exercised that option, the Vans would receive additional options.

The Van Sweringens were consummate salesmen and convinced a number of Cleveland's leading citizens to join their development syndicate. After exercising a few of the options, they bought the entire property of 1,400 acres, which they later expanded to 4,000 acres.

The Van Sweringen brothers had learned during an earlier venture that transportation was critical to successful suburban development, but the president of the Cleveland Railway Company rejected as impractical their proposal that the company contribute an extension to the existing railway line to serve the new Shaker Heights community. As a result, they decided to build their own railroad.

First, they identified a ravine in which the railroad tracks could run without hindrance of any grade crossings and then began to buy the needed land. Eventually, it was necessary for them to purchase an entire railroad (called the Nickel Plate) for $8.5 million to complete the right-of-way. In addition, they acquired four acres of land in downtown Cleveland's Public Square to construct a terminal for their new commuter railroad.

By June 1929, they had spent more than $2 million on their development of Public Square, including a new railroad station, a 36-story office tower, a department store, and a hotel. By then, over 15,000 people lived in Shaker Heights, on land valued at more than $80 million.[11]

The Birth of Industry Trade Associations

The vigorous spirit of reform and modernization that characterized the early 20th century paralleled the tremendous growth and institutional development of the real estate industry through the movement for "professionalization." Many elements of the flourishing real estate business organized trade associations to upgrade standards of practice; to isolate, ostracize, and, where possible, eliminate unsavory activities; and to cooperate with the public sector and other segments of the business world and the general public to protect the interests of real estate and enhance its political stature and economic viability.

The National Association of Realtors® (NAR), for example, was established in 1908 to seek government licensing of the brokerage business. Operating through local boards of Realtors®, the NAR lobbied for public regulation of all participants in the larger industry combined with self-policing of smaller and more select groups of members. The NAR promoted real estate education and research and played a role in many public policy issues, from urban planning to property taxa-

tion. Its Home Builders and Subdividers Division was a national leader in the formulation of federal housing policy in the 1920s and 1930s.

Two other groups organized during this period were the Building Owners and Managers Association (BOMA International) and the Mortgage Bankers Association of America (MBA). BOMA represented the owners and property managers of the rapidly growing number of skyscrapers and other large commercial buildings in central cities, and later also in the suburbs. Its focus was on professional training for management combined with a unified voice for relevant public policy issues. The MBA was originally called the Farm Mortgage Bankers Association, but it adopted an urban focus and assumed a new name during the early 1920s. At that time, mortgage bond houses and mortgage lending companies—allied with real estate brokers, developers, and life insurance companies—were rapidly evolving and expanding the variety of capital financing instruments available to acquire and develop property. The MBA later increased its national prominence with the advent of the federal government's new housing finance system in the 1930s and 1940s.

Finance

In real estate more so than in most other investments, capital costs are generally high relative to current incomes; therefore, the means of financing is a critical factor in the ability to engage in transactions and in the likely success or failure of projects. To compensate for the first problem, real estate is normally a valuable physical asset that makes excellent collateral for securing loans. Thus, while cash equities have always been important in financing real estate, increasingly during the past two centuries, new institutions were created and methods devised to establish real estate as a highly leveraged form of enterprise operating chiefly on borrowed funds. Easily available credit has usually fueled real estate booms as well as excessive speculation and overbuilding. Conversely, when lenders turn off the spigot, tight money becomes the bane of the industry, leading at times to decreasing supply, declining sales, falling prices, rising defaults and foreclosures, and illiquid markets—as was the case most recently in 1991 and 1992.

An important source of credit has always been sellers, including landowners and building owners, subdividers, and speculative builders. Sellers "taking back paper" in the form of land contracts, purchase-money mortgages, second mortgages, assumables, and a host of other "creative financing" instruments, all of which permit purchasers to buy now and pay later, have been significant players in the history of U.S. real estate markets. Beginning in the 1880s, subdivider William E. Harmon launched what became a successful enterprise by selling subdivision lots with as little as a 5 percent downpayment and the rest due in small monthly installments.

Before the advent of the Federal Housing Administration (FHA), mortgage insurance, and Veterans Administration (VA) home loan guarantee programs, "builders' mortgages" were an essential component in the sale of one- to four-unit housing. Developers acquiring acreage from farmers and other rural landowners often negotiated complex transfers of ownership and repayment schemes in an attempt to bridge the gaps of time and cash flow. Brokers also entered the field; many real estate sales firms maintained mortgage and loan departments as a service to their clients and helped generate a greater volume of sales (and thus sales commissions) and additional profits from the loan business itself.

Another traditional supplier of funds for real estate has been networks of local investors, including direct financing from friends, relatives, and wealthy individuals, lending through the vehicle of a trust company or mortgage company, and providing equity capital by forming or joining syndicates and limited partnerships. Richard Hurd, most famous today for writing the classic *Principles of City Land Values* in 1903, for many years headed the Lawyers Mortgage Company in New York City, gathering money from prosperous investors and then making first mortgage loans on commercial and residential real estate that was strictly limited to high-quality rental buildings or "income properties" in the best locations.[12] Hurd's instincts for good value and his low-risk strategy led to a successful track record in loan safety and relatively high yields.

In contrast to Richard Hurd, mortgage bond houses such as S.W. Straus flourished during the 1920s by selling securities backed by the frequently overinflated values of new office and apartment buildings. Before the 1929 stock market crash, funds flowed into mortgage bond sales, and securities dealers arranged for highly speculative new construction simply as a minor detail associated with issuing and selling more bonds. After the crash, even the most optimistic appraiser had to admit that the buildings were grossly overvalued; not only did the borrowers default for lack of sufficient tenants to generate cash flow, but the bond houses themselves also went bankrupt and left vast numbers of investors with little or nothing of what had often been promised as a guaranteed high yield and timely return of principal and interest.

Throughout the 19th century and up to the 1920s, the main source of financing for home mortgages was private individuals who operated mainly through the various methods described in the preceding paragraphs. Since that time, financial institutions have played the dominant role in all types of real estate finance; indeed, the growth of these institutions is an important part of the story of real estate development. Chapters 4, 5, and 6 examined how these financial intermediaries operate today. This chapter looks at their histories to obtain a clearer perspective on their contemporary decision making.

Commercial banks are the oldest of the institutions that have been involved in making both construction loans and mortgage loans. These banks have participated heavily in real estate lending, often to the point of insolvency during periods of economic and financial crisis. Financial "panics" and banking problems were so common in the 19th century that when the federal government introduced national bank charters in the 1860s, the charters expressly prohibited urban real estate mortgage lending. State-chartered commercial banks were under no such constraints, however, and continued to be major real estate lenders. National banks were permitted to get back into urban mortgages beginning in 1916, and they expanded real estate lending significantly during the 1920s.

Because commercial banks relied primarily on short-term deposits to obtain funds for lending, they generally preferred and were often required to lend for short terms, either through construction loans or through mortgages on properties for as little as one year. Until well into the 1930s, most bankers considered a three- to five-year mortgage loan to be both long term and risky. Normally, though, short-term mortgages were renewable; in fact, borrowers simply assumed that they could keep rolling the loans over for years to come. When the market turned down and the banks got into trouble, however, lenders called the loans or refused to refinance them, often forcing borrowers into default and foreclosure. Historically, the system of real estate credit has been far more unstable than it is even in today's volatile world.

Life insurance companies have always been important players in real estate, both as owners and as lenders. Since the mid-19th century, 25 to 50 percent of life insurance companies' investment portfolios have been in real estate assets. Life insurance companies have traditionally been involved in financing and purchasing large-scale projects such as office buildings, shopping centers, and apartment complexes. Beginning in the 1920s, some life insurance companies also entered into home mortgage lending.

Mutual savings banks have also been major real estate lenders. Located primarily in the northeastern United States, mutual savings banks were significant institutions in some cities. Nationally, however, their role and influence in residential lending was eclipsed by the advent of savings and loan associations. Also called building and loan associations, homestead associations, cooperative banks, and thrift institutions, S&Ls evolved in the mid-19th century specifically to promote homebuilding and homeownership for people of modest incomes. Savings were pooled through monthly savings plans, and money was loaned for the construction or purchase of one- to four-family dwellings. Though S&Ls charged higher interest rates than other mortgage lenders in order to pay a higher return to their depositors, their loan terms were more favorable in two ways: higher leverage—they lent up to 75 percent of the property's appraised value when most other lenders advanced only 40 percent or 50 percent on first mortgages; and longer terms—S&Ls used amortized monthly loan repayment plans for up to 12 years while most other lenders used nonamortized balloon mortgages with semiannual interest payments and the entire principal due in one to five years.

By the 1920s, S&Ls had emerged as the leading residential lender among financial intermediaries, particularly for single-family homes. Life insurance companies and commercial banks dominated commercial and industrial real estate lending. While syndications, mortgage companies, and a variety of other noninstitutional lenders remained important, the major trend in real estate lending was the increasing role of financial institutions, especially in the field of housing. For example, the institutional share of residential mortgage debt increased from less than half during the 1890s to two-thirds by 1912. The total percentage of owned houses that were mortgaged rose from 25 percent in 1890 to nearly 40 percent in 1920 and to more than 50 percent in New England and the Mid-Atlantic states, where the larger financial institutions were concentrated. More and more, "sweat equity" was being supplanted in real estate by a debt-driven system that encompassed entrepreneurial producers and institutional financiers.

The Great Depression and World War II

The long boom of the 1920s came to an abrupt end when the stock market crashed in October 1929. Though most people believed that the economic downturn was only a temporary setback—that prosperity was just

Soup lines formed in major cities across the country to feed the many unemployed workers during the Great Depression.

around the corner—in fact the Great Depression was the longest and most severe economic depression in our nation's history. Starting in 1929, output and employment fell steadily for four straight years, finally hitting bottom in 1933. At the low point, one out of every four people was out of work, desperately seeking but unable to find any kind of job.

The bubble had burst on the real estate boom even before the stock market crash, though many eager speculators had not realized that they were in for such a hard landing. Most real estate markets had reached their peak in 1926, the same year that the Florida land boom collapsed. Investment in real estate, construction, property sales, and values had been slowly spiraling downward since 1926. Real estate activity, though declining in most markets, was still continuing at a high level relative to the early 1920s or the previous decade, and, in certain categories such as construction of new urban office and apartment buildings, the markets still appeared to be flourishing.

By the late 1920s, however, the speculative craze for subdivision lots was abating, and many of the legions of people that had bought on credit in anticipation of rapid and profitable resales were defaulting on their loans and property tax assessments. A major disaster loomed. Soon most of the mortgage bond issues were in default and foreclosure, with many bondholders losing their capital, leading to widely publicized investigations of fraud and corruption during the 1930s, similar to the S&L collapse in the 1980s. As banks increasingly faced a crisis of liquidity after 1929, they refused to make new real estate loans or to refinance existing ones, often calling in loans to be repaid immediately. That approach was self-defeating because it brought the further collapse of markets and the failure of thousands of banks. Millions of depositors lost much or all of their savings.

Through 1931, new investment, development, sales, and leasing continued in many markets, and real estate entrepreneurs kept hopes alive; in the following year, however, everything began grinding to a halt, and bankruptcy became the normal state of affairs. Financing was unavailable, and real estate plummeted in value. Much of the market was frozen, flooded with for-sale and rental properties that no one wanted—even at heavily discounted prices and rents. By 1933, nearly half of all home mortgages were in default and 1,000 properties were being foreclosed each day. Annual construction starts of new housing had dropped by more than 90 percent from the record-breaking peak of 937,000 units in 1925 to the dismal trough of 93,000 units in 1933.

Into this escalating crisis stepped the federal government, at first gingerly under President Herbert C. Hoover—with considerable prodding in 1931 and 1932 from the Democratic Congress—and then forcefully under the New Deal of President Franklin D. Roosevelt. Failing banks and securities markets were reorganized and stabilized as federal deposit insurance and a new regulatory apparatus helped restore the public's and investors' confidence. Public works programs were initiated on a massive scale that dwarfed any previous peacetime federal spending, with billions of dollars to employ millions of jobless workers in building and rebuilding the nation's infrastructure—roads, bridges, tunnels, highways, dams, power plants, airports, waterways and ports, railroad and transit lines and terminals, parks, playgrounds, schools, health clinics, community centers, civic administration buildings, public housing, and a host of other facilities.

The ever-changing and -expanding alphabet soup of federal agencies—the RFC, PWA, CWA, WPA, TVA, and many others—played key roles in financing, contracting with, and mobilizing state and local governments and the private sector. Collectively, this effort built a better economic future while putting people immediately to work and stimulating the rebirth of economic activity and growth. In many real estate markets during the worst years of the 1930s, government-supported development and redevelopment projects were the only action in town. These mainly federal public works initiatives helped encourage two forms of entrepreneurship that flourished during the New Deal: the powerful public works manager, best symbolized by New York's Robert Moses (see profile), and the large-scale private contractor, exemplified by California's Henry J. Kaiser (see profile).

Bailing Out the Financial Institutions

Public works was only one of the strategies New Dealers used to revive both the general economy and one of its most important sectors: the construction and development industry. By 1933, the field of private

Profile **Robert Moses**

Robert Moses directed the construction of parks and parkways for the state of New York beginning in the 1920s. In 1933, Mayor Fiorello LaGuardia appointed him parks commissioner for New York City. During the New Deal, LaGuardia lobbied in Washington for billions of dollars in federal public works funds, and Moses built many of the projects, including the complex and expensive Triborough Bridge, which opened in 1936. As chair of the Triborough Bridge Authority, Moses discovered that semi-independent public authorities could amass considerable long-term power so long as the authority's management continued to control an activity that generated sufficient revenue to repay debt and accumulate a surplus. These authorities could successfully finance their operations through the sale of bonds and then retire those bonds through a dedicated revenue source, such as bridge tolls. (In the early days of the Triborough, the federal Reconstruction Finance Corporation was the only willing bond buyer, though later private investors bought the bonds.) Moses's extensive multibillion dollar development activities as head of several authorities for more than three decades helped establish public authorities as critical organizations in the real estate field. During the early 1970s, for example, under the leadership of Austin Tobin, one of Robert Moses's most powerful competitors among public authority chief executives, the Port Authority of New York and New Jersey built the massive twin office towers of the World Trade Center in lower Manhattan, at that time the world's tallest buildings. ∎

Profile **Henry J. Kaiser**

Henry J. Kaiser was a general contractor who built public works. Initially a road builder for governments in the western United States and Canada, in 1930 he put together a consortium of six large construction firms and successfully obtained the federal contract to build the massive Hoover Dam on the Colorado River in southern Nevada.

Beginning in 1933, Kaiser established a close working relationship with U.S. Secretary of the Interior Harold L. Ickes, who was one of a handful of key New Deal officials controlling the federal public works purse strings and dispensing billions of dollars in government contracts. During the 1930s, Kaiser-led teams won federal contracts to build both the Bonneville and the Grand Coulee Dams, in addition to doing part of the work on the San Francisco–Oakland Bay Bridge and constructing Oakland's Broadway Tunnel and several other large projects. Headquartered in Oakland, California, Kaiser achieved national recognition as a shipbuilder during World War II and as a manufacturer

of cement, gypsum, aluminum, chemicals, steel, automobiles, cargo planes, and jeeps.

During the war, Henry Kaiser built a substantial amount of emergency housing for the workers who were flocking to Richmond, California, Portland, Oregon, and Vancouver, Washington, to construct Kaiser's "liberty ships" for the U.S. Navy. After the war, Kaiser became interested in mass-producing houses and formed, in 1945, a partnership with Fritz Burns, a major southern California developer. Their new company, Kaiser Community Homes, built thousands of small, inexpensive, two- and three-bedroom single-family detached houses on the West Coast until it ceased production in 1950. During the mid-1950s, Henry Kaiser retired as chief executive of Kaiser Industries, remarried, and moved to Hawaii, where he became a major developer of resort hotels, recreational subdivisions, houses, shopping malls, golf courses, and convention centers until his death in 1967 at the age of 85. ∎

---

housing had suffered an almost complete collapse, and the entire system of residential financing that had grown so rapidly during the 1920s with its crazy quilt of land contracts, second and third mortgages, high interest rates and loan fees, short terms, balloon payments, and various other high-risk and speculative practices had come crashing down like a house of cards. In the wake of this panic of defaults and foreclosures, the federal government intervened to transform the rules of the financial game and move the sale and construction of private housing out of the doldrums.

The first federal actions in housing finance focused on bailing out the savings and loan associations. S&Ls had mortgaged 4.35 million properties during the 1920s, lending out more than $15 billion to homebuilders and purchasers. By the early 1930s, thousands of these institutions were insolvent as a result of bad loans, overvalued properties, and the inability to raise sufficient new capital. President Hoover and the Congress responded to the crisis by establishing the Federal Home Loan Bank System in 1932, which merged and reorganized bankrupt S&Ls, encouraged the creation of new federally chartered S&Ls that would be better capitalized and more strictly regulated, and, most important, provided vitally needed liquidity for federal- and state-chartered thrifts, helping to free them from their traditional dependence on short-term commercial bank credit. Two years later came the Federal Savings and Loan Insurance Corporation, which greatly strength-

ened the attractiveness of S&Ls to savers by insuring deposits and helping to standardize the management of thrift institutions. S&Ls also were granted a series of income tax and regulatory benefits in exchange for the requirement that they continue to lend money primarily for residential mortgages (a requirement that remained in force until the Reagan Administration's monetary "reforms" of 1982).

Other dramatic structural changes occurred in the 1930s. The federal government created the Home Owners' Loan Corporation (HOLC) in 1933 and the Federal Housing Administration in 1934. The HOLC refinanced more than $3 billion of shaky or defaulted mortgages and introduced long-term (15-year) self-amortizing loans to many borrowers who were not familiar with the idea.

The Rise of the Federal Housing Administration

While the HOLC was a temporary bailout operation that stopped making loans in 1936, the FHA was a permanent program that launched a revolution in housing finance. The FHA's mutual mortgage insurance system reduced the investment risk for lenders and brought the twin S&L principles of long-term amortization of mortgage loans and high loan-to-value ratios into the world of commercial banks, life insurance companies, mutual savings banks, and mortgage companies

—institutions that had not previously used such underwriting practices. The FHA's initiatives encouraged lenders to increase the first mortgage loan-to-value ratio to an unprecedented 80 to 90 percent, to extend the length of the loan repayment period to 20 and 25 years, to eliminate second mortgages, and to lower interest rates and total loan origination fees significantly.

Among its many reforms, the FHA rationalized, standardized, and improved methods and practices of appraisal, universalized the use of title insurance, required the lender's monthly collection of property taxes and property insurance as part of the loan payments, and helped popularize other methods for stabilizing real estate transactions and financing procedures. The FHA's insured mortgages became a standardized product and a safe investment that helped establish a nationwide mortgage market in place of previously idiosyncratic and localized submarkets. The entire home mortgage lending system began to shift from lending primarily on the security of the property in the event of foreclosure to lending mainly based on the borrower's projected income and ability to repay without default—a major conceptual change.

The FHA also promoted cost-efficient production of small houses and affordable homeownership for middle-income families. The FHA's conditional commitment enabled subdivision developers and merchant homebuilders to obtain debt financing for the large-scale construction of new residential neighborhoods and communities, complete with finished houses and full installation of improvements and ready for immediate occupancy by people who were able to buy with modest savings because they qualified for FHA-insured mortgages. The FHA model of real estate development represented a dramatic advance over the previous methods of subdividing and selling unimproved lots that had been fairly common in the 1920s.

The FHA's property standards and neighborhood standards helped improve the minimum level of quality in the design, engineering, materials, equipment, and methods of land development and housing construction. The FHA's Land Planning Division encouraged private planning by developers and builders and public planning by state and local governments to ensure the coordination of accessible transportation, recreational facilities, utilities, services, and land uses through comprehensive plans, official maps, zoning laws, requirements for setbacks, and regulations for subdivisions. The Land Planning Division also played a key national role in reshaping the design of suburban housing tracts, upgrading the use of deed restrictions for private planning and development, and reorganizing and extending the role of local and metropolitan public planning.

In addition, the FHA introduced new techniques for analyzing market demand and using stricter underwriting criteria to limit overbuilding and excessive subdividing. This element of market control was explicitly aimed at eliminating "curbstone" subdividers and "jerry-builders" and replacing them with community builders. More sophisticated market analysis and greater market control became necessary as a result of the FHA's primary emphasis on long-term financing of large numbers of homes in newly developed neighborhoods. FHA underwriters needed to know before development began that the market commanded a sufficient number of potential buyers for the planned houses, and that purchasers' incomes, market demand, and property values would either remain stable or rise over the 25 years the mortgages would be insured. The FHA's "risk-rating system" weighed several factors affecting the supply of and demand for housing, including patterns of urban employment, distribution of income, population growth, changes in the housing stock, formation of households, the locational dynamics of residential neighborhoods, and future land uses and property values.[13]

Within two years of the FHA's creation, new federal and state laws to stabilize and restructure the commercial banking system, along with the creation of the Federal Deposit Insurance Corporation in 1933, enabled commercial banks to participate in the FHA's program. Life insurance companies and mutual savings banks also took advantage of FHA insurance. They acted as primary lenders, and also purchased and sold standardized and relatively low-risk FHA-insured loans. FHA-insured mortgages made possible the 1938 creation of the Federal National Mortgage Association (Fannie Mae). Fannie Mae, capitalized by the federal government's Reconstruction Finance Corporation (RFC), initiated a strong secondary market for FHA-insured mortgages, purchasing loans from primary lenders to provide them with both the liquidity to make new loans and additional income gained through the retention of servicing fees. This national secondary mortgage market helped smooth out the fluctuations in real estate business cycles as well as compensate for geographic differences in the availability of mortgage funds. Fannie Mae was particularly vital to the growth of modern mortgage banking companies, many of which started their high-volume businesses in the 1930s and 1940s based mainly on making FHA-insured loans for resale to Fannie Mae or to a life insurance company, a savings bank, or another group of lenders and investors.

The FHA's underwriting guidelines strongly favored new housing over existing homes, suburban locations over central-city sites, entire subdivisions over scattered building lots, single-family houses over apartments, and Caucasians over African Americans. For older cities and racial minorities, these policies were inequitable, discriminatory, and disastrous. But for the growth of white, middle-class suburbs, they were crucial. Though the FHA did insure mortgages on suburban garden apartments, its overall policy helped reverse the late 1920s trend toward increased construction of apartment buildings and instead boosted large-scale homebuilding and suburban homeownership.

By the late 1930s, the U.S. economy and housing markets were reviving, and the FHA was insuring more than one-third of all new homes; 98 percent of the FHA's insured mortgages were on single-family detached houses in new suburban subdivisions. The FHA's highest volume was in California, where the country's suburban future was already under construction in the late 1930s. Fred Marlow, who headed the FHA's southern California office from 1934 to 1938, and Fritz Burns formed a private development company and, beginning in 1942, built more than 4,000 FHA-insured houses in a new southwest Los Angeles subdivision called West-

chester. The purchasers of the houses were primarily workers in the nearby and rapidly growing aircraft industry. Westchester became a model for postwar suburban tract housing, and Fred Marlow and Fritz Burns both served as presidents of the National Association of Home Builders.

Housing after the Great Depression

While construction of new homes finally began rising after the long slump, much of the older housing stock was badly deteriorated and getting worse as a result of overcrowding, lack of maintenance, and other direct effects of the Great Depression. In 1937, President Roosevelt declared in his second inaugural address that "one-third of a nation [was] ill-housed, ill-clad, and ill-nourished."

In 1919, Edith Elmer Wood, a talented housing reformer with a PhD in political economy from Columbia University, wrote *The Housing of the Unskilled Wage Earner,* an eloquent book documenting the problems of low-income shelter and arguing for government aid

Housing in a low-income Washington, D.C., neighborhood circa 1937.

as part of a positive solution. In 1935, the federal Public Works Administration (PWA) under Harold Ickes published Wood's *Slums and Blighted Areas in the United States.* Wood demonstrated in considerable detail that more than 36 percent of the American people were living in very substandard housing. In her 1919 book and in her *Recent Trends in American Housing,* published in 1931, Wood described various private, philanthropic, and public sector efforts to build decent and affordable housing in many areas of the country.[14] Except for New York City and a handful of other cities, however, substantial government involvement did not begin to emerge until the early 1930s. The collapse of the private housing industry opened the way for public support and programs to stimulate employment and economic activity in urban real estate development.

Starting with RFC loans for limited-dividend housing companies building apartments at moderate rentals, the federal government established the PWA Housing Division in 1934 and the U.S. Housing Authority (USHA) in 1937 to support the removal of the worst slum dwellings and their replacement with brand new publicly owned rental housing. Under USHA's formula, local governments owned the housing, which was built by private contractors. Local authorities borrowed the funds by selling 40-year tax-exempt bonds to private investors, and the federal government repaid the principal and interest on the bonds through annual contributions. Operating costs of the housing were to be paid by the local government through rents collected from the tenants. By the time that World War II interrupted and changed the nature of the public housing program to providing temporary shelter for war workers, USHA and its predecessors had already produced more than 100,000 units of decent, safe, and sanitary dwellings in low-rise buildings. These well-constructed and attractively landscaped buildings provided a welcome new environment for many low- and moderate-income families.

Nathan Straus, chief administrator of USHA from 1937 to 1941, had been an early pioneer of private, limited-dividend housing development in New York City. During 1934 and 1935, he developed Hillside Homes in the Bronx, which was the largest private housing development built with a federal loan from the PWA. Clarence Stein served as the architect for Hillside Homes, and Starrett Brothers and Eken were the general contractors. The 26-acre project consisted of low-rise and garden apartments for 1,400 families and included landscaped interior garden courts, a public school, a large central playground, clubrooms, a nursery school, a community center, and other recreational facilities. Straus, though initially a private developer,

authored *The Seven Myths of Housing* in 1941, a spirited defense of America's public housing programs.[15]

Rockefeller Center

A major private development that tore down several blocks of older tenement housing was Rockefeller Center in New York City, one of the few big projects during the 1930s that was not publicly funded or subsidized. Rockefeller Center stands as the forerunner of today's large-scale urban mixed-use developments and continues to be among the best known and most successful of such projects.

Rockefeller Center's original parcel of land between Fifth and Sixth Avenues and 48th and 51st Streets belonged to Columbia University, which leased it for 46 years to John D. Rockefeller, Jr., in October 1928 at an annual rent of nearly $4 million—ten times the existing rental yield from the site. The Rockefeller family lived on 53rd Street near Fifth Avenue and already owned a great deal of property in the neighborhood. In autumn 1928, New York City was in the midst of the real estate boom that preceded the stock market crash, and Rockefeller was extremely optimistic about his prospects for redeveloping the area. He originally planned to build a new Metropolitan Opera House on the site. The directors of the opera company wanted to relocate from their 45-year-old facility at 40th Street and Broadway because of encroachment by the garment industry. Ironically, the opera company eventually turned down Rockefeller's many appeals to become the centerpiece of his ambitious real estate venture, preferring to remain in place until the mid-1960s, when it finally moved to a new opera house built as part of the massive urban renewal project called Lincoln Center for the Performing Arts.

The Sixth Avenue portion of Rockefeller's site was considered a blighted area in 1928 because of the elevated railroad tracks running along the avenue. By 1939, a new Sixth Avenue subway was constructed and the elevated tracks removed, opening up new opportunities for private redevelopment. The Rockefeller Center site was extraordinarily large, and it was highly uncertain how all the land could be redeveloped and space occupied in the marketwide context of economic depression, falling rents, and rising vacancies. Teams of architects worked for several years on many different schemes, both with and without the opera house as a focal point. The buildings were planned in a relatively unified architectural theme of style and materials, enhancing the new and unusual image of a mixed-use center within a single development project. Innovative design features included the addition of private streets to cut up the long east-west blocks and the creation of the first privately developed public plaza in the city, which today houses the world's most famous outdoor ice skating rink.

Lacking the high culture of opera, Rockefeller turned to mass culture as his best prospect for attracting commercial tenants to this untested location. By the mid-1930s, he had filled the 70-story RCA Building (now called the GE Building)—his main high-rise office tower—with radio, motion picture, and vaudeville businesses, including RCA, RKO, and NBC, that were thriving even during the Great Depression. He also developed on Sixth Avenue his own entertainment facility for the general public, the Radio City Music Hall, as well as the Center Theatre for Opera and large-scale musical shows. Magazine, news service, and book publishers also gravitated to new office buildings in Rockefeller Center. On the Fifth Avenue side, Rockefeller constructed low-rise structures for international retail and office tenants, taking advantage of proximity to prestigious retailers across the street. By the early 1940s, the development had clearly succeeded as a desirable location for corporate office space, and since the 1950s, Rockefeller Center has expanded to the west across Sixth Avenue, with tall office buildings and major tenants ranging from Time-Life to McGraw-Hill to the Rockefeller family's own Exxon. At the same time, travel agents at street level, below-ground retail shops, and a tightly controlled and well-maintained environment all helped turn what was initially a risky, speculative, expensive, money-losing venture into the premier private real estate development of the Great Depression decade.

The Professionalization of Real Estate Development

Two new private organizations, both spin-offs of the National Association of Realtors®, emerged from the crucible of economic crisis and political reform that characterized the 1930s. The Urban Land Institute started as a small, elite organization of primarily large commercial and residential developers. ULI was charged with focusing on education and research, public policy issues, and improving standards and practices of private development. Initially, ULI organized into two key subgroups. The Central Business District Council sponsored a series of studies on urban decentralization and urged federal, state, and local government officials to establish and provide funds for urban renewal, urban highways, and other programs to redevelop physically and revitalize economically the commercial core of older central cities. The Community Builders Council, which sponsored ULI's *Community Builders Handbook,* published

in 1947, concerned itself with promoting high-quality, large-scale residential and commercial development in suburban areas.[16]

The National Association of Home Builders (NAHB) was formed in 1943 to lobby the federal government during wartime to allow the continued private development of for-sale and rental housing with the aid of FHA mortgage insurance. Some government policy makers favored limiting new housing to public construction and ownership during the wartime emergency, arguing that such an approach would be more cost-efficient and easier to manage in the context of allocating scarce resources for the war effort. The Home Builders Emergency Committee, led by Hugh Potter, a former lawyer and judge who developed River Oaks in Houston, fought for publicly subsidized housing for war workers to be built and owned by the private sector. In the end, a compromise permitted the development of housing under both public and private ownership. In the process, the Home Builders and Subdividers Division of NAR split from the parent organization and merged with a completely separate group called the National Home Builders Association. Together, the two groups became NAHB, with Fritz Burns of Los Angeles as the founding president of the new organization, which grew from an initial 1,300 members to more than 25,000 in less than a decade.

During World War II, the real estate industry in certain locations received an enormous economic boost from the surge in demand for new construction, land, and space in existing buildings. Yet many ventures not directly related to the war economy were put on hold for the duration, and some entrepreneurs eagerly awaited peacetime. Many people were apprehensive, fearing a replay of the Great Depression after the soldiers and sailors returned home and the production of so many new guns, tanks, ships, and planes was no longer necessary. Others were more optimistic, seeing a wave of growth precipitated by the rising disposable incomes and pent-up consumer demand that was accumulating during the war, when most people were earning much more than during the previous decade but were unable to spend their new wealth because a great deal of U.S. production capacity was diverted to the global battlefields. By 1948, the optimists were proved correct in their predictions, and the postwar suburbs—dependent on the automobile, homeownership, and a consumer boom—were in full swing.

Summary

Expansion in the real estate industry characterizes most of the period from the end of the 19th century through the first half of the 20th century. Aggressive downtown commercial development and residential movement to the suburbs changed the face of the nation's cities and metropolitan regions.

The growing involvement of the public sector reinforced the private development process, and the changes in lending policies brought about by the creation of the FHA made residential development easier and dramatically increased the number of homeowners in the United States.

Chapter 9 looks at postwar development trends and how the real estate industry evolved into its present situation.

Terms

- Central business district (CBD)
- City Beautiful movement
- Community builders
- Comprehensive planning
- Federal Housing Administration (FHA)
- Federal National Mortgage Association (Fannie Mae)
- Garden city
- Greenbelt
- Industrialization
- Mortgage
- Public Works Administration (PWA)
- Skyscraper
- Steel frame construction
- Subdivision controls
- Trade association
- Zoning

Review Questions

8.1 What happened to downtowns as transportation allowed people to move farther and farther out of the city?

8.2 Discuss the history of the skyscraper—its construction, its symbolism, and how it shaped cities.

8.3 Discuss the role of the downtown department store at the turn of the century.

8.4 What was the City Beautiful movement?

8.5 What was a garden city and how did the movement evolve?

8.6 How did real estate trade associations come about?

8.7 How did the advent of creative financing change real estate markets in the United States?

8.8 What strategies were used in the New Deal to revive the Great Depression economy?

8.9 What was the role of the Federal Housing Administration in financing housing and homeownership?

8.10 Why was Rockefeller Center such an important project?

Notes

1. Adna Ferrin Weber, *The Growth of Cities in the Nineteenth Century: A Study in Statistics* (New York: Macmillan, 1899), p. 1.

2. Paul Goldberger, *The Skyscraper* (New York: Alfred A. Knopf, 1981), p. 7.

3. Kenneth Turney Gibbs, *Business Architectural Imagery in America, 1870–1930* (Ann Arbor, Mich.: UMI Research Press, 1984), p. 45.

4. Ibid.

5. Ibid., p. 54.

6. Earle Shultz and Walter Simmons, *Offices in the Sky* (Indianapolis: Bobbs-Merrill, 1959), pp. 33–34.

7. *Golden Book of Wanamaker Stores* (Philadelphia: John Wanamaker, 1911), p. 47.

8. Marc A. Weiss and John T. Metzger, "Planning for Chicago: The Changing Politics of Metropolitan Growth and Neighborhood Development," in *Atop the Urban Hierarchy*, ed. Robert A. Beauregard (Totowa, N.J.: Rowman & Littlefield, 1989), pp. 123–51.

9. Thompson-Starrett Company, "A Census of Skyscrapers," *The American City*, September 1929, p. 130. See also Marc A. Weiss, *The Rise of the Community Builders: The American Real Estate Industry and Urban Land Planning* (New York: Columbia Univ. Press, 1987); and Marc A. Weiss, "Skyscraper Zoning: New York's Pioneering Role," *Journal of the American Planning Association*, Spring 1992, pp. 201–12.

10. Ebenezer Howard, *Garden Cities of Tomorrow* (London: Faber & Faber, 1945). See especially the introductory essays by Lewis Mumford and Frederic Osborn; and Marc A. Weiss, "Developing and Financing the 'Garden Metropolis': Urban Planning and Housing Policy in Twentieth-Century America," *Planning Perspectives*, September 1990, pp. 307–19.

11. Eugene Rachlis and John E. Marqusee, *The Land Lords* (New York: Random House, 1963), pp. 60–86.

12. Richard M. Hurd, *Principles of City Land Values* (New York: Real Estate Record and Guide, 1903).

13. Marc A. Weiss, "Richard T. Ely and the Contribution of Economic Research to National Housing Policy, 1920–1940," *Urban Studies,* February 1989, pp. 115–26; Marc A. Weiss, "Marketing and Financing Homeownership: Mortgage Lending and Public Policy in the United States, 1918–1989," *Business and Economic History,* 1989, pp. 109–18; and Weiss, *The Rise of the Community Builders.*

14. Edith Elmer Wood, *The Housing of the Unskilled Wage Earner* (New York: Macmillan, 1919); *Recent Trends in American Housing* (New York: Macmillan, 1931); and *Slums and Blighted Areas in the United States,* Public Works Administration, Housing Division Bulletin No. 1 (Washington, D.C.: U.S. Government Printing Office, 1935).

15. Nathan Straus, *The Seven Myths of Housing* (New York: Alfred A. Knopf, 1941).

16. Community Builders Council, *The Community Builders Handbook* (Washington, D.C.: ULI–the Urban Land Institute, 1947).

Chapter 9

Post–World War II to the Present

For the duration of World War II, most new private construction was put on hold except for industrial and residential development directly related to the war effort. On the heels of a decade-long economic depression, most U.S. real estate markets were badly underbuilt by 1945. In particular, the demand for housing was pressing. Eleven million servicemen and -women were returning home to communities where few unoccupied houses were available. By 1947, more than 5 million families had either doubled up with other families in overcrowded dwellings or were occupying temporary shelters. New housing construction quadrupled to a half million homes in 1946, but production fell far below demand, and newly deregulated housing prices were skyrocketing.

After a bumpy start, the homebuilding industry eventually rose to the challenge. With government assistance in the form of mortgage financing, new highways and infrastructure, permissive zoning and planning, and other tools, housing starts reached an all-time high of more than 1.5 million new units by 1950, mostly single-family homes to accommodate the new suburban baby boom.

Against this backdrop of postwar economic growth, this chapter explores the evolution of the real estate industry since World War II, examining:

- Suburbanization and the postwar boom;
- The office building boom;
- Urban renewal;

This chapter was written and updated by Marc A. Weiss, PhD, Public Policy Scholar, Woodrow Wilson Center, Washington, D.C.

- The expansion of interstate highways and the growth of the suburbs;
- The urban crisis in race, housing, and neighborhoods; and
- The 1970s through the 1990s.

Suburbanization and the Postwar Boom

In 1944, Congress prepared for postwar growth by passing the Servicemen's Readjustment Act—the "GI Bill"—which established both the Veterans Administration and the VA home loan guarantee program. Under this program, an eligible veteran could obtain a low-interest, highly leveraged mortgage loan to buy a home, in some cases with no downpayment. In the original legislation, homeownership loan guarantees were available only to veterans for the first two years following their return to civilian life, but by 1946 the housing shortage became so severe that Congress soon extended the program for ten years. Billions of dollars were authorized for the FHA, VA, and Fannie Mae during those postwar years, most notably in the landmark Housing Act of 1949, which declared as a national goal "a decent home and a suitable living environment for every American family."

The production of housing reached an unprecedented volume. Fifteen million homes and apartments were built in the 1950s, more than double the number in the 1940s and more than five times the 1930s total. With two-thirds of the housing constructed in the rapidly expanding suburbs, many central cities began losing population after 1950.

Inexpensive two-bedroom Levittown homes made it possible for families to purchase a home with little money down and low monthly payments—a real boon to World War II veterans who were starting over in the late 1940s and early 1950s.

Formerly agricultural land was subdivided into sub-urban tracts on a grand scale all over the United States. The greatest growth occurred in the Sunbelt states, especially California, Texas, and Florida—new centers of what President Eisenhower called "the military-industrial complex."

The FHA's and VA's promotion of large-scale home-building and the availability of mass financing through life insurance companies, S&Ls, mutual savings banks, and other sources led residential developers to grow rapidly in size as the entire housing industry dramatically increased total production.

By 1949, 10 percent of the builders constructed 70 percent of the homes, 4 percent of the builders constructed 45 percent of the homes, and just 720 firms built 24 percent of the homes. These figures reflected a radical change from the prewar years, and they were to continue changing during the 1950s with the large homebuilders further expanding in size, scale, and volume. Part of the postwar change in the real estate industry can be attributed to the experience gained during the war, when the federal government encouraged and subsidized residential developers to mass produce private housing for war workers.

The biggest of all the homebuilders immediately after the war was Levitt & Sons, developers of Levittown, New York. Levittown was the country's largest private housing project at the time. The first homes were completed in fall 1947, and, by the early 1950s, Levitt & Sons had built 17,500 homes on 4,000 acres of potato fields in Hempstead on central Long Island, about 30 miles east of New York City. *Time* magazine devoted a cover

story to Levittown in July 1950, calling the firm's president, William Levitt, "the most potent single modernizing influence in a largely antiquated industry."[1] The Levitts priced most of their newly built homes at $7,990—$1,500 less than any of their competitors—and still managed to earn a $1,000 profit on every home sold.

Abraham Levitt and his two sons William and Alfred started in the housing business on Long Island in the late 1920s, building individual luxury houses and, later, a small subdivision called Strathmore-at-Manhasset. During World War II, the Levitt firm entered into government contracts to construct 2,350 homes for war workers in and around Norfolk, Virginia; what the Levitts learned about high-volume methods of production became the basis for their postwar planning and development. At Levittown, William Levitt turned the entire development into a mobile assembly line, with teams of workers moving from house to house to perform 26 specific, repetitive tasks. Everything was carefully programmed and tightly controlled. The Levitts bought materials in bulk, producing them to their own specifications. Subcontractors were required to work only for them; Levitt specially trained and managed construction crews. Materials were preassembled in central facilities and delivered to each construction site just in time for that day's set of repetitive assignments. The emphasis was on speed, and, at peak production, homes in Levittown were completed at the astounding rate of 35 per day.

With an advance commitment from the FHA to insure mortgages on thousands of homes, the Levitts were able to obtain the credit they needed to construct houses and to develop roads, sewers, parks, schools, swimming pools, a shopping center, and other facilities. Levitt simplified the sales transaction to two simple half-hour steps that made purchasing easy for people who had never before owned a home. Many of the purchasers were veterans who could move in with no downpayment other than $10.00 in closing costs and then pay $56.00 a month for principal, interest, taxes, and insurance, considerably less than the monthly rent for a comparable apartment. The two-bedroom homes came equipped with modern appliances, and the quarter-acre lots offered plenty of room for expansion. Regrettably, the Levitts restricted their American Dream to whites only. Before the civil rights movement of the 1960s, restrictive practices were common among most new housing developments. Even the FHA and VA—two federal government agencies—actively supported discriminatory policies against racial minorities.

Levitt & Sons built two other Levittowns, both in the suburbs of Philadelphia: in Bucks County, Pennsylvania, in the early 1950s, and in Willingboro, New Jersey, in the late 1950s. They built the last of their large housing projects, Belair, in Bowie, Maryland, during the early 1960s. The Levitt style of mass-produced community development had its share of critics who disdained the communities' architectural and social conformity, which were best characterized during the 1950s by John Keats's *The Crack in the Picture Window* and William H. Whyte's *The Organization Man*.[2] While many other big developments flourished during the postwar years, the original Levittown in Hempstead, Long Island, still stands as an American cultural symbol of postwar housing construction.

New York City's Postwar Office Developers

A surge in office building construction in Manhattan occurred a few years after the end of World War II. New demand began to fuel a long-dormant market. New York City led the nation in the production of office space by a significant margin. Harold and Percy Uris alone developed almost 9 million square feet of office space in Manhattan from 1947 to 1962, which was twice as much as that developed in the entire city of Chicago during the same period.[3]

Most of this office construction was undertaken by family organizations led by the second or third generation in the business. Several of these families had gained significant experience before the war by developing large apartment buildings. The move to office buildings was triggered as much by the continued imposition of wartime rent controls on apartment buildings as by the demands of the commercial and financial sectors.

Family-owned office developers viewed themselves as long-term investors. They constructed buildings with the intention of holding them in the family portfolio for an indefinite period. Often, sites were assembled over extended periods of time and warehoused until the appropriate moment to build. Before demolishing the existing buildings on a site, these office developers either allowed the leases to expire or compensated tenants for surrendering the remainder of their term.

Project financing was usually simple in concept. The office developers secured a long-term mortgage commitment or "takeout," often from an insurance company. This commitment served as security for a construction loan from a commercial bank. After constructing the building and satisfying any leasing requirements, the office developers transferred the loan to the long-term lender. The developers or a few passive investors usually provided the needed equity capital.

In addition to the Uris family, major office developers included family firms such as Durst, Fisher, Rudin, Tishman, Kaufman, and Minskoff. They developed long-term trust relationships with suppliers, contractors, and professionals that were also family-operated businesses. Of that group, none were more significant than the architectural firm of Emery Roth & Sons. The Roth firm had worked for some of New York's office developers at the turn of the century, and succeeding generations of family firms turned to Roth when they moved from apartment to office development.

Urban Renewal

Even though suburbanization hit the country like a tidal wave in the 1950s, the movement of population and employment away from central cities was already evident three decades earlier. While downtown development flourished in most cities during the 1920s, the neighborhoods surrounding the central business district, sometimes called "the zone of transition," had stopped growing and started to deteriorate. Once the Great Depression took root, development in most central cities ground to a halt, a condition that continued in the commercial core through World War II and into the years immediately after. By the mid-1950s, many U.S. cities had not seen a single new office building constructed in nearly 30 years. Most of these cities were also losing large numbers of manufacturing jobs after the growth spurt induced by the war. Railyards, factories,

The American Dream—a typical FHA-financed residential subdivision in San Diego circa 1964.

and warehouses were abandoned, with little demand for new occupancy. Many old houses and apartments in the zone of transition fell into poor physical condition and lacked tenants. Offices, retail stores, hotels, and restaurants all suffered from declining markets and vitality. Civic leaders feared that the heart of the city would die a slow economic, political, and cultural death.

The remedy proposed by many downtown business, real estate, and civic groups was first called district replanning, then urban redevelopment, and, finally, urban renewal. The idea was to rebuild centrally located slums and blighted areas—clear away old and underused commercial and industrial structures, move out poor and minority residents, and tear down their housing—replacing them with shiny new office towers, convention centers, hotels, shopping malls, and luxury housing. Local governments would use their powers of eminent domain to condemn and acquire the land, demolish the structures, replan and redevelop the area with new infrastructure and public amenities, and sell the land at a discount to private developers who, with tax subsidies and other financial inducements, would invest in and construct new privately owned developments.

Initially, state and local governments operated urban renewal programs. One of the most ambitious efforts

was the Pittsburgh "Renaissance," which was spearheaded by a coalition of corporate executives headed by Richard King Mellon, scion of the family that owned Gulf Oil, Alcoa, and Mellon Bank, and by Mayor David Lawrence, an energetic New Deal Democrat. Working through the Allegheny Conference on Community Development, state and city officials and private sector leaders devised a master plan that guided the rebuilding of downtown's "Golden Triangle" as well as part of the nearby Lower Hill neighborhood, which was largely populated by African Americans. Several new high-rise office buildings, a state park, two parkways, a convention center, a sports arena and stadium, luxury apartments, and a mix of other new public and private development projects replaced the older buildings that had previously occupied one of downtown Pittsburgh's key sites.

The main obstacle to extensive state and local urban renewal was its high public cost. Local taxpayers balked at the magnitude of the funding needed for full-scale renewal, although occasionally subsidies provided sufficient economic incentive in the form of real estate tax abatements for large investors and developers to bear the direct expenses. Such was the case with the Metropolitan Life Insurance Company's Stuyvesant Town and Peter Cooper Village, two massive private residential redevelopment projects built on Manhattan's East Side during the 1940s. Drawing on the precedent of the 1930s, when the federal government had for the first time granted billions of dollars for public works to state and local governments to rebuild the infrastructure and amenities of central cities, several key lobbying groups demanded that Washington pay for urban renewal through a federal grant program. Title I of the Housing Act of 1949 created such a program, which was strengthened and modified by the Housing Act of 1954 and by many subsequent legislative enactments. Under Title I, the federal government paid anywhere from two-thirds to three-fourths or more of the "writedown," the total direct public subsidy minus the revenue from the sale of land to private redevelopers.

By the 1960s, the impact of Title I was apparent in the form of new private and public buildings in many central cities throughout the nation. Most of these development projects brought needed new investment into the urban economy. They helped create jobs, increase the tax base, improve the physical, cultural, and recreational environment, modernize the use of urban land, and add attractive structures as well as public open spaces.

Some efforts at clearance, however, merely produced holes in the ground but no new development; projects such as St. Louis's notoriously nicknamed "Hiroshima Flats" cleared sites that failed to attract bids from private developers. These sites became a more blighting influence on the community than the buildings that had been demolished. Urban renewal projects also meant dramatic displacement of small businesses and of low- and moderate-income residents. Unless they owned property, those who were displaced received no compensation and, in most cases, little or no relocation assistance —either in the form of money or new facilities or dwellings. Even when relocation housing was available, it was seldom located in the same neighborhood. Between 1949 and 1967, for example, 400,000 residential units were demolished under Title I, but only 10,000 new public housing units were built on urban renewal sites. By the middle 1960s, such statistics led to outcries of "Negro removal" and considerable controversy. As a result, the program underwent substantial improvement during 1968 to 1970 but was abolished in 1974.[4]

With the power of suburbia's attraction and the long period of downtown stagnation uppermost in their minds, lenders, investors, and users of downtown space were very cautious during the 1950s and early 1960s. Therefore, despite all the financial incentives, most local governments found it difficult to persuade private developers to participate in downtown renewal efforts. One successful high-risk developer who bucked the conservative mood and plunged headfirst into the urban renewal program in cities all across the country was William Zeckendorf (see profile).

In the early days of urban renewal, the largest investors, lenders, and, in many cases, joint venture developers of projects were the country's leading life insurance companies. They had emerged from the war with tremendous amounts of cash to invest, and real estate assets appeared to offer a good economic return. Companies such as Equitable, which developed the Gateway Center office complex in Pittsburgh's Golden Triangle; New York Life, the developer of Chicago's Lake

Profile **William Zeckendorf**

As head of Webb & Knapp, William Zeckendorf was America's best-known national developer in the 1950s and 1960s, buying and selling land and existing buildings in and near many large cities and constructing major projects from Mile High Center and Court House Square in Denver to Roosevelt Field Mall on Long Island to Plâce Ville-Marie in Montreal to Century City in Los Angeles. He assembled the land for the site of the United Nations in New York and achieved distinction in urban design through the work of his chief architect, I.M. Pei. His most aggressive efforts were federally subsidized urban renewal projects. Beginning in the 1950s, Webb & Knapp built L'Enfant Plaza, a mixed-use office complex, the Town Center apartments, and Waterside Mall shopping center in Washington, D.C. In Philadelphia, Zeckendorf developed the Society Hill Towers and townhouses near the waterfront of the historic city and restored many of Society Hill's colonial rowhouses. Webb & Knapp, using the talents of architects I.M. Pei and Henry Cobb, won the contract to redevelop Society Hill through a design competition. Webb & Knapp also won design competitions to build the University Gardens apartment complex in the Hyde Park neighborhood of Chicago and an even larger project in Pittsburgh's Lower Hill area. In New York, where Webb & Knapp had its headquarters, Zeckendorf and Pei teamed up to develop three major Title I urban renewal residential developments in Manhattan: Park West Village, Kips Bay Plaza, and Lincoln Towers. Zeckendorf was also involved with downtown redevelopment planning in Cincinnati, St. Louis, San Francisco, Cleveland, and Hartford. ∎

Meadows racially integrated middle-income apartment complex; Prudential, which built and occupied the main office tower in Boston's Prudential Center; and Metropolitan Life and John Hancock were all players in the urban renewal game in various cities. They developed corporate office skyscrapers, shopping facilities, and residential towers and townhouses.

The Expansion of Interstate Highways and the Growth of The Suburbs

Though urban renewal was controversial for displacing residents and businesses and received much attention for its efforts to reshape central cities, it was dwarfed by the impact of the interstate highway program on the urban landscape. Downtown corporate interests lobbied heavily for the federal government to fund the interstate highway program, which was initiated in 1956. They wanted to bring these new superhighways into the heart of the nation's cities. It was to be the last, best hope for downtown. New expressways radiating in all directions from the central core were expected to bring workers, shoppers, tourists, and middle-class residents to urban downtowns while reducing traffic congestion on city streets and improving speed and accessibility. In the process of building this grand and expensive automobile-based transportation system, displacement decimated inner-city communities and created many new land use patterns. "One Mile," Robert Caro's dramatic chapter on New York City's Cross-Bronx Expressway in *The Power Broker,* paints a vivid portrait of the human drama behind a small portion of the vast network of urban interstate highways.[5]

Ironically, the downtown expressways turned out to be two-way streets that allowed city businesses and residents to leave as well as to enter the center city, thereby disappointing the most ardent advocates of urban renewal. Together with the suburban beltways and highways that surrounded and bypassed the urban core, the interstates that radiated from the cities' centers opened up a new frontier of suburbanization, and many hallmarks of downtowns—office buildings, department stores, and hotels—moved or expanded to rapidly growing developments near the interchanges of two or more major suburban transportation arteries.

The Growth of Suburban Shopping Centers

Even before the federal interstate highway program was launched, state and local highways in the suburbs offered promising locations for a new type of large-scale development project, the shopping center. By 1954, total retail sales in suburban centers already exceeded the retail sales volume in major central cities. Though antecedents to the modern shopping center existed before the war—J.C. Nichols's Country Club Plaza in Kansas City, Hugh Prather's Highland Park Shopping Village in Dallas, and Hugh Potter's River Oaks Center in Houston—these centers were built primarily to serve existing communities. It was only after World War II that construction of the first freestanding regional shopping centers—not tied to any specific residential development—drew patrons from a wide geographic area.

By the early 1950s, shopping centers were springing up on the periphery of cities everywhere, from Cameron Village in Raleigh, North Carolina, to Poplar Plaza in Memphis, Tennessee, to Shopper's World in Framingham, Massachusetts, near Boston. One of the most widely heralded of the new suburban malls was the Northgate Shopping Center, about 20 miles from downtown Seattle. Developed by Allied Stores and opened in 1950, Northgate featured a large Bon Marché department store as the anchor tenant. Smaller stores flanked what at that time was considered a major innovation in design: a central outdoor ground-level pedestrian mall with an underground truck tunnel that hid deliveries and removal of solid waste. Surrounding the mall was the necessary sea of parking spaces, and it was considered a bold step to turn the mall storefronts away from the automobile traffic and parking lots. In 1954, Northland Center outside Detroit, developed and anchored by J.L. Hudson's department store, opened as the largest regional shopping center at that date and the first to offer attractive amenities and open space. *Architectural Forum* even compared Northland, which was designed by Victor Gruen, to Rockefeller Center.[6]

Two years later, another department store company, Dayton's of Minneapolis, built Southdale Center, the first fully enclosed, heated, and air-conditioned suburban shopping mall. Located in Edina, Minnesota, Southdale was also designed by Gruen, America's leading shopping center architect, who had won critical acclaim for Northland and later went on to design nearly 100 other malls. To block the threatened construction of a nearby competing mall and thus reduce the risks to its expensive project, Dayton's broke with previous shopping center development practices by inducing another department store, Donaldson's, to come to Southdale as a second anchor. Southdale set new standards for the design, construction, leasing, and management of shopping malls. Other department store chains and speculative shopping center developers quickly followed the new trends.

Before 1956, Southdale, Minnesota, was farmland. But in 1956, Dayton's opened Southdale Center, the first fully enclosed, heated, and air-conditioned suburban shopping mall.

The year after Southdale opened, James Rouse, an independent developer, built the fully enclosed Harundale Mall in the Baltimore suburbs. In 1961, Rouse and Victor Gruen teamed up to design and develop Cherry Hill, a 78-acre shopping center in the Philadelphia suburb of Delaware Township, New Jersey. The shopping center became such a successful focal point and symbol of the suburban area's economic and cultural life that township residents later voted to change the community's name to Cherry Hill.

Many of the early shopping centers proved to be highly popular and profitable, and, over the past three decades, those with available land have expanded their retail square footage as well as the number of stores and the number and size of department store anchors. The total number of shopping centers in the United States has grown exponentially, from a relative handful at the end of the war to 7,000 at the beginning of the 1960s to more than 43,000 by 1998, including several hundred large regional malls and a host of different types of smaller centers. In 1954, the International Council of Shopping Centers was formed to represent developers, owners, and managers of this innovative suburban phenomenon; by 1998, ICSC represented more than 38,000 members.

The Growth of Suburban Industrial Parks

The decentralization and suburban growth fostered by the new highway system influenced more than the location of housing and retail centers. Industry and commerce also began moving to suburbia to locate near major transportation arteries. Manufacturing plants that

had previously depended mainly on railroad lines now relied more heavily on trucking. They found highway-accessible suburban locations, whose land costs and rents were cheaper than inner-city sites, to be increasingly available for expansion or relocation. In the 1950s, industrial parks, office parks, research and development parks—with full utilities, plenty of parking, access roads, attractive landscaping, and, occasionally, nearby services—sprouted across suburbia, particularly near the interstate highways. Cabot, Cabot & Forbes Company of Boston earned a national reputation for successfully developing many of these projects.

Cabot, Cabot & Forbes (CC&F) was an old-line real estate investment management company for Boston's Brahmin elite. In 1947, 26-year-old Gerald Blakely convinced senior partner Murray Forbes to hire him to develop suburban industrial parks. The role of MIT and Harvard in pioneering new science and technology for the war effort suggested that the Boston area could become a significant center of research and manufacturing for electronics and related industries. Blakely also assumed that engineers and scientists then moving to the expanding residential suburbs farther out from the city would appreciate shorter commuting times to nearby industrial and office parks. He focused his development strategy on Route 128, a circumferential state highway then under construction west of Boston in a semicircle about 12 miles from the center of the city.

Blakely acquired land in Needham and Waltham—two suburban towns along Route 128. It took several years to raise the necessary private financing, win support from local governments for the required zoning changes, and convince the state government to build the

Profile **Trammell Crow**

Initially a leasing agent for existing warehouse space, Trammell Crow began building new warehouses in 1948 in Dallas's 10,000-acre Trinity Industrial District along the Trinity River. A federally funded flood control construction program in 1946 had rendered this area, formerly considered an undesirable floodplain, newly ripe for development when Crow first approached the industrial district's owners, John and Storey Stemmons, to negotiate a deal to obtain land. The Stemmons brothers decided to go into partnership with Crow. With financing from several local banks and from such life insurance companies as Pacific Mutual and Equitable, Crow and the Stemmons brothers developed more than 50 warehouses over the next two decades. Working with different partners, Crow built another 40 warehouses in the Trinity Industrial District and branched out to build warehouses in Denver, Atlanta, and many other cities. Crow has been a partner in constructing tens of millions of square feet of warehouse space—more than any other single developer—ranging from speculative multi-tenant facilities to custom- built, single-tenant projects.

In his travels to find tenants for his inventory of warehouse space, Crow became fascinated by Chicago's massive 24-story Merchandise Mart, built by Marshall Field in 1934 as the world's largest wholesale showroom facility and featuring more than 4 million square feet of space. By the mid-1950s, Crow launched a new plan to build trade marts in the Trinity Industrial District. Over the next three decades, the Dallas Market Center became Crow's largest and best-known development. The project became feasible in 1955 when John and Storey Stemmons donated 102 acres of land to the state of Texas for a planned interstate highway with service roads for the Trinity District, making the site for Crow's trade center just two blocks from an on/off ramp and a short ten- to 15-minute commute to downtown Dallas and the airport. The highway (I-35), known in Dallas as the Stemmons Freeway, opened in 1959.

Rather than build one enormous, multipurpose structure like the Merchandise Mart, Trammell Crow's strategy was to build an entire complex of attractive and modern buildings —one structure at a time—that would specialize in specific product lines. In partnership with the Stemmons brothers, Crow constructed the Dallas Decorative Center in 1955 for decorators and the design trade, then developed the Homefurnishings Mart in 1957 for the furniture and fixtures business, the Trade Mart in 1960, the Apparel Mart in 1964, the World Trade Center in 1972, and the Infomart in 1984 for the high-tech information industry. He also built the Market Hall in 1963, which was the largest privately owned exhibition center in the United States, and the 1,600-room Loew's Anatole Hotel, which opened in two stages in 1979 and 1981. This hotel has so many amenities and facilities that it helped turn the Dallas Market Center into a focal point for nighttime activity and added to the center's attractiveness as a location for conducting business and holding conventions and trade shows.

Trammell Crow entered the hotel business through his association with architect-developer John Portman of Atlanta. This team built the Atlanta Decorative Arts Center in 1960 and over the next two decades developed two huge urban renewal projects, Peachtree Center in Atlanta and, together with David Rockefeller, Embarcadero Center in San Francisco. Both projects involved the construction of multiple high-rise office buildings and the development of a large Hyatt Regency Hotel. Beginning in 1960 with the opening of the Trade Mart in Dallas, Crow included large indoor atrium lobbies in his buildings. The atrium lobby has since become a standard feature of Crow's wholesale market centers, office buildings, hotels, apartment buildings, and even industrial parks. Portman, as chief architect, achieved public recognition for the large atrium lobbies in the Atlanta and San Francisco Hyatt Regency Hotels, and the ensuing publicity accorded this innovative hotel design helped set off a wave of similar developments during the boom in downtown and suburban hotel construction that ebbed and flowed during the 1970s and 1980s. ■

---

appropriate highway interchanges and access roads. In the mid-1950s, Cabot, Cabot & Forbes finally opened three large facilities: the New England Industrial Park in Needham, the Waltham Industrial Center, and the Waltham Research and Development Park. All three centers were soon fully occupied, and CC&F was quickly searching for more sites to capture a major share of the rapid economic growth then taking place around Route 128.

By the mid-1960s, Cabot, Cabot & Forbes had built 13 of the 19 industrial parks along Route 128. It also developed the 800-acre I-95 Industrial Center farther away from Boston near I-495, Technology Square in Cambridge near MIT, industrial parks in Pennsylvania and

A typical motel outside Washington, D.C., in the early 1950s.

California, and several office buildings and shopping centers. Gerald Blakely became a millionaire, and CC&F acquired assets worth hundreds of millions of dollars, all from an initial investment of several hundred thousand dollars for land acquisition and site planning. In 1967, the National Association of Industrial and Office Properties (NAIOP) was formed to represent developers, owners, and managers of such parks.

With manufacturing comes distribution and wholesale trade; for developers, that means warehouses and showrooms. Trammell Crow, the country's largest developer of the postwar period, started out as a specialist in providing space for industry's needed storage and wholesaling facilities, building millions of square feet of warehouses and trade marts in his hometown of Dallas and across the country. As the U.S economy grew, especially in the Sunbelt, so did Crow's ambitious development, construction, and leasing activities (see profile).

Hotel and Motel Development

The growth of the interstate highway system and the wave of postwar suburbanization also dramatically affected the hotel business. Before the late 1940s, most hotels were located in the center of cities and towns. The exception was resort hotels located near lakes, rivers, oceans, mountains, and other vacation destinations. Large hotels almost always command a prominent site in the city or town center, from the Astor family's Waldorf-Astoria in Manhattan to Henry Flagler's Royal Poinciana in West Palm Beach. When the primary mode of transportation was by railroad, hotels served travelers through their proximity to train stations.

Beginning in the 1920s, "roadside inns" opened up along major thoroughfares to accommodate automobile drivers, but this type of lodging was usually small and nearly always a local mom-and-pop business. Further, roadside inns quickly acquired a seedy image, denounced by FBI Director J. Edgar Hoover in 1940 as "dens of vice" whose main clientele was the "hot pillow trade."[7]

In 1952, Kemmons Wilson and Wallace Johnson opened the nation's first Holiday Inn "hotel courts" in Memphis, with clean rooms, free parking, modest prices, and a respectable family image bolstered by the widely advertised offer of free accommodations for children under 12 when accompanied by their parents. The Holiday Inn hotel chain expanded rapidly during the 1950s and 1960s, initially building inns along highways and taking advantage of key locations on the new interstate system. Holiday Inn later moved into urban areas and resort communities and, by the 1980s, became the world's largest hotel chain.

The earliest hotel chains such as Hilton and Sheraton evolved from large downtown hotels that, in general, were independently owned and managed. But, with the 1950s explosion of motels, motor hotels, and motor inns at freeway exits and interchanges and near airports, chains such as Ramada Inn, Howard Johnson's, and TraveLodge quickly proliferated, as did cooperative referral organizations such as Best Western and Friendship Inns that represent large groups of independently owned hotels and motels. By 1954, the number of motel rooms in the United States exceeded the number of hotel rooms for the first time, and, by 1972, the nation had twice as many motel rooms as hotel rooms.

Not only did the focus of new development shift from the center of town to the outskirts; much more of the growth occurred in the Sunbelt states and the intermountain West than in the Northeast and Midwest. In 1948, more than half of all hotel rooms in the United States were located in the Northeast and Midwest. By 1981, the south Atlantic states along the coast from Virginia to Florida claimed nearly one-quarter of all U.S. hotel rooms, with another 40 percent located in the rest of the Sunbelt and the Rocky Mountain states. In addition, the size of hotels and motels grew steadily larger; between 1948 and 1981, the number of properties decreased slightly while the number of rooms grew by 35 percent. At the same time, different product types emerged, with hoteliers offering conference centers, budget motels, residence suites, and a multitude of other new categories. Unfortunately for the industry, all this expansion and competition led to a dramatic decline in average occupancy rates, which fell from 85 percent in 1948 to less than 65 percent in 1997, according to the American Hotel and Motel Association.

Probably the most important changes in the lodging industry were the entry of investors into the business and the reemergence of many large chains, such as Hilton, Hyatt, Marriott, and Sheraton, as contract management firms. The many new and complicated methods by which hotels and motels are owned and operated have created an opening for real estate developers in speculative hotel development, both for individual projects and as components of mixed-use developments. Some developers also own and operate hotels, motels, conference centers, and resorts as a long-term investment, although many more are involved on a shorter-term basis in the construction and sale of such properties. Today, hotels and motels are considered a key sector of the real estate development industry, and most of the growth and interest in hospitality business investment has taken place in the half century since the dawn of the postwar suburban age.

The Urban Crisis: Race, Housing, And Neighborhoods

In 1957, the editors of *Fortune* magazine published a book entitled *The Exploding Metropolis.* The title referred primarily to the burgeoning postwar suburbs, but the volume also included articles on downtowns, central cities, and rising racial conflict. A chapter on "the enduring slum" concluded with an ominous statement: "One way or another, we will continue to pay plenty for our slums."[8] Written at the time of the bus boycott

in Montgomery, Alabama, led by the Reverend Martin Luther King, Jr., and the first stirrings of the civil rights movement, the words proved a perfect introduction to the 1960s and the title of the book a prologue for the events that would unfold in our cities during the decade. Along with the migration of white middle-class homeowners to the suburbs, another massive urban migration was taking place: African Americans were moving to central cities in record numbers. The African American population in northern and southern cities was growing rapidly, and, particularly in many of the older industrial cities of the North, the new immigrants from the rural South overflowed the boundaries of established and highly segregated ghetto areas. Three million African Americans migrated from the South to the North and West in the 1940s and 1950s; by 1960, two-thirds of that population was concentrated in the 12 largest cities. The percentage of African Americans in Chicago, for example, jumped from 8 percent in 1940 to nearly 25 percent in 1960 (and 40 percent in 1980).

The unfortunate legacy of racism cast a cloud over this dynamic process of urban growth and change. Newly arrived African Americans were forced in many cases to live in overcrowded, overpriced, poor-quality housing simply because they were restricted from buying or renting in many white neighborhoods. When they did attempt to break through the "color line," African Americans frequently met with verbal intimidation and physical violence. In response, many metropolitan areas launched interracial antidiscrimination movements for "open housing." At the same time, however, most cities were beginning to lose industrial jobs, either to the suburbs or from the entire metropolitan region. As a result, new rural-to-urban migrants during the 1950s and thereafter had fewer economic opportunities than their predecessors. In fact, the competition for jobs with existing residents intensified and contributed to racial tensions. Finally, most city government agencies, bureaucracies, and politicians proved unreceptive to these African American newcomers, who were often denied access to adequate municipal services and political representation. In particular, schooling became a volatile issue, with numerous battles fought over racial desegregation.

Other groups of "new minorities" also gained a foothold in some cities during this period, most notably Puerto Ricans in New York City, Cubans in Miami, and Mexican Americans in many communities, especially in Texas, Arizona, Colorado, and California. By the 1970s and 1980s, large numbers of Hispanic Americans from Central and South American countries and a dramatic influx of Asian Americans, including Chinese, Japanese, Koreans, and Vietnamese, had become major forces in U.S. urban life. What came to be called the "urban crisis" of the 1960s, however, largely revolved around the economic and social injustice suffered by African Americans.

The battle grew increasingly heated throughout the 1950s and 1960s, with violent skirmishes in the 1950s exploding into full-scale rebellion during the 1960s. Local police, white workers, and white residents directed much early violence against their African American neighbors and coworkers. Later, African Americans fought back, battling in the streets with law enforcement officials, including the National Guard, looting stores, and burning or vandalizing buildings and cars, usually in their own neighborhoods. Long hot summers of riots descended on U.S cities, from New York's Harlem in 1964 and Los Angeles's Watts in 1965 to Detroit and Newark in 1967 and dozens of other cities in 1968 in the wake of the assassination of Dr. Martin Luther King, Jr. In all, nearly 200 people were killed and 20,000 people arrested nationwide, with property damage estimated in the hundreds of millions of dollars.

Eventually, many concerned citizens mobilized to address the interconnected set of problems that had helped spawn dissatisfaction and disorder. The most obvious inequity was the legally and officially sanctioned segregation and discrimination that had long pervaded U.S. life. Beginning in the 1940s, the powerful political coalition and moral force of the civil rights movement finally began to sweep away many discriminatory barriers through a series of federal, state, and local laws and court decisions. In 1962, President John F. Kennedy issued an executive order banning racial discrimination in federal housing programs, and, after President Kennedy's assassination the following year, President Lyndon B. Johnson carried through on a host of successful legislative efforts, including the landmark Civil Rights Act of 1964 and the Voting Rights Act of 1965.

To solve the underlying problems, however, legal rights had to be supplemented by economic and social action. In 1960, the Ford Foundation launched its Gray Areas Program to foster the revitalization and redevelopment of urban neighborhoods with minority populations, simultaneously trying to improve housing, social services, employment training, jobs, business opportunities, crime prevention, and public education. These pilot projects paved the way for a vast array of public efforts, from the many programs and organizations grouped under the War on Poverty starting in 1964 to the comprehensive neighborhood-based Model Cities Program of 1966. One of the most innovative public/ private partnerships was the creation of community development corporations (CDCs), entrepreneurial institutions that attempted to combine the best features of business investment and management with government services and citizen participation.

In 1967, the Ford Foundation worked with New York's two U.S. Senators, Robert F. Kennedy and Jacob K. Javits, to establish the Bedford-Stuyvesant Restoration Corporation in a predominantly African American neighborhood of Brooklyn. A combination of public and private nonprofit funding plus for-profit activity has

Washington, D.C., after the 1968 riots. The destruction of the inner city was extensive, and evidence of it remains more than 30 years later.

Figure 9-1

Community Development Corporations: Building Bridges to Prosperity

The harsh economic and social changes that have ripped at the fabric of our nation's central cities and inner-ring suburbs have not caused these communities to give up hope. Many have reclaimed their neighborhoods and begun the process of renewal by building bridges to mainstream economic opportunity.

As the federal government's support for urban development and housing initiatives diminished during the 1980s, corresponding growth occurred in private nonprofit community development corporations and other community-based development organizations to help fill the gap. These groups built and managed affordable housing and created jobs by developing neighborhood shopping centers, incubator buildings for small businesses, industrial parks and other facilities, along with recreation and services such as community medical clinics, preschools, and employment training and placement centers to serve local needs.

To support this growing movement of more than 4,000 CDCs that currently create over 20,000 affordable homes and apartments and thousands of jobs every year, state and local governments expanded funding for community-based development efforts, as did private foundations, corporations, and banks. In the 1990s, the federal government redirected additional resources for neighborhood developers through programs such as Low-Income Housing Tax Credits, Community Development Block Grants, HOME Investment Partnerships, Empowerment Zones, and Enterprise Communities (see Chapter 15 for more detail).

In addition, today such national intermediaries as the Neighborhood Reinvestment Corporation, the Local Initiatives Support Corporation (LISC), the Enterprise Foundation (founded by well-known real estate developer James Rouse), and the National Community Development Initiative provide technical and financial assistance to community-based groups for economic development and affordable housing. Nationwide advocacy and community organizing groups such as Citizen Action, ACORN (Association of Community Organizations for Reform Now), and the Industrial Areas Foundation also work to expand grass-roots community development activities. These growing national initiatives have been supplemented by local partnerships in most cities—New York, Los Angeles, Chicago, Atlanta, Baltimore, Boston, Cleveland, Detroit, Miami, Denver, Kansas City, Houston, Washington, D.C., and many more—to mobilize funds and management expertise for community development activities. For example:

- In Newark, New Jersey, the New Community Corporation partly owns a profitable, high-volume supermarket in an area all but abandoned by private business. New Community emerged from the ashes of the 1967 riots to restore the spirit and fabric of life in the Central Ward, starting with building or renovating 3,000 affordable homes and apartments for 7,000 residents. Altogether, New Community runs a variety of businesses providing 1,600 jobs and operates job-training services for area residents and major employers, placing 1,000 low-income people every year in full-time employment. New Community's successful efforts at revitalization have brought private investment in homes and businesses back into central Newark, ranging from homeownership and a successful business loan fund to the first major new shopping center in decades.

- Headquartered in San Francisco, BRIDGE Housing Corporation is one of America's largest builders of affordable rental housing and for-sale homes. Founded in 1983, this nonprofit enterprise has developed and managed more than 8,000 affordable homes and apartments throughout the San Francisco Bay Area and southern California. BRIDGE has won many awards for developing high-quality, mixed-income residences that increase the amount of affordable housing for low- and moderate-income families and senior citizens, expand homeownership, and improve communities. In the mid-1990s, BRIDGE launched a $320 million statewide partnership with financing from World Savings, HUD, major California banks, and two California public employee pension funds. ∎

---

helped many other CDCs grow and mature since the 1960s in a wide variety of neighborhoods that are home to diverse ethnic and religious groups. Today, thousands of CDCs and other types of neighborhood development organizations exist in U.S. cities and rural areas, building and managing affordable housing, health clinics, office and industrial parks, and shopping centers; and providing preschool education, child care, job training and placement, and a host of other family and community services. Much of today's minority and urban political, business, and philanthropic leadership has emerged from these organizations and movements. Esteban Torres, who founded The East Los Angeles Community Union (TELACU) in the 1960s to serve a rapidly growing Hispanic population, was elected to the U.S. Congress from east Los Angeles in 1982. Franklin A. Thomas, who headed the Bedford-Stuyvesant Restoration Corporation for many years, was named president and chief executive officer of the Ford Foundation in 1979.

The Federal Government's Response To the Urban Crisis

One major response to the 1960s urban crisis was the 1965 creation of the federal government's cabinet-level U.S. Department of Housing and Urban Development. Robert C. Weaver, a lifelong activist for better-quality affordable housing and a strong opponent of racial discrimination, was appointed secretary of HUD, becoming the first African American member of a U.S. president's cabinet. In 1961, President Kennedy appointed Weaver to head the Housing and Home Finance Agency (HHFA), HUD's predecessor. Before then, Weaver had served as the New York State rent administrator. Under Weaver's direction as HHFA administrator and then as HUD secretary, federal involvement in subsidized housing changed dramatically. Since the 1930s, the federal government's housing focus was largely limited to mortgage insurance and guarantees and the secondary mortgage market, mostly for the benefit of middle-income homeowners but also to foster the development of middle-income suburban rental apartments. In encouraging private development, these activities received active support from the real estate development industry. The other emphasis at that time concentrated on public housing for low- and moderate-income families. Public housing was a small program nationwide, directed primarily to larger cities, and was extremely unpopular within the real estate community. Some of the original base of support for public housing in the 1930s and 1940s had dwindled, the result of rising affluence and increasing racial tensions. Catherine Bauer, one of public housing's most famous advocates, wrote in 1957 that "public housing, after more than two decades, still drags along in a kind of limbo, not dead but never more than half alive."[9]

By the late 1950s, the incredible postwar demand for new suburban single-family houses had largely been satisfied, and builders and developers began searching for new products and markets. One potential market yet to be tapped was individuals and families whose incomes were still too modest to afford new homes and apartments priced at the lower end of the private market. Such households could, however, be served by the private sector if public subsidies were available. Proponents of low-income housing began to view the sub-sidized public/ private approach as a way to break what Catherine Bauer called "the dreary deadlock of public housing."[10] On the other side of the barricades, the National Association of Home Builders (NAHB), recognizing the economic potential of this new business opportunity for its members, reconsidered its position and became a key supporter of federal subsidies to produce privately owned housing for moderate-income families.

With NAHB's backing, the federal government launched new affordable housing programs in the 1960s, including the Section 221(d)(3) program (below-market mortgage interest rates), the Section 202 program (housing for the elderly), and several others. These programs generally served a target market of people with somewhat higher incomes than public housing residents. By the 1970s, these assisted housing programs were producing a large volume of new rental apartments. In addition, passage of the landmark National Housing Act of 1968 set forth the enormously ambitious goal of producing 600,000 subsidized homes and apartments each year for ten consecutive years. The 1968 act included both a program to assist the production of rental housing (Section 236) and a subsidy program to reduce the cost of mortgage interest to encourage homeownership for low- and moderate-income families (Section 235). Both programs expanded rapidly in the early 1970s but ran into problems, ranging from poor management and outright fraud to the economic recession and inflated oil prices of 1973. In 1974, the Section 236 program was replaced by yet another variant, the now-familiar Section 8 New Construction and Substantial Rehabilitation programs. (The Section 8 program is discussed in Chapter 15.)

Particularly during the 1960s and 1970s, these programs helped produce literally hundreds of thousands of new homes and apartments, many of good quality. Unfortunately, the federal government drastically cut back most of these programs during the 1980s, entirely eliminating some and reducing others by as much as three-fourths of their annual budget compared with the late 1970s.

State and local governments as well as philanthropic institutions and nonprofit organizations have contributed resources to the nation's complex system of housing production. Some for-profit builders have made development of rental housing and homeownership for low- and moderate-income families a major component of their business. For example, HRH Construction Corporation, under the leadership of Richard Ravitch in the 1960s and 1970s, developed more than 25,000 affordable apartments, including Waterside, an attractive high-rise residential complex built in Manhattan in 1974 on a platform overlooking the East River. HRH is now owned

Profile **Abraham Kazan**

Perhaps the biggest of all of America's private builders of affordable housing was Abraham E. Kazan. Kazan was a Jewish immigrant from Russia who joined the Amalgamated Clothing Workers, one of the newly emerging labor unions of the early 20th century. Kazan helped organize a credit union and a union-sponsored bank to make financing more available for affordable rental housing and homeownership. In the 1920s, his union was instrumental in passing the New York State housing law that provided subsidies for moderate-income rental apartments. Kazan formed the Amalgamated Housing Corporation in 1927 and, with property tax abatements under the new state law, built the first two affordable developments: Amalgamated Houses in the Bronx and Amalgamated Dwellings on the Lower East Side of Manhattan. These historic landmark residential complexes were financed primarily by the

Metropolitan Life Insurance Company and the Amalgamated Bank. Both developments were structured as limited-dividend cooperatives to make the attractively designed new housing permanently affordable for moderate-income working families.

In 1951, Abraham Kazan formed the United Housing Foundation, a nonprofit organization that built numerous large-scale cooperative housing developments in New York City during the 1950s, 1960s, and 1970s. His final project was Co-op City, which, with over 15,000 apartments, is still the largest private housing development in the United States. All told, Kazan constructed more than 33,000 cooperatively owned affordable apartments in over half a century of real estate development. Today, the United Housing Foundation and other institutions like the National Cooperative Bank help to carry on his legacy. ■

---

by Starrett, another large builder and owner of affordable housing developments, the most notable of which is the massive Starrett at Spring Creek in Brooklyn.

Development Movements in Inner-City Neighborhoods

As the wholesale clearance and displacement associated with urban renewal grew increasingly controversial and expensive in the 1960s and early 1970s, many community activists and urban policy makers searched for alternative methods to save and improve the existing housing stock. Their goal was to preserve and revitalize the fabric of neighborhood life for existing residents and businesses. Over time, the idea of neighborhood conservation and housing renovation gained popularity as reflected in new government programs, such as Section 312 home rehabilitation loans, Federally Assisted Code Enforcement, and Community Development Block Grants (CDBGs), to assist the revitalization process.

One of the biggest stumbling blocks was "redlining" —real estate lenders' refusal to lend money on properties in older inner-city neighborhoods inhabited by people with modest incomes—and property insurance companies' denial of homeowners insurance in those neighborhoods. Whites were as negatively affected by redlining as nonwhites; although whites normally had an easier time obtaining a mortgage to buy a house in the suburbs, those who chose to remain in the inner cities often could not even get a home improvement loan.

For many years, the federal government redlined properties through the FHA and VA, but, by the late 1960s, various legislative and policy directives led to reform of this harmful practice. After these reforms, the FHA and VA became the only available sources for home loans in many inner-city neighborhoods. Most private lenders and insurers, however, including banks, insurance companies, S&Ls, and mortgage companies, continued redlining. In the 1960s and 1970s, a movement emerged to reverse this tide.

Gale Cincotta, a housewife and PTA leader in the west side Chicago neighborhood of Austin, helped lead a crusade for community stabilization and improvement. She began her efforts with the discovery that commercial banks and thrift institutions were taking millions of dollars in deposits from local residents but refusing to lend even thousands of dollars to those very same customers. Cincotta's neighborhood battle against redlining and in support of "greenlining" united people across racial, ethnic, religious, and geographic boundaries—all could agree to help preserve their own communities. Starting with the Organization for a Better Austin, Cincotta later helped establish the Chicago Reinvestment Alliance and the National People's Action, which led to city, state, and federal intervention and eventually to a variety of neighborhood lending and fair insurance agreements with banks, thrifts, and insurance companies. These agreements have helped bring needed loan and grant money and homeowners insurance back into long-ignored communities where existing property owners are eager to reinvest and upgrade their homes and where for-profit and nonprofit developers are ready and willing to rebuild homes, apartments, and stores.

From Gale Cincotta's movement came two key national laws: the Home Mortgage Disclosure Act (HMDA) of 1975 and the Community Reinvestment Act (CRA) of 1977. Both laws discourage redlining and encourage affirmative lending. A related initiative is the federal government–supported Neighborhood Reinvestment Corporation, which promotes conservation of communities through the successful Neighborhood Housing Services plan pioneered on the north side of Pittsburgh in the mid-1970s. Congress and the federal financial regulatory agencies strengthened the Community Reinvestment Act in 1989. President William J. Clinton and Comptroller of the Currency Eugene Ludwig further strengthened the CRA in 1994. Congressional amendments to the Fair Housing Act in 1992 plus subsequent civil court rulings have helped reduce property insurance redlining. The Community Reinvestment Act played an essential role in expanding available capital for neighborhood development in the 1990s.

The Downtown Revival

While residents of inner-city neighborhoods were struggling to pump economic life into their communities and physically improve their immediate surroundings, corporate and civic leaders were engaged in an identical process focused on the areas around the central business districts of their respective cities. Most downtowns

that experienced real estate booms during the 1920s languished for the next two or three decades without any significant new development. The postwar urban renewal and interstate highway programs were designed to jump-start the process of downtown development through the combination of land assembly, public improvements, and public subsidies. By the 1960s, these government programs were beginning to yield results. The growth of the service economy and the white-collar workforce stimulated the construction of new office buildings, and the rising incomes and changing lifestyles of both young and old led to new investment in retail development and, in some cities, even the construction and renovation of downtown housing.

In 1985, the Urban Land Institute published a survey conducted by the Real Estate Research Corporation that documented the long hiatus in office building development in 24 of the country's biggest cities from the 1920s to the 1950s, followed by massive growth from the late 1960s to the mid-1980s.[11] The survey documented the completion of new, privately owned, large high-rise office buildings (100,000 square feet or more) located in central business districts. In some cases, no office towers had ever been built in these cities before the postwar years; in most other cases, major cities lived through several decades without any development of these tall symbols of progress and prosperity. The following list documents the lean years for construction of urban office skyscrapers:

- Atlanta—before 1961;
- Baltimore—1929 to 1963;

Figure 9-2

Greenlining Neighborhoods with Community Development Financing

Over the past 25 years, many community development financial institutions have emerged in cities across the country. These diverse organizations—banks, credit unions, community loan funds—provide vitally needed capital and credit to revitalize neighborhoods. The Shorebank Corporation of Chicago, owner of the South Shore Bank, was one of the first of these organizations, offering a full range of residential, commercial, and consumer loans, deposit banking services, venture capital for small businesses and real estate development, job training, and social services to communities traditionally underserved by lending institutions. Since 1974, Shorebank has made more than 12,000

development loans and equity investments for over $700 million to residents and businesses in South Shore, Austin, and other neighborhoods of Chicago. Shorebank operates community development banks in Cleveland, Detroit, Portland, Oregon, Seattle, and rural areas in Arkansas, Michigan, and Washington, and is also working as a financial adviser in Baltimore, Denver, Louisville, Los Angeles, and other cities. President Clinton and Congress recognized the importance of greenlining neighborhoods in 1994 by passing the Community Development Financial Institutions Act, creating a $415 million CDFI fund to support new and existing community development lenders. ∎

- Boston—1930 to 1966;
- Chicago—1934 to 1957;
- Cleveland—1928 to 1964;
- Dallas—1921 to 1943;
- Denver—before 1957;
- Detroit—1929 to 1962;
- Fort Worth—1930 to 1969;
- Houston—1929 to 1960;
- Los Angeles—before 1964;
- Miami—before 1967;
- Minneapolis—1929 to 1960;
- New York City (downtown)—1933 to 1956;
- New York City (midtown, excluding Rockefeller Center)—1931 to 1950;
- Newark—1930 to 1962;
- Philadelphia—1931 to 1968;
- Pittsburgh—1933 to 1950;
- St. Louis—before 1970;
- St. Paul—1931 to 1973;
- San Diego—before 1963;
- San Francisco—before 1955;
- Seattle—1929 to 1969;
- Tampa—before 1971;
- Washington, D.C.—before 1970.

During the past three decades, these cities made up for the long drought in office tower development. From 1970 through 1983, for example, the central business districts of these cities added 627 new, privately owned high-rise office buildings of more than 100,000 square feet, for a total of over 340 million square feet of new office space! The most active downtown office markets during this 14-year period were New York City, Chicago, San Francisco, Houston, Washington, D.C., Denver, Boston, Los Angeles, Dallas, Philadelphia, Atlanta, and Seattle. Many of these—and other—cities experienced an accelerated volume of office tower construction after 1983 and for much of the remainder of the 1980s.

Along with the growth of office space and high-rise office buildings came a gradual revival in the fortunes of retail space, with large department stores partially eclipsed by new specialty multistore shopping malls. The early 1970s success of Chicago's Water Tower Place, an enclosed vertical mall with two department store anchors and 130 retail stores on seven levels, led to similar developments in other cities. Boston's Copley Place, for example, was developed by the Urban Investment and Development Company, the same firm that built Water Tower Place. A similar innovative development is the TrizecHahn Company's Horton Plaza in San Diego, an architecturally distinctive vertical downtown shopping mall that is not fully enclosed to take advantage of the city's year-round dry and temperate climate.

Even more widely publicized was the success of the tourism-, entertainment-, and food-oriented "festival marketplaces" that relied exclusively on specialty shops rather than on department store anchors. Unquestionably, the leading developer in this field is the Rouse Company, headed in the 1970s by its charismatic founder James Rouse. The first two such marketplaces, both surprisingly successful for a new concept attempted in what were considered unfavorable locations, were Boston's Faneuil Hall, opened in 1976, and Baltimore's Harborplace, opened in 1980. *Time* magazine was so enthusiastic about the impact of these two developments on the revitalization of urban downtowns that it featured James Rouse on its cover in 1981 under the heading, "Cities Are Fun!"[12] By 1990, the Rouse Company was operating 14 such centers in cities around the country, the largest being Pioneer Place in Portland, Oregon. James Rouse's last venture, the Enterprise Development Company, which he established in 1982 as a revenue-generating venture to help finance affordable housing and community development through his Enterprise Foundation, has also developed and operates several festival marketplaces. Interestingly, many downtown projects, including Horton Plaza and the various central-city retail and mixed-use centers developed by the Rouse Company and the Enterprise Development Company, were urban renewal projects whose initial costs were heavily subsidized by their city governments.

The fundamental idea of the festival marketplace—that the urban shopping experience is "fun"—accelerated in the 1980s and 1990s with the development of urban entertainment centers. These complexes combine retail stores with entertainment activities ranging from cinemas to skating rinks to roller coasters. In many cases, the stores themselves are designed for play, ranging from Niketown to Dave & Buster's to the Sharper Image to the Discovery Channel Store. The entertainment venues include a ferris wheel at Navy Pier in Chicago and a variety of sports from batting practice to golf practice at New York's Chelsea Piers to an amusement park at the Mall of America just outside Minneapolis. Many of these new urban entertainment centers highlight the joys of strolling along to view and enjoy the crowds and action, and some have made that aspect the most prominent feature of their names, such as Third Street Promenade in Santa Monica, Coco Walk in Coconut Grove near Miami, and Universal CityWalk near Universal Studios close to Los Angeles. Some of these new centers have an ethnic appeal, like Harlem *USA* in New York City or Jump Street *USA* in Philadelphia. The notion of re-creating city street life as a key aspect of shopping and entertainment first expressed by Disneyland in California and Disney World in

Faneuil Hall consists of 160 stores and 219,000 square feet of gross leasable retail space housed in three 536-foot-long converted industrial and public market buildings, all of which were originally built before 1826.

Florida is being imitated not just by many urban development projects, but even in suburban retail malls, where the look and feel of "Main Street" is becoming increasingly popular.

The Wave of New Communities

James Rouse was also heavily identified with another key trend of the 1960s and 1970s: the attempt to create new large-scale, mixed-use communities as an alternative to both big crowded cities and suburban sprawl. Beginning in the early 1960s, a Rouse Company subsidiary called Community Research and Development secretly purchased more than 16,000 acres of mostly contiguous farmland in Howard County, Maryland, halfway between Baltimore and Washington, D.C., and began planning and building the new community of Columbia. Rouse convinced his main lender, the Connecticut General Life Insurance Company (CIGNA), to provide financial backing for the massive community development project, beginning with the cloak-and-dagger operation of land acquisition that involved several hundred transactions.

Rouse assembled a team of distinguished city planners and social scientists to advise him on how to produce a better design for urban living. They devised such innovations as a prepaid community health insurance plan, a minibus system, shared multipurpose community facilities for worship, recreation, and other uses, and a focus on quality education and active community participation. Although Columbia endured financial hard times with the collapse of its homebuilding program during the national economic recession from 1973 to 1975, it survived to become a thriving community of 75,000 people.

Built around residential villages and created lakes, Columbia has a "downtown" that features a regional shopping mall (owned and operated by the Rouse Company), office centers, entertainment and cultural facilities, and branches of five colleges and universities. The community, intended to accommodate both residential villages and business centers, includes various industrial and office parks that employ nearly 60,000 people—not all residents of Columbia.

Housing is targeted to a wide range of income groups and includes numerous subsidized, moderate-income rental apartments. Racial integration, one of Rouse's explicit goals, has been achieved through a policy of nondiscrimination: nearly one-fourth of Columbia's population is African American. The Rouse Company also helped launch a successful homebuilding firm, Ryland Homes, which now operates nationwide but is still headquartered in Columbia.

Columbia was just one of a wave of new communities privately developed during the 1960s and 1970s. Most of these efforts were concentrated in Sunbelt climates, especially California, Texas, and Florida, though many other states were also represented. Some of the developments were associated with resource-based corporations such as oil companies that already owned large amounts of land—for example, Reston, Virginia, previously owned by Gulf Oil and now by Mobil, and Friendswood, Texas, owned by Exxon. Other new communities such as Las Colinas, Texas, evolved from large agricultural and cattle ranches. Several developments in California were the legacy of the Spanish land grants, whose massive, contiguous, undeveloped acreage survived into modern times under single ownership.

California ranches that became new urban centers in the past few decades include Thousand Oaks, Valencia, Laguna Niguel, Mission Viejo, Rancho Santa Margarita, and, the biggest of them all, the Irvine Ranch. Owned by the Irvine Company, the ranch consisted of more than 100,000 acres, nearly one-fifth of all the private and public land in Orange County. By the early 1960s, postwar suburbanization and the construction of two interstate highways brought metropolitan growth to the northern boundaries of the Irvine Ranch. The Irvine Company hired architect William Pereira to design a master plan for the new city of Irvine to be built around a new campus of the University of California. Irvine is still growing rapidly today, home to 130,000 people and 170,000 jobs. In addition to the city of Irvine, land originally part of the Irvine Ranch was developed for urban uses in Newport Beach, Laguna Beach, Costa Mesa, Tustin, and several other communities in central Orange County.

Additional types of new communities developed since the 1960s include retiree- or adult-oriented centers such as Leisure World in Florida, California, and other states; recreation-oriented subdivisions and second-home communities in many areas of the country; and urban "new-town-in-town" mixed-use residential complexes in some big cities. Because the initial costs of land acquisition, planning, infrastructure, and development are high and take many years to pay back through sales and leasing of land and buildings, one lesson learned from these types of developments is that they require strong, long-term financial investment to succeed. Eventually, prices appreciate substantially once a critical mass of the community is developed, but time and patient investors are necessary ingredients. The federal government's New Communities Program, managed by HUD in the 1970s, sponsored developers who, for the most part, were too thinly capitalized and received woefully inadequate operating support from HUD. Consequently, most of the HUD-supported new community projects went bankrupt. One exception is the Woodlands, a HUD-supported new community near Houston owned for nearly three decades by the Mitchell Energy and Development Corporation. The Woodlands was able to draw from both the corporate resources of its parent firm during a time of high profits and from the substantial personal commitment of the company's owner and chief executive, George Mitchell, to build the town of his dreams.

Certainly the single most catalytic development was the entry of the Disney Corporation into central Florida. In 1965, Disney purchased 27,000 acres of undeveloped swampland near Orlando and began to develop Walt Disney World, including the Magic Kingdom and EPCOT Center. Two years later, Florida's legislature created Disney's own private government, the Reedy Creek Improvement District, which enjoys full powers of taxation, borrowing, servicing, regulation, and development. Disney's intention was to control the pace and type of development surrounding its main facilities, something the company had been unable to do with its 250-acre Disneyland in Anaheim, California. Despite Disney's careful plans, the overwhelming response to the East Coast theme park set off a wave of speculation, population and employment growth, and real estate development in the greater Orlando metropolitan region that has not subsided even three decades later. On opening day in December 1971, cars were backed up for 15 miles on the new interstate highway to enter the Magic Kingdom.

Today, Disney continues to expand, building a motion picture and television theme park and studios (together with MGM), a wild animal park, many distinctively designed resort hotels by well-known architects such as Michael Graves and Robert A.M. Stern, a major shopping center called Downtown Disney, office buildings, recreation facilities, and housing, including the whole new communities of Lake Buena Vista and Celebration. For a time, Disney was heavily involved in residential development throughout Florida, acquiring the Arvida Company, a major land development and homebuilding firm now owned by the St. Joe Company. Disney is currently concentrating its development plans for Florida entirely on metropolitan Orlando. The result of Walt Disney's choice of a sleepy spot on a map is that Orlando today boasts 90,000 hotel rooms, more than any metropolitan region in the United States except Los Angeles and New York, and one of America's busiest airports. Metropolitan Orlando's population increased by 50 percent during the 1980s, and by 20 percent in the 1990s.

The heavy investment in new communities and large-scale development at the periphery of big, established central cities led to a new phenomenon in the 1970s and 1980s—the growth of "urban villages," "edge cities," "suburban megacenters," "technoburbs," and "growth corridors." These concentrations of super regional shopping malls, office and industrial parks with enormous quantities of space, major highway interchanges, and low- to medium-density housing are often located in more than one government jurisdiction and create a prime activity area away from the traditional central-city downtowns. Some of these new suburban mixed-use developments have grown around a large suburban shopping center, such as Tysons Corner, Virginia, or Woodfield Mall in Schaumburg, Illinois. In other cases, a highway such as Route 1 in the vicinity of Princeton, New Jersey, or I-285 north of Atlanta has been the focal point. The image of these centers ranges from the corporate office complexes headquartered in Fairfield County, Connecticut, to the research and industrial parks of Silicon Valley in Santa Clara County, California. Nearly every major metropolitan region now has multiple suburban central business districts that compete with and often surpass the older urban downtowns.

Real estate developers have played major roles in planning and creating these large-scale mixed-use complexes away from the traditional central business districts, from J.C. Nichols's Country Club Plaza in Kansas City to William Zeckendorf's Roosevelt Field on Long Island and Century City in Los Angeles. One of the best-known recent projects is Gerald Hines's development of the Post Oak–Westheimer area as Houston's main high-end retail center and a thriving location for office space and hotels. In 1969, Hines opened the Galleria shopping center, a mixed-use facility that now contains 2.5 million square feet of retail space and four department store anchors. The project also includes two large Westin Hotels and three major office buildings. The 25-story Post Oak Tower office building in the Galleria, completed in 1973, was at that time one of only two Houston office towers with more than 500,000 square feet of space located outside downtown. In 1983, Hines built the 64-story, 1.6 million-square-foot Transco Tower in the Post Oak area. Transco Tower, designed by New York architects Philip Johnson and John Burgee, is the world's tallest office building located outside a large city's central business district. Gerald Hines Interests has been among the biggest commercial developers in the United States (and abroad) during the past three decades, with major office buildings, shopping centers, and hotels in Houston and many other cities on its list of credits, including Atlanta, Boston, Chicago, Detroit, Minneapolis, New York, and Washington, D.C. The Galleria–Post Oak center, which continues to be Hines's trademark project, has had a major national impact on retail and mixed-use development.

The 1970s through the 1990s

Real estate development has always been a cyclical industry. Since the 1930s, economists such as Homer Hoyt, Roy Wenzlick, Clarence Long, Leo Grebler, and Manuel Gottlieb have been collecting data and analyzing historical patterns of the ever-changing rise and fall in the volume of real estate activity and the value of property.[13] Downturns may be caused by general economic recessions or depressions, changes in money markets that restrict the supply or drive up the cost of money, and overbuilding that generates too many buildings competing for too few tenants or buyers. Upturns may be caused by a significant increase in demand as a result of population, employment, and income growth; changes in money markets that lead to a plentiful supply of relatively low-cost financing; and speculative responses to rapidly increasing rents, prices, profits, and perceived values.

The past three decades have seen a great deal of cyclical fluctuation precipitated by a wide variety of factors. A boom in the late 1960s and early 1970s fueled by strong economic growth, military spending, and modest inflation heralded a bust from 1973 to 1975 that

The Woodlands, which opened in 1974, is a HUD-supported planned new community on 25,000 acres of heavily forested land 27 miles north of downtown Houston. Pictured here is the Woodlands country club, with industrial buildings in the background.

was induced by the shock of quadrupled oil prices, double-digit inflation, and a severe economic recession. A boom in the late 1970s stimulated by the entry of a large portion of the baby boom generation into housing and job markets gave way to a crash in the early 1980s caused by extremely high interest rates and a contraction in financing, combined with high unemployment and a severe economic recession. In the mid-1980s, money flowed freely again, job growth was strong, and real estate development took off on a speculative binge that by 1990 was squeezed by extraordinarily high vacancies, low occupancies, large unsold inventories, falling prices, rents, and yields, and the most defaults, foreclosures, and bankruptcies since the Great Depression. Yet, by 1993 and 1994, relatively low mortgage interest rates and rising job growth led to a new boom in home sales and residential construction. In 1994, single-family housing construction starts reached 1.2 million homes, the highest total since 1978. By 1997, the national homeownership rate reached

Gerald Hines Interests's mixed-use development, the 64-story Transco Tower and the 2.5 million-square-foot Galleria, created a completely new suburban-style business district outside Houston's downtown.

a new all-time high of 65.7 percent, surpassing the previous record set in 1980. It set another record in 1998, reaching 66.3 percent.

As always, this pattern displayed much variation. Within a metropolitan area or a multistate region, some neighborhoods and communities flourished while others languished. In the early 1980s, Dallas continued to thrive while Houston was in a decline— but, by the late 1980s, both cities' fortunes began to reverse. Throughout the decade and all across the country, shiny new office towers and shopping centers coexisted with abandoned housing and the homeless. Cycles also varied between regions. Beginning in the mid-1970s, the Southwest boomed while the Northeast stagnated, both affected by the dramatic rise in energy prices. In the 1980s, energy prices fell substantially, and the Southwest sank while the Northeast rose again. In addition to the prime factor of geographic location, the relative fortunes of real estate differ cyclically by product type. During the late 1980s, when office buildings and hotels were generally overbuilt in most markets, developers and investors turned to residential apart-

ment buildings and industrial warehouses. By the late 1990s, Class A downtown office buildings and luxury hotels had once again become "hot" properties.

The massive population influx of the postwar baby boomers who reached adulthood and formed separate households, the shift in population growth from the Frostbelt to the Sunbelt, the substantial increase in single and divorced households, and the rise in the numbers, income, and wealth of senior citizens all had a major impact on housing development. The housing industry responded by building and rehabilitating a record volume of homes and apartments in the 1970s and maintaining high production through much of the 1980s. Condominiums as a new form of individual apartment ownership burst onto the scene in the early 1970s, accounting for a significant portion of new and converted multifamily housing.

Prices, especially of single-family homes, rose rapidly in many markets as demand outran supply, with the costs of new and existing housing and developable land outpacing the previous two decades' increase in household income. The gap in wealth between home-owners and renters widened, and both longstanding tenants and newly formed families, taking advantage of the anticipated appreciation in equity and the available tax benefits, strained their resources to rush into homeownership before prices escalated higher. Mostly on the East and West Coasts at various times from the mid-1970s to the late 1980s, housing sales and prices rose and fell in successive waves of speculative frenzy followed by recessionary panic. Construction of multi-family housing received a major boost in the early and mid-1980s when the Economic Recovery Tax Act of 1981 provided for syndications, accelerated depreciation, passive losses, and other income tax benefits. The reduction of these benefits under the Tax Reform Act of 1986 immediately triggered a significant reduction in investment in and development of new rental housing as well as a rapid decline of the syndication industry. The importance of congressional actions and federal administrative and judicial decisions highlighted by these tax laws encouraged major real estate firms to strengthen the National Realty Committee as a vital Washington lobby.

Contributing to the instability and wide cyclical swings of the last three decades was the impact of a higher level of general price inflation than most U.S. citizens had ever experienced in combination with revolutionary changes in capital markets and real estate finance. The easy availability of relatively low-cost, fixed-interest, long-term residential mortgages at a time of rapidly rising interest rates in the late 1970s, for example, helped finance and encourage the boom in homeownership. It also led to the near insolvency of savings and loan institutions. Under deregulation, thrifts began to compete for funds from 1980 to 1982 by paying interest on deposits that was higher than the interest they received on much of their mortgage loan portfolios. This disaster of deregulation was followed by another in 1982, when S&Ls were permitted to move away from home mortgage lending and into commercial real estate markets, to engage in equity deals, to purchase "junk bonds," and to get involved in many high-risk ventures while bearing no risk of failure to depositors, because all their deposit accounts were federally insured for up to $100,000 each. A combination of corruption in some cases, poor judgment in others, and bad luck from cyclical downturns, especially the massive real estate depression of the late 1980s in the energy-producing states, led to widespread bankruptcy among S&Ls. Consequently, as of 1989, the government began taking over much of the thrift industry. The federal Resolution Trust Corporation, created to handle the S&L debacle, entered the 1990s as the owner of real property worth many billions of dollars. Indeed, the RTC became a major force in the future fortunes of the real estate industry as it sold off its vast property holdings during the first half of the 1990s.

The collapse of many thrifts, the difficulties experienced by a large number of commercial banks, and tighter federal regulations on real estate lending meant that, in the early 1990s, developers faced considerable challenges financing new projects. By the mid-1990s, a mood of cautious, selective lending prevailed, especially for commercial development. This pattern was a complete reversal of the dominant trend in the 1980s, when highly leveraged nonrecourse debt from financial institutions was plentiful and many developers rushed to construct new space, often without sufficient demand for occupancy at projected rents or sale prices.

While the decline of the thrifts left a temporary vacuum for financing new commercial development, it has had little impact on financing home purchases because of the past three decades' dramatic growth in securitization and mortgage banking and the rapid expansion of the secondary mortgage market. Through the medium of large government-backed agencies such as Fannie Mae, Freddie Mac (Federal Home Loan Mortgage Corporation), and Ginnie Mae (Government National Mortgage Association) and a host of private securities firms, mortgage companies have been able to draw capital from a wide range of institutional investors. Insurance companies, pension funds, depository institutions, and global investors now participate in the secondary mortgage market. These new sources of capital provide ample funds for primary lenders and borrowers, though

often at higher real interest rates than before deregulation, when funds for housing loans were partially sheltered from competition on the capital markets.

Pension funds, life insurance companies, opportunity funds, and other institutional investors have also begun playing a much greater role as lenders, purchasers, and joint venture partners for both new development and the acquisition, refinancing, and redevelopment of existing properties. Since the 1970s, the growth of real estate investment funds has generated a new industry in which financial advisers play an increasingly prominent role in development and management. At the same time, real estate is becoming more professionalized. New trade associations, such as the Pension Real Estate Association, the National Council of Real Estate Investment Fiduciaries, and the National Association of Real Estate Investment Trusts, signal the financial and organizational changes recently experienced by the real estate industry.

In particular, real estate investment trusts have grown rapidly in recent years, drawing billions of dollars into real estate investment from the public capital markets and reflecting the burgeoning expansion of the stock market and mutual funds in the mid-1990s. Total market capitalization of 119 publicly traded REITs in 1990 was less than $9 billion; by 1998, the number of publicly traded REITs tracked by its national association had nearly doubled to 210, and their collective share value had skyrocketed to about $142 billion. Most of these REITs provide equity financing for the acquisition and development of real estate. (See Chapter 6 for more details.)

An important recent source of debt capital for real estate development has come through the dramatic increase in commercial mortgage–backed securities, rising from less than $5 billion issued in 1990 to nearly $45 billion issued in 1997 and again in 1998. With total market capitalization of $180 billion, securitization and the secondary mortgage market are bringing global capital to commercial real estate, just as they have been doing for financing of residential homeownership since the 1980s.

A related change is the increasing involvement of large corporations in real estate. Most industrial and commercial firms have traditionally ignored the profit potential of the land and buildings they own and use. Beginning in the 1960s, however, many resource-based companies, such as the railroad, forestry, oil, mining, and agricultural giants that owned surplus land, entered the real estate business to develop everything from rural recreational subdivisions to urban mixed-use complexes. The federal government also encouraged corporate entry into the high-volume production of housing through

Figure 9-3

Real Estate Securities

The development industry's constant need for capital and the average citizen's desire for a "piece of the action" have combined over the years to create a market for real estate securities. The health of that market has varied with conditions in both the real estate and securities markets. Today's alphabet soup of REITs and REMICs had its genesis in the 19th century.

One of the earliest issuers of publicly held securities in real estate was the American Real Estate Company. Organized in 1888 with capital of $100,000, the company fueled its growth by selling almost $15 million of bonds and "certificates" on an installment basis throughout the United States. Unfortunately, a downturn in the metropolitan New York market in 1914 led to bankruptcy and eventual liquidation.

In 1925, Fred F. French financed construction of Tudor City, a 12-building project with 2,500 apartments in midtown Manhattan, by selling $50 million of preferred stock. French made a gift of one share of common stock with each share of preferred stock that was purchased. The preferred stock was to be redeemed after ten years. French retained a share of common stock for each share issued to the public. In addition, he obtained mortgage financing in an amount equal to 50 percent of the total project cost.

Harry Black, president of the George A. Fuller Company and builder of the Flatiron Building, founded the United States Realty and Construction Company in 1903 with capitalization of $66 million, $30 million in preferred stock and $33 million in common stock—-the largest publicly held real estate organization of the time. In early 1929, Black extended French's financing concept by issuing stock for the total cost of the construction of each new building, altogether eliminating the use of mortgage financing.

Public participation in mortgage debt financing became big business in the first third of the 20th century. Both guaranteed and plain (nonguaranteed) mortgage bonds were issued. Typically, a bond issue covered a single development project. Commercial banks and title insurance companies guaranteed repayment of principal and interest on the bonds. By 1931, mortgage bonds accounted for more than 17 percent of total urban mortgage debt. Unfortunately, with the onset of the Great Depression, more than 60 percent of those bonds defaulted.

The importance of real estate securities was recognized in early 1929 by the Real Estate Board of New York's creating the New York Real Estate Securities Exchange. Exchange members included 500 traders who generated a volume of $309 million in 1930. A victim of the chaos in the securities markets, the exchange ceased operating during the 1930s.

The stock market crash of 1929 had a devastating impact on real estate securities. Over 80 percent of the real estate corporations listed in Moody's *Manual* in 1929 had either reorganized or disappeared completely from that publication six years later.

HUD's Operation Breakthrough. With the failure of many of these 1960s commercial and residential developments, however, corporations withdrew to safer and more familiar business activities. But the threat of hostile takeovers and leveraged buyouts financed by undervalued real estate, played out against the cost-conscious era of international competition in the 1980s, led to renewed interest among many major companies to use their real estate assets more intensively and productively, manage them more effectively, and sell to or enter into joint ventures with developers more frequently. This interest is reflected in the growth of a key professional organization, the National Association of Corporate Real Estate Executives. (Chapter 21 addresses both the pension fund and the corporate perspective.)

The growing presence of large institutions in real estate was matched by the growing size of many development firms. As early as the 1960s, large national developers emerged in the homebuilding field, including Kaufman & Broad, Centex, Ryan Homes, National Homes, Ryland, and U.S. Home. Similarly, shopping center developers such as Edward DeBartolo, Melvin Simon, Alfred Taubman, Ernest Hahn, and James Rouse went national. In the 1970s and 1980s, they were joined by nationwide office developers such as Trammell Crow, Gerald Hines, John Galbreath, Lincoln Property, the Urban Investment and Development Company, and Tishman Speyer, along with major life insurance companies such as Prudential, Metropolitan, and Equitable and several large Canadian development firms, including Olympia & York, Cadillac Fairview, and Trizec-Hahn. Many of the largest developers built office, retail, hotel, industrial, apartment, and mixed-use projects. The entry of the Canadians into the U.S. development market also signaled a trend toward international development, as many major North

The 1950s dawned with a renewed vigor for real estate development as well as with a significant increase in both personal and corporate income taxes. These elements combined to propel a new breed of real estate syndicators. Louis Glickman, Harry Helmsley, Marvin Kratter, Lawrence Wien, and others were in the forefront of syndicators offering limited partnership interests to the general public. Both new construction and acquisition of such famous structures as the Chrysler Building and the Empire State Building were included in this wave of real estate equity syndication. Eventually, many of the individual syndicates were combined as investors traded their interests for shares in new publicly owned companies.

During this period, well-known real estate firms participated in the parade for stock ownership. Among them were Webb & Knapp, Arvida, the Uris brothers, and Kaufman & Broad. They joined a handful of pre-Depression survivors such as City Investing, Starrett, and Tishman.

In particular, a boom in the public offerings of single-family homebuilders occurred in the 1960s. The difficulty in raising financing for each individual development project, along with a 1966 credit crunch, swelled the ranks of publicly traded homebuilding companies to 41 by 1972.

In 1960, passage of the Real Estate Investment Tax Act permitted the formation of real estate investment trusts. Each shareholder would be taxed as if investing in a partnership, yet the REIT had limited liability and other features similar to a corporation. Most of the new REITs were formed between 1968 and 1973, and many were mortgage trusts rather than equity trusts. They often borrowed heavily in the short-term money markets while lending for longer time periods. A decline in the fortunes of the real estate market and a steep increase in short-term interest, because rates in the mid-1970s resulted in the collapse or reorganization of many REITs.

The 1980s witnessed a return to public limited partnerships. This time, the underwriters and promoters were mainly large stock brokerage and investment banking firms such as Merrill Lynch. The Tax Reform Act of 1986, however, changed the rules of the game sufficiently to make these investments unattractive to the typical investor, because real estate losses could no longer be used to offset ordinary earned income.

The 1990s saw the explosive rebirth of REITs, although the new breed consists mostly of equity ownership trusts rather than the mortgage debt trusts that were popular in the 1960s. In addition, recent enabling legislation has made it easier for pension funds to invest in these securities. Further, Wall Street reentered the mortgage market through the vehicle of mortgage-backed securities. These instruments are used primarily in the residential field, and they are steadily increasing in importance in financing commercial real estate development and investment. ■

American developers looked to Europe for new projects and prospects in the 1990s.

One profound change that began with the movement for neighborhood participation in the 1960s and accelerated after Earth Day in April 1970 was a growing concern for the effects of real estate development on the natural, physical, and human environment. The 1969 National Environmental Policy Act and its various state equivalents led to public regulators' and legislators' use of environmental impact reviews to decide whether proposed development projects should be approved. The 1966 National Historic Preservation Act helped focus attention on conserving existing structures rather than permitting their demolition to make way for entirely new developments. These and many other new federal, state, and local laws and practices—growth controls, sewer moratoriums, impact fees, linkage payments—all slowed the approval process and added to the costs of public and private real estate development in many communities.

In the 1970s, 1980s, and 1990s, California, which in the 1950s and 1960s was considered a developer's paradise for obtaining public infrastructure and services along with fast and favorable regulations, became an embattled and difficult state in which to build new projects, with active protests by citizens, strict and time-consuming regulatory processes, and extensive and costly taxes and fees. This change in the political scene helped reduce overbuilding, especially residential development, but it also contributed greatly to the rapid escalation of housing prices. Clearly, supply could no longer keep pace with demand.

The California syndrome was repeated in the Northeast during the housing boom of the mid-1980s. In some cases, developers joined the ranks of civil rights and affordable housing activists to attack exclusionary zoning and other related practices. The New Jersey State Supreme Court's *Mount Laurel* decisions mandated regional fair share housing, and Massachusetts's statewide "anti-snob" zoning law attempted to deal with the exclusionary practices of many suburban towns. NAHB, HUD, ULI, and other public and private organizations have searched for solutions that lower housing costs through regulatory reform.

Part of the problem is that all levels of government have trimmed their expenditures for roads, bridges, and a vast array of other needed infrastructure and services. The tax revolt of the 1970s and 1980s led to reduced maintenance and the neglect of vitally needed replacement and expansion of key facilities. In the context of overburdened infrastructure, new private development often appears to exacerbate traffic congestion, air and water pollution, crowded schools, and other undesirable environmental outcomes without generating sufficient tax revenues to improve overall conditions. Developers find themselves increasingly involved in public relations campaigns and public policy initiatives to build support for proposed projects. They work with local residents, business and civic groups, community leaders, and government officials to gain project approvals based on agreements to pay for a greater share of public facilities and amenities and to mitigate the perceived negative effects of proposed development.

During the 1990s, this form of cooperation and negotiation renewed the search for cooperative physical and financial solutions that meet society's needs for adequate and affordable housing, attractive and livable environments, and dynamic and efficient urban economic development. These solutions included "smart growth" initiatives designed to reduce suburban sprawl by reinvesting in existing developed urban and suburban areas; increasing residential and commercial densities, particularly around transit stations and other key transportation crossroads; and preserving agricultural and recreational land and open space. Many states and localities are now working on smart growth management efforts, ranging from Maryland to Oregon, Florida to New Jersey, Vermont to Tennessee, and many more. Under the leadership of President William Clinton and Vice President Albert Gore, the President's Council on Sustainable Development emerged as a major forum for promoting smart growth in states, regions, and communities across the country.

Another sign of the growing interest in sustainable development and smart growth was the rise of a new organization, the Congress for the New Urbanism. New urbanists—architects and planners such as Peter Calthorpe and Andres Duany, public officials such as former HUD Secretary Henry Cisneros and Milwaukee's Mayor John Norquist, civic leaders like Henry Richmond of the National Growth Management Leadership Project and Robert Yaro of New York's Regional Plan Association, plus an increasing number of real estate developers such as Robert Davis of Seaside, Florida, and Henry Turley of Memphis, Tennessee, and real estate investors including Jonathan Miller of Lend Lease and Christopher Leinberger of Arcadia—captured the public's imagination with community planning and design that bring back the best in traditional neighborhoods of the old "walking cities" in America and Europe combined with new ways of organizing daily life in a rapidly changing world. Architect-planners like Ray Gindroz are applying principles of the new urbanism in developments ranging from upscale environments such as the Disney Company's new community of Celebration near Orlando, Florida, all the way to inner-city low-income neighborhoods like Park Du Valle in Louisville, Kentucky.

According to a 1996 publication from HUD, *New American Neighborhoods:*

> The fundamental idea of new urbanism is to view the neighborhood as a coherent unit, where adults and children can walk to nearby shopping, services, schools, parks, recreation centers, and in some cases, to their own jobs and businesses; where civic centers can serve as focal points for community activity; where streets and blocks are connected with pedestrian walkways and bicycle paths; where public transit is readily available to connect with other neighborhoods and communities throughout the metropolitan region; where automobiles are convenient to use but do not dominate the most visible aspects of the urban landscape with traffic congestion and massive parking lots; and where houses are built closer together, with front and back porches and yards, grouped around tree-shaded squares, small parks, and narrow streets with planting strips. Such pedestrian-friendly environments help facilitate positive community spirit and emphasize neighborhood safety and security. The goal of the new urbanism is to promote diverse and livable communities with a greater variety of housing types, land uses, and building densities—in other words, to develop and maintain a melting pot of neighborhood homes serving a wide range of household and family sizes, ages, cultures, and incomes.[14]

Along with the new urbanism has come a new regionalism. As metropolitan areas grow far beyond the boundaries of their central cities, the need for increased regional cooperation and coordinated metropolitan economic development strategies has become vital and urgent. The "new economy" that has emerged is knowledge- and information-based, technology- and communications-intensive, and globally oriented, and it places a premium on the competitiveness of metropolitan regions to generate investment, jobs, and prosperity. For communities and regions to succeed in the global marketplace, fundamental factors of economic activity—including quality of the metropolitan transportation and infrastructure systems, education and workforce development, research and technology, the physical and social environment, and financing and capital formation—have to be strong.

Establishing technology centers has also been seen as a means of generating prosperity for many regions—from Austin, Texas, to Akron, Ohio. Creating the necessary climate of innovation and entrepreneurship depends on public/private collaboration across governmental boundaries and jurisdictions involving cities, suburbs, counties, states, and even nations where regions cross international borders, such as Buffalo and San Diego. In addition, metropolitan initiatives in cities from Portland, Oregon, to Jacksonville, Florida, focus on environmental preservation and restoration. Many of these initiatives also address key issues of poverty, racial and ethnic divisions and disparities, and rebuilding inner-city and inner-suburban neighborhoods with modest success and many challenges. Americans will increasingly see themselves as citizens of metropolitan economies, and the search for solutions to designing more effective governance and implementing successful regional collaboration will grow even more pressing in the 21st century.[15]

Summary

This chapter has described and analyzed the growth of a mature, modern, and professional real estate development industry with more complex sources of financing and greater sophistication in relating to government and the general public. In the half century since World War II, developers have increasingly specialized in different product types—offices, shopping centers, industrial parks, hotels, and housing. They have built larger and more efficient organizations and faced tough economic challenges such as inflation and recession. Sensitivity to racial, ethnic, and environmental issues has become much more important. The new global economy will bring changes in real estate development even more dramatic.

Terms

- Civil Rights Act of 1964
- Community development corporation (CDC)
- Community Reinvestment Act (CRA)
- Festival marketplaces
- GI Bill
- Gray Areas Program
- Greenlining
- Industrial parks
- Junk bonds
- Limited partnership
- Military-industrial complex
- Model Cities Program of 1966
- National Housing Act of 1968
- Neighborhood development organization
- Neighborhood Reinvestment Corporation
- New communities
- New urbanism
- Power of eminent domain
- Redlining
- Syndicator
- Takeout
- Title I
- Urban entertainment center
- Urban renewal
- VA home loan guarantee program
- Veterans Administration
- Voting Rights Act of 1965
- War on Poverty

Review Questions

9.1 How and why did homebuilding production methods change after World War II?

9.2 Describe the urban renewal efforts of the 1950s and 1960s.

9.3 How and why did retailing change in the 1950s and 1960s?

9.4 What spurred the urban crisis of the 1960s and what housing-related programs were initiated because of it?

9.5 What is a CDC and what is its role in community building?

9.6 What is a new community?

9.7 Real estate is always said to be a cyclical business. What are some of the financial cycles that have occurred since 1970?

9.8 Describe the growth of real estate securities from 1888 to their current form as REITs.

Notes

1. "Housing: Up from the Potato Fields," *Time,* July 3, 1950, p. 67. See also Marc A. Weiss, *The Rise of the Community Builders: The American Real Estate Industry and Urban Land Planning* (New York: Columbia Univ. Press, 1987).

2. John Keats, *The Crack in the Picture Window* (Boston: Houghton Mifflin, 1957); and William H. Whyte, Jr., *The Organization Man* (New York: Simon & Schuster, 1956).

3. Tom Schactman, *Skyscraper Dreams: The Great Real Estate Dynasties of New York* (Boston: Little, Brown, 1991), p. 218.

4. Marc A. Weiss, "The Origins and Legacy of Urban Renewal," in *Federal Housing Policy and Programs: Past and Present,* ed. J. Paul Mitchell (New Brunswick, N.J.: Rutgers Univ. Center for Urban Policy Research, 1985), pp. 253–76; and Ann R. Markusen, Annalee Saxenian, and Marc A. Weiss, "Who Benefits from Intergovernmental Transfers?" *Publius: The Journal of Federalism,* Winter 1981, pp. 5–35.

5. Robert A. Caro, *The Power Broker: Robert Moses and the Fall of New York* (New York: Random House, 1974), pp. 850–94.

6. "Northland: A New Yardstick for Shopping Center Planning," *Architectural Forum,* June 1954, pp. 102–19. The article begins, "This is a classic in shopping center planning, in the sense that Rockefeller Center is a classic in urban skyscraper-group planning, or Radburn, N.J., in suburban residential planning." On Northland and Victor Gruen, see also Howard Gillette, Jr., "The Evolution of the Planned Shopping Center in Suburb and City," *Journal of the American Planning Association,* Autumn 1985, pp. 449–60.

7. Kenneth T. Jackson, *Crabgrass Frontier: The Suburbanization of the United States* (New York: Oxford Univ. Press, 1985), p. 254.

8. Daniel Seligman, "The Enduring Slums," in *The Exploding Metropolis* (Garden City, N.Y.: Doubleday, 1957), p. 132.

9. Catherine Bauer, "The Dreary Deadlock of Public Housing," *Architectural Forum,* May 1957, p. 140.

10. Ibid.

11. Real Estate Research Corporation, *Tall Office Buildings in the United States* (Washington, D.C.: ULI–the Urban Land Institute, 1985).

12. "He Digs Downtown: For Master Planner James Rouse, Urban Life Is a Festival," *Time,* August 24, 1981, pp. 42–53.

13. See, for example, Clarence D. Long, Jr., *Building Cycles and the Theory of Investment* (Princeton, N.J.: Princeton Univ. Press, 1940); Homer Hoyt, *The Urban Real Estate Cycle: Performances and Prospects,* Technical Bulletin No. 38 (Washington, D.C.: ULI–the Urban Land Institute, 1950); Roy Wenzlick, *The Coming Boom in Real Estate* (New York: Simon & Schuster, 1936); Leo Grebler, David M. Blank, and Louis Winnick, *Capital Formation in Residential Real Estate: Trends and Prospects* (Princeton, N.J.: Princeton Univ. Press, 1956); Manuel Gottlieb, *Long Swings in Urban Development* (New York: National Bureau of Economic Research, 1976); and Marc A. Weiss, "The Politics of Real Estate Cycles," *Urban Land,* March 1992, pp. 33–35.

14. Henry G. Cisneros and Marc A. Weiss, *New American Neighborhoods: Building Homeownership Zones to Revitalize Our Nation's Communities* (Washington, D.C.: U.S. Department of Housing and Urban Development, 1996), pp. 5–6. See also Peter Katz, *The New Urbanism: Toward an Architecture of Community* (New York: McGraw-Hill, 1994); and Marc A. Weiss, "Neighborhood Diversity," in *Charter of the New Urbanism,* ed. Congress for the New Urbanism (New York: McGraw-Hill, 1999), pp. 89–96.

15. See, for example, Henry G. Cisneros, ed., *Interwoven Destinies: Cities and the Nation* (New York: W.W. Norton, 1993); Rosabeth Moss Kanter, *World Class: Thriving Locally in the Global Economy* (New York: Simon & Schuster, 1995); Henry G. Cisneros and Marc A. Weiss, *America's New Economy and the Challenge of the Cities: A HUD Report on Metropolitan Economic Strategy* (Washington, D.C.: U.S. Dept. of Housing and Urban Development, 1996); Henry G. Cisneros and Marc A. Weiss, "The Wealth of Regions and the Challenge of Cities, *The Regionalist,* Winter 1997, pp. 42–45; Richard Monteilh and Marc A. Weiss, *The Economic Resurgence of Washington, DC: Citizens Plan for Prosperity in the 21st Century* (Washington, D.C.: District of Columbia Department of Housing and Community Development, 1998); and David Rusk, *Inside Game/Outside Game: Winning Strategies for Saving Urban America* (Washington, D.C.: Brookings Institution Press, 1999). The special issue of *The Regionalist* published in winter 1997 is devoted to Initiatives for America's Regions, with 20 key articles by metropolitan leaders and experts.

Bibliography

The Colonial Period to the Late 1800s

Abrams, Charles. *Revolution in Land*. New York: Harper, 1939.

Akin, Edward N. *Flagler: Rockefeller Partner and Florida Baron*. Kent, Ohio: Kent State Univ. Press, 1988.

Blackmar, Elizabeth. *Manhattan for Rent, 1785–1850*. Ithaca, N.Y.: Cornell Univ. Press, 1989.

Dumke, Glenn S. *The Boom of the Eighties in Southern California*. San Marino, Calif.: Huntington Library, 1944.

Ely, Richard T., and George S. Wehrwein. *Land Economics*. New York: Macmillan, 1940.

Fogelson, Robert M. *The Fragmented Metropolis: Los Angeles, 1880–1930*. Cambridge, Mass.: Harvard Univ. Press, 1967.

Friedricks, William B. *Henry E. Huntington and the Creation of Southern California*. Columbus: Ohio State Univ. Press, 1992.

Gates, Paul W. *History of Public Land Law Development*. Washington, D.C.: U.S. Government Printing Office, 1968.

Hartog, Hendrik. *Public Property and Private Law: The Corporation of the City of New York in American Law, 1730–1870*. Chapel Hill: Univ. of North Carolina Press, 1983.

Hoyt, Homer. *One Hundred Years of Land Values in Chicago: The Relationship of the Growth of Chicago to the Rise in Its Land Values, 1830–1933*. Chicago: Univ. of Chicago Press, 1933.

Hurd, Richard M. *Principles of City Land Values*. New York: Real Estate Record and Guide, 1903.

Jackson, Kenneth T. *Crabgrass Frontier: The Suburbanization of the United States*. New York: Oxford Univ. Press, 1985.

——. *The Encyclopedia of New York City*. New Haven, Conn.: Yale Univ. Press, 1995.

Keating, Ann Durkin. *Building Chicago: Suburban Developers and the Creating of a Divided Metropolis*. Columbus: Ohio State Univ. Press, 1988.

Lubove, Roy. *The Progressives and the Slums: Tenement House Reform in New York City, 1890–1917*. Pittsburgh: Univ. of Pittsburgh Press, 1962.

Moehring, Eugene P. *Public Works and the Patterns of Urban Real Estate Growth in Manhattan, 1835–1894*. New York: Arno Press, 1981.

Platt, Harold L. *City Building in the New South: The Growth of Public Services in Houston, Texas, 1830–1910*. Philadelphia: Temple Univ. Press, 1983.

Rachlis, Eugene, and John E. Marqusee. *The Land Lords*. New York: Random House, 1963.

Real Estate Record Association. *A History of Real Estate, Building, and Architecture in New York City*. New York: Real Estate Record and Guide, 1898.

Reps, John W. *The Making of Urban America: A History of City Planning in the United States*. Princeton, N.J.: Princeton Univ. Press, 1965.

Riis, Jacob. *How the Other Half Lives: Studies among the Tenements of New York*. New York: Scribner's, 1890.

Robbins, Roy M. *Our Landed Heritage: The Public Domain, 1776–1936*. 2d ed. Lincoln: Univ. of Nebraska Press, 1976.

Robinson, W.W. *Land in California: The Story of Mission Lands, Ranchos, Squatters, Mining Claims, Railroad Grants, Land Scrip, Homesteads*. Berkeley: Univ. of California Press, 1948.

Rosen, Christine Meisner. *The Limits of Power: Great Fires and the Process of City Growth in America*. New York: Cambridge Univ. Press, 1986.

Sakolski, A.M. *The Great American Land Bubble: The Amazing Story of Land-Grabbing, Speculations, and Booms from Colonial Days to the Present Time*. New York: Harper, 1932.

Smith, Arthur D. Howden. *John Jacob Astor: Landlord of New York*. Philadelphia: Lippincott, 1929.

Taylor, George R. *The Transportation Revolution, 1815–1860*. New York: Harper, 1968.

Thomas, Dana L. *Lords of the Land: The Triumphs and Scandals of America's Real Estate Barons from Early Times to the Present*. New York: Putnam's, 1977.

Vanderblue, Homer B. "The Florida Land Boom." *Journal of Land and Public Utility Economics* 3:2 (May 1927): 113–31.

———. "The Florida Land Boom." *Journal of Land and Public Utility Economics* 3:3 (August 1927): 252–69.

Warner, Sam Bass, Jr. *Streetcar Suburbs: The Process of Growth in Boston, 1870–1900*. Cambridge, Mass.: Harvard Univ. Press, 1962.

Weiss, Marc A. "Real Estate History: An Overview and Research Agenda." *Business History Review* 63:2 (Summer 1989): 241–82.

———. *The Rise of the Community Builders: The American Real Estate Industry and Urban Land Planning*. New York: Columbia Univ. Press, 1987.

Wolf, Peter. *Land in America: Its Value, Use, and Control*. New York: Pantheon, 1981.

Wright, Carroll D. *The Slums of Baltimore, Chicago, New York, and Philadelphia*. Seventh Special Report of the Commissioner of Labor. Washington, D.C.: U.S. Government Printing Office, 1894.

Wyckoff, William. *The Developer's Frontier: The Making of the Western New York Landscape*. New Haven, Conn.: Yale Univ. Press, 1988.

The Late 1800s to World War II

Beito, David T. *Taypayers in Revolt: Tax Resistance during the Great Depression*. Chapel Hill: Univ. of North Carolina Press, 1989.

Bishir, Catherine W., Charlotte V. Brown, Carl R. Lounsbury, and Ernest H. Wood III. *Architects and Builders in North Carolina: A History of the Practice of Building*. Chapel Hill: Univ. of North Carolina Press, 1990.

Blackford, Mausel G. *The Lost Dream: Businessmen and City Planning on the Pacific Coast, 1890–1920*. Columbus: Ohio State Univ. Press, 1993.

Burgess, Patricia. *Planning for the Private Interest: Land Use Controls and Residential Patterns in Columbus, Ohio, 1900–1970*. Columbus: Ohio State Univ. Press, 1994.

Caro, Robert A. *The Power Broker: Robert Moses and the Fall of New York*. New York: Random House, 1974.

Colean, Miles L. *American Housing: Problems and Prospects*. New York: Twentieth Century Fund, 1944.

Community Builders Council. *Community Builders Handbook*. Washington, D.C.: ULI–the Urban Land Institute, 1947.

Cranz, Galen. *The Politics of Park Design: A History of Urban Parks in America*. Cambridge, Mass.: MIT Press, 1982.

Cromley, Elizabeth Collins. *Alone Together: A History of New York's Early Apartments*. Ithaca, N.Y.: Cornell Univ. Press, 1990.

Davies, Pearl Janet. *Real Estate in American History*. Washington, D.C.: Public Affairs Press, 1958.

Eskew, Garnett Laidlaw. *Of Land and Men: The Birth and Growth of an Idea*. Washington, D.C.: ULI–the Urban Land Institute, 1959.

Ewalt, Josephine Hedges. *A Business Reborn: The Savings and Loan Story, 1930–1960*. Chicago: American Savings and Loan Institute, 1962.

Fisher, Ernest M. *Urban Real Estate Markets: Characteristics and Financing*. New York: National Bureau of Economic Research, 1951.

Foster, Mark S. *Henry J. Kaiser: Builder in the Modern American West*. Austin: Univ. of Texas Press, 1989.

Gibbs, Kenneth Turney. *Business Architectural Imagery in America, 1870–1930*. Ann Arbor, Mich.: UMI Research Press, 1984.

Goldberger, Paul. *The Skyscraper*. New York: Knopf, 1981.

Golden Book of Wanamaker Stores. Philadelphia: John Wanamaker, 1911.

Grebler, Leo, David M. Blank, and Louis Winnick. *Capital Formation in Residential Real Estate: Trends and Prospects*. Princeton, N.J.: Princeton Univ. Press, 1956.

Howard, Ebenezer. *Garden Cities of Tomorrow*. London: Faber & Faber, 1945.

Hoyt, Homer. *The Structure and Growth of Residential Neighborhoods in American Cities*. Washington, D.C.: Federal Housing Administration, 1939.

Hubbard, Theodora Kimball, and Henry Vincent Hubbard. *Our Cities Today and Tomorrow.* Cambridge, Mass.: Harvard Univ. Press, 1929.

Hurd, Richard M. *Principles of City Land Values.* New York: Real Estate Record and Guide, 1903.

Jackson, Kenneth T. *Crabgrass Frontier: The Suburbanization of the United States.* New York: Oxford Univ. Press, 1985.

——. *The Encyclopedia of New York City.* New Haven, Conn.: Yale Univ. Press, 1995.

James, Marquis. *The Metropolitan Life: A Study in Business Growth.* New York: Viking, 1947.

Kahn, Judd. *Imperial San Francisco: Politics and Planning in an American City, 1897–1906.* Lincoln: Univ. of Nebraska Press, 1979.

Klaman, Saul B. *The Postwar Rise of Mortgage Companies.* New York: National Bureau of Economic Research, 1959.

Krinsky, Carol Herselle. *Rockefeller Center.* New York: Oxford Univ. Press, 1978.

Lotchin, Roger W. *Fortress California, 1910–1961: From Warfare to Welfare.* New York: Oxford Univ. Press, 1992.

Mayer, Harold M., and Richard C. Wade. *Chicago: Growth of a Metropolis.* Chicago: Univ. of Chicago Press, 1969.

Morton, J.E. *Urban Mortgage Lending: Comparative Markets and Experience.* Princeton, N.J.: Princeton Univ. Press, 1956.

Rabinowitz, Alan. *The Real Estate Gamble: Lessons from 50 Years of Boom and Bust.* New York: AMACOM, 1980.

Schactman, Tom. *Skyscraper Dreams: The Great Real Estate Dynasties of New York.* Boston: Little, Brown, 1991.

Schaffer, Daniel. *Garden Cities for America: The Radburn Experience.* Philadelphia: Templc Univ. Press, 1982.

Scott, Mel. *American City Planning since 1890.* Berkeley: Univ. of California Press, 1969.

Shultz, Earle, and Walter Simmons. *Offices in the Sky.* Indianapolis: Bobbs-Merrill, 1959.

Starrett, William A. *Skyscrapers and the Men Who Build Them.* New York: Scribner's, 1928.

Stein, Clarence S. *Toward New Towns for America.* New York: Reinhold, 1957.

Stern, Robert A.M., Gregory Gilmartin, and Thomas Mellins. *New York, 1930: Architecture and Urbanism between the Two World Wars.* New York: Rizzoli, 1987.

Straus, Nathan. *The Seven Myths of Housing.* New York: Knopf, 1944.

Taylor, Waverly, Hugh Potter, and W.P. Atkinson. *History of the National Association of Home Builders of the United States.* Washington, D.C.: National Association of Home Builders, 1958.

Teaford, Jon C. *The Unheralded Triumph: City Government in America, 1870–1900.* Baltimore: Johns Hopkins Univ. Press, 1984.

Thompson-Starrett Company. "A Census of Skyscrapers." *American City* 41 (September 1929): 130.

Walker, Robert A. *The Planning Function in Urban Government.* Chicago: Univ. of Chicago Press, 1950.

Ward, David, and Olivier Zunz. *The Landscape of Modernity.* New York: Russell Sage, 1992.

Weber, Adna Ferrin. *The Growth of Cities in the Nineteenth Century: A Study in Statistics.* New York: Macmillan, 1899.

Weiss, Marc A. "Density and Intervention: New York's Planning Traditions." In *The Landscape of Modernity: Essays on New York City, 1900–1940,* ed. David Ward and Oliver Zunz. New York: Russell Sage Foundation, 1992.

——. "Richard T. Ely and the Contribution of Economic Research to National Housing Policy, 1920–1940." *Urban Studies* (February 1989): 115–26.

——. *The Rise of the Community Builders: The American Real Estate Industry and Urban Land Planning.* New York: Columbia Univ. Press, 1987.

Willis, Carol. *Form Follows Finance: Skyscrapers and Skylines in New York and Chicago.* Princeton, N.J.: Princeton Architectural Press, 1995.

Wood, Edith Elmer. *The Housing of the Unskilled Wage Earner.* New York: Macmillan, 1919.

——. *Recent Trends in American Housing.* New York: Macmillan, 1931.

——. *Slums and Blighted Areas in the United States.* PWA, Housing Division Bulletin No. 1. Washington, D.C.: U.S. Government Printing Office, 1935.

Woodbury, Coleman. *The Trend of Multifamily Housing in Cities in the United States.* Chicago: Institute for Economic Research, 1931.

Worley, William S. *J.C. Nichols and the Shaping of Kansas City: Innovation in Planned Residential Communities.* Columbia: Univ. of Missouri Press, 1990.

Wright, Gwendolyn. *Moralism and the Model Home: Domestic Architecture and Cultural Conflict in Chicago, 1873–1913.* Chicago: Univ. of Chicago Press, 1980.

Post–World War II to the Present

Abrams, Charles. *The City Is the Frontier*. New York: Harper & Row, 1965.

Alterman, Rachelle, ed. *Private Supply of Public Services: Evaluation of Real Estate Exactions, Linkage, and Alternative Land Policies*. New York: New York Univ. Press, 1988.

Barrett, Wayne. *Trump: The Deals and the Downfall*. New York: Harper Collins, 1992.

Bauer, Catherine. "The Dreary Deadlock of Public Housing." *Architectural Forum* (May 1957): 140.

Beauregard, Robert A., ed. *Atop the Urban Hierarchy*. Totowa, N.J.: Rowman & Littlefield, 1989.

Boyte, Harry C. *The Backyard Revolution: Understanding the New Citizen Movement*. Philadelphia: Temple Univ. Press, 1980.

Bratt, Rachel G. *Rebuilding a Low-Income Housing Policy*. Philadelphia: Temple Univ. Press, 1989.

Breckenfeld, Gurney. *Columbia and the New Cities*. New York: Ives Washburn, 1971.

Caro, Robert A. *The Power Broker: Robert Moses and the Fall of New York*. New York: Random House, 1974.

Checkoway, Barry. *The Politics of Postwar Suburban Development*. Berkeley: Univ. of California, Childhood and Government Project, 1977.

Cisneros, Henry G., ed. *Interwoman Destinies: Cities and the Nation*. New York: Norton, 1993.

Cisneros, Henry G., and Marc A. Weiss. *America's New Economy and the Challenge of the Cities*. Washington, D.C.: U.S. Dept. of Housing and Urban Development, 1996.

———. *New American Neighborhoods: Building Home-ownership Zones to Revitalize Our Nation's Communities*. Washington, D.C.: U.S. Dept. of Housing and Urban Development, 1996.

———. "The Wealth of Regions and the Challenge of Cities." *The Regionalist* (Winter 1997): 42–45.

Congress for the New Urbanism. *Charter of the New Urbanism*. New York: McGraw-Hill, 1999.

Downs, Anthony. *The Revolution in Real Estate Finance*. Washington, D.C.: Brookings Institution, 1985.

Edel, Matthew, Elliott D. Sclar, and Daniel Luria. *Shaky Palaces: Homeownership and Social Mobility in Boston's Suburbanization*. New York: Columbia Univ. Press, 1984.

Eichler, Ned. *The Merchant Builders*. Cambridge, Mass.: MIT Press, 1982.

———. *The Thrift Debacle*. Berkeley: Univ. of California Press, 1989.

Feagin, Joe R., and Robert Parker. *Building American Cities: The Urban Real Estate Game*. Englewood Cliffs, N.J.: Prentice-Hall, 1990.

Fisher, Ernest M. *Urban Real Estate Markets: Characteristics and Financing*. New York: National Bureau of Economic Research, 1951.

Frantz, Douglas. *From the Ground Up: The Business of Building in an Age of Money*. Berkeley: Univ. of California Press, 1993.

Frieden, Bernard J., and Lynne B. Sagalyn. *Downtown, Inc.: How America Rebuilds Cities*. Cambridge, Mass.: MIT Press, 1989.

Friedman, Lawrence M. *Government and Slum Housing: A Century of Frustration*. Chicago: Rand McNally, 1968.

Garreau, Joel. *Edge City: Life on the New Frontier*. New York: Doubleday, 1992.

Gelfand, Mark I. *A Nation of Cities: The Federal Government and Urban America, 1933–1965*. New York: Oxford Univ. Press, 1975.

Goldberger, Paul. *The Skyscraper*. New York: Knopf, 1981.

Goldenberg, Susan. *Men of Property: The Canadian Developers Who Are Buying America*. Toronto: Personal Library, 1981.

Goodkin, Lewis M. *When Real Estate and Homebuilding Become Big Business: Mergers, Acquisitions, and Joint Ventures*. Boston: Cahners Books, 1974.

Gottlieb, Manuel. *Long Swings in Urban Development*. New York: National Bureau of Economic Research, 1976.

Grebler, Leo. *Large-Scale Housing and Real Estate Firms: Analysis of a New Business Enterprise*. New York: Praeger, 1973.

Grebler, Leo, David M. Blank, and Louis Winnick. *Capital Formation in Residential Real Estate: Trends and Prospects*. Princeton, N.J.: Princeton Univ. Press, 1956.

Griffin, Nathaniel M. *Irvine: Genesis of a New Community*. Washington, D.C.: ULI–the Urban Land Institute, 1974.

Haar, Charles M., and Jerold S. Kayden. *Zoning and the American Dream: Promises Still to Keep*. Chicago: Planners Press, 1989.

Hayden, Dolores. *Redesigning the American Dream: The Future of Housing, Work, and Family Life*. New York: Norton, 1984.

Hays, R. Allen. *The Federal Government and Urban Housing: Ideology and Change in Public Policy.* Albany: State Univ. of New York Press, 1985.

Hays, Samuel P. *Beauty, Health, and Permanence: Environmental Politics in the United States, 1955–1985.* New York: Cambridge Univ. Press, 1987.

Helper, Rose. *Racial Policies and Practices of Real Estate Brokers.* Minneapolis: Univ. of Minnesota Press, 1969.

Hoyt, Homer. *The Urban Real Estate Cycle: Performances and Prospects.* Technical Bulletin No. 38. Washington, D.C.: ULI–the Urban Land Institute, 1950.

Jackson, Kenneth T. *Crabgrass Frontier: The Suburbanization of the United States.* New York: Oxford Univ. Press, 1985.

———. *The Encyclopedia of New York City.* New Haven, Conn.: Yale Univ. Press, 1995.

Kanter, Rosabeth Moss. *World Class: Thriving Locally in a Global Economy.* New York: Simon & Schuster, 1995.

Katz, Peter. *The New Urbanism: Toward an Architecture of Community.* New York: McGraw-Hill, 1994.

Keats, John. *The Crack in the Picture Window.* Boston: Houghton Mifflin, 1957.

Lachman, M. Leanne. *Decade to Decade: U.S. Real Estate Adapts to Revolution in Finance and Demographic Evolution.* New York: Schroder Real Estate Associates, 1988.

Laventhol & Horwath. *Hotel/Motel Development.* Washington, D.C.: ULI–the Urban Land Institute, 1984.

Lo, Clarence Y.H. *Small Property versus Big Government: Social Origins of the Property Tax Revolt.* Berkeley: Univ. of California Press, 1990.

Long, Clarence D., Jr. *Building Cycles and the Theory of Investment.* Princeton, N.J.: Princeton Univ. Press, 1940.

McMahan, John. *Property Development.* 2d ed. New York: McGraw-Hill, 1989.

Mayer, Martin. *The Builders: Houses, People, Neighborhoods, Governments, Money.* New York: Norton, 1978.

Moehring, Eugene P. *Resort City in the Sunbelt: Las Vegas, 1930–1970.* Las Vegas: Univ. of Nevada Press, 1989.

Mollenkopf, John H. *The Contested City.* Princeton, N.J.: Princeton Univ. Press, 1983.

Monteilh, Richard, and Marc A. Weiss. *The Economic Resurgence of Washington, DC: Citizens Plan for Prosperity in the 21st Century.* Washington, D.C.: D.C. Dept. of Housing and Community Development, 1998.

Morgan, George T., Jr., and John O. King. *The Woodlands: New Community Development, 1964–1983.* College Station: Texas A&M Univ. Press, 1987.

Plunz, Richard. *A History of Housing in New York City: Dwelling Type and Social Change in the American Metropolis.* New York: Columbia Univ. Press, 1990.

Portman, John C., and Jonathan Barnett. *The Architect as Developer.* New York: McGraw-Hill, 1976.

Real Estate Research Corporation. *Tall Office Buildings in the United States.* Washington, D.C.: ULI–the Urban Land Institute, 1985.

Robin, Peggy. *Saving the Neighborhood: You Can Fight Developers and Win.* Washington, D.C.: Preservation Press, 1993.

Rusk, David. *Inside Game/Outside Game: Winning Strategies for Saving Urban America.* Washington, D.C.: Brookings Institution Press, 1999.

Sabbagh, Karl. *Skyscraper: The Making of a Building.* New York: Viking Penguin, 1990.

Seligman, Daniel. "The Enduring Slums." In *The Exploding Metropolis*, by the editors of *Fortune*. Garden City, N.Y.: Doubleday, 1957.

Sigafoos, Robert A. *Corporate Real Estate Development.* Lexington, Mass.: Lexington Books, 1976.

Sobel, Robert. *Trammell Crow, Master Builder: The Story of America's Largest Real Estate Empire.* New York: Wiley, 1989.

Teaford, Jon C. *The Rough Road to Renaissance: Urban Revitalization in America, 1940–1985.* Baltimore: Johns Hopkins Univ. Press, 1990.

Trump, Donald J., with Tony Schwartz. *Trump: The Art of the Deal.* New York: Random House, 1987.

Walsh, Annmarie Hauck. *The Public's Business: The Politics and Practices of Government Corporations.* Cambridge, Mass.: MIT Press, 1978.

Weaver, Robert C. *The Urban Complex: Human Values in Urban Life.* Garden City, N.Y.: Doubleday, 1964.

Weiss, Marc A. "Developing and Financing the 'Garden Metropolis': Urban Planning and Housing Policy in Twentieth Century America." *Planning Perspectives* (September 1990): 307–19.

———. "Marketing and Financing Homeownership: Mortgage Lending and Public Policy in the United States, 1918–1989." *Business and Economic History* (1989): 109–18.

———. "The Origins and Legacy of Urban Renewal." In *Federal Housing Policy and Programs: Past and Present*, ed. J. Paul Mitchell. New Brunswick, N.J.: Rutgers Univ. Center for Urban Policy Research, 1985.

——. "The Politics of Real Estate Cycles." *Urban Land* 51:3 (March 1992): 33-35.

——. *The Rise of the Community Builders: The American Real Estate Industry and Urban Land Planning.* New York: Columbia Univ. Press, 1987.

——. "Skyscraper Zoning: New York's Pioneering Role." *Journal of the American Planning Association* (Spring 1992): 201–12.

Weiss, Marc A., and John T. Metzger. *Neighborhood Lending Agreements: Negotiating and Financing Community Development.* Cambridge, Mass.: Lincoln Institute of Land Policy, 1988.

Weiss, Marc A., and John W. Watts. "Community Builders and Community Associations: The Role of Real Estate Developers in Private Residential Governance." In *Residential Community Associations: Private Governments in the Intergovernmental System.* Washington, D.C.: U.S. Advisory Commission on Intergovernmental Relations, 1989.

Wenzlick, Roy. *The Coming Boom in Real Estate.* New York: Simon & Schuster, 1936.

Whyte, William H., Jr. *The Organization Man.* New York: Simon & Schuster, 1956.

Zeckendorf, William, with Edward McCreary. *The Autobiography of William Zeckendorf.* New York: Holt, Rinehart & Winston, 1970.

Some of the best ideas seem so simple that people assume they appear like the proverbial light bulb over cartoon characters' heads. Unfortunately, that "ah, ha!" experience is rare. Instead, most ideas are a combination of intuition, interest, creativity, and deliberate, rigorous market research. Developers need new ideas so their firms can stay in business. Sometimes opportunities result from the developer's deliberate efforts. At other times, an almost unconscious processing of information leads to ideas for the next development. At still other times, opportunities seem to present themselves from nowhere.

No matter how the ideas for the next development come about, developers have to know when to go ahead with those ideas or when to abandon them before too much time and money are invested in a losing proposition. The next three chapters look at the formation of ideas in general and in the context of development in particular (stage one) and how and when the decisions are made to refine the idea and move forward (stage two). Market research is a critical element in the decision-making process, just as it is throughout the entire development process.

Part IV
Ideas

Chapter 10

Stage One: Inception of an Idea

With the historical evolution of the public/ private partnership clearly in mind, we are ready to move forward with stage one of the development process—inception of an idea. Of all the activities that constitute real estate development, generating successful prospective ideas for projects should be the least mechanical and most creative. The excitement of identifying an unfilled human need and creating a product (and a marketing campaign) to fill it at a profit is the stimulus that drives development—even if the product is as technically uncomplicated as self-storage units or pads for mobile homes. The best ideas result in products that serve the user well and add value to the community, and doing it at a profit is part of what distinguishes good development from poor development. It is not possible to manage your way out of a bad development idea, so everything that follows is predicated on getting stage one right.

Where do developers get their ideas? How do they know which ideas deserve further analysis and which do not? No magic formula exists for generating good development ideas, because everyone receives different information and processes it differently. The spark comes from the way different pieces of information are put together to solve a problem—as well as from the quality and uniqueness of the information itself. One thing that *is* certain is that developers generally need background information to make the most of good ideas. Such information, along with experience, results in what is often called "a feel for the market." This feel does not earn the developer any money, but, without it, a developer is likely to lose money and do a disservice to the community.

Although generating development ideas might often be thought of as unpredictable and intuitive, in truth, a portion of generating ideas is methodical and calculated. Developers need to plan future projects to keep their firms in business. Thorough market research has become as important as a developer's drive to complete a project. Successful developers are rigorous in their planning but not so regimented as to lose the creative spark.

Little human experience and observation go to waste when players try to understand real estate markets. Developers, members of the development team, investors, regulators, and policy makers can be most effective and successful if they look at all knowledge (history, current conditions, and forecasts) as potentially useful when envisioning new projects. In a sense, the development players unconsciously perform market research during almost all their waking moments when they read, drive, eat, play, meditate, or interact with other people. They also perform more structured market research when they rigorously analyze the regional economy and local population growth, employment figures, zoning provisions, traffic counts, occupancy rates, and consumer surveys. Curiosity, interest, and observation enhance the formal approaches to generating ideas.

This chapter explains a developer's need to understand the total marketing concept: 1) finding out what customers want, 2) producing it, and 3) persuading customers to purchase or rent it. It provides a decision framework in which the development team's creative juices can flow productively into an idea that will become reality.

Although marketing and market research underlie every stage of the development process, the basics of marketing and market research are highlighted at four points in the development process (see Figure 10-1).

As a starting point to the eight stages of the development process, this chapter covers the following topics:

- The different motivations behind ideas;
- The back-of-the-envelope pro forma;
- Generating ideas through strategic decision making and market research;
- Techniques for generating ideas;
- Words of warning and signposts; and
- Risk control during stage one of the real estate development process.

The two case studies introduced in Chapter 1 are continued, illustrating stage one of the development process.

Different Motivations behind Ideas

Although idea inception is usually the fuzziest stage in the real estate development process, it can also be the most enjoyable stage—even for individuals who are compulsive about order. Simply put, it is exciting to think about creating a new built environment. In fact, a developer frequently devotes 20 to 30 percent of the time required for a project to idea inception. Every new insight serves as a catalyst, which, when melded with the developer's background and experience, generates

still more ideas. In this way, the developer moves through stage one of the development process.

This chapter characterizes developers as professionals constantly involved in informal brainstorming; they search their background and current experience for an idea that offers potential. During the development process, however, ideas emerge in many different ways. For example, developers often discover a site looking for a use. For one reason or another, the owners of a particular parcel, whether public or private, want the site to be developed, thereby creating possibilities for the developer. Sometimes the site is already developed and the existing structure needs to be redeveloped. Perhaps a building stands on the site and must remain, but the owner is seeking a new use for the building. Or perhaps the existing building will be expanded or additional buildings built on the site. Alternatively, developers might encounter a use looking for a site, which is frequently the case when corporations want to expand, introduce a new product, or restructure their operations, thereby creating a need for constructed space. Finally, powerful forces of the capital market might be at work, setting capital to look for a development opportunity.

In all three cases, the developer must have the background—relevant experience in development and familiarity with the latest changes in the industry—to be able to respond to the stimulus. Successful developers also have extensive contacts who can function as a sounding board for new ideas and suggest potential members of the development team.

Figure 10-1

Market Principles and Market Research Pervade the Development Process

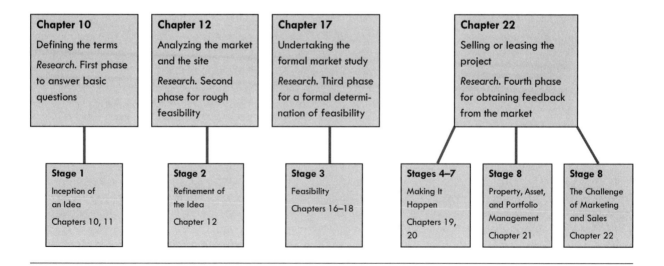

Profile **James J. Chaffin, Jr.**

President, Chaffin/Light Associates
Snowmass Village, Colorado
Spring Island, South Carolina

Jim Chaffin is a cofounder (with James W. Light) and president of Chaffin/Light Associates, a firm that specializes in developing resort and recreational communities. For 30 years, Chaffin has been involved in the development of communities across the country, beginning with the Sea Pines Company at Hilton Head Island, South Carolina (Sea Pines Plantation, Hilton Head Plantation, Amelia Island, Florida, Kiawah Island, South Carolina, Palmas del Mar, Puerto Rico, Brandermill in Richmond, Virginia, and many more). With his partner Jim Light, he has gone on to develop Snowmass Village in Colorado, the Semiahmoo resort in Washington, Spring Island and Callawassie Island in South Carolina, and most recently the Roaring Fork Club near Aspen, Colorado. Chaffin is active in several professional and community organizations, including ULI, the National Real Estate Advisory Council of the Trust for Public Land, the Board of Managers of the University of Virginia, and local arts and education groups.

Generating Ideas for New Projects

Chaffin believes that the process for generating new ideas should be both systematic and creative. "To have one without the other is a big mistake. Developers should know the fundamentals of market analysis and be able to dream." Even though some poor ideas are successful because of circumstance or market aberrations, Chaffin believes that developers who are aware of the economic, social, political, and environmental conditions of the global community will come up with the best product ideas or "create the most stimulating places for people to live and work."

Now that Chaffin has a solid track record as a developer, he finds that many deals come to him. Well over half his opportunities involve a site that somebody wants developed, about 20 percent come about because he or his partner has an idea that demands a site, and another 10 percent represent capital coming to the firm in search of an investment.

Chaffin/Light's newest project is Roaring Fork Club near Aspen, Colorado. This golf and hunting club is designed with sustainability in mind. A very limited number of homes are planned, and an environmental trust has been established to ensure the continuation of environmentally sensitive practices in the area.

Chaffin's starting point in the process of generating ideas is to think about his previous experience. "Who have been my customers in the past? What did they expect? Was I able to deliver? What have I learned from those experiences?" The next step is to examine the economic, sociographic, and demographic trends of the area and analyze demand. "Start with the fundamental questions. Who are my potential customers? How many? How fast will they respond? Who else is competing for the same customers and how are they doing? And so on."

From Sea Pines to Spring Island

Like many major recreational community developers of his generation, Chaffin got his start working with Charles Fraser (the same Fraser of Fraser Morrow Daniels) at Sea Pines Plantation on Hilton Head Island, South Carolina.

continued on next page

Jim Chaffin, Jr., a resort and recreational developer responsible for Snowmass Village, Colorado, Spring Island, South Carolina, and Semiahmoo in Blaine, Washington, among others, believes that the best development ideas come from creative dreaming balanced by knowledge of the industry and trends—economic, sociographic, psychographic, and demographic.

Even though the developer is typically the driving force during the subsequent stages of development, landowners, space users, or sources of capital are periodically the catalysts for development ideas. For example, organizations such as railroads and paper companies that own vast tracts of land have created development subsidiaries to plan and develop selected sites. Many

That project set new standards for recreational communities by putting aside 1,200 of the development's total 5,200 acres for open space, establishing architectural controls on building design, protecting environmentally sensitive areas, and developing extensive outdoor amenities such as golf courses, tennis courts, marinas, and walking/cycling trails.

Chaffin then went on with his partner Jim Light (also a former employee of Sea Pines) to develop resort and private club communities in the Colorado Rockies, the Pacific Northwest, southern California, and the South Carolina coast. Their interest in conservation led to Spring Island, a 3,000-acre high-end golf/residential island community off the coast of South Carolina. The Spring Island Company has preserved one-third of the island and with it a plethora of wildlife, including bald eagles, wood storks, deer, quail, fox squirrels, and a 600-acre live oak forest. "When I visited the island for the first time Thanksgiving weekend 1988, I was awed by its natural beauty and so frustrated to know that the original developer had approvals to build 5,500 homes on the island that when the developer couldn't fulfill his options, we decided to grab it." Chaffin and Light have developed a total of 410 lots on the island, thereby preserving the project's most important amenity—nature. They also created the nonprofit Spring Island Trust to maintain a 1,000-acre nature preserve and manage a staff of working naturalists and their nature laboratory, supported by a 1.5 percent transfer fee on the sale of all lots to perpetuity.

Although Chaffin's associates thought he was a little idealistic to undertake Spring Island and cautioned him to wait until he was approaching retirement before indulging himself in such a project, he went ahead based on his knowledge of the market and his gut feeling. "I really had a feeling that people were moving back to basic values. Families wanted to be outdoors in a real place, sharing real experiences and safe adventures." His goal was to complete a high-quality project that is sustainable and ecologically sound and to set an example for other developers. The community has received many national awards for its environmental stewardship, and it has been financially successful ("striking a balance between environmental sensitivity and economic sensibility"). Several developers are already using Spring Island as a model for developments in other locations.

The Chaffin/Light team's current project is Roaring Fork Club near Aspen, Colorado. A family fly fishing and golf club, the project has limited residential development to 45 log cabins, sensitively located around the golf course and along 1.75 miles of "golf medal" fishing waters. Similar to Spring Island, Roaring Fork Club has established a 501(c)(3) environmental trust for environmental programs in the Roaring Fork Valley.

Advice for Would-Be Developers

"I think a liberal arts education with a graduate degree in business or law or real estate is most beneficial to a developer for several reasons. Developers have to be able to communicate well. They have to be interested in the entire planet and must be aware of what's going on in the world, to be good observers and listeners so they can see and hear what the market is telling them. They need discipline and passion, persistence and courage, all with a healthy dose of humility. We're all deal junkies. We look at a deal and think that we can make it work. But no matter how great the opportunity, you have to be able to admit not having the capital, personnel, experience, or energy to take on a project that's not right for you. And for that you need discipline and rigor."

Chaffin's strongest advice to students: "Don't ever think you are as smart as everybody thinks you are during the good times because you're not going to want to believe you're as dumb as they think you are during the bad times." ∎

---

large corporations have established real estate units or subsidiaries to develop space as well as to manage their leased space. Some have gone so far as to spin off a separate company to develop and manage their extensive real estate holdings. Although the initial push comes from many sources, eventually someone (inside or outside the corporation) must take charge and become the developer.

It is, of course, possible for an idea—a purely entrepreneurial idea—to spring from the developer's own imagination. Often, however, a combination of motivations triggers a development idea. John Portman, for example, generated the idea for a new form of development in his initial Hyatt Hotel from his belief that interior space could be designed to serve people better and that the existing hotel market could be expanded if space served people in new ways. He applied his idea to urban renewal sites in Atlanta and San Francisco (see Chapter 14) to create new uses appropriate for the sites. When developer Joseph Alfandre acquired 352 acres outside Washington, D.C., he knew he wanted something different from the typical suburban communities that were being re-created across the United States. No land planning firms he went to could satisfy his desire to do something unusual on the site he called Kentlands. Then he met architect and planner Andres Duany, with whom he conducted a seven-day charrette to develop design and planning principles for the site. With participation from citizens and political bodies, the developer and architect came up with a surprisingly dense neotraditional site plan on a modified grid system with no culs-de-sac or on-street parking, and shared open space that defines the character of the community.[1]

Although an initial idea may be rough, James Graaskamp's "situs"—all the ways a project affects its surrounding environment as well as all the effects of that environment on the project—is the key concern. The type of project must generally fit the location, which, in turn, must fit the tenant and fit the financing. Ultimately, this fit usually reshapes the original idea, as

demonstrated in the next several chapters. And when "fit" and "reshaping" are being considered, it is important not to lose sight of ethical obligations. As the pressures of the development process intensify, the developer must remain alert to any moral hazards lurking in the substructure.

The Back-of-the-Envelope Pro Forma

Stage one of the development process ends when the developer tests the new idea with a "back-of-the-envelope" pro forma—a simple comparison of value and cost. At this stage, ideas are not sufficiently refined to be subjected to the type of detailed analysis that incorporates computerized discounted cash flow. And because most ideas generated at this stage are never carried out, the developer cannot justify the expenditure of a great deal of money or time to analyze each idea's preliminary feasibility.

To prepare a quick pro forma, the developer typically uses his concept of the target tenant to estimate how much rent the tenant might be willing to pay for a particular type of space with appropriate services in a particular location. The projection consists of a rough estimate of income per square foot and operating expenses per square foot without detailed attention to

The developer's idea for the American Visionary Art Museum (AVAM) in Baltimore, Maryland, was to promote self-taught artistry and to demonstrate that creative architecture combined with social objectives can have a positive effect on the community. The 33,000-square-foot AVAM—a ULI 1998 Award for Excellence winner—was built on a formerly contaminated industrial site and combines new construction with the adaptive reuse of an existing industrial building in Baltimore's Inner Harbor.

the level of tenant improvements, cost escalations, length of lease, and the many other factors that become important during the later stages of development decision making. The next step is to multiply the project's leasable square feet by the estimated revenue per square foot. The developer then subtracts the projected operating expenses and multiplies by ten (the inverse of a 10 percent cap rate). This back-of-the-envelope pro forma follows the same format as the one introduced in Chapter 6. It differs only in the level of detail. The rough estimate of value thus inelegantly generated is then compared with a rough estimate of cost, which at this point typically is projected from estimates of what the land might sell for plus site development costs and construction costs per square foot of the proposed structure. If value exceeds cost, at least based on the rough numbers, the idea remains viable. If cost exceeds value, it is back to the drawing board.

For example, consider a project with 200,000 leasable square feet. If expected annual market rental rates were $18.25 per square foot for the proposed tenant and a 93 percent occupancy rate were appropriate, then the owner would collect $16.97 per square foot ($18.25 × 0.93). If expected operating expenses totaled $7.30 per square foot annually for this type of project, then $9.67 ($16.97 – $7.30) represents the project's anticipated net income per square foot. Multiplying $9.67 by 200,000 square feet of leasable space yields $1,934,000 of net income per year. Capitalizing it at 10 percent ($1,934,000 ÷ 0.10) results in a value of $19,340,000. If the land for this project costs $4,000,000, expected site development costs are $500,000, and construction per square foot costs about $95.00 ($19,000,000), then developing the project would total about $23,500,000. The projected cost thus exceeds the value, and the developer would need to search for another site, a higher paying tenant, or, most likely, a better idea.

Like most research-driven activities, the vast majority of ideas do not pass muster. Thus, most of the time, stage one ends with the best possible device to control risk: the decision to stop. The prospect of a "no-go" decision is a fact of life and a natural part of the development process. But the compensation for nine ideas that die on the back of the envelope is one good idea worth refining in stage two.

It is important to note, too, that when developers calculate a back-of-the-envelope pro forma and it looks like a go, it is not a guarantee that the idea will live beyond the next stage. Developers are dreamers, and everything to this point is a rough estimate. Once other players become more closely involved—which occurs upon completion of the back-of-the-envelope

pro forma—they may temper the dream with realities that make it impossible to go ahead with the project.

Generating Ideas through Strategic Decision Making and Market Research

The rise of large development companies, corporate real estate departments, and large numbers of professionals with extensive university training has accelerated the application of strategic planning to the creative side of real property development. This trend is noteworthy given that the public often views developers as freewheelers unfettered by bureaucracy. In fact, as shown in Figure 10-2, market research is a strategic tool applied throughout the development process. Although the specifics of strategic planning are beyond the scope of this book, all members of the development team should appreciate strategic planning's overall framework and aim.

Strategic planning consists of formulating goals (ends) and determining courses of action (using the associated means available) to achieve these goals. The choice of a project affects the development company's organization, and, before deciding on projects, developers should think about how large an organization they want to control, the extent of desired vertical or horizontal integration (the amount of structure they are willing to accept), and the talent, ambition, and money available to the organization. Any idea selected for implementation becomes de facto part of an organizational strategy; in fact, developers can identify specific projects and locations and consider those choices part of the organizational strategy they want to pursue. Ideally, developers should think beforehand about how a particular project might fit into a strategy for their organization. In other words, to use marketing research effectively for a project, developers should have a clear idea of why they want to undertake the project and how much of their money, personnel, and reputation they are willing and able to commit to it. (Note how Graaskamp's 25-year-old definition of feasibility fits easily into a strategic planning framework.)

Organizational strategies differ in detail and formality, depending on the size and focus of the development company. Small developers may have a strategy that exists only in their heads. In contrast, the development arm of a large corporation must usually prepare an organizational strategy for its real estate business that fits into the larger corporate strategy. In such an environment, fairly rigid procedures for making a go/no-go

Figure 10-2
Market Research in the Real Estate Development Process

Stage	Market Research Provides
1 Inception of an Idea	Background for brainstorming, initial information for a back-of-the-envelope pro forma
2 Refinement of the Idea	Specific input for refining the rough idea
3 Feasibility	Input for rigorous market analysis to convince all participants in the process that the development is a feasible project and feasible for them personally
4 Contract Negotiation	Supporting information needed for hard negotiations between the different participants in the process
5 Formal Commitment	Support material for legal documentation
6 Construction	The basis for planning marketing tactics and adapting to changing market conditions during construction. Marketing feedback loop is critical.
7 Completion and Formal Opening	Current market data for implementing the operating plan and ongoing marketing effort
8 Property, Asset, and Portfolio Management	Input for all capital expenditure decisions, leasing and re-leasing, and eventually repositioning the project

decision must be followed. In development, it is hard to separate the strategic idea from the team that will try to implement it. Consequently, it is usually good practice to move quickly from the *what* of the idea to the *how*. To keep the text as readable as possible, however, this chapter focuses on the *what* of strategic planning, with the *how* to follow in subsequent chapters.

Techniques for Generating Ideas

Ideas often appear to arise intuitively; however, certain formal techniques can be used to stimulate creativity. Of the various formal techniques, brainstorming, the nominal group process, the Delphi method, environmental scanning, focus groups, and surveys (or a combination of the types) are those most frequently used to generate and test development ideas. These techniques are sufficiently systematic and precise to help generate ideas without making exorbitant demands on limited time and money.[2]

Brainstorming is a group (or individual) exercise devoted to producing the largest possible number of creative ideas during a given period of time. To encourage an atmosphere of creativity, the group or individual initially accepts every idea, no matter how unusual. Whether pursued in a group or individually, brainstorming should follow several rules: write down every idea, defer judgment on the value of ideas, list as many ideas as possible, and, most important, look for combinations of listed ideas. After a brainstorming session is completed, the development team can study the lists more closely and select the most promising combination of ideas for potential projects.

The *nominal group process* is a technique for establishing priority among ideas identified by a group. It can be used to analyze in more detail ideas generated through brainstorming and is particularly useful when a development team is responsible for achieving consensus about goals and courses of action to achieve those goals. A facilitator lists, clarifies, and screens opinions based on the group's preferences. Members then submit a written, confidential vote on the various alternatives. Preferred projects emerge from the process. The usefulness of nominal group process depends on the developer's willingness to work with a group—

Figure 10-3

The Park and Garage at Post Office Square

This unusual public/private development has transformed an unsightly parking structure in downtown Boston into a major community asset—a much-needed downtown public open space and new underground parking garage. The project eliminated the blight of a badly deteriorated above-grade parking structure, increased the total volume of parking by replacing 750 above-grade spaces with 1,400 underground spaces, and, most important, increased the scarce resource of public open space in a dense urban area. The creative collaboration of public and private interests created a project that dramatically improves the public realm and at the same time provides great utility and value to property owners, tenants, and workers in the surrounding area.

Development Process and Financing

For many years, Boston's financial district was dominated by an aging parking structure in the center of Post Office Square. In 1983, a group of 19 Boston business and civic leaders—primarily nearby property owners and tenants led by Norman Leventhal of the Beacon Companies—formed Friends of Post Office Square (FOPOS) and developed a plan to replace the decrepit parking structure with a combination public park and underground parking garage.

The first effort was to structure a public/private partnership between the city of Boston—including strong involvement from the mayor's office—and FOPOS. Once the partnership was formed, the participants cooperated in finding solutions to a wide variety of problems they encountered in moving the project forward. For example, the existing garage was built in 1954 on city-owned land with a lease that ran until 1994. The garage owner fought the proposal until 1987, when he agreed to a buyout of his lease.

Under the terms of the public/private partnership, the $75 million project was financed entirely from private funds with an unusual approach, a stock offering. Improvements were funded with $930,000 of shareholders' initial contributions to FOPOS, an offering of preferred stock that raised $29.25 million, and debt financing of $60 million now held by Fleet Bank of Massachusetts. The preferred stock offering (450 shares) linked each stockholder's investment ($65,000 per share) with long-term parking rights in the new garage (one space per share was reserved at market rates). The total project funding of $90 million exceeds project costs, and the excess funding is held in reserve in a line of credit.

The city of Boston receives substantial financial benefits from the deal. First, the project pays property taxes. Second, all net cash after debt service will accrue to the city, with a portion dedicated to the maintenance of neighborhood parks; all the operating costs of the park and garage are funded from proceeds of the garage. Third, once all the debt and equity are repaid, ownership of the project will revert to the city. Fourth, the city has received $1 million for its ownership interest in the site.

Planning and Design

Participants reached a consensus on the program and design for this highly visible project by implementing comprehensive planning and programming. The mayor appointed the Program Development and Design Review Committee to formulate the design program for the park, participate in the selection of a designer, and generally advise FOPOS on the development. The diverse group included design professionals, community open space advocates, businesspeople, and public officials.

The park is primarily an open lawn with an overstory canopy of large deciduous trees. Brick walkways and plazas surround one large lawn area at the park's center, and seven smaller green areas are located at the edges. Two garden pavilions mark the South Plaza and a ground-level elevator structure that provides access for the handicapped. Constructed of copper and glass, the eastern pavilion provides escalator access to the lower-level lobby

---

usually the development organization or a larger development team that includes outside consultants—to establish priorities among project ideas. The nominal group process is often used in public sector development efforts where consensus is critical.

The *Delphi method,* first used to analyze military strategies and the impacts and implications of new technologies, offers a formal approach for bringing expert opinion to bear on a research question. Developers can use the technique to gather the informed opinions of market experts about a complex question. One obvious real estate application is in forecasting the supply of and demand for different kinds of space. Aiming for a consistent set of answers, the developer prepares a set of questions for a diverse group of experts, perhaps a politician, a market researcher, and a broker. After examining the

The focal point of the park is a fountain/sculpture of copper and green glass located near the north end of the park and surrounded by rich plantings and low granite seat-walls.

Bill Horsman

for the parking garage and the elevators to the parking levels. The western structure houses a year-round café.

A copper and green glass fountain/sculpture located near the north end of the park is surrounded by rich plantings and low granite seat-walls. A 143-foot-long trellis, supported by 26 granite columns, provides a shaded promenade that runs along the eastern edge of the central lawn and connects the North and South Plazas. The trellis is covered by a rich assortment of vines and plantings and is lit at night with thousands of miniature lights. Seating in the park is designed to accommodate as many as 1,000 people during peak hours: 20 wooden garden benches under the trellis and in the South Plaza, 35 steel benches in the park and along its perimeters, and 700 linear feet of sculptural granite seat-walls provide a large number of park users with different types of spaces. The park uses more than 125 varieties of plants for its horticultural display, chosen to celebrate the change of seasons.

The Park at Post Office Square is surrounded by four one-way streets, and auto ingress to and egress from the garage are provided on both the east and west sides of the park; entrances are separated from exits to ensure smooth traffic flow, which was a significant problem for the previous garage. The parking garage's design features a gracious main lobby with high-quality finishes and fresh flower arrangements and spacious and well-lit parking levels with colorful graphics. Each parking floor is organized around a central elevator core that is distinguished by colorful neon and is easily visible from anywhere on the parking level. The parking floors are laid out on flat grids carefully planned for easy perpendicular parking. An internal express ramp is located at the north end of the garage to move motorists between levels. ■

Sources: ULI Project Reference File, Vol. 24, No. 3, January–March 1994; and *Urban Parks and Open Space* (Washington, D.C.: ULI–the Urban Land Institute, 1997).

experts' independent forecasts, the developer can prepare more structured and close-ended questions and then ask the experts to compare their views with others and to consider revising their opinions. The process may require several rounds of review. If the process is successful, the developer can elicit a single, coherent picture of the environment under study. Developers find the Delphi method attractive when the questions are com-

plex, the experts are dispersed and few in number, or antipathy exists within the proposed development team.

Environmental scanning is a systematic way for developers or a development team to monitor the local, regional, national, and global environments and to predict the possible implications of environmental events. For example, a developer engaged in a large-scale project with a lengthy completion period might consider

Market research estimated that Viejas Spring's proximity to San Diego's airport would attract 2 million visitors annually to the 187,000-square-foot open-air retail/entertainment center. Natural materials invoke the style of the local Kumayaay Indians, and the distinctive sun-shaped design and colorful illumination are meant to capture the attention of inbound tourists flying over the site.

the implications of a recession on the project's feasibility. Scanning can be simplified by identifying a few readily available, easily interpreted indicators for monitoring environmental events. Examples include the prime interest rate or quarterly changes in the GDP. The developer or team specifies the events and the actions they would trigger and often writes scenarios used for playing out various implications and the results of alternative courses of action. Although environmental scanning is widely used and highly recommended for strategic organizational planning, it is a time-consuming way to generate project ideas. Although it is included here for reference, it is more commonly used in stage three with computerized sensitivity analysis.

Focus groups are most often used for modifying a proposed project to meet the desires of a potential consumer group, although they are sometimes used to generate ideas for future developments. Focus groups have one primary advantage over other processes: they allow the free flow of thoughts that can sometimes generate a wide range of interesting ideas.

Focus groups typically comprise eight to 12 people who meet for about two hours. A moderator leads a discussion according to a set of carefully prepared questions or objectives, but he must be flexible enough and sufficiently knowledgeable about the topic to know when to delve deeper. The moderator must also be trained to avoid steering the group to affirm preconceived notions. Critics of focus groups say that the technique is not rigorous and that its results can be misleading if the wrong participants are chosen. When focus groups are used to search for ideas that will subsequently be tested, however, these weaknesses are not critical.

Surveys are another tool used by developers to generate ideas for new products and projects and to modify projects that are underway. Many times surveys are given to residents or tenants in the developer's existing projects to assess customer satisfaction. Or they are given to prospective customers who visit or call the sales office for information. Developers can put together a profile of probable customers and the kind of product they want, their willingness to pay for it, and so on. The advantage of this method is that the profile is generated by sales center traffic—people who have already shown a certain amount of interest by making the effort to gather information about the development.

All these generic techniques can be modified to fit the particular situation. So long as the developer enters into these activities with an open mind and is not merely looking for confirmation of an initial idea, new ideas and reshaped ideas will emerge.

Words of Warning and Signposts

Although many basic principles of market research can be applied to real estate development, a few caveats apply.

Test Marketing a New Idea

One traditional form of market research—test marketing a new product—generally does not work in real estate development, for real estate products are expensive, large, physically fixed to a location, and long-lasting. Thus, developers cannot simply test a new concept in hotel design by building a hotel and inviting a sample group of guests to try it. Once a large project is built, the developer is committed—at least to the part already built.

Not surprisingly, developers kick a lot of tires, show friends a lot of sketches and photographs, and visit other cities and countries to get ideas. Increasingly, they build projects in what appear to be uneconomically small phases, allowing market response to shape the later phases. But because products are so expensive, good market research is particularly important. Trial and error is seldom a viable method of proving the market.

Using Research to Make Decisions

Successful developers have been able to cope with too little relevant information, too much data, inaccurate data, and rapidly changing conditions—somehow managing to synthesize successful new ideas from insights gained from imperfect sources. Sometimes the idea is a small change in familiar elements—perhaps developing a fairly standard 300-unit apartment complex but with slightly larger master baths in a new city. Sometimes the idea is a startling new combination of elements such as Chelsea Piers Sports and Entertainment, a 30-acre sports and film center located on New York City's Hudson River on four giant finger piers. The piers house a sports center, ice-skating rinks, a gymnasium, a rock-climbing wall, a park, restaurants, and golf—every kind of recreational facility in a city with limited space.[3]

But behind almost all these ideas lies some form of market research.

Given the difficulties of obtaining just the right data at just the right moment, the market research effort initiated in stage one must be even more organized and coordinated in subsequent stages of the development process.

Risk Control during Stage One of the Real Estate Development Process

Pragmatic developers can take several steps to reduce risk in stage one of the development process. Knowing when to hedge your bets is a big part of a developer's longevity.

- *Know yourself.* Developers who carefully evaluate their own capabilities (financial and intellectual) will be better situated to deal with the pressures of development. It is helpful to have well-positioned contacts in financial institutions, in groups of prospective tenants, and in construction companies. A large liquid net worth is also usually helpful. Ideas that can be successfully executed by one developer may be less viable for another. If your net worth is in the six figures and you have no construction experience beyond garden apartments, you would be stretching to attempt a $50 million high-rise residential tower without strong development partners to fill the gaps.
- *Know your image.* Often the public perception of a developer is that of gunslinger (without the white hat). Successful developers often see themselves as risk averse and functioning more like movie producers. By drawing on several individuals' talents, they package ideas and create a product intended to satisfy society's needs for space. Aspiring developers should understand both what a developer does and how the public views the development profession. If you keep the public perception firmly in mind from the beginning, you will be more likely to dot all the i's so that your idea is appropriately documented to win the support of others.
- *Know your team.* Self-perception and public perception are a useful background for self-preservation. Developers must determine the quality of all participants in the development process at an early juncture. During stage one, as developers decide on a general type of project, a general location, and a general type of tenant, they must also think about players they might recruit for the development team to

Figure 10-4

Big Ideas: Petronas Towers

The age of the skyscraper was born in the United States in the late 19th century, made possible by the advent of structural steel frame construction and workable electric elevators. Until recently, the United States held the distinction of being home to most of the world's tallest buildings. Today, however, fewer than half of the ten tallest buildings in the world are located in this country. Spurred by rapid industrialization and economies that surged through much of the 1990s, most new construction of tall buildings has been taking place in Asia and the Pacific Rim.

The current record holders, following a controversial decision by the Council on Tall Buildings, are the 1,483-foot-high Petronas twin towers in Kuala Lumpur, Malaysia. The buildings are owned by Midciti Resources Sdn Bhd, a joint venture of the Malaysian gas and oil company Petronas and KLCC Holdings Sdn Bhd. Petronas is also the primary occupant of the buildings, taking up about three-fourths of the leasable office space.

Completed in 1996, the 88-story twin circular structures were developed as an integral part of Kuala Lumpur City Center, a 100-acre site in the heart of Kuala Lumpur's Golden Triangle being developed as a city within a city to provide an economic heart for Kuala Lumpur. The towers will serve as a gateway to the project that, when completed, will provide 18.8 million square feet (1.75 million m^2) of office, retail, hotel, residential, and entertainment space as well as a 50-acre public park.

The towers were designed by Argentina-born architect Cesar Pelli and, unlike some other recent Asian skyscrapers, attempt to reflect a uniquely Malaysian design and the dominant Islamic culture. The design of the buildings is based on geometric principles typical of Islamic architecture, the complexity of which serves to represent the incomprehensibility of Allah. Two interlocked squares

Designed by Cesar Pelli & Associates, the twin 88-story structures of Petronas Towers in Kuala Lumpur enclose 4.5 million square feet (420,000 m^2) of space.

form an eight-pointed star over which eight semicircles are superimposed to create a 16-sided figure. The steel spires atop the building are meant to resemble the minarets of a mosque. At the same time, the buildings'

make the development possible. People who demonstrate both excellent track records and financial strength and are easy to work with will reduce long-term risk. Naturally, such people often cost more. Risk reduction is seldom free. The developer must decide what costs are justified from the perspective of reducing risk.

- *Coordinate.* From the beginning, developers must coordinate the activities and functions of the individuals involved in the process. This task becomes even more critical in later stages when the team

adopts a more managerial role. Even at the beginning, however, developers must talk to—not just read about—contractors, subcontractors, potential tenants, city managers, and community groups. A team should function more smoothly than a collection of talented free agents.

- *Keep current.* To the extent that developers stay current in their reading and networking, they are more likely not to move beyond stage one when available information suggests an idea is not feasible, economically or otherwise. Trends in the national economy, modernity is reflected in their glass and stainless steel cladding. The windows were designed as continuous horizontal ribbons encircling each floor. Overhanging shades protect against sunlight. Inside, the towers incorporate a *surau*, or prayer room, to allow workers to pray while kneeling toward Mecca. The design of the buildings' interior spaces emphasizes the use of local materials and patterns.

Each cylindrical structure measures 150 feet (46 m) in diameter and rests on 16 reinforced concrete columns around its perimeter. Narrower 44-story towers flank the north face of each taller tower, visually reinforcing the buildings' function as a gateway. A 160-foot (50-m) glass and steel skybridge connects the towers at the 41st and 42nd floors. The towers narrow slightly as they rise, being set back at levels 60, 73, 82, and 85. Each tower was constructed by separate independent general contractors, one Japanese and one Korean, in an attempt by the developer to create competition and achieve lower costs and faster deliveries.

The designers of Petronas Towers and other recent high-rise developments have turned to high-strength concrete instead of steel frame as the primary structural material for the construction of tall buildings because of its ability to absorb more external forces and to reduce sway.

The controversy surrounding naming Petronas Towers the world's tallest buildings stems from the Council on Tall Buildings's decision to include the buildings' spires in calculating their height, reasoning that they are integral to the buildings' design. Conversely, using the same reasoning, the council does not include the Sears Tower's radio antennas. Thus, Petronas Towers supplanted the Sears Tower as the world's tallest buildings, even though the Sears Tower's roofline is 100 feet higher than those of Petronas Towers.

In response to the controversy, the Council on Tall Buildings announced there will now be four official categories for measuring the height of a building: 1) height to structural or architectural top; 2) height to top of antenna; 3) height to top of roof; and 4) height to highest occupied floor. Category one, currently claimed by Petronas Towers, is still considered to be the most relevant measure. The Sears Tower still maintains the record in categories three and four. Petronas Towers' reign as the tallest buildings may be short lived, however, as even taller buildings are already being designed.

The World's Ten Tallest Buildings[a]

1.	Petronas Tower 1 (Kuala Lumpur)	1,483 feet
2.	Petronas Tower 2 (Kuala Lumpur)	1,483 feet
3.	Sears Tower (Chicago)	1,450 feet
4.	Jin Mao Building (Shanghai)	1,380 feet
5.	World Trade Center One (New York City)	1,368 feet
6.	World Trade Center Two (New York City)	1,362 feet
7.	Empire State Building (New York City)	1,250 feet
8.	Central Plaza (Hong Kong)	1,209 feet
9.	Bank of China Tower (Hong Kong)	1,209 feet
10.	T & C Tower (Kaoshiung, Taiwan)	1,140 feet

[a]**As measured from the sidewalk level of the main entrance to the structural top of the building, including spires, but not radio or television antennas or flagpoles. Heights are rounded to the nearest integer.**

Source: Council on Tall Buildings.

---

supply conditions, the political climate, and tax laws can shift quickly and interact in unexpected ways. Reading newsletters and attending local and national meetings cannot guarantee profits, but keeping abreast of major events can help minimize financial losses.

■ *Behave ethically.* Personal relationships and ethics are critically important parts of the development process because it is often difficult to rely on the courts for a speedy resolution when problems arise. In development, time is money—a lot of money—and

developers lack the luxury of time to stop and sue. The stronger the personal relationships and business ethics of all those involved, the safer the development for all concerned, including the general public.

As a new entrant in the Research Triangle Park market,[4] Fraser Morrow Daniels relied heavily on formal inquiry, as Whit Morrow describes in the continuing case study. The company's market research and definition of a target market reflect the steps outlined in this chapter, but the steps are not clearly defined. As Fraser

Morrow Daniels learned more about emerging trends in the market, the firm synthesized the information and moved back and forth between market research and planning tactics to revise the initial concept.

⠿ Europa Center

Whit Morrow Explains the Genesis of an Idea

Analyzing Market Opportunities

Why did we form a new company to undertake new ventures in a new area, and what made us choose the Research Triangle area? What did we consider in picking our products, and how did we structure our company in that environment?

The area as a whole was attractive to us; it was an area where we would personally want to live and work. We looked at several factors: growth and diversity in employment, demographics, infrastructure, government regulations, prices, product supply, availability of financing, politics (different from the regulatory environment, it is the attitude in the area, what people are thinking, what will happen when the bulldozer starts), labor supply, and quality of the natural environment.

With all those factors in mind, we started looking at the whole Research Triangle area. It was a new business environment, unlike Atlanta, for example, which is a big city with a beltway and all the traditional factors that go along with working in a fairly steady, predictable business environment. In the Research Triangle, four small cities—Raleigh, Durham, Chapel Hill, and Cary—make up the metropolitan area.

We tried to develop an overall business strategy for the 1980s and the 1990s. We looked not just at population growth but also at changing segments. Census data showed that the area was growing at a higher rate than the national average. We took what was happening in the national economy and national population statistics and compared it with local data.

Researching and Selecting Target Markets

Then we looked at Raleigh/Durham to see how the trend was playing out there. Who was moving there? Which market segments, defined by age group, were being built for shopping opportunities, for housing? What effect did those trends have on the homebuilding market and other segments?

We found that local job growth and diversification were probably the best mix of any area we looked at in the

country. The factors driving the local economy were universities, state government, and growth in Research Triangle Park, where high-tech businesses were growing rather than being overbuilt or dying out. What those factors told us was that that marketplace was the place to be if we wanted to be in the development business for the next 15 to 20 years.

Developing a Marketing Strategy

Next question. What do we do and where do we do it? The first factor we started looking at was who else was doing what in the marketplace. Who were the major players? Who had been around for a long time building office buildings and shopping centers? Where were they located? We wanted to put things on a map and decide where the opportunities were. We wanted to combine that information with our analysis of infrastructure.

I went to the local map store and asked for a map of the Research Triangle area and was shocked to find that none were available anywhere. I went to the Council of Governments for the six-county area. All it had were county road maps pieced together—without even the cities on it —a map of the water supply, and a map that had schools on it but basically nothing else. No one had put together all the nitty-gritty details that are necessary for the area as a whole, making it such a peculiar opportunity for real estate development.

The Research Triangle area was also different because it had 750,000 people spread over three or four cities, which together have all the activity equivalent to one major city that attracts businesses. Individually, however, the cities are small towns. The competitors we found in this marketplace were people like the Yorks, who had started the Cameron Village shopping center 40 years earlier in Raleigh. The Davidson and Jones construction company had been building buildings for the universities and the state government. And some big companies, like IBM, had built their own campuses or leased space in other buildings.

This was a key finding. No active, competitive, national speculative office building developer was operating in the area. Nobody had gone out on a limb and built a building and hoped to fill it because of growth in the office population. There had been only companies doing it for themselves and local builders building for existing committed demand. As of 1983, the supply was 100,000 square feet and absorption was 100,000 square feet—totally unlike any other place in the country with a population of 750,000.

Our next stop was the local chambers of commerce to talk to the people who were promoting business activity and pushing development. Raleigh's chamber had all the statistics on Raleigh and knew all about Raleigh's beltway, how long it would take to get the outer beltway built, and

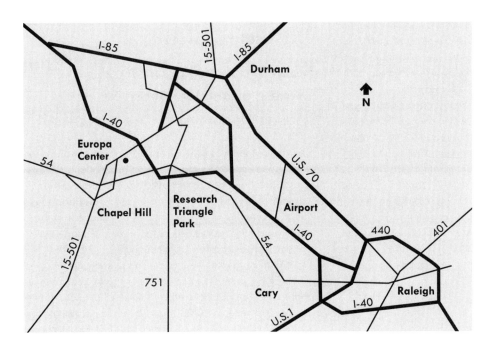

Europa Center is located on the U.S. 15-501 corridor, 1.5 miles west of I-40.

some other statistics as well. Durham's chamber had all its statistics, although it still had somewhat of an inferiority complex because Durham had been just a tobacco town and isn't beautiful. In Chapel Hill, the chamber of commerce represented about 2 percent of the community's population. The university represented one part, retirees another part, and residents who commuted to jobs in other parts of the Triangle the rest of the community. So Chapel Hill's chamber was basically of no help. And people there didn't even want to talk about development.

So we were, in a sense, real pioneers (along with many other people, as it turned out) in a new business environment ripe for plucking. The people there had all their assumptions about the way it was: "Nobody's going to live in Durham. Nobody's going to move to Durham." They told us about the last developer that tried to build houses on the south side of Durham in 1972, on Highway 54 near Research Triangle Park. That developer went bankrupt. Total failure.

Well, some other newcomers realized that it was not possible to buy a nice house next to a swimming pool and tennis court, despite the high rate of growth. They took a chance and bought 750 acres at dirt-cheap prices south of Durham in the same location that had failed ten years earlier near Research Triangle Park. Boom! Woodcroft was born, selling 2,000 housing units over a two-year period. That's how rapidly this business environment was changing.

It's hard to imagine, but at that time the individual chambers of commerce had no concept of a unified MSA. They were individual communities, fighting among themselves for recognition. So we took the U.S. Geological Survey maps and pieced them together to make a big map. It

was the only detailed topographic map available of the whole area, and it was ten feet long. Standing back from it, anyone could see that a very strong link would develop between the east and west sides of the community (Raleigh to Chapel Hill) with the completion of I-40 as well as a great deal of opportunity in the middle that did not exist before because of cars backed up on two-lane Highway 54. Simple things became apparent: Research Triangle Park had no restaurants, it shuts down at 5:00 at night, there's only one hotel, and nightlife is as boring as it can be.

These ideas are very simple. The infrastructure changed: the airport built a real runway and the number of flights quadrupled. American Airlines put a hub there. Research Triangle Park accelerated from a very steady 4 to 5 percent increase over the 20 years from 1960 to 1980 to 20 percent increases every year for the next five or six years. And in the middle of this abundant land, the federal government and the state were spending oodles of money on the highway systems, and the airport was reaching huge capacity.

At the Raleigh chamber of commerce, the chief concern was developing Raleigh's outer fringe—trying to force development to the east side of Raleigh, exactly the opposite direction from Research Triangle Park. In Durham, most of the power brokers live north of town, also opposite from the Park, and the north side of Durham was being developed. Even some bright, forward-thinking people said that the solution was a replication of Research Triangle Park in that area and proposed Treyburn, a mixed-use project on 5,500 acres northeast of Durham. But the natives still thought of Durham and Raleigh and Chapel Hill as separate cities—even though a multimillion dollar interstate highway runs right through the area between Durham and Chapel Hill within eight minutes of the heart of the Park.

Thus, we had an obvious strategy: buy 100 to 200 acres to build office buildings. With the growth we saw and the communities' coming together, we foresaw the need for a large amount of office space. The old absorption rate of 100,000 square feet per year would change. In fact, we noticed that in 1983, 500,000 square feet of office space had been used (with some businesses building their own space on top of that). Population growth, demographics, and infrastructure combined to tell us that someone could take advantage of a big opportunity. We did just that, buying 100 acres of land to develop office space. As it turned out, we were not alone in our astute observations.

continued on page 209

Like Europa Center, Museum Towers is a fairly standard product. It didn't stretch the boundaries in creativity; it didn't require years of research to come up with the idea. It was a straightforward look at the market and the location. But what was ultimately built was not what Dean Stratouly intended to build.

▌▌▌ Museum Towers

Dean Stratouly Explains the Genesis of an Idea: Analyzing Market Opportunities

The original site was 4.11 acres and was actually three lots. We had intended to subdivide the property and develop it as a hotel and apartment building. The proposed development would have consisted of a 420-unit apartment building complex, a 207-suite hotel building, and a total of 696 parking spaces. The city's preferred usage was housing, including affordable housing.

When the market went to hell in the early nineties and we were basically sitting on the property, we changed our plans when we got the opportunity to sell the hotel parcel. So, in 1996 we sold 50,000 square feet to E.F. Institute for Cultural Exchange for $5.25 million for its North American headquarters (the company is based in Sweden). The institute built a ten-story office project containing 250,000 gross square feet—159,000 square feet of office space, a restaurant on the first floor, and 132 parking spaces.

The site of Museum Towers is in the middle of a vibrant region with excellent access to Cambridge and the west end of downtown Boston.

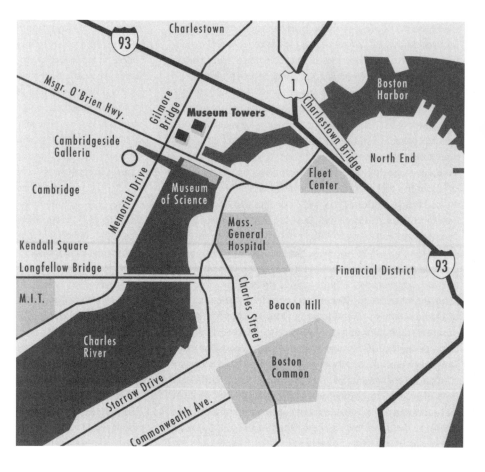

After we gave away an acre to the state for the park and a small strip to the city for roads, we ended up with a site of 2.07 acres.

The housing vacancy rate in Boston has been low for a long time, so the market was ripe for a new product. At the same time, at least three other major projects were on about the same schedule as we were—Cronin's Landing and the Village at Bear Hill in Waltham and University Park at MIT. Some others were permitted and being constructed, and several others were still waiting for approvals. When a major real estate research firm identified Boston as the third best market in the country for apartment investment and development, people started taking notice. Only San Francisco and Orange County, California, were rated better markets.

But other things contributed to the interest in multifamily housing here. For one thing, the state eliminated rent control in 1996—which affected about 17,000 units in Boston alone. The unemployment rate in Cambridge was very low throughout the 1990s and was about 2 percent in 1999. The state also made some big tax cuts in favor of business and investment. In addition, the high-tech economy was great and the overall job market (education, medicine, and financial services in addition to technology) strong. Cambridge has always attracted entrepreneurs and innovators because of its highly educated workforce. Moody's rates the Cambridge government "Aa1." The vacancy rate was less than 2 percent, and interest rates were at historic lows. We had a site that had waited nearly ten years. What more do you need?

So for this project, the idea wasn't a big light bulb going off in my head. It was market driven, because my original idea was different from what we ended up with. Developers gotta be flexible.

continued on page 210

Summary

Inception of an idea is the first stage in the development process. Several techniques are available for generating ideas: brainstorming, the nominal group process, the Delphi method, environmental scanning, focus groups, and surveys. Ideas come from several different motivations and inspirations, but, regardless of the source, ideas must be tested quickly with a back-of-the-envelope pro forma. Ideally, idea generation is integrated into the development company's strategic planning by using market research to add rigor to the process. Regardless of the level of rigor or the techniques employed, several potential pitfalls can derail even the

most promising proposed project. Accordingly, formal consideration of risk control is necessary even during the first stage of the development process.

From the beginning (stage one), the developer is the ultimate responsible party. He doesn't have to do every job (not even generating ideas), but he is responsible for each job's getting done well. A developer must maintain the mindset of a "do-er" rather than a consultant. Strategic planning is useful, but the developer has to make it happen.

Stage one is clearly the most important stage of the development process. Although weak leadership and poor management can ruin a good development idea, the converse is not true. Strong leadership and great management can't save a bad idea. Remember, Napoleon lost at Waterloo because fighting everyone at once was a bad idea.

The best risk control technique is "don't." Moreover, everyone will tell you to "stay within the boundaries of the market." On average, this is good advice, but the boundary shouldn't be the market just as consultants see it today. Rather, the boundary should be set where the market will be upon completion of the development. The developer can use examples from other times and other places (along with current local market rents) to estimate future demand.

Terms

- Back-of-the-envelope pro forma
- Brainstorming
- Delphi method
- Environmental scanning
- Focus groups
- GDP
- Nominal group process
- Situs
- Strategic planning
- Subsidiaries
- Total marketing concept

Review Questions

10.1 What are the three most common motivations from which ideas for new developments emerge?

10.2 Describe a back-of-the-envelope pro forma and what it is used for.

10.3 What are some of the formal techniques that developers can use to generate ideas?

10.4 Describe the techniques of risk control that developers can use at this stage. How do they help developers hedge their bets?

10.5 In the Europa Center case study, describe how Fraser Morrow Daniels went about assessing the need for commercial development in the Research Triangle Park area. Was the situation he described common?

10.6 Summarize the advice developer James J. Chaffin, Jr., gives to would-be developers. Do you agree or disagree with his advice?

10.7 Developer Dean Stratouly describes a fairly straightforward approach to assessing what to build on the Museum Towers site. Do you think developers use this approach more frequently to come up with ideas?

Notes

1. For a more complete description of Kentlands, see *ULI Project Reference File,* Vol. 24, No. 6, October–December 1994.

2. The references at the end of this part provide excellent descriptions of basic techniques for generating ideas (although not in the context of real estate development).

3. For a more complete description of Chelsea Piers, see Alexander Garvin and Gayle Berens, *Urban Parks and Open Space* (Washington, D.C.: ULI–the Urban Land Institute, 1997), pp. 126–33; and Michael D. Beyard et al., *Developing Urban Entertainment Centers* (Washington, D.C.: ULI–the Urban Land Institute, 1998).

4. The Research Triangle of North Carolina includes the cities of Raleigh (the state capital), Durham, Chapel Hill (the location of Europa Center), and Cary. Research Triangle Park, the University of North Carolina at Chapel Hill, North Carolina State University (in Raleigh), and Duke University (in Durham) are all located in this metropolitan area.

Chapter 11

Market Research: A Tool for Generating Ideas

Because market research is fundamental to the generation of ideas—the starting point for all development—it is useful to look in depth at how market research fits with the total marketing concept taught in basic marketing courses. By taking such an approach, this chapter adds structure to the material developed in the preceding chapter.

Before starting any project, developers should understand the market. The market is defined as *users* of a type of property (e.g., light industrial), *buyers* (players in the capital market), and *tenants* (players in the space market) located in a geographic area. A strong overall market does not necessarily equate with a good opportunity for development. Neither does a weak market mean that a good idea cannot be implemented. In other words, a good market from the perspective of demand may be oversupplied; at the same time, a good idea may prove successful in a low-growth market. Although poor implementation can undermine the most promising opportunities in any market, understanding the market is a necessary prerequisite to generating ideas. Flawless implementation (stages four through eight) cannot redcem a bad idea.

Those involved in marketing must develop a dynamic marketing strategy—one that continues to evolve. One key aspect is recognizing that planning never stops; it must be continuous because products, markets, the development organization, the competition, and the environment continue to change. Marketing is a continuous cycle that accumulates knowledge through a sequence of activities: market analysis, market positioning, product design, marketing sales planning, and evaluation of market response.[1] By building on this cumulative experience, developers can better understand today's market dynamics and hone in on tomorrow's market.

This chapter discusses the elements involved in looking at a market by focusing on:

- The basics: what are markets, the marketing concept, and market research?
- What marketers (and developers using marketing) do throughout the development process; and
- The connection between market research and development ideas in stage one of the development process.

After reviewing marketing basics, we return to stage one of the development process.

The Basics: Marketing and Market Research

Developers are always vulnerable to the field of dreams syndrome by too often assuming that "if you build it they will come." Even experienced developers, because of their past successes, might assume that their next project will be successful just because they are building it; that is, "their" supply will create its own demand. Such an assumption sometimes holds for hot recording stars and clothing designers but rarely applies to real estate development. As one developer said when asked at what point in his career he finally felt safe being on his own, "You're never safe."

Real estate developers, like all businesspeople, need to pay close attention to their customers. Peter Drucker, the grand master of management consultants, underscores this point by defining marketing as adopting the customer's perspective on any given business. In the same vein, marketing specialist Philip Kotler argues that marketing should not be narrowly construed as the process of selling products but more broadly understood as satisfying human wants and needs. In today's highly competitive real estate industry, developers who pay careful attention to markets fare far better than those who do not.

Although it is obvious that deals driven by the marketplace tend to be the most successful, examples abound of deals executed for reasons other than simply satisfying current market demand. Until 1986, when tax reform eliminated several provisions favorable to real estate, incentives in the federal tax code prompted a number of otherwise uneconomic developments. When financing was readily available, many dubious projects were developed because some participant in the process benefited even if the project did not succeed. Further, some projects were developed to realize the dream of a particular developer, who paid scant attention to the market.

If any such non-market-driven projects were successful in the past, it is best to consider them as flukes rather than as useful models for future practice. When developers can persuasively demonstrate that they have identified customers with unfilled wants and needs, they can use the collected market information to garner public support and financial backing for a project. When the project is not justified by the market but is considered socially necessary, as in the case of housing for the very poor (see Chapter 15), developers should understand the extent of the subsidy required.

The following overview of marketing principles draws heavily from Philip Kotler's well-known marketing textbook,[2] which sets forth the following key marketing concepts:

- Marketing is a social and managerial process by which individuals and groups obtain what they need and want through creating, offering, and exchanging products of value with each other.
- Marketing occurs because humans have needs, wants, and demands, some of which can be satisfied by products (goods, services, and ideas).
- If people have a choice among products, their choice will usually be guided by their notion of value and their expectation of satisfaction.
- Although products can be obtained in several ways —producing them ourselves, coercion, begging, or exchange, for example—most of us acquire goods by exchange. Therefore, most of us become specialists in producing particular products, which we trade for other things we need.

- A market consists of all the potential customers sharing a particular need or want who might be willing and able to engage in exchange to satisfy that need or want. The size of that market depends on how many people share the need or want, have resources that interest others, and are willing and able to offer those resources in exchange for what they want.
- A marketer is someone seeking one or more prospects who might engage in an exchange of values.
- Marketing management is the process of planning and executing the conception, pricing, promotion, and distribution of goods, services, and ideas to create exchanges with target groups that satisfy customers' and organizations' goals.

The word "market" can be used in a variety of ways. Historically, markets were places where buyers and sellers met—typically the town center or the farmer's market.[3] Today, businesspeople usually use the word to refer to different ways of grouping customers, including geographic location (the Pacific Northwest, the Midwest), demographic profiles (yuppies, empty nesters), and product types (Internet users). The concept also includes groups such as labor markets or donor markets not comprising customers. Economists refer to both buyers and sellers when describing markets in terms of supply and demand, while marketing professionals (the people who try to convince us to buy a Buick instead of a Lexus) consider the sellers as the industry and the buyers as the market.

Industry and market, sellers and buyers are linked in four ways. Sellers send 1) goods or services produced by industry and 2) communications to the market; in return, they receive from the buyers 3) money and 4) information. In essence, marketing is the activity that turns the crank: potential transactions become real transactions when people are stimulated to exchange money (or something else of value) for something they want or need.

People—employees—create and manage marketing campaigns to achieve a company's objectives—no less in real estate development companies than at Microsoft or General Foods. In theory, marketing objectives ought to be part of most management functions, including, for example, the construction process. In practice, however, the task of finding and keeping customers is at times left solely to the marketing staff—which, in real estate development, means leasing agents or salespeople. As in any company, projects are more successful when the people marketing the product understand how the product is produced and financed and can communicate what they learn from dealing directly

The low-key strategy for marketing the 145-unit neighborhood of "semi-custom" homes in the Vintage Oaks development in Palo Alto, California, emphasized community and media relations over advertising. No off-street signs or banners were used, and the information center had the professional feel of an architect's office. The developer saved more than $1.5 million in merchandising and carrying costs by building just one model and using computers for a "virtual walk-through."

with the customers to those producing and managing the project. It is the developer's job to ensure that such feedback occurs regularly throughout the development process.

The Marketing Concept: Serving The Potential Customer

"Putting the customer first" became a business cliché during the 1980s as U.S. companies sought ways to regain customers lost to our international trading partners, notably Japan. One phrase that characterizes "putting the customer first" is the "marketing (or total marketing) concept";[4] that is, a company achieves organizational goals by determining the needs and wants of its target customers and then tries to satisfy those needs and wants better than its competitors. This approach should be the foundation of any business. In fact, surprisingly often and for their own reasons, companies put other interests ahead of customers' interests. In contrast with the "marketing concept," these narrower interests can be characterized as the "production concept," the "product concept," the "selling concept," or simply a "short-term, self-centered approach."

The production concept supports sales by keeping prices down through efficient production and wide distribution. The product concept emphasizes continual improvements in product quality, at least from the engi-

neer's perspective. The selling concept focuses on sales and promotional efforts to stimulate consumers' latent demand, as in "we've got it, why don't you pay for it?" Although "getting it built" and/or "protecting yourself" may be worthy objectives, they should serve, not supplant, the developer's primary purpose—identifying customers and competitively satisfying their needs. Efficiently produced, well-advertised sites for single-family houses do not earn a profit and do not improve a community unless they satisfy customers' needs for such sites.

The marketing concept includes these widely heard slogans:

- "Meeting needs profitably."
- "Find wants and fill them."
- "Love the customer, not the product."
- "Putting people first" (British Airways).[5]

The renovation and expansion of the retail and food concessions at Portland International Airport was directed by extensive market research. Until 1994, concessions were handled by a master concessionaire, who offered traditional food and beverages. Market research studies showed that passengers wanted quicker service, higher-quality food, wider selection, and competitive pricing. Demographic surveys also showed that airport passengers have higher incomes and more education than the average tricounty resident, thus supporting the decision to feature upscale specialty retail shopping.[6]

Classic Marketing Strategy

A marketing strategy is a detailed plan for meeting marketing objectives; it includes a clear statement of the target market, measurable objectives for serving that market, a marketing budget (a critical part of the project's overall feasibility), and the marketing mix. In classic marketing terms, the marketing mix includes the four Ps: product, place, price, and promotion.

In real estate, *product* refers to property type—apartment buildings, offices, warehouses, for example—which are further distinguished by quality, brand, packaging, and services. Quality (features, options, and style) relates to the project's architecture, construction, layout, and finishes. Brand names may be equivalent to the developer's reputation or the class of an office building (A, B, C, D). Packaging a real estate product refers to the physical features, functions, and benefits added to the given type of property to make it appeal to particular customers—extra electrical outlets or extensive landscaping, for example. Services represent the developer's commitment to ongoing property management, such as providing security and janitorial service.

Place is the project's location. (In classic marketing, place refers to channels of distribution, coverage, loca-tions, inventory, and transport.) In marketing real property, many people still believe the three key factors are location, location, and location.[7] This entire book is about providing space with appropriate services at a fixed location.

Price includes special allowances for space customized by the tenant (for example, $30.00 per square yard for carpet or mahogany paneling in the senior partner's office), renewal options, expense pass-throughs, and other comparable terms. Payment period and credit terms are particularly important because real property is an expensive, long-lived asset.

Promotion refers to the elements of advertising and selling that are readily identified with real estate marketing (covered in detail in Chapter 22). It should not, however, obscure the importance of the other three Ps in setting strategy.

A winning strategy is consistent across all four Ps. Part of implementing a strategy is the specification of planning tactics, which require a finer analysis of the elements in the marketing mix, particularly the timing and costs of each. In smaller developments, strategy and tactics tend to blend together. In larger projects, the distinction is clearer. The overall development team sets strategy while the marketing staff works out the tactics.

Finally, the developer must implement and control the marketing strategy. Skillful management is required to staff, monitor, and control implementation of

The developers of Bridge-court in Emeryville, California, catered to the area's youthful market of professionals, artists, and staff from nearby universities by designing affordable industrial loft apartments. Forty percent of the 220 units are below-market-rate rentals, and the rent-to-own housing concept allows renters to buy units after 15 years.

the marketing plan. Controlling creative planning and active selling without stifling the staff's initiative is critical to successful implementation. Planning cannot change the product too frequently (construction costs jump disproportionately with even small changes) and sales people motivated by commissions cannot promise too much future service (for example, extra security), or operations after the development is complete will not be profitable.

Research provides the input for analyzing marketing opportunities and selecting target markets. Ideally, the development team never stops gathering market intelligence, continually using new information to reposition the project as change occurs.

Stimulating and Managing Demand

Good marketers do more than offer customers products they already know they want. They also seek to create new demand by making customers aware of new needs and/or by creating dissatisfaction with old products that may be dated in the face of new technology.

Employers, for example, have been slow to recognize how the lifestyle requirements of the workforce can be satisfied in the workplace and thus help attract a more skilled and dedicated office staff. Nonetheless, some developers have undertaken marketing efforts that respond to workers' (not just industrial) concerns.

Dissatisfaction with Existing Space

Dissatisfaction with existing space occurs whenever new needs are discovered or, more simply, whenever standards are raised. The most typical example occurs when the design of a more prestigious office development—with all the latest features and finishing details—is unveiled. The notion of what constitutes Class A office space can change overnight, forcing managers of existing space to upgrade their own buildings or change the classification to Class B, which means less prestigious tenants and lower rents.

Strategic developers not only beat the bushes for new customers and stimulate demand, but also manage demand—its level, timing, and composition—to achieve a company's objectives. Even so, demand can be very "lumpy"; that is, large numbers of tenants often enter markets during boom times and occupy space under the terms of similarly structured leases. When those leases expire, large numbers of tenants look to relocate to new space, exacerbating the lumpiness of demand. It may seem that every large legal, accounting, and financial firm wants to upgrade space at one time. But a lease-by-lease analysis can permit marketers to track the vol-

ume of potential relocators. Astute developers strive to manage lumpy demand by matching the timing of new construction with the expiration of leases.

What Marketers (and Developers Using Marketing) Do

Those who market a product must first analyze market opportunities by paying careful attention to the macro and micro levels of the market. The macro level includes the major forces that influence society and institutions: technology, tastes, demographics, sociocultural developments, political attitudes, legal structures, and economic trends. The micro (or industry) level includes both current and potential suppliers, customers, and competitors as well as the public that regulates or influences the market.[8]

With an understanding of macro- and microlevel markets, marketers then research and select target markets with, at a minimum, good information on customers who have purchased or leased a similar real estate product in the past. Developers also collect market intelligence on potential consumers and competitors. They can go even further and pursue one or more forms of research described in the next section of this chapter—research on market conditions and on trends exhibited by past, present, and future users.

Laguna West in Sacramento is an example of a lakefront residential new urbanist development that changed its original development plan in response to the results of market research. The original plan called for a variety of attached housing with a somewhat urban character. Research showed that California homebuyers preferred single-family homes, even on very small lots, over attached homes.[9]

Different from Toothpaste

Attention to classic notions of marketing helps bring greater structure and discipline to real estate development. But the real estate product differs substantially from standard mass-produced and nationally advertised products. Four major differences predominate.

■ *The real estate product is highly differentiated.* It serves several functions of different space users and is produced in more variable styles than most common household products. Above all, the real estate product is distinguished by the importance of location. Unlike all other products, people cannot take real estate home. Instead, the customer must move to the product, which offers a distinctive location.

- *Constraints on supply are far more variable with regard to real estate.* Unlike in mass manufacturing, the local vagaries of site availability and political entitlements often control the volume of competing supply and direct the developer's opportunities.

- *Market data are much less certain in the case of real estate.* Developers lack the finely structured data banks of corporate America, although recent years have seen significant improvements (as described in Part I and more clearly detailed in Part VI). Nevertheless, the uniqueness of different locations and market niches, combined with the volatility of local economies and construction cycles, implies that developers must work hard to know their markets.

- *Most projects must be custom-tailored and cannot be mass-produced or mass-marketed.* Without the economies of scale of a Procter & Gamble or a Ford Motor Company, developers cannot create their products as efficiently as corporate giants. Indeed, developers must rely on a fuller array of senses to craft their products artfully.

The Search for Segmentation

Developers seek to identify market segments—whether defined socially, spatially, or behaviorally. Historically, real estate development has been a spatially segmented industry: most developers worked in only a few locations and constructed only one or two product types. Since the 1950s, however, developers' geographic scope and product mix have increased with the size of their companies. Now, in addition to serving a variety of geographically and functionally segmented markets, developers search for important socioeconomic and behavioral distinctions among potential customers. Research into these different factors identifies target market segments that usually consist of a distinctive combination of people, lifestyles, purchasing power, and place. Identifying new markets or niches within established markets is the most crucial application of marketing research to real estate development. The underpinnings of the research into market segments include sociology and urban history, again demonstrating the interdisciplinary nature of real estate development.

Marketing for Entitlements

One area where the marketing of real estate diverges most distinctly from the marketing of other products is the effort that must be devoted to securing local political approvals. Whereas toothpaste manufacturers must seek the approval of only the federal Food and Drug Administration, real estate developers must often run their product through a maze of local regulations. In the process of running through the maze, they are required to engage in societal marketing.

The concept of societal marketing extends the idea of marketing beyond company profits and consumer satisfaction to collective or societal satisfaction. By definition, real estate is a long-lived asset in a fixed location; however, meeting only space users' needs is not sufficient. Developers must satisfy at least some of the needs of neighbors and regulators and should consider government their partner. A community will ultimately alter the development approval rules to the detriment of the project owner if a project does not serve the community well (another way to view the "constraints" in Graaskamp's definition of feasibility—see Chapter 16).

As described more fully in Chapter 14, developers need to make certain that their projects respond to government's overall plans for the community—and plans include those developed by a number of community, county, regional, and state agencies. The most relevant plans are land use and zoning plans, but others that may be equally important in particular development situations include transportation, economic development, and environmental plans and policies. Local political approval is generally binding, although plans issued by higher-level agencies can be influential and should not be disregarded.

Marketing is required to sell the idea of the project to the responsible government authorities. How well does the proposed project support the intent, if not the letter, of the community's general plan or of regional comprehensive plans? It is important to recognize that the plans developed by various agencies often conflict with one another and express a variety of opposing objectives. For example, local land use plans may not accommodate the goal of creating jobs, or the land use map may not have been updated to reflect new transportation corridors, or environmental protection may be better served by the proposed project than by alternatives in other locations. In addition, skilled developers know that the members of decision-making bodies are often not of a single mind and that even individual decision makers subscribe to a variety of goals and objectives that are at times internally inconsistent. The marketer's task is to help the various participants recognize the relative merits of the project, and it is, of course, the developer's job to be sure that the marketer accomplishes this task.

Recognizing that the entitlement authorities represent customers to be "sold" on a project, experienced developers have learned that marketing should address local authorities' needs and desires from the beginning of project design. A series of negotiations often transpires as developers seek to tailor their projects to regulators' expectations. Public relations experts recommend that developers organize their project marketing along the lines of a political campaign to ensure neighbors' and officials' acceptance of the project. Careful research into public opinion is essential in the effort to gain acceptance.[10] It is far better to identify and address community concerns early during the project approval process than to face an angry audience in a public hearing before the responsible authorities. Elected officials are much more comfortable when the electorate is at ease with a project.

The Connection between Market Research and Development Ideas

With this general review of marketing fundamentals and the role of marketing as it applies to the development process, we can now return to stage one. Good ideas flow from specific sources with specific knowledge of the industry and its markets. Developers need to understand themselves, their company, the competition, the other players who help build and finance projects, the regulatory and socioeconomic environment, and, most important, potential clients. Where does this knowledge come from? Practical experience, reading, and formal inquiries into specific topics are all important sources of knowledge.

When entering a new market where they have little or no experience, developers obviously assume added risk. To limit risk, developers must pay special attention to assessing their position in the marketplace as well as to the realism of their goals and objectives. As the case study of Europa Center continues, Whit Morrow describes Fraser Morrow Daniels's search for a site and the impact of detailed market research on the company's initial strategy.

⁂ Europa Center

Whit Morrow on Competition and Risk

People who were buying land in the Research Triangle area started doing so based more on politics than on the economics of the area. And they started speculating on land prices a little bit, so that the situation got to be very competitive. The obvious strategy was to buy 100 to 200 acres in and around Research Triangle Park and to build

ten or 12 buildings over 15 years. We were just hell-bent-for-leather to develop there. We had bids in on four or five pieces of land, but the politics of the area made us uncomfortable, so we got setbacks and height amendments.

Within a year, while we were trying to buy land, at least 15 or 20 other people—with more money, more staff, more power, and more connections than we had—dived right into the marketplace. Every time we identified 100 acres to buy, three other people were bidding on it, trying to buy it.

So we stopped, looked at our company, and looked at our capacity. We didn't have 500 banks trying to give us money or 2,000 employees. We were a tiny company—five or six people. So what could we do in that highly competitive business environment?

We totally shifted our strategy from becoming a big organization and doing 15 office buildings and a big office park and making our first profits on the fifth building to being a little organization. We acknowledged who we were and what the real competitive market was. We decided instead to buy ten acres and build one or two buildings. We based our profit projections on a modest goal and not on what we were going to do over a ten-year period.

We focused on the I-40 extension corridor from Research Triangle Park to the U.S. 15-501/I-40 intersection just east of Chapel Hill and looked at the major intersections closest to the population centers. There were really just two centers: Durham and Chapel Hill. And we weren't alone. We identified 23 different projects that came on line or were about to come on line during the three-year period that it takes to get something started.

In 1984 when we moved our company to the area, we wanted to be associated with the Research Triangle area. Therefore, we did not want our office in Raleigh, Durham, or Chapel Hill. We wanted to be in Research Triangle Park or on the edge of the park. We tried to lease office space, but no suitable space was available. We got into about 4,000 square feet of crummy space at $14.50 a square foot. In 1989, if I had wanted to rent office space around the park, at least 500,000 square feet was available at a net effective rent of about $12.00 per square foot for Class A space.

In 1986, a lot of money was available to build office buildings in Research Triangle Park. Many banks would put up exactly what you needed, build the building, and finance all the tenant improvements on the day the building opened. And there was no shortage of potential tenants. Looking ahead, we saw that the competitive environment would be different in three years. We asked five or six banks for an extra million dollars or more to carry the finished building through the leasing period. We held out for the extra financing for a long lease-up period that lasted two years.

My partner, Charles Fraser, was unwilling to sign a guarantee that he was the sole source of that extra million dollars, and we knew the banks would not lend it to us. So Charles decided to give up half his projected profit in exchange for a financial partner who would share the risk with us. It is important for a company entering this kind of environment to ask what its staying power is, what its risk profile is, and how much of a chance it is willing to take. How much do you really believe your projections? We decided to involve a financial partner in this office venture to put up money to buy the land and to guarantee an extra million dollars if we needed it.

Any time you have a great idea that takes several years to implement, you won't be the only one there, even if you're first. Furthermore, other companies have different risk profiles. Our risk profile was such that we could not stand the heat if it came to a competitive environment with 17 projects all targeted to the same market. It was a matter of survival for us.

In a three-year cycle, your potential tenants have to recognize you. The site with only one building must be attractive. You can't sell somebody a 100-acre parcel with the promise of a lake and trails; the site has to be right today. So the difference between us and some of the other players was that when we switched from 100-acre purchases at $50,000 an acre to ten-acre tracts at five times that amount per acre, the economics changed a little bit, too. You do not have to carry all that land, but you do have to pay more for the one piece that's currently available. So our strategy changed from finding a good site that we could market over ten years to one of finding a site that people stumble over every hour today—and we were willing to pay a lot for that.

continued on page 226

Dean Stratouly's experience was a little different. Boston was a completely different kind of market, and his company approached things differently. In both cases, however, both developers had to take a look at their firms and their firms' capacity and develop a strategy for going forward.

▌▌▌ Museum Towers

Getting Started

Once I settled in Boston, I got a job with an architecture/engineering firm that had within its client pool something called a "real estate developer." Don't forget that I was coming from the nuclear power plant business, where projects cost billions of dollars and take ten to 12 years to complete and a very sophisticated group of people are involved in economics, design, and construction. So when I started dealing with our client who was the real estate developer, I was surprised at how little he knew about the design and construction process and how unsophisticated his approach was to market and location decisions.

It was all fairly ad hoc—you know, the market seems good, that's a good location, let's see if we can put something up. Very much back of the envelope. This particular developer and I struck up a relationship that grew from our firm's providing him services to my doing some consulting for him to our actually becoming partners. In 1980, we started working on a project together that went extremely well, and I decided to leave the architecture/engineering firm and go do this development stuff.

I joined with Ed Berry in 1980. Ed had two partners locally and a relationship with several guys in New York, one of whom is my current partner. I actually started in this business with a company that we called the Russia Wharf Company, because we were redeveloping a historic project that had been the site where the trade came in from Russia to Boston. We started the project the year that Russia invaded Afghanistan and Russia wasn't very popular in the U.S. I was standing on the corner of Congress Street and Atlantic Avenue in downtown Boston, ready to sprint across that street. It was a hot August day, and a big crowd of people were getting ready to make the dash. A couple of tourists noticed the Russia Wharf sign, and one said, "Look at this! The Russians are everywhere—even in Boston."

I walked into the office and said to my partner, "We've got to change the name of this Russia thing." Since we were on Congress Street, we decided to call it the Congress Group. We needed to make the decision fairly quickly, because we had just acquired our next project and we needed names for the partnerships.

In 1982, Ed and I bought out the other partners. Everything we did from 1980 to 1986 included equity participation from a group in New York. We had an agreement that all of our projects would be financed with this group of individuals of high net worth, who had access to other individuals with high net worth. Then in late 1986, Ed and I split up Congress Group, and my current partner in New York and I re-formed Congress Group Ventures and went on in 1986 to do the stuff we have done for the last ten or 12 years.

continued on page 227

Watching experienced developers at work leaves the impression that real estate development is much more an art than a science. But formal research requires patient and systematic investigation to discover the facts and principles pertinent to the subject of inquiry. How does such a time-consuming process relate to generating good development ideas?

Consider the creativity of jazz musicians whose improvisations prompt critical acclaim. Their music appears spontaneous; they create it as they go. In fact, the apparent freedom and ease of play stem from years of study and practice. Through practice, they have mastered the techniques of their instrument and of jazz forms. Through study, they have come to understand the relevant principles. By reading about the principles or listening to the interpretations of great jazz players, they refine their knowledge of the medium. Thus, freedom and discipline and improvisation and technique interact. In fact, creativity and logic generally work together.

Structured research provides the discipline, fuels the logic, helps set the criteria, and to some extent even prompts the intuition by which people respond creatively to events occurring around them. Most successful real estate developers have at one time or another engaged in careful, systematic study of specific markets and property types. In addition, they have tested ideas for projects by planning, building, and leasing space. Thus, even in cases where the inception of an idea appears to be a flash of brilliance—something truly original—the idea can often be traced to the interplay of past study and analysis of widely known facts and basic principles. The new idea is usually a reworked combination of known elements. More typically, good development ideas replicate to a great extent previously tried ideas that are tailored to a particular niche.

Structured Market Research and Successful Generation of Ideas

The condition of the market is generally described in terms of the supply of and demand for space. To keep abreast of short- and long-term aspects of the market, developers and real estate professionals must read market forecasts and talk to people familiar with the national and local economies. Knowledge about both supply and demand is necessary background for the generation of ideas, stage one of the development process. Knowledge should begin with a very broad, national picture, because financing is national (and increasingly international), some tenants are national, and some contractors are national. Knowledge should also include a regional, local, and even neighborhood picture of current conditions. At that level, developers ask themselves how comparable properties are performing and what trends are emerging.

Simply collecting a wealth of data will not aid the developer's decision-making process. Too often, marketing research is served up by the pound when only an ounce of insight is needed. Data must be carefully selected and placed in a meaningful framework that links the proposed project with the market and connects the present with the future.

One simple model can help: a four-square design that links present and future and property and market (see Figure 11-1). Every market study seeks knowledge of the likely future success of a specific proposed project. Yet almost all of the currently available data pertain to the present market as a whole. The challenge, then, is to make the relevant connections from the macrolevel present to the property's microlevel future.

Most valuable to the developer are trend data, which measure changes over the past decade and over the decade to come. Relevant changes include employment growth and income levels, age structure of the population, industrial structure, and supply configurations. These macrolevel trends should be collected for the nation, metropolitan region, and local area. Macrolevel forecasts are available from several sources (see Chapters 17 and 18) and can be used to develop useful forecasts of local supply and demand. Because forecast data are especially scarce, they should be the first subject of inquiry. Limitations associated with those data (variables and categories) can then guide the search for comparable data covering historical trends. Forecast data also help the developer brainstorm about the real estate needs of the future.

The collected macrolevel data (the material covered in Chapter 2) that describe broad market conditions must then be related to the microlevel needs of a proposed project. If the project does not exist at present, the developer obviously cannot study it; however, the developer can identify comparable projects for review. Successful as these examples may have been, the key question to answer is how well a comparable project lines up with the forecasted trends. Are a project's space users drawn from categories projected to increase faster or slower than average? How rapidly is the competitive supply likely to increase? What would happen to the comparable property if it simply floated with the forecasted trends?

Answers to these questions provide a simple and efficient (albeit rough) market analysis that is entirely appropriate for this stage of the development process. Forecasts of job growth and demographic estimates of age, sex, and income distribution are useful for segmenting markets and projecting the emerging requirements for types of space. The developer then translates the forecasts into an absorption schedule to see whether it satisfies the financial requirements of the proposed project by converting total growth into segmented

Figure 11-1

Interrelating the Two Essential Dimensions of Market Studies

	Present	**Future**
Macro **(Market)**	**Current and Historical** ■ Supply by Broad Segment ■ Demand Characteristics 　■ Preferences 　■ Income 　■ Tenant Types ■ Absorption and Vacancies ■ Rents and Value (cap rates)	**Market Forecasts** ■ Supply by Segment—Lagged Interaction with Demand ■ Demand Characteristics 　■ Employment Growth 　■ Population Growth 　■ Space Needs (derived from employment and population growth) ■ Absorption and Vacancies ■ Rents and Value (cap rates)
Micro **(Individual Property)**	**Subject Property and Comparables** ■ Unit Size and Quality (features, functions, and benefits) ■ Demand Characteristics 　■ Preferences 　■ Income 　■ Tenant Types ■ Operating Expenses (adjusted for services provided) ■ Absorption and Vacancies ■ Rents and Value (cap rates)	**Future Performance of Subject Property** ■ Prospective Rents ■ Operating Expenses ■ Absorption and Vacancies ■ Net Operating Income ■ Market Value 　　　　　　　　　(**Goal**)

Adapted from Dowell Myers and Kenneth Beck, "A Four-Square Design for Relating the Two Essential Dimensions for Real Estate Market Studies," in *Appraisal, Market Analysis, and Public Policy in Real Estate: Essays in Honor of James R. Graaskamp*, ed. James R. DeLisle and J. Sa-Aadu (Boston: Kluwer Academic Publishers, 1994), pp. 259–88.

space needs and needs into absorption by applying an estimated capture rate (see Chapter 17 for details).[11]

Assessing Future Supply Competition

Supply-side considerations are the most uncertain of all. Developers can gather aggregate data on the existing national supply of types of space distinguished by use, size, location, function, style, and overall quality, and they can note vacancy rates in the existing stock. National figures are available from large brokerage firms such as Coldwell Banker, Grubb & Ellis, and Cushman & Wakefield, while regional financial institutions and local brokerage firms can often supply additional details for specific markets.

Developers should be aware, however, that vacancy rates are difficult to measure. Some space is unoccupied but committed under signed leases with occupancy scheduled to start at a later date, some space is rented but not fully occupied, some space is subleased, and several other variations are possible. And, alas, owners of buildings with large vacancies do not always truthfully report vacancies to people who gather data about them. The key question is what percentage of the space is actually used by tenants, not what part is being paid for, because in slow markets, for example, some tenants lease more space than they need in anticipation of expected future expansion. If these tenants already hold excess space, they are less likely to lease new space when the economy rebounds.

Data on the amount of space currently under construction and the expected completion date are also critical to analyzing the supply in any market. "Announced" space may or may not be built, but space already under construction will probably be completed and should be included in the estimate of supply.

Beyond knowing the current local supply, the vacancy rate in the existing supply, the volume of space under construction, and announcements of space to be built, developers also need a feel for the local legal and political environment. How easy is it to initiate a new project? Local zoning ordinances place legal constraints on the volume and location of new space. The easier it is to build and the shorter the political lead time, the faster the market will respond to tight conditions. While it is harder to develop in tightly regulated markets, development risk is reduced when regulations are tighter, thus insulating an ongoing project from new competition.

Another factor that affects the local supply of space is the physical. How much "unbuilt" capacity does the market have? The concern in this case is how much land (or air rights) is available for a particular use. Only certain locations can accommodate certain needs. Drainage, topography, and soil conditions prohibit development in some areas. Infrastructure is an increasingly important constraint (see Chapter 13). Again, these factors measure the likely ease with which new competition can enter the market.

In sum, knowledge of supply begins with knowledge of existing space, current vacancies in that space, and new space already in the pipeline. Knowledge also includes legal and political considerations (not only current zoning but any potential zoning changes as well). Physical constraints—mountains, lakes, and the like—give developers a perspective on today's supply and on the potential to increase that supply over time. Development is a forward-looking endeavor. Developers who limit their analyses to only the first dimension—current supply—are likely to come up short.

Asking the Great "How Come?"

Successful development responds to the needs of space users and, to a lesser extent, to the requirements of government and citizens/neighbors. The successful project highlighted in the profile of Ross Perot, Jr., shows how developers effectively use information about the market and good ideas to satisfy diverse interests. Products, places, people, and capital add up to many useful areas of inquiry.

Once the developer and the marketing staff believe that they have arrived at a good choice for a proposed development, they must still ask one nagging question: How come no other developer has stumbled across this fine opportunity? Is something wrong with the idea? Why do we see the opportunity more clearly than others? Asking such a skeptical question brings added discipline to the marketing process. The question is especially important for out-of-town developers who may be less knowledgeable about local politics and market trends but more sophisticated about development in general.

In Chapter 10, Whit Morrow explained how others had overlooked the Research Triangle, which was viewed as separate small towns rather than as a single region. Growth had been sluggish in the past, but more recent indicators suggested that the area was poised for development. As Morrow's comments in this chapter attest, the opportunity quickly had become too obvious and eventually was discovered by a number of other developers as well.

As part of their research, developers must identify and recognize the competition so they can position their own product competitively to reach the target market. Better price, quality, and location are obvious attributes of competing real estate products. Only slightly less important are reputation, expertise, and financial depth.

Simply discovering a development opportunity is not enough. For the development firm to prevail, it may also need to secure the best site or come up with the best design or arrange the earliest loan commitment or obtain needed entitlements or secure the key anchor tenant or develop the best marketing plan before other developers come up with the same idea. More often, the successful developer integrates several key advantages and builds all decisions around the total marketing concept. When a developer follows a systematic marketing approach, an objective evaluation will likely reveal when the developer does have a competitive edge and is thus well advised to proceed.

Summary

The importance of marketing principles and market research to real estate developers, particularly in highly competitive markets, cannot be overemphasized. Marketing begins long before the leasing of space—and even before design of the product; it begins with the marketing concept—the notion that any business should start with the needs and wants of customers and satisfy those needs and wants competitively.

Market research is the investigation into needs and wants (demand) and into products and competitors that might satisfy those needs and wants (supply). While usually thought of as formal, focused, and sys-

Profile **Ross Perot, Jr.**

Chair, Hillwood Development Corporation
Dallas, Texas

Ross Perot, Jr., likes to think big. The Dallas native and son of the two-time presidential candidate is chair of Hillwood Development Corporation, a firm that has been making headlines for its big vision and its big projects, such as the 18,000-acre Alliance Airport and Business Park in Fort Worth, Texas.

Thinking Big

Perot has led Hillwood since it was founded in the 1980s. He decided to get involved in the real estate business, a field that had always appealed to him, after graduating with a bachelor's degree in business administration from Vanderbilt University and serving for $8^{1}/_{2}$ years in the U.S. Air Force.

The firm began as a traditional real estate development company, developing land for more than 20 residential projects in the north Texas market and elsewhere. Since then, however, Perot has taken Hillwood into more ambitious and complicated terrain. The company's first major project was the Alliance Airport and Business Park in Fort Worth. Working closely with the Federal Aviation Administration, the Texas Department of Transportation, and the city of Fort Worth, the Alliance Development Corporation, a subsidiary of Hillwood, successfully created one of this country's largest and most advanced facilities for commercial, industrial, and transportation firms. The project features outstanding access to highways, rail lines, and air routes, along with advanced fiber-optic telecommunications infrastructure. The result is that Alliance offers substantial savings in transportation costs, and, with its triple-freeport status, the firms located there are exempt from certain state and local taxes. As global trade increases and as the economic effects of the North American Free Trade Agreement become stronger, the Alliance development is perfectly suited to helping companies succeed in these new market conditions. Initially, some people were skeptical about the prospects for such a large project, but so far Alliance has seen

over $2 billion of investment, has created more than 14,000 jobs, and is home to 14 *Fortune* 500 companies.

One of Hillwood's current projects is equally ambitious. The downtown Dallas project, named Victory, will involve the redevelopment of 65 acres of blighted industrial land into a mixed-use complex of entertainment, office, retail, and residential uses. Once completed, the project will feature 4 million square feet of office space, 1,000 residential units, and 600,000 square feet of retail space. The mile-long development site will be anchored by a new 20,000-seat arena for the Dallas Stars hockey team and the Dallas Mavericks basketball team. Perot hopes that the Victory development will bring vitality to downtown Dallas and that the project will connect downtown with other active neighborhoods, including the Market Center and Design District. Perot has said that he would like Victory to become "the model for inner-city revitalization."

Building Teams

Perot points out that building teams is an essential part of creating successful developments, particularly for projects like Alliance or Victory. For each project, Hillwood attempts to bring together firms that have outstanding professional skills, reputations for honesty, and a solid knowledge of local conditions. Perot says that "ideas are precious" and that "you need to keep things fresh." For the Victory project, Hillwood held design charrettes with top firms so that it could gather ideas and test the firms as potential partners. In its role as master developer, Hillwood marries its own expertise and ability to execute complex projects with the specialized knowledge of outside firms. Moreover, Hillwood works closely with local governments and community groups to ensure support for the project.

The Challenge of Urban Redevelopment Projects

Urban redevelopment sites can be especially difficult to develop, no matter how skilled the development team. In

---

tematic, market research for generating development ideas involves a large informal component made up of experience, observation, reading, conversation, and interdisciplinary analysis. Prudent developers equip themselves to undertake both types of inquiry. The generation of ideas, marketing, and market research embrace both intuitive and rational elements. Successful devel-

opers are able to integrate the intuitive with the rational. Formal knowledge of marketing principles and market research enhances the use of both faculties.

This chapter has taken a broad view of marketing and market research as befits the earliest of the eight stages of the development process. Chapter 12 covers refining the project idea and sharpens the focus of the

Victory, the new Dallas arena and mixed-use project, is intended to link the city's vital core districts: the booming Uptown area, the Dallas central business district, the West End Historic District, the Market Center, and the 60-acre Arts District.

the case of the Victory project, the site for more than 100 years had been an industrial area that included a railyard, a power plant, and a meat-packing plant. Not surprisingly, the site required extensive environmental remediation. Perot notes that these problems kept the site from being redeveloped earlier, despite its outstanding location and potential. Thus, it was essential for Hillwood to work with the city government to clean up the site. Another challenge was the size and the political profile of the project. Although public opposition arose over the city of Dallas's financial support (through taxes on hotel rooms and rental cars) for the new arena, the public ultimately approved the financing plan in a referendum. For Perot, the politics of the development process proved frustrating at times, even though he knew that political opposition to projects can be a part of the real estate business.

Measuring Success

With the Victory project in the construction phase, Perot can step back to consider how far his company has come in the past decade. Hillwood would be judged a successful firm by anyone's standards, but for Perot the real satisfaction comes from driving through one of the firm's residential communities and seeing families enjoying their neighborhoods, or thinking about all the economic benefits that a development like Alliance has generated. As he says, "If you do it right, your projects can have a big impact on the community." Although all development projects have to make financial sense, it is the feeling of pride in a good project that matters most to Perot. Visionary real estate developers are great assets to their communities, whether they are small or whether they think big like Perot. ∎

---

market research effort. Chapters 17 and 18 show how focused market research results in a formal market study, which constitutes one component of the feasibility analysis. If a developer formally commits to the project idea in stage five, then the market study (which has evolved in stages one through four) becomes a building block in the marketing plan that drives sales

or leasing in stages six through eight (Chapters 20 through 23).

Market research supports real estate development through all its stages. Useful research can be both broad (including global, national, and regional economies) and highly focused (for example, checking the traffic counts along a main artery that serves a site). Little of a developer's total experience and knowledge go to waste when searching for new ideas.

Terms

- Absorption
- Amenities
- Forecast data
- Four Ps: product, place, price, promotion
- Lumpy demand
- Macro trends
- Marketing strategy
- Micro trends
- Segmentation
- Societal marketing concept
- Supply and demand

Review Questions

11.1 Describe Philip Kotler's attitude toward the customer and how that affects marketing principles.

11.2 Describe the differences in the marketing concept, the production concept, the product concept, and the selling concept.

11.3 What are the four Ps, and how do they fit into a classic marketing strategy?

11.4 What are the four major differences between marketing real estate and marketing traditional products?

11.5 What is societal marketing, and why are real estate developers forced to engage in it?

11.6 In the Europa Center case study, Whit Morrow discusses his company's reasons for moving to the Research Triangle Park area. How did his company go about setting its strategy for the type of development company it would be, where it would concentrate its efforts, and what kind of development it would focus on?

11.7 Ross Perot, Jr., has a familiar name and access to money. Do those factors ensure success for a developer?

11.8 How do the marketing concepts of supply and demand apply to this stage of the development process?

Notes

1. Donald L. Williams and Sally M. Dwyer, "A Marketing Revolution," *Urban Land,* March 1994, pp. 28–31.

2. Philip Kotler, *Marketing Management: Analysis, Planning, and Control,* 9th ed. (Englewood Cliffs, N.J.: Prentice-Hall, 1997).

3. For more information on the role of such markets today, see T.M. Spitzer and H. Baum, *Public Markets and Community Revitalization* (Washington, D.C.: ULI–the Urban Land Institute, 1995).

4. Kotler, *Marketing Management.*

5. Ibid.

6. *ULI Project Reference File,* Vol. 27, No. 16, October–December 1997.

7. The authors prefer the following three key factors: location, location, and timing (see Chapter 23 for more details).

8. Required reading for anyone attempting to understand the structure of an industry are Michael Porter, *Competitive Strategy: Techniques for Analyzing Industries and Competitors* (New York: Free Press, 1980); and Michael E. Porter, *Michael E. Porter on Competition* (Cambridge, Mass.: Harvard Business School Press, 1998).

9. For a more complete description of Laguna West, see *ULI Project Reference File,* Vol. 24, No. 11, July–September 1994; and Mark C. Eppli and Charles J. Tu, *Valuing the New Urbanism* (Washington, D.C.: ULI–the Urban Land Institute, 1999).

10. See Debra Stein, "Taking the Guesswork out of Winning Community Support," *Urban Land,* October 1991, pp. 2–5; Debra Stein, *Winning Community Support for Land Use Projects* (Washington, D.C.: ULI–the Urban Land Institute, 1992); Debra Stein, *Making Community Meetings Work* (Washington, D.C.: ULI–the Urban Land Institute, 1996); and David Godschalk et al., *Pulling Together: A Planning and Development Consensus-Building Manual* (Washington, D.C.: ULI–the Urban Land Institute, 1994).

11. Dowell Myers and Philip Mitchell, "Identifying a Well-Founded Market Study," *Appraisal Journal,* October 1993, pp. 500–8.

Chapter 12

Stage Two: Refinement of the Idea

The Fraser Morrow Daniels development company, because it was interested in entering a new geographic area and developing products outside its previous expertise, undertook an extraordinary amount of market research when it moved into North Carolina's Research Triangle Park area. The firm set out to answer the basic questions raised by Chapter 10: Where do we work and what do we develop? For Fraser Morrow Daniels, stage one of the development process concluded with the decision to work in the Research Triangle and to develop several property types, including an office park. In contrast, Dean Stratouly set out to develop multifamily housing and a hotel, but problems with acquiring approvals and a subsequent economic downturn stalled the project, which ultimately resulted in a smaller site for high-rise multifamily housing.

As noted earlier, most ideas don't survive beyond stage one; they succumb to qualitative limitations (such as image), or they die in red ink on the back-of-the-envelope pro forma. But, occasionally, the developer's back-of-the-envelope figures show promise, and the development idea continues to generate interest. When that happens, the process moves to stage two: refinement of the idea.

This chapter elaborates on the following activities of stage two:

- Objectives of stage two;
- A more detailed scanning of the environment;
- Choosing the site;
- Deciding what can be built on the site: initial design feasibility;
- Negotiating for the site;

- Discussing the project with other players;
- Segmenting the market and differentiating the product;
- Financial feasibility; and
- Risk control during stage two.

The chapter concludes with a discussion of the factors involved in deciding to move ahead with Europa Center and what became Museum Towers.

Objectives of Stage Two

Considering the complexity of what happens in stage two, "refining the idea" is a deceptively simple phrase. The intent is clear: the developer's idea must either evolve into a particular project design associated with a specific piece of land or be abandoned before extensive resources are committed to the concept. Finding and acquiring a site and making an initial determination of legal and physical feasibility are the primary objectives in stage two. Once the developer meets these objectives, another physical objective is specifying the project, that is, moving from the idea of building office space to a preliminary design for a 100,000-square-foot, four-story office building with more specific features, functions, and benefits.

Associated with these primary physical objectives are marketing, financial, and management objectives, which combine with the physical objectives to allow the developer to feel reasonably confident of the project's feasibility at the end of stage two. This comfort level permits a significant increase in "resource com-

The developer of Stoney Brook in Danville, California, overcame the community's antidevelopment sentiment by changing the bulky mass of high-density townhouses in the original design to clustered single-family detached homes. The community accepted the new design, which was built to the same scale and style of the surrounding neighborhood.

mitment" during stage three. During stage three, the developer must demonstrate feasibility to all participants in the development process. In stage two, however, it is the developer who must become convinced of the project's feasibility, because it is largely his funds that will be expended (i.e., put at risk) during stage three to convince the other participants of the project's viability.

Several key concepts underlie site selection, the first of stage two's physical objectives.

First, finding the right site is crucial. In the United States, land typically represents anywhere from 10 to 30 percent of a project's total cost. In some markets, the cost of residential lots represents over 50 percent of the median price for new and existing houses. Although many legally and physically feasible sites where a structure could be constructed might be available, one site will often be preferable in the eyes of a prospective tenant. Location is the key to realizable rent: a better site might generate 10 percent, 20 percent, or even 50 percent more rent, depending on the particular components of value. Because it costs roughly the same amount to construct a given building on any of the physically possible sites (barring any unusual natural features that must be accommodated), the increase in rent is said to be attributed to the land. Given that the other physical costs are fixed across competing sites, experts point

to "operating leverage" for any particular use of a selected site.

The developer must exercise great care in the site selection process. In many urban areas, a distance of only a few blocks might separate vastly different neighborhoods. Thus, selection of the optimal site provides the greatest positive divergence between cost and value.

Further, at this point, the developer's profit motive often conflicts with the desire to control the level of financial commitment early in the development process. This dilemma leads to a Catch-22: the developer must tie up a site early, before fully demonstrating its feasibility, to capture the maximum profit on the land, yet to do so he must spend money, increasing his financial exposure. Clearly, minimizing outlays of cash in the early stages is a prime method of controlling risk, but the developer who waits to tie up land until he can demonstrate its physical, legal, political, and economic feasibility may have to pay a premium (and others may be willing to pay more). If the developer purchases the land outright only to discover that the idea proves infeasible, he may have to resell the land at a considerably lower price. Consequently, developers typically use some type of an "option to buy" to tie up a site during stage two.

In any development undertaking, the public sector is the developer's partner in site selection. Public sector officials enforce the rules, while the body politic determines how the rules will change in the future. (The developer can try to influence change, for example, by lobbying for a rezoning.) Zoning regulations reflect the public partner's general position regarding development. Today, zoning in most jurisdictions grants a developer the right to present a proposed site plan, though it does not necessarily allow the developer to develop retail or office space. Zoning practices vary across jurisdictions. In Florida, for example, statutes require a municipality to prove the existence of adequate infrastructure before a plan for development is approved. In downtown San Francisco, a 1986 voter initiative (Proposition M) set limits on the overall amount of allowable development—only 450,000 square feet a year through 1998 and no more than 950,000 square feet annually after that. A developer's proposal for the "best use" for a given space must be weighed against other developers' ideas for the site. In general, the time required today for project approval often extends the development period to the point that developers must either risk more of their own money (if it is available) or seek the equivalent of venture capital to fund the project during planning and approval. (Remember from Chapter 3 that increasing demands for venture funding is a primary evolutionary change in the real estate development process.)

In many areas of the United States, the influence of well-organized neighborhood groups intent on having a direct say in development in their community has grown significantly. Incurring the opposition of such groups almost certainly affects planning and approval. At a minimum, developers facing community opposition will likely experience substantial delays and significant expenses for engaging the services of additional professionals (primarily attorneys and planners) to help them work with the community.

In the process of finding a site and specifying a proposed project, developers must undertake the following tasks simultaneously:

- Scanning the environment for significant forces— possible competitors, government jurisdictions, political power bases;
- Choosing the site;
- Analyzing the market, that is, the areas or neighborhoods within the market that might offer an appropriate site;
- Setting market, physical, legal, and political criteria for the proposed project;
- Analyzing possible sites to identify the site that best satisfies the criteria;
- Determining initial design feasibility;

- Negotiating for the selected site and structuring a contract (usually one that constitutes an option) to secure the site;
- Discussing the project with elected and appointed officials and city planners to ascertain their interests and any possible constraints on the project;
- Analyzing the competition—competing development companies and competing projects—and refining the subject development to maximize its competitive position;
- Continuing to refine financial feasibility—periodically retesting the back-of-the-envelope numbers for financial feasibility and undertaking preliminary projections of the timing of cash flows over the development period, remembering the importance of level two feasibility; and
- Controlling risk during idea refinement—testing the design's preliminary feasibility by discussing with engineers, architects, land planners, contractors, and/or financial sources a project design that fits the prospective tenant market.

Completion of these tasks culminates in a decision to move the idea to stage three (formal feasibility), rework the idea, or abandon the idea.

The process of refining the idea is complex not only because so many activities are involved in identifying the right use for the right site, but also because the activities must be carried out simultaneously and interactively. (Figure 12-1 captures this complexity in two dimensions.) The answer to the overarching question —is this idea feasible in this area?—is conditioned on the answers to many other questions posed at about the same time but not always answered quickly, completely, or at all. Therefore, refining the idea is typically not a straightforward process. Developers must tolerate some disorder, uncertainty, and risk as they try to bring an idea to physical reality. Each development requires a slightly different approach. Sometimes developers press hard and commit more resources. In other situations, developers let certain political pressures "work themselves out" before proceeding. Still, at some point, the developer must acquire land, make contact with other potential members of the development team, and undertake initial project design; typically, these activities occur during stage two of the development process. Although there are often good reasons to deviate from the sequence outlined in the eight-stage model—for example, one site might be far superior to all others and the owner will sell only for cash—it is important to remember that developers frequently incur penalties through increased risk or decreased reward when tasks are completed too far out of the logical sequence of the development process.

Figure 12-1

Activities Involved in Refinement of the Idea

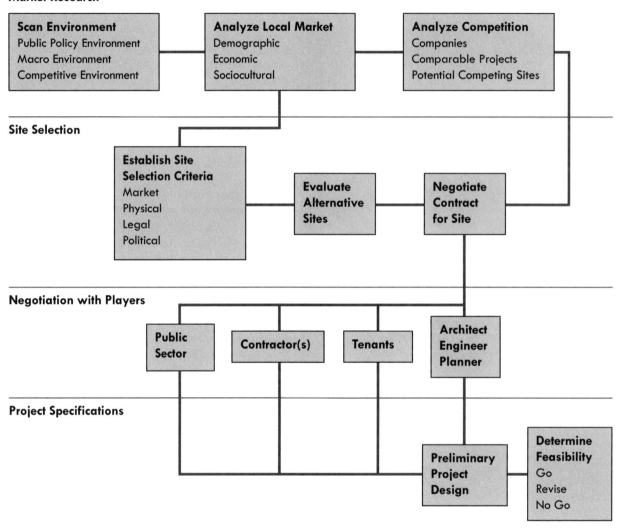

Market Research

Scan Environment
Public Policy Environment
Macro Environment
Competitive Environment

Analyze Local Market
Demographic
Economic
Sociocultural

Analyze Competition
Companies
Comparable Projects
Potential Competing Sites

Site Selection

Establish Site Selection Criteria
Market
Physical
Legal
Political

Evaluate Alternative Sites

Negotiate Contract for Site

Negotiation with Players

Public Sector

Contractor(s)

Tenants

Architect Engineer Planner

Project Specifications

Preliminary Project Design

Determine Feasibility
Go
Revise
No Go

A More Detailed Scanning of The Environment: Competitors And Governments

Home-grown developers know the projects, financial depth, and political clout of their competitors in the local market, but newcomers must identify the competition as well as determine what the market wants. Further, all developers—whether home-grown or newly arrived —need to understand the ways in which trends in local politics and regulations are likely to affect the via-

bility of their projects. They need to forge relationships with city officials, politicians, and the general public. Indeed, understanding the human and organizational sides of a market is as important to formulating successful development ideas as understanding the physical patterns of infrastructure, interactive land uses, and urban growth patterns.

It is important to recall that Fraser Morrow Daniels perceived an excellent opportunity to build speculative office space in the Research Triangle in the early 1980s when almost all space in the area was build-to-suit by local developers. This same opportunity, however, also attracted to the market a flock of much larger out-of-town developers. Thus, as the competitive situation changed rapidly in the mid-1980s, Fraser Morrow Daniels had to reassess its ability to compete with other newcomers. After evaluating the competition, Fraser Morrow Daniels realized that its own capacities were not the same as those of the other, larger players. Therefore, the firm abandoned its plans to build an office park and instead looked for a niche to fill with one or two office buildings on a smaller site.

Similarly, Fraser Morrow Daniels recognized the various climates for development in the different political jurisdictions within the Research Triangle market. The city where the firm ultimately chose a site posed the greatest political and legal difficulties of the four major Triangle cities for developers wanting to work quickly. Nonetheless, Fraser Morrow Daniels's accurate perception of the city's regulatory climate guided the company's site selection: any site would need to have the appropriate zoning already in place to avoid substantial delays.

Learning about competitors, governments, regulatory frameworks, and politics is an ongoing process for developers. In a dynamic real estate market, competition, regulation, and politics are all subject to continuous change. One developer might perceive an opportunity to develop apartments in one submarket, only to find that an established apartment developer with solid political connections and a favorable public image is already planning such a project. Unless the new entrant can clearly distinguish its project from those of established developers, the newcomer might be well advised to find another submarket.

Alternatively, a developer might find an opportunity, only to confront rigid opposition from the public sector. The market for apartments might exist simply because residents successfully opposed previous project proposals. Or the local council or planning board might decide to limit apartment construction as a strategy for avoiding adverse fiscal impacts. In other instances, constraints on building could represent more subtle impediments to development. Overlong project review might prevent a developer from retaining site control at an affordable price. Infrastructure might appear to be adequate, but other planned projects scheduled for completion before the developer's proposed project could consume available service capacity and lead to moratoriums on new development. And impact fees (see Chapter 13) can reduce the project's profitability.

The Culture of Urban Growth Patterns

Even harder to explain than the role of transportation, technology, immigration, and economic opportunity in shaping U.S. cities is the culture or personality of a city and how that personality influences what gets built. In many cases, a city's ability to foster a climate of entrepreneurship is central to its growth.

The success story of the last several decades is Los Angeles. Other than its benign climate, Los Angeles can boast few natural advantages. In 1880, the city was on its way to nowhere, its ports were inferior to those of San Francisco and other western cities, and, most important, it had no water. Urban historians such as Roger Lotchin, who have studied the evolution of Los Angeles, often attribute the city's remarkable growth to an entrepreneurial spirit among its leaders—the people who organized the California Institute of Technology, the people who brought water to Los Angeles in 1900 via the first 250-mile aqueduct, and the people responsible for the Colorado River Compact in 1928 and eventually the Hoover (now Boulder) Dam.[1] Los Angeles exists because people made it happen. In today's urban environment, cities can still make it happen, and a sense of history can enhance any developer's appreciation of the entrepreneurial opportunities awaiting discovery (see Chapters 7 through 9).

Models of urban growth provide developers with a useful framework for understanding a city's current patterns of land use and indicate to some extent the future direction of change. These theoretical urban models focus on where growth takes place and how different land uses interrelate. For several reasons, people and firms cluster in concentrations rather than spreading uniformly over the territory. One major reason is to minimize the "friction of distance." Because resources are needed to move people, goods, and information, agglomerations can reduce the costs of moving and handling goods, thereby fostering economies of scale. Because cities are agglomerations of people and activities, all cities reduce some of these transfer costs. Most large cities evolved around nodes where transportation lines met (often a break or transfer between modes of transportation such as water to rail).

People congregate to pursue economic opportunities that are less available at lower social and physical densities. The modern city has taken on economic functions that overshadow the historically important reasons of defense, religion, government, and local trade. The new telecommunications infrastructure often locates at existing transportation hubs (large cities or their newly developing suburban areas near regional airports) to profit from existing large markets, thereby strengthening existing urban centers. The Internet backbone generally has been built to connect existing population concentrations, although there are differences in access that will materially affect cities' competitiveness.

Urban Economic Theories

When searching for a site, developers can organize the sea of existing data by using three simple theories of urban economics: concentric zone theory, axial theory, and sector theory. *Concentric zone theory* holds that, assuming no variations in topography or transport corridors or limits on land supply, cities grow in concentric rings, with the most intensive uses located at the center. Over time, more competitive land uses replace less competitive uses, which move outward from the center. Generally, land values decline the farther land is located from the central, most intensive uses. The concentric zone theory held up fairly well until the early 1900s and the advent of new transit options. Consequently, it explains best the original shape of our older cities.

Axial theory came next and accounts for development along transportation corridors, which typically radiate outward in several directions from the city center. Over time, advances in transportation systems and improvements in transport technology have changed the patterns of access in many cities and, consequently, land values. Transportation routes usually form paths along which development locates as new areas become accessible. Activity still locates efficiently, but it is commuting time rather than physical distance that drives location.

Sector theory holds that because geographic features and differential access exist in the real world, waves of development tend to move outward from the center, forming wedge-shaped sectors (like a pie cut into wedge-shaped pieces) that follow the path of least resistance and lower costs.

Careful analysis of the development of particular cities over many years often reveals a sectoral pattern of growth, possibly overlain by the more recent network of circumferential highways that have created new suburban nodes. In fact, during the late 19th and early 20th centuries, Homer Hoyt (the originator of the sector theory) based his general model of urban sectors on such an evolution of U.S. cities.[2]

Atlanta is a good example of a city with no major geographic restrictions preventing concentric spread. In fact, the railroad line and its terminus established the original city center, which still serves as the CBD. As strong north/south corridors developed in response to the influence of the rail lines, the first upper-income residential area expanded to the north of downtown on physically attractive land. Over many years, the higher-income residential areas continued to be developed northward, forming a wedge-shaped sector moving outward to the northeast and northwest. The major industrial zone moved outward south of downtown and today extends to Hartsfield International Airport and the

Fulton County stadium. The lower, flatter industrial zone also happens to be downwind of the northern residential areas. In fact, many cities with prevailing winds from northwest to southeast have evolved with higher-income residences located in the northwest and industrial uses situated in the southeast.

As the perimeter highway around Atlanta developed, new nodes of office and retail development sprang up. Primarily north of downtown, these nodes formed the base point of new sectors that pushed Atlanta's urban fringe farther out and created a multicentered pattern and many more new "edge cities."[3]

Clearly, no simple theory can fully explain the richness of our urban environments. Still, the developer who is well grounded in models of urban growth can have a competitive advantage in finding appropriate sites. These straightforward models make it easier to assimilate new data and forecast future land uses.

The models are also helpful for understanding transitions that result in the replacement of one land use with another. In Atlanta, for example, developers have purchased entire residential subdivisions with the express purpose of redeveloping the land more intensively for nonresidential uses. Redevelopment of parts of existing sectors is another useful insight enjoyed by those who can organize facts by combining these and other urban economic theories.

By using the theories of urban growth, developers should have a better grasp of the long-term development potential of any site they are considering. Whit Morrow, unlike many competitors, viewed the cities that make up the Research Triangle as a converging market area and assumed that office growth would spread beyond Research Triangle Park (the center of the triangle formed originally by three cities) along the transportation corridors, especially I-40. Because he had compiled a list of planned office buildings for the entire Research Triangle market rather than for any one of the individual cities (Raleigh, Durham, Chapel Hill, and Cary), whose spatial distinctions were weakening, Morrow also projected the coming oversupply of office space earlier than most competitors.

Choosing the Site

Developers find sites in various ways. One obvious way is by keeping abreast of real estate listed for sale. In addition, developers (or other members of the in-house development team) often study zoning and tax maps for prospective parcels, examine deed records, and then approach owners of property not listed for sale. The grapevine is yet another source: an attorney might happen to mention over lunch that a competitor is strapped for cash.

The truth is that developers love real estate, are fascinated by it, and think about it a lot of the time. They go to professional meetings to get new ideas and more background. They regularly take time wherever they are visiting to "kick the tires." They get out, talk to people, and see sites, creating a specific database in their heads.

Publicly available (at a price) databases are another source of real estate information. Today, some developers use Geographic Information Systems (GISs) to look at a city on a computer screen by first calling up a map

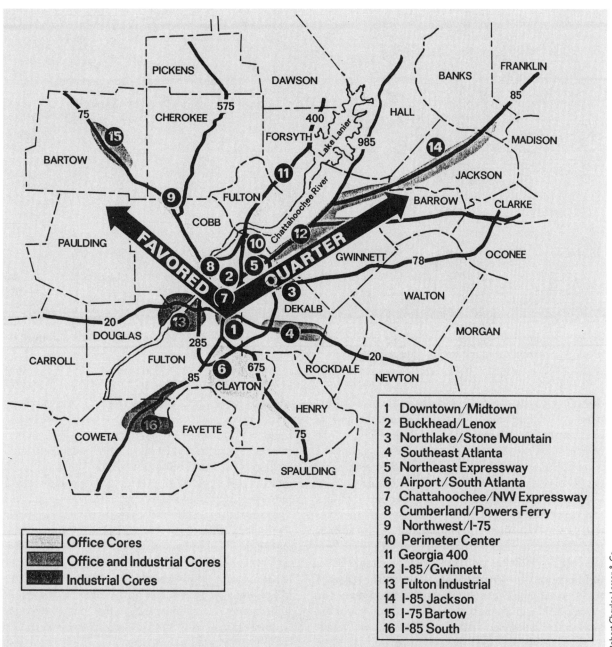

1 Downtown/Midtown
2 Buckhead/Lenox
3 Northlake/Stone Mountain
4 Southeast Atlanta
5 Northeast Expressway
6 Airport/South Atlanta
7 Chattahoochee/NW Expressway
8 Cumberland/Powers Ferry
9 Northwest/I-75
10 Perimeter Center
11 Georgia 400
12 I-85/Gwinnett
13 Fulton Industrial
14 I-85 Jackson
15 I-75 Bartow
16 I-85 South

Office Cores
Office and Industrial Cores
Industrial Cores

Robert Charles Lesser & Co.

Christopher Leinberger uses his "favored quarter of growth" theory for Atlanta to show how metropolitan cores develop in increasingly distant locations. Central cities are the first-generation cores; second-generation cores were built in the 1960s within the beltway. Third-generation cores, built in the 1970s and 1980s, and the newer fourth-generation cores (Georgia 400 and Oakwood/Gwinnett) are located outside the beltway. Since 1983, almost 80 percent of Atlanta's net employment growth has taken place in the third- and fourth-generation cores.

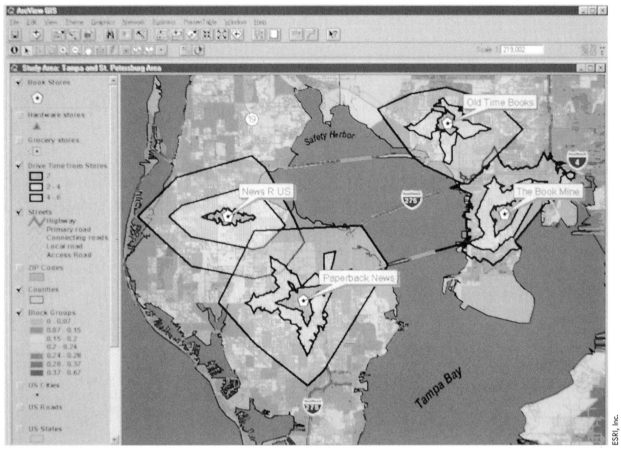

Various computer databases are available to assess different geographic and spatial elements. This program combines demographic and marketing data to help locate potential development sites.

of the nation, state, region, and city and then zooming in on a particular point. The complete GIS contains all property tax records, Multiple Listing Service records, census records, recent crime statistics, water and sewer records, transportation arteries, and possibly even satellite photography. Ideally, viewers are able to use the GIS to go back and forth in time to see how development evolved. Parts of such an ideal GIS exist in many cities today. Although the technology and underlying information exist for GISs in nearly all cities, the time and expense of gathering (and "proofing") the information in the appropriate format has resulted in slower progress than hoped. Optimistic forecasters had predicted that by 2000, comprehensive GISs would be common. Now, forecasters are looking at 2002 as a more likely time period but with the systems available to everyone via the Internet (again, at a price).

The two main GIS models are spatial interaction models and spatial diffusion models. Currently, through spatial interaction models (also known as gravity models), users have the capability of, for example, fore-casting traffic flows, store patronage, and shopping center revenue as one means of assessing the desirability of a retail site. Spatial diffusion models can help predict population movement, growth or decay of neighborhoods, or the development of new neighborhoods and the rate of absorption. Such models allow developers to visualize complex spatial information.[4]

Despite the evolution of advanced computer models, technology will not replace old-fashioned tire kicking. Developers work in an uncertain world, and to anticipate emerging trends, they will continue to rely on personal contacts—with people and sites. More important, developers recognize the advantages of imperfect information and will not readily give up any advantage by freely transferring all their insights and information to publicly available databases.

As developers begin to narrow their search to several specific sites, they move from a demand-centered view of the location to a site's physical and legal dimensions. One approach to analyzing a site is to look for binding constraints—reasons for excluding a site. For ex-

Figure 12-2

Factors in Site Selection

Zoning
- Legal use of the site
- Restrictions on density and layout
- Contiguous land uses
- Likelihood of obtaining variances

Physical Features
- Size
- Soils
- Topography
- Hydrology (floodplains, subsurface water)

Utilities
- Sewage (usually most constraining factor)
- Water (important constraint in certain parts of the United States, particularly the Southeast and Southwest)
- Computer lines, fiber optics, cable television, telephone, gas, oil, electricity; usually readily available except in large-scale projects

Transportation (all modes)
- Transportation linkages
- Traffic
- Availability of public transportation
- Especially important in determining access and in evaluating ingress, egress, and visibility of alternative sites

Parking
- Usually needed on site; therefore, competes with the building for land
- If site cost per square foot is less than cost of structured parking, surface parking is warranted (and vice versa)

Environmental Impact
- Adverse impacts on air, water, and noise levels
- Amount and type of waste project will generate
- Other areas of concern, including historic districts, parks, open space, trees, wildlife habitats

Government Services
- Police and fire service
- Garbage collection
- Schools, health facilities, and other government services
- Impact fees, property taxes, and permit fees

Local Attitudes
- Defensive (How powerful are antidevelopment forces?)
- Neutral (What social costs does the project impose? What are the benefits to the locality? Is the project in the public interest?)
- Offensive (What are local attitudes toward growth and how can they be used to help shape, refine, and specify the project to be built?)

Price of the Land
- Cost of land, including acquisition and site development

Demand and Supply
- Population growth, trends, and projection
- Employment
- Income distribution and probable change
- Existing and planned supply
- Competitive environment

Source: Modified from material in G. Vincent Barrett and John P. Blair, How to Conduct and Analyze Real Estate Market and Feasibility Studies (New York: Van Nostrand Reinhold, 1988). Used with permission.

ample, when Fraser Morrow Daniels began looking at possible office sites in Chapel Hill, it identified zoning as one binding constraint. Any site for consideration needed to have the appropriate zoning already in place; a rezoning in Chapel Hill would have been too difficult, costly, and time-consuming. Even though the site for Europa Center met the zoning requirement, Fraser Morrow Daniels found the land only after stepping back, rescanning the environment, and revising its criteria for site selection. Other binding constraints face developers: traffic (too much or too little), access, infra-

structure, and adequate space for parking, for example. Figure 12-2 summarizes major factors to consider in site selection.

In the continuation of the case study, Fraser Morrow Daniels narrows its search for a site and focuses on the Europa Center site because it eliminated uncertainties about zoning and hastened the development process. In making its decision, the company weighed the competitive edge of controlling the right site against the risk of the large financial commitment required by the outright purchase of an expensive parcel.

⦂⦂⦂ Europa Center

Back to the Drawing Board

We wanted to build west of Research Triangle Park and somewhere strategically close to the I-40 extension. We studied every single intersection in the area of I-40 and all the land around it. We collected tax maps and called landowners to ask if they wanted to sell their land. We talked to all the brokers and went after pieces of land that weren't for sale, because everything that was for sale was priced too high or was poorly located.

As part of that process, we discovered the Europa Center site, which was owned by the developers of the Hotel Europa. At first when the owners offered us the land for $250,000 an acre, we said it was three times more than we wanted to pay and what anybody else was paying. But the owners assured us it was a site with great potential and that they wanted to sell it to someone who would develop an attractive building. They had already turned down Kmart, which was willing to pay the price, but the city did not want a discount store on the site. In fact, the site had been for sale several times for different purposes. The owners tried to convince us that with I-40 going through, the site was worth $250,000 an acre, but we still said no.

Instead, we went back to our site selection criteria and looked at the overall market and what was already built on Durham–Chapel Hill Boulevard toward Chapel Hill. In addition, we looked at other factors, such as the demographics and the office/business neighborhood. No other office buildings existed there except for Eastowne (11 two-story office buildings), but Blue Cross/Blue Shield was just up the street from the Hotel Europa. We conceded that the project might fit as an office/business complex. We talked to some potential tenants who were interested in moving into an attractive building near their present location (Eastowne Park). Some potential tenants said they would like a place that was between Durham and Chapel Hill so they could combine offices. That kind of feedback pointed us toward the intersection of I-40 and Durham–Chapel Hill Boulevard (U.S. 15-501).

We were committed to developing an office building somewhere between Durham and Chapel Hill close to that intersection, and things kept coming back to the Europa site. We justified the high price by saying it would mean only $0.80 a square foot more in rent.

But what about the politics in Chapel Hill? We had heard dozens of horror stories.

We decided we would go ahead with the project only if we didn't have to ask for any approvals. The site was already zoned for office buildings, and the planning board had already approved some proposed office buildings for construction. We thought the Europa site would be easy because the planning board had already blessed it, the city council had already blessed it, and we didn't have to do anything to get a site plan approved. We decided to pursue the site.

Then we started looking at the competition and the marketing significance of that competition. North Raleigh had a lot of activity and a lot of land. Downtown Raleigh had a lot of space. Downtown Durham was trying to give away land for office buildings. But in Chapel Hill, a fight broke out at every turn with anybody who wanted to develop commercial or office buildings. Every other piece of land that had been zoned for offices was already built on. Eastowne, across from Blue Cross/Blue Shield on Durham–Chapel Hill Boulevard, had two small tracts of land left, about an acre and a half each, for office buildings. So we figured we would be the only game in town for the foreseeable future. The possibility that competitors could enter the market and attract the same tenants was relatively small.

At that time, a McDonald's restaurant was proposed in front of the site on U.S. 15-501 as an upscale building with an inconspicuous sign. And the Hotel Europa was one of the more attractive buildings in town. The project we had in mind would also be an attractive building to fit our image of the company. The Europa site became, in all our analyses, the best site available: it satisfied all our criteria for our company profile, the market profile, and the competitive environment.

The only real unknown was the political environment. We could not purchase the land contingent on certain conditions. The seller would not allow it. We had to buy the land with the existing zoning.

The planning board and city council said informally that our idea looked good and advised us to proceed with project design; they would then decide. Accordingly, we purchased the land for $5.00 per square foot (in late 1985). Several people around town chuckled. The Hotel Europa was in deep financial trouble at that time, badly needed the money, and, we discovered later, probably would have sold the land to us for $3.50 a square foot. But we had justified the price in our minds and paid the asking price.

continued on page 228

Whit Morrow and his team spent a lot of time thinking about the political situation. Dean Stratouly did, too. For many developers, a city's political climate is as important as the appropriateness of the site and the vibrancy of the market.

▌▌▌ Museum Towers

The Site

We bought the site, which was 4.11 acres, in October 1987 with the belief that Cambridge would become hot. The site was on the river but in an unattractive industrial area. You have to understand what was happening in the market at that time. This marginal piece of land was put on the market for $10.5 million. Three companies were chasing it, and the day I bought it, one of the other bidders ran into the president's office with a check for $1 million and said, "Whatever Stratouly's giving you, put this million on top of it." It was a lot of money, reflective of the market at the time, and way overpriced. Just after we bought it, the stock market took the largest percentage drop in history. Timing is everything.

This site was at the corners of Somerville, Charlestown, and Cambridge, an area known as North Point. A high-end residential product wasn't conceivable there ten years ago. When we purchased it, the site contained a bottling company with more than 400 people working in it. The company wanted to move to a new location and so decided to maximize the investment it had made in real estate.

The city of Cambridge had put a moratorium in place that was to expire in December 1987. We agreed to voluntarily extend the moratorium while they rezoned the area, provided that we controlled the rezoning process so the city wouldn't try to kill us. The moratorium was put in place because of a neighborhood reaction against the amount of development going on in East Cambridge.

The zoning that had been there was good old-fashioned zoning designed to allow you to do what you want—big FAR (floor/area ratio), no height restrictions—it was great.

But the city began to panic after I bought the land. They figured out that we were here, other developers were over there, and then another developer tied up another piece of land and the next thing they knew, the city was confronted with the fruits of its own success, which would result in more development on the riverfront. The North Point district is made up of about 70 acres of land with 13 different landowners, ranging from a husband/wife team to Boston & Maine Railroad. Their knowledge and understanding of real estate matters was all over the map, so we organized all the landowners and spent one year and 17 days rezoning the full 70 acres. And it was torture. That was the balance of 1987, all of 1988, and into 1989.

The amount of fighting was unbelievable because we had to divide the land and put roads in certain areas—through buildings and properties—so we had to do land swaps. Then some people complained that their land would be less valuable, and so on. It was unbelievable.

We needed a vote from the city council, but before we could get to the council, we had to get the landowners and two neighborhood groups to agree on a master plan. Then we had to get the planning board to agree on the master plan before it could be presented to the city council. Eventually we succeeded.

And then the world stopped moving. Boston's economy went into a high-speed nosedive, and everything ground to a halt.

At the same time I was working on this site, we had several other projects underway: 42 acres on the Southeast Expressway in the middle of permitting a 4 million-square-foot biomedical research center, the American Express Building in Providence, Rhode Island, a condominium project in New York City, a ten-acre parcel in Cambridge off the Massachusetts Turnpike, and a project in Connecticut.

We bought our development site. I didn't take an option because I don't believe in options when the entitlement lead time is hard to measure and potentially very long. It took us until 1991 to get our permits. Between then and 1998, when the project was completed, we hung on. We wrote a lot of checks—thousands of dollars—begging for equity, trying to get someone to believe in our project and not take us for a ride. The area was nothing but warehouses and railroad cars. The river was basically inaccessible from the site. And we had promises from the state that it would build a park along the river. But we didn't know if those promises were real.

At the time, no one was buying land, so we couldn't have really sold it for a reasonable price. Land was like leprosy then—untouchable.

continued on page 238

The Site's Physical Characteristics

An appropriate site is not simply the gross number of square feet but, more important, the number of *buildable* square feet with the appropriate configuration. Ten acres may be more usable than 40 acres, for example, if part of the 40 acres is located in a floodplain or if the 40 acres is configured as one long, narrow strip along the side of a mountain. This fact may seem obvious, but owners of large tracts do not always invest in land planning as readily as they invest in a qualified architect to design a building and prepare its specifications.

Soils further help determine a site's potential for development; soils must exhibit adequate load-bearing capacity for the structures the developer plans to construct. In many areas, soils are not a problem, but would-be developers should not take soil conditions for granted. First, even where soils are generally suitable for construction, special conditions such as abandoned land-fills may create problems that even long-time residents have forgotten. Second, newcomers in town should talk to more than one knowledgeable local broker, builder, banker, geologist, or soils engineer about soil conditions. The developer does not want to learn after the deal is closed that poor bearing qualities (or the soil's expansion and contraction properties or the amount of rock or the underground water patterns) well known to local builders will add extra costs in excavation and foundation work.

Other considerations include hazardous wastes and possibly even the requirements for an archaeological survey. Unless specified otherwise in the land sale contract, it is the purchaser's responsibility to remove hazardous wastes to a safe place (see Chapter 19), and the expense can be ruinous. Many cases warrant elaborate and costly hazardous waste studies that must be conducted by environmental professionals. In stage two, however, the developer must hold down major cash outlays and make careful tradeoffs between expenditures and the assumption of risk. Ideally, the developer structures contracts that allow him to back out of a purchase if significant pollution is discovered. Even with such contracts, however, the developer is still out of pocket the cost of the environmental study.

Some government agencies require an archaeological survey. If a survey turns up artifacts, archaeologists may then have to excavate the area by hand, possibly delaying development for months. This possibility is not as great in urban and suburban areas as the likelihood of discovering hazardous wastes, but developers should nonetheless be aware of it. Even in New York City, when an African American cemetery was discovered on a site in lower Manhattan, construction of a federal courthouse was delayed until a decision could be reached about the proper means of dealing with the remains.

Developers should also consider a site's ties to the surrounding infrastructure. How far is the site from water and sewer service? Where is major road access possible? Increasingly, developers need more than access to water and roads; they need to ascertain whether the local municipality can and will provide sufficient water and sewer infrastructure and surrounding road capacity. In more intensively used areas, a city may properly deny access from certain directions to any given site. And such denial can turn an otherwise attractive site into an infeasible one—despite high demand, and ideal topography, parcel configuration, and soils.

Twenty-five years ago, developers who had access to needed municipal services could expect the city to deliver them. No longer. More and more, developers

absorb some or all of the costs of constructing adequate infrastructure (see Chapter 13). In the case of Europa Center, for example, the planning board and the town staff identified traffic and traffic control as major concerns.[5] Fraser Morrow Daniels strove to allay the city's fears and solve the traffic problem by volunteering to realign the affected intersection. Dean Stratouly of Museum Towers had to provide all utilities, rebuild an intersection, build roads within the development, and then give it all to the city. Today, developers must be concerned with a municipality's ability to provide essential services and their own ability to afford the related fees.[6]

⠿ Europa Center

Anticipating Exactions

During our negotiations with the town of Chapel Hill, many questions arose about traffic and traffic control, a major concern of the planning board and the town staff. We knew some improvements were needed in the intersection of U.S. 15-501 and Europa Drive, primarily because of all the recent residential development nearby on Erwin Road and increased traffic between Durham and Chapel Hill. For our project to work well, we needed some traffic control signals and some adjustments in turning lanes, and we volunteered to perform the entire amount of work for $50,000. That's not a normal anticipated cost of development.

Most cities in the past have done that work themselves because they wanted economic growth. In Chapel Hill, the situation was different. We volunteered to do the work, knowing that it would otherwise not get done. We needed to allay the town's fears, and we needed to solve an anticipated traffic problem.

The North Carolina Department of Transportation completed the work, and we paid for it. It realigned the whole intersection, not just a turning lane into our project. And we managed to find a way to do it that didn't cost as much as some of the other alternatives.

continued on page 238

The Site's Legal Characteristics

Another consideration is the permitted intensity of use. Thus, a site may be zoned for multifamily housing but at such a low number of dwelling units per acre that, given development costs, the idea is infeasible. Assuming variations in allowable densities, the analysis of

Figure 12-3

Analysis of Alternative Sites Based on Permissible Density

Alternative Site Number	Size (Acres)	Allowable Number of Dwelling Units per Acre	Price	Price per Square Foot	Price per Dwelling Unit
1	3.0	25	$561,900	$4.30	$7,492
2	2.5	18	$350,650	$3.22	$7,792
3	3.2	21	$510,175	$3.66	$7,592

likely sale prices based on permissible density (e.g., price per multifamily dwelling unit rather than on-site price per square foot) provides a more logical framework. Figure 12-3 provides an example of these two methods of comparison. Obviously, the prices per dwelling unit are much more tightly clustered than are the prices per square foot of site area.

Developers must look at current zoning for both the tract under consideration and the surrounding parcels as well as at the flexibility of current zoning and the possibility of major changes. The way developers work with the city within the existing rules or to change those rules and the way developers of competing sites influence the legal/political process are important considerations. A town or a neighborhood can be a potent force. Politics can create opportunities just as easily as obstacles. Finding a way to get what you need, given the particular political climate, is one way developers "add value."

Beyond zoning, subdivision regulations are usually in place not only in metropolitan areas but also in "extraterritorial jurisdictions," that is, in areas that a city may eventually annex. (Some states permit the enactment of subdivision regulations for all areas.) Subdivision regulations generally specify the quality of the needed infrastructure. Developers must meet those requirements if they plan to dedicate that infrastructure to the city, which, in turn, is expected to provide ongoing maintenance. In most cases, developers prefer to dedicate infrastructure to avoid the costs of lifetime maintenance and eventual reconstruction.

Besides subdivision regulations, building codes can slow development if building inspectors are unfamiliar with innovative designs and technologies. The ideal building code specifies a particular standard, not a particular material. In some cities, materials suppliers have occasionally managed to write their particular products into the building code, a practice that can be an especially difficult issue for manufactured housing whose construction takes place far from the installation site. Highly rigid building codes restrict a developer's creativity in fitting a product that satisfies consumers' needs to a particular location.

Initial Design Feasibility

In larger developments or in smaller developments on difficult sites, developers customarily determine the feasibility of project layout before committing large sums of money to site acquisition. Determining the feasibility of the layout requires engineering and architectural information that may include the results of soils tests, exact grade measurements, a look at setbacks combined with various projected land and building configurations, and projections of space for parking and other requirements.

The problem with major design issues, including the feasibility of project layout, is that developers must, for the first time in the eight-stage development process, engage outside consultants—often a land design professional, an architect, and possibly engineers—to survey the site to determine whether it satisfies development objectives. The associated outlays increase the developer's financial exposure if the project should ultimately prove infeasible.

The investigation begins with the ground. In many areas, a soils engineer must determine the soil's load-bearing capacity and address problems related to groundwater and stormwater runoff. Changing the direction of water can be extremely expensive, but ignoring drainage can be disastrous. Soils and mechanical engineers, working as part of the development team (for a fee), often go beyond a simple determination of physical viability to suggest better ways to handle problems. The soils engineer, the architect, and sometimes the grading subcontractor can advise the developer on how to work with the grade of a site—from designs that use

Figure 12-4

A Site Looking for a Use

Mission Bay is currently the largest mixed-use redevelopment project underway in San Francisco and for some 20 years has been a site searching for its highest and best use. The former railyard is a 303-acre site outside downtown San Francisco in the South of Market neighborhood, a burgeoning area, that for two decades has been the source of many plans, none of which have proceeded.

As early as 1981, community opposition and market forces dashed plans for 40-story high rises to be constructed on the site. Two votes in the late 1980s rejected proposals to bring baseball South of Market along the waterfront. Then in 1991, the owner of most of the site, Catellus Development Corporation (a spin-off of the Santa Fe Pacific Corporation), obtained approvals to go ahead with the high rises, but a weak economy stopped those plans. In 1995, Catellus sought a new scaled-down plan and began once again to seek approvals from the city.

The time seemed right to try again as the South of Market neighborhood boomed with the new Museum of Modern Art, the Yerba Buena projects, the expanded convention center, the growth of restaurants and nightlife, and the opening of the Embarcadero Promenade, a 2.5-mile-long, 25-foot-wide pedestrian zone built along the river after the elevated Embarcadero freeway was damaged in the Loma Prieta earthquake and ultimately torn down.

With Catellus acting as master developer, the centerpiece of the proposed Mission Bay project is the Giants's new baseball stadium, Pacific Bell Park, built on city-leased land with $300 million of private funds (the first privately financed ballpark since the early 1960s). The park was planned to be easily accessible by foot (it's located a very short distance from the financial district), by ferry, by train, and by light rail (a nearby recently completed station connects to the subway). In addition, some 5,000 dedicated parking spaces as well as scattered sites throughout the neighborhood are available to fans, although acceptance of the plan was contingent upon efforts to reduce use of motor vehicles as much as possible. This compromise came about primarily after 19 meetings with citizens who voiced concern about traffic and noise.

The master developer, Catellus Development Corporation, holds one of the largest portfolios of developable land in the western United States, including 167 acres of the site. The University of California at San Francisco (UCSF) owns 42 acres, and the city and port of San Francisco own the remaining 94 acres. It is expected that the development will include a mix of mid-rise and high-rise housing units (4,300 market rate and 245 affordable); 5 million square feet of office, research and development, and biotechnology space complemented by the 2.65 million-square-foot (about 43-acre) expansion of the UCSF campus; 250,000 square feet of entertainment retail space adjacent to the ballpark; 500,000 square feet of neighborhood- and community-supporting retail space; and a 500-room hotel. It is also proposed that an additional 1,455 units of affordable housing will be developed by several different developers. ∎

---

the existing grade to create a specific image to engineering solutions that permit development on difficult grades to finding more cost-efficient ways to cut, adjust, and bank the land.

Moving beyond the developer's initial idea of building configuration, the architect lays out an initial building footprint on the site and, given intended access points, determines whether or not the building and its associated parking can be placed on the site. The layout must honor all setbacks specified in the local subdivision regulations without compromising the image the developer hopes to create; at the same time, it must ensure tenants' satisfaction with the final product.

In some cases, assistance from architects, engineers, land planners, and/or subcontractors can be obtained without paying for it upfront. Large developers who generate a great deal of business can call on professionals they have previously engaged and expect some services at deferred costs. Although astute developers minimize costs and capitalize on past relationships appropriately, successful developers also know when to spend additional dollars. The developer's role is to decide which items require additional investment as a means of controlling risk.

In most cases, the primary design contract is executed with an architect. The contract establishes a relationship that usually continues for the duration of the project. Figure 12-5 provides suggestions about what to expect from an architect, what not to expect, and how to select an architect.

During the process of selecting the site and defining the physical product that fits the client to the site,[7] it is wise to remember that urban land value relies more on the land's visibility and proximity to customers and

Figure 12-5

Working with an Architect

What to Expect from an Architect

1. Quality design that satisfies the owner's program.
2. Timely answers to the owner's requests and suggestions.
3. Alternative suggestions and schemes during the early phases of the project; an architectural problem never has only one solution. An open mind to requests for modifications of the project when necessary.
4. Sensitivity to and understanding of zoning and building codes, environmental issues, and other government restrictions.
5. An understanding of construction costs relating to particular types and uses of buildings.
6. Ability to interact constructively with government agencies, and to understand the positions of groups opposing the project.
7. Ability to be a team player, joining and frequently meeting with owners, consultants, and others who contribute to the project.
8. Suitable graphic presentations that portray the project in its best light to government agencies and local interest groups.
9. Good (not perfect) construction documents that are well coordinated with documentation from other consultants.
10. Architectural supervision throughout the construction of the project, with field reports on each site visit; it is easier to respond to a contractor's questions on the job than to make serious corrections later.
11. Timely and accurate processing of all paperwork—change orders, bulletins, pay requests, and final certifications as required by lenders (with the wording not in conflict with what an architect is allowed to sign under professional liability insurance).

What Not to Expect

1. Cut-rate fees, free services, or work on "spec"; quality service with the proper amount of time spent by experienced professional personnel requires proper remuneration; if a large, upfront payment is a problem for the developer, deferred payments should be an option.
2. The ability to design *anything;* special consultants with proper training and experience should be used for traffic, parking, interiors, graphics, landscaping, and so on.
3. A guarantee of the contractor's work; architects cannot guarantee work over which they have no control or have not put in place.
4. Work on a fixed fee before the program and final scope of the project are determined.
5. Changes by the owner without affecting the architect's fee, construction costs, and schedule.
6. Detailed, highly accurate cost estimates unless a professional cost estimator is on staff or has been retained to perform such work.

How to Select an Architect

1. An architect should not be hired on the basis of aesthetics alone. The most attractive project can be totally unsuccessful in terms of financial performance, profitability, and quality of construction.
2. An architect or the key person on staff who will manage the project should be highly experienced in the specific project type.
3. An architect should not be hired based on an extensive portfolio of renderings of unbuilt projects.
4. You should talk to the owners and/or users of other projects the architect has designed to determine the project's success and the architect's responsiveness throughout the project.
5. It is essential that the owner can relate to and respect the individual assigned to the project.
6. The owner should make sure the architect's current workload allows for the required attention to the project and its on-schedule completion. ■

Source: **Adapted from Charles Kober, the Kober Group, Santa Ana, California.**

services than on its inherent productivity (the soil's fertility, coal reserves, or timber stands, for example). Thus, when developers evaluate alternative sites, they carefully consider access to residences and businesses, pedestrian and vehicular traffic flow, and/or proximity to any off-site amenities that make the site more or less attractive to prospective customers.

Sites also have links to competitive supply. A site's physical and legal characteristics limit the volume of space that can be built. Surrounding land uses might include competing projects that determine how long a developer can expect to enjoy a spatial monopoly at a given site. Thus, in considering the proper scale for a project, developers must screen competing sites.

The site's slope and the challenge of fitting a regulation size ballfield within a city block required a creative architectural solution at the Durham Bulls Athletic Park in Durham, North Carolina. The steep slope was transformed into a grassy outfield berm able to accommodate 2,200 spectators, and a 24-foot outfield wall compensated for the size constraints.

Negotiating for the Site

At this point, the developer faces a Catch-22. Although the site meets the development firm's criteria and is probably feasible physically, legally, and politically, it has yet to be subjected to a complete feasibility study. In an effort to keep down the initial investment, the developer does not want to purchase the land. At the same time, however, the more the idea for development becomes public and takes shape, the more money the current landowner is likely to ask for the land. Thus, assuming the refined idea and subsequent feasibility study may prove positive, the developer's objective is to obtain the right to buy the land at "today's price" without committing a great deal of money.

The most obvious solution is an option. Ideally, the developer would like to pay $1.00 for the right to buy the land at today's stated price at any time over the next five years. Regrettably, owners are not enthusiastic about tying up their land for a long time without significant remuneration. Thus, depending on the landowner's objectives and the attractiveness of the site, negotiations might lead to a tradeoff between the developer's desire to pay as little as possible for the option with as long a lead time as possible and the owner's desire to receive a large payment for a short option period.

An option agreement is a complex document. Even in the most straightforward transaction, the option, if exercised, becomes a contract of sale and legally drives the entire process of land purchase. Accordingly, the option must specify all necessary requirements for the transfer of title from the seller to the buyer, including any details about financing by the seller such as release clauses and subordination agreements that facilitate

subsequent financing.[8] The option almost always grants the buyer the opportunity to examine the quality of the seller's title as well as time to arrange financing, permits, and, possibly, zoning. The agreement must not only specify the price and any warranties in the deed (and any possible deed restrictions), but it should also include escape clauses based on the results of environmental or engineering tests.

The option is a forward-looking agreement that should be as complete as possible and anticipate future actions and reactions to those actions. If the developer, for example, needs a rezoning to permit construction of the proposed project on the chosen site, the option agreement might contain a clause specifying that the developer has 120 days to propose the change to the town council and that the option will run until 90 days or one year after the council's decision, whichever comes first.

As with all real estate contracts, the economic content of the option agreement is in theory very flexible; the developer is limited only by the extent of his imagination. In fact, the agreement might not, strictly speaking, be an option. For example, in a low-downpayment, nonrecourse purchase, the developer actually buys the property but with 95 + percent financing provided by the seller, and the seller's only recourse is to the property. In economic terms, this particular arrangement differs little from paying 5 percent of the asking price for an option.

At times, it can be useful to include landowners in the development process. Sometimes landowners want to take a long-term equity position in a developed structure. At other times, when the seller owns surrounding parcels, that can be the incentive needed to encourage the participation of the landowner as a financer of the development. Developers should use their imagination to create an appropriate investment vehicle for their given development by taking careful account of their own financial resources and desires, the availability of outside financing, the city's requirements, the position and needs of the landowner, and, always foremost, the needs of prospective tenants.

Discussing the Project with Other Players

Developers do not work in isolation. They talk to other industry professionals and community members who might be affected by the proposed development, thereby both refining the idea further and initially planning its tactical implementation.

Contractors

In the project's early stages, developers need to determine how many people in the area have the expertise needed to construct the project. Some general contractors take on all types of projects; others specialize in one type of project or another. In a dynamic market, developers must also determine how many of the general contractors have the time to construct another project. In addition, the business cycle affects the quality of available building tradespeople. Construction workers tend to move up the line during a boom period when ample work is available. In other words, the rough carpenter becomes a finish carpenter, the finish carpenter becomes a superintendent, and the superintendent becomes an independent general contractor. As the business cycle peaks, construction costs thus escalate and quality may suffer.

From the perspective of marketing, contractors can outline for developers the typical functions and features as well as the quality of materials and finishes in comparable buildings in the market area. Typically, contractors will also estimate the cost of construction; their input is one of the critical elements in both the informal feasibility in stage two and the formal feasibility in stage three.

Tenants

During this stage, developers begin discussions with a range of possible tenants to determine users' specific requirements and to refine the general idea of market demand established during stage one. As the idea becomes better defined and tied to a particular site, developers must begin serious discussions with likely tenants,

for they may find that the initially targeted users do not want what is proposed. Designing a project with desired features, functions, and benefits is much more cost-effective than adding such items to a completed structure. Conversely, developers can eliminate items tenants do not need enough to justify the cost.

The focus on marketing at this stage is to tailor the product to make sure it serves customers' needs. Refining an idea and then formally determining its feasibility are the critical links between a good idea and fully occupied space. During this stage, the developer moves from a general use to a specific project design and starts to construct a marketing strategy for eventual execution by the sales and leasing staff.

Property Managers

Early in the process, the developer should begin working with a property manager knowledgeable in the particular field. This input is even more critical when a proposed project will involve extensive, ongoing services. Keeping tenants satisfied requires good management, and good management requires a building realistically designed to accommodate people and their day-to-day needs. Property managers who specialize in a particular type of operation can be most valuable in helping to avoid a costly design mistake and planning design features that will make the building easier to manage while reducing operating costs. Experienced managers can advise the developer about appropriate floorplans, layout, and specific equipment or features.

Lenders

Because most developments require some type of outside financing, developers should usually contact potential lenders and investors at an early stage. A typical sequence begins with discussions with permanent lenders—institutions that might want to finance the project for the long term and are willing to take the long-term market risk or at least some portion of it (see Part II for a more detailed review of the process).[9] Lenders have preferences; some finance only certain types of projects and others finance projects only in certain ways. To obtain the most advantageous and compatible source of financing, developers may rely on their knowledge of financial markets, or they may obtain assistance from a mortgage banker. Hiring a mortgage banker represents an additional expense and does not relieve the developer of the responsibility of making financial decisions. Developers must still choose the appropriate source of financing and the appropriate structure for the particular transaction.

Developers also need a lender to finance construction. The construction lender assumes the risk that the project will not be completed on time and within budget; it does not typically assume the long-term market risk (which is assumed by the permanent lender and the equity investor). So long as the project is built according to plans and specifications, the construction lender generally has a "takeout" in the form of a permanent loan commitment.

At this early stage, developers seek merely an understanding of lenders' interests in the geographic area and type of project and, most important, of any specific guidelines lenders have, such as parking requirements that exceed city minimums or sprinkler systems that go beyond code requirements. By determining their interests at this stage, developers can often refine a project to increase the number of potential lenders, heighten lenders' interest, and, it is hoped, lower financing costs.

In addition to facilitating project financing, lenders can help developers understand the market. Local lenders, often knowledgeable of local tenants' needs and preferences, frequently apply useful rules of thumb that bear on the project's feasibility.

Investors

Developers might also want to discuss the project with long-term equity investors, those who take the higher risk position. In recent years, the most common long-term equity investors in real estate capital markets are pension funds, real estate investment trusts, wealthy individuals, and syndicates of less wealthy individuals. Many other long-term investors, however, such as insurance companies and major corporations, have become involved in the real estate development process at different times in the capital market cycle. By anticipating some of the equity investors' needs at an early stage, developers can refine their ideas more effectively.

An important issue is whether to bring in equity investors at the beginning or end of the development process. Early equity investors typically want more because they assume some of the development risk, but the early involvement of equity investors reduces the risk to permanent and construction lenders, thereby lowering the cost of debt financing. Depending on a developer's financial position, the nature of the project, and lenders' demands, a developer must, at least by stage three, decide when to involve outside equity investors. Typically, the longer a developer can wait, the higher his potential profits. Just as developers can use a mortgage banker to help them determine the shape of debt financing, they can also seek outside counsel on equity investments. For larger projects, the counselor might be a national or international investment banker, for medium projects a regional investment banker, and for smaller or tax-oriented projects a local syndicator. Although specialized assistance may increase the developer's awareness of options, it does not replace the developer's responsibility for making decisions.

Higher-Risk Investors

Because the development process now takes longer than ever before, many projects today involve a period that requires something resembling "venture capital" and, consequently, a class of investors distinct from traditional real estate equity investors. Developers must often command substantial upfront capital or otherwise demonstrate the ability to secure it. Money for expenditures before construction is the hardest kind of money to raise and also the most expensive. Traditionally, venture capitalists have not financed real estate development. Those who do, however, are a relatively few wealthy individuals. The other source is "opportunity funds" managed by Wall Street firms and independent investment boutiques. Because venture capital is so costly, developers want to rely on as little as possible as late as possible—another reason for keeping early cash investment requirements to a minimum.

The Public

Possibly the most important player developers must talk to at this stage is the general public, as represented by government, neighborhood associations, and other advocacy groups. The public sector is always the developer's partner in a long-lived investment that requires substantial infrastructure. The developer must "sell" the project and its benefits to both elected and appointed public officials and to relevant citizen groups, with the hope that, by the end of stage two, the public will have a favorable impression of the project.

Public officials can offer suggestions that enhance the value of the finished project and, more important, speed approval time. Just as lenders and investors exhibit different preferences and concerns, so do government officials and agencies. Developers should investigate regulators' desires and how the project might satisfy public needs in various jurisdictions. Sources of information on local policy and politics include newspapers, the municipality's master plan, elected and appointed officials, other developers working in the local market, political consultants who specialize in the local market, and public meetings where multiple groups express their opinions.

Figure 12-6

Office Market Segmentation

Stage Two: Refinement of the Idea

Analyze competing projects and developers to determine what is selling or leasing.

Consider trends creating demand for more specialized uses.

Consider trends changing locational requirements for key tenant groups.

Define segments based on users' needs, for example, large floorplates, low rent, central city versus suburban location.

Compare potential supply and development controls across spatial submarkets.

Remember the goal: to capture a share of the market by differentiating the product from competitors' products and to satisfy the demand for space of a particular group of users (a market segment).

Understand potential space users in order to target marketing and promotion.

Keep an open mind: remember that a differentiated product could lead to the discovery of a new product to serve a changing market.

Stage Three: Feasibility

Forecast demand and supply to gauge overall market conditions in the metropolitan area and quantify submarket conditions.

Specifically designate the key characteristics for describing products: location, size, physical features, price, quality, age, and amenities.

Relate characteristics to differences among space users to define relatively homogeneous segments of space users.

Use careful assessment of supply and demand in each market segment to forecast rents, inventory, absorption, and vacancies for each segment over the next three to five years.

Adapted from: **David E. Dowall, "Office Market Research: The Case for Segmentation,"** *Journal of Real Estate Development,* **Summer 1988, pp. 34–43.**

Whether as regulators or codevelopers (see Chapter 14), public officials seek to protect the public interest. Understanding the public (the development site's neighbors and the public at large) is an important aspect of market research. Although tenants rent space or buy units, the public is exposed to the physical asset created by the developer as part of the long-lived built environment. Savvy developers want to satisfy the public—or local citizens might not let developers serve their intended customers. The public is primarily concerned about the project's appearance, its fit to the land, its compatibility with surrounding land uses, its impact on the community in terms of on- and off-site costs, and its benefits, such as taxes generated, jobs created, and new amenities and services offered.

Paula Collins, chief executive officer of Western Development Group Companies, learned early on the importance of working with the community at all levels. As her profile indicates, time spent with the public is a good business decision as well as a means of controlling risk.

Segmenting the Market and Differentiating the Product

After introducing the project to others involved in the development process and evaluating their responses, developers must decide whether the project is worth taking to stage three, the formal determination of feasibility. It is at stage three that the emotional and financial stakes go up. Before then, however, the developer initiates some more detailed market research. (Figure 12-6

Profile **Paula R. Collins**

Chief Executive Officer, WDG Ventures, Inc.
San Francisco

Paula R. Collins is a founding principal and chief executive officer of WDG Ventures, Inc., a real estate development and urban planning consulting firm founded in 1981. Historically, the firm's focus has been on the development of residential, commercial, and mixed-use projects in the San Francisco Bay Area. More recently, WDGV has been involved in larger-scale urban entertainment projects such as Sony's Metreon and the Fillmore Renaissance project.

A cum laude graduate in urban studies of Mount Holyoke College, Collins received her master of city planning degree from the Massachusetts Institute of Technology in 1975. She has a wealth of experience in the development industry, from project conceptualization to economic and fiscal impact analysis to management responsibility for large-scale office, industrial, residential, and urban entertainment developments. Collins has primary responsibility for overseeing the design, construction, marketing, and leasing of the firm's development projects. She serves on numerous boards, is active in civic organizations, is a director of Bayview Federal Bank, the California State Automobile Association, and BRIDGE Housing Corporation. Her business partner is her husband, Charles Collins, a Harvard-trained lawyer and graduate of MIT.

Hands-On Management

WDGV prefers to focus its development activities in the San Francisco area because the firm's partners have a hands-on style that requires senior management's direct involvement in all aspects of project operations—from the formation of new investments through property and portfolio management. "Combining the unique set of skills and experience of senior management is what we believe creates a superior product," says Collins.

Profitability through Partnership with the Public Sector and Local Community

The firm's projects are the result of forging effective public/ private partnerships focused on creating well-designed,

profitable real estate that energizes its surroundings and serves as a catalyst for economic revitalization. Although profit is important, "the professional orientation of the partners is sincere community involvement." WDGV's mission is realized by investing early, concentrating on projects that will answer a strong demand, assuming risks commensurate with targeted investment returns, including the public sector as an active participant, and working with community-based nonprofit organizations.

Collins stresses that any development strategy must emphasize the community's total environment—social and economic. "You can't ignore the community," she says. "You wouldn't want to because you want the community to be a user group. Literally from the day we decide to work on a project, we go to neighborhood meetings, organize our own meetings, take people through our conceptual plans, and encourage the involvement of the surrounding business community."

The recently opened Sony Metreon, a four-level, 350,000-square-foot entertainment complex at Yerba Buena Gardens, offers an example of the firm's approach to development. The project, located on the last parcel of a ten-acre site adjacent to the Yerba Buena Gardens, includes 15 theater screens, the city's first IMAX® theater, four theme restaurants, entertainment-based shopping venues, and various interactive attractions. As with many San Francisco neighborhoods, the people who live and work near the Metreon project are highly political and active regarding development issues. "It's not whether you should achieve consensus, it's *how* you achieve it," says Collins. Collins and the development team met with residents to gain their input on seating, landscaping, and park space. "We wanted the project to be perceived as user-friendly and a positive addition to what everybody views as their backyard."

WDGV also worked closely with the San Francisco Redevelopment Agency (SFRA) to satisfy design requirements and support the surrounding institutions. As part of the required development approvals, WDGV negotiated an

---

distinguishes between market research during stages two and three.) The more thorough the research, the more precisely developers can define their market niche and reduce risk. (Unfortunately, quality research is not usually free, so the developer must decide how much research is appropriate for the particular project at each stage in the development process.)

While talking with other players, developers continually think about who will use the proposed space and how the public will react to the project. By narrowing the choice of sites, developers find that they are better able to define the relevant market areas for the project. They need to move from the broader idea of building apartments in Madison, Wisconsin, for example, to the nar-

Metreon, Sony's new urban entertainment destination in San Francisco, is 350,000 square feet of eateries, a multiplex cinema with a 3-D IMAX® theater, stores, and entertainment attractions.

agreement between Sony, the tenant, and the SFRA to include local minorities and minority firms in the construction of the building and provision of services. WDGV also created a system to identify those firms. Additionally, the ground lease payments for the site will go to support the maintenance of all the facilities at Yerba Buena Gardens. The project is expected to attract up to 8 million people each year, half of them tourists.

Looking to the Future
Collins hopes to see increased racial and gender diversity among senior managers and industry shareholders. She comments, "I run across very few for-profit developers who are either African Americans or women. Access to capital

is critical in changing that situation. Our numbers among the ranks of technical consultants, especially in architecture and engineering, are growing but not fast enough. As an owner, I understand the benefits of using talented professionals to create successful real estate. I get special satisfaction out of demonstrating that, contrary to some anti–affirmative action rhetoric, a diverse workforce is an advantage, not a concession. Often when touring our projects, I listen first to the accolades on speedy approvals, design quality, and profitability before I tell them who did it—a Latino architect, a female plumber, or African American subcontractors, for example. The quality of our projects speaks volumes." ■

rower plan of building 225 one- and two-bedroom units in three-story garden apartments located on the northwest corner of Midvale Boulevard and Mineral Point Road targeted to single persons and couples earning over $40,000. How do developers accomplish this task?

They consider the features, functions, and benefits offered by the competition. In searching for the win-

ning strategy that will capture the greatest market share at the highest price, developers move back and forth between considerations of supply and demand. During this process, they segment demand and differentiate their own product from the competing supply. In fact, when considered in terms of market research, refining an idea can be viewed as the interactive process of segmenting the market and differentiating the product.

In an effort to keep costs down, developers often perform much of the market research during stage two. The discussions with other professionals are only one component; other parts of the research effort include making telephone calls to see who has vacant space, driving around to inspect competing projects, delving through public records, and checking the newspaper for announcements of new projects. All this information goes into the developer's database and provides insight into the existing supply, the characteristics of space users, and unmet needs (demand).

For Fraser Morrow Daniels, researching the converging segments of the Research Triangle Park market required two years of analysis to break out segments of the market and to define supply and demand fully. Location emerged as a key feature in developing Europa Center in the Research Triangle office market.

▚ Europa Center

Segmenting the Market

In selecting a site, we had to seek first-class, gold-plated sites that would win out at even rental rates in a competitive market. Developers who succeed are those whose sites are good right now, today. Tenants don't want to move to the middle of the wilderness where customers don't come. Renting office space in an office environment is only 2 to 5 percent of your business budget. People will pay $0.75 per square foot more to get an office space if it's the right space for their business. Being a pioneer is not necessarily good.

In deciding which land to buy, we had a choice between land selling at $1.00 a square foot ($45,000 to $50,000 an acre) and $5.00 a square foot ($250,000 an acre, the Europa site next to the Hotel Europa). The less successful and less visible land was cheaper, but is the Europa land five times more valuable than the other land? Who knows? What is the bottom line?

The land component per square foot of building area turned out (at $5.00 per square foot) to be $0.80 per square foot in the building rental rate—$16.80 instead of $16.00 per square foot to put somebody on a site next to the Hotel Europa rather than three blocks away behind a sewer plant. For $0.80 a square foot in the rental rate, can you add that much more value from the tenant's point of view? If you're building only one building, absolutely.

To help us make our decision, we looked at the office buildings in the area to assess how much space was available, what quality it was, how much space was being built,

what kind of tenants leased space there, who was likely to move, who was not. We listed every building in every segment of the market on a computer printout. Our list had 500 buildings. A Chapel Hill undergraduate worked for me for four hours a day after school for two years calling owners, agents, and tenants and asking how many square feet of office space they had. It's this kind of nitty-gritty detective work you have to do for the project coming up three months from now.

continued on page 240

Like Fraser Morrow Daniels, Dean Stratouly took a chance on a site in a developing but promising area. But in both cases, the developers looked at many factors and potential risks and rewards before proceeding.

▚ Museum Towers

Researching and Selecting Target Markets

The site is located in a "North Point Residential, Office, and Business Zoning District" or NP/PUD-6 District, also known as a planned unit development district. This district was established to provide a transition from the industrial sector to a mixed-use area. Residential uses are permitted and so are hotel/motel, retail, entertainment, recreational, office, industrial, transportation, and utility uses. The property meets the requirements of the PUD except for the maximum height, which is 50 feet. Museum Towers obtained a special permit from the city of Cambridge in June 1989 to go up to 24 stories.

The location is somewhat isolated, but the improvements have made a big difference. If everything else—the park and infrastructure improvements—goes according to plan, the location should become more popular. This kind of revitalization is not unprecedented in the Boston area. A project at the Charlestown Navy Yard, for example, Constitution Quarters, is a luxury rental apartment constructed in a neighborhood that wasn't known as a luxury market. But that project's done well because of the quality of the building. Cambridge has two new rental developments—Church Corner and Kennedy Lofts—in the Central Square area, which isn't exactly a desirable neighborhood. But both those projects have done very well, beyond expectations.

We figured that with the apartment rent, storage unit rent, parking fees, and retail rental, the project had a potential annual income of over $12 million.

continued on page 345

Financial Feasibility

An ongoing function during refinement of the idea is to translate all the collected information and completed analyses into a framework that relates potential risks and rewards to the developer's objectives. As noted in Chapter 1, developers rarely build projects for money alone. They need to address each goal explicitly and determine how the project may need to be modified to meet that goal.

Typically, developers continually revise the initial back-of-the-envelope analysis as they refine the idea. Refinement means better estimates of hard and soft costs and better projections of revenues and expenses. The pro forma does not have to be sophisticated. During refinement of the idea, the developer should listen and talk to knowledgeable people and potential tenants, not beat a spreadsheet to death.

During stage two, however, financial feasibility goes a critical step beyond stage one: developers must begin estimating cash flows during the development period. Can the developer finance the project through startup? It hardly matters that the project's value exceeds cost if the developer cannot survive to completion. A key part of the analysis at this stage is figuring out how much startup capital is needed and where it will come from.

Risk Control during Stage Two

The method of acquisition can itself be a means of controlling risk during stage two. Because a developer seeks to limit financial exposure before formally committing resources to a project, controlling the site through an option or a low-downpayment, nonrecourse, seller-financed purchase is one way to minimize exposure in stage two.

Any option and/or purchase agreement should ideally (from the developer's perspective) contain contingency clauses and specify that protective warranties will be included in the deed. Developers should ensure that the seller has provided all possible guarantees to the title's quality. Beyond that, the other terms of the sale (which should be included in any option) can help limit the developer's risk. One common provision, for example, stipulates that the developer will receive the downpayment and/or option amount back with no further responsibility if appropriate zoning cannot be obtained.

In most real estate transactions, constructive notice to the general public takes place by recording the instrument. The first instrument executed typically is the option agreement to acquire the land. So long as it is in proper form and, in most states, notarized, it can be recorded. Recording this agreement places it in the chain of title and thus gives notice to all others of the developer's right to the land. At times, this step can be particularly helpful in reducing the possibility that a landowner will execute subsequent contracts that use the land for purposes other than the developer's intent.

Release clauses and/or subordination clauses in the option or purchase agreement are also useful techniques for controlling risk. A release clause is common in a seller-financed mortgage; essentially, it allows a borrower or developer to obtain a first lien on a portion of the land by paying a portion of the note. For example, if a developer purchases 100 acres for $10,000 an acre, a release clause might provide that any one of ten ten-acre parcels included in the overall tract could be released from the lien if the developer makes a $150,000 payment. Thus, if the developer wants to begin the development with a ten-acre site and needs a first lien for the construction lender, the original purchase money mortgage could be removed from that ten-acre site with a payment of $150,000 as opposed to payment of the entire note for $1 million.

Subordination clauses accomplish a similar objective while providing developers with even greater risk coverage. They too must be written into any option agreement so that they are subsequently included in the seller's financing. An agreement to subordinate by the seller (lender) is a promise to move from a first lien position to a second lien position under specified circumstances. For example, a seller who owns thousands of acres in a particular area and wants to encourage a particular developer to develop one site within that area might agree to subordinate its claim of financing on that one site to the bank's construction financing. Thus, when the purchase closes, the seller (lender) will have a first lien. When the developer begins construction and needs to give the construction lender a first lien, the seller then agrees to move to a second lien position. Subordination is superior from the developer's perspective because it enhances his ability to borrow money. From the construction lender's perspective, the landowner's subordinated interest looks almost like equity in that it is an investment that is paid after the bank's loan. In effect, if the landowner subordinates its claim, the land serves as collateral for the development, even though the developer has not yet paid for it.

In addition to eliminating the uncertainties associated with a site's availability, developers can control risk by helping to ensure that a project is acceptable to the community. If developers can show from the beginning that the development plan fits or coordinates well with the city's master plan, fewer time-consuming delays are likely.

Informally presenting the project to city officials and building inspectors to elicit their responses can eliminate potential opposition later in the process. Not only do such officials become more committed to the project, but, like other participants, they too make suggestions that the developer can incorporate into the proposed idea. It is important to note, however, that elected officials sometimes leave office during the time required for the approval of large projects. Therefore, it behooves developers to seek approvals and opinions in writing. Although documentation does not always secure a developer's position against changes in policy and rules during the process, it does help.

More and better market research is another technique for controlling risk, but, as noted earlier, it can be expensive. The best risk control technique in stage two is to keep down the invested time and dollars so that the option of stopping remains viable.

⣿ Europa Center

Weighing the Pros and Cons

The site of Europa Center appeared to fit the bill: location on the major transportation artery connecting the two cities and adjacent to the highest-quality hotel at that time in Chapel Hill or Durham (see map in Chapter 10). The land was well configured and nearly rectangular, with a pond that represented an amenity, not a problem. Access was not perfect but was possible.

The fact that the site was nearly ready for development fit with our evaluation of the overall Research Triangle Park market; although long-term prospects were good, substantial new construction was coming on line soon, and it was thus important to bring the project to fruition as soon as possible. We had already invested heavily in both research and creating an image and wanted to recapture some of those costs through a series of developments, one of which was Europa Center.

We had done an excellent job of overall background research on the Research Triangle market and had worked hard at producing a positive image in the community, but we were still taking a chance with the Europa site. Although ideally situated in the middle of growth, close to major transportation arteries, physically attractive without major constraints on construction, and appropriately configured, the location had not traditionally projected an image of quality in the community. Though located next to the most expensive hotel in the area, the hotel was only four years

old and had already been through one foreclosure caused by lower-than-expected average rates and surprisingly low summer occupancy. Near the site on the east side was a subsidized housing project and, farther to the northeast, low-income retirement housing. With McDonald's and new car dealers on the south and west, the site offered excellent potential but would require substantial marketing and operating expertise to ensure a successful project. We chose particularly high-quality architecture and construction to try to influence the market's perception of the project.

continued on page 342

Summary

Stage two in the development process involves what many people call "real" real estate, further refining the idea generated during stage one. Toward the end of stage two, the rough idea is linked to a specific site that is legally, politically, and physically capable of supporting that idea. Moreover, the developer, through a series of conversations, believes that one or more general contractors will be available to construct the project, that tenants will be interested, that lenders will want to lend money, and that equity interests can be attracted to the project.

By this time, the developer has probably decided whether the development idea is feasible. Nonetheless, a formal feasibility study is often necessary to convince other participants, such as investors, lenders, tenants, and the public sector. Although 99 out of 100 ideas generated in stage one fail the back-of-the-envelope pro forma test, the pass rate is higher in stage two. Perhaps one in three or maybe even two in five ideas pass this stage. If the refined idea still seems feasible, the developer takes it to stage three, at which point financial and emotional commitments become greater.

Terms

- Archaeological survey
- Axial theory
- Concentric zone theory
- Extraterritorial jurisdiction
- Floodplain
- Geographic Information System (GIS)
- Lien
- Multiple Listing Service (MLS)
- Option agreement

- Product differentiation
- Sector theory
- Submarket
- Subordination clause
- Urban economics
- Venture capital

Review Questions

12.1 Describe some of the key concepts involved in site selection and how developers go about assessing potential sites.

12.2 How did Fraser Morrow Daniels go about choosing the site for Europa Center? How did the firm justify paying so much more than market value?

12.3 What is the Catch-22 developers face when they find a site that meets their initial criteria but that has not yet been subjected to a thorough feasibility analysis?

12.4 What services can architects provide to developers at this stage of the development process?

12.5 Why does Paula R. Collins's development company work so closely with the public?

12.6 What are "market segmentation" and "product differentiation?" Why are they important in the real estate development planning process?

12.7 How can developers control risk during stage two?

12.8 In Dean Stratouly's description of rezoning, the situation sounds extremely stressful and aggravating. But this is one of his first steps in a long development process. What is the impetus for him to continue the project?

Notes

1. Roger W. Lotchin, *The Martial Metropolis: U.S. Cities in War and Peace, 1900–1970* (New York: Praeger, 1984). See also Marc A. Weiss, *The Rise of the Community Builders* (New York: Columbia Univ. Press, 1987), Chap. 4.

2. For a fuller discussion of these and other urban economic concepts, see Charles H. Wurtzebach and Mike E. Miles, *Modern Real Estate,* 5th ed. (New York: John Wiley & Sons, 1994).

3. For more information about the definition and growth of edge cities, see Joel Garreau, *Edge City: Life on the New Frontier* (New York: Anchor, 1992).

4. For more information on GISs, see Grant Ian Thrall and Allen P. Marks, "Functional Requirements of a Geographic

Information System for Performing Real Estate Research and Analysis," *Journal of Real Estate Literature,* January 1993, pp. 49–61; and Allen P. Marks, Craig Stanley, and Grant Ian Thrall, "Criteria and Definition for the Evaluation of Geographic Information System Software for Real Estate Analysis," *Journal of Real Estate Literature,* July 1994, pp. 227–41.

5. For a good look at traffic in America, see Anthony Downs, *Stuck in Traffic: Coping with Peak-Hour Traffic Congestion* (Washington, D.C.: The Brookings Institution, 1992); Robert T. Dunphy, *Moving beyond Gridlock* (Washington, D.C.: ULI–the Urban Land Institute, 1997); and Robert Burke Cervero, *The Transit Metropolis: A Global Inquiry* (Washington, D.C.: Island Press, 1998). Developers should never underestimate the potential for protest against proposed developments simply because of the traffic the developments will generate or the traffic residents think will be generated. Traffic has become a headache for most residents of urban areas. From 1975 to 1990, the total number of miles traveled annually by vehicles rose 61.9 percent. From 1990 to 1997, vehicle miles traveled increased 18.6 percent, for a total of 2.5 trillion vehicle miles traveled daily in the United States.

6. Impact fees can undermine a pro forma and are a major factor in site selection. Thus, they are the subject of heated debate in some states. In Florida and California, for example, impact fees in some cities rose 300 to 400 percent in one year. In one extreme case, Tampa's impact fee was calculated at several million dollars for a 500-bed hotel; at the same time, no impact fee was levied outside the city. Nonetheless, public services must be paid for, and the rule that those reaping the benefits should pay the costs is probably a good one (see Chapter 13).

7. See Grant Ian Thrall et al., *Real Estate Market Analysis* (Washington, D.C.: ULI–the Urban Land Institute, forthcoming); and John Clapp, *Handbook for Real Estate Market Analysis* (Englewood Cliffs, N.J.: Prentice-Hall, 1987), for a useful way of relating site selection to the process of refining the project design to fit the local market.

8. The many items likely to be specified are covered in most elementary textbooks and more completely in Robert Kratovil and Raymond Werner, *Real Estate Law,* 10th ed. (Englewood Cliffs, N.J.: Prentice-Hall, 1992), or William D. Lusk and Harold F. French, *Law of the Real Estate Business,* 5th ed. (Homewood, Ill.: Richard D. Irwin, 1984).

9. See James H. Boykin and Richard L. Haney, Jr., *Financing Real Estate,* 2d ed. (Englewood Cliffs, N.J.: Prentice-Hall, 1993), for an excellent description of these different lenders; Charles H. Wurtzebach and Mike E. Miles, *Modern Real Estate,* 5th ed. (New York: John Wiley & Sons, 1994), for a discussion of real estate finance in general; and publications by Goldman Sachs real estate research and Lehman Brothers real estate research for current discussions of financing terms and financial innovations.

Part IV

Bibliography

Inception of an Idea

Anthony, Robert N., and Vijay Govindarajan. *Management Control Systems.* 9th ed. Homewood, Ill.: Irwin, 1997.

Boykin, James H., and Richard L. Haney, Jr. *Financing Real Estate.* 2d ed. Englewood Cliffs, N.J.: Prentice-Hall, 1993.

Cervero, Robert Burke. *The Transit Metropolis: A Global Inquiry.* Washington, D.C.: Island Press, 1998.

Delbecq, Andre L., Andrew H. Van de Ven, and David H. Gustafson. *Group Techniques for Program Planning.* Middleton, Wis.: Green Briar Press, 1986.

Downs, Anthony. *Stuck in Traffic: Coping with Peak-Hour Traffic Congestion.* Washington, D.C.: The Brookings Institution, 1992.

Dunphy, Robert T. *Moving beyond Gridlock.* Washington, D.C.: ULI–the Urban Land Institute, 1997.

Edmonds, Holly. *The Focus Group Research Handbook.* Lincolnwood, Ill.: NTC Business Books, 1999.

Garreau, Joel. *Edge City: Life on the New Frontier.* New York: Anchor, 1992.

Godschalk, David, et al. *Pulling Together: A Planning and Development Consensus-Building Manual.* Washington, D.C.: ULI–the Urban Land Institute, 1994.

Kratovil, Robert, and Raymond Werner. *Real Estate Law.* 10th ed. Englewood Cliffs, N.J.: Prentice-Hall, 1992.

Krueger, Richard A. *Focus Groups: A Practical Guide to Applied Research.* 2d ed. Thousand Oaks, Calif.: Sage, 1994.

Linstone, Harold A. *Multiple Perspectives for Decision Making: Bridging the Gap between Analysis and Action.* Englewood Cliffs, N.J.: Prentice-Hall, 1994.

Linstone, H.A., and M. Turoff, eds. *The Delphi Method: Techniques and Applications.* Reading, Mass.: Addison-Wesley, 1975.

Lotchin, Roger W. *The Martial Metropolis: U.S. Cities in War and Peace, 1900–1970.* New York: Praeger, 1984.

Lusk, William D., and Harold F. French. *Law of the Real Estate Business.* 5th ed. Homewood, Ill.: Irwin, 1984.

Malizia, Emil E., and Edward J. Feser. *Understanding Local Economic Development.* New Brunswick, N.J.: CUPR Press, 1999.

Morgan, David L., ed. *Successful Focus Groups: Advancing the State of the Art.* Thousand Oaks, Calif.: Sage, 1993.

Stewart, David, and Prem N. Shamdasani. *Focus Groups: Theory and Practice.* Thousand Oaks, Calif.: Sage, 1990.

Weiss, Marc A. *The Rise of the Community Builders.* New York: Columbia Univ. Press, 1987.

Wurtzebach, Charles H., and Mike E. Miles. *Modern Real Estate.* 5th ed. New York: Wiley, 1994.

Market Research

Aaker, David A., V. Kumar, and George S. Day. *Marketing Research.* 6th ed. New York: Wiley, 1998.

Bajozzi, Richard P., ed. *Advanced Marketing Research.* Cambridge, Mass.: Blackwell Publishers, 1994.

———. *Principles of Marketing Research.* Cambridge, Mass.: Blackwell Publishers, 1994.

Barrett, G. Vincent, and John P. Blair. *How to Conduct and Analyze Real Estate Market and Feasibility Studies.* 2d ed. New York: Van Nostrand Reinhold, 1988.

Blankenship, Albert Breneman, George Edward Breen, and Alan F. Dutka. *State of the Art Marketing Research.* 2d ed. Lincolnwood, Ill.: NTC Business Books, 1998.

Churchill, Gilbert A., Jr. *Marketing Research: Methodological Foundations.* 7th ed. Fort Worth: Dryden Press, 1999.

Churchill, Gilbert A., Jr., and J. Paul Peter. *Marketing: Creating Value for Customers.* 2d ed. Blacklick, Ohio: Irwin Professional Publications, 1998.

Clapp, John. *Handbook for Real Estate Market Analysis.* Englewood Cliffs, N.J.: Prentice-Hall, 1987.

Drezner, Zvi, ed. *Facility Location: A Survey of Applications and Methods.* New York: Springer Verlag, 1996.

Graaskamp, James A. *Fundamentals of Real Estate Development.* Washington, D.C.: ULI–the Urban Land Institute, 1981.

———. "Identification and Delineation of Real Estate Market Research." *Real Estate Issues* 10:1 (Spring/Summer 1985): 6–12.

Kotler, Philip. *Marketing Management: The Millennium Edition.* 10th ed. Upper Saddle River, N.J.: Prentice-Hall, 1999.

Kotler, Philip, and Gary Armstrong. *Principles of Marketing.* 8th ed. Englewood Cliffs, N.J.: Prentice-Hall, 1998.

Kotler, Philip, et al. *Marketing Places: Attracting Investment, Industry, and Tourism to Cities, States, and Nations.* New York: Free Press, 1993.

Kress, George J., and John Snyder. *Forecasting and Market Analysis Techniques: A Practical Approach.* Westport, Conn.: Greenwood Press, 1994.

Lehmann, Donald R., and Sunil Gupta. *Marketing Research.* Reading, Mass.: Addison-Wesley, 1998.

Lilien, Gary L., Philip Kotler, and K. Sridhar Moorthy. *Marketing Models.* Englewood Cliffs, N.J.: Prentice-Hall, 1991.

Milder, N. David. *Niche Strategies for Downtown Revitalization: A Hands-On Guide to Developing, Strengthening, and Marketing Niches.* New York: Alexander Communications Group, 1998.

Myers, Dowell, and Philip Mitchell. "Identifying a Well-Founded Market Study." *Appraisal Journal* 61:4 (October 1993): 500–8.

Peter, J. Paul, and Jerry C. Olson. *Consumer Behavior and Marketing Strategy.* 5th ed. New York: Irwin, 1998.

Porter, Michael E. *Competitive Strategy: Techniques for Analyzing Industries and Competitors.* New York: Free Press, 1980.

———. *Michael E. Porter on Competition.* Cambridge, Mass.: Harvard Business School Press, 1998.

Ratcliff, Richard. *Real Estate Analysis.* New York: McGraw-Hill, 1961.

Raymondo, James C. *Population Estimation and Projection: Methods for Marketing, Demographic, and Planning Personnel.* Westport, Conn.: Greenwood Press, 1992.

Russell, Cheryl. *The American Marketplace: Demographics and Spending Patterns.* 4th ed. Ithaca, N.Y.: New Strategist Publications, 1999.

Spitzer, T.M., and H. Baum. *Public Markets and Community Revitalization.* Washington, D.C.: ULI–the Urban Land Institute, 1995.

ULI–the Urban Land Institute. *ULI Market Profiles: 1999.* 3 vol. Washington, D.C.: Author, 1999.

———. *ULI Market Profiles: 2000.* 3 vol. Washington, D.C.: Author, forthcoming 2000.

Vernor, James D., ed. *Readings in Market Research for Real Estate.* Chicago: American Institute of Real Estate Appraisers, 1985.

Williams, Donald L., and Sally M. Dwyer. "A Marketing Revolution." *Urban Land* 53:3 (March 1994): 28–31.

The authors of this textbook are relentless in emphasizing that the government is always a partner in any real estate development. Whether it's a residential development, an office building, a business park, a recreation center, a museum, or a shopping mall, no developer can accomplish his goal without taking on the government as a partner. Development professionals should never underestimate the importance of that relationship—whether a formal public/private partnership or simply zoning and land use policies that affect what and how development can be implemented.

Because of the importance of this issue, we devote all of Part V to it. Chapter 13 explores the role of the public sector as it relates to zoning, land use policy, impact fees, financing infrastructure, and the like. Chapter 14 examines all varieties of partnerships that cities have formed with private entities to accomplish development and revitalization goals. And Chapter 15 looks at affordable housing—what it is, why we need it, and some of the financing issues involved in its production. Even though we could have focused in depth on many different types of development, we chose affordable housing, because the number of homeless and the number of persons living in substandard and unaffordable housing continue to increase in virtually every area of the country.

Part V
Planning and Analysis: The Public Roles

Chapter 13
The Roles of the Public Sector

Historically, the United States has relied on spontaneous economic forces (the "free market system" or "free enterprise") to carry out urban development. The right of private individuals to own and determine how they will use real estate has been a cherished and constitutionally protected tradition. But even in the free market, the public sector has always been a strong force in establishing the rules of the development game. Government statutes and court decisions provide the legal framework for landownership and contractual understandings. Government policies and programs support development by planning and securing the funding for underlying infrastructure. Government regulations prescribe standards to guide the character and location of private development.

In many communities and in many ways, public officials and agencies are intensifying their involvement in the development process. Some developers and builders expected the real estate recession of the late 1980s and early 1990s to stimulate local governments' easing of restrictions and requirements as a means of rekindling economic growth and development. In addition, the property rights movement, successful in enacting restraining legislation in many states and some favorable court decisions, was viewed as a cautionary factor in local regulation of development. Although that scenario may have played out in some regions and communities, especially in rural areas welcoming development, most communities have strengthened rather than weakened public guidance of the development process.

Citizens in Las Vegas, Nevada, and Phoenix, Arizona, for example, recently mounted campaigns to establish growth boundaries around their urban areas. Public officials in communities that generally favor growth, such as Cary, North Carolina, and Wichita, Kansas, have considered adoption of growth management techniques. Prince William County, Virginia, one of the booming jurisdictions in the Washington, D.C., region, has shifted its stance from vigorously supporting development to restrictive measures. Although communities like these are not necessarily adopting drastic restrictions on growth, they are focusing more than ever on the public impacts of development. Meanwhile, communities with long-established growth management programs, such as Fort Collins, Colorado, have tightened development restrictions and standards.

Overlooked during the market slump was the expanding constituency of interests in most regions who are pressing for greater restrictions on growth and higher standards of development. Environmentalists, quality-of-life advocates, NIMBYists of every kind, have influenced public attitudes toward community development. Virtually nationwide, growth is blamed for congested highways, overcrowded schools, loss of valued natural qualities, and other impacts on communities' quality of life and fiscal stability. Today developers can expect heightened public scrutiny and stricter guidance of the development approval process to avoid or at least mitigate the impacts of development.

The roles of the public sector as regulator of private development and provider of needed facilities and services are constantly evolving. In recent years, many local governments, constrained by limitations on their powers of taxation and by voters' changing attitudes

---

This chapter was written by Douglas R. Porter, president, The Growth Management Institute, Chevy Chase, Maryland.

toward development, have shifted much of the burden of financing infrastructure to the private sector. Some communities have imposed limits on development in response to voters' wishes to slow or even stop growth. Environmentalists and other interest groups have persuaded governments to adopt more rigorous standards and complex requirements to protect specific areas, natural features, and historic buildings. As always, the real estate industry functions within a climate of changing public/private responsibilities and goals.

For that reason, developers increasingly find themselves working closely with government officials to ensure that their projects meet public objectives for development. In almost every local jurisdiction, developers encounter official public plans, zoning and subdivision requirements, and other policies and regulations that affect their development plans. Increasingly, too, state governments are stepping into the land development process to make additional demands on both local governments and developers. If developers are to succeed in their endeavors, they must anticipate public needs and desires for private development and seek to mesh the interests of private development with public goals and requirements.

This chapter examines the following important roles of governments as they affect the development process and the development industry:

- Regulator of private development; and
- Provider of needed facilities.

The chapter's central theme is that real estate development is a shared process in which the public and private sectors continually interact for their mutual benefit.

The Public Sector as Regulator

Developers usually first come in contact with local government regulations early in stage two of the development process, even before acquiring a site. Those contacts increase in frequency and intensity as proposed projects are subjected to intensive scrutiny throughout the development approval process as it leads to final permits for construction and occupancy. Along the way, developers must deal with public expectations for development that are framed in comprehensive plans and zoning ordinances and satisfy public standards and requirements for development that are expressed in subdivision regulations and building codes. In addition, developers may find their projects affected by growth management ordinances and provisions that can postpone or restrict development. The extent to which devel-

opers understand the regulatory process and its components can spell success or failure for their proposals.

The Legal Foundation for Public Regulations

State and local governments' regulation of land development is based on the police power—the requirement of government to protect the health, safety, and general welfare of citizens. Oddly, the police power is not a constitutional power of the federal government except in cases of interstate commerce, land held in federal ownership, and private land subject to major federal public works such as dams and irrigation systems. Rather, the police power is reserved for the states, which usually delegate that authority to local governments.

Most states enacted enabling legislation in the 1920s and 1930s to give local governments the police power (authority) to regulate real estate development for purposes of health, safety, and general welfare. Since then, local officials have grown accustomed to thinking of these regulatory powers as theirs by right. They believe that regulations affecting the growth and character of their communities should be determined and administered by local governments. Developers also have tended to support local control of development in the belief that state governments are too removed from the realities of development in local areas. Increasingly, however, states are moving to reassert a role in managing the development process.[1] A reminder of state prerogatives in land use control occurred in Fairfax County, Virginia, in 1990, when the state legislature rescinded part of the county's downzoning of industrially zoned land. Although the Fairfax case is unusual, it illustrates the ultimate legal power of states to regulate development.

Courts recognize the legal rights of local governments to exercise the police power, but they are also concerned with safeguarding private property rights. The history of land use law in the United States describes the working out of an uneasy—and continuously evolving—balance between the rights of local governments to protect the public health, safety, and general welfare and the rights of individuals to unfettered enjoyment of private property. That balance has shifted over the years as courts have expanded their interpretation of "health," "safety," and "general welfare" to include aesthetic and other concerns. The courts also have tended to grant local governments wide latitude in adopting legislation under the police power. Under the doctrine of "legislative presumption of validity," the courts give great deference to regulations that are properly enacted by local governments, generally holding the regulations valid unless clearly proven otherwise. Local governments' use of the police power to regulate land devel-

Figure 13-1

Some Important Land Use Cases

Welch v. Swasey, 214 U.S. 91 (1909). The U.S. Supreme Court upheld Boston's height restrictions within districts.

Hadacheck v. Sebastian, 239 U.S. 394 (1915). The U.S. Supreme Court upheld as a proper exercise of the police power a city ordinance that prohibited the continuation of brick manufacturing within designated areas as a nuisance to nearby residents.

Village of Euclid, Ohio v. Ambler Realty Co., 272 U.S. 365 (1926). *Euclid* was the first U.S. Supreme Court case to uphold zoning as a valid form of regulation of the police power.

Golden v. Planning Board of Town of Ramapo, 285 N.W.2d 291 (N.Y. 1972). This case is one of the first and most important cases upholding regulations for timing, phasing, and quotas in development generally and in Ramapo specifically, making development permits contingent on the availability of adequate public facilities.

Southern Burlington County NAACP v. Mt. Laurel Township, 336 A.2d 713 (N.J. 1975) and 456 A.2d 390 (N.J. 1983). In these two cases, the state court ruled that Mt. Laurel Township and other New Jersey municipalities must provide for development of a fair share of lower-cost housing and imposed court oversight of the process.

Avco Community Builders, Inc. v. South Coastal Regional Commission, 132 Cal. Rptr. 386, 553 P.2d 546 (1976). The California Supreme Court held that Avco did not have vested rights to develop a property despite having secured local approvals and expending more than $2 million. The decision led directly to the state Development Agreements Act.

Penn Central Transportation Co. v. New York City, 438 U.S. 104 (1978). The U.S. Supreme Court upheld New York City's imposition of landmark status on Grand Central Station as a justifiable regulation that required no compensation, thus preventing construction of an office building over the station.

Kaiser Aetna v. United States, 444 U.S. 164 (1979). The U.S. Supreme Court upheld the owners of a private lagoon in their claim that a taking had occurred when they were forced to allow public use of the lagoon.

Agins v. City of Tiburon, 447 U.S. 255 (1980). This case was one of a series in which the U.S. Supreme Court held that the cases were not "ripe" for a decision, usually meaning that the plaintiffs had not exhausted the administrative procedures that might have resolved their complaint before going to court.

First English Evangelical Lutheran Church of Glendale v. the County of Los Angeles, 482 U.S. 304 (1987). This decision was the first by the U.S. Supreme Court claiming that a regulatory taking of property can require compensation to the owner, even if the regulation has only a temporary effect.

Nollan v. California Coastal Commission, 483 U.S. 825 (1987). The U.S. Supreme Court ruled that the California Coastal Commission had not established an appropriate connection between a requirement for an exaction and the cited public objective for the exaction.

Lucas v. South Carolina Coastal Council, 112 S. Ct. 2886 (1992). The U.S. Supreme Court ruled that damages are due in the relatively rare situations in which a government entity deprives a landowner of "all economically beneficial uses" of the land.

Dolan v. City of Tigard, 114 S. Ct. 2309 (1994). The U.S. Supreme Court ruled that the government has the burden of justifying permit conditions requiring dedication for which the property owner is not compensated. ■

opment therefore has grown considerably in scope and application.

Two early U.S. Supreme Court cases, *Welch v. Swasey* in 1909 and *Hadacheck v. Sebastian* in 1915, established the right of local governments to regulate development. (All references to court cases in this chapter can be found in Figure 13-1, listed chronologically.) A major judicial step supporting regulation of the police power occurred in 1926, when the U.S. Supreme Court, in *Euclid v. Ambler Realty,* upheld zoning as a valid form of regulation. Through countless court decisions since then, the courts have consistently upheld the right of local governments to regulate land use and development so long as they establish a legitimate public interest and follow due process in adopting and administering regulations. Indeed, under the police power, governments may severely limit private property owners' rights to use their property. In appropriate circumstances, governments may legally curtail or prohibit development to preserve floodplains, wetlands, sand dunes, and habitats of endangered species, and they may restrict the amount or height of development to protect erodible hillsides, mountain views, access to beaches, solar access, and other public interests.

Rights to use the police power are, however, constrained by court decisions and limits self-imposed by local governments. The question of just how restrictive regulations can be continues to vex developers and public officials. If regulations are too restrictive, they may be viewed as a "taking" of private property without compensation, which is prohibited by the Constitution. Two famous U.S. Supreme Court decisions in 1987 and another in 1992 sounded warnings to local governments about overly expansive use of the police power. In *Nollan v. California Coastal Commission,* the Court ruled that the commission had not established an appropriate connection between a regulation and the public interest when it required property owner Patrick Nollan to allow public access along his beach frontage to provide public views of the ocean. The Court indicated that, in future cases of this type, it would more closely scrutinize government actions to ensure that regulations were properly related to public purposes. Then, in *First English Evangelical Lutheran Church of Glendale v. the County of Los Angeles,* the Court ruled that if regulations are found to be so restrictive as to constitute an effective taking of property, then the public authority may be required to compensate the owner as if it had actually taken title. (In this case, however, a state court later determined that the regulations, which prevented the rebuilding of structures destroyed by a flood in a floodplain, were not a taking.)

In 1992, in *Lucas v. South Carolina Coastal Council,* the U.S. Supreme Court held that a taking had occurred and that damages were due because the council's regulations against beachfront development deprived Lucas of all use of his two lots on the ocean. These decisions demonstrate the necessity of governments' regulation of development following strict rules, with due caution for the rights of private property owners.

The other, perhaps more widely significant, brake on governments' use of the police power is public opinion as expressed in the political arena. Many U.S. citizens own property and place great store in their rights to use it. It is not surprising, therefore, that public officials, when deciding to regulate land use and development, usually attempt to allow property owners a reasonable economic use of their property. Public officials' attitudes toward this issue, however, vary considerably from state to state. What might be considered reasonable regulation in California or Colorado might be anathema in Virginia or Texas.

Thus, local governments have a great deal of latitude in determining how to regulate development. State enabling legislation provides a starting point and court decisions erect a legal framework, but final decisions often depend on the attitudes and perspectives of the public officials making them.

The Local Regulatory Process

Cities, counties, and other local governments undertake to regulate development according to state enabling statutes and, in some cases, in conformance with home rule charters granted by the state. The mainstays of local governments' regulatory programs are comprehensive plans, zoning ordinances, subdivision regulations, and capital improvement programs. Many communities adopt additional measures to manage growth and development.

A *comprehensive plan* describes the desirable ways in which a community should develop over a ten- to 20-year time frame. A plan usually consists of written development goals and policies, supplemented by maps, that provide guidelines for local officials as they make decisions about the quality, location, and amount of development. Depending on state enabling statutes, comprehensive plans may be either merely advisory in nature or legally binding on public decisions. Comprehensive plans may also include more detailed plans for specific development elements such as housing and infrastructure systems or for particular areas of importance such as central business districts and historic neighborhoods.

Zoning ordinances are the most widely used form of land use regulation. They establish a variety of districts, depicted on maps, and spell out requirements and standards for permitted uses of land and buildings, the height and size of buildings, the size of lots and yards around buildings, the supply of parking spaces, the size and type of signs and fences, and other matters within each district. When a local government adopts a zoning ordinance, every property within the government's jurisdiction is designated for a specific district, and the property's use is regulated by the ordinance provisions for that district. The ordinance also establishes procedures for changing zoning. (Figure 13-2 describes a number of special zoning approaches that may be incorporated into local ordinances.) Developers should be sure to check the current zoning for properties they wish to develop as well as procedures for rezoning.

Subdivision regulations provide public control over subdivisions of land into lots for sale and development. They contain requirements and standards regarding the size and shape of lots; the design and construction of streets, water and sewer lines, and other public facilities; and other concerns such as protecting environmental features. The regulations require all subdivision developers to obtain approval of detailed plans before they can record and sell lots. (Figure 13-3 presents a typical set of requirements and procedures for subdivision plan approval.)

Capital improvement programs are adopted by local governments to provide a construction schedule for planned infrastructure improvements; they also identify the expected sources of funds to pay for the improvements. Usually updated each year for a multiyear period, the capital improvement program is a guide to when and where improvements will be made. From the developer's perspective, the capital improvement program provides a useful indication of longer-term plans but is typically conclusive only about infrastructure improvements that are to be funded over the next year.

In addition to these basic forms of regulation, various growth management techniques have gained favor with many local governments. These techniques tend to provide more direct public control over the amount, type, timing, location, and quality of development than traditional planning and zoning. Many types of growth management techniques are in use today. They range from more precise standards for development to actual restrictions on the amount of development that may take place. In San Diego County, California, for example, most municipalities impose some type of limit on the amount of growth that will be permitted

---

Figure 13-2

Selected Zoning Innovations

Planned unit development. An optional procedure for project design, usually applied to a fairly large site. It allows more flexible site design than ordinary zoning by permitting options or relaxing some requirements. A PUD frequently permits a variety of housing types and sometimes other uses as well. Usually a PUD includes an overall general plan that is implemented in phases through specific subdivision plans.

Cluster zoning. Zoning provisions that allow groups of dwellings on small lots to be located on one part of a site, thereby preserving open space and/or natural features on the remainder of the site. Minimum lot and yard sizes for the clustered development are reduced. Like PUDs, cluster site designs are subject to more detailed reviews.

Overlay zoning. A zoning district, applied over one or more other districts, that contains additional provisions for special features or conditions such as historic buildings, wetlands, steep slopes, and downtown residential uses.

Floating zones. Zoning districts and provisions for which locations are not identified until enacted for a specific project. Such zones are used to anticipate certain uses, such as regional shopping centers, for which locations will not be designated on the zoning map until developers apply for zoning. Floating zones usually require special review procedures.

Incentive zoning. Zoning provisions that encourage but do not require developers to provide certain amenities or qualities in their projects in return for identified benefits such as increased density or rapid processing of applications. Incentives are often used in downtown areas to gain open space, special building features, or public art in connection with approved developments.

Flexible zoning. Zoning regulations that establish performance standards and other criteria for determining appropriate uses and site design requirements rather than prescribing specific uses and building standards. Performance provisions are rarely applied to all zoning districts but are often used for selected locations or types of uses (e.g., PUDs).

Inclusionary zoning. Zoning that requires or encourages construction of lower-income housing as a condition of a project's approval. Provisions may include density or other bonuses in return for housing commitments and may require housing on site or allow construction at another site.

Transferable (or transfer of) development rights (TDRs). A procedure that permits owners of property restricted from development to recoup some lost value by selling development rights to developers for transfer to another location where increased densities are allowed. TDRs are often used to preserve buildings of historic or architectural importance and sometimes to preserve open space or farmland. ∎

Figure 13-3

Tentative Map Submittal Requirements

City of Walnut Creek, California, Community Development Department

Author's note: Walnut Creek's subdivision process, as set out in its "Subdivision Guidelines," suggests that applicants first review the city's general plan and zoning regulations, then consider submission of a preliminary proposal for review by the city's Development Review Team before a formal application. Once an application is submitted to the Community Development Department, it is assigned to a staff planner, who reviews it for completeness and acts as liaison throughout the approval process. The department sends a copy of the tentative map to all affected public agencies, utilities, school districts, and other city departments for comment. An environmental assessment determines whether an Environmental Impact Report must be prepared. The proposal also may be referred to the Design Review Commission for comment. Planning and engineering staffs will prepare a written staff report analyzing the land use, traffic, and other impacts of the proposal, and including comments and recommendations received from other agencies. The Planning Commission schedules a public hearing on the proposal, with public notice. The staff presents its report and recommendations, and the applicant and other interested persons may respond. The Planning Commission approves, approves with conditions, denies, or postpones a decision to a later hearing. The decision can be appealed to the city council. Following approval, the Design Review Commission must approve final plans for structures, and a final map and improvement agreement must be submitted to the Engineering Division for final approval by the city council. The approved final map is filed with the County Recorder.

The tentative map shall be prepared in a manner acceptable to the Community Development Department and shall be prepared by a registered civil engineer or licensed land surveyor. The tentative map shall be clearly and leg-

ibly drawn on a single 600 mm × 90 mm (24" × 36") sheet and contain not less than the following:

- A title, which shall contain the subdivision number, subdivision name, and type of subdivision.
- Name and address of legal owner, subdivider, and person preparing the map, including registration or license number.
- Sufficient legal description to define the boundary of the proposed subdivision.
- Date, north arrow, scale, contour interval, and source and date of existing contours.
- Existing and proposed land uses and zoning districts.
- A vicinity map showing streets, highways, adjoining jurisdictions, adjoining subdivisions, and other data sufficient to locate the proposed subdivision and show its relation to the community.
- Existing topography of the proposed site and at least 30 meters (100 feet) beyond its boundary, including but not limited to:
  - Existing contours at 600-mm (2-foot) intervals if the existing ground slope is less than 10 percent and at not less than 1,500-mm (5-foot) intervals for existing ground slopes greater than or equal to 10 percent. Contour intervals shall not be spread more than 46 meters (150 feet) apart. Existing contours shall be represented by dashed lines or by screened lines;
  - Type, circumference, and dripline of existing trees as defined by Chapter 8 of Title 3 (Preservation of Trees on Private Property) of the Walnut Creek Municipal Code. Any trees proposed to be removed shall be so indicated;

---

each year. In the 1980s, citizens' initiatives in San Francisco and Seattle succeeded in capping the amount of development that may occur each year in the downtown areas of those cities.

A popular regulatory technique that goes beyond traditional planning and zoning is the use of requirements for "adequate public facilities." Such regulations make development contingent on the existence of adequate capacity in the local infrastructure systems that will serve new development. Developers covered by such requirements could find their proposals grinding to a halt. In some places, developers can provide such infrastructure to move forward with development—though at a higher

cost. When the service capacity problem is a congested major highway, however, developers may choose to defer development until the government constructs more capacity. (Figure 13-4 describes some of the more common types of growth management techniques.)

Regulations adopted by local governments establish procedures that require property owners and developers to obtain zoning, building, and eventually occupancy permits. Applications must be submitted for these permits, usually with supporting documentation. If the type of development is allowed "by right," according to the permitted zoning for the property, an administrative official can approve the zoning permit withou

- The approximate location and outline of existing structures identified by type. Structures to be removed shall be so marked;
- The approximate location of all areas subject to inundation or stormwater overflow and the location, width, and direction of flow of each watercourse;
- The location, pavement, and right-of-way width, grade, and name of existing streets or highways;
- The widths, location, and identity of all existing easements;
- The location and size of existing sanitary sewers, fire hydrants, water mains, and storm drains, and the location of fire hydrants. The approximate slope of existing sewers and storm drains shall be indicated. The location of existing overhead utility lines on peripheral streets, fire hydrants, and street lights;
- The location of the 60, 65, and 70 community noise equivalent level contours, if any; and
- Other such data as may be required by the Community Development Department.
- All proposed improvements, including:
  - The location, grade, centerline radius, and arc length of curves, pavement, right-of-way widths, and names of all streets. Typical sections of all streets must be shown. Proposed private streets shall be so indicated;
  - The location and radius of all curb returns and culs-de-sac;
  - The location, width, and purpose of all easements;
  - The angle of intersecting streets if such angle deviates from a right angle by more than four degrees;
  - The approximate lot layout and the approximate dimensions of each lot and of each building site.

Engineering data must show the approximate finished grading of each lot, the preliminary design of all grading, the elevation of proposed building pads, the top and toe of cut-and-fill slopes to scale, and the number of each lot;
- Proposed contours at 600-mm (2-foot) intervals must be shown if the existing ground slope is less than 10 percent and not at less than 1,500-mm (5-foot) intervals for existing ground slopes equal to or greater than 10 percent (a separate grading plan may be submitted);
- Proposed recreation sites, trails, and parks for private or public use;
- Proposed common areas and areas to be dedicated to public open space; and
- The location and size of sanitary sewers, water mains, and storm drains, and the location of fire hydrants. Proposed slopes and approximate elevations of sanitary sewers and storm drains shall be indicated.
- The name or names of any geologist or soils engineer whose services were required in the preparation of the design of the tentative map.
- All lettering size shall be print of legible size.
- If the subdivider plans to develop the site in units, the proposed units and their proposed sequence of construction shall be shown.
- The Community Development Department may waive any of the above tentative map requirements if the location and nature of the proposed subdivision or existing documentation demonstrate that a waiver is justified. The

continued on next page

further action. If the proposed development is allowed only under certain conditions or requires a change in zoning, special hearings and other procedures are necessary, some of which can take months or even years. Zoning changes may also require revisions in comprehensive plans, thus extending the process even further. (Figure 13-5 illustrates typical procedures that many communities follow.)

As development regulations become more complicated and convoluted, developers face many decisions about making their way through the permitting process. Frequently, to develop a marketable product or to maximize their investment, developers request changes in the adopted plans or zoning or turn to special procedures that allow alternative uses or more flexible design treatment. A request for changes or special procedures usually exposes a project to closer scrutiny by public officials and the general public and often creates opportunities for public officials to require additional contributions of amenities or infrastructure.

The use of these special "discretionary" procedures has grown in recent years. In part, this growth has occurred because public officials have discovered that they can control the size and quality of development more directly through case-by-case reviews than through written regulations. In part, developers have found

Figure 13-3

Tentative Map Submittal Requirements (continued)
City of Walnut Creek, California, Community Development Department

Community Development Department may require other drawings, data, or information as deemed necessary.

Accompanying Data and Reports: The tentative map shall be accompanied by the following data or reports:

- A list of potential street names for any unnamed street or alley. The Community Development Department shall submit the list to the Street Naming Committee for comment and recommendations. Those comments and recommendations may be included in the staff report to the Planning Commission.
- A preliminary soils report prepared in accordance with the city's Grading Ordinance shall be submitted. If the preliminary soils report indicates the presence of critically expansive soils or other soil problems that, if not corrected, could lead to structural defects, the soils report accompanying the final map shall contain an investigation of each lot within the subdivision. The City Engineer may require additional information or reject the report if it is found to be incomplete, inaccurate, or unsatisfactory.
- A preliminary title report showing the legal owners at the time of filing the tentative map.
- Preliminary engineering, geology, and/or seismic safety reports (prepared in accordance with guidelines established by the Community Development Department) if the subdivision lies within a "medium-risk" or "high-risk" geologic hazard area, as shown on the maps on file in the Community Development Department. If the preliminary engineering, geology, and/or seismic safety report indicates the presence of geologic hazards or seismic hazards that, if not corrected, would lead to structural defects, an engineering, geology, and/or seismic safety report shall accompany the final map,

and it shall contain an investigation of each lot within the subdivision.

- The subdivider shall obtain from the school districts involved their intention, in writing, concerning the necessity for a school site and/or facilities, if any, within the subdivision and shall present this information to the Community Development Department prior to the consideration of the tentative map by the Planning Commission.
- The subdivider shall provide additional data and information, and deposit and pay such fees as may be required for the preparation and processing of environmental review documents.
- If applicable, the subdivider shall submit a tree removal permit application in accordance with Title 3, Chapter 8 of the Municipal Code, and/or an arborist's report.
- If applicable, the subdivider shall submit any information required under Section 10-1.1206 for a vesting tentative map.
- Any other data or reports deemed necessary by the Community Development Department.
- If there will be displacement of persons residing in the existing residential units, applicant shall submit a relocation plan according to Title 9, Chapter 15 of the Municipal Code.

Plans:
- For minor subdivisions, 13 copies must be submitted and folded to approximately 9" × 11".
- For major subdivisions, 35 copies must be submitted and folded to approximately 9" × 11".
- Any other data or reports deemed necessary by the Community Development Department. ■

Source: **City of Walnut Creek, "Tentative Map Submittal Requirements," 1998.**

---

regulations too restrictive and thus request special procedures that permit greater flexibility. But special interest groups and citizens' groups have also discovered that such procedures open opportunities for participating in decisions (see Figure 13-6 for an example). Developers increasingly find that they must spend almost as much time coming to terms with neighborhood or special interest groups as with the public officials charged with project approval. In many instances,

developers must employ consultants and prepare special studies to respond to questions and demands from such groups. Developers in many communities have had to become (or hire) public relations experts to have their projects approved.[2]

Depending on the circumstances, however, developers may find the results worth the effort, especially if their projects draw favorable public attention in the process. In fact, more than one developer has been able

Figure 13-4

Major Techniques for Managing Growth

Urban growth boundary/urban service limit. Boundaries established around a community within which the local government plans to provide public services and facilities and beyond which urban development is discouraged or prohibited. Boundaries are usually set to accommodate growth over ten to 20 years and are intended to provide more efficient services and to protect rural land and natural resources. Communities in Oregon, Florida, Colorado, Maryland, and California use boundaries extensively.

Designated development area. Similar to an urban growth boundary in that certain areas within a community are designated as urbanized, urbanizing, future urban, and/or rural, within which different policies for future development apply. Used to encourage development in an urbanizing area or redevelopment in an urbanized area.

Adequate facilities ordinance. A requirement that approvals for projects are contingent upon evidence that public facilities have adequate capacity for the proposed development. When facilities are found inadequate, development is postponed, or developers may contribute funds to improve facilities.

Extraterritorial jurisdiction. Power of local governments in some states to plan and control urban development outside their boundaries until such areas can be annexed. Such controls may also be effected through intergovernmental agreements, such as between a city and a county.

Affordable housing allocation. A requirement in some states that local governments must plan to accommodate a fair share of all housing types geared to regional housing needs. Targets can then be met through various programs to encourage or mandate lower-income housing (see "inclusionary zoning" in Figure 13-2).

Growth limit. Establishment of an annual limit on the amount of permitted development, usually affecting the number of building permits issued and most often applied to residential development. Such limits require a method for allocating permits, such as a point system (see below). Limits may be adopted as either an interim or a permanent measure.

Growth moratorium. Temporary prohibition of development based on an immediate need to forestall a public health, safety, or welfare problem such as lack of sewage treatment capacity or major traffic congestion. A moratorium may apply to one or more types of development communitywide or in a specific area. Moratoriums typically remain in effect for one to three years to allow time for the problem to be solved, but they may last for many years.

Point system. A technique for rating the quality of proposed developments by awarding points according to the degree to which projects meet stated standards and criteria. Typically, the various factors are weighted to reflect public policies. Point systems are frequently used in flexible zoning and with techniques to limit growth. ∎

---

to use "required" amenities as major marketing tools. When one project in Florida was required to retain an eagle habitat, the developer's marketing materials featured the habitat as the project's centerpiece. Many developers have learned to use required stormwater retention ponds and stream buffers as natural features that add value to adjoining development. Developers who must safeguard stands of trees usually find that lots near wooded acres command substantially higher prices.

A time may come, however, when the local regulatory process needs to be rethought and reorganized. Communities have frequently formed task groups, comprising both public and private interests, to review existing regulations and procedures and to recommend ways to "streamline" them. Complex or overlapping requirements and lengthy, bureaucratic procedures can

be simplified to reduce wear and tear on both the public and private sectors in the permitting process. At the same time, design and construction standards can be brought in line with community objectives, particularly if reducing housing costs is a concern.[3]

State Regulatory Actions

Although state governments delegate most regulation of land use and development to local governments, states have always exercised some control over development. For example, states typically build most of the major highways and roads on which so much development depends and preserve large amounts of open space in state parks and conservation areas. In addition, to preserve water quality, most states regulate municipal

Figure 13-5

Typical Procedures for Development Approval

This figure outlines a "generic" process used by many communities for subdivision plan review, rezoning, or comprehensive plan amendments.

Concept Phase	Developer	■ Identifies site, defines preliminary development concept ■ Evaluates feasibility of concept with consultants ■ May test ideas with citizen groups
Preapplication Phase	Developer	■ Prepares basic descriptions of proposed project, including location, types of uses, general densities, public facilities ■ Meets with public staff to discuss concept, define initial issues, determine appropriate approval procedure
	Public Staff	■ Checks conformance of proposal with official plans and regulations ■ May test preliminary concept with other agency staff
Application Phase	Developer	■ Prepares reports, drawings, plans for application
	Public Staff	■ Routes application to other agencies ■ Meets with developer to resolve questions, problems ■ Initiates official notice of upcoming public hearing(s) to public, adjacent owners
	Developer	■ Prepares final plans
	Public Staff	■ Prepares final report and recommendations to public officials
Public Decision Phase	Public Officials	■ Conduct one or more public hearings at which developer presents plans (perhaps before multiple agencies)
	Public Officials, Staff, and Developer	■ Propose modifications or conditions necessary for approval
	Public Officials	■ Approve, approve with conditions, or deny application

and individual water supply and sewage treatment systems and have enacted various environmental laws that affect where and how urban development will take place. A number of states, for example, have adopted environmental protection acts similar to the federal act that requires many major projects to undergo environmental evaluations. State powers of taxation and now infrastructure spending also play a significant role in community development.

In general, such state agencies pursue these programs without much coordination among agencies or between state and local agencies. In the past ten to 15 years, however, a number of states have enacted more specific statutes—in the form of growth management laws—to control urban development. The first wave of such

laws appeared in the early 1970s, primarily as an outgrowth of the environmental movement. Legislatures in Vermont, Oregon, California, Florida, Colorado, Rhode Island, North Carolina, and Hawaii enacted laws that were intended to curb the excesses of urban growth and to protect natural resources. Ten years later, most of those laws were found wanting because they had either failed to achieve their objectives or had stirred up unproductive controversies.

A second wave of state growth management acts began with Florida's 1985 enactment of a sweeping new law aimed at strengthening previous requirements for local planning and requiring state-level planning. Florida's law was quickly followed by actions in Vermont, Maine, Rhode Island, New Jersey, Georgia,

Figure 13-6

The (Sometimes Circuitous) Road to Project Approval
Colorado Place, Santa Monica, California

The Becket Group, a well-known, 55-year-old California firm engaged in architecture and engineering (Welton Becket Associates) and real estate development, assembled a 15-acre property in Santa Monica, California, with the intention of building a new headquarters and a first-rate mixed-use development, including its own offices, to be called Colorado Place.

Becket planned the Colorado Place project entirely within existing regulations and Santa Monica's adopted general plan. The firm spent about a year and a half in discussions with city officials and in the planning and design process to bring the project to the point of financing, with signed leases for 85 percent of the office space.

Three weeks after construction began in 1981, the newly elected city council imposed a building moratorium that stopped all construction. Becket then discovered that under California law the firm's development rights were not vested beyond the ability to complete the footings.

With the project's financing imperiled, Becket proposed that the city enter into a development agreement pursuant to California law. The city responded positively, recognizing the massive project's substantial benefits in terms of employment, property taxes, user fees, and favorable redevelopment in a somewhat blighted area of the city. In subsequent negotiations, two of the city's specific aims were to exact a commitment to low- and moderate-income housing and to downscale the project in response to neighbors' complaints.

Ultimately, the parties reached a development agreement, reducing the size of the project by one-third and lowering building heights in the first phase of development. The agreement also called for Becket to build or furnish 50 units of low- and moderate-income housing, a 3.5-acre public park, a daycare center and its equipment, an art and social services fee of 1.5 percent of land and development costs, and programs for affirmative action, job training, energy conservation, traffic and emissions abatement, and street improvements. Phase I was completed in January 1984.

With Phase II about to start, financing became a critical issue, primarily because of cost overruns in Phase I induced by the moratorium and a month-long strike by carpenters. In June 1984, Becket announced the indefinite postponement of Phase II and, in January 1985, sold Colorado Place to Southmark Pacific, a subsidiary of the Dallas-based Southmark Corporation. Five months later, Southmark announced its intention to seek substantial changes in the agreement inherited from Becket. At that point, the city refused to consider any proposed changes. The developer then sued the city for failing to fulfill its obligations under the agreement, and the primary neighborhood group broke off talks with the developer. The project reached an impasse but, after repeated attempts at renegotiation, the city and the developer reached a tentative out-of-court settlement in May 1986, and Southmark continued to negotiate revisions to the agreement as new problems and new demands

continued on next page

Washington, and Maryland. All the acts set state goals for development and require local plans, state agency plans, and, in some cases, regional plans to be consistent with these goals. Requirements for consistency mean, in essence, that public plans for future development must meet the spirit and intent of the state goals. In addition, most state acts require local governments to formulate follow-up programs to implement the plans. (Figure 13-7 summarizes the requirements of Florida's growth management law.)

In the growth management states, once a local plan has been reviewed or approved by a state agency and the community has adjusted its zoning and other regulations to the new plan, development approvals and permits proceed in a traditional manner. The states expect that the laws will improve the quality of develop-

ment regulations and the predictability of the development approval process because all local governments are required to plan according to specified standards and procedures and are required to back up plans with solid implementation programs. Certainly in Oregon, which has the most extensive experience with state growth management, builders generally support the law. On the negative side, the resulting multiple layers of plans and bureaucracies may breed a sluggish and somewhat inflexible approval process that is slow to adjust to rapidly changing market conditions and/or emerging technologies.

In summary, state and local regulation of development promises to become more, not less, complex and generally more restrictive. Developers, in addition to their knowledge of the physical, financial, and economic

Figure 13-6

The (Sometimes Circuitous) Road to Project Approval (continued)

Colorado Place, Santa Monica, California

arose. At the same time, the soft leasing market caused the developer to delay construction. Nonetheless, approval of the new plan appeared imminent—at least until it was threatened by a citywide no-growth movement, in which civic activists demanded suspension of all major construction projects in Santa Monica, including Colorado Place.

Despite opposition, completion of Colorado Place received narrow approval in September 1987 after Southmark agreed to pay an additional $5 million in fees for traffic improvements and to build an on-site sewage treatment plant. Three months later, the amended agreement was finally approved.

By 1986, Southmark had completed three commercial office buildings in the project, now renamed MGM Plaza, representing about 500,000 square feet of space. Because of the soft office market, however, further construction of office, retail, housing, and hotel space was put on hold.

In 1990, Southmark, faced with a soft office market in its home base, Texas, and elsewhere, sold Colorado Place to prominent office developer Maguire Thomas Partners, which was based in Los Angeles and had built extensively in downtown and other parts of the region.

Upon acquisition, the new owners chose to renegotiate the development agreement with the city of Santa Monica. The planned hotel, retail space, and 50 housing units were replaced with three additional office buildings totaling 500,000 square feet, which would incorporate about 40,000 square feet of space for neighborhood-serving retail shops and restaurants. The renegotiated development agreement allowed the developers to drop the on-site sewage treatment facility and build a 3.5-acre public park on the site originally planned for housing. The park, which includes landscaped areas and tennis and basketball courts, is open to the public but maintained by Maguire Thomas Partners. In addition, MGM Plaza includes a child care center open for use by the public and MGM Plaza employees.

As of early 1999, the project was completely built out, with approximately 1 million square feet of commercial and office space. MGM Plaza is totally leased and commands some of the highest commercial rents in west Los Angeles, as high as $3.20 per gross square foot. Three additional office developments totaling over 900,000 square feet of new office space are under construction adjacent to MGM Plaza, strengthening the importance of this area as an office site. ■

Sources: **David O'Malley and Richard F. Davis, "Development Agreements: Colorado Place, Santa Monica, California," in *Working with the Community: A Developer's Guide,* by Douglas R. Porter, Patrick L. Phillips, and Colleen Grogan Moore (Washington, D.C.: ULI–the Urban Land Institute, 1985); Rita Fitzgerald and Richard Peiser, "Development (Dis)agreements at Colorado Place," *Urban Land,* July 1988, pp. 2–5; and Jay Stark, director of development, the Lee Group, Los Angeles.**

factors of development, will have to become more skillful at working with public officials and the general public to complete their projects successfully. As detailed in Chapter 16, the increased complexity and restrictiveness lengthens the early stages of the development process and often increases the amount of capital needed before traditional construction financing is available.

Public/Private Roles in Planning And Financing Infrastructure

Governments generally play a major role in planning, financing, and constructing the capital facilities that provide essential services for the general public. For several reasons, providing infrastructure for community development is viewed as a primary government function. First, many facility systems, such as roads and water and sewer lines that serve large areas and benefit many people, must be closely interrelated. Second, some public facilities and services such as schools should be made available even to people who cannot afford to pay their direct costs. Third, governments frequently expand infrastructure systems to support economic development.

The private sector is also heavily involved in providing capital facilities. Sometimes, public facilities and services such as toll roads and water supply and distribution are owned and/or operated by private companies or semipublic authorities. In addition, developers of real estate projects are usually required to plan, finance, and build roads and other infrastructure necessary to support proposed development within—and frequently outside—project sites. Therefore, planning and financing infrastructure have traditionally been joint responsibilities shared by the public and private sectors. The particular ways those responsibilities are shared have changed over time and vary to some extent among specific types of facilities. In recent years, for example, a greater share of the burden of designing and constructing capital facilities has been shifted to the private sector, as overall public expenditures for capital facilities have failed to keep pace with increases in either economic activity or population. In fact, federal and state capital expenditures per capita have been falling steadily since 1977, leaving local governments to take up the slack. Local governments, in turn, are beset with rising costs for social services and taxpayer revolts against increased taxes to pay for expanding infrastructure systems. Consequently, these governments are turning to the private sector to "make development pay for itself"—a favorite phrase in rapidly growing communities.

Public/private participation in planning and financing facilities also depends on the type of infrastructure system involved. Funds for major highways, for example, come chiefly from federal and state gasoline and other vehicle-related user taxes, whereas minor highways are usually funded from state and local tax sources, with some contributions from developers of projects adjoining the roads. Local streets are usually financed and built by developers, although local governments generally assume responsibility for maintaining them so long as they are built to the standards specified in the subdivision ordinance.

In contrast, major water and sewer facilities are usually financed by bond issues repaid by fees and charges imposed on consumers, plus some additional funding from federal and state grants. Local water and sewer systems are usually financed and installed by developers who must sometimes pay a hookup or tap-in fee as well to help fund major improvements such as trunk lines.

In these times of fiscal restraint, public officials and developers are experimenting with many forms of public/private planning and financing of infrastructure. It is not surprising, therefore, that developers may encounter a variety of approaches to providing infrastructure for their projects.

Sources of Public Capital Funds

Local governments obtain capital for infrastructure improvements from their annual budgets, from the issuance of municipal bonds, and from state and federal funding programs. Often several sources are combined to fund improvements. Construction or reconstruction of major streets, for example, is frequently financed

Figure 13-7

Summary of Requirements in Florida's Local Government Comprehensive Planning and Land Development Regulation Act
(Adopted in 1985, Amending the 1975 Act)

Each county and municipality must conform its comprehensive plan to state goals and the requirements of the act within a specified time period, or the plan will be prepared by the regional planning body. All plans shall include a capital improvement element, and no development permits shall be issued unless public facilities are adequate to serve the proposed development.

The coastal zone element of each plan must meet new and tougher requirements.

The state Department of Community Affairs must review and approve local plans according to rules drafted by the department and approved by the legislature.

All plans must be reviewed every five years.

Land development regulations must be adopted to implement the plan within a specified time period after the plan is approved. ∎

from annual budgets, but revenues earmarked for street projects also flow from fuel, motor vehicle, and other taxes and from state and federal funding programs that collect revenues from some of the same sources. Improvements in municipal water supply systems are often financed from revenue bonds repaid through user fees, although general revenues and general obligation bonds may be used instead.

For long-term investments in capital improvements, local governments often depend on funds derived from the issuance of general obligation bonds or revenue bonds. General obligation bonds are backed by the full faith and credit of the municipality and thus carry a fairly low interest rate. Revenue bonds are repaid from specified sources of revenue, usually fees and charges for services, and carry a somewhat higher interest rate. Interest rates for both types of public bond issues are lower than rates for privately issued bonds, however; bondholders find municipal bonds attractive because the interest income earned on the bonds is generally tax free. In addition, investment bankers have invented a large variety of general obligation and revenue bonds to suit various local government needs and/or the conditions of today's bond market.

The $14 million renovation and expansion of the 80,000-square-foot concession and retail area of the Tom Bradley International Airport in Los Angeles was a public project funded with airport revenue bonds. Live palms, neon lights, reflecting materials, and large storefront windows capture the feel and energy of Los Angeles.

Bonds are repaid from several revenue sources. For many years, the basic source was property taxes, but by the mid-1980s, property taxes had dropped to less than half (47 percent) of all revenues collected from local sources, and their decline as a share of all local revenues continues today. In their stead, sales and income taxes and various types of excise taxes, fees, and charges have gained significance. Excise taxes or taxes on specific types of uses or activities, such as those on aircraft landings and hotel rooms, help fund airport improvements and convention centers. User fees and charges are much favored sources of revenue for many capital facilities because consumers pay them for services rendered. Many communities now rely on a variety of fees and charges, including landfill charges, fees for use of recreation areas, automobile license fees, and public parking charges. In addition, especially for large-scale systems such as transit and regional parks, communities often earmark increases in sales taxes to pay for improvements.

Impact Fees and Exactions

One type of fee that is increasingly imposed on development projects is the impact fee. (Other terms are "systems development charges" and "development impact fees.") Impact fees are one form of a variety of exactions that require developers to contribute to the provision of public facilities related to their developments. Variously termed "exactions," "extractions," "proffers,"

and other names, these contributions may include dedication of land, construction of facilities, or payment of fees to be used for the construction of public facilities. The importance of this financing approach has increased over the past decade or two as more local governments turn to the private sector to fund infrastructure improvements.

Often, subdivision regulations require developers to fund, build, and dedicate for public use the basic facilities required for residents and tenants of a new development, such as local streets, sewer and water lines, drainage facilities, and parks and recreational facilities. Many jurisdictions also require developers to fund selected improvements to major streets within or at the borders of their projects or at nearby intersections. In addition, it is not unusual for subdivision ordinances to require developers to provide drainage improvements in the general area of the proposed project and to reserve sites for schools. Such requirements usually include standards for determining the appropriate size and character of the facilities.

Impact fees are a fairly new form of exaction. More and more communities impose impact fees because they help pay for project-related facilities located beyond the bounds of development projects. For example, developers often must pay hookup or tap-in fees to connect their projects to water and sewer systems; such fees are used to improve trunk lines, pumping stations, treatment plants, and the like outside the project site. Impact fees also pay for large parks and recreational areas that serve residents of many developments, major highway sections and interchanges, drainage systems, schools, and many other types of facilities. The ordinances that impose such fees normally spell out methods for calculating them, thereby permitting developers to determine their expected payments in advance. Most communities allow developers to build facilities directly to offset required fees.

Impact fees can range from a few hundred dollars to many thousands of dollars. A survey of 33 jurisdictions conducted by the Center for Governmental Responsibility at the University of Florida found that impact fees in 1997 averaged $11,856 per house for single-family houses, $9,118 per unit for multifamily housing, more than $1,883 per 1,000 square feet of industrial space, more than $3,038 per 1,000 square feet of general office space, and more than $4,207 per 1,000 square feet of retail space (see Figures 13-8 and 13-9). Not surprisingly, fees had increased substantially since a previous survey in 1988—and local governments continue to raise fees. It is not uncommon for rapidly growing communities to levy fees of $5,000 to $10,000 and more for a single-family house.

A few communities have adopted special types of fees, often called "linkage fees," which are intended to assist in financing housing programs and other community needs. The most widely known and most stringent program is San Francisco's Office Housing Production Program, which requires developers of downtown office buildings of over 50,000 square feet of floor space to pay fees for improvements to transit, housing, public art, child care, and public open space. Jersey City, New Jersey, requires developers of all new projects to contribute to affordable housing.

Although exactions and fees may be specified in regulations, many jurisdictions also negotiate with developers to exact other contributions. Such exactions become possible when developers request a rezoning or the use of special procedures, such as planned unit developments, that require approval by a board or legislative body. Public officials (and neighborhood groups) often find that negotiations present an excellent opportunity for requesting additional contributions from developers. Legally, developers are obligated to offer only facilities and improvements that primarily benefit their developments, but developers pressed to move forward with a project often agree to other contributions as well, including such offerings as scholarships for neighborhood youths and relandscaping of neighborhood parks.

Fees and exactions raise three major issues that deserve consideration: legal constraints, equity, and administrative concerns.

Figure 13-8

National Average Impact Fees by Type: 1997

	Single-Family House (Unit)	Multifamily Housing (Unit)	General Industry (1,000 Square Feet)	General Office (1,000 Square Feet)	General Retail (1,000 Square Feet)
Roads	$1,288	$825	$727	$1,594	$2,423
Parks	966	797	209	209	209
Utilities	829	849	200	306	391
Water and Sewer	5,063	4,113	Varies	Varies	Varies
Schools	2,179	1,078	270	270	280
Public Facility	251	151	48	118	158
Solid Waste	781	923	256	192	385
Public Safety	259	235	58	81	200
Libraries	240	147	115	268	161
Total	$11,856	$9,118	$1,883+	$3,038+	$4,207+

Note: **The survey found that actual fees ranged widely; road fees for single-family homes, for example, varied from $86.00 to $5,276. Total fees for single-family homes ranged from $1,192 to $39,216. The highest total fees by type ranged from $5,685 for general industry to $39,216 for single-family homes.**

Source: **National survey conducted by James Nicholas, professor, Growth Management Studies, University of Florida, 1997.**

Figure 13-9

Range of National Average Impact Fees by Type: 1997

	Single-Family House (Unit)	Multifamily Housing (Unit)	General Industry (Per 1,000 Square Feet)	General Office (Per 1,000 Square Feet)	General Retail (Per 1,000 Square Feet)
Roads					
Maximum	$5,276	$4,216	$2,950	$14,095	$8,370
Minimum	86	69	31	5	209
Average	1,288	825	727	1,594	2,423
Median	1,070	621	619	1,337	2,373
Parks					
Maximum	$5,746	$4,329	$404	$404	$404
Minimum	100	79	14	14	14
Average	966	797	209	209	209
Median	562	433	209	209	209
Utilities					
Maximum	$2,350	$2,350	$381	$841	$976
Minimum	160	123	58	104	72
Average	829	849	200	306	391
Median	600	552	213	220	291
Water and Sewer					
Maximum	$12,423	$12,423	Varies	Varies	Varies
Minimum	536	395	Varies	Varies	Varies
Average	5,063	4,113	Varies	Varies	Varies
Median	4,155	3,217	Varies	Varies	Varies
Schools					
Maximum	$3,440	$1,700	$280	$270	$280
Minimum	135	33	270	270	280
Average	2,179	1,078	270	270	280
Median	2,022	1,005	270	270	280
Public Facility					
Maximum	$2,259	$849	$218	$518	$621
Minimum	26	26	7	17	17
Average	251	151	48	118	158
Median	71	70	30	65	131
Solid Waste					
Maximum	$5,460	$5,460	$490	$490	$650
Minimum	64	61	54	54	54
Average	781	923	256	192	385
Median	220	323	260	160	450
Public Safety					
Maximum	$1,262	$1,230	$847	$1,093	$4,954
Minimum	36	39	8	10	20
Average	259	235	58	81	200
Median	188	181	26	47	120
Library					
Maximum	$1,000	$412	$115	$268	$161
Minimum	49	38	115	268	161
Average	240	147	115	268	161
Median	160	117	115	268	161
Total					
Maximum	$39,216	$32,969	$5,685	$17,979	$16,416
Minimum	1,192	863	557	742	827
Average	11,856	9,118	1,883	3,038	4,207
Median	9,048	6,519	1,742	2,576	4,015

Source: **National survey conducted by James Nicholas, professor, Growth Management Studies, University of Florida, 1997.**

Public and private infrastructure improvments—such as streets, sidewalks, lighting, and landscaping—were financed through tax increment financing in the mixed-use development of East Pointe, Milwaukee, Wisconsin.

Legal Constraints

The extent to which local governments can demand contributions from developers, and for what purposes, has generated a considerable amount of litigation in state and federal courts. Three constitutional guarantees—just compensation for taking property, equal protection under the law, and due process—limit local governments' powers to require exactions. Exactions must be clearly related to a public purpose, they must be applied equally to all types of development and not have an exclusionary effect, and they must not be imposed in arbitrary and capricious ways. Under the police power that allows local governments to regulate land development, exactions must be necessary for protecting health, safety, and public welfare.

The general test, applicable in virtually all states, is that exactions should bear a "rational nexus" to a development's impacts on local public facilities. That is, a local government may, for example, require a developer to improve a certain road intersection if the developer's project will generate enough traffic to warrant the improvement. The local government cannot, however, legitimately require developers to pay for improvements to distant intersections that will seldom serve traffic generated by the developer's project.

The legal foundation for impact fees is more complicated than for other forms of exactions. First, it must be established that fees are allowable under the police powers granted by the state to the local government rather than defined as a form of tax for which specific state authorization is usually required. Then, assuming that the state deems impact fees allowable, calculation and administration of fees must meet stiffer criteria than

for tax revenues. To avoid double taxation, the amounts of fees should take into account regular taxes that property owners will pay for public improvements and must not include funds needed to correct existing deficiencies (for which existing residents are responsible). In administering impact fee programs, local governments must expend collected fees within a reasonable time for facilities that will benefit the developments that paid the fees.

Equity Considerations

Exactions raise some issues about who should pay for infrastructure improvements. At one time, it was assumed that the general community should be responsible for funding major infrastructure systems, while developers should be primarily responsible for facilities needed on their development sites. But that simple division of financial responsibility is breaking down. Urged by taxpayers, public officials are increasingly concerned with ensuring that developers contribute to overcoming any adverse impacts of new development on the capacity of the community's public facilities. In response, developers point out that past generations of residents benefited from wide public sharing of infrastructure costs and that many citizens besides those in their projects, including future generations of users, benefit from the improvements.

Another issue concerns government services financed on the basis of ability to pay: that is, people who earn more should pay more. Elementary and secondary education, for example, is normally considered important enough to society as a whole that it is financed largely by property tax revenues that reflect levels of personal income. Which capital facilities should be financed in this way and which should be targeted for payment by specific fees is a continuing issue. The question becomes more complex when considering the fact that much infrastructure confers value on property it does not directly serve: a good park system, for example, improves everyone's property values in addition to offering direct benefits to park users.

Administrative Concerns

Exactions and fees pose two administrative concerns: the general lack of administrative guidelines or rules for determining exactions and the difficulties inherent in the use of impact fees. As noted earlier, many exactions of land or improvements, especially those located off the development site, are negotiated during project approval procedures. Seldom do guidelines exist to determine the appropriate types or amounts of exactions, to suggest how financial responsibilities should be shared among public and private interests, or to guide negotiations. As a result, developers often complain of extortionary exactions unrelated to the impacts of their projects; at the same time, public officials frequently believe that developers escape contributing enough.

These problems are supposedly solved in large part by relying on impact fees whose requirements call for predictable measures of impact and specified payment amounts. It takes expert knowledge, time, and effort to create legally sound and politically stable fee programs, however. Once enacted, impact fee programs require correctly calculated fees to be collected for each project and timely expenditures to be made for the construction of facilities that benefit fee payers. Cities such as San Diego that use impact fees as a major financing mechanism employ a full-time staff to administer fee programs.

Fees and exactions as a method for obtaining private contributions of needed public facilities should not be viewed as a panacea; such contributions rarely cover all the costs of required infrastructure. Instead, fees and exactions should be employed as one of several sources of revenue within an overall public program of financing capital facilities. In this context, however, they may generate essential funds that permit development to proceed. In effect, developers "pay to play."

Indeed, infrastructure improvements funded by fees and exactions often add market value to the projects they serve. Public requirements for open space or drainage, for example, usually enhance the value of many building sites. Environmental features preserved from development often become valuable amenities for residents and tenants in the surrounding area. Other benefits relate to management of the development process. Developers who have paid impact fees enjoy

greater assurance that needed public facilities will be built. Further, developers who construct facilities have a significant amount of control over the timing and quality of those facilities and can make certain that facilities are in place when they need them. For these reasons, fees and exactions may prove to be a net benefit to many developments.

Special Taxing Districts

Special taxing districts are another means of planning and financing infrastructure. Districts are especially useful in providing specific services to targeted users. They may encompass one or more development projects, in a single neighborhood or local jurisdiction, or across several jurisdictions. Several types of districts exist, including districts for single purposes such as constructing roads, building junior colleges, and promoting soil conservation. In a number of states, districts can be formed to supply almost all the facilities and services required to serve new development.

Special districts are established according to state legislation that spells out requirements for initiating, financing, and operating specific types of districts. For this reason, types of districts vary considerably from state to state and even within states. States may allow local governments to establish districts (in the form of assessment districts or public improvement districts) to levy a special tax on property owners who will benefit from improved facilities. Such districts may be governed by special boards or commissions, but their budgets and actions are usually subject to the local government's review and approval. In many cases, the city or county governing board will simply name its own members as the district board. Alternatively, property owners, including developers, who wish to establish a financing mechanism for capital facilities may petition either a local government or a state agency to establish a district, which then often functions as an independent authority. Special taxing districts are allowed in all states but are particularly numerous in some states, including Illinois, Texas, California, Florida, and Pennsylvania.

Special taxing districts are especially useful to developers. Creation of a district circumvents the need to tax existing residents for facilities required for new development and spreads the costs of improvements over a targeted group of owners for a repayment period of 15 to 20 years. Districts are also invaluable in developing areas where local governments have little incentive, administrative capacity, or financial resources to fund infrastructure.

One type of special district popular in several states is a tax increment financing (TIF) district. TIF districts obtain revenues from earmarked taxes raised only from new development to finance capital improvements. Assessments are based on net increases over the existing property tax base. For this reason, TIF districts are often used for redevelopment areas.

Establishing special districts requires a considerable amount of time and talent. A district must be initiated according to specific state provisions relating to the voting powers of the property owners involved, organization of the managing board, types of facilities to be constructed, and financing plans and revenue sources. Securing financing involves the services of bond counsels, underwriters, rating agencies, and insurers. Planning and undertaking infrastructure construction and managing the district demand still other specialties. In any case, special taxing districts offer a useful alternative to local government financing of infrastructure (see Figure 13-10).

Privatization

In recent years, many local governments have experimented with the use of private companies to build and operate public facilities. It is not a new idea: private water companies, private solid waste disposal facilities, and private transit companies are not uncommon. Semiprivate authorities manage many toll roads and bridges. Special taxing districts that provide basic services are often managed by private companies under contract to the districts. In many small- and large-scale developments, community associations own and manage recreational and other facilities.

Figure 13-10

The Lely Resort Community Development District

In 1983, the Lely Development Corporation planned to develop a golf/residential community and destination resort on 2,892 acres in Florida's Collier County, just 12 miles southeast of Pelican Bay. The development was to include 10,150 housing units, 1.1 million square feet of commercial space, and various education, conference, and recreation facilities. To provide basic infrastructure and services, the corporation decided to establish a community development district.

First, corporate staff met with county staff and elected officials to determine the extent of their support for the proposal—not a technical requirement but a political necessity as districts are rarely established over the objections of local governments in Florida. Then the developers petitioned the governor and cabinet, sitting as the Florida Land and Water Adjudicatory Commission, to establish a community development district under Chapter 190 of the Florida statutes. The petition included the signed consent of all landowners in the proposed district, a legal description of the property involved, a map, and an economic impact statement. After an administrative hearing and a report by the hearing officer, the petition was granted and the district established by rule making. Costs for the government staff to consider district establishment were largely offset by the $15,000 filing fee.

The Lely Resort Community Development District is governed by a five-member board initially elected by district landowners voting according to acreage. By agreement with county officials, the board includes one member nominated by the county, a former county administrative offi-

cial. According to Florida law, the board will be elected by landowners (one person/one vote) after six years and when 250 electors own property in the district.

The Lely district is responsible for financing and constructing arterial roads and subdivision streets, water and sewer trunk lines, a master drainage system, bikeways, sidewalks, street lighting, landscaping, and entranceways. The district issued $33 million in revenue bonds for the first phase of construction. Debt service is provided through special assessments imposed on all benefiting properties.

The district retains close working relationships with the county government. The county tax collector collects district assessments under contract to the district. Once constructed, the water and sewer lines were dedicated to the county utility system for operation. The county also retains the power to assume responsibility for other district functions if it can demonstrate its ability to deliver comparable services at an equal or lower cost than the district. The district, on the other hand, frees the county from responsibility for planning and managing most on-site public facilities, and the district's debt service requirements do not count against the county's cap on millage.

In 1992, the district had completed about 80 percent of the planned facilities and launched the second phase of construction in mid-1993. ■

Source: **Douglas R. Porter et al.,** *Special Districts: A Useful Technique for Financing Infrastructure,* **2d ed. (Washington, DC: ULI– the Urban Land Institute, 1992), p. 51.**

Proponents of privatization claim that private companies provide superior service at lower cost (partly the result of more efficient management but also because of lower wage scales). Public officials, however, often worry that private companies may make unreasonable profits or fail to provide equal, adequate service to all residents. Private firms also have had trouble raising the significant amounts of capital required to launch a new facility. Perhaps for these reasons—despite a great deal of interest in privatization and some highly publicized examples—the nation has not seen a rush to convert public facilities and services to private operation.

Planning, Design, and Construction

Planning and design of infrastructure improvements may be carried out by public agency staffs or by contractors employed by public agencies. Developers usually employ consultants to lay out and design the improvements required in their projects, although the engineering drawings are subject to public approval. Design and construction standards for facilities are specified by public agencies for individual public works projects or, in the case of development projects, laid out in subdivision regulations. In the latter case, the subdivision drawings indicate the standards of construction for each type of facility. Before proceeding with construction, developers are usually required to post a bond to ensure the satisfactory completion of the facilities. During construction, public inspections determine that facilities adhere to standards. Usually the completed facilities are then dedicated to the local government for public use, although they may become the responsibility of a community or homeowners' association organized to manage the common facilities.

Summary

Developers should expect to interact closely with public officials and administrators in the course of achieving their objectives. Developers must understand and adhere to regulations, rules, and established public procedures in selecting sites, designing projects, and carrying out construction. In addition, they can take advantage of optional regulatory approaches that offer special project or design opportunities. Thus, both personally and through trusted consultants, developers should acquire a keen knowledge of local regulations affecting development.

This principle also holds for the provision of needed infrastructure to support proposed developments. Especially as more communities attempt to shift the costs of infrastructure to the private sector, developers are advised to keep abreast of facility and financing requirements and options that can have an important effect on a project's bottom line.

In both cases, developers find it good business practice to know local public officials and administrators and to participate in community decision making regarding future development. Developers can lend their special understanding of the practical aspects of development to discussions about new comprehensive plans, rezoning, annual capital improvement programs, and other public actions that directly affect the climate for development in their communities. At the end of the day, successful development requires the meshing of public and private objectives.

Terms

- Capital improvement program
- Comprehensive plan
- Discretionary
- Enabling legislation
- Exaction
- General obligation bond
- Growth management techniques
- Impact fees
- Linkage fees
- Police power
- PUD
- Rational nexus
- Revenue bond
- Special taxing district
- Subdivision regulations
- Taking
- Tax increment financing (TIF)
- Zoning ordinances

Review Questions

13.1 What is the police power and how is it enforced? Who has a stronger obligation in the exercise of the police power—the federal government or the states? Why?

13.2 What are the mainstays of local governments' regulatory programs and how do they affect development?

13.3 What is the role of the state in regulating development?

13.4 What does the popular phrase—make development pay for itself—mean? How does that attitude manifest itself?

13.5 What are the main sources of capital for infrastructure improvements?

13.6 Discuss how legal constraints, equity, and administrative concerns affect fees and exactions.

13.7 What are special taxing districts?

Notes

1. See Douglas R. Porter, "The States: Growing Smarter?" in *Smart Growth: Economy, Community, Environment* (Washington, D.C.: ULI–the Urban Land Institute, 1998), pp. 28–35.

2. See Debra Stein, *Winning Community Support for Land Use Projects* (Washington, D.C.: ULI–the Urban Land Institute, 1992); and Douglas R. Porter, Patrick L. Phillips, and Colleen Grogan Moore, *Working with the Community: A Developer's Guide* (Washington, D.C.: ULI–the Urban Land Institute, 1985).

3. Two publications by the American Planning Association provide helpful advice on streamlining techniques and reviews of standards: John Vranicar, Welford Sanders, and David Mosena, *Streamlining Land Use Regulations* (Chicago: APA Press, 1980); and Welford Sanders, Judith Getzels, David Mosena, and JoAnn Butler, *Affordable Single-Family Housing: A Review of Development Standards,* Planning Advisory Service Report No. 385 (Chicago: APA Press, 1984).

Chapter 14

Meshing Public and Private Roles In the Development Process

Development in the United States has traditionally occurred through a conventional process in which the public and private sectors perform independent functions and therefore tend to remain at arm's length from one another. As a general rule, simple projects in strong markets have historically followed conventional modes of development, and any mix of function between the public and private sectors has been seen as a conflict of interest on the part of local government. As detailed in preceding chapters, the public sector was expected to perform the functions of regulation and broad planning, providing the needed services—schools, roads, water, sanitation, fire and police protection—to support new development. The private developer originated projects based on information about the market and formulated a specific plan for a project with public policy in mind—all without the public's direct involvement in stages one and two of the process. Consequently, the public sector did not assume any of the entrepreneurial risks or absorb any project-specific costs typically borne by the private sector.[1]

This development scenario underwent a dramatic transformation in the late 1970s with a proliferation of new-style real estate projects defined by their special public/private status. Variously referred to as partnerships, joint developments, codevelopments, or just public/private deals, these projects have reshaped the conventional development process by expanding the public sector's traditional sphere of activity. In a number of ways—as developers, lenders, equity investors, land lessors, and, in selected cases, operators—public agencies have become more active in the development arena and, in so doing, have assumed new risks.

Several forces contributed to the public sector's heightened engagement in the development process. In particular, cutbacks of federal urban aid in the 1980s pushed local governments to innovate and improvise to meet their city planning and economic development objectives.[2] At the same time, local pressures compelled local governments to search for new sources of funds after a rash of tax-cutting referenda (beginning in 1978 with California's Proposition 13) made raising taxes or going to the voters for approval of new bond issues a political risk. In an environment of fiscal restraint and rising land values during the 1980s, local governments came to view development as a strategic resource that could be harnessed to revitalize downtowns, capture hidden land values, finance needed infrastructure, stimulate economic growth, and generate jobs. Even during the first half of the 1990s, when property markets were experiencing severe distress, public/private development lost none of its appeal as a strategy of economic development, although the deals were certainly fewer in number and harder to put together.

The authors are indebted to Lynne B. Sagalyn, PhD, Earle W. Kazis and Benjamin Schore director, MBA Real Estate Program, and professor, Graduate School of Business, Columbia University, for her extensive revisions to this chapter.

Portions of this chapter appeared in Chapter 8 of John R. White, ed., *The Office Building: From Concept to Investment Reality* (Chicago and Washington, D.C.: Counselors of Real Estate, Appraisal Institute, and Society of Industrial and Office Realtors®, 1993).

This chapter looks at the changing nature of inter-actions between government and private developers and the character of their joint projects. In particular, it examines:

- The objectives of public/private development;
- The process involved in forming public/private partnerships; and
- The practical problems and policy issues associated with public/private development.

The Objectives of Public/ Private Development

Each decade since the 1940s has seen the promulgation of federal, state, and local public policies aimed at stimulating the development of projects that would otherwise not occur. The ways in which government has sought to influence private investment decisions span a wide spectrum of policy approaches. At one end of the continuum are "carrot-oriented" regulatory actions (incentive zoning and transfer of development rights) and programmatic assistance (tax abatements) through which local government provides subsidies to attract desired types of private investment. With these policy approaches, the benefits of public assistance are available to all who meet the qualifying conditions of entitlement.

At the other end of the continuum are more active public intervention strategies that rely on bargaining and custom-tailored negotiations with private firms over the terms and conditions of individual projects. In this instance, selective processes of competition rather than prescribed incentives determine private firms' access to development opportunities.

Intervention in the market has successfully stimulated urban revitalization in center-city and suburban downtowns, inner-city neighborhoods, and waterfront districts through the development of mixed-use projects, retail centers, commercial buildings, stadia and convention centers, and residential clusters. Several cities have earned acclaim for their joint public/private efforts—Baltimore, San Antonio, Milwaukee, Philadelphia, New York, Boston, Indianapolis, San Diego, and Cleveland, among others. Each city has developed its own method of leveraging private investment to stimulate revitalization of that city's economy. Some more "entrepreneurial" local governments have, through their own initiative and their willingness to take risks, become joint venture partners with private developers on some projects.

Baltimore, for instance, has entered into several joint venture agreements, both for the revitalization of its well-known Inner Harbor and for other large and small development projects. Coldspring, for example, is an in-town planned community developed at the instigation of Baltimore's Department of Housing and Community Development (HCD). In addition to complete master planning and overall coordination, HCD provided land, infrastructure, parks, public facilities, and financing in an agreement with the F.D. Rich Housing Corporation in 1978. In meeting its goals for the site, which was the last large undeveloped tract in the city, HCD specified the exact form of development that was to occur and limited the developer's profit to 10 percent. Assuming a role as senior partner in Coldspring, HCD succeeded in meeting goals for affordable housing and other aims for the site. Both risk and reward for the developer were considerably lower than in conventional private developments.[3]

In another early initiative, the Philadelphia Redevelopment Authority entered into a joint venture in 1974 with the Rouse Company to develop the Gallery, a downtown retail/office project incorporating many of the attractive features of suburban shopping malls. Private developers were not interested in the site because of the perceived risk in revitalizing the Market Street area and the large number of funding sources involved. Acting as both joint developer and general contractor, the redevelopment authority provided $18 million toward two-thirds of the costs of the shell. The Rouse Company provided $20 million in equity for the project, covering one-third of the costs of the shell in a 99-year ground lease arrangement under which Rouse also finished the space and sublet it.[4] Within a few years of the Gallery's opening in 1977, city officials initiated an expansion of the project, which included a second retail phase (Gallery II), an office tower (One Reading Center), and a parking garage linked to transit improvements.

Public/private efforts in San Antonio led to the successful redevelopment of a deteriorated historic structure in the Alamo Plaza historic district. The San Antonio Local Development Commission (LDC) worked with a developer to couple special financing (an urban development action grant [UDAG] and matching funds from the LDC) with local tax incentives (a five-year reprieve on property taxes for renovated historic structures) to make feasible development of a hotel on the site of a former medical building. The terra cotta facade of the Gothic revival structure was preserved, and the new use —the Emily Morgan Hotel—capitalized on San Antonio's burgeoning tourist trade.[5]

The success of early efforts spawned a second wave of public/private projects, many of which were even more ambitious in scope, such as the Brooklyn-based MetroTech complex (see Figure 14-1), or sought to

Figure 14-1

MetroTech Center—Economic Development in Brooklyn

MetroTech Center is a large-scale commercial, academic, and high-tech complex situated on a ten-block, 16-acre site in downtown Brooklyn. Developed through a partnership of the city of New York, Polytechnic University, and Forest City Ratner Companies, the $1 billion project represents the fused interests of public and private capital investment.

Formally initiated in 1982 after several years of preliminary feasibility study by the city's public development agency (in response to Polytechnic's pressing concerns about the deteriorating environment around the school and its negative impact on recruiting faculty and enrolling students), the development of the MetroTech project was

continued on next page

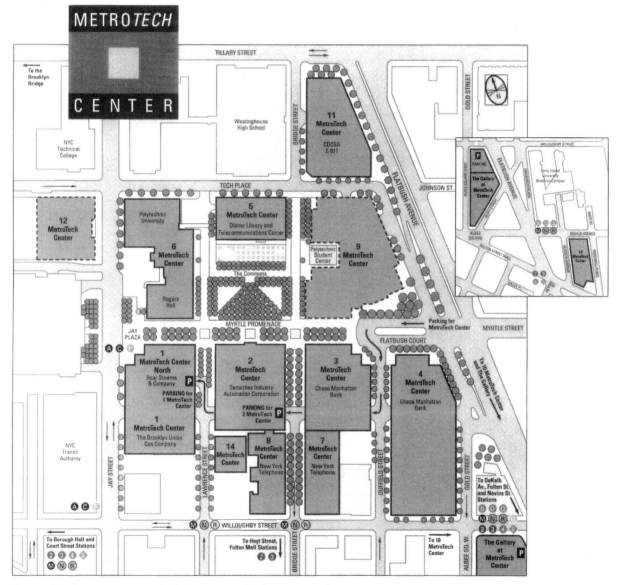

The ten-block, 16-acre MetroTech Center required a variety of innovative approaches to develop this dense, intensely urban mixed-use project.

Figure 14-1

MetroTech Center—Economic Development in Brooklyn (continued)

part of then-Mayor Koch's so-called "outer-borough strategy," which sought to foster development of back-office space in areas beyond Manhattan. Through public development incentives, the city aimed to retain jobs that might otherwise be lost in corporate moves beyond the city's boundaries.

The city's investment took shape in two distinct forms. The first consisted of traditional redevelopment assistance for land acquisition, relocation, demolition, and infrastructure needed to ready the site for private development. The second consisted of an aggressive economic development package of tax incentives, discretionary benefits, and energy cost savings designed to lower occupancy costs for corporate tenants. According to the developer's projection, the package would result in a $5.00 to $15.00 per square foot rental cost advantage over Manhattan for new construction.

In combination with strong private investment, the development succeeded in attracting a critical mass of corporate tenants. The tenants occupying the first phase of the complex include the Chase Manhattan Bank, the Securities Industries Automation Corporation, Brooklyn Union Gas, and the district headquarters of the Internal Revenue Service.

In addition, as part of its obligations to the public development partnership, Polytechnic University built a new library and a Center for Advanced Telecommunications Technology (under the sponsorship of New York State) and renovated existing academic space. In all, the master plan calls for 8.1 million square feet of space in eight new and three renovated buildings—a significant presence with the capacity to become the third node in New York, following the commercial centers of downtown and midtown Manhattan. The MetroTech complex of six buildings totaled around 2.5 million square feet of office space as of early 1999.

MetroTech Center was one among a handful of large-scale public/private ventures started by big cities across the nation in the 1980s. Such projects were not going to develop by themselves. Private developers could not have gone it alone. The scale was too large and the risks too great. In the case of MetroTech Center, even with public support from New York City and New York State and a UDAG, private financing was unavailable from domestic sources. Credited with transforming Brooklyn's downtown, MetroTech Center stands as visible testimony to the strength of public/private partnerships. ∎

---

extend the public/private model beyond downtown to meet neighborhood needs for long-undersupplied services, particularly retail space, as in the case of the Vermont-Slauson Shopping Center in south central Los Angeles (see Figure 14-2).

Over time as public/private projects developed strong performance records, public agencies, universities, school districts, and port authorities continued to expand the ambitions of their development activities, embarking on high-visibility public/private development ventures to build sports arenas, cultural facilities, and entertainment complexes. Entertainment-based projects such as San Francisco's Metreon (see Figure 14-3)—the centerpiece of the city's most ambitious redevelopment project, Yerba Buena Center, an 87-acre mixed-use project in South of Market—can be said to constitute a third wave of public/private projects.

Public/private projects are markedly diverse in scope. For any city, individual characteristics and history determine the types of projects and forms of assistance that best meet local public goals. Generally speaking, public entrepreneurship is most beneficial in the case of complex projects proposed for weak

markets if a city can capitalize on its resources and use incentives to make a real estate project feasible for both public and private participants. In contrast, in strong markets, the public sector may be presented with select opportunities to capture benefits from the rising values of publicly owned land.

Although the majority of public/private projects have involved revitalization efforts directed toward the urban cores and distressed neighborhoods of the nation's cities, in the 1980s the strength of local real estate markets prompted some suburban governments to enter into public/private development. A case in point is Fairfax County, Virginia. In 1987, the county board of supervisors entered into a development partnership with the Charles E. Smith Company and the Artery Organization Partnership to build a new $83.4 million government center on 100 acres of existing county land at no cash outlay to taxpayers. Instead of floating bonds for the project, the county swapped 116 acres of its adjoining land (which would be zoned for commercial and residential development) in exchange for tenancy (and ultimately building ownership after 75 years), $24.6 million in cash, and $16.6 million in other forms of compensation. The county had bought 183 of those acres for $4.1 million in 1979, and the 116 acres involved in the land exchange were valued at $42 million.[6]

Value capture as a fiscal objective distinguishes another set of public/private projects, typically those initiated by public transit agencies, which, as a residual of their primary function, often control desirable development parcels. The Washington Metropolitan Area Transit Authority, for example, manages transit-related site development through its joint development program, which was a pilot started in 1969 and then expanded in 1981.

From the perspective of city planning or real estate, joint development of transit-related sites often seeks close coordination of residential and commercial development at transit stations.[7] From the perspective of transit, joint development aims to meet many goals—generation of additional sources of revenue, increased rail ridership, enhanced convenience for riders, a public amenity, and architectural distinction through direct physical connections between private building entrances and rail stations.

Whether for urban revitalization, economic development, or value capture, the growth of public/private development initiatives has been fostered by a shift in public values favoring entrepreneurial behavior. Further, the broad definition typically accorded "public purpose" provides a rationale that allows every type of public agency to become involved in real estate development: local governments, redevelopment authorities, transit agencies, port authorities, school districts, quasi-public development corporations—even the U.S. General Services Administration, the U.S. Navy, and the U.S. Postal Service.

San Antonio's Emily Morgan Hotel, a significant rehabilitation involving public/private efforts.

The Process Involved in Forming Public/Private Partnerships

Public/private partnerships dramatically redefine the traditional roles of the public and private sectors in the development process. In such ventures, joint participation by the public and private sectors is a prerequisite to developing a project in which each partner shares risks and benefits. Even though joint efforts involve many steps similar to conventional development, they differ in several ways:

- Business agreements between private firms and government detail the terms and conditions of development and involve the private sector in the public planning process much earlier than is traditionally the case, even under conventional urban renewal.

- Relatively limited public resources are used (leveraged) to attract larger amounts of private investment for community and economic development.
- Public commitments of financial resources to a project engender concerns about public accountability and create expectations for financial returns in exchange for the risks taken.
- The active involvement of the public, private, and community sectors creates more complex sets of public/private interactions.
- Public objectives (including community goals, design criteria, affirmative action, and hiring residents) must be considered in addition to private objectives.[8]

Public/private partnerships offer many advantages. Developers anticipate a more cooperative regulatory environment when a government agency is their part-

Figure 14-2

Vermont-Slauson Shopping Center

A prototype for inner-city neighborhood retail services, the Vermont-Slauson Shopping Center is a 154,021-square-foot (gross leasable area) community center developed as a public/private joint venture. The project occupies a 9.7-acre site in south central Los Angeles—a high-density, inner-city area characterized by low incomes and a high crime rate. Anchoring the development are two major tenants—a discount department store (Kmart) and a supermarket (Boys). Other tenants include a drugstore, two shoe stores, several restaurants and fast-food places, and a U.S. post office. With the help of exceptional security measures, the center has operated successfully since its opening in fall 1981. In the first full year of operation (1982), sales averaged $239 per square foot, and the center is still performing well at 100 percent occupancy.

Public funding for the $8.2 million project totaled approximately $5 million, including a $1.5 million Economic Development Administration grant, a $2.5 million UDAG, and $1 million from the city of Los Angeles. Private investment totaled approximately $2.2 million; in addition, Sears donated a portion of the shopping center site, which was valued at $1.2 million.

Since the 1920s, Sears had served as the anchor for retail activities in the community. In 1977, following a number of unprofitable years, Sears abandoned its location. Concerned about the negative impacts of the closing on area retailing, local merchants approached the city of Los Angeles to explore possible solutions. When Sears indicated a willingness to donate its property to a nonprofit group, the city two years later established the Vermont-Slauson Economic Development Corporation (VSEDC).

The city commissioned an economic study and an architectural study on the site's development potential, focusing on the reuse of the Sears building. In 1978, the city approached the Alexander Haagen Development Co. about developing retail space at that site. The firm determined that, although the Sears building was structurally sound, it was obsolete from the standpoint of merchandising and recommended demolition of the structure and of several other buildings so that an entirely new retail center could be created on the site.

To develop the new community shopping center, Haagen Development (as general partner) and VSEDC (as limited partner) formed a limited partnership. VSEDC became the recipient of the federal and city grants and holds title to the property; Haagen Development holds a 90-year ground lease. The developer negotiated the various deals necessary to complete the land assembly, which was funded with the use of city block grant funds and completed without reliance on eminent domain. Sixty percent of the center's profits (following a defined return on investment of private sector money) flows to VSEDC and 40 percent to

---

ner.[9] Developers perceive government entities as more apt to approve and often to accelerate the approval process for those projects in which public agencies have an investment. For the public sector, public/private partnerships afford more control over projects throughout the development process and enable cities to achieve a variety of social objectives, for example, affirmative action, use of minority contractors, and the creation of jobs for low-income residents. Public/private projects, however, typically involve increased public review and comment, specific contracting requirements, and attention to political concerns. Under most conditions, the receipt of public monies and the participation of a public partner also mean greater disclosure than that common in a private project. At the same time, politically active pressure groups are more likely to be a problem for private developers as a result of the publicity that usually accompanies public/private ventures.

Figure 14-4 describes how two levels of government worked together to execute the cleanup and redevel-opment of New York's 42nd Street, long known for its reputation as a center for vice, crime, pornography, and sleaze. In reviewing Figure 14-4, consider the private developer's perspective in terms of how different types of active public support may be enlisted, how many different constituencies may become involved in a project, and how a model of the development process takes on great importance in the complex world of public/private development.

Strategic Decisions in the Implementation Of Public/Private Projects

In implementing a public/private project, the public sector faces five fundamental tasks:

- Selecting a developer;
- Determining the terms and conditions of the opportunity for development, including forms of public assistance;

the private developer, who operates the center. VSEDC plans to use its proceeds for further development of the local community.

Adequate security was the primary concern in the planning and design of the project; it also affected the cost structure for the center. The site is surrounded by a six-foot-high wrought-iron fence, with access limited to two entrances and exits. These gated access points are locked at 11:00 p.m. and reopen at 5:00 a.m.; each access point has its own gatehouse for security personnel. Within the center, a uniformed, armed security force is on duty 24 hours a day, seven days a week. The 17-person force is supplemented by a two-person patrol assigned to an eight-hour day shift by the Los Angeles Police Department. The extra security has been a critical factor in the center's success, although the center's unusual common area expenses (the annual costs of security approximate $1.95 per square foot) had to be offset by lower-than-normal rents. Nevertheless, the project's public funds ensured its economic viability despite below-market rents.

Experience has revealed that, for a public/private partnership to operate smoothly and efficiently, elected public officials must, at the outset of the project, clearly document what they want to accomplish and make certain that all public agency staff members are aware of and adhere to the stated objectives. A clear specification of

objectives helps expedite government review and approval, thereby avoiding major delays and cost overruns for the private developer.

From the perspective of the private developer, working in partnership with the public sector meant delays in funding, extensive contractual and sign-off requirements, frequent progress reporting, and complex bidding procedures. Decisions about what appeared to be comparatively simple items, such as the type of perimeter fencing around the site, stretched into a lengthy process.

The decline of good-quality, competitively priced retail services in inner-city neighborhoods is a longstanding, well-documented trend for which numerous causes have been cited. Combining private development expertise, public financing, and a community economic development initiative, the Vermont-Slauson Shopping Center represents an example of the successful return of retailing to inner-city areas. It also stands as a model neighborhood public/ private initiative. ■

Source: ULI–the Urban Land Institute, "Los Angeles: Vermont-Slauson Shopping Center," in *Inner-City Economic Development: Successful Projects in Distressed Urban Neighborhoods,* ULI Research Working Paper Series No. 632 (Washington, D.C.: Author, April 1994).

- Negotiating disposition and development agreements;
- Resolving problems and conflicts that arise throughout the development process; and
- Monitoring performance responsibilities and payments of project revenues due over the life of the agreement.[10]

From a strategic perspective, some of the decisions a city must make in the early stages of planning a public/private venture (often when city decision makers are least informed about a project's development potential or are still evaluating possibilities) ultimately come to shape both the agenda for negotiations and the tools available for managing the initiative. One such decision concerns the process of selecting a developer. The choice is typically between an auction-bid competition or a development-prospectus competition through which a parcel is offered for disposition and a developer selected on the basis of comprehensive re-

sponses to a request for qualifications (RFQ) or a request for proposals (RFP). For nearly all public/private ventures, the RFQ/RFP has been the preferred option; the auction-bid approach generally offers government less flexibility in controlling the development process and less control over the composition of the benefits package.[11]

In attracting private developers' interest and specifying the ground rules for participation in the project, the RFP sets the stage for future implementation of the project. The RFP can be short and open-ended or long and detailed with respect to a project's land uses, design guidelines, and business terms; regardless of the RFP's length, however, it requires the public entity to assess its specific objectives for the project with an eye to broadly defining the character of the private development, identifying public roles and available types of assistance, structuring a set of project-specific planning conditions and business points to which developers must respond, and providing for an orderly and

Figure 14-3

Metreon in Yerba Buena Gardens

Metreon is a 360,000-square-foot entertainment/retail complex in Yerba Buena Center—an 87-acre mixed-use development in San Francisco's South of Market neighborhood. Yerba Buena Center is an undertaking of the San Francisco Redevelopment Agency, which has sought to ensure that the privately developed entertainment/retail center complements the other cultural and commercial uses in the ten-acre megablock dubbed Yerba Buena Gardens and provides revenue to the agency for operating and maintaining public spaces there.

The four-level entertainment/retail center shares the megablock with several other facilities: a 5.5-acre public park known as the Esplanade, the Visual Arts Center (52,000 square feet), the Performing Arts Theater (48,000 square feet), and two visually prominent cafés, as well as subsurface facilities for the nearby George R. Moscone Convention Center and the Marriott Hotel ballroom. On the adjacent blocks, the San Francisco Museum of Modern Art (200,000 square feet) was completed in January 1995, and plans are underway for a Jewish arts museum (to be put in a rehabilitated building across from MOMA) and a Mexican arts museum on Mission Street. In 1998, a three-acre children's center opened with an indoor ice-skating rink, a carousel (which was rescued from Playland at a Long Beach mall), a plaza with a small garden and playground, a 12-lane bowling alley, the Zeum multimedia teaching complex, a child development center, W Hotel, and other facilities. Multiple office developments are underway or newly completed in adjacent neighborhoods.

The Yerba Buena neighborhood was part of an early 1960s large-scale urban renewal project and had been in decline when the redevelopment effort started. Largely because of the redevelopment effort of the past decade, the area has turned the corner and a rich mix of urban uses—including Class A development of many types—has recently come into being.

The agency's 1992 RFPs identified two goals for the entertainment/retail center. The agency's primary objective was to create a mix of entertainment and related uses that would complement the area's cultural uses and enliven the neighborhood day and night. Its second objective was to establish a reliable, long-term revenue stream that could be used to operate and maintain the public facilities in Yerba Buena Gardens.

The city required that development proposals for the 120,000-square-foot site be for a project of at least 200,000 square feet that would include a cinema complex no smaller than 45,000 square feet and at least one other destination use encompassing a minimum of 30,000 square feet. These minimum requirements were believed essential to achieve the critical mass that would draw the project's diverse constituencies—the residents of the city and the Bay Area, the 210,000 downtown workers, and San Francisco's 13 million annual visitors, including more than 1.3 million conventioneers.

The agency believed that an expensive design competition would deter many developers from participating in the process and did not require competing developers to submit designs or allow developers to associate with an architect. The agency and the selected developer would jointly choose the project architect.

The challenge of design was to achieve a number of important objectives in the face of some complex development constraints—construction over the Marriott's underground ballroom, ingress/egress complications, venting problems, and the need to provide vehicular access to the Esplanade, the Marriott, and the convention center—while not compromising the marketability of the entertainment/retail center. Those objectives included:

- Creating a high-caliber design that would hold its own with world-class designs in the neighborhood—Romaldo Giurgola's Esplanade, Fumihiko Maki's Visual Arts Center, James Stewart Polshek's Performing Arts Theater, and Mario Botta's Museum of Modern Art.
- Developing entrances through the entertainment/retail center to the Esplanade that would welcome pedestrians coming from the office and retail core north of Market Street, from the convention center, and from the more than 1,000 residential units (many inhabited by older people) in the South of Market area.
- Harmoniously blending the eastern edge of the project with the western edge of the Esplanade, which is on a sloping grade.
- Activating commercial life on the Fourth Street frontage and along the edge of the Esplanade.
- Bringing sunlight into the Esplanade and mitigating prevailing winds.

The project's conceptual design was coordinated closely with the agency and the major retail tenants and was completed in summer 1994, at the same time that negotiation of business terms was concluded. After numerous delays, construction of the entertainment center, with

The ten-acre megablock dubbed Yerba Buena Gardens is an undertaking of the San Francisco Redevelopment Agency, which sought to ensure that the privately developed entertainment/retail center complements the other cultural and commercial uses in the project and provides revenue to the agency for operating and maintaining public spaces there.

Sony Retail Entertainment (a division of Sony Corporation of America) as its master tenant, began in May 1997 and was completed in mid-1999. From Sony's standpoint, the project is an attempt to seize the high ground in technology-based entertainment attractions. Sony Retail Entertainment will develop and operate some of the attractions in the center, sublease space to other tenants, and develop and operate some attractions as joint ventures with other entities.

The developer for Metreon is Yerba Buena Entertainment Center LLC, an entity 85 percent owned by Millennium Partners of New York and WDG Ventures of San Francisco (see the profile of developer Paula Collins in Chapter 12) and 15 percent by Sony Retail Entertainment. Millennium Partners is a New York–based entity that developed a similar retail/entertainment center as part of its 800,000-square-foot Lincoln Square residential/retail complex in Manhattan. WDG Ventures is a San Francisco–based and minority-controlled firm with almost 20 years of development experience. Its close familiarity with the approvals process in San Francisco and with the many interest groups in the city was an important asset for a development group whose other partner is based in New York.

The developer built Metreon in 3.3 acres of leased air space above the ballroom of the San Francisco Convention Center. The lease expires in mid-2046, with the right of the land tenant to renew for two additional periods of 18 years each. The agency will receive both fixed and contingent compensation as consideration for the lease. According to the agency's economic adviser, Keyser Marston Associates, Inc., the total present value of the income streams in the lease is $21.5 million, of which $15.6 million is accounted for by fixed (minimum-risk) forms of compensation. The balance is attributable to the potential receipt of percentage rent. This revenue will provide the agency with funds to operate and maintain the public spaces of Yerba Buena Gardens. ∎

Sources: **Robert Wetmore and Helen L. Sause, "Striking a Public/Private Deal,"** Urban Land, **January 1995, pp. 25–28; Robert J. Wetmore and Helen L. Sause, "Sony Entertainment Center Breaks Ground,"** Urban Land, **August 1997, pp. 24–25; and Gina Mackintosh, freelance writer.**

clearly understood procedure for evaluating proposals. These tasks are roughly analogous in timing to the activities in stages one through three of the conventional development model. (Most of the detail covered in Chapters 10, 11, 12, 16, 17, and 18 is relevant background for preparing the RFP.)

The level of specificity for each of these elements is often a matter of market conditions. For example, when

---

Figure 14-4

42nd Street at Times Square: Marshaling Public and Private Resources for a Transformation

One of the most visible examples of redevelopment that took advantage of public and private resources is New York's 42nd Street at Times Square—or the *new* 42nd Street as bespeaks its radical transformation in perception and reality. The emergence of the new 42nd Street has become a worldwide symbol of renewed optimism about the dynamics of city life in general and public/private projects focused on entertainment in particular. Long associated with a lengthy list of urban ills, conditions of social depravity, vice and high crime rates, and the easy availability of every form of sexual pleasure, West 42nd Street today is a vast construction site rapidly on its way to reemerging as New York's prime entertainment mecca, a drawing card for families, out-of-towners, and native New Yorkers alike.

When fully redeveloped by the turn of the century, this historic one-block stretch of midtown Manhattan, also the nexus of the city's transportation system since 1904 when the first of several subway lines to converge on Times Square was completed, will be the new home for corporate tenants such as Condé Nast Publications and Reuters, as four new office towers with more than 4.1 million square feet of space rise on corner sites at 42nd Street on Seventh Avenue and Broadway. Already operating are three newly renovated theaters—New York's art nouveau masterpiece, the 1,800-seat New Amsterdam now operated by Disney; the city's first theater dedicated to children's programming, the 500-seat New Victory Theater; and the 1,821-seat Ford Center for the Performing Arts (refashioned from the combined Lyric and Apollo theaters) designed for musical productions. Joining these theaters, on the north side of 42nd Street, will be the new home for the Roundabout Theater Company and rehearsal studios for nonprofit arts groups (in the old Selwyn Theater) and E-Walk, a 193,000-square-foot entertainment/retail center that includes a 13-screen, 100,000-square-foot Sony/Loews theater complex and a 45-story hotel. Rising on the south side of 42nd Street in the space of three other theaters (the Empire, Harris, and Liberty theaters) is a 335,000-square-foot retail project that will include a 25-screen AMC multiplex cinema, the 60,000-square-foot Madame Tussaud's wax museum, and other retail attractions. The Times Tower, the 26-story tower built by the *New York Times* that gave the district its name and became its symbolic heart, now houses a new Warner Bros. store (across from the Disney store) in addition to being a billboard of electronic signs and a

The emergence of the new 42nd Street at Times Square has become a worldwide symbol of renewed optimism about the dynamics of city life in general and public/private projects focused on entertainment in particular.

the market is weak and the site untested, attracting the attention of qualified developers may require a detailed prospectus and thorough feasibility study. Conversely, when the market is strong, less documentation may be needed, but correspondingly more attention must be devoted to other matters, particularly the detailed terms and conditions for the contemplated business deal. Differences in market dynamics, site character-

---

visual entry point for the eight-block stretch of Broadway—from 42nd Street to 50th Street—ablaze with a new generation of flashing neon, kinetic lights, and supersigns.

This vast transformation and cleanup of 42nd Street—a saga of stops and starts, 47 lawsuits, continual controversy, and market reversals over the course of nearly 20 years since the public/private project was initiated by the public sector—has been a joint undertaking by an unusually powerful coalition between the city and state. Under a memorandum of understanding signed in 1980, the city of New York and the state of New York through the entrepreneurial public development entity, the Urban Development Corporation (UDC), agreed to cooperate in the redevelopment of the 42nd Street block between Broadway and Eighth Avenue. The compelling force of this institutional coalition came from the singular combination of three powers only UDC could bring to the deal-making process: the police power of eminent domain to condemn land (the city's public development arm did not have clear statutory authority to undertake the power, and, though the city did, its process was viewed as terribly cumbersome and relatively slow), the legal status (as would-be landowner) to negotiate customized tax agreements for commercial projects, and a distinctive statutory power to override local land use regulations.

As part of the agreement, UDC accepted the lead role of implementing agency for the project. The city retained the rights of approval on financial terms and changes to UDC's *General Project Plan,* which governed the redevelopment land use program. Most significant, the public approvals that are the legal ballast to the project were undertaken pursuant to state regulations and therefore did not go through the city's traditional lengthy approval process.

In city-state agreements executed in 1988, 1991, and 1994, UDC agreed to transfer its interest and obligations to a wholly owned subsidiary whose sole activity would be development of the 42nd Street Development Project (42DP). Thus, although UDC was the original condemning authority, title to the properties lies with 42nd Street Devel-

opment Project, Inc. In addition, the city in 1988 created an independent nonprofit organization, the New 42nd Street, Inc., and charged it with long-term oversight of the renovation and ongoing operations of 42nd Street's historic theaters.

As the implementing agency, 42DP has been responsible for day-to-day management of the project (including property management, condemnation, relocation, and fee and fixture trials) as well as development of the plan, marketing, attracting tenants, and negotiations with developers. The city retained consent rights on all "material" actions by 42DP and UDC. 42DP's core activities have been funded through UDC, and were repaid directly by developers or will be reimbursed through developers' revenues related to site development.

From the perspective of implementation, at least two structural characteristics distinguish this project from other large-scale public/private efforts in the nation. The first was the city's policy mandate that it take no direct financial risk for the costs of acquiring, through condemnation, the 13-acre project area. It managed to do so through an innovative public/private deal structure designed to shift that risk to private developers (principally Prudential Insurance Company as the money partner behind Times Square Center Associates, the joint venture that held the development rights for the four office tower sites). The second was the public coalition between the city and state that was instrumental in carrying out the city's financial mandate and acting as a political bulwark against constant opposition that continuously delayed condemnation and troubled implementation of the project. In turn, when the real estate market collapsed in the early 1990s and effectively killed the initial concept of office/mart/hotel for the project, the leadership and resources of 42DP, in concert with the staying power of the public/private coalition, provided the basis for rescripting the project. It was a rare second chance for any large-scale redevelopment project. This new plan, with its clear and timely focus on entertainment-based activity, reinforced the historic and enduring thematic attraction of 42nd Street at Times Square. ■

istics, a given project's public objectives, and the legal alternatives available for designating developers are all important considerations when selecting a developer and thus make generalizations about the "best" approach inappropriate.[12]

When land for the public/private development is publicly owned, a second strategic decision is whether to sell or lease the parcel. A sale can generate substantial upfront revenues for use in other public projects, eliminate the risk of future nonpayment,[13] and, under certain conditions, promise higher dollars for the public treasury than lease arrangements. In terms of controlling land use, restrictive covenants can be attached to property deeds as a condition of sale, as was the case with urban renewal dispositions. As a means for managing the development of large-scale public/private projects, however, many big cities have found that leasing affords more strategic advantages.[14]

Los Angeles's disposition of the land underlying California Center is illustrative. The last remaining parcel in the city's long-running Bunker Hill urban renewal project, the 8.75-acre site was also the only large parcel of land left in downtown when the Community Redevelopment Agency solicited development proposals in 1979. After two moribund decades, the market in downtown Los Angeles heated up, and to capture the benefits of its position as landowner, the agency decided to offer the parcel on a long-term lease basis. The RFP called for a mixed-use project of 3.5 million to 4.4 million square feet with a substantial allocation to housing uses; a major public benefits package, including a new, free-standing structure for the Los Angeles Museum of Modern Art, which was to form the focus of the entire development; and an adjacent 1.5-acre central park as well as other pedestrian open spaces to be provided, owned, and maintained by the developer. These public amenities would not substitute for direct financial returns—which, according to the RFP, should reflect prevailing market practices and include provisions for inflation-protected rents, escalations pegged to rising property values, and profit-sharing participations.[15]

Forms of Assistance

The nature of public investment in projects has taken the form of subsidies for land redevelopment and such capital improvements as infrastructure, parking garages, transit systems and stations, public amenities (e.g., outdoor plazas, pedestrian malls, other open space), and complementary facilities such as convention centers and stadia. Such improvements ready a site for private development, provide needed amenities, and/or create an improved programmatic environment in

which a project is more likely to succeed. Indirect—or softer—forms of assistance designed to improve project feasibility can be passed on to developers in several ways: through density bonuses, government agencies' commitments or guarantees to lease space in a new development, transfers of development rights, land and/or building exchanges, air rights transfers, regulatory relief from zoning and building codes, reduced processing time for project approvals, coordinated design of projects in an area, arbitration of any disputes that might arise, and work with or organization of neighborhood and business groups. These public actions typically do not require an outlay of public money but provide the developer with savings in time and money, reduced risk, or increased opportunities for development (see Figure 14-5).

After the cutbacks in federal aid in the late 1970s, cities received fewer categorical aid dollars from Washington with which to fund their projects, yet they continued to support projects through the issuance of tax-exempt bonds—at least until the 1986 Tax Reform Act curtailed the use of such bonds for private-purpose projects. Continually pushed to rely more and more on local resources, cities established a broad inventory of incentive tools and financing techniques from which to fashion their assistance packages: tax increment financing, special assessment districts, tax abatements, dedication of sales or special-purpose taxes, UDAG loan paybacks, eminent domain, land writedowns, land swaps, ground leases, lease/purchase arrangements, second mortgage financing, loan guarantees and credit enhancements, loan subsidies, capital improvements, leases for office space, and value-creating tradeoffs based on zoning bonuses.[16]

In return for the increased risk associated with providing substantial assistance, the public sector can take a direct financial stake in projects to secure a specified percent of a project's cash flow (a pseudo-equity interest) through such mechanisms as participatory leases and profit-sharing agreements.

Although used with some frequency in the past, profit-sharing agreements have not produced substantial revenues for many cities. In one study of 16 cities that structured project financing around profit-sharing arrangements, only three projects were generating any cash for the city as of 1988.[17] The economic logic of the subsidy in many downtown or inner-city neighborhood projects works against a big return. To kick off a project, the city invests funds early in the development process. Then, so as not to burden the project before it reaches an economically viable operating position, profit-sharing revenues typically are structured as triple-net revenues, with the city last in line to receive any

Figure 14-5

Strategies and Incentives for Public Assistance

Strategies for Enhancing the Risk/Return
Relationship of Private Investment
- Reduce capital costs
- Absorb demands for new or improved infrastructure
- Lower operating costs
- Increase opportunity for development
- Reduce debt service burden
- Reduce predevelopment risk of approval
- Enhance availability to private capital

Direct Financial Assistance
Land Assembly
- Acquisition
- Demolition
- Relocation
- Writedowns

Capital Improvements
- Infrastructure
- Parking garages
- Open space and amenities
- Programmatic facilities

Grant Assistance
- Cost sharing of private improvements
- Payment for predevelopment studies

Debt Financing
- Direct loans
- Below-market interest rates
- Loan guarantees
- Credit enhancements

Indirect Assistance
- Zoning or density bonuses
- Transfer of development rights
- Transfer of air rights
- Regulatory relief from zoning and building codes
- Reduced processing time for project approvals
- Quick take by eminent domain
- Design coordination in public/private projects
- Below-cost utilities if publicly owned
- Arbitration of disputes that might arise
- Government commitments to rent space

Financing Strategies
Intergovernmental Grants
- Community development block grants
- Section 108 guaranteed loans
- State economic development grants

Local Debt Financing
- General obligation bonds
- Revenue bonds
- Industrial development bonds

Off-Budget Financing
- Lease/purchase agreements
- Ground leases
- Land/building swaps
- Property tax abatements

Dedicated Sources of Local Funds
- Special district assessments
- Tax increment financing
- Earmarked sales or special-purpose taxes
- Reuse of UDAG loan paybacks

General Budget Revenues

---

cash flow. In other words, the cost-revenue account is likely to be negative for many years. Such was the case in Boston, where officials waited 17 years before realizing any profit from Faneuil Hall Marketplace. In that project, the city acts as a limited development partner, sharing a percentage of the development's net cash flow in lieu of collecting property taxes and relying on conventional lease terms.[18]

Notwithstanding the evidence to date, sharing profits affords cities other nonfinancial benefits. Although large public subsidies are always potentially controversial, profit-sharing arrangements in effect provide a political solution to the buy-high/sell-low problem of writing down the cost of redevelopment. They offer political protection to city officials vulnerable to charges of giving away too much. Even if the anticipated revenues are small or expected far in the future, a financial agreement to share returns is perceived as a sign that the city is acting responsibly and effectively.[19]

Cities aim to be pragmatic in packaging assistance. Their objective is to create combinations of incentives that make a real estate investment feasible for both the public and private participants. In this case, feasibility means overcoming serious obstacles and problems—

land assembly, negative impacts of the surrounding area, excessive or premium costs, heavy upfront capital investments—that inhibit private development or renovation. Through diverse and numerous means, the public assistance package reconfigures the risk/return relationship of private investment through one or more financial tactics: reducing capital costs, absorbing the demands for new infrastructure, lowering operating costs, or reducing debt service burdens.

In determining whether significant levels of public assistance for development and financing will be required, public officials typically proceed through several steps.

1. Determine total development costs by project component.
2. Determine the level of private financing available (see Chapter 6) by:
   ■ Estimating the income-producing capacity of the project;
   ■ Capitalizing net operating income;
   ■ Determining loan value;
   ■ Determining available equity financing; and
   ■ Calculating total private funding capacity.
3. Identify the gap between project costs and available private resources.
4. Structure assistance to close financing gaps and to gain reasonable project returns.[20]

Although the terms and conditions of public aid are tailored to the needs of individual projects, local governments structure assistance within the framework of three widely held (if informal) general policy principles:

1. Public aid should be delivered through cost-sharing mechanisms.
2. Investment of public dollars requires a return for risk taking apart from increased collections of property taxes, based on some form of loan recapture or profit participation in future project revenues.
3. The timing and conditions of public commitments should be linked to specific private obligations and responsibilities that must be performed.

In each instance, the public sector seeks to create binding ties in the form of mutually dependent commitments and business interests that establish incentives for the completion of an economically viable project. Generous upfront subsidies can carry risky projects through the first uncertain years, but experience has shown that they cannot turn weak projects into successful ventures. Beyond the task of making development feasible, the hard part of crafting public/private deals is finding ways to ensure the efficacy of public investment in joint development ventures. When deciding on the measures to apply in helping developers close financing gaps, public entities must define and measure the public risk of and reward for their actions (see Figure 14-6).

Cities and states today have become more sophisticated about claims of benefits from private projects and are acting accordingly by critically scrutinizing the cost/benefit ratio attached to projects with large subsidies. One area where this scrutiny is most visible is the provision of publicly subsidized financing for stadia and arenas, especially when voters are being asked directly—through the ballot box—to pay the price. If voters want stadia, they often don't want to shoulder the costs or subsidize a team's owner, so voters' rejections of referenda on stadium-financing questions are not unusual. A "no" vote on stadium financing is not always the final word, however, and therein lies a big part of what is a nationwide fierce, tough, and controversial debate over municipal assistance to sports stadia.

With increasing regularity, sports franchises have used their monopoly-type power to pressure governments for a new or substantially refurbished stadium; the present stadium may be too old or too small or without the amenities, luxury boxes, and suites that raise the revenue to develop a top team. Alternatively, city officials may actively seek a franchise when the city has no sports team, or it may view an additional franchise as an element of its economic development strategy for downtown, in particular. In either case, cities have to figure out how much and in what form they should contribute to the building of a new stadium for a privately owned team, or risk losing that team to other cities who seem (at least during the heat of negotiations) only too willing to promise team owners a new stadium. Despite the trend toward public financing, the San Francisco Giants's new stadium, Pacific Bell Park, and the new MCI Center, a professional sports arena in downtown Washington, D.C., were built entirely with private funds.

The political stakes of such debates are high, with pros and cons targeting both economic and strategic issues (see Figure 14-7). Economists continue to cast doubt on the monetary benefits cities reap from subsidizing new stadia. Heavy public financial assistance is highly controversial, so how the public assistance package is put together is key to the political acceptance of a city's decision making. Sports stadia may rely on specialized types of "export" taxes, such as hotel and motel taxes, car rental taxes, or a tax on visiting athletes; cities also have created sports lotteries and put in place

Figure 14-6
Analyzing Financial Returns to the City

To accomplish goals for revitalization, cities are increasingly bargaining for better terms on paying back loans, lease arrangements, and land writedowns, and are requiring higher percentages of net cash flow for the risk they are taking in development. Their negotiating prowess, however, has resulted in increasingly complex deals, rendering financial analysis more complex as well.

Arizona Center, for example, is an 18.5-acre, $515 million mixed-use development in downtown Phoenix that will ultimately feature 1.9 million square feet of office space, 450,000 square feet of retail shops, a 600-room hotel, a three-acre garden park, and parking for approximately 5,400 vehicles. Phases I and II, already completed, include two office buildings totaling about 750,000 square feet, 150,000 square feet of specialty retail shops, the garden park, and two parking structures. Completion of these portions of the project in November 1990 followed the city's RFP in May 1986 and selection of the Rouse Company of Columbia, Maryland, and the Phoenix Community Alliance, a private nonprofit developer, in August 1986 as the entities with whom the city would enter into exclusive negotiations. By December 1986, the city council was requested to approve the right to negotiate a disposition and development agreement with the developers based on the following terms. (The terms are as described in a memorandum of understanding between the city of Phoenix and the Rouse Company dated December 19, 1986, and might not reflect the terms of the final deal.)

Terms of the Agreement
1. *City's contribution.* Acquiring 1.85 acres through eminent domain. Vacating 4.71 acres of public right-of-way (streets and alleys). Subordinating its interest in the land and buildings to any project financing.

   City's return. Land to be leased to the developer for 60 years for rental payments totaling the sum of 1) the debt service required to retire land acquisition bonds for the 1.85 acres; and 2) participation in cash flow as follows: 8 percent on any cash invested by the city in the 600-space garage plus 7 percent on the value of the 4.71 acres in vacated streets and alleys so long as that amount does not exceed 17 percent of operating cash flow after certain defined expenses and returns to the developer and the city (the 8 percent on the garage). After the 15th year, the developer has the right to purchase the city's fee interest, in which case the 17 percent return would increase to 27 percent. If the developer does not exercise this right, however, the percents remain the same.

2. *City's contribution.* Abating all real estate property taxes for eight years. Making best efforts to obtain tax-exempt bonds or certificates of participation to finance the developer-funded garden park as well as certain improvements to traffic, sewer, water, and storm sewer systems to be built by the developer with tax abatements.

   City's return. Upon the sale or refinancing of office buildings other than those built during Phases I and II, the city receives an amount equal to the capitalized tax abatement provided on those buildings after the payment of defined expenses and returns. Further, the project is to be completed according to the approved development plan, with the developer to fund the garden park as well as certain improvements to off-site traffic; the sewer, water, and storm sewer systems; and dedicated tax abatements toward repayment of bond obligations if the city does obtain financing. The developer is also to work with the Public Transit Department to develop an incentive program encouraging ridership on public transit and in carpools, and to develop a participation plan for including minority and women

continued on next page

---

a "temporary" sales tax or surcharge on an existing sales tax to partially finance stadium construction, in addition to the many other forms of assistance listed in Figure 14-5. The private side of the equation offers a number of special sources of funds: corporate sponsorships, stadium-naming rights, luxury boxes and charter seats, as well as concession rights, advertising revenues, and parking fees.[21]

The terms of assistance and conditions of development contained within public/private agreements are complex. This complexity reflects the many tradeoffs made during the course of negotiations in which the public's set of objectives is reconciled with both its limited resources and the demands of private investment. Similarly, the roles adopted by the public sector —broker, facilitator, lessor, builder, lender, investor— reflect both the range of multifaceted issues (bureaucratic, financial, political) to be addressed and the conditions in local real estate markets at the time those roles are defined.

Figure 14-6

Analyzing Financial Returns to the City (continued)

business owners in the project. Future abatements are to be used to fund additional parking, maintenance of the garden park, and incentives for hotel and department store development.

3. *City's contribution.* Making the best efforts to obtain financing for the 600-space garage to be owned and operated by the city. (The parking requirement has been reduced based on calculations of shared parking.)

   City's return. Eight percent return on any cash invested if the city obtains financing (see number 1 above).

4. *City's contribution.* Making best efforts to ensure certain traffic improvements, including the maintenance of two key streets as high-volume, two-way arterials, relocation of certain diagonals, and modification of travel on key avenues to improve public transit. Making best efforts to extend streetscaping.

   City's return. No specific return.

5. *City's contribution.* Conveying ownership of the garden park.

   City's return. The developer builds and maintains the garden park.

6. *City's contribution.* Rezoning the entire parcel, permanently waiving the permit requirements for outdoor activities, and changing the High-Rise Residential Incentive Overlay Zone, among others.

   City's return. No specific return, but, on an overall basis, the project is expected ultimately to employ 10,500 people and be valued at $515 million.

A careful reading of these terms, even summarized as they are, indicates the deal's complexity. In fact, the cover memorandum that accompanied the memorandum of understanding appears to have misstated the deal in assuming that, for example, the city's participation in cash flow would automatically increase to 27 percent in the 16th year, when in fact that event would occur only if the developer chose to exercise its option to purchase.

Analyzing Potential Returns

A city should consider several questions when analyzing the potential returns on a deal such as this one:

- What are the opportunity costs associated with the tax abatement on property of potentially rising value? Can increases in property values for areas surrounding the subject property be projected?
- How does the city account for its costs related to the project, including soft administrative costs?
- How critical to the city is the developer's purchase of the property? (It is the purchase that triggers an increase in the percentage of participation in cash flow.)
- Not counting the value of social goals such as minority employment, what is the net present value of the city's investment in the project? Have long-term financial pro formas been developed so that such value can be calculated? What discount rate should be used in calculating the net present value of the city's investment?
- What value should be placed on the projected new jobs to be generated by the project?
- What is the procedure, if any, for renegotiating any portions of the deal in the event of unforeseen circumstances?

Cities like Phoenix—and many others—are fine-tuning their skills in analysis and negotiation to leverage public dollars for revitalization. As the competition for public money increases and deals become more complex, however, cities will need to hone these skills even more to use resources as wisely as possible. ■

Sources: **Phoenix Community Alliance, "Central Phoenix Project Update, Summer 1990"; and "City Council Report," cover memorandum, December 19, 1986, describing the memorandum of understanding for the project and memorandum of understanding between the city of Phoenix and the Rouse Company, December 19, 1986.**

Organizations and the Public/ Private Process

As public/private ventures have evolved, the involvement of state and local organizations has expanded in innovative ways. Various types of government structures, including an array of quasi-public government bodies, development corporations, and city departments with expanded functions, have been organized to handle public/private development. Public/private development is frequently organized under a quasi-public institutional structure that permits an organization to operate with greater flexibility and fewer restrictions than a city agency involved in development. Though partially publicly funded, a quasi-public development organization can conduct negotiations in private—a par-

Figure 14-7

The Pros and Cons of Publicly Subsidized Financing for Sports Stadia and Arenas

Pros—New stadia:
- Foster local economic growth,
- Generate new jobs and new taxes,
- Stimulate spending in neighborhood restaurants, bars, and hotels,
- Create spillover opportunities for real estate development,
- Meet local citizens' desires for entertainment and pride of place for local sports team ("consumption value").

Cons—New stadia:
- Are poor economic development generators, as most empirical studies have shown, because:
  - The projected economic impacts rarely materialize,
  - Stadium-related jobs are often seasonal and pay low wages,
  - They only change the way people spend money on entertainment rather than generate new revenue,
  - The value of publicly subsidized financing is often distorted in economic studies,
  - The costs typically exceed the benefits;
- Cities have more pressing needs—schools, transit, infrastructure—for scarce public funds.

Three questions economic studies need to answer:
- How do the costs of a proposed stadium compare with its benefits? Who benefits and who pays?
- What is the impact of a new stadium on local per capita income?
- What is the likely impact of a new stadium on the rate of growth of the local economy?

Common critiques of economic studies:
- Impact or cost/benefit studies are rarely commissioned by "independent" players, and the results typically are consistent with the positions (pro or con) of their sponsors.
- Estimates of benefits (direct revenues and spillovers) are imprecise because data are limited and assumptions suspect or optimistic.

Coors Field in Denver, Colorado, is a traditional-style urban ballpark designed to complement the red brick buildings of historic LoDo.

- Multipliers—one of the key variables of any economic impact analysis—used by most studies are based on decades-old data.
- Econometric studies of economic impacts are also suspect, because economists disagree on methodological approach and conceptual models for measuring impacts are weak. ∎

For an informed discussion, see David C. Petersen, *Sports, Convention, and Entertainment Facilities* (Washington, D.C.: ULI–the Urban Land Institute, 1996); and Roger G. Noll and Andrew Zimbalist, eds., *Sports, Jobs, and Taxes: The Economic Impact of Sports Teams and Stadiums* (Washington, D.C.: Brookings Institution Press, 1997).

---

ticularly useful feature as developers are reluctant to negotiate when the details of their financial dealings are made public. Examples of quasi-public organizations are the Centre City Development Corporation in San Diego and the Milwaukee Redevelopment Corporation (see Figure 14-8).

The Centre City Development Corporation (CCDC) was created in 1975 in connection with the increasingly complex redevelopment of the Horton Plaza project, San Diego's first post–World War II investment in a badly deteriorated downtown. As the city's sole representative in such activities as condemnation, relocation, land acquisition, and negotiations with private developers, CCDC played an aggressive role in an extensive planning process that involved 13 contract revisions with developer Ernest W. Hahn, Inc.[22]

A dedicated and specialized public development partner is crucial. The many responsibilities carried out by the public partner—brokering regulatory approvals, negotiating with other public agencies, shepherding the development proposal through the environmental impact and community review processes, and providing financial assistance—can expedite progress through the inevitable hurdles encountered by these projects.

Figure 14-8

Milwaukee Redevelopment Corporation

The Milwaukee Redevelopment Corporation (MRC) is a private, nonprofit corporation working with the local government on major civic projects, particularly the revitalization of downtown; it is a "quasi-private" entity. Though a private organization with a board of directors comprising chief executive officers of major area corporations, the MRC works closely with the city and county governments.

The MRC was established in 1973 as a limited-profit development company and raised $3 million in seed money by selling stock to more than 40 Milwaukee-based firms. Even though shareholders were told not to expect a rapid or market rate of return on their investment, the MRC reorganized as a nonprofit corporation in 1983 to reflect its actual performance. Operating funds now come from membership dues rather than from the sale of stock. Any return from the MRC's development partnerships is reinvested in civic projects.

In its first two years of operation, the MRC met with business and government leaders to identify priorities and to establish an agenda for downtown revitalization. Among the targeted priority districts was the central retail area west of the Milwaukee River. A three-pronged strategy involved the development of a hotel, a regional retail center, and an office building.

To develop the hotel, the MRC made a cash equity investment in the project, while the city participated in landscaping and the construction of a skywalk. For the office building, the MRC optioned much of the land, and the city assembled a portion of the land. For the retail center, the MRC forged a coalition with the city and the Rouse Company—developer of the retail center—and developed the entire $70 million project. It provided more than $16 million of the equity, purchased two of the buildings used in the redevelopment, acquired other land in the project area, and executed a lease of the retail space with the Rouse Company.

Since its first three projects, the MRC has continued its work downtown. It became a joint venture partner in the development of the 354-unit Yankee Hill, the first major housing development in downtown Milwaukee in 20 years.

Completed in 1988, Yankee Hill is a market-rate rental project. The MRC is also working with the Mandel Group and WISPARK, the local electric utility's real estate subsidiary, to develop a 20-acre project on the edge of downtown that will include more than 600 housing units. The development also includes a successful 40,000-square-foot supermarket and 17,000 square feet of neighborhood retail services. In partnership with the Trammell Crow Company, the MRC participated in the redevelopment of a historic building as the new home of the Milwaukee Repertory Theatre. As part of the project, the city restored the historic Pabst Theater, while Trammell Crow developed an adjoining hotel and office complex.

As compensation for its involvement in various projects, the MRC negotiates a percentage of the cash flow from the project as well as a percentage of the residual sales proceeds. A negotiated fee is also sometimes part of the MRC's share of the deal.

The MRC has used both informal and formal processes to initiate deals. The theater project exemplifies the informal process. With the project still in the conceptual stage, Jon Wellhoefer, executive vice president of the MRC, contacted Trammell Crow to see whether he had any interest in the project. A similarly informal process guided the work with the Rouse Company on the Grand Avenue.

A more formal process involving a request for proposals brought about the Yankee Hill project. Letters to more than 60 local and national developers resulted in "something of a beauty contest" in which finalists submitted plans for the project in a competitive selection process. Both processes have worked well for Milwaukee.

The MRC's agenda includes joint development of downtown housing, entertainment projects, improvements to the Grand Avenue area, participation in the new convention center, and assistance to the county in the development of a research park. ■

Source: ULI—the Urban Land Institute, *Downtown Development Handbook*, 2d ed. (Washington, D.C.: Author, 1992), p. 10.

And more so than with other types of development, the risks of public/private development are political. Gauging both the level of political commitment to carry through with a project and the government's ability (in financial matters and personnel) to deliver on agreements is central to a developer's qualitative assessment of project feasibility.

Practical Problems and Policy Issues

Shared Decision Making

The public interests at stake in joint venture projects draw governments into the management of development and the details of decision making associated with stages four through seven of the conventional development process—decisions typically left to the private sector. As cities share more of a project's financial risk, they ask for more control. When, for example, public interests take charge of developing parts of a project, as was the case in the $95 million mixed-use Town Square project in which the city of St. Paul, Minnesota, built a park on the third level of a retail mall, it is clear that shared control is the most practical way to proceed. In that instance, while it was possible to settle some of the major issues early in the development process, St. Paul could not anticipate all the details well in advance of actual construction. Further, the demands of mutually dependent construction schedules that overlapped in time and space ruled out the hands-off control style of urban renewal. For St. Paul to cut a straightforward deal, prepare and transfer the property, and then merely monitor the developer's performance until the project was completed according to plan would have been practically impossible. The deal in St. Paul was an implied agreement to share both design and management decisions throughout the development period and to cope with problems by renegotiating any earlier understandings. Frequent trips back to the bargaining table helped move the project beyond unexpected obstacles.[23]

The ground lease form of land disposition similarly creates an ongoing business relationship. For the developer, leasing minimizes the upfront capital investments and makes more efficient use of taxable deductions; for the government agency, retaining ownership of the land allows the public to benefit from rising land values through lease payments and percentage rents, thereby capturing the residual value of the built improvements. Alongside these benefits, however, lies the potential for conflict and tough lease negotiations, especially if the RFP does not include a sample lease

document that sets out terms and conditions affecting the developer's bid.

Structuring a ground lease that is acceptable to a long-term lender is the developer's major concern. In strong markets, government often does not subordinate the land; for reasons of both business and policy, public officials generally want participation in project revenues above a base fixed rent. To control its exposure to the political as well as business risks of assuming a proprietary interest in a private investment, the public sector seeks tight lease conditions and, through participation formulas, protection against charges that the developer is earning a "windfall." Both positions present problems to institutional lenders seeking protection from the potential loss of control through foreclosure by the government fee owner.[24]

The city of Orlando's negotiations with Lincoln Property Company for the development of a new 245,000-square-foot city hall, a public park and plaza, 1 million square feet of commercial office space, ancillary retail space, and associated parking provide an example of the complexity and shared decision making that characterize public/private projects (see Figure 14-9).

The practical problems of implementing public/private development rule out anything but an active role in project decision making for the public sector. Attempting to anticipate upfront all conditions that might arise in the course of development would not only extend the process indefinitely, but also be unrealistic. Reconciling initial differences, finding efficient cost-sharing arrangements, coordinating public and private construction schedules, recasting the deal when crisis threatens the project, and managing the process in light of public review all call for flexibility in responding to the economic and political events that often challenge public/private projects. For private developers, participation in a public/private development means changing normal business practices to accommodate the demands of a politically accountable partner.

Conflicts and Accountability

As the public sector has become more involved in making deals, concerns have surfaced about its objectivity in regulating development. At a ULI policy forum in 1988, leading experts in the field of public/private development questioned whether public/private development leads to a conflict of interest for the public sector. Participants noted that the dual role of the public sector creates a two-hat dilemma: the potential conflict of interest inherent in the public sector's role as both land seller and land regulator. At its simplest, the conflict arises because a city's goals in selling versus regulating land

Figure 14-9
Orlando's City Commons

As Orlando's government outgrew its 1950s-vintage city hall, city operations were scattered among a number of buildings, resulting in inefficient service to the public. The city also faced escalating rental costs in privately owned buildings. Although Orlando could finance a new city hall without resorting to immediate tax increases or bond referenda, the mayor and the city council wanted to rely on an alternative scheme of funding.

To achieve that objective, the city chose to lease its land to a private firm, requiring the development of a large project designed to include significant commercial elements. The ground rents from the private development would partially offset the costs of constructing the city hall, and the developer could be persuaded to subsidize the costs of certain on-site amenities. Capitalizing on a strong market and a prime location, the city negotiated simultaneously with three finalists over six months. During that time, the competition even included the final details of the development and lease documents. Despite the extra time and effort, city officials believe that the benefits to the city, which also holds a reversionary interest in the project, were greatly enhanced. The important points of the final agreement with Lincoln Property Company, the developer, are as follows:

- The city retains fee simple title to approximately 2.5 acres of land (of the total seven-acre site) where the new city hall and a park/plaza will be constructed. The city will own the building outright in the conventional manner. (The city would have been willing under certain circumstances to rent the city hall from a developer to facilitate financing of the private portion of the project.)
- Lincoln Property Company is paid a negotiated development fee on performance of a guaranteed fixed-price contract to demolish the old building and construct the new city hall and park/plaza. This mutually satis-

factory arrangement gave Lincoln the opportunity to achieve some economies of scale in constructing a larger project. Lincoln is known for its cost-effective construction management, giving the city confidence in its ability to complete the project successfully.

- Lincoln and the city will jointly plan and design the project. Lincoln pays the planning costs and manages the process, assuming that the overall project conforms to the development practices of the private sector.
- Lincoln agrees to rent the remainder of the seven-acre site from the city in two phases—one beginning in 1992 and the other in 1996. The term for each parcel of land is 75 years. The city conservatively estimated and developed projected ground rents and equity participation to equal the city's bond service for the new city hall and the park/plaza within ten to 12 years.

Upon execution of the ground leases for the private phases, Lincoln will reimburse the city for the entire cost of the planned $1.8 million park/plaza and for two-thirds of the cost of demolishing the existing city hall.

This project underscores the complexity of joint public/private development. The developer not only has to handle the complexities of a large-scale project but also must meet the government's many requirements: extensive public interaction, review and input from the community, the need to respond to several government constituencies, and compliance with statutory provisions regulating the selection and use of consultants, contractors, and other services. All these requirements mean that for a project to succeed, it must have true potential for development. ∎

Source: Lewis Oliver and Eric Smart, "Orlando's City Commons: A Model Public/Private Venture," *Urban Land,* January 1990, pp. 21–25.

---

are potentially at odds and the city's role as seller might improperly influence its regulatory role (see Figure 14-9).[25] The following questions should be considered in examining whether such a conflict exists:

- Is the city overlooking longer-range public interest goals?
- Can cities make good deals, especially when bargaining with sophisticated private parties?
- Are regulatory concessions given away too cheaply?

- Are planners as deal makers focusing on short-term real estate development rather than on long-range comprehensive planning?
- Can traditional notions of due process be fulfilled when deals are hammered out behind closed doors?

The potential for conflict of interest is great, especially when real estate markets are strong. So far, however, conflicts have surfaced only infrequently, particularly given the large number of public/private projects. The

Figure 14-10

The Columbus Circle Project

The Columbus Circle project, initially a 4.5-acre development on the site of the old Coliseum on the southwest corner of New York City's Central Park, is an example of a court's characterization of a development transaction as a cash sale for a zoning bonus. That characterization reflected the trial judge's fundamental unease with New York City's dual role. In 1985, Boston Properties won a city-sponsored competition to develop the site. The design would have produced one of the biggest private buildings in the world, a 925-foot-high structure with 2 million square feet of office space, street-level shops, cinemas, several hundred luxury condominiums, and a 300-room hotel. The deal between the city and Boston Properties exchanged the publicly owned site (the Metropolitan Transit Authority is the parent owner of the parcel) and permission to exceed the zoning by 20 percent for a payment by Boston Properties of $455.1 million and a commitment of up to $40 million for improvements to the nearby Columbus Center subway station. With the bonus, the allowable floor/area ratio increased from 15 to 18, allowing 2.7 million square feet to be built. The city would have realized about $100 million in taxes each year.

The Municipal Art Society, watchdog of the city's physical environment, filed suit, along with the metropolitan chapter of the American Planning Association and the New York Parks Council, asserting that the city's financial stake in the sale tainted the approval process and that environmental analysis of traffic and light and air quality was not adequate. In late 1987, the judge found that the city had exchanged density bonuses for money. The pivotal issue was the contractual clause that allowed Boston Properties to cut its payment by $57 million should the city withhold the bonus of 448,500 square feet. In the decision *(Municipal Art Society of New York v. City of New York, 522 N.Y.S. 800,803–04 [S.Ct. 1987])*, the judge wrote that "government may not place itself in the position of reaping a cash premium because one of its agencies bestows a zoning benefit upon a developer. Zoning benefits are not cash items."

Donning the hat of entrepreneur, the city attempted to generate the highest income from the sale of public land while simultaneously approving the use of a discretionary density bonus as part of its regulatory function. The singularity of the city's pecuniary motives was evident in the timing of its actions. The city incorporated the initial proceeds into the fiscal year 1987 budget before final approval of the sale and thus appeared to have granted the bonus to help balance the budget. Equally damaging was the city's RFP, which stated that the purchase price offered would be "the primary consideration" and that the developer would be required to "apply for and use its best efforts to obtain the maximum 20 percent subway bonus."

The intended disposition of the Coliseum site collapsed on itself under deteriorating market conditions and the withdrawal of the project's lead office tenant and joint venture partner. (Although efforts continued throughout the late 1980s and early 1990s to salvage the deal, the politics remained difficult. An agreement reached in the mid-1990s that would have allowed a scaled-down project to go forward also collapsed.) Nevertheless, the Columbus Circle case exemplifies the tension between the regulatory responsibility of a city and its entrepreneurial zeal in disposing of its property. It poses questions about priorities. Is good planning sacrificed when cities have a financial stake in a project? Does an inherent conflict of interest exist when the public sector wears two hats as developer and regulator? ■

Sources: Richard F. Babcock, "The City as Entrepreneur: Fiscal Wisdom or Regulatory Folly?" in City Deal Making, ed. Terry Jill Lassar (Washington, D.C.: ULI–the Urban Land Institute, 1990), pp. 23–29; and Lynne B. Sagalyn, "Public Development: Using Land as a Capital Resource," Working Paper (Cambridge, Mass.: Lincoln Institute of Land Policy, 1992).

Columbus Circle project (see Figure 14-10) stands out as a notable exception. Another instance of conflict of interest arose with the government center project in Fairfax County, Virginia (already described). In this case, the county was accused of selling the land at too low a price to develop its new building. Critics said the county should have held onto the land (which rose substantially in value after the trade) and sold bonds to finance the government center. The issue to consider is a question of public stewardship. Does gaining income for the city through the disposition of city-owned land further the public interest?[26]

Public/private deal making also poses difficult issues of political and financial accountability. With development agreements too complex to work out in public forums, meetings must be held behind closed doors. But for a local government to grant formal approval, the city council needs to understand the agreements; nonetheless, council members are not briefed on the choices and tradeoffs that are factored into the decision-making process. The complexity of public/private deals also underscores the importance of balancing the need to provide timely information to both council members and the public against the need to protect the city's effectiveness in ongoing negotiations with private developers. In practice, the city council typically faces the choice of accepting a deal as it is or running the risk that a rejection would mark the council as the spoiler of a project that has been years in the making.

Ideally, a full accounting of costs and benefits should accompany the evaluation of a deal; with several different agencies involved in negotiations and cost sharing, however, it is often hard to track all the direct costs and indirect subsidies. Certain aspects of a deal are simply too difficult to value. Although design amenities, subway improvements, and below-market loans can be valued by referencing market equivalents, other benefits such as employment preferences and environmental mitigation commitments have no obvious market prices. These differences make it hard to standardize evaluation techniques and to define the value of tradeoffs in a public/private deal. As a result, public officials must devote substantial time and resources to effectively communicating the objectives of public/private development and to disclosing public commitments, risks, and expected returns.

Summary

The shift to public/private development evolved from the efforts of local government to manage the redevelopment process with greater control than that afforded by regulatory strategies and arm's length relationships with private developers. The success of public/private development has made it an important strategy for stimulating local economic development and financing selected items of capital infrastructure. It is also a means of implementing complex redevelopment projects. The highly visible record of public/private projects in the 1980s reshaped the landscape of downtowns across the country. The tangible results of this type of development approach contrasted sharply with the legacy of political controversy, acres of cleared but eerily vacant land, and years of frustration that had resulted from failed urban renewal projects developed under a strategy of command and control. The strong record offers tangible evidence that the public/private approach is a pragmatic solution to the earlier bureaucratic problems that beset the federal urban renewal program, proving that it is a strategy extremely well suited for coping with the complexity and risks of attracting the types of projects officials have wanted to revitalize their cities. Consequently, city governments, public authorities, and other special-purpose agencies have strong incentives to continue forging relationships with developers who understand, from observation and experience, how to play by the new rules.

The public financing environment for public/private development is tougher today, however. On the public side, local government continues to operate on its own. The 1986 revisions to federal tax legislation cut back the availability of tax-exempt financing for private-purpose projects, while budget cutbacks in discretionary spending have reduced even further the funds available for domestic programs. On the private side, during the first half of the 1990s, depressed fundamentals of supply and demand in most product markets, as well as an overall lack of capital for the industry in general meant that development opportunities were few and far between. Yet these conditions—the need for inventive responses to fiscal pressures and shared resources for risky ventures—were not unlike those that gave rise to widespread use of the public/private strategy. High-priority public/private projects did succeed in getting off the drawing boards, particularly when political support and leadership were present.

The future is likely to differ in the scope and focus of urban public/private development activity—in the type and locus of such project initiatives. Building on past experience, much of which was concentrated on large-scale building of downtowns, cities are likely to focus more on smaller-scale projects targeted at rebuilding neighborhoods and a continued strategy of seeking job-based economic development. In turn, there is little reason to expect that the drive for off-budget financing of public infrastructure and civic amenities among suburban governments will abate. Land-owning public authorities as well are likely to continue to pursue efforts to capture value through joint development. Hence, even if the market is more demanding, the motives for pursuing public/private development remain strong. That fewer opportunities may exist will only make that handful of opportunities the intense focus of limited resources for both public and private sector players.

Given that the management of development from the public perspective is so difficult, public bodies should do everything within their power to facilitate strong and consistent management. Particularly important is coordinating all public agencies to avoid undue time delays.

Terms

- Disposition and development agreement
- Financing gap

- Investment tax credits
- Joint development
- Land leasing
- Leveraging
- Municipal bonds
- Public/private development
- Quasi-public
- RFP
- RFQ
- UDAG
- Urban renewal
- Value capture

Review Questions

14.1 What are the opportunities for working in a public/private partnership for a city? For a developer? What are some of the practical problems or points of tension in such a business relationship?

14.2 Describe the five key decisions the public sector faces in implementing a public/private project.

14.3 Why is city assistance, both financial and organizational, needed to facilitate public/private development projects?

14.4 The Vermont-Slauson Shopping Center is considered a prototype for neighborhood retailing services in inner-city locations. What are the special issues that such a shopping center faces, and how did the Vermont-Slauson Economic Development Corporation deal with them?

14.5 What are some of the financial techniques that cities can use and have used to accomplish their goals for revitalization and for reducing their risk?

Notes

1. Robert Witherspoon, *Codevelopment: City Rebuilding by Business and Government* (Washington, D.C.: ULI–the Urban Land Institute, 1982).

2. See Lynne B. Sagalyn, "Explaining the Improbable: Local Redevelopment in the Wake of Federal Cutbacks," *Journal of the American Planning Association,* 1990, pp. 429–41.

3. For a more complete description of Coldspring, see *ULI Project Reference File,* Vol. 9, No. 9, April–June 1979.

4. For a more complete description of the Gallery, see *ULI Project Reference File,* Vol. 8, No. 4, January–March 1978.

5. For a more complete description of the Emily Morgan Hotel, see *ULI Project Reference File,* Vol. 16, No. 20, October–December 1986.

6. Richard F. Babcock, "The City as Entrepreneur: Fiscal Wisdom or Regulatory Folly?" in *City Deal Making,* ed. Terry Jill Lassar (Washington, D.C.: ULI–the Urban Land Institute, 1990), pp. 9–43; and Ralph J. Basile, Jim Furr, and Charles Thomsen, "Leveraging Privatization in Real Estate Development," *Urban Land,* January 1987, pp. 6–11.

7. ULI–the Urban Land Institute with Gladstone Associates, *Joint Development: Making the Real Estate–Transit Connection* (Washington, D.C.: ULI–the Urban Land Institute, 1979).

8. Witherspoon, *Codevelopment,* pp. 8–9.

9. Babcock, "The City as Entrepreneur," p. 14.

10. For a detailed discussion of the steps involved in the process of joint development, see Witherspoon, *Codevelopment.*

11. Empirical studies of auction dispositions for housing in both Boston and New York, for instance, revealed critical limitations—low levels of rehabilitation investment and immediate property tax recidivism. See Christine A. Flynn and Lawrence P. Goldman, *New York's Largest Landowner: The City as Owner, Planner, and Marketer of Real Estate,* Report for the Fund for the City of New York, 1980; and H. James Brown and Christopher E. Herbert, "Local Government Real Estate Asset Management," unpublished report for Lincoln Institute for Land Policy Seminar, September 1989.

12. See Witherspoon, *Codevelopment,* p. 18; and ULI–the Urban Land Institute, *Downtown Development Handbook,* 2d ed. (Washington, D.C.: Author, 1992), pp. 41–43, for an extended discussion.

13. The infusion of cash can be duplicated with prepayment of rent, and the risk of nonpayment can be nearly eliminated with the purchase of a riskless government security, as was the case for Copley Place, a large-scale mixed-use project in Boston.

14. See Lynne B. Sagalyn, "Leasing: The Strategic Option for Public Development," Working Paper (Cambridge, Mass.: Lincoln Institute of Land Policy, 1993); Robert Wetmore and Chris Klinger, "Land Leases: More Than Rent Schedules," *Urban Land,* June 1990, pp. 6–9; and Lynne B. Sagalyn, "Negotiating Public Benefits: The Bargaining Calculus of Public/Private Development," *Urban Studies,* December 1997, pp. 1955–70.

15. Community Redevelopment Agency of the City of Los Angeles, "Development Offering: Remaining 8.75 Acres of Bunker Hill, Downtown Los Angeles," September 1979.

16. See ULI, *Downtown Development Handbook,* 2d ed., pp. 55–70.

17. Bernard Frieden and Lynne B. Sagalyn, *Downtown, Inc.: How America Rebuilds Cities* (Cambridge, Mass.: MIT Press, 1989).

18. Lynne B. Sagalyn, "Measuring Financial Returns When the City Acts as an Investor: Boston and Faneuil Hall Marketplace," *Real Estate Issues,* Fall/Winter 1989, pp. 7–15.

19. Lynne B. Sagalyn, "Public Profit Sharing: Symbol or Substance?" in *City Deal Making,* ed. Lassar, pp. 139–53.

20. See ULI, *Downtown Development Handbook,* 2d ed.

21. David C. Petersen, *Sports, Convention, and Entertainment Facilities* (Washington, D.C.: ULI–the Urban Land Institute, 1996).

22. See Jacques Gordon, "Horton Plaza, San Diego: A Case Study of Public/Private Development," Working Paper No. 2 (Cambridge, Mass.: MIT Center for Real Estate Development, 1985).

23. See Frieden and Sagalyn, *Downtown, Inc.,* pp. 140–42, for a more complete description of Town Square; and *ULI Project Reference File,* Vol. 11, No. 15, July–September 1981.

24. In the case of percentage rent, lenders hesitate because they fear a reduction in the amount of income to be capitalized when a large percentage of the income stream is committed to a ground lessor. In the event of foreclosure, the valuation impact would be substantial unless the lessor had agreed to subordinate the percentage provision in the lease. For a detailed case discussion, see ULI, *Joint Development,* pp. 76–81.

25. Lassar, *City Deal Making,* p. 3.

26. Ibid.

Chapter 15

Affordable Housing

For most U.S. citizens, adequate housing is no longer an important issue. Most are well housed, and the problems confronting those who are not—except in the case of the homeless—are not highly visible. Some critics, however, say that the United States is rapidly becoming a nation of housing haves and have-nots. The number of homeless is escalating beyond any city's ability to care for them, and young married couples who in the past could always plan on buying a small starter home must now defer that dream because of the sky-rocketing costs of housing and financing. Although the inflation in housing prices is well below the double-digit inflation that characterized the 1970s and early to mid-1980s and the overall affordability indices indicate benign conditions, the lower tier of house prices nonetheless remains high by historical standards.

This chapter introduces and looks at the concept of affordable housing through the lenses of both the public and private sectors. This type of development, formerly infeasible for private developers without massive direct government subsidies, can now be quite attractive to private developers as the result of a combination of new tax and risk-sharing incentives. The chapter also discusses the nature and extent of the problem of affordability, outlines some current activities and policy considerations, and discusses ongoing public and/or private efforts to increase the supply of affordable housing (see Figure 15-1). It looks in depth at the following topics:

- A definition of affordable housing;
- The evolving roles of federal, state, and local governments, and of the private sector;
- Low-income rental housing; and
- Affordable ownership housing.

A Definition of Affordable Housing

Because it is so broad, the term "affordable housing" might mean different things to different people. Some define affordable housing generally as housing that has not risen rapidly in price over the last several years. Others think of affordability in terms of houses that young people entering the housing market for the first time can buy. Some might equate affordability with rental rather than with for-sale housing, and still others consider affordable housing synonymous with government-subsidized housing or even with public housing. In fact, the term encompasses a wide spectrum of housing types, housing prices, and housing occupants.

As a general rule, housing can be considered affordable for a low- or moderate-income household if that household can acquire use of that housing unit (owned or rented) for an amount up to 30 percent of its household income.[1]

The standard for determining affordability in federal housing programs is also used by mortgage lenders as one important criterion in qualifying buyers of market-rate housing for mortgage loans. Home sellers and their real estate agents generally do not seriously consider potential homebuyers if the price of a home is more than two and one-half to three times a prospective borrower's

---

This chapter was written by Mary Boehling Schwartz, former senior practice associate, ULI, based on a chapter written for the first edition of this book by Diane R. Suchman, consultant.

Figure 15-1

Public Policy Issues

Several key policy issues must be addressed in formulating a response to the extensive, complex, and difficult problems associated with affordable housing.

Achieving a Consensus for Action

The problem must be recognized and its key components and priority needs agreed to, including what, if any, responsibility the public must assume.

Allocating Scarce Resources

How should scarce funds be allocated to provide assistance? Who should receive assistance, how much, and in what form? What are reasonable goals? Should few households be provided with sufficient resources, or should the same dollar amount be stretched or leveraged to reach a greater number of households with smaller subsidies?

Roles and Responsibilities

What are the appropriate roles for the federal, state, and local governments and for the private sector, including non-profits? What impact will devolution—the passing down of responsibility from the federal to state governments—have on the production of affordable housing and vouchers for families who need to obtain market-rate housing? How and to what extent should the poor be empowered to decide for themselves how their needs can best be met? How can the participation of the parties be encouraged, sustained, and coordinated?

Related Issues

Maximization of financial resources. We must identify, generate, and/or tap additional sources of funding and find ways to leverage available funds. We must find the means to streamline and simplify the financing of low-income housing so that an efficient and replicable delivery system can be established.

Supporting physical and social services. Without supportive services and programs for revitalization, physical shelter deteriorates rapidly and does little to improve the lives of the poor. Related issues such as inadequate income, education, job training, drug counseling, security, and medical and social services must be addressed if goals for housing are to succeed.

Populations with special needs. Certain population groups—the elderly, the disabled, single-parent households, rural households, immigrants, the homeless—have special needs that cannot be adequately met by policies and programs designed for more typical populations.

Preservation of low-income housing. The preservation of low-income housing is particularly critical through 2002, when contracts between owners and HUD on federally subsidized housing units expire. What incentives can Congress extend to owners to ensure that the units are not converted to market-rate housing with rents pushed beyond the reach of the nation's low- and moderate-income households? How can the debt on these properties be restructured to make it financially feasible for owners to maintain them in the low-cost housing stock while at the same time minimizing the claims to the FHA fund? Once constructed and operating, how can low-income housing be preserved to ensure its long-term affordability and to avoid rapid deterioration and decay? Where will funds for operation and maintenance come from? Where will funds for capital expenditures come from? How can commitments to long-term affordability best be ensured?

Responsiveness versus efficiency. How can the tension between the need for local solutions and responsiveness to social goals and the need for systemization and efficient production be resolved?

Subsidies for middle- and upper-income owners. As many advocates of low-income housing point out, the groups receiving the largest federal subsidy are middle- and upper-income homeowners—through the income tax deduction for interest paid on home mortgages. The U.S. Office of Management and Budget estimates that the revenue forgone to the U.S. Treasury as a result of the deductibility of mortgage interest on up to $1 million in principal on home mortgage debt will exceed $297 billion between 1999 and 2003.* The elimination of this deduction has been a major part of the housing policy debate for decades, leading to the capping of the mortgage interest deduction in the late 1980s. Although its complete annihilation is extremely unlikely, the subsidy will likely be the subject of lively debate well into the future. Other substantial subsidies to middle- and upper-income owners include the deductibility from federal income taxes of state and local property taxes on owner-occupied homes, estimated to be $100.5 billion between 1999 and 2003, and the exclusion of capital gains on home sales, estimated to be $51 billion between 1999 and 2003.* This latter subsidy will be even deeper in future years as legislation that passed in 1997 virtually eliminated the payment on any capital gains on home sales for most taxpayers. ■

*U.S. Office of Management and Budget, *Budget of the U.S. Government, Fiscal Year 1999: Analytical Perspectives*, p. 91.

income, with this two and one-half to three times standard derived from the 30 percent ratio.

According to the 30 percent standard, then, the term "affordable housing" can apply to any income group. As a practical matter, however, discussions of public policy usually restrict affordability to:

- Low-income rental housing—housing that requires subsidies for production or for occupants or both to make it affordable to low- and very-low-income households; or
- Affordable ownership housing—market-rate, unsubsidized housing for moderate-income households, particularly first-time buyers, and subsidized ownership housing for low- and moderate-income homebuyers.

A social problem occurs when a gap exists between the cost of housing and what those in need of housing can afford to pay. All indicators of expenditures and household budgets show that the largest share of a low- to moderate-income household's earnings goes toward housing. Because housing is generally the first claim on income, households with limited incomes often cannot afford other necessities, like food, medication, insurance, and savings. Affordable housing can increase the amount of household income available for these other necessities.

The 30 percent definition for affordable housing suffers from serious limitations when applied to low-income households. The 30 percent standard ignores variations in the size of families. An individual with an income of $15,000 per year might be able to find adequate market-rate housing within the 30 percent standard, while a family of eight with the same income might not. (It must be noted, however, that although the affordability standard does not consider family or household size, the income limits for household eligibility for U.S. Department of Housing and Urban Development [HUD] programs are adjusted from a four-person base according to household size. Additional adjustments to income limits for program eligibility reflect unusually high- or low-income areas or high or low housing costs.) Other sliding scale standards of affordability for low- and moderate-income households base the share of income that a household can comfortably spend on housing on both the size and income of the household. HUD programs, however, do not use the sliding scale standards—perhaps because of the difficulty in administering programs tied to so many definitions of affordability.

From the perspective of public policy, another problem with the 30 percent standard in determining whether a given geographic area contains an adequate supply of affordable housing is that the standard compares only numbers of households at various levels of income with

The Knolls, located in Orange County, California, is a public/private effort that transformed this once blighted neighborhood into 260 units of rehabilitated affordable townhouse apartments. By issuing tax-exempt financing, selling tax credits, and using a combination of grants and low-interest loans from the Orange County Redevelopment Agency, the project achieved a 17 percent return on investment in its first year.

The 8,000-square-foot recreation center at Eden Palms Housing in San Jose, California, contains a daycare center, computer lab, teen lounge, and multipurpose room for residents' use. The developer, Eden Palms Associates, used a $550,000 affordable housing grant and federal low-income housing tax credits to generate $12 million in equity to provide 145 units of affordable rental housing.

numbers of housing units at the prices or rents these households can afford. It fails to consider that the notion of access to housing also implies a certain amount of choice in housing types and locations so that various needs, particularly the commute to work, can be accommodated. Studies have shown that minority households of the same income level as nonminority households often pay higher prices for housing because of limited access and choice. Thus, a simple comparison of the number of households at a given income level with the number of housing units that households at these income levels can afford is inadequate in capturing the problem of affordability faced by many minority households as a result of discrimination in housing markets. Nonminority low- and moderate-income households are also susceptible to limited housing choices and limited access, often because of a community's preconceived negative notions about those households. These forms of discrimination, whether overt (and blatantly illegal) or covert (and difficult to document in court), are beyond the scope of this chapter. It is important to keep in mind that discrimination or "steering" by sellers, real estate agents, brokers, leasing agents, lenders, mortgage insurers, or the secondary market can limit the effective supply of housing available to certain households. More subtly, affluent communities might rely on socially and legally acceptable arguments to fight the development of nearby lower-cost housing, even though the underlying force behind their arguments could in fact be veiled racial discrimination.[2]

Although the provision of all types of affordable housing requires a creative search for reduced costs at every step of the process, increasing the supply of low-income rental housing usually demands that governments and

developers generally seek below-market financing and direct subsidies as well as take advantage of available tax expenditure programs, such as low-income housing tax credits and municipal tax-exempt bonds. To produce affordable ownership housing, on the other hand, the general approach is to minimize the direct costs of development: land, land development, and construction. These differences are explored throughout this chapter.

Changing Roles

The Federal Government

In the early part of the 20th century, production of housing at all levels was considered an activity of the private sector. The federal government's role was limited to expediting mortgage lending associated with homeownership. From the Great Depression through 1980, however, the history of the federal government's involvement in housing—through financial assistance to producers and occupants, direct production, tax incentives, insurance and credit programs, specialized thrift institutions, the creation of a secondary market, and neighborhood revitalization programs—was one of expanding responsibility. Especially during the 1970s, federal housing programs supported massive production of low-income housing.

Housing policy shifted dramatically beginning in the late 1970s. Between 1978 and 1990, the federal government systematically dismantled its housing production programs and withdrew funding support for affordable housing. Federal authorizations for housing dropped by 70 percent between 1978 and 1989 (see Figure 15-2).

The government's retreat from affordable housing is more clearly revealed in HUD's budget when the effect of inflation is removed. In 1978, at the peak of federal spending for housing, the budget authority reached $73.8 billion. By 1980, direct spending for housing was only $54.1 billion, but, by 1990, spending dropped to only $13.7 billion—less than one-fifth its 1978 level.

This trend has now reversed. The National Affordable Housing Act (NAHA) of 1990 renewed the federal government's commitment to housing, as evidenced in Fig-

Figure 15-2

Federal Spending for Housing: 1976 to 2003

(Billions of Dollars)

Year	Current Dollars		Constant (1998) Dollars	
	Budget Authority	Outlays	Budget Authority	Outlays
1976	$19.5	$ 3.2	$51.4	$ 6.3
1977	28.6	3.0	70.0	7.3
1978	32.3	3.7	73.8	8.4
1979	24.8	4.4	52.3	9.2
1980	27.9	5.6	54.1	10.9
1981	26.9	7.8	47.5	13.7
1982	14.6	8.7	24.1	14.4
1983	10.5	10.0	16.5	15.7
1984	12.7	11.3	19.2	17.1
1985	26.9	25.3	39.4	37.0
1986	11.6	12.4	16.6	17.7
1987	9.9	12.7	13.7	17.5
1988	9.7	13.9	13.0	18.7
1989	9.6	14.7	12.3	18.9
1990	11.1	15.9	13.7	19.6
1991	19.7	17.2	23.3	20.3
1992	19.7	18.9	22.7	21.7
1993	21.2	21.5	23.7	24.1
1994	21.1	23.9	23.1	26.1
1995	15.3	27.5	16.3	29.3
1996	16.4	26.8	17.1	27.9
1997	11.7	27.8	12.0	28.3
1998*	19.8	28.8	19.8	28.8
1999*	20.4	28.8	20.0	28.2
2000*	24.2	29.2	23.2	28.0
2001*	25.1	29.1	23.6	27.3
2002*	26.3	28.8	24.2	26.5
2003*	27.5	28.7	24.8	25.8

*Estimated.

Note: HUD's budget authority in a given year is the budget that Congress passes in that year; funds are then appropriated based on the congressionally approved budget. Funds appropriated to HUD each year are actually spent over five- to 20-year periods. Thus, outlays can actually rise while budget authority is declining, which is what happened during the 1980s.

Source: National Low-Income Housing Coalition calculations of housing data contained in U.S. Office of Management and Budget FY 1999 Budget CD-ROM, Tables 3.2 and 5.1.

Figure 15-3

Tax-Exempt Bond Financing

Tax-exempt bonds issued by state or local governments have helped finance the development of low-income multifamily housing. Issuers sell bonds to investors whose income from such investments is exempt from federal—and, in most cases, state—income taxes. Consequently, issuers can market bonds at lower-than-conventional interest rates. Issuers usually seek a bond rating from one of the rating agencies (Standard & Poor's or Moody's, for example) whose credit rating further reduces the interest rate payable on the debt. Issuers might also use some form of credit enhancement to obtain a higher rating based on the credit enhancer's credit from the rating agencies. Such credit enhancement is also needed to provide liquidity if the debt is variable rate. For example, the bond issue could be secured by either a letter of credit or bond insurance. A letter of credit gives the bonds the same rating as the bank issuing the letter.

The Tax Reform Act of 1986 restricts the range of private uses eligible for tax-exempt funding and reduces the annual volume of bonds that may be issued for the remaining permitted uses. Most private-purpose bonds, including bonds for ownership and rental housing, are subject to unified state-by-state volume ceilings equal to the greater of $50.00 per resident or $150 million. That is, they are subject to the unified private activity bond volume cap. Therefore, housing must compete with alternative private uses, like economic development projects and student loans, for this limited resource. Before passage of the Tax Reform Act of 1986, multifamily housing bonds were not limited, while the separate cap for mortgage revenue bonds was

higher in many states than is the unified volume cap on bonds for all permitted private activities combined. Projects financed with tax-exempt bonds that use low-income housing tax credits are subject to this unified private activity bond volume cap rather than to the volume cap for tax credits (discussed in Figure 15-4). As a result of increasingly fierce competition for tax credit allocations, project owners have opted for tax-exempt financing to avoid the "beauty contest." Now, even tax-exempt bond allocation has become more competitive.

Under the Tax Reform Act of 1986, public agencies may issue a tax-exempt bond if a Section 501(c)(3) tax-exempt entity uses the proceeds for its exempt purposes and complies with other restrictions. Such an organization can use the bond proceeds to develop or acquire housing that it will own. The bonds are not subject to the volume cap applicable to most multifamily bonds. Each Section 501(c)(3) organization can use up to $150 million of bonds issued for housing on its behalf. The bonds tend to sell at an interest rate that is about 25 basis points lower than other tax-exempt bonds, as interest on the bonds is not a tax preference subject to the alternative minimum tax. One potential disadvantage of these bonds, however, is that these projects do not qualify for low-income housing tax credits. ■

Source: **Updated from Diane R. Suchman et al.,** *Public/Private Housing Partnerships* **(Washington, D.C.: ULI—the Urban Land Institute, 1990), p. 15.**

---

ure 15-2. Between 1989 and 1993, federal authorizations for housing (current dollars) rose from $9.6 billion to $21.2 billion—an increase of 120 percent. HUD's budget shows a flattening during the mid-1990s as HUD restructured many of its multifamily programs to reduce the risk and restore the financial soundness of its loan portfolio.

Some of the losses in federal spending for housing are expected to be restored into the new millennium. By 2003, HUD's budget authority is expected to reach nearly $28 billion (current dollars)—a level not achieved since 1980.[3] Nonetheless, the funding levels for housing are uncertain and subject to the vagaries of congressional appropriations. What *is* fairly certain is that the levels of the late 1970s will not soon be reached again, as the federal government turns more toward tax expen-

diture programs, state and local government programs, and the private sector for the provision of affordable housing.

Although HUD generally operates through direct spending programs, the U.S. Department of the Treasury was arguably even more instrumental in the provision of affordable housing, through its tax expenditure programs, during the 1990s. Private developers competed fiercely for allocations from two tax expenditure programs: tax-exempt bonds (see Figure 15-3) and low-income housing tax credits (see Figure 15-4). With increasing use of tax-exempt bonds and the tax credits to finance low-income rental housing, losses to the Treasury accruing to housing expenditures will increase into the new millennium. Between 1999 and 2003, the

Figure 15-4

Low-Income Housing Tax Credits: Changing the Project Economics

To encourage production of low-income housing, the Tax Reform Act of 1986 authorized a ten-year federal income tax credit for investments in mixed- or low-income rental housing to replace the abolished incentives of the Economic Recovery Tax Act (ERTA) of 1981. Incentives for the real estate sector under ERTA included accelerated depreciation rates for real property, shorter useful lives, five-year amortization of expenses for rehabilitation, and a full write-off of interest and taxes during the construction period. By 1986, the economy had recovered and ERTA was no longer needed to stimulate the economy. Not wishing to eliminate the positive side effect ERTA had on the production of affordable housing, lawmakers introduced the low-income housing tax credit in the 1986 tax legislation.

The tax credit offers investors one of two levels of benefit. Over a ten-year period, it returns either 70 percent or 30 percent of the costs (present value of total eligible development costs) of the investments in qualifying units, depending on the size of the credit. For properties placed in service in 1987, the credit percentages were fixed at 9 percent (credit against federal income tax liability) for eligible expenditures in new buildings and at 4 percent for eligible expenditures in existing buildings or buildings constructed using 50 percent or more of tax-exempt bond financing (see Figure 15-3). Investors receive the credit annually for ten years. The size of the credit can be fixed or can float until the time the property is placed in service, and is based on an average of federal interest rates. Therefore, actual rates may vary; that is, the 9 percent credit may actually be 8.65, and the 4 percent credit may actually be 3.71, for example.

The pool of credits is limited. Each state receives an annual allocation of tax credits that represents $1.25 per capita. States can also receive additional credits through a reallocation of a national pool of unused credits at the end of each year. Unused credits, however, are becoming very scarce. Developers/investors must apply to state hous-

ing finance agencies, or other designated allocators of the credits, in a competitive process, demonstrating that their proposed properties meet an array of federal requirements for setasides and rent restrictions. Tax credit properties that are more than 50 percent financed with federally tax-exempt housing bonds do not need to apply for tax credit allocation but do need to receive volume cap bond allocations for the issuance of the bonds (see Figure 15-5).

An important caveat pertains to investors who do not intend to maintain the property in the low-income stock over the long haul. If the elected percentage of units for low- and very-low-income tenants is not maintained for 15 years, the tax credit investor must pay interest and a penalty and repay part of the tax savings of the credits (which is also considered preference income for the alternative minimum tax).

Applying the Low-Income Housing Tax Credit to the Multifamily Rental Property in Figure 15-5

For a property to qualify for the credit, one of two set-aside requirements must be met. At least 20 percent of the units must be set aside for very-low-income families (those earning 50 percent or less of the area median income), or at least 40 percent of the units must be reserved for other low-income families (those earning less than 60 percent of the area median income). The proportion of eligible development, rehabilitation, and acquisition costs that qualifies as the basis for the credits is called the *applicable fraction* and is determined by the lower of the following calculations:

$$\frac{\text{Number of very-low- and low-income occupied units}}{\text{Total units}}$$

or

$$\frac{\text{Square footage in low- and very-low-income units}}{\text{Total residential square footage.}}$$

continued on next page

total revenue loss is expected to be nearly $12 billion for the tax credit program and nearly $10 billion for the tax-exempt bonds for rental housing and mortgage revenue bonds combined. The estimates are high because expectations are that private developers will use these programs extensively in the coming years. (Figure 15-5 discusses the economics of a typical multifamily rental project as affected by the programs discussed in Figures 15-3 and 15-4.)

State and Local Governments' Expanding Roles

Devolution in housing is occurring at a rapid rate, with the federal government's looking increasingly to state and local governments to provide decent and affordable housing for the populace. Project-based Section 8 federal programs for new construction and substantial rehabilitation have been dead since the early

Figure 15-4

Low-Income Housing Tax Credits: Changing the Project Economics (continued)

Because 80 percent of the units (square footage, as all units are the same size) in the prototypical 100-unit multi-family housing development in Figure 15-5 were reserved for households with incomes below 60 percent (but above 50 percent) of the area median family income and the remaining 20 percent of the units were reserved for house-holds with incomes below 50 percent, the setaside require-ment is met, and even exceeded, and the proportion of eligible costs that qualifies for the tax credit is determined as follows:

$$\frac{[80 \text{ units reserved for low-income families}] + [20 \text{ units reserved for very-low-income families}]}{100 \text{ total units}} =$$

100% of total development costs.

Calculating the Credit Based on the Qualified Basis of the Property

Certain items are subtracted from the total development cost to arrive at the eligible basis on which to calculate the tax credit. Some of these items include land costs (which are not depreciable), costs to develop any commercial space in the project, ineligible soft costs, grants, federal loans, and capitalized operating expenses (marketing ex-penses, deficit escrows, for example). Assume the developer of the hypothetical project in Figure 15-5 is not pursuing grants or federally subsidized financing and there are no ineligible soft costs. (In actuality, there would be some soft costs and likely some form of federal subsidy that must be subtracted from the development cost to arrive at the eli-gible basis. Thus, these numbers are for illustration only.) Further, assume that land cost constitutes 15 percent of the total development cost of $9,133,261. The amount of credit allocated to the property would then be calculated as follows:

Total Development Cost	$9,133,261
− Land Cost (15% of Total Development Cost)	− $1,369,989
= Eligible Basis[a]	= $7,763,272
× Applicable Fraction	× 100%
= Qualified Basis for Credit	= $7,763,272
× Percentage for New Building	× 0.09
= Yearly Income Tax Credit	= $698,694.

[a]Developers who produce affordable rental housing in difficult develop-ment areas (metropolitan and nonmetropolitan counties where construction, land, and utility costs are high relative to incomes) and qualified census tracts (census tracts in which at least 50 percent of the households have incomes less than 60 percent of the area median gross income, per HUD) may claim a higher eligible basis (130 percent of ordinary basis).

If the property in Figure 15-5 were an existing prop-erty, the calculation for the credit would be as follows:

Eligible Basis	$7,763,272
× Applicable Fraction	× 100%
= Qualified Basis for Credit	= $7,763,272
× Percentage for Existing or New Federally Subsidized Building	× 0.04
= Yearly Income Tax Credit	= $310,530.

In the case of both the 9 percent and 4 percent credits, the $7,763,272 of the eligible basis can also be depreci-ated, though over 27.5 years at the straight-line rate of 3.92 percent, as the Tax Reform Act of 1986 eliminated accelerated depreciation schedules.

The yearly income tax credit of $698,694 (or $310,530 in the case of the 4 percent credit) can be used to reduce tax liability on both wages and portfolio income when an investor is considered an active participant rather than a passive investor as defined by tax law. Loss limitations on passive income then mean that typical investors are cor-porations that are not subject to such limitations.

1980s. Many state and local governments have picked up the slack and now administer similar programs. Still, the federal government has the ability to redistrib-ute resources effectively, while states and localities can draw only from within their own boundaries. As Anthony Downs of the Brookings Institution observed, "If local jurisdictions tax the rich to serve the poor, the rich can —and often do—move elsewhere."

Although not all states and localities have yet risen to the challenge of devising or identifying resources for housing, the range of responses to date demonstrates determination, creativity, and considerable success in tapping into existing resources and/or creating new ones. Indeed, data from the American Housing Survey for the United States for 1987, 1989, 1991, 1993, 1995, and 1997 suggest that state and local governments are grad-

Computing the Maximum Annual Tax Credit Based on Need

Calculating the annual tax credit based on the eligible basis alone can cause properties to capitalize excess development fees by leveraging more debt and equity than are actually needed to make the project economics work. In fact, most developers/investors are able to secure subsidized or conventional loans, find equity investors, and/or receive federal grants to make the project economics work. These sources of financing all lower the amount of equity required and thus the amount of the credit needed to make the numbers work. To prevent excess capitalization, the IRS requires developers/investors to compute the "equity gap." The "maximum sufficient annual credit" then would be that credit just necessary to fill this gap in financing.

Take the property in Figure 15-5, for example, with its financing gap after accounting for the maximum supportable loan (or, alternatively, the total equity required) of $6,498,320. Further, assume that equity interests command the hypothetical price of $0.70 per credit dollar.[b] The calculation of the equity gap and maximum sufficient annual tax credit would be as follows:

Total Equity Required	$6,498,320
× Percent of Qualified Units	× 100%
= Equity Required for Qualified Units (Equity Gap)	= $6,498,320
÷ Investor Price per Credit	÷ $0.70
= Total Ten-Year Credit Stream	= $9,283,314
÷ Number of Credit Years	÷ 10
= Maximum Sufficient Annual Credit	= $928,331.

As the maximum sufficient annual credit is higher than the tax credit, the tax credit of $698,694 is allowed.

[b]The determination of tax credit prices is based on the present value to an investor of a $1.00 tax credit some time in the future. Clearly, an investor would be unwilling to pay $1.00 today for a $1.00 tax credit tomorrow or, more important, ten years in the future because of the risks (interest rate risk, inflation risk, etc.) involved. How much less is determined by the market, largely by the yields on alternative investments, expectations of cash flows on the property, and so forth. Prices are negotiated between developers and tax credit investors.

Determining the Amount of Equity That Can Be Raised

How much equity can be raised with this $698,694 annual credit? The amount is calculated as follows:

Annual Tax Credit Amount	$698,694
× 10-Year Stream of Credit	× 10
× Investor Price per Credit	× $0.70
= Equity Investment	= $4,890,858.

Closing the Gap

Will the equity be sufficient to close the financing gap on the property in Figure 15-5? The calculation of the remaining financing gap, after accounting for the equity that can be raised by selling tax credits, is as follows:

Loan	$2,634,941
+ Tax Credit Financing	+ 4,890,858
= Total Financing	= $7,525,799
÷ Total Development Cost	÷ $9,133,261
= Financing as Percentage of Total Development Cost	= 82%
100% − Financing as Percentage of Total Development Cost = Financing Gap	= 18%.

Although the financing gap has been narrowed considerably from 71 percent to 18 percent by the sale of ownership interests in the tax credit property, it has not been eliminated altogether. Therefore, the developer may need

continued on next page

ually assuming larger roles in the provision of housing for their poorest households. The number of poverty-level renters assisted through rent reductions attributable to state and local subsidies rose from 314,000 in 1987 to 380,000 in 1995.

The history of state and local governments' assistance to poverty-level homeowners has been less straightforward. In 1987, state and local housing programs provided assistance to 220,000 poverty-level homeowners; by 1991, the number of assisted poverty-level homeowners had risen to 314,000. By 1997, however, only 263,000 poverty-level homeowners used lower-cost mortgages available from state and local housing programs. Whether this reduction represents a retreat by state and local governments as they increasingly target limited resources to the neediest renting households

Figure 15-4

Low-Income Housing Tax Credits: Changing the Project Economics (continued)

to look for more favorable loan terms or some public subsidies, or put up the equity himself to finance the project. (The role of subsidized financing in closing the gap is discussed in Figure 15-3.)

If, on the other hand, the price of tax credits were higher than the $0.70 hypothesized above, then it is possible that the gap could be eliminated altogether. Now, calculate the amount of equity that can be raised if the price of tax credits rose to $0.93.

Annual Tax Credit Amount	$698,694
× 10-Year Stream of Credit	× 10
× Investor Price per Credit	× $0.93
= Equity Investment	= $6,497,854
+ Loan	+ $2,634,941
= Total Financing	= $9,132,795
Total Development Cost	$9,133,261
Total Financing as Percentage of Total Development Cost	100%

Thus, at any price above $0.93 per tax credit dollar, the financing gap will be closed. It must be noted, however, that this price is unrealistic, and it was used only to illustrate how, at the right price, tax credit financing can close the gap. In actuality, the market price of tax credits ranges from around $0.70 to $0.76.

Outlook for the Program

The regulations governing use of the credit are complex and discouraged its early application. In recent years, however, a better understanding of the applicability of the credit has augmented the low-income housing stock. According to the National Council of State Housing Finance Agencies, more than 100,000 low-income housing units have been produced annually since 1989. Altogether, more than 800,000 units of low-income housing have been developed, rehabilitated, or acquired since 1986. Estimates by the U.S. General Accounting Office are somewhat lower. Between 1992 and 1994, GAO estimates that 172,000 units, or roughly 60,000 units per year, in 4,100 projects were financed with tax credits.

Because the tax credit is a tax expenditure rather than an annual revenue appropriation, it is less susceptible to the vagaries of the congressional budget process, arguably making it a more stable source of funding for the production of affordable housing than various HUD programs. The Office of Management and Budget estimated that in 1997 the loss of revenue to the Treasury as a result of the credit was $2.3 billion, about the same as the loss of revenue from the exclusion from taxes of interest on owner-occupied mortgage subsidy bonds ($1.75 billion) and rental housing bonds ($810 million) combined. (It is important to note that this loss is small when compared with the drain on the Treasury of nearly $50 billion attributable to the deduction for home mortgage interest available to all homeowners.) Congress has extended the tax credit indefinitely. A continuing healthy economy, flourishing tax revenues, and the successful track record of the low-income housing tax credit bode well for its continuation. ■

Sources: Adapted from *Financing Multifamily Housing Using Section 42 Low-Income Housing Tax Credits*, ULI Research Working Paper Series No. 654, August 1996; and *Budget of the United States Government: Analytical Perspectives—Fiscal Year 1999*, U.S. Office of Management and Budget.

---

or the decrease is attributable to waning demand cannot be discerned from the data.

State and local government activities and legislation can actually impede rather than promote the provision of affordable housing if left unchecked. Overregulation can drive up land and production costs, pushing home prices and rents out of reach of low-, moderate-, and, in some cases, middle-income households. Zoning can often exclude certain households from living in given areas. But when state and local zoning and land use regulations, such as the slow-growth initiatives springing up around the country, impede rather than promote affordable housing, the federal government can dangle carrots before states and localities. A central requirement of the NAHA calls for all jurisdictions wishing to participate in many federal housing programs and ultimately to receive federal housing assistance to develop a Comprehensive Housing Affordability Strategy (CHAS). Funds are distributed based on the relative housing needs of the participating jurisdictions as illustrated in the strategy. Proposed federal legislation will go even farther by demanding an impact analysis of all proposed state and local land use regulations on the supply of affordable housing. The carrot of federal monies will undoubtedly go a long way toward increasing state and local government involvement as state governments vie for limited federal resources.

Private Sector Initiatives

The private sector is increasingly being called on to pinch-hit, and many participants have stepped up to the plate. Spurred on by low-income housing tax credits and tax-exempt rental housing bonds, for-profit developers are finding many opportunities in the development of affordable housing.

The challenges are also great. As can be seen in Figures 15-3, 15-4, and 15-5, getting an affordable housing project to fly can test even the savviest financier. Meeting the challenge, nonprofit housing developers such as community development corporations (CDCs) are producing record numbers of affordable homes, often in conjunction with for-profit developers. Many charities and foundations, including the Fannie Mae Foundation, the Freddie Mac Foundation, the Ford Foundation, and Habitat for Humanity, have made affordable housing a primary cause. Financial institutions have pooled resources through various consortia for the purpose of making community development and mortgage loans in distressed communities. Players in the secondary mortgage market, through their purchases of loans secured by homes in inner cities, minority neighborhoods, and affordable housing, have been instrumental in expanding the supply of mortgage credit. New products being developed by the secondary market along with adaptation of underwriting guidelines to meet the needs of nontraditional buyers have gone a long way toward expanding opportunities for homeownership.

Low-Income Rental Housing

The Working Definition of Low Income

"Low income" is generally defined according to criteria used to determine whether a household is eligible for government housing assistance. In most cases, according to HUD:

- A four-person household with an income less than 50 percent of the local area median family income is considered "very low income"; within this category, a four-person household with an income less than 30 percent of the local area median family income is considered "extremely low income";

- A four-person household with an income from 50 percent to 80 percent of the local area median income is considered "other low income"; and
- A four-person household with an income from 80 percent to 95 percent of the local area median income is considered "moderate income."

Given that median income differs by locality, a household with a fixed income could fall within different defined categories of income in different areas of the country. The percentages vary somewhat along with variations in family size. Using a standard of "relative deprivation" ensures that a certain proportion of households will, by definition, always fall into each of the designated categories. Generally speaking, however, extremely low-income and very-low-income households cannot compete effectively for market-rate housing, and, in many locations in the Northeast, on the West Coast, and in Hawaii, moderate-income households face the same plight.

HUD's definition of low income is not generally as low as another common measure of economic deprivation—the "poverty line," which is defined by the U.S. Census Bureau in terms of a household's ability to purchase a hypothetical "market basket" of goods and services. (The poverty line is used to determine eligibility for certain kinds of government assistance other than housing.) Assuming that the median income for an area is $41,600 (equivalent to HUD's 1996 median family income for the United States for a family of four), a family would be considered very low income by HUD's standard if it earned less than $20,800. Under the Census Bureau's definition of poverty level, however, a family of four would be considered very poor if it earned less than $16,036. In most areas of the United States, the income ceiling for HUD is one-third higher than that of the Census Bureau.[4] Thus, more households are classified as poor under HUD's definition.

These measures do not, however, take into consideration other aspects of a household's financial situation: ownership of assets and equity in a home (which may be significant in some groups such as the elderly); government assistance such as food stamps, Medicare, and housing assistance (although Aid to Families with Dependent Children is taken into account when calculating income); and employer-provided benefits such as payments for health insurance premiums (which can add significantly to an employee's total compensation package).

The Nature and Extent of the Problem

The problem of affordable rental housing is most serious for renters at the tail end of income distribution. Accord-

Figure 15-5

The Economics of a Typical Multifamily Rental Project

This information describes the economics of a prototypical 100-unit multifamily rental development with rent restrictions that meet the requirements of Section 42 low-income housing tax credits. To qualify for the tax credit, either 20 percent of units must be set aside for families earning 50 percent or less of the area median family income or 40 percent of units must be set aside for families earning 60 percent or less of the area median family income. In practice, most owners set aside all units for low-income households at restricted rents to maximize the credit. Rents are restricted on the low-income units to provide a yearly maximum rental amount of 30 percent of the applicable area median income adjusted for family size and including a utility allowance.

Fair market rents for units as determined by HUD vary by the number of bedrooms. HUD specifies that for every 1.5 individuals in the family, housing must include one bedroom.

The following example assumes that the developer will accommodate a family of four in all units; therefore, all units have three bedrooms. In actuality, the developer would likely build units with varying numbers of bedrooms to accommodate families of different sizes. The numbers are for illustration only; in actual cases, costs may be higher or lower.

Assumptions Underlying the Prototype for Rent-Restricted and Unrestricted Cases

Number of Three-Bedroom Units	100
Median Income (U.S. median for four-person family)	$41,600
Percentage of Units Set Aside for Low-Income Families	
@ 50% of median income	20%
@ 60% of median income	80%
Annual Operating Expenses (including taxes, excluding debt service)	$337,200
Annual Operating Expenses per Unit (including taxes, excluding debt service)	$3,372
Total Development Cost (including land)	$9,133,261
Total Development Cost per Unit (including land)	$91,333
Loan Maturity	30 years
Interest Rate on 30-Year Loan	7.7 percent

The Rent-Restricted Case

The developer must first determine the maximum amount that can be charged on the restricted units, which loosely reflects the tenant's ability to pay. The maximum amount depends on median family income, which in this case is $41,600; the percentage of the median income that the family earns, which in this case is between 50 and 60 percent for other low-income families and below 50 percent for very-low-income families; the HUD-determined maximum share of income that should be allocated for housing expenses by low- and very-low-income families, which in this case is 30 percent; and the typical cost of utilities, which in this case is assumed to be $80.00 per month.

Maximum Rent That Can Be Charged

Percent of Median Income	Annual Income	Monthly Income	30 Percent of Monthly Income	Allowance for Utilities	Income Available for Rent
100	$41,600	$3,467	$1,040	$80	$960
60	$24,960	$2,080	$624	$80	$544
50	$20,800	$1,733	$520	$80	$440

Thus, the maximum rent the developer/owner/landlord can command for units reserved for low-income families is $544 per unit and $440 per unit reserved for very-low-income families. Next, the developer/owner/landlord must calculate how large a loan he can afford based on expected rental income and expenses. That is, how much money will the developer have to pay for debt service? It is important to note that lenders require some "cushion"; commercial banks and syndicators often require a debt service coverage ratio (net operating income/debt service) as high as 1.3 to cover unexpected expenses. In this example, we assume a debt service coverage ratio of 1.15, which can be found in underwriting requirements for some affordable housing programs, although it is a very liberal debt service coverage ratio.

---

ing to *The State of the Nation's Housing, 1999,* the number of very-low-income renters grew by 13.5 percent between 1985 and 1995, driven largely by the growth in poor single-parent families. In comparison, the number of renters with very high incomes fell by 5 percent. Low-income renters are concentrated in center cities, many in inner cities. Thus, they are disproportionately affected by high crime rates, low educational attainment, and other ills of urban life.[5]

Low-income households rely heavily on government programs to secure housing that is both affordable and adequate. Thus, the fact that the number of assisted hous-

Operating Income and Expenses

	Per Month	Per Year
Rental Payments		
20 units @ 50% of median = 20 × $440	$8,800	$105,600
80 units @ 60% of median = 80 × $544	43,520	522,240
Gross Income from Rent	$52,320	$627,840
Less 5% Vacancy Allowance	$2,616	$31,392
Less Operating Expenses (including taxes)	$28,100	$337,200
Net Operating Income	$21,604	$259,248
Debt Service Coverage Ratio	1.15	1.15
Net Rent Available for Debt Service		
(Net Operating Income/1.15)	$18,786	$225,433

Finally, the developer/owner/landlord can use this information to calculate the present value of the stream of debt service payments, assuming a 30-year loan at an interest rate of 7.7 percent. The present value of this income stream is the maximum amount that a lender would be willing to lend; that is, it is the maximum loan amount supportable from the rent. The calculation is as follows.

Maximum Loan Amount (Based on Net Rent Available for Debt Service)*

Required Inputs:

Net Rent Available for Debt Service	$225,433
Interest Rate (per year)	7.7%
Loan Term (years)	30

Formula for Calculating Present Value of Net Rent:

$$(\text{Net Rent Available}) \times \left[\frac{1 - (1 + \text{Interest Rate})^{-\text{Loan Term}}}{\text{Interest Rate}} \right]$$

$$= \$225{,}433 \times \left[\frac{1 - (1 + 0.077)^{-30}}{0.077} \right]$$

Present Value of Net Rent = Maximum Loan Amount = $2,634,941

*Most computer spreadsheets will calculate the present value easily if the user simply supplies the required inputs.

The difference between the total development cost and the maximum loan amount is the financing gap.

Financing Gap

Total Development Cost	$9,133,261
Loan Able to Be Supported from Rental Income	$2,634,941
Loan as Percentage of Total Development Cost	0.29
Financing Gap	$6,498,320
Financing Gap as Percentage of Total Development Cost	0.71
Financing Gap (per unit)	$64,983

Thus, the net rent of $225,433 supports a loan of $2,634,941, which is less than one-third of the cost to develop the project. The financing gap is $6,498,320 for the entire project, or about $64,983 per unit. Clearly, this financing gap without considerable government subsidies would make the project infeasible.

Closing the Gap

Rent subsidies can reduce the gap considerably. The maximum rent that the landlord is allowed to charge tenants— $440 per month and $544 per month—for tenants earning 50 percent and 60 percent of the area median family income, respectively, can be supplemented by federal government subsidies. On units receiving Section 8 rental assistance, HUD pays the difference between the maximum allowable rent and the fair market rent for the area (as determined by HUD). In some cases, the subsidized rents are nearly the same as or higher than market-determined rents. Such additional subsidies can reduce the financing gap, or eliminate it altogether, for the multifamily housing development. Because of reduced availability of Section 8 funding, however, tax credit and other investors in multifamily housing should not base the feasibility of the project on obtaining this type of assistance unless they are sure it will be available.

continued on next page

---

ing units fell for the first time in the history of government programs is particularly disturbing. Between 1995 and 1998, some 65,000 rental units receiving HUD subsidies were taken off the market because they were demolished or converted to market-rate rental units (17,000 such units in 1998 alone, with a total of 30,000 since 1996).

Shrinking Supply

After 40 years of steadily increasing rates of homeownership, the proportion of households that own their own homes dropped steadily from a peak of 65.6 percent in 1980 to a stabilized rate of around 64 percent in 1997. But the effects of the booming economy

Figure 15-5

The Economics of a Typical Multifamily Rental Project (continued)

Another type of subsidy that can close or eliminate the financing gap is an interest rate subsidy. Some government programs offer below-market interest rates that can narrow or eliminate the financing gap that occurs in rent-restricted affordable multifamily housing development. Sensitivity analysis can be performed to determine whether there is any rate that will close the gap. In the case of this development, no interest rate is low enough to close the financing gap, so it may take a complex web of financing to make the project feasible.

Many developers have come to rely on low-income housing tax credits to make a project feasible. In this case, the multifamily development qualifies for the tax credit because all of its units are reserved for families earning below 60 percent of the area median family income.

The Unrestricted Case

The following analysis shows the process by which a developer determines the feasibility of a multifamily rental property without rent restrictions. This simplified example assumes that 100 percent debt financing is available, which, of course, is rarely the case. The prototype and assumptions regarding operating expenses, development costs, and loan terms are the same as in the rent-restricted case.

Essentially, the developer takes the total cost of the project—the amount of loan required—and calculates what the debt service payment would be on that loan, given the interest rate and loan term. The calculation of debt service is as follows:

Debt Service on $9,133,261 Loan (total development cost) *

Required Inputs:

Loan Amount	$9,133,261
Interest Rate (per year)	7.7%
Loan Term (years)	30

Formula for Calculating Debt Service Payment:

$$\text{Loan Amount} \times \left[\frac{\text{Interest Rate}}{1 - (1 + \text{Interest Rate})^{-\text{Loan Term}}} \right]$$

$$= \$9,133,261 \times \left[\frac{0.077}{1 - (1 + 0.077)^{-30}} \right]$$

Debt Service Payment (per year) = $781,404

Debt Service Payment (per month) = $65,117

*Most computer spreadsheets will calculate the debt service payment easily if the user simply supplies the required inputs.

The monthly debt service payment, coupled with monthly operating expenses, provides total expenses the developer/owner/landlord would have to cover each month, providing a minimum rent that the developer must charge to make the project feasible.

	Per Month	Per Year
Debt Service Payment (on a 30-year, 7.7% loan)	$65,117	$781,398
Operating Expenses	28,100	337,200
Total Expenses	$93,217	$1,118,598
Minimum Rental Income Required to Meet Expenses	$93,217	$1,118,598
Minimum Rent Required per Unit	$932	$11,186
Minimum Rental Income Required to Meet Expenses Allowing for 5% Vacancy	$97,877	$1,174,528
Minimum Rent per Unit (assuming all units command same rent)	$979	$11,745

Note how this calculation compares with the rent-restricted case. In the former case, the developer knows that he can command only $52,320 in monthly rental income. In the latter case, the developer knows that he must set rents so that they are at least sufficient to cover operating expenses and debt service, even when 5 percent of the units are vacant, which translates into roughly $97,900 in monthly rental income, or $979 per unit per month. In the latter case, if the developer/owner/landlord contends that $979 a month is above the rent level that can be supported in the area, he may abandon the project solely on financial grounds. ∎

Sources for Assumptions: Median Income—HUD's 1996 Income Limits and Section 8 Fair Market Rents; Annual Operating Expenses and Utility Allowances—ULI's *Dollars & Cents of Multifamily Housing, 1997*, Table 4-37; Development Cost—1993 development cost of $8,467,000 for similar project inflated using Construction Cost Indexes per *Engineering News-Record*, March 30, 1998; Interest Rate—Federal Housing Finance Board's *Monthly Interest Rate Survey* of effective rates on loans closed.

could be felt in 1998, when homeownership increased to a record 66.3 percent. Despite the robust spending on building and remodeling ($300 billion in 1998) and increased homeownership, the gap between minority and white homeownership rates has not lessened noticeably.

The languishing homeownership rate of the mid- to late 1980s forced policy makers to take a hard look at the inventory of low-cost rental housing. The argument goes this way: If households cannot rent housing that is affordable enough to allow them to save for down-payments, then fewer households will be able to purchase in the future and the homeownership rate will fall. Between 1974 and 1995, the number of affordable rental units (both subsidized units and unsubsidized units renting for less than $300 in 1989 dollars) declined throughout the United States. In the Northeast, the number of affordable units declined from nearly 2.5 million to 2 million, in the South, from just over 3.5 million to about 3.4 million, and in the West, from 1.75 million to just under 1.5 million. The Midwest actually showed a small increase, from about 2.3 million to 2.4 million.[6]

The discontinuation of the federal government's newer production programs, particularly Section 8 New Construction, Substantial Rehabilitation, and Moderate Rehabilitation, during the 1980s contributed to the decline. A shift in the focus of federal government policy away from the production of rental housing units toward the provision of housing certificates and vouchers that enable eligible households to obtain private sector housing has reduced new production of subsidized rental homes.

Losses resulting from cuts in new production programs are exacerbated by the loss of existing housing units built under the early federal production programs (Section 221(d)(3) and Section 236 programs). Contracts between private owners of housing built under these programs during the 1960s and 1970s are expiring. If contract rents fall below the basic costs of maintenance and operation, private owners of assisted units built under these programs will disinvest in their property, thereby accelerating the removal of units from the inventory of affordable housing. As competition for developable land increases, property owners demolish existing low-income housing projects or convert them to other uses when time limits expire. Owners of assisted units also upgrade and convert units, raise rents, and, in effect, remove additional units from the affordable stock.

Budget cuts and HUD's restructuring of the multi-family housing program will likely continue to take their toll on subsidized units. Legislation designed to preserve "threatened" project-based Section 8 housing at rents consistent with local markets may cause additional hemorrhaging. Section 8 contract rents in many areas are currently above market rents. As contracts expire and HUD aims to get contract rents more in line with market rents before renewal, some property owners may not renew at the lower rent levels, opting instead to remove their units from the stock of low-cost assisted units.

Public housing is also problematic. According to a report by HUD's Office of Policy Development and Research, tenants in public housing in 1997 waited, on average, nearly one year for a public housing unit to become available. Nonetheless, 10 percent of public housing units are vacant as public housing authorities await funding from HUD to undertake needed maintenance.[7] Indeed, many of the units in public housing projects desperately need repair and modernization. HUD's analysis of the 1993 American Housing Survey revealed that nearly 12 percent of the public housing stock in which very-low-income renters reside was structurally inadequate because of low initial construction standards and/or poor maintenance.

In addition, certain local regulatory measures discourage developers from building lower-cost, market-rate rental housing. Rent controls, in particular, are a major disincentive to the production of affordable rental housing.[8] Exclusionary zoning, too, limits the production of affordable housing by allowing only the production of low-density, single-family housing within areas zoned for it. The frustrating length and difficulty of the permitting process for higher-density housing adds substantially to the cost of producing housing and deters many otherwise willing developers of multifamily housing from entering the market.

Increasing Need

At the same time the size of the low-income housing stock has declined, the number of poor households needing such housing has grown. In 1985, 8.6 million very-low-income renting households received no housing subsidies. By 1995, that number grew 14 percent to 9.8 million, exceeding the roughly 11 percent growth rate in households in general. Of the 9.8 million unassisted very-low-income households, nearly 6 million, or 61 percent, faced severe housing problems—1.3 million lived in inadequate housing, and 4.7 million spent over one-half of their meager incomes for rent. The problem is even more pronounced when focusing on extremely low-income households. Of the 5.2 million unassisted extremely low-income renter households, 4.3 million, or 83 percent, experienced serious housing problems— 3.6 million paid more than one-half their incomes for rent, and 725,000 lived in inadequate housing.[9] Thus, while some low-income renting households were able to find decent, affordable housing in the unsubsidized sector, the vast majority face substantial barriers.

The most dramatic and visible manifestation of the increasing need for low-cost rental housing, however, is the growing number of homeless individuals and families lining the streets of every major U.S. city. In 1990, for the first time, the U.S. Census Bureau sent enumerators to locations typically associated with the homeless population, including emergency shelters, shelters for runaway, neglected, and homeless youth, various street locations, and shelters for abused women, to try to develop a sense of the magnitude of the problem. As part of its standard enumeration, the Census Bureau also attempted to count persons who do not live in typical households but instead reside in homes for unwed mothers, drug/alcohol treatment centers, agricultural workers' dormitories on farms, group homes for the mentally ill, and other nonhousehold living arrangements. According to the 1990 Census of Population and Housing, nearly 460,000 persons were found at these locations. And although the Census Bureau cautions that the data undeniably underestimate the number of homeless, it is difficult to know the magnitude of the undercount.[10]

Proponents of a decennial sampling rather than a head count of the population and housing units say that sampling guarantees a more accurate count of the homeless, immigrants, minorities, and other populations difficult to enumerate. Better representation of these groups will give them better representation in Congress as district lines are redrawn and thus better access to federal program funding. The U.S. Supreme Court struck down the use of sampling for enumeration for Census 2000.

Current Efforts to Assist Low-Income Renter Households Obtain Affordable Housing

Federal Government Activities

Federal government subsidies for rental housing fall into two broad categories—supply side and demand side. Supply side subsidies are given to developers/owners to produce housing that is affordable to low- and moderate-income households. Demand side subsidies are provided to eligible households to seek housing in the private market. During the early 1980s, the federal government began shifting toward demand side subsidies.

The Section 8 Rental Voucher Program and Rental Certificate Program are the two largest demand side programs active today. The programs have different implications for households and for developers/owners.

Under the certificate program, households are restricted to finding accommodations that rent for no more than the fair market rents established by HUD. Fair market rents vary by metropolitan area (or county for nonmetropolitan areas) and by number of bedrooms and, in theory, reflect typical asking rents for apartments in the area. HUD makes an assistance payment to the developer/owner that equals the difference between what the household can afford (30 percent of its income) and the fair market rent. Developers/owners participating in the Section 8 rental certificate program cannot charge more for their units than the fair market rents.

Under the voucher program, a voucher-assisted family is free to choose a unit at any rent level. The assistance payment by the public housing authority on behalf of the household is fixed, however. So if the household chooses an apartment that rents for more than the payment standard established by the public housing authority for the area, which is similar to HUD's fair market rents, it may need to spend more than 30 percent of its income to do so. Developers/owners participating in the voucher program are not restricted in the rents they can charge, although they are subject to other regulations.

Detractors of demand side subsidies believe that housing markets are inefficient and that income-related housing allowances rather than subsidies for new production may be insufficient in spurring developers to supply housing that is affordable for the nation's low- and moderate-income families. In any event, most production (supply side) programs provide few units that are affordable for low-income households without additional demand side rental subsidies. The two types of subsidies can be used together quite effectively.

The most significant federal supply side activities in support of housing, which augment the certificate and voucher programs, are:

■ The Home Investment Partnership Act program (HOME), which include grants from the federal government to states, localities, and Native American tribes, based on relative housing need, as demonstrated in the participating jurisdiction's CHAS. Private developers or agencies in these participating jurisdictions can then apply for and receive funds in the form of equity investments and interest-bearing or non-interest-bearing loans for the provision of affordable housing, primarily through rehabilitation of existing structures, but also through new construction in some cases. All housing developed with HOME funds must serve low- and very-low-income families. (HOME funds have been used extensively to provide housing for low-income elderly renters, as discussed in the following section. HOME funds can also be used to provide assistance to first-time homebuyers to purchase homes at below-market interest rates.)

- Locally allocated community development block grants (CDBGs);[11]
- Supportive housing finance programs, including the mortgage loan purchase programs of the federally chartered secondary mortgage market players—the Federal National Mortgage Association (Fannie Mae), the Federal Home Loan Mortgage Corporation (Freddie Mac), and the Government National Mortgage Association (Ginnie Mae)—FHA and VA traditional mortgage insurance and guarantee programs, FHA's recent risk-sharing programs,[12] and Rural Housing Services/Rural Development (formerly Farmers' Home Administration [FmHA]) subsidies for rural housing programs;
- Low-income housing tax credits, administered by states and local governments and allocated to developers in an increasingly competitive process, to encourage private investment in low-income housing as authorized by the Tax Reform Act of 1986 (see Figure 15-4);
- The historic properties/older buildings tax credit, which, though amended by the Tax Reform Act of 1986, is still in effect and may be used in producing low-income housing;
- Fair market incentives to encourage private owners to keep affordable that housing built with federal assistance and originally designated as affordable; and
- Public housing.

Shifting Focus to the Elderly and Populations With Special Needs

The federal government shifted its focus during the 1990s from affordable housing for the low-income population in general to housing for the growing number of low-income elderly and special needs populations. In 1996, at least 1.4 million elderly individuals nationwide needed but did not receive housing assistance. The two main programs designed to alleviate the housing problems faced by the nation's elderly include Section 202 supportive housing for the elderly and HOME investment partnerships.

According to a 1998 report by the General Accounting Office, Section 202 projects, which number more than 1,400, provided homes for nearly 48,000 elderly residents between 1992 and 1996. Under the Section 202 program, capital advances are made to eligible, private, nonprofit sponsors to finance the development of rental housing with supportive services for the elderly. The advance to the sponsor, who may work with a private, for-profit developer, is interest-free and does not have to be repaid so long as the housing remains available for very-low-income elderly persons for at least 40 years. HUD compensates the developer/owner for the difference between the operating costs of the units built under the program and the amount the resident can afford to pay, which, according to program rules, is about 30 percent of income.[13]

The HOME program, which began several years after Section 202, nonetheless provides housing assistance to nearly 21,500 low-income elderly households. Unlike the Section 202 program, housing built with HOME funds is not limited to elderly residents. Another major difference between the two programs is the sources of financing for the projects built under the programs. Financing for housing built under the HOME program typically comes from many sources, including grants from state or local housing programs, conventional bank mortgages, and proceeds from syndication of low-income housing tax credits. Financing for projects built under Section 202 is much simpler, with HUD's capital advance being the only significant source of funds for most projects.[14]

The 1990s also ushered in increased funding for programs geared toward populations with special needs. Similar to the Section 202 program, Section 811, supportive housing for persons with disabilities, provides interest-free capital advances to nonprofit private organizations that do not have to be repaid so long as the housing built with program funds remains available for the intended program beneficiaries for 40 years. Like the Section 202 program, the nonprofit sponsor may work with a for-profit developer with certain restrictions.

The shelter plus care (S+C) program, another example, provides grants on a competitive basis to states, local governments, and Native American tribes. These grants are to be used to provide rental assistance and support services for homeless people with disabilities, primarily those with serious mental illness, chronic problems with alcohol and/or drugs, and AIDS and related diseases.

State and Local Activities

State administration of federal programs has enabled state agencies to develop a sound base of experience. In fact, many state programs are modeled after now-unfunded federal initiatives. For example, the Massachusetts community development action grant (CDAG) program, which was patterned after the now-unfunded federal urban development action grant (UDAG) program, helps finance site improvements in distressed areas in an effort to make housing and economic development projects feasible.[15]

Most state housing- and economic development–related activities are administered by state housing finance agencies (HFAs), which oversee both multifamily rental and single-family ownership programs. HFAs generally receive and administer the federal allocation of low-income housing tax credits and tax-exempt bond authority, which are in great demand by private developers of affordable multifamily housing (see Figures 15-3 and 15-4). HFAs also oversee allocations from federal HOME funds.

Although each state has specific programs, they include some common elements: below–market interest rate financing for new construction, acquisition, and/or rehabilitation of affordable housing; below–market rate financing for construction or rehabilitation of housing for populations with special needs; and loan guarantees to qualified lenders for affordable and special needs housing. Many HFAs, including the California HFA, participate in a risk-sharing pilot program with the FHA. Under risk-sharing programs, FHA assumes up to 50 percent of the default risk on affordable multifamily rental housing. The creditworthiness of the HFA is consequently "enhanced" such that investors will accept lower interest rates on the HFA's bonds. The lower interest rates may be passed on to the developers in the form of low-cost financing. This system is similar to passing on to developers the cost savings from the sale of tax-exempt bonds over taxable bonds in the form of below–market rate financing.

In response to restrictions imposed by the Tax Reform Act of 1986 (TRA 1986) on the type of private activities eligible and the volume of tax-exempt bond financing (which is the thrust behind the below–market rate financing programs), states began experimenting with a variety of programs and funding techniques, including:

- Off-budget funding vehicles such as housing trust funds to produce housing and assist occupants; in New Jersey, for example, proceeds from a statewide realty transfer tax are put into a housing trust fund to which developers of affordable housing can apply for funds;
- State tax credit programs such as California's and Connecticut's efforts to piggyback state credits on federal low-income housing tax credits;
- Revised building codes and housing standards to reduce costs and to facilitate production; and
- Simplified procedures, requirements, and delivery systems for the production of subsidized housing.

Many of today's state-administered programs are derived from HUD demonstration programs. For example, under the Demonstration Disposition Program, the Massachusetts HFA oversees the management, construction, renovation, and ultimate sale to low- and moderate-income buyers of more than 2,000 rental units from HUD's portfolio of foreclosed properties. The properties will provide affordable housing at 11 scattered-site housing developments in several inner-city neighborhoods in Boston. When such demonstration programs prove successful, they are often made permanent or extended indefinitely.

Local governments, often through local HFAs, have been experimenting with many other creative approaches tailored to community resources and opportunities, including:

- Using real estate taxes and new sources of revenue (such as fees on new developments and community loan funds) as well as tax-exempt or taxable bond financing to support low-income housing;
- Donating or otherwise making available surplus, publicly owned land at low cost or through land lease arrangements;
- Using linkage programs or regulations that require contributions to the development of low-income housing as a condition for obtaining approvals for other types of development;
- Using inclusionary zoning or requirements to mandate a set percentage of housing units for low-income households in new market-rate communities, often with the sweetener of a density bonus;
- Providing credit enhancements such as mortgage insurance, letters of credit, or funding reserves that reduce risks and make investment in low-income housing more secure for private developers or investors and often make lower interest rates possible;
- Using local housing vouchers, as in Pennsylvania and Maryland;
- Employing land use concessions and flexible zoning provisions, subdivision ordinances, density allowances, building code requirements, and waivers or reductions of fees to add value to a project;
- Fast-tracking the approval process to save developers time and money;
- Using funds creatively, as in San Francisco's use of linkage payments to fund loan origination fees;
- Forgiving or abating real property taxes; and
- Allocating funds repaid for UDAGs to low-income housing.

Private Sector Participants

Private sector participants include nonprofit and for-profit developers, banks and other financial institutions (such as insurance companies and pension funds), trade unions, foundations, and other philanthropic groups. The anticipated users of low-income housing are also participants in the process, though the extent of their

Evergreen Hills Apartments in Macedon, New York, benefited from the developer's attention to detail when seeking to blend the 150 multifamily rental units with the surrounding community of single-family homes. The project was funded with a variety of private and state funds for affordable housing, and is targeted to families and seniors with incomes at or below 50 or 60 percent of the area median income.

participation varies from place to place and often from project to project. (See Figure 15-6 about the Mercado Apartments for a discussion of an affordable rental apartment project that sought the community's and users' support from the beginning.)

Private development entities typically produce and often manage low-income housing. In some cases, for-profit private developers construct low-income housing either exclusively or in conjunction with other market-rate developments through linkage programs or in fulfillment of inclusionary zoning requirements.[16] Because of their entrepreneurial approach, for-profit developers are generally more efficient producers of housing, but they require sufficient incentives to enable them to make a profit and monitoring to ensure that they fulfill the public purpose.

In today's environment, incentives for for-profit developers are fewer than in the past, as the accompanying profile of developer Thomas Safran illustrates. Safran's strong commitment to building affordable housing has enabled him to continue his work even when the resolution of funding and zoning issues requires years of hard work and patience to proceed.

Some housing markets are not strong enough to permit linkage or inclusionary zoning programs to operate effectively. For this reason, as well as the current preference for grass-roots, bottom-up decision making and implementation, governments and private funders are increasingly looking to nonprofit developers, primarily community development corporations. Between 1960 and 1990, CDCs developed on the order of 20,000 to 30,000 affordable housing units per year, accounting for a total of 736,600 housing units or 14 percent of all federally assisted housing units.[17] A survey by the Afford-

able Housing Network of New Jersey, a statewide association of CDCs, revealed that in 1996 alone, member CDCs had produced 11,000 affordable housing units and had another 5,500 units under development. Nonprofit community-based developers typically know and understand firsthand their communities' needs and resources and generally enjoy a strong local political base and community support. They tend to be accountable to the community and demonstrate a long-term commitment to low-income housing. In particular, according to Neil Mayer of the Berkeley (California) Office of Economic Development, neighborhood-based organizations "need not be cajoled into choosing troubled neighborhoods in which to pursue their efforts." Further, they are less likely to displace current residents and more likely to involve neighborhood people in their work.[18] For these reasons, they have an advantage when seeking certain charitable and public funds.

Such groups, however, are often hampered in their effectiveness by several factors. Most CDCs have small, often overworked staffs with limited experience or technical capability, especially in the areas of financial feasibility analysis and financial packaging. In addition, CDCs are frequently undercapitalized, waiving development fees even when they are allowed. As a result, CDCs suffer chronic shortfalls in operating revenues needed for predevelopment and ongoing operating costs.

Spurred in part by the requirements of the Community Reinvestment Act of 1977 (CRA),[19] banks, insurance companies, and pension funds provide financing for the development of low-income housing. In addition, some private organizations have created special programs that set aside funds for low-income housing proj-

Figure 15-6

The Mercado Apartments: More Than Housing

The Mercado Apartments complex in San Diego is the realization of a 25-year-old dream to construct affordable housing in a community blighted by neglect and poor planning policies. In the early 1960s, Barrio Logan was a thriving community, but the construction of I-5 and the Coronado Bay Bridge bisected the community, resulting in a depleted housing stock and families renting housing through absentee landlords. Lack of consistent zoning, political apathy, and years of neglected environmental regulations continued the course of devastation. Residents did not leave, however, and the neighborhood remained a cultural center for the Latino community.

In 1990, the San Diego Redevelopment Agency created the Barrio Logan redevelopment area, allowing use of tax increment funds to develop the Mercado Apartments, the first major residential development in Barrio Logan in more than 50 years. In addition to providing 144 units of new affordable housing for low-income families, the Mercado Apartments, whose motto is "More Than Housing," is a major effort to build community.

In designing the Mercado Apartments, the architect worked closely with community groups and neighbors to develop a design strategy that respected and promoted their lifestyle, their traditional housing types, and the objectives of their community plan. At the suggestion of the community, the architect designed units that draw inspiration from Mexican urban townhouses and courtyard bungalow housing of the early 1930s and 1940s. Extensive use of flat roofs with varied parapet lines and shallow barrel tile accents recall a familiar architectural style. Private interior courtyards promote pedestrian circulation, with direct access to all the apartments. Each courtyard provides an outdoor space for gathering, visiting, and other passive activities.

The architect's larger mission was to promote community pride, which had been missing for decades; a secondary mission was to fill a social and physical gap in the urban fabric. Thus, the development needed to create a new sense of vitality.

The architect oriented the homes toward the street, unlike most conventional suburban developments; the orientation toward the public areas is further enhanced by generous front porches, front entry doors, and private second-floor balconies, from which residents can keep watch over their neighborhood. Divided into two smaller areas, parking is located toward the interior of the development to minimize its impact on pedestrian circulation. Landscaping uses a combination of drought-tolerant plants and low-maintenance ground cover to maximize aesthetics while minimizing cost. Paths and walkways encourage interaction, and the project complements the neighborhood's existing street grid.

By any measure, Mercado is a success.

Financially, simplified architectural elements and building infrastructure kept costs to $39.00 per square foot. At $86,000 per unit, the project is one of the most affordably built residential developments in San Diego, and one of the lowest-priced rental tax credit properties in California. Inexpensive materials, such as aluminum windows, stucco, and flat roofing with tile accents helped keep costs down. Placing bathroom plumbing in common walls and minimizing mechanical ducting also minimized costs. This value engineering, however, did not compromise quality. Exterior designs are still beautiful, and the spacious interiors feature wood cabinets and tile countertops.

In terms of social success, 144 families now live in affordable, uncrowded, safe conditions. Not squeezed by exorbitant rents, these families are in a better position to save some of their limited incomes in individual development accounts, individual retirement accounts, and other vehicles to be used to purchase first homes, send children to college, pay medical expenses, and so forth. Social scientists agree that a holistic approach is necessary when providing affordable housing, and at Mercado Apartments, more than 40 children are in Head Start slots, with 48 children receiving Home-Based Start educational services. More than 50 individuals have been trained to be entrepreneurs and 200 counseled in starting and developing a business. Job training and development services are also available for adults in the area. ∎

---

ects, while several insurance companies have initiated social investment programs that provide limited amounts of specially targeted funds for low-income housing.

Some banks, following the lead of the South Shore Bank of Chicago, aggregate and hold in low- and non-interest-bearing accounts funds deposited by individu-

als, government agencies, and foundations. These so-called "linked deposits" are earmarked for investment in community development projects. Because the South Shore Bank is insured by the Federal Deposit Insurance Corporation, depositors assume no real risk on linked funds used for community projects.

Intermediaries are private sector organizations that raise and distribute funds and provide various kinds of technical support for (usually nonprofit) developers of low-income housing. Intermediaries can include public/private housing partnerships such as the Boston Housing Partnership or the Cleveland Housing Network, both of which operate locally to support nonprofit community-based developers. They might also include private national organizations such as the Local Initiatives Support Corporation (LISC), a nonprofit corporation created in 1979 by the Ford Foundation; the Enterprise Foundation, established by developer James Rouse in 1982; and the Housing Assistance Council.

Another national intermediary of note is the Neighborhood Reinvestment Corporation (NRC), a congressionally chartered public nonprofit corporation formed in 1978 to revitalize deteriorating urban neighborhoods and to promote affordable housing. The NRC's Neighborhood Housing Services (NHS) program—which involves local residents, business leaders, and governments—and 239 other local partnerships form the NeighborWorks system and receive small grants of seed money from the NRC. One of the NHS program's more important contributions to spurring the production of low-income housing was the creation of its local government secondary market, which enables the delivery of loans to low-income borrowers who cannot satisfy standard underwriting criteria.[20] Flexible underwriting criteria are now becoming more prevalent, primarily because of support from Fannie Mae and Freddie Mac.

Corporations sometimes make direct contributions to developers or housing partnerships that specialize in low-income housing, indirect contributions to intermediary organizations, and in-kind donations of goods, property, and expert time. Corporations and other large employers such as Fannie Mae and Freddie Mac often initiate special programs designed to assist their employees in obtaining housing in expensive localities. "Employer-assisted housing programs," designed to enable employees to live near their jobs, can take the form of assistance with downpayments, low-interest mortgages, equity sharing, rent subsidies, or contributions to local communities' efforts to develop affordable housing.

Finally, foundations invest in low-income housing developments through such vehicles as program-related investments (PRIs).[21] They have also been the chief supporters of intermediary organizations, including many local housing partnerships. Moreover, foundations provide grant money directly to nonprofit, community-based housing developers and to housing partnerships.

Limitations on Financing

The credit crunch during the early 1990s brought production of affordable rental units to a virtual standstill for years. For a time, entire categories of typical multifamily lenders and guarantors stopped providing financing. The investment criteria for lending institutions that did extend multifamily credit became highly standardized and stringent, and effectively dried up sources of financing for all but the plainest vanilla projects. But by the mid-1990s, happy days for the production of affordable housing returned. Financing has largely resumed for the development of multifamily housing, especially financing for low-income tax credit properties.

Financing affordable rental housing can be quite complex. The essence of the problem of financing low-income housing is the need to fill the "affordability gap"—the difference between shelter costs and what a family can afford to pay (see Figure 15-5). The size of the gap and thus the magnitude of the problem vary with locality.

Financing low-income housing is complicated by the fact that no single source of subsidies is available that can on its own make a project financially feasible. Resources available for financing low-income projects are fragmented and vary according to different types of projects and locations. Projects typically require funds from many sources, and it is not unusual for five or six sources of funds to support a single project such that funds from one source become the basis for securing commitments for funds from other sources.

In addition, because each provider of funding has its own social agenda and underwriting criteria, financing arrangements must be flexible enough to respond to the various requirements. The resulting financing packages are time-consuming and expensive to structure and require sophisticated financial expertise. Because they are tailored to a particular project, time, and place and involve local resources, the packages are typically unique to the projects they support and therefore not replicable from place to place or even from project to project within the same city.

Affordable Ownership Housing

The second aspect of what is commonly termed "the affordability problem" is the increasing inability of households of moderate means—especially young households—to purchase a home. The problem has crept steadily up the income ladder. In addition, the 1980s were a time when household incomes began to polarize: the proportion of households with higher incomes and the proportion of households with lower incomes increased, while the proportion in the middle declined.

Profile **Thomas L. Safran, Affordable Housing Developer**

Award-winning Los Angeles affordable housing developer Tom Safran is a product of the late 1960s, when his native Chicago was a hotbed of political activity and an urban crisis was percolating all across America. Safran knew when he was in college that he wanted to do something to help our failing cities. After completing his undergraduate degree at Trinity College in Hartford, Connecticut, he went back to Chicago to enroll at the University of Chicago in political science and urban studies. In the summer before his second year, Safran took a year's internship at HUD in Chicago and Washington, D.C., that extended into almost five years. He eventually ended up in southern California, where he worked as a consultant to several housing authorities and, at the same time, began work on his MBA at the University of California at Los Angeles.

At UCLA, while delivering a presentation on developing a hypothetical project using the newly created Section 8 program funds, Safran was struck with the notion that perhaps he could undertake such a project. But never having worked in the private sector, he knew he was not a savvy deal maker. In fact, he had no idea how to structure a deal or how to tie up a piece of property, which was his first goal. Somehow, though, with only $1,000, Safran managed to tie up a piece of property that no one else had been able to claim simply because he persuaded the owner to consider his offer. Safran worked with the property owner to bring him into the deal and relocate him. With the final piece of the puzzle in place, Safran built his first project.

That was the beginning of Safran's 20-plus years in the development of affordable housing. Since that time, Thomas Safran & Associates has developed more than 2,075 units of affordable rental housing for seniors and families—projects that are known for their attention to design. Although Safran maintains sole proprietorship, he depends heavily on his 14-person staff in the office and 20 on-site resident managers to maintain the quality that he seeks in everything he does. He believes that properly managing HUD projects takes a special kind of person. When hiring staff members, Safran says, "I look for people who have a passion for what they're doing. I also require a certain sensitivity in my employees toward the people they're serving. My employees can't be in this business just for making money. They must be interested in what we do and how we do it. We're providing housing for the same people as public housing authorities are, but we're committed to doing it better."

Safran has a keen interest in design and believes that low-income housing does not have to be unattractive. His awards attest to Safran's point—the 1978 Exceptional Design Award from the Inglewood Planning Commission for his first project; the 1980 Honor Award for Project Design from HUD for Ponderosa Village; the 1983 Hollywood Beautification Award for Multifamily Residential and Residential Landscaping for Hollywood Fountain North; the 1993 National Award of Merit in Project Design for the Strathern Park Apartments; the 1995 ULI Award for Excellence in the small-scale residential category. And the list goes on.

Safran's commitment to quality design helps him attract quality low-income residents as well as "sell" affordable housing, especially family developments, to communities that would not otherwise accept them.

Good Management Is Key

Safran's group puts great stock in good management. Resident managers are hired during project construction so that they will develop a commitment to a given project. As a result, they go the extra step in selecting good residents. And good residents are critical to a project's success.

Selecting tenants begins with a careful screening, including thorough background checks of job history and rent history that cover at a minimum the past two residences. Managers also visit every potential resident's current home with all family members present to develop a sense of the household's attitude toward home and family. In addition, residents must sign lease agreements that some might consider particularly strict. The agreements clearly limit the number of occupants in a unit and precisely define "occupant" and "visitor." The agreements also forbid any kind of illegal drug use. Ground rules are very stringent. Family units are subject to inspections twice a year, senior units once a year. Income is recertified annually. Without question, resident managers' concern has paid off. Thomas Safran & Associates exhibits a remarkably low delinquency collection rate, ranging from 0.1 to 1 percent.

Day-to-day issues and decisions rest with the resident managers and the vice president of property management, who oversees the resident managers. In response to some difficult lessons learned over the years, Safran himself approves all new resident managers as well as all evictions for reasons other than nonpayment of rent.

The Deal Maker

Despite his apparent success, the next project is not always clearly waiting for Safran. His main role within the organization is that of deal maker; he creates and initiates new

The transition from run-down housing to an attractive home is not uncommon in the work done by Thomas Safran & Associates and other affordable housing developers.

projects. But the deal-making function depends on so many other factors that, at any one time, Safran might have three or four potential deals in the works. Indeed, some of them might fall through because of a lack of appropriate funding, a jurisdiction's reluctance to give approvals for the type of project proposed by Thomas Safran & Associates, or a variety of other reasons.

Developing affordable housing requires the careful selection of neighborhoods. Safran tends to stay out of neighborhoods plagued with problems block after block after block; however, he likes to go into areas where a cluster of problem properties is surrounded by decent buildings. On occasion, Safran or his staff has had to deal with gangs or displacement problems, but such matters are all part of the social environment that is unavoidable for developers of affordable housing.

Safran prefers to develop the types of property with which he feels most competent, namely, affordable housing for families and the elderly. He has no interest at this time in expanding his activities to market-rate housing or single-room occupancy housing, for example. "But the competition is much tougher than it used to be. A lot of private developers are looking for opportunities, particularly in southern California, where, until recently, the office market dried up, and they saw affordable housing as a wide-open market."

Safran calls himself a limited-profit developer. He neither earns as much money as the typical private developer

nor assumes as much personal risk, but he also does not have nonprofit status and the advantages that can come with it. Nonetheless, he is convinced that a frequently mistaken assumption holds that nonprofit sponsors are inherently better suited to developing affordable housing than "greedy" private developers. The perception is that nonprofits and community-based groups will stay around and take care of their buildings, while private developers will either abandon them or turn them into market-rate housing after 20 years.

"The best part of what I do is create a home, a nice environment. I like to help upgrade neighborhoods and provide homes for people. I think a good home environment can turn around lives in some cases." Safran believes that his success is partly the result of an ability to blend a strong business sense with a social conscience.

Tenacity is another requisite for Safran's work. "I spend a lot of time figuring out ways to get around obstacles. You also need creativity and vision to see the possibilities where others might not. One of my staff once said that the best lesson he learned working in this office is that no means maybe and maybe means yes. That pretty well describes what it takes."

The Complications of Financing Affordable Housing
"Probably the hardest thing about this type of development is coordinating the endless varieties of approvals and

continued on next page

financing. It can be numbing to get a deal together because of the inconsistencies from one group to the other," says Safran. Because financing is generally layered, the developer has to meet standards (legal, occupancy, design, and more) for each source of funding.

Safran likes to use his favorite project, Strathern Park in the Sun Valley section of Los Angeles, as an example of the complexity of financing. This $25.5 million project, which provides 241 apartment units to low- and very-low-income residents, was completed by layering seven different sources of funding. First, the Los Angeles CRA funded a land acquisition loan for $4.3 million. This loan, in addition to more than $2 million in seed money that Safran advanced to the project, financed the acquisition of the project as well as many predevelopment costs.

Upon funding of the $7.8 million construction loan from Wells Fargo Bank, the CRA's land loan was taken out by $5.2 million in loan funds from HUD's housing development action grant program (HoDAG), which was administered jointly by the CRA and the Los Angeles Housing Preservation and Production Department. At the same time, the CRA funded a long-term gap loan for $6.3 million, to be disbursed along with the conventional construction loan.

During the predevelopment phase of the project, the developer received an allocation of 9 percent federal low-income housing tax credits from the state, which were syndicated through the Boston Financial Group, bringing a total of $7.8 million in equity investment to the project. A portion of this capital was made available to the project at the start of construction. The remaining amounts were contributed to the project on completion of construction, on permanent loan funding, and after a period of stabilized occupancy.

After completion of the project, the construction loan was taken out by a combination of investors' equity and a long-term $6.2 million first trust deed loan from the California Community Reinvestment Corporation. The

$5.2 million HoDAG loan (second trust deed) and the CRA's $6.3 million gap loan (third trust deed) remained in place, payable out of surplus cash flow.

Financing Sources

	Amount
Preconstruction Sources	
Seed Capital from the Developer	$2,000,000
Land Acquisition Loan from the CRA	4,300,000
Total	$6,300,000
Construction Sources	
Partial Equity from Tax Credit Investor	$3,900,000
Permanent Gap Loan from the CRA	6,300,000
HUD HoDAG	5,200,000
Wells Fargo Construction Loan	7,800,000
Total	$23,200,000
Permanent Sources	
Full Equity from Tax Credit Investor	$7,800,000
Permanent Gap Loan from the CRA	6,300,000
HUD HoDAG	5,200,000
California Community Reinvestment Corporation	6,200,000
Total	$25,500,000

Lark Ellen Village is another example of the type of project for which Safran feels best suited. Lark Ellen Village, just 15 miles east of downtown Los Angeles, will provide affordable housing for nearly 88 seniors (and spouses) and 34 families. The site originally housed a ten-story convalescent care facility that was demolished to accommodate the two-story Cape Cod complexes now in place. This $13.5 million project was the result of a combination of public and private financing with equity generated by the sale of tax credits.

One striking difference, notes Safran, between the financing of Lark Ellen Village and Strathern Park is the

The Definition of Affordable Ownership Housing

The definition of affordable ownership housing has long divided analysts in the housing, real estate, academic, and government communities. Several mathematical expressions or affordability indices for homeownership have emerged in an attempt to summarize the relationship among home prices, household incomes, and the structure of mortgage financing costs.

Affordability indices generally fall into two broad categories. The first category embraces individual household affordability indices, which measure whether a specific type of buyer can afford a specific home (see Figure 15-7). The second broad category of indices encompasses market measures of housing affordability that can be divided into two subcategories: the share of homes within a specific market that a typical household can afford and the share of households that can afford a typical home in a particular allocation of tax credits. The 9 percent tax credit for expenditures in new structures was getting increasingly difficult to obtain, so Safran was forced to restructure the entire deal when the Tax Credit Allocation Committee denied his original request. Fierce competition for tax credit allocations gave birth to a new lottery system, under which, Safran determined, it would be exceedingly difficult to obtain an allocation. (Only about one in five projects was funded under the new system.) Rather than reapplying, Safran opted instead to apply for the 4 percent tax credit and "go the tax-exempt bond financing route." Because the IRS requires that at least 50 percent of the eligible basis be paid for by tax-exempt bonds, a B-bond or bridge loan for $268,146 was put in place for a period of one to four years to satisfy this requirement. Edison Equity will take out the B-bond later.

The West Covina Redevelopment Agency has committed $4,270,000 to the project. This loan, which will be available at the start of construction, will also provide permanent financing. The 40-year loan bears a 3 percent interest rate and requires "residual receipts" debt service payments for 50 percent of the cash flow, only to the extent that cash flow is available after payment of all operating expenses, reserve contributions, and senior mortgage debt. In addition to this amount, Bank of America provided a 9.25 percent, 12-month construction loan for $7,510,000.

Permanent financing included a commitment for a 6.75 percent, 40-year loan for $5,399,000 from the California HFA to the project sponsor. The project will generate sufficient rental income to meet the required annual debt service of $390,849 on this loan. The loan, along with the $254,959 Affordable Housing Program loan from the Federal Home Loan Bank, an additional pay-in of tax credit equity for $3,476,208, and an owner equity contribution of $35,114, will repay the construction loan. The construction loan, obtained at the start of construction from the West Covina Redevelopment Agency, will remain in place and will be secured by a second deed of trust.

Financing Sources

	Amount
Construction Sources	
West Covina Redevelopment Agency	$4,270,000
Bank of America	7,510,000
Federal Home Loan Bank—Affordable Housing Program	254,959
Deferred Fees	749,576
Edison Equity	650,746
Total	$13,435,281
Permanent Sources	
West Covina Redevelopment Agency	$4,270,000
California HFA	5,399,000
Tax Credit Investor Equity	3,476,208
Owner Equity	35,114
AHP	254,959
Total	$13,435,281

Overcoming Obstacles

Despite the difficulties—financial, gang-related, and social—Safran feels confident that Thomas Safran & Associates is doing important work; in fact, he encourages other developers to try their hand at the development of affordable housing. "Our company has a credo: 'Our goal is to enhance the world in which we live and enrich the lives of the people who reside in our buildings.' I live by it and my staff has to live by it. To me, integrity in this business is essential. My word is everything. Public agencies have to trust me and want to do business with me. I think that should be true for every developer, but it might be more important in this type of development because so many people's well-being is affected.

"There's always going to be a need for housing, especially affordable housing. I encourage people to explore this type of development because it involves a lot of reward and opportunity. You have to limit your financial expectations, but the internal reward can be tremendous." ■

market—the housing opportunity index (HOI) (see Figure 15-8).[22]

The Nature of the Problem

In many areas of the country—the Chicago metropolitan area, the New York/New Jersey/Connecticut suburbs, the Boston metropolitan area, Hawaii, and much of California, for example—the price of an average house is well beyond the means of households with area median incomes. Buying a home is difficult for many families, particularly for renter households headed by females without a spouse present—a household type becoming more prevalent in today's society. According to a 1991 report by the U.S. Census Bureau, renter families headed by females are virtually locked out of homeownership, with nearly 98 percent unable to afford the purchase of a median-priced home with either conventional or FHA financing. By 1995, the situation deteriorated further, with 98.4 percent of renter families headed

Figure 15-7

Housing Affordability for the United States: 1970-1997

How to read this chart: In 1996, the family earning the median income of $42,300 had 130.5 percent (127 percent for the fixed index and 140 percent for the ARM [adjustable-rate mortgage] index) of the income needed to qualify for a conventional loan covering 80 percent of the price of a home priced at the national median of $118,200 at the prevailing average interest rate of 7.7 percent. (For the composite index, the interest rate used in the calculations is an average of the fixed and adjustable rates. For the fixed index, the interest rate used in the calculation is the average of the interest rates on conventional mortgages with fixed interest rates only. For the ARM index, the interest rate used in the calculation is the average of the interest rates on conventional mortgages with adjustable rates only.)

Year	Median-Priced Existing Single-Family Home	Mortgage Rate[a]	Monthly Principal and Interest Payment	Payment as Percent of Income	Median Family Income	Qualifying Income[b]	Affordability Indices		
							Composite	Fixed	ARM
1970	$23,000	8.35%	$140	17.0%	$9,867	$6,697	147.3	147.3	147.3
1971	24,800	7.67	141	16.5	10,285	6,770	151.9	151.9	151.9
1972	26,700	7.52	150	16.2	11,116	7,183	154.8	154.8	154.8
1973	28,900	8.01	170	16.9	12,051	8,151	147.9	147.9	147.9
1974	32,000	9.02	206	19.2	12,902	9,905	130.3	130.3	130.3
1975	35,300	9.21	232	20.2	13,719	11,112	123.5	123.5	123.5
1976	38,100	9.11	248	19.9	14,958	11,888	125.8	125.8	125.8
1977	42,900	9.02	277	20.7	16,010	13,279	120.6	120.6	120.6
1978	48,700	9.58	230	22.4	17,640	15,834	111.4	111.4	111.4
1979	55,700	10.92	422	25.7	19,680	20,240	97.2	97.2	97.2
1980	62,200	12.95	549	31.3	21,023	26,328	79.9	79.9	79.9
1981	66,400	15.12	677	36.3	22,388	32,485	68.9	68.9	68.9
1982	67,800	15.38	702	35.9	23,433	33,713	69.5	69.4	69.7
1983	70,300	12.85	616	30.1	24,580	29,546	83.2	82.0	85.6
1984	72,400	12.49	618	28.2	26,433	29,650	89.1	84.6	92.1
1985	75,500	11.74	609	26.2	27,735	29,243	94.8	89.6	100.6
1986	80,300	10.25	563	23.0	29,458	27,047	108.9	105.7	116.3
1987	85,600	9.28	565	21.9	30,970	27,113	114.2	107.6	122.4
1988	89,300	9.31	591	22.0	32,191	28,360	113.5	103.6	122.0
1989	93,100	10.11	660	23.1	34,213	31,662	108.1	103.6	114.3
1990	95,500	10.04	673	22.7	35,581	32,286	110.2	107.2	119.1
1991	100,300	9.30	663	22.1	35,939	31,825	112.9	109.9	124.2
1992	103,700	8.11	615	20.1	36,812	29,523	124.7	120.1	145.0
1993	106,800	7.16	578	18.8	36,959	27,727	133.3	128.4	154.9
1994	109,900	7.47	613	19.0	38,782	29,419	131.8	122.2	149.5
1995	113,100	7.85	654	19.3	40,611	31,415	129.3	123.7	140.0
1996	118,200	7.71	675	19.2	42,300	32,402	130.5	127.0	140.0
1997	124,100	7.68	706	19.3	43,920	33,910	129.5	126.6	140.5

[a]Effective rate on loans closed on existing homes from the Federal Housing Finance Board.

[b]Based on current lending requirements of the Federal National Mortgage Association using a 20 percent equity downpayment.

Sources: Reprinted with permission from National Association of Realtors®, *Home Sales Yearbook: 1990* (Washington, D.C.: Author, 1991); and National Association of Realtors®, *Real Estate Outlook: Market Trends and Insights* (Washington, D.C.: Author, 1998). The information contained in this table is for the reader's internal use only and may not be further reproduced by the reader except as authorized under Title 17 of the United States Code.

by females unable to afford a median-priced home using either method of financing.

This situation is not unique to households headed by females, however. More than 93 percent of renter families headed by males without a spouse present were likewise unable to afford to purchase a home in 1991; by 1995, the share rose to nearly 96.5 percent. Even among married-couple renter families, which commonly have two incomes, nearly 90 percent were unable to afford a typical home in both years using conventional financing. There was little improvement using FHA-insured financing: 88 percent were still unable to afford a typical home.[23]

The result was a decline in the rate of homeownership between 1980 and 1990—the first decline in 40 years. In the early 1990s, the homeownership rate began to rebound in response to historically low mortgage rates and a rapidly expanding economy. By 1997, the homeownership rate reached its 1980 peak. Still, the overall figures mask glaring differences among household types. Young households—those aged 25 to 34, historically the age of first-time homebuyers—have been most affected by the affordability problem, with their rate of homeownership well below 1980 peaks. Older households have fared better, as evidenced by the substantial increase in their homeownership rates between 1980 and 1997 (see Figure 15-9). The increase in homeownership rates among the elderly is primarily the result of a shift in national wealth toward the elderly and of a healthier elderly population. Also important is market acceptance of different variants of reverse mortgages, which allow elderly households to tap into the equity in their homes. They can use the proceeds for the costs of operating and maintaining their homes, in-home care, and other services that help them remain in their homes longer.

The incidence of the homeownership affordability problem is uneven, varying considerably among housing markets. The first reason relates to *demand*. During the 1980s, the maturing of baby boomers created a surge in demand for entry-level houses. At the same time, the decentralization of employment to suburban locations translated into increased demand for workers' housing in suburban areas. In addition, the number of households as a proportion of the population increased dramatically during the 1970s and 1980s as more people remained single well into their adult lives. Some observers believe that as baby boomers age and create continuing strong demand for move-up housing, the entry-level housing they can be expected to vacate will create affordable housing for the next generation of first-time buyers, namely, households lower on the income ladder. To be sure, this "moving up" of boomers has already begun.

The second major contributor to the affordability problem is *financing*. Except for those with the deepest pockets, housing producers need financing to undertake a real estate project. They need predevelopment financing to pay for land acquisition, feasibility studies, site planning, and so on, and construction financing to pay for all the hard and soft costs of actually preparing the site and building the homes. Mortgage financing must also be available to homebuyers to purchase the homes, as over 90 percent of homes are sold with mortgages. High interest rates, limited sources of funding, or other unfavorable terms then thwart the production of affordable housing. Indeed, unfavorable financing terms and high interest rates of the late 1980s and early 1990s played a great part in the decline in affordability, particularly for young first-time homebuyers. With enactment of FIRREA in 1989, residential developers faced additional concerns for a period, specifically with regard to restrictions on the amount of loans that can be obtained for land acquisition and, more generally, on sources of capital for development. That period of high interest rates and stringent underwriting criteria has passed, but financial cycles will continue to create difficulties.

The Community Reinvestment Act (CRA) strongly encourages loans for the construction, rehabilitation, and purchase of homes in low- and moderate-income areas, and banks that do not meet their obligations to these underserved communities face stiff penalties under CRA.

A third issue is related to the concern that *overregulation* was a primary culprit in the diminishing supply of affordable housing, which was strongly supported by the findings of the 1990 Advisory Commission on Regulatory Barriers to Affordable Housing. Since those findings were published, state and local governments have passed many new regulations, despite the growing body of evidence that overregulation decreases the supply of affordable housing. For example, house prices in Austin, Texas, in recent years have risen sharply in response to the increased cost of developing in Travis and Williamson Counties as a result of government fees and other regulations designed to discourage growth. Prince William County, in the Washington, D.C., area, designated one-half of the county as "rural" and charges developers nearly five times as much to develop in the "rural" areas.

Regulation schemes share some common elements:

- The rationing of building or sewer, water, and utility connection permits;
- Limitations on the amount or location of developable land through the establishment of urban limit

Figure 15-8

Housing Opportunity Index

How to read this chart: During the fourth quarter of 1997, the family earning the median income of $46,900 in Kokomo, Indiana, could qualify for a conventional 30-year fixed-rate mortgage with a 10 percent downpayment on 95.3 percent of homes that sold in Kokomo during that quarter. During that same quarter of 1997, the family earning the median income of $64,400 in San Francisco could qualify for a mortgage on only 18.7 percent of the homes sold in San Francisco during that quarter.

Metropolitan Areas	1997 Fourth Quarter HOI	1997 Median Income ($000)	1997 Fourth Quarter Median Price ($000)	Affordability Rank	
				National	Regional
Northeast					
Most Affordable Areas					
Binghamton, NY, MSA[b]	84.8	41.0	70.0	6	1
Vineland-Millville-Bridgeton, NJ, PMSA[c]	83.4	43.0	85.0	11	2
Utica-Rome, NY, MSA[b]	83.0	37.2	65.0	12	3
Jamestown, NY, MSA[c]	81.9	36.0	58.0	18	4
Nashua, NH, PMSA[c]	81.7	59.6	119.0	21	5
Least Affordable Areas					
Danbury, CT, PMSA[c]	54.6	74.8	219.0	168	36
New Bedford, MA, PMSA[c]	54.3	40.9	128.0	170	37
Lowell, MA-NH, PMSA[b]	51.6	59.1	185.0	174	38
New York, NY, PMSA[a]	49.5	47.3	155.0	177	39
Jersey City, NJ, PMSA[b]	46.9	44.7	135.0	179	40
Midwest					
Most Affordable Areas					
Kokomo, IN, MSA[c]	95.3	46.9	79.0	1	1
Elkhart-Goshen, IN, MSA[c]	86.6	46.1	98.0	3	2
Duluth-Superior, MN-WI, MSA[c]	85.9	40.6	77.0	4	3
Rockford, IL, MSA[b]	84.8	47.1	85.0	6	4
Lima, OH, MSA[c]	83.5	42.3	70.0	10	5
Least Affordable Areas					
Benton Harbor, MI, MSA[c]	65.8	42.6	90.0	124	35
Chicago, IL, PMSA[a]	64.4	55.8	143.0	131	36
Detroit, MI, PMSA[a]	61.1	53.3	123.0	144	37
Ann Arbor, MI, PMSA[b]	56.7	58.1	148.0	161	38
Fargo-Moorhead, ND-MN, MSA[c]	55.6	43.8	118.0	166	39

lines and zoning of insufficient amounts of vacant land for residential use;

- "Exclusionary zoning" that allows only very-low-density development on residential land;
- Excessive subdivision regulations, such as unnecessarily high standards for grading and drainage, street spacing or width, pavement thickness, curb and sidewalk design, lighting, utility mains, or other physical improvements to the site;
- Requirements that developers construct, or pay fees for the construction of, infrastructure beyond what is required for the specific project;

Metropolitan Areas	1997 Fourth Quarter HOI	1997 Median Income ($000)	1997 Fourth Quarter Median Price ($000)	Affordability Rank National	Affordability Rank Regional
South					
Most Affordable Areas					
Baton Rouge, LA, MSA[b]	87.4	42.6	92.0	2	1
Lakeland-Winter Haven, FL, MSA[b]	85.1	37.2	77.0	5	2
Wilmington-Newark, DE-MD, PMSA[b]	84.7	57.6	125.0	8	3
Melbourne-Titusville-Palm Bay, FL, MSA[b]	84.2	44.5	87.0	9	4
Beaumont-Port Arthur, TX[b]	82.6	40.9	74.0	16	5
Least Affordable Areas					
Raleigh-Durham-Chapel Hill, NC, MSA[a]	57.8	52.3	150.0	156	65
Charlotte-Gastonia-Rock Hill, NC-SC, MSA[a]	57.5	47.3	138.0	157	66
Austin-San Marcos, TX, MSA[a]	57.3	48.6	129.0	159	67
Laredo, TX, MSA[c]	43.0	27.3	88.0	181	68
Brownsville-Harlingen-San Benito, TX, MSA[b]	38.4	24.9	83.0	185	69
West					
Most Affordable Areas					
Anchorage, AK, MSA[b]	82.8	58.6	133.0	15	1
Bakersfield, CA, MSA[b]	76.2	37.7	87.0	48	2
Modesto, CA, MSA[b]	73.8	41.0	114.0	64	3
Riverside/San Bernardino, CA, PMSA[a]	69.5	44.8	119.0	100	4
Reno, NV, MSA[b]	68.3	52.5	145.0	110	5
Least Affordable Areas					
San Jose, CA, PMSA[a]	32.9	70.2	288.0	189	41
Salinas, CA, MSA[b]	31.9	45.6	185.0	190	42
Portland-Vancouver, OR-WA, PMSA[a]	26.9	46.3	155.0	191	43
Santa Cruz-Watsonville, CA, PMSA[c]	25.9	55.2	245.0	192	44
San Francisco, CA, PMSA[a]	18.7	64.4	325.0	193	45

[a]Denotes population above 1,000,000.
[b]Denotes population between 250,000 and 1,000,000.
[c]Denotes population below 250,000.
Source: Reprinted with permission from *Housing Economics* (Washington, D.C.: National Association of Home Builders, 1998).

- The imposition of fees or exactions in excess of actual costs associated with a new development;
- Complex and time-consuming permitting procedures that increase developers' holding costs and risk exposure; and

- Environmental regulations that, for example, control air pollution, protect water supplies, limit the demand for water, preserve wetlands and endangered species, and manage and require the removal of toxic wastes.[24]

Figure 15-9

Homeownership Rates

(Percent)

Age	1980	1983	1986	1990	1993	1993[a]	1997
Under 25	21.3	19.3	17.8	15.3	15.0	14.9	18.3
25 to 29	43.3	38.2	36.1	35.9	34.6	34.1	35.5
30 to 34	61.1	55.7	54.1	51.5	51.0	50.6	52.0
35 to 39	70.8	65.8	64.2	63.1	62.9	62.6	62.5
40 to 44	74.2	74.2	69.3	70.4	68.7	68.4	69.4
45 to 54	77.7	77.1	75.6	76.1	75.2	75.1	75.4
55 to 64	79.3	80.5	81.0	80.4	79.6	79.6	79.7
65 to 74	75.2	76.9	77.6	78.7	79.9	79.6	82.3
75 and Over	67.8	71.6	70.3	71.0	74.0	73.9	75.4
Total	65.6	64.9	63.8	64.1	64.5	64.1	65.7

[a]Data were revised in 1993 to reflect changes in sample, survey, and weighting methodologies as well as rebenchmarking from 1980 Census of Population and Housing weights to 1990 weights.
Source: Harvard University, Joint Center for Housing Studies, from U.S. Census Bureau data. Data for 1980 are from *American Housing Survey for the United States for 1980;* other years are based on *Current Population Surveys* (March 1983 through 1997).

Increased construction costs are also a factor in the rising cost of homeownership. Individual dwellings are affected by height limits and requirements for setbacks and site coverage as well as by specifications for construction materials or standards that are unnecessarily restrictive when other, less expensive alternatives would suffice.

Issues

Housing and land development regulations are enacted to serve legitimate public purposes, such as protecting a community's health and safety. Yet it is ironic that "excessive" regulations may produce adverse effects in the communities they are supposed to protect. Indeed, some regulations, particularly ones regarding minimum lot size and the ratio of house to lot size in certain neighborhoods, often have the effect of excluding low- and moderate-income families from moving in. Low-density development is often another outcome of excessive regulation. Where low-density development is widespread, dwelling costs tend to be higher and individuals' dependence on automobiles for transportation greater. The results are high infrastructure costs, increased traffic congestion, high levels of energy use, increased air pollution, and shortages of certain categories of (lower-wage) labor.

One of the most pervasive and difficult issues confronted by communities seeking to encourage the pro-

duction and purchase of affordable houses is the lack of political will among leaders in support of affordable housing, coupled with affluent neighborhoods' resistance to including lower-cost housing in their communities. Even though no reductions in property values resulting from the inclusion of moderately priced dwellings in expensive neighborhoods have been documented, housing is usually the largest single expenditure for any household; thus, homeowners are highly motivated to protect and enhance their investment. And people apparently prefer to live among others of similar or higher incomes.

Encouraging the Production of Affordable Housing

Affording homeownership involves two primary difficulties: making the downpayment and meeting the monthly payments. Federal housing programs as well as innovations by private mortgage lenders are geared toward helping households overcome either or both of these two barriers. Traditional FHA mortgage insurance, by insuring mortgage lenders against loss from defaults, has expanded the pool of mortgage money available to households who would not qualify under conventional underwriting standards. Because HUD insures up to 97 percent of the first $25,000 of home value, 95 percent of the value between $25,000 and $125,000, and 90 percent of the value above $125,000, private financial institutions are willing to make mortgages that require low downpayments. FHA-insured loans then significantly lower the downpayment barrier. Interest rates on FHA loans are also lower, thereby reducing monthly payments below those required with conventional financing. The Veterans Administration has a similar loan guarantee program. Private mortage insurance companies perform a function similar to the FHA and VA in lowering the downpayment required by lenders, although downpayments are still higher than those required under the FHA insurance and VA guarantee programs.

Low-income households qualify for the HOPE Homeownership of Single-Family Homes program. Under this program, HUD makes planning and implementation grants to private nonprofit organizations, public agencies, and cooperative associations. The recipient organizations can then use funds to help homebuyers purchase properties owned or held by HUD, VA, Rural Housing Services/Rural Development, state or local governments, and scattered-site single-family properties owned by public housing and Native American housing authorities. Properties are made available to low-income households at affordable prices and favorable financing terms, thus overcoming both the downpayment and monthly payment obstacles.

Private mortgage lenders have also developed new products to make homeownership more affordable. Nontraditional mortgage instruments such as adjustable-rate mortgages (ARMs) or graduated-payment mortgages (GPMs) may make possible lower monthly payments than those required by fixed-rate mortgages, assisting those prospective homebuyers who cannot afford the monthly payment for a fixed-rate mortgage.

Many new savings incentives have been introduced in recent years to address the problem of downpayments for all prospective homebuyers. For example, first-time homebuyers can now make withdrawals from qualified individual retirement accounts without incurring a tax penalty if the withdrawn contributions and earnings are used for a downpayment on a first home.[25]

Tax savings, by reducing its real cost, encourages homeownership. Homeowners of all income levels are allowed to exclude from income for federal income tax purposes interest paid on mortgages for primary and secondary residences as well as real estate property taxes paid to state and local governments. To the extent that they hold greater amounts of mortgage debt, upper- and middle-income homeowners receive a disproportionate share of the subsidy from the mortgage interest and property tax deductions. But low-income homeowners benefit as well.

Various groups have demonstrated that reductions in the cost of housing production can be achieved through regulatory reform. Through the Joint Venture for Affordable Housing, HUD and the National Association of Home Builders (NAHB) demonstrated the cost savings that could be realized by updating or eliminating certain regulations governing residential land development and construction. Working with builders constructing houses ranging from $30,000 to $60,000 in 18 communities nationwide, HUD and NAHB documented cost savings of $855 to $15,647 per unit as a consequence of regulatory reform. Among the 18 communities, cost savings averaged about 15 percent.

Regulatory reforms have taken several forms, including:

- Zoning for higher densities;
- Encouraging PUD zoning and clustering of housing units;
- Allowing zero-lot-line zoning;
- Basing subdivision ordinances and requirements for infrastructure on anticipated needs rather than on set standards;
- Streamlining the entitlement/permitting process;
- Modifying building codes to allow the use of less expensive building materials and more flexible construction standards; and
- Waiving fees.

Communities can also enable the production of lower-cost housing by promoting alternative building types, such as manufactured housing. In 1994, the cost per square foot of manufactured homes was less than one-half the cost of site-built homes.[26] Modular housing units, which are generally 90 to 95 percent complete when delivered to the site, have been used successfully, especially on infill sites, to construct inexpensive housing quickly and efficiently. Much of the cost savings comes from standardization, efficient land use and construction, and reduced construction time, which translates into savings in carrying costs. Not surprisingly, the building trades have typically opposed modular housing because it requires less on-site labor; in addition, building inspectors may find that modular housing is complicated to inspect. Even the building trades, however, are now realizing that the highly skilled labor force required in certain cost-cutting production techniques will be a boon to training and wages in the industry.

Favorable court rulings in litigation involving exclusionary zoning and antidiscrimination have gone a long way to ensure that this type of housing is not arbitrarily excluded from planned residential developments. Moreover, the secondary market supports this type of housing through various new products. The next step is for such housing to be included as a viable alternative to site-built housing in any jurisdiction's CHAS. Many states have already adopted sophisticated planning legislation, which recognizes affordable housing as an element of the comprehensive plan.[27]

Summary

The need for affordable housing for moderate- and low-income households is great and will continue to expand. Aging baby boomers will swell the ranks of retirees, many of whom will be living on fixed incomes, who are unable to keep pace with ever-increasing housing costs. The polarization of incomes will continue to widen the gap between the housing haves and have-nots, with more middle-income households pushed toward the have-nots. Production of affordable housing, albeit increasing, is still unable to keep up with the growing demand. Existing affordable housing is being lost as homes "filter up" and landlords command higher rents, or deteriorating as landlords do not undertake necessary maintenance because rents are unable to cover even operating expenses.

Housing is a continuum, and when renting households at its lower end are unable to secure decent housing at affordable rents, reverberations are felt throughout the market. The pool of prospective first-time homebuyers diminishes as renting households are squeezed by high rents and unable to save for downpayments. Thus, the young renting households who in a previous time would have moved up to homeownership continue to rent. Current homeowners with considerable equity in their homes move up to large, well-appointed homes, thereby widening the gap between the housing haves and the have-nots.

Federal, state, and local initiatives for affordable rental and ownership housing have met with mixed success. For example, the 1990 NAHA incentives offered to private owners of federally subsidized housing to maintain their properties in the affordable rental stock when contracts expired were very expensive. Thus, the preservation incentive program was stopped and no new funds were appropriated before the losses stopped. In contrast, the low-income housing tax credit (a federal tax expenditure program administered by the states) has proved to be a tremendous incentive for private developers, with roughly 60,000 units of affordable housing being built annually in recent years using the credits. State programs that provide below–market rate financing to developers to build affordable housing and purchasers to buy affordable housing have also been successful, with over 650,000 units of affordable housing produced and 2 million mortgage loans made since the beginning of the program in the 1970s.

Private sector participants are stepping up to the plate, too. For-profit and nonprofit developers, such as CDCs, are increasing their production of affordable rental and ownership housing, spurred on by new tax incentives. Individual financial institutions are forming affiliates that specialize in community development lending, including mortgage loans for affordable housing. Financial institutions are pooling resources in loan consortia to make mortgage loans for affordable housing. Life insurance companies and pension funds are putting money in economically targeted investments. Affordable housing is climbing to the top of many foundations' and charities' social agendas.

To achieve the goal of the Housing Act of 1949 of "a decent home and suitable living environment for every American," all participants in the development process will need to be ever more creative.

Terms

- Community development block grant (CDBG)
- Community Reinvestment Act of 1977
- Demonstration programs
- Exclusionary zoning
- Fannie Mae
- FDIC
- FHA
- FIRREA
- Freddie Mac
- Ginnie Mae
- Housing vouchers
- HUD
- Linked deposits
- Market-rate housing
- National Affordable Housing Act of 1990 (NAHA)
- Rent control
- Risk sharing
- Special needs program
- Tax Reform Act of 1986
- Urban development action grant (UDAG)

Review Questions

15.1 Define affordable housing. Why is there confusion when it comes to identifying what affordable housing is?

15.2 Why is owning a home becoming increasingly difficult for many families?

15.3 Discuss the role of state and local governments in providing housing and the type of programs and techniques they use.

15.4 Define low income.

15.5 Discuss various programs for low-income housing.

15.6 How does the private sector participate in providing low-income housing?

15.7 What are some of the factors affecting the cost of housing?

15.8 What are some of the regulatory reforms that have encouraged the production of affordable housing?

Notes

1. Thirty percent was selected because the U.S. Department of Housing and Urban Development uses this standard in its determinations of affordability for most of its housing programs. (Until 1981, HUD's standard of affordability was 25 percent of income.)

2. Racial discrimination in housing and credit markets has again ascended to the top of the housing policy agenda. See Katherine L. Bradbury, Karl E. Case, and Constance R. Dunham, "Geographic Patterns of Mortgage Lending in Boston, 1982–1987," *New England Economic Review,* September/October 1989, pp. 3–30. The authors used data on loan applications required to be kept by lenders subject to the Home Mortgage Disclosure Act and concluded that discrimination was pervasive among mortgage lenders in Boston. Subsequent studies similarly concluded that many barriers exist for minorities seeking mortgage credit; see Alicia H. Munnell, Lynne E. Browne, James McEneaney, and Geoffrey Tootell, "Mortgage Lending in Boston: Interpreting HMDA Data," Working Paper (Boston: Federal Reserve Bank of Boston, 1992); Robert B. Avery, Patricia E. Beeson, and Mark S. Sniderman, "Cross Lender Variation in Home Mortgage Lending," Working Paper (Cleveland: Federal Reserve Bank of Cleveland, 1992); and James H. Carr and Isaac F. Megbolugbe, "The Federal Reserve Bank of Boston Study on Mortgage Lending Revisited," Fannie Mae Working Paper (Washington, D.C.: Fannie Mae, 1993). Such studies, however, are not without their detractors, including Nobel laureate economist Gary Becker, who indicates that the studies fail to reveal adverse impacts of discrimination.

3. Cushing N. Dolbeare, *At a Snail's Pace: FY95* (Washington, D.C.: Low-Income Housing Information Service, 1994); and calculated by National Low-Income Housing Coalition from data contained in OMB's FY 1999 Budget CD-ROM, Tables 3.2 and 5.1. Figures for 1998 through 2003 are OMB estimates of direct spending for housing.

4. ULI calculations based on data contained in U.S. Department of Housing and Urban Development, "1993 Income Limits for Low-Income and Very-Low-Income Families under the Housing Act of 1937," HUD 21B (3-80), GPO no. 871 902; and U.S. Census Bureau, *Poverty in the United States, 1992.* Current Population Reports, Series P60-185 (Washington, D.C.: U.S. Government Printing Office, 1993).

5. *The State of the Nation's Housing, 1999* (Cambridge, Mass.: Harvard University, Joint Center for Housing Studies, 1999).

6. Ibid.

7. U.S. Department of Housing and Urban Development, *A Picture of Subsidized Households, 1997, www.huduser.org.*

8. Anthony Downs, *Residential Rent Controls: An Evaluation* (Washington, D.C.: ULI–the Urban Land Institute, 1988), p. 6.

9. *The State of the Nation's Housing, 1999.*

10. U.S. Census Bureau, "Fact Sheet for 1990 Decennial Census: Counts of Persons in Selected Locations Where Homeless Persons Are Found," CPH-L-87 (Washington, D.C.: U.S. Government Printing Office, 1992).

11. Since their authorization in 1974, CDBGs have provided a flexible source of funding for community and economic development. HUD gives CDBGs to qualified cities and counties on the basis of entitlement; smaller cities and towns compete for project-specific funds through state governments. Money may be used for projects in which 70 percent of the beneficiaries are low- and moderate-income households and for programs that eliminate slums and blight and serve "urgent community needs."

12. The FHA has introduced several risk-sharing demonstration programs, which are similar to traditional mortgage insurance except that FHA shares the risk, rather than assumes the entire risk, of loss from mortgage defaults with state and local housing finance agencies (in the case of the credit enhancement program) and with qualified lenders (in the case of the reinsurance program).

13. U.S. General Accounting Office, *Housing for the Elderly: Information on HUD's Section 202 and HOME Investment Partnerships Programs,* Report No. GAO/RCED-98-11, November 1997.

14. Ibid.

15. Michael A. Stegman and J. David Holden, *Nonfederal Housing Programs: How States and Localities Are Responding to Federal Cutbacks in Low-Income Housing* (Washington, D.C.: ULI–the Urban Land Institute, 1987), p. 75. UDAGs are grants from the federal government to cities for economic development; the cities then lend the money to private developers. As the loans are repaid, the city can use the accumulated funds in different ways. In Cleveland, for example, according to ULI member David Goss, repaid UDAGs are used in much the same way as funds from CDBGs.

16. Housing linkage programs, in which approvals for non-residential construction are conditioned upon the applicant's direct provision of market-rate and/or affordable housing or payment of fees for housing in lieu of such provision, flourish during periods of strong commercial construction activity. As a result, housing linkage programs virtually came to a halt with the lull in office construction in the late 1980s and early 1990s. Despite the resumption of office construction during the mid-1990s, mandatory linkage programs have not reached the importance they had during the 1980s.

17. Christopher Walker, "Nonprofit Housing Development: Status, Trends, and Prospects," *Housing Policy Debate,* Vol. 4, No. 3, pp. 369–414.

18. Neil S. Mayer, *Neighborhood Organizations and Community Development: Making Revitalization Work* (Washington, D.C.: Urban Institute Press, 1984), p. 3.

19. Congress passed the Community Reinvestment Act (CRA) in 1977 to encourage banks to invest in their local communities. The CRA affects state-chartered banks, bank holding companies, federal S&Ls, savings banks, state-chartered savings institutions, S&L holding companies, and national banks. It requires covered institutions to prepare a statement of their investment in the community at least once a year. The statement must outline the types of credit offered by the institution to the community. The appropriate supervisory agency (the Board of Governors of the Federal Reserve System, the Federal Deposit Insurance Corporation, the Office of Thrift Supervision, or the Office of the Comptroller of the Currency) rates each covered institution under its purview according to specific guidelines regarding reinvestment in the communities that the institutions are supposed to be serving.

The Financial Institutions Reform, Recovery, and Enforcement Act of 1989 (FIRREA) amended the CRA to give the public access to regulators' examination assessments and CRA ratings. Over the years, the focus of the CRA has shifted from the identification of community needs, which are now assumed, to the actual performance of the financial institutions. Enforcement is a large element of the legislation as it currently stands.

20. Neighborhood Reinvestment Corporation, "New Local Government Secondary Market to Aid Low-Income Residents; Cincinnati Proposes First Sale," news release, June 9, 1988; and Mary K. Nenno and George S. Colyer, *New Money and New Methods: A Catalog of State and Local Initiatives in Housing and Community Development,* 2d ed. (Washington, D.C.: National

Association of Housing and Redevelopment Officials, 1988), pp. 62–63.

21. The Ford Foundation instituted PRIs in 1968. PRIs are not grants but rather investments made by a foundation from its endowment or annual earnings. Investments can take the form of loans, loan guarantees, or equity investments. Detailed information on foundations' activities in housing and community development is available from the Foundation Centers in New York, Washington, D.C., Cleveland, and San Francisco.

22. Mary Boehling Schwartz, "Checking the Nation's Vital Signs: Homeownership Affordability Measures (Part II)," in *Real Estate Outlook* (Washington, D.C.: National Association of Realtors®, 1991), pp. 22–30.

23. Howard A. Savage and Peter J. Fronczek, *Who Can Afford to Buy a House in 1991?* U.S. Census Bureau, Current Housing Reports H121/93-3 (Washington, D.C.: U.S. Government Printing Office, 1993); and *Who Can Afford to Buy a House in 1995?* U.S. Census Bureau, Current Housing Reports H121/97-1. See the Census Bureau's Web site, *www.census.gov,* for current information.

24. These categories of regulation were developed by Ira S. Lowry in conjunction with ULI-sponsored research conducted in May 1990 on the relationship between the restrictiveness of regulatory environments and housing costs.

25. Another example of a vehicle that encourages saving, particularly by low- and moderate-income households, is the individual development account (IDA). The theory behind IDAs is that, given the right financial incentives, low-income households will save money. Among the major incentives to save is matching funds provided by public and private sources, which can exceed $10.00 for every $1.00 saved. Indeed, many states have lifted limits on savings and added provisions to exclude money in IDAs in determining eligibility for welfare, thereby eliminating this disincentive for lower-income households to save. See *Ford Foundation,* "Downpayments on a Dream," Winter 1998, pp. 4–7.

26. S. Mark White, "State and Federal Planning Legislation and Manufactured Housing: New Opportunities for Affordable, Single-Family Shelter," *The Urban Lawyer,* Spring 1996, pp. 263–91.

27. Ibid.

Part V
Bibliography

The Public Roles

Alterman, Rachelle, ed. *Private Supply of Public Services: Evaluation of Real Estate Exactions, Linkage, and Alternative Land Policies.* New York: New York Univ. Press, 1988.

Anton, Thomas J. *American Federalism and Public Policy: How the System Works.* Philadelphia: Temple Univ. Press, 1989.

Babcock, Richard. *The Zoning Game.* Madison: Univ. of Wisconsin Press, 1966.

Babcock, Richard, and Charles L. Siemon. *The Zoning Game Revisited.* Cambridge, Mass: Lincoln Institute of Land Policy, 1985.

Barrows, Richard L. *The Roles of Federal, State, and Local Governments in Land Use Planning.* Washington, D.C.: National Planning Association, 1982.

Basile, Ralph J., Jim Furr, and Charles Thomsen. "Leveraging Privatization in Real Estate Development." *Urban Land* 46:1 (January 1987): 6–11.

Bollens, John C. *Special Purpose District Government in the United States.* Berkeley and Los Angeles: Univ. of California Press, 1957.

Brower, David J., David R. Godschalk, and Douglas R. Porter, eds. *Understanding Growth Management.* Washington, D.C.: ULI–the Urban Land Institute, 1989.

Colman, William G. *State and Local Government and Public-Private Partnerships.* New York: Greenwood Press, 1989.

Diamond, Henry L., ed. *Land Use in America.* Washington, D.C.: Island Press, 1996.

Dowall, David E. "Making Land Development Work: The Process and Critical Elements for Success." *Real Estate Finance* 6:3 (Fall 1989): 15–26.

Downs, Anthony. *Urban Affairs and Urban Policy.* Northampton, Mass.: Edward Elgar, 1998.

Fisk, Donald, Herbert Kiesling, and Thomas Muller. *Private Provision of Public Services: An Overview.* Washington, D.C.: Urban Institute Press, 1978.

Frank, James E. *The Costs of Alternative Development Patterns.* Washington, D.C.: ULI–the Urban Land Institute, 1989.

Frieden, Bernard, and Lynne B. Sagalyn. *Downtown, Inc.: How America Rebuilds Cities.* Cambridge, Mass.: MIT Press, 1989.

Haar, Charles. *Land Use Planning: A Casebook in the Use, Misuse, and Re-Use of Urban Land.* 4th ed. Gaithersburg, Md.: Aspen Publishers, 1989.

Haar, Charles M., and Jerold S. Kayden. *Landmark Justice: The Influence of William J. Brennan on America's Communities.* Washington, D.C.: Preservation Press, 1989.

Jackson, Richard H. *Land Use in America.* New York: Halsted Press, 1981.

Judd, Dennis R., and Paul Kantor. *The Politics of Urban America: A Reader.* 2d ed. Boston: Allyn & Bacon, 1998.

Kelly, Eric Damian. *Managing Community Growth: Policies, Techniques, and Impacts.* Westport, Conn.: Praeger, 1993.

Landis, John, Robert Cervero, and Peter Hall. "Transit Joint Development in the U.S." Berkeley: Univ. of California, Institute of Urban and Regional Development, August 1992.

Lassar, Terry Jill. *Carrots & Sticks: New Zoning Downtown.* Washington, D.C.: ULI–the Urban Land Institute, 1989.

——. *City Deal Making.* Washington, D.C.: ULI–the Urban Land Institute, 1990.

Levitt, Rachelle L., ed. *Cities Reborn.* Washington, D.C.: ULI–the Urban Land Institute, 1987.

Levitt, Rachelle L., and John J. Kirlin, eds. *Managing Development through Public/Private Negotiations.* Washington, D.C.: ULI–the Urban Land Institute and the American Bar Association, 1985.

McBee, Susanna, et al. *Downtown Development Handbook.* 2d ed. Washington, D.C.: ULI–the Urban Land Institute, 1992.

Moffitt, Leonard C. *Strategic Management: Public Planning at the Local Level.* Greenwich, Conn., and London: JAI Press, 1984.

Musgrave, Richard A., and Peggy B. Musgrave. *Public Finance in Theory and Practice.* 3d ed. New York: McGraw-Hill, 1980.

Nelson, Arthur C., ed. *Development Impact Fees.* Chicago: Planners Press, 1988.

Palumbo, Dennis J. *Public Policy in America: Government in Action.* 2d ed. New York: Harcourt Brace Jovanovich, 1997.

Paumier, Cyril B., et al. *Designing the Successful Downtown.* Washington, D.C.: ULI–the Urban Land Institute, 1988.

Payne, Geoffrey. *Making Common Ground: Public/Private Partnerships in Land for Housing.* London: Intermediate Technologies, 1999.

Petersen, David C. *Sports, Convention, and Entertainment Facilities.* Washington, D.C.: ULI–the Urban Land Institute, 1996.

Pierre, Jon. *Partnerships in Urban Governance: European and American Experience.* New York: St. Martins Press, 1998.

Porter, Douglas R. *Managing Growth in America's Communities.* Washington, D.C.: Island Press, 1997.

——. *Profiles in Growth Management.* Washington, D.C.: ULI–the Urban Land Institute, 1996.

——, ed. *State and Regional Initiatives for Managing Development: Policy Issues and Practical Concerns.* Washington, D.C.: ULI–the Urban Land Institute, 1992.

Porter, Douglas R., Susan Jakubiak, Ben C. Lin, and Richard Peiser. *Special Districts: A Useful Technique for Financing Infrastructure.* Washington, D.C.: ULI–the Urban Land Institute, 1992.

Porter, Douglas R., Patrick L. Phillips, and Colleen Grogan Moore. *Working with the Community: A Developer's Guide.* Washington, D.C.: ULI–the Urban Land Institute, 1985.

Porter, Douglas R., et al. *Flexible Zoning: How It Works.* Washington, D.C.: ULI–the Urban Land Institute, 1988.

Reilly, William K., ed. *The Use of Land: A Citizens' Policy Guide to Urban Growth.* New York: Thomas Y. Crowell Co., 1973.

Roddewig, Richard J., and Christopher J. Duerksen. *Responding to the Takings Challenge: A Guide for Local Officials and Planners.* Chicago: Planners Press, 1989.

Sagalyn, Lynne B. "Explaining the Improbable: Local Redevelopment in the Wake of Federal Cutbacks." *Journal of the American Planning Association* 56 (1990): 429–41.

——. "Leasing: The Strategic Option for Public Development." Working Paper. Cambridge, Mass.: Lincoln Institute of Land Policy and A. Alfred Taubman Center for State and Local Government, Kennedy School of Government, Harvard Univ., 1993.

——. "Measuring Financial Returns When the City Acts as an Investor: Boston and Faneuil Hall Marketplace." *Real Estate Issues* 14:2 (Fall 1989): 7–15.

——. "Public Development: Using Land as a Capital Resource." Working Paper. Cambridge, Mass.: Lincoln Institute of Land Policy and A. Alfred Taubman Center for State and Local Government, Kennedy School of Government, Harvard Univ., 1992.

Scott, Randall W., David J. Brower, and Dallas D. Miner, eds. *Management and Control of Growth: Issues, Techniques, Problems, and Trends.* 5 vol. Washington, D.C.: ULI–the Urban Land Institute, 1975.

Seidenstat, Paul. *Contracting Out Government Services (Privatizing Government).* Westport, Conn.: Praeger, 1999.

Snyder, Thomas P., and Michael A. Stegman. *Paying for Growth.* Washington, D.C.: ULI–the Urban Land Institute, 1986.

Solnit, Albert. *Project Approval: A Developer's Guide to Successful Local Government Review.* Belmont, Calif.: Wadsworth, 1983.

Sonenblum, Sidney, John J. Kirlin, and John C. Ries. *How Cities Provide Services: An Evaluation of Alternative Delivery Structures.* Cambridge, Mass.: Ballinger, 1977.

Squires, Gregory D., ed. *Unequal Partnerships: The Political Economy of Redevelopment in Postwar Amer-*

ica. New Brunswick, N.J.: Rutgers Univ., Center for Urban Policy Research, 1989.

Stein, Debra. *Winning Community Support for Land Use Projects.* Washington, D.C.: ULI–the Urban Land Institute, 1992.

Stone, Clarence N., and Heywood T. Sanders, eds. *The Politics of Urban Development.* Lawrence: Univ. of Kansas Press, 1987.

ULI–the Urban Land Institute, with Gladstone Associates. *Joint Development: Making the Real Estate–Transit Connection.* Washington, D.C.: Author, 1979.

Vranicar, John, Welford Sanders, and David Mosena. *Streamlining Land Use Regulations.* Chicago: APA Press, 1980.

Wetmore, Robert. "Bidding the Public Property: Guidelines for Developers." *Urban Land* 50:5 (May 1991): 8–13.

Wetmore, Robert, and Chris Klinger. "Land Leases: More Than Rent Schedules." *Urban Land* 50:6 (June 1991): 6–9.

Williams, Norman, Jr., and John M. Taylor. *American Planning Law: Land Use and the Police Power.* Rev. ed. Deerfield, Ill.: Clark Boardman Callaghan, 1988. Orig. pub. 1974. Periodic revisions and updates.

Witherspoon, Robert. *Codevelopment.* Washington, D.C.: ULI–the Urban Land Institute, 1982.

Affordable Housing

Atlas, John, and Ellen Shoshkes. *Saving Affordable Housing: What Community Groups Can Do and What Government Should Do.* Orange, N.J.: National Housing Institute, 1997.

Avery, Robert B., Patricia E. Beeson, and Mark S. Sniderman. *Cross Lender Variation in Home Mortgage Lending.* Working Paper. Cleveland: Federal Reserve Bank of Cleveland, 1992.

Bogdon, Amy, Joshua Silver, Margery Austin Turner, Kara Hartnett, and Matthew VanderGoot. *National Analysis of Housing Affordability, Adequacy, and Availability: A Framework for Local Housing Strategies.* Washington, D.C.: U.S. Department of Housing and Urban Development, 1994.

Bradbury, Katherine L., Karl E. Case, and Constance R. Dunham. "Geographic Patterns of Mortgage Lending in Boston, 1982–1987." *New England Economic Review* (September/October 1989): 3–30.

Burchell, Robert W. "Preservation Actors, Past and Present: A Trip through the Players from 1960 to 2000 and Beyond." *Housing Policy Debate* 2:2 (1991): 413–38.

Burnham, Richard. *Housing Ourselves: Creating Affordable, Sustainable Shelter.* New York: McGraw-Hill, 1998.

Carr, James H., and Isaac F. Megbolugbe. "The Federal Reserve Bank of Boston Study on Mortgage Lending Revisited." Working Paper. Washington, D.C.: Fannie Mae, 1993.

Case, Karl E. "Investors, Developers, and Supply Side Subsidies: How Much Is Enough?" *Housing Policy Debate* 2:2 (1991): 341–56.

Council of State Community Affairs Agencies. *State Housing Initiatives: The 1988 Compendium.* Washington, D.C.: Author, 1988.

Dalaker, Joseph, and Mary Naifeh. *Poverty in the United States: 1997.* Current Population Reports P60-201. Washington, D.C.: U.S. Census Bureau, 1998.

Dolbeare, Cushing N. *At a Snail's Pace: FY95.* Washington, D.C.: Low-Income Housing Information Service, 1994.

——. *Out of Reach: Why Everyday People Can't Find Affordable Housing.* Washington, D.C.: Low-Income Housing Information Center, 1989.

Downs, Anthony. *A Reevaluation of Residential Rent Controls.* Washington, D.C.: ULI–the Urban Land Institute, 1996.

Ford Foundation. *Affordable Housing: The Years Ahead.* New York: Author, 1989.

Friedrichs, Juergen. *Affordable Housing for the Homeless.* New York: Walter de Gruyter, 1988.

Hamilton Securities Group. *A Report on the Multi-family Mortgage Industry.* Washington, D.C.: National Multi Housing Council & National Apartment Association, 1994.

Hecht, Bennett L., et al. *Managing Affordable Housing: A Practical Guide to Creating Stable Communities.* New York: Wiley, 1996.

Hughes, James W., and George Sternlieb. *The Dynamics of America's Housing.* New Brunswick, N.J.: Rutgers Univ., Center for Urban Policy Research, 1987.

Joint Center for Housing Studies, Harvard Univ. *The State of the Nation's Housing, 1999.* Cambridge, Mass.: Author, 1999.

Jones, Tom, William Pettus, and Michael Pyatok. *Good Neighbors: Affordable Family Housing.* Melbourne, Australia: Images Publishing Group, 1997.

Kelly, Christine, Donald C. Kelly, and Ed Marciniak. *Nonprofits with Hard Hats: Building Affordable Housing.* Washington, D.C.: National Center for Ethnic Affairs, 1988.

Leonard, Paul A., Cushing N. Dolbeare, and Edward B. Lazere. *A Place to Call Home: A Crisis in Housing for the Poor.* Washington, D.C.: Center on Budget and Policy Priorities/National Low-Income Housing Information Service, 1989.

Lifland, Carol M., Gregory J. Karns, and Amy H. Wells. *Summary of Legal Developments in 1993 Affecting the Real Estate, Construction, and Financial Services Industries.* Los Angeles: Cox, Castle, & Nicholson, 1994.

Linneman, Peter, and Susan Wachter. "The Impact of Borrowing Constraints on Home Ownership." *AREUEA Journal* 17:4 (Winter 1989): 389–402.

Malpezzi, Stephen. "Housing Prices, Externalities, and Regulation in U.S. Metropolitan Areas." *Journal of Housing Research* 7:2 (1996): 209–41.

Mayer, Neil S. *Neighborhood Organizations and Community Development: Making Revitalization Work.* Washington, D.C.: Urban Institute Press, 1984.

——. "Preserving the Low-Income Housing Stock." *Housing Policy Debate* 2:2 (1991): 499–533.

Munnell, Alicia H., Lynne E. Browne, James McEneaney, and Geoffrey Tootell. "Mortgage Lending in Boston: Interpreting HMDA Data." Working Paper. Boston: Federal Reserve Bank of Boston, 1992.

National Council of State Housing Agencies. *The HFA Program Catalog.* Washington, D.C.: Author, 1991.

National Housing Task Force. *A Decent Place to Live.* Washington, D.C.: Author, 1988.

Nenno, Mary K., and Paul C. Brophy. *Housing and Local Government.* Washington, D.C.: International City Management Association, 1982.

Nenno, Mary K., and George S. Colyer. *New Money and New Methods: A Catalog of State and Local Initiatives in Housing and Community Development.* 2d ed. Washington, D.C.: National Association of Housing and Redevelopment Officials, 1988.

Ramsey, Rey. *Developing Affordable Housing: A Practical Guide for Nonprofit Organizations.* 2d ed. New York: Wiley, 1999.

Sanders, Welford, Judith Getzels, David Mosena, and JoAnn Butler. *Affordable Single-Family Housing: A Review of Development Standards.* Planning Advisory Service Report No. 385. Chicago: APA Press, 1984.

Savage, Howard A. *Who Can Afford to Buy a House in 1993?* Current Housing Reports H121/97-1. Washington, D.C.: U.S. Census Bureau, 1997.

Schwartz, David C., Richard C. Ferlauto, and Daniel N. Hoffman. *A New Housing Policy for America: Recapturing the American Dream.* Philadelphia: Temple Univ. Press, 1988.

Schwartz, Mary Boehling. "Checking the Nation's Vital Signs: Homeownership Affordability Measures. Part II." *Real Estate Outlook.* Washington, D.C.: National Association of Realtors®, 1991.

Stegman, Michael A. "The Excessive Costs of Creative Finance." *Housing Policy Debate* 2:2 (1991): 357–73.

——, ed. *Housing and Economics: The American Dilemma.* Cambridge, Mass.: MIT Press, 1970.

Stegman, Michael A., and Diane R. Suchman. *State and Local Affordable Housing Programs: A Rich Tapestry.* Washington, D.C.: ULI–the Urban Land Institute, 1999.

Struyk, Raymond J. "Preservation Policies in Perspective." *Housing Policy Debate* 2:2 (1991): 383–411.

Struyk, Raymond J., Margery Austin Turner, and Makiko Ueno. *Future U.S. Housing Policy: Meeting the Demographic Challenge.* Washington, D.C.: Urban Institute Press, 1988.

Suchman, Diane R., et al. *Public/Private Housing Partnerships.* Washington, D.C.: ULI–the Urban Land Institute, 1990.

U.S. Census Bureau. *Fact Sheet for 1990 Decennial Census Counts of Persons in Selected Locations Where Homeless Persons Are Found.* Washington, D.C.: U.S. Government Printing Office, 1992.

U.S. Conference of Mayors. *Partnerships for Affordable Housing: An Annotated Listing of City Programs.* Washington, D.C.: Author, 1989.

U.S. Department of Housing and Urban Development. *American Housing Survey for the United States in 1995.* Washington, D.C.: U.S. Government Printing Office. Series published biannually.

——, Office of Community Development and Planning. *Building Public-Private Partnerships to Develop Affordable Housing.* Washington, D.C.: U.S. Government Printing Office, 1996.

U.S. Department of Housing and Urban Development, Office of Policy Development and Research. *The Location of Worst-Case Needs in the Late 1980s: A Report to Congress.* Washington, D.C.: Author, December 1992.

——. *Priority Housing Problems and "Worst Case" Needs in 1989: A Report to Congress.* Washington, D.C.: Author, June 1991.

U.S. General Accounting Office. *Housing for the Elderly: Information on HUD's Section 202 and HOME*

Investment Partnerships Programs. Report No. GAO/ RCED-98-11. Washington, D.C.: U.S. Government Printing Office, 1997.

Van Vliet, Willem. *Affordable Housing and Urban Redevelopment in the United States.* Thousand Oaks, Calif.: Sage, 1996.

Walker, Christopher. "Nonprofit Housing Development." *Housing Policy Debate* 4:3 (1993): 369–414.

Wallace, James E. *Modeling the Future Status of HUD-Insured Multifamily Rental Property.* Report for the Office of Policy Development and Research, U.S. Department of Housing and Urban Development. Contract HC-5838. Cambridge, Mass.: Abt Associates, 1992.

White, S. Mark. "State and Federal Planning Legislation and Manufactured Housing: New Opportunities for Affordable, Single-Family Shelter." *Urban Lawyer* 28:22 (Spring 1996): 263–91.

The following organizations can provide information about affordable housing:

American Institute of Architects
1735 New York Avenue, N.W.
Washington, DC 20006
(212) 626-7300
www.aiaonline.com

American Planning Association
1313 East 60th Street
Chicago, IL 60637
(312) 955-9100
www.planning.org

Association of Local Housing Finance Agencies
1200 19th Street, N.W., Suite 300
Washington, DC 20036
(202) 857-1197
www.alhfa.org

Center on Budget and Policy Priorities
820 First Street, N.E., Suite 510
Washington, DC 20002
(202) 408-1080
www.cbpp.org

Center for Community Change
1000 Wisconsin Avenue, N.W.
Washington, DC 20007
(202) 342-0567
www.communitychange.org

Council of Large Public Housing Agencies
1250 I Street, N.W., Suite 901A
Washington, DC 20005
(202) 638-1300
www.clpha.org

Council of State Community Development Agencies
444 North Capitol Street, N.W., Suite 224
Washington, DC 20001
(202) 624-3630

The Enterprise Foundation
10227 Wincopin Circle, Suite 500
Columbia, MD 21044
(410) 964-1230
www.enterprisefoundation.org

Fannie Mae
3900 Wisconsin Avenue, N.W.
Washington, DC 20016-2892
(202) 752-7000
www.fanniemae.com

Ford Foundation
320 East 43rd Street
New York, NY 10017
(212) 573-5000
www.fordfound.org

Freddie Mac
8200 Jones Branch Drive
McLean, VA 22102-3110
(800) 424-5401
www.freddiemac.com

Habitat for Humanity
121 Habitat Street
Americus, GA 31709
(912) 924-6935
www.habitat.org

Housing Assistance Council
1025 Vermont Avenue, N.W., Suite 606
Washington, DC 20005
(202) 842-8600
www.ruralhome.org

Joint Center for Housing Studies of
  Harvard University
79 John F. Kennedy Street
Cambridge, MA 02138
(617) 495-7908
www.gsd.harvard.edu/jcenter

Local Initiatives Support Corporation
733 Third Avenue, 8th Floor
New York, NY 10017
(212) 455-9800
www.liscnet.org

Mortgage Bankers Association
1125 15th Street, N.W.
Washington, DC 20005
(202) 861-6500
www.mbaa.org

National Association of Counties
440 First Street, N.W., Suite 800
Washington, DC 20001
(202) 393-6226
www.naco.org

National Association of Home Builders
1201 15th Street, N.W.
Washington, DC 20005
(800) 368-5242
www.nahb.com

National Association of Housing and
    Redevelopment Officials
1320 18th Street, N.W.
Washington, DC 20036
(202) 429-2960
www.nahro.org

National Association of Realtors®
700 11th Street, N.W.
Washington, DC 20001
(202) 383-1000
nar.realtor.com

National Coalition for the Homeless
1012 14th Street, N.W., Suite 600
Washington, DC 20005-3410
(202) 737-6444
nch.ari.net

National Community Development Association
522 21st Street, N.W., Suite 120
Washington, DC 20006
(202) 293-7587
www.ncdaonline.org

National Congress for Community Economic
    Development
1030 15th Street, N.W., Suite 325
Washington, DC 20005
(202) 289-9020
www.ncced.org

National Council of State Housing Agencies
444 North Capitol Street, N.W., Suite 438
Washington, DC 20001
(202) 624-7710
www.ncsha.org

National Housing Conference, Inc.
815 15th Street, N.W., Suite 538
Washington, DC 20005
(202) 393-5772
www.nhc.org

National Housing Trust
1101 30th Street, N.W., Suite 400
Washington, DC 20007
(202) 333-8931
www.nhtinc.org

National League of Cities
1301 Pennsylvania Avenue, N.W.
Washington, DC 20004-1763
(202) 626-3000
www.nlc.org

National Low-Income Housing Coalition
1012 14th Street, N.W., Suite 610
Washington, DC 20005
(202) 662-1530
www.nlihc.org

National Multi Housing Council
1850 M Street, N.W., Suite 540
Washington, DC 20036-5803
(202) 974-2300
www.nmhc.org

National Trust for Historic Preservation
1785 Massachusetts Avenue, N.W.
Washington, DC 20036
(202) 588-6000
www.nthp.org

Neighborhood Housing Services of America
1970 Broadway, Suite 470
Oakland, CA 94612
(510) 832-5542
www.nhsofamerica.org

Neighborhood Reinvestment Corporation
1325 G Street N.W., Suite 800
Washington, DC 20005-3100
(202) 376-2400
www.nw.org/nrc

U.S. Census Bureau
Housing and Household Economic Statistics
   Division
4700 Silver Hill Road
Suitland, MD 20746-2401
(301) 457-3199
www.census.gov

U.S. Conference of Mayors
1620 I Street, N.W.
Washington, DC 20006
(202) 293-7330
www.usmayors.org

U.S. Department of Agriculture
Rural Development Agency
1400 Independence Avenue, S.W., Room 206W
Washington, DC 20250
(202) 720-4581
www.rurdev.usda.gov

U.S. Department of Housing and Urban
   Development
Office of the Secretary
451 Seventh Street, S.W.
Washington, DC 20410
(202) 708-0417
www.hud.gov

U.S. General Accounting Office
Resources, Community, and Economic
   Development Division
441 G Street, N.W.
Washington, DC 20548
(202) 512-9824
www.gao.gov

United Way of America
701 North Fairfax Street
Alexandria, VA 22314-2045
(703) 836-7100
www.unitedway.org

Urban Institute
2100 M Street, N.W.
Washington, DC 20037
(202) 833-7200
www.urbaninstitute.org

ULI–the Urban Land Institute
1025 Thomas Jefferson Street, N.W., Suite 500-W
Washington, DC 20007-5201
(202) 624-7000
www.uli.org

Planning and analysis form the heart of this textbook. All the preceding material sets the stage for making the big decisions. Now the developer must take a hard look at the data to see whether they support the idea. No matter how strong a gut feeling developers may have about a proposed project, instincts are not enough for making the go/no go decisions. Development involves the cooperation of many different entities, and each must be informed with sufficient data about the level of risk involved in the project.

Chapter 16 defines and outlines a holistic version of the feasibility study—the most important decision aid and management tool in the development process. The developer uses it to evaluate the idea across all dimensions of the project—physical, legal, market, and financial—and to assemble the development team. The feasibility study remains a living document that is constantly revised throughout stages four through seven of the process.

Chapter 17 covers the most important element of the feasibility study—market analysis. Properly collected and validated data are critical components of insightful market research and help establish a connection between supply and demand trends and forecasts for the competitive marketplace and property-specific cash flow and valuation assumptions. Chapter 18 helps the analyst appreciate the data and looks at various data sources and forecasting models.

Part VI
Planning and Analysis: The Market Perspective

Chapter 16

Stage Three: The Feasibility Study

Although developers probably have a strong intuitive feel for a project's ultimate viability based on the results of activities that occur during stage two, typically they must still formally demonstrate the project's viability to other participants. The formal demonstration of viability is the goal of stage three—the feasibility study. If the project survives refinement of the idea (stage two), then it is more likely to be a viable project than the rough idea that survived stage one. During stage three, developers commit additional dollars to the project to perform more detailed analyses along several dimensions. Consequently, a strong intuitive positive feeling for the project is necessary coming out of stage two to induce the developer to make the additional financial commitment. At the end of stage three, developers can still decide not to undertake a project, but at a significantly higher cost than at the end of stage two. The cost goes beyond dollars—it includes relationships, time, reputation, and credibility.

Development is more than a series of numbers gleaned from the marketplace; it involves entrepreneurial energy and creativity as well. Still, even the most creative, intuitive developers who bring to the marketplace new concepts of space (over time with associated services) benefit from running all the numbers and systematically addressing all the issues. In addition to serving as a marketing tool to bring all the members of the proposed development team together, the feasibility study is an important management tool providing multiple forms of risk control over several subsequent stages of the development process.

This chapter begins with a comprehensive definition of feasibility and then moves to the initiation of the feasibility study and an overview of the market study. The market study is so critical that Chapters 17 and 18 are devoted exclusively to its preparation. The present chapter discusses other traditional elements of the feasibility study, newer topics under the broad headings "the enterprise concept" and "the notion of venture capital," and techniques to control risk during stage three. It covers the following major topics:

- The definition of feasibility;
- Initiating the feasibility study;
- An overview of the market study;
- Preliminary drawings;
- Initial construction and total cost estimates;
- Lenders and investors;
- Building permits and other government considerations;
- The value statement and formal estimate of feasibility;
- The Europa Center feasibility study, including financial estimates and a pro forma;
- The enterprise concept;
- The notion of venture capital;
- Level two feasibility; and
- Techniques of risk control during stage three.

In thinking about the feasibility study, certain broad principles should be kept in mind.

1. Among its other uses, the feasibility study is an excellent organizational tool. It brings together everything about the development in a consistent format, usually

by using a computer program to facilitate sensitivity analysis. As the development moves through the eight stages, the feasibility study is continually modified, with estimates becoming increasingly concrete over the passage of time.

2. The developer should produce one feasibility study, with relevant sections for each participant in the development process. He probably does not want to share the details of the equity financing with the contractor or the lead tenant, but he does want to be certain that all the assumptions in the equity section are internally consistent with the assumptions in the building cost and leasing sections. The developer should not prepare an independent feasibility study for each participant, even though each must be induced to make an individual commitment. A single feasibility study for the entire project allows the individual participants to achieve the development goal collectively.

3. A complete feasibility study is an extensive undertaking. To ensure its full benefit, the study should not end with a mere finding of "satisfaction," i.e., a determination that the project's value exceeds the cost of making the development "feasible." Rather, the feasibility study should be considered an optimization tool. By using computer-aided sensitivity analysis, the developer should examine every major decision and every significant feature, function, and benefit of the proposed project to see whether it is the *best* plan, not simply an acceptable plan.

4. The eight stages of the development process provide a convenient and logical framework within which to explore the many interactive aspects of real estate development. In fact, the feasibility study might not always be clearly delineated at the third stage of the development process. It might start during refinement of the idea, and final design might spill over into the fourth stage—contract negotiation. Like the entire development process, the feasibility study should be seen as inherently interdisciplinary.

The Definition of Feasibility

The best definition of feasibility remains the one that renowned real estate educator James A. Graaskamp advanced in his classic 1972 article, "A Rational Approach to Feasibility Analysis": "A real estate project is 'feasible' when the real estate analyst determines that there is a reasonable likelihood of satisfying explicit objectives when a selected course of action is tested for fit to a context of specific constraints and limited resources."[1]

Each phrase of Graaskamp's long definition is important. First, feasibility never demonstrates certainty. A project is feasible when it is reasonably likely to meet its goals; even favorable results from a feasibility study cannot guarantee a project's success.

Second, feasibility is determined by satisfying explicit objectives that must be defined before initiating the feasibility study. It is not just a matter of satisfying the developer's explicit objectives, though such objectives may be the initial driving force. The other players have objectives that must be met, the most important of which are the objectives of the public sector partner and the final user.

Third, the definition talks about a selected course of action and testing it for fit. In other words, logistics, particularly timing, matter. It is not simply a question of whether or not an idea might work; rather, it is a question of whether a particular plan for turning an idea into bricks and mortar is likely to work within a specific time frame.

Fourth, the selected course of action is tested for fit in a context of specific constraints, which include all the legal and physical limitations enumerated in stage two of the development process. In addition to the obvious constraints associated with both the public sector's involvement and the land itself, people and capital are limited. For a project to be feasible, it must be feasible given the amount of capital and number of people to be dedicated to the project, according to a specific course of action at a particular time.

This broad definition of feasibility goes far beyond the simple idea of value exceeding cost. When the word "constraints" is pushed into the ethical dimension (as suggested by Graaskamp), then both personal and social ethics as well as formal legal and physical constraints must also be satisfied.

Initiating the Feasibility Study

The feasibility study is the formal demonstration that a proposed project is or is not viable. In addition to maps, pictures, and résumés, a typical feasibility study includes an executive summary, a market study, preliminary drawings, cost estimates, information about terms and sources of financing, government considerations, and the estimate of value.

Depending on the size and complexity of the development, the feasibility study can vary dramatically in length, scope, and cost. At one extreme, if the project is a duplex in an area already developed with other duplexes and is to use architectural drawings from a previously built project and the same contractor and lender, then the feasibility analysis is a simple activity

While the developers of Avenel in Potomac, Maryland, Natelli Communities Limited Partnership, were conducting their feasibility study, the Washington Suburban Sanitary Commission targeted the land for an advanced wastewater treatment facility. The developers brokered an agreement that accommodated the treatment plant while using its buffer zone for the location of the community's famous golf course.

that involves the new market information described in Chapters 10 through 12 applied to a proven course of action. In other words, new market data are used to project rent and absorption, with most other factors refined modestly from preceding developments. In such a simple case, developers would probably choose to perform the feasibility study with in-house staff at limited cost.

This simple case contrasts sharply with a 5,000-acre planned community and industrial park. Such a community includes several types of developed real estate and requires extensive infrastructure as well as above-ground construction. Because the project is likely to take many years to complete, the recognition of long-term trends is more important—even for designing the first stage of the project. An idea for a complex, expensive, long-term project often results in a complex, expensive feasibility study that involves at least one and possibly more outside professionals, such as architects, land planners, soils engineers, hazardous waste experts, and even public relations consultants. More than one architect might be used to specify designs for key facilities as well as any architectural constraints for projects slated to be constructed by outside builders.

Because the relationship between developers and local governments is more dynamic and complex than in the past, interaction with and involvement of various government bodies will probably be substantial from the outset. In some jurisdictions, developers use political consultants who function like pollsters to test the local political waters and then help prepare and deliver the developer's message.

Likewise, market analysis and tenant relations are more complex because of the possibility that people will move to the location not simply from within the city, but also from around the country and possibly from around the world. The developer must coordinate all the professionals and ensure that they are all talking about precisely the same project so that they can collectively determine its feasibility.

For the developer who chooses to use an outside analyst to produce the feasibility study, numerous specialized companies and professional organizations are available to perform the work. Locally owned and operated appraisal firms or national firms with local or regional offices can be commissioned to perform a feasibility study. Likewise, most large accounting firms and major business consulting companies offer this service.

Because various state and federal regulatory agencies oversee the lenders who bear a portion of the risk in major developments, affected financial institutions are usually required to include some feasibility work as one of the items they examine in underwriting the loan. An outside feasibility study prepared by a well-respected firm meets this requirement. By the latter part of the 1980s, for example, Rule R-41c (Appraisal Policies and Practices of Insured Institutions and Service Corporations) required lenders to mandate that appraisals of development projects constitute more than simply a collection of a few comparable facts illustrating current conditions. Instead, lenders are required to formally estimate a project's "highest and best use" based on a schedule of space absorption over time. Further, as a measure of risk control, appraisers must estimate the "as is" value of partially completed projects as well as their projected values upon completion. (See Chapter 6 for more information.)

Although the government hoped to end the unsubstantiated assertions of financial feasibility and property values that led to many financial disasters during the 1980s, more recent regulatory attitudes have placed a greater burden on lenders. Regulators no longer spell out what lenders must demand of appraisers and other market analysts. Rather, lenders are required to demand whatever analyses are necessary in the particular situation—a Catch-22 for most lenders. If they do not require substantial analysis by an independent party and a loan subsequently goes into default, then the regulators will fault them for not performing sufficiently detailed due diligence. Lenders, on the other hand, do not know ahead of time what level of analysis is adequate to avoid loan losses. They don't want to put too much cost burden on their customers (developers/borrowers), but they want to leave a paper trail in case problems develop later.

Before examining each individual component of the feasibility study, it is instructive to consider all the components as a single unit. An analysis of the collective items listed below yields an answer to whether or not an idea is feasible, using Graaskamp's broad definition of feasibility.

The Essentials:
- Executive summary
- Maps
- Photographs of the site
- Renderings
- Electronic valuation model derived from market study
- Documented cost projections—Marshall & Swift, R.S. Means, or F.W. Dodge plus a supporting contractor's estimate
- Time line
- Résumés.

The Critical Analytic Elements:
- Idea and target market for the project, from the big picture down to an absorption schedule for today in the particular market niche—progressing from world to nation to region to city to neighborhood to site;
- A careful enumeration of the target market—number of people, their tastes, their income—tied to the specific idea;
- Identification of appropriate comparable properties (the competition) along with the major features, functions, and benefits of each;
- The foregoing information tied into a discounted cash flow model;

28 State Street, a 40-story office building in the center of Boston, underwent a $45 million renovation. The new design, by Elkus/Manfredi Architects, re-created the 1968 building by adding three tiers of underground parking, a new HVAC system, heightened ceilings, and an elliptical split-level lobby using curved wood and glass walls to achieve a high level of architectural quality.

- A sensitivity analysis to move from feasible to optimal, with an individual evaluation of each component of the plan;
- A review of risks in the optimal configuration, with appropriate select risk control techniques;
- Confirmation that the project is feasible for each participant (see "Level Two Feasibility" below).

An Overview of the Market Study

The market study is the most crucial item in a feasibility analysis. It analyzes all the long-term global, national, regional, and local trends that were initially identified during refinement of the idea in stage two. These trends are now formally brought to bear on the existing local situation as the analyst projects an absorption schedule for the project. This task is so important that real estate market studies for various property types are the entire focus of Chapters 17 and 18.

The first step in a market study is an examination of national economic conditions (including international influences) and projected long-term trends as well as careful consideration of the characteristics of the region, locality, neighborhood, and site. Long-term national trends are often extremely important to the site. It has been well documented, for example, that, nationally, the types of jobs available and types of job seekers in central cities are mismatched.[2] The United States has moved increasingly away from the strong back (manufacturing) and toward the strong mind (information processing) in numbers of available jobs. Entry-level jobs for high school dropouts that used to be available in manufacturing have declined drastically in inner cities; jobs involving information processing have increased in number but are out of reach for dropouts.[3]

This national trend is particularly apparent in certain regions and is directly relevant to development in many central cities. Developers of office space in central cities may find that prospective tenants worry about their ability to attract needed high-level secretarial help at a given location. At the same time, suburban retail developments might have difficulty finding individuals willing to take lower-paying positions at fast-food restaurants and retail shops. In both cases, the lack of available workers may decrease the value that prospective tenants place on a proposed project. Market analysts should not lose sight of such important national trends as they project operating numbers for a specific site, and they must remember that even modestly sized projects have two- to five-year time horizons for planning, construction, sales, and leasing, thus increasing the importance of sound forecasting.

As a second step, market analysts investigate comparable properties to determine the features, functions, and benefits of those properties that are important to the market. Because market analysis is expensive, the proposed development should benefit from the insights gained by the analyst in studying comparable projects. Knowing the value that space users place on particular features can help developers specify the key features of the proposed development. If the best leasing in the area has been achieved by an office building that has no health club but more parking than the competition, then extra parking is more important than a health club; thus, the subject property should be designed accordingly.

Third, the market study always concludes with projected absorption schedules for the market segment and for the specific property. How many units at what price over what time period will the target market be likely to absorb? It is necessary to segment the market carefully by defining all the features, functions, and benefits of comparable projects to be able to predict the overall absorption rate for the market segment. The developer can then attach value to the distinctive features of the subject property and compare it with the market to estimate the proposed development's capture rate and expected rents.

Preliminary Drawings

If an idea's viability is established (at least in the developer's mind) in stage two, more money must usually be committed to drawings in stage three. Preliminary drawings show exterior elevations and specify rentable square feet or salable units, parking, type of HVAC systems, and the like. Part of this work was done in stage two, but the formal feasibility study requires drawings much closer to final design plans than those needed for stage two.

Although different architects and engineers can be used for the initial architectural layout and the final construction drawings, it is usually more efficient to use the same architect and engineer throughout the entire process. Such consistency reduces the learning curve involved in bringing in new players and prompts their commitment to and understanding of the development team's objectives. Developers usually find it difficult to specify the level of sophistication (read "out-of-pocket costs") needed of the architect and engineer and the amount of their time to use at each stage. The more complex and innovative the job, the more important it is to hire competent professionals and bring them into the process earlier. On the other hand, for simpler projects that are much like other projects and on sites much like other sites, it is probably not cost-efficient to bring in Frank Gehry or I.M. Pei with a full team of supporting engineers. The developer must decide on the quality, quantity, and timing of design talent.

Overall, high-quality design is becoming much more important as more communities implement design standards. High-quality design can go a long way toward the successful leasing and management of the finished project. Landscaping is also increasing in importance. A creative landscape architect can enhance and beautify an already striking project and, when necessary, mask previous design errors. Some cities, like Bilbao, Spain, have centered economic development plans around striking architecture. The unusual architecture and high style of the new Bilbao Guggenheim, designed by Frank Gehry, was expected to bring perhaps 500,000 visitors to Bilbao the first year. Instead, it brought 1.36 million visitors and $160 million in revenue to the former shipbuilding town that few ever visited. The city's solution to its economic decline was culture and design, and, in addition to the museum, it is building a concert hall and a sports arena, all designed by internationally renowned architects.

Although the selection of architectural support often reflects a project's distinctiveness or complexity, it can also complement the developer's experience or reputation. In selecting architects for Europa Center, Fraser Morrow Daniels balanced the high cost of a well-established firm against its lack of development experience in the local office market.

▦ Europa Center

A Key Hiring Decision

The next step after justifying the cost of the land was to decide which architects and construction companies to use —major decisions for our company. People in the business of building offices usually have long working relationships with architects and ask for five or six bids. Our company had no history of building major office buildings, but all our lenders told us that putting up office buildings was quite simple compared with the complicated resort development we had done earlier and that it ought to be relatively easy for us.

What I wanted to do, even if it cost more money, was to hire the best, most experienced architect that I knew we could trust and the best construction company with a record of getting the job done—even if its prices weren't the best going. Our choice was the architectural firm Cooper Carry & Associates from Atlanta, which has built many office buildings.

As the Europa Center case study demonstrates, outside professionals can bring valuable experience to the development team and reduce risk when a development company lacks experience in a certain type of project or has not yet established a good track record with local government bodies. As specialists, architects play a crucial role in the development process, but they cannot design the project unless they are aware of other players' activities and objectives. To be successful, the final product must be marketable, manageable, and cost-effective. Communication and feedback among the members of the development team are essential from the beginning, because preliminary drawings must compare and trade off three basic items: marketing appeal

(the project's eye appeal to prospective tenants), the project's physical cost, and the ease of ongoing management. A beautiful building that costs too much to construct and is difficult to manage is not a successful development. On the other hand, a low-budget project could be both visually unappealing and difficult to manage and therefore even less successful. Optimal results occur when property management (described in Chapter 21) is combined with the factors discussed in this chapter and with the concepts of marketing discussed throughout the text. The development team's clear communication of marketing information to the architect stimulates the design of manageable space that is attractive to prospective tenants.

A balance among marketing appeal, cost, and ease of management cannot be achieved without fitting the project to a specific site; after all, the primary distinguishing characteristic of real estate is its specific, unchangeable location. A project that fits one site well is often far less successful when replicated on a second site. Fitting the project to the site requires creativity and is frequently a time-consuming process, but it is an invaluable device for controlling risk. Early refinements in the design can prevent the development of structures that cannot be managed or leased. Good planning can also reduce or eliminate opposition from the public sector. During the development of preliminary drawings for Europa Center, the building's design underwent many changes to satisfy the requirements of the developers and Chapel Hill's city council.

▦ Europa Center

Working with the Architect

Designing the project was another delicate process, because we did not have a lot of money. The architects designed the whole building for $250,000 for a chance to participate in the project, even though they would not be paid until after we got a loan funded. They had to prepare fairly complete working drawings of the whole building so that we could put it out for bids to contractors and get a firm, guaranteed maximum price. The architects did all that work before we got our construction loan.

We gave the architects general parameters: design something distinctive and relatively conservative that reflects the architecture and style of the Hotel Europa. It should be heavy on landscaping, should not remove any of the existing trees (we knew in Chapel Hill that saving the seven or eight remaining trees on the site was critical), and should not fill in the small pond (a landmark that people

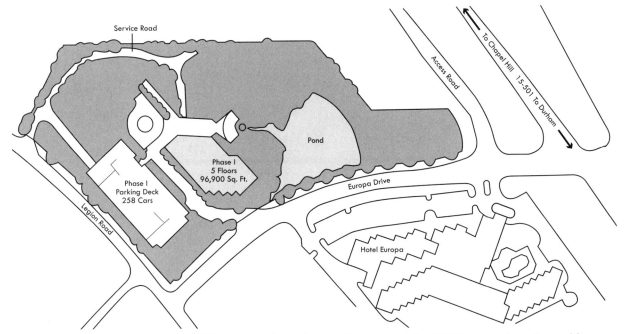

Phase I of Europa Center contains 96,900 square feet of space (approximately 92,700 square feet of rentable space) and 258 parking spaces in a parking deck with covered access. Landscape amenities include an abundance of trees and a pond.

valued). We wanted to concentrate the building on the back of the site.

We asked the architects, based on the 50 buildings they had designed before, what the best, most compatible design for this site would be. The architects came back with about five plans and told us the only way we could get a cost-effective amount of square footage for the $5.00 per square foot we had paid for land would be to fill in the pond, cover it over with asphalt, and build a building there. They recommended a seven-story building.

We went back to the planning board and the town council informally and asked whether the architects' proposed plan could work. They said it wouldn't and told us to have the architects redesign the building to take into consideration the trees, the pond, and the site's general aesthetics.

Again we had to justify cost. Either we had to build a smaller building, build surface parking, and keep the pond, or we had to build the amount of square footage that it took to justify $5.00 per square foot for the land and build structured parking. Economically, structured parking is borderline unless you've paid about $6.00 or $7.00 per square foot for land. Based on just one building analysis, we would have been better off to build one building on this site, make less money, and buy another piece of land somewhere else for a second building; the cost of the land for the second building would be cheaper than the incremental cost of building the parking deck. But we could not identify another site that was as good as this one for

a second building. The logical solution would be to put the parking somewhere else, not under ground. We decided, however, that we would be better off paying the extra price, building a five-story building, adding another $0.70 a square foot to the rental rate, building structured parking, and getting 200,000 square feet of building on the site.

So we gave the architects some very tight boundaries to work within, all based on economics. They came up with a building [described in the accompanying site plan and specifications] that fit the shape of the site, reflected the architecture of the Hotel Europa, and preserved the pond and landscaping nearest the major frontage road. It took about an extra three months in the process.

The relationship with the city was complex, simply because the town council and planning board staunchly supported Chapel Hill's no-growth climate. The planning board, concerned about the building's height, wanted to see what the site would look like after construction and asked us to put up balloons that would delineate the building's top floor. The day the board was to visit the project, the wind was blowing at 20 miles an hour. We brought four high-rise cranes to the site, one for each corner, and had ribbons stretched across the tops of the cranes to outline the top of the proposed five-story building. It worked, although balloons clearly would have been cheaper. The cost of delay and rescheduling the council's site visit, however, would have been greater than the cranes.

Building Specifications

Location
U.S. 15-501 and Europa Drive

Building Size
Total gross square feet, Phase I—96,900
Total rentable square feet, Phase I—92,700

Suite Sizes
Approximately 1,000 square feet to full floor (approximately 18,860 square feet); capability of expansion in Phase II to a contiguous floor area of approximately 40,000 square feet.

Parking
258 spaces in an open-air parking structure consisting of one on-grade parking level and two elevated levels.

Elevator
Two custom hydraulic elevators in the entrance lobby; interiors of cabs finished with raised-fabric wall panels with polished stainless steel accents, carpeted floors, and polished stainless steel 9.5-foot ceiling with recessed downlighting.

Standards

Partitioning
All partitions to be drywall construction using $1/2$-inch gypsum wallboard over two $1/2$-inch metal studs; tenant allowance to be one linear foot of partitioning per 10 square feet of usable area; of this linear footage, 20 percent will be soundproofed.

Wall Finishes
Interior walls will be finished with standard vinyl covering, with tenants' choice of colors; upgraded finishes available.

Ceiling
Suspended $5/8$-inch acoustical fireguard tile with recessed edge in exposed two-foot by two-foot grid.

Electrical Lights
Two-foot by four-foot, three-lamp, lay-in fluorescent energy-saving lamp and ballast fixture with parabolic louver diffuser; one per 83 square feet of usable area.

Power Outlets
One duplex wall outlet per 100 square feet of usable area.

Light Switches
One double-pole switch per 300 square feet of usable area.

Telephone Outlets
One outlet per 150 square feet of usable area, wall mounted in interior partitions.

Floor Covering
Standard carpet is 30-ounce tufted cut-pile nylon commercial carpet installed by direct gluedown, with colors to be selected by tenant and upgraded carpet available; vinyl asbestos tile is 12 inches by 12 inches by $1/8$ inch, available for kitchen and storage areas; four-inch vinyl cove base standard.

Entry Door
One single, full-height, three-foot-wide, solid-core door in an aluminum frame, with hardware to include lockset, wall stop, and automatic closer; one set of double-entry doors provided for leased premises larger than 3,000 usable square feet.

Interior Doors
One single, full-height, three-foot-wide, solid-core door in an aluminum frame with passage set hardware; one per 225 square feet of usable area (including entrance door).

Window Covering
One-inch blinds with Top-Lok feature or equal provided at all fixed exterior windows.

Heating and Air Conditioning
Multiple-zone, variable-air-volume system using heat reclaim with thermostatically controlled zones; distribution for each zone uses ceiling diffusers; one supply per 150 usable square feet and one return per 200 usable square feet.

Space Planning
Layout and design services that provide blueprints for construction will be furnished at no cost by the landlord.

Graphics
One tenant identification and suite number sign to be provided by landlord at entry door; one listing on building directory to be provided by landlord on interior building directory; all graphics standard throughout building.

Floor Loading
70 pounds per square foot, including wall partitions.

continued on page 348

Museum Towers

Working with the Architect

Museum Towers is not a "high-design" project. When all the adjoining public work is complete, it will have tremendous views and a very convenient location. With those attributes, we didn't think we needed to overpay on design. We did spend a considerable amount of time with interior design people, making sure that the kitchens and baths were superior to the older competition, but the project won't win any design competitions.

Building Specifications

Location
Eight and Ten Museum Way (formerly 15 Monsignor O'Brien Highway), Cambridge, Massachusetts, in the North Point neighborhood, directly across the Charles River from the west end area of downtown Boston.

Lot Size
Total parcel area—90,169 square feet (2.07 acres)

Building Size
Total gross square feet—618,710
Total rentable square feet—410,444

Units
Total number of units—435
Average square feet per unit—944
Mix of units—four studios, 180 one-bedroom units, 251 two-bedroom units

Parking
490 spaces in a 103,200-square-foot underground garage.

Museum Towers is located close to several main arteries and two subway lines.

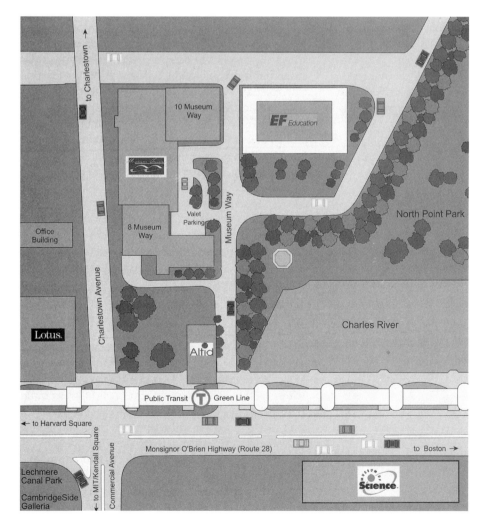

Common Area/Mechanical
88,566 square feet

Retail Space
2,500 square feet

Health Club
14,000 square feet

Tenant Storage Space
200 units

Elevators
Six high-speed elevators, three in each tower, that travel at the rate of 700 feet per minute.

Windows
Combination of awning windows, fixed windows, and sliding doors with insulated glass in aluminum frames.

Standards

Partitioning—Wall Finishes
Gypsum wallboard with plaster.

Ceilings
Gypsum wallboard with skim coat of plaster and sprayed, textured finish. Suspended acoustical tile in commercial areas.

Floors
Poured concrete.

Electrical Lights
Incandescent and fluorescent.

Floor Coverings
Carpeting in unit living and common areas; resilient tile in the storage, janitor, and utilities areas; ceramic tile in the bathrooms; sheet vinyl in the kitchens.

Exterior Doors
Combination of metal and glass in metal frames.

Exterior Unit Doors
Solid wood.

Interior Unit Doors
Hollow-core wood, bifold and six panel.

HVAC
Individually controlled water source heat pumps with circulated warm and cool water from a central system.

Hot Water
Individual electric units in each unit.

Utilities
Sewer and water—City of Cambridge
Electricity and natural gas—Commonwealth Energy

Trash Removal/Disposal
Trash chutes on each floor.

Life Safety Systems
High-rise fire alarms and smoke detectors, emergency lighting, sprinkler system, stair pressurization, and smoke exhaust systems.

Security
Twenty-four-hour concierge service along with card access security systems. Closed-circuit television with videotape surveillance in each building.

continued on page 348

Space is created for people, not vice versa. Moreover, space that appeals to people can generate a new market in the future beyond the demand indicated in the market study. Today, heightened interest in the functionality and aesthetics of constructed space leads to research into the value created by outstanding architecture and specifically addresses the question of whether or not buildings that clearly are design landmarks (or are particularly attractive) bring a higher return to the developer and investor.[4] Whether or not such research eventually proves that greater returns accrue to "great" architecture, developers find some lenders and investors want to be associated with "big names."

Besides being concerned about how a building fits its site and serves its intended tenants, developers also need to think about how a building blends into the urban setting. For example, Pittsburgh—with its many corporate headquarters buildings, three rivers, and mountains—has been said to have one of the most stunning skylines of any major U.S. city. In contrast, other writers have characterized Dallas as "a bunch of buildings screaming at each other." Dallas's cityscape seems less to bring together a harmonious group of different buildings than to show different buildings that compete with each other. The lesson is that an individual building may appear attractive in isolation but, once built, must interact with its surroundings. Context is an important element of design.

Truly great architecture synthesizes the elements of context and design. Size and scale, massing and setbacks, landscaping, circulation in the parking area, lighting, stylistic details, relationships, image, range of difference —not to mention form and materials—are all important within what is usually referred to as "the context of the building." Likewise, foreshadowing and the entry, contrast and consistency, form and space relationships, volume, ordering systems, edges in transition, activity areas, levels, circulation in movement, the building's footprint, human scale, surfaces and materials, varied elements, ornamentation and color, and landscaping are important design considerations.

For a nonarchitect, this list may sound like an expensive set of intangible combinations. The ideal way for most individuals to learn about architecture is to visit great buildings and to study how their architecture fits with the city and how the space functions for those who inhabit it. It is probably one of the most enjoyable parts of kicking tires in the real estate business.

Initial Construction and Total Cost Estimates

The estimate of the cost to construct the project should include the land, usually optioned or contracted for in stage two, the needed infrastructure, and the planned improvements to the land. In large, complex developments, both the latter requirements can be extremely expensive. Off-site infrastructure costs, whether assumed voluntarily or imposed on the developer by regulation,

must be combined with on-site costs of water, sewers, streets, and the like to obtain an estimate of the total cost of infrastructure. Beyond needed infrastructure, the basic development costs are the land and the physical improvements to it that are necessary to bring the site to a condition that is ready for above-ground construction. In Tokyo, where a hectare of land (about 2.5 acres) can sell for more than a small ranch in Montana, land is usually the costliest item; in the United States, the greatest cost is usually attributable to the construction of the building—the bricks, mortar, and labor necessary to build the space.

Although it is easy to list cost categories, it is difficult to estimate the dollars associated with those costs. The cost of the land will probably be known after stage two, though with some variability for more complex options, lease fees, subordination agreements, and the like. In most cases, the most difficult cost to estimate accurately is infrastructure. Without extensive borings, it is difficult to know where rock is located and hence how expensive it will be to route pipe around it. And even with the advice of the best soils engineer, sometimes the handling of water is more expensive than expected. Every experienced developer can relate war stories about problems encountered during construction—and underestimating the cost of infrastructure often heads the list.

Above ground, readily accessible guides are available for estimating construction costs. The guides break down cost elements and include monthly updates for inflation as well as adjustments for the geographic location of the proposed development.[5] The breakdown

The architects of Calakmul—a 397,000-square-foot office building in a suburb of Mexico City—created the illusion of a single pyramid appearing as three in succession and a structure of a sphere within a cube. The building's "smart" design employs fully automated functions, uses energy-efficient construction materials, and has a network of pluvial trays to catch and recycle rainwater.

between materials and labor or at least their components is usually based on square feet or linear feet. Other above-ground improvements—for example, parking lots, trees, lights, and signs—are often categorized under landscape architecture.

Developers should use standard industry cost guides to compile in-house cost projections to compare with local general contractors' estimates. In-house cost projections should yield an estimate that is close to general contractors' own cost estimates. When a significant difference occurs, the developer needs to recheck the figures and discuss them in more detail with the general contractors. If discrepancies remain, they must at least be explainable.

At times, the estimating process requires the developer to meet with individual subcontractors. For example, if an unusual amount and type of glass is to be used in a particular project, the developer might find it advisable to discuss with the glass subcontractor the specifics underlying the cost estimates used in the feasibility study. Information gleaned from talking to contractors and subcontractors helps redefine and improve parts of the project so that the proposal becomes more attractive to tenants, less expensive to construct, more cost-effective to operate, or some combination of the three. During the initial solicitation for construction bids, Fraser Morrow Daniels used the suggestions of three contractors to revise the architects' preliminary drawings. The accompanying section of the case study reveals the motivation for selecting the contractor for Europa Center. Although selection of the architect was based on reputation, cost entered more heavily into the selection of the contractor.

▦ Europa Center

The Tradeoffs in Choosing Players

We put the design out to bid to three different contractors. We reviewed the project in detail with each one, incorporating some of their suggestions for saving money, got a final price, and then chose the construction company based on price as well as on the firm's reputation for finishing jobs. In this case, we violated one of our own rules. To save $200,000 on the cost of construction, we picked the company that had a less solid reputation than the others (although all three companies were good ones). In this way, we reached the base construction price; later, we had to negotiate the parking deck, which wasn't yet designed.

continued on page 353

Dean Stratouly tries to never make tradeoffs when it comes to choosing the people who will be working with him.

▦ Museum Towers

Choosing Players

I can't tell you how important it is to work with people you trust. If you're trying to make a decision about buying a building or a permitting issue or cooling towers, you have to be able to look at people and understand something about their personality, how credible they are. You have to get a sense of who they are and what their agenda is and where they're trying to go compared with where you're trying to go.

I'm fortunate because I've had the same project team for 20 years. The same mechanical engineer, electrical engineer, plumbing engineer, structural engineer. I've got one lead law firm. Even in the office, I need to be sure that everybody who works for me is working toward the same goal. I tell them that everybody has to do what's necessary to make sure we meet our pro formas. If you expect to come to work at nine o'clock and go home at five o'clock Monday through Friday, it's the wrong place to be.

Loyalty is a big piece of it. Trust is a big piece of it. And the loyalty and trust start off with capability. My construction guy, for example, is one of the best in the business. In the early eighties, I fired a construction company and hired another one that had a young assistant project manager. The project manager and the assistant manager both came to the meeting. The project manager was so full of himself, but the assistant project manager was a straightforward guy. So I hired them on the condition that the assistant would be the project manager. We've been together ever since. There was something about the way he answered questions that made me trust him. I hired him after he finished that project, and he's been with us ever since.

He's stuck with me, too. In 1989, we had 55 people in the company; by 1992, we were down to seven people, and then I had to cut everybody's salary by 20 percent. I know that my construction guy was offered several jobs, one of which would have doubled his salary, but he said he helped me get into this mess and he'd help me get out. That kind of loyalty you can't buy.

I make mistakes every day—some really big ones sometimes. It doesn't do me any good to have well-paid people on staff telling me what I want to hear. People need to know that they're going to get treated fairly and not see their heads roll when they deliver unpleasant news to me. My construction guy and I fight. You should see the fights sometimes. But I trust him.

continued on page 408

For Europa Center, the changes prompted by the contractor's suggestions rippled through to the cost estimates, thus demonstrating that the feasibility study should not be considered a static document. Rather, the study should be continually refined to reflect changes in both the physical project and market conditions.

Beyond the costs of land with improvements and above-ground construction, an estimate of total costs involves a substantial amount for marketing, financing, preparing taxes, insurance, and other administrative costs. Depending on the type of project, marketing could start months or even years before completion. Market research should start even earlier. Postconstruction costs for operations during initial periods of moderate occupancy are part of the total marketing cost. Advertising, commissions, and special concessions to tenants during the initial leasing period usually represent the major portion of the costs of marketing the development.

Lenders charge fees. Long-term lenders charge a commitment fee for the promise to replace the construction lender. Construction lenders typically charge origination fees (points) and certainly charge interest over the period of a loan. Additional points may be payable on the permanent loan at closing.

Local governments expect to collect property taxes throughout the development process, making such taxes another very real cost of development. Insurance should include fire and extended coverage in addition to various forms of liability coverage. Accounting costs and a variety of overhead costs should also be included in the overall cost estimate. The inclusion of both overhead and a development fee over and above overhead costs indicates that the developer is planning to draw some profit during the construction period. (See "Level Two Feasibility" later in this chapter.)

Most estimates of marketing, borrowing, property taxes, insurance, and administrative costs can be based on experience and a projection of future trends. It is possible, for example, to know what market brokerage fees are, to estimate the amount of media time needed for advertising and the cost of that time, and, based on trends in the marketplace, to project leasing periods, an essential part of accurately estimating the cost of initial periods of low occupancy. Likewise, estimates of financing costs can be based on a combination of projected construction time and projected interest rates.

Overall, past experience can be helpful in estimating costs for a standard product in a familiar location. Looking at the history of recent comparable developments can provide updated information, allowing a developer to adjust for recent changes. Clearly, it is important to plan for the impact of any changes in tax law, any changes in public policy, and evolving market conditions.

Finally, costs for contingencies should be included for every project. In an uncertain world, where feasibility is only "reasonably likely" and not guaranteed, it is important to set aside funds for unexpected costs and cost overruns. Because the total cost estimate is based on several other estimates, it is important to provide contingency funds commensurate with project risk. In a standard development, 5 percent might be adequate; in complex mixed-use redevelopments, 10 percent may not be sufficient.

Although each development will have features specific to it, a typical cost estimate might include the following elements:

- Land cost
- Site development costs
- Design fees
    - Architecture
    - Engineering
- Hard costs
    - By category
    - Labor and materials
- Permitting costs
- Financing costs
    - Permanent loan commitment fees
    - Construction interest
    - Construction loan fees
- Marketing costs
    - Promotion
    - Advertising
    - Leasing commissions
    - Brokers' fees
- Preopening operating costs
- Legal fees
- Accounting costs
- Field supervision (inspection) costs
- Overhead
- Contingencies
- Development fees.

Ideally, each estimate is confirmed by market data. Some items, such as land costs, may be based on contracts or options. The largest item, hard costs, should be confirmed by comparison with 1) the cost of similar projects; 2) cost estimation services; and 3) the prospective general contractor.

Profile **Jerry Speyer**

President and CEO, Tishman Speyer Properties
New York, New York

Jerry Speyer is president and chief executive officer of Tishman Speyer Properties, a global real estate company established in 1978. Based in New York City, the company has offices in the United States, Europe, South America, and Asia. Tishman Speyer employs more than 500 people in its real estate division and several thousand more in its services division, which provides expertise in building maintenance, mostly to properties owned or managed by Tishman Speyer. Since its founding, the company has developed or acquired more than 36 million square feet of commercial space. The market value of Tishman Speyer's portfolio totals an estimated $10.5 billion.

Fluent in German, Speyer graduated in 1962 from Columbia College with a degree in German literature. In 1964, he earned his MBA from Columbia Business School and in 1966 began working at his father-in-law's company, Tishman Realty, one of the few publicly traded real estate companies at that time. In the mid-1970s, with the unfavorable tax treatment of public companies at that time, the family decided to convert the company back to private ownership. To avoid double taxation of shareholders, the company had to liquidate all its assets and services. Speyer's business acumen and training were instrumental in maximizing the liquidation value of the stock. The company was split along discipline lines into three different companies, with Speyer and his father-in-law forming Tishman Speyer Properties in 1978.

On Development and Management

Speyer sees real estate as having two distinct yet interdependent aspects. The real estate business, particularly the development process, requires a blend of both art and science, imagination and practical restraint. According to Speyer, "It's not one or the other; real estate requires a lot of creativity with a significant amount of diligence and discipline applied." When considering the company's tremendous growth from a core group of ten to 15 people to the multinational corporation it is today, Speyer points to a few key factors: "great partners, being well capitalized, and making sure the skill set required for every transaction is in place."

The management structure of Tishman Speyer Properties today is organized along five divisions: development and investment, business affairs, property management, asset management, and compensation/personnel. Although Speyer is involved in most major decisions, management of the company is fairly decentralized, with day-to-day operations run largely by the head of each division. Management consultants are regularly used to organize each of the company's divisions "to keep them sharp and efficient." Says Speyer, "We do what we know how to do. Our consultants help us to manage doing those things better."

Overbuilding and Overseas Development

Tishman Speyer came into being just as the real estate boom of the 1980s was revving up, and the firm soon developed and acquired properties nationwide. By the mid-1980s, Speyer perceived that the market was quickly becoming overbuilt and began to prudently divest much of the company's portfolio. As a result, Tishman Speyer avoided much of the calamity that befell many developers when the commercial property market crashed in the late 1980s. The company emerged healthy from the real estate recession well positioned for the market comeback of the 1990s.

While development opportunities in the United States were diminished because of the real estate recession, Speyer turned his attention to development overseas. Political turmoil had unraveled a deal in China, but Speyer also began to look toward Europe. The fall of the Berlin Wall brought new development opportunities in Europe, particularly in Germany. In 1988, Speyer was approached to develop the MesseTurm office building in Frankfurt after the original developer bowed out. In partnership with Citicorp/Citibank and the Kajima Corporation, Speyer took over development of the building.

With the basic design of the building and the development rights already in place, the challenge for Tishman Speyer was to acquire a ground lease, forge the development partnership, and revisit some of the design issues to make the building more efficient and profitable. The first two tasks required a thorough study of German law and considerable consultation with local law and accounting firms. In revisiting the design of the building, Tishman Speyer could only make modifications, not wanting to take the building through the approval process again. These modifications included designing a simpler frame, employing a more efficient elevator system, revamping the HVAC system, and using a less expensive facade that still recalled many of the architecturally significant buildings in Frankfurt. The result of these and other changes was an increase in rentable space, a shortened construction schedule, and a reduction in capital costs. The MesseTurm is a slender 72-story, 680,000-square-foot (net rentable area) world-class office tower that rises 842 feet into the air, making it the tallest office building in Europe. The building has become an instant landmark in Frankfurt, appearing on postcards and posters for the city.

Since developing the MesseTurm, Tishman Speyer has opened offices in several international markets, including Paris, London, Berlin, Frankfurt, and São Paulo. The company's success overseas has been the result of careful planning and a thorough understanding of the aspects of each market. When developing in a foreign market, says Speyer, "It's always important to spend a lot of time doing reconnaissance work, learning about the market and its culture. You can't just parachute in and expect to be successful overnight."

Acquisitions

In addition to properties his company has developed, Speyer is equally well known for some of his company's acquisitions. In 1997, Tishman Speyer formed an $800 million joint real estate venture with the Travelers Insurance Company, which Speyer's company oversees. Some of the more famous recent acquisitions have been in New York and include the famed but long-neglected Chrysler building and a portion of the landmark Rockefeller Center.

Speyer approaches acquisitions with the same savvy and intensity as a development project. "Both development and acquisition projects are challenging. There are quite meaningful projects in both of those categories for us." Some of that savvy is evident in the acquisition of the 1.2 million-square-foot Chrysler building.

Speyer was able to acquire the Chrysler building by first negotiating for the land lease on which the building stands. The Cooper Union, a tuition-free educational institution that owns the land, depends on revenues from the land lease to support scholarships for students. Acquisition of the Chrysler building also included acquisition of the nearby Kent building, an unremarkable 32-story structure built in 1951 at the eastern end of the same block, and four brownstones in between.

Speyer was able to make a superior offer to Cooper Union by devising a way to make space in the Kent building more efficient. The elevator core of the building was located at one end of the structure. Breaking through one of the brownstones allowed the elevator core to be moved to the center of the new structure, increasing the amount of leasable space. Speyer plans to envelop the Kent building and the smaller commercial buildings into a larger Chrysler complex.

Towering over the low-rise exhibition and meeting halls of the Messe Frankfurt (Frankfurt fairgrounds), the slender, campanile-like MesseTurm marks the east end of the fairgrounds, where it connects with the classical 1909 festival hall and a new exhibition hall/entrance pavilion, also designed by Murphy/Jahn.

Speyer is also overseeing the redevelopment of Rockefeller Center, another New York City landmark, of which he is part owner. Since taking over management of the venerable facility in May 1996, Speyer has seen vacancies drop from 20 percent to just 2 percent. A $100 million redevelopment of the property now underway will include a retenanting of the retail space and the development of new restaurants in an effort to reinvigorate the property and spark new interest among locals and tourists. While embarking on needed changes, Speyer is cognizant of the need to balance change against the historical significance of the complex. In a recent New York Times magazine article, Speyer notes, "There's a culture in each of these buildings that's really important to respect. We're staying away from anything that's faddish." ■

Lenders and Investors

The preliminary discussions with lenders and investors that began in stage two now progress to a much more formal level. Based on initial reactions, the developer is close to finding the most appropriate permanent lender, construction lender, and, possibly, development-period equity investor and/or joint venture partner. In stage three, the developer presents lenders and investors with more specific information about the target market, design and costs of the project, and the financial structure of the proposed transaction. At this point, the developer uses the project's estimated value to encourage participation. Permanent lenders look at their prospective return and the associated risk. This exercise usually involves a projected debt service coverage ratio, a loan-to-value ratio, and an estimation of the project's ability to maintain value through long-term appeal in a particular market.

Construction lenders usually prefer a simple project designed and built by highly skilled individuals with whom they have experience. If developers always followed lenders' guidelines, however, their profit (value minus cost) would likely be slim indeed. Lenders want both low risk (often interpreted as "it's been done before") and high interest rates with many loan fees. Lenders have been known to deviate from their general preferences—but only for logical reasons and usually only if those reasons are supported by a high-quality feasibility study.

To find the appropriate financiers for a proposed development, developers must know lenders' and investors' particular needs, their histories, their self-images, and the current preferred mix for their portfolios. Accordingly, developers work to minimize the costs of financing (see Chapters 4 through 6) and maximize their flexibility by minimizing the number of rules and other constraints imposed by lenders in the loan documents.

Why does a particular investment fit one lender better than another? On the surface, the answer is fairly straightforward. Larger life insurance companies typically finance larger projects developed by national firms. Regional life insurance companies and some commercial banks are more likely to finance smaller, more local projects. Many commercial banks, because of their predominantly short-term sources of funding, are more typically construction lenders on safer projects. S&Ls, which formerly took equity positions more easily than commercial banks, were once more likely to make higher-risk construction loans that involved equity participation. That situation has changed substantially, however, and the remaining solvent S&Ls have become more cautious lenders.[6]

Recall the typical sequence presented in Chapters 4 through 6. Usually, the developer first lines up the largest, lowest-cost permanent loan possible. This permanent loan is the "takeout" for the construction lender. The difference between the total project cost and the available financing is the required equity. If the developer doesn't have (or doesn't want to risk) much money, he needs an equity investor for the development period.

The critical concept is matching the right lender/investor to the particular development. With recent consolidation in the financial markets, financial supermarkets from the merger of Bank America/NationsBank to GE Capital now typically engage in a variety of real estate loans through subsidiaries and affiliates, if not directly. Again, a mortgage broker might be hired to help developers deal with the financial community. As with the selection of an architect and an engineer, the more complex and crucial the financing arrangement, the more skilled developers or their agent must be in dealing with the financial community. Developers don't have to arrange financing; instead, they could hire Goldman Sachs and get first-rate assistance. Even with a top national investment banker on the team, however, it remains the developer's job to make the project happen, and financing is critical to that outcome.

Building Permits and Other Government Considerations

During stage three, it is important not to forget the most important partner in the development process—the government. Government agencies are responsible for issuing the necessary building permits for the project. In some areas, obtaining permits is a highly political process. Developers who misjudge the local political environment or suggest a project that does not fit the community's long-term interests can have difficulty even if they technically meet the letter of the law (see Chapters 13 through 15 for more detail).

Clearly, some representatives of local government need to be involved in the determination of feasibility. If the regulators understand all the pressures on the development and how the development meets both public and private objectives, they will more than likely support the project and be less likely to delay the development approval process. Often, municipal staff are technically well trained and will accept the development concept so long as it fits with the city's master plan. If the public sector is recruited early in the development process and is fully committed to the concept, it is less likely to throw up time-consuming roadblocks as the process unfolds.

Successful developers must not ignore the political side of government. Elected officials representing the public at large and individuals representing particular interest groups may mount a challenge even if a project benefits the overall jurisdiction. In many areas, the political environment has become a nightmare for developers who fail to anticipate the power of opinions strongly held by small groups. Projects endorsed earlier by elected officials may suddenly lose support when officials respond to an unexpected public outcry. Successful developers have learned to work with citizens and local governments to address citizens' concerns such as unwanted traffic and possibly to make some concessions. Through the feasibility study, developers can see at an early stage of the development process the full impact of requested concessions.

Turnover in public offices can pose other problems for developers when projects conflict with the platforms of newly elected officials. When administrations change, earlier approval of a project does not necessarily guarantee that the newly elected officials will be good partners. For Europa Center, an election in Chapel Hill had considerable impact on Fraser Morrow Daniels's project. At that point in the process (well into stage three), the company was in a vulnerable position. It had committed a great deal of time and money to specify a project and obtain approval, but construction had not yet started.

▦ Europa Center

Politics and Changing the Rules in Midstream

After we chose a contractor and spent a great deal of money to design the building, one political uncertainty in the process jumped up and bit us. An election in Chapel Hill in November 1985 brought new players to the game. The people who were elected vowed that no more tall buildings would be built in town and that they would lower the density of everything. We thought that wouldn't matter because our project had already been approved and we had bought the land. But we found out otherwise. If the new officials' proposals went through, the amount of time that it would take to put the new limits and restrictions in place would have been about three months. So we had three months to begin construction, for we found out that if the project was not under construction, all of the approvals were dead. There we were with a set of financial calculations based on 200,000 square feet of building and a parking deck, already having been through planning re-

view and site planning and in the final stages of bidding with the contractors, with only three months to begin building without any financing. We really had to scramble. About the middle of February, the town fathers decreed that any project not under construction on April 15 probably would fall under the new rules instead of the old ones.

continued on page 405

Some developers have taken the route of working with governments through public/private development. This partnership can be particularly complicated but ultimately rewarding.

The Value Statement and Formal Estimate of Feasibility

The result of the market study is an estimated schedule of leasing or sales for the proposed development that projects rent, occupancy, and expenses over the leasing period or sales period and number of units over the sellout period. During the feasibility study, developers must ensure that the marketing staff is planning to sell the same product that the builders are planning to construct, which in turn is the same project that the public sector is expecting to review and that lenders/investors are planning to finance.

It is also critical that projected rents or sales are based on truly comparable projects. A well-prepared feasibility analysis always includes a comparison grid in the section discussing the market study. Whether the project is for sale or for lease, the attributes of value of the comparable projects must be explicitly laid out on the grid, which shows the specific adjustments for differences between the comparable projects and the subject project, i.e., the proposed development. The comparison must be sufficiently rigorous to give readers confidence in the estimate of how the market will receive the subject property's features, functions, and benefits. The larger the adjustments the analyst must make to the comparables, the more likely that some error has been or will be made and the greater the need for a larger budget for contingencies and/or a higher risk premium in the discount rate. In other words, truly unique development ideas for which no real comparable projects exist are considered risky, and the developer thus should have more reserves.

The grid that shows comparable factors should be used interactively with the grid for the proposed project to modify the project according to which features, functions, and benefits are justified by costs in relation to current supply and demand in the particular market.

Figure 16-1

Expected Case Analysis of Chapel Hill Office Building

	Year 2	Year 3	Year 4	Year 5	Year 6	Year 7	Year 8	Year 9	Year 10	Year 11
Assumptions										
Rentable Square Feet	92,700	92,700	92,700	92,700	92,700	92,700	92,700	92,700	92,700	92,700
Rent per Square Foot	$17.50	$18.03	$18.57	$20.24	$20.84	$21.89	$22.98	$24.13	$25.34	$26.60
Escalation (percent)	0.00	0.03	0.03	0.09	0.03	0.05	0.05	0.05	0.05	0.05
Vacancy (percent)	0.05	0.05	0.05	0.05	0.05	0.05	0.05	0.05	0.05	0.05
Operating Costs per Square Foot										
Utilities	$1.35	$1.42	$1.49	$1.56	$1.64	$1.72	$1.81	$1.90	$1.99	$2.09
Janitor	0.70	0.74	0.77	0.81	0.85	0.89	0.94	0.98	1.03	1.09
Maintenance	0.50	0.53	0.55	0.58	0.61	0.64	0.67	0.70	0.74	0.78
Security	0.25	0.26	0.28	0.29	0.30	0.32	0.34	0.35	0.37	0.39
Professional Fees	0.48	0.50	0.53	0.56	0.58	0.61	0.64	0.68	0.71	0.74
General Escalation (percent)										
Utilities	0.00	0.05	0.05	0.05	0.05	0.05	0.05	0.05	0.05	0.05
Janitor	0.00	0.05	0.05	0.05	0.05	0.05	0.05	0.05	0.05	0.05
Maintenance	0.00	0.05	0.05	0.05	0.05	0.05	0.05	0.05	0.05	0.05
Security	0.00	0.05	0.05	0.05	0.05	0.05	0.05	0.05	0.05	0.05
Professional Fees	0.00	0.05	0.05	0.05	0.05	0.05	0.05	0.05	0.05	0.05
General	0.00	0.05	0.05	0.05	0.05	0.05	0.05	0.05	0.05	0.05
Fixed Costs per Square Foot										
Property Taxes	$0.51	$0.54	$0.56	$0.59	$0.62	$0.65	$0.68	$0.72	$0.75	$0.79
Insurance Escalation (percent)	0.09	0.09	0.10	0.10	0.11	0.11	0.12	0.13	0.13	0.14
Property Taxes	0.00	0.05	0.05	0.05	0.05	0.05	0.05	0.05	0.05	0.05
Insurance	0.00	0.05	0.05	0.05	0.05	0.05	0.05	0.05	0.05	0.05
Management Fee (percent)	0.02	0.02	0.02	0.02	0.02	0.02	0.02	0.02	0.02	0.02
Leasing Fee (percent)	0.00	0.00	0.00	0.00	0.00	0.00	0.00	0.00	0.00	0.00
Cost of New Tenants										
Percent of Space Turned Over	0.00	0.00	0.00	0.10	0.10	0.10	0.00	0.00	0.00	0.00
Square Foot Turnover	0.00	0.00	0.00	9,270	9,270	9,270	0.00	0.00	0.00	0.00
Allowance per Square Foot	$10.00	$10.00	$10.00	$10.00	$10.00	$10.00	$10.00	$10.00	$10.00	$10.00
Cost (000)	$0.00	$0.00	$0.00	$93.00	$93.00	$93.00	$0.00	$0.00	$0.00	$0.00
Rent for First Month	$0.00	$0.00	$0.00	$17.00	$17.00	$18.00	$0.00	$0.00	$0.00	$0.00

Once the project's final amenities have been chosen, the analyst derives the expected prices (or rents) from the grid and generates the projected cash flows.

As seen from the pro forma for Europa Center (Figures 16-1 through 16-3), the process is straightforward: potential revenues minus vacant space equals gross revenues minus operating expenses equals net operating income. The difficulty comes in making reasonable assumptions for each of the elements. (See Chapters 4 to 6 for information on the mechanics of these statements.)

Since the change in the tax laws in 1986, it has become more common to base the value side of the feasibility analysis on pretax cash flows. Under such a scenario, the net operating income plus an estimate of residual value

Figure 16-2

Europa Center Pro Forma

	Year 2	Year 3	Year 4	Year 5	Year 6	Year 7	Year 8	Year 9	Year 10	Year 11
Revenues										
Gross Potential Rent	$1,622	$1,671	$1,721	$1,876	$1,932	$2,029	$2,130	$2,237	$2,349	$2,466
Less Allowance for Vacancies	81	84	86	94	97	101	107	112	117	123
Effective Gross Rent	$1,541	$1,587	$1,635	$1,782	$1,835	$1,928	$2,023	$2,125	$2,232	$2,343
Cash Expenses										
Operating Costs										
Utilities	$125	$131	$138	$145	$152	$160	$168	$176	$185	$194
Janitor	65	68	72	75	79	83	87	91	96	101
Maintenance	46	49	51	54	56	59	62	65	68	72
Security	23	24	26	27	28	30	31	33	34	36
Professional Fees	44	47	49	52	54	57	60	63	66	69
Field Costs										
Property Taxes	47	50	52	55	57	60	63	67	70	73
Insurance	8	9	9	10	10	11	11	12	12	13
Leasing and Management	31	32	33	35	36	38	40	43	45	47
Cost of New Tenants	0	0	0	110	110	111	0	0	0	0
Total Cash Expenses	$389	$410	$430	$563	$582	$609	$522	$550	$576	$605
Cash Income before										
Depreciation	$1,152	$1,177	$1,205	$1,219	$1,253	$1,319	$1,501	$1,575	$1,656	$1,738
Debt Service @ 9.5%	996	996	996	996	996	996	996	996	996	996
New Income	$156	$181	$209	$223	$257	$323	$505	$579	$660	$742

is discounted to a present value. As explained in Chapters 4 through 6, the discount rate is taken from the marketplace. In the case of a major national project, the rate may be derived from published property indices.[7] For smaller projects, local appraisers and financial institutions maintain records of returns from comparable projects. Feasibility is a forward-looking concept, and historic returns are merely a guide to what investors require for a current project. Hence, in preparing the feasibility study, the analyst looks at historical numbers and then adjusts them for the expected inflation rate as well as for any other projected changes in market conditions that may affect the relative risk of the subject property. Once a discount rate has been determined in this manner, the analyst should confirm it by questioning investors who are actively seeking the type of project proposed for development.

By using the estimated discount rate, the analyst reduces projected operating flows to a current value

that incorporates everything that can be known about the project. In other words, all the information about the market, the quality of the space relative to the competition, future trends, and the risks associated with all the projections are brought back to one value at one point in time. The analyst then compares this value with the total cost estimated earlier (see Figures 16-1 through 16-4).

A project satisfies Graaskamp's definition of feasibility if the value (adjusted for risk) exceeds the total cost, where the total cost includes all the logistics as well as all the items necessary to satisfy the legal, physical, and ethical rules and where the developer commands the financial and human resources necessary to bring the project to fruition. Thus, the developer uses both appropriately defined value and completely specified costs to determine formal feasibility.

After estimating the value based on net operating income, the analyst should construct an after-financing

Figure 16-3

Europa Center Case Study

	Total	Q1	Q2	Q3	Q4	Q5	Q6	Q7	Q8	Q9	Q10	Q11	Q12
Percent Leased by Quarter—Occupied		0	0	0	0	25	15	15	10	10	10	5	5
Percent Leased by Quarter—Full Rent		0	0	0	0	0	15	15	20	20	15	5	5
Capitalized Expenses (000)													
Land Purchase and Startup	$1,000	$1,000											
Maximum Construction Cost, Including Site Development	4,985	1,246	$1,246	$1,246	$1,247								
Hard-Cost Contingency	200				200								
Financing Fees (2%)	190	145						$45					
Construction Interest (11.5%)	379	11	40	75	113	$140							
Leasing Deficit	457					120	$100	80	$60	$45	$30	$15	$7
Design and Engineering (5%)	275	138	69	68									
Tenant Finishes ($12)	1,112	0	0	0	0	278	167	167	111	111	111	86	81
Leasing (5%)	308	0	0	0	0	77	46	46	31	31	31	23	23
Management (4%)	253	45	45	45	45	45	28						
Legal and Inspection Fees	20	10	5	5									
Soft-Cost Contingency	160	40	40	40	40								
Total Capitalization	$9,339	$2,635	$1,445	$1,479	$1,645	$660	$341	$338	$202	$187	$172	$124	$111

and after-tax scenario to show how all the participants fit into the project. Ideally, the sum of the parts should be greater than the whole. In other words, if tax benefits occur, they should accrue to the appropriate investor.[8]

Once the entire cost and all the value statements have been determined, the developer should run a sensitivity analysis to see whether some feature of the project can be improved. For example, a slight increase in operating costs may be justified if it substantially lowers the project's total cost. If the cost and income statements are set up on a simple computer spreadsheet, it is easy to check the tradeoff between operating costs and visual appeal, between construction costs and management costs, and so on. By using sensitivity analyses, a feasibility study moves beyond a static accounting system and becomes a dynamic planning tool.

One important caveat is in order. Computer spreadsheet models are often used to force feasibility: it is easy to change a number here or there to produce a value that exceeds costs by an appropriate amount. But forcing the numbers will surely come back to haunt a developer during the highly stressful stage six of the process and/or during the very long life of stage eight.

Figure 16-4

Cost Estimates for Europa Center

Land (Phase I)	$1,000,000
Building (Phase I)	4,985,000
Hard-Cost Contingency	200,000
Financing Fees (2%)	190,000
Construction Interest (11.5%)	379,000
Leasing Deficit (net 36 months)	457,000
Design and Engineering	275,000
Tenant Finishes	1,112,000
Leasing (5%)	308,000
Management (4%)	253,000
Legal and Inspection Fees	20,000
Soft-Cost Contingency	160,000
Total Cost	$9,339,000

The Europa Center Feasibility Study

In the development of Europa Center, stage two gradually slid (rather than suddenly lurched) into stage three. The architect, from an independent firm, was involved in both stages, because architecture was not one of Fraser Morrow Daniels's in-house capabilities. Moreover, with Fraser Morrow Daniels being new to office development, the firm chose the best architect to minimize risk and establish credibility. The developer focused on fitting the building to its site and surroundings (a political as well as design decision). By acquiring a highly buildable piece of land and using the highest-quality architect, the developer hoped to realize savings by avoiding construction cost overruns and permitting delays.

The case study focuses on the tradeoff among costs, rents, and operating efficiency. Fraser Morrow Daniels intended to capitalize on the existing market for office space without creating something particularly special—a high-quality development but not a unique development. The developer worked closely with the city because the city fathers were known to be difficult. As a result, the relationship was a dynamic one. In this case, the developer came close to fast-tracking construction simply to avoid losing building permits.

The Enterprise Concept

More and more frequently, development involves the combination of an operating business and the construction of physical space. In today's customer-focused markets, it is increasingly important that the space specifically fit the user's needs—and continue to do so over its life. In other words, some of the considerations that were always important in running a hotel are becoming more important in running a warehouse. Is a merchandise mart, for example, a real estate project or an operating business? Is Trammell Crow's Infomart in Dallas a real estate project or a business? Because such projects involve constructed space that can satisfy a range of users, all the standard questions about real estate development apply. The constructed space is, however, specially oriented toward the functioning of a particular business, and if that business fails, the next best use will often generate a far lower rent from the next user. Consequently, traditional real estate feasibility analysis is interwoven with modern business planning.

Operations management is assuming a more important role in all phases of real estate—and is critical as the developer considers the complex combination of real estate development and the ongoing needs of a business and the customers of that business. The *enterprise concept* is a view of the development process as a living, breathing organism with ongoing problems of cash management, just like an operating business. For a proper feasibility study, it is necessary to decide how much of the ongoing business risk is "developmental" and how much will be passed on to tenants or to long-term investors. The part passed on generally reduces the developer's risk so long as the lease agreements and tenants' credit are both strong and/or the role of the permanent investor is unconditional. The more a building is combined with significant management operations such as a hotel, where food, beverage, and other services are critical to realizing income, the more complex the feasibility study. Two kinds of questions are involved: 1) How crucial is the operating management to the project's long-term success? And how good is the management (on a relative basis) selected for this development? and 2) Is the developer or the tenant responsible? Or has the developer passed this risk on through an unconditional presale to a long-term investor? A hotel exemplifies the enterprise concept, but if a net lease with Hyatt is in effect for 99 years, the developer is creating an investment that will receive bondlike returns. Alternatively, if the developer plans to own and operate the hotel, the development investment is considerably riskier.

The more small, short-term tenants involved, the more the development must be seen as an operating business. The active marketing required in such circumstances must focus on the ongoing "business aspects" of the project. As players involved in the development process have come to realize the importance of seeing the whole enterprise, feasibility studies have changed significantly. Some feasibility studies look more like formal business plans than traditional descriptions of the value and cost of constructed space.

The Notion of Venture Capital

Another aspect growing in complexity is the increasing likelihood of the need for the real estate equivalent of "venture capital." For a 5,000-acre combined residential and industrial development, for example, two to six years might elapse between the time the developer moves from stage two to the beginning of construction in stage six. During that time, the formal feasibility study is undertaken, much of the design work is done, extensive government relations are worked out, and long-term tenant relations are negotiated. All these phases require out-of-pocket cash the developer must pay out during this period. Consequently, the source of operating money becomes an extremely important consideration. Because the amount of money may be large and because developers usually take great pains to minimize the amount of their own money involved before commitment, substantial front-end dollars from other sources may be needed.

In such a situation, it is probably appropriate to judge this interim period—the period between the end of stage two and the beginning of stage six (construction)—as more of a "venture capital period" than as a traditional real estate financing period. The dollars invested may be substantial. Further, a great deal of risk is associated with the investment because of uncertainties as to whether the project, whose exact size and value are unknown, will ever be undertaken. Consequently, investors during this period look for extraordinarily high returns, not unlike traditional venture capitalists. An extended venture capital period changes the investor's, the lender's, and even the developer's traditional roles. (We are not suggesting that such financing comes from venture capitalists but that this financing comes from higher-risk investors—like venture capitalists—and is usually noticeably expensive.) All the traditional players are still important, but the need for venture capital financing introduces an additional level of complexity. If the project does not proceed to stage six, the investors do not receive a low return. In fact, they lose all their money. After all, plans for an infeasible development have no resale value.

The astute developer uses as much of the less expensive financing (e.g., commercial banks) as possible and as little of the expensive financing (e.g., venture capital) as possible.

The development company is a business, and its collection of development projects must be structured so that the development company remains viable. Thus, to keep the development company solvent, the developer may at times need to trade longer-term profits (the percentage of the difference between value and cost) for higher immediate development fees and for a way to mitigate the need for large amounts of venture capital.

During Europa Center's development, Fraser Morrow Daniels was also attempting to secure approval for a condominium hotel, also in the Research Triangle area. Located close to a state university, the hotel was projected to attract persons attending events associated with the school, so an operating "tie in" was needed. In addition, the project was to be located in a historic section of town, further complicating political issues, traffic congestion, and even physical construction. Fraser Morrow Daniels, a relatively small developer working in a relatively small town, had over $2 million invested in the project before the city finally approved it. (Obviously, much more money would be involved in a complex project in Manhattan!) Think about how the providers of the capital reacted when the project proved infeasible despite the eventual political approvals. The developer chose not to move to stage four, leaving the investor with $2 million worth of plans for a project that would never be built.

Level Two Feasibility

The failed Research Triangle hotel leads us from an awareness of the financing problems associated with

a lengthening venture capital period to a specific focus on the developer's solvency. (Enhanced environmental awareness, more politically active interest groups, and the enterprise concept are several factors that serve to lengthen this venture capital period.) The project may eventually be feasible, but the developer wants to eat every day. It is instructive to think of the project's feasibility as level one and the developer's position as a participant in the process as level two (refer again to Appendix A). The developer must be concerned with the level two perspective of every participant in the development process.

Although a given project might appear feasible, that is, value substantially exceeds cost, the level one relationship is a necessary but not sufficient condition. All participants in the process must see a similar relationship between the value to them of participating in the process and the cost of their participation. If, at any point in the process, any participant suddenly finds that its level two participation ceases to be "feasible," the whole project may be endangered. Despite legal obligations to perform, most people become less enthusiastic about even the most exciting project when their participation starts to cost money rather than generate the expected profit. As an ongoing risk control technique, the developer uses the feasibility study not just at level one but also to think about each participant's level two perspective. The electronic spreadsheet should first show overall project feasibility calculations (level one feasibility) and then the cash flow position of each primary participant, particularly the developer himself (level two feasibility). The developer tries to anticipate problems so as to have sufficient flexibility in keeping the development team together.

Techniques of Risk Control During Stage Three

Several techniques are available to control risk during stage three. The most common ones follow:

1. Feasibility analysis is clearly a major technique of risk control, which will be used throughout the remainder of the development process. The more time and effort that go into estimating all revenues and costs, the more likely it is that the development decision will be sound. In almost all cases, the better the forecast, the less risk involved in the development. On the other hand, the feasibility study for a large project is expensive and time-consuming. Overdoing the feasibility analysis is a waste of money that can

seriously extend the length of the development process—much to the detriment of the developer. How much is enough but not too much? That is where the developer's judgment comes into play.

2. The financing arranged during stage three critically affects the sharing of project risks. Different lenders and equity investors have different preferences. The construction lender wants early equity contributions, a floating-rate loan with strict procedures for dispensing funds, and both the developer's and any equity investors' guarantee of personal liability. The developer, however, prefers a cap on the interest rate, easy procedures for requesting payments, no personal liability, and the right to contribute his own cash after the bank puts up its cash. How these desires are traded off depends on the quality of the project, the relative strength of the lender and the developer, and current conditions in the money markets. In a lender's market, the developer may have to toe the line. When financing is readily available from many sources, lenders are more likely to accommodate developers' desires.

Permanent lenders likewise must consider certain interests in the tradeoff between risks and returns. Adjusting the principal balance for inflation (and/or getting an equity participation) moves some of the inflation-centered risk out of the lender's portfolio. The higher the debt service coverage ratio and the lower the loan-to-value ratio, the more likely it is that the lender will be paid on schedule and, in the event of default, collect the total loan balance. Investors also bring their own perspectives to the financing arrangement. They want to make their cash contributions late and receive assurance that, in the event of the need for additional cash, the shortfall would be made up by the developer or the lenders. Certainly, investors do not want to be personally liable, but they do want to maximize their after-tax returns.

3. A formal review of the architect's design plan by operating, marketing, and construction professionals as well as by public officials is critical in controlling risk. A formal review by all players in stage three will make stage four's negotiations much easier.

4. The developer must check to ensure that utilities and other infrastructure are available. Even though a project is legally feasible and publicly desirable, the city might be unable to provide sewer, water, or other infrastructure services. The developer must begin discussions early, document meetings, and, whenever possible, obtain formal commitments for public facilities and services.

5. When considering all the costs of infrastructure for a project, developers try to go beyond negotiations for "permissions" and ask the city for concessions in return for providing it with something of value. A joint venture with other private sector users or with the general public, which is a beneficiary of the development, might be both possible and appropriate. Sometimes when sharing costs is not possible, the developer finds it feasible to acquire some of the surrounding land and capture some of the increased value that results from the development (unfortunately, doing so increases risk, but the return may justify the incremental cost).

The idea is not to forget the concept of *situs*—the interactions of a project with surrounding sites and the impact of those surrounding uses on the subject property.[9] This principle is basic to real estate. No site operates in isolation. In a competitive world, it is useful to share costs and, at times, to capture some of the benefits of the development on surrounding land. It is not always possible, but it is useful to consider the possibility.

A graphic example of the impact of situs is the difference between the development of Disneyland in Anaheim, California, and Disney World in Orlando, Florida. At Anaheim, all the peripheral "action" accrued to the benefit of others. Recognizing this loss of profitable opportunities, the huge site acquired for the Magic Kingdom has allowed Disney to reap much of the benefit of additional development that feeds on the central theme park's facilities.

6. The developer must check to make sure that a building permit has been issued to the chosen contractor; in addition, in some cities, it is important to make sure that subcontractors have obtained the appropriate permits. In their haste to get a job, contractors sometimes overlook certain rules or promise something that the company cannot legally deliver. Further, it is wise to ensure that both contractors and subcontractors are properly licensed to do the work. Checking details is a good way to control risk.

7. It is often useful to provide structural warranties in the architect's contract. (Some people even consider insuring the contract when the architectural firm is small.) After the windows fell out of the John Hancock building in Boston, it became obvious to many developers that they personally were not adequately prepared to undertake a final review of all the technical aspects of construction. Warranties from the architect, suppliers, and builders and a guarantee that all participants have sufficient financial worth to make a lawsuit worthwhile mean that the developer has a remedy in the event of disaster. Although it is seldom a good idea to stop development for a lawsuit, the potential for a successful lawsuit often en-

courages players to perform up to their commitment. The more concrete the legal documentation of responsibilities, the easier it is to convince individual players that serious problems will result if they fail to perform. Thus, structural warranties and, more important, clearly drawn contracts can be tools for negotiating from strength. These possibilities must be anticipated during stage three's economic discussions; if they are not, stage four's legal negotiations will be far more difficult.

Summary

The definition of feasibility presented in this chapter is noticeably broad. It begins with a formal definition of the development's objectives, which may involve money, ego, civic enhancement, and other related items. The defined objectives are then tested for fit in the context of specific market, legal, physical, and ethical constraints as well as limited financial and human resources. A project is feasible when it is reasonably likely (almost never certain) that its objectives can be achieved in a particular situation.

The primary task in the feasibility analysis is to produce a sound market analysis, one that culminates in a projection of net operating income for the subject property over the relevant time frame. Based on these projections, the developer estimates value for the project by using discounted cash flow analysis. A project is said to be feasible when that value exceeds all the projected costs of development.

The feasibility analysis is more than a technique for controlling risk during stage three of the development process. Once completed, the formal feasibility study is the sales tool used to bring together all the different players needed to fulfill the objectives of development. During stages four through seven, the feasibility study is constantly refined; it remains probably the single most important management tool in the development process.

Terms

- Enterprise concept
- Feasibility analysis
- Floor loading
- Formal feasibility
- Market study
- Operating efficiency
- Optimization tool
- Preliminary drawings
- Sensitivity analysis
- Takeout
- Value statement
- Venture capital

Review Questions

16.1 Define feasibility.

16.2 What is a feasibility study, and why is it necessary for a development?

16.3 What is a market study?

16.4 What is the role of the architect at this stage of the development process?

16.5 How do developers know whether general contractors' estimates of construction costs are appropriate?

16.6 What is the value statement?

16.7 Describe some of the techniques that can be used to control risk during stage three.

16.8 Describe how developer Jerry Speyer approaches development projects in markets outside the United States.

16.9 Why was it critical that construction of Europa Center begin by April 15?

16.10 Both Dean Stratouly and Jerry Speyer talk about the importance of finding good partners. Both of them are very experienced, however, and have developed many projects. How does a new developer starting out find the right partners?

Notes

1. James A. Graaskamp, "A Rational Approach to Feasibility Analysis," *Appraisal Journal,* October 1972, p. 515.

2. See, e.g., Boston Consulting Group, *The Business Case for Pursuing Retail Opportunities in the Inner City* (Cambridge, Mass.: Initiative for a Competitive Inner City, 1998); and John Kasarda, "America's Changing Commercial Real Estate Markets: Population, Jobs, and Investment Performance to the Year 2000," in *Real Estate Investment Strategy: A Year 2000 Perspective* (New York: Prudential Realty Group and Univ. of North Carolina, 1989).

3. Kasarda, "America's Changing Commercial Real Estate Markets."

4. See, e.g., M. Atef Sharkawy and Joseph Rabianski, "How Design Elements Create and Enhance Real Estate Value,"

Real Estate Review, Summer 1995, pp. 83–86; and Kerry Vandell, "Will Good Design Pay? The Economics of Architecture and Urban Design," in *Real Estate Investment Strategy: A Year 2000 Perspective* (New York: Prudential Realty Group and Univ. of North Carolina, 1989).

5. Information is available from, for example, Marshall & Swift and the McGraw-Hill Construction Information Group (a network including *Architectural Record, Design-Build, Engineering News-Record,* F.W. Dodge, and Sweet's Group), found at all major appraisal firms and in some public libraries and now available online *(www.construction.com).*

6. Charles H. Wurtzebach and Mike E. Miles, *Modern Real Estate,* 5th ed. (New York: John Wiley & Sons, 1995); and James H. Boykin and Richard L. Haney, Jr., *Financing Real Estate,* 2d ed. (Englewood Cliffs, N.J.: Prentice-Hall, 1993) describe all the lenders (and their analytic techniques) in considerable detail. Lehman Brothers, Morgan Stanley Dean Witter, PaineWebber, and Salomon Smith Barney publications describe the more current bells and whistles that attract certain larger lenders to particular transactions.

7. For example, the NCREIF Property Index, published quarterly by the National Council of Real Estate Investment Fiduciaries, Chicago.

8. See Wurtzebach and Miles, *Modern Real Estate,* for an in-depth illustration of calculations.

9. Richard Andrews, *Urban Land Economics and Public Policy* (New York: Free Press, 1971).

Chapter 17

Market Analysis: Collecting, Validating, and Understanding Market Data

If you can't "buy" the assumptions as presented, you cannot afford the real estate product about which those assumptions were made, no matter how "good" the site and "attractive" the building.

—James A. Graaskamp

The technique of real estate market analysis forms the basis for the assumptions that are made about the future value of a real estate development. If a developer cannot defend the cash flow projections with a defensible system of analysis and reasonable data inputs, the feasibility of the entire development will be unsubstantiated and largely based on hope that there will be tenants to lease the building, rental rates will return a sufficient cash flow to service the debt, and the type of space proposed is what the market desires.

Real estate market analysis is an important risk management technique in that it provides the backup for the set of assumptions used in the cash flow analyses and therefore reduces or at least delineates the riskiness of projected cash flows. Thus, the market study functions as the backbone of the real estate development process by providing the critical inputs to the feasibility analysis discussed in Chapter 16. Before proceeding to the increasingly sophisticated econometrics applied to forecasting (Chapter 18), this chapter looks at the nuts

---

Mark J. Eppli, PhD, professor, George Washington University, made extensive revisions to this chapter, which was originally written by Lloyd Lynford, *REIS Reports.*

and bolts of data collection, verification, and analysis. Specifically, the chapter covers:

- Market analysis as a process—market studies, marketability studies, and market analysis as part of feasibility;
- Data collection and validation—validating supply data, and understanding and validating demand data;
- Defining the relevant market and the competitive submarket, and market disaggregation; and
- Presenting research.

Market Analysis as a Process

Market analysis is the identification and study of the market for a particular economic good or service.[1] Markets are created at the intersection of market participants' needs and desires (demand for space) and characteristics and amenities of the built environment (supply of space).

Real estate markets can be subdivided into different property types: office, retail, residential, hotel, and industrial, among others. Each property type can be further segmented into smaller markets by location and functionality. Market segmentation is the process of identifying and analyzing submarkets of a larger group of property markets. For instance, office markets can be segmented into CBD and suburban, retail markets can be segmented into regional malls and strip retailing, and residential can be segmented into single-family housing and multifamily housing.

Most real estate market analyses include both a *market study* and a *marketability study.*

Market Studies

Market studies report and analyze aggregate supply and demand data. Aggregate data assist the developer in understanding the effective supply of and demand for space of a broadly defined user group.

Supply analysis is carried out using data from local, regional, and national providers. Analysis of the supply of competing projects takes into consideration the following factors:

- Inventory and quality of existing space;
- New construction of space (under construction and proposed);
- Features, functions, and benefits of existing and proposed space; and
- Overall vacancy rate and characteristics of vacant stock;
- Recent absorption of space (including types of tenants);
- Market rents (and the reasons rents differ across locations and by quality of space); and
- Lease terms and concessions (i.e., free rent, tenant improvement allowances, etc.).

Whereas supply analysis looks at the projects that could be construed as competition, *demand analysis* investigates the potential users of the space. Potential space users are usually identified by analyzing the expected needs and preferences of users as well as the expected changes in needs and preferences. An analysis of regional demographic, employment, or income data is often the first step in a demand analysis, because changes in population, workforce, or income levels drive demand for most new space. It is somewhat difficult to provide a "generic" list of the critical factors to be included in a demand analysis, because users' needs can differ greatly. Still, most demand analyses include some important inputs:

- Population and population changes;
- Employment and employment changes;
- Income and income changes; and
- Other macroeconomic and local factors.

When assessing the anticipated demand for different types of space, it is clearly important to assess existing population, employment, income, and other macroeconomic and local factors. What is frequently more important to real estate developers is how these numbers change over time. Existing demand generally fills existing space, but changes in the factors listed above often create demand for new space.

Marketability Studies

Most market analyses also include a marketability study. The marketability study usually covers a specific property and identifies the property's demand attributes. Thus, the developer can adapt the real estate product, price, and merchandising appeal to better fit the market and attract a group of users with particular behaviors or preferences. Marketability studies generally include four steps:

1. Profile the space user to be served by the development.
2. Identify the revenue unit, i.e., the space over time with associated services.
3. Fully define the product in terms of features, functions, and benefits.
4. Delineate pricing strategy, including sales logistics.

The marketability study refines the aggregate findings of the market study for the subject project. Through the marketability study, the set of income assumptions (rental rates, rental growth rates, and space absorption rates) is generated for the specific development within the confines established for the market study.

The market analyst should be able to establish a connection between trends in supply and demand in the competitive marketplace and cash flow assumptions for the specific property. The analysis can be enhanced by postponing early judgment on conclusions about the specific property and instead focusing on 1) collecting market data at the most highly disaggregated levels available; 2) validating the integrity of the data; 3) constructing multiple data series[2] that pertain to a variety of assumptions influencing performance of the property (supporting the sensitivity analysis described in Chapter 16); and 4) rigorously defining the submarket where the subject property will compete after the data have been analyzed.

Market Analysis as Part of Feasibility

Recall at this point where the market analysis fits into the eight-stage model of real estate development described throughout this book: after the developer initially tests and refines the project idea, a market analyst undertakes systematic research to make sure the developer's assumptions are realistic.

Market studies bracket the questions to be answered, and marketability studies focus the analysis. These studies provide the "top-line" revenue estimates used in financial feasibility analysis that substantiate estimates of NOI. Better studies also indicate the degree of confidence that the estimates deserve and therefore help developers set an appropriate premium for risk in the discount rate.[3]

As Figure 17-1 shows, market research is conducted for the benefit of different players at different stages of the development process. It is helpful to know who performs the analysis at each stage of development as well as each player's objectives. In stages one and two, for example, developers take the lead in analyzing the market, albeit informally. In stage three, developers often ask a market analyst to formally evaluate the subject project and then use the market study, marketability study, and financial feasibility analysis to make the final decision on the project's viability. The developer might also commission and present the results of an economic impact analysis to garner public support for the project.

In stage four, developers negotiate the contracts needed to build a project that appears feasible. At this point, other participants must reach their final decisions about whether or not the market will support the project as proposed and, consequently, how likely they are to achieve their individual objectives (level two feasibility). Lenders are required to underwrite loans to determine the project's expected market value in accordance with accepted professional standards. Investors often commission appraisals as part of the process of studying and analyzing all the issues—financial, environmental, and other related attributes—of a project or property ("due diligence"). Like other participants in the process, they must decide whether the proposed project's estimated value justifies their participation. Major tenants often employ in-house market analysts or outsource firms to assess competing sites. Even local governments may want assessments of the project from their particular perspectives before committing their support.

In many areas, the public sector is being called on to sponsor market studies and help rationalize proposed development or redevelopment projects. Although the public sector's in-house capability or resources to hire market analysts are often limited, the public sector has a legitimate role in providing reliable information about expected demand. Sound market analysis can improve planning and zoning practices, guide the provision of development incentives, and reduce the social costs of overbuilding by accommodating growth while protecting a community's environment and quality of life.

Data Collection and Validation

Practitioners and academicians often bemoan the inadequacies of market data and the data's inconsistent methodologies, terminology, and collection procedures,

biases, and outdatedness. But many real estate textbooks that clearly recognize the limitations of available data do not provide suggestions for overcoming these shortcomings. This section shows how existing data can be made more useful by obtaining additional data, particularly from reluctant sources, or deciphering and reconciling the data to directly address the critical decisions regarding feasibility and investment (see the bibliography at the end of Chapter 18).

Weaknesses in the data do not necessarily represent a fatal flaw in its applicability. For those market analysts willing to expend the effort to ask appropriate questions and to review and adjust the data as required, many sources of professionally compiled market data can offer useful insights. Although the data may not be individually compelling, the fully analyzed composite may provide the foundation for successful decision making. This section discusses what needs to be done to get the best possible information. In a price-inefficient market like real estate, getting the best possible information from all data sources can be very rewarding.

Properly collected and validated data are critical when making assumptions that bridge the past with the future, which involves:

- Data collection;
- Validating real estate market supply data; and
- Understanding and validating real estate market demand data.

This work will allow the market analyst to define the relevant submarket and present persuasive conclusions about that submarket.

Data Collection

Real estate traditionally has been a private industry, and, despite its recent more public incarnations in the form of REITs and commercial mortgage–backed securities, it continues to be intensely private. Some people believe that relevant information is almost impossible to obtain and/or that sources willing to volunteer information fabricate their responses. The truth is that obtaining information from private sector real estate sources, typically brokers, developers, appraisers, and consultants, requires more finesse than working with public sector data sources. Persistence is often the most important factor in success.

One key to effective private or public sector research is to know as much as possible before making contact with a prospective source. For example, before calling a local brokerage firm to request a market report, the analyst should try to obtain any press reports that

Figure 17-1

Market and Economic Studies

Type of Study	Question to Be Answered	User	Provider	Focus	Development Preexisting or Assumed
Appraisal	What is the value of this improved or unimproved site?	Property owner Investor Lender	Appraiser	Subject property (improved or unimproved site)	Maybe
Cost/Benefit Analysis	What is the net value of this project to the public?	Government agency	Economist	Public investment in the project	Yes
Analysis of Economic Base	What is the outlook for near-term growth for this city/metropolitan area?	Planning agency	Urban analyst[b]	Economy of the city or metropoli-tan area	No
Analysis of Economic Impact	What is the economic impact of this development on the surrounding area?	Government agency	Urban analyst	City or market area	Yes
Study of Highest and Best Use	What is the optimal use of this site?	Investor Property owner Lender	Appraiser Market analyst	Subject parcel of land	No
Land Use Study	What is the pattern of land use in this geographic area?	Planning agency	Planner	All parcels of land in the jurisdiction	No
Market Study	What is the demand for and supply of this type of property in this market area?	Developer	Market analyst	Market area that includes the sub-ject project	Maybe
Marketability Study	What prices, sizes, functions, and features are required to capture a market share?	Developer	Market analyst	Subject property compared with all competing projects	Yes
Financial Feasibility Analysis	What financial return is attain-able for this project, given con-straints on development?	Developer Investor Lender	Real estate investment analyst	Private investment in the project	Yes

[a]If market prices are used, the study of highest and best use becomes an elaborate feasibility analysis that considers alternative projects. If social values are used, the study of highest and best use becomes a cost/benefit analysis in which the user has the same objective function as society as a whole.

[b]Urban analysts include regional scientists, economic geographers, or city planners.

Estimation of Value (or Return on Investment)	Sources of Value Estimates	Estimates of Absorption	Estimates of Market Capture	Estimates of Project's Timing	Description of Conditions for Success	Stage in Development Process
Yes	Market prices Replacement cost Present worth (DCF)	Yes	Maybe	No	No	4 and 8
Yes	Social values[a] (DCF)	Yes	Yes	Yes	No	1 or 2
No	NA	No	No	No	No	3
No	NA	No	No	Yes	No	3
Yes	Market prices or social values[a] (DCF)	Yes	Yes	No	No	3 and 8
No	NA	No	No	No	No	1 or 2
No	NA	Yes	Maybe	Maybe	No	3
No	NA	Maybe	Yes	Yes	Yes	3
Yes	Market prices Present worth (DCF)	No	No	Maybe	Yes	3

Note: Market and feasibility studies may contain an economic base study, a market study, a marketability study, and a financial feasibility analysis. Market and marketability studies are often combined.

Source: Based on original classifications in Anthony Downs, "Characteristics of Various Economic Studies," *Appraisal Journal*, July 1966, pp. 329–38.

summarize some of the report's findings. Even better, the analyst should be armed with findings from competitive firms. If it is not clear that a particular report is generally available, the analyst should avoid beginning the conversation by asking for the material and should instead inquire about the contents of press accounts by focusing on methodology and terminology. After establishing a dialogue with an information source and demonstrating respect for that source, the market analyst may find the contact more willing to share information as well as some underlying raw data or insights.

Another way to pry data from reluctant sources is to offer to exchange data. Assuming that the analyst is gathering data from multiple sources and plans to clean and organize the data, the contact may be interested in receiving an excerpt from the analyst's report in exchange for available data. Or, in some cases, earlier reports prepared by the analyst may be of interest to the contact. It is important to try to obtain a level of detail from each contact beyond what is generally available. If a contact's report addresses the market or submarket, the analyst should ask for the supporting detail about buildings. When an analyst demonstrates professional behavior and offers to share data, the information flow will usually improve. The worst that can happen is that the contact will say "no."

It is critical to remember that a successful real estate researcher must possess the skills of an investigative reporter. Interpersonal skills and persistence often represent the critical distinction between turning out stale, repackaged market analyses and producing reports that literally crackle with proprietary information and insight.

Validating Real Estate Market Supply Data

Why must and how does an analyst validate what is often conflicting data about supply? Not until the data have been validated does the market analyst have a defensible set of assumptions for cash flow analyses. As an analyst's research becomes more focused on a specific project, some unique property characteristics may force the market analyst to narrow the focus of research. Nevertheless, an analyst can usually compile a strong profile of metropolitan or submarket supply by attending to the seven market factors noted earlier:

- Inventory and quality of existing space;
- New construction of space (under construction and proposed);
- Features, functions, and benefits of existing and proposed space;

- Overall vacancy rate and characteristics of vacant stock;
- Recent absorption of space (including types of tenants);
- Market rents (and the reasons rents differ across locations and by quality of space); and
- Lease terms and concessions (i.e., free rent, tenant improvement allowances, etc.).

All these indicators carry import as snapshots of current market conditions. When viewed over time, these same indicators reveal the trends that will have a significant impact on cash flows for the development and should drive investment decisions.

Multiple analyses by time period are also vital in assessing the credibility of real estate market data or, in other words, in performing an audit. An *audit* is a formal examination and verification process whose objective is to confirm that a data set has been compiled with accuracy, logic, and internal consistency. In accounting, audited financial statements are typically considered more credible when they reflect multiple years of a company's financial results. Reconciliations can be performed and changes in financial conditions traced back to the source.

Similarly, the real estate market analyst must obtain multiple years of market data and array the information so as to ensure internal consistency. For example, the annual change in total inventory should equal that year's new completions minus deletions. Likewise, absorption should equal the net change in occupied space. Unfortunately, in much market research, many of these key indicators appear to "float" from year to year, thereby obscuring actual trends. The reason for the frustrating shifts in data can most often be traced to inconsistencies in the survey sample. For example, often the precise definition of geography and/or quality for the particular market fluctuates, thus changing the mix of buildings included in the sample. The analyst must recognize variability in the sample and take steps to adjust the data accordingly.

Two of the most important market fundamentals—absorption of space and rent—influence future cash flows, and the analyst must therefore devote considerable effort to ensuring the integrity of these data. Absorption is particularly vulnerable to misstatement based on changes in the survey sample. By implication, any data about absorption not supported by corresponding data on inventory and occupied space should be subjected to more intense scrutiny. Data about changes in rental rates are also highly sensitive to variations in the survey sample. In quantifying percentage changes in rent levels, the analyst must hold the building sample as constant as

Market research conducted by the developers of Silver Mill Resort, Keystone-Intrawest LLC, in Keystone, Colorado, found that a substantial number of baby boomers were seeking moderately priced second homes at mountain resorts. The developers responded by building 130 fully furnished condominium units that were designed slightly smaller to make them more affordable for their target customers.

possible between each survey point, even if it means sacrificing a large number of observations. Three questions are critical in auditing real estate supply data:

1. What are the limits of the sample survey (i.e., geographic size of the market, minimum building size, etc.)?
2. How has the sample changed over time (understanding sample changes is critical when creating historical trend analyses)?
3. What are the quality of and amenities in the surveyed buildings?

The analyst's ability to answer these questions depends heavily on his skill as an investigative reporter.

Recognizing that net absorption is one of the most incorrectly defined and poorly understood market concepts, the market analyst must make a special effort to distinguish the varying measures of market demand typically lumped under the heading "absorption." Net absorption is defined as total space leased less space vacated less space added to the market. Frequently, state-ments of gross leasing activity, which usually represent a brokerage firm's estimate of all leases signed in the market during a given time period, are labeled net absorption. Similarly, the leasing of space in new developments is often included in net absorption, while newly constructed space is not. Although both total leasing and leasing in new buildings are insightful market measures and necessary in certain types of property-specific analyses, they should not be confused with net absorption.

Given the importance of precisely measuring a market's or submarket's net absorption, the market analyst must avoid the perils typically associated with building-level data and aggregate market statistics. Optimally, analysts should look behind the absorption estimates quoted in reports and attempt to create their own estimates based on data by building. This procedure calls for determining the most accurate and comprehensive inventory (often through combining multiple surveys and sources) and making appropriate adjustments for building size, double-counted buildings, and excluded buildings that should be included in the sample.

Thirty percent of the residents of the Fountains at La Cholla in Tucson, Arizona—a rental congregate housing and assisted living community—are called "snow birds," because they moved to Tucson from colder northern states. The management found that the residents themselves were their best marketing source and that most of the snow birds chose the Fountains because they had a close relative living there.

Understanding and Validating Real Estate Market Demand Data

The demand for real estate space is generally a function of job creation, household formation, and/or income generation. For instance, the primary source of demand for office/industrial space is white- and blue-collar employment, demand for residential housing depends more on household formation, and demand for retail space depends more on income generation. All types of space demand also depend on local economic growth, wage rates, and other economic and noneconomic forces that make a location competitive or desirable.

Additionally, the competitive role of a local or regional economy within the national or global economy must be examined. Within a town or city, nodes of employment, commercial centers, or residential areas must be accessible to garner a sufficient share of the metropolitan market. The ebb and flow of metropolitan economies and areas within them is continuous; such flows show the combination of interdependence and competition that generates change and affects long-term profitability for a real estate development. Thus, both competition and cooperation among people and firms affect a locale's economic viability. Naturally, the spa-

tial arrangements within an area (situs) are important in influencing firms' profitability and local residents' well-being.

Demand for space is also influenced by varying tax structures, interest rates, and financing requirements to the extent that these factors affect space users' available resources. Employment, demographics, and income are the primary direct influences on the demand for space (for a more detailed discussion of economic forecasting, see Chapter 18).

Employment and Demographic Forecasts
It is important to thoroughly understand the underlying methods of collecting the many types of available economic and demographic data for analysis of the real estate market. For example, depending on the application, employment data gathered at "place of work" or "place of residence" may be significant. A common mistake is the inadvertent integration of the two, often made by relying on occupational employment data from the Bureau of the Census (gathered at place of residence) and industry-group data from the Bureau of Labor Statistics (gathered at place of work).

Economic and demographic forecasts also vary in quality. Nonetheless, even the most prestigious sources, such as Data Resources, Inc. (DRI), Regional Financial Associates, Inc. (RFA), and Wharton Econometrics (WEFA), should be examined for their underlying assumptions. In addition, the analyst should compare data from these sources with current actual data (for example, the Bureau of Labor Statistics [BLS] for employment data) to determine whether a forecast is consistent with current conditions in an MSA[4] and then validate data against alternative forecasts.

To make informed judgments about the future, market analysts must examine trends. Forecasts of population, households, income, or employment form the basis for forecasts of a market area's space absorption. The key is to recognize patterns and how these factors change over time. For example, one trend in the late 1990s saw an increasing number of single adults purchasing their own homes, thereby forming new households and significantly affecting the demand for new housing units. Studying historical trends to understand how absorption has changed relative to indicators of demand for space leads to better-informed forecasts of demand for a given market and eventually for a specific development.

Economic Forecasts

Forecasts of key economic and demographic indicators[5] are critical components of any market analysis. Forecasts of absorption and growth in rents must be linked with forecasts of the growth rate from the demographic, employment, or other demand drivers for the proposed development. Viewed in this light, all demographic and economic forecasts should receive a level of scrutiny equal to that often reserved for capitalization and discount rates.

Market analysts are typically not in a position to build sophisticated models of regional or MSA economies. They can, however, obtain substantial analytic leverage by studying the models and assumptions of others. Good market analysts try to determine whether projections make sense. For example, are income forecasts supported by emerging changes in the local economy? Or are forecasted rates of in-migration sustainable, given the availability of properly zoned and serviced land?

Market analysts make their own projections of population, jobs, and income based on analyses prepared by government agencies, universities, and other private institutions. Rather than making original forecasts for cities or metropolitan areas, analysts are usually advised to check and refine existing forecasts, which are frequently available at no cost from local, regional, state, and federal agencies or for a modest fee from for-profit sources. Part of being a good market analyst is developing familiarity with the appropriate sources of infor-

mation.[6] Savvy analysts collect and compare estimates from several sources, but the analyst's central job is to make reasonable estimates for subareas or market segments for which no projections exist.

As a general rule, analysts should compare all local estimates with regional or national averages. For example, analysts frequently use location quotients, which take the percentages of the workforce employed in each major industry sector in the locality and divide them by the percentage of the workforce employed in the industry sector nationally. Thus, a location quotient equal to 1.0 shows that a local industry's percentage share of total employment in the MSA is the same as that industry's national share. Industries with location quotients of less than 1.0 are underrepresented in a particular market relative to the nation. Those with location quotients greater than 1.0 show an overrepresentation or account for the locality's economic specialization. In local economic analysis, learning how a market differs from the region or nation is as important as knowing the absolute values. Comparisons with reference areas in either the same locale or other parts of the country can help the analyst understand the macro forces that are at work behind observed local outcomes.

In the comparison of forecasts, an outlier forecast[7] is often as interesting as a consensus forecast, because it challenges the analyst to identify the reasons accounting for the deviation. Variability among forecasts may indicate greater market volatility and warrant an increase in the risk premium in the discount rate or can be modeled in wider-ranging sensitivity analyses.

Population Forecasts

In forecasting population, births and deaths are relatively easy to estimate. Estimates of migration, however, can be difficult to predict. It is also difficult to aggregate population properly into consuming units as required in residential or retail studies. Regional planning agencies often provide demographic and economic information, which is also available from the Bureau of the Census. Subscription services collect, analyze, and sell census information. (Increasingly, this information is available on line and in multiple formats.)

Good analysts check the details. They might, for example, look at recent utility hookups and telephone installations to estimate whether household migration is slowing or accelerating. Usually such data are highly reliable. In some areas where cable television is heavily subscribed, cable installations can also be used to gauge recent migration. National moving companies are a useful source of current information on interstate moves. At one time, for example, it was impossible to rent a moving van in Louisiana, because out-migration was so great that moving companies could not keep enough vans and trucks on hand to satisfy demand.

The most easily available and comprehensive information on population is usually the decennial census of the United States, which is mandated by law to take place every ten years. As the sole source of actual socioeconomic data on individuals and households by small geographic areas (census tracts and census blocks in metropolitan areas or minor civil divisions elsewhere), census figures provide excellent benchmarks. Census information is available on line, on CD-ROM, in major libraries, and in most city or county planning departments. The government regularly updates population estimates based on the most recent census (which is far less detailed and comprehensive than the decennial census), indicating the increment of population or employment that has either moved into or out of a community. Estimates of migration are the primary source of information about population and labor force changes.

Income and Employment

The same sources that provide information on population and income also provide information on employment. Most of the published figures ultimately depend on estimates developed by the U.S. Departments of Commerce and Labor. For example, the Bureau of Labor Statistics publishes employment statistics for metropolitan areas monthly in *Employment and Earnings*. For nonmetropolitan areas, the Economic Research Service (ERS) of the U.S. Department of Agriculture makes available numerous county-level studies free or at nominal cost. The local office of the state employment security commission tracks current employment, at least those workers covered by unemployment insurance.

The BLS uses a disaggregated input-output model to forecast national employment. Based on estimates of final demand for goods and services and estimates of productivity, the BLS generates industry-specific estimates. Using BLS estimates as control totals, the Bureau of Economic Analysis (BEA) of the U.S. Department of Commerce disaggregates the estimates to state and metropolitan areas with a combination of location quotient, shift-share, and economic base analyses plus some well-informed judgments. The National Planning Association (NPA) also publishes proprietary estimates for counties, metropolitan areas, and states based on BEA and BLS figures. The BEA performs more comprehensive analyses but publishes forecasts only every five years. The NPA revises forecasts biennially but publishes less comprehensive analyses. Additionally, several firms provide proprietary short-term forecasts for states and, in some cases, for counties and metropolitan areas.

Annual subscriptions range up to $35,000 and are now available on line.

One method of checking for consistency between population and employment estimates is to compute and examine the employment-to-population ratio over time. A second way to audit the data is to compare the employment-to-population ratios with national averages.[8] By using decennial or annual estimates, analysts can determine whether the ratio is constant, trending up, or trending down. With the ratio and the trend, analysts can then compare projections of population with projections of employment. Although the two factors are interdependent, job growth tends to lead population growth. If the ratio for future projections is out of line with the past, it is worth taking the time to figure out how to adjust one or both projections.

For example, it might be reasonable to find that labor force participation rates for a locality are gradually decreasing and that the average age of the city's population is gradually increasing. If so, the employment-to-population ratio will decline over time. If independent projections of employment and population yield ratios that change erratically over time, the projections may need to be revised; at the least, the assumptions need careful checking.

Although it is difficult to come up with reliable forecasts of metropolitan-level employment, public sources such as city or regional planning agencies and state government are often as good as any source for employment forecasts. Local economic development authorities may offer useful insights, although they tend to be a bit optimistic on their area. Local community leaders can add information about an area's economic opportunities and problems that the top-down models (models that begin with aggregate data and then disaggregate the data down) never capture.[9] It is therefore wise to complement top-down employment projections with bottom-up models (models that begin with disaggregate data and aggregate the data up). Additionally, market analysts may want to interview major employers, local bank executives, university researchers, economic development officials, and others to sample expert opinion.

Another use of the bottom-up approach is to examine the details of the employment base: the age of facilities in the area, the credit ratings of major employers, and the product mix generated by employers in the community. Some communities manufacture products on the leading edge in a particular industry. Some products face stiff local or foreign competition, while others sell in less competitive markets. For office or industrial market analyses that emphasize employment forecasts, analysts should look within an area's major industries to understand the mix of goods or services produced in the market and local firms' relative competitiveness.

Why devote so much effort to forecasting population, income, and employment for a metropolitan area? Market analysts use local and regional forecasts to establish the baseline figures for the demand for space. Thus, they must comprehend the regional economy's future direction. Because the demand for space is derived from market demographics, employment, and income, concise and validated estimates of these factors are critical inputs to the market analysis.

Defining the Relevant Market

Unlike the market for most consumer goods, real estate competes principally in its own locationally constrained and functionally defined submarket. Hence, proper definition of the submarket and then accurate disaggregation to that submarket are essential to accurate projections.

Defining the Competitive Submarket

With audited supply data (preferably built up from building-level information) and objective demand forecasts of population, households, income, and employment in hand, the market analyst can focus on data in the subject property's neighborhood for the marketability study. Most competitive submarkets have a narrowly defined area from which demand is drawn and competition (supply) is located. Depending on the type of property, market analysts must generate specific forecasts of employment, population, households, or income for this narrowly defined market area.

Although analysts have traditionally been forced to approximate market areas by using census tracts, ZIP codes, or county boundaries because of data limitations, emerging GIS technology, or electronic mapping, is liberating real estate decision makers from relying on arbitrary boundaries. GIS is a combination of data, software, and geographic analysis that allows the creation of maps and sophisticated analysis that has a tremendous amount of potential for real estate. Examples of GIS data include county property assessment files, geodemographic information, traffic volume counts, and projections of absorption rates. Property assessment files include all of a property's characteristics used by property tax assessors to arrive at assessed values as well as latitude and longitude coordinates of the property. Geodemographic information includes hundreds of census year demographic measurements, such as income, education, race, and family composition, as well as

projections to present and future years. Traffic volume count is a key data input for making judgmental decisions for commercial real estate. The most important data available are U.S. road networks in digital format, first digitized in 1990 and available from the U.S. Bureau of the Census as TIGER/Line data. TIGER/Line data, when combined with appropriate software, allows for the assignment of latitude and longitude coordinates based on a property's address. GIS software has often been referred to as a "spatial spreadsheet." Early in the 1990s and before, GIS software was very expensive and difficult to use. Today, commercial software is based on Microsoft Windows, more user friendly, and available from a variety of sources, and ranges in price from $100 to several thousand dollars.

GIS is not limited to desktop computers. The Internet has made geographic technology quite commonplace.[10] A real estate agent might post the location of a listing on the Internet, and if someone interested in that listing types in his home address, the Internet-based GIS software draws a map of the best route from the prospect's home to the address of the listing. Internet-based GIS also makes available maps of the neighborhood's geodemographic and housing characteristics.[11]

Whether analysts are armed with elementary analysis tools or sophisticated electronic mapping technologies, their knowledge of the market's vehicular and mass-transit patterns, natural barriers, competitive projects, and economic and demographic profiles is of critical importance in defining property submarkets.

The definition of a competitive market area for a marketability study is best discussed in terms of property type. A marketability study usually begins by identifying and profiling the space user who will demand the benefits offered by the project. The next step is to locate where those potential consumers live and work as well as whether reasonable access exists to the subject site and how the potential space users will overcome any "friction of distance." Competitive space suppliers in the market area must also be profiled, including amenities offered.

For instance, residential development establishes locations from which the local population has access to jobs and local goods and services. The metropolitan area or labor market area therefore represents the overall housing market area. Market analysts, however, devote most attention to submarkets that are distinguished by the specific nature of demand or the differences among housing units, such as age, structure, or neighborhood characteristics (supply). On the demand side, tenure, location, and amenities distinguish major market segments. Preferences for tenure allocate demand to owners or renters. Adding preferences for locations and amenities leads to more refined market segments for which data might not be easily available but are of critical importance. For the marketability study, the market area where the subject project is located receives the most attention, but competitive supply almost always exists in other locations. As a result, residential market areas are often noncontiguous areas within the same labor market or metropolitan area. Residential developments in different sections of the metropolitan area often compete to attract the same in-migrants or local homebuyers and renters who are moving up.[12]

In retail analysis, submarkets are created of consumers living or working near the retail site. Retail trade areas are typically segmented into primary, secondary, and tertiary areas and are defined in most instances in terms of drive time and the category of goods offered. For example, the primary trade area for neighborhood shopping centers may be limited to a five- to ten-minute drive, and the secondary and tertiary trade areas will not extend much farther than the primary trade area. Super regional shopping centers, however, may have primary trade areas extending up to 20 minutes from the site and secondary trade areas of up to 40 minutes, while the tertiary trade area could extend up to and beyond an hour in some areas.

Office market areas often assume one of two forms: local services or export services. Local services such as routine medical or dental care characterize market areas similar to retail trade areas because of their orientation to local residents; local consumers visit service providers to receive services. In contrast, export services are characterized by large, noncontiguous service areas. Customers do not visit export service sites. Rather, information flows to and from the sites, and service providers (for example, accountants, architects, engineers) usually travel to deliver services to customers at their locations. Therefore, a complete office development marketability study must clearly define space users as local service providers or export service providers. Whether office space users are local or export service providers, access to a qualified labor pool, related business services, and transportation is essential.

Industrial trade areas are also noncontiguous, as most manufacturers export products to regional, national, or international markets. Unlike retailing operations, which compete for the same customers from within their overlapping trade areas, industrial tenants generally sell to different customers in dispersed locations. Nonetheless, they might well compete for local infrastructure, labor, intermediate goods or services, and properly zoned industrial land.

Hotel guests reside somewhere outside the locality rather than near the accommodations. The large majority of guests therefore pass through a locality rather than permanently residing there. Like retail centers and offices, hotels compete for sites at highly accessible transportation nodes or key destinations. Although it is difficult to define a hotel's market area by a market's characteristics, hotel demand can be disaggregated by weekday versus weekend guests, business guests versus vacationers, and conference travelers, airline employees, and so on to better estimate new demand.

For each product type, many different factors must be considered in market and marketability analyses. (The bibliography for Part VI contains many resources for different property types and different situations.)

Market Disaggregation into Competitive Submarkets

The research and valuation committees of the National Council of Real Estate Investment Fiduciaries (NCREIF) have established an articulate and well-reasoned general premise and goal for real estate market analyses:

> The Market Analysis content of an appraisal report should provide data concerning both the historical and prospective relationships between supply and demand information. In addition, this information should form the basis for assumptions set forth in the Income Approach. These issues are all interrelated, and the appraisal report should demonstrate a consistency of rationale between the issues. . . . The appraisal report must maintain a flow of logic addressing the interplay of these factors when developing investment assumptions.[13]

To develop "a consistency of rationale" and "a flow of logic," it is critical for the analyst to select the appropriate level of data disaggregation for the type and use of the proposed development. In fact, different levels of market data or selected qualitative or quantitative classifications may reveal information on distinct aspects of the subject's historical, current, and prospective performance. Three of the most powerful levels of data disaggregation are for the metropolitan area, the competitive submarket, and the peer group. Each level of disaggregation has a specific analytical purpose and/or relationship to the performance of the proposed development.

The Metropolitan Area Market

Most market analyses rely heavily or even exclusively on data for the MSA in formulating property-specific assumptions, but relying solely on data for the MSA does not sufficiently pinpoint the competitive forces that most directly influence the proposed development's pace of absorption and rental rates. Nonetheless, analysis of the MSA is an essential first step in developing sound market-driven assumptions. To the extent that an MSA represents a well-defined economic unit, virtually any analysis of the area's economic and demographic base (the primary drivers of demand) will benefit from the use of comprehensive historical, current, and forecast data for the metropolitan area.

Likewise, an attempt to focus exclusively on the economic activity of a submarket is likely to ignore many of the factors for the metropolitan area that either promote or discourage growth throughout the metropolitan area and overlook the richest sources of demand side data. Moreover, MSA demand forecasts represent the baseline data to compare and contrast market share benchmarks and capture rates for individual submarkets.

The value of developing trends and forecasts for the MSA also extends to supply side indicators, particularly new construction and change in rents. Because information on new construction projects is often limited to the near term, a well-developed annual time series that presents a submarket's historical share of metropolitan construction can be extremely useful in developing longer-term forecasts of construction in the submarket. With respect to assumptions for rental growth rates, metropolitan trends and forecasts are a necessary check on any forecasts developed for a submarket and a peer group market. It is likely that any one submarket's significant deviation from the average metropolitan rental growth rate will be corrected in the intermediate term or that the submarket's share of absorption and construction will adjust appropriately.

The Competitive Submarket

The definition of a competitive submarket or trade area, "a geographical area surrounding the subject site that will provide a substantial portion of the customers for the real estate project,"[14] has received considerable attention in the literature. Hence, a submarket's trends in supply and demand should have a more direct impact than metropolitan trends on the performance of the subject property. As a result, a strong case can be made for relying heavily on submarket trends and forecasts in the development of property-specific cash flow assumptions. Although the characteristics of the subject property and/or peer group may justify a modification in the submarket research, trends in supply and demand in a well-defined submarket determine more precisely the parameters in which individual buildings can shift rental rate pricing and lease terms.

The Peer Group Market

Before discussing the value of peer group analysis, it is important to address the limitations that can often

accompany market statistics by property class. For instance, property-type quality measures such as Class A or Class B office space market segments are often arbitrarily defined. Sometimes market classification measures are used to justify not using a part of the space inventory that is difficult to measure. Although some properties are competitive within a given classification, the most rigorous method for establishing specific parameters of a competitive position is from the bottom up, or by taking the inventory of the individual buildings that constitute the primary and secondary levels of competition.

A determination of the physical, locational, or economic factors that distinguish the subject's proper classification can be made after completing the peer group analysis. Thereafter, individual peer buildings can be ranked according to comparability with the subject development. At the same time, distinctions among properties can be evaluated and priced. These often subtle distinctions are critical factors in refining net effective rents, rental growth rates, and leasing concession assumptions used in the discounted cash flow analysis.[15]

In other words, peer group analysis is central to defining the subject property's market niche from which submarket trend analysis can be used to project future change in the niche's performance. Moreover, if the analyst can obtain historical trend data on the performance of the peer group, he can conduct a comparative analysis to ascertain market share and to quantify differentials in growth rates. If the peer group history is sufficiently extensive, the analyst may be justified in adjusting the absorption and rent growth assumptions based on the historical premium or discount recorded by the peer group.

Presenting the Research And Conclusions

The material in this chapter has thus far portrayed the tasks of gathering and validating market data that are essential components of a process that yields greater insight into a project's marketability for both the market and the specific project. Once the data have been obtained, cleaned, and reconciled, no one way is available to present findings and conclusions that speak equally well to all audiences. Despite that admission, information should usually be arrayed in a way that conveys the process of discovery to the reader of a market analysis (see Figure 17-2 for a generic outline of items to be covered in a market analysis report).

This chapter places considerable emphasis on developing time-series analyses at multiple levels of mar-

Figure 17-2

A Generic Outline of Market Analysis to Be Adapted for Specific Situations

 I. Executive Summary
   A. Goals and objectives
   B. Methods of analysis, key assumptions, risk factors
   C. Recommendations—go/no go/postpone/improve project
 II. Overview
   A. National (or global) economy and key growth areas
   B. Regional economic outlook
   C. Local economy
   D. Market delineation and site analysis
 III. Analysis of Demand
   A. Projected overall demand
   B. Analysis of absorption
 IV. Analysis of Supply
   A. Survey of existing stock, past trends, and future supply
   B. Analysis of existing zoning and possible changes
   C. Consideration of business cycle and building cycle to compare projections of supply and demand
 V. Analysis of Competition
   A. Features, functions, and benefits of the project in relation to the competition
   B. Analysis of market segmentation
 VI. Analysis of Capture Rate
   A. Based on analysis of the competition, estimated total absorption and absorption schedule by market segment and projected market share to account for the distinct features and competitive advantages that should attract customers and tenants
   B. Final estimate of market capture rate, projected leases or sales per period, specification of price and total time to complete leases or sales ■

---

ket disaggregation in the belief that historical trends communicate a sense of variability, and thus risk, that analyses relying on a single point in time cannot. Therefore, the construction of trend analysis is viewed as perhaps the most important means of communicating the market study's results. Specifically, the analyst should pay attention to peaks and troughs of market performance and other measures of market cyclicity, such as the levels of construction, absorption, vacancy, and rent growth that were recorded during the most dynamic periods of market and economic expansion and severe economic contraction. The same analysis should be performed for all demand indicators. Given that annual data can fluctuate significantly and distort apparently meaningful trend analysis, the construction of time slices in two-, three-, and/or five-year increments may be helpful. To the extent that sensitivity analyses are employed, these historical benchmarks represent a far more intuitive and factual approach to alternative future scenarios than simply varying assumptions by specified percentages.

Another important technique for conveying the quality of market research results is not to hide all the warts and contradictions in the data. Although market analysts are hired typically in part to resolve many of the thorniest research problems and to present lucid findings and conclusions, exposing the reader to "contradictions" in the data and explaining their resolution can add dynamism and integrity to the report.

Summary

This chapter has emphasized the market researcher's responsibility to engage in data collection and validation in the context of market and marketability analyses. Data on the real estate space markets (supply) and on employment, population, and income (demand drivers) are critical to the process. Understanding collection methodologies, reconciling contradictions of multiple data sources, and aggregating/disaggregating data are critical.

Ultimately, the process of data collection and validation yields a data set that supports the two critical analytic links without which the market analysis enterprise is doomed to the irrelevancy of "background" information: the connections between the macromarket and the subject property, and the connections between historical trends and future performance. Armed with the requisite data and capable of forging vital analytic connections, the market analyst can determine what the data are saying and how to present findings in a compelling manner to support critical assumptions underlying cash flow analysis. The data as formed in market and marketability studies are the heart and soul of the feasibility analysis.

Terms

- Absorption
- Aggregated data
- Audit
- Bottom-up approach
- Consensus forecast
- Data series
- Decennial census
- Demographic indicators
- Disaggregated data
- Due diligence
- Econometric forecasting models
- Location quotient
- Net absorption
- Outlier forecast
- Primary source
- Secondary source
- Top-down approach

Review Questions

17.1 What are some of the problems data gatherers are likely to encounter?

17.2 What are the seven basic factors the market analyst should consider when auditing real estate supply or demand data?

17.3 Why are two of the most crucial data space absorption and rent changes? What kind of judgments does the market analyst make based on that information?

17.4 Why is it crucial for market analysts to gather data for several time periods?

17.5 Why must an analyst devote attention to ensuring the accuracy of absorption rates and the growth and decline of rental rates?

17.6 What are some of the factors that influence market-driven demand?

17.7 What are some of the resources analysts can use for forecasting population, income, and employment growth or decline?

Notes

1. Appraisal Institute, *The Appraisal of Real Estate,* 11th ed. (Chicago: Author, 1996), p. 58.

2. A data series is a grouping of aggregated information in an order or arrangement that typically shows a progression or relationship.

3. Stage three (the feasibility study) considers the full range of legal, physical, market, and financial dimensions. The market study and marketability study evaluate the subject project in relation to the market. The financial feasibility analysis estimates risks and rewards for developers, investors, and lenders.

4. A metropolitan statistical area consists of a central city with a population exceeding 50,000, the county(ies) in which it is located, and other contiguous counties that are metropolitan in character and socially and economically integrated with the central city.

5. Demographic indicators are vital statistics on human populations that typically refer to size, density, distribution, and other significant characteristics. For real estate markets, vital statistics include population, households, and income, among others. Refer to Chapter 2 for more information on demographics.

6. Lists of sources are easily obtained from the World Wide Web. In print, they are available in Grant Ian Thrall et al., *Real Estate Market Analysis* (Washington, D.C.: ULI–the Urban Land Institute, forthcoming); G. Vincent Barrett and John P. Blair, *How to Conduct and Analyze Real Estate Market and Feasibility Studies* (New York: Van Nostrand Reinhold, 1988); John Clapp, *Handbook for Real Estate Market Analysis* (Englewood Cliffs, N.J.: Prentice-Hall, 1987); Neil Carn, Joseph Rabianski, Ronald Racster, and Maury Seldin, *Real Estate Market Analysis: Techniques and Applications* (Englewood Cliffs, N.J.: Prentice-Hall, 1988); and C.F. Sirmans, *Data Sources for Real Estate Market Analysis* (Glastonbury, Conn.: Pension Real Estate Association, 1994).

7. An outlier forecast is one of a group of projections that differs substantially from all others in the group as well as from the group average.

8. See Thrall et al., *Real Estate Market Analysis;* and Barrett and Blair, *How to Conduct and Analyze Real Estate Market and Feasibility Studies.*

9. A top-down approach to analysis first focuses on aggregated results. A bottom-up approach typically refers to developing an analysis based on the most disaggregated data available.

10. See Susan Thrall and Grant Ian Thrall, "Desktop GIS," in *Geographical Information Systems: Principles, Techniques, Management, and Application,* ed. P.A. Longley et al. (New York: John Wiley & Sons, 1998).

11. For more details about GIS, see Grant Ian Thrall, "Applications of GIS to Real Estate and Related Industries," *Journal of Housing Research,* Vol. 9 (1998), pp. 33–59; Thrall and Thrall, ibid.; and Grant Ian Thrall and Juan Del Valle, "The Calculation of Retail Market Areas: The Reilly Model," *Geo Info Systems*, 1997, pp. 46–49.

12. More detailed discussions are found in Thrall et al., *Real Estate Market Analysis;* and Carn et al., *Real Estate Market Analysis.*

13. National Council of Real Estate Investment Fiduciaries, "Market Analysis in the Valuation Process," unpublished white paper (Chicago: Joint Valuation/Research Committees, 1994).

14. Clapp, *Handbook for Real Estate Market Analysis.*

15. Although gathering the information is difficult, analysts need to measure effective rent, which is contract rent minus concessions such as rent-free periods, above-average tenant improvements, moving allowances, and lease assumptions, among others. See Robert P. Tunis, "The Negotiation Differential: A New Approach to Office Market Analysis," *Real Estate Review,* Winter 1989, pp. 49–55.

Chapter 18

Data Sources Supporting Market Studies

Chapters 16 and 17 demonstrated the role of the market study as part of the feasibility analysis and the role of the entire feasibility study as a primary management tool during the development process.

Although Chapter 17 looked at the logic of the market study, this chapter focuses on the secondary sources available to analysts preparing market studies. Beyond in-house resources and the primary research done by the development team, the developer has a plethora of information sources available, most of them on line. Generally speaking, these secondary sources provide background material for the study. Primary research is then used to supplement and tailor secondary sources to fit the market study for the proposed development.

Generally, two types of secondary information are available in the marketplace. The first set of sources focuses on the basic supply and demand fundamentals in the metropolitan statistical area markets. These providers (described later in this chapter) estimate employment growth, income changes, and other variables of *demand* as well as enumerate new projects under construction, the *supply* side. Supply and demand are the fundamental building blocks of a market study.

The second general type of secondary sources uses some subset of supply and demand vendors, along with proprietary technology, to forecast rent growth or value growth, or to estimate the general attractiveness of a particular property type in a particular market.

Chapter 18 is intended to help analysts fully appreciate the data and use it properly. It:

- Describes the forecasting models and methods used by the providers of the fundamental supply and demand information;

- Describes and explains the primary sources of supply and demand data and the vendors of fundamental supply and demand forecasts; and
- Explains the providers of real estate–specific forecasts, i.e., people forecasting growth in rents and value.

It is not enough merely to list the providers and their methods: the quality of their forecasts must be assessed as well ("Providers of MSA Rankings," later in this chapter, addresses these issues). Because these "end providers" rely on the suppliers of fundamental supply and demand forecasters, who themselves rely on government statistics and long-term economic trends, Appendix C is provided to give a longer-term perspective on demographic fundamentals. Appendix C (at the end of this book) augments much of the demographic material in Chapter 2, which sets the basic framework for all real estate analysis. Such information is typically not explicitly included in a market study, because it is common to all market analysis. But the analyst undertaking the market study needs to understand the longer-term perspective to properly use current information and forecasts from the secondary sources evaluated here.

Forecasting Models and Methods

All real estate investors use forecasts, and investors should thus understand how the forecasts are constructed. In all economic models, supply and demand jointly determine price. In real estate, supply adjusts with an extensive lag so that it is always somewhat out of balance. The key to understanding differences across the models is understanding which elements of demand drive the final forecast.

This chapter begins with a brief review of the generic supply and demand model and then extends it for use in determining prices for commercial real estate.

Suppose we are interested in the price of an agricultural commodity, corn, for example. The basic model may take the following form:

$$Q_D = a + bP + cY$$
$$Q_S = d + eP + fW$$

$$Q_D = Q_S$$

where Q represents quantity and D and S indicate demand and supply, respectively. The model states that quantity demanded (Q_D) is a function of price P and income Y and quantity supplied (Q_S) is a function of price P and weather W. The third equation indicates that we assume the market for corn "clears" and what is observed is a market-clearing price and a single market-clearing quantity. Thus the two *endogenous* variables, i.e., variables determined by the model, are price and quantity. The two *exogenous* variables, i.e., variables determined outside the model, are income and weather. This model is in *structural form;* that is, we have written down the model in the basic form in which we think the variables of the model interact when endogenous variables are allowed to be determined by other endogenous variables. We can always solve the equations for the two endogenous variables (since the market is assumed to clear):

$$P = g + hY + iW$$
$$Q = j + kY + lW$$

where price and quantity are now simply functions of the two exogenous variables. This is the *reduced form* of the model.

Remember that exogenous variables are determined outside the system, but as is clear from the reduced form, they are the true determining factors for the variables of interest: price and quantity. Thus, the assumptions users make about these variables or the forecast supplier makes about these variables are absolutely crucial to the accuracy of the forecast. We return to this point in the next section when we examine the key assumptions that major forecasting services make about important exogenous variables in macromodels of the U.S. economy, such as interest rates and oil prices.

We now extend this simple model to one in which MSA-level returns or prices can be determined. First, define the following set of variables:

Q_{Sti}^* : The desired supply or inventory of properties at time t in MSA i.

Q_{Sti} : The actual inventory at time t in MSA i.

Q_{Dti} : The demand for space at time t in MSA i.

P_{ti} : The generic price for a property at time t in MSA i.

X_{ti} : Demand side variables measured for the MSA or county, such as employment and per capita income.

N_t : National variables, such as interest rates and inflation rates.

ε_{ti} : Disturbance terms used to indicate that even a very-well-specified model cannot capture all the relevant factors.

Supply Side

The supply side of the model recognizes that desired supply and actual supply are often different. The following equations model this fact.

$$Q_{Sti}^* = \alpha + \beta P_{ti} + \gamma N_t + \varepsilon_{ti} \qquad (1)$$

The above equation states that the desired supply at time t is a function of the price that can be obtained for properties and national-level variables that may influence the ability to provide the space. In this simple model, we assume that current desired supply is a function of current price; the model is straightforward to incorporate lags on price in the equation (more on this subject later).

Real estate is different from many commodities, because a long lag exists before properties can be produced to take advantage of price increases. The following partial adjustment equation recognizes this lag:

$$Q_{Sti} = \lambda Q_{Sti}^* + (1 - \lambda)Q_{S,t-1,i} \qquad (2)$$

This equation states that the actual quantity of space supplied at time t in MSA i is a function of the *desired* supply at time t and *actual* supply at time $t-1$. The λ is a positive constant between zero and one that captures the speed with which suppliers can supply new properties. If properties could be built within a single time period (say a year or a quarter), the λ would be equal to one and we would have actual supply equal to desired supply. At the other extreme, $\lambda = 0$ means that no adjustment can take place at all. A λ between zero and one recognizes that the lag resulting from the need to acquire the land, obtain the necessary permits, prepare plans, and physically construct the building may require several time periods. The size of λ is undoubtedly different for different property types. For example, one would expect that the λ for office buildings in the CBD is probably closer to zero than the λ for apartments.

Equation 1 contains the empirically unobservable variable Q_{Sti}^*. Therefore, we substitute Equation 1 into Equation 2 to obtain:

$$Q_{Sti} = \lambda\alpha + \lambda\beta P_{ti} + (1 - \lambda)Q_{S,t-1,i} + \lambda\gamma N_t + \lambda\varepsilon_{ti} \quad (3)$$

Demand Side

The demand side of the market is represented by Equation 4:

$$Q_{Sti} = \delta + \varsigma P_{ti} + \theta X_{ti} + TN_t + \varepsilon_{ti} \quad (4)$$

where we hypothesize that in addition to price, demand is determined by national variables such as interest rates, the consumer price index (CPI), and economic conditions in the MSA, such as unemployment rates.

So far, we have specified two equations with three unknowns: quantity of space demanded, quantity supplied, and price. If we impose the condition of equilibrium that the market must clear in every period (quantity demanded is equal to quantity supplied), we can solve Equations 3 and 4 for price and quantity (as $Q_{Sti} = Q_{Dti}$). For example, the price equation takes on the following form:

$$P_{ti} = \pi_1 + \pi_2 Q_{S,t-1,i} + \pi_3 X_{ti} + \pi_4 N_t + \upsilon_{ti} \quad (5)$$

The new coefficients are linear combinations of the coefficients in the separate demand and supply equations, and the disturbance term incorporates the disturbance terms in both equations. Equation 5 states that the price of a property is determined by national, MSA, and county economic conditions and lagged supply.

A straightforward extension of the model allows either desired supply or quantity demanded to be a function of lagged price. It is easy to justify lagged price in either equation because of the time involved in property development on the supply side and relocation time on the demand side. Regardless of where lagged price is introduced, the reduced form of the equation is modified as follows:

$$P_{ti} = \pi_1 + \pi_2 Q_{S,t-1,i} + \pi_3 X_{ti} + \pi_4 N_t + \pi_5 P_{t-1,i} + \upsilon_{ti} \quad (6)$$

where price in the current period is now a function of price in the preceding period. Note that this equation requires us to have complete data, because for each MSA in the data set at each point in time, we must observe both a current and a lagged price. Depending on the data source, this requirement could be problematic,

On Dewees Island, South Carolina, the market responded well to the developer's efforts to emphasize living in harmony with the island's environment. Homes nest within the island's abundant flora, and low-impact amenities emphasize an outdoor lifestyle on this 1,206-acre private oceanfront retreat.

because it may not be possible to construct an accurate price for each MSA for each point in time as a result of the relatively slow turnover of commercial real estate properties. If complete data are not available, we can substitute for lagged price in Equation 6 as follows:

$$P_{ti} = \pi 1^* + \sum_{k=1}^{K}\pi 2_k^* Q_{S,t-k,i} + \sum_{k=0}^{K}\pi 3_k^* X_{t-k,i} + \sum_{k=0}^{K}\pi 4_k^* N_{t-k} + \upsilon_{ti}^* \quad (7)$$

where * indicates that the coefficient or disturbance term in Equation 7 is a linear combination of coefficients and disturbances in Equation 6. Equation 7 states that current price is a function of a weighted average of past supply, demand, and national-level variables.

In the literature, both structural equation models (CB Richard Ellis/Torto-Wheaton Research, Property & Portfolio Research, and *REIS Reports*) and reduced-form models (Case and Shiller) have been used. Figure 18-1 illustrates the tradeoffs between the two forms.

Figure 18-1

Tradeoffs in Reduced-Form and Structural-Form Equations

	Reduced Form (Equations 5, 6, or 7)	Structural Form (Equations 3 and 4)
Pros	■ No endogenous explanatory variables, which means that simpler methods can be used in estimation. ■ Forecasting future returns requires only values for variables that are exogenous to the model.	■ The model is more intuitive, and we can understand the pathways through which variables influence price.
Cons	■ Estimated coefficients represent combinations of coefficients from the structural equations model, which may make interpretation more difficult.	■ It is more difficult to estimate ¥, although some forecasting services ignore the simultaneity of the model and use simple methods, such as ordinary least squares, to estimate structural coefficients. ■ The model produces forecasting equations for both price and quantity; however, reduced-form equations for quantity can be obtained simply by replacing price on the left side of the reduced form.

Primary Sources of Demand Data

This section provides an overview of demand side forecasts at the MSA level, starting with a review of U.S. macromodels, as the major forecasting services all must ensure consistency between their macromodel forecasts and regional and MSA-level forecasts. Although there are several smaller competitors, the three major producers of demand side forecasts are the WEFA Group, RFA (Regional Financial Associates), and DRI (Data Resources Inc./F.W. Dodge Company). Major differences can be found in their methodology, but all start with a macromodel for the U.S. economy and then produce regional and MSA-level forecasts. Instead of presenting details about the individual models, this chapter presents instead a generic macromodel that will help us understand the types of data needed and the types of assumptions that must be made. In addition, this section discusses one of the major sources of data for MSA-level forecasts, BLS employment statistics by MSA, the relationship between two major surveys conducted by BLS, and information on demand side variables.

U.S. Macromodels

The theoretical basis of most macromodels is Keynesian or neo-Keynesian theory, which allows both monetary (the Federal Reserve) and fiscal (government spending and taxation) policy to play a role in the workings of the model; that is, the actions of regulators and spending by the federal government affect all the critical variables. These models show how national price levels, output, employment, and interest rates can be manipulated by policy initiatives. Keynesian or neo-Keynesian theory attempts to explain the interrelationship between aggregate demand for goods and services and aggregate supply. Consider the aggregate demand side of the model. The basic equations are in the following form:

$$\frac{M^D}{P} = L(Y,r)$$

where M^D is nominal money demanded, P is the price level, Y is output, and r is the interest rate. This equation states that the real demand for money is a function of the level of output for the economy and interest rates. The money supply M^S is determined by the Federal Reserve through control over key interest rates and open market operations (the buying and selling of government securities). In equilibrium, the money market must clear (money supply = money demand), which means that, for fixed prices, output and interest rates must adjust to the clear market. The Keynesian LM curve (the liquidity-preference relationship between money and income) shows the combinations of interest rates and output that are market clearing. Thus, the Federal Reserve and its exogenous manipulation of the money supply have their effect through the money demand and supply relationship.

The second equation in the system is a very familiar relationship:

$$Y = C(Y) + I(r) + G + X(Y^f, \pi) - Z(Y, \pi)$$

where output is assumed to be a function of consumption C, investment I, government expenditures G, exports X (which are a function of foreign output Y^f and exchange rates π), and imports Z (which are a function of domestic output Y and exchange rates π). If exchange rates, foreign output, and government expenditures and taxation are assumed to be exogenous to the system, then the standard Keynesian IS curve (the investment savings curve) shows the combination of output levels and interest rates that causes the product market to clear Y—the equality to hold in the above equation. Thus, we see that government fiscal policy works through the IS curve. For example, an exogenous increase in government expenditures must cause a shift in the equilibrium combinations of output and interest rates.

When the IS and LM curves are combined, the intersection of the two curves determines equilibrium output and interest rates for the fixed-price level. When price is varied, the aggregate demand curve is determined (equilibrium combinations of output and price levels).

The supply side of the system involves equilibrium in the labor market, where the level of real wages and employment levels are determined by the intersection of labor demand and supply schedules. Output on the supply side is determined by a production function relationship between employment and output.

Finally, the intersection of the aggregate demand and supply schedules determines equilibrium output and price. We see from the above system that the major exogenous variables in the system are government expenditures and taxes (as y must also equal $c + s + t$), money supply, exchange rates, and foreign output. The major endogenous variables are output, prices, interest rates, investment, consumption, savings, wage rates, and employment. Clearly, the levels of these important endogenous variables depend on the levels of the exogenous variables, which are typically assumed by the various forecasting services and are the driving force in their forecasts.

The faith that a user puts into a macroforecast is, to a large degree, a function of the faith the user has in the underlying assumptions. To understand the assumptions behind the forecasts of three major data providers—RFA, WEFA, and DRI—we asked each to provide a list of its five most important exogenous variables and current assumptions about these variables (see Figure 18-2).

First, note that DRI provided a bonus variable and there are actually six variables in that case. Next, note that three variables are common across the three providers: the federal funds rate,[1] exchange rates, and growth in foreign GDP. Although the variables are common, the assumptions made about them are quite different. RFA assumes that the federal funds rate will stay the same, while WEFA expects it to increase and DRI expects it to decrease. All three expect depreciation in the U.S. dollar from the third quarter of 1998 to the third quarter of 1999, but the rates are dramatically different. The alignment between the assumed growth of foreign GDP is closer, but the spread of 0.7 percent between the high and low (RFA at 2.8 percent and DRI at 2.1 percent) is still quite substantial.

Demand was greater than anticipated for the 121-unit mixed-use condo/hotel at Whistler Ski Resort in British Columbia. The project was marketed as the "first and the last" residential location to be built at the base of the two mountains at Whistler Resort. The project sold out in one hour at prices much higher than expected.

Rob Melnychuk

Figure 18-2

The Five Most Important Forecast Assumptions

	RFA	WEFA	DRI
Federal Funds Rate	(1998.3) 5.5%	(1998.3) 5.5%	(1998.3) 5.5%
	(1999.3) 5.5%	(1999.3) 6.0%	(1999.3) 4.8%
West Texas Intermediate Crude Price	(1998.3) 15.30		
	(1999.3) 19.40		
Change in Federal Government Consumption Expenditures, 1998.3 to 1999.3	2.7%		−0.1%
Change in Trade-Weighted Dollar Exchange Rate 1998.3 to 1999.3	−9.7%	−4.5%	−3.7%
Change in Trade-Weighted Dollar Exchange Rate 1998.3 to 1999.3 for Developing Countries			13.3%
World Real GDP Growth, Excluding U.S.	(1998.3) 1.6%	(1998.3) 1.7%	(1998.3) 1.7%
	(1999.3) 2.8%	(1999.3) 2.3%	(1999.3) 2.1%
U.S. Change in Inventory (in real billion $)		(1998.3) 64.0	
		(1999.3) 82.4	
Producer Price Inflation Rate		(1998.3) 1.8%	
		(1999.3) 2.7%	
Change in Total Fixed Investment for Rest of World			5.2%

Both RFA and DRI make assumptions about federal government expenditures, but RFA expects growth in the expenditures, while DRI expects a slight decline. The other variables are unique to one forecasting service or another. The two that are specific to WEFA typically would be considered endogenous in a standard Keynesian system; WEFA actually does estimate equations for them, but they start the forecasting process with the subjective judgments given above.

So, who is right? Unfortunately, we cannot answer that question at this time, and much of the answer will depend on unforeseen world events. The important point is that all three major suppliers will share this information with you, and you can make your own judgment about the reasonableness of their assumptions, keeping in mind the likely divergence in assumptions across suppliers.

Two Sources of Employment Data

The move from a macromodel to a regional or MSA model involves a variable of critical importance — employment growth measured at the appropriate level of aggregation (either region or MSA). It is one of the most important endogenous variables the government forecasts, and actual employment growth from quarters before the forecast period are the major exogenous variables. Government is the ultimate source of all employment data, and most of the numbers that users assume to be *actual* are probably estimates. All major forecasting services rely on data from the Bureau of Labor Statistics to produce their forecasts of employment growth by MSA. The BLS conducts two primary surveys, Current Employment Statistics and Employment and Wages Covered by Unemployment Insurance, and all major services use both surveys in their forecasts.[2]

Current Employment Statistics

The survey of current employment statistics is a payroll survey frequently referred to as the "790 survey," because the reporting form used is BLS form 790. The survey is administered monthly to a sample of approximately 390,000 business establishments nationwide. The primary statistics derived are estimates of employment, hours, and earnings down to the level of MSA. This huge sample asks all establishments with more than 250 employees to participate; a representative sample of smaller firms also participates. Nearly 40 percent of the total nonfarm population is represented in the survey. Respondents extract the needed information from payroll records they are required to keep for a variety of reasons.

Bias adjustment factors (a mathematical correction that compensates for any biases that might occur in survey work) are used primarily to adjust for the inability of the survey to capture the entry of new firms. The bias adjustment uses the universal coverage provided by the ES-202 data (described next) to provide an adjustment factor.

Employment and Wages Covered by Unemployment Insurance

Commonly called the "ES-202 program," the survey of employment and wages covered by unemployment insurance is a cooperative effort of the BLS and the employment security agencies of the 50 states, the District of Columbia, Puerto Rico, and the Virgin Islands. The ES-202 program is a comprehensive and accurate source of employment and wage data, by industry for the nation, states, and counties. Providing a virtual census of nonagricultural employees and their wages, it also covers about 47 percent of all workers in agricultural industries.[3]

Benchmarking Employment Data

Not surprisingly, a tradeoff exists between the two sources of employment data. The 790 data are timely, as the lag between the time the data are collected and when they are released is only one month. It is a survey, however, and is subject to sampling error and possibly bias in coverage. The ES-202 data provide a virtual census, but because of the complexity of the data, the lag between collection and release is 15 months.

The BLS therefore benchmarks (corrects preceding forecasts using new, more detailed information) the 790 figures to the ES-202 figures in March each year. For example, in March 1998, the BLS benchmarked employment statistics for April 1996 through February 1997. Estimates based on the new benchmark were also released at that time for the period after the benchmark, April 1997 through February 1998.

Primary Sources of Supply Data

Figure 18-3 presents information on the major suppliers of supply side information. See Figure 18-4 for a description of CoStar, one of the services available. As shown in the figure, F.W. Dodge maintains by far the

Figure 18-3

Supply Side Forecasts

Service	Web Site	Comments
CB Richard Ellis/Torto-Wheaton Research	www.cbcommercial.com/twr	Maintains a database for new construction for 50 to 60 MSAs, depending on the property type (office or industrial). The supply forecast is generated as part of the process of modeling structural equations.
F.W. Dodge	www.mag.fwdodge.com	Maintains database on building stock and building starts. The forecast of starts is updated monthly, the stock forecast yearly. Forecasts for 31 building types are produced for 3,105 counties. MSA forecasts can be obtained by a simple summation from the county database.
Merrill Lynch	www.ml.com	Obtains a list of all projects currently in the construction pipeline from local commercial real estate brokers. Data for 33 MSAs for office space and 43 MSAs for apartments are currently available.
Realty Information Group (CoStar)	www.rig.com	Provides analyses of availability and vacancies for office and industrial properties for 15 MSAs.
Construction Market Data Group	www.cmdg.com	Provides mainly lead information on new construction projects for contractors. The group has 15 years of construction history and is considering marketing this information.

Figure 18-4

CoStar: A Product of Realty Information Group

One information provider, among many, is Realty Information Group, Inc., based in Bethesda, Maryland. It offers building-specific information to the U.S. commercial real estate industry and related industries. The company has created a proprietary database—called CoStar—through internal development and strategic acquisitions detailing office and industrial space in the United States. The company also has developed a portfolio of multimedia software products with Internet connectivity that allows clients to access the database.

The database, the result of more than ten years of research, tracks available space floor by floor and suite by suite in increments as small as 100 square feet. CoStar archives valuable historical information, including leasing, occupancy, rental rates, and ownership. It also contains detailed information on tens of thousands of commercial real estate companies that own, lease, and manage properties.

CoStar includes hundreds of data fields providing substantive information as well as digitized photographs and floor plan images for individual commercial buildings in the major metropolitan markets throughout the country. This highly complex database is a real-time information system comprising interrelated tables containing such categories as location, site, and zoning information, building characteristics, availability of space, tax assessments, ownership, comparable space for sale, mortgage and deed information, for-sale information, and income and expense histories.

CoStar allows office and industrial real estate professionals to analyze leasing options, market conditions, and competitive property positions, and to produce multimedia presentations. A companion product—CrosTrac—allows them to identify the most likely tenants to fill vacant space, find tenants needing representation for their space needs, and undertake business-to-business marketing.

Realty Information Group's clients use CoStar to find leasing options in office and industrial buildings. Users can query CoStar with any combination of pertinent criteria. Clients also use CoStar to analyze market conditions by calculating up-to-the-minute vacancy rates, absorption

rates, or average rental rates. Thus, clients can gauge the balance between supply and demand and track market trends. Clients can also keep abreast of their competitors' market share and how competitors are positioning their properties. CoStar also has a news wire that keeps clients informed of late-breaking commercial real estate news, such as major deals signed, acquisitions, and ground breakings.

CoStar allows users to create professional presentations for clients, complete with high-resolution, digital color photographs and aerial photos of commercial buildings, in minutes using a desktop computer and color printer. The user can export and edit reports, photos, and floor plans in popular software packages such as Microsoft Word, Power Point, WordPerfect, Excel, and Lotus 1-2-3.

CoStar's convenience and utility are best displayed in the **Query Listings** mode. This function of CoStar allows the time-starved commercial real estate broker to instantly come up with a list of potential spaces for a client. For instance, let's say that Bill Clinton needs 25,000 square feet of contiguous space and that he wants to keep a Pennsylvania Avenue address in Washington, D.C. CoStar allows the user to survey the buildings in this submarket.

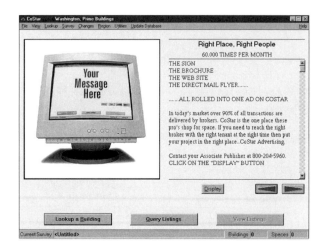

On the main screen, click on **Query Listings.**

---

most comprehensive database, and this discussion focuses on Dodge's methodology and accuracy. Some users find Dodge's forecasts more effective for large cities than for small cities. The database includes quarterly information on square feet of stock and starts from 1970 to the present for 31 building types in 3,105 counties. The

amounts of the stock for most property types are estimates, as a comprehensive census of existing stock exists only for federally owned structures, higher education facilities, and housing. For other building types, proxies had to be developed. The most important source of data used to develop the proxies has been the U.S.

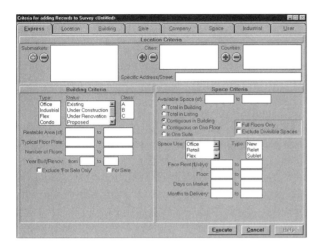

An express query screen appears that displays a single card featuring the most popular search criteria used to help you perform a fast survey. Begin by adding a city to the survey by clicking on the **plus sign (+)** under **Cities** in the upper center portion of the screen.

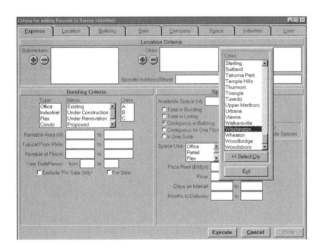

Highlight **Washington** under **Cities.** Then click on **Select City.** Click on **Exit** when you're finished.

In the box **Specific Address/Street,** type in Pennsylvania.

Under **Building Criteria** in the lower left half of the screen, highlight **Office** under **Type.**

Under **Space Criteria** in the lower right half of the screen, click in the first box next to **Available Space (sf)** and enter 25,000. Press the Tab key, and the cursor will move to the next box, where you type the number 26,000 (the narrowest range of spaces meeting the client's requirement). Then click in the button next to **Contiguous in Building,** and then on **Execute.**

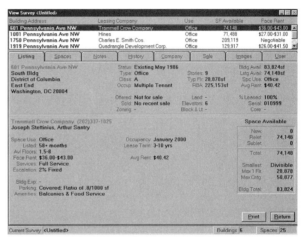

CoStar will show you how many buildings were found and how many spaces in those buildings match your criteria (the bottom line of the screen in the lower right corner). When you highlight a specific address, it brings up the results for that building. ■

Department of Energy's survey first conducted in 1979 and then updated in 1983.[4]

Dodge tracks starts through a network of more than 1,300 Dodge Reporters, who obtain information from building permits and other sources. Projects are tracked through a "project life cycle" that includes preplanning,

planning, final planning, negotiations, bidding, award, start, and construction.

In addition to these data, Dodge produces an econometrically generated forecast (the REAPS [Real Estate Analysis and Planning Service] forecast) for the top 58 MSAs for both starts and stock, and a shift-share forecast for smaller MSAs. The company uses a structural demand and supply model with a focus on predicting change in supply rather than change in price. Data requirements are basically the same as those required for a model that predicts returns, and demand side information comes from DRI. After deriving the econometric forecast, Dodge adjusts it up or down depending on "pipeline" information about potential building starts from the Dodge Reporters.

Providers of MSA Rankings for Commercial Real Estate Investment Purposes

Real estate forecasts use other people's supply and demand forecasts, but they arrive at conclusions using very different methodologies and obtain very different rankings of MSAs. This section provides a survey of suppliers of MSA forecasts of prices or rents for at least one property type. Some suppliers produce an explicit forecast, such as a forecast of growth in rents, while others simply rank MSAs for a specific property type on the basis of demand and supply side variables hypothesized to be important for a specific property type. Figure 18-5 presents brief sketches of the suppliers, and the rest of this section provides more detail on seven suppliers who rank MSAs for office properties, allowing us to compare forecasts for the MSAs that are common across the seven suppliers.

As shown in Figure 18-5, RFA seems to dominate the demand side of the market, with almost 50 percent of suppliers using some type of data from RFA. Only three suppliers provide an explicit forecast using regression methods (Korpacz is survey based). Two suppliers rely on the change in rent as their major dependent variable (CB Richard Ellis/Torto-Wheaton Research and *REIS Reports)*, and one relies on returns (Property & Portfolio Research).

How divergent are the forecasts? The answer to that question is based on actual forecasts from late 1997 or early 1998 (before the latest benchmarking of employment data by BLS) for seven of the suppliers. Thus, the forecast from PaineWebber, for example, is from November 1997 rather than the more current June 1998, because the June forecast would use the newly benchmarked data.

The following details on the suppliers provide a comparison for office space only, although most of the suppliers provide forecasts for several property types. (The description and analysis provided here do not constitute an endorsement but are only for information purposes.)

CB Richard Ellis/Torto-Wheaton Research (Spring 1998)

CB Richard Ellis/Torto-Wheaton Research estimates structural equation models for office, industrial, retail, and apartment space. The structures and data sources differ somewhat by property type. In all cases, the ultimate dependent variable is a standardized rent that is calculated based on information from CB Richard Ellis. The modeling approach is structural so that, in addition to rent, the company forecasts absorption, vacancy rates, and, for some property types (office among them), completions of new space. The company estimates a separate equation for each of 54 MSAs and provides forecasts of rental growth.

On the *supply side,* the major variable is that CB Richard Ellis provides historical data on the inventory of office space. Completions are known with certainty from the CB database for one year out; completions beyond one year are forecast as part of the model. On the *demand side,* RFA provides historical data and a two-year forecast of office employment, using the categories "finance/insurance/real estate" (FIRE) and "other office" employment.

PaineWebber (November 1997)

PaineWebber produces an index of attractiveness that can be used to rank the top 80 MSAs. It also provides ranks for REITs based on their exposure in the various MSAs. Currently, rankings are available for office, retail, and industrial property types, but the company expects to add apartments and storage categories in the near future. The basic methodology for the three property types is similar.

On the *supply side,* both historical and forecast data come from Dodge. On the *demand side,* data from CB Richard Ellis are used for historical vacancy rates for 57 MSAs, and estimates of vacancy rates from RFA are used for the remaining MSAs. Projected changes in the vacancy rate are obtained from the use of RFA's forecasts of office-occupying employment.

The rating system is based on two factors: 1) the difference between the current office vacancy rate and the natural vacancy rate for the MSA; and 2) the forecast change in the vacancy rate relative to its natural rate in the next year.

Guilkey-Miles Space Market Index (First Quarter 1998)

The Space Market Index is created in the same way for office, retail, warehouse, and apartment properties.

Figure 18-5

Demand and Supply Models That Rank the Attractiveness of MSAs

Models That Calculate an Explicit Return Forecast

Service	Address	Features
Property & Portfolio Research	www.ppr-research.com	Produces forecasts of market return (both total and appreciation) for office, retail, apartment, and warehouse properties for 60 MSAs. Demand side variables are from RFA, supply side variables from Dodge, dependent variable from NCREIF.
Korpacz and Associates	www.korpacz.com	Produces forecasts of market rental growth for office, retail, industrial, apartment, and hotel properties based on surveys of investors.
CB Richard Ellis/ Torto-Wheaton Research	www.cbcommercial.com/twr	Produces forecasts of market rental growth for office, retail, apartment, and industrial properties for 40 to 60 MSAs. Demand side variables are from RFA, supply side variables from CB Commercial.
REIS Reports	www.reisreports.com	Produces forecasts of market rental growth for apartment, retail, and office properties for both rental growth and vacancy rates for the top 50 MSAs. Demand side data are from RFA, and supply side data are based on its own surveys.

Services That Produce an Index of MSA Attractiveness

Service	Address	Features
Jacques Gordon (*Wharton Real Estate Review,* Fall 1997)		Produces an index of CBD office market strength for 36 MSAs. Major demand side source is Cognetics; no real supply side variables.
Williams Lavitt & Company	www.williams-lavitt.com	Trend index (RealTrenDex^{TM}) compares growth patterns of 150 U.S. cities for retail, commercial office, and single- and multi-family housing properties. Data sources are *Emerging Trends, Viewpoint,* and Heitman research.
Real Estate Research Corporation (RERC)	www.rerc.com	Uses a survey to determine attractive property types; provides limited information by MSA.
PaineWebber (in partnership with RFA)	www.painewebber.com	Produces forecasts for office, retail, and industrial space. Forecasts for apartments and storage facilities are in process. Uses supply data from Dodge (both history and forecast) and demand data from RFA (both history and forecast) to determine the relative attractiveness of the top 80 MSAs. Also uses data from CB Richard Ellis for occupancy rates for 52 MSAs for industrial and office space.

continued on next page

Figure 18-5

Demand and Supply Models That Rank the Attractiveness of MSAs (continued)

Service	Address	Features
Merrill Lynch	www.ml.com	Produces an index for offices and apartments for 33 MSAs that incorporates demand and supply characteristics. Supply side statistics come from government statistics and telephone interviews, demand side variables from RFA.
Guilkey-Miles Space Market Index	Fidelity Real Estate Group Fidelity Management & Research 82 Devonshire E15C Boston, MA 02109	Produces an index for office, retail, apartment, and warehouse space for 113 MSAs. Uses RFA for the demand side and Dodge for the supply side.
Morgan Stanley Dean Witter	www.dwdean.com	Provides ratings of individual REITs for office, industrial, retail, and apartment space. Does not rank MSAs but provides rankings generated by *REIS Reports*. Uses occupancy rate data from CB Richard Ellis.
Lehman Brothers	www.lehman.com	Produces an index for apartments for 43 MSAs. Supply side information from government statistics, demand side information from WEFA. Produces an office index for 42 MSAs, using supply side vacancy rates from CB Richard Ellis and demand side employment growth from DRI.
Salomon Smith Barney	www.smithbarney.com	Produces an index for apartments for 53 MSAs, using supply side statistics from the government and demand side demographic data from RFA.

An average yearly growth rate for the past two years and a one-year forward forecast is calculated for growth in both employment and supply. The index is simply the ratio of employment growth to supply growth. The Space Market Index was created by the authors as a simple method of compressing demand and supply statistics to a single number to get a quick read on demand and supply pressures for an MSA. Even though some data sources are common, the Space Market Index and the proprietary Fidelity Management and Research econometric models are quite different. The internal Fidelity model uses two additional major data sources, an explicit dependent variable, and a regression framework for forecasting.

The Space Market Index, on the *supply side,* uses Dodge data for both history and forecast and, on the *demand side,* RFA nonagricultural employment data for both history and forecast.

Property & Portfolio Research (First Quarter 1998)

This model estimates separate equations for returns on NOI and capital value, which are then summed to create a total return. The historical return series comprises national statistics from NCREIF, but the company plans to begin using regional NCREIF data. After the regression coefficients are estimated, forecasts for MSAs are obtained by plugging MSA demand and supply variables into the estimated regression model.

On the *supply side,* Dodge data on contract awards are used for historical data, and future construction is estimated as part of the structural equations model. On the *demand side,* the model uses "office-using employment," which is determined as a different percentage of total employment based on characteristics of the MSA. The data are from RFA.

Figure 18-6

Correlations of the Rankings of 20 MSAs

	Guilkey-Miles	Merrill Lynch	Paine-Webber	Jacques Gordon	REIS Reports	CBRE/Torto-Wheaton	Property & Portfolio
Guilkey-Miles	1.0						
Merrill Lynch	–.06	1.0					
PaineWebber	–.27	.52	1.0				
Jacques Gordon	–.06	.76	.29	1.0			
REIS Reports	.13	.71	.54	.56	1.0		
CBRE/Torto-Wheaton	.41	–.04	–.19	.23	.36	1.0	
Property & Portfolio	–.16	.15	.66	.06	.25	–.10	1.0

Merrill Lynch (January 1998)

Merrill Lynch combines forecasts of the demand for and supply of office space to yield projected vacancy rates for each of 33 MSAs. *Supply side* information comes from Merrill Lynch's own survey, and vacancy rates come from CB Richard Ellis. On the *demand side,* employment forecasts are from RFA.

REIS Reports (First Quarter 1998)

REIS Reports has historical information for each MSA from primary surveys plus secondary data sources. It gathers its own rent and vacancy information for 50 MSAs and estimates MSA-specific regression models that can be used to produce forecasts. It estimates a four-equation structural model (percentage change in occupied stock, percentage change in inventory, growth in real asking rent, and inverse root of the percentage difference between asking and effective rents).

On the *supply side, REIS Reports* obtains information on completions by screening local trade journals and permit clearinghouses. RFA provides history and forecasts for office employment on the *demand side.*

Jacques Gordon (Fall 1997)

Jacques Gordon has created an index of attractiveness for 36 MSAs for office properties. The index uses data on 11 variables from a wide variety of sources. For example, employment data are from Cognetics. Gordon uses "quality of life" data on such factors as public transportation, culture, and crime rates. He also uses information on the number of *Fortune* 500 firms located in the MSA along with the number of government employees to develop

an "anchor" rating for the CBD. He does not appear to use supply side information.

The correlations in Figure 18-6 were generated by taking whatever prediction the supplier provided (typically vacancy rate or rental growth) and ranking the MSAs for each service. Restricting the information to MSAs common across all seven services reduced the number of MSAs to 20. These 20 MSAs were then re-ranked, and simple correlations were calculated. Figure 18-7 presents the top and bottom five MSAs for each supplier.

What conclusions can be drawn from this exercise?

1. As can be easily seen in either figure, there is widespread disagreement in the MSA rankings.
2. This widespread disagreement exists even though six of the seven suppliers use some form of demand side data from RFA. The different suppliers obviously "massage" the data very differently.
3. Even when both the demand and supply side data sources are the same (RFA and F.W. Dodge for Guilkey-Miles, PaineWebber, and Property & Portfolio Research), the numbers are quite different.

This last observation leads to an important point about the relative advantage of indices compared with a methodology that uses an explicit dependent variable in a regression analysis. Note that the Guilkey-Miles index is formed by the ratio of change in employment to change in supply; thus, if we double our forecast for employment growth for an MSA and also double the forecasted increase in supply, the index and the rank of the MSA relative to other MSAs are unchanged. The underlying assumption is that the demand and supply factors should have equal weight in the ranking of MSAs.

Figure 18-7

Top and Bottom Five MSAs

Rank	Guilkey-Miles	Merrill Lynch	Paine-Webber	Jacques Gordon	REIS Reports	CBRE/Torto-Wheaton	Property & Portfolio
1	Houston	San Francisco	Boston	New York	San Francisco	New York	Atlanta
2	Boston	Boston	Austin	San Francisco	New York	San Francisco	Boston
3	Los Angeles	Seattle	Denver	Washington, D.C.	Seattle	Dallas	Phoenix
4	San Francisco	Austin	Seattle	Boston	San Diego	Phoenix	Seattle
5	Philadelphia	Cincinnati	Charlotte	Seattle	Boston	Houston	Denver
16	Atlanta	Cleveland	New York	Dallas	Philadelphia	St. Louis	Indianapolis
17	Washington, D.C.	Indianapolis	Philadelphia	Indianapolis	Indianapolis	Columbus	Los Angeles
18	Austin	Houston	Cincinnati	St. Louis	Cleveland	Austin	Cleveland
19	Columbus	Los Angeles	Indianapolis	Houston	Los Angeles	Boston	Washington, D.C.
20	Charlotte	Dallas	Los Angeles	Los Angeles	Charlotte	Cleveland	New York

If we have an explicit dependent variable such as rent growth or appreciation return, we can use regression methods to develop the relative weight demand and supply side factors should have in forecasting returns rather than make a subjective judgment. For example, suppose that regression methods were used to estimate the following relationship:

$$R = 1.5 + 2xE - 1xS.$$

This equation states that return R is a function of a constant, employment growth E, and growth in supply S. If employment growth and supply growth in an MSA are both 3 percent, our estimated return would be 4.5 percent, because, in this example, the demand side factor is twice as important as the supply side factor. It is important to note that this weighting scheme was determined empirically rather than by using subjective judgment about the relative importance of the two factors, as must be done when no explicit dependent variable is available. In other empirical work, Guilkey and Miles have found that the relative weights for the demand and supply variables differ dramatically by property type, and so it is probably the case that suppliers that have a reasonable dependent variable have an advantage over suppliers that must rely on indices.

Summary

A major question we set out to answer is "how accurate are the forecasts?" We can say one thing with cer-

tainty: given the divergence in information, forecasts clearly cannot all be accurate. So how should the analyst choose which supplier to use? Here are some general guidelines:

1. Buying real estate is expensive relative to buying forecasts, and so you should buy more than one forecast. In making your decision, you should certainly diversify across demand suppliers. If you are buying a forecast that uses F.W. Dodge for the supply side, keep in mind that Dodge uses DRI data for its forecasts and take that fact into account in diversification.

2. Remember that the whole forecasting process starts at the macro level with someone's subjective judgment on a few key exogenous variables. All services will provide you with their list of variables and assumptions, leaving you to judge for yourself whether the assumptions are reasonable.

3. You should probably choose suppliers that have an explicit dependent variable that is of interest to you over suppliers that create indices. Using regression methods to weight the relative importance of the demand and supply side factors reduces the amount of subjectivity in the forecast.

4. If your potential supplier has been producing forecasts for a number of years, it should be able to provide you with measures of forecast accuracy similar to Figures 18-6 and 18-7 for the demand and supply side variables. It is important to note that some of the suppliers listed in this chapter that use regression methods estimate MSA-specific regression models with the dependent variable a function of its own

lagged value plus demand and supply variables. These models are simply time series models—and relatively short time series models at that. Therefore, you should not be impressed by r-squareds of 90 percent or higher. This information is relatively easy to obtain. You should be more interested in the cross-sectional performance of MSAs (i.e., at any particular time, do you want to buy a building in Dallas or San Francisco?). This calculation is a lot harder to do well, resulting in relatively low r-squareds.

5. Employment data for MSA-level forecasts, which undergo wholesale revision in March every year, are critically important. It is important to understand how fast these data are incorporated into your supplier's forecast. Experience shows that there is a three- to four-month difference in the speed with which BLS data are incorporated into the various demand side forecasts.

And it is important to remember that, whether you are buying a final forecast based on regression methods or an index, either implicit or explicit weights are used to combine the supply and demand variables. These weights—whether objectively obtained by regression methods or set subjectively—are based on historical information ("forecasting the past with ever greater precision," as the cartoon goes). Clearly, if the future relationship between demand and supply variables changes in some fundamental way, then regardless of how well our model fits the past, our forecast for the future will be imprecise. For example, if we feel that technology will fundamentally alter the amount of warehouse space that is needed by drastically reducing inventories, then we may need to adjust our forecast accordingly.

Terms

- Aggregate supply
- Benchmark
- Bias adjustment factors
- Endogenous variables
- Equilibrium
- Exogenous variables
- Keynesian (neo-Keynesian)
- Lag
- Linear combinations
- Supply and demand
- Weights

Review Questions

18.1 How does real estate differ from most other commodities, and how do supply and demand models accommodate that difference?

18.2 Explain the difference between structural-equation models and reduced-form models.

In Irving, Texas, market analysis showed that many young professional singles and families wanted both a custom home design and the convenience of a multifamily residential community. The Grand Venetian filled the market niche by providing an upscale community with a classic design and amenities such as tanning beds, a spa, ATMs, a business center, a dry cleaners, and an art gallery.

Steve Hinds

18.3 Describe the roles that monetary and fiscal policy play in macroeconomic models.

18.4 How does a user deal with the different assumptions that different data providers use when making their forecasts?

18.5 The text states that the government is the ultimate source of employment data and that most of the data are estimates rather than actual numbers. What implication does this observation have for a forecaster?

18.6 In the correlations using the seven data services, all the forecasts differ. How does a user make sense of those differences and decide which one is "correct"?

Notes

1. The federal funds rate is the rate of interest that banks charge each other for loans. The Federal Reserve can change this rate through open market operations, and it has been a major policy target in the past.

2. Very complete information about the surveys can be obtained from the BLS Web site *(www.bls.gov)*.

3. Bureau of Labor Statistics, *Handbook of Methods* (Washington, D.C.: U.S. Government Printing Office, 1997), Chap. 5.

4. Detailed information on how the benchmark numbers for the stock were calculated for each building type can be obtained from F.W. Dodge.

Part VI
Bibliography

Feasibility Studies

Angelo, Rocco M. *Practical Guide to Understanding Feasibility Studies.* East Lansing, Mich.: American Hotel and Motel Association, 1985.

Barrett, G. Vincent, and John P. Blair. *How to Conduct and Analyze Real Estate Market and Feasibility Studies.* 2d ed. New York: Van Nostrand Reinhold, 1988.

Beals, Paul. "Rehabilitating Hotel Feasibility Studies." *Real Estate Review* 24:1 (Spring 1994): 58–60.

Brecht, Susan, and James F. Sherman. *Retirement Housing Markets: Project Planning and Feasibility Analysis.* New York: Wiley, 1991.

Building Owners and Managers Association International and ULI–the Urban Land Institute. *What Office Tenants Want: 1999 BOMA/ULI Office Tenant Survey Report.* Washington, D.C.: Author, 1999.

Burrough, P.A., and Rachael McDonnell. *Principles of Geographical Information Systems.* Rev. ed. New York: Oxford Univ. Press, 1998.

Campbell, Burnham O. *Population Change and Building Cycles.* Urbana: Univ. of Illinois, Bureau of Business and Economic Research, 1966.

Canestaro, James C. *Refining Project Feasibility.* 3d ed. Blacksburg, Va.: The Refine Group, 1989.

Carn, Neil, Joseph Rabianski, Ronald Racster, and Maury Seldin. *Real Estate Market Analysis: Techniques and Applications.* Englewood Cliffs, N.J.: Prentice-Hall, 1988.

Carter, Charles C. "Assumptions Underlying the Retail Gravity Model." *Appraisal Journal* 61:4 (October 1993): 509–18.

Castle, Gilbert, ed. *GIS in Real Estate.* Chicago: Appraisal Institute, 1998.

Clapp, John M. *Handbook for Real Estate Market Analysis.* Englewood Cliffs, N.J.: Prentice-Hall, 1987.

Clapp, John M., Mauricio Rodriguez, and Grant Thrall. "How GIS Can Put Urban Economic Analysis on the Map." *Journal of Housing Economics* 6:4 (December 1997): 368–86.

Clapp, John M., and Stephen D. Messner, eds. *Real Estate Market Analysis: Methods and Applications.* Westport, Conn.: Greenwood Press, 1988.

DeMers, Michael. *Fundamentals of Geographic Information Systems.* New York: Wiley, 1997.

Downs, Anthony. "Characteristics of Various Economic Studies." *Appraisal Journal* 34:7 (July 1966): 329–38.

Fanning, Stephen, and Jody Winslow. "Guidelines for Defining the Scope of Market Analysis in Appraisal Assignments." *Appraisal Journal* 56:10 (October 1988): 466–76.

Featherston, J.B. "Approaching Market Analysis in a New Economic Environment." *Journal of Real Estate Development* 1:4 (Spring 1986): 5–10.

Fouts, Mickey E., and James C. Canestaro. "The New Realities of Development Project Feasibility." *Urban Land* 49:2 (February 1990): 6–9.

George, Vernon. "Market Feasibility." In *Financing Income-Producing Real Estate,* ed. Eric Stevenson. Washington, D.C.: Mortgage Bankers Association, 1988.

Graaskamp, James. *A Guide to Feasibility Analysis.* Chicago: Appraisal Institute, 1970.

Haddow, David F. "Making the City Overview Meaningful." *Appraisal Journal* 52:1 (January 1984): 48–52.

Hanna, Karen, and R. Brian Culpepper. *GIS in Site Design: New Tools for Design Professionals.* New York: Wiley, 1998.

Hartzell, David, and Emil Malizia. "Market Analysis for Investors: A Special Breed of Real Estate Market Research." *Urban Land* 48:1 (January 1989): 6–8.

Huff, David L. "Defining and Estimating a Trade Area." *Journal of Marketing* 28:7 (July 1964): 34–38.

Jarchow, Stephen P., ed. *Graaskamp on Real Estate.* Washington, D.C.: ULI–the Urban Land Institute, 1991.

Johnson, L.M. "Feasibility Study." *Real Estate Today* 12:8 (August 1979): 10–13.

Marks, Alan, Craig Stanley, and Grant Thrall. "Criteria and Definitions for the Evaluation of Geographic Information System Software for Real Estate Analysis." *Journal of Real Estate Literature* 2:2 (1994): 227–24.

Martin, Vernon, III. "Nine Abuses Common in Pro Forma Cash Flow Projections." *Real Estate Review* 18:3 (Fall 1988): 20–25.

Messner, Stephen D., et al. *Analyzing Real Estate Opportunities.* Chicago: Realtors® National Marketing Institute, 1985.

Perkins, B. "Why Real Estate Feasibility Analyses Have Not Worked." *Real Estate Review* 9:3 (Fall 1979): 33–37.

Peterson, K. "Snapshot Feasibility Analysis." *Real Estate Review* 9:3 (Fall 1979): 88–89.

Roddewig, Richard J., and Jared Shales. *Analyzing the Economic Feasbility of a Development Project: A Guide for Planners.* Planning Advisory Service Report No. 380. Chicago: American Planning Association, 1983.

Rushmore, Stephen. *How to Perform an Economic Feasibility Study of a Proposed Hotel-Motel.* Chicago: American Society of Real Estate Counselors, 1986.

Siegel, Richard A. "Market Structures and Market Studies." *Journal of Real Estate Development* 1:3 (Winter 1986): 30–34.

Sirmans, C.F. *Data Sources for Real Estate Market Analysis.* Glastonbury, Conn.: Pension Real Estate Association, 1994.

Stevens, Robert, and Philip K. Sherwood. *How to Prepare a Feasibility Study: A Step-by-Step Guide Including Three Model Studies.* Englewood Cliffs, N.J.: Prentice-Hall, 1982.

Thrall, Grant Ian. "Applications of GIS to Real Estate and Related Industries." *Journal of Housing Economics.*

FannieMae: Washington D.C., 1998. *Research* 9 (1998): 33–59.

Thrall, Grant, and Juan del Valle. "The Calculation of Retail Market Areas: The Reilly Model." *Geo Info Systems* 7:4 (1997): 46–49.

Thrall, Grant Ian, et al. *Real Estate Market Analysis.* Washington, D.C.: ULI–the Urban Land Institute, forthcoming.

Thrall, Susan, and Grant Ian Thrall. "Desktop GIS." In *Geographical Information Systems: Principles, Techniques, Management, and Application,* ed. P.A. Longley et al. New York: Wiley, 1998.

Vandell, Kerry D. "Market Analysis: Can We Do Better?" *Appraisal Journal* 56:7 (July 1988): 344–50.

Weiss, J.M. "Deductibility of Marketing and Feasibility Studies." *Management Accounting* 63 (April 1982): 60.

Young, G.I.M. "Feasibility Studies." *Appraisal Journal* 38:7 (July 1970): 376–83.

Zaddack, Gerald N. "Real Estate Applications for GIS: A Review of Existing Conditions and Future Opportunities." *Real Estate Issues* 23:4 (1999): 13–19.

Real Estate Market Studies

Adams, Harold L., and David Parham. "Repositioning the Office Building." In *ULI on the Future: Reinventing Real Estate.* Washington, D.C.: ULI–the Urban Land Institute, 1995.

Anderson, Austin. "Common Pitfalls in Real Estate Market Research." *Real Estate Finance* (Spring 1989): 77–81.

Appraisal Institute. *Real Estate Market Analysis: Supply and Demand Factors.* Chicago: Author, 1993.

Becker, T.J. "Hottest Hits in Single-Family Housing." *Urban Land* 55:2 (February 1996): 25–28.

Beyard, Michael D. *Business and Industrial Park Development Handbook.* Washington, D.C.: ULI–the Urban Land Institute, 1988.

Beyard, Michael D., and W. Paul O'Mara. *Shopping Center Development Handbook.* 3d ed. Washington, D.C.: ULI–the Urban Land Institute, 1999.

Birnkrant, Michael. "Shopping Center Feasibility Study: Its Methods and Techniques." *Journal of Property Management* 35:6 (November/December 1970): 272–79.

Bookout, Lloyd, et al. *Residential Development Handbook.* 2d ed. Washington, D.C.: ULI–the Urban Land Institute, 1990.

Cameron, Christine. "How to Select, Use, and Interpret Real Estate Market Statistics." *Skylines* 17:1 (January 1992): 30–31.

Carn, Neil, et al. *Real Estate Market Analysis: Techniques and Applications*. Englewood Cliffs, N.J.: Prentice-Hall, 1988.

Christensen, Marvin, and Kenneth Ackerman. "Warehouse/ Distribution Facilities: Emerging Industry Trends and Future Market Implications." In *ULI on the Future: Creating Tomorrow's Competitive Advantage*. Washington, D.C.: ULI–the Urban Land Institute, 1996.

Clapp, John M. *Dynamics of Office Markets: Empirical Findings and Research Issues*. Washington, D.C.: Urban Institute Press, 1993.

Coldwell Banker Commercial/Torto-Wheaton Services. *Office Outlook*. Boston: Author, annual.

Danielsen, Karen, et al. *Multifamily Development Handbook*. Washington, D.C.: ULI–the Urban Land Institute, 1998.

Del Casino, Joseph J. "A Risk Simulation Approach to Long-Range Office Demand Forecasting." *Real Estate Review* 15:2 (Summer 1985): 82–87.

DeLisle, James. *Appraisal, Market Analysis, and Public Policy in Real Estate: Essays in Honor of James A. Graaskamp*. Boston: Kluwer Academic Publishers, 1994.

Dilmore, Gene. *Quantitative Techniques in Real Estate Counseling*. Lexington, Mass.: Lexington Books, 1981.

DiPasquale, Denise, and William C. Wheaton. "The Market for Real Estate Assets and Space: A Conceptual Framework." *AREUEA Journal* 20:2 (Summer 1992): 181–97.

Dowall, David E. "Office Market Research: The Case for Segmentation." *Journal of Real Estate Development* 3:1 (Summer 1988): 34–43.

Eppli, Mark J., and Monty J. Childs. "A Descriptive Analysis of U.S. Housing Demand for the 1990s." *Journal of Real Estate Research* 10:1 (1995): 69–86.

Fanning, Stephen, Terry Glisson, and Thomas Pearson. *Market Analysis in Valuation Appraisals*. Chicago: Appraisal Institute, 1994.

Fisher, Jeffrey. "Integrating Research on Markets for Space and Capital." *American Real Estate and Urban Economics Association Journal* 20:1 (1992): 161–80.

Fisher, Jeffrey D., and R. Brian Webb. "Current Issues in the Analysis of Commercial Real Estate." *AREUEA Journal* 20:2 (Summer 1992): 211–27.

Gause, Jo Allen, et al. *Office Development Handbook*. 2d ed. Washington, D.C.: ULI–the Urban Land Institute, 1998.

Goodman, Jack. 1998. "The Multifamily Outlook." *Urban Land* 57:11 (November 1998): 38–41.

Goodman, John L., Jr., and Stuart A. Gabriel. "Why Housing Forecasts Go Awry." *Real Estate Review* 17:3 (Fall 1987): 64–71.

Grenadier, Steven R. "Local and National Determinants of Office Vacancies." *Journal of Urban Economics* 37:1 (January 1995): 57–71.

Hughes, William T., Jr. "Determinants of Demand for Industrial Property." *Appraisal Journal* 62:2 (April 1994): 303–9.

Jones, Gareth. *Methodology for Land and Housing Market Analysis*. Cambridge, Mass.: Lincoln Institute of Land Policy, 1994.

Kellough, W.R. "The Appraiser and Feasibility Analysis." *Canadian Appraiser* 37:2 (Summer 1993): 39–42.

Kelly, Hugh F. "Forecasting Office Space Demand in Urban Areas." *Real Estate Review* 13:3 (Fall 1983): 87–94.

Kenney, Michael D. "Market Studies for Real Estate Projects." *NAIOP News* 17:12 (December 1985): 28–32.

Kimball, J.R., and Barbara Bloomberg. "Office Space Demand Analysis." *Appraisal Journal* 55:10 (October 1987): 567–77.

McBee, Susanna, et al. *Downtown Development Handbook*. 2d ed. Washington, D.C.: ULI–the Urban Land Institute, 1992.

Messner, Stephen D., Irving Schreiber, and Victor L. Lyon. *Marketing Investment Real Estate*. 3d ed. Chicago: Realtors® National Marketing Institute, 1985.

Mier, Robert, and Wim Wiewel. *Analyzing Neighborhood Retail Opportunities: A Guide for Carrying Out a Preliminary Market Study*. Planning Advisory Service Report No. 358. Chicago: American Planning Association, 1981.

Myers, Dowell. *Analysis with Local Census Data: Portraits of Change*. Boston: Academic Press, 1992.

———. "Demographic Waves and Retail Development." *Urban Land* 46:5 (May 1987): 2–5.

———. "Extended Forecasts of Housing Demand in Metropolitan Areas." *Appraisal Journal* 55:4 (April 1987): 266–78.

———. "Housing Market Research: Time for a Change." *Urban Land* 47:10 (October 1988): 16–19.

Myers, Dowell, and Phillip S. Mitchell. "Identifying a Well-Founded Market Analysis." *Appraisal Journal* 61:4 (October 1993): 500–8.

Prudential Realty Group and University of North Carolina. *Real Estate Investment Strategy: A Year 2000 Perspective*. New York: Author, 1989.

Rabianski, Joseph. "Market Analyses and Appraisals: Problems Persist." *Real Estate Review* 24:4 (Winter 1995): 45–49.

———. "A New Tool for Hotel Market and Financial Analysis." *Real Estate Review* 25:1 (Spring 1995): 37–41.

Real Estate Research Corporation. *Emerging Trends in Real Estate.* Chicago: Author, annual.

Roca, Rueben. "Market Research for Shopping Centers." In *Basic Research Procedures,* ed. William J. McCollum. Washington, D.C.: International Council of Shopping Centers, 1987.

Scott, J.F. "Importance of Feasibility Studies in Site Selection and Disposition of Industrial Properties." *Journal of Property Management* 45:1 (January 1980): 39–40.

Society of Industrial and Office Realtors®. *Comparative Statistics of Industrial and Office Real Estate Markets.* Washington, D.C.: Author, 1993.

Tunis, Robert T. "The Negotiation Differential: A New Approach to Office Market Analysis." *Real Estate Review* 18:4 (Winter 1989): 49–55.

Vernor, James D., ed. *Readings in Market Research for Real Estate.* Chicago: Appraisal Institute, 1985.

———. *Shopping Center Appraisal and Analysis.* Chicago: Appraisal Institute, 1993.

Weisbrod, Glen, and Karl Radov. "The Seven Deadly Sins of Retail Market Studies." *Urban Land* 47:2 (February 1988): 21–25.

White, Pip. "Residential Housing Market Analysis: A Turning Points Model." *Property Tax Journal* 10:2 (June 1991): 147–56.

Wilson, Donald C. "Highest and Best Use Analysis: Appraisal Heuristics versus Economic Theory." *Appraisal Journal* 63:1 (January 1995): 11–26.

Wincott, D. Richard, and Glenn R. Mueller. "Market Analysis in the Appraisal Process." *Appraisal Journal* 63:1 (January 1995): 27–32.

Witten, G. Ronald. "Capital Markets' Need for Reliable Real Estate Market Forecasts." *Urban Land* 51:7 (July 1992): 33–35.

Wofford, Larry E. "Significant Trends Affecting Office and Industrial Real Estate: A 21st Century Perspective." *Appraisal Journal* 55:1 (January 1987): 94–107.

The diverse, creative work that goes into starting a development comes together in stages four, five, six, and seven.

During stages four and five, the nitty-gritty negotiations and detailed agreements are completed, allowing the project to begin. Many decisions are made that will affect how well and how quickly the development is completed. By the time a developer reaches stage six—construction—his commitment to a project is nearly irreversible, because the decision to back out from that point on would result in a tremendous financial and professional loss.

Now the developer moves from the role of creator/promoter to that of manager, ensuring that time and budget are as tightly controlled as possible, accounting for the performance and payment of all the players in the process. Stage seven—completion and formal opening—is the initial test of how well everything was done. In this stage, users begin their assessment of the development, from the building itself to the services and amenities.

Part VII
Making It
Happen

Chapter 19

Stages Four and Five: Contract Negotiation and Formal Commitment

S tage three of the development process—the formal feasibility study—brings together all previously completed research and projections into summary statements of value and costs. If the project is feasible, its estimated value will exceed costs (broadly defined). With documentation indicating that the project is feasible, the developer has the necessary information to assemble the development team. Thus, the feasibility analysis serves as a sales and negotiating tool and as a coordinating device in stage four, contract negotiation. During stage four, contracts are arranged to implement the decision to proceed with the project; during stage five, these contracts are executed.

A detailed agreement should be negotiated with and documented for each member of the development team. The developer must ensure that all the different aspects of the project are covered by the collection of individual contracts and that the various relationships among players are clearly defined. Because many of the contracts are contingent on one another, stage five represents the joint execution of the contracts negotiated in stage four.

Contracts are another method of controlling risk. They set forth the rules for the physical, financial, marketing, and operating activities that will occur during construction, formal opening, and operation (stages six, seven, and eight, respectively). If all contracts are properly drawn and are consistent with one another, then the collective risk of all members of the development team is reduced—which does not mean that a naive participant will necessarily benefit from tightly drawn contracts that might favor others. With proper structuring of the contracts, the developer will be able to spread the risks appropriately among the participants.

A major transition occurs in a development as it moves from stage three to stage six; stages four and five are thus the last opportunity to back out before major construction costs are incurred. During stage four, negotiations ensure that the idea is still feasible as all details are confirmed in a set of formal contracts that make the details explicit and as free of ambiguities as possible. Once the documents are executed in stage five, most of the players no longer retain the option to walk out of the deal. In reality, of course, it is still possible to quit, but the pain can be intense and costly after contracts have been executed. During the earlier stages, developers are primarily idea generators and promoters. As the process moves toward construction, however, the developer's role becomes that of primary negotiator who brings together all the members of the team. And in stage six, the developer's role shifts to manager of the development team.

This chapter covers the following issues involved in contract negotiation (stage four) and formal commitment (stage five):

- Arranging financing;
- Environmental issues;
- Decisions about design and contractors;
- Decisions about major tenants;
- Decisions about equity;
- The government as partner; and
- Commitment, signing contracts, and initiating construction.

The authors are indebted to the law firm of Cox, Castle & Nicholson LLP, Los Angeles, for its contributions to this chapter.

Stage Four: Contract Negotiation

Like the other stages of the development process, everything interacts in stage four. For example, the players do not negotiate financing without first considering the impact of the timing of financing on construction. Because so many different elements must be clarified and potential problems identified at this stage, the discussion that follows covers a variety of issues. It begins with construction and permanent financing and some recent innovations in financing. It then moves to the handling of hazardous materials and other environmental concerns; consideration of contracts with architects, engineers, and contractors; leases with tenants; and equity contracts with financial partners during the development period and long-term equity investors.

Keep in mind as you read about stage four that, because of their many interactions, the topics are covered in a somewhat arbitrary fashion. Nowhere are these interactions more evident than in the financing arena. For example, environmental concerns must be satisfactorily addressed; acceptable architects, engineers, and contractors must be located; preleasing or presales of a significant amount of space may be required; and the identity and dollar contributions of any financial partners during development and long-term equity investors must be firm before the commitment for permanent financing is signed. The fewer uncertainties that exist, the less risk to the lender and the better the financing rates and terms to the developer/borrower.

The market study (Chapters 17 and 18) and the investment analysis contained in the feasibility study (Chapter 16) are part of the raw material for the loan application. Historically, developers began arranging financing by seeking a permanent lender and obtaining a permanent loan commitment, and then finding a construction lender and negotiating a construction loan. Currently, it is more often the case that developers seek a construction loan without prearranging the takeout of the construction loan by a permanent loan. Given both the historical context and current customs and practices, this analysis of financing issues begins with a discussion of construction lending and then focuses on permanent financing. The discussion of construction lending includes a discussion of dynamics between construction lenders and permanent lenders.

Arranging Financing:
The Construction Lender

As noted, construction lenders[1] historically made development loans conditioned upon the developer's obtaining a commitment from a so-called permanent lender;

the permanent lender would provide assurance to the construction lender that, if the project is built on time, the construction lender's loan will be paid off at a certain time. With a permanent loan commitment in hand, the construction lender does not have to assume market or other long-term risk.

The degree to which the construction lender relies on the permanent lender's commitment is a factor of both the construction lender's internal practices and the willingness of lenders to issue commitments for takeout finance. Some construction lenders rely on the permanent loan commitment for repayment. Depending on the construction lender's internal practices, it will either not lend more than the permanent loan's initial funding amount unless and until the economic conditions for subsequent permanent fundings are satisfied or, more problematic for the developer, until each condition of the permanent loan commitment, short of completion of the improvements, is satisfied. Other construction lenders may agree (with the permanent lender) that the portion of the construction loan not covered by the initial permanent loan funding will be placed into a subordinate position on the project, subject to repayment upon the satisfaction of the conditions for the subsequent funding.

Given the relationship between the construction loan and the permanent loan, anticipating what the permanent lender will require for loan approval thus can represent a threshold for obtaining the construction loan. The most crucial part of the feasibility study (discussed in stage three) for long-term lenders is the market analysis. Most long-term lenders look at the feasibility study submitted by the developer and then adjust it according to their own perceptions of the market. Sophisticated permanent lenders maintain a substantial database on the markets in which they lend money. They underwrite the loan—that is, they analyze the market, the cost of the proposed project, and the demand for the project—based on community needs.

Depending on the state of the market, many construction lenders may not require permanent commitments as a condition of loan approval. Even without the express requirement, however, construction lenders typically expect that they will be paid off in a short time frame and therefore still usually view their risk as short term.

Short-term loans tend to come from institutions with shorter-term liabilities in their portfolios. Balancing asset and liability maturities reduces the institution's risk. For that reason, commercial banks are the leading construction lenders. With thousands of commercial banks across the country, the institutions are more likely to be located close to a given project; accordingly, they are able to supervise construction and reduce risk

Construction lenders that are not located near a project often engage local construction disbursement agents to supervise the project in the lenders' absence.

Given the lender's time horizon, a construction lender focuses on the developer's experience and reputation, the professionalism of the architect, the reputation of the general contractor, the complexity of the project, and other immediate risks specific to the project. The more complex the project and the more inexperienced the developer and other participants in the process, the greater the risks to the construction lender.

For major projects, it is not atypical for a number of lenders to provide construction financing. A single lender may not want to assume the multimillion dollar risk inherent in a large project. The structures for such an arrangement are varied, ranging from a traditional loan participation arrangement in which a lead lender commits to make the loan and seeks out loan participants who have no direct relationship with the developer, to an agency lending arrangement in which each lender executes its own commitment with the developer and one of the lenders is appointed as the agent to act on behalf of all lenders in dealing with the developer. The latter option is riskier for the developer, as no lender agrees to fund any shortfall that may arise as a result of one lender's failure to fund its share of the loan.

The interest rate on a construction loan typically varies and is most often tied to some index, generally the lender's prime rate or LIBOR (London interbank offered rate). Depending on the index, the lender typically charges a spread over the index from one to two points (for a prime-based lender) to as much as four points (for a LIBOR-based lender). Because these indices can be volatile in a rapidly changing market, a risk exists that the interest reserve in the construction loan may not be large enough to accommodate unanticipated increases in the interest rate.

The conditions under which the developer is permitted to draw down the construction loan can be the source of a great deal of negotiation. Typically, the developer and construction lender agree on a line-item budget for the project (usually from the feasibility study), with draws advanced against that budget. Many lenders do not permit draws against a particular line item if, in the opinion of the lender's consultants, the draws will leave insufficient funds in the line item to complete that portion of the project. Most lenders, however, permit the developer to use a portion of the "contingency" line item in the budget to cover a shortfall or to move any savings in other line items into a deficient line. If neither of these devices is available, the loan may become "out of balance"; that is, sufficient funds will not be available to complete the project. The lender may then require the developer to deposit sufficient funds with the lender to bring the loan into balance; the lender will disburse the developer's funds first.

Alternatives available to developers who do not care to place their cash with the lender include providing the lender with additional security, such as a letter of credit, to ensure that sufficient funds will always be available to complete the project. A developer typically puts up additional cash or provides the additional security if 1) the developer believes he will ultimately achieve substantial cost savings when bringing the loan into balance, or 2) the anticipated value of the project justifies a potential infusion of cash. Clearly, construction lenders need to keep a close watch on the entire construction process.

Arranging Financing: The Permanent Lender

As noted, construction lenders sometimes require a permanent lender to "preapprove" certain of the closing conditions in the permanent loan commitment. The permanent lender provides longer-term capital than the construction lender and thus assumes some of the project's longer-term market risks.

Historically, the developer and lender expected financing to remain in place through one or more market cycles. Under those conditions, permanent loans ran for 30-year terms on a fixed-rate, fully amortized basis. More recently, the permanent lending community has attempted to limit the market risk it is willing to accept. The result has been shorter loan terms "ballooning" (coming due) in five to ten years but still with 30-year loan amortization schedules. Further, interest rates on some loans now are adjusted periodically so that the lender is somewhat insulated from (and the developer exposed to) major shifts in interest rates.

Competition is a key consideration for permanent lenders. The astute permanent lender analyzes the post-development market needs of the community, comparable projects under construction, and sites that, while not under construction, offer the potential for long-term competition. Permanent lenders are concerned with the project's ability to sustain cash flows sufficient to pay operating expenses and debt service over the term of the loan at the same time they need to anticipate potential demand for the project at the date of any balloon payment, thereby minimizing the risk that no replacement financing will be available.

The development and project management team plays a major role in the lender's decision making. The permanent lender looks to the leasing and management capabilities of the developer or, if these services are not to be provided by the developer, to the management company to be engaged by the developer. Specifically, the permanent lender is interested in any management contract that the developer proposes to execute and the capability and experience of the management company. Understandably, the long-term management track record of the developer and/or management company is a prime consideration for the permanent lender, as poor management can adversely affect collateral value.

As the lender analyzes the proposal in light of its understanding of the market, it also determines whether the loan fits into its portfolio. Most lenders have crafted diversification strategies that require diversification by region, product type, developer, and tenant. Further, many lenders attempt to match permanent loan receipts (assets) on the one hand with payment obligations (liabilities) on the other. For example, if an insurance company has guaranteed a certain yield to a pension fund as part of an investment contract for a defined period of time (referred to as a GIC, or guaranteed investment contract), the lender will attempt to match the term of the pension investment contract (liability) with the term of the permanent loan (asset).

Once the lender decides to make a loan on the project, it either issues a commitment letter or accepts the developer's application for financing. Both the letter and the application typically include loan amount, interest rate, terms of the loan, and a period of time within which the loan must be closed, i.e., funded by the lender. In short, in the context of the so-called takeout loan, both documents provide that the lender will make the described loan within a certain time, say, 12 to 36 months in the future, upon the satisfaction of certain terms and conditions. Such conditions usually include completion of the project in accordance with approved plans and specifications, satisfaction of any leasing requirements, and proof of acceptable title insurance and an ALTA (American Land Title Association) survey.

The precise economic terms of a loan depend on the availability and cost of financing in the capital markets generally, and other market conditions that bear on the relative bargaining strength of the parties. Often, the amount of the permanent loan is funded in stages according to the ability of the project to achieve certain leasing levels. The major portion of the loan is funded upon satisfaction of physical construction. Additional amounts are funded as leases are signed for more than preestablished rates and with tenants of acceptable quality.

Arranging Financing: The Mezzanine Lender

Conventional financing, i.e., construction financing or permanent financing, does not always fund all develop-

ment costs. Typically, construction loans fund only 50 to 70 percent of development costs, and permanent loans are usually for an amount equal to and in some instances slightly more than the construction loan. Rarely, however, is the permanent loan sufficient to permit the developer to recoup all of his equity investment.

In the past, developers used a variety of equity structures (partnerships, syndications, private placements, and so on) to raise the shortfall to complete the development. (A discussion of equity structures follows.) In recent years, however, a new source of funding has become available: mezzanine financing.

Originally, mezzanine financing typically was used for speculative developments where the goal was to sell the project in three to five years. Now, mezzanine financing is used in a variety of circumstances where a developer wants to get his equity investment out earlier or wishes to obtain financing in lieu of equity, thereby minimizing his risk.

Basically, the mezzanine lender makes a loan to the developer or the equity holders in the development (i.e., the partners, members, or shareholders) in an amount ranging from 75 percent to as much as 100 percent of the shortfall between the construction lender's (or permanent lender's) loan and the total costs of development. For example, assume that the total costs for a particular development are $10 million and that the developer can obtain $7.5 million in construction financing. As an alternative to raising the $2.5 million in equity, a developer might consider obtaining mezzanine financing for a substantial portion, and possibly all, of the required equity investment.

Mezzanine lending is inherently riskier than conventional lending. The mezzanine lender usually requires the loan to be secured by a subordinate deed of trust. More often than not, however, the "senior lender" (i.e., either the construction lender or the permanent lender) will not permit a junior encumbrance, and the mezzanine lender is forced to secure the loan with a pledge of the equity in the developer. In either event, the mezzanine lender's security is less secure than the first priority lien granted to the conventional lender.

The inherent risk underlying mezzanine financing translates into higher borrowing costs, which sometimes come in the form of loan fees. Further, mezzanine loans typically carry higher interest rates than conventional development loans. Moreover, in addition to higher standard loan costs, mezzanine lenders typically require a share of the profits. So-called "participation interests" usually amount to both a share of the project's net operating income (if any) until the project is sold or the mezzanine loan is otherwise repaid, and a percentage of the profits from the sale (i.e., the net proceeds after payment of the development loan, repayment of the principal amount of the mezzanine loan, and a return of any cash equity contributed by the developer). As an incentive to developers to finish projects on time and to lessen the risk to mezzanine lenders, mezzanine lenders generally require that their percentage of participation interest increases over the term of the loan.

Although comparatively more expensive than conventional development financing, mezzanine financing may be more palatable than traditional equity alternatives. Some developers may prefer to rely on an additional lending relationship than to rely on partnerships and the inherent fiduciary relationships that arise when partnerships are involved.[2]

Fraser Morrow Daniels had no financing for Europa Center and was under pressure to begin construction before Chapel Hill's new rules restricting a building's height and density took effect.

⦂⦂ Europa Center

Financing and a Quick Move to Contract Negotiation

We beat the April 15 deadline by starting construction before the completion of financial negotiations. But we traded one kind of risk for another.

It takes a long time to execute documents and to get the contractor and the architect to agree on all the final details —how they will proceed, order materials, get the grading subcontractor to come out and start bulldozing. The financial negotiations were not quite finished on April 15, but we had our site plan approved and we started clearing ground on April 14.

We called the town fathers and told them they wouldn't see a lot of building soon but that we were starting. We just didn't want to get caught on a technicality because of the political environment. If we had missed the deadline, our building would have become a three-story building instead of a five-story building and 120,000 square feet in two phases instead of 200,000 square feet. Under those circumstances, we would have lost money on the day we started.

To get funding for Europa Center, we needed a financial partner—on this project the Centennial Group, a group partially composed of former Sea Pines people who managed a fund that they created. It was a publicly held stock company that has invested in various projects around the country. They put $2 million into the Europa project. For that, they got 50 percent of the deal. Financing was arranged through Investor S&L out of Richmond, which had a work-

ing relationship with the Centennial Group from previous development deals. Centennial as a financial partner brought more to the table than just money; it also brought a reputation and a working relationship with a lender. We funded the research, planning, purchase negotiations, staff, and so on before the joint venture and were partially reimbursed in the joint venture agreement. So we had a small initial dollar risk: $50,000 to $100,000 partially reimbursed.

We invest time and money on many ideas that never come to fruition. For every project we end up working on, we may have spent time and money on ten other ones that didn't happen. We usually wouldn't get to the stage of having invested $50,000 or $100,000 on a project that wasn't going to go anywhere. But we may spend $10,000 to $15,000 or $20,000 many times before we ever get to a project that works.

The financial models we used included a little section called "capitalized expenses"—the capital cost of building a project. It's a list covering the relative cost of doing things in a project like this. The land purchase is half of the $2 million land price, because this model is for one building (the first phase of two). Centennial holds land for the second phase for the Park Forty project and for Europa, accruing interest on it. When we use it, it will be a separate calculation. But as far as the bank is concerned, it's $1 million for land, and Centennial and our group together have another million dollars invested in another piece of land.

Our financial partners ended up bearing the risk of that million in addition to the other million for the second phase. The lender agreed to fund everything else on the list, so instead of $9,339,000, the lender loaned us $8,339,000. We negotiated the construction price of $4,985,000 with the construction company building the building. It included an allocation for the parking deck. The parking deck was not yet fully designed, so we estimated the cost and had some money allocated for it.

To attract a lender, we had to pay fees up front—in this case, 1.5 percent in the beginning and another 0.5 percent for an extension of the amount they were lending, which is about $200,000. We budgeted for interest on the construction loan at 11.5 percent during construction; fortunately, during the process, the interest rate went down.

The next item was a deficit in leasing over the 36 months of funding for the project. That amounted to $457,000 that we had to fund for operating the building while no rent was being paid and for paying the interest on the empty space. The budget also included normal design and engineering costs, the cost of finishing space for tenants at $12.00 a square foot, leasing commissions for the leasing agent, salaries for the developer's staff, and some other soft costs, for a total capitalization of about $9,339,000.

The management fee in the budget is the 4 percent development fee. The construction company handles construction management. We got $250,000 in fees during the construction period and the leasing period—$15,000 a month over about 17 months. After it ran out, that was all we got until we made some profit on the building.

The S&L made us an open-ended construction loan with an extension period. There was no takeout on the deal. The S&L also agreed to fund the deficit during leasing, which doesn't normally happen. The agreement stated that we would lease the office building in Chapel Hill gradually over two years after the building was finished; that's 100,000 square feet over two years, with the first tenant moving in the first day the building is completed and then not filling the building for two years afterward.

We projected that we would lease 25 percent of the building to rent-paying tenants during the first quarter after construction, then 5 percent a month, then about 3 percent a month. That meant getting four or five tenants to move in when the building was completed and then one or two small tenants requiring 3,000 to 5,000 square feet a month for the remaining year and a half.

Thirty-six months of the leasing period includes the 12 months of construction, so the deficit item in the loan is funding for the 24 months after the completion of construction. That seemed reasonable to us, and we didn't see any major competition for our project. The extension of I-40 from Research Triangle Park to U.S. 15-501 was scheduled to open about the same time our building was scheduled to be completed.

But what happens if that amount is not enough? What happens if we have to come up with another million dollars? We decided that it was a good insurance policy for us to have an extra million dollars lined up before we executed the agreement on the loan. We said the two 50/50 partners jointly should be willing to give up 30 percent of the project, leaving each with 35 percent. All the third party had to do was guarantee with a letter of credit or something else that it would have the money available to lend if we didn't meet the schedule for leasing and construction costs and other things.

Instead of having to get a third party to come in as an investor, Centennial decided it would do it. The agreement was as follows: the million dollars that Centennial had put up to purchase the land was not funded by the bank. So instead of $9,339,000, the bank funded $8,339,000, and the million dollars was left in the deal, essentially as a line of credit to be used if leasing did not go according to plan. We ended up with a 65/35 deal, with Fraser Morrow Daniels receiving 35 percent and Centennial 65 percent of the project's profits.

When you calculate how much it costs to operate the building versus how much rent you're collecting, the occu-

pancy figure drives the cost of operating the building. And the number of rent-paying tenants drives the revenue side. Our revised model gave us the $9,339,000 capital cost over three years from when we started—a building 95 percent occupied at $17.00 per square foot two years out. If you rent the office space today and get six months of free rent, then start paying at $16.00 per square foot, your rent escalates after a year by 5 percent and after another year by another 5 percent and you're paying about $17.50 by the time we would sell or refinance the building.

What it cost to get from a raw piece of land to a fully occupied, income-producing building two years after construction, including all the interest carrying costs, was $9,339,000 total. The construction cost was $5 million, the land was $1 million, and tenant finishes, interest, marketing, and commissions were $3.3 million. With conventional financing, owning an office building that leases at these rates provides a relatively marginal return to the building owner.

The capital cost is what we have to pay back when we sell the building. The selling price is a function of net rental income after operating costs and before debt service. When you build an office building, basically it's always for sale. Our expected profit was $2.2 million, and we expected to get 35 percent of that $2.2 million at the end.

continued on page 425

New Sources of Development Financing

The evolution of global financial markets continues apace. From the perspective of real estate development, several things have happened over the last few years that have created new opportunities. Specifically, we have seen further consolidation in banking, volatile behavior from the large life insurance companies, and a clear if not dominant lending presence established by Wall Street.

During the 1990s, considerable consolidation, particularly among the large banks, reduced the number of depository institutions in this country. In the 1980s, no one would have thought that North Carolina National Bank would become NationsBank and eventually acquire Bank of America. It has been a period of rapid evolution at the top of the American commercial banking business. The new financial giants are clearly aggressive and determined to serve a bigger part of the overall financial community than commercial banks have traditionally served.

From the perspective of real estate, this change means that the larger financial institutions are now financial supermarkets. They make construction loans, they originate permanent loans and sell them to others, and, in general, they continue to look for new ways to generate fees through service to their customers. Clearly, developers can explore multiple options with large commercial banks. As always, it is the overall cost of financing that is the developer's concern, not just interest rates and loan amounts.

Life insurance companies have traditionally been a major source of financing for commercial real estate. As pointed out in Part II, life insurance companies have invested in residential lending and commercial lending, and have held extensive portfolios of commercial real estate equity. The introduction of risk-based capital rules in the early 1990s gave big insurance companies the incentive to move away from equity ownership. They have done so but have also maintained a significant position in commercial real estate lending. Unlike banks, life insurance companies have remained focused on commercial lending and avoided construction lending.

The big change for large life insurance companies has been the reintroduction of correspondent programs, i.e., subcontracting some of the loan origination work to outside firms to be able to maintain a national presence without the full cost of staff in multiple markets. The new correspondent firms are very cost efficient, which allows the life insurance companies (through them) to make not just very large loans, but also small loans. Thus, small developers as well as large developers now have access to the pools of savings managed by large life insurance companies.

The most exciting new source of financing comes from Wall Street. As explained in Part II, many commercial loans now are packaged and securitized, allowing real estate borrowers to reach a much larger audience of investors. The S&L crisis in the late 1980s brought about the packaging of existing loans and loan portfolios held by defunct S&Ls, and thus began the securitization trend. It has progressed today to where the vast majority of new commercial mortgage–backed securities (CMBSs) come from "conduit programs."

Conduit loans are originated specifically to be securitized. Some conduit loans are originated by Wall Street lenders. In addition, to increase loan pools, Wall Street firms also have correspondent relationships with mortgage bankers located around the country. The local mortgage brokers originate loans under terms specified by the investment banks, with the loans then pooled by the investment banks (with the investment banks' own loan portfolios) and securitized.

This conduit structure allows developers to tap a vast new array of investors for financing through the Wall Street–operated local conduit. The loans usually are nonrecourse to the developer (that is, the lender may look only to the collateral for recovery) and are very competitively priced, often much lower than conventional loans. Further, conduit lenders generally hold themselves out as able to close quickly.

Although attractive, conduit loans also come with exacting rules for "documenting" loans, as loan originators do not intend to be the ultimate investor/lender. In particular, conduit lenders require complex lock-box agreements and have stringent insurance requirements. Further, in an effort to protect the real property security from the developer's creditors, conduit lenders insist that the developer's company be structured in a certain way (so-called bankruptcy-remote, single-purpose entities), which may result in higher costs of transaction for the developer.

Conduit lenders also need to answer to the investors' need for long-term stability with regard to the income stream of the loan pool. As a consequence, conduit lenders also use a variety of provisions to protect the income stream by restricting prepayment of the loans.

The first such method is a prohibition against prepayment of the loan for some but not all of the term. Depending on the term of the loan, the so-called "lock-out" period ranges from one year from the date of funding (for short-term loans) to as much as seven to ten years from the date of funding (for longer loans). Although not a problem for every developer, developers need to consider whether or not these restrictions materially affect their exit strategy.

The second such method is the requirement that a premium accompany the prepayment. One form of prepayment premium—the so-called "yield maintenance" premium—is the amount that, when added to the principal amount of the loan and invested in Treasuries with a term equal to the remaining term of the loan, gives the conduit lender an amount equal to the payments the lender would have otherwise received during the term of the loan. Alternatively, the lender may require a "spread maintenance" premium, which takes into consideration that the interest rate on the loan carries an interest rate "spread" approximating the conduit lender's profit and that mere reinvestment of the prepaid loan amount will not necessarily fully compensate the lender. Thus, upon prepayment, the developer must actually make up the lost profit (which, depending on the term and amount of the loan, can be significant).

Finally, conduit lenders may prohibit any prepayment but nevertheless permit the developer to obtain a release of the real property collateral if the developer purchases replacement collateral that will provide the same income stream as the loan over the term of the loan. When the real property collateral is replaced with so-called "defeasance collateral," typically U.S. Treasuries, the loan remains outstanding, but the borrower has obtained a release of the property from the conduit lender's lien. To obtain a similar income stream, however, the developer must purchase a significant amount of U.S. Treasuries that (because the interest rate of the Treasuries is typically below the interest rate of the loan) exceeds the loan amount and may actually have a value in excess of collateral for the real property. This requirement, for obvious reasons, severely limits the developer's ability to release the underlying real property collateral.

The CMBS market originally was a vehicle for placement of permanent loans with fairly safe loan-to-value ratios and high-quality real estate products as collateral. As the market has changed, new programs (most notably, short-term "interim" loans) entered the scene, thereby allowing for conduit loans for riskier ventures, such as lesser-quality real estate or loans to borrowers who intend to make significant improvements.

The one drawback with the CMBS market is that CMBS lenders need to undertake secondary market offerings to move their loans off their books. Until recently, these securitizations were "fixed" at the closing of the offering; that is, CMBS lenders could not move new loans into a previously securitized pool of loans. The fixed nature of the securitized loan pools limits the ability of CMBS lenders to make construction loans. In particular, loans that have as collateral undeveloped or partially developed land are too risky for the public markets.

In 1998, the CMBS market introduced the FASIT (financial asset securitization investment trust) structure, which allows for "postclosing" placement of loans into securitized loan pools. Thus, CMBS lenders now have an exit strategy for construction loans, and conduit lenders can make the construction loan and hold it until the property is sufficiently developed to permit placement into an existing FASIT.

It is not yet clear how large a loan volume will be committed through the FASIT structure. Further, the market volatility experienced by many conduit lenders in the latter half of 1998 likely will reduce the number of conduit lenders and make the remaining lenders more cautious. Ultimately, some believe that the acceleration of conduit lending in general and construction loans destined for FASITs will decrease.

Market volatility also should give developers reason to pause in considering conduit loans. As many developers discovered in the latter half of 1998, the need to respond to the constantly changing Wall Street environment often resulted in "last-minute" changes to the loan terms, with some loans being denied during the final stages of internal review. In some instances, when developers had no backup financing, acquisition and development opportunities were lost.

Notwithstanding the latent uncertainty of the CMBS market, most believe that CMBSs are a permanent fixture in real estate financing. Clearly, as opportunities for permanent loans become less profitable, the CMBS market will turn to development and likely provide a potentially huge new source of construction financing.

The Common Thread in All Forms of Financing

A developer must ensure that all the financing options are explored, by himself or a member of the development team or a third party retained to obtain the financing. Although new financing techniques are always cropping up, one thing remains true—whoever is seeking the financing should try to stand in the lender's shoes. Only when the developer is able to anticipate all the ways the lender may be compensated (interest rates, points, participation, and so on) and appreciate any nonmonetary objectives (compliance with new regulations, civic duties, among others) the lender may have is the developer able to obtain the lowest overall cost of financing with the fewest restrictions. Finally, it remains important to fit the financing not just to the lending institution's financial and nonmonetary objectives, but also to its self-image. Most institutions, for example, picture themselves as experts in certain areas or dedicated to leadership in certain fields. When a project "fits" the lender's self-image, the lender tends to stretch a little to get the business. Likewise, individual loan officers have self-images, and the smart borrower fits the financing to the individual loan officer as well as to the institution.

▥ Museum Towers

Financing

The way our company is set up, I'm the person who takes the lead in fighting with public officials and neighborhood groups. My partner lives in New York, and he's involved in every project but in a very different way from my involvement. He talks to the players on the phone, he reads everything, and he provides good counsel and financial support. He's excellent at dealing with the facts. He doesn't deal with tenants or permitting agents. He deals with the banks, the lawyers, the lawyers in the banks, and that's it. He's the first one to admit that if he were running the company on a day-to-day basis, we would never get anything permitted. Nothing would get built. And we'd have no tenants. His temperament and ego wouldn't allow him to sit through the public hearings. Being called an asshole and a liar in public on a nightly basis just doesn't sit well—nor should it—but it is what it is.

When we first financed the project, we got low-risk money—prime plus one. Not bad. But then, in 1994, we were forced to restructure the debt. I don't know if I can tell the story without crying. From 1990 to 1994 were the worst four years of my life. Everything had changed in real estate. You couldn't borrow money. The money you did borrow was outrageously expensive: you could borrow it from loan sharks on the North End of Boston for less. We found out we were close to getting construction of this project financed; in fact, Chase Manhattan Bank held the existing land mortgage that had financed cost overages (beyond our initial equity) up to this date (when you carry a project for years, the preconstruction costs are huge). We struck a deal on a repayment plan. But unbeknownst to us, while we were spending another $1 million to redesign and re-permit the project, they sold the mortgage. The group they sold it to was a collection of bright, talented lawyers and finance people. You know how the guys on the North End that lend you money might come at you with baseball bats? Finance guys come at you with legal fees. It's the same thing. It's just slower and more painful the way they do it on Wall Street.

We spent eight months negotiating with our new lender, and it was a bare-knuckles fight. It's situations like this when you learn how good your partner really is and what you're made of. It was war.

The day before Thanksgiving, my wife called me in tears. She said the sheriff had just showed up at the house and left a bunch of boxes. I went home to my pregnant wife and two giant boxes. It's one thing to fight with me—it's another thing to get my wife and kids into it. So we got the largest law firm in Boston, which has some equally nasty litigators to represent them. We had nasty people on both sides. And the battle began. It was awful, but some of my greatest moments were in this fight. At one point, we met with their attorney, a good ol' boy, very calm and tranquil but a shark. He is like getting cut with a razor blade—deep, fast, seemingly not painful, but you bleed to death anyway. So he approached the problem by ac-knowledging that he realized that I didn't have any money, that it was really my partner who did, and that it wasn't worth suing me. So he suggested that they take me out of the deal, but that I continue working for them. I told him that I wasn't interested in that kind of deal. He said, "Dean, we can make your life really miserable." I said, "I can make your life equally miserable. That land in Boston, without the permits, is worth nothing. And you know who controls those permits? Me. And you'll never see those permits." They hired local counsel and discovered that in fact I did control some of the permits and that the others would be difficult for them to get. In the end we got our money, but

it was $3 million more than we were settling on with Chase. It was a horrible experience.

Once everybody had established his position and they understood what we had, they were reasonably prag-matic. To them it was just another transaction, just another restructuring: it was nothing personal like it was for my part-ner and me. We got the deal to work, and they made a ton of money on it. In the end they were decent guys. In fact, when we did a press announcement about Museum Towers, I got a handwritten note from the guy that runs the firm. Decent.

There are a couple of banks that to this day I hold some personal malice toward. That experience has given me a whole new view on working with lenders. Just like lenders want to know who their borrowers are, well, guess what: I want to know who the lender is. I won't allow the wholesale sale of our notes. We've walked away from three deals because they wouldn't give us the right of approval. That's a big difference in how we do business.

Of course, paying the original lender was just part of the story. We needed a construction loan. The Boston mar-ket had improved dramatically, and our now fully entitled land was very valuable. Still, we weren't able to get a con-struction loan to cover all the remaining costs. (Fleet Bank agreed to a floating rate, roughly 8 percent, on a $55 mil-lion first lien.) We found a higher-risk mezzanine lender to provide a participating second lien. For an expected total return of 21 percent, the Fidelity Real Estate Group closed the gap between the value of what we had created (our real cash invested was much larger) and what the lower-cost first lien holder would provide. The gap financing was expensive, but we felt that keeping most of the upside was the smart thing to do.

continued on page 415

Environmental Issues

Awareness of the environment increased dramatically in the 1970s as the courts took an active role in protect-ing the nation's natural resources. As noted in the dis-cussion of stages one, two, and three, developers should be vitally interested in determining whether the prop-erty violates any environmental protection laws. Such laws apply to contamination of the environment by hazardous or toxic materials, protection of our shrink-ing wetlands, and protection of the species of flora and fauna classified as endangered or threatened. Indeed, several federal and state laws profoundly affect real estate development. Two federal laws stand out: the Superfund and the Clean Water Act. Lenders, devel-

Hazardous Wastes: Now Everyone's Concern

In response to environmental contamination problems that were perceived to be no less than a crisis, Congress enacted the Comprehensive Environmental Response, Compensation, and Liability Act of 1980 (CERCLA), commonly referred to as the Superfund law. The Superfund law was adopted not only to provide funding for at least a portion of the cleanup of the nation's worst toxic waste sites, but also to establish powerful legal tools to allow both regulatory agencies and in some cases private parties adversely affected by contamination either to force the responsible party to undertake a cleanup program or to recover costs if the cleanup is undertaken by the claimant. Under Superfund and now the Superfund Amendments and Reauthorization Act of 1986 (SARA), present owners and certain past owners of land contaminated with hazardous substances can be liable for the entire cost of cleanup, even if the disposal of the material was legal at the time, even if the owner had nothing to do with the disposal, and even if the disposal occurred years before passage of the Superfund law. Mere ownership, not culpability, is enough to establish liability.

Superfund's all-inclusive liability scheme caught many developers and lenders off guard. In 1985, for instance, Shore Realty Corporation as well as its principal stockholder were each held responsible for cleaning up hazardous wastes on land only recently purchased, even though the corporation had neither owned the property at the time the wastes were dumped nor caused the release of toxins.[3] The court did not need to rely on the traditional (and often difficult) process of "piercing the corporate veil" to find the stockholder liable. Instead, it relied on a principle included in the Superfund legislation to determine that the stockholder had enough of a role in managing the hazardous materials after the corporate acquisition to qualify as an "operator." According to the background summary included in the court opinion, the cleanup was estimated to cost more than Shore Realty paid for the property.

In another case, U.S. v. Fleet Factors, which has become probably the leading case involving a lender's liability adjudicated under Superfund, a lender was deemed responsible for cleanup costs after foreclosing on contaminated property. The court held that the lender retained the "capacity to manage" the hazardous materials.[4] As a result of that case, lenders over the next several years commonly would not originate a loan for commercial or industrial property unless the property received a clean bill of environmental health. In an attempt to ameliorate the harsh results of the Fleet Factors decision, the U.S. Environmental Protection Agency (EPA) adopted regulations to clarify the secured-lender exemption language included in Superfund, but, in early 1994, the federal Circuit Court of Appeals for the First District invalidated the regulations. The EPA shortly thereafter announced it was considering an appeal of the ruling, and the Clinton administration's proposed reauthorization bill for Superfund in 1994 would have resolved the issue but was not passed by Congress. Finally, legislation in 1996 eliminated the "capacity to manage" test of Fleet Factors, and, as a result, lenders have now returned to the marketplace although still typically demanding a thorough environmental investigation as a condition of loan approval.

In response to the excessively onerous provisions of the Superfund law, SARA created a defense for so-called "innocent landowners," that is, landowners who did not know and had no reason to know that the property they purchased was contaminated. To qualify as an innocent landowner, purchasers must prove that they made all appropriate inquiries into previous uses of the property to uncover any possible evidence of contamination. Moreover, if contamination is subsequently found after acquisition, the landowner is required to exercise "due care" in dealing with it. Unfortunately, neither Congress nor the EPA has yet established standards for what constitutes sufficient due diligence, thus leaving members of the real estate community in a quandary; accordingly, real estate professionals must take steps to meet the vague standards of due diligence with no guarantee that they will be absolved from liability should contamination later be discovered. Over the years, some standardization in the investigation has evolved as a result, in large measure, of a procedure published by the American Society for Testing and Materials, ASTM E-1527, which has established the current custom and practice for such investigations.

Even if a landowner qualifies as an innocent purchaser, the problem of contaminated property may only have begun. Contaminated property probably cannot be sold except at a discount related to the cost of cleanup. Further, if a public health threat is associated with the contamination (e.g., poisoned drinking wells), the exculpation against cleanup costs provided by the Superfund to an innocent purchaser may very possibly prove ineffective as a shield from tort liability if the facts indicate a breach of duty to the public by the owner of the property where the problem has originated.

opers, buyers, and sellers have all been touched by these and other far-reaching laws (see Figure 19-1).

Figure 19-1

A Return to Love Canal

In the late 1970s, more than 900 families were evacuated from their homes in the Love Canal neighborhood of Niagara Falls, New York. The Federal Emergency Management Agency (FEMA), under emergency orders from then President Carter, evacuated residents of the area because hazardous chemical wastes that had been dumped in Love Canal by the Hooker Chemical Company from 1947 to 1954 posed a health threat. During that time, approximately 22,000 tons of liquid chemical wastes were dumped in the canal. Nevertheless, in the 1950s, homes, streets, and utilities were constructed adjacent to the canal to accommodate the postwar baby boom. The basements and sewer lines that were built breached the canal's concrete walls several times.

Until the 1970s, the community was peaceful, but then unusually high precipitation caused the water table within the canal to rise, and contaminants in the canal spread into the local groundwater, basements of nearby homes, and local sewer lines. Before long, residents of the Love Canal neighborhood began to complain of an increase in medical ailments, including birth defects, miscarriages, respiratory problems, and cancer. The federal government declared the ten square blocks surrounding Love Canal a disaster area in 1978 and evacuated the residents. Although the ailments reported by Love Canal residents have never been definitively tied to the chemicals, state and federal officials were concerned that further exposure to the chemicals could pose a serious health threat if the residents remained.

In 1980, the Love Canal Area Revitalization Agency (LCARA) was created by New York State as a public benefit corporation to revitalize the area; at the same time, the federal government purchased the homes from the Love Canal residents because it was unclear how or when the contamination could be cleaned up. That same year, the emergency at Love Canal led Congress to enact the Comprehensive Environmental Response, Compensation, and Liability Act (CERCLA), also known as the Superfund law.

LCARA was responsible for holding the titles of the homes that were evacuated and purchased by the federal government. More than 200 homes were demolished in the early 1980s because of contamination. The remaining 239 abandoned homes in LCARA's possession were in various stages of deterioration.

In 1983, Love Canal was placed on the Superfund National Priority List, and environmental remediation of the site began. Cleanup included building a treatment system in the canal to pump out leachate (contaminated water), covering the canal with a permanent high-density polyethylene cap, and severing the canal's sewer lines from the rest of the community.

Once the remediation was complete, the EPA conducted a habitability study that was released in 1988. That same year, LCARA began work on a master land use plan for the area, completing it in 1990. The land use plan followed the thrust of EPA's habitability study by recommending that two-thirds of the land was suitable for residential use and the remaining one-third for industrial/commercial use.

The entrepreneurial creativity of LCARA in revitalizing the area is demonstrated by the agency's creation of a revolving fund to rehabilitate the vacant homes. LCARA sold the homes that were in the best condition first and plowed the proceeds from sales back into the structures that were the most deteriorated so it could maintain cash flow to complete rehabilitation. Rehabilitation involved stripping homes to their shell and installing new roofs, siding, windows, and hot water heaters, and painting exteriors.

As part of the revitalization effort, Love Canal was renamed Black Creek Village. As of mid-1998, LCARA had sold 230 of the 239 homes in its inventory. In the beginning, buyers were offered a 20 percent discount from the appraised market value of each home. The discount was eventually phased out, and, by 1997, all the homes in LCARA's inventory were sold for their full appraised value, despite a slump in the local real estate market. Property values have climbed as the sales of homes have increased. Local real estate appraisers estimate that the value of homes in Black Creek Village rose from 70 percent of the value of comparable properties in 1990 to about 95 percent as of mid-1998.

Lending institutions were initially reluctant to approve mortgages for prospective homebuyers in the former Love Canal neighborhood. To assuage the banking community's concerns about the environmental viability of the area, LCARA met directly with officials at the FHA in 1992, presenting them with the findings of the habitability study. This scientific documentation of the area's environmental health convinced officials at the FHA to begin insuring mortgages in Black Creek Village in 1992, and people began returning to Love Canal, once the subject of intense scrutiny by the media and environmental watchdog groups. ∎

Most real estate lenders have developed their own standards that generally require purchasers to conduct what has come to be known as a "Phase I environmental audit," which sometimes goes well beyond the requirements of the ASTM procedure. The ASTM procedure is typically implemented by conducting, for example, a background check on previous uses and owners of the property, a visual inspection of the site, a review of aerial photographs and insurance maps of the property (if such historical records are available), and a careful review of regulatory agency records. In the event that any steps in the initial review indicate the possibility of contamination, the purchaser will likely be advised to physically sample the soils and possibly the groundwater to fully investigate the site's environmental condition.

Many states have enacted laws intended to require investigation and cleanup of hazardous waste sites within their borders. Among others, California has adopted its own version of legislation modeled after the federal Superfund. New Jersey has enacted legislation that has earned a reputation as perhaps the toughest body of hazardous waste laws in the country. Some state laws impose penalties if the landowner does not address the requirement for cleanup; for example, if the state of California cleans up a site after failure of a responsible party to comply with a cleanup order, then, under state law, the responsible party or parties may be assessed treble damages and the state may place a lien on the property to recover its costs. Many state enactments provide for the imposition of a lien to allow the jurisdiction that conducted the remediation to recapture the public monies spent for the cleanup, thereby avoiding a windfall to the owner (that is, the restoration of market value to the previously contaminated site). A handful of those states have adopted so-called "superlien" laws that give the state claim priority over all other liens.

Asbestos

Asbestos was used extensively for decades to insulate, fireproof, and soundproof all kinds of buildings, particularly commercial and industrial buildings. In the mid-1970s, however, following mounting evidence that asbestos posed significant health risks (particularly lung cancer), the EPA adopted regulations that for all practical purposes ended the use of asbestos materials in newly constructed buildings. Nevertheless, the EPA has estimated that more than 500,000 office buildings and more than 200,000 apartment buildings still contain asbestos. Depending on the condition of the asbestos in those buildings, owners may be sitting on a time bomb of future asbestos remediation and management in-place costs.

Asbestos is a natural, fibrous material mined from the earth and found in numerous locations around the world, including the United States, Canada, South Africa, and the former Soviet Union. Its mere presence in buildings does not necessarily pose a hazard; only when it exists in a "friable" condition—that is, when it can be crumbled by hand pressure, thereby causing its fibers to become airborne—does it pose a danger. When they are inhaled, the tiny asbestos fibers may lodge in the lungs, which, research indicates, can lead to lung disease such as asbestosis and cancer. Fear of asbestos-induced illness and the potential resulting claims has made bankers and investors wary of buildings containing asbestos. Many lenders and investors can be expected to buy buildings containing asbestos only if the properties are offered at prices low enough to make asbestos remediation procedures (such as encapsulation or removal) economically feasible.

In the mid-1980s, Congress enacted the Asbestos Hazard Emergency Response Act (AHERA) to address the concern related to risks created by asbestos used in the construction of public schools. The program required all schools to be inspected by certified inspectors trained under guidelines established by the EPA. It further mandated preparation of a "management plan" if asbestos were identified. Commercial building owners have not yet been brought within a regulatory net similar to AHERA, but under the Clean Air Act, asbestos must be handled in a health-protective manner before a building is demolished. Building owners and managers may, however, face common law liability as a result of claims by persons exposed to asbestos. Relatively recent regulations promulgated by the Occupational Safety and Health Administration (OSHA) now impose duties on commercial building owners to safeguard employees against the risk associated with on-site asbestos.

A few states have adopted regulations governing buildings containing asbestos. In California, for instance, owners and lessees of buildings containing asbestos must inform their employees and certain other persons of the location and condition of asbestos in the building, the results of any studies to monitor the air, and any potential health risk stemming from exposure to asbestos.

In response to investors' jitters, many owners of buildings containing asbestos have spent considerable sums of money removing asbestos. Widespread removal of asbestos from buildings, however, may not only be exceedingly expensive, but also exacerbate the problem by increasing the level of airborne fibers and the associated health risks. In the 1980s, the mere presence of

As part of the renovation of 1251 Avenue of the Americas in Manhattan, all asbestos was removed from the 54-story building at a cost of $45 million. The abatement was performed with minimum disturbance to tenants, and throughout the program, building occupancy never dropped below 75 percent.

asbestos panicked many people, but by the mid-1990s, science and the law came closer together so that asbestos became an understandable and manageable problem in redevelopment.

Wetlands

Not too long ago, bogs, swamps, and marshes—commonly known as "wetlands"—were considered nuisances. Developers and farmers alike were encouraged to convert these "worthless" areas into productive uses. Until 1985, the federal government subsidized farmers for draining, plowing, and planting wetlands. Today, however, the situation has changed. After centuries of mistreatment, wetlands are now valued for their enormous environmental and economic importance.

Wetlands are one of the earth's most productive natural ecosystems and can outproduce even the most groomed and pampered Iowa cornfield. They have an extraordinary ability to shelter fish and wildlife, cleanse polluted and silt-laden water, and protect against floods. Over half of North American ducks nest in wetlands in the north central United States and southern Canada. And about two-thirds of U.S. shellfish and commercial sport fisheries rely on coastal marshes for spawning and nursery grounds.

As our understanding and appreciation of wetlands expand, so do the number and scope of federal and state laws to protect them. Under Section 404 of the Clean Water Act, for instance, developers must first secure a permit from the U.S. Army Corps of Engineers (the Corps) before building in wetlands. This permitting process has become controversial for a number of reasons.

- First, there is the problem of what constitutes wetlands. Using the complex federal definition, land that would appear to be dry to a layperson may constitute wetlands subject to the permitting process. A related problem is federal jurisdiction over dry washes in the Southwest: is a two-foot-wide wash that carries water only after a rare rainfall a water of the United States? Development in wetlands (or nonwetland waters) without a permit can lead to substantial fines and, in some cases, jail time.
- Second, there is no way to obtain judicial review of the Corps's determination that wetlands or other waters are present except by first seeking a permit or else by defending against an enforcement action that seeks to punish a landowner for developing in wetlands without a permit.
- Third, the permitting process itself is complicated, involving a minimum of three federal agencies (the Corps, the EPA, and the Fish and Wildlife Service), and time-consuming (a recent study indicated that the average time to obtain an individual permit was 373 days). As a result, most applications for permits are withdrawn because of the complexity, time, and cost involved.
- Finally, the Corps usually issues a permit on the condition that the developer mitigate any adverse impacts on wetlands stemming from the development. In addition, a growing number of states have adopted wetlands protection laws that are more stringent than the federal laws.

Ten years ago, only a few states had enacted laws protecting wetlands; now, over half the states have wetlands laws on the books, and the list is growing.

Before receiving a permit to develop on wetlands, developers must first demonstrate that, for so-called non-

The developers of Brasstown Valley Resort in Hiawassee, Georgia, took great care to minimize the impacts of development. Only one acre of wetlands in the 500-acre development was disturbed, and the project actually created a net increase in wetlands, improved the trout habitat along the streams, and was responsible for an increase in rare and sensitive plant species as a result of the sanctuaries that were established.

water-dependent uses such as a mall or a housing development, no practicable, nonwetland sites exist. (Water-dependent uses include, for example, marinas and ports.) Furthermore, both the Corps of Engineers and state regulators generally require developers to minimize adverse effects on wetlands and to compensate for any wetlands lost by restoring or creating wetlands nearby. This process is generally referred to as "wetlands mitigation."

Wetlands mitigation, particularly creating wetlands, has been controversial. Wetlands are complex, dynamic ecosystems, and early attempts to create them yielded mixed results. Environmentalists argued that artificially created wetlands could scarcely be considered adequate substitutes for natural wetlands. More recently, a number of successes have occurred, particularly in the context of "mitigation banks," and the Corps has gained substantial experience in how to write and enforce permit conditions that will ensure successful mitigation and provide fallback systems and other provisions to protect the environment in case the mitigation is not as successful as hoped. Even with these improvements in mitigation, however, federal permitting for projects involving wetlands or other waters of the United States remains very problematic, and prudent developers will avoid such sites if at all possible.

Our Environmental Future

In April 1990, the world celebrated the 20th anniversary of Earth Day. As one communist government after another fell in eastern Europe, the world became aware of a harsh reality that had only been suspected for some time: pollution in eastern Europe far surpassed the western world's wildest expectations. Cesspools of toxic chemicals forced entire towns to move; factories spewed such enormous amounts of toxins that young children had to wear masks because of the extreme danger of cancer. With these revelations and the catastrophe at Chernobyl, we have finally realized that the environment is a global issue, not just a national, state, local, or neighborhood one.

Real estate development no longer occurs in a vacuum away from environmental realities. Savvy developers foresaw that the new involvement of communities would lead to more and more interest from citizens in environmental issues. As a result, they began to publicize their efforts to save trees and ponds and other natural amenities associated with new developments. Businesses and developers have also started to work with governments to find acceptable compromises.

One case in Kenosha County, Wisconsin, illustrates how a business and a conservation group collaborated with the state to further ecologically sound development. The Des Plaines River originates in the farming country of southeast Wisconsin and winds its way south before entering the Chicago metropolitan area. WISPARK, a subsidiary of the Wisconsin Energy Corporation, is developing a corporate park in Kenosha County that will include a 1,460-acre industrial/business park and a 600-acre conservation area on the Des Plaines River floodplain. In addition, a 100-acre lake, formerly a gravel pit, lies immediately northwest of the business park.

The site was ideally located midway between Chicago and Milwaukee, one mile north of the Illinois border and only 1.5 miles from I-94, but it had one drawback: the Des Plaines River prevented direct access to the interstate. County Highway Q ran part of the way through the parcel but stopped short of the river. The missing link was completed in 1988, when the state of Wisconsin, Kenosha County, and WISPARK built a bridge and two miles of highway. Construction involved filling several acres of wetlands and floodplain. In exchange, WISPARK created more than 30 acres of wetlands through a 1.2:1 mitigation agreement and several acres of floodplain, and donated more than 500 acres of wetlands and floodplain to the Nature Conservancy of Wisconsin. The developer also gave the Nature Conservancy money for stewardship of the land. In addition, the town of

Pleasant Prairie built a 200-acre public park on land donated by the Wisconsin Electric Company.

The solution worked to everyone's satisfaction, but it took a great deal of time and effort to achieve it. Developers and businesses can no longer afford not to anticipate potential community responses to environmental issues; they must work with government agencies to mitigate possible unpleasant effects, no matter how lengthy the process.

For many development projects, environmental issues are a routine but often complex part of the project. Museum Towers was built on an old industrial site located on the "tidelands" of a river, and the environmental issues took many years to work through.

▌▌ Museum Towers

Environmental Issues

Although there are no wetlands on the site and it's not within a designated 100-year floodplain, the environmental issues were murder.

We tried in the late 1980s and early 1990s to win approval for our apartment complex. But much to my dismay, MEPA (Massachusetts Environmental Policy Act) exercised jurisdiction over the project, which meant we had to do a full environmental statement. Basically, it forces you to go to a multitude of different state agencies, commissions, and authorities. It opens up Pandora's box. On top of that, the Chapter 91 Division of Waterways exercised jurisdiction, claiming that the site was filled land and that the project was located in "historical tidelands" of the Charles River, so they had jurisdiction that could not be usurped by MEPA. It was like going to a football game and watching all the guys pile on the little running back. The process dragged on so long that, by the time we got the approvals, the market had changed and our project was no longer commercially viable.

About 65 percent of Boston is landfill. It used to be a series of islands interconnected by strips of land. Boston's Back Bay used to be a bay where ships anchored. The North End, where Boston started, was about half its current size. The filling of titled land, marshes, and wetlands was granted by the King of England in the 1600s and 1700s. These licenses were granted for the creation of facilities to support commerce. The theory was that the reduction of access to the water and marshes was justifiable because the creation of commerce created a benefit that inured to the body politic on a greater basis.

Fast-forward to the late 1970s and early 1980s, and all the lawyers in the commonwealth of Massachusetts are

North Point Park conveys a positive environmental message and is a great amenity for Museum Towers as well as for the city of Cambridge.

challenging developers because they don't have fee simple title—they have licenses. So it was decided that our buildings were a change of use of the "historical tidelands," because that's not what they were originally designated as; therefore, we had to go through a new permitting process to establish that what we wanted to do with this real estate addressed the spirit of the original license—to create commerce or to create a benefit for the public good. They declared that the project proposal constituted a "non-water-dependent use of tidelands," and we had to prove that our project serves a proper public purpose and provides a net public benefit to the rights of the public in the tidelands. I submit that this process is absolutely irrational, irresponsible, and exploitative.

In the middle of all this, the planning board in the city of Cambridge exerted autonomy that it may or may not have had, and the city council tried to get its name on whatever projects it could to keep politically active. And two state entities were at war with each other: MEPA tried

to demonstrate that it was the ultimate permitting agency within the state government, and the Chapter 91 Division of Waterways said that, when it came to waterfronts, it had all the authority. Then a new complication arose when the executive secretary of transportation and construction for the state said that the land was previously owned by the railroad and the railroad never got a signoff from the state transportation group. Under Massachusetts General Law 4054A, you have to get a release from the state transportation secretary to change property that was originally designated as transportation dependent to use it for non-transportation-related property. So then the circle widened to include the city of Cambridge, the planning board, MEPA, Chapter 91, and the executive office of transportation and construction.

They all wanted a piece of us. Not a small piece, but a big piece, and they all wanted the other guy to go first so they could come in and really chew us up. We spent an inordinate amount of time juggling and dancing among all these groups. And MEPA forces you to go to every involved agency, each with its own agenda. For example, Health and Human Services wanted a big low-income housing component. The Massachusetts Business Commission (MBC) wanted parks. Transportation wanted roads. It just kept going and going. So we took on all four groups in parallel and just tried knocking them off one at a time. Then we had to do an Environmental Notification (ENF), a special permit application.

Let me tell you, that was 1988 and a lot of other stuff was going on in the city of Cambridge. The secretary of transportation wanted to put in a river crossing from Federal Island to Cambridge. He was having a hard time getting it through, so he suggested that if I help him get the river crossing, he'd help me.

It gets more complicated. A lot of our troubles went back to the time when railroads were big. Railroads were given the power of eminent domain all over the country, so they could come in and, with compensation for you, take your home, your farm, and your business, because they were building a railroad system. The concept was the loss to an individual was secondary to the gain of the entire body politic. So the railroads amassed huge landholdings, and when the railroads started cutting back, they went into the real estate development business. But the commonwealth of Massachusetts intervened and forced the railroads to go through the commonwealth with all their deals. As the regulator of transportation systems, the commonwealth had the right to decide whether the land should remain a transportation-related use or whether the short-term gain the railroads got on the real estate would hurt the long-term public transportation network. The secretary of transportation is given three bites at the apple. First, the railroad had to notify Transportation when they put the land on the market. The state can take it then. Second, before the title is transferred, the railroad had to go back to the commonwealth, when it can take the land at the same price. Third, and most difficult, is that when the local building department is going to issue a building permit, the new owner has to go back to the secretary of transportation and he has to approve the building permit. In our situation, that's the point where he wouldn't give us the approval—unless we could work with him on getting the river crossing. Of course, the city of Cambridge wanted us to do the opposite. They wanted us to work against him.

MEPA was unbelievable. We did an ENF, a draft environmental impact statement, a final environmental impact statement, a supplemental final environmental impact statement, and a supplemental supplemental environmental impact statement.

But in 1998, by the time our project was built, the state began easing some of the environmental burdens on developers. The idea is that the reform efforts will ensure a faster review process among state agencies, eliminate filing of the same forms with different agencies, and stuff like that. In theory, things that took months or years to get approved will now take only a few weeks.

If I were buying this site today, without permits, I'd pay only $1 million. But it took $3.5 million just in permit costs.

continued on page 426

Decisions about Design And Contractors

By the time they enter stage four, developers will have at least preliminary drawings of the project, and it will be necessary to make final arrangements with the architect and other design professionals, including engineers. At some point, and certainly before the architect draws final plans, a contract must be drafted to establish the formal relationship between the developer and the architect.

It is often useful and necessary to designate the architect as the responsible party for all design matters, as developers have difficulty closing the permanent loan unless someone is professionally responsible for the quality of all work. Thus, the contract with the architect drives related contracts with other design professionals.

Most architects prefer to use the American Institute of Architects (AIA) standard contract (B-141), which was revised in 1997 (see Figure 19-2). Of course, developers must be careful not to execute the AIA contract blindly. Like all contracts in stage four, it must be negotiated and executed so that all parties agree to produce the appropriate product, with risks and responsibilities clearly defined. The AIA standard contract is frequently modified to add items not covered, such as responsibility for errors and omissions insurance, indemnification, and any expanded scope of services. In fact, lenders might require several changes to the contract. What is omitted from the standard AIA contract is as important as what is included.

Because the contract was drafted by AIA, it clearly protects the architect in various ways. Therefore, developers have a strong incentive to negotiate and change the standard AIA contract. Only some preliminary budgeting (estimating costs) is included in the basic services portion of the standard AIA contract; any other budgeting must be paid for in addition to the basic price of architectural design. Indeed, the current version of the AIA contract specifies that public hearings and interior layouts are excluded from the basic contract price. If developers want any of these services, they need to be clear about whether or not they will pay extra for them. Under the AIA contract, architects also have the right to notify developers of their need for certain additional services. If the developer does not respond promptly, the architect has the right to do the work and bill the developer for those services.

Insurance of any kind (such as errors and omissions insurance, commercial general liability insurance, or worker's compensation insurance) is not included in the AIA standard contract. Of course, the cost of insurance varies with the coverage required. Developers should note these facts and determine the proper amount of insurance and the appropriate carrier.

In the current version of the AIA contract, the architect can make decisions binding on the developer and the contractor regarding disputes between the parties. Unless the developer or the general contractor takes specific actions to challenge the architect's decision, such decisions will be binding.

Figure 19-2

AIA Document B-141-1997

**Standard Form of Agreement between Owner and Architect
With Standard Form of Architect's Services**

where the basis for payment is the COST OF THE WORK PLUS A FEE with a negotiated guaranteed maximum price

1997 EDITION

THIS DOCUMENT HAS IMPORTANT LEGAL CONSEQUENCES; CONSULTATION WITH AN ATTORNEY IS ENCOURAGED WITH RESPECT TO ITS COMPLETION OR MODIFICATION.

AIA Document A201-1997, General Conditions of the Contract for Construction, is adopted in this document by reference.

This document has been approved and endorsed by the Associated General Contractors of America.

**Article 1.1
Initial Information**
This is a new Article in which the parties describe or identify, if known at the time of contract execution, certain information and assumptions about the Project, such as the physical, legal, financial, and time parameters and key persons or entities with the Project. It includes project parameters and project team (including designated representatives of the architect and the owner).

**Article 1.2
Responsibilities of the Parties**
The Owner's and the Architect's responsibilities now have been combined and placed in one Article.

**Article 1.3
Terms and Conditions**
This new Article encompasses the former Articles Five through Nine in the 1987 Edition and includes Cost of the Work, Instruments of Service, Change in Services, Mediation, Arbitration, Claims for Consequential Damages, Miscellaneous Provisions, Termination or Suspension, and Payments to the Architect.

**Article 1.4
Scope of Services and Other Special
Terms and Conditions**
This new Article enumerates all documents that make up the agreement between the Owner and the Architect, including the Standard Form of Architect's Services, unless another scope of services is indicated, and provides a blank space to describe any other terms and conditions that modify the agreement.

**Article 1.5
Compensation**
Compensation includes basis of compensation computation, services to be included, how to calculate payments for change in services, and reimbursable expenses.

**Article 2.1
Project Administration Services**
This new Article describes administrative services that the Architect performs at various intervals throughout the life of the Project, including submittal of design documents, project presentation requirements, project schedule updates, attendance at project meetings, filing documents, and other such tasks.

The contract does not specify the exact form of certification that will be required to be executed by the architect regarding the quality of the work (certification will be needed when the permanent loan is closed). Thus, the developer must specify the form in the contract so that problems will not arise at closing.

The standard contract specifies that the plans drawn belong to the architect, not to the developer, even though the developer has paid for them. This provision should be changed to give the developer ownership rights to the plans, provided the developer makes payment to the architect in accordance with the contract.

A provision in the AIA contract prohibits assignment of the contract to any other developer without obtaining the architect's consent. This provision should be deleted, for if the original developer cannot perform, the lender might want another developer to step in and finish the project to salvage the lender's position. This provision, if not eliminated, could seriously affect project financing.

Article 2.2
Supporting Services
Formerly contained in Article Four, Owner's Responsibilities, of the 1987 Edition of B141, this Article includes the responsibilities to furnish services or information relating to the program, land surveys, and geotechnical engineering.

Article 2.3
Evaluation and Planning Services
This new Article lists certain predesign services to be performed by the Architect, such as evaluation of the Owner's budget, schedule, and site for the Project.

Article 2.4
Design Services
This Article describes the normal design disciplines (normal structural, mechanical, and electrical engineering services) included in the agreement and contains provisions defining and describing Schematic Design Documents, Design Development Documents, and Construction Documents.

Article 2.5
Construction Procurement Services
Article 2.5 of B-141-1997 delineates in greater depth than in the previous edition of B-141 the Architect's services relating to the Owner's procurement of the contract for construction and covers the competitive bidding process and negotiated proposals.

Article 2.6
Contract Administration Services
The Architect's Contract Administration Services now are further divided into six subcategories: General Administration; Evaluations of the Work; Certification of Payments to Contractor; Submittals; Changes in the Work; and Project Completion.

Article 2.7
Facility Operation Services
This new Article provides for two meetings between the Architect and the Owner (or the Owner's Designated Representative): one promptly after substantial completion to review the need for Facility Operation Services, and the second before the expiration of one year from the date of Substantial Completion to review the building's performance.

Article 2.8
Schedule of Services
A new feature of B-141-1997, this Article enables the parties to fill in a specific number of submittal reviews, site visits, and inspections to determine Substantial Completion and final completion that will be performed before the Architect incurs a Change in Services and to specifically designate any other services that form part of the agreement between the Owner and the Architect.

Article 2.9
Modifications
Similar to Article 12 of the 1987 Edition of B-141, this Article provides a blank space for modifications the parties wish to make to the provisions of the Standard Form of Architect's Services.

Source: **The American Institute of Architects, 1735 New York Avenue, N.W., Washington, D.C. 20006. Used with permission.**

Profile **David M. Schwarz**

President and CEO, David M. Schwarz/Architectural Services, Inc.
Washington, D.C.

David Schwarz has been a practicing architect for more than 20 years. He founded his firm, David M. Schwarz/Architectural Services, in 1978, four years after completing his Master of Architecture degree at Yale University. The firm now employs 35 people and has offices in Washington, D.C., and Fort Worth, Texas. What sets Schwarz apart is his commitment to designing places that are oriented to their users and that respect the history and context of the area where they are located. Besides lecturing widely on the importance of blending the old and the new in architecture, Schwarz has been able to put his ideas into practice by designing everything from stadia and performing arts venues to a master plan for a 135-acre new town. While he has worked on many projects in the Washington, D.C., area, Schwarz has also done a significant amount of work in other states, notably Texas.

Designing in the Lone Star State
With well over 40 commissions in Texas, Schwarz has played a major role in shaping the future of cities such as Dallas and Fort Worth. Schwarz was responsible for the Sundance Master Plan, which will guide the redevelopment and revitalization of 60 square blocks in downtown Fort Worth. In the downtown area alone, Schwarz has designed or redeveloped the Cook Children's Medical Center, the city's central library, the conversion of a department store to residential lofts, a Barnes & Noble bookstore, and a school. One of the projects, Sundance West, is a 12-story mixed-use building that includes retail stores and an 11-screen movie theater, with apartments above. While the project was being planned, many people doubted that anyone would want to live in downtown Fort Worth. But the project has been a tremendous success. When Schwarz began his work in Fort Worth, "You couldn't find anyone on the street after 4:30. Now you can't find a parking space." By combining attractive designs and a mixture of uses, and by preserving some of the area's historic facades,

Schwarz has helped to make downtown Fort Worth a treasured destination for the city's residents and visitors alike.

Bass Hall
The Nancy Lee and Perry R. Bass Performance Hall is perhaps Schwarz's greatest accomplishment in downtown Fort Worth. The centerpiece for downtown Fort Worth's renaissance, the hall will serve as the home for the Fort Worth Symphony, Opera, and Ballet, as well as the quadrennial Van Cliburn International Piano Competition. Ed Bass, chair of the Board of Performing Arts, told Schwarz that he wanted a building that would last 300 years, just like the great performance halls of Europe. Schwarz produced a stunning building that combines the human scale with a definite sense of grandeur. The site, a 200-foot by 200-foot downtown city block, imposed a number of design constraints. As a result, backstage sits practically on the southern property line, while the last row of seats is only a corridor away from the northern property line. Still, the building, which opened in April 1998, has won widespread praise from the public, and it has succeeded in bringing people together to enjoy the arts in downtown Fort Worth.

The Ballpark at Arlington
Schwarz also designed a remarkable performance venue of a different kind. The Ballpark at Arlington has been the home of the Texas Rangers baseball team since 1994. Like Camden Yards in Baltimore, the Ballpark at Arlington draws on a number of elements of traditional stadium design as well as provides a host of modern amenities to create a special place for America's pastime. The red brick walls outside the building feature friezes depicting scenes from Texas history. The playing field has real grass, and the seats provide great sight lines as well as a real sense of intimacy with the game. Although he never previously designed a stadium, Schwarz was chosen in a nationwide

---

The construction contract (the contract with the general contractor) usually follows the architect's contract fairly directly. Thus, it is important to determine at this stage whether disputes are to be handled by mediation, arbitration, or litigation. Architects often prefer arbitration, although some developers often fare better using at least the threat of litigation as a negotiating point. It is beneficial to the developer to have the same

procedures for resolving disputes in all the developer's contracts.

A provision in the construction contract makes it possible to retain a portion of the money due the contractor based on work completed but withheld to ensure final completion. That provision must be coordinated with the loan agreement. The developer must be able to draw down the amount of money owed on the construction contract.

competition; his development team created a place that fans and players alike have embraced.

Designing for People

Despite his success, some architects have criticized Schwarz for being too populist and for not making his designs avant-garde. Schwarz rejects these criticisms, saying, "Our measure of success is whether or not people like it or use it." Although he believes it is important to understand the client's goals, Schwarz also believes that "the passive user is just as much a part of" his constituency. Schwarz's work reflects a belief that architecture plays an important role in fostering community. About his work in Southlake, Texas, a suburb of Dallas, Schwarz says, "The community had no focus. In our planning, we created a town square where

the community could come together on a casual basis." He believes a great degree of interest exists in American cities and downtowns as places for social interaction. Schwarz's work tries to support this trend in designing plans and buildings that offer people richness, complexity, and diversity.

For Schwarz, the best part about being an architect is the variety in his job. "It gives me the opportunity to learn about lots of things that I otherwise wouldn't know." Schwarz believes that architects and designers just entering the field must have a real passion for architecture. He also believes that they need to understand the past, because "understanding our roots is very important in moving toward a more coherent future." Schwarz is a prime example of how to successfully integrate the past and the future in his work. ■

Although everything should be tailored to fit the specific development, developers are generally well advised to guard against the designation of allowances, as opposed to fixed prices, for certain budgeted items in the construction contract. Allowances such as $20,000 for carpeting rather than a fixed price can lead to serious problems in stage six. With allowances, a set amount can be drawn from the construction lender. If costs

exceed this amount, serious financial pressures can result, as the developer, rather than the lender, is responsible for costs in excess of the allowance. (See Figure 19-3 for items that must be considered in a construction contract.)

Drafting the design contract typically requires advance thought about the construction contract. For example, developers can designate their in-house staff as the

Figure 19-3

Checklist for Construction Contracts

	Owner	Architect	Contractor

1.0 Program Development

1.1 Project requirements, including design objectives, constraints and criteria, space requirements and relationships, flexibility and expandability, special equipment, and systems and site requirements

1.2 Legal description and a certified survey; complete, as required

1.3 Soils engineering; complete, as required

1.4 Materials testing, inspections, and reports; complete, as required

1.5 Legal, accounting (including auditing), and insurance counseling, as required

1.6 Program review

1.7 Financial feasibility

1.8 Planning surveys, site evaluations, environmental studies, or comparative studies of prospective sites

1.9 Verification of existing conditions or facilities

2.0 Construction Cost

2.1 Budget and funds

2.2 Estimate of probable costs

2.3 Detailed estimates of construction cost

2.4 Control of design to meet fixed limit of construction cost

3.0 Design

3.1 Schematic

3.2 Design development

3.3 Consultants: structural, mechanical, electrical, special

4.0 Construction Documents

4.1 Final drawings and specifications

4.2 Bidding information, bid forms, conditions of contract, and form of agreement between owner and contractor

4.3 Filing for government approvals

4.4 For use in construction

4.5 On-site maintenance of drawings, specifications, addenda, change orders, shop drawings, product data, and samples

5.0 Bidding

5.1 Obtaining bids or negotiated proposals

5.2 Awarding and preparing contracts

5.3 Documents for alternate, separate, or sequential bids; extra services in connection with bidding, negotiation, or construction before completion of construction documents

6.0 Administration of Construction Contract

6.1 General

6.1.1 Owner's representative

6.1.2 Periodic visits to the site

	Owner	Architect	Contractor
6.1.3 Construction methods, techniques, sequences, procedures, safety precautions, and programs			
6.1.4 Contractor's applications for payments			
6.1.5 Certificates for payment			
6.1.6 Document interpretation/artistic effect			
6.1.7 Rejection of work; special inspections or testing			
6.1.8 Shop drawings, product data, and samples			
6.1.8.1 Submittals			
6.1.8.2 Review and action			
6.1.9 Change orders			
6.1.9.1 Preparation			
6.1.9.2 Approval			
6.1.10 Closeout			
6.1.10.1 Date of substantial completion			
6.1.10.2 Date of final completion			
6.1.10.3 Written warranties			
6.1.10.4 Certificate for final payment			
6.1.11 Coordination of work of separate contractors or by owner's forces			
6.1.12 Services of construction manager			
6.1.13 As-built drawings			
7.0 Schedule			
7.1 Design schedule			
7.1.1 Development			
7.1.2 Maintenance			
7.2 Construction schedule			
7.2.1 Development			
7.2.2 Maintenance			
8.0 Payment			
8.1 Basic design services			
8.1.1 Accounting records			
8.2 Construction (the work)			
8.2.1 Progress payments			
8.2.2 Final payment			
8.3 Evidence of ability to pay			
8.4 Secure and pay for necessary approvals, easements, assessments, and changes for construction, use, or occupancy			
9.0 Construction			
9.1 General			

continued on next page

Figure 19-3

Checklist for Construction Contracts (continued)

	Owner	Architect	Contractor
9.2 Labor, materials, and equipment			
9.3 Correlation of local conditions with requirements of the contract documents			
9.4 Division of work among subcontractors			
9.5 Right to stop work			
9.6 Owner's right to carry out work			
9.7 Review of contract documents for errors, inconsistencies, or omissions			
9.8 Supervision and direction of the work			
9.9 Responsibility to owner for errors and omissions in the work			
9.10 Obligation to perform the work in accordance with contract documents			
9.11 Provide and pay for all labor, materials, equipment, tools, machinery, utilities, transportation, and other facilities and services for the proper execution and completion of the work			
9.12 Enforce discipline and good order among those employed on the job			
9.13 Warranty for all materials and equipment			
9.14 Sales, consumer, and use taxes			
9.15 Secure and pay for all permits, fees, licenses, and inspections			
9.16 Compliance with all laws, ordinances, regulations, and lawful orders			
9.17 Employment of superintendent			
9.18 Cutting and patching			
9.19 Cleaning up			
9.20 Communications			
9.21 Payments of all royalties and license fees; defense against suits and claims			
9.22 Indemnification; hold harmless			
9.23 Award of subcontracts			
9.24 Owner's right to perform work and award separate contracts			
9.24.1 Award			
9.24.2 Mutual responsibility			
9.24.3 Cleanup dispute			
10.0 **Miscellaneous**			
10.1 Performance bond, labor, and material payment bond			
10.2 Tests			
10.3 Protection of persons and property			
11.0 **Insurance**			
11.1 Contractor's liability insurance			
11.2 Owner's liability insurance			
11.3 Property insurance			
12.0 **Changes in the Work**			
13.0 **Uncovering and Correction of Work**			

Source: **G. Niles Bolton, architect, Atlanta, Georgia.**

primary builder of the project; those who come from a general contracting background often take this approach. Most developers, however, rely on outside construction contractors for much of their work. Like all aspects of the development process, many variations are possible, depending on the developer's in-house skills.

Bidding versus Negotiations: Fixed Price versus Cost Plus

The developer and general contractor can reach agreement on a construction contract in several ways. The two ends of the spectrum are bidding and negotiation. In the case of bidding, the developer puts out plans and specifications to general contractors in the local area who are considered technically and financially qualified and asks them to supply one set price or a base price with additions per unit for certain items that cannot be fully planned in advance. For example, an office building might require a price for the building plus a certain amount per linear foot for interior walls. Not until leasing is completed will the developer know how many linear feet of walls are needed. In the bid itself, the contractor promises to perform the job according to plans and specifications for one cost plus a certain amount per foot for the amount of interior walls subsequently requested by the developer.

At the other end of the spectrum is the arrangement in which the developer negotiates with one general contractor, agreeing that the general contractor will perform the work and bill the developer for either a fixed price or a cost plus a certain profit margin.

Clearly, developers prefer a fixed-price contract while contractors prefer a cost-plus agreement without a guaranteed maximum price. Consequently, many jobs fall somewhere between the two extremes. It is common for a developer to negotiate with only one contractor and to obtain a "not-to-exceed price" based on the contractor's estimate of cost plus a reasonable profit margin. If the cost of the work plus the reasonable profit margin come in below the not-to-exceed price, then the developer and contractor can share any such savings.

Fraser Morrow Daniels negotiated a similar agreement with the contractor for Europa Center. For the developer, a cost-plus-fee contract with a guaranteed maximum price is preferable to a fixed-price contract (where the fixed price equals the guaranteed maximum price). With a cost-plus-fee contract, the developer receives the benefit of any savings (unless the contract provides otherwise); with a fixed-price contract, the contractor reaps any savings only if the actual cost of construction is less than the amount of the fixed price.

▦ Europa Center

Construction Costs

The contractor gave us a guaranteed maximum price, and the agreement stated that if actual costs came in under that price, the contractor could keep half of what it saved us. The negotiations were so tight that I was certain savings would not occur.

During construction, the contractor builds the project exactly as it is drawn. If you change anything, a step or a rail or a nail, it's extra and, in some cases, much extra. We have learned over the years that even though a project can be improved by changing it during the process, it costs about four times as much as improving it before building starts. So you live with it the way it is bid except for critical omissions or safety features. We added a $200,000 contingency to cover just such possibilities.

continued on page 432

In reality, most developments involve a great deal of the unknown, even after completion of the formal feasibility study. Often, marketing feedback during construction requires change orders. Thus, the developer is to some extent exposed to renegotiation, no matter how tightly the original construction contract is drawn. On jobs that tend to require few change orders and where public scrutiny is more intense, bidding is most common. Projects involving the federal, state, or local government, where the plans are set firmly in advance and no formal marketing occurs, are usually "bid." The bid process satisfies the public's need to know that the price is fair. Formulating a bid requires the contractor to spend considerable time motivating subcontractors to submit their bids, consolidating the bids, and submitting the complete bid package to the developer. When contractors have some clout, i.e., when they have plenty of other work, they might even refuse to bid on smaller jobs. At other times, they might bid high on the theory that they do not need the work but will obviously benefit if they are awarded the contract at the high price. In such situations, developers who have established long-term relationships with quality contractors might find it preferable to negotiate directly with one contractor.

Typically, the developer and the general contractor sign one contract, and the general contractor and various subcontractors sign another set of contracts. The developer negotiating a contract with the general contractor might, however, also demonstrate concern about the quality of the subcontractors. Depending on the job's complexity, certain subcontractors might play key roles in construction. In such situations, developers might specify in the bid package or during negotiations for a cost-plus contract that particular subcontractors be used and/or specific trade contractors be bonded.

Developers can negotiate directly with key subcontractors with whom they have a good relationship. In such situations, the developer might negotiate a price with subcontractors and then ask the various possible general contractors for a bid, requiring a particular subcontracted job to be performed by a specified subcontractor. The general contractor is then relieved of the difficulty of, first, finding a subcontractor to perform the job and, second, motivating the subcontractor to take the bidding seriously. Consequently, general contractors might be more willing to submit a bid, assuming that they respect the particular subcontractor's work. As with many aspects of the process, no hard and fast rules exist. In the absence of rules, therefore, developers must devise the process that best serves their needs.

▌▌▌ Museum Towers

Construction Costs

The construction company we chose to build Museum Towers was Suffolk Construction Company, a Boston-based group.

The total estimated cost to complete the project was, by category:

Land	$8,100,000
Hard Costs	53,600,000
Soft Costs	9,500,000
Project Administration	1,500,000
Loan Fees	1,800,000
Contingency	2,900,000
Construction Interest	7,600,000
Interim Rents	(7,000,000)
Total	$78,000,000

Financing

Construction Loan	$55,000,000
Mezzanine Loan	$16,500,000
Borrowers' Equity	$6,500,000*
	$78,000,000

*Credited—actual amount invested was higher.

continued on page 442

Fast-Track Construction

During periods when interest rates are inordinately high or when the project must be completed rapidly to satisfy a tenant or the government, the developer could find it beneficial to engage in fast-track construction. The idea is to have as many steps underway at the same time as feasible. One possibility is to start excavation as soon as the architect has completed the general layout and to start building the structure before the interior design has been completed. Fast-track construction always involves the developer in negotiating a cost-plus contract. When it works, fast-track construction can help the developer beat competitors to the marketplace and reduce interest costs. When coordination of activities is weak, however, the results can be disastrous. Another problem with fast-track projects is adjusting the contract price to reflect the final "for-construction" plans and specifications. The contractor's leverage increases greatly if work begins before reaching an agreement on the final price.

A classic illustration of fast-track construction out of control concerns a retail development south of Mexico City. Given Mexico's high interest rates, fast-track construction is not uncommon. Mexico's volcanic subsurface soils, however, can pose serious problems for construction. In this case, with the project half finished, the architect realized that it would be difficult to complete the project according to the original plans and within the original budget. The foundation work specified by the architect had been constructed before all the building plans were completed, yet the foundation would not support the optimal structure and the architect was not sure how to remedy the problem. Though the developer could have brought a lawsuit against the architect, lawsuits are usually poor recourse for problems encountered under the pressure of constructing a building on time. With the high interest costs in Mexico, accelerating the opening was critical. Thus, the developer had to knock out that portion of the foundation that did not fit the new plan (which he decided to complete with a second architect). The additional cost placed considerable stress on construction financing.

Bonding

Bonding is a guarantee of either completion and/or payment. The city might require developers to provide a bond to prove that they have the capacity to complete the infrastructure. The developer might ask the contracting firm to provide a bond to prove that the general contractor has the wherewithal to complete the job. When issuing a bond, a surety company examines the credibility of the individuals or institutions to be bonded. The assessment covers both their capacity to do the work and their financial substance. Bonds are the most common form of guarantee, although alternatives such as a letter of credit or depositing assets in escrow can be used. Bonds enable the developer or general contractor to ask a surety company to stand behind the nonperforming firm in a lawsuit.

During stage four, a developer might want the general contractor to be bonded if he fears that the contractor might not be able to perform or cannot muster the financial resources to pay a judgment in the event of a lawsuit. Federal, state, and local government contracts often require the general contractor to be bonded. Often, though, government agencies do not have the personnel to monitor construction yet want to ensure that taxpayers' dollars will not be lost.

Bonding has several different connotations. Completion bonds and payment bonds, for example, differ markedly. In the case of a completion bond, the surety guarantees that the project will be completed according to the contract, including the plans and the cost. A payment bond ensures that the surety will pay all valid claims for work performed and materials supplied arising from the project. Thus, a payment bond prevents any claims for mechanic's liens, while a completion bond provides that the project will be completed notwithstanding the default or bankruptcy of the contractor.[5] In the event of a lawsuit in which the developer successfully secures a judgment against the general contractor, the surety on the payment bond is liable for that judgment. In this situation, the surety can use all the defenses available to the general contractor. If the developer has caused part of the problem, it might not be able to collect on the bond. Most developers believe that when they are forced to call on a bonding agent, they will lose some money for time lost and higher interest rates. Thus, bonding provides some, albeit not complete, protection.

The final decision in design and construction is whether to go with architectural supervision of the construction or have a member of the development team supervise construction. Either way, someone representing the developer must regularly inspect construction and certify compliance with design specifications and the construction contracts. Construction lenders are vitally concerned about the quality of this work, as they will substantiate the draws made under the construction loan agreement as construction progresses. Likewise, architects want to be sure their ideas are properly translated into constructed space, and the general contractor wants to get paid. Consequently, provision for construction supervision is part of several of the contracts negotiated in stage four and signed in stage five.

Decisions about Major Tenants

Since stage one of the process, the developer has had an idea of the primary tenant and/or tenant mix anticipated for the project. In the case of a for-sale project, the developer has had some idea of the end customer. That idea is refined in stage two and further formalized in stage three. In stage four, the developer must make the final decision. Possibly by applying sensitivity analysis to the pro forma numbers from the feasibility study, the developer decides how much space to allocate to major tenants and when to sign them on.

The first question pertains to major tenants. Large tenants ranging from regional mall anchors (major department stores) to tenants occupying several full floors in an office building to industrial tenants occupying a significant amount of space, say, 50,000 square feet or more, know their power and drive a hard bargain. Thus, the greater the number of major space users (particularly those with prominent names) the developer signs, the less the net rent (rent after consideration of concessions for tenants, impact of unusual expense stops, and the like). On the other hand, large tenants draw other tenants. A regional mall is not usually possible without several anchor department stores. Signing the anchors is usually the key to drawing smaller tenants and convincing lenders of the project's long-term viability. From the developer's standpoint, however, the more space the major tenants lease, the lower the average rent per square foot.

In regional malls, developers might actually give away space to the anchor tenants and earn all their return from smaller tenants. This practice is not unreasonable, as it is the advertising and name recognition of the major tenants that draw customers to the mall and thus provide the smaller tenants' livelihood. The critical decision is what percentage of the space should be allocated to major tenants. On the one hand, it is usually safer to reserve more space for major tenants. On the other hand, it is more lucrative to recruit a large share of smaller tenants if they "stay and pay."

In addition to deciding what percentage of space to allocate to major tenants (and all gradations between major and minor tenants), developers must decide when to sign tenants. (Of course, lenders' preleasing requirements, discussed in Chapter 6, often reduce the developer's flexibility in this regard.) Tenants signed early in the process commit to something they cannot see as well as to a possibly uncertain future opening date. To induce tenants to make an early commitment, developers must offer some concession, perhaps a rent concession or a choice location.

From the developer's perspective, signing a tenant early has certain advantages. The more tenants that sign early, the lower the vacancy rate if the market becomes less robust or the project less inviting after construction. Although early leasing is a way to reduce risk, it also requires greater concessions to tenants.

After making decisions about the advance signing of tenants and the number of major tenants, developers must specify the general conditions desired in other leases. What is involved is not just rent per square foot, which varies with location, the amount of space required, and other considerations. Developers must also decide who pays what portion of which operating costs, the amount of tenant improvement allowances, and who provides what services. For example, who pays for carpeting and other interior features? If the developer pays, the rent is typically higher. Often developers give the tenant a certain improvement allowance; the tenant then pays whatever additional amount is necessary for upgraded fixtures beyond the amount specified in the lease. From a lender's perspective, tenant allowances are attractive because money spent on permanent interior improvements creates additional collateral for the first lien on the project. Given that the developer typically negotiates the first lien, it is often easier to include in those negotiations a certain tenant allowance and pass it along to tenants. The alternative is for tenants to borrow the necessary funds. Smaller tenants frequently find it difficult to finance improvements because their lenders cannot consider the improvements as collateral.

Ongoing operating guidelines are also important. What services will the landlord provide? How often will the bathrooms be cleaned? How fast will the elevators travel? What kind of security will be provided? In many projects, particularly shopping centers, tenants also have obligations. What are the minimum hours of operation? How much cooperation is necessary for joint promotions? All these items must be negotiated before the execution of leases to ensure that the total marketing effort for the project matches the expectations specified in the feasibility study. Although the landlord would like higher rents with more expenses passed on to tenants and fewer allowances, the market may not tolerate such terms. Few tenants may be willing to sign before seeing more of the project, particularly if the market is overbuilt, the developer inexperienced, the project unusual, or the location unproved. Further, although the landlord may hope to pass escalations in operating expenses through to

tenants, tenants hope for just the opposite; in fact, market conditions may reduce the developer's strength in the negotiation.

At this point, developers must also decide whether leasing is to be handled by in-house staff or outside contractors. For some types of projects and some locations, it is preferable to use outside leasing agents, at least in part. In other cases, such as leasing (or sale) of retirement housing, the product is so unusual and complex that developers often do well to have the needed talent on staff, where they can monitor it more closely.

The developer is accountable for all these decisions and for seeing that the corresponding documents are properly drafted. If the developer concludes that the numbers in the feasibility study cannot be met, stage four is the last chance to get off the wagon.

Decisions about Equity

The difference between project costs and what can be financed is the required development equity. The ideal project is one whose value is so far above cost that the developer can obtain a low loan-to-value ratio loan and still secure a sufficiently large loan to cover all costs, including a development fee, major reserves to cover any operating deficits before lease-up, and a large reserve for contingencies. When a lender finances a real estate development project, however, it usually relies on such conservative underwriting criteria that it nearly always requires a significant equity investment by the developer. Only a truly great idea gets 100 percent debt financing.

When developers cannot finance the entire project through debt, they must find additional sources of capital. Three basic alternatives are possible: developers provide the necessary equity from their own funds or their firm's funds, they bring in an outside equity investor for the development period, or they establish a joint venture with the lender in which the lender also gets part of the equity in return for a greater loan amount and/or contribution of equity beyond the loan amount. These three approaches have numerous variations, all of them compensating investors according to the risk associated with their contribution to equity.

In its deal for Europa Center, Fraser Morrow Daniels ended up with a 65/35 split with Centennial. A small development company, Fraser Morrow Daniels traded off a share of ownership and potential monetary rewards to share the risk inherent in leasing a new product—Class A office space in a new location—and to provide the additional equity necessary to attract construction and permanent financing for the project

A large portion of the MCI Arena in downtown Washington, D.C., was constructed underground to maintain the scale of the adjacent buildings while meeting the arena's size requirements.

(i.e., the equity that Fraser Morrow Daniels was either unable or unwilling to invest).

When developers lack the resources for equity or choose to allocate their funds differently, they usually consider the participation of outside investors and joint venture partnerships or limited-liability companies (LLCs) or partnerships (LLPs). Before the 1986 changes to the tax law, long-term real estate investment provided substantial tax benefits, because losses induced by depreciation could essentially be offset against an investor's ordinary income. In such a world, it made more sense for wealthy individuals to invest in real estate projects. With the revision to the tax laws in 1986, however, fewer tax benefits became available. As a result, developers must develop projects that are economically viable, i.e., provide an acceptable rate of return to investors before taxes. After 1986, pension funds and other institutional investors replaced real estate tax syndications as the primary source of long-term equity capital

In structuring an outside equity deal, developers extend the cash flow forecast from the feasibility study to include income taxes and debt service for each participant in each financing alternative. Potential tradeoffs can be exceedingly complex. Often, the amount of the developer's profits and exposure to risk changes materially, depending on the source of permanent debt and equity financing. It takes experience, and the discounted cash flow analysis introduced in Chapter 5, for the developer to decide on the optimal structure for any required equity. Taking advantage of the feasibility study's electronic spreadsheet as an optimization tool, the developer performs sensitivity analyses on revised cash flows,

using alternative forecasts of future events to determine the impact of each scenario on the various cash flows. Experience comes into play in specifying likely scenarios. For example, just how likely is the combination of interest rates 10 percent lower, an increase in local demand with the relocation of a major employer to the area, and a steady competitive supply as a competing property owner chooses not to expand? It takes experience and "feel" to estimate the likelihood of alternative scenarios.

If the market is hot and the developer is financially able, it is usually most rewarding to build the project with the developer's own funds and then sell it upon completion. At that time, the final investor, attracted by lower risk because the development process is over, should be willing to pay a higher price.

Before tax reform in 1976, 1981, and 1986, the development period offered substantial tax advantages through the deduction of construction interest, property taxes, and operating and marketing expenses before opening. With the elimination of various tax benefits, however, it has become more difficult to entice investors to invest early.

The development-period equity joint venture requires the developer to give away a share of the profits to the investor partner along with some control over decisions concerning the development, ownership, and ultimate disposition of the project. With the tightening of the capital markets in the 1990s and the emphasis today's investors place on the internal rate of return generated by the project, developers are frequently required to provide the investor with what is often referred to as a "priority return or yield" on the investor's money before "profits" are shared between investor and developer. This priority is often expressed as both an internal rate of return threshold and a minimum dollar amount. Eventually, after the outside investor has received its "priority return," the developer begins to receive distributions, including yield on its capital, return of its capital, and, then, a split of cash flow. The split of cash flow is often disproportionate to the relative percentage of capital invested by the developer and investor; that is, the developer's percentage share of back-end cash flow is greater than the relative percentage of capital invested by the developer—often referred to as the developer's "promote."

A hybrid of debt and equity financing for a developer often takes the form of a participating or convertible mortgage. Under this structure, the "lender" not only receives the stated interest amount but also either a right to a certain portion of the project's cash flow (i.e., the participating loan) or a right to convert its debt into equity in the project and thereby participate in the profits (i.e., a convertible loan). The participation, for example, could be 20 percent of gross revenues over a certain amount, 50 percent of net operating profit, or any other variation. Typically, permanent lenders receive not only a periodic additional payment but also some percentage of the proceeds from the final sale or any intervening refinancing.

With a joint venture, participation from the outset is more common. Long-term lenders or investors may be induced to invest money before the project is built, thereby reducing the amount of cash the developer needs. Sophisticated long-term lenders know the value of such a commitment and are likely to negotiate a more advantageous split of the rewards in exchange for assuming additional risk. The more developers can guarantee in terms of construction costs, completion dates, and leasing, the higher the percentage of rewards they will be able to retain.

The Government as Partner

Developers are well advised to collaborate with their public partner—the local municipality—throughout the early stages of development. In stage four, as the developer is negotiating and finalizing contracts with all the key players on the development team, it would be extremely advantageous if the developer were able to "contract" with the municipality where the project is located.

The contract with the municipality would, among other things, confirm the parties' understanding regarding the project's entitlements, fees, exactions, and dedi-cations for which the project will be responsible, and the right of the developer to develop the project in accordance with the municipality's rules, regulations, and policies, such as the local zoning ordinance, as those rules existed on the date of the "contract."

Unfortunately, not all municipalities permit these types of contracts. In some municipalities, however, state law permits a developer to enter into a "development agreement" with the local municipality. Under such an agreement, a developer is assured of the right to proceed with the development of the project during the term of the development agreement, and is assured that the development may be developed in accordance with the rules, regulations, and official policies of the municipality that were in effect on the date the development agreement was entered into. For a large project that will be developed in phases, this type of assurance is essential and is frequently required by the developer's lender(s). A number of states, including Arizona, California, Colorado, Florida, Hawaii, Maryland, Minnesota, and Nevada, permit development agreements in one form or another.

A developer's right to proceed with development of the project without being concerned about having the rules change is known as a "vested right." Until a developer has obtained a vested right, the possibility exists that the local rules could change and preclude the developer from proceeding as planned. Achieving a vested right to develop varies from state to state. In some states, merely pulling a building permit vests the developer's right to proceed with the development for a period of time equal to, at least, the life of the building permit.

In Massachusetts, for example, the developer's interests are vested if a building permit has been issued *and* construction starts within six months. Also in Massachusetts, so long as a plat for a new subdivision is filed before a rezoning hearing, zoning is frozen for a period of eight years. Downzoning is therefore not an immediate risk once the plat is filed. In other jurisdictions—California, for example—no vested right is obtained to complete construction of a project until a building permit is obtained and substantial work has been undertaken and liabilities incurred in good faith reliance on that building permit. A grading permit would not satisfy this standard for vested rights.

In formalizing the relationships among parties, particularly the local municipality, developers should not lose sight of the changing face of the urban landscape. Projects that began as industrial distribution centers have become high-tech office parks and in the process made their owners extremely wealthy.

Evolving land uses are usually stimulated by growth in surrounding areas, public restrictions on the development of other land, and other forces prompting change. Although the stimulus might come from the outside, developers can create the possibility of change. Developers who realize the inevitability of change and provide as much flexibility as possible in design, tenant selection, financing, and entitlements are most likely to enjoy the benefits of "second-order effects."

The fine print in the contracts and entitlements negotiated during stage four greatly affects the flexibility to change. Developers should not ignore the details in their contracts *or* in the conditions to their entitlements, because those "details" can end up either restricting or maximizing the developer's flexibility. Developers should make every effort to ensure future flexibility when drawing up agreements and when reviewing conditions to their entitlements.

Stage Five: Commitment— Signing Contracts and Initiating Construction

Several of the contracts negotiated during stage four can be contingent on other contracts. It is common for the permanent lender to be unwilling to make a commitment until certain major tenants have signed a commitment. The construction lender's agreement is often contingent on a permanent loan takeout. Developers do not want to make a commitment to a contractor until they have the funds available to pay for construction, and major tenants do not want to sign a contract until they are sure the developer has sufficient money and staff to complete the project.

Hence, many of the parties examine contracts in which they are not direct participants but that are necessary for them to realize their own objectives. It is often necessary to have different contracts executed simultaneously. Regardless of whether the contracts are executed sequentially or simultaneously, most must be fairly firmly negotiated before any are signed. And a series of events must happen as the contracts are signed.

In stage five of the process, the contracts negotiated in stage four are executed. If outside investors are involved, agreements documenting the formation of entities such as partnerships or other relationships typically must be signed and filed with governmental jurisdictions. In larger projects, a public offering registered with the federal Securities and Exchange Commission might be involved. To complete the financial arrangements, the permanent loan commitment must be signed and the fee paid; similarly, the construction loan agreement must be signed and that origination fee paid.

The contract with the general contractor is signed, while the general contractor signs a series of contracts with the subcontractors.

The local jurisdiction is also involved. If possible, permits are obtained in stage three or at least early in stage four, but negotiations in stage four often cause changes that require renegotiation with the city. In larger projects (and increasingly in smaller projects), local governments require impact fees and/or major off-site improvements before approving a development. These agreements must also be finalized in stage five.

As for marketing, the preleased space requires a formally executed lease, with memoranda of some (usually major) leases recorded. If an outside leasing agent or sales agent is used, a listing agreement or at least a memorandum of understanding may be necessary. A memorandum describes the type of space to be leased or sold and the conditions under which the transaction is to occur.

To close the construction loan, the developer probably will have to close on the option to buy the land and/or pay off any land loan in the event the land has already been purchased. This step is necessary to ensure that the construction lender's loan will be a first lien on the property.

On the administrative side, insurance for the construction period must be put in force—liability, fire, and extended coverage; an update on title insurance; and the like. At the same time, the developer switches to a more formal accounting system. Up to this point, the developer has probably simply aggregated all the costs associated with the project, but now a formal budget and cash controls are necessary. The budget comes from the feasibility analysis (as amended by negotiations in stage four), receives the construction lender's blessing, and becomes part of the procedure to draw down funds as construction proceeds. It is also the basis of the contract with the general contractor.

Cash controls require a look at the budget to compare funds expended and funds committed in the original plans while keeping a careful eye on remaining funds. The construction lender uses a similar procedure to keep track of the draws by the developer to fund construction.

Most important, the developer must institute some type of control mechanism for the development itself, either by directing the architect to perform a certain amount of supervision or employing an on-site construction manager. The general contractor must also use some type of formalized process for control. The most common methods are the program evaluation and review technique (PERT) and the critical path method (CPM), both of which are available for use on personal computers.

⊞ Europa Center

Initiating Construction

We formalized the relationship that had been negotiated with the S&L. Final negotiations were tough because both the S&L and Centennial were initially unwilling to expand the loan to cover the extensive leasing period we sought. When things started to get tight, it became obvious that different members of the development team had different goals. The firm's senior partner did not want to lose his established net worth, while the younger members did not want to lose an opportunity. All members of the team realized their respective positions, however, and held firm in their negotiations with the lender/financier, eventually obtaining the desired $1 million reserve for the leasing period.

We negotiated the price of construction, dealing seriously with three potential general contractors and finally obtaining a contract that did not need to be bonded because of the general contractor's quality. The architect's judgment played a central role throughout, but we did not turn over final decisions involving rent, costs, and operating efficiency to the architect. And because quality construction was very important to us and local builders did not

have much experience with Class A office buildings, we added a partner to the team to supervise construction for a salary plus a small percentage of the profits.

continued on page 437

Summary

Once the project is officially deemed feasible in stage three, the development team can move toward formalizing all the relationships necessary to implement the plan. During stage four, detailed relationships are negotiated, possibly leading to some changes in the plan as a result of the negotiations. And in stage five, the contracts negotiated in stage four are executed.

During stages four and five, although it is still possible for the developer to determine that the project is not feasible, it is far more expensive than it was earlier to pull out of the project. Developers who frequently arrive at stage four and decide to stop find that they have accumulated a tremendous amount of uncovered overhead. Nonetheless, failure to stop when the signals indicate a stop in stages four and five can cause disaster in stages six, seven, and eight. Developers use the feasibility study done in stage three as a management tool

The vision of Europa Center the developers and architects sold to the financiers so that they could begin construction.

during stages four and five. They should be particularly careful to ensure that 1) the overall project remains feasible after all the contracts are negotiated; and 2) none of the participants in the process have lost level two feasibility through contract negotiation.

Terms

- AHERA
- AIA allowances
- Asbestos
- Bonding
- CERCLA
- Clean Air Act
- Clean Water Act
- Commitment letter
- Construction loan
- Convertible loan
- CPM
- Draw down a loan
- Ecosystems
- EPA
- Fast-track construction
- Friable
- Guaranteed investment contract (GIC)
- Hazardous waste
- Mitigation
- Participating loan
- Permanent loan
- PERT
- Phase I environmental audit
- Prime rate
- SARA
- Superfund
- Surety company
- Takeout
- Wetlands

Review Questions

19.1 How do contracts help control risk?

19.2 What are the options for developers who do not have permanent financing committed before construction begins?

19.3 What is the difference between the risks taken by a construction lender and those taken by a permanent lender?

19.4 What is mezzanine financing, and why is it usually expensive money?

19.5 What are some different types of equity investment vehicles?

19.6 Describe the financing obtained by the developers of Europa Center.

19.7 What is the Superfund legislation, and why is it of concern to landowners and purchasers?

19.8 What is wetlands mitigation, and what is the controversy surrounding it?

19.9 Describe the contract a developer must sign with an architect and some of the issues that should be negotiated.

19.10 What are two primary ways in which a developer hires a general contractor?

19.11 How do allowance items in a construction contract allocate risk?

19.12 What occurs in stage five? Why is stage five so heavily dependent on what decisions are made in stage four?

Notes

1. Additional detail about permanent and construction loans and lenders is provided in Chapters 4 and 6.

2. The interested student should use the material in this chapter and the financial logic developed in Chapters 4 through 6 as bases for exploring the professional real estate journals (e.g., *Real Estate Review, Real Estate Finance, Real Estate Finance Journal,* and *National Real Estate Investor*) for new ideas that can be modified to fit a proposed development.

3. See *New York v. Shore Realty Corporation,* 759 F.2d 1032.

4. See *U.S. v. Fleet Factors,* 901 F.2d 1550 (1990).

5. A mechanic's lien is a lien on property that comes about when a worker claims to have been unpaid. Lenders find liens troublesome because they often take effect as of the first day the subcontractors furnished labor, but they appear in the title (the legal recorded history of ownership) only when filed at some subsequent date. To avoid such potential clouds on a title, some lenders use title companies as disbursing agents, particularly in states with especially strong statutes covering mechanic's liens.

Chapter 20

Stages Six and Seven: Construction, Completion, And Formal Opening

Stage six—construction—differs in one key way from all other stages covered so far: time becomes even more crucial. At stage six, the developer is more exposed to multiple uncertainties, most of them potentially expensive. Unlike earlier stages of development, when a well-structured option may keep the developer's cash contributions to a minimum, the developer is now significantly committed—with cash, guarantees, and human resources—to the development project. Once the general contract has been executed and construction commences, it is not possible to stop or make major modifications without incurring serious financial consequences. Even when developers have arranged non-recourse financing and are entitled to receive substantial development fees, their reputations—and usually a lot more—are on the line.

During the earlier stages, particularly during stages four and five—contract negotiation and formal commitment—the specific rules governing the relationships among the parties were formalized and their obligations defined. Once the agreements are signed and construction begins, the developer's focus shifts toward project management. The crucial items to be controlled are time, quality, and budget. The developer must ensure that all players perform their jobs on time and deliver quality work and that all costs are carefully and continuously monitored. Although the feasibility study remains an important management tool allowing the developer to quickly evaluate potential reactions to changing market conditions, the contracts negotiated

in stage four and signed in stage five have created binding obligations, so changes now are almost certainly more cumbersome and expensive to implement.

This chapter covers two stages in real estate development: project construction (stage six) and the project's completion and formal opening (stage seven). Specifically, it considers:

- The continuing interaction among major players;
- Building the structure;
- Drawing down the construction loan;
- Leasing space and "building out" the tenant space;
- Landscaping and exterior construction;
- Phased development;
- Potential problems that might arise during stage six;
- Completion and formal opening; and
- Risk control techniques during stages six and seven.

Stage Six: Construction

In stage six, the developer (along with the other players now formally committed to the project) takes a major financial leap and begins the process of construction. Making life even more exciting is the high degree of uncertainty that remains part of the process in even the most exhaustively planned and fully contracted developments.

The Continuing Interaction among Major Players during the Construction Process

A developer's role as manager does not end and may well intensify with the hiring of a general contractor to oversee construction. The developer must still manage

The authors are indebted to Edward F. Cassidy, AEW Capital Management, and Chris Carney, Fidelity Real Estate Group, for their contributions to this chapter.

the general contractor and the other members of the development team. By carefully selecting a team of experienced professionals and by establishing formal relationships during stages four and five, the developer is better able to coordinate the working relationship among the design, construction, marketing, financial, operations, and public sector players during stage six. Coordinating the players through the construction process is especially important in complex multiphase or mixed-use developments, which often involve multiple designers and builders, many different users, and several chances for the general public to express its opinion and have an impact on the process. The developer—subject to approval rights of lenders, investors, and tenants—is the final arbiter among all the players and is responsible for making the final decision when a tough judgment is needed.

During the construction phase, so many players are involved that much of the process focuses on coordination and collaboration. For example, the architect will most likely work with his own team of design professionals, which could include a lighting designer, an acoustical consultant, a structural engineer, a mechanical engineer, and an interior design professional. The general contractor will probably coordinate a team of professionals, which could include labor unions, materials suppliers, equipment rental companies, various insurers and financiers, project engineers, estimators, the architecture and design professionals, and a team of subcontractors. And don't forget the team of public sector professionals—municipal inspectors, health inspectors, life safety inspectors—who will also have an interest in the development.

During the early stages of construction, Fraser Morrow Daniels encountered problems arising from poor on-site supervision. To correct the problem, the firm hired a professional experienced in construction management in the Research Triangle market. As both construction manager and partner in the project, he certainly cost more than his predecessor, but the predecessor was not getting the job done.

Developers can provide on-site management in several ways. In some instances, the architect who designed the project examines the work at various stages and certifies that it has been performed according to plans and specifications. Another approach is to hire an in-house project manager, typically an architect or engineer with a construction background who remains on site and, among other things, monitors the general contractor's performance throughout the process.

Twenty years ago, substantial reliance on architectural supervision was common. With today's more complex jobs and a more competitive environment, however, periodic supervision by the architect is often insufficient. On larger jobs, most developers hire or arrange for someone who is on site all the time and is responsible for dealing with both the general contractor and the design team. The more complex the job, the more frequent and unusual the problems that are likely to arise. And as problems occur, somebody must be available to make decisions quickly. Either the developer himself or some member of the staff must be there to work with the general contractor.

Construction lenders are especially interested in the arrangements for supervision and oversight of project construction. Periodic sign-offs, usually once a month, by the architect or the developer's project manager are required when the contractor asks for money and the developer requisitions a draw on the construction loan. Construction lenders (and occasionally institutional partners and permanent lenders) also inspect the construction work, but their presence reinforces rather than replaces technical reviews.

Project Manager

The project manager—whether an architect, in-house construction professional, or in-house engineer—should be experienced in the type of project under construction. Without such experience, the project manager could miss opportunities to intercept and reduce the inevitable conflicts that arise as the general contractor attempts to minimize costs, the operating and marketing people clamor for changes to make the structure more functional, and the architect tries to retain a certain aesthetic concept. In an ideal situation, most conflicts would have been resolved in stages three, four, or five, but changes are often necessitated by market shifts or unanticipated construction problems encountered during stage six. An experienced and effective project manager will be able to maintain a sense of cooperation and mutual achievement among the development team as the various inevitable conflicts are resolved.

Marketing Manager

Unless all the tenant space is preleased or the building has a single tenant (the case of the construction of a public hospital, for example), marketing is an ongoing activity. Simultaneously with initiation of construction, the marketing strategy is implemented in full force. As detailed in subsequent chapters, this strategy usually involves advertising (which means photographs must be taken), coordination of the sales force (which is responsible for meeting with prospects and selling or leasing space), and site visits by prospects.

Among the sales and leasing manager's responsibilities is providing feedback gathered by interacting

The parking deck for Phase I of Europa Center just after construction. Designed to accommodate close to 300 cars, the parking deck was eventually cloaked by attractive landscaping.

with potential tenants to the rest of the development team. As space is leased or sold, it often becomes clear that certain aspects of design fare better in the marketplace than others. Ideally, the original overall design offers enough built-in flexibility that, during the development process, interior configurations, color schemes, and other features can be changed to suit the market as tenants' preferences are expressed and become clear (and change over time). The design for Europa Center stressed both current appeal to tenants and future flexibility. With each decision it faced, Fraser Morrow Daniels considered the tradeoff between immediate cost benefits and longer-term impacts.

Europa Center

The Building Itself

Europa Center has a high ratio of usable space compared with the core utility and common areas (85 percent), and we maximized the amount of window space for tenants. Everyone likes windows and extra corner offices. It costs a little bit more for construction, but I don't think it affects utility costs very much.

Almost all of the mechanical systems in a well-designed multitenant building offer a lot of flexibility for different heating and cooling requirements in different zones throughout the day. We used high-efficiency glass for comfort and energy cost control. We used the best elevators so that we could move people more efficiently; in a five-story building with 20,000-square-foot floors, a lot of people need to move up and down. The building also has two separate sets of stairs; a freight elevator is planned in the second building.

We had to decide how much telecommunications and electronics capability to put in the building. Initially in looking at office building development, we thought we should

build a state-of-the-art building with built-in computer systems (a so-called "smart" building), but we learned in talking with others that 80 or 90 percent of tenants won't pay for that extra cost: they don't yet know how to use the systems and don't want them. The best thing to do is to build flexible conduit space and wiring into the building so those systems can be added as they become economically feasible for tenants. We got clearance for a satellite dish on the roof. Such decisions gave us flexibility about how to use the building in the future.

We also did some special on-site landscaping, changing the land plan to increase some landscaped areas. We sank the parking deck into the ground at significant cost so that it would have a low profile and be hidden by earth berms and trees. That probably cost us an extra $50,000 to $100,000. We'll landscape it so that some marginal leasing benefit might be possible. We liked that from the standpoint of design, but it was more expensive. We would have to increase rent to pay for the added costs, but which pocket could we take it out of? In a very competitive market, we probably would not recover the extra rent.

Later, the building will be more valuable because of that decision. The building is more valuable because of the parking deck. Period. The alternative to a parking deck to serve a fairly large building like Europa Center would have been to cover the entire site with asphalt.

continued on page 442

Financial Officer

The development team's financial officer manages the project's budget, pays all the bills, and, beyond hard construction, ensures compliance with the plan's overall economics. Financial officers must also be sure that insurance coverage is exactly what is required, that the marketing manager is staying within budget, and so on. They also manage the relationship with the construc-

Profile **Robert Silverman**

Chair, The Winter Group of Companies, Inc.
Atlanta, Georgia

Bob Silverman is chair of the Winter Group of Companies, with headquarters in Atlanta. Winter is a diversified real estate and construction company with divisions specializing in general construction, environmental remediation, real estate development, and property management.

After college at Dartmouth and an MBA from Columbia, Silverman began his professional career as a systems analyst with IBM in Schenectady, New York, but his career took a sharp turn when he was faced with taking over his father-in-law's construction company in 1968. Although he knew nothing about the construction industry when he began, Silverman now says that was an asset. It caused him to hire talented people to work in the field while he focused on applying his skills as a systems analyst to building construction, pioneering the use of technology to optimize project management. Although "people laughed the first few years," never thinking that technology and computers could have a place in the construction industry, the practice proved successful and Silverman eventually wrote a paper delivered at the National Academy of Sciences titled, "A Multidisciplinary Team Approach to Building Construction."

By the mid-1970s, the construction market in Schenectady and central New York was in a tailspin and Silverman began looking for a market he believed was poised for growth. Against the advice of many skeptics, Silverman chose Atlanta, seeing it as a city with great promise and being intrigued by the combination of southern grace and Yankee energy that seemed to result from the diverse population that had migrated to Atlanta. With just $25,000 of his own and another $25,000 from an investment partner, Silverman in 1978 purchased the name and assets of the nearly bankrupt A.R. Winter Construction Company in Atlanta. Silverman served as president of that company, which evolved into the Winter Group of Companies, Inc., working for select national clients and concentrating in the Southeast. There he found himself shut out of much of the market by the existing good old boy network. The company built a local reputation slowly, breaking into the market from the outside by winning bid contracts and working for companies from outside Atlanta.

Much of the firm's work at that time included renovating regional malls, a practice that prompted the creation of Winter Environmental Services. The advent of more stringent environmental laws created a demand among Winter's clients for a firm with the capability for both construction and remediation. Knowing nothing of this field either, Silverman followed his earlier business model, hiring a president to head the division and highly qualified people in the field, and using his managerial skills to optimize their performance. By 1983, Silverman bought out his initial investment partner.

Silverman made the move into development in the late 1980s after noticing a declining number of historic buildings in Atlanta, a market not known for having a strong tradition of preservation. In 1988, Silverman purchased the Carriage Works, a four-story, 110,000-square-foot brick structure built at the turn of the century that was originally home to the Atlanta Buggy Company, and Winter Properties was born. The building was located in a depressed and dangerous area of the city but strategically close to downtown and the Georgia Tech campus. Silverman envisioned converting the facility into loft apartments. But after 32 banks turned him down for financing, Silverman began renovating the building for office use out of pocket and moved his company into the facility. Finally, the company found a bank to finance completion of the building.

At about the same time, Silverman had purchased a historic warehouse near the Carriage Works. He sold the building at cost to the Nexus Contemporary Arts Center, which had recently lost its space in an abandoned school. The Winter Group has always been a strong supporter of the arts, donating 10 percent of after-tax profits to cultural endeavors. Silverman also offered Nexus parking. The arts center lent an ambience to the area and to the Carriage Works building, the lobby of which serves as an art gallery. The Carriage Works building then leased quickly, its non-cookie-cutter space featuring exposed bricks and timbers attracting high-tech tenants eager for an alternative to bland office developments and a location near the university. Later, when Microsoft was interested in renting space in the building, no tenants would agree to have their leases bought out.

Silverman soothed tenants' concerns about security by erecting a perimeter wall around the site and providing 24-hour security. Winter and others have since redeveloped several nearby properties for both residential and commercial uses. The once derelict area has emerged into an eclectic community of high-tech and arts-oriented residents and businesses. Says Silverman, "We educated this market about preservation. And each time a building is restored a miracle happens." People drawn to these types of projects love the sense of community that develops,

Bass Lofts, a three-story former high school built in the 1920s, offers distinctive living space to the city of Atlanta's rapidly growing population of young professionals. Additional two-level units were developed in the adjacent gymnasium as well as 30 new units in a separate building.

according to Silverman, who adds that the National Trust for Historic Preservation is now becoming aware of this community-building byproduct of restoration.

Winter Properties has since completed several more historic preservation projects both around the Carriage Works building and in other areas of the city. The company has also successfully repositioned office properties of more recent vintage. Its most recent project, Bass Lofts, is the conversion of a former high school, built in the 1920s, into 133 luxury apartments, a project Silverman had in mind since he first strolled the neighborhood 17 years earlier. The project has been extremely successful, with rents achieved higher than the predevelopment pro forma.

Today Silverman focuses mainly on business development and spends much of his time speaking, teaching, and "always taking seminars." And, even with a proven track

record of successful developments, Silverman still finds rejection to be the most difficult part of his job. "It's difficult when a project won't get done because someone doesn't share your vision. Rejection is one of the toughest things in life no matter the context."

Silverman believes that Winter is well positioned for the future, thanks largely to its conservative approach to development. "We look for at least a 20 percent return across the board for any project." And although exhibiting a strong commitment to city and community, "we are businesspeople first," says Silverman. "We even encourage our engineers to pursue business degrees." With its track record, the company now finds financing easier to obtain. Silverman also sees a "return to normalcy" in the real estate industry, with interest rates and cap rates reaching more sustainable levels. ∎

tion lender, permanent lender, and all project investors. Whenever feedback from the marketing staff or the architect suggests changes and the project manager is asked to estimate the cost of the suggested alternative, financial officers at the same time must determine whether the increment in value justifies the additional cost and whether the lender or the equity investor can be convinced to increase its financial commitment to the project to cover the additional costs.

Property Manager

The property manager, who ideally participated during the design stages, should also be involved during construction. As the marketing representative suggests changes and the construction manager responds with alternatives, the property manager should ensure that the proposed changes do not compromise the building's long-term manageability. Particularly when financing becomes tight, short-term decisions to solve financing problems—often referred to as "value engineering"—can cause long-term trouble. The property manager is responsible for ensuring that short-term solutions to problems during construction do not unduly complicate any important aspect of property and asset management (see Chapter 21). The future property manager, or some other member of the development team, should maintain positive relations with the various city regulatory bodies during construction. The orchestration of physical inspections by regulatory agencies as work proceeds (usually coordinated by the general contractor and the project manager) is only one aspect of managing government partners. Most development projects have several more points of contact—from shared policing of the construction site to new municipal bus stops.

Building the Structure

As noted earlier, the general contractor typically contracts with a variety of subcontractors to accomplish the physical work and provide the needed equipment. These efforts usually involve installing the building's major systems, including the electrical, plumbing, and HVAC systems. Subcontractors are also typically engaged for excavation, foundation and concrete work, framing, drywall, roofing, trim, painting, and other specialty trades, although general contractors may be able to provide these functions from their in-house staffs. In high-rise construction, the structural components are more difficult and the systems more complex, but the same principle applies. Although the general contractor manages the subcontractors, the project manager represents the developer's interests with the general contractor. At the same time, the developer makes sure that construc-

tion is coordinated with the ongoing marketing effort and that construction and marketing are covered by the available financing without sacrificing long-term management efficiencies.

Subcontractors vary dramatically in the size and organizational sophistication of their companies. Some subcontractors for mechanical systems are large regional or even national firms with sophisticated management procedures and accounting controls. By contrast, the masonry subcontractor or the painter could be one woman and her nephew with a few tools in the back of a pickup truck. The general contractor must choose the appropriate subcontractor for the job at hand, remembering that it is expensive to hire someone more skilled than necessary and imprudent and dangerous to hire someone less skilled than necessary. The appropriate subcontractor must have the time and resources to do the job when needed, be financially solvent, have appropriate insurance, and should have earned the general contractor's trust based on reputation, past relations, and the possibility of future business. Depending on the relationship between the developer and the general contractor, the developer's in-house construction expertise, and the needs of the project, the developer sometimes hires individual subcontractors directly, often to lock in a price or a slot in the subcontractor's schedule. Regardless, developers are ultimately responsible, so it behooves them to know how the general contractor is handling the tradeoff between quality and experience versus availability and low cost.

The general contractor's most important task is properly scheduling the different subcontractors' work and then making every effort to maintain that schedule. Although everyone appreciates the difficulty involved in putting on a roof before the walls are up, it is also difficult to know exactly how long it will take to put the walls up when the weather turns inclement. Because most construction is performed outdoors in uncertain weather conditions, even the most reliable subcontractors can easily fall behind schedule. If one task falls behind, the next subcontractor may be committed to another job when the previous subcontractor has finally completed its task. Thus, four days of heavy rain can throw a schedule far more than four days behind. The general contractor must be flexible enough and forceful enough to make certain that subcontractors adjust their other schedules as necessary.

Drawing Down the Construction Loan

Lenders, not surprisingly, are reluctant to pay their entire share of the cost of a development up front before the collateral has been created. In fact, they normally provide funds only as construction progress is demonstrated. Similarly, the developer is not required to pay the general contractor before the work is performed, although general contractors and subcontractors are reluctant and often unable to wait until the completion of all construction and final inspections before receiving any payments. In most construction contracts, the parties agree that the developer will pay for the work program as it progresses while retaining a set amount—often between 5 and 10 percent of the cost of construction—until the end of the job. Thus, for a $100,000 construction job with a provision for 10 percent retainage that is 20 percent complete, the general contractor has earned a $20,000 payment but would receive only $18,000, with the developer retaining $2,000 until completion. And only upon "satisfactory" completion does the general contractor (and through him the subcontractors) receive the amounts retained. "Satisfactory" means that all provisions of the agreement between owner and general contractor have been met and accepted by the architect, the building officials, and the developer. Thus, retainage is a major device that ensures completion in accordance with plans and specifications. It is also partial protection for the developer against default by the general contractor.

The paperwork involved in drawing down funds from the construction lender typically follows a clearly delineated path. Periodically, often every two weeks on smaller projects or every month on larger jobs, the subcontractor submits an invoice for work completed. The general contractor then compiles invoices from all the subcontractors and, often with input from the architect and the project manager, examines the subcontracted work to ensure that the percentage of work claimed has been completed according to the plans and specifications. If discrepancies arise, the general contractor works them out with the subcontractor(s) and eventually sends an invoice to the developer for the combined total of all subcontractors' draw requests plus the general contractor's fee and other markups and eligible costs. In this way, individual subcontractors can be paid by the end of the month for the work completed minus the amount for retainage.

The project manager (or the architect) verifies to the developer and the lenders that the total invoice submitted by the general contractor agrees with the contract between the general contractor and the developer, that the work has been completed, and that it meets plans and specifications. At this point, the approved invoices are sent to the developer's financial officer. The financial officer combines the invoice for construction costs (the hard costs) with various other "soft costs" associated with the development—insurance, property taxes,

interest on the construction loan, marketing costs, and general administrative overhead, for example—and then submits a total figure to the construction lender.

The loan agreement with the construction lender typically stipulates that the lender will provide funding as needed to cover the costs so long as the costs are within budget. Thus, the financial officer uses the budget originally defined in the feasibility study and refined during stage four to produce a monthly draw request that ties to the original budget, summarizing costs to date, the amount for the relevant period, and the remaining balance available for completion, typically for each item in the cost budget. (During stage four, the developer argued for as few categories as possible to achieve more flexibility in moving funds around while the lender favored more categories to increase control.)

The construction lender verifies that the request from the developer is in accordance with the loan agreement and that all participants (the architect or project manager, the general contractor, and the financial officer) have initialed the request. The lender might decide to inspect the construction to ensure that the project is proceeding as the draw request indicates. Finally, the construction lender verifies that the development appears to be on time and within budget for both hard and soft costs.

Assuming that all requirements are satisfied, the construction lender deposits funds in the developer's account for the total amount of the draw. The financial officer then writes a check to the general contractor, who in turn pays the various subcontractors. Disbursements for soft costs are also made directly to the appropriate vendors and service providers.

One risk control device that lenders often use is to disburse funds only through title companies. In such cases, subcontractors exchange lien waivers for their appropriate draw checks. The title company can thus ensure that all subcontractors have acknowledged payment before funds are disbursed, thereby protecting the lender from mechanic's liens filed by unpaid subcontractors.

Mechanic's liens are liens on the property that arise when a contractor goes to court to seek help in collecting payment for construction work. To protect workers (considered to be at risk relative to big institutions), the law provides that mechanic's liens take effect when the work is done, not when the lien is filed. Thus, the lender could lose the coveted first lien position to a previously unrecorded claim. Laws that apply to mechanic's liens vary significantly by state, and the developer is well advised to engage legal counsel familiar with applicable local laws.

The length of time from the billing cutoff date (usually the last day of each month) until funds are disbursed to the subcontractors can be critical. If the elapsed time between performance of the work and payment for the work becomes too long, a significant burden is imposed on the subcontractors.

For example, suppose a subcontractor submits a bill at the end of each month, that each month's average billing is $50,000, and that payment is received on the 15th of the following month. Under this scenario, the subcontractor must finance its work for one and one-half months or, in this example, in the amount of $75,000. This burden can be minimized by making payments more often, perhaps twice a month, or by speeding the approval and payment process so the waiting time is reduced to perhaps one week rather than 15 days. But the principle is the same: every contractor and subcontractor must be financially able to carry a portion of the work until the disbursement of funds.

Leasing Space and "Building Out" The Tenant Space

Even with extensive preleasing before construction, some space usually remains unleased at the initiation of construction and therefore must be marketed during construction. Ideally, tenants would pay rent on every square foot of the building on the day the project opens. One cost item in the pro forma, however, is usually an operating deficit for the period immediately after construction until the building is sufficiently leased and occupied to cover debt service and all operating expenses.

A major goal of most developers is to capture this leasing reserve. If total costs include the cost of funding a deficit and the deficit does not materialize because the building is fully leased and occupied when it opens, then the budget item moves from the cost column directly into profits. Fraser Morrow Daniels, for example, planned to give up 15 percent of its share in Europa Center's profits to obtain a leasing reserve of $1 million, and Whit Morrow hoped the company would never need that reserve. As it happened, the firm could not lease the building during construction because prospective tenants were unfamiliar with the benefits of the proposed Class A office space. Compounding this problem was the disappearance of the planned leasing reserve.

⠿ Europa Center

Leasing during Construction

We anticipated signing some leases immediately after the building was completed—mostly small professional firms and service firms—but expected that it would take two

full years to fill the building. And because of rent concessions that had emerged as standard in the marketplace, we were not sure when those tenants would begin paying rent. Whether we use free rent or extra tenant improvements is always a consideration. The cost of tenant improvements may add to the building's value; free rent doesn't do anything except induce tenants to move in.

And we ended with no convenient million dollars to draw on if necessary. Investors S&L bought Centennial and required that million dollar cushion in equity. Despite a valid loan contract, the bank negotiated a more secure position as part of the acquisition and absorbed the real million. We then expected to require some additional prorated contribution of capital from the partners, with a possible renegotiation of partnership shares—an eventuality that was not anticipated going into the project. But if you examine almost any real estate development deal today, the amount of profits that actually ends up with the person who generated the original idea for the project is usually a lot less than anticipated at the outset. [Authors' note: In this case, failure to anticipate all the project-level implications of the acquisition put the project in jeopardy.]

What would I do differently if I had it to do over again? Bargain for another million. Be more explicit about the long-term contingencies for which money would be used. And continue to reexamine them during negotiations for financing. The feeling that we would be more cooperative, I think, put less pressure on us to spell out every contingency and every detail in a 200-page agreement.

continued on page 448

Museum Towers had the advantage of an extremely favorable market and skilled professional marketers. Yet they did not achieve 100 percent occupancy, and leasing for the most expensive units was much slower than expected.

⠿ Museum Towers

Leasing during Construction

The rental housing market in the Boston area has been extremely strong for quite some time. With a vacancy rate less than 2 percent in 1998, rents increased across the board at a rate of 5 to 10 percent annually in the late 1990s. Renters in this market have been waiting for something new for a long time, at least ten years.

Developers have to have a bit of what we call "snake oil salesmanship." Real estate development projects require a lot of selling, at every step. You gotta sell to your banks,

The marketing campaign for Museum Towers emphasized location and views.

to your partners, to the tenants, to the public, to the leasing guys so they can sell it to others. And a lot of this selling goes on while the building is being constructed, so you have to convince everyone that they're going to like what they see before they see it. It's not always easy, so as a developer, you really have to believe in your product.

On the other hand, selling real estate is like selling anything. You need a complete marketing plan and the right people to execute it. As of June 1999, we had made only one major error. We are 70 percent leased but had planned to be 90 percent leased by that time. Essentially all of the lower-priced units are leased, but we probably held out for too high a rate in the best units. Overall, the market's strength has allowed us to be above pro forma revenue, which is clearly good. But if we hadn't been quite so aggressive on rates for the best units, we would have had more income during construction.

continued on page 445

In addition to a leasing reserve, the lender's agreement might provide for floor and ceiling loan amounts; for example, the total amount of the loan will be only x dollars until y percent of the building is leased, at which time the remaining amount will be funded. If such a provision is found in the permanent loan, the construction lender typically lends only the floor amount, which will be assessed as the permanent or takeout lender's minimum commitment. Usually this

scenario requires the developer to put up whatever funds, beyond the floor loan, are needed before starting construction. This type of loan provision places extreme pressure on the developer. If marketing does not proceed according to schedule, the developer will, at some point, have drawn down the full floor amount of the loan, which can cause problems. The developer may have to provide funds "out of pocket" for the balance. As construction progresses, it is difficult to tell participants to stop and wait a month until more space is leased. Construction must continue as scheduled, or costs will surely escalate. Meanwhile, money might not be available to pay the general contractors and subcontractors, who will not be sympathetic with the marketing staff's failure to meet the leasing expectations. The lender will not fund an amount above the floor until the additional leasing occurs—and the pressure mounts.

Developers can cover such funding shortfalls themselves or induce outside investors to cover them. But once a project is in trouble, it is much harder and more expensive to secure additional funding.

The lease for office space in a major downtown building covers long-term financial and operating concerns as well as such physical details as the location of interior walls, the number of electrical outlets and plumbing fixtures, and the type of carpeting. Thus, the leasing agent's negotiations directly influence the construction crew's work and what must be financed.

When the market is overbuilt, as it was in the late 1980s, most developers claim to be driven almost exclusively by their customers' demands: if the customer wants it, they will find a way to provide it. Responding to such demands is not a simple task, however, for the requests must be incorporated into the development process in the proper sequence, and they must be financed. If the lender will not fund interior physical improvements after the fact, the pressure mounts a little more.

Landscaping and Exterior Construction

The initial feasibility study likely included at least one line item in the budget for landscaping, which is becoming increasingly important in marketing a project. In the past, if the building's design was not appealing, creative landscaping could cover or at least detract from major flaws. Today, however, landscaping has assumed a different and more integral role.

Landscaping is now viewed more as an enticement to tenants. It helps create an environment that will appeal to future employees, particularly in markets where labor is in short supply. Creative landscaping distinguishes a project from the competition and therefore

The development concept for the R.R. Donnelley Building in Chicago was to create a Class A office building using the highest quality materials and craftsmanship to attract large and financially secure tenants. The project's richly finished pocket park featuring landscaped planters and a "Villa D'Este" stair is just one of the exterior landscaping details adding to the building's beauty and market competitiveness.

Steinkamp/Ballogg Chicago

can accelerate leasing. In addition, marketing specific, visible environmental features can go a long way toward attracting clients and making a project acceptable to neighbors.[1]

In this context, landscaping covers a wide range of additions to the environment. In a development of less expensive single-family houses, it might involve only spreading topsoil, seeding it, and planting a few shrubs. A major downtown mixed-use project might involve porches, decks, walkways, street furniture (such as benches, lighting, and signs), intensively planted areas, and even some works of art. (Art, both interior and exterior, has become more than a novelty.)

Many developers of large commercial projects are now nearly as careful about selecting a landscape architect as they are about selecting a building architect. Office and industrial parks in particular are exploiting some of the most innovative trends in landscape design to gain quicker market acceptance.

For a variety of reasons, landscaping typically is completed late in the construction process. From a design perspective, landscaping treatment can respond to a different mix of tenants from that originally envisioned, adding an element of flexibility for the developer. From an operational standpoint, once in place, landscaping must be maintained. If installed too early in the construction process, landscaping materials will likely be vulnerable to destruction by construction vehicles still on site. Further, the appropriate maintenance personnel will not yet be on staff.

Phased Development

For a large development, construction is likely to proceed on several buildings at the same time, with different stages of the development process in progress at once—perhaps infrastructure planning (stage three) on one large tract and the construction of individual buildings (stage six) elsewhere. While such large-scale developments have several economic, social, and aesthetic benefits, they often require ten to 20 years to complete. During that period, hundreds of less ambitious individual projects could be built, each with its own development process.

The developer may construct the individual buildings in phases as the market warrants. Perhaps an entrance to an office park is installed at the outset, followed by roads and amenities as dictated by the market. Sometimes, each parcel of a large tract is sufficiently distinct to require its own development process. In such cases, the developer moves through all eight stages for one parcel even though another parcel may be in stage three and still another in stage one.

For a development of single-family houses, the builder/developer may acquire lots from the land developer, assemble all members of the team, and then move immediately to stage six. For small developers, stage six will last perhaps 90 to 180 days for one house. Alternatively, the developer could build several houses in sequence to keep subcontractors working efficiently—for example, having plumbers move from one house to the next without ever leaving the site. For these large developers, stage six could last six months to several years.

▊▊ Museum Towers

Initiating Construction

Construction of Museum Towers used the PERI forming system, the same system used to erect the Petronas Towers in Kuala Lumpur, Malaysia, the world's tallest buildings. The PERI system, developed in Weissenhorn, Germany, is a formwork and scaffolding system. Basically, a shore or support beam is put up, another beam is put on top, and a modular panel follows. When the panel is stripped out, the system comes out in pieces and is reassembled on another floor. The walls of the towers were constructed using the TRIO system, which is a modular system that uses clamping mechanisms rather than nut-and-bolt attachments. The SKY-DECK system was used for the building's slabs.

The PERI system allows construction to go at a rate that's three or four times faster than a conventional construction system. It's also lightweight and safer than most other systems.

It isn't cheap, but building in Boston never is and we needed to minimize the time we had to pay the 20+ percent interest on the mezzanine debt.

continued on page 488

Potential Problems

Because of unforeseen problems, Fraser Morrow Daniels lost about three months at the beginning of Europa Center's development and a few more months at the end. The construction company was partially responsible for several of the early delays. For instance, when the lobby was under construction, some of the granite pieces and some of the special marble from Italy arrived in the wrong size. On-site cutting and fitting of those pieces required additional time. Fabric panels for the lobby walls were missing, and some of the exterior signs arrived late. Although developers cannot fore-see all the impediments to construction, they should assume that *some* will occur and know how to manage them. A careful developer preserves some portion of "float" in the project schedule as a hedge against unforeseen delays.

The circumstances described in the following illustration did all occur on the same project, but to keep this text a manageable length, the illustration is condensed. Still, such problems are likely to plague most developers at some point during their career. Imagine then, the development of a tennis village designed to be one of the premier tennis facilities in the world. Located on a 200-acre site within an established resort, the project has been designed in phases, the first phase containing the main clubhouse, the central tennis courts, a small hotel, and 50 townhouses. In subsequent phases, another 300 townhouses and more tennis courts will be added.

The financing negotiated for the project allows the developer, who is putting up $500,000, to borrow up to $24.5 million as needed. The $25 million thus available will cover the initial cost of the central courts, the 70-room hotel, the clubhouse, and the first 50 townhouses, and then become a revolving loan fund.

Under the arrangement, the developer will pay back the $24.5 million as he sells the first 50 townhouses. Assuming the units sell for $250,000 each, as projected in the feasibility study, 50 units will generate $12.5 million. This money will then be available for the developer to draw down again to continue building townhouses. Accordingly, the project involves a certain amount of financing on the courts/hotel/clubhouse (which will eventually be repaid from a permanent loan and the transfer of the amenities to the property owners) and a revolving amount that allows the developer to continue building townhouses, so long as the first units sell. The developer realizes no profit from the first group of townhouses, which are priced to induce the first residents to buy into a novel concept. He does, however, receive a development fee on the first phase and expects to profit handsomely on subsequent phases as he increases the price but not the cost of the remaining 250 townhouse units. If the developer stays within the time and cost budgets forecast in the pro forma, the financing package will remain intact and produce substantial profits down the road. If marketing slips or construction is delayed, problems will arise.

As the developer of this project, you are six months from completion of the clubhouse, the hotel, the stadium tennis courts, and the first 50 townhouses. The marketing staff tells you that the two-bedroom units are sold out but that the one-bedroom units, which are essentially the same size but feature a balcony, are not selling at all. The first 50 units were planned to include 25 two-

Creative developers can turn perceived problems into opportunities. The Hualalai Development Company used the hard black lava rock covering the site in the design of the scenic Jack Nicklaus golf course, part of Hualalai at Historic Ka Upulehu, in Kailua-Kona, Hawaii. The lush green fairways contrast beautifully with the black lava and blue ocean.

bedroom units and 25 one-bedroom units, but now the marketing staff suggests changing most of the 25 one-bedroom units to two-bedroom units. The construction manager tells you that the additional walls and minimal additional electrical service needed for the change will require $450,000 total, or $18,000 per unit. You agree to the change, remembering $625,000 allocated in the budget for contingencies.

Then it rains in what should have been the dry season—every day for two weeks. Because the subcontractors' other commitments are also backing up, rescheduling proves to be difficult and the project is now four weeks behind schedule. Moreover, the rescheduling will cost some money. The subcontractors want incentive compensation to return promptly to the project, and the interest meter will now run for a full additional month. The added expense will likely total $325,000. What to do?

The solution to the second problem is to approach the construction lender and claim, in an appropriately humble manner, that an act of God has wiped out the amount set aside for contingencies (the original $625,000 minus $450,000 for 25 conversions to two-bedroom units left only $175,000). The construction lender, who is your partner in the development process, should understand that events beyond your control sometimes require a little more cash.

If the lender goes along with your request, however, he also puts himself in a difficult position. The original financing provides a permanent takeout loan on the clubhouse, stadium tennis courts, and hotel for $12 million (predicated on completion of construction according to plans and specifications). If the cost overrun is allocated to these facilities, then the lender has loaned more than the agreed-upon $12 million, which is tied to his

estimate of value for the improvements. What is the source of payment for the additional funding? If the lender allocates the excess amount to the townhouses, he must believe that the sale price will be sufficient to cover the loan. In other words, he must assume a little more risk or believe that the price can be higher than projected in the original feasibility study. He decides, based on your charm, to allocate the excess to the townhouse units, believing that they can be sold at a somewhat higher price than specified in the feasibility study.

Two weeks later, the marketing staff returns, highly upset. Architectural costs for this particular job were kept to a minimum, and your in-house project manager finalized the site plans and managed the process. But, as the job began, the general contractor noted a large quantity of rock at the end of the site where the first phase of townhouses was to be located. Working with your project manager, he determined that if the units were relocated slightly closer to the outlying tennis courts, which were in the center of each cluster of units, far less rock would have to be moved and costs could be kept to a minimum. The project manager approved the new location of the units, and the development team was pleased because a potential problem had been solved expeditiously with only a slight shift in design and no increase in site costs.

Regrettably, when the units were moved closer, the end units with the attractive bay windows ceased to look out toward the mountains and looked instead into another bedroom window 12 feet away. According to the marketing staff, these units could not be sold for any amount close to the projected price and would have to be rented instead. Normally, you cannot expect to limit the price cut to 10 percent on a luxury item when the item has a flaw that is obvious to even the most unsophisticated consumer. If the end units, eight of them in this first phase, are kept as rental rather than for-sale units and the $12.5 million townhouse construction loan for the townhouses is not fully paid back as planned, you will be short of cash as development continues. You might have to develop in smaller phases (fewer townhouses in each), which would be inefficient and raise your construction costs.

But your troubles do not stop here. Two weeks before the scheduled grand opening, another deluge of rain falls, and a second flaw in the redesign is discovered. With the units now located closer to the tennis courts, the stormwater runoff cannot be fully absorbed by the original drainage system, and the units on the lower side of the courts flood. The flood ruins the drywall and carpeting in ten units that had been scheduled to close in two weeks.

In addition to the costs of replacing the drywall and carpeting, you must find a solution to the drainage problem. Working with your in-house engineer and the general contractor, you identify a solution that will cost $160,000 ($70,000 for new materials and other miscellaneous repairs and $90,000 to install a new "Mediterranean" drainage system on the lower side of the tennis courts). Unlike the money involved in the no-view/ no-sale units, the $160,000 is needed now. The end of the construction period is near, and not much leeway is left to shift expenditures between budget categories, even if the lender would permit it. You have already asked nicely at the bank and received more money for a problem that was an act of God and not your fault. What do you do now? If you show weakness, the lender may "deem itself insecure" (a provision in most new construction loans that allows foreclosure before default if the lender decides that there is no way for you to finish successfully).

Assuming you solve that problem, the project advances to the week before the scheduled grand opening. It is August in the Southwest, and the beautiful landscaping is brown. Apparently, the landscape contractor assumed that the property manager would take responsibility for landscape maintenance. Somehow the property manager did not get the signal, and $100,000 worth of plants are dead. Your high-end buyers will not go to closing with dead shrubs, and if you back off the grand opening, you could lose existing presales; that is, people who previously agreed to buy might decide they do not want to buy a unit in your development. How do you solve the problem? Remember that, as the developer, everything is ultimately your responsibility. In each stage of the development process, we have discussed risk control techniques. Which would have been appropriate for this development situation?

Stage Seven: Completion and Formal Opening

Training the operations staff, connecting the utilities, beginning the on-site operations, final marketing of the development, the grand opening, tenants' moving in, and a transition in financing from the construction loan to the permanent loan all constitute stage seven —completion and formal opening.

Operations personnel are brought to the site before the grand opening. Their job is to make sure that tenants get the space with associated services specified in the lease agreement. The amount of time the operations people spend on site depends on their functions and on the project's size and type. In a convention hotel, for example, some marketing people may join the operations staff two years early.

The marketing people, working with the operations personnel, handle activities before the opening— advertising, promotion, VIP parties, and the like. It is often good business to throw a party to thank the people who have helped you. In the process, you generate some long-term good will in the community and the market, and use the opportunity to invite potential customers to visit the development. Before the party, however, the utilities must be connected, which means all obligations to the city must have been met. Building inspectors must ensure that final items were installed according to code. Assuming that city inspections are only an annoying technicality can result in cancellation of the party. The government is always your partner.

Suppose that, during the final stages of construction, a pipe on the 25th floor bursts and water seeps in and damages key components of the fire alarm system. A fire inspection is scheduled in two days and tenants are moving in two days after that, but now the alarm system must be rewired—a process that will take longer than two days. Rescheduling the inspection will force a delay of at least two weeks even if the city inspector, whom you've been cultivating since stage three, bends over backward to be helpful. What do you tell tenants who plan to move in next week?

During the construction phase, all the interior finish work specified by tenants must be completed, and the marketing staff must coordinate work with the tenants so that the new occupants can move in and be ready to operate in their new space. With the tenants occupying and paying rent on their new space, the permanent loan may be closed and the construction lender repaid.

In addition, a shift might occur from the developer as the controlling equity interest to a new long-term equity investor. The new investor might have in-house management personnel, rely on outside property management companies, or hire the developer as manager. In fact, the developer in many cases stays on as a partner with the new investor. Even with this arrangement, a significant part of the risk shifts from the developer, who has now completed the development, to the long-term investor.

▦ Europa Center

Leasing and Opening the Project

By December 1987, things were going much more smoothly for us. Europa Center was complete and had opened in November with a well-attended party. One-third of the building was committed, and we expected the building to be 50 percent leased by the end of January 1988.

The market was better. We had been pushing sales hard and pricing space competitively. Our base rate was $15.00 to $15.50 instead of the projected $17.00—about 12 percent under original projections. We used a combination of free rent and tenant improvements, so it will take us a little longer—two years—to reach the amount on the pro forma. We expected to be fully leased by summer 1988 and for everyone to be paying rent by 1989.

We committed 13,000 square feet to an executive business center for small but high-profile tenants. Basically, it offers space plus services for a one-person office: a 200- to 300-square-foot office, a common reception area, and secretarial, telephone answering, and copy services. Tenants can even rent office furniture. It's ideal for companies with just one person in the region. Costs to tenants are about twice the base rate for space alone, and the arrangement has been very profitable for us.

One thing we found in this extremely competitive market is that almost nobody would lease space before the building was complete. Another thing we learned is that a lot of prospective tenants didn't know what Class A meant. We had to attract them to the VIP party to make them aware of our project. Our opening party in November was attended by 450 people. We started planning two months ahead in conjunction with the chamber of commerce's Business After Hours program. With all that lead time, we were able to convince the chamber to hold graduation for its leadership training class there. It makes sense to hold this type of function in an office building expected to be a major part of the business community.

We wanted to get two points across about the building: it's exciting and it's elegant. So we hired party consultants instead of planning it ourselves. They put a baby grand piano and a pianist in the lobby and a huge stream of

silver balloons from the first to the third level of the atrium. We served shrimp and beverages and had a steady stream of people from 4:30 p.m. to 9:00 p.m. All kinds of people came—including some town planners and some local political figures.

continued on page 450

Risk Control Techniques during Stages Six and Seven

Under pressure to keep construction and marketing on schedule and costs within budget, developers seek the best means of controlling risk. Some possible risk control techniques follow:

1. Retainage, discussed earlier, and performance bonds are useful methods of controlling construction risk. Retainage allows the developer to hold back cash to ensure the contractor's satisfactory completion of work. A surety company's guarantee of completion or performance of a general contractor's contract reduces the developer's risk by providing a "deep pocket." (Unfortunately, even such guarantees do not eliminate the time risk.) Likewise, a bonded general contractor reduces the city's risk when infrastructure is involved.

2. Union relations are an important consideration. Sensitivity to the unions and to construction workers in general can only benefit the developer. On a high-rise project in Manhattan, the entire construction process can be stopped by one person—the worker who runs the construction elevator. If that person belongs to a union different from that of any of the other workers and decides to strike, the other workers cannot get to their jobs, even if they are willing to cross the one-person picket line.

3. Architectural supervision and/or construction project management are obviously important risk control techniques. In addition to supervising the general contractor, developers can require contractors to include warranties in their contracts. Beyond promises of structural integrity, which can be the basis of subsequent lawsuits, developers should also check that subcontractors have the necessary licenses to perform the specified work and that they are paid a reasonable amount for what is expected of them. Unless the developer is one step ahead of a potential issue, the subcontractor with a problem could eventually become the developer's problem.

4. Liability, fire, and extended insurance coverage are basic to controlling risks. For insurance to

The Bayou Place was once a convention center until it was turned into an entertainment complex in downtown Houston. More than 28,000 people paid $50.00 to attend the grand opening gala, providing substantial revenue for the developer as well as generating millions of dollars in free media coverage.

work, developers must be covered for what might happen, and the insurance must be in force at the right time.

5. By focusing on critical events, PERT and CPM and similar program management systems are useful techniques for managing time and thus controlling risk. Several software packages are now available to perform critical path analysis for construction. (See the bibliography for Part VII for descriptions of these operations research techniques.)

6. Preleasing and presales reduce the risk of initial high vacancies. Careful attention to the tenant mix also helps reduce risk. If tenants "fit" together or if one tenant draws others, fewer problems with long-term vacancies are likely.

7. For small tenants, insurance covering lease guarantees or some type of letter of credit is another possible risk control technique. Depending on the strength of the market, it might be possible to obtain high rent from a small tenant and some type of outside guarantee that the tenant will be able to pay the rent. Although this type of insurance is relatively uncommon, some form of guarantee for a smaller and newer tenant's performance is common. The guarantee can range from the tenant's designation of a cosigner to the occupant's completing a portion of the finish work, thereby enhancing the commitment to the space.

8. Net leases, expense stops, and escalations are all important devices to control risk for long-term investors, and developers should structure leases with these possibilities in mind. When market condi-

tions permit, developers should make sure that they are not the first to absorb all the pain in the event of rapid inflation.

9. The operating agreement negotiated with tenants during the leasing process is another risk control technique. By controlling how tenants relate to one another and to the building, developers can help ensure both long-term operating viability and a minimum of maintenance problems.

10. From an administrative perspective, good internal controls, particularly the accounting system, are critical during the development process.

11. It is essential to involve the operations professionals in project planning and to involve them in the project early. Otherwise, initial operation of the facility could be less efficient—and more expensive—than it should be. Poor service can establish an image that will be expensive to change later.

When evaluating each of these techniques, it is helpful to keep in mind the fundamental things that can be done to reduce risk; in concept, there are six basic ways to reduce risk:

1. Avoid risk by stopping in stage one, two, or three before much money is committed.

2. Increase the research and know more about the possibilities by completing a more substantial feasibility study in stage three.

3. Engage in some form of "loss prevention," the most obvious of which is a competent development team assembled in stages four and five.

4. Transfer a potential loss to other players through the contracts negotiated in stage four.
5. Combine and diversify to reduce the pain of large losses by buying insurance for stages six through eight.
6. Assume risks. Even after adopting these five strategies, the developer must assume some amount of residual risk. Developers are the type of people who can live and work in risky environments. Successful developers price all risks and accept (i.e., allow a residual risk) only when costs justify it.

::: Europa Center

After Construction

The physical construction of Europa Center went reasonably smoothly—which was to be anticipated because we hired a very talented and experienced architect, hired and paid well a construction supervisor, fully explored in advance all regulations with the relevant public officials, and bought a site that presented few physical problems.

Although the construction was smooth, marketing was anything but. In 1987 and 1988, the Research Triangle area continued to be highly overbuilt, like many other sections of the country. More important, approximately eight months earlier, an office tower with more than 200,000 square feet—huge by the area's standards—was completed only four miles away on the southeastern side of Durham at the other end of U.S. 15-501. The earlier completion of another Class A office building that was also pursuing tenants with business in both Durham and Chapel Hill was a serious problem for us. Although we tried to woo tenants already committed to the other building, our late arrival in the market allowed the other developer to pre-sign larger tenants. Even highly attractive rental concessions could not cause them to change their minds. And inducing them to jump after signing would involve buying out existing leases for a substantial period of remaining time.

Europa Center officially opened with 15 percent occupancy, and the leasing reserve was therefore critical. To spur activity in the building, we entered into a joint venture with another promoter for an executive office suite. That joint venture took another 20 percent of the building but certainly did not reduce our risk because we were equity partners in the venture. Despite the fact that risks were not reduced, the need for activity in the building made the joint venture a logical decision. [Authors' note: Even though plans for an executive office suite were prepared, they were never executed and the idea did not take hold until much later.]

Interior construction at Europa Center.

The city fathers loved Europa Center when it opened. It was attractive to anyone thinking of moving to town because the prices looked very reasonable for the space available. The public sector partner was happy; the neighbors around it were happy. The question was how much longer the lender would be tolerant.

continued on page 482

Summary

The physical structure is built during stage six of the development process, requiring constant interplay among the construction, marketing, financial, government, and operating personnel. The developer's role shifts with the move to stage six: he becomes less a promoter and more a manager. Time becomes the critical element of risk. It takes an extremely competent manager to coordinate all the activities that unfold simultaneously during stage six.

Stage seven encompasses the activities associated with completion and the formal opening and requires considerations involving the public sector, tenants, the interior layout, operations personnel, and a shift in financing to long-term investors. Stage seven is the end of the active phase of real estate development and sets the stage for asset and property management—stage eight.

Terms

- Construction manager
- Draw request
- Escalation
- General contractor
- HVAC
- Lien waiver
- Mechanic's lien
- Phased development
- Retainage

Review Questions

20.1 How does stage six differ from the first five stages?

20.2 What is the role of the developer in managing the construction process? How does it differ from the role of the project manager?

20.3 Why is appropriate scheduling particularly important for the project manager?

20.4 Describe the process of drawing down the construction loan.

20.5 How does good landscaping add to the value of a project?

20.6 What are the elements of stage seven? Who assumes the risk at this point in the process?

20.7 Describe some of the risks inherent in stages six and seven and some ways to avoid them.

20.8 Summarize the various risk reduction strategies available to the developer.

20.9 The developer profiled in this chapter, Robert Silverman, took a lot of risks by going into a "bad" neighborhood close to downtown Atlanta and engaging in historic preservation at a time when few in the city knew what it was. How did he handle the financial, professional, and personal risks involved, and what was the outcome?

Note

1. An interesting landscaping trend is toward xeriscaping, in which ongoing maintenance costs are minimized because the landscape architect chooses native plants that are well adapted to the locale. Originally geared to arid sections of the country, xeriscaping is nonetheless well suited wherever control of landscaping maintenance and water use is important. See Connie Ellefson, Thomas Stephens, and Douglas Welsh, *Xeriscape Gardening* (New York: Macmillan, 1992).

Part VII
Bibliography

Contract Negotiation and Formal Commitment

AIA Contract Documents. Washington, D.C: American Institute of Architects. Updated regularly.

Barstein, Fred, ed. *Bowker's Real Estate Law Locator, 1988.* New York: Bowker, 1988.

Becker, Mitchell W., and Robert F. Cushman. *Construction Industry Joint Venture Formbook.* New York: Wiley, 1992.

Culbertson, Alan N., and Donald E. Kenney. *Contract Administration Manual for the Design Professions: How to Establish, Systematize, and Monitor Construction Contract Controls.* New York: McGraw-Hill, 1983.

Currie, Overton A., Neal J. Sweeney, and Randall F. Hafer, eds. *Construction Subcontracting: A Legal Guide for Industry Professionals.* New York: Wiley, 1991. With 1996 supplement.

Cushman, Robert F., G. Christian Hedemann, and Peter J. King. *Construction Contractor's Handbook of Business and Law.* New York: Wiley, 1992.

Friedman, Milton R. *Contracts and Conveyances of Real Property.* 5th ed. New York: Practising Law Institute, 1991. With 1995 supplement.

Hagman, Donald G., and Julian C. Jürgensmeyer. *Urban Planning and Land Development Control Law: Practitioner's Edition.* 2d ed. St. Paul, Minn.: West Publishing Co., 1986.

Harris, Richard. *Construction and Development Financing: Law, Practice, Forms.* Vol. 1. Boston: Warren, Gorham & Lamont, 1987.

Holtzschue, Karl B. *Real Estate Contracts.* New York: Practising Law Institute, 1988.

Krol, John J. *Construction Contract Law.* New York: Wiley, 1993.

Levin, Paul. *Construction Contract Claims, Changes, and Dispute Resolution.* 2d ed. Reston, Va.: ASCE Press, 1998.

Living with Environmental Law. Boston: Massachusetts Continuing Legal Education, 1984.

O'Leary, Arthur F. *A Guide to Successful Construction: Effective Contract Administration.* Rev. ed. Anaheim, Calif.: BNI Building News, 1997.

Senn, Mark A., ed. *Negotiating Real Estate Transactions.* 2d ed. New York: Wiley, 1993. With 1997 cumulative supplement.

Stein, Steven G.M. *Construction Law.* New York: Matthew Bender & Co., 1995.

Stokes, McNeill. *Construction Law in Contractor's Language.* 2d ed. New York: McGraw-Hill, 1990.

Sweeney, Neal J., and Overton A. Currie. *1997 Wiley Construction Law Update.* New York: Wiley, 1997.

Sweet, Justin. *Legal Aspects of Architecture, Engineering, and the Construction Process.* 6th ed. Pacific Grove, Calif.: Brooks/Cole, 1999.

———. *Sweet on Construction Industry Contracts: Major AIA Documents.* 3d ed. Vol. 1 & 2. Gaithersburg, Md.: Aspen, 1996. With 1997 supplement.

Werner, Raymond J., and Robert Kratovil. *Real Estate Law.* 10th ed. Englewood Cliffs, N.J.: Prentice-Hall, 1992.

Wiley Law Publications. *Construction Industry Contracts: Legal Citator and Case Digest.* New York: Wiley, 1988. With 1994 supplement.

Construction, Completion, and Formal Opening

Albern, William F., and M.D. Morris. *Factory-Constructed Housing Developments: Planning, Design, and Construction.* Boca Raton, Fla.: CRC Press, 1997.

Alfeld, Louis Edward. *Construction Productivity: On-Site Measurement and Management.* New York: McGraw-Hill, 1988.

Allen, Edward. *Fundamentals of Building Construction: Materials and Methods.* 3d ed. New York: Wiley, 1999.

Bart, Jahn. *Residential Construction Problem Solver.* New York: McGraw-Hill, 1998.

Bernstein, Harvey M., and Andrew C. Lemer. *Solving the Innovation Puzzle: Challenges Facing the U.S. Design and Construction Industry.* New York: ASCE Press, 1996.

Birnberg, Howard G. *Project Management for Building Designers and Owners.* 2d ed. Boca Raton, Fla.: CRC Press, 1999.

Brock, Dan S. *Field Inspection Handbook: An On-the-Job Guide for Construction Inspectors, Contractors, Architects, and Engineers.* New York: McGraw-Hill, 1986.

Bynum, Richard T., and Daniel L. Rubino. *Handbook of Alternative Materials in Residential Construction.* New York: McGraw-Hill, 1999.

Chew, M.Y.L. *Construction Technology for Tall Buildings.* River Edge, N.J.: Singapore Univ. Press, 1999.

Cushman, Robert F. *Construction Change Order Claims.* New York: Wiley, 1994. With 1997 supplement.

Cushman, Robert F., and John P. Bigda. *The McGraw-Hill Construction Business Handbook.* 2d ed. New York: McGraw-Hill, 1985.

Cushman, Robert F., and Peter J. King. *Construction Owner's Handbook of Property Development.* New York: Wiley, 1992.

Cushman, Robert F., and P.J. Trimble, eds. *Construction Project Forms Book.* New York: Wiley, 1994.

Dietrich, Norman L. *Kerr's Cost Data for Landscape Construction, 1994.* 14th ed. New York: Van Nostrand Reinhold, 1994.

Dines, Nicholas T. *Time-Saver Standards: Site Construction Details Manual.* New York: McGraw-Hill, 1999.

Dodge Manual for Building Construction, Pricing, and Scheduling. New York: Dodge Building Cost Services, annual.

Ellefson, Connie, Thomas Stephens, and Douglas Welsh. *Xeriscape Gardening.* New York: Macmillan, 1992.

Fisk, Edward R. *Construction Project Administration.* 6th ed. Englewood Cliffs, N.J.: Prentice-Hall, 1999.

Harris, Cynthia M. *Dictionary of Building Construction.* New York: McGraw-Hill, 1992.

Harrison, Henry S. *Houses: The Illustrated Guide to Construction Design and Systems.* 3d ed. Chicago: Real Estate Education Co., 1998.

Hornbostel, Caleb. *Construction Material: Types, Uses, and Applications.* 2d ed. New York: Wiley, 1991.

Horowitz, Joseph. *Critical Path Scheduling: Management Control through CPM and PERT.* Melbourne, Fla.: Krieger Publishing, 1980.

Illston, John M. *Construction Materials: Their Nature and Behavior.* 2d ed. New York: Chapman & Hall, 1993.

Kerzner, Harold. *Project Management: A Systems Approach to Planning, Scheduling, and Controlling.* 6th ed. New York: Wiley, 1997.

Landphair, Harlow, and Fred Klatt, Jr. *Landscape Architecture Construction.* 3d ed. Englewood Cliffs, N.J.: Prentice-Hall, 1998.

Levitt, Raymond Elliott, and Nancy Morse Samelson. *Construction Safety Management.* 2d ed. New York: Wiley, 1993.

Levy, Sidney M. *Project Management in Construction.* 2d ed. New York: McGraw-Hill, 1994.

Loftus, Jack. *Project Management of Multiple Projects and Contracts.* London: Thomas Telford, 1999.

McMullen, Randall. *Dictionary of Building.* Pontiac, Mich.: G.P. Publishing, 1991.

Moder, Joseph J., Cecil R. Phillips, and Edward W. Davis. *Project Management with CPM, PERT, and PRECEDENCE Diagramming.* 3d ed. Middleton, Wis.: Blitz Publishing Co., 1995.

O'Brien, James J. *Construction Inspection Handbook: Total Quality Management.* New York: Chapman & Hall, 1997.

——. *Preconstruction Estimating: Budget through Bid.* New York: McGraw-Hill, 1994.

O'Brien, James J., and Frederic L. Plotnick. *CPM in Construction Management.* 5th ed. New York: McGraw-Hill, 1999.

Palmer, William J., William E. Coombs, and Mark A. Smith. *Construction Accounting and Financial Management.* 5th ed. New York: McGraw-Hill, 1995.

Palmer, William J., James M. Maloney, and John L. Heffron. *Construction Insurance, Bonding, and Risk Management.* New York: McGraw-Hill, 1996.

Peurifoy, R.L., William Burt Ledbetter, and Cliff J. Schexnayder. *Construction Planning, Equipment, and Methods.* 5th ed. New York: McGraw-Hill, 1996.

Rogers, Leon. *Basic Construction Management: The Superintendent's Job.* 4th ed. Washington, D.C.: Home Builder Press, 1999.

Rosen, Harold J. *Construction Specifications Writing: Principles and Procedures.* 4th ed. New York: Wiley, 1999.

R.S. Means Co. *Means Illustrated Construction Dictionary.* Kingston, Mass.: Author, 1991.

——. *Residential and Light Commercial Construction Standards.* Kingston, Mass.: Author, 1998.

——. *R.S. Means Residential Cost Data.* 16th annual ed. Kingston, Mass.: Author, 1996.

——. *Square Foot Costs: Residential, Commercial, Industrial, Institutional.* 20th annual ed. Kingston, Mass.: Author, 1998.

Rubenstein, Harvey M. *A Guide to Site Planning and Landscape Construction.* 4th ed. New York: Wiley, 1996.

Stitt, Fred A. *Construction Specifications Portable Handbook.* New York: McGraw-Hill, 1999.

Trauner, Theodore J., Jr. *Managing the Construction Project: A Practical Guide for the Project Manager.* New York: Wiley, 1992.

Trauner, Theodore J., Jr., and Michael H. Payne. *Bidding and Managing Government Construction.* Kingston, Mass.: R.S. Means Co., 1988.

Waier, Phillip R., and Thomas J. Atkins. *Building Construction Cost Data, 1999.* Kingston, Mass.: R.S. Means Co., 1999.

Woodward, John F. *Construction Project Management: Getting It Right the First Time.* London: T. Telford, 1997.

In the final stage of the development process, value takes on a different meaning from its earlier one. Value now comes from the long-term viability of a project, which is heavily dependent on the quality of ongoing management and marketing or sales. Although the developer initially provides value by matching an idea to a site and seeing the process of constructing an attractive, efficient building through, the asset and property managers must continue to increase the value that is already there through management of the project and its users.

At this point, the development team and the development—the product—are tested. Until now, there was no way to test the product the way other consumer goods are tested. There's no inexpensive way to go back and tweak the original design or start over because a test group doesn't like the product. That's why everything to this point must be done carefully and thoroughly. That care must continue into the final stage of the process, which eventually involves repositioning, renovation, and possibly even redevelopment.

Part VIII
Making It Work

Chapter 21

Stage Eight: Property, Asset, and Portfolio Management

Managing real estate assets, from the completion of development (or property acquisition) through its life cycle, including renovations and eventual disposition, is the responsibility of the property, asset, and portfolio managers—the real estate management triad. Although the functions of the management triad are interrelated and overlapping, they are collectively essential to maximizing the value of the real estate.

Property management focuses on the day-to-day operation of the asset. By maintaining a detailed understanding of the submarket where the asset competes (its situs), the property manager implements the strategic directives developed by the asset manager to satisfy the portfolio manager's objectives.

Asset management broadens the focus of property management beyond one physical facility and its tenants to several different properties that employ a variety of property managers. The asset manager manages the property managers, monitoring their performance and guiding them in developing strategic plans for their properties to maximize the assets' values—from the portfolio manager's perspective—within the submarkets where the properties are located.

Broader yet is real estate portfolio management. It includes understanding and directing the owner's investment objectives, evaluating the performance of the asset managers, deciding on the capital improvements recommended by the asset managers as necessary to maintain the asset's physical structure and competitive position, managing assets to maximize risk-adjusted portfolio returns, and orchestrating acquisitions and dispositions.

Early in this text, real estate development was defined as a process that ultimately takes an idea and transforms it into bricks and mortar. Once the development is complete, it is up to the management triad to deliver the future cash flows envisioned in the feasibility study and to maintain the structure so as to protect the project's long-run profitability. To accomplish this task, the real property management triad must focus on one key reality: customers ultimately create value; bricks and mortar are only tools to satisfy customers.

Asset management describes the process of adding value to existing real estate investments. In this context, real estate profits are created in three basic ways: buying extremely well (either from the developer or the owner of an existing property), operating a property to maximize the present value of cash flows over the holding period, and selling at the right time. Asset managers oversee all three activities on behalf of individual or institutional investors and, in effect, serve as de facto property owners.[1]

The triad should work together to add value. Sometimes a single individual may perform two (or even all three) of the asset management functions. Still, the three functions are distinct; therefore, it is instructive to cover stage eight by thinking of property, asset, and portfolio management as separate but inherently interrelated functions.

Throughout stages one through seven, we have emphasized the importance of anticipating stage eight of the real estate development process. In this chapter, we discuss in detail the following topics:

■ The enterprise concept espoused by James A. Graaskamp, which explores the concept of a building as a dynamic business—not just bricks and mortar—competing in an ever-changing market;

- A definition of the real property management triad and its increasing importance in real estate development;
- The fundamentals of real estate management from the perspective of development;
- The transition from property development to asset management and the development of a strategic plan for the asset;
- Management's role in implementing the strategic plan—the heart of this chapter;
- The influence of the public sector in the management of real estate projects;
- Intelligent buildings as a tool to enhance the effectiveness of property and asset management;
- Training for property, asset, and portfolio managers to ensure that the individuals responsible for the assets are properly prepared and capable; and
- The corporate real estate director.

The Enterprise Concept and Continuing Management of The Developed Asset

The enterprise concept, as originally espoused by James A. Graaskamp, portrays real estate as an enterprise and thus sets the stage for more aggressive management. Long considered one of the most innovative thinkers among real estate academicians, Graaskamp campaigned for years for a change from the concept of real estate as bricks and mortar to the concept of a building as an operating entity, that is, a living, breathing business with a cash flow cycle similar to any other operating business. He suggested that developers should expect a world in which buildings are like businesses. Businesses continually need to redefend their market positions and to seek new niches in the marketplace. From the standpoint of development, the enterprise concept means not only that marketing must be ongoing but also, in all probability, that the structure itself will have to change over time to meet new needs of the marketplace.

Since 1993, Graaskamp's concept has been gaining currency among the real estate community as it responds to the explosion of REITs. For example, Alex. Brown Realty Advisors (now part of Jones Lang LaSalle), in its October 1993 issue of *Real Estate Stocks Monitor,* proposed a REIT valuation model that prices REIT shares as an ongoing operating business rather than solely on the net asset value of real estate assets in the REIT, that is, as they would be priced in a typical private market portfolio. This approach to valuing a collection of properties as more than the sum of their parts under-

scores the importance of recognizing that most development projects will be part of an ongoing operating business rather than merely an independent collection of bricks and mortar.[2]

The notion of treating real estate assets as a business is important, because operating businesses must continually change to remain viable. IBM, for example, is a different company today from what it was ten years ago. Microsoft was barely a company 15 years ago. Although it is true that real estate projects have a long life and a fixed location, it is also important to note that the needs they serve vary over time. If real estate developers see that they are creating an ongoing business, not simply bricks and mortar, they will be more likely to incorporate into their projects the design flexibility needed for long-term operating success in a changing environment.

The enterprise concept is not new; it is just more important now than ever before. That is why the framework established earlier in this text focused on the extended venture capital period, level two feasibility, and a tighter tie to the business operations of prospective tenants. These aspects are all contemporary components of Graaskamp's enterprise concept.

An example of the enterprise concept in action is the Showplace Square development in San Francisco's South of Market (SoMa) District. The Showplace is a design mart where interior designers bring their upscale clients for a glass of wine and the opportunity to browse through hundreds of thousands of square feet of home furnishings, from pillows to furniture. The development originated in a cluster of abandoned industrial buildings when the initial developer, Henry Adams, saw the opportunity to use the space to satisfy a new need in the market. In the early 1980s, the SoMa neighborhood was a pioneering location; now it's a trendy market that's become known as Multimedia Gulch. For it to survive the twists and turns of the neighborhood, Showplace Square has required ongoing operations savvy. Bill Poland, the current developer, senses that the critical element for success in the ongoing development of this part of the city is viewing the real estate as an operating business. Satisfied tenants need customers and products, and, to draw customers and products, the developer promotes trade shows, frequently at a loss. To maximize profits and create a "sense of place," the developer has used the vast facilities for weddings and other social functions in the evenings and on weekends. Showplace Square is very much a business and thus requires extensive management. The real estate is central but is not the only element: quality basic services and creative management make the Showplace a successful business enterprise and hence a successful development.

Profile **James A. Graaskamp**

Former Chair and Professor, Department of Real Estate and Urban Land Economics
University of Wisconsin at Madison

The late Jim Graaskamp was a hero and mentor to his students and others who knew him. At the time of his death in 1988, the wheelchair-bound quadriplegic professor was the driving force behind the real estate program at the University of Wisconsin at Madison. Crippled by polio since his teens, Graaskamp, who turned lecture notes with a stick held in place with his teeth, viewed his handicap as a "materials-handling problem."

His disability, however, did not prevent him from earning a PhD in 1964, teaching real estate, encouraging new theories of real estate, and consulting through his Landmark Research company. Well-known for his articulate and spellbinding speeches, he was also often an outspoken critic—with many critics of his own—on national and local land use policies, often taking very unpopular positions.

Graaskamp understood that, in a world of change and uncertainty, determining a course of action is more important than merely pricing assets. Graaskamp was a visionary in the field of real estate with a strong system of ethics. He believed that the developer's profit should be the secondary motivation for a development project. For if a project fails, the negative consequences do not stop with the investor. In fact, Graaskamp wrote that a project should not be viewed as solvent if society has been shortchanged in its development. He conceptualized a real estate development process that would maximize the benefits not for just a few individuals, but for the greater society.

Feasibility analysis—the determination of what makes sense and why—was Graaskamp's major contribution to the real estate field. He developed methods for solving problems based on the tenet that, because the key characteristic of real estate is its location, most real estate problems are unique to the particular site. In response, he developed the microanalytical approach to real estate problem solving, in which the issues are defined in terms of the specific location, the individual developer, the micromarket, and other characteristics of the project.

According to Graaskamp, the real estate feasibility process should attempt to answer the following four questions:

1. *What is it that we are doing?* The three possibilities are a site in search of a user, a user in search of a site, or an investor seeking a development opportunity. If beginning with the site, the site's attributes should determine the project. Beginning with a user requires identifying a site that matches the user's requirements. When start-

ing with an investor, the investor's objectives are the crucial element.
2. *For whom are we doing it?* Realizing that development occurs for many reasons beyond simply maximizing the investor's income, Graaskamp believed that it is important to understand the individual developer's goals.
3. *To whom are we doing it?* This question addresses understanding the market to adapt the product to its needs.
4. *Will it fly?* More than just the narrow concern of "will it sell?" this question seeks to explore broader issues regarding the project's viability.

Graaskamp expanded upon the traditional concept of highest and best use with the more idealistic "most fitting use," in which the land use is measured by its optimization of consumer satisfaction, cost of production, impact on third parties, and, finally, profit to the investor. He also defined the more pragmatic "most probable use," described as less than the most fitting use but constrained by political factors, short-term solvency, and the state of real estate technology.

Although better known for the spoken word than for his writings, Graaskamp authored *The Fundamentals of Real Estate Development,* published by ULI in 1981. In addition, his life and work were the inspiration for ULI's 1991 book, *Graaskamp on Real Estate,* and James R. Delisle's 1994 book, *Appraisal, Market Analysis, and Public Policy in Real Estate: Essays in Honor of James A. Graaskamp.* Clearly, James A. Graaskamp was, and continues to be, an influential force in real estate thinking. ∎

Sources: **James A. Graaskamp,** *Fundamentals of Real Estate Development* **(Washington, D.C.: ULI—the Urban Land Institute, 1981); Stephen D. Jarchow, ed.,** *Graaskamp on Real Estate* **(Washington, D.C.: ULI—the Urban Land Institute, 1991); and Mike Miles and Mark Eppli, "The Graaskamp Legacy,"** *Real Estate Finance,* **Spring 1998, pp. 84–91.**

Figure 21-1

The Relationship among Property Managers, Asset Managers, and Portfolio Managers

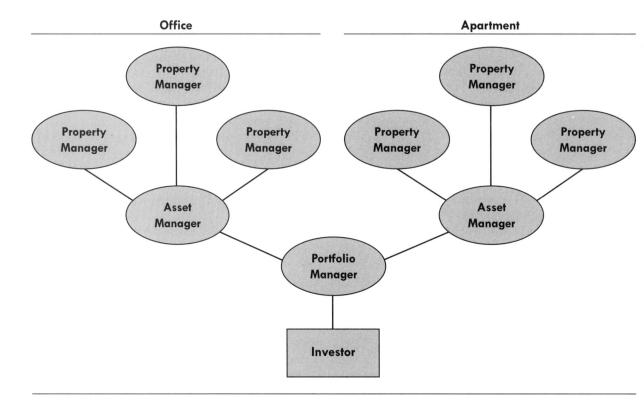

A more straightforward example is Chase Heritage in the Washington, D.C., metropolitan area. When originally developed by Trammell Crow Residential in 1986, Chase Heritage was a Class A residential apartment community that competed effectively in its submarket in the northern Virginia suburbs. Over time, however, new competitors such as Cascades, Saddle Ridge, and University Heights entered the submarket, presenting the developer with the problem of how to maximize the asset's value while simultaneously trying to compete effectively in the community's dynamic submarket in the Ballston corridor. The possible choices were to maintain the property in its existing condition and to compete with older properties with less favorable rental rates or to invest in the project (that is, update apartment color schemes, improve and replace apartment features that dated the community, and enhance the landscaping, common areas, and recreational facilities). The owner decided to make the investment. As of May 1994, the property was competing effectively (with respect to both rental rates and occupancy) with the newer rental apartment communities that have entered the submarket. By 1999, the Ballston corridor was becoming a minicity much like midtown Atlanta. As the submarket evolves, the project (now part of the Avalon-Bay REIT) must continue to evolve as a business where situs is critically important.

Developers are charged with planning and constructing space. If they do so with asset management in mind, the building will serve society's needs better over the long run, increasing the likelihood of profitable operation. Even if the developer is not a long-term owner, he must be concerned about long-term profitability. The developer's return frequently comes in the form of a fee plus some participation in the value created through the process of development. The creation of value results when the expected future benefits that will accrue to an investor exceed costs. And those long-term benefits are maximized when the property functions well after opening (stage seven) and is expected to continue to perform well over its long expected economic life (stage eight). The prospective future owners (investors) in the development are interested in how the constructed space and the management provided by the developer will perform over the long term, and they price the investment accordingly.

The Real Estate Management Triad

Against the backdrop of Graaskamp's enterprise concept, this section explores the roles of the real estate management triad. Although property management is at the heart of the traditional management function, asset and portfolio management have expanded the broad management function to include a much greater range of challenges in response to both changes in the economy and society's demands for constructed space. The roles of the property manager, asset manager, and portfolio manager are interrelated. In a small "portfolio," the same person may even play all three roles.

Figure 21-1 shows the relationships between and among property managers, asset managers, and the portfolio manager for a large real estate portfolio. Every portfolio is different, and the relative roles of the property managers, asset managers, and portfolio manager may expand or contract depending on the composition of the portfolio and the experience and capabilities of the professionals occupying the positions.

In this example, property managers are located on site and are the primary link with the rent-paying customer. (On-site property managers may also be known as site managers.) Their main role is to provide immediate service to the tenants and to protect the property's ongoing revenue and cash flow streams.

In contrast, asset managers are typically located off site and are usually responsible for several different properties. Asset managers may specialize by property type, geographic location, or both (such as office buildings in New York City or apartments in the Midwest). Even with such specialization, they have a broader perspective than the on-site property manager. The asset manager "manages" the property managers as the owner's (investor's) representative. More specifically, the asset manager hires, fires, and coordinates property managers as he monitors the properties' performance. He develops the strategic plans with input from the property managers, with an eye toward meeting the investor's objective for returns over the asset's holding period.

Because property managers often find it more lucrative to manage the best, most up-to-date properties (as they tend to have fewer problems), they are usually interested in spending money on upgrades. Asset managers serve property owners by making sure that recommended capital expenditures add more to value than they cost.

Finally, the portfolio manager defines and implements a portfolio investment strategy based on the goals and risk/return parameters of the investors in the portfolio of properties. The portfolio manager oversees acquisitions, asset management, dispositions, and reinvestment decisions as well as supervises cash management and reports to clients. In a large portfolio, the portfolio manager may strive to diversify the portfolio by property type or location to reduce the portfolio's overall risk exposure. (Part II discussed modern portfolio theory, offering significant detail through the evolving literature on real estate finance.) Figure 21-2 highlights the major responsibilities of the property manager, the asset manager, and the portfolio manager.

Figure 21-2

Major Responsibilities of the Management Triad

Property Manager
- Tenant relations and retention
- Rent collection
- Control of operating expenses
- Financial reporting and record keeping
- Maintenance of property
- Planning capital expenditures
- Crisis management
- Security issues
- Public relations

Asset Manager
- Development of property strategic plan
- Hold/sale analysis
- Review of opportunities to reposition properties and to provide justification for major expenditures
- Monitoring property performance
- Managing and evaluating the property manager by comparing property performance to peer properties in the particular submarket
- Assisting in tenant relations

Portfolio Manager
- Communicating with investors and setting portfolio goals and investment criteria
- Defining and implementing portfolio investment strategy
- Overseeing acquisitions, dispositions, asset management, and reinvestment decisions
- Accountable for portfolio performance
- Client reporting and cash management

Just as asset managers make sure that the capital expenditures recommended by property managers are a good investment, portfolio managers must coordinate with the various asset managers to balance cash needs across the entire portfolio. They must also decide when to sell a property. Asset and property managers may fall in love with their properties and not want to sell. Further, they might lose their jobs if the properties are sold to new investors who want to employ their own management team. Portfolio managers are judged on portfolios' performance and are thus far less likely to fall in love with individual properties.

By structuring all operations to maximize the value of investors' real estate portfolios, effective managers of real estate assets should reflect a willingness to respond to changing market needs and to accommodate investors' and owners' needs. The more active investment management of pension funds and the growth of REITs have brought about a heightened awareness of the need to manage clients' positions as well as their real property assets. Portfolio managers work with investors to determine both investment objectives and the types of properties that, in combination, satisfy those objectives.

The Fundamentals of Real Estate Management from the Perspective of Development

As indicated in Figure 21-2, the basic functions of property management include establishing a management plan, creating a budget tied to that plan, marketing and leasing space, collecting rent, monitoring and responding to tenant issues, maintaining accounting and operating records, directing and performing preventive and remedial building maintenance, supervising staff and contract personnel, addressing risk management –related issues, coordinating insurance, managing real and personal property tax valuations, and generally preserving the project's value day to day.

The management plan determines the ease with which many of the other property management functions can be performed. From the beginning, the management plan is based on an evaluation of the property's competitive position in the market and the owner's explicit needs. Therefore, the management plan must clearly identify the project's competitive position, and the details of the plan must be consistent with the property's ability to provide the space over time and associated services necessary to compete effectively in the market. If the services are inconsistent with the market's desires, the project is not likely to generate maximum net operating income over time. For example, providing services of no value to tenants increases expenses without a commensurate increase in lease rates. As a result, the property's value is not maximized. The management plan must be well documented to ensure that the needs and responsibilities of all those involved in operating the development are consistent.

From the developer's standpoint, the feasibility study provides the basic analyses needed to assess the strengths and weaknesses of the property as it serves its target market. The feasibility study also provides a detailed analysis of the competition and thus permits a particular property to be evaluated point by point compared with its competitors. During the development process, developers should use this comparison to identify cost-efficient changes in the initial development plan. Changes are justifiable if they make the property more competitive (higher rents) or more efficient to operate (lower costs) by an amount that more than offsets the incremental development costs.

Maintaining good tenant relations, collecting rent, paying the bills, re-leasing space, handling maintenance schedules, conserving energy, providing security, supervising personnel, and coordinating insurance are all critically important property management functions; anticipation of these tasks can help create a better development project. Security, for example, is a critical concern of many tenants, and initial design dramatically affects security. For example, the proper placement of exterior lights and of entranceways that are clearly visible from the street makes property management easier. Some older residential buildings in deteriorating central cities are nearly impossible to secure fully because of their mazes of hallways, sudden unlighted corners, and other features that could have been designed differently to provide for better and more cost effective operating management had the developer foreseen the need. Further, decisions made during the development process can seriously affect insurance. For instance, older buildings that lack modern sprinkler systems typically pay high insurance premiums.

As contracts are negotiated and executed and construction begins, property management becomes increasingly important. In stages four and five, the various participants' roles in the development process are formalized in executed contracts. Before contracts are signed, however, tenants specify the features, functions, and benefits they expect as part of ongoing property management. As part of the cost of the structure, contractors specify all the features they are committed to build. Property managers must determine that they will be able to provide the level of service tenants expect at the costs specified in the operating pro forma based on the structure designed by the architect and to be built by the contractor. Certainly the financial arrangements (debt and equity) must be capable of funding the structural features necessary for adequate property management. Thus, even in stages four and five, all players are concerned about effective property management.

During construction (stage six), the remaining space is leased, the loan drawn down, the structure built, and, in the case of commercial buildings, changes made to accommodate future tenants' needs. Property management is a consideration when any changes are contemplated. Although tenants may want a certain feature, the developer must estimate the initial cost and any increment in ongoing operating expenses to determine whether the change is logical in terms of prospective tenants' and investors' long-term needs.

Consider, for example, the review of a prospective lease between the operator of movie theaters and the owner of a mall under development. Normally, such an operation would be freestanding or have its own entrance. In this instance, however, a movie theater was not originally envisioned as part of the mall, and no separate entrance or remaining outparcel is available. The leasing agent, however, has considerable interior space that must be leased and thus pushes for the movie theater to be inside the mall. The construction manager favors the change, because one tenant with one set of operating systems (lighting and so on) would take a major portion of the remaining space. The architect revises pedestrian flow through the mall to determine whether other stores would benefit from the presence of theater patrons. Should the developer approve the arrangement?

Not necessarily. The property manager reviews the revised leasing plan and points out related problems. Not only will janitorial costs escalate, but nighttime security will also become a major problem because the theater will be open well after other stores close. The costs incurred to solve these problems exceed the difference between the rent the theaters would pay and the lower rent expected from the next-highest-paying prospective tenant. Quickly considering the discounted cash flow model introduced in Chapter 5 and detailed in the feasibility study, the developer understands that the movie theater, at this stage of this project, will not "create value." When the developer carefully evaluates all the longer-term issues, particularly operating management, the highest "present value" development results. The feasibility study is now a tool for sensitivity analysis, with costs as the critical variable.

During stage seven of the development process, the property management team shifts from an advisory role to an operating role. At that time, the management plan must be formalized so that when the management team takes over at the close of stage seven, a plan is available that matches the asset's position in the marketplace as it has evolved during the construction period to the investor's needs, which may also have evolved during the construction period. The developer is responsible for ensuring that the initial management plan is established and implemented.

In establishing the initial management plan, developers must consider the image conveyed by the physical structure initially and over time. Clearly, project architecture makes a statement about the property. For better or worse, this statement is conveyed by the end of stage seven. Accordingly, the management plan cannot ignore the marketplace's initial perception of the structure. New colors and innovative promotions can alter the initial impression, but the basic design remains a major factor in determining what is operationally possible.

Closely related to end users' initial perception is the issue of continuing maintenance. A building designed to standards for residential construction should not be maintained like a commercial building. A heavy volume of foot traffic, for example, can quickly wear down a structure that has been built to residential standards, regardless of the intensity of property management. In contrast, a structure built to more demanding standards allows greater flexibility in terms of the volume of foot traffic and the intensity of property management. But designing flexibility into a project usually costs something —either in construction dollars or operating efficiency— and this tradeoff requires the developer's consideration.

Site maintenance is another area that can be significantly affected by the various decisions made during the design and development process. It not only involves the daily maintenance of the project, but also considers the ongoing preventive and nonroutine maintenance necessary to ensure preservation of the value of the real estate asset throughout its useful life. Design and development decisions that do not consider both daily and long-term site maintenance are likely to generate additional operating expenses that will reduce the asset's net operating income. It is therefore critical that all aspects of project maintenance be considered and that the property management personnel be involved to ensure that daily operating issues are properly evaluated.

If, for instance, clear light fixtures are installed in the common areas in a manner that causes the fixtures to collect dirt, they will require more frequent cleaning; as a result, housekeeping costs will rise. If the landscaping plan calls for excessive seasonal plants or time-consuming maintenance, the costs associated with either in-house or contract landscaping will necessarily increase. If in an apartment community the proper utility cutoffs necessary to isolate a single unit are not installed, then it will be difficult and time-consuming to perform normal maintenance. In addition, emergency repairs may be delayed and result in damage to other apartments and inconvenience to residents. Similarly, installation of a single, double-wide parking garage door instead of two single-wide doors may inhibit not only the maintenance of the doors but also ingress and egress in the event repairs are needed.

Some of these examples may lead to significant increases in operating costs if the development team makes the wrong decisions. The examples are, however, only a few of the many areas that may alter the costs associated with on-site maintenance. Actual experience in property management is invaluable when attempting to identify decisions that may have an unfavorable effect on operating expenses. It is therefore critical to consider these issues throughout the design and development process and to involve the property management personnel in the process as early as possible.

The Transition from Property Development to Property Management

The graph in Figure 21-3 depicts the stages in the life of a real estate project. The first stage—the subject of most of this text—is the development period. As the shortest period in the life of a real estate project, the development period for some small industrial or residential projects may last less than one year from project conception to completion and opening. On the other hand, the development period for large mixed-use projects or planned unit developments may span years. According to a development project's pro forma, the income and value of the project would be expected to grow as space is leased to tenants, because the risk of vacancy is decreased (unless, of course, the space is leased at lower rents than anticipated).

When the project is physically complete and the building's occupancy has attained its fair share of the market, the project is considered to be "stabilized." The length of the period to stabilize varies by property type, market conditions, and the quality of the asset and its management. The Empire State Building, for example, took nearly a decade to reach stabilization but has now been operating in a stabilized mode for about 60 years. In contrast, some poorly conceived and constructed projects go into decline the moment they are completed; that is, they never attain stabilization. When a project reaches stabilization, it typically becomes fully the responsibility of property and asset man-

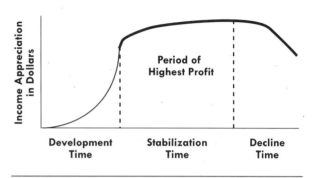

Figure 21-3

Real Estate Project Life Cycle

agers. Until that time, the developer remains very active working with the management group as part of the development team.

The developer's profit is calculated at the end of the development period as the difference between the developer's total cost and the project's market value. The market value can be either the sale price to the new owner or a market-derived figure for the value of the project if the developer retains ownership of the project. Slow lease-up (a long period to stabilization) increases costs (prestabilization operating losses) and may reduce value at stabilization; that is, lower-quality tenants than anticipated must be signed or prospective rents lowered.

The end of the development period is the day of reckoning for the developer. Did the developer create value or not? If so, how much? If not, why not?

Development companies are often capital-constrained and desire to recover their capital and profit from a project as early as possible. Thus, level two feasibility is a vital concern. From the developer's perspective, maximizing development period profit means keeping construction costs as low as possible for the product type constructed and then completing the project as quickly as possible to minimize the opportunity cost of capital.

The asset manager is as interested in the value of the completed project as the developer. Why? Although the value upon completion of construction determines the profit and potential incentive compensation for the developer, it also provides the baseline for measuring the performance of the property and asset managers in the future. After all, it is their charge to "add" value to the real estate. To the extent that the developer is credited with creating value in excess of what the property is truly worth, the property, asset, and portfolio managers will be starting their job from a deficit position, an unhappy predicament for them. As a result, even if the property is simply transferred from one group within a real estate company to another (from development to asset management), it is still incumbent upon the asset manager to sign off on the value of the property as if it were involved in a sale.

Handing Off the Project to Asset Management

At the time the project is sold or transferred to the asset manager, the transition is accompanied by a "transfer package" that clearly establishes the benchmark for measuring management's future performance. The documents in the transfer package vary with the size and complexity of the project but might include:

- A brief narrative describing the status of the project at transfer and any major outstanding issues. All significant construction-related documents should be incorporated into the report (including "as-built" drawings and certificates of occupancy).
- A comparison of actual results with pro forma results. All significant variances, both positive and negative, should be explained. Categories would include the construction budget by line item, the length of the development period, the status of leasing and rental rates, and net operating income and cash flow generated during the development period.
- The value of the project and assumptions used to arrive at that value (discount rate, capitalization rate, rental growth rate, vacancy rate, and so on).
- The total cost of development and any outstanding items that remain to be completed.
- The calculation of the profit created by the developer.

In an ideal world, the handoff from the developer to the management team would be simple. The asset and property managers have tracked the project during its development period and have had the opportunity to provide input into project design and the marketing strategy; as a result, there are no surprises at project completion. In reality, however, a project rarely follows its pro forma exactly during the development period. The reasons are many and may range from increases in project scope to changing market conditions. The transfer package is thus a mechanism that enables all parties involved in the throes of a development project to take a step back and objectively measure where the project stands in the marketplace. As such, the transfer package is the first step in developing the initial strategic management plan for the property.

Developing a Strategic Plan For the Property

Let us revisit the graph of a real estate project's life cycle (Figure 21-3) and consider two projects during the development period: one that performed significantly worse than its pro forma and one that performed significantly better than its pro forma. If, in a project's initial stage of life, the project were stunted or experienced unusually prolific growth, what does the experience of the development period portend for the future? Where will the project stabilize? What can the asset manager do about it?

Let's first consider the case in which a project performed significantly worse than its pro forma during the development period (see Figure 21-4). Unfortunately, in the mid- to late 1980s, many projects fit into this category, as a burst of new construction activity rapidly increased the supply of space in many markets and simultaneously caused a fall in effective rents, substantially lowering the expected net income of new projects. The Europa Center exemplifies a property that fell short of its pro forma, owing to dramatic changes in market conditions. But changing market conditions are only one reason a project falls short in the development period. Poor project design, an incorrect reading of users' requirements, an inaccessible location, or poor construction management can also cause a project to miss the mark. At this stage, the challenge for the asset manager is to determine whether there is a way to reestablish the project on the originally an-

Figure 21-4

Variations in Real Estate Project Life Cycle

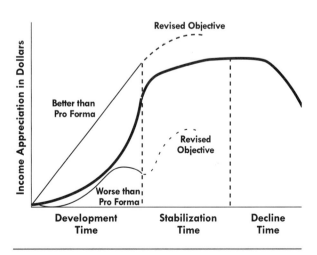

ticipated growth curve or to revise expectations downward in light of current market realities.

Ironically, a project that performs better than its pro forma during the development period can also present problems for an asset manager. Consider an apartment development program created by the Prudential Insurance Company's PRISA II commingled pension fund real estate account in conjunction with several leading, high-quality apartment developers such as Trammell Crow Residential. As background, it is important to recall that the 1986 Tax Reform Act eliminated the tax benefits of syndicators and abruptly ended the extreme overbuilding of apartments. Nationwide, construction of multifamily units dropped by 75 percent from 1985 to 1992. At the same time, the real estate credit crunch that accompanied the restructuring of the banking and savings and loan industries translated into little demand among traditional lenders for financing new apartment construction, even in those markets where demand for high-quality apartments outstripped supply.

PRISA II responded to this inefficiency in the capital markets by developing a program to purchase to-be-built apartment communities in exchange for a financial return higher than what would be available from acquiring a top-quality existing apartment community at market prices. PRISA II's projects would be constructed in such locations as Princeton, New Jersey, Phoenix and Tucson, Arizona, Salt Lake City, Utah, and Albuquerque, New Mexico. As the demand for high-quality apartments exceeds supply in those markets (in 1994, occupancy levels were running 97 to 99 percent), the initial lease-up and rental growth exceeds the pro forma on all these projects during the development period. Not surprisingly, the asset manager questions whether this growth can be sustained over the long run. Are regulatory controls in the local markets sufficient to prevent a repeat of the apartment overbuilding of the early 1980s? Or is it more probable that once the capital markets reach a new equilibrium, apartment construction will relapse to the boom-and-bust cycle historically typical of real estate?

Figure 21-5 summarizes the major elements of the real estate strategic planning process, with the concept of property life cycle as background. Using such tools as the transfer package, the asset manager must define the opportunities and problems facing a property. This situational analysis is not performed in a vacuum. In fact, in compiling the necessary information, property and asset managers should seek out a wide variety of local experts and written reports. The next step is to evaluate the existing objectives (stated or implied) for the property and to revise them based on current information. In short, is the developer's concept for the

Figure 21-5

Property Strategic Planning Process

Define and Analyze Property Problems And Opportunities
- Physical description of property
- Operating history
- Market conditions
- Property strengths and weaknesses compared with competition

Evaluate and Revise Objectives Based On Current Information
- Local market/competition
- Investor needs
- Tenant requirements
- Portfolio and other considerations

Consider Alternatives and Generate a Plan to Meet Objectives
- Review major decision points
  - Hold or sell?
  - Rehabilitate?
  - Change the use of the building?
  - Change the tenant mix?
  - Change the manager/leasing agent?
- Create a new pro forma for the property based on the plan

Implement the Plan
- Staffing
- Marketing program
- Operating budget
- Capital program

property still valid or does it need to be recast? Variables that precipitate a revision of the original objectives might include changes in local market competition, tenant requirements, or portfolio considerations (investors' needs).

Once the property's situational analysis is performed in context with the revised objectives, the asset and portfolio managers are then in a position to examine the various possible alternatives for the property's future. The real estate management team must agree on the preferred direction for the property as reflected in a new pro forma. The pro forma provides a picture of the property that, in effect, is painted with numbers and serves as a guide to the property and integrates all the major factors that shape a property's future. Even though the numbers in the pro forma are at best only educated guesses, they still play a central role in providing a road map for where the asset managers would like to take the property. In the absence of a clear, articulated vision, the property will be subject to the arbitrary whims of the marketplace and is unlikely to meet its full potential.

In the case of newly constructed apartments in Phoenix that were leasing at a rate in excess of the pro forma rate, for example, the best choice for maximizing the owner's return over the short run might be to sell the property while investors' interest in apartments in the Southwest remains high. On the other hand, in the case of a slow-to-lease office building designed for large corporate tenants, the asset and portfolio managers may decide to redirect the leasing strategy by pursuing smaller local firms that may represent a higher credit risk but offer better long-term opportunities for growth. Each case demands a pro forma that logically and consistently supports the property's strategic direction.

Management's Role in Implementing the Strategic Plan

Once the plan has been agreed upon, the next step is implementation. For the plan to be credible, the resources devoted to implementation must be commensurate with the goal in mind. If an office building is only 15 percent occupied at the end of the development period, for example, and the goal is to reach 80 percent occupancy within a year, a fully staffed leasing team consisting of aggressive agents armed with a full complement of marketing tools will probably be required. The four main elements in the implementation of a strategic plan are 1) staffing, 2) the marketing program, 3) the operating budget, and 4) the capital program.

Staffing

As discussed in the section on the enterprise concept, commercial real estate is at its core a service business and, unless the staff at a property is properly trained and fully understands the objectives for the property, it is unlikely to manage the property satisfactorily. The appropriate quantity and quality of staff at a property must be continually evaluated. The marketing, operating, and capital budget components of strategic plan implementation are then reviewed again with the staff that will operate the property.

The Marketing Program

The marketing program—designed both to attract new customers and to retain existing customers—is critical in implementing a property's strategy. It involves not only personnel but also advertising, promotional events, commission schedules, and other factors explored further in Chapter 22.

Ongoing marketing and leasing beyond initial occupancy are typically the responsibility of the property manager. For a small multifamily project, ongoing marketing might involve little more than showing available apartments to prospective tenants. For larger multifamily assets, marketing might include the creation of collateral materials, the development of effective property signs, the negotiation of contracts with prospect referral firms, the development and placement of advertising copy, the coordination of cooperative advertising with local businesses to attract customers similar to those residing at the community, and the creation of corporate outreach programs targeted to areas that have traditionally provided residents for the community. In these instances, it is critical that the property management firm demonstrate its ability to track both the source and quality of the prospects generated from its marketing efforts.

For example, if during the course of a year the $15,000 spent on advertising in the *Washington Post* generates 23 leases, the advertising cost per lease is approximately $652. Likewise, if the $6,800 spent annually on advertising in the *Apartment Shopper's Guide* generates an average of 32 leases, the cost per lease for this method of advertising is approximately $213. Such information is critical in attempting to ensure that marketing dollars are spent as effectively as possible. The developer must carefully consider advertising strategies when identifying the property management firm best able to maximize the project's value.

For larger commercial projects, ongoing marketing can be more complex, and the property manager might cooperate with outside brokerage firms to achieve objectives of leasing. In a major office building, for example, property managers would be responsible for advertising, showing the property, approving all final leases, and possibly leasing some of the space themselves. Outside brokerage firms might develop prospects, handle negotiations, show the property, and review prospective leases.

Regardless of the size of the property and who handles the ongoing marketing, rental concessions and tenant allowances (which were extremely important in the initial construction budget) must be included in the operating budget as well as in the pro forma to allow for an evaluation of long-term investment returns. Initial valuations of properties often include rent adjustments for inflation and improving marketplaces, but it is a major error not to include the tenant allowances and/or rent concessions necessary to attract tenants during the transition period. Developers are always concerned with making sure that value exceeds cost, and value is a function of projected cash flow. Accurately projected cash flows must therefore include all ongoing costs of marketing the space, including brokerage commissions, rental concessions, and tenant allowances. In other words, from the feasibility study to the operating budget, the bottom line should be effective rents, not the higher asking rents.

The Operating Budget

Once the property's place in the market is matched to the owner's needs, the management team develops a management plan that is converted to dollars to create a budget. The operating budget is typically based on the first year of the new pro forma, which is spelled out in greater detail than subsequent years. From the developer's perspective, the budget is identical to the top portion of the pro forma income statement used in the feasibility study. From the property manager's standpoint, the property is expected to provide the cash flow projected by the pro forma (assuming the budget is met). Thus, projections of net operating income are derived from projected gross revenues, projected vacancies, and projected expenditures for real estate taxes, fire and extended insurance coverage, payroll, marketing, utilities, maintenance, management, replacements, and other expenses. Adjustments for debt service and income taxes after net operating income are not traditional concerns of property management and therefore are not necessarily included in the property manager's operating budget.

The process of creating a budget for the property is time-consuming, tedious, and extremely important. Each revenue and expense line item from the property's chart of accounts must be carefully considered and detailed to ensure that all potential revenues and expenses are accurately recognized. Overstating revenues and/or understating expenses can result in financial projections that are overly optimistic; understating revenues and/or overstating expenses can result in financial projections that are overly pessimistic. In either case, the developer will be misinformed and will likely make inappropriate investment decisions.

Optimistic projections of net operating income may result in the development of projects that cannot succeed financially. Many of the real estate assets that failed during the 1980s were derived from financial pro formas that contained overly optimistic and unrealistic assumptions. Revenues were shown to increase at rates that, while achieved in the past, could not be substantiated by the market conditions projected for the future. Similarly, likely expenses were not properly recognized. The result was the development of assets that could not produce the income required to satisfy their financial obligations. These developments severely hampered, and sometimes even curtailed, the operations of historically successful companies. Likewise, projections of net operating income that are overly conservative because of ill-conceived or inaccurate revenue and expense projections may cause the developer to forgo profitable development opportunities.

The importance of creating a realistic and accurate operating budget cannot be overemphasized. The potential ramifications of overstating or understating net operating income for the project are severe. The most effective method for ensuring that errors are not incorporated into the development's operating budget is to require:

- Asset and property managers to be involved as early as possible in the development process. Asset and property managers are the individuals who are most knowledgeable of the costs and complications of managing a stabilized project. They are also the individuals most capable of generating realistic operating pro formas.
- The development of detailed assumptions that describe each line item in the operating budget. By generating detailed assumptions, all individuals who assess the financial feasibility of the development will be able to comment on the logic of the financial projections and to ensure that the assumptions are internally consistent (e.g., if 50 percent of the apartments in a residential apartment community are expected to turn over annually and be leased to new residents at higher rental rates, then the associated apartment turnover costs must be included in the operating expenses).
- The actual operating results of similar development projects in similar locations, to be used as the basis for the creation of the pro forma financials. Many line items in the operating budget cannot be accurately projected without operating experience. New developments obviously lack a history on which to base projections. Therefore, compelling evidence and logic are a prerequisite to any deviation from actual historical operating results associated with similar projects.

After a thoughtful budget has been created from the management plan, an examination of the details of the operating budget early in the development process can allow the developer to make necessary adjustments to the project to avoid serious errors. For example, some highly decorative floors in shopping centers are visually appealing but difficult to maintain. Likewise, certain types of lighting are attractive but require replacement more frequently than other types. During the development process, developers must trade off the marketing appeal of certain design features against long-term operating costs.

Although industry averages are a reasonable starting point in considering the feasibility of development projects, what counts in the final analysis is the cost of building and operating a particular property relative to what the market will pay for the features, functions, and benefits provided by that property. An accurate budget is critical to providing the developer with the information necessary to make informed decisions. In fact, the developer's role goes beyond the initial tradeoff between direct costs and revenues to more subtle questions related to longer-term property management. All decisions, including long-term management considerations, should be based on the present value of the expected revenues and expenses.

The Capital Program

The initial capital program often receives little attention, especially in the case of a new project, which ideally should need few additional capital expenditures. In practice, however, most projects—even well-conceived new projects—require some additional capital investment either to remedy construction or design deficiencies not covered by warranties (such as inadequate drainage in a parking lot) or to meet expanded tenant requirements (such as demand for additional carports or garages in an apartment project). From the perspective of the property's life cycle, it is important to note that the upkeep of a commercial real estate building and its basic components is predictable (in the same way that a maintenance program for a new car is predictable). Accordingly, a ten-year schedule of capital expenditures should be created at the time a property is acquired.

Figure 21-6 is a graph of the repair and replacement schedule for three major components of an office property—the roof, the cooling tower, and the elevators. These capital projects would be considered base building maintenance. Other projects involve tenant improvements related to re-leasing space as the initial terms of tenants' leases roll over. Additional capital expenditures may arise as a result of changes in government regulations or market requirements. Life safety improvements, new security systems, asbestos removal, energy management programs, and retrofits to provide im-

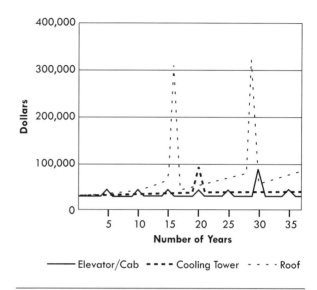

Figure 21-6

Long-Term Capital Budget Program

proved access for the disabled are all examples of programs that have emerged in recent years but were not originally incorporated into developers' pro formas. Although property and asset managers must be careful not to overimprove a facility and drain a property's cash flow through excessive capital expenditures, a property must be maintained at the market standard if it is to have an extended useful life. Further, scheduled preventive maintenance projects are usually less costly and less disruptive to tenants over the long run than crisis-driven emergency repairs.

The Ongoing Planning Process

Dwight D. Eisenhower once said, "Plans are useless, but planning indispensable." That statement is particularly appropriate for real estate strategic plans. In many cases, as a result of changes in market conditions and tenants' requirements, a property strategic plan may become obsolete a short time after it is prepared. Property strategic plans should be reviewed at least annually and more frequently if circumstances dictate. Ideally, asset and portfolio managers should look at the property with fresh eyes each year and ask themselves, "If we didn't already own this asset, would we acquire it again today? If not, why not?" By forcing the property to be "reacquired" each year, the asset manager invigorates the planning process and sloughs off the inertia so often endemic to the property management business.

The Property Management Contract

A property management contract provides a framework for the relationship between the property manager and the owner. It specifies which management services will be paid for by the owner and which by the property management firm. It determines who pays employees, who can authorize certain expenditures, who is responsible for keeping certain records, who is responsible for maintaining insurance coverage, who handles advertising and promotion, and how much the property manager is paid. The budget quantifies the management plan and ensures that the interests of owners and tenants are expressed consistently. Just as they must be alert to general contractors' bids that do not include all essential cost items, developers must also scrutinize management plans and budgets to ensure they do not promise services that cannot be delivered for the fee quoted. Only when the capabilities of the property management firms are thoroughly scrutinized and the management contract negotiated and committed to paper can developers be certain that a qualified person is ready to perform all specified services at the price quoted.

Unless a building is designed for a single tenant who will both own and use the facility, developers are typically responsible for hiring the first property manager. (Portfolio managers are usually brought on later by the long-term owner.) Many developers have subsidiary companies that perform the service; others hire independent property managers. The length of the management contract varies depending on the prospective owner's desires and the nature of the project. The more the property management firm engages in initial marketing and other operations that exceed basic property management requirements, the more likely it is that the contract will cover a long period. A performance contingency in longer-term contracts often allows the owner to replace the manager should the property not perform according to budget or to some agreed-upon percent of the budget. Figure 21-7 depicts the elements of a standard management agreement.

Figure 21-7

A Standard Management Agreement

Article 1	Properties
Article 2	Commencement Date
Article 3	Manager's Responsibilities
Article 4	Insurance
Article 5	Financial Reporting and Record Keeping
Article 6	Owner's Right to Audit
Article 7	Bank Account
Article 8	Payment of Expenses
Article 9	Insufficient Gross Income
Article 10	Sale of a Property
Article 11	Cooperation
Article 12	Compensation
Article 13	Termination
Article 14	Subsidiaries and Affiliates
Article 15	Notices
Article 16	Nonassignables, etc.

Schedules

A	Property Identification, Compensation Schedule, and Leasing Commission
B	Leasing Guidelines
C	Monthly Report Forms
C-1	Chart of Accounts
D	Reimbursable Employees
E	Subsidiaries and Affiliates
F	Insurance Certificate

The Influence of the Public Sector in the Management of Real Estate Projects

As discussed continually throughout this book, the public sector plays an active role in development because of the people-intensive nature of the product. Stage eight is no exception; the enactment of new legislation and promulgation of new regulations obviously demand compliance. Properties and buildings not only provide space for tenants, but also offer employment opportunities for a significant number of people. In its efforts to ensure that all individuals are treated fairly and that the environment is preserved for the long term, the public sector frequently enacts "rules" that apply to real estate assets. These rules often affect the ongoing operating expenses of the project, requiring modifications to existing structures or generating liabilities that the owner, property manager, asset manager, and portfolio manager must be prepared to address.

The real estate industry actively attempts to ensure that new legislation and regulations achieve the desired public purpose without creating undue hardships for the owners of real estate assets. Industry groups such as the National Multi Housing Council, the National Apartment Association, the National Realty Committee, and the Urban Land Institute make sure that all interested parties understand the ramifications of the various rules adopted by the public sector. Legislation that appears to target a specific public purpose frequently creates unintended burdens that are less than desirable.

Two recent pieces of federal legislation—the Americans with Disabilities Act (ADA) and Title IV of the Clean Air Act of 1990—have had an immediate effect on both the methods and costs associated with managing real estate projects. In its most general sense, the ADA prohibits discrimination against disabled persons with respect to employment, public services, and public accommodations and services operated by private businesses. Its intent is to provide persons with disabilities with accommodations and access equal to, or similar to, those available to the general public (see Figure 21-8). Title IV of the Clean Air Act of 1990 addresses protection of atmospheric ozone and mandates the recycling, production phaseout, and elimination of ozone-depleting compounds during the next 30-plus years. In addition, as of July 1992, the act prohibits the release of chlorofluorocarbons (CFCs) into the atmosphere during the maintenance, servicing, and disposal of refrigeration equipment.

Although both these acts address critical issues that face society, they also create costs for the development process and the subsequent ongoing operation of real estate projects. New developments are required to include costly equipment, while existing projects must undertake retrofit and maintenance activities to ensure compliance with the new guidelines. Expanded training is necessary for both management and maintenance personnel, as even innocent noncompliance may result in costly fines.

The impact of the public sector on the planning, design, feasibility analysis, and operation of real estate projects is evident and reinforces the importance of the involvement of both the asset manager and the property manager throughout the development process. The asset and property managers, like other members of the development team, should interact regularly with the public sector during the development process, setting up the vital working relationship that will (of necessity) exist during stage eight.

Intelligent Buildings

Although the smart house with robots and electronic voices that was projected early in the computer age has

Figure 21-8

The Americans with Disabilities Act

The Americans with Disabilities Act was signed by President George H. W. Bush in July 1990. Its objective is to provide persons with disabilities with access equal to, or similar to, that available to the general public. Title III affects places of public accommodation, including commercial real estate. The law also affects alterations to existing properties subsequent to January 26, 1992. Residential real estate is excluded from the ADA as it is already covered by the Fair Housing Act of 1988. Significantly, the ADA is civil rights legislation—not a building code.

The law is administered and enforced by the U.S. Department of Justice. Congress incorporated a provision into the ADA stating that "good faith efforts" and "attempts to comply" should be considered in enforcing this law. The Department of Justice has identified a compliance plan as a "good faith effort" when accompanied by constructive actions. Priorities in a compliance plan include entryways, routes from entryways to public places, restrooms, and public facilities such as telephones and drinking fountains. The cost of complying varies significantly from property to property, depending on specific building conditions and original project design. For additional insights into ADA compliance, see "ADA Compliance Guidebook," published by the Building Owners and Managers Association International. ∎

not yet become the norm, in just a short time building systems and controls have become dependent on increasingly sophisticated integrated electronic systems. From computer-aided design programs to security systems, almost every aspect of the development of a project is affected by new technology.

Intelligent buildings "combine two previously separate sets of technologies through an information network: . . . the building management technologies (building automation), [which] control such systems as heating and air conditioning, and the information technologies (office automation), which control communications operations."[3]

From a developer's perspective, intelligent buildings offer high-tech features whose costs must be included in the feasibility study. Potential benefits come from both additional revenues generated by the automated technologies billed to tenants and from reduced operating expenses generated by cost savings from the building's technologies.

An intelligent building combines appropriate high-tech features and innovative design. Accordingly, architects and electronic technology experts must work together with market analysts to achieve maximum benefit. The overall impact on tenant operations is the central consideration. High-tech features and high-tech design are useful only when they provide benefits that the users of the space will pay for; high-tech features should not be included simply because they are innovative, creative, or available. Redundant fiber optics are essential for a few tenants, but for a greater cost than most tenants will pay for.

The long-term impetus toward intelligent buildings is clear. As we become an information society and try to maintain global competitiveness, we must increase office productivity. Automation increases general office productivity through the use of word processors, electronic mail, facsimile modems, and electronic filing systems. At the same time, most of these devices require some changes in building design and technology —more space, more electrical circuits, greater cooling capacity, and so on. The truly smart building facilitates the adoption of innovations and provides flexibility over the long term.

Smart technology enhances a building's security by allowing the use of computer-controlled access cards and keys for the building and elevators. Motion detectors can be installed in common areas to trigger a video monitoring system. In some new multifamily facilities, a visitor can access the building by highlighting a resident's name on a computer screen. The computer then notifies the resident, who can view the visitor on a closed-circuit screen before permitting entry. Fire detection systems can now be operated by a micro-processor chip that runs on a computerized network, requiring much less wiring than a centrally controlled system. Safety systems can now instruct all elevators to go to the first floor and stay there in the event of a fire. Overall operation of elevators is now potentially more efficient, if planned appropriately.

Among the potential cost savings offered by an intelligent building is the increased monitoring sophistication of HVAC systems. The addition of personal computers and other electronic equipment often causes a building's temperature to rise. An automated system responds to temperature changes to avoid costly overheating of computer equipment without unduly cooling other parts of a building. Energy efficiency is also increased through simple occupancy sensors that turn off lights when employees are out of their offices for longer than 20 or 30 minutes.

These changes affect developers in that they need to plan for flexibility, networking within a building, networking with other locations, and monitoring overall building performance while allowing individuals in multitenant buildings to monitor their own space. Admittedly, these benefits are achieved at a certain cost. For any particular market, developers must decide how intelligent to make a building.

Offering tenants the opportunity to share such services is a possibility property managers should consider to reap additional profits. If the target market is a variety of smaller users, jointly provided information services—from telecommunications to client/server computing—might be more efficiently provided for all tenants through a central facility. If so, the building might have an additional profit center—additional profit for the developer who seizes the opportunity.

Office buildings built to a specific tenant's needs have been the most successful intelligent buildings, but such an approach is not always possible. For Europa Center, Fraser Morrow Daniels compromised in favor of maximum flexibility by providing the necessary wiring conduits but not the high-tech communications systems, because tenants would not pay for such services. Still, future installation is feasible at reasonable cost. In Museum Towers, Dean Stratouly installed four high-speed telecommunications lines and a broadband cable-ready outlet in every apartment.

191 Peachtree Street in downtown Atlanta uses computer-based environmental controls for its HVAC and life safety systems. Access to the 50-story, 1.2 million-square-foot tower is monitored and controlled by advanced electronic systems.

Training Property, Asset, and Portfolio Managers

The capabilities of the management triad must be of primary concern to the developer. During implementation of the management plan, capable management is critical to achieving the results specified in the operating budget. Only well-trained personnel can succeed in the competitive and complex marketplace. Management personnel need certain functions and skills.

Property Managers

Property managers and on-site property personnel have long had an erratic professional reputation, yet they are integral to the successful performance of the development project. Typically, large commercial buildings have employed engineers as property managers, while individuals with less training (who are often the secondary wage earners in a family) have frequently managed multifamily housing. These property managers are often responsible for assets that generate considerable revenues, expenses, and net operating income, but they have often undergone little formal training before assuming their responsibilities.

As developers have come to realize the importance of property management, they have placed greater emphasis on identifying individuals capable of performing the necessary management tasks. At the same time, more training opportunities have emerged, including programs offered by several associations. The best-known association is the Institute of Real Estate Management, an affiliate of the National Association of Realtors®, which offers a designation as *certified property manager* (CPM). Other designations are available for on-site resident managers, including *accredited resident manager* (ARM) and *certified apartment manager* (CAM).

The Building Owners and Managers Association International produces an array of statistics on office building operations similar to the analyses of apartment income and expenses produced by the Institute of Real Estate Management. The International Council of Shopping Centers generates its own statistics, while the Urban Land Institute publishes operating results for shopping centers. All of these organizations seek to enhance professionalism in the field and to provide data that can be used in feasibility studies and long-term operating budgets.

In addition, the various professional programs aim to familiarize managers with the use of a systematic approach to record keeping, the best ways to anticipate and respond to tenants' needs, strategies for negotiating leases, legal responsibilities to tenants, and sales/marketing techniques. Because real estate management involves meticulous attention to detail, techniques for tracking the many functions of building management are often best learned in professional training courses.

Courtesy of David M. Schwarz/Architectural Services

An exquisite concierge desk for the lobby of an office building in Washington, D.C. Concierges in commercial office buildings function much like concierges in hotels, providing tenants with theater tickets, dry-cleaning services, photographic reproduction services, restaurant recommendations, and so on.

Asset and Portfolio Managers

A variety of companies offer real estate investment management services. A few are subsidiaries of development companies; others are independent investment managers or subsidiaries of major financial institutions. The largest group of portfolio managers is probably pension fund investment managers who are members of the National Council of Real Estate Investment Fiduciaries (NCREIF), the Pension Real Estate Association (PREA), or the National Association of Real Estate Investment Managers (NAREIM). In addition to providing advice on managing a portfolio and acquiring and disposing of properties, these companies manage real estate assets for their pension fund clients. This group of asset and portfolio managers—the "who's who" in the business—often hires local property management firms to take care of traditional functions but retains for its own firms the supervisory role in asset management and the other aspects of portfolio management.

Profile **Lizanne Galbreath**

Managing Director, Jones Lang LaSalle
New York, New York

Lizanne Galbreath began her real estate career with the real estate division of Chemical Bank, where she worked as a financial analyst. In 1984, after receiving an MBA from the Wharton School of the University of Pennsylvania, she joined her grandfather's firm, the Galbreath Company, and worked as a broker in the leasing and new business department. In 1995, she became chair and CEO of the Galbreath Company, a firm that had developed more than 60 million square feet of property and had 90 million square feet of commercial space under management. The Galbreath Company employed more than 3,000 people nationwide. In the late 1980s, as vice chair, she took over responsibility for the New York office and the firm's expansion along the East Coast.

In 1997, with the industry in a consolidation mode, Galbreath structured a merger with LaSalle Partners, an international full-service real estate firm. The merger created one of the largest real estate firms in the world, managing more than 200 million square feet of office, industrial, and retail property nationwide. In late 1999, LaSalle Partners merged with Jones Lang Wootton to become Jones Lang LaSalle. Galbreath is the managing director, client services group, of Jones Lang LaSalle in New York City.

Trump International Hotel and Tower
With the development of the Trump International Hotel and Tower, LaSalle will complete one of the most successful developments of the 1990s in New York City. In 1993, the Galbreath Company along with the General Electric Pension Trust and the Trump Organization formed a joint venture partnership to redevelop the 650,000-square-foot Gulf & Western Building on Columbus Circle, former headquarters of Paramount Communications. As a result of the predevelopment feasibility study, the partnership converted the building into a mixed-use development,

two-thirds of it containing superluxury residential condominiums and the rest a 168-unit all-suite hotel.

The first phase of the redevelopment involved the abatement of more than 600,000 square feet of sprayed-on asbestos fireproofing, and the removal of all mechanical systems, and plumbing, electrical, and sanitary waste risers. After the building was stripped to its steel frame, a series of concrete shear walls was poured to stiffen the building. The old curtain wall was removed and a new one, designed by renowned architect Philip Johnson, installed. In less than 18 months, the project was completed on time and on budget. Both the residential apartments and hotel units were sold as condominiums, achieving the highest prices in U.S. history.

Additionally, a 175-seat restaurant, awarded four stars by the *New York Times,* the highest rating in the city, was constructed in the building.

Consolidation
Galbreath believes that the national and international consolidation of real estate companies provides firms with a larger geographic reach with which to serve clients globally, and a larger base of business to support the growing technological and service demands being placed on service firms today.

In merging her own firm with LaSalle, Galbreath sought a company with a compatible culture, a strong capital base to support further growth and consolidation, the capabilities to service Galbreath's existing clients, and a team of top-notch professionals that would embrace Galbreath employees.

Through the merger, says Galbreath, her firm has acquired a deeper pool of expertise to draw upon to ensure excellent execution of transactions, and a broader geographical reach to service existing and new clients in

---

Thus, it is their charge to be sure that their clients invest in the right types of properties and in the right markets and that those properties are managed to achieve the maximum benefit for the client. Typically, the individuals who handle asset and portfolio management in investment management companies are university trained in management, finance, or law. Through seminars and professional literature made available by the three associations noted earlier, these professionals continue to enhance and develop their skills.

The Corporate Real Estate Director

Fifteen years ago, chief executive officers (CEOs) often considered real estate management one of the less important corporate functions. Today, they recognize that the major part of their balance sheets is in real estate and that, in an often harshly competitive world, management of those fixed assets is critical to a firm's success. Real estate at market value is estimated to account for 25 to 40 percent of a corporation's assets. Not only is real

more locations. The merger has also afforded more technological and selling support as well as increased opportunities to grow the business and learn from others.

Communication Skills

Galbreath believes the most important skill for success in the real estate industry is the ability to communicate effectively with clients and employees. "Good communication, both internally and externally to clients, is imperative. As firms grow, employees still need to be and feel part of a team, not lost in a bureaucratic jumble." She adds, "Communicating with others in the industry can be complicated because the personalities are entrepreneurial, motivated, and aggressive—which are all necessary for success. The difficulty is to challenge people and direct them toward opportunities. You must maintain enough control to run a successful business, but not so much to hinder their goals, creativity, and entrepreneurial spirit."

Consolidation can be a help and a hindrance in this regard, according to Galbreath. Although a need exists to guard against employees' and clients' being lost in a bureaucratic shuffle, her firm's merger has relieved some of the burden of the day-to-day operations of running a company and has allowed her to focus more time on clients and strategy. Still, she adds, "I miss the family nature of a smaller company and the flexibility to react on a dime to opportunities." ∎

To achieve a high level of architectural quality, Philip Johnson was hired to design the exterior of Trump International Hotel and Tower in Manhattan, using bronze colored glass and stainless steel. Trump Tower's new development concept of merging commercial hotel and individual condominium unit ownership required complex and innovative management, legal, and marketing strategies.

---

estate important from a cost/value perspective, but access to the right space in the right location with the appropriate features, functions, and benefits is also critical to the firm's operating performance and its employees' quality of life.[4]

A detailed understanding of the value of a corporation's real estate is extremely important as the corporation attempts to minimize its cost of space while meeting all of its space needs. Indeed, the cost of space for many businesses is second only to the cost

of its payroll. In the early 1990s, businesses devoted considerable effort to reducing operating costs, and the corporate real estate director was a big part of the process. An accurate assessment of the value of the corporation's real estate assets can help ensure that the assets are properly reflected on the balance sheet. Effective asset management helps increase the value per share and minimize the potential for corporate takeovers aimed at acquiring businesses for their real estate holdings.

To address these concerns effectively, the corporate real estate director must be involved in the decisions on building capacity and layout in the same manner that the property manager, asset manager, and portfolio manager contribute to the design of a traditional development. Corporate real estate directors often chair site selection committees. They assist in decisions to lease or buy space and in the search for financing. They work with the firm's operating management team to create the best organization for the continuing management and monitoring of real estate assets. They also lead in creating a management information system for this purpose. They work to identify surplus or underused real property and seek ways to reuse those assets. They negotiate on the company's behalf in the leasing or purchasing of space. They initiate suggestions for alternative ways of owning or leasing real estate, such as the opportunity to create a joint venture if the company does not want to create its own development business but still wants to take advantage of its financial strength to reap the rewards of equity participation.

CEOs also know that the flexibility to react to changing market conditions is often hampered by the ownership of long-term assets in fixed locations. The empty steel mills in Pittsburgh are a prime example. Pittsburgh, with its beautiful downtown skyline, still has large vacant, corporate-owned buildings inside the central city because of the poor market for large, old industrial space.

Small wonder that real estate is suddenly receiving far greater attention in both the popular press and professional organizations such as the National Association of Corporate Real Estate Executives (NACORE), the National Association of Industrial and Office Properties (NAIOP), and the Industrial Development Research Council (IDRC).

Given that corporations are the major users of space, developers need to understand corporations' requirements for the use of the real estate asset. Accordingly, developers need to include in the development plan features that are important to corporate users.

The rate of change in business has increased rapidly, leading to growing unpredictability from a CEO's perspective—in essence, to faster product obsolescence. Further, globalization and integrated just-in-time production systems have complicated planning. Real estate is fixed, almost indefinitely, but what CEOs now need most is flexibility because they cannot forecast future events with great certainty.

Modern technology has greatly affected the space requirements of corporations in many ways. Telecommuting, the facsimile machine, electronic mail, voice mail, the personal computer in every office, and other technological innovations have transformed the way companies work. At the same time, public policy mandates often accentuate technology's impact. Under the Clean Air Act, major employers are required to cut back the number of employees who commute to work during peak-hour periods as a means of reducing air pollutants, thereby providing a further impetus to nontraditional work locations and schedules for employees.

In response to the changing business and work environment, many major corporations have downsized their employment base in recent years and in turn have trimmed back their real estate requirements by selling off excess corporate holdings and cutting back on space leased from others. To improve efficiency in managing their real estate exposure, many companies have turned to external professional real estate companies. Real estate "outsourcing" enables corporations to avail themselves of expertise in a variety of areas that may not be available in house (such as life safety or engineering) and allows the corporate real estate office to maintain a lean staff. For example, Trammell Crow as a developer and LaSalle Partners (now Jones Lang LaSalle) as an investment manager have been leaders in forging alliances with major corporations such as United Parcel Service and Exxon to assist in efficiently managing corporate real estate holdings.[5]

The need for flexibility translates into the need to build general-purpose real estate rather than special-purpose industrial or headquarters office buildings. An interesting parallel is that the major new real estate investor, the pension fund, also wants to invest in general-purpose real estate. If the prime tenant ceases to be a tenant, general-purpose real estate is clearly easier to release. From a corporate perspective, a smaller version of a general-purpose building also reduces the break-even point by lowering fixed costs. Although in many ways corporate real estate is an ordinary development situation (thus a good place to use the eight-stage model and the other tools covered in this text), it is complicated by larger issues of corporate strategy and concern for shareholders' earnings.

As the United States moves to a world with fewer middle managers and more subcontractors as partners, space needs likewise change. Successful developers will be those who correctly anticipate the changes in corporate requirements and build space to fit the new relationships.

Summary

- The triad of real estate management—property, asset, and portfolio managers—provides critical functions for ensuring that real estate projects maximize their value. The role of the various real estate managers cannot be overestimated, and the involvement of these individuals throughout the development process is essential.

- As espoused by James A. Graaskamp, the real estate asset must be viewed as more than just bricks and mortar. The project must be recognized as a dynamic business enterprise operating in an ever-changing and increasingly competitive marketplace.

- The role of asset and portfolio management in real estate continues to expand and evolve. Although asset managers' fundamental involvement and interaction with the property manager remains a priority, the portfolio manager is assuming a much more active role in the development and/or acquisition of assets, the positioning of the product throughout its life cycle, and the timely disposition of the asset. These responsibilities serve to enhance the value of individual assets to long-term investors.

- Effective property management continues to be fundamental for both maintaining and enhancing the value of real estate projects. The detailed nature of property management requires a thoughtful and structured approach that includes early involvement in the development process, detailed management plans and budgets, consistent attention to day-to-day operations, and the flexibility to adjust to changing market conditions.

- Because of the people-intensive nature of real estate projects, the public sector plays an active role in asset and property management. New legislation and regulations are promulgated almost daily, and their effects on property can be costly from the perspective of both initial development costs and ongoing operating expenses. Proactive involvement in understanding rules and regulations by both the development and management teams is essential.

- Intelligent office buildings raise the level of sophistication required of real estate managers and complicate the design and development process. Although the potential benefits of these new technologies cannot be ignored, thorough analysis of the cost/benefit relationship must be considered before implementing these rapidly changing technologies.

- The importance of the property manager and on-site personnel to the real estate project's long-term financial success cannot be overemphasized. Effective, ongoing training is critical to ensure that these individuals continue to perform effectively in an increasingly competitive and demanding marketplace.

- Real estate and/or office space is an important component of the business management side of most corporations. In the past, CEOs frequently viewed these assets as necessary evils. Today, however, the value and importance of effective management of company real estate is gaining recognition and has heightened the importance and involvement of the corporate real estate director in the day-to-day operation of the business. This additional scrutiny has created opportunities for capable developers who are able to provide flexible solutions to satisfy the corporation's requirements.

Terms

- Asset manager
- Corporate real estate
- Effective rent
- Enterprise concept
- Intelligent building
- Management plan
- Marketing program
- Portfolio manager
- Property life cycle
- Property management contract
- Property manager
- Property strategic plan
- Transfer package

Review Questions

21.1 Describe the differences in the property, asset, and portfolio managers' functions and how they are interrelated.

21.2 How does a property manager use a management plan?

21.3 Why is the involvement of a property manager early in the development process ideal?

21.4 What are some of the potential problems facing an asset manager, even in good markets?

21.5 What are the four main elements of a strategic plan? Discuss each one.

21.6 Why is it so important to create a realistic and accurate operating budget?

21.7 What issues does the property management contract spell out?

21.8 What is the impact of smart technology on buildings? How do you think it will change management and development in the future?

21.9 Why is real estate such an important asset to corporations?

Notes

1. Richard Kateley and M. Leanne Lachman, *Asset Management: The Key to Profitable Real Estate Investment* (Chicago: Real Estate Research Corporation, 1985), p. 2.

2. Alex. Brown & Sons, *Real Estate Stocks Monitor,* October 1993.

3. Michelle D. Gouin and Thomas B. Cross, *Intelligent Buildings* (Homewood, Ill.: Dow Jones–Irwin, 1986), pp. 2–3.

4. See a discussion of quality-of-life issues in Christopher B. Leinberger, "Flexecutives: Redefining the American Dream," *Urban Land,* August 1994, pp. 51–54.

5. Steve Bergsman, "Changes in Corporate Philosophy Dictate New Directions for Their Real Estate Department," *National Real Estate Investor,* March 1993, pp. 28–36.

Chapter 22

The Challenge of Marketing And Sales

Sales and/or leasing represent the culmination of the development team's entire efforts. It behooves the developer, like any businessperson, to take a broad view of marketing, including research, analysis, and design, to meet the customer's needs, put together an integrated sales effort to convince the target market that the product meets its needs, and then develop a feedback loop so that customers' reactions can be used to regularly reposition the product and the sales effort. Earlier chapters have covered market research, analysis, and design. This chapter focuses on the last two components of marketing—sales and/or leasing plus the feedback loop.

Every type of property presents its own marketing challenges; in fact, every project is distinguished by certain characteristics that the developer is trying to sell or lease. Covering all the different facets of even the major property types goes beyond what can be achieved in one chapter; therefore, we use two especially challenging property types—residential subdivisions and a major mall—to illustrate the basic principles of sales and leasing, respectively, and then provide references for the other property types. Although every sales or leasing challenge is unique (because every real estate project is unique), some commonalities exist among all of them. Just as we covered the basics of market analysis, design, financing, management, and public policy in earlier chapters, here we review the basics of sales (and sales management) from the perspective of development. This chapter may be the least academic one in this book, but it is far from the least important.

This chapter was originally written by William N. Webb, Amelia Island, Florida.

Marketing professionals and salespeople should be firmly grounded in the primary components of business education: finance, marketing, production, and management. They must thoroughly understand finance so that they can competently advise prospects of alternative financial structures for proposed lease transactions. Further, more basic understanding of finance is necessary for brokers to analyze the variety of financial structures that the developer may impose on them. Both marketing professionals and brokers also need to understand the financial aspects of feasibility analysis to know which tenant proposals may be acceptable to the developer/investor. The principles that guide the formulation and implementation of the marketing strategy, including market research and techniques for determining space use, must be second nature to anyone contemplating a successful career in marketing and sales. After all, sales (or leasing) is the final step in the overall marketing process, which began in stage one. Understanding the specific product type as well as its design and production (the construction process) is a prerequisite to selling the product knowledgeably and successfully. In development, leasing or sales almost always starts before the project is complete and often before construction begins. As a result, the marketing representative is often involved in changing plans during construction to meet tenants' needs. Finally, the ability to empathize with and lead people, a general management skill, is crucial to the sales process.

The marketing specialists on the development team, including the leasing and sales agents, may be employees of the developer or third parties who provide services under contract. Even when using outside specialists, the developer is not relieved of making decisions related to marketing; calling the plays is still the developer's responsibility. In small developments, developers themselves may perform much of the marketing function.

The challenge of selling real estate is the focus of this chapter. For the most part, the word "sales" is used broadly to include both leasing and selling. Ideally, if members of the development team do a good job at research and product design, sales and leasing can be a relatively straightforward exercise. But even if research and product design were nearly perfect, the team must still identify and convince prospects of the project's merits. Getting a lease signed takes a similar effort as that required to get a sales contract signed. The overriding purpose in both cases is finding and convincing prospects that a particular development better meets their space needs than any other available product. For shopping centers, marketing also includes convincing the prospective tenant's customers to shop at a particular center.

This chapter moves from getting started and managing sales to actually selling the product. It examines:

- Coordinating marketing and sales;
- The marketing plan and budget;
- Targeted advertising;
- Public relations;
- On-site promotions;
- Merchandising the product;
- Relations with real estate agents;
- Educating the sales staff;
- Sales operations;
- Building the sale;
- Follow-up; and
- Accepting the challenge of marketing and sales.

Rarely does any project—no matter how well conceived and executed—generate its own market. In our continuing case study, Fraser Morrow Daniels, for example, turned to an outside firm to lease Europa Center.

::: Europa Center

Leasing Space

There's a major question about who will lease your building for you, especially in the Research Triangle area, where the market was just forming. We chose a national organization, Cushman & Wakefield, which leases only office space, because we anticipated that the competition for tenants would be cutthroat. In a highly competitive environment, the tenants run the show anyway. If the company listing your space leases it, it will cost 4 percent of the value of the lease. If it is cobrokered with another company, you pay 6 percent of the value of the lease, including the cobrokerage fee. We budgeted 5 percent, because we figured that we or the leasing company could generate tenants for half the space and that the other half would be cobrokered.

The leasing process works mostly like this. The leasing company identifies tenants—trying to find businesses that

The pond and trees the developer left on the site enhanced the appeal of Europa Center and were used in the marketing program.

are expanding or moving to the area or that could be talked out of a current lease that still has a year to run. Once the leasing agents have a prospect, they come to us and say, "This is how your building stacks up against other buildings. You're this much nicer, your location is this much better, and your rent is $1.00 higher. The tenant needs a loading dock; here's what it values. What will it take to get that tenant here rather than to one of the other three buildings it could move into?" Then we try to guess what the other buildings have to offer and decide how low we can go to beat them out.

Then the leasing agent says, "To get that tenant, I think we'll have to give them a lower rate and six months of free rent. They can't afford to pay for any extra finishes, but they need an extra $3.00 a square foot for nice surroundings. We should offer an extra $3.00 per square foot that we pay for, and I think we can get them. Or we should offer free electricity on weekends rather than charging extra." Then we say, "We're not comfortable with six months of free rent; give them four." Or we might say, "That's a great tenant. We really want them because we think they'll attract more tenants. Let's give them 18 months of free rent. They're really beneficial to the building. Let's pay something to get them in there."

After the building was 30 percent leased, more people came to us and asked to be in the building, instead of the other way around. Getting started is very tough, but the subsequent leasing is usually easier.

By April 1989, Europa Center was more than 80 percent leased. Most of the tenants were local professional companies that have been in Chapel Hill and Durham for some time. Virtually all the tenants moved up from substandard space to our space. A few companies had expanded and just needed more space. A couple were startup companies, and some were controlled and located in other parts of the country but used Europa Center as their Chapel Hill office.

Asset management and ongoing leasing are strong considerations for building owners. All the existing tenants had different lease contracts with different terms, different rates, and different escalation clauses. When overbuilding and high vacancy rates are common, tenants can pretty much get what they want by shopping around. Building owners become more and more willing to conform to a tenant's needs, first with lower prices or lower escalations and later with higher tenant allowances and a lot of special things you probably wouldn't want to fool with in a better market.

Once a building is finished and occupied, the building owner or building manager worries about the electricity, the water bill, parking, elevator maintenance, and indoor and outdoor landscaping—all the things that are essential to keeping the tenants happy and the building looking good. Because a lot of different tenants have leases with varying lengths, some leases are always coming up for renewal or people are moving out. Leasing in a building like Europa Center is a continuous process.

continued on page 506

Coordinating Marketing and Sales

The experience of builders and developers has shown that a systematic approach to marketing and sales tends to produce superior results. Just as the construction of a new building requires the coordinated assembly of many components, the successful selling or leasing of that building depends on the combination of marketing and sales activities (see Figure 22-1).

Guided by market research and controlled by a strategic plan and the budget, each individual activity plays an important role in satisfying potential users. Developers must guide and support a coordinated system if the efforts of individual sales and leasing professionals are to collectively produce maximum results. Ideally, every member of the development team understands how each activity is designed to contribute to the success of the overall sales program so that sales and leasing agents will have the support they need from design, construction, finance, and property management.

The marketing and sales process begins with market research, the goal of which is to project the absorption rate of the project (through stabilization and transfer to continuing property management) based on the supply of and demand for similar products in a specified market area (see Chapters 17 and 18). In retail properties, market research also projects the potential sales volume that the various tenants can expect, the corresponding rent levels that the developer can achieve, and the merchandise/tenant mix that is necessary to optimize sales and therefore rents.

The Marketing Plan and Budget

Developers like to estimate the cost of marketing, leasing, and sales in terms of the total dollar amount that will suffice to complete project leasing or selling. Given that the overall costs of several development components lend themselves to fairly accurate estimates, it is easy to understand a developer's preference for precisely estimating the costs of marketing, leasing, and sales. As a practical matter, however, developing a hard-and-fast number for marketing and sales expenses is much more

Figure 22-1

Performance System for Successful Real Estate Marketing and Sales

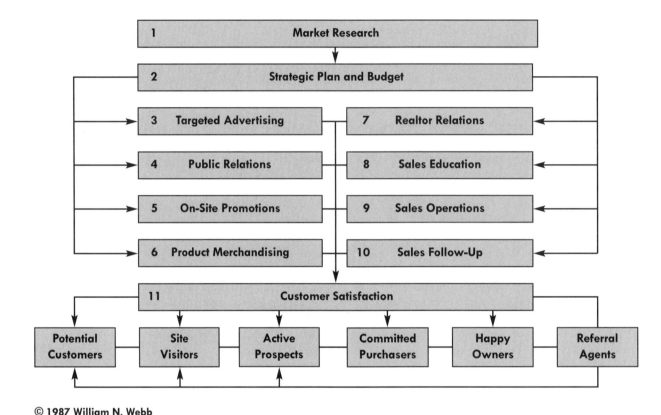

© 1987 William N. Webb

difficult than, for example, deriving estimates for the cost of light fixtures.

Nobody can forecast accurately just how much marketing and sales effort a particular project will require. Everyone would probably agree that the marketing team should at least attempt to achieve the rate of absorption projected in the market research. The challenge is to figure out what is necessary to reach that goal.

At least two methods of budgeting have proven useful in making projections; they both start with a marketing plan. As early as possible in the development process, the developer and/or the marketing staff should begin formulating a plan to promote the product to the target market. In retail development, the plan includes an analysis of merchandise mix that targets the needed retail categories and proposes retailers who fit within each category. From the beginning, any plan should be committed to writing to encourage logical thought and thorough analysis.

Based on earlier market research, the plan typically begins with a description of both the real estate itself and the target market. It includes statements about how the product will attract the target market and the customer and how the marketing and sales staff should reach out to that market. As the development progresses, each category should be expanded with a list of specific, productive activities. To ensure that no promising prospects go overlooked, a comprehensive checklist of activities appropriate to a wide range of products and markets is an appropriate starting point.

The first step in budgeting involves compiling a reasonable cost estimate for each marketing activity on the list. In the beginning, spare no expense and assume no corners will be cut. Encourage brainstorming to develop new ideas. Then total the cost. It should be wildly excessive.

Start paring down the total by going back and scrutinizing every item. Each activity should justify itself; delete ones that do not. Presumably, only the strongest ideas will survive, which is the purpose of this method of budgeting—casting the net as wide as possible, keeping only the best of what is caught.

Some of the items such as building a sales or customer information center might be one-time investments that will last for the life of the program. Other one-time investments include a grand opening event for the tenants and the community at large. Other items, such as brochures that may have to be replaced periodically, are consumables. Others such as media charges recur periodically and will keep mounting as the marketing effort intensifies.

To estimate the grand total, it is necessary to predict how long it will take to lease the project. Market research has predicted an absorption rate. How hard to push (how much to spend per month) to achieve that rate is a judgment call. As a result, the second budgeting method provides a cross-check of the estimate.

The second method, particularly relevant in subdivision sales, starts with a question: How many new prospects/contacts will have to be generated to achieve the predicted absorption rate necessary to reach stabilization? The answer depends on two factors: the rate of converting new prospects/contacts to completed transactions, which is affected by numerous variables, not the least of which is the effectiveness of the sales staff; and how much space will be absorbed by each completed transaction. In residential marketing, each buyer generally absorbs one dwelling. In the case of commercial properties, market research predicts the number of square feet absorbed per tenant. For retail tenants in particular, standard building size and lease terms are known before the marketing process is initiated.

How much will each new prospect/contact cost? It depends on how contacts are made, the quality of the project's location, and, in some respects, the project's anchor tenant. Commercial real estate marketing relies heavily on active prospecting: members of the sales and leasing team make direct contacts with parties likely to be interested in the new project. For retail centers, agents contact the retailers identified in the category analysis contained in the market study. (In some markets, tenants are represented by their own agents, whose services demand remuneration and add to total costs.) Marketing is intended primarily to support agents' efforts, generating some leads along the way. In residential marketing, prospecting is rare, and salespeople depend on advertising to motivate prospects to come to the sales office.

It is critically important that the productivity of marketing and sales activities be continuously measured against leases produced or sales closed. Incorporating the list of budget line items directly into the accounting system is crucial. In that way, total return on marketing dollars expended can be tracked with some precision. It is also important to use continuing market research to measure effectiveness and to pick up on changes in the project's trade area that affect marketing efforts. In addition, it is essential to request feedback from the sales team and prospects. As the team develops a track record, its experience can replace the original projections for the remainder of the sales (leasing) effort.

Just gathering information is not enough. In this information age, data are readily available. Knowing how to handle the data and use information to benefit the developer is a special skill that cannot be underestimated (see Figure 22-2). As you can see, coordinated marketing and sales is an optimization exercise within the broader optimization that is continually occurring throughout the development process. This broader optimization uses the whole feasibility study, as explained in Chapter 16.

Targeted Advertising

The market research's definition of the target market should include information about where potential prospects are located. Once the appropriate form of advertising has been chosen (radio or newspaper, for example), advertising should be purchased in the geographic areas where the target market is located.

The market research provides ideas for the creative content of the advertising message. Often, an outside advertising agency is responsible for writing advertising copy and producing a logo and accompanying graphics for the property. The agency also purchases media space or time for advertising. It is not usually advisable, however, to leave to the advertising agency exclusively determination of the target market or establishment of an appropriate marketing budget. These factors are the responsibility of the marketing specialist (or the developer). Larger developers typically employ their own in-house marketing staffs, research staffs, and advertising professionals. In this case, it is entirely appropriate to use in-house resources simultaneously with outside professionals.

Deciding on the best mix of media is an important component of targeted advertising. The target market itself should suggest which media would be most productive. Even with the availability of the Internet for advertising, newspaper advertising is still the traditional medium of choice across the nation for real estate, regardless of product type. If newspaper advertising is judged appropriate for both the product and the target market, the next task is to select the newspapers in which to advertise. That decision is based on what the target market is likely to read.

Deciding where in each newspaper to place the advertisement is also critical. A basic principle to follow

Figure 22-2

Market Intelligence and Marketing

The intelligence process—the practice of transforming data into useful knowledge—is not a widely understood tool in real estate companies. Most companies fail to realize the value of organizing for gathering data and creating useful information from the collected data. As a result, they are drowning in data and regurgitated data printouts.

Intelligence systems are the key to long-term business success in the information age. Such systems gather an abundance of information and use technology to record, retrieve, and analyze it. The product is knowledge that is readily available to the right persons at the right time. The intelligence organizations of nations have long used intelligence systems, and businesses of all kinds increasingly are adopting such systems.

Marketing in particular requires a disciplined, step-by-step intelligence process. In the coming years, marketing will succeed only when relevant information is extracted from a sea of data, when patterns are recognized early so that the business can act before its competition does, and when market knowledge is used to its full advantage in strategies for specific properties as well as for the overall business.

The intelligence process is a business's early warning system. It is essential for implementing the marketing strategy. It is the most powerful business tool available today.

Business intelligence in general and market intelligence in particular are already making a difference for a few in the real estate industry. Before too long, intelligence systems will become an industry standard.

Data Handling Systems

Easily customized databases, Geographic Information Systems, and graphic presentation systems are increasingly available in combination. The growing ability to customize software applications means that past intermediaries now can be eliminated from the development process. Thus, people who are intimately familiar with real estate marketing can produce custom software applications for specific properties. Increasingly, real estate owners, managers, and salespeople will have access to varieties of user-friendly and productive marketing, sales, and management support systems that they can only wish for today. (See, e.g., Charles Tallman, "The Uses of Database Marketing," *Urban Land,* June 1993, p. 33.)

A prospective customer tracking system created by Dwyer Williams for USX Realty Development's Swan Point residential community in southern Maryland is an example. This database application tracks prospects from initial contacts through selling efforts to sale and postsale follow-up. It supplies sales personnel with current data on prospective customers as well as with follow-up reminders. It provides management with reports on weekly activity, prospect status, and marketing and sales effectiveness. And it generates extensive prospective customer data, which are immediately available to market analysts.

Information correlation software, an evolving tool that is currently less fully developed and less competitively priced, combined with low-priced, PC-based computing power will enable real estate practitioners to monitor a wide range of data sources—from newspapers to specialized databases—to gather useful information on markets, potential

---

is to place advertising where interested customers will look for it. Communicating with an interested audience actively seeking information about a product is much more useful than attempting to capture the attention of someone with no initial interest in the product. The goal is to design and place an advertisement powerful enough to induce response.

Magazines and trade publications are another medium often used to advertise real estate. In many communities, some magazines survive almost exclusively on real estate–oriented advertising, particularly for residential developments in rapidly growing communities. Local and statewide business magazines are natural choices for developers of almost all types of income-producing

properties. Both residential and commercial developers may find opportunities in magazines targeted to area newcomers. Product-specific trade publications are another medium for advertising property developments, particularly in the retail sector, where players are fewer and their interrelationships well established.

Compared with newspapers, magazines have longer cycles and may deliver more highly targeted readers. The print quality of magazines is also much higher, especially if the magazines frequently include full-color photographs. For particularly attractive developments, these factors can be compelling inducements. Public service publications, such as the local guide to radio and television symphony broadcasts, can sometimes customers, economic conditions, and competitors in the context of specific properties and market objectives.

The possibility of drawing on the right information at the right time (or of one's competitor having the right information at the right time) boggles the mind—especially when the information is available at an acceptable price without the need to hire and manage a room full of jargon-spouting technocrats.

A Successful Example
Leasing at Banner Place—a 286,000-square-foot office building in Dallas's suburban Park Central market—shot from 64 percent to 85 percent when a collaborative marketing approach was instituted. The time was 1992 and 1993, when the Dallas office market was experiencing continuing difficulties: 74 percent occupancy at an average lease rate of $13.90 in early 1992 and $12.18 in late 1993. At the beginning of this period, Banner Place was 64 percent leased at quoted lease rates of $11.00 to $13.50, including expenses of $5.97. Announced tenant departures were expected to pull occupancy down to around 40 percent. At the end of 1993, Banner Place was 87 percent leased at lease rates of $10.00 to $12.00 and the same expense level. The lower lease rate reflected the building's market position and general market conditions. No net negative leases were executed.

Why these results? The owner (USX Realty Development), the property management/leasing firm (Transwestern Property Company), the marketing adviser (Dwyer Williams), and the building's tenants collaborated on making Banner Place a building that responds to today's business needs. Several factors contributed to improved performance:

- Tenant retention programs that worked;
- Improved market intelligence that anticipated changing market directions and identified vulnerable competition;
- A marketing and repositioning strategy based on the reality of the marketplace and Banner Place's relative position in it;
- A marketing plan based on this strategy with a detailed action schedule for all marketing and leasing functions;
- Aggressive building management that succeeded in making improvements to the building while not increasing tenant expenses;
- Continuing discussion with tenants and lost prospects to gain their perspectives on Banner Place's management, leasing, and performance; and
- Active owner interaction with tenants and prospective tenants on a business-to-business basis.

The intelligence gathering, repositioning strategy, and marketing plan all relied on teamwork and collaboration with customers and potential customers. The effort has paid off not only in the building's substantial recovery in the face of difficult market conditions but also in its strategic positioning for further improvement as the Dallas office market changes. ■

Source: **Donald L. Williams and Sally M. Dwyer, "A Marketing Revolution,"** *Urban Land,* **March 1994, p. 28.**

---

make sense when trying to establish a certain tone for a development.

Radio and television offer tremendous impact, though generally at commensurate cost, particularly in major metropolitan markets. They are especially useful for the short-term support of a special event, such as a grand opening. Many metropolitan areas have radio stations targeted to just about any imaginable profile of residential buyers. The growing popularity of cable television offers creative possibilities for business-oriented developments.

Where available, outdoor billboards are a natural for advertising real estate. They can include directions to the project—crucial to a product that depends on location. The challenge is to find available boards along roads used by the target market and to develop an appropriate advertising campaign.

Direct mail is the most highly targeted advertising medium. The careful selection of recipients means that wasted exposure is minimized. This efficiency makes multiple exposures feasible, which is why most successful direct-mail campaigns feature repetitive mailings. When the advantage of rapid print production is added, direct mail becomes even more attractive. Thorough market research of the trade area, perhaps carried out in conjunction with the market research conducted by a potential development's anchor tenant, can focus a direct-mail campaign to the point where different mailers are sent to households based on previous shopping

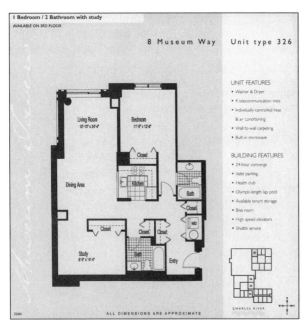

A floorplan and a grid showing where in the building the apartment is located are available for every apartment in the **Museum Towers** buildings.

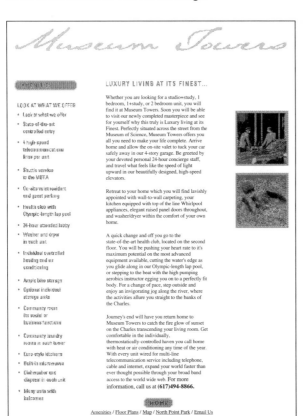

Web sites can assist consumers and owners in the marketing process. Owners can save money on printed material, and consumers can educate themselves about the project and its competition before touring the property.

purchases. Such highly focused marketing is used extensively by catalog retailers and is gaining importance within the shopping center industry as a whole.

More and more, the Internet is becoming a popular advertising medium. Prospective customers can view floorplans, see videos of available apartments, see various advertised rates, and then E-mail or telephone the marketing department for more information or to set up an appointment. In addition, most newspapers now have all their classifieds on line, and potential customers can search all the ads by listing the features they most desire in an apartment or home.

Most real estate companies now have Web sites with their listings and contact information. Photographs of the properties often accompany the ads, which is rarely the case in newspaper ads. Several other rental and leasing clearinghouses can also be found on the Web. Like *www.rent.com,* these Web sites allow users to search by type of property desired and location, making follow-up easy. Web sites provide a relatively low-cost means of marketing and providing up-to-date information for potential users.

Whatever the medium of choice, the marketing team should take care to fully estimate the costs and benefits of using that medium in a marketing campaign.

In the case of Museum Towers, Dean Stratouly knew his limitations in marketing and leasing and hired professionals to help develop a strategy for leasing space in a pioneering location.

▌▌▌ Museum Towers

Developing a Marketing Strategy

We hired Doerr Associates of Winchester to do our marketing. I'm a developer, not a marketing person, so I think it's really important to use the professionals that know what they're doing. Doerr has been around for more than 25 years, and we hired them to develop advertising strategies, direct-mail campaigns, and printed brochures and other material. We put ads in the *Boston Globe* that were designed to appeal to the "hip" professional crowd. We also developed our own Web site *(http://www.museumtowers.com)* and advertised on Rent.Net. From the beginning, the *Boston Globe,* a very traditional apartment leasing tool, brought the greatest number of prospective tenants.

We developed a marketing slogan—Rent the Apartment; Own the City—that we put on billboards, on line, on our collateral marketing materials. We paid a lot of attention to the amenities and special features, and marketed them heavily. We made some decisions about which

A model apartment with a view of the Charles River is an effective leasing tool for Museum Towers.

amenities to include based on a focus group of renters who lived within two miles of Museum Towers. The washer and dryer in each unit, which were recommended by the focus group, have been a real boon to our marketing. High-speed elevators and security were also important. So we got elevators that travel 700 feet per minute, a 24-hour concierge staff, and valet parking. Every apartment has four high-speed telecommunications lines and a broadband cable–ready outlet from *MediaOne*. We run a shuttle in the morning and evening to the three closest subway stops —Lechmere, Kendall Square, and North Station.

But we also have a 15,000-square-foot health club with an indoor two-lane lap pool, which cost over $2 million to build. It's two floors with treadmills, cross-trainers, stairmasters, lifecycles, weights, aerobics, spin classes—you name it.

Plus we offer 200 units for tenants' storage and park-ing—both of which are hard to find in this market. We've even got a housekeeping service and furniture rentals. There's also a nice courtyard for our renters to use.

Cambridge is a great market for high-end renters. The average household income is about $57,000, compared with the national average of about $46,000.

continued below

Public Relations

Targeted advertising must be reinforced by a coordi-nated public relations effort. It is useful to think of public relations as untargeted promotion aimed at the public at large, with the best generator of positive public relations the quality of the development itself.

Almost all real estate development today generates some ill will among people who live near the project, fos-tering movements such as NIMBY (not in my back yard) and BANANA (build absolutely nothing anywhere near anything). Opponents might see the development as damaging the environment, generating excess traffic on local roads, or negatively affecting the value of their own property. The sensitivity with which such concerns are handled can make or break a project.

Because government is always the developer's part-ner and must ultimately answer to the people, it must respond to any negative concerns with great care. None-theless, developers are usually best positioned to address those concerns. Thoughtfully receiving feedback from government and the people shows respect for the pub-lic interest. Developers have some latitude in initiating changes as a result of that feedback. Few actions of a developer can be more effective in generating favor-able public relations than demonstrating responsible concern for the community and corresponding flexi-bility during the development process.

The local government was heavily involved in the development of Museum Towers, which required the de-veloper to include some non-market-rate units.

▮▮ Museum Towers

Setting Rental Rates

A total of 33 units, or 7.5 percent of the units, are for low- or moderate-income renters. The subsidized units include 15 one-bedrooms and 18 two-bedrooms. Although the ten-ants have to be qualified by the Cambridge Housing Author-ity, we're working very closely with CHA to screen the ten-ants, most of whom will be Section 8 certificate holders.

The law allows these units to be 110 percent of allowed Section 8 rents adjusted for utilities or, in this case, $772 for one-bedrooms and $920 for two-bedrooms. The remaining subsidized units will be available to tenants earning 80 percent of the median income. These tenants will pay 30 percent of their gross income, with an estimated rent of $722 for the one-bedroom units.

Estimated Annual Gross Income from Apartment Rentals

	Per Square Foot	Per Unit	Total
Market Units	$2.55	$2,433	$977,918
Affordable Units	$1.06	$838	$27,640
Total			$1,005,558
Annualized (x 12)			$12,066,696

Rent Schedules

	Total	Unit Size (Square Feet)	In-Place Rent/Per Square Foot	Current Market Rent Range/ Per Square Foot
Market Units				
Studio	3	720	$1,225–1,400/ $1.70–1.94	$1,390–1,490/ $1.93–2.07
1 Bedroom/1 Bath				
Floors 2–9	61	646–864	$1,200–1,585/ $1.59–2.17	$1,300–1,775/ $1.63–2.43
Floors 10–19	37	701–864	$1,485–2,000/ $2.12–2.85	$1,650–2,050/ $2.16–2.92
Floors 20–24	25	701–864	$1,975–2,075/ $2.82–2.96	$1,975–2,600/ $2.66–3.38
Subtotal	123	646–864	$1,200–2,075/ $1.59–2.96	$1,300–2,600/ $1.63–3.38
1 Bedroom & Study/1 Bath				
Floors 2–9	9	864–889	$1,300–1,635/ $1.47–1.89	$1,425–1,675/ $1.60–1.94
Floors 10–19	16	864	$1,545–2,055/ $1.79–2.38	$1,725–2,200/ $2.00–2.55
Floors 20–24	9	862–864	$2,150–2,410/ $2.49–2.79	$2,050–2,650/ $2.37–3.07
Subtotal	34	862–889	$1,300–2,410/ $1.47–2.79	$1,425–2,650/ $1.60–3.07
2 Bedrooms/2 Baths				
Floors 2–9	30	1,044–1,337	$1,800–2,300/ $1.65–2.10	$1,925–2,360/ $1.72–2.20
Floors 10–19	110	1,044–1,095	$2,045–2,760/ $1.91–2.54	$2,120–2,905/ $1.95–2.70
Floors 20–24	52	1,072–1,210	$2,700–4,000/ $2.47–3.35	$2,615–4,150/ $2.39–3.47
Subtotal	192	1,050–1,210	$1,800–4,000/ $1.65–3.35	$1,925–4,150/ $1.72–3.47
Total	352	936	$2,023/ $2.16	$2,198/ $2.35

	Total	Unit Size (Square Feet)	In-Place Rent/Per Square Foot	Current Market Rent Range/ Per Square Foot
Totals by Floor				
Floors 2–9	103	646–1,337	$1,200–2,300/ $1.47–2.07	$1,300–2,360/ $1.60–2.43
Floors 10–19	163	701–1,095	$1,485–2,760/ $1.79–2.85	$1,650–2,950/ $1.95–2.92
Floors 20–24	86	701–1,210	$1,975–4,000/ $2.47–3.35	$1,975–4,150/ $2.37–3.47
Affordable Units				
Studio	0	–	–	–
1 Bedroom/1 Bath	14	636–714	$587–801/ $0.86–1.15	$700–729/ $1.01–1.15
1 Bedroom & Study/ 1 Bath	1	1,083	N/A	$900/ $0.83
2 Bedrooms/2 Baths	18	1,050–1,092	$721–908/ $0.66–0.85	$736–908/ $0.68–0.84
Subtotal	33	906	$763/ $0.84	$812/ $0.90
Corporate Units				
Studio	1	720	$1,500/ $2.08	$1,540/ $2.14
1 Bedroom/1 Bath	7	636–714	$1,500–2,000/ $2.14–2.85	$1,500–2,050/ $2.14–2.92
1 Bedroom & Study/1 Bath	1	1,076	$1,975/ $1.84	$2,000/ $1.86
2 Bedrooms/2 Baths	41	1,072–1,095	$1,950–2,450/ $1.80–2.26	$1,955–2,425/ $1.80–2.24
Subtotal	50	1,023	$1,964/ $1.92	$2,043/ $2.00
Total	435	944	$1,920/ $2.04	$2,075/ $2.20

continued on page 491

Given that government is so important in the development process, a well-conceived public relations program provides relevant agencies and officials with the comprehensive information they need to discharge their responsibilities efficiently. Taking the initiative to raise and resolve potentially difficult issues can sometimes avert distressingly contentious public confrontations.

Another component of a well-crafted public relations program is generating positive editorial exposure for the development plans. The potential impact of such exposure derives from the power of the implied third-party endorsement. Editorialists can offer favorable comments, which, if uttered by a developer, would appear self-serving. The best single generator of prospects' visits to a sales center selling new homes is a feature article with photographs in the local newspaper's real estate section.

No matter the type of property involved, the opportunities to benefit from positive editorial exposure abound. The secret is simply to develop professional friendships with the individuals who write the articles or editorials—reporters for the business section of the newspaper and editors of state or local business magazines. An often overlooked fact is that reporters and editors must meet tough deadlines with interesting copy day after day and week after week. The time will come during the life of any real estate development when developers and their professional friends will be able to help one another—but only if developers do their part in advance by developing working relationships with the press.

Yet another component of the public relations program is a newsletter published by the development company. Newsletters allow developers to tell their own story in their own way while preserving some of the impact of an implied third-party endorsement. It makes relatively little difference whether the newsletter is elaborate or inexpensive; what does make a difference is the frequency with which the newsletter is published. Newsletters should be short, newsy, factual, and light and include photographs of interesting people. No single issue will take over the market; it is more a question of building an overall positive image for the endeavor one small step at a time. Newsletters are likewise useful in reaching the target market and staying close to public officials.

On-Site Promotions

The principle of on-site promotions is to induce members of the target market—whether tenants or potential customers—to visit the site. The goal is to stage an interesting event on the property to attract prospects who might otherwise not visit the project.

Perhaps the most obvious on-site promotion of a new development is the grand opening. Developers should invite to the opening citizens and government officials they met as part of the public relations program as well as representatives of the extended development team. Developers should also invite principal or potential prospects. In many areas, a chamber of commerce function is a worthwhile on-site promotion. The primary and secondary trade areas' customers should be included, along with area retailers and anchor tenants, corporate real estate managers, and merchants.

Not only should the physical features of a building be used as a sales tool, but the quality and depth of the

property's tenancies should also be distinctly attractive to the target market. Allowing the market to experience firsthand a project's features, functions, and benefits can be a great sales tool.

A city agency asked Museum Towers to donate land to a park that will abut the property. What was originally seen as a concession to the city in the negotiations is being marketed as an amenity.

▌▌ Museum Towers

The Park as a Marketing Tool

North Point Park is a 40-acre park that, under the direction of the Metropolitan District Commission, was scheduled to be completed in 2000. The idea of the park was first presented to the public in 1986. It's all part of the Metropolitan Park System's plan to connect the edges of the city. The Boston and Cambridge Esplanades will be connected along the river to HarborPark and the Freedom Trail. Along the way are large-scale engineering works, such as bridges, dams, pumping stations, locks, and viaducts, that will all be set off and beautified with parkland and water elements. Seven miles of new pathways will be available along the Charles River.

The Metropolitan District Commission held public hearings and various meetings and worked closely with the New Charles River Basin Citizens Advisory Committee to solicit ideas, attitudes, and expectations about the park.

The land that the park is on was part of the site that we owned and donated to the state. Somewhere during this development process, I got religion and said, yes, I want to give up an acre of my land to parks, yes, I want to have my site cut in half by a road, yes, I want to set aside 7.5 percent of my project for low-income housing, yes, I want to build my own utilities, yes, I want to rebuild an intersection, yes, I want to build two separate towers instead of one, yes, I want to build towers that are not as tall as I'd like, yes, I want to build a restaurant that has to be open to the public certain hours. I love being a developer.

But the park will come up around one building and wrap around the other building, right up to the health club. We have to give the roads to the city. In the end, the park will be a huge asset to the project. It will be for passive use, with trails. It'll link with other bike trails. There will be a canoe house and some kiosks. I expect the restaurant I was forced to build will also benefit from the park.

continued on page 512

Merchandising the Product

Merchandising the product encompasses all the visual impressions associated with the project (other than those clearly stated in advertising or editorials). It extends not only to brochures and stationery but also to everything that prospects might see in support of a sales presentation on or off site.

When a building's architectural design has been carefully planned, it should be a primary component of product merchandising. Entrances to most real estate developments are consciously designed to give the impression that the individuals who live, work, or shop in those places are people of substance. An impressive entrance can help sales in at least two ways. First, creating a favorable impression makes prospects feel better personally. Second, an attractive entrance can impress visitors—whether friends, employees, suppliers, or even competitors.

The same phenomenon holds true for other elements of the site design. Landscaping, street and parking layout, and signs all play a part in fostering the idea that the subject development is worthy of consideration and worth the asking price.

A sales or leasing information center could be a major component in merchandising different product types. Such a facility should be an artful blend of pleasing aesthetics and efficiency. From the prospect's point of view, approaching, entering, and lingering in the information center should be a pleasant, nonthreatening experience. Achieving this effect is a responsibility best assigned to a competent designer experienced with sales centers.

The efficiency of a successful sales center, however, is best left to marketing and sales experts. Depending on the specific characteristics of the product, certain displays and graphic sales aids will be required to underscore the points stressed in the sales presentation. The design of each individual display, the message it conveys, and its placement within the facility should support the presentation to the maximum extent possible. Each design therefore requires the cooperation of the sales staff who know what they want, the graphic artist who understands design, and the interior designer who wants each presentation to please prospects and to fit within a consistent design theme. For retail developments, the quality of both anchor tenants and national tenants, project layout, visibility from major roadways, and access play a significant part in merchandising the center not only to other retailers but also to the shopping public. In other words, marketing centers may be essential to selling homes, but the successful leasing of a regional mall, community shopping center, or neighborhood center depends on location and other tenants.

For some products, particularly new houses, furnished models that show a sample of the finished product are effective. Two principal schools of thought concern the effect that should be created. One school says, "Visitors who come here will not forget where they saw this purple wallpaper!" The other says, "Gee, honey, it looks so comfortable. We could move in here this afternoon."

A logo and a name for a development are essential for any marketing plan. The entry to the Hamptons in Tampa, Florida, introduces an arrowhead motif, which is carried throughout the community to preserve the site's Native American history.

The final elements to consider in product merchandising are naming the project and developing a consistent image through a logo and the promotional color scheme. Successful names reinforce the project's attractiveness to the target market and should reflect the same attributes as well-designed entranceways. They should be impressive and dignified without intimidating prospects, yet still convey warmth (see Figure 22-3).

With the project's name determined, it is often useful to design a distinctive logo consistent with the impression the developer is trying to convey to the target market. Designing logos is a matter for commercial artists. Once the logo is chosen, it should be used consistently without alteration. The same holds true for the promotional color scheme. It is important to specify colors based on a standard system and to use only those colors in promotional pieces. Absolutely consistent presentation is central to building market awareness of the product.

Relations with Real Estate Agents

Knowing local real estate agents who specialize in a specific property type is critical, regardless of whether the developer employs an in-house sales staff or an outside agency. In today's real estate markets, many tenants are represented by their own broker. Alternatively, successful brokers know about local market conditions and often have advantageous access to prospects. In the retail real estate business, retailers often rely on their own internal real estate staff and thus entirely avoid third-party brokers.

The influence of local real estate agents in commercial sales and leasing is powerful. Expanding companies establishing operations in a new area are likely to view as essential the help of a knowledgeable local agent, whether they are seeking office, warehouse, manufacturing, or retail space. Even for companies that have operated in an area for some time, the assistance of local agents frees executives to pursue their primary responsibilities.

If sales and leasing are handled by in-house staff, the developer has far more direct control. If the in-house staff is arrogant and internally focused, however, it will be harder to create a productive relationship with any third parties needed to complete sales. Brokers are not easily excited by new products unless they are convinced they can sell the property quickly and easily. Therefore, convincing real estate agents that they can make money by introducing prospects to the subject property can pose a challenge to the developer.

Publishing a special newsletter for real estate agents is one approach to the problem. Even better, the developer can visit the brokerage offices that serve the target market, making presentations intended to sell brokers themselves on the value of the product and to get to know the brokers as individuals. Frequently, the most efficient approach of all is to examine local records to determine which individual agents are the leaders in selling the specific property type. Highly personal approaches to these high achievers can sometimes produce extraordinary results.

A real estate agent relations program is not likely to go far until local agents are convinced that the developer's representatives will treat their prospects courteously and professionally. Equally important, agents want assurance that developers will pay full commissions quickly with checks that will not be returned for insufficient funds. Time and time again, proper and timely financial remuneration of cooperating brokers is the primary reason that agents bring prospects to a developer's property. To the extent that the developer can help agents build a stronger relationship with their clients, local agents will become more enthusiastic about introducing their clients to the developer.

Educating the Sales Staff

By its very nature, the real estate sales process is characterized by rejection and failure. Attempted sales far surpass completed sales, and the number of prospects far surpasses the number of buyers. Many more selling days end in defeat than in victory. Keeping salespeople contented and motivated thus becomes a challenge. The traditional means of dealing with morale issues has been to compensate salespeople on the basis of commissions. The rationale is that the possibility of a substantial carrot will inspire superior effort. A more consistent approach, however, is to build the sales force's professional capability through continuing education. Two benefits occur. First, the salesperson's professional skills are enhanced. Second, enhanced professional skills almost always bring a corresponding increase in self-confidence, motivation, and sales or leases (and translate into obvious benefits for the developer). Whether relying on in-house staff or an outside agency, a wise developer takes advantage of these benefits by making sure that continuing sales education is an integral part of the marketing and sales system.

To sell a product well, an agent must fully understand the product. Recognizing this fact, most developers provide some type of orientation program for new agents. It would be difficult to go too far in this endeavor, for every detail about the project's design and excellence that can be communicated to salespeople

Figure 22-3

Celebration

Celebration, a town of approximately 4,900 acres near Orlando, Florida, is being developed by the Celebration Company, a subsidiary of the Walt Disney Company. The company is striving to make Celebration an education-minded, health-conscious place to live, work, and play. Ground was broken in March 1994. The residential sales and rental program began in November 1995, and the first residents moved in by June 1996, followed by the opening of the downtown district in November that year. Buildout is expected to take ten to 15 years.

Marketing and Sales Strategy

Robert Charles Lesser & Co., based in Los Angeles, undertook initial market studies for the community in the late 1980s. Lesser's research indicated a strong market for primary housing for young families and empty nesters, second homes, and retirement homes. Rather than deal with all these markets in Phase I, Disney decided to focus on the primary-home market, as it provided the greatest support for the school and health campus. During Phase I, covenants prohibited use of the houses for second homes. The first phase where houses can be used seasonally is Phase IV—North Village—which includes housing products targeted for second-home and retirement markets and allows houses to be rented out.

Although the company placed no national advertising, the national press was keenly interested in the project, generating a high level of interest among consumers. Because demand was so strong, the company held a drawing to establish priority for purchasing the 351 lots and leasing the 123 apartments. Five thousand people attended the Founders Day drawing in 1995, and 1,200 prospective residents put down deposits.

The Celebration Preview Center functions as an information center and headquarters for Celebration Realty, which handles all home sales. The center's ground floor houses exhibits, a video presentation, a model of the community, and an interactive computer display. Visitors with strong interest are escorted to the realty and design center on the second floor, where sample home designs and floorplans are displayed. From there, they tour model homes. Showcase Village, a collection of three models, highlights innovative building technologies and displays the latest products from suppliers and participants. Each house employs a different energy-efficient method of construction.

To build the houses for Phase I, Disney selected eight premier local homebuilders and two high-quality national homebuilding companies. Builders are free to set their own prices and margins. Disney undertook extensive research to determine the mix of product types. The company analyzed market growth, absorption by price point, and house and lot size. The research resulted in a master plan for a community that would appeal to a variety of buyers and create a vibrant town. Selling prices in all categories appear to carry a premium of at least 10 to 15 percent above comparable homes in other local master-planned communities. The estate homes are lowest in demand, perhaps because some builders set sale prices well above the recommended $500,000.

General Business Strategy

Over the years, Disney's goal has been to maintain the special values and high quality that have been Disney hallmarks while always embracing new ideas. The company tries to look at the familiar in new ways, seeing change as the essence of creativity. The company is structured like most development firms, with a general manager, a marketing division, a sales division, a residential development division that works with builders, and a financial and operations division responsible for financial planning, asset management, apartment leasing, and building maintenance. What distinguishes the company's structure from most is its new business development division, whose role is to establish strategic alliances and to work with strategic alliance partners.

---

becomes ammunition for use with prospects. Most developers also acknowledge that any real estate sale or leasing transaction could well take the prospect or the developer into unfamiliar financial territory. For this reason, the agent must be able to act as a financial guide, leading the prospect to a rational and comfortable decision among possibly confusing and conflicting financing alternatives.

The need to provide education for salespeople about the specific skills of selling is less well understood. The profession of selling is built on the ability of salespeople to establish clear and compelling communication with prospects. Most often, sound communication is based on establishing as much personal rapport as possible with the prospect as soon as possible. Prospects who feel comfortable with their sales agent and are convinced that

Celebration's 18-acre downtown district features apartments, shops, offices, restaurants, a movie theater, small parks, public plazas, and a lakefront promenade. Designed on the assumption that streets belong to people, not cars, most parking is placed in lots behind buildings.

The Walt Disney Company

The Celebration Company believes that other developers can replicate almost everything about the community, including the town center and the creation of public/private partnerships for information technology, education, and health. At the same time, however, the company acknowledges that it would be considerably more difficult for most developers than it was for Disney to undertake so much advance research and development. The special circumstances that made it possible were that Disney owned the land, had access to substantial financial resources, and was also able to tap into strong market demand. Nevertheless, the company points out that it has a pro forma for each element of the project and that every element is programmed to generate an appropriate return over time. Further, building the infrastructure through community development districts helped the economic equation greatly.

The strategic alliances with corporate partners proved beneficial to all involved. Celebration's alliances bring industry leaders together to help create the special components that form the town's cornerstones. Since the alliance process was initiated in 1992, alliances have typically evolved through several steps: research and identification of potential partners, information sharing, letters of understanding, an operations plan, formal agreements, operations, vision, and alliance expansion. The last step often results in the identification of new products and opportunities for Disney, creating value that the company did not have in the past. The alliances often create synergistic relationships. As the partners were brought together with the common purpose of creating community, they were asked to focus not only on their own areas but also on the entire town. ∎

the agent is sincerely interested in their point of view are much more likely to buy or lease the product.

Building rapport with prospective buyers generally requires breaking down the prospect's emotional defenses against the sale of an item. Prospects usually perceive themselves at risk, believing that a negotiation could be critically important to them. They want to get as much information as possible from the sales agent

without revealing too much about themselves, their needs, and their motives. The sales agent's challenge is almost the opposite. Building rapport with the prospect requires the agent to learn as much as possible about the prospect as an individual.

Many training courses devote time to classifying personalities that enable salespeople to identify a prospect's comfortable style of behavior. Reading the prospect's verbal and nonverbal cues in the first few moments allows the agent to place that individual into one of a number of behavioral categories and to adapt his own normal style of behavior to the prospect's behavior to lower defensive barriers. The assumption is that different behavioral types are interested in and motivated by distinctly different elements of the product.

Another body of useful knowledge is negotiation techniques. If the prospect perceives the two parties to be involved in negotiation from the outset, then they are. Many of the lessons that have been learned during negotiations, either between nations or between management and labor, are directly applicable to negotiations in real estate sales and leasing. Understanding where power comes from and how to use it can give salespeople a tremendous advantage. Likewise, understanding classic maneuvers and how best to counter them can make some of the toughest situations appear elementary.

All these techniques apply to the general objective of fostering improved communication between the participants involved on either side of a real estate sales presentation. They are adaptations of techniques that are one foundation of an education in business management. Including them in the education of sales agents can expand team members' professional capabilities.

Defining the target market and creating a product specifically suited to it are fundamental to successful real estate sales. Although market research defines the target market in economic and demographic terms, understanding the psychographic profile of target markets is a well-established principle in marketing consumer products that is directly applicable to marketing real estate. Just as traditional demographic analysis allows salespeople to group customers on the basis of age, sex, income, and family size, psychographic analysis allows the sales force to segment the overall population into groups that share the same general outlook on life. (This approach helps in retail leasing, because it becomes possible to lease to the appropriate tenants whose merchandise or line of business fits the needs of the trade area's particular psychographic groups.)

Knowing what customers want as individuals allows sales agents to present the product so that it meets needs customers may not even perceive they have. This principle is the basis of psychographic marketing: creating products (or leasing to tenants who sell products) that meet the strongly felt needs of an identified target market segment and then presenting those products to that target so that their unrealized needs are satisfied just as their explicit needs are met. The psychographic profile represents an extremely powerful component of marketing knowledge that salespeople can use to great effect.

Sales Operations

Sales operations is where the rubber meets the road in marketing and sales. It is here that individual prospects and sales representatives convert the space that has been created into revenue. Organizing to accomplish this task is a critical activity itself, and perhaps the developer's most fundamental decision is whether to conduct sales operations with an in-house staff, under contract to an outside agency, or through some combination of the two.

Each has its advantages and disadvantages. Use of in-house staff enables the developer to exercise more control over the specifics of how the task is accomplished. The developer has the power and authority to supervise sales and leasing representatives directly, setting their daily priorities and requiring adherence to specific procedures. But these very advantages carry their own costs in terms of financial obligations and management.

Perhaps these obligations are the reason so many developers find it advantageous to contract with an outside brokerage agency for sales and leasing. A relatively simple negotiation between a developer and a broker sets in motion a continuing effort in which the developer may be somewhat less involved. The agency is presumed to command special expertise in handling a particular type of product in a particular market and to employ a competent and motivated staff. (The developer's administrative burden is reduced dramatically, especially in subdivision sales, where the agency is paid from the proceeds of actual sales. In the case of leasing, commissions are paid from property operations or construction and development loans.)

In sales operations, one of the principal differences between commercial and residential sales is the extent to which active prospecting takes place. In commercial developments, developer's representatives normally identify potential individual members of the target market and contact them directly to initiate the sale. Alternatively, developer's representatives may contact members of the brokerage community who enjoy exclusive leasing arrangements with prospective tenants.

An enterprising salesperson should spend some time calling on a developer's current clients to see whether they are content or might be thinking of expanding or relocating their facilities. Lack of attention could send current clients to a competing project. Existing relationships with current tenants offer a great advantage to the developer who is not concerned about eroding occupancy in one building to increase it in another. When the same developer controls both existing and prospective leases, timing the move is not overly worrisome. In fact, it is not uncommon for an asset manager to manage investments for multiple clients. Although in such cases

This furnished room in a model home was an effective marketing tool for the Addison Reserve in Palm Beach County, Florida. The developers transformed a flat tomato field into a luxury golf community set among rolling hills and lakes.

moving tenants between buildings can create serious conflicts of interest, keeping up with existing tenants' needs is still a good idea. Care should be taken, therefore, to investigate any conflicts of interest adequately before engaging an asset manager or a brokerage firm.

The sales staff should also compile a list of firms that fit the profile of the target market and then seek them out. They need to find out whom the targeted firms do business with and to note what other businesses are located nearby. They should also call on nearby businesses that are already related by location to the primary product to be sold.

If it works, advertising will generate inquiries from additional potential occupants. Inquiries indicate an existing interest and must receive prompt attention. Calling on interested parties who are responding to advertising is relatively easy. Calling on current customers and following up on responses to advertising are, however, never enough to cover the target market adequately. For the remaining potential occupants, "directed prospecting" (also known as "cold calling") is the only approach. Reaching someone new is often the key to extraordinary success in real estate sales.

In retail centers, successful prospecting includes scouring the market for successful "local" tenant prospects who can expand their businesses. Although most leasing for regional malls has shifted to national tenan-cies, good local tenants are always desirable. Constant vigilance and a review of competitive projects can uncover diamonds in the rough.

Successful prospecting requires some preparation. The salesperson must target the prospect, identify the key person within the organization, make an appointment with that person, and convince the individual the development will meet his needs. Even then, a considerable amount of time might pass before the contact yields a sale. Patience and follow-up are needed before the effort eventually bears fruit.

Building the Sale

Once the salesperson has identified an interested prospect, the challenge shifts to making a successful sales presentation. Whether the objective is generating a signed lease or an authorized purchase agreement, a planned rather than improvised presentation is always preferable, regardless of property type. The agent must identify the prospect's needs and convince him that the proffered product will meet those needs, ensuring that the value delivered is at least equal to the price.

Finally, the salesperson must ask for the order. It is this final part of the process that many salespeople find so difficult; it always seems to be too soon to ask. The best salespeople eliminate this stress from the decision-making process by following a planned sequence for the presentation that guarantees delivery of all needed information in a logical order as well as opportunities for ample feedback from the prospect. If the salesperson has followed the sequence and delivered all the necessary information, the prospect will want the agent to ask for an order. If the prospect is not ready to proceed, he already would have found a way to terminate the process.

Follow-Up

Effective follow-up is essential for any sales transaction. Few sales are closed in the first meeting, and good salespeople work patiently with identified prospects.

In residential sales, following up on presales is intended to encourage return visits to the sales center. The agent should follow a prearranged schedule of written and telephone contacts, based on the number of days that pass since the prospect's first visit to the sales center. Generally speaking, these contacts should be friendly and not oriented toward sales. For commercial properties, the same general idea holds, though with one major exception: the intensity of follow-up should increase as the expiration date of the prospect's present lease approaches.

Reaching an agreement does not mean that follow-up should cease. One of the most important functions a sales or leasing professional can perform is to hold the deal together between signing and moving in. In Florida, for example, the signing of a purchase agreement for a new condominium merely signals the beginning of a 15-day period during which the purchaser can cancel the deal at any time for any reason. This law, reflecting government's continuing role as the developer's partner, merely acknowledges that once people make a decision, they often have second thoughts. It is up to the sales agent to anticipate this event and to take steps to prevent its occurrence.

After the tenant moves in, follow-up shifts to ascertaining that the space has been delivered in acceptable condition. Given the effort and expense of creating a synergistic marketing and sales system, it makes sense to try for more than a one-time contact with a prospect who is never seen or heard from again. It makes no sense to shepherd a prospect to an agreement only to have the deal fall apart. Likewise, it is of limited benefit to put a prospect into space the team has worked so hard to create only to have him become unhappy. The most efficient way to avoid these unfortunate circumstances is systematic and sensitive follow-up by salespeople.

Accepting the Challenge of Marketing and Sales

In successful development operations, people come to work early, work hard, move fast, and stay late. Salespeople who are not immediately productive are quickly gone. If salespeople want to avoid failure, they might consider the following suggestions:

1. Learn the property type, tenant market, customer, and trade area. Thoroughly understand the market research. Read the feasibility study very carefully. Look at comparable facilities; shop the competitors. Understand access, visibility, and road patterns. Review the plans and specifications for each building under construction. Walk around the property, preferably with someone who can explain its features, functions, and benefits.
2. Know the development company's history and its current financial condition. Look for statements of its operating philosophy and plans for the future. In retail development, visit tenants' existing units. Understand their business.
3. Read recent leases and/or purchase agreements, which demonstrate how business is conducted and with whom. Differences among recent agreements indicate areas of frequent negotiation.
4. Get to know the company's principal suppliers.
5. Estimate where the financial pressures will be felt in the organization. Compare the current status of the project with the projections included in original plans. Pressure will most assuredly be directed toward operations that are behind schedule, including marketing and sales.
6. Get to know the players on the team. Who controls what in the company? Who is reliable? Where are the territorial lines that should not be crossed?
7. Find out the current status of the relevant local market and any apparent market trends. Know how the market is doing and how it is important to potential customers. The local press is a great place to start on both counts.
8. Most important, be professional from the beginning. Work hard. Tell the truth. Never stop learning.
9. And never sell all the lakefront property first.

Summary

Few people are born salespeople, but many people can learn marketing, and everyone—whether a consumer or supplier of space—should understand what makes space appealing, marketable, and valuable to its users. Although many aspects of this discipline are common to all property selling and leasing, distinct aspects are associated with each property type. We have illustrated a few of the major differences with the examples of regional mall leasing and subdivision sales throughout the chapter. More detail on aspects of the other property types is available in course format from the primary trade organizations, including the International Council of Shopping Centers (ICSC), the American Hotel and Motel Association (AHMA), the National Association of Industrial and Office Properties (NAIOP), the National Association of Realtors® (NAR) and its numerous subsidiaries, the Building Owners and Managers Association (BOMA) International, and ULI–the Urban Land Institute.

Terms

- Absorption
- Anchor tenants
- Broker
- Cold calling
- Demographics
- Merchandise mix
- National chain tenants
- Prospecting
- Psychographic profile
- Target market
- Trade area

Review Questions

22.1 What four elements of business should marketing personnel be familiar with and why?

22.2 Define the ultimate goals of market research.

22.3 Describe the two principal methods of developing a marketing budget.

22.4 What are the primary advertising media employed by the real estate industry? Give a description of each, including positive and negative aspects.

22.5 Museum Towers has a Web site advertising the property to potential tenants. How does that kind of advertising differ from a print ad or a direct-mail campaign? What are some of the advantages and disadvantages?

22.6 Why is it important for the developer to maintain a strong public relations campaign with government officials?

22.7 What is the single most important reason for tenant brokers to bring prospects to a developer's facility?

22.8 How does knowledge of psychographic profiles assist the developer in design, construction, operations, and leasing of a project?

22.9 Should asset managers be concerned with a developer's or broker's existing client base? Why or why not?

22.10 After a lease is signed or a sale closed, the developer's marketing efforts should cease. True or false? Comment.

Chapter 23

A Note about the Future

There can be no fully appropriate summary or conclusion to a book about real estate development, because society's needs for built space are continually evolving. We offer instead a note about the future.

Decisions about the development of real property are critical to our society's future functioning. Indeed, the largest share of the nation's wealth is invested in real property, and the built environment has a major impact on almost everyone's life. The better the development decisions made today, the better tomorrow's built environment will be. The eight-stage model of the real estate development process discussed throughout this text is a flexible strategic tool that allows developers to make better decisions today—to see the whole while focusing on a particular decision.

The logic behind the eight-stage model is clearly financial, but the motivation comes from the market. Development involves complex marketing, financial, political, and production tasks as well as many different kinds of interpersonal relationships. Still, all of the activity is in response to particular market segments and the consumers in those segments whose preferences are constantly changing.

A complete understanding of the development process is impossible without a historical perspective, for history allows us to understand where we have been and how we have arrived at the present. As such, history is a useful tool for predicting the future. Development is a forward-looking activity based on knowledge and experience drawn from the past. Because constructed space can be expected to last for several decades, a long-term historical perspective is important in anticipating what society will demand over the next several decades.

This chapter about the future discusses several topics:

- A contemporary perspective on the past;
- How best to think about what will be in the future;
- Several issues that could be critical in developers' consideration of the future; and
- A return to Graaskamp's complete definition of feasibility and concern for "what ought to be."

Along the way, we pay a final visit to Europa Center and Museum Towers.

A Historical Look at the Future of Development

The long view—from the past and into the future—yields a portrait of recurring patterns as well as entirely new circumstances. For example, the fact that real estate development slowed from its dizzying pace of the mid-1980s is certainly not a new phenomenon. Real estate is traditionally a cyclical business, and it has always experienced the inevitable busts that follow the booms. What was different about the 1980s was the extent of overbuilding. Typically, during the downturns of the past four decades, the development pendulum would swing back again within a few years. This time, however, the supply of available office space, hotel rooms, strip shopping centers, and residential condominiums compared with projected demand was so excessive that it took over half a decade to restore balance in some markets. Nevertheless, although overbuilding was far more extensive in the 1980s than in the 1950s, 1960s, or 1970s, the situation was still far better than at the beginning of the 1930s. With the economic impact of the Great Depression, supply was so much greater than demand that virtually no new private office buildings were constructed in many urban areas for more than 20 years.

One important difference between earlier cycles—all the way back to the 18th century—and contemporary circumstances is that the more severe real estate crashes from the 1790s to the 1930s were generally accompanied by a major panic in the financial system. Today, with the S&L crisis now history and new regulatory safeguards in place, America's financial system is quite stable. Indeed, pension funds and other forms of institutional ownership have introduced an added element of stability that was missing during the 1930s, when the widespread default of privately insured mortgage bonds led to a long-term withdrawal of private capital from real estate. New financial institutions and global investors will continue to bring many structural changes to real estate development in the 21st century as they did during the 1990s.

Sometimes history repeats itself. The financial instruments of the 1980s such as mortgage-backed securities resemble the innovations of the 1920s, while the development ideas and practices of the 1990s included a return to traditional street grids in suburban subdivisions and nostalgic Main Street storefront designs for new shopping centers. Yet at the same time, recent and projected demographic patterns of a rapidly aging population and the formation of nontraditional households (such as single-parent families) combined with the challenge of a newly defined set of environmental problems suggest that we will witness the creation of more radically different forms and processes of development than ever before. The prospects for a genuine renaissance in the design and use of space—for a rebirth of the visionary aspects of real estate development—loom large. Further stimulating these prospects is the continuing restructuring and increasing professionalization within the real estate industry. Certainly, the growth of university graduate school education in real estate development should enhance physical and institutional innovations. New development will continue to dot the landscape, because people will continue to demand more types of space in new locations. The competition will be tough, because many of the scared warriors of the 1980s and 1990s want another chance, while a host of new players with new ideas await their turn.

How Best to Think about the Future

Timing is obviously critical in all investment but particularly in development period investment. From an analytical perspective, the time horizon determines what type of research is needed to support the various elements of investment strategy.

The performance of short-term investments in most real estate markets (property type and geographic location) is controlled by idiosyncratic events—rebuilding after a hurricane, corporate relocations, the advent of new technology, and so on. The performance of intermediate-term investments is controlled more by industry mix and whether or not the drivers of the local economy are doing well nationally. And long-term performance, most fundamentally value growth, is more a function of relative costs—a productivity-adjusted measure, so workforce skills, agglomeration benefits, and existing infrastructure all matter. Quality of life is also a critical component of locational decision making. Cost advantages (quality adjusted) lead to a more rapidly growing local economy and growth in per capita income, the major drivers of changes in real estate value.

In most markets, existing conditions are "fairly" priced as soon as they become widely known. Therefore, what matters in investment performance is forecasting change. Whether concerned with minute-to-minute pricing (lease decisions) or three-year forecasts (when to start Phase II of a project), the astute developer focuses on change.

Future changes involve two kinds of judgment:

- Learning from the past (while monitoring the contemporary situation). This kind of judgment is econometric and data intensive. Most of the market material covered in this text deals with judgments based on documentable current conditions and historic relationships.
- Estimating what may be different in the future.

Although learning from the past is something every professional tries to do, estimating what may be different in the future is more subjective and often difficult for decision makers. Everyone will admit it is critically important not to "straight line" a forecast, but that doesn't mean everyone will agree on how to draw the curves. Different curves are what create the development horse race. It is not a matter of guessing the date of "the big one" in California. Rather, it is a matter of looking at the reactions to and interactions among existing trends—which can be done without a crystal ball. All investors do it implicitly, but the best ones do it explicitly as well.

A Few Things That Could Be Critical

The Changing Workplace

New office buildings are bulking up with the latest high-tech gadgets, particularly where information technology is concerned. The old rat's nest of cubicle-clogging wires has given way to compatible outlets. At the offices of the Equitable Life Assurance Society in New York, for example, workstations were wired with state-of-the-art Category 5 cable, which can handle the high-speed voice, data, and video communications used in shared computer networks. Fiber-optic cable, an even more expensive carrier, is used between floors at Equitable.

In Manhattan's growing Silicon Alley, another office building successfully lured two communications-oriented tenants by offering ready-to-use Rate Adaptive Digital Subscriber Line (RADSL) service. The service automatically adjusts bandwidth rate to compensate for circuit noise. The new tenants attracted by the RADSL service include Dynamo Development, Inc., a software firm, and Tri Star Web, Inc., which operates a World Wide Web hosting service.

Information technology now accounts for the largest segment of the U.S. corporate capital budget, even surpassing real estate. That means buildings offering state-of-the-art equipment are at the top of the list for managers of computer-intensive offices. Other attractive features include heavier and more reliable power and high-tech security and building management systems.

The impact of technology on office location poses another concern, but again the trends are debatable. High-tech communications obviously facilitates the decentralization of office jobs; indeed, in recent years, employment growth outside metropolitan areas has been increasing for the first time in a long time. Moreover, high-tech communications should continue to spur new office development in second-tier cities where back-office operations have been a growing office user in recent years.

Technology and Industrial Real Estate

"Just-in-time" delivery strikes the same fear among industrial space providers that "virtual office" does among office owners—that their product will soon become obsolete. Just-in-time delivery extends the production line to suppliers and arranges for the delivery of materials just as they are required, eliminating the need for intermediate warehousing and reducing the volume of on-site inventory. Despite the logic of just-in-time delivery, the need for warehouse space has not changed —at least not yet.

The consensus among economists is that the ratio of inventories to business sales, a key indicator of an inventory-efficient economy, has remained unchanged. An easy explanation might be that the new technologies for enhancing the efficiency of inventorying have not been applied. In fact, an Ohio State University survey found that only 14 percent of responding companies were making serious attempts to adopt the new inventory techniques. A more complex explanation might be that the increasing globalization of the economy and a stronger reliance on subcontracting demand a greater flow of intermediate goods for each final good produced, thereby actually increasing the need for storage.

In addition, although the growing sophistication of information systems required in state-of-the-art warehousing is admittedly making some warehouse operations obsolete, it is also opening up new business opportunities for others. One firm that has taken the plunge into the new technology is the Fritz Companies, the nation's largest customs broker, which moved aggressively into warehousing and distribution in 1988 through acquisitions and internal expansion. Fritz handles Asian goods for Sears Roebuck & Company, shipping them through China and Hong Kong into a warehouse in Carson, California, and then to nine Sears distribution centers. According to Jim Fitzhugh, Fritz's southern California regional manager, if a company cannot deliver such integrated services, "somebody else will soon take your customer."

Hotels: Networking versus the Net

The digerati, claiming that much commercial travel and certainly the need for face-to-face conventions would be rendered obsolete by advanced communications, erred when they predicted that hotels, particularly those catering to business travelers, would soon become relics of the jet age. In fact, hotel occupancies and conference attendance have both increased recently. At the same time, communications technology has been advancing at an astonishing pace with the explosion of Internet use. All this activity seems to be the product of a vigorous economy and a healthy resistance to replacing meet-space with cyberspace. Indeed, industry spokespeople report that an unexpected benefit of Internet use is the growing desire of people who connect in on-line communities to gather face to face.

Of necessity, hotel services have had to keep pace with the growing technological sophistication of business users; fax machines are virtually universal and the room as workstation will soon follow. A recent example is a kiosk installed in the San Diego Marriott that features a high-capacity ISDN (integrated services digital network) connection, enabling users to send and receive E-mail. Can roboconcierges be far behind? Not if an experiment at the MainStay Suites in Plano, Texas, proves successful. Guests can check in electronically and receive a magnetic room key at a kiosk.

The hotel sector is also set to be connected to the Internet. Hilton Hotels Corp. recently rolled out a new feature for its guests—public Internet access stations in 15 major business lodges around the country, with more to come. And a firm called @Home Network, Inc., has formed a partnership with the Fourth Communications Network, Inc., to link hotels throughout the United States to the Internet, starting with the San Francisco Bay Area. The two companies will provide Internet access directly to hotel rooms and will set up Internet kiosks in hotel lobbies.

Retail.com

The migration of retailers into cyberspace—prime examples are bookseller Amazon.com, which has no stores, and Egghead Software, which decided to close all stores in favor of going entirely on line—has caused some to wonder whether stores as we know them are outmoded. Yet today, nonstore shopping—catalogs, telemarketing, television, and the Internet—accounts for a mere 3 to 4 percent of retail sales, with on-line sales only a fraction of that.

During the last decade, however, the growth in nonstore sales sharply outpaced in-store sales. An estimate by Bear Stearns pegs Internet sales at about 10 percent of the retail market by 2010, a potentially large hit. And retail analyst Gary London predicts that "the big-box retailer, whose main reason for being is [its] ability to stock many goods under one roof, will become a vestigial remnant of an old way of shopping."

Shopping centers can fight back by working from their strengths. For example, many people consider retail mall shopping a social and sensory experience that cyberspace cannot duplicate. Moreover, shopping center operators have remedied many of the deficiencies that once turned shoppers away, such as inconvenience and fear of crime. Andrew Halliday, former vice president of Simon Property Group, identifies the biochemical power of the salesperson and emphasizes "the mall as medium," with expanded boundaries to include interactive marketing, electronic commerce, and sophisticated entertainment. Further, a better understanding of the customer can allow the mall retailer to customize inventories with greater precision.

One of the first of a new generation of "wired" malls, the 210,000-square-foot Promenade at Westlake opened at the end of 1996 in Thousand Oaks, California. The mall's fiber-optic network allows tenants to take advantage of the latest communications systems to speed information to their home offices and goods and services to their customers, according to developer Rick H. Caruso. The developer envisions "tapping the fiber-optic network for interactive kiosks to provide our customers with information and services beyond what is physically available at the Promenade."

Technology in the Home and The Community

The wild card in determining technology's effect on residential real estate is telecommuting, the extent to which a worker is no longer bound to live reasonably close to work. Although 1990 Census data reported that 20 million people work from home—a broad category that includes telecommuters—only 5 percent were full-time at-home workers.

Working at home in addition to the office is a growing trend; at least half of renters living in upscale apartment communities work at home some of the time, according to recent M/PF Research surveys. In neighborhoods near high-tech centers, such as northwest Austin, as many as two-thirds of upscale apartment households reportedly own computers. A computer setup, however, requires more space—typically a separate room for an office—and multiple telephone lines. Many new apartments are being outfitted with ultra-high-speed T-1 line Internet connections and power more typical of business users. A recent trend in larger multifamily buildings is the offering of an advanced fiber-optic network that provides telephone, Internet, and cable services from one source.

New planned communities also offer opportunities for incorporating advanced technology. At Montgomery, the first wired community in the Toronto market, accessibility to a fiber-optic cable permitted the developer to promote a special feature. All houses and businesses were wired, and surveys showed that one-half of buyers intended to do paid work at home, double the national average. Interestingly, surveys of buyers showed that although the technology was attractive, it ranked fourth in purchasers' decisions, behind quality of the house, neighborhood, and value.

What Ought to Be

If you believe that everything you hear about the future is important and just about to happen, then you may qualify as the world's most gullible person. Even the authors of this text do not agree with all the suggestions made in this one chapter. We do agree, however, that one of our most important jobs is to think about dealing with the brave new world we all inhabit. What follows is a demonstration of how the mythical Clinton Bidwell combines rigorous thought about the future with personal inspiration to produce rules for living. Clearly, you must adopt them (or not) for yourself based on updated facts, reinterpreted trends, anticipated reactions to those trends, and your own personal ethics.

- *Rule 1.* Do business only with people who are pleasant. In fact, as you get older, add to that only people who are fun. After all, people will be the critical resource, and you don't want any unnecessary negatives.
- *Rule 2.* Do not get locked into a narrow educational path unless you want to be a research physicist. If you want to be something else, breadth is important and your best work may well occur when you are over 35, unless you're a computer nerd, in which case you're over the hill at 28. Continued learning is facilitated by a broad educational background.
- *Rule 3.* You should measure personal success by a self-defined quality of life. Otherwise, you will be the victim of the "reaction syndrome" and end up in the wrong club. More important, you will end up a wimp, which leads to Rule 4.
- *Rule 4.* Your self-worth should be measured by what you can give away. With the breakdown of the traditional political system (as exemplified by presidential impeachment) and a general increase in confusion (the U.S. House of Representatives), it is incumbent on anyone who wants to have a meaningful life to contribute something to the neighborhood where he lives, if not to the region and the world.
- *Rule 5.* Education must get better. Yours is the first generation of high school graduates to have a poorer education (at the median) than their parents. Continuing education is a must. With a graduate degree, you are only an average player. Moreover, the half-life of information is short and getting shorter.
- *Rule 6.* We should not segment things into little boxes. Breakthroughs come at the interfaces. Your continuing education shouldn't be all in the same field. Real estate is an interdisciplinary field, and the successful player needs an understanding of many different aspects of life—sociological, psychological, architectural, and historical—as well as of business and politics.
- *Rule 7.* Do not trust economists. In an information society, you can give it away and still have it. This fact does not fit well in traditional economic models.
- *Rule 8.* Think globally, act locally. Watch Washington for destabilizing activities, but make it happen in your own world, which is probably your neighborhood or your city.
- *Rule 9.* It should be knowledge and eventually wisdom, not information, that we seek. There are already more newsletters in the real estate area than anyone could read on a regular basis. Beyond that, an incredible array of facts and information is at your disposal through the Internet. The challenge is to develop the conceptual framework that allows you to process this sea of information into knowledge, especially the knowledge needed to act and the wisdom to know when to run.
- *Rule 10.* Always fully segment your markets. Do not get trapped into measuring the MSA exclusively when you are dealing with a world of neighborhoods. Remember that we all live not in one neighborhood but rather in a series of neighborhoods. One is for our work environment, another for our social environment, and there are possibly many more, depending on the different facets of our lives. When you are building space, you are satisfying the needs of people who themselves function in a series of probably overlapping neighborhoods. Consideration of the census tract is an easy first pass but not the whole story.
- *Rule 11.* Overall, expect continued growth in the United States. It is one of the few countries both developed enough to be comfortable and open enough economically to provide opportunity. Therefore, the best and brightest (and their money) will continue to come. Entrepreneurial immigrants create a brain-drain toward America that will make tomorrow's United States an exciting place.
- *Rule 12.* Remember that only change is constant in this life. This recognition will continue to force a search for spiritual certainty that will, in turn, have an impact on other aspects of our lives. Given that people, not capital, are the critical resource, the search for meaning will become increasingly important to development trends.
- *Rule 13.* Do not fool yourself into believing that MBA thinking (adjusting available data) is real thinking. Even the latest accounting rules drive through the rear view mirror, and appraisal practices still ignore most of the big issues that we have discussed in this chapter. If you are a little right on the future, it can make up for a lot of smaller mistakes. No amount of getting it right in the present can make up for a major miss on future trends.
- *Rule 14.* In the future, you need partners—not suppliers, not customers, not acquisition targets—but partners. And partnerships should not be based solely on long legal agreements but rather on reciprocally fair deals oriented toward mutual interests and maintained in an atmosphere of good will (bad news for lawyers).

A Final Look at Europa Center And Museum Towers

Whit Morrow and Dean Stratouly, the developers who were profiled throughout this text, shared their real life with readers, reminding them, first, that real estate development is an art and, second, that it requires some luck. In working out the interactive design and construction of Europa Center, Morrow was slowed down, allowing his competitor (University Tower, which was eventually foreclosed on by its lender) to fill the same market niche first with two substantial projects. In a modest market niche, Fraser Morrow Daniels's Class A building had no fallback position; thus, the firm was both unlucky and a step behind in reaching the market.

Today, Whit Morrow is a senior executive with a medical laboratory and prefers an environment in which professionalism counts more than art or luck.

⠿ Europa Center

A Final Word from Whit Morrow

Europa Center was sold in early 1989 to a Chapel Hill family that has been a great benefactor of the community. The price was market at this stage of development, allowing the existing owner/financial institution to come close to breaking even and giving the new investor significant long-term benefits.

No profits were available for distribution to partners. It was disappointing for us, but when I look at the building, I think I would have done the project anyway because it was interesting and exciting. Our final product is gorgeous. It's the best office building in town. Everything about Europa Center is right.

It is very difficult to have a short-term perspective about real estate and still make money. After we build a project and it's occupied, there is no reason for people to continue to pay us to be involved in it, so we have to move on to different projects. As a small company, we didn't have the equity position for long-term projects. Profits from building management are not significant for a company like ours. It would have been nice to have developed ten buildings and to have ended with a continuing source of income from managing all ten, but that's not the situation we were in.

The building's capital structure, financing, and ownership evolved in a way that was not conducive to long-term ownership. We made the decision to sell the building to an investor whose objective was to manage the building over the long term, which was different from our objectives. A company with a different financial structure might value long-term growth more than immediate cash. Banks and small development companies like ours are not in a position to take advantage of the long-term benefits of owning a

Europa Center has the advantage of many corner offices, providing much light for occupants.

The completed Phase I of Europa Center.

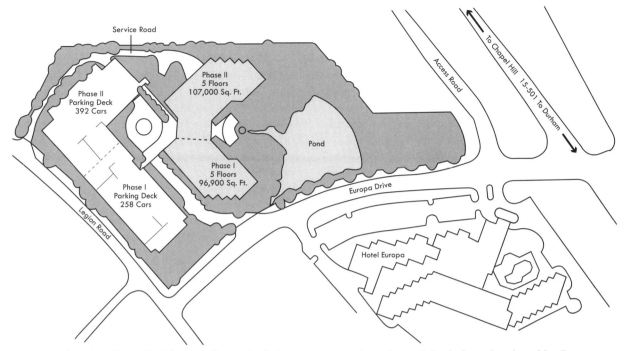

Site plan showing Phase II of Europa Center, built by new owners based on original plans developed by Fraser Morrow Daniels. Phase II contains an additional 107,000 square feet of office space and accommodates an additional 392 cars.

building, even though a project might be worth considerably more ten years from now than it is today.

The lender decided that it wanted to sell the building to recover its money. A lending institution that owns a property values it differently because of the accounting rules associated with lending. It has to depreciate and write things off and maintain reserves against potential losses, so that owning a building is not as valuable to that institution as it might be to some other type of institution. In fact, owning the building negatively affected the lender's ability to lend money. The lender knew it could make a greater profit over the short term by lending money rather than by managing a building.

I have very mixed emotions about the sale of Europa Center. Although the long-term prospects for ownership are excellent, we had evolved to a point where the lending institution had full control. It was more advantageous to the lender to sell than to hold the property for future marginal gain. Instead of selling the building, we might have restructured the financing such that we would have maintained ownership by merely replacing the lender. But a separate question arises about whether or not our small company could have properly structured itself to stay involved. In my judgment, it worked out better to sell the building outright and not to enter the building management business.

The new investor occupied the remaining 20 percent of the first building and immediately began construction of the approved second phase, a 107,000-square-foot building. The town managers or citizens had no objections; they now regard Europa Center as attractive and beneficial to the community. The local leasing market is better, and today Europa Center has no competition from new buildings. With other highly respected occupants in place (particularly the new investor and related subsidiaries), prospective tenants now feel secure that Europa Center is a fine building in a superior location. The completed site is truly spectacular.

The story of Europa Center does not end with its sale in 1989, however. The new owner has since built a second phase of the project and has his own perspective on the situation, as described in the following discussion.

⠿ Europa Center[1]

The New Owner's Perspective

Although Europa Center was initially well conceived, the project was generally perceived by the market as an unsuccessful venture by the time it was offered for sale. This image posed a dilemma for prospective tenants. The original developers were offering attractive lease terms to fill the building, but the uncertainty of the future ownership of the building added some risk to the agreements. When Investors S&L decided to sell the project "as is," the new owner purchased the building with the intention of holding it as a long-term investment, recognizing numerous benefits in the building. For one, it was the first and only true Class A space in Chapel Hill. It was well built and offered attractive amenities to a small market with no previous Class A space. Moreover, it was approved for more than 100,000 square feet of additional space. The new owner felt comfortable that the market could bear a second phase of this type of attractive project.

Europa Center was purchased for $11 million, which included the land and building from Phase I and the additional land originally intended for Phase II. As a result of the longstanding relationship between the new owner and his capital sources, an unsecured line of credit was available for both the purchase and the subsequent development of Phase II.

The new owner brought in a team of on-site managers from Allen & O'Hara of Memphis. The team leader then served as the owner's representative during the development of Phase II. The presence of the new on-site management to deal with the day-to-day issues and the sale of Europa Center to a respected and well-known member of the community changed the business community's perceptions such that the building leased up rather quickly, going from about 65 percent occupancy at the time of purchase to almost 100 percent within six to eight months.

Construction of Phase II

Soon after the purchase, plans were made to start Phase II. An Atlanta architectural firm, Cooper Carry & Associates, was retained to design Phase II; it had been the original architectural firm for Europa Center and had created the footprint for Phase II. As approvals from the city had been negotiated during Phase I, the second building could get started quickly. The architects prepared drawings for a building of 107,863 gross square feet (99,751 of it rentable space), a three-story atrium connecting the two phases, and an expansion of the parking deck from 258 to 650 spaces.

The owner offered the construction contract to Allen & O'Hara, with which he had worked on previous projects. Based on past experience, he was confident that the firm could complete the project on time and within budget. The total cost of construction of Phase II was estimated at slightly more than $11 million. That amount covered the hard costs of the building and parking deck, architectural and engineering fees, development fees, hard- and soft-cost contingencies, leasing commissions, and interest; it also included approximately $2 million for tenant improvements. These

costs were significantly higher than for Phase I, but nearly four years had elapsed since Phase I had been planned. The cost also included the addition of a three-story atrium and the substantial expansion of the parking deck to more than double its original size. Construction financing was based on an unsecured line of credit at the prime interest rate minus 1 percent. The interim financing remained in place through lease-up and was subsequently rolled into long-term fixed-rate financing in early 1994 at a time when commercial mortgage rates were the lowest in more than 30 years.

Construction took approximately one year. Having the construction information available from Phase I simplified the job somewhat; overall, the job progressed smoothly. Excavation revealed several soil types, necessitating an increase in the size of a few footings, some to more than 20 feet wide. A fair number of unexpected boulders were also encountered. Neither problem required significant expense to rectify.

Expansion of the parking deck proceeded without problems, using the same contractor from Phase I. Precast concrete was used in both phases.

During initial management of the project, the owner noticed what appeared to be a limitation in the capacity of the electrical heating system. If the system went down for any lengthy period, it would take as long as four or five days to get back up to normal ranges. The system was designed to incorporate heat gain from all sources, including solar gain, gain from the presence of people, and gain from lights. After long discussions with the architect and engineers, the owner decided to use the same type of electrical heating system in Phase II as in Phase I, even though managers would be required to monitor the system closely and to use setbacks to make sure the temperature does not fall below predetermined levels.

Although no major problems were encountered in construction, several incidents related to birds caused headaches for a while. For example, construction of the three-story atrium connecting the two buildings necessitated removal of the temporary end wall of Phase I. During construction, that wall was covered with visqueen, but, unbeknownst to the contractor, pigeons gained entry through the visqueen and nested in the space above the ceiling tiles on nearly every floor. The pigeon noises that could be heard throughout the project gave away the birds' presence. The problem was easily solved when the atrium was closed and the birds could no longer gain entry.

After Phase II was completed and being leased, the managers noticed that flocks of large crows were perching on the window ledges and pecking at the window caulking until an edible chunk could be torn loose. The caulking manufacturer, initially refusing to admit that birds liked the compound, eventually acknowledged it and agreed to change the formula. The windows were recaulked and that problem disappeared.

The only major delay during construction was on the interior finish work. The atrium was to be finished with a combination of Canadian and Italian granite. Although the granite was preselected from both countries, the Italian quarry experienced a labor strike just before shipping. When the strike was settled, the granite was shipped, but for some reason, the marble had to go through quarantine and could not be delivered. The result was a two-month delay. And because the Canadian and Italian granites were to be mixed in the atrium, the finish work had to be deferred until all the granite arrived on site.

Given the quality of the building and the image projected by Europa Center, the new owner decided during completion of the project to provide excess landscaping. The original landscape subcontractor went bankrupt during Phase II construction, leaving plants that had been paid for but not delivered and an irrigation system that had not been completely installed. In addition, the subcontractor had not provided adequate drainage for the trees that were to be placed in circular planters near the building entry. The general contractor took responsibility for the problem and brought in another subcontractor, thereby minimizing the financial impact. Unfortunately, the lack of proper drainage for the trees in the circular planters required replacement of four of the trees within the first two years of operation. But the attention to landscaping detail has made Europa Center a particularly attractive project. Overall, the construction process for Phase II lasted about 13 months, and the contractor was able to bring the project in on time and on budget.

Marketing and Leasing

When the property was purchased in 1989, Phase I was about 65 percent leased at an average lease rate of about $13.50 to $14.00 per square foot. The market for office space during that time was slow, primarily as a result of overbuilding in the area during the late 1980s. The recently completed University Towers, a 200,000-square-foot office building in south Durham, had an occupancy rate of about 30 percent then, and the owners were extending attractive lease terms to fill the building. It was not uncommon to receive one year's free rent on a five-year lease in addition to a generous amount for tenant improvements. Another new project, the Quadrangle, a campus-style office facility also located in Durham, was about 25 percent occupied. The Chapel Hill market is very small, so the addition of new space has a tendency to oversupply the market quickly. Further, in that small market, tenants generally prefer to see the space they are going to lease; accordingly, preleasing is somewhat more difficult than in larger cities, such as Raleigh.

The three-story atrium connecting Phases I and II of Europa Center, finished with Canadian and Italian marble.

By the time construction began on Phase II, the market was beginning to improve slightly, and it continued to improve slowly from that point. The improvement in the market during this time was largely a result of the lack of capital for new construction during the early 1990s. Most banks and S&Ls had withdrawn from the construction lending business and were not interested in making speculative development loans. In addition, because the market was already overbuilt, few developers were interested in starting a new project in a down market. But that very lack of new office construction meant that Europa Center was well positioned to take advantage of the market as it improved.

Securing tenants for Europa Center in such a soft market was not easy. The fact that Phase I was complete provided a slight advantage during the construction of Phase II, because prospective tenants had a sense of what the new space would look like. The new owner and his long-term commitment were also major selling points. Nonetheless, the marketing team followed several leads and knocked

The entrance to the now successful Class A office building profiled in this textbook.

on a lot of doors while Phase II of Europa Center was under construction.

By the time construction of Phase II was nearly complete, almost all the remaining space in Phase I had been leased and about 10 to 15 percent of Phase II preleased, but there were no anchor tenants for Phase II. Instead, the tenants were mostly local companies that wanted to locate in Class A space or small offices with regional or national affiliations. Tenants occupied from 600 square feet to more than 10,000 square feet, but most located in 4,000- to 5,000-square-foot spaces.

With the market far from robust during that period, space was preleased at rates of about $14.00 per square foot, with tenant improvement allowances of approximately $12.00 to $14.00 per square foot. The real improvement in the market during that period materialized in the area of free rent; instead of providing one year's free rent on a five-year lease, the marketing team was able to secure three- and five-year leases with only three to five months of free rent. Even with the slightly improved market, lease rates of $14.00 per square foot would not support the

capital budget imposed by the acquisition of the project, at least over the short run.

As the project was nearing completion in early 1991, the new owner expressed concern about the pace of leasing for Phase II. He felt that a brokerage firm with national exposure would be needed to attract major tenants. As a result, he signed a one-year contract with a large national brokerage firm that specializes in the leasing of office space and kept on Allen & O'Hara as property managers that assisted in leasing the building. Over the next year, occupancy in Phase II increased from about 15 percent to approximately 30 percent. Allen & O'Hara was instrumental in securing a few small tenants over the course of the year; the new leasing company was not successful in leasing any new space in the building. In fact, a couple of potential tenants were lost to other space represented by the same brokerage company.

At the expiration of the listing contract at the beginning of 1992, Allen & O'Hara reassumed its position as primary leasing agents for the project. By then, the market had improved considerably, and the leasing momentum had picked up. New leases were signed at $15.00 to $16.00 per square foot, and free rent was no longer necessary to attract tenants. By the end of 1992, Phase II was about 70 percent occupied, and it took only an additional six months or so to bring the building to 90 percent occupancy.

Even though leasing was progressing well, a few locations in the building proved difficult to lease. One such space, at the back of the terrace-level atrium, encompassed approximately 1,500 square feet. The space had limited visibility and was ill suited for configuration as offices. Alternative uses were explored at length until the need emerged for on-site food facilities. At the owner's suggestion, the firm negotiated a deal with a local restaurant operator for approximately 1,200 square feet of space, thus providing a viable solution to otherwise difficult-to-lease space.

Another difficult area to lease was a wedge-shaped space comprising about 3,000 square feet on the fifth floor over the atrium. This space had a limited number of windows and was therefore unacceptable to the vast majority of tenants looking for quality space in a building such as Europa Center. Given the difficulty in leasing this space, the owner made the space available as executive suites. The idea was an instant success. Many regional or national companies wanted a presence in the area but could not justify the expense associated with staffing an office. The executive suite satisfied the need for small amounts of high-quality space in a Class A building. The suites leased instantly, and a waiting list developed for those offices. Interestingly, a previous Phase I tenant had leased a large amount of space from the original developer for use as executive offices, but for some reason, the space was never developed into suites.

Final Thoughts

By the end of 1994, the entire building was approximately 95 percent leased. Leases at that time were being signed at rates of about $18.00 per square foot, with a $5.00 per square foot tenant improvement allowance. Free rent was no longer incorporated into any of the leases. It took several years for the project to lease at rates projected by the original developer. Europa Center illustrates one of the key issues associated with the development of real estate—the cyclical nature of the product. Even though few developers consider a recession or slowdown in the market when conducting their initial financial analysis of a project, real estate has been shown to suffer large swings in performance, just like any other asset class.

Since 1995, the market in Chapel Hill has tightened considerably. Occupancy at Europa Center now hovers near 100 percent and rents average $21.00 to $22.00 per square foot. Most of the older, below-market leases have been turned over. New leases offer no rental concessions or tenant improvement allowance, save some minor painting. Tenants pay for their own interior buildouts. Exten-

sive marketing has not been necessary, as turnover has been quite low and additional space is in demand from existing tenants. In fact, one of the biggest challenges currently facing management is finding room for expansion of tenants.

With the emergence of a strong market and increased demand for space, management has discontinued the executive suite program in favor of a single tenant. As the market has tightened, the less optimal space offered as executive suites has become more desirable. Because of the additional management and furniture leasing costs associated with offering several executive suites, the owner achieves a higher return by leasing to a single tenant. The program was, however, an excellent short-term strategy for leasing unused space.

The managers have made an effort to keep the tenant mix diverse. Beyond protecting the owner against the impact of the sudden departure of a large tenant, a diversity of tenants also avoids the perception that the building is controlled by any single tenant. The largest tenant at Europa Center controls less than 14 percent of the space.

The owner and managers are pleased with the results achieved at Europa Center. This Class A project was well conceived by the original developers; it is very attractive and offers all the amenities necessary for today's office market. The extensive landscaping and attention to quality throughout the building have served the project well. The value of one amenity in particular, the parking deck, is becoming increasingly apparent over time. As the office market in Chapel Hill continues to mature, parking has become a valuable commodity, one not enjoyed by many other new office developments in the area. Indeed, the owner considers the development of the parking deck to be as much of a coup as the development of the office building itself. Although parking on the deck is currently unrestricted, management feels that it may eventually be necessary to reserve parking on the deck for tenants and visitors to Europa Center.

Large-scale upgrades of the property have not been necessary. An electronic security system has been installed, eliminating the need for a graveyard shift of security personnel. Guards are still on the premises weekdays from 7 a.m. to 11 p.m and on Saturday from 9 a.m. to 2 p.m. At all other times, the building is accessible with electronic key cards. The investment in the system was recouped in only one year. Utility upgrades have been provided to individual tenants as needed by the utilities, and management has brought in an Internet service provider, giving tenants the option to connect to the Internet. ∎

The owner continues to view Europa Center as a long-term asset. Several other properties in the area have been flipped into REIT portfolios, a prospect the owner does not currently entertain. Europa Center continues to stand as the premier Class A office in the Chapel Hill market. Although other new office buildings have been developed, none boast the scale and amenities of Europa Center. Its position at the top of the market is fairly secure, as Europa Center now enjoys a certain amount of insulation from competition. Because of the high regulatory barriers to entering the market, it is unlikely that comparable space will be developed in the near term.

Museum Towers is in a slightly less stable position than Europa Center because of its short history as a built project. The buildings, located in a part of the city that is still somewhat new as a residential neighborhood, are not fully occupied. Still, the project is expected to be successful, and the developer and lender are optimistic about the potential to make money on it.

▌ Museum Towers

A Final Word from Dean Stratouly

Somebody asked me if I expect to make money from this project. Well, if I look at all the money spent over the dura-tion of this project, back to 1987, we will make a little, maybe break even to slightly positive. If we look at the project from the time I restructured the debt in 1994 to the time when we dispose of the project, we'll do well.

With everything that was going on, it wasn't really until 1996 that I could start looking again at acquiring other land. In 1997, I actually began putting some deals together. In the early nineties, like a lot of developers, we were doing management work for banks just to eke out enough money to meet payroll. So many guys during that time continued to talk about putting together deals. And either they were being taken advantage of by the guys on Wall Street or they were overdosing on Prozac, because there was nothing going on.

The thing that scares me about development now is that there's a whole new generation of developers who don't know what "down" means. I was pretty naive when I started in 1980, but I had been around a little bit. I watched the nuclear power plant industry collapse around me. When I left, we were turning into spare parts salesmen; there hadn't been a new plant sold in years.

Now, when things are good, nobody thinks the real estate business can collapse again. Well, it can. It's a very fragile business. If you're in this for the money, you're not going to be successful at it. I love this business. I really do. I even loved it when I was failing. It's like racing a sail boat and colliding. It's an adrenaline rush. Keeps you on edge.

Museum Towers is not a high-design project, but its location and amenity package have made it a very competitive property.

The desirable location of Museum Towers was a big factor in the ease with which it sold.

It's hell for spouses though. One minute you have money and the next you don't.

No two days are the same. I love the construction, the machines, the mud. I even enjoy the negotiations with the banks. When I started out, I had this vision of building a national real estate company that would do design, development, marketing, property management, finance— the whole nine yards. The next thing I knew, I was sitting in an office with 50 employees and I was two or three people removed from the actual piece of real estate. I wasn't particularly happy. I'd have staff meetings once a week, project update meetings once a week, but I was running people not building buildings. Now I'm back to being a real estate developer.

A Final Comment from the Lender/Investor

Beginning in late spring 1999, Museum Towers was being marketed for sale by Fallon Hines & O'Connor, a Trammell Crow company. After looking at the first round of bids, we expected the project to sell for about $112 million, which would provide us with a profit slightly larger than the anticipated 20 percent. Dean Stratouly would do very well at that price, at least over the last three years that we invested with him. He did a good job and we have financed (as equity partner) another of his projects—the renovation of an old Raytheon Plant in Wayland, Massachusetts.

The property was actually sold on August 19, 1999, to Clarion, which is institutional capital but not a REIT. The purchase price was $108 million, or $248,000 a unit, $4 million less than we had hoped, but even at $108 million, it's a big win for the developer. At the time it was sold, Museum Towers was 85 percent occupied. At 15 percent vacancy, the capitalization rate was higher than the hoped-for 7 percent vacancy. The cap rate of 7.25 percent was based on stabilized NOI, which is 93 percent occupancy. That's quite a low cap rate, which obviously wasn't achieved.

In the end, everyone went away pretty happy, despite the fact that REITs were off when the property was on the market. But there was still a buyer for it because of its excellent location and the perceived potential for the future. ■

Summary

This chapter only touches on what future developers need to consider as they think about upcoming development opportunities. If readers come away with only one piece of advice from this chapter, it should be to read as widely as possible and to talk to as many different kinds of people as possible. Keeping attuned to cycles and always looking for a new way to fill customers' needs can give developers an edge that spells the difference between a successful and a marginal development.

Although developers cannot continuously focus on broad societal trends, given the demands of their daily operations, over the long run such trends and changes account for the biggest differences between successful and less successful developments. As providers of space over time with associated services, developers should continuously respond to the needs and wants of consumers. Sensitivity to underlying shifts in preferred locations, commuting habits, customs and cultural orientation, and household characteristics is critical to effective decision making. The developer's first job is to anticipate what society will want from the built environment —one of the most exciting, challenging, and rewarding tasks in our society.

Review Questions

23.1 How can looking at the past help us in thinking about the future? Was the overbuilding of the 1980s an anomaly?

23.2 How has the trend toward "development's paying its own way" affected developers?

23.3 What are Bidwell's rules for living? Do you agree with them? How realistic are they?

23.4 How did developer Whit Morrow end up not owning Europa Center? Why was it sold by the financial institution?

23.5 Describe the new owner's assessment of the Europa Center project as a whole. What was particularly attractive to the owner?

23.6 Why was construction of Phase II of Europa Center so much more expensive than Phase I? Were there any major construction problems?

23.7 What is the advantage to the developer of Museum Towers to sell so soon after the development is complete? What is the advantage to holding onto the project? What goes into making the decision to hold or not hold?

23.8 Do you believe, like Dean Stratouly, that it's dangerous for new developers who haven't ever experienced the down cycle in real estate?

23.9 The authors offer one piece of advice to readers —read as widely as possible and talk to as many different kinds of people as possible. Why would it be beneficial for a developer to follow that advice? Are there any possible pitfalls?

Note

1. This update on Europa Center was compiled by Brian Ciochetti, PhD, assistant professor, University of North Carolina at Chapel Hill, and supplemented by David Mulvihill, director, information services, ULI.

Part VIII

Bibliography

Asset and Property Management

Albert, J.D., and W. McIntosh. "Identifying Risk-Adjusted Indifference Rents for Alternative Operating Leases." *Journal of Real Estate Research* 4:3 (1989): 81–94.

Apgar, M., IV. "Discovering Your Hidden Occupancy Costs." *Harvard Business Review* 71:3 (May/June 1993): 124–36.

Bachner, John P. *The Guide to Practical Property Management.* New York: McGraw-Hill, 1991.

Banning, Kent. *Residential Property Management Handbook.* New York: McGraw-Hill, 1992.

Bell, Michael. "The Importance of Sound Fixed Asset Management." *Industrial Development* 156:1 (January/February 1987): 11–13.

Briggs, Mary M. "Real Estate Opportunities for Institutional Investors." *Real Estate Finance Journal* 5:3 (Winter 1990): 67–71.

Brown, H. James, and Christopher E. Herbert. "Local Government Real Estate Asset Management: The New England Experience." *Land Lines* (December 1989): 1–2.

Brown, Robert Kevin. "Corporate Asset Management: Hidden Profits in Real Estate." *Valuation Research* (Fall/Winter 1985).

———. *Corporate Real Estate: Executive Strategies for Profit-Making.* Homewood, Ill.: Dow Jones–Irwin, 1979.

Brown, Robert Kevin, Paul Lapides, and Edmond P. Rondeau. *Managing Corporate Real Estate: Form and Procedures.* New York: Wiley, 1994.

Brown, Robert Kevin, et al. *Managing Corporate Real Estate.* New York: Wiley, 1993. With 1995 supplement.

Building Owners and Managers Association International and ULI–the Urban Land Institute. *The Changing Office Workplace.* Washington, D.C.: Author, 1986.

Camdon, Barbara. "Real Estate Investment Strategies." *Urban Land* (September 1997).

Cammarano, Nicholas. *Real Estate Accounting and Reporting: A Guide for Developers, Investors, and Lenders.* New York: Wiley, 1996.

Chan, S.H., G.W. Gau, and K. Wang. "Stock Market Reactions to Capital Investment Decisions: Unifying Evidence from Business Relocation." Paper presented at a meeting of the American Real Estate and Urban Economics Association, January 1993.

Cushman, Robert F., and Neal I. Rodin, eds. *Property Management Handbook: A Practical Guide to Real Estate Management.* New York: Wiley, 1985.

Darragh, Alexander J., and Elizabeth K. Bell. "The Role of Investment Research in Corporate Real Estate Firms." *Real Estate Review* 22:1 (Spring 1992): 87.

Dasso, Jerry, W. Kinnard, and Joseph Rabianski. "Corporate Real Estate: A Course Outline and Rationale." *Journal of Real Estate Research* 4:3 (1989): 35–46.

DeCarlos, Joseph W. *Property Management.* Englewood Cliffs, N.J.: Prentice-Hall, 1996.

Dober, Patrick. "Creating Value from Property Management." *Urban Land* (November 1996).

Downs, James C., Jr. *Principles of Real Estate Management.* 13th ed. Chicago: Institute of Real Estate Management, 1994.

Fabozzi, Frank. "The Gains from Corporate Selloffs: The Case of Real Estate Assets." *AREUEA Journal* 19:4 (1991): 567–83.

——. *The Handbook of Asset/Liability Management.* Rev. ed. Burr Ridge, Ill.: Probus, 1995.

Felson, Marcus, and Richard B. Peiser. *Reducing Crime through Real Estate Development and Management.* Washington, D.C.: ULI–the Urban Land Institute, 1998.

Ferguson, William J. "Compensating Institutional Tenant Representatives and Asset Managers." *Real Estate Review* 21:4 (Winter 1992): 9.

Flegel, Douglas D. "Disposing of Surplus Corporate Real Estate." *Real Estate Review* 21:4 (Winter 1992): 53.

Glascock, J.L., W.N. Davidson III, and C.F. Sirmans. "An Analysis of the Acquisition and Disposition of Real Estate Assets." *Journal of Real Estate Research* 4:3 (1989): 131–40.

Goodman, Daniel, and Richard Rusdorf. *The Landlord's Handbook: A Complete Guide to Managing Small Residential Properties.* 2d ed. Chicago: Dearborn Financial, 1999.

Gordon, Paul A. *Seniors' Housing and Care Facilities: Development, Business, and Operations.* Vol. 1 and 2. 3d ed. Washington, D.C.: ULI–the Urban Land Institute, 1998.

Greig, D. Wylie, and Michael S. Young. "New Measures of Future Property Performance and Risk." *Real Estate Review* 21:1 (Spring 1991): 17.

Grogan, Bradley C. "Managing Property." *Urban Land* (March 1999): 34–37.

Hickman, Ron. "Institutional Investors and the Residential Market." *Real Estate Finance Journal* 5:3 (Winter 1990): 72–76.

Hines, M.A. *Global Corporate Real Estate Management: A Handbook for Multinational Businesses and Organizations.* Westport, Conn.: Greenwood Press, 1990.

Hoffman, J.J., M.J. Schniederjans, and G.S. Sirmans. "A Multi-Criteria Model for Corporate Property Evaluation." *Journal of Real Estate Research* 5:3 (1990): 285–300.

Holden, Meg Parker. "The Nation's Portfolio of Institutional Grade Real Estate." *Real Estate Review* 22:4 (Winter 1993): 36–46.

Hudson-Wilson, Susan, and Charles H. Wurtzebach. *Managing Real Estate Portfolios.* Homewood, Ill.: Dow Jones–Irwin, 1993.

Hyatt, Wayne S. *Protecting Your Assets: Strategies for Successful Business Operation in a Litigious Society.* Washington, D.C.: ULI–the Urban Land Institute, 1997.

Iezman, Stanley L., and Nicole A. Ihlenfeld. "Real Estate Asset Management." *Real Estate Review* 21:2 (Summer 1991): 58.

Irwin, Robert. *Handbook of Property Management.* New York: McGraw-Hill, 1986.

Jussim, Seth E. "The City of Chicago Looks at Its Real Estate." *Urban Land* 48:11 (November 1989): 21–23.

Kateley, Richard, and M. Leanne Lachman. *Asset Management: The Key to Profitable Real Estate Investment.* Chicago: Real Estate Research Corporation, 1985.

Kyle, Robert C., Floyd M. Baird, and Marie S. Spodek. *Property Management.* 6th ed. Chicago: Dearborn Trade, 1999.

Lawrence, P.R., and Jay R. Lorsch. *Organization and Environment: Managing Differentiation and Integration.* Rev. ed. Cambridge, Mass.: Harvard Univ. Press, 1986.

Lax, D.A., and J.K. Sebenius. *The Manager as Negotiator.* New York: Free Press, 1986.

Louargand, Marc A., and Sandra Lambert. *Transformation: The Evolution of the Property Management Industry.* Working Paper 64. Cambridge, Mass.: MIT Center for Real Estate, 1996.

Lusht, Kenneth M., and Darryl Farber. "Technical Change and the Changing Technical Infrastructure: Implications for Real Estate Investment." Paper prepared for Prudential Real Estate Investors. May 1994.

McIntosh, W., D.T. Officer, and J.A. Born. "The Wealth Effects of Merger Activities: Further Evidence from Real Estate Investment Trusts." *Journal of Real Estate Research* 4:3 (1989): 141–56.

McMahan, John. *Property Development.* 2d ed. New York: McGraw-Hill, 1989.

Managing the Office Building. Chicago: Institute of Real Estate Management, 1985.

Managing the Shopping Center. Chicago: Institute of Real Estate Management, 1983.

Manning, Christopher. "Leasing versus Purchase of Corporate Real Property: Leases with Residual Equity Interests." *Journal of Real Estate Research* 6:1 (1991): 79–86.

Moody, Frank. "What Institutions Need and Expect from an Asset Manager." *Real Estate Finance Journal* 5:3 (Winter 1990): 90–92.

O'Mara, Martha A. *Managing Corporate Real Estate and Facilities for Competitive Advantage.* New York: Free Press, 1999.

Nourse, Hugh O. "Corporate Real Estate Ownership as a Form of Vertical Integration." *Real Estate Review* 20:3 (1990): 67–71.

——. *Managerial Real Estate: Corporate Real Estate Asset Management.* Englewood Cliffs, N.J.: Prentice-Hall, 1990.

——. "Real Estate Flexibility Must Complement Business Strategy." *Real Estate Review* 21:4 (Winter 1992): 25–29.

——. "Using Real Estate Asset Management to Improve Strategic Performance." *Industrial Development* 155:3 (May/June 1986): 1–7.

Nourse, Hugh O., and D. Kingery. "Survey of Approaches to Disposing of Surplus Corporate Real Estate." *Journal of Real Estate Research* 2:1 (1987): 51–60.

Pagliari, Joseph L., Jr. *Handbook of Real Estate Portfolio Management.* New York: McGraw-Hill, 1995.

Parker, Rosetta E. *Housing for the Elderly: The Handbook for Managers.* Chicago: Institute of Real Estate Management, 1984.

Patterson, Mark W. *Real Estate Portfolios: Acquisition, Management, and Disposition.* New York: Wiley, 1994.

Paulson, M.F., and J.M. Rooney. "Benchmarking in the Corporate Real Estate Function." *Industrial Development Research Foundation* (January 1991).

Pearse, Richard W., and Keith F. Maxfield. "Living with the Americans with Disabilities Act." *Real Estate Review* 22:3 (Fall 1992): 85.

Pederson, Rick. "Establishing a Real Estate Asset Management System." *Management Information Services Report* 21:4 (April 1989): 1–12.

Pittman, R., and J. Parker. "A Survey of Corporate Real Estate Executives on Factors Influencing Corporate Real Estate Performance." *Journal of Real Estate Research* 4:3 (1989): 107–20.

The Property Manager's Relationship with Developers and Lenders. Chicago: Institute of Real Estate Management, 1986.

Pugash, James Z. "Increasing Institutional Investments in Single-Family Home Building." *Real Estate Review* 22:4 (Winter 1993).

Rappaport, A. *Creating Shareholder Value: A Guide for Managers and Investors.* Rev. ed. New York: Free Press, 1997.

Redman, A.L. "The Financing of Corporate Real Estate: A Survey." *Journal of Real Estate Research* 6:2 (1991): 217–40.

Redman, A.L., and J.R. Tanner. "The Acquisition and Disposition of Real Estate by Corporate Executives: A Survey." *Journal of Real Estate Research* 4:3 (1989): 67–80.

Roulac, S.E. "Real Estate as a Strategic Resource." *Chief Financial Officer International* (1986): 317–21.

Roulac, S.E., and N. Roberts. "Strategic Priority: Unlock Corporate Real Estate Values." *Real Estate Outlook* (Spring 1990).

Rutherford, R. "Empirical Evidence on Shareholder Value and the Sale-Leaseback of Corporate Real Estate." *AREUEA Journal* 18:4 (1990): 522–29.

Rutherford, R., and H.O. Nourse. "The Impact of Corporate Real Estate Unit Formation on the Parent Firm's Value." *Journal of Real Estate Research* 3:3 (1988): 73–84.

Rutherford, R., and R. Stone. "Corporate Real Estate Unit Formation: Rationale, Industry, and Type of Unit." *Journal of Real Estate Research* 4:3 (1989): 121–30.

Sagalyn, Lynne B., ed. *Cases in Real Estate Finance and Investment Strategy.* Washington, D.C.: ULI–the Urban Land Institute, 1999.

Schimpff, Carol R., and Robert M. Fair. "The Emerging Science of Real Estate Asset Management." *Real Estate Finance Journal* 5:1 (Summer 1989): 10–16.

Schuck, Gloria. "Outsourcing in the 1990s: Managing Corporate Real Estate Consultants." *Site Selection* 36:4 (August 1991): 1–5.

Shearer, Kenneth A., ed. *The Investors' and Owners' Guide to Office Building Management.* Homewood, Ill.: Irwin, 1991.

Silverman, Robert A., ed. *Corporate Real Estate Handbook: Strategies for Improving Bottom-Line Performance.* New York: McGraw-Hill, 1987.

Sladack, J.A. "A Corporate Client's View of Narrative Appraisal Reports." *Appraisal Journal* 59:2 (1991): 276–79.

Soens, Margaret A., and Robert Kevin Brown. *Real Estate Asset Management: Executive Strategies for Profit Making.* New York: Wiley, 1994.

Tregoe, B.B., and J.W. Zimmerman. *Top Management Strategy: What It Is and How to Make It Work.* New York: Simon & Schuster, 1980.

ULI–the Urban Land Institute and Building Owners and Managers Association International. *What Office Tenants Want: Building Features, Amenities, and Services.* Washington, D.C.: Author, 1998.

Veale, Peter R. "Managing Corporate Real Estate Assets: Current Executive Attitudes and Prospects for an Emergent Discipline." *Journal of Real Estate Research* 4:3 (1989): 1–22.

———. *Managing Corporate Real Estate Assets: A Survey of U.S. Real Estate Executives.* Cambridge, Mass.: MIT, Laboratory of Architecture and Planning, 1988.

Walters, William, Jr. *The Practice of Real Estate Management for the Experienced Property Manager.* Chicago: Institute of Real Estate Management, 1979.

Weimer, A.M. "Real Estate Decisions Are Different." *Harvard Business Review* 44:6 (November/December 1966): 110–12.

Wheaton, William C., and Raymond G. Torto. "The Prospect for Rebound in the Commercial Real Estate Market." *Real Estate Review* 21:4 (Winter 1992): 91.

Wise, David W. "Reorganizing Real Estate Enterprises for a New Economic Regime." *Real Estate Review* 22:2 (Summer 1992): 49.

Zeckhauser, Sally, and Robert Silverman. "Rediscovering Your Company's Real Estate." *Harvard Business Review* 61:1 (January/February 1983): 111–17.

Organizations

Institute of Real Estate Management
430 North Michigan Avenue
Chicago, IL 60611-4090
(312) 329-6000
www.irem.org

NACORE International
440 Columbia Drive, Suite 100
West Palm Beach, FL 33409
(407) 683-8111
www.nacore.com

National Association of Real Estate
   Investment Managers
11755 Wilshire Boulevard, Suite 1380
Los Angeles, CA 90025-1531
(310) 479-2219
www.nareim.org

Pension Real Estate Association
95 Glastonbury Boulevard
Glastonbury, CT 06033
(860) 657-2612
www.prea.org

Periodicals

Journal of Portfolio Management (quarterly). New York: Institutional Investor.

Journal of Property Management (bimonthly). Chicago: Institute of Real Estate Management of the National Association of Realtors®.

National Real Estate Investor (monthly). Regular column on asset management. Atlanta: Communications Channels, Inc.

Real Estate Finance Journal (quarterly). New York: Warren, Gorham & Lamont.

Sales and Marketing

Arnold, Alvin L. *The Arnold Encyclopedia of Real Estate.* 2d ed. New York: Wiley, 1993.

———. *Real Estate Investor's Deskbook.* 2d ed. Boston: Warren, Gorham & Lamont, 1994.

Brown, Donald R., and Wendell G. Matthews. *Real Estate Advertising Handbook.* Chicago: Realtors National Marketing Institute, 1981.

Calero, Henry H., and Bob Oskam. *Negotiate the Deal You Want.* New York: Dodd, Mead & Co., 1983.

Cyr, John E., Joan M. Sobeck, and Laurel D. McAdams. *Real Estate Brokerage: A Management Guide.* 5th ed. Chicago: Dearborn Trade, 1999.

Daly, Herman E., and John B. Cobb, Jr. *For the Common Good.* 2d ed. Boston: Beacon Press, 1994.

Hines, Mary Alice. *Marketing Real Estate Internationally.* New York: Quorum Books, 1988.

Karrass, Chester L. *Give and Take: The Complete Guide to Negotiating Strategies and Tactics.* Rev. ed. New York: Harper Business, 1993.

———. *The Negotiating Game: How to Get What You Want.* New York: Harper Business, 1992.

Karrass, Gary. *Negotiate to Close.* New York: Simon & Schuster, 1987.

Kasemodel, Therese F. *Word Marketing: How to Empower Real Estate Advertising through the Proper Choice of Words.* Grafton: Blue Rose Studio, 1996.

Kennedy, Danielle, and Warren Jamison. *How to List and Sell Real Estate in the 21st Century.* Englewood Cliffs, N.J.: Prentice-Hall, 1999.

McCurry, Leta. *Commercial Real Estate: An Introduction to Marketing Investment Properties.* Englewood Cliffs, N.J.: Prentice-Hall, 1990.

McKenna-Harmon, Kathleen, and Laurence C. Harmon. *Contemporary Apartment Marketing: New and Innovative Methods That Work.* Chicago: Institute of Real Estate Management, 1993.

Merill, David, and Roger Reid. *Personal Styles and Effective Performances.* Radnor, Pa.: Chilton Book Co., 1983.

Messner, Stephen D., et al. *Marketing Investment Real Estate.* 3d ed. Englewood Cliffs, N.J.: Prentice-Hall, 1986.

Mitchell, Arnold. *Nine American Lifestyles.* New York: Macmillan, 1983.

Mitchell, Jan. *Sales and Marketing Checklist.* Washington, D.C.: Home Builders Press, 1997.

Morrison, William F., and Henry H. Calero. *The Human Side of Negotiation.* Melbourne, Fla.: Krieger, 1994.

National Association of Industrial and Office Properties. *Marketing Office and Industrial Parks.* Arlington, Va.: Author, 1983.

Nierenberg, Gerard I. *The Complete Negotiator.* New York: Berkley, 1991.

——. *Negotiating the Big Sale.* New York: Berkley, 1993.

Parker, David F., and Charles C. Clark. *Marketing New Homes.* 2d ed. Washington, D.C.: Home Builders Press, 1999.

Passerini, Edward. *The Curve of the Future.* Dubuque, Iowa: Kendall/Hunt Publishing Co., 1992.

Reyhons, Ken. *Strategic Planning for the Real Estate Manager.* 3d ed. Chicago: Realtors® National Marketing Institute, 1993.

Roberts, Duane F. *Marketing and Leasing of Office Space.* Rev. ed. Chicago: Institute of Real Estate Management, 1986.

Senn, Mark A. *Commercial Real Estate Leases: Preparation and Negotiation.* 2d ed. New York: Wiley, 1990. With 1997 supplement.

Shashaty, Andre. *Marketing Housing to an Aging Population.* Washington, D.C.: Home Builders Press, 1991.

Shenkel, William M. *Marketing Real Estate.* 3d ed. Englewood Cliffs, N.J.: Prentice-Hall, 1994.

Stefaniak, Norbert J. *Real Estate Marketing: Developing a Professional Career.* West Allis, Wis.: Walker-Pearse, 1998.

Wenner, S. Albert. *Marketing Your Shopping Center.* New York: International Council of Shopping Centers, 1987.

The Future

Aburdene, Patricia, and John Naisbitt. *Megatrends for Women: From Liberation to Leadership.* New York: Fawcett, 1993.

Hudnut, William H., III. *Cities on the Rebound: A Vision for Urban America.* Washington, D.C.: ULI–the Urban Land Institute, 1998.

Naisbitt, John. *Global Paradox: The Bigger the World Economy, the More Powerful Its Smallest Players.* New York: William Morrow, 1994.

——. *Megatrends.* New York: Warner Books, 1988.

Naisbitt, John, and Patricia Aburdene. *Megatrends 2000.* New York: Avon Books, 1991.

ULI–the Urban Land Institute. *ULI on the Future.* Washington, D.C.: Author. Annual.

Periodicals

American Demographics (monthly). Ithaca, N.Y.: American Demographics.

Emerging Trends (monthly). New York: Real Estate Research Corporation and The Equitable.

Fast Company (bimonthly). Boston: Net Company.

Future Economic Trends (weekly). Santa Barbara, Calif.: Economic Behavior Institute.

Futurist (bimonthly). Bethesda, Md.: World Future Society.

Omni (monthly). New York: Penthouse International.

Appendices
and Index

Appendix A

The Real Estate Game: Level One and Level Two

The real estate game is played on two levels. Level one of the game is about valuing the productive capacity of the property itself. At level one, we try to determine how well the space over time with associated services (the package being sold to the user of the real estate) serves the particular marketplace. How well it serves is determined by the rent it generates, and we have the tools (discussed in Chapter 5) to convert that expected rent to an estimate of value. This is valuation at level one of the game, and most of this textbook is written about level one.

At level two, we look at the many individual players of the game and evaluate the revenue—not only to the project but also to the individual players. Why is this distinction between level one and level two important? Simply put, when conflicting goals drive different players, the system can go haywire. For example, the United States is thought to have the most efficient capital markets in the world. How then could we have produced the multihundred billion dollar S&L crisis? At level one of the game, a vast number of projects were built that made no economic sense; that is, no rational person would have expected the marketplace to pay enough rent for the space over time with associated services to justify the cost of some of these projects. How could these projects have been built when at level one many made no economic sense? If careful analysis had indicated that these properties would cost more than they were worth, then why did the S&Ls finance them?

The answer lies in the distinction between level one and level two. As noted, public policy with regard to the S&L industry changed dramatically in the 1980s. The S&Ls were in trouble at that time because they were lending long and borrowing short. They were borrowing from savers and lending on fixed-rate mortgages. When interest rates went up, their costs adjusted upward (they were flexible in the short term), but their revenues did not because they lent long term with no short-term flexibility. The political fix to this problem was to allow S&Ls to enjoy the benefits of diversification across more types of investments and across more geographic regions. The logic behind this "solution" was that diversification reduced risk and would improve the S&Ls' position. This logic was fallacious, and the real reason behind the new initiative was Congress's refusal to spend the money to fix the S&L program that existed at the beginning of the 1980s. Rather than appropriate the needed funds, Congress gave S&L entrepreneurs something like a blank check. Owners of S&Ls could speculate with taxpayers' money, generating funds with high-yielding certificates of deposit, which were federally insured, and then making aggressive investments. This action was justified by citing benefits from new opportunities for diversification, but the resulting lending policy actually increased risk.

Look at level two of the game and think about the S&L entrepreneurs' position. Would they make low-risk investments or high-risk investments? Because many S&Ls were already slightly under water at the time, a low-risk investment would have been sure death. With a high-risk investment, they had at least a possibility that things would go well. So at level two, it became quite clear what the entrepreneurs would want to do with the S&Ls—buy junk bonds and invest in speculative real estate. In essence, go for it. They had very little to lose because the taxpayers were footing the bill. This is an oversimplified explanation, but it makes the point. If you want to understand the S&L crisis, you can't do it exclusively at level one (the real estate) but must also look at level two (the players and the rules).

The structure of the game looks very similar for both level one and level two. We begin by estimating revenues that can be generated from the marketplace, and we subtract the operating expenses necessary to provide the services that were promised to the marketplace. The result is a projection of net operating income, which can be translated into cash flow and valued using the discounted cash flow method. The difference is that, at level one, we value the rents to the building, and, at level two, we value the salaries, fees, bonuses, stock options, and other compensations that the individual players receive. For the S&Ls, the associations' position looked very risky as they moved into more speculative investments. The decision makers and owners had less to lose (taxpayers had provided deposit insurance) and a lot to gain (bonuses, stock options, dividends, and more), however, if the speculations worked out well. In fact, many of the more speculative real estate loans involved large "origination" fees that translated into immediate dividends for the S&L owners. Thus, many of these people won even if the investment did not work out. Hence, the decisions that lost so much money for the associations (level one) were really very rational for the owners (level two).

Appendix B

Compound Interest and the Discounting Process

Compounding

Interest is payment for the use of money. *Compound interest* is no more than interest paid on interest. For example, construction loans are structured to pay the lender interest on the sum of the cash advanced and the accumulated interest. Permanent loans also pay the lender compound interest, often monthly.

For many years, savings institutions compounded interest semiannually or quarterly, thereby raising the effective annual interest rate by a small fraction. More recently, banks located where competition for funds is great have been compounding interest daily. Compounded daily, an annual interest rate of 7.75 percent actually pays 8.10 percent on the initial investment at the end of a full year. Compound interest is calculated by computing the interest on the balance at the end of every interest period (whether daily, monthly, quarterly, or otherwise). Many books carry tables with compound interest already calculated, and calculators and computers can do the calculations quickly and easily.

The calculations for compounding are straightforward. Suppose, for example, that a savings association pays interest at the rate of 8 percent, with the interest calculated once each year. A dollar invested (deposited) in a savings account yields $1.08 at the end of the year. Thus, on the day the dollar is deposited, its future value (FV) in one year is equal to its present value (PV) compounded for one (n) year:

$$FV = PV\,(1 + i)^n$$
$$= \$1.00\,(1 + .08)^1$$
$$= \$1.08.$$

Suppose you had $100 to invest today in a savings account that pays 10 percent interest for the next three years. If the interest is compounded annually and deposited into the account, the account would grow as follows:

$100.00   Initial investment in the savings account
+10.00   10% interest for Year 1 credited to the savings account at the end of Year 1.

The example to this point describes simple interest. In the second year of the deposit, however, 10 percent interest would be paid not merely on the $100 original deposit but also on the $10.00 earned as interest during Year 1. Thus, the interest earned in the second year amounts to $11.00 ($110 × .10 = $11.00); this example illustrates compound interest. Carried forward two additional years, your account contains $133.10:

$110.00   Savings account balance at the end of Year 1
+11.00   10% interest for Year 2 credited to the savings account at the end of Year 2

$121.00   Savings account balance at the end of Year 2
+12.10   10% interest for Year 3 credited to the savings account at the end of Year 3

$133.10   Savings account balance at the end of Year 3.

We can calculate the future value quickly using the formula:

$$FV = PV\,(1 + i)^n$$
$$= \$100\,(1.10)^3$$
$$= \$133.10.$$

Another and easier way to arrive at this answer is to use the financial function keys on your calculator. Key in –100 (because it is a cash outflow for the saver) and press the *PV* key, key in 10 and press the *i* key, key in 0 and press the *PMT* key (on some calculations this step is unnecessary), and key in 3 and press the *n* key. Then press the *FV* key and the calculator will display 133.10 as the correct answer, assuming you have set the calculator to round the displayed answer to two decimal places. This operation can be represented more uniformly by showing the following keystrokes:

–100	*PV*	
10	*i*	
0	*PMT*	(not necessary with all calculators)
3	*n*	
	FV	133.10.

We will continue to use this notation when presenting keystrokes for financial calculators throughout the remainder of the book.

Discounting

The opposite of compounding is *discounting,* when the compounded present value is known and we solve for future value. When discounting, the future value is known, and we solve for the present value. Suppose a business associate has promised to pay you $10,000 (future value, *FV*) in one lump sum at the end of three years. The question is what would you be willing to accept today (present value, *PV*) for that promise? The answer is a function of the discount rate (*i*) and how long you must wait for the payment (*n*). The formula is the opposite of the formula for future value.

$$PV = FV \times \frac{1}{(1 + i)^n}$$

$$= \$10,000 \times \frac{1}{(1 + .10)^3}$$

$$= \$7,513.15$$

Using the calculator,

10,000	*FV*	
10	*i*	
3	*n*	
0	*PMT*	
	PV	–7,513.15.

This example shows that at a discount rate of 10 percent, you would accept $7,513.15 today for the expectation of $10,000 in three years. Stated another way, at a 10 percent discount rate, you would be indifferent to receiving $7,513.15 today or the right to receive $10,000 three years from today.

A test of this answer, which also demonstrates the reverse relationship between compounding and discounting, is to calculate the future value of placing $7,513.15 in the savings account at an annual compound interest rate of 10 percent. If our present value of $7,513.15 is correct, the savings account should yield a balance of $10,000 after three years.

$$FV = PV (1 + i)^n$$

$$= (\$7,513.15) (1 + .10)^3$$

$$= \$10,000$$

The Mortgage Constant

When using discounting for investment analysis, we ask what an expected future amount is worth today. Borrowers and lenders ask a different question: What is the amount that must be paid each month (or other period) to repay both the principal and the required interest? The total of the principal plus interest is the amount of periodic debt service, and the debt service as a percentage of the original loan is called the *mortgage constant (MC).*

The *MC* is sometimes called the "installment to amortize," because it is the periodic debt service payment necessary to amortize a loan of $1.00 completely without resorting to a balloon payment. If you know the loan amount and the debt service payment, you can calculate the mortgage constant by dividing the periodic debt service by the loan amount. You then express the result as an annual figure by multiplying the quotient by the number of periods per year.

Most of the time, however, the debt service payment is unknown and must be calculated. The constant is always the debt service payment for a loan of $1.00 expressed on an annual basis. The formula for the mortgage constant is as follows:

$$MC = \frac{i}{1 - \dfrac{1}{(1 + i)^n}}$$

where *i* is the interest rate, and *n* is the number of payments to amortize the loan.

To illustrate the use of this formula, assume a 9.5 percent loan to be amortized over 30 years, with monthly payments.

$$MC = \left[\frac{i}{1 - \frac{1}{(1 + i)^n}}\right] \text{ (payments per year)}$$

$$= \left[\frac{\frac{.095}{.2}}{1 - \frac{1}{\frac{(1 + .095)^{360}}{.2}}}\right] \text{ (12)}$$

$$= .100903$$

Once the constant is calculated, it is multiplied by the loan amount to calculate the annual debt service payment. For a $1 million loan, the annual debt service (total of 12 monthly payments) would be $100,903.

When using a calculator to solve for the mortgage constant, first key in –1 and press the *PV* key, 9.5 ÷ 12 = and press the *i* key, 30 × 12 = and press the *n* key, and 0 and press the *FV* key. When you press the *PMT* key, you find the monthly constant (0.008408542), which is then multiplied by 12 to obtain the annual constant (0.100902505), as follows:

–1	*PV*
9.5 ÷ 12 =	*i*
30 × 12 =	*n*
0	*FV*
	PMT × 12 = 0.100902505
or	10.0902505. . .%.

Some calculators have keys that automatically convert annual interest and payments into their monthly equivalents.

Each periodic debt service payment consists of two parts: 1) interest for the preceding period on the outstanding amount of the loan at the beginning of the period, and 2) partial payment of principal (amortization). In the early years of a level-payment amortizing loan, the largest portion of the periodic payment is interest. As the loan principal is gradually reduced while the periodic payment remains constant, however, the amount of interest declines (as interest is calculated only on the outstanding balance). At the same time, the portion of the total payment that goes to amortize the loan principal gradually increases (see Figure B-1).

Note that changes in either the term (repayment period) or the interest rate will change the mortgage constant. If the term remains the same, then

- *The higher the interest rate, the higher the constant;* or
- *The lower the interest rate, the lower the constant.*

Figure B-1

Example of Three-Year Amortization

How much interest and principal will the borrower pay in the first three years on a $40,000, 12 percent interest, 25-year amortizing loan with an annual debt service payment of $5,100?

First-Year Interest	$40,000 × 12% = $4,800
First-Year Amortization	$5,100 – $4,800 = $300
Loan Balance after First Year	$40,000 – $300 = $39,700
Second-Year Interest	$39,700 × 12% = $4,764
Second-Year Amortization	$5,100 – $4,764 = $336
Loan Balance after Second Year	$39,700 – $336 = $39,364
Third-year Interest	$39,364 × 12% = $4,724
Third-Year Amortization	$5,100 – $4,724 = $376

Clearly this process would be very time-consuming for the 25th year. In practice, actual calculations are performed by using calculators or computers with preprogrammed routines. Note that as payments are made, the ratio of principal to interest increases.

If the interest rate remains the same, then

- *The longer the repayment period, the lower the constant;* or
- *The shorter the repayment period, the higher the constant.*

Because the mortgage constant is no more than the debt service payment for a loan of $1.00, it is possible to use the same technique to calculate the debt service payment on any loan. Consider, for example, a single-family home loan of $200,000. Assume the loan carries a 9.25 percent interest rate and requires monthly payments over 15 years to fully amortize the loan. Using a financial calculator, you compute the monthly payment as follows:

–200,000	*PV*	
9.5 ÷ 12 =	*i*	
15 × 12 =	*n*	
0	*FV*	
	PMT	2,058.38.

The loan requires a monthly payment of $2,058.38 to pay the required interest and fully amortize the loan over the next 15 years. For a 30-year loan, the only change necessary is to increase the 180 (15 × 12) periods in *n* to 360 and then recalculate *PMT*. The result is $1,645.35 each month, or $413.03 less than for the 15-year loan. Of course, payments would be made for twice as long.

A Longer-Term Perspective On Demographics

Despite turmoil in global financial markets and economies, the U.S. economy's performance was nothing short of stellar in the middle to late 1990s. Economic expansion in the 1990s, as of the end of the decade, was the second longest expansion in the nation's economic history—only the expansion of the 1960s was longer. In many regards, the most recent expansion is the most impressive. Although the expansion of the 1960s was fueled by spending related to the Vietnam War and Great Society programs, the expansion of the 1990s occurred despite substantial fiscal restraint as the federal government successfully turned a yawning budget deficit into a surplus.

The economy's strength is most evident in the labor market. Since the expansion began, some 18 million jobs have been created, and despite considerable hand-wringing among policy makers and analysts, the quality of those jobs has been relatively high. The proportion of the labor force at work was at a record high as of 1999, and the 4.6 percent jobless rate was near a generational low. Unemployment was low from coast to coast. In 1999, jobless rates were at or below 3 percent in metropolitan areas as varied as Atlanta, Boston, Dallas, Denver, Detroit, Minneapolis, Seattle, and the San Francisco Bay Area. And despite the strongly expanding economy and low unemployment, inflation remained at bay. Consumer price inflation slowed to near 1.5 percent, and producer prices fell.

The economy's unprecedented performance appears to be more than simply the result of the fortuitous confluence of several fleeting events. A number of structural or long-term changes in the U.S. economy have lifted long-term growth in labor productivity, raised competitive pressures on businesses and labor, and enhanced the economy's ability to adjust to any imbalances and shocks that ultimately undermine expansions.[1] This so-called "new economy" is thus able to grow more quickly and at higher rates of capacity without engendering inflationary pressures. Moreover, the new economy will experience longer expansions and shorter and milder recessions (see Figure C-1).

Structural Changes in the Economy

The most significant structural changes shaping the new economy include a heightened pace of technological change, increasing globalization, ongoing deregulation of key sectors, a changing process of financial intermediation, and the aging of the population. This appendix begins by considering each change and then looks at significant implications of those changes for investors in commercial real estate.[2] Both the structural changes and their most obvious implications are "deep background" for the market study. With an understanding of these issues (as well as the models and methods covered in Chapter 18), analysts will be better able to correctly analyze the plethora of market data available.

Technological Change

Nowhere is the quickening pace of technological change more evident than in advances in semiconductor technology. Intel formally introduced the 286 chip,

The authors are grateful to Mark Zandi, Regional Financial Associates, who prepared this appendix.

Figure C-1

Shorter Recessions and Longer Expansions

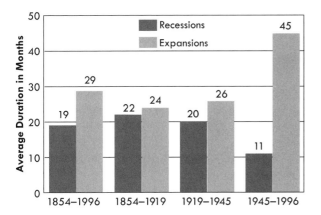

Source: **National Bureau of Economic Research.**

which had an initial speed of 1 million instructions per second (MIPS), in early 1982.[3] The power of succeeding generations of chips, which have been introduced nearly every three years, has grown quickly. The top of the line is currently the Pentium III, which operates at about 500 MIPS (but by the time this book is published will probably no longer be in that position).

The sophistication of computer software has also advanced significantly. Microsoft introduced Windows 3.1 in 1992 and Windows NT and 95 in 1995, all of which heightened the acceptance of PC (personal computer) technology. The pace of technological change remains heated. The next-generation chip from Intel and Hewlett-Packard, the Merced chip, expected in 2000, could deliver twice as much speed as the Pentium III.[4]

The fast pace of technological change has likely raised the long-term trend for growth in productivity.[5] New computer and telecommunication technologies allow for the quick completion of previously insurmountable tasks, and they induce businesses to invest more aggressively (see Figure C-2). Businesses that fail to invest strongly lose their competitiveness, because their capital does not embody the gains in efficiency offered by the newest technology. Note, for example, the significant increase in the depreciation rate for capital equipment during the past quarter century. Since the early 1970s, the average useful life of capital equipment has fallen from 15 years to 12 years.

Technological advances have also reduced fluctuations in the business cycle by reducing the historically dramatic shifts in investment. In the recessions of the first quarter century after World War II, collapsing investment in inventory accounted for nearly all of the decline in real GDP. During the last quarter of the 20th century, however, changes in inventory became an increasingly smaller proportion of overall economic activity. In the 1990–91 downturn, only one-half of the decline in real GDP was the result of falling inventories. Technology is reducing the role of inventory shifts in shaping the business cycle by reducing the inventories that businesses need to hold relative to sales. This phenomenon occurred through the adoption of inventory management techniques such as just-in-time inventorying and materials resource planning, which have been made possible by advances and strong investment in computer, scanner, and telecommunications technology.

Globalization

The U.S. economy is increasingly globally oriented as a result of greater trade, direct investment, and foreign immigration. The sum of exports and imports of goods and services—a good measure of the openness of the economy—will soon account for nearly one-third of GDP, up from one-fifth of GDP at the start of the 1990s,

Figure C-2

Increased Investment as a Result of Accelerated Technological Innovation
(Real Investment in Information-Processing Equipment as a Share of GDP)

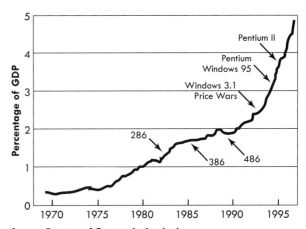

Source: **Bureau of Economic Analysis.**

Figure C-3

Accelerated Economic Globalization

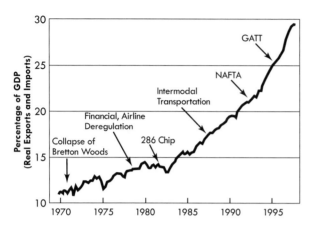

Source: Bureau of Economic Analysis.

and one-tenth of GDP in the mid-1970s (see Figure C-3). The liberalization of trade laws and international financial deregulation, from the collapse of the Bretton Woods fixed–exchange rate agreement in the early 1970s to the more recent passage of NAFTA and GATT (General Agreement on Tariffs and Trade), have contributed to the globalization of the economy. Improvements in transportation, distribution, and communications technology and infrastructure have also stimulated trade.

Globalization has heightened competitive pressures on businesses and labor.[6] U.S. manufacturers who compete in a global marketplace are unable to raise prices and are in some cases forced to cut prices to remain competitive when the dollar rises in value. This effect is evident from the current outright decline in producer prices and only modest gains during the 1990s. Labor is also struggling with foreign competition. Compensation for labor has been constrained not only for those working in globally competing industries, but also among less-skilled and -educated workers who directly compete with foreign immigrants.

The more global U.S. economy is also less cyclical. U.S. recessions during the last quarter of the 20th century would have been substantially more severe if international trade were not as important to the economy. In the nadir of the 1973–1975, 1980, and 1990–1991 recessions, for example, year-over-year decline in real GDP growth would have been as much as 1 percentage point greater if not for an improving trade balance. A deteriorating trade balance also reined in the economy dur-

ing the boom periods of expansions, forestalling wage and price pressures and thus subsequent downturns.

The trade balance generally moves countercyclically, as U.S. and world economies are often at different stages in their business cycles. In the U.S. recession year of 1991, for example, the Mexican and Japanese economies expanded by more than 3 percent, and the German economy grew by more than 5 percent. In contrast, when the U.S. economy was surging in 1994, the Japanese economy hardly grew, and the German economy was quickly decelerating.

The countercyclical changes in the trade balance are also supported by procyclical changes in the value of the dollar. The dollar generally appreciates when the U.S. economy is strong and interest rates are rising, and depreciates when the economy is weak and rates are moving lower.

Deregulation

A growing number of industries have been deregulated since the mid-1970s. In the 1970s, government deregulated the energy and transportation industries. In the 1980s, it was the financial services industry and, in the 1990s, the telecommunications and electric utility industries (see Figure C-4). In some regards, the health care industry was also deregulated in the 1990s by government's efforts to induce Medicare and Medicaid recipients into managed care. Deregulation was jumpstarted by the tumultuous economy of the 1970s, and

Figure C-4

Deregulation of Key Sectors of The Economy

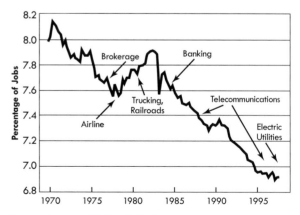

Source: Bureau of Labor Statistics.

it has been fueled by new technologies and the competitive pressures introduced by globalization.

Deregulation has unleashed competitive forces that have constrained inflation and prompted increased innovation and investment. Consumer prices for electricity, for example, are falling sharply as the electric industry gears up for deregulation.[7] In 1998, prices were down nearly 4 percent from the year before, the fastest rate of decline in more than 50 years. RFA ultimately expects electric utility deregulation to reduce electricity prices by some 20 percent from what they otherwise would have been.[8]

The explosion in financial innovation and investment since the early 1980s is a direct result of deregulation. Homebuyers, for example, can pick from a veritable smorgasbord of mortgage loans from a surfeit of lenders. In the mid-1980s, the only available mortgage was a 30-year, fixed-rate mortgage, and the only choice was whether to borrow from the local S&L or a bank.

Securitization

Another ongoing change shaping the new economy is the boom in financial securitization.[9] Securitization is a fundamental change in the process of financial intermediation. Historically, households deposited their savings in commercial banks and thrift institutions. The banks and thrifts in turn invested those savings by making loans to other households and businesses. Lending by banks and thrifts is increasingly being supplanted by securitization. In the process of securitization, loans made to individual households and businesses are combined with other loans into a so-called pool of loans. A financial security that is backed by the interest and principal paid on the pool of loans is originated and sold to a wide range of investors. Securitized lending, which began only in the late 1970s, will soon account for one-fifth of all lending (see Figure C-5).[10]

The rapid growth in securitization has reduced the constraints on the availability of credit to households and businesses. The lack of available credit has historically been a major factor contributing to fluctuations in the business cycle: witness the severity of the California and Northeast recessions early in the 1990s. Those downturns were exacerbated by the lack of bank lending during the credit crunch.

Securitization also results in the more efficient allocation of capital, which can be seen in comparing the U.S. economic experience of the late 1990s with that of Asia. Until late 1998, for example, the rapidly growing nations of Asia were considered examples of how high rates of saving would result in strong investment and thus rapid growth. The contrast with the United

Figure C-5

A Change in the Process of Financial Intermediation

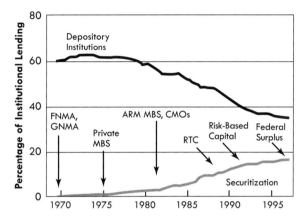

Source: Federal Reserve Board.

States, where saving rates were the lowest in the world, was striking. It is now apparent, however, that the ample savings of the Asian nations were squandered on unproductive investments. A few government and bank officials made investment decisions, not prices determined in an efficient marketplace. Despite the poor saving rate in the United States, the efficient allocation of scarcer savings has resulted in highly productive investments and an economy that in 1999 was the envy of the world.

The Aging Population

The economy's exceptional performance is also in part the result of the aging of the population. Baby boomers, born in the 20 years following World War II—from 1945 through 1964—account for by far the largest generation, or approximately one-third of the population (see Figure C-6). Where the baby boomers are in their life cycle is thus a significant determinant of a wide range of economic activity.[11]

In 1998, the boomers were between the ages of 33 and 53—the ages in which workers are their most productive and saving rates are highest. Workers' productivity generally rises until age 50 as workers gain experience, training, and education. It declines thereafter as workers approach retirement and their health begins to deteriorate. Saving rates also rise and peak for those between the ages of 45 and 54. According to the Consumer Expenditure Survey, households in this age group saved well over 10 percent of their income in 1996.[12] Households under 25 years old and over 65 had negative saving rates. Older households obviously save more of their income in anticipation of retirement. Higher rates of saving also enhance the economy's productivity, as the increased savings lower the cost of capital for businesses and thus prompt greater investments by businesses.

Implications for Investors in Commercial Real Estate

Implication 1. The New Economy Is Valid but Overstated

The theory of the new economy accurately postulates that because of a number of ongoing structural economic trends, underlying growth in productivity has accelerated in recent years. Moreover, the business cycle is somewhat longer and less volatile than in the past. Real estate investors should thus reasonably expect to enjoy stronger and more stable growth in the demand for commercial space. Although the new economy is certainly impressive, its virtues are likely overstated.[13] The economy's growth potential—or the rate of growth consistent with a stable jobless rate and inflation—is not that much greater today than a decade ago, and although business cycles will likely be less pronounced than in the past, they are alive and well. Real estate investors should thus not base current investment decisions on the belief that the economy's recent stellar performance will be the norm in the future.

It is important to recognize that, although underlying gains in productivity have likely accelerated in recent years, they have accelerated only modestly. Moreover, even though growth in productivity has accelerated, growth in the labor force is decelerating. The result is that the economy's long-term potential growth is not much higher currently than it was at the beginning of the 1990s—witness the increasingly tight labor market. Indeed, each time the economy has expanded above a 2.5 percent rate during the current economic expansion, the jobless rate has consistently fallen (see Figure C-7).

The acute shortage of labor, if not soon alleviated, will ultimately erode the "labor anxiety" that has allowed the economy to expand so strongly without engendering wage and price pressures. Labor costs are now on

Figure C-6

The Aging Population: Distribution of Live Births as of 1997

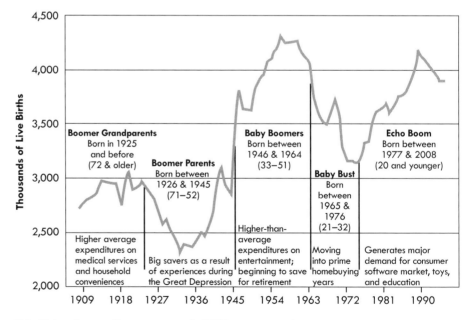

Note: Values in parentheses are ages in 1997.
Source: Vital Statistics.

Figure C-7

Potential Growth of the Economy

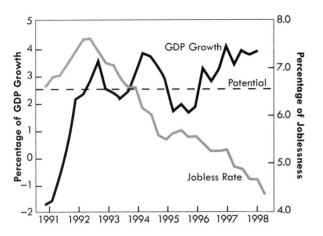

Sources: **Bureau of Economic Analysis, Bureau of Labor Statistics.**

the rise, which will ultimately put pressure on businesses to raise their prices more aggressively.

The new economy also has a dark side. The distribution of income is increasingly more skewed, as better-skilled and -educated workers are flourishing, while less-skilled workers suffer from declining real incomes.

The risks to the new economy are now more likely to come from overseas (such as the Asian economic crisis) and thus more difficult to identify, assess, and respond to.

The new economy has also not done away with those "animal spirits" that historically have led to the speculation resulting in the excesses that ultimately undermine expansions. These excesses are arguably apparent in the stock market today, where price-earning ratios are near record highs despite the global financial and economic turmoil and growing prospects for weak, if not declining, corporate profits.

Implication 2. The New Economy Has Wide-Ranging Implications for Regional Economies

Those regions that have relatively low cost structures, that are more reliant on high-tech activities, and that are globally oriented have the most positive long-term prospects for economic growth. Regions with relatively high cost structures and large deregulating industries will expand more slowly.

A key implication of the new economy is that high-tech industries and the regions with a large concentration of high-tech activities will experience relatively strong growth. This fact is evident in the heretofore relatively strong job gains experienced in metropolitan areas where high-tech industries account for a disproportionate share of all jobs.

Areas dominated by the high-tech industry face risks, however. The rapid pace of technological change can leave today's high-tech winners tomorrow's losers. Consider the impact of the switch from minicomputers to PCs beginning in the late 1980s and the effect it had on Boston's economy, which at the time was home to some of the largest minicomputer producers. High-tech businesses are also a relatively volatile industry, enjoying fantastic growth in the good times but significant losses when conditions are weaker. At the start of the 1990s in the midst of the last recession, for example, high-tech metropolitan areas significantly lagged the rest of the nation. The recent global economic downturn has also had its most profound impact on the U.S. economy to date as a result of its impact on high-tech industries.

Given the importance of increasing globalization in forming the new economy, those regions that are more globally oriented stand a better chance of doing well. Metropolitan areas with an oversized dependence on exports have experienced relatively strong growth more recently.

Greater links with overseas economies also present economic risks. The Mexican peso crisis in late 1994 and the subsequent severe Mexican recession constrained growth in the nation's Southwest in 1995. The more recent currency crisis in Asia and ongoing economic malaise in Japan will limit trade from the West Coast. Canada's difficulties with Quebec secessionists and Europe's move toward a monetary union also present significant economic challenges to those regional economies in the Northeast and Midwest that trade most heavily with those international economies.

The ongoing deregulation of key sectors of the economy is also influencing the new regional economy. As competition is introduced into formerly regulated industries, the industries go through a wrenching restructuring and, at least initially, downsizing. Mergers and acquisitions wracked the commercial banking industry for much of the 1990s and will continue well into the new century. AT&T and the baby Bells have experienced a number of restructurings as they have geared up for competition in the long distance and local phone markets. Electric utilities are also just beginning to reorganize as they prepare for a deregulated market. Those regions with a relatively high concentration of jobs in these industries have suffered. Job growth in metropolitan areas that have more than double the national share of employment in these industries have barely kept pace with growth in other metropolitan areas in the current expansion.

Deregulation also presents economic opportunities to various regional economies. Bank consolidation has been a boon to Charlotte, North Carolina, for example, as BankAmerica (formerly NationsBank) and First Union have grown rapidly in size. The explosive growth in monoline credit card banks, which has come in part from the deregulation of the financial services industry, has fueled growth in Wilmington, Delaware, home to MBNA and BancOne's First USA. Deregulation of telecommunications has resulted in strong gains in the industry in Washington, D.C, as exemplified by MCI's growth, and in Kansas City, home of Sprint. Deregulation of the electric utilities will also ultimately benefit some regions enormously as that industry consolidates.

The heightened competitive environment characterizing the new economy also suggests that relative regional business costs will be increasingly important in determining regional economic performances. Businesses that have trouble raising prices to maintain earnings growth and profit margins are instead focusing on lowering their cost structures. One of the easiest ways to do so is to expand and relocate into areas of the country where costs are relatively low. Advances in computer, telecommunications, and transportation technologies also allow businesses to take advantage of regional cost differentials. Moreover, the economy is increasingly producing high-tech and information-based products and services that have very low transportation costs, if any, and can thus be located almost anywhere. This situation contrasts with most traditional manufactured goods, which have high transportation costs and are more likely produced near where they are ultimately consumed or near a port for easy movement.[14]

Regional economies that will be relatively successful in the new economy are found in all areas of the nation. Examples include, but are not limited to, central New Jersey and the northern Virginia suburbs of Washington, D.C., in the Northeast; Raleigh, North Carolina, and Dallas and Austin, Texas, in the South; Minneapolis in the Midwest; and Denver and Sacramento in the West.

Implication 3. Variations in Regional Economies Are Abating

Perhaps the most important, but least recognized, hallmark of the new regional economy is that, although significant differences will continue in regional economic performances, they will be much less pronounced than in the past. From Boston to the San Francisco Bay Area, for example, the nation's regional economies are experiencing expanding payrolls and low and falling unemployment. Regional economies are struggling in some areas, but they are relatively small and geographically dispersed.[15]

The widespread strength of regional economies is unprecedented. Each national expansion of the last quarter of the 20th century saw significant regional economies in recession. In the early 1970s, California's economy was struggling under the weight of cuts in the defense budget as the Vietnam War came to a close. In the mid-1970s, economies in much of the nation's Southeast were contracting as a result of a severe real estate market downturn. During the late 1970s and early 1980s, the industrial Midwest's economy reeled as the region's manufacturing industries restructured and downsized. The most substantial peak-to-trough job decline of a metropolitan area occurred in Detroit during that period as the auto industry severely cut payrolls. In the mid-1980s, the resource-dependent economies of the Southwest and Farm Belt struggled when oil, agricultural, and other commodity prices collapsed. In the late 1980s and early 1990s, the Northeast's and California's economies experienced severe downturns as a result of defense cuts, a downturn in the real estate market, and downsizings at corporations headquartered in the regions.

Patterns of regional economic growth in the late 1990s also appeared to be increasingly similar. The formerly high-flying regions of expansion in the South and much of the West began experiencing much slower growth. Las Vegas, the nation's fastest-growing metropolitan area in the 1990s, saw growth slip from a boom-like 14 percent job growth rate in the middle of the decade to merely torrid growth of half that at the end. In contrast, the nation's weaker regional economies are experiencing much stronger growth. The Northeast's economy is expanding at close to the national average, and California is now one of the fastest-growing states in the nation. Both regions suffered through debilitating downturns earlier in the 1990s.

The seeming convergence of regional economic performances is borne out statistically. During the national expansions of the 1970s and 1980s, the standard deviation of job growth across states was well over 2 percent (compared with 1.7 percent during the expansion at the end of the 1990s). A similar story is told by the standard deviation of job growth across the nation's metropolitan areas. In the 1970s and 1980s expansion, the standard deviation of metropolitan area job growth was well over 6 percent (compared with less than 2 percent at the end of the decade).

Figure C-8

Regional Economic Diversity Over Time

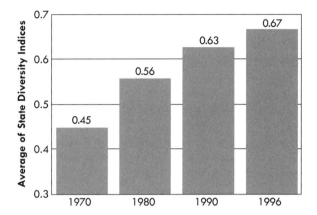

Note: A diversity index of 1.0 indicates that a state has the same business mix as the nation.
Sources: Bureau of Labor Statistics, Regional Financial Associates.

The increasing similarity in regional economic performances is in part the result of tighter labor markets across the nation. Fully 90 percent of the nation's metropolitan areas have jobless rates below the national average of 4.6 percent. An astounding one-third of metropolitan areas have jobless rates below 3 percent, and an increasing number of metropolitan areas have jobless rates below 2 percent. Only the New York metropolitan area, with a jobless rate of close to 7 percent, has any significant slack remaining in its labor market. Less unemployment means fewer reasons for people to move, and regional migration flows have slowed considerably. The net outflow of residents from California to the rest of the West has stopped, for example, as the state's economy has improved. Shifting migration patterns have significant impacts on regional economies. Outflows from California exacerbated that state's downturn, for example, while stimulating the booming economies of the Mountain West and Pacific Northwest.

The structural or longer-term factors shaping the new economy are likely more important, however, in the increasing similarity of regional economic performances. The principal reason for the declining variability of regional economic performances is that regional economies are beginning to look more like each other. As businesses have become more footloose, prompted by the need to control costs, and allowed to move by technological advances, they are locating in previously far-flung regions. For example, financial services are locating in Des Moines, Charlotte, and Jacksonville; chip manufacturing in Austin, Texas, and Albuquerque; PC manufacturing in Sioux Falls, South Dakota, and Houston; computer software in Salt Lake City and Seattle; and telemarketing in Omaha.

Figure C-8 illustrates the increasing diversity of regional economies, showing the average economic diversity of states as defined by an index that measures how similar each state's business mix is to the national business mix.[16] In 1970, the average state diversity index was only 0.45. By 1980, the average had risen to 0.56, and, in 1996, the average state diversity index rose to 0.67. By this measure, state economies have become nearly 50 percent more diverse in less than two decades.

Deregulation is also leading to more similar regional economic performances. The deregulation of the transportation, energy, electric utility, and telecommunications industries is eroding differences in regional economic advantages and disadvantages. This phenomenon will soon be seen for the cost of electricity as deregulation of that industry results in falling electric rates in the Northeast and California. Current regional differences in electricity costs are substantial. In much of New England, commercial electric rates are close to 50 percent above the national average, while the Pacific Northwest enjoys rates that range from 30 to 40 percent below the national average. California illustrates the influence of different costs of electricity on relative regional business costs. If the state were able to reduce its rates for electricity to the national average, for example, then its total relative business costs would fall from being 7 percent above the national average to near the national average.

Deregulation of the financial services industry has also been instrumental in smoothing out differences in regional economic performances. Historically, the cost of financial capital varied considerably across the nation, as the availability and cost of funds in regions depended on the deposits collected by intermediaries in those regions. Moreover, lenders would extend credit to businesses and households in a relatively small geographic area. If those borrowers got into trouble, the lenders' ability to make other loans would be seriously impaired, thus exacerbating any regional economic problems. With financial deregulation, however, capital markets are no longer regional but international. Businesses and households in any region can borrow just as easily from their local thrift as from a European pension fund or a Japanese insurance company.

Financial deregulation has significantly reduced variations in the cost of borrowing across regions. The standard deviation of mortgage rates across five broad regions of the nation during the 1990s as measured by Freddie Mac, for example, was cut in half during the decade. Differences in mortgage borrowing costs across regions have clearly narrowed as regional mortgage markets have become increasingly linked to global financial markets. Other borrowing costs are affected as well.

The globalization of the economy has also reduced variations in regional economic performances. As regions sell an increasing share of the goods and services they produce overseas, they are less susceptible to the impact of changing domestic fiscal and monetary policies or other domestic shocks. During the last recession in 1990/1991, continued strong exports were instrumental in mitigating the downturn. In California, for example, the peak-to-trough decline in real gross state product (GSP) in the last recession was 3.2 percent. Without robust exporting by the state's manufacturers and agricultural concerns during the period, however, real GSP would have fallen by 5.5 percent.[17] With few exceptions, international trade cushioned the blow of the last recession on regional economies.

Implication 4. Real Estate Markets Will Be Less Cyclical

Historically, commercial real estate markets eventually turn speculative in good economic times, with builders putting up space that is not preleased. Doing so ultimately results in significant overbuilding and an eventual collapse in new building.

A downturn in the real estate market almost always plays a significant part in broader economic downturns. During the five recessions of the last quarter of the 20th century, weaker building was responsible for an average of one-sixth of the decline in peak-to-trough GDP, more than three times greater than the contribution of commercial building to GDP. The drop in building during the 1990/1991 recession was similar in magnitude. The most significant decline in building was during the 1974/1975 recession, when it accounted for one-third of the decline in GDP. The severe real estate collapse of that period was in large part the result of the speculative investing and developing of the REITs of that day.

The impact of weak real estate markets on a recessionary economy goes well beyond that resulting simply from reduced building. Most notable is the effect that falling real estate values have on the balance sheets of financial intermediaries. As commercial property prices fell during the last recession, commercial banks, thrifts, and insurance companies experienced enormous losses on their commercial real estate loan portfolios. In the early 1990s, for example, commercial real estate loans accounted for just under one-half of all noncurrent assets at commercial banks. Such loans accounted for only one-tenth of total bank assets. Losses were so high during that period that many institutions experienced significant shortages of capital, and many failed. The result was the so-called credit crunch of the period. Problems in commercial real estate limited the ability of consumers and businesses to borrow, thus crimping their spending and investing and severely exacerbating that downturn.[18]

Weak real estate markets are even more important in exacerbating some of the most severe regional economic downturns. In the very severe recession that wracked Boston's economy in the early 1990s and shaved 12 percent from the metropolitan area's job base, losses in construction accounted for almost one-fifth of all jobs lost, whereas construction accounted for only 4 percent of all jobs at the start of the metropolitan area's downturn. Other notable examples include the Houston recession in the wake of the mid-1980s energy price collapse in which more than one-fourth of all jobs lost were in construction, and the Atlanta recession of the mid-1970s when close to one-third of jobs lost were construction jobs.

The rapid securitization of commercial real estate through the REIT and CMBS markets reduces the chances that future real estate market cycles will be as pronounced as those experienced historically. A significant impact of the REIT and CMBS markets is that an ever-larger share of real estate assets is priced daily in public equity and fixed-income markets. (Private real estate pricing through appraisals is done infrequently and is not publicly available.)

The most significant advantage of public real estate markets over private real estate markets is that more information is available regarding market conditions of various types of property. In public real estate markets, it is easier to know who is planning to develop what properties where and when. This knowledge should dissuade development in markets that are heating up and guide investment toward markets that are less active. In privately held real estate markets, it is much more difficult to know what other developers are planning and thus more likely that too much or too little building will occur.

Information is also more quickly disseminated and prices more quickly discounted in public markets than in private markets. Public market prices appear to lead changes in real estate cash flows. Prices for public REITs hit their nadir in 1990, for example, while cash flow did not reach its trough until three years later. Private real estate prices, however, appear to follow or even lag cash flows. Public market prices should also respond more quickly if underlying property market conditions deteriorate, which would raise the cost of capital and thus slow future property development more quickly, making it less likely for severe overbuilding to occur.

Management of real estate by REITs should also be more responsive to changing market conditions than private management. REIT managers have better incentives to make correct decisions about purchasing, holding, and managing real property, because they generally have a large stake in the ownership of the REIT through stock ownership and options. Providing the same incentives to private asset managers, in contrast, has long been an issue plaguing institutional investors.

Although the excesses that have historically characterized commercial real estate are less likely to develop, there are reasons to suspect that real estate cycles are not simply a thing of the past. Public ownership of real estate is still relatively small. Approximately one-fourth of the more than $1.7 trillion in public and private real estate equity and debt outstanding is publicly traded.[19] Although private investors are benefiting from the information provided in the quickly expanding public markets, they still have less information and poorer incentives and are thus still likely to make speculative investment and development decisions.

Public real estate markets are also not immune to speculative excesses. The mood in the REIT and CMBS market went from rampant euphoria in 1997 to abject pessimism in 1998. In 1997, REIT stocks traded at substantial premiums to the value of their properties. The higher prices prompted a flood of new and follow-on stock offerings. Wall Street paid large premiums, providing ample cash to REITs in anticipation of future growth in assets and cash flow. As of early 1999, REIT stock prices had fallen some 15 to 20 percent from their peaks, all but ending the flow of public equity capital into the real estate market. This situation in turn prompted lower real estate prices and a curtailment of new development.

Investors' demand for CMBSs has changed as dramatically. In 1998, demand from investors was seemingly insatiable, driving yields down to what seemed like paper-thin premiums over comparable Treasury securities. Spreads on investment-grade CMBSs shrank to 60 to 90 basis points. The narrowing on non-investment-grade CMBS spreads was even more significant. BB-rated CMBSs were trading only 200 basis points over Treasuries, roughly equivalent to spreads on comparably rated plain-vanilla corporate bonds. Early in 1999, CMBS spreads more than doubled, effectively shutting down the market. Investors' willingness to provide ample and cheap capital was replaced seemingly overnight with an unwillingness to provide any capital at any price. This change in sentiment cannot be explained by any change in fundamental current or prospective real estate market conditions.

Even if public real estate markets militate against the most egregious speculation, the long lead times required for many construction projects—including land acquisition, financing, design, permit approvals, and construction—will ensure that real estate remains subject to significant booms and busts. The time it takes to plan and build an office building without an unusual disruption can be as long as three years. During the time that the building process is in motion, economic conditions and thus the demand for that space can change substantially. Buildings that began development in the late 1980s in southern California were being completed when that economy was suffering from severe job losses. Development times for other types of commercial property are shorter, but they are long enough to make it difficult for developers to avoid making decisions to build at what in hindsight appears to be a poor time in the market.

Implication 5. Office Absorption Will Weaken

The national office market enjoyed steadily improving conditions in the late 1990s. According to CB Commercial, the office vacancy rate was cut in half, from close to 20 percent at the start of the 1990s to well below 10 percent in late 1998. Vacancy rates in 1999 were as low as they have been since the early 1980s, and office rents and prices rose at a double-digit pace as a result. The price for office space was up 25 percent from its nadir and was only 10 percent below its peak in the late 1980s.

The improvement in the office market was driven by weak new construction and robust absorption of office space. Driving office absorption was surging job growth. Since the current expansion began in the early 1990s, the economy has generated some 18 million jobs, or 2.5 million jobs per year.

The year 1999 was expected to be a key transition year for the office market, however, as the supply of new office space was again expected to outstrip the absorption of new space. This view is based on the clear acceleration in building activity, which was expected to continue into early in the new century and, more important, a sharp deceleration in absorption.

Behind the expectation for weaker office absorption is the nation's exceedingly tight labor market. With little unemployment, job growth must soon slow to equal growth in the labor force. Given growth in the working-

Figure C-9

Growth in Labor Force and Employment

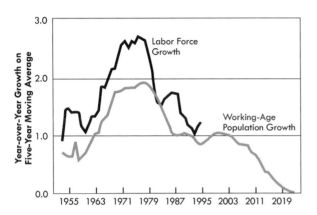

Sources: **Bureau of Labor Statistics, U.S. Census Bureau.**

age population of just over 1 percent per year, the labor force can consistently grow only close to 1.25 percent per year. The difference in growth between the labor force and the working-age population is the result of an ongoing expected increase in the labor force participation rate. Greater increases in participation are possible but seem unlikely, given that participation is already at a record high two-thirds of the civilian noninstitutional population.[20] With growth in the labor force of only 1.25 percent per year, job growth will ultimately be cut in half from its current growth rate of 2.5 percent.[21]

Job growth will remain weak for the next quarter century by the standards of the past quarter century as a result of the ongoing slowing in the growth of the working-age population. As baby boomers begin to retire in approximately 2010, growth in working-age population will slow from 1 percent per year currently to one-half that rate, according to Bureau of the Census projections (see Figure C-9). Moreover, growth in working-age population will come to a virtual halt by 2025. Growth in the labor force will slow as well, albeit perhaps not as dramatically, because the retirement age will likely be extended further and because even those of retirement age increasingly may decide to continue working as labor-starved businesses become more aggressive in inducing them to stay on payrolls. Weaker job growth will be a significant constraint on absorption of office space. Whether or not the supply of new office space slows commensurately is the most significant long-term risk to the office market.

Implication 6. Changes in the Financial Services Industry Will Affect Absorption Of Office Space

A substantial long-term shift in the demand for office space has begun as a result of dramatic changes in the financial services industry. The industry, which includes depository institutions such as commercial banks and S&Ls, investment banks, mutual funds, finance companies, and insurance companies, is the most important source of office demand. The industry is in the throes of consolidation, particularly among depository institutions. Each week, announced mergers have gotten larger, culminating in the megadeals that combine Citicorp with Travelers, Bank of America with NationsBank, and First Chicago NBD with BancOne. This trend has resulted and will continue to result in significant job cutting and thus weaker office absorption (see Figure C-10).[22]

But while depository institutions have been shedding payrolls, nondepository institutions continue to expand aggressively. Since the start of the 1990s, employment at depository institutions declined by approximately 250,000 jobs, or 10 percent, of all jobs at depository institutions. Jobs at nondepository institutions rose by 400,000 jobs, or 50 percent.

Most, but not all, regions with a significant number of jobs at depository institutions will experience weaker office absorption. Columbus, Ohio, home to BancOne, for example, stands to lose banking jobs. Those areas that are home to large and growing institutions will experience flourishing office demand. Even these areas are at risk, however, as no institution appears too large

Figure C-10

Trading Places in Financial Services

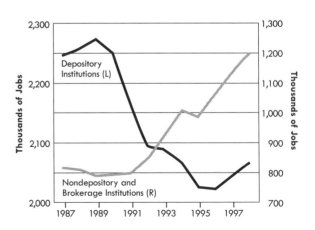

Source: **Bureau of Labor Statistics.**

538 Appendix C

to be part of an acquisition. San Francisco, for example, stands to lose jobs as a result of the merger of Bank of America and NationsBank. Moreover, not all regions losing banking jobs will experience weaker growth in financial service jobs, as gains at nondepository institutions more than compensate for the lost jobs in banking. First Union's acquisition of CoreStates Bank is resulting in lost banking jobs in Philadelphia, for example, but this loss is being offset by significant job gains at companies such as mutual fund giant Vanguard and credit card companies.

Depository institutions are consolidating and nondepository institutions expanding because of the same forces driving the new economy. Financial service companies are making increasingly massive investments in sophisticated information technology—hardware and software—needed to manage their businesses efficiently. Costs associated with making computer systems compatible with dates of the new millennium (the Y2K problem) are enormous and may be contributing to the decision of some institutions to join with others with greater financial resources.

The high fixed costs associated with investments in technology also heighten the substantial economies of scale and scope in financial services. Consumer and mortgage lending, for example, requires significant and costly marketing, customer support, account management, and servicing operations. Adding new customers spreads the large fixed costs associated with these activities across more customers—the definition of economies of scale. Significant economies of scope also exist. For example, the same database of information about customers can be mined to discern the best prospects for different bank products or who is most likely to default on a loan.

Consolidation is also the result as commercial banks struggle to maintain growth in revenues. Banks' profitability is strong because of the strong economy and low interest rates, cost cutting, and, outside their credit card portfolios, stellar credit quality. Recent commercial bank acquisitions of investment banks, brokerages, and, most recently, insurance companies are in large measure a bet that they will be able to cross-sell other financial services to their existing customers and their own banking services to the customers of those other financial institutions.

Recent regulatory changes have also been a catalyst for the consolidation of the financial services industry. Interstate banking became a reality in the 1990s, opening up significant opportunities for commercial banks to expand geographic boundaries that had been in place since the Great Depression. The quickest and most cost effective way to do so is through acquisitions. To some

degree, the way interstate banking grew helped to shape today's banking winners. North Carolina, for example, long allowed its banks to expand elsewhere in the nation but did not allow outside banks to do business in the state, supporting the expansion of two current banking powerhouses, NationsBank and First Union.

The effective demise of many of the restrictions between cross-ownership among commercial banks, investment banks, and insurance companies embodied in the Glass-Steagall Act of 1933 (which restricted most U.S. commercial banks from engaging in underwriting or performing investment banking activities) has also stimulated consolidation in the financial services industry. Bank regulators have increasingly permitted the nation's largest commercial banks to raise the revenues allowed from investment banking activities. Banking reform legislation to put an official end to Glass-Steagall has yet to make it through the legislative process, although the Citibank-Travelers marriage put added pressure on lawmakers to fashion a compromise.

Commercial banks have the wherewithal to make acquisitions, as they are capital rich. The equity-to-capital ratio for FDIC-insured institutions rose to a record 8.3 percent in 1998. With ample capital, banks are eager to put it to work making loans and earning fees. Many of the banks' acquisitions in the investment banking, brokerage, and mutual fund industries, in contrast, are capital poor and unable to expand as quickly as profit opportunities present themselves. Banks also find such acquisitions attractive, as many of the targets are able to attract significant savings from former bank depositors.

Heightened competitive pressures are also inducing consolidation. The increasingly global market for financial services is resulting in increasing competition between domestic and foreign institutions. European and, until more recently, Japanese institutions are increasing their presence in the United States. Most of these foreign institutions are already the size of the U.S. institutions that will result from the recent megadeals. Moreover, if U.S. institutions want to compete overseas, they will need the size and scope they are now aspiring to.

Competition among financial institutions is also rising at home as a result of the boom in financial securitization. Securitization raises competition in the financial services industry, as it breaks down the barriers to entry in the financial intermediation process. Smaller finance companies can quickly set up shop and make loans by originating loans and then quickly selling them to players in the securitized loan market. It is no longer necessary to have a large branch network to raise the deposits to then turn around and make a loan. Nimble finance companies are thus able to quickly exploit any extraordinarily profitable lending opportunity.

All the forces that have resulted in the current rush of mergers and acquisitions will remain in place for some time to come. The economies of scale and scope in the industry are compelling and will only rise with the increasing fixed costs associated with investments in technology and efforts to expand globally. Competition in the industry will remain intense as barriers to global competition fall and the process of financial securitization continues to erode the market share of depository institutions in the process of financial intermediation. Regulatory hurdles will also continue to fall, as Glass-Steagall will ultimately be repealed. The 9,000 or so commercial banks in existence today will be cut at least in half a decade from now.

Implication 7. Downtown Office Markets Will Shine

Prospects in the nation's downtown office markets are as strong as they have been in over a decade. In fact, the anticipated weakening in the national office market will be most pronounced in suburban office markets, partly because of the rush of new office supply that was expected to be completed at the end of the 1990s

in the suburbs. According to F.W. Dodge, of the approximately 170 million square feet in office space started in 1997, most of which was completed in 1998, less than 10 percent was in the nation's downtowns. Large office markets such as Chicago, Philadelphia, and Detroit have experienced essentially no building downtown, while building in New York, Houston, and Los Angeles remained relatively inconsequential.

Moreover, downtown office markets are not likely to experience the same sharp deceleration in absorption expected in the nation's suburbs. Economies of central urban areas are improving somewhat. Jobs in the urban core rose in 1998 for the sixth consecutive year, with job growth in 1998 well over 2 percent, the strongest growth since 1984 (see Figure C-11).

The stronger job gains in urban cores are partly the result of available labor. If any labor supply remains, it is in the central urban cores of the nation's cities. The reform of the nation's welfare system, which induces those previously on welfare rolls into jobs, prompted some of the increased availability. Businesses needing workers will increasingly be willing to hire the less-skilled and -educated labor force of the urban cores.

Figure C-11

Job Growth in the Nation's Urban Cores

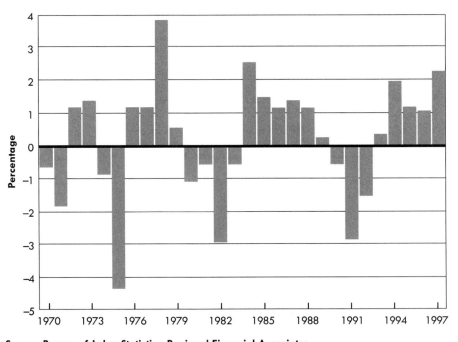

Sources: **Bureau of Labor Statistics, Regional Financial Associates.**

A number of long-lasting forces may also be at work supporting the growth prospects of central cities.[23] Many of the nation's largest and most important universities and research centers are located in urban cores. These institutions are instrumental in providing the labor and technical expertise used in the strongest-growing high-tech activities. Many high-tech activities also benefit from being closely located to each other, which many urban cores can offer. These so-called agglomeration economies are particularly important for the most sophisticated research conducted by high-tech firms. Although technological changes have broken down the agglomeration economies in production-oriented activities, they have heightened the agglomeration economies involved in research and development and design.

Central cities are also home to an urban area's most important physical infrastructure, including seaports, airports, rail hubs, and road systems. This infrastructure is particularly important in a global economy, which raises the volume of goods and number of people moving from place to place. Many city governments have also successfully reduced tax burdens and have become more proactive in promoting economic development, helping central cities win an increasing number of contests to attract large and high-profile businesses.

But despite their expected economic revival, central cities are not expected to outperform suburban economies. The share of jobs in central areas is expected to continue falling, just not as quickly as during the last quarter of the 20th century. Data constructed by Regional Financial Associates based on information from the BLS indicate that the share of jobs in central areas fell from 31 percent to near 26 percent during the 1990s. Moreover, not all central cities will fare as well. Most central areas that have large concentrations of employment at depository institutions, for example, will continue to substantially lag growth in the suburban ring.

Implication 8. Demographics Will Boost Multifamily Housing

The demand for multifamily space is set to rebound, after languishing for much of the 1990s. Throughout the 1980s, absorption of multifamily housing approached 400,000 units per year. During the 1990s, annual absorption was closer to 300,000 units. But absorption is expected to rebound as a result of a number of demographic and other factors.

The expected acceleration in multifamily household formation is the result of an increase in the number of persons in their prime renting ages, the first increase

Figure C-12

Growth in Renter Cohorts

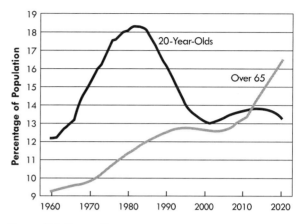

Source: **U.S. Census Bureau.**

since the mid-1980s (see Figure C-12). (Renter age groups include those between the ages of 20 and 29 and a portion of those over the age of 65.) The long steady decline of those in their prime renting years has been a substantial and long-running constraint on demand for multifamily housing. In the 1970s, population growth in these cohorts averaged just under 3 percent per year. Growth slowed in the 1980s to near 1 percent, and, in the 1990s, the number of persons declined at a nearly 1 percent annual rate.

The stronger expected increase in the number of multifamily households is also the result of continued strong foreign immigration, which will account for an increasing proportion of U.S. population growth. Foreign immigrants generally have relatively low rates of home-ownership in the first few years of their residence in the United States. According to the Joint Center for Housing Studies at Harvard University, the homeownership rate among immigrants is substantially below that of native-born residents early during their residence in this nation. Immigrants that were between the ages of 25 and 34 and in this country an average of five years, for example, had a homeownership rate of 24.2 percent in 1980, compared with a homeownership rate of 57.4 percent for native whites. Nearly 1 million foreign immigrants come to the United States each year, accounting for nearly one-third of national population growth.

Multifamily housing demand is also expected to receive a boost as the factors wane that currently support the soaring demand for single-family housing. There is currently not a single constraint on the single-family housing market: the economy is enjoying healthy gains in jobs and personal income, and unemployment is at a generational low. Stellar conditions in the labor market have resulted in record high consumer confidence. Fixed mortgage rates near 7 percent are also low by historical standards. With strongly rising incomes and low mortgage rates, housing affordability is as high as it has been since the early 1970s. According to the National Association of Realtors®, a household earning the median income can afford to purchase 135 percent of the median-priced house at prevailing mortgage rates.

Households not only have strong income; the soaring stock market has lifted household wealth. An estimated $5 trillion in stockholders' wealth was created just from 1995 to 1998[24]—equal to approximately $50,000 per household. Confident households that are working for increasing pay and benefiting from strongly rising net worth make very willing homebuyers.

Mortgage lenders are also very willing to extend mortgage loans to homebuyers. Competition among lenders has induced many to lower the points and fees they charge on loans. Average mortgage loan costs are currently near 125 basis points, compared with more than 200 basis points at the start of the 1990s. The explosion in affordable and so-called subprime lending also allows many prospective homebuyers to purchase homes for the first time. Affordable loans have very low downpayments and are made to homebuyers with relatively low incomes. Making such loans has been a priority for the Clinton administration, Fannie Mae, and Freddie Mac. Subprime loans are made to borrowers with blemished credit histories who would not qualify for more traditional mortgage loans.

Both willing households and lenders are reflected in the soaring rate of homeownership. The proportion of households that own their home is at a record, greater than two-thirds of all households and up nearly 2 whole percentage points in just two years (1997 and 1998). Homeownership has risen across all regions of the nation and across all demographic and ethnic groups.

Each factor fueling the demand for single-family space will likely remain in place, but likely to a lesser degree than recently. Job and income growth are expected to slow, mortgage lenders will turn less aggressive as losses rise in response to their more recent lowering in loan standards, and, given recent rising house prices, housing affordability will decline. It is also reasonable to expect that stock prices will not continue to rise at the rate experienced in recent years. Tax policy that has long favored single-family housing also appears to be turning less favorable. Recent changes in the capital gains treatment of homeowners' equity, for example, will make it easier for homeowners to sell their homes at younger ages and become renters.[25]

Figure C-13

The Effect of Demographics On Retailing

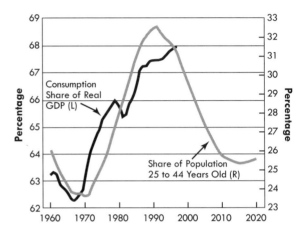

Sources: **U.S. Census Bureau , Bureau of Economic Analysis.**

Implication 9. Demographics Will Create a Drag on Retailing

Demographic trends were favorable to retailers during the last quarter of the 20th century, when the large baby boom generation was in its principal buying ages between 25 and 44. Households are first formed during these ages and thus homes and all the things that go into them are purchased. Consumer spending as a share of GDP rose, along with the share of the population in this age cohort (see Figure C-13).

But the baby boomers are now aging into their prime saving years. Based on data from the BLS Survey of Consumer Expenditures, the saving rate is at its highest for families headed by those between 45 and 54 years old. Not surprisingly, this cohort is also when family earnings peak. Saving rates are also relatively high for families headed by those aged 55 to 64. In contrast, saving rates are negative for families headed by those less than 25 years old and over 65. Those under 25 are likely to borrow to finance their spending beyond their incomes, while those over 65 are likely to sell accumulated wealth to pay for their spending.

To gauge how much the boomers have added and will likely add to the saving rate, a demographically weighted saving rate was constructed, with the weights equal to the share of all households headed by persons of the various age groups. Saving rates by age are assumed to remain constant at their 1995 rate. Figure C-14 shows the change in the demographically weighted

Figure C-14

Contribution of the Aging Population to the Saving Rate

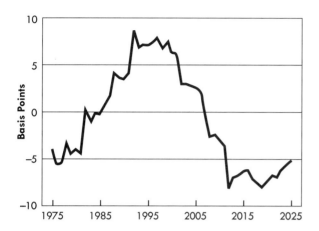

Sources: U.S. Census Bureau, Regional Financial Associates.

saving rate for 1975 through 2025. It represents the contribution that the changing age composition of the population has had and will have on the national saving rate.

The aging of the boomers began to lift the saving rate beginning in the mid-1980s, adding an average of five basis points each year over the next decade. In other words, if the population had not aged during the decade, the saving rate in 1997 would have been close to 50 basis points (five basis points times ten years) lower than its actual 4 percent. As the figure illustrates, the aging of the population will add another 50 basis points to the saving rate over the next decade. The aging of the boomers will thus ultimately lift the saving rate by a full percentage point. Growth in consumer spending will consequently weaken relative to overall growth in the economy. If the historical relationship depicted in Figure C-13 is any guide, then the consumption share of GDP will fall back close to its early 1970s level over the 15 years to 2010.[26]

Implication 10. Upscale Retailers and Housing Will Perform Best

Retailers, homebuilders, and landlords that cater to lower-income households will experience particularly weak demand, largely because of the ongoing skewing of the distribution of income and wealth in the new economy. According to the Census Bureau, share of total income for the top quintile of income distribution in-

creased sharply from 1976 to 1996 (see Figure C-15), while it declined for each of the other quintiles.

Real average annual family incomes for those families in the bottom quintile of income distribution declined by 0.8 percent per year from 1976 to 1996. Real family incomes in the second quintile also declined. In contrast, those families in the top two quintiles experienced substantial real gains in income, and families in the top 5 percent of income distribution experienced a whopping 2 percent per year increase in real incomes. The skewing of income distribution from 1976 to 1996 toward upper-income groups is a sharp reversal of the narrowing in income differentials that occurred in the years after World War II and the early 1970s. During those periods, real incomes for families in the bottom quintile of income distribution rose by 3 percent per year, while real incomes for families in the top 5 percent rose by only 2.4 percent per year.

The most important factors that account for skewing of income distribution include technological change, which has enhanced the value of highly skilled and educated labor in comparison with less-skilled and -educated labor, increased globalization, and shifts in fiscal policy with respect to equity objectives.

Technological change and the impact it has had on the value placed on highly skilled and educated labor in comparison with less-skilled and -educated labor are the most important factors explaining the skewing of income distribution. Businesses' enormous and increasingly rapid investments in high-tech equipment during the last quarter of the 20th century raised the demand for skilled labor with the ability to use the new technologies effectively relative to unskilled labor without that ability. Moreover, the slower growth of the college-age population since the early 1980s has reduced the growth in the supply of highly educated labor. Returns to education have soared as a result. The earnings of college-educated labor rose from approximately 140 percent of the earnings of high school–educated labor in the early 1970s to nearly 160 percent in the late 1990s. The differential in earnings between college-educated individuals and high school dropouts rose by even more.

Moreover, the increased openness of the U.S. economy to the world economy during the last quarter of the 20th century also contributed to the skewing of income distribution. Increased globalization led to the skewing of income distribution, because the value of goods and services in which the United States has a comparative advantage and the labor that produces them, namely high-tech products, was enhanced. Further, the value of goods and services in which the United States has a comparative disadvantage, namely products that use low-skilled labor, was depressed.

Figure C-15

The Ongoing Skewing of Income Distribution

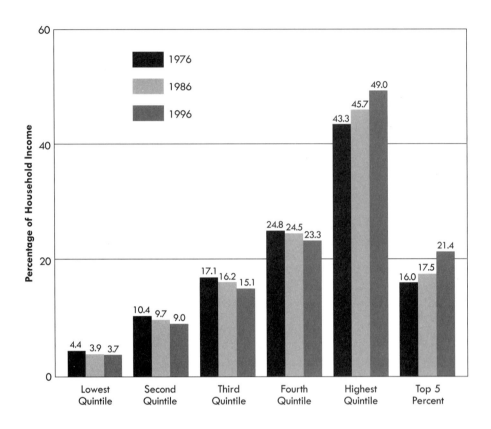

Source: **U.S. Census Bureau.**

Also contributing to the skewing of income distribution was a shift in the objectives of fiscal policy that deemphasized efforts to support the income and well-being of lower-income groups. The shift in emphasis began in the early 1980s during the Reagan administration, largely through changes in tax laws that clearly favored upper-income households. Although programs that largely benefited lower-income groups were not dramatically changed during the early 1980s, the large increases in defense outlays during that decade resulted in the large budget deficits that placed enormous pressures on current policy makers to curb the growth of or eliminate such programs.

The factors that led to the skewing of income distribution over the last quarter of the 20th century will remain in place well into the 21st century. The low cost of capital, ample financial resources, and the heightened pace of technological change are expected to foment continued strong investment by U.S. businesses in high-tech capital, further enhancing the value of labor that can

employ that capital effectively relative to those that cannot. Technological change and an increasingly propitious political environment will also support the continued globalization of the U.S. economy. Lower-skilled U.S. workers will be at an increasing disadvantage, while highly skilled U.S. workers will benefit as demand for the goods and services they produce grows. Slower growth in Medicaid and cuts in the earned income tax credit and in welfare programs will also continue to hit low-income groups hard.

In an attempt to maintain their living standards in the face of falling incomes, lower-income households have been avid borrowers. According to the Survey of Consumer Finance, last conducted by the Federal Reserve in 1995, debt burdens—equal to the proportion of after-tax income devoted to principal and interest and consumer installment and mortgage debt—were relatively high and rising for families with incomes of less than $50,000 annually.[27] In contrast, debt burdens were relatively low and falling for those families with greater incomes. Families with the highest annual incomes—those greater than $100,000—had debt burdens in 1995 that were approximately one-half those of families making the lowest annual incomes, less than $10,000.

Lower-income families already have the most serious difficulty making payments on their debt. More than one-fifth of families with annual incomes of less than $50,000 experienced at least one period of delinquency greater than 60 days in 1995, according to the Survey of Consumer Finance, compared with less than 5 percent of families with annual incomes greater than $50,000. Those who file for bankruptcy are also relatively poor. The Center for Credit Research found in a recent survey of filers that the median income of Chapter 7 filers was less than $18,000 annually and that of Chapter 13 filers was less than $24,000, compared with national median household income of $36,000.

Lower-income groups have also not benefited to a significant degree from the recent increase in stock and housing values. According to the 1995 Survey of Consumer Finance, less than one-third of households earning less than $50,000 annually owned some stock directly or indirectly, and the median value of those holdings was close to $6,000. In contrast, approximately three-quarters of households earning more than $50,000 annually owned some stock, whose median value was nearly $50,000.

Notes

1. See "The Next Recession," *Regional Financial Review,* November 1997, for a detailed discussion of the imbalances and shocks that have undermined economic expansions since World War II.

2. There are clearly many implications of the new economy on real estate markets that are not considered in this appendix, but those considered are deemed to be some of the more important ones.

3. MIPS increasingly is no longer the convention used in the computer industry to measure the power of computers. Intel uses SPECint and SPECfp measures for the Pentium family of processors, for example, but does not provide a comparable measure for earlier generations of chips.

4. See "Investment Boom or Bust," *Regional Financial Review,* October 1995, for a discussion of the pace of technological change and its impact on investment and the economy.

5. A comprehensive review of the literature on the impact of technological change on productivity and economic growth is provided in J. Fuhrer and J. Sneddon Little, "Technology and Growth: An Overview," *New England Economic Review,* November/December 1996, pp. 3–26.

6. See G. Borjas, R. Freeman, and L. Katz, "How Much Do Immigration and Trade Affect Labor Market Outcomes?" *Brookings Papers on Economic Activity,* no. 1, 1997, pp. 1–90.

7. See M. White, "Power Struggles: Explaining Deregulatory Reforms in Electricity Markets," *Brookings Papers on Economic Activity,* 1996, pp. 201–68.

8. The recent decline in the electricity consumer price index is also partly the result of the plunge in energy prices. See "The Economic Impact of Electric Utility Deregulation," *Regional Financial Review,* September 1996, for a detailed description of the impact of deregulation.

9. See "The Securitization of America," *Regional Financial Review,* February 1998, for a detailed description of the causes and impacts of financial securitization.

10. Based on data from the Federal Reserve Board's flow of funds accounts. More than one-half of residential mortgages, one-fourth of consumer loans, and one-sixth of commercial mortgage–backed securities are securitized.

11. A comprehensive and readable description of the life cycle theory of consumption is provided in D. Wilcox, "Household Spending and Saving: Measurement, Trends, and Analysis," *Federal Reserve Board Bulletin,* January 1991, pp. 1–17.

12. The Consumer Expenditure Survey is conducted annually by the Bureau of Labor Statistics.

13. The best-known supporters of the theory of the new economy include *Business Week,* Deutsche Bank Chief Economist Ed Yardeni, and, to a lesser degree, Federal Reserve Board Chair Alan Greenspan. Academic economists are generally more skeptical of the new economy. Perhaps the most vocal detractor of the theory is MIT professor Paul Krugman, who provided a strong critique of the theory in "How Fast Can the Economy Grow?" *Harvard Business Review,* July/August 1997.

14. A more thorough discussion of this argument is provided in M. Zandi and W. Basel, "The High Price of High Costs," *Research in Urban Economics,* Vol. 10, 1996, pp. 17–44.

15. Regional economies that are currently struggling include the District of Columbia, Hawaii, and the area extending from Providence, Rhode Island, to Buffalo, New York.

16. More specifically, diversity is defined as:

$$\text{Diversity} = 1/S[(E_{ij}/E_{usj})^*E_{ij}]$$

where E_{ij} is the share of employment in three-digit SIC (Standard Industrial Classification) industry j in state i and E_{usj} is the share of employment in three-digit SIC industry j in the nation. The diversity measure is bounded between 0 and 1, with 1 indicating that the state has the same industrial structure as the nation. Diversity measures for 1995/1996 range from 0.16 in the District of Columbia and 0.17 in Nevada to 0.83 in Illinois, Missouri, and Pennsylvania. The mean state diversity is 0.69.

17. The aid provided by international trade to regional economies was likely even more pronounced as import growth slowed dramatically during the last recession. This trend supported import-competing industries throughout the nation. Just how important it was to regional economies is not known, however, as regional import data are unavailable.

18. One of the first and clearest links between the real estate market collapse and the credit crunch is provided in Richard Syron, "Are We Experiencing a Credit Crunch?" *New England Economic Review*, July/August 1991.

19. This information is based on data for year-end 1997 from the Roulac Group and published in *Investment Property & Real Estate Capital Markets Report* by Institutional Real Estate, Inc.

20. The BLS defines noninstitutional population to include those over age 16 residing in the 50 states and the District of Columbia who are not inmates of institutions and who are not on active duty for the armed forces.

21. Federal Reserve Chair Alan Greenspan also advanced this argument in July 1998 during testimony on the Humphrey-Hawkins bill before Congress.

22. The ongoing job cuts at depository institutions have recently been masked by the soaring stock market and booming residential housing market, which have induced the entire industry to hire employees aggressively. Neither the stock market nor the mortgage market can reasonably be expected to maintain these kinds of gains for long, however.

23. See M. Porter, "The Competitive Advantage of the Inner City," *Harvard Business Review,* May/June 1995, pp. 55–71.

24. Based on data from the Federal Reserve Board's flow of funds accounts.

25. The on-again, off-again political discussion regarding the flat tax, which under many forms would reduce or eliminate the deduction for mortgage interest, may also signal changing attitudes with respect to homeownership.

26. The new economy will also affect the demand for retail space through a number of other conduits, including but not limited to the expected explosive growth in electronic commerce.

27. According to the Census Bureau, the median household income in 1995 was less than $35,000 per year, while the average household income was close to $55,000.

Appendix D
Glossary

Absorption schedule. The estimated schedule or rate at which properties for sale or lease can be marketed in a given locality; usually used when preparing a forecast of the sales or leasing rate to substantiate a development plan and to obtain financing.

Agglomeration. Concentration of commercial activity within a given area, tending to have a synergistic effect by increasing diversity, specialization, and overall business activity. In the context of urban sprawl, an overlapping of population and government jurisdictions.

AHERA (Asbestos Hazard Emergency Response Act). Legislation passed in 1986 that requires all public schools to be inspected for asbestos by certified inspectors and mandates the preparation of a management plan if asbestos is identified.

Amenity. Nonmonetary tangible or intangible benefit derived from real property (often offered to a lessee), typically, swimming pools, parks, valets, and the like.

Amortization. The periodic writing off of an asset over a specified term. Also the periodic repayment of debt over a specified time.

Anchor tenant. The major chain(s) or department store(s) in a shopping center, positioned to produce traffic for the smaller stores in the facility.

Appraisal. An opinion or estimate of value substantiated by various analyses.

Architect. Primarily a designer of buildings and supervisor of construction. All states require architects to be licensed under laws governing health, safety, and welfare.

Asset manager. A person who balances risk and reward in managing investment portfolios, including, but not limited to, real property and improvements. Asset managers either oversee property management or are responsible for it themselves.

Attached housing. Two or more dwelling units constructed with party walls (for example, townhouses, cluster houses, stacked flats).

Audit. In real estate development, the assessment of the credibility and reliability of real estate market data.

Axial theory. A theory of land use development that suggests that land uses tend to develop in relation to time-cost functions of transportation axes that radiate from the central business district.

Binding constraint. Legally enforceable limit on the allowable development on a given site.

Bonding. A guarantee of completion or performance, typically issued by an insurance company that will back up the bonded party in any lawsuit. In real estate, contractors, for example, are often bonded as assurance that they will complete the work.

Bottom-up approach. An approach to developing an analysis based on the most disaggregated data available.

Break-even ratio. In finance, the point at which total income is equal to total expenses.

Broker. A person who, for a commission, acts as the agent of another in the process of buying, selling, leasing, or managing property rights.

Brokerage. The business of a broker that includes all the functions necessary to market a seller's property and represent the seller's (principal's) best interests.

Building efficiency ratio. The ratio of net leasable area to gross leasable area.

Build to suit. Construction of land improvements according to a tenant's or purchaser's specifications.

Building Owners and Managers Association International (BOMA). A trade association of owners and managers of apartment and office buildings.

Buildout. Construction of specific interior finishes to a tenant's specifications.

Capital. Money or property invested in an asset for the creation of wealth; alternatively, the surplus of production over consumption.

Capital improvement projects. Investments in infrastructure such as roads, bridges, and ports.

Capital market. Financial marketplace in which savings (from individuals, companies, or pension funds) are aggregated by financial intermediaries and allocated to real investors.

Capitalization. The process of estimating value by discounting stabilized net operating income at an appropriate rate.

Capitalization rate (cap rate). The rate, expressed as a percentage, at which a future flow of income is converted into a present value figure.

Capture rate. Forecasted rate of absorption within a targeted market segment for a proposed project, based on an analysis of supply and demand.

Central business district (CBD). The center of commercial activity within a town or city; usually the largest and oldest concentration of such activity.

CERCLA (Comprehensive Environmental Response, Compensation, and Liability Act of 1980). Legislation adopted to provide partial funding for the cleanup of environmentally contaminated sites by requiring the party responsible for the contamination to undertake cleanup efforts or provide compensation for cleanup costs; also known as the Superfund Law.

Codevelopment. Term that refers to the combined development of real estate by the private sector and government, where the public sector assumes risks or costs normally borne by private developers.

Commercial paper. Short-term negotiable financial instruments, usually unsecured, such as promissory notes, bank checks, bills, and acceptances.

Commercial real estate. Improved real estate held for the production of income through leases for commercial or business use (for example, office buildings, retail shops, and shopping centers).

Commitment letter. A written agreement by a lender to loan a specific amount of money at a specified interest rate within a particular period of time.

Community builder. One who engages in the platting and improvement of subdivisions.

Community Development Block Grants (CDBGs). Federal grants received by cities based on a formula that considers population, extent of poverty, and housing overpopulation and that may be used for a variety of community development activities.

Community development corporations (CDCs). Entrepreneurial institutions combining public and private resources to aid in the development of socioeconomically disadvantaged areas.

Community Reinvestment Act (CRA). Legislation enacted in 1978 that directs federal agencies with supervisory authority over depository lenders to consider a lender's record in serving local credit needs when making decisions about the expansion plans of depository institutions.

Comparable property. Another property to which a subject property can be compared to reach an estimate of market value.

Compound interest. Interest that is earned and immediately added to principal, thereafter itself earning interest.

Comprehensive planning. Long-range planning by a local or regional government encompassing the entire area of a community and integrating all elements related to its physical development, such as housing, recreation, open space, and economic development.

Concentric zone theory. Urban development theory that holds that because mobility is paramount to community growth, land uses tend to be arranged in a series of concentric, circular zones around a city's central business district.

Concession. Discount given to prospective tenants to induce them to sign a lease, typically in the form of some free rent, cash for improvements furnished by the tenant, and so on.

Condominium. A form of joint ownership and control of property in which specified volumes of air space (for example, apartments) are owned individually while the common elements of the building (for example, outside walls) are jointly owned.

Consensus forecasts. Forecasts in reference areas either in the same locale or in other parts of the country that support the findings of a particular forecast.

Construction lender. Entity or individual providing interim financing during the construction phase(s) of the real estate development process.

Construction loan. A loan made usually by a commercial bank to a builder to be used for the construction of improvements on real estate and usually running six months to two years.

Contingent interest. A form of equity participation by lenders enabling them to receive an additional return if the income property securing the loan exceeds its projected profit or cash flow goals.

Convenience goods. Items typically purchased at the most convenient locations. They are usually not very expensive or long-lasting, and their purchase involves little deliberation. Convenience goods are distinguished from shoppers goods when performing retail market studies.

Convertible loan. A loan in which the lender, in addition to receiving a stated interest rate, reserves the right to convert its debt on a project to equity and thereby participate in the profits.

Covenant. A restriction on real property that is binding, regardless of changes in ownership, because it is attached to the title. Used generally in covenants, conditions, and restrictions (CC&Rs).

Critical path method (CPM). A network analysis method that graphically displays the activities involved in completing a project and shows the relationship between the activities. This display can graphically show how a delay in one activity will affect other activities.

Debt service. Periodic payments on a loan, with a portion of the payment for interest and the balance for repayment (amortization) of principal.

Debt (service) coverage ratio. The ratio of the annual net operating income of a property to the annual debt service of the mortgage on the property.

Deed restrictions. Private form of land use regulation using covenants or conditions placed on the title to a property, e.g., minimum lot sizes.

Delphi method. A project analysis tool in which a group of diverse experts is presented with a set of questions on a particular topic. The responses are then compared among the group and more refined questions developed, the ultimate goal of which is the development of a single, coherent response.

Demand deposits. Shorter-term deposits, such as checking accounts, that banks typically put into relatively short-term investments.

Demographics. Information on population characteristics by location, including such aspects as age, employment, earnings, and expenditures.

Density. The level of concentration (high or low) of buildings, including their total volume, within a given area. Often expressed as a ratio, for example, dwelling units per acre or floor/area ratio.

Department of Housing and Urban Development (HUD). A cabinet-level federal department responsible for carrying out national housing programs, including Federal Housing Administration subsidy programs, home mortgage insurance, urban renewal, and urban planning assistance.

Detached housing. A freestanding dwelling unit, normally single-family, situated on its own lot.

Developer. One who prepares raw land for improvement by installing roads, utilities, and so on; also a builder (one who actually constructs improvements on real estate).

Development fee. Compensation paid to a developer in return for managing a development project on behalf of a client such as a corporation or public sector agency.

Development process. The process of preparing raw land so that it becomes suitable for the erection of buildings; generally involves clearing and grading land and installing roads and utility services.

Development team. The range of participants engaged by a developer, both public and private, to assist in the planning, design, construction, marketing, and management of a development project.

Discounted cash flow. Present value of monies to be received in the future; determined by multiplying projected cash flows by the discount factor.

Downzoning. A change in the zoning classification of property from a higher use to a lower use (e.g., from commercial to residential).

Draw. The lender's release of construction loan funds in accordance with set procedures for providing portions of the total amount as each stage of construction is satisfactorily completed.

Due diligence. A forthright effort to investigate all reasonable considerations in a timely manner, as in the case of earlier waste disposal on a parcel of land.

Econometrics. The application of statistical methods to the study of economic data and problems.

Ecosystem management. Management of the interrelationships among the biological members of a community and their nonliving environment.

Effective rent. Rental income after deductions for financial concessions such as no-rent periods during a lease term.

Eminent domain. The power of a public authority to condemn and take property for public use on payment of just compensation.

Enabling legislation. Legislation typically delegated to local government that specifies the police power the state is giving to the local government. Cities, counties, and other local governments undertake planning, zoning, and additional forms of development regulation according to state enabling statutes.

Enterprise concept. The idea that encouraging private enterprise will facilitate economic revitalization or other socioeconomic goals. Encourages owners to look at real estate as another type of private enterprise.

Entrepreneur. A venture capitalist; one who accepts personal financial risk in business ventures.

Environmental scanning. The surveying of a variety of indicators in order to gauge the overall business, economic, social, political, or financial conditions that could affect a project's development.

Equity. That portion of an ownership interest in real property or other securities that is owned outright, that is, above amounts financed.

Equity kicker. A provision in the loan terms that guarantees the lender a percentage of the property's appreciation over some specified time or a percentage of income from the property or both.

Escalation clause. A provision in a lease that permits a landlord to pass through increases in real estate taxes and operating expenses to tenants, with each tenant paying its prorated share. Also a mortgage clause that allows the lender to increase the interest rate based on the terms of the note.

Estoppel letter. A written statement made by a tenant, lender, or other party establishing certain facts and conditions with regard to a piece of real estate.

Eurodollars. U.S. dollars deposited in European foreign banks and used as a medium of international credit.

Exactions. Fee or payment-in-kind required of a developer by a local jurisdiction for approval of development plans, in accordance with state and local legislation regarding the provision of public facilities and amenities.

Exclusionary zoning. Zoning practices such as large lot requirements and minimum housing sizes that serve to exclude from a community, intentionally or not, racial minorities and low-income persons.

Fast-tracking. A method of project management in which construction of a project actually begins before all details are finalized.

Feasibility study. A combination of a market study and an economic study that provides the investor with knowledge of both the environment where the project exists and the expected returns from investment in it.

Federal Home Loan Mortgage Corporation (Freddie Mac). Subsidiary of the Federal Home Loan Bank System (FHLBS) established in 1970 to act as a secondary mortgage market for savings and loan associations that are members of the FHLBS.

Federal Housing Administration (FHA). Federal agency created by the 1934 National Housing Act that insures residential mortgages originated by private lenders on properties and borrowers meeting certain minimum standards and requirements.

Federal National Mortgage Association (Fannie Mae). A quasi-private corporation chartered by the federal government to function as a secondary market for residential mortgages.

Fee simple absolute. The most extensive interest in land recognized by law. Absolute ownership but subject to the limitations of police power, taxation, eminent domain, escheat, and private restrictions of record.

Fee simple determinable. Fee simple ownership that terminates on the happening (or failure to happen) of a stated condition. Also referred to as a "defeasible fee."

Festival marketplace. A specialty retail center incorporating aspects of old marketplaces, including significant public spaces and a variety of activities.

Financial Institutions Reform, Recovery, and Enforcement Act of 1989 (FIRREA). A comprehensive legislative act designed to overhaul the regulatory structure of the thrift industry.

FIRE (fire/insurance/real estate). An employment classification used by the Department of Labor when analyzing the service industry.

Floodplain. Land adjacent to rivers and streams subject to overflow and flooding.

Floor amount. Initial portion of a floor-to-ceiling mortgage loan, advanced when certain conditions—for example, construction of core and shell—are met.

Floor/area ratio. The ratio of floor area to land area, expressed as a percent or decimal, that is determined by dividing the total floor area of the building by the area of the lot; typically used as a formula to regulate building volume.

Floor load. The weight that the floor of a building is able to support if such weight is evenly distributed, measured in pounds per square foot.

Focus group. Market analysis tool in which a moderator presents a set of carefully prepared questions to a group, usually eight to 12 people, in order to collect detailed and specific information on consumer attitudes and preferences.

Foreclosure. The legal process by which a mortgagee, in case of a mortgagor's default, forces sale of the mortgaged property to provide funds to pay off the loan.

Formal feasibility. Formal demonstration through the use of quantitative, objective data that a proposed project is or is not viable.

Friable. Material able to be crushed or pulverized by hand pressure such that the particles become airborne; used to describe different types of asbestos.

Garden apartments. Two- or three-story multifamily housing featuring low density, ample open space around buildings and convenient on-site parking.

Garden city. Movement begun in late 19th century Europe that sought to counter the rapid, unplanned growth of industrial cities by constructing self-contained planned communities emphasizing environmental reform, social reform, town planning, and regional planning.

General contractor. Person or firm that supervises a construction project under contract to the owner; also known as the "prime contractor."

General obligation bond. Municipal bond backed by the full faith and credit of the issuer as opposed to being backed by a particular project.

Government National Mortgage Association (Ginnie Mae). Agency of the Department of Housing and Urban Development (HUD) that operates as a participant in the secondary mortgage market, guaranteeing privately issued securities backed by pools of FHA or VA mortgages.

Gray Areas Program. Program launched by the Ford Foundation in 1960 to foster the revitalization and redevelopment of communities in minority areas.

Greenbelt. Area of undeveloped, open space that serves as a buffer between developed areas.

Gross income multiplier. Rule-of-thumb calculation to estimate the value of residential property, derived by dividing the sale price of comparable properties by their gross annual or monthly rent.

Gross leasing activity. The sum of all leases signed during a given time period, including renewals and leases signed in new buildings.

Ground lease. A long-term lease on a parcel of land, separate from and exclusive of the improvements on the land.

Growth management. The public sector's control over the timing and location of real estate development by various means, including legislative and administrative.

Growth path. The area of a city where development, price appreciation, and user or tenant demand are the greatest.

Guaranteed investment contract (GIC). A written guarantee to an investor of a certain yield for a defined period of time.

Hard costs. In new construction, includes payments for land, labor, materials, improvements, and the contractor's fee.

High rise. Tall building, skyscraper, usually more than ten stories.

Highest and best use. The property use that, at a given time, is deemed likely to produce the greatest net return in the foreseeable future, whether or not such use is the current use of the property.

Homesteader. A person residing on public land and establishing a homestead for the purpose of acquiring legal title to the land.

HVAC system. A building system supplying heating, ventilation, and air conditioning.

Impact fee. Charge levied (on developers) by local governments to pay for the cost of providing public facilities necessitated by a given development.

Income kicker. A provision in loan terms that guarantees the lender's receiving a portion of gross income over an established minimum, for example, 10 percent of the first year's gross rent receipts.

Industrial park. A large tract of improved land used for a variety of light industrial and manufacturing uses. Users either purchase or lease individual sites.

Inflation risk. The risk that inflation will reduce the purchasing power of monies lent.

Infrastructure. Services and facilities provided by a municipality, including roads, highways, water, sewerage, emergency services, parks and recreation, and so on. Can also be privately provided.

In-sample out-sample analysis. Market analysis technique in which the analyst strives to hold samples constant between surveys conducted at different points in time.

Institute of Real Estate Management (IREM). An affiliate of the National Association of Realtors® whose purpose is to promote professionalism in the field of property management.

Intelligent building. A building that incorporates technologically advanced features to facilitate communications, information processing, energy conservation, and tenant services.

Internal rate of return (IRR). The discount rate at which investment has zero net present value (that is, the yield to the investor).

International Council of Shopping Centers (ICSC). An international trade association for owners, developers, and managers of shopping centers.

IPO (initial public offering). The first offering of stock on a previously privately held company.

Joint venture. An association of two or more firms or individuals to carry on a single business enterprise for profit.

Junk bond. Any bond (a long-term debt obligation of a corporation or a government) with a relatively low rating. The lower the rating, the more speculative or risky the investment. Returns can be much higher than for a less speculative investment, however. Bonds are rated by credit-rating companies, the best known being Standard & Poor's.

Land development. The process of preparing raw land through clearing, grading, installing utilities, etc., for the construction of improvements.

Land planner. Individual who specializes in the allocation of desired land uses within a particular site in order to maximize the site's value and utility, striving for efficient internal traffic circulation, well-placed uses and amenities, and adequate open space.

Lease. A contract that gives the lessor (the tenant) the right of possession for a period of time in return for paying rent to the lessee (the landlord).

Lease concession. A benefit to a tenant to induce him to enter into a lease; usually takes the form of one month or more of free rent.

Lease-up. Period during which a real estate rental property is marketed, leasing agreements are signed, and tenants begin to move in.

Leverage. The use of borrowed funds to finance a project.

LIBOR (London interbank offered rate). An interest rate frequently used as an index in adjustable mortgage loans; most often the interest rate on three- or six-month Eurodeposits.

Lien. The right to hold property as security until the debt that it secures is paid. A mortgage is one type of lien.

Limited partnership. A partnership that restricts the personal liability of the partners to the amount of their investment.

Linkage. Typically, a payment to a municipality for some needed development that is not necessarily profitable for a developer (say, low-income housing) in exchange for the right to develop more profitable, high-density buildings (say, commercial development).

Loan placement analysis. The decision by a lender to hold a loan or to sell the loan in the secondary market, or the decision not to make a loan if the lender is unwilling to hold it and no secondary market exists.

Loan-to-value (LTV) ratio. The relationship between the amount of a mortgage loan and the value of the real estate securing it; the loan amount divided by market value.

Location quotient. Market analysis tool used to compare local workforce estimates with national averages, derived by taking the percentages of the workforce employed in each major industry group locally and dividing them by the percentages of the workforce employed in the industry groups nationally.

Low rise. A multistory building, usually in outlying areas, with fewer than ten stories.

Maquiladora. In Mexico, a manufacturing plant that temporarily imports capital goods duty free and then ships finished goods out of the country as exports. Most are located near the U.S. border.

Market niche. A particular subgroup within a market segment distinguishable from the rest of the segment by certain characteristics.

Market research. A study of the needs of groups of people to develop a product appropriate for an identifiable market niche.

Market study. An analysis of the general demand for a single real estate product for a particular project.

Marketability risk. The risk that a lender will be unable to sell a loan in a secondary market.

Marketing research. The study of factors that will satisfy the needs of target customers and convince them to buy or rent.

Marketing study/marketability study. A study that determines the price or rent appropriate to market a project successfully.

Mechanic's lien. A claim that attaches to real estate to protect the right to compensation of one who performs labor or provides materials in connection with construction.

Mechanistic model. A forecast method that is based on research indicating generalized algorithms that can be applied to a given property type across all markets.

Metropolitan statistical area (MSA). An urban area containing multiple political jurisdictions grouped together for purposes of counting individuals by the Census Bureau.

Miniperm loan. A short-term loan (usually five years) meant to be an interim loan between a construction loan and a permanent loan. A miniperm loan is usually securitized like any other loan; the interest rate could be less onerous than a construction loan but not as favorable as a permanent loan.

Miniwarehouse. A building, usually one story, subdivided into numerous small cubicles intended to be used as storage by families or small businesses.

Mixed-use development. A development, in one building or several buildings, that combines at least three significant revenue-producing uses that are physically and functionally integrated and developed in conformance with a coherent plan. A mixed-use development might include, for example, retail space on the ground floor, offices on the middle floors, and condominiums on the top floors, with a garage on the lower levels.

Monetary policy. The actions and procedures of the Federal Reserve System meant to control the availability of loanable funds.

Money market instruments. Investment tools such as U.S. Treasury bills and commercial paper employed by money markets.

Money markets. Name given to financial markets employing short-term investment instruments that mature in one year or less.

Mortgage. An instrument used in some states (rather than a deed of trust) to make real estate security for a debt. A two-party instrument between a mortgagor (a borrower) and a mortgagee (a lender).

Mortgage banking. The process of originating real estate loans and then selling them to institutional lenders and other investors.

Mortgage loan constant. Percentage of the original loan balance represented by the constant periodic mortgage payment.

Move-up housing. Typically, larger, more expensive houses that homeowners buy as their incomes increase. First homes, or "starter homes," are generally modestly sized and priced. As purchasers' incomes increase, they "move up" into larger, more expensive housing.

Multifamily housing. Structures that house more than one family in separate units (apartments). Can be high rises, low rises, garden apartments, or townhouses.

National Association of Housing Redevelopment Officials (NAHRO). Professional association of agencies and private officials involved in publicly assisted housing and community development activities.

National Association of Industrial and Office Properties (NAIOP). Trade association representing the interests of commercial real estate developers, owners, and managers.

National Association of Realtors® (NAR). The largest real estate organization in the country and probably in the world. Members are entitled to use the designation "Realtor."

National Housing Act of 1968. Legislation that created several programs designed to encourage the production and rehabilitation of low-income housing.

Neighborhood. A segment of a city or town with common features that distinguish it from adjoining areas.

Neighborhood Reinvestment Corporation. A public, nonprofit corporation created by law in 1978 that uses congressional appropriations to encourage public/private partnerships in the interest of revitalizing older urban neighborhoods.

Net absorption. The change in square feet of occupied inventory over a specified period of time, including the addition or deletion of building stock during that period of time.

Net operating income (NOI). Cash flow from rental income on a property after operating expenses are deducted from gross income.

Net present income. The value of an income-producing property at a given discount rate, minus the original investment cost.

Nominal group process. A decision-making technique used to set priorities for ideas generated by a group.

Nonrecourse loan. A loan, which in the event of default by the borrower, limits the lender to foreclosure of the mortgage and acquisition of the real estate, i.e., the lender waives any personal liability by the borrower.

Office building. A building or area of a building leased to tenants for the conduct of business or practice of a profession, as distinguished from residential, commercial, or retail uses.

Open market operations. The buying and selling of government securities by the Federal Reserve System; a tool for controlling the availability of loanable funds.

Operating budget. A budget, usually prepared a year in advance, listing projected costs of maintenance and repair for a building.

Operating expense ratio. The ratio of operating expenses to either potential gross income or effective gross income.

Operating expenses. Expenses directly related to the operation and maintenance of a property, including real estate taxes, maintenance and repair, insurance, payroll and management fees, supplies, and utilities. Debt service on mortgages or depreciation is not included.

Opportunity cost. The return on capital invested in a particular asset compared with the return available from alternative uses of that capital.

Option. The right given by the owner of property (the optionor) to another (the optionee) to purchase or lease the property at a specific price within a set time.

Origination fee. A charge made by the lender at the inception of the loan to cover administrative costs.

Outlier forecast. A forecast in a group of projections that differs substantially from all others in the group as well as from the group average.

Participation loan. A mortgage wherein one or more lenders have a share in a mortgage with the lead or originating lender.

Passive investor. An investor who seeks no active role in construction or operation of a building but merely seeks to invest funds to earn a return. Institutional investors, such as pension funds, are typically passive investors.

Pass-through. Lease provision whereby certain costs flow through directly to the tenant rather than to the owner (for example, property tax increases on a long-term lease).

Pass-through certificate. An investment instrument in which the periodic debt service payments on a package of mortgage loans are paid out (passed through) to the investors owning the instrument.

Peer group. Those properties most directly comparable to and competitive with a subject property.

Pension fund. An institution that holds assets to be used for the payment of pensions to corporate or government employees, union members, and other groups.

Permanent lender. A financial institution undertaking a long-term loan on real estate subject to specified conditions (for example, the construction of improvements).

PERT (program evaluation and review technique). A technique that provides project managers with a flowchart representing construction schedule times. Includes a critical path that indicates the activities that must be completed on time so as not to delay completion.

Planned unit development (PUD). Zoning classification created to accommodate master-planned developments that include mixed uses, varied housing types, and/or unconventional subdivision designs.

Points. An amount charged by the lender at the inception of a loan in order to increase the lender's effective yield. Each point equals 1 percent of the loan.

Police power. The right of government to regulate property in order to protect the health, safety, and general welfare of citizens.

Portfolio. A collection of varied investments held by an individual or firm. Real estate is often among those investments.

Preliminary drawings. Architectural renderings of a project showing definite project dimensions and volumes and including such items as exterior elevations, rentable square feet or salable units, parking, and the type of HVAC system.

Prepayment or callability risk. The risk that a borrower will pay off a loan before it has matured, thus depriving the lender of additional interest payments.

Present value. The current value of an income-producing asset, estimated by discounting all expected future cash flows over the holding period.

Prime rate. The lowest interest rate charged to the largest and strongest customers of a commercial bank for a short-term loan.

Profitability ratios. A set of single-period ratios that indicate the capacity of a project to produce income relative to the capital investment required to obtain that income.

Pro forma. A financial statement that projects gross income, operating expenses, and net operating income for a future period based on a set of specific assumptions.

Property life cycle. The three periods in the life of a building—the development period, the stabilization period, and the decline period.

Property manager. An individual or firm responsible for the operation of improved real estate. Management functions include leasing and maintenance supervision.

Psychographic profile. A detailed description of a group that goes beyond personal data, such as place of residence, and includes more psychological aspects, such as interests and levels of aspiration.

Purchasing power. The financial means (including credit) that people possess to purchase durable and nondurable goods.

Rational nexus. A reasonable connection between impact fees and improvements that will be made with those fees. Jurisdictions must be able to justify the fees they charge developers by showing that the fees will be spent on improvements related to the development. For example, a fee of $25.00 per square foot charged for a shopping center might not be justifiable if it is to be used for building an addition to the local elementary school. It might be justified, however, if it will be used to improve roads near the shopping center because of the additional traffic that the shopping center is likely to generate.

Real estate development. The process of converting undeveloped tracts of land into construction-ready parcels and/or components of the built environment.

Real estate investment trust (REIT). An ownership entity that provides limited liability, no tax on the entity, and liquidity. Ownership is evidenced by shares of beneficial interest similar to shares of common stock.

Real estate mortgage investment conduit (REMIC). An issue of publicly traded debt securities backed by a fixed pool of mortgages that can be used as a pass-through entity for federal income tax purposes.

Realtor®. A member of the National Association of Realtors®. "Realtor" is also a generic term used to describe professionals involved in selling property.

Recourse loan. A loan offering no protection to the borrower against personal liability for the debt, thus putting the borrower's personal assets at risk in addition to any collateral securing the loan.

Redevelopment. The redesign or rehabilitation of existing properties.

Redlining. The practice of denying loans or insurance coverage to residents within a specific geographic area, usually low-income inner-city neighborhoods.

Reliability. The ability to remain consistent under repeated tests.

Rent control. Limitations imposed by state or local authorities on the amount of rent a landlord can charge in certain jurisdictions.

Repos. Short-term repurchase agreements between financial institutions.

Resolution Trust Corporation (RTC). A mixed-ownership government corporation created by Congress to manage failed thrift institutions and their holdings.

Retainage. A portion of the amount due under a construction contract that the owner withholds until the job is completed in accordance with plans and specifications; usually a percentage of the total contract price.

Revenue bonds. Bonds issued by municipalities and backed by specific fees or service charges.

Risk. The possibility that returns on an investment or loan will not be as high as expected.

Risk control techniques. Stages in the development or construction process at which the developer can discontinue or modify operations in light of new circumstances.

Risk-free interest rate. A short-term, base interest rate calculated before various risk premiums are added; approximated by the rate on U.S. Treasury bills.

Rural Housing Services/Rural Development. Agency (formerly Farmers' Home Administration) of the Department of Agriculture that provides credit to farmers and nonfarm businesses in rural areas as well as guaranteeing and insuring certain loans.

Savings and loan (S&L) association. A type of savings institution that is the primary source of financing for one- to four-family homes. Most S&Ls are mutual (non-stock) institutions.

Secondary mortgage market. The market in which existing mortgages are bought and sold: conventional loans by Freddie Mac and Fannie Mae, FHA and VA loans by Fannie Mae, and special-assistance (HUD-regulated) loans by Ginnie Mae.

Sector theory. Land use development theory that postulates that land uses tend to develop along transportation corridors outward from the city center, forming wedge-shaped sectors that follow the path of least resistance and lowest costs.

Securitization. The pooling of mortgages for securities offerings.

Security. Evidence of ownership, such as stocks or bonds.

Segmentation. The classification of a population group into segments for the purpose of identifying marketing subgroups.

Sensitivity/analysis. A cost/benefit examination of the various features and aspects of a real estate development project, such as operating costs, amenities, management costs, visual appeal, etc., and the impact of adjustments to them on the value of the project.

Setback. The part of zoning regulations that restricts a building to within a specified distance from the property frontline or edge of the public street; thus, the structure must be set back a given number of feet from the frontline.

Shoppers goods. Items purchased after some degree of deliberation or shopping around. Generally, they are differentiated through brand identification, the retailer's image, or the ambience of the shopping area. Such purchases are made less often, and the product is typically more durable and expensive.

Shopping center. Integrated and self-contained shopping area, usually in the suburbs. Classified as neighborhood (30,000 to 100,000 square feet and providing convenience goods and personal services), community (100,000 to 500,000 square feet and providing a wider range of goods), regional (about 500,000 square feet with one or two department store anchors), and super regional (1 million plus square feet with three or more department store anchors).

Single-family housing. A dwelling unit, either attached or detached, designed for use by one family and with direct access to a street; does not share heating facilities or other essential building facilities with any other dwelling.

Single-point-in-time analyses. Analyses of market performance and various demand indicators, such as construction levels, absorption, vacancy, and rent growth, recorded at only one point in time.

Situs. The total urban environment in which a specific urban land use on a specific land parcel functions and with which it interacts at a specific time. More simply, location.

Societal marketing concept. The idea that a real estate project has an effect on more than just the users of the product and therefore must be marketed to the collective satisfaction of neighbors and regulators.

Soft costs. Outlays for interest, origination fees, appraisals, and other third-party charges associated with real estate development.

Special taxing districts. Districts established by local governments, in the form of assessment districts or public improvement districts, in which a special tax is levied on property owners in order to fund public improvements that will directly benefit those owners.

Stabilization. In appraisal, the use of one year's typical property income and expenses and annualized capital reserve expenditures to represent each year's income stream.

Steering. The illegal practice of directing prospective homebuyers or renters away from neighborhoods of different racial or ethnic composition.

Strip mall. A shopping center with a linear configuration and located on a highway or major street along which development has sprawled outward from a town or city center.

Subcontractor. An individual or company that performs a specific job for a construction project pursuant to an agreement with the general contractor.

Subdivision. Division of a parcel of land into building lots. Can also include streets, parks, schools, utilities, and other public facilities.

Subdivision controls. Development restrictions placed on parcels within a recorded subdivision.

Submarket. A geographic area surrounding a site that will provide a substantial portion of the customers for a real estate project.

Subordination clause. Clause in which one party agrees, under certain conditions, to yield its priority to another mortgagee.

Suburbanization. The movement of development to the suburbs created by the overflow effect of cities and by the automobile, which improved access to the inner city.

Surety company. A company that guarantees the performance or debt of another in case of default.

Sustainable site design. The process of developing landscaping features amenable to a project's location, climate, and environmental surroundings, thus requiring less maintenance.

Syndication. The process of acquiring and combining equity investment from multiple sources (for example, syndicating units in a limited partnership).

Takeout commitment. The permanent loan commitment for a project to be constructed.

Taking. The acquisition or seizure of land without just compensation or the application of police power constraints so restrictive as to prevent any viable use of the land.

Tax increment financing (TIF). A type of special district financing in which tax revenues raised only from new development, as assessed by the net increase over the existing property tax base, are earmarked to fund capital improvements.

Taxation risk. The risk that changes in tax laws will adversely affect taxes on the interest of a loan or will undermine the value of the underlying loan collateral.

Temporary financing. Short-term financing, usually for land acquisition, preconstruction infrastructure, and construction of improvements.

Tenant. One who rents from another.

Tenant allowance. A cash payment made by the developer to a tenant (usually in an income property) to enable the tenant, rather than the developer, to complete the interior work for the leased premises.

Tenant mix. The combination of various types of tenants in a leased building.

Term or maturity risk premium. Risk premium charged by lenders to compensate for the opportunity costs of long-term loans.

Time-series analyses. Analyses of market performance and other measures of market cyclicity, such as construction levels, absorption, vacancy, and rental growth recorded during periods of market expansion and contraction.

Time-value-of-money concept. The idea that because money is assumed to earn interest, a dollar today is worth more than a dollar at some future date.

Title. Evidence of ownership of real property, often used synonymously with the term "ownership" to indicate a person's right to possess, use, and dispose of property.

Title company. A company that examines titles to real estate, determines whether they are valid and any limitations on the title exist, and, for a premium, insures the validity of the title to the owner or lender.

Title I. FHA-insured property improvement or rehabilitation mortgage.

Top-down approach. An approach to developing analysis based on the use of aggregated data first.

Total marketing concept. The process of determining consumer desires, producing a product to match those desires, and persuading the consumer to purchase or rent that product.

Townhouse. Single-family attached residence separated from another by party walls, usually on a narrow lot offering small front- and backyards.

Trade area. Geographic area from which a retail facility consistently draws most of its customers.

Tranche. Multiple classes of tiered bond or security ownership, interests issued by real estate mortgage investment conduits (REMICs).

Transfer package. Documentation compiled at the time a project is sold or transferred to an asset manager that attempts to measure objectively the project's standing in the marketplace in order to provide a benchmark for the asset manager's future performance.

Underwriters. Persons employed by mortgage lenders and charged with making recommendations on loan approvals or disapprovals based on their knowledge of the applicant's creditworthiness and the quality or value of any collateral to secure the loan.

Urban Development Action Grants (UDAGs). Program of grants begun in 1977 and administered through the Department of Housing and Urban Development for the revitalization of distressed urban areas; program has been unfunded since the mid-1980s.

Urban economics. Economic concepts applied in the context of a particular urban area.

Urban renewal. Process of the physical improvement and redevelopment of an area through government action or assistance.

Validity. Execution with proper legal authority.

Value. With ratio at which commodities or services exchange; the power of one commodity or service to command other commodities or services in exchange.

Value capture. With regard to the joint development of transportation facilities, it is the government purchase, management, or control of land adjacent to these developments that allows the public to share in the potential financial and community development benefits that would not otherwise be possible.

Variance. In general, the difference between expected results and actual results. Statistically, "variance" refers to the square of the standard deviation. Can be used as a measure of risk.

Venture capital. Funds available for investment at risk i to a profit-seeking enterprise.

Veterans Administration (VA). An independent agency of the federal government that administers the veteran benefit programs intended to help returning veterans adjust to civilian life.

Warehouse. A building that is used for the storage of goods or merchandise and that can be occupied by the owner or leased to one or more tenants.

Workout. Negotiated arrangements between a lending institution and a developer unable to fulfill a loan agreement.

Writedown. A deliberate reduction in the book value of an asset, typically made because of changes in market conditions, deterioration of properties, loss of tenants, and the like.

Xeriscaping. Landscaping that thrives with little or no water.

Yield curve. The relationship between the yield on an instrument and the number of years until it matures or comes due.

Zone of transition. Neighborhoods surrounding the central business district of a city.

Zoning. Classification and regulation of land by local governments according to use categories (zones); often includes density designations as well.

Index

appraisals/appraisers, 47–48, 85, 145, 366–67

appreciation, 71

approvals, 4, 39, 46, 48, 51, 256, 257–58, 352–53. *See also* regulation

architects, 14, 39–41, 116, 231, 417–19, 441. *See also* design; development team; landscape architects; players

Arizona, 160, 430

Arlington, Texas, 420–21

Army Corps of Engineers, U.S., 413, 414

Artery Organization Partnership, 272

Arvida Company, 168

asbestos, 412–13

Asbestos Hazard Emergency Response Act (AHERA), 412

Asian Americans. *See* race/ethnicity

Asian Pacific region, 20

ASLA. *See* American Society of Landscape Architects

asset management, 5, 7, 459, 460–63, 466–69, 470, 474–76. *See also* eight-stage model; management

Associated Builders and Contractors (ABC), 46

Associated General Contractors (AGC), 46

assumables, 140

Astor family, 159

Astor, John Jacob, 114, 130, 131

At Home Network, Inc., 504

Atchison, Topeka, and Santa Fe Railroad, 123

Atlanta, Georgia; air pollution in, 47; Centennial Olympic Park in, 42, 43; construction in, 438–39; department stores in, 131; downtown in, 165, 166; history of development in, 131, 158; intelligent buildings in, 474; location of, 31; new communities around, 168; population in, 29; skyscrapers in, 165; urban economic theories applied to, 222; urban renewal in, 189

attorneys, 48

Austin, Texas, 319, 504

automobiles, 31, 32

Avco Community Builders, Inc. v. South Coastal Regional Commission (1976), 249

Avenel (Potomac, Maryland), 339

axial theory, 222

back-of-the-envelope pro forma, 189–90

balloon-frame method, 118

balloon mortgages, 142, 403

Ballpark at Arlington (Texas), 420–21

Baltimore, Maryland; downtown in, 165, 166; history of development in, 118, 119, 133, 134; public/private partnerships in, 270; shopping centers in, 157; skyscrapers in, 134, 165; slums in, 119

Bank of America, 406

Bank America/NationsBank, 352

banks, 66, 67, 141. *See also type of bank or specific bank*

Banner Place (Dallas), 487

Barcelona, Spain, 43

Bass Brothers, 94

Bass, Ed, 420

Bass Lofts (Atlanta), 439

Bass Performance Hall (Fort Worth), 420, 421

Bauer, Catherine, 138, 163

Bayou Place (Houston), 449

Bear Stearns, 504

Bedford-Stuyvesant Restoration Corporation, 161, 163

Belair project (Maryland), 153

Best Western, 159

bidding/negotiation process, 39, 46, 425–26. *See also* eight-stage model

Bilbao Guggenheim (Spain), 341–42

Bing, Alexander, 137, 138

Bing, Leo, 137

Birmingham, Alabama, 121

Black Creek Village (Love Canal), 411

Black, Harry, 134

blacks. *See* race/ethnicity

Blakely, Gerald, 157, 158

Blockbuster, 20

BOMA International. *See* Building Owners and Managers Association International

Bon Marché department store, 156

bonding, 426–27

bonds; as financing for capital improvement, 114; and history of development, 114, 133, 143, 147; performance, 448; tax-exempt, 298

Bonneville Dam, 144

"Boosterism," 114

Border City (Mojave Desert), 124

Boston Housing Partnership, 312

Boston, Massachusetts; and affordable housing, 310, 312, 317; apartments in, 130, 135; department stores in, 131; downtown in, 166; "Emerald Necklace" around, 44–45; environmental issues in, 415–17; history of development in, 129, 130, 131, 132, 133, 134, 135; parks in, 132; public/private partnerships in, 270, 281; regulation in, 133; rental housing in, 442; skyscrapers in, 129, 134, 165

Bowie, Maryland, 153

brainstorming, 191

Brasstown Valley Resort (Hiawassee, Georgia), 414

Breakers Hotel (West Palm Beach, Florida), 122, 123

BRIDGE Housing Corporation, 162

Broadway Tunnel (Oakland, California), 144

brokers; mortgage, 73; real estate, 48, 140

Brookfield, Illinois, 118–19

Brookline, Massachusetts, 118

Brooklyn, New York, 132, 161, 164, 270–72

Brooks, Peter, 129, 130

Brooks, Shepherd, 129, 130

Brown, Floyd, 136

Brown, Nathan, 131

Bucks County, Pennsylvania, 153

budget; and formal commitment, 431; long-term capital, 471; for marketing, 483–85; operating, 470–71

Buffalo, New York, 113, 132

"builders' mortgages," 141

building codes, 115, 133

Building Owners and Managers Association International (BOMA), 85, 140, 475

building permits, 352–53

buildings; functional efficiency of, 40; intelligent, 473–74

Bunker Hill (Los Angeles), 280

Bureau of Economic Analysis, U.S., 66–67, 372

Bureau of Labor Statistics, U.S., 27, 370, 371, 372, 384, 385, 388, 393

Burgee, John, 169

Burnham, Daniel, 129, 130, 133

Burns, Fritz, 144, 146, 148

buydowns, 98

Dewees Island, South Carolina, 381
Diagonal Mar (Barcelona, Spain), 43
Dickens, Charles, 110, 111
Dillard's, 20
direct costs, 82
discount rate, 12, 87
discounted cash flow (DCF), 81, 82, 83, 84, 86–87, 465
discounting, 83. *See also* discount rate; discounted cash flow
discrimination, 139, 146, 153
disintermediation, 98
Disney Corporation, 168, 174, 494–5
Disney World (Orlando, Florida), 166–67, 168, 359
Disneyland (Anaheim, California), 166–67, 168, 359
dissatisfaction with existing space, 207
district replanning, 154
Doerr Associates, 488
Dolan v. City of Tigard (1994), 249
Donaldson's department store, 156
downpayments, 115, 118, 141, 153
Downtown Disney (Florida), 168
downtowns, 155, 156, 160–69. *See also* center cities; central business districts
draws, 76, 440–42
DRI. *See* Data Resources, Inc.
Drucker, Peter, 203–4
DSCR. *See* debt service coverage ratio
du Pont family, 136
Duany, Andres, 174, 189
Duff and Phelps, 73
Durst, 153
Dwyer Williams, 486, 487
Dynamo Development, Inc., 503

Earth Day, 173, 415
East Coast Lines, 123
East Los Angeles Community Union, The (TELACU), 162–63
economic base analysis, 366–67
economic development, 32, 38
economic forecasts, 371
economic impact analysis, 366–67
Economic Recovery Tax Act (1981), 170
Economic Research Service (ERS), 372
economic studies, 366–67. *See also type of study*
economic theories, urban, 222
economics, "new," 174–75

economy; balance sheet of U.S., 67; national U.S., 20–22; underground, 26. *See also* income/revenue
EDAW (consulting firm), 42–43
Eden Palms Housing (San Jose, California), 296
Edina, Minnesota, 156
Egghead Software, 504
eight-stage model, 5, 6, 7, 51, 52, 501. *See also specific stage*
EIRs (environmental impact reports), 46
Eisenhower, Dwight D., 152
EISs (environmental impact statements), 46
elderly. *See* aging population
elevators, 128, 129
Elkus/Manfredi Architects, 340
Ellicott, Joseph, 113–14
Embarcadero Center (San Francisco), 158
"Emerald Necklace" (Boston), 44–45
Emery Roth & Sons, 153
Emily Morgan Hotel (San Antonio), 270, 273
eminent domain, 154
Empire State Building (New York City), 135, 136–37, 466
Empire State Company, 136
employment; data about, 372–73, 384–85, 393; forecasts of, 370–71; growth in, 26–27; by major industry, 28; and national economy, 21–22; office, 27; and shape of cities, 32
Emporium, The (San Francisco), 131
empowerment zones, 162
endogenous variables, 380, 383
engineers, 40–41. *See also type of engineer*
Enterprise Communities, 162
enterprise concept, 357, 459, 460–63, 464
Enterprise Development Company, 166
Enterprise Foundation, 162, 166, 312
entitlements, marketing, 208–9
entrepreneurs, 4, 38, 115, 142, 143. *See also* developers
environment, and refinement of idea, 220–22
environmental consultants, 46
environmental engineers, 41

environmental issues, 45, 137, 409–17, 473
Environmental Protection Agency, U.S. (EPA), 410, 411, 412, 413
environmental scanning, 193–94
equations, reduced and structural form of, 380, 381–82
Equitable life Assurance Society Building (New York City), 503
Equitable Life Insurance Company, 128, 155, 158, 172
equities; closer look at, 69–75; data about, 66, 67; decisions about, 428–30; and financing decisions, 82; and forms of ownership for real estate, 69–71; and impact fees and exactions, 263–64; and infrastructure considerations, 263–64; rate of return on, 89. *See also* equity investors
equity investors, 10, 20, 82, 89
equity kickers, 49
Ernest W. Hahn, Inc., 285
ES-202 program, 385
escalation, 449
ethics, 14, 197
ethnicity. *See* race/ethnicity
Euclid, Ohio v. Ambler Realty Co. (1926), 249
Europa Center (Chapel Hill, North Carolina); architect for, 342–44; building specifications for, 344; buildings for, 13; as case study, 4; and competition, 209–10; construction of, 425, 432, 436, 437, 442, 445, 450, 508–9; contracts for, 405–6, 425; costs for, 13, 349, 356, 425; design of, 13, 508; development company for, 7–8; and equity decisions, 428–29; exactions for, 229; feasibility study for, 337, 356–57; final thoughts about, 505–12; financing of, 13, 405–6, 428–29, 508; formal opening of, 448, 450–51; and inception of idea, 198–200, 209–10; and intelligent buildings, 474; joint venture shares for, 13; land for, 13; leasing of, 442, 448, 482–83, 509–11; location of, 13; market segmentation for, 238; marketing of, 450–51, 482, 509–11; new owner's perspective on, 507–11; players for, 342, 348; politics of building, 353; preliminary drawings

for, 342–44; pro forma for, 354–56; pros and cons for, 240; refinement of ideas for, 226, 228, 238, 240; and risk, 209–10 ; site selection for, 225, 226, 228; size of, 8; strategic plan for, 467; summary about, 13; tenants for, 509–10, 511; and venture capital, 358

Europe, 20, 118, 173

Evergreen Hills Apartments (Macedon, New York), 311

exactions, 47, 228, 260–64

exit strategies, 5, 99

exogenous variables, 380, 383, 392

expense stops, 449

Experience Exchange Report, 85

Exxon Corporation, 167

factory towns, 121

Faga, Barbara, 42–43

Fair Housing Act, 165, 473

Fair Lawn, New Jersey, 138

Fairfax County, Virginia, 248, 272, 289

Fairfield County, Connecticut, 168

Fairmount Park (Philadelphia), 131

Fallon Hines & O'Connor, 513

family-operated businesses, 153

Faneuil Hall (Boston), 166, 281

Fannie Mae. *See* Federal National Mortgage Association

Fannie Mae Foundation, 303

Farm Mortgage Bankers Association, 140

farms, 18, 19, 30, 114–15

FASIT (financial asset securitization investment trust), 408

F.D. Rich Housing Corporation, 270

FDIC. *See* Federal Deposit Insurance Corporation

feasibility; and characteristics of developers, 8; continuing check on, 35; definition of, 52, 338, 355; design, 229–32; and eight-stage model, 51; formal estimate of, 353–56; for individual development team members, 52; level two, 358, 466; and management, 466; and market analysis as process, 363–65; and marketability studies, 364. *See also* eight-stage model; feasibility study; financial feasibility

feasibility study; appraisers' roles in, 47; and approvals and regula-

tion, 352–53; and definition of feasibility, 338, 355; and enterprise concept, 357; and formal commitment, 431; and formal estimate of feasibility, 353–56; and Graaskamp's contribution to development, 461; importance of, 11–12; initiating the, 338–40; and intelligent buildings, 473; and investors/lenders, 352; and management, 464, 465; and market study, 340–41; and marketing, 498; and prelimary drawings, 341–47; and risk, 358–60; and sales/leasing, 498; and value statement, 353–56; and venture capital, 357–58. *See also specific project*

Federal Deposit Insurance Corporation (FDIC), 67, 143, 145, 312

Federal Emergency Management Agency (FEMA), 411

federal government; and affordable housing, 296–99, 308–9; and highway expansion, 156; and history of development, 110, 111, 114, 124, 140, 141, 143, 144, 147; housing expenditures of, 297; and innovations in financing, 74, 98; as land owner, 18; in post–World War II years, 151, 152; as primary financial market, 66; and professionalization in real estate industry, 140, 148; and public/private partnerships, 280; and refinement of idea, 220–22; and savings, 65; and single-family housing, 98; and urban crisis, 162, 163–64; and urban renewal, 155. *See also specific agency or department*

Federal Home Loan Bank System, 144

Federal Home Loan Mortgage Corporation (Freddie Mac), 171, 309, 312

Federal Housing Administration (FHA), 18, 141, 144–46, 148, 151, 152; and affordable housing, 309, 310, 317, 319, 322, 323; discrimatory policies of, 146, 153; and urban crisis, 164

Federal National Mortgage Association (Fannie Mae), 145, 151, 171, 309, 312

Federal Reserve System, 66, 67, 72

Federal Savings and Loan Insurance Corporation, 144

Federal Transit Administration, 39

federally assisted code enforcement, 164

fee simple transactions, 110

fees; and opportunity funds, 94. *See also type of fee*

FHA. *See* Federal Housing Administration

Fidelity Management and Research, 63, 390

Fidelity Real Estate Group, 100

Field, Marshall, 158

Filene's (Boston), 131

final users, 51

financial asset securitization investment trust (FASIT), 408

financial feasibility, 239, 366–67

financial institutions, 19, 143–44. *See also specific institution or type of institution*

financial markets; link between real estate and, 63–64. *See also specific market*

financial officer, 437, 440

financial players, 48–50. *See also specific player*

financial system, intuitive model of overall, 64–66

financing; of affordable housing, 298, 309–10, 311–13, 315–16, 317, 319, 322–23; basic principles of, 93; and characteristics of developers, 8; common thread in all forms of, 408; and contract negotiations, 402–6; "creative," 141; cycle of, 75–77; drawing down, 76, 440–42; and eight-stage model, 7; and equity, 82, 428–30; by FHA, 144–46; and financial theory, 81–92; and globalization, 7, 52; and history of development, 114, 122, 134, 140–42, 145; importance of, 75; of infrastructure/improvements, 114, 255–66; innovations in, 93–102; institutional setting for, 63–80; and length of development period, 52; making decisions about, 81–92; and market study, 12; mezzanine, 404–6; new sources of, 406–8; in post–World War II years, 152, 153; and public/private partnerships, 255–66; by railroads/railroad barons,

gross domestic product (GDP), 21, 75, 194
Gross, Samuel E., 118–19
Grossdale. *See* Brookfield, Illinois
ground leases, 112–13, 114
growth, techniques for managing, 255
Grubb & Ellis, 212
Gruen, Victor, 156, 157
guaranteed investment contract (GIC), 404
Guilkey-Miles Space Market Index, 388, 390, 391, 392
Gulf & Western Building (New York City), 476
Gulf Oil Corporation, 167

Habitat for Humanity, 303
Hadacheck v. Sebastian (1915), 249
Hahn Company, 166
Hahn, Ernest, 172
Halliday, Andrew, 504
Hamptons (Tampa, Florida), 491
Harborplace (Baltimore), 166
Hare, S. Herbert, 138
Harlem (New York City), 11, 161
Harlem *USA* (New York City), 166
Harmon, William E., 141
Hartsfield International Airport (Atlanta), 222
Harundale Mall (Baltimore), 157
Harvard University, 157
Haskell, Llewellyn, 116, 117
Hastings, Thomas, 122–23
Hawaii, 144, 256, 303, 317, 430
hazardous waste, 410–12
Hempstead, New York, 152, 153
highest and best use study, 366–67
Highland Park Shopping Village (Dallas), 156
highways, interstate, 156–60
Hillside Homes (Bronx), 147
Hilton Hotels Corp., 159, 160, 503–4
Hines, Gerald, 169, 172
Hispanics. *See* race/ethnicity
historical data, 12, 68
history of development; colonial period to late 1800s in, 109–26, 177–78; and future of industry, 501–2; and Great Depression, 142–46, 178–80; from late 1800s to 1920s, 127–40, 178–80; in 1940s, 146–50, 178–80; in post–World War II years, 151–53, 180–82; and public sector, 132–34; Roaring

Twenties in, 134–40, 178–80; and urban renewal, 153–56, 180–82
Holabird and Roche, 130
HOLC. *See* Home Owners' Loan Corporation
Holiday Inns, 159
Holland Land Company, 113–14
Homberg, Simon, 124
Home Builders Emergency Committee, 148
Home Builders and Subdividers Division (NAR), 140
Home Insurance Building, 129
Home Investment Partnership Act (HOME), 308–9, 310
HOME Investment Partnerships, 162
Home Mortgage Disclosure Act (HMDA) (1975), 165
home mortgages, 141. *See also* Federal Housing Administration
Home Owners' Loan Corporation (HOLC), 144
homebuilding, trends in, 18
homeowners' associations, 138
homeownership, 18–19, 22, 25, 322
homes, technology in, 504
Homestead Act, 110
Hooker Chemical Company, 411
Hoover, Herbert C., 143, 144
Hoover, J. Edgar, 159
Hoover Dam (Nevada), 144, 221
HOPE Homeownership of Single-Family Homes, 323
Horton Plaza (San Diego), 166, 285
Hotel Ponce de Leon (St. Augustine, Florida), 122–23
hotels/motels, 130–31, 134, 158, 159–60, 168, 503–4
households, 25–26
housing; federal spending for, 297; and future of development industry, 504; and GDP, 21; after Great Depression, 146–47; and history of development, 120, 121, 127, 142–47; and national economy, 21; in post–World War II years, 151–53; recent trends in American, 147; rental, 303–8; seven myths of, 147; of unskilled wage earners, 146; and urban crisis, 160–69; value of, 21; working class, 121. *See also* affordable housing; multifamily housing; residential property; single-family

housing; *specific person, project, agency, or organization*
Housing Act (1949, 1954), 151, 155, 324
Housing Assistance Council, 312
housing codes, 115, 133
Housing and Home Finance Agency (HHFA), 163
Housing Opportunity Index (HOI), 317, 320–21
Housing and Urban Development, U.S. Department of (HUD), 66, 162, 163, 168, 172, 174; and affordable housing, 295, 297, 298, 305, 307, 308, 309, 310, 322, 323
Houston, Texas, 30, 134, 156, 166, 168–69, 170
HOV (high-occupancy vehicle), 46
Howard, Ebenezer, 136–37
Howard Johnson Motels, 159
Hoyt, Homer, 169, 222
HRH Construction Corporation, 163–64
Hualalai Development Company, 446
Hualalai at Historic Ka Upulehu (Hawaii), 446
HUD. *See* Housing and Urban Development, U.S. Department of
Hudson department store, 131, 156
Hunt, Richard Morris, 130
Huntington, Collis P., 123, 124, 125
Huntington, Henry E., 122, 123–25, 130
Huntington Beach, California, 124
Huntington Land and Improvement Company, 124
Huntington Museum and Library, 124
Hurd, Richard, 141
HVAC (heating, ventilation, and air conditioning), 39, 40, 85
Hyatt Hotels, 158, 160, 189

Ickes, Harold L., 144, 147
Idaho, 18
idea, inception of; and back-of-the-envelope pro forma, 189–90; case studies about, 197–201, 209–10; and competition, 209–10, 212–13; and market research, 190–91, 203–16; motivations behind, 186–89; and risk control, 195–97; as stage one in development process, 185–203; and strategic decision

making, 190–91; and techniques for generating ideas, 191–95; test marketing of, 195; and words of warning and signposts, 195. *See also* eight-stage model

idea, refinement of; activities involved in, 220; case studies about, 226, 227, 228, 238, 240; and culture of urban growth patterns, 221–22; and discussion with other players, 233–35; and environment, 220–22; and financial feasibility, 239; and government, 220–22; and initial design feasibility, 229–32; and market segmentation, 235–39; objectives of, 217–20; and product differentiation, 235–39; and risk, 239–40; and site negotiation, 232–33; and site selection, 222–29; and urban economic theories, 222. *See also* eight-stage model

Illinois, 28, 264. *See also* Chicago, Illinois

image; of architects, 39; and design, 14; of developers, 9; know your, 195; of landscape architects, 44; and risk control, 195

immigration, 18, 22, 23, 24, 27, 29

impact fees, 260–64, 431

improvements, 23, 114, 115, 120, 251–52, 431. *See also* infrastructure

incentive zoning, 251

incentives, and affordable housing, 299–302, 322–24

inclusionary zoning, 251

income kickers, 49

income/revenue; data about, 372–73; and demographic trends, 25–26; and financial theory, 83, 85–91, 93; and forms of ownership for real estate equity markets, 69; and innovations in financing, 93; and market study, 12; mediam household, 25–26; and property value, 83. *See also type of income*

Indianapolis, Indiana, 270

Industrial Areas Foundation, 162

Industrial Development Research Council (IDRC), 478

industrial parks, 121–22, 157–58

industrial property; in cities, 121–22; and demographic trends, 27; financing for, 142; and future of

development industry, 503; and history of development, 121–22, 127, 142; ownership of, 19; programs and policies promoting, 18; and property management, 122; and technology, 503; and transportation, 121–22; and urban renewal, 154

industrialization, 121–22, 127, 132

industry trade associations, 140

inflation, 75, 83, 94

Infomart (Dallas), 357

information technology, 32, 53, 174–75, 502–3

infrastructure; administrative concerns about, 264; construction of, 266; design of, 266; equity considerations about, 263–64; financing of, 255–66; and history of development, 109, 114, 115, 118, 125, 127, 132–33, 134, 138; and impact fees and exactions, 260–64; legal constraints concerning, 263; planning of, 266; and population, 29; programs and policies promoting, 19; and public/private partnerships, 255–66; source of public capital funds for, 259–60; and special taxing districts, 264–65; and urban renewal, 154, 155. *See also* improvements

inner cities; development movements in, 164–65; slums in, 119–20. *See also* center cities

Institute of Real Estate Management, 475

institutional investors/lenders, 5, 19, 75–76, 94, 142

Institutional Real Estate, Inc., 66, 67

insurance companies, 53. *See also* life insurance companies; *specific company*

insurance coverage, 431, 448–49

intelligent buildings, 473–74

interest; and construction loans, 72; "contingent," 49; and debt financing, 82; and debt markets, 71; and debt servicing, 84, 85; and FHA, 145; and financial theory, 82, 84, 85; and history of development, 145; and innovations in financing, 98; and single-family housing, 98; and takeout commitments, 76. *See also type of loan or type of rate*

interim loans. *See* construction loans

International Council of Shopping Centers, 157, 475

International Garden City Association (London), 136

international projects, 10, 43. *See also specific project*

Internet, 51, 488, 503–4

investment bankers, 96–97

investors; allocating savings to, 65–66; capital flows for, 67; as capital market, 65; and CMBSs, 97; and debt financing, 82; and equity decisions, 430; and feasibility study, 352; and FHA, 145; and financial theory, 82, 83; guarantees to, 36; high-risk, 234; and history of development, 110, 113, 115, 117, 124, 135, 141, 145, 147; and innovations in financing, 95–96, 97; long-term equity, 49–50; and offshore opportunities, 20; and property value, 83; and refinement of idea, 234; and REITs, 95–96; and tax legislation, 18; traditional commercial, 97–98; and urban renewal, 155. *See also specific investor or type of investor*

Investors S&L. *See* Centennial Group

Irvine, California, 167–68

Irvine Company, 167–68

Irvine Ranch (California), 167–68

Jack Nicklaus golf course (Hawaii), 446

Jacques Gordon, 389, 391, 392

Japan/Japanese, 19, 52, 94, 160, 205

Javits, Jacob K., 161

J.C. Nichols Company, 138

JCPenney, 20, 22

Jefferson, Thomas, 111

Jenney, William LeBaron, 117, 118, 129

Jersey City, New Jersey, 261

Jin Mao building (Shanghai, China), 41

JMB Realty, 168

John Hancock Building (Boston), 359

John Hancock Insurance Company, 156

Johnson, Lyndon B., 161

Johnson, Philip, 169, 477

Johnson, Wallace, 159

Joint Venture for Affordable Housing, 323

Marriott Hotels, 503
Marshall Field's (Chicago), 131
Marshall & Swift, 340
Maryland, 257, 310, 430. *See also* Baltimore, Maryland
Massachusetts, 110, 310, 415–17, 430. *See also* Boston, Massachusetts; Cambridge, Massachusetts; Museum Towers
Massachusetts Business Commission (MBC), 417
Massachusetts Environmental Policy Act (MEPA), 415–17
Massachusetts Institute of Technology (MIT), 157
master plans, 41, 44
Mayer, Neil, 311
MBA. *See* Mortgage Bankers Association of America
MC. *See* mortgage constant
MCI Center (Washington, D.C.), 282, 429
mechanical engineers, 40
mechanic's liens, 441
Mellon, Richard King, 154
Memphis, Tennessee, 156, 159
Mercado Apartments (San Diego), 311, 312
Merchandise Mart (Chicago), 158
merchant homebuilding, 116
Merrill Lynch, 53, 94, 385, 390, 391, 392
MesseTurm (Frankfurt, Germany), 350–51
Metreon (San Francisco), 272, 276–77
Metropolitan Life Insurance Company/Tower, 128, 129, 135, 154–55, 156, 172
Metropolitan Opera House (New York City), 147
Metropolitan Pier and Exposition Authority, 38
metropolitan statistical area (MSA); and availability of data, 51–52; land in, 17–18; market data about, 371, 374–75; and market study, 374–75; population in, 18, 27–30; and rankings for commerical property, 388–92
MetroTech complex (Brooklyn), 270–72
Mexico, 20, 110, 426
mezzanine financing, 404–6
MGM Studios, 168

Miami, Florida, 22, 52, 123, 130, 160, 166
Microsoft, 63, 96, 204
migration, 27–30, 127
Miller, Jonathan, 174
Milwaukee Redevelopment Corporation, 285, 286
Milwaukee, Wisconsin, 270, 285, 286
miniperm loans, 73, 75. *See also* specific project
Minneapolis, Minnesota, 131, 134, 156–57, 166
Minnesota, 430. *See also* Minneapolis, Minnesota
Minskoff, 153
Miralles, Enric, 43
Mission Bay (San Francisco), 121
Mission Viejo, California, 167
Mitchell Energy and Development Corporation, 168
Mitchell, George, 168
mixed-use projects, 44, 47, 160
Mobil Oil Corporation, 167
Model Cities Program, 161
moderate rehabilitation program, 307
Monadnock Block (Chicago), 130
monetary policy, 72
money markets, principles of, 71–72
Montauk Block (Chicago), 130
Montgomery, Alabama, 160
Moody's, 73
Morgan Stanley Dean Witter, 53, 94, 390
Morris, Robert, 111, 113
Morrow, Whit, 4, 37–38, 197–200, 209–10, 213, 222, 226, 505–7. *See also* Europa Center; Fraser Morrow Daniels
Mortgage Bankers Association of America (MBA), 140
mortgage banking companies, 66, 73, 74, 97, 144–45
mortgage brokers, 73
mortgage constant (MC), 84–85, 89
mortgage guarantee programs, of VA, 18
mortgage insurance, 18, 141
mortgage life insurance, 71
mortgages; data about, 66; and history of development, 141. *See also* secondary markets; *specific type of mortgage*
Moses, Robert, 143
Mount Laurel decision, 174

MSA. *See* data; metropolitan statistical area
Muldavin, Scott, 66
multifamily housing, 115, 131, 304–6, 311, 393, 469. *See also* apartment
multinational corporations, 20
Multiple Listing Service, 224
Mumford, Lewis, 138
Murphy/Jahn, 351
Museum Towers (Cambridge, Massachusetts); building specifications for, 345–46; buildings of, 14; as case study, 4, 8; and CMBSs, 97; construction of, 426, 442–43, 445; costs for, 14, 426; design of, 488; and environmental issues, 415–17; final thoughts about, 512–13; financing of, 97, 98, 99, 408–9; and inception of idea, 200–201, 210; and innovations in financing, 97, 98–100; and intelligent buildings, 474; land for, 14; leasing of, 442–43; location of, 14; marketing of, 488, 489–90, 491; players for, 348–49; preliminary drawings for, 345–46; and refinement of idea, 223, 228, 238; rental rates at, 489–90; and site selection, 228; size of, 98; summary of, 13–14; targeting markets for, 238
Mutual Life Insurance Company, 128
mutual savings banks, 66, 142, 144–45, 152

NAHB *See* National Association of Home Builders
naming projects, 492
NAR. *See* National Association of Realtors
Natelli Communities Limited Partnership, 339
National Affordable Housing Act (NAHA) (1990), 297, 324
National Apartment Association, 473
National Association of Corporate Real Estate Executives (NACORE), 172, 478
National Association of Home Builders (NAHB), 146, 148, 163, 174, 323
National Association of Industrial and Office Properties (NAIOP), 159, 478

National Association of Insurance Commissioners, 73

National Association of Real Estate Investment Managers (NAREIM), 475

National Association of Real Estate Investment Trusts, 66, 171

National Association of Realtors (NAR), 139, 140, 148, 475

National Association of Security Dealers/American Stock and Bond Exchanges, 66

National Community Development Initiative, 162

National Council of Architectural Registration Boards (NCARB), 39

National Council of Real Estate Investment Fiduciaries (NCREIF), 171, 374, 390, 475

national economy, 20–22

National Environmental Policy Act (1969), 173

National Growth Management Leadership Project, 174

National Historic Preservation Act (1966), 173

National Home Builders Association, 148

National Homes, 172

National Housing Act (1968), 163

National Multi Housing Council, 473

National People's Action, 164

National Planning Association (NPA), 372

National Realty Committee, 170, 473

National Society of Professional Engineers, 41

National Trust for Historic Preservation, 439

NationsBank, 406

Native Americans, 18, 109, 308, 309, 323

Nature Conservancy of Wisconsin, 415

Navy Pier (Chicago), 38, 133, 166

Navy, U.S., 144, 273

NCARB. *See* National Council of Architectural Registration Boards

Needham, Massachusetts, 157–58

Neighborhood Housing Services (NHS) program, 312

Neighborhood Reinvestment Corporation (NRC), 162, 165, 312

neighborhoods. *See* communities/neighborhoods

net operating income (NOI), 63, 81–82, 83–84, 86, 87, 88, 89, 90, 364–65. *See also specific project*

Nevada, 18, 28, 144, 430

New American Neighborhoods (HUD), 174

new communities, 167–69

New Communities Program (HUD), 168

New Community Corporation, 162

New Construction and Substantial Rehabilitation programs, 163

New Deal, 143, 144

New England Industrial Park (Needham, Massachusetts), 158

New Jersey, 143, 174, 256, 310, 311, 317, 412

new regionalism, 174–75

new urbanism, 174–75

New York Bond Exchange, 66

New York City; affordable housing in, 163–64, 317; African American cemetery in, 228; apartments in, 130, 135; department stores in, 131; downtown in, 166; environmental issues in, 413; foreign ownership of real estate in, 19; future of development industry in, 503; highways in, 156; history of development in and around, 112–13, 114, 116–17, 119, 120, 123, 128–29, 130, 131, 132, 133, 134, 135, 137, 147, 155; hotels in, 130, 131, 159, 168; information technology in, 503; land in, 17; office properties in, 153, 503; population in, 22, 27, 29; public parks in, 132; public/private partnerships in, 270, 274, 278–79; race/ethnicity in, 160, 161; reform in, 120; regulation in, 133; risk in, 448; site selection in, 228; skyscrapers in, 128–29, 134, 166; slums in, 119; urban crisis in, 163–64; urban renewal in, 154–55; zoning in, 137

New York City Housing Development Corporation, 11

New York Evening Post, 129

New York Life Insurance and Trust Company, 113, 155–56

New York Regional Plan Association, 174

New York State, 28, 113, 143

New York Stock Exchange, 63, 66

New York Times, 129

New York Tribune, 128–29

New York World Building (New York City), 129

Newark, New Jersey, 161, 162, 166

Newport Beach, California, 124, 168

Newport, Rhode Island, 122

Nexus Contemporary Arts Center (Atlanta), 438

niche marketing, 25

Nichols, Jesse Clyde, 136, 137, 138, 139, 156, 168

Nicholson, John, 111

Nickel Plate Railroad, 140

NIMBY, 247

NOI. *See* net operating income; *specific project*

Nollan v. California Coastal Commission (1987), 249, 250

nominal group process, 191–92

Norfolk, Virginia, 152

Norquist, John, 174

North American Free Trade Agreement (NAFTA), 20

North Carolina National Bank, 406

North Carolina, regulation in, 256

North General Hospital (Harlem, New York City), 11

North Point Park (Cambridge, Massachusetts), 98

Northgate Shopping Center (Seattle), 156

Northland Center (Detroit), 156

Nyland (Lafayette, Colorado), 49

Oak Hall (Philadelphia), 131

Oakland, California, 118

Occupational Safety and Health Administration (OSHA), 412

Office Housing Production program (San Francisco), 261

office property; capitalization rates for, 87; and demographic trends, 27; expected case analysis of Chapel Hill, 354; financing for, 141, 153; forecasting demand and supply for, 30; and future of development industry, 502–3; and history of development, 128–30, 134, 135, 141, 153; as intelligent buildings, 474; management of, 469; market segmentation for, 235; marketing of, 469;

Prather, Hugh, 156
preleasing, and final users, 51
prelimary drawings, 341–47
prepayments, 75, 77, 407
President's Council on Sustainable Development, 174–75
price, 206
Price Club, 20
primary loan markets, 66
prime interest rate, 72, 76
Prince William County, Virginia, 247
Princeton, New Jersey, 168
PRIs. *See* program-related investments
private markets, components of, 64
private sector; and affordable housing, 303, 310–13; developers of, 36–38; goals of, 3; and history of development, 133–34; as land owner, 18; office employment in, 27; and ownership of commercial and industrial real estate, 19; and regulation, 133–34. *See also* public/private partnerships
privatization, of infrastructure, 265–66
pro forma, 189–90, 466, 467, 468–69, 470, 471
product; differentiating of, 235–39; as highly differentiated, 207–8; merchandising the, 492–93; and refinement of idea, 235–39
professionalization, 144, 148, 502
profits, 36
program evaluation and review technique (PERT), 431, 449
program-related investments (PRIs), 312
project manager, 436, 441, 446
projects; administration of, 39; custom tailoring of, 208; life cycle of, 466, 467, 468, 471
Promenade at Westlake (Thousand Oaks, California), 504
promotion, 12, 206–7
property (collateral) value estimating, 82–84. *See also* collateral
property insurance, 145
property managers/management; compensation for, 50; and construction stage, 440, 447; contracts for, 472; and coordinating marketing and sales, 483; and enterprise concept, 460–63; functions of, 440, 459, 463; and fundamen-

tals of management, 464–66; and history of development, 122; importance of, 5, 7; and industry, 122; in-house, 50; and management fundamentals, 464–66; outside, 50; and professionalization of real estate industry, 140; and refinement of idea, 233; and relationship to asset managers and portfolio managers, 459, 463–64; as source of operating expense information, 85; and strategic plan, 467–71; training of, 474–75; transition from development to, 466–69. *See also* eight-stage model; management
Property & Portfolio Research, 388, 389, 390, 391, 392
property, productivity of, 81–82. *See also* level one
property taxes, 114, 145
property values; and capital improvements, 114; and CBDs, 127; and debt servicing, 84; estimating, 82–84; and FHA, 145; and financial theory, 82–84, 85–91; and history of development, 109, 114, 124–25, 127, 130, 134, 145; principles of city, 141
Proposition M (San Francisco), 219
Prospect Park (Brooklyn), 132
Prudential Insurance Company, 128, 156, 172, 468
public corporations. *See* C corporations
public entrepreneurs, 38
public housing, 155, 163
public markets, components of, 64
public policy, and affordable housing, 294, 322
public/private partnerships; conflicts and accountability in, 287–90; contracts with, 430, 431; decision making in, 287; examples of, 36; financial returns to cities in, 283–84; and financing, 255–66; forms of assistance in, 280–84; goals and objectives of, 3; and infrastructure, 255–66; and marketing, 489, 490; objectives of, 270–73; and organizations, 284–87; and planning, 255–66; practical problems and policy issues in, 287–90; process involved in forming, 273–85; and public developer, 38–39; stra-

tegic decision in implementation of, 274–80; summary about, 290; and technology, 175; and urban crisis, 161–62
public relations, 50–51, 489–91
Public Relations Society of America, 50
public sector; and capital improvements, 114; changing of rules by, 10–11; and defining real estate development, 4; developers of, 38–39; as equity partner, 10; goals of, 3; and history of development, 114, 132–34; increased pressure for, 53; and management, 472–73; and market study, 12; modern role of, 132–34; as participant on development team, 51; as partner in development process, 10–11, 53; and refinement of idea, 234–35; roles of, 247–68. *See also* federal government; local government; public/private partnerships; regulation; state government
Public Square (Cleveland), 140
public works, 133, 134, 143, 144
Public Works Administration (PWA), 143, 147
PUD (planned unit development), 251, 323
Pulitzer, Joseph, 129
purchase commitment, 50
purchase-money mortgages, 76, 140
PWA (Public Works Administration), 143, 147

Quadrangle (Durham, North Carolina), 509

race/ethnicity; and African American cemetery in New York City, 228; and FHA/VA discrimatory policies, 146, 153; and globalization, 7; and history of development, 146; income by, 26; and Levitt homes, 153; and new communities, 167; and population growth, 24–25; in post–World War II years, 153; and regional and metropolitan shifts, 26, 27; and urban crisis, 160–69; and urban renewal, 154, 155–56
Radburn, 137–39
Radio City Music Hall (New York City), 148

railroad barons, as developers, 122–25

railroads, 30–31, 120–25, 127. *See also* transportation

Raleigh, North Carolina, 156

Ramada Inn Hotels/Motels, 159

"Ramble" (natural park), 116

Rancho Santa Margarita, California, 167

Raskob, John Jacob, 137

rate of return on total capital (ROR), and financial theory, 88–89

Ravitch, Richard, 163

Raytheon Plant (Wayland, Massachusetts), 513

RCA Building (New York City), 148

Reagan, Ronald, 144

real estate agents, 116, 493

Real Estate Analysis and Planning Service, 387–88

Real Estate and Building Journal, 119

Real Estate Capital Markets Report, 66

real estate companies, publicly traded, 52–53

real estate industry; as American tradition, 109–14; critical issues for, 502–4; cyclical nature of, 22, 501–2; future of, 501–14; importance to national economy of, 20–22; in post–World War II years, 151–53; professionalization of, 144, 148, 502

real estate investment trusts (REITs); and asset management, 460, 465; and capital flow, 66, 68; capitalization of, 95, 96; and characterizing developers, 7; and CMBSs, 97; and commercial property, 95; conversions to, 71; data about, 66, 365, 388; decline/collapse of, 68, 95; and development between 1970s and 1990s, 171; equity, 95; as form of ownership for real estate equity markets, 71; and innovations in financing, 94, 95–96, 97, 99; and investors, 95–96; and management, 71; market value of, 53; mortgage, 95, 97; and national economy, 21; and opportunity funds, 94, 96; and ownership of commercial and industrial real estate, 19; rapid growth of, 71; and rent, 96; and taxes, 71, 95; and Wall Street, 96

Real Estate Research Corporation (RERC), 165, 389

Realty Information Group, Inc., 385, 386–87

REAPS (Real Estate Analysis and Planning Service), 387–88

Reconstruction Finance Corporation (RFC), 143, 145, 147

redevelopment, 5, 38, 161

Redondo Beach, California, 124

Reedy Creek Improvement District, 168

refinancing, 77, 118

reform; during Reagan administration, 144; and history of development, 116, 137, 138, 140

Regional Financial Associates, Inc. (RFA), 51–52, 371, 382, 383, 384, 388, 389, 390, 391

regional planning, 137

Regional Planning Association of America, 138

regionalism, "new," 174–75

regulation; and affordable housing, 319–22, 323; of apartments, 153; and capital improvements, 114; and developers' characteristics, 37; and feasibility, 352–53; and GDP, 21; and history of development, 114, 120, 133–34, 143; and innovations in financing, 97; legal foundation of, 248–50; by local government, 250–66; and market study, 12; and offshore opportunities, 20; in post–World War II years, 153; and private sector, 133–34; and public sector as partner, 10; and public sector as regulator, 51, 248–50; and reports to regulators, 71; by state government, 255–58. *See also* approvals

Regulation Q, 98

REIS Reports, 388, 389, 391, 392

REIT market capitalization, 96

REITs. *See* real estate investment trusts

REMICs (real estate mortgage investment conduits), 74–75

remodeling, 5

rent; and advance signing of tenants, 428; and affordable housing, 303–8, 311; and financial theory, 81–82, 85–91; and financing cycle, 76–77; and ground leases,

112–13; and history of development, 112–13, 119–20, 147; and innovations in financing, 94, 96; low-income, 303–8; and opportunity funds, 94; and permanent loans, 76–77; and productivity of property, 81–82; and REITs, 96; and slums, 119–20

repayment, 76, 145

request for proposals (RFP), 275, 280, 287

request for qualifications (RFQ), 275

research; in decision making, 195. *See also type of research or study*

Research Triangle Park (North Carolina), 197, 213, 217, 220–21, 222, 238, 358, 436

residential property; and history of development, 114–20; and landscape architects, 44; marketing of, 486; sales/leasing of, 486, 496–97, 498; and subdivisions, 114–20. *See also* apartments; housing; multifamily housing; single-family housing

Resolution Trust Corporation (RTC), 7, 74, 94, 171

Reston, Virginia, 167

retail property; and coordinating marketing and sales, 483; employment in, 27; and future of development industry, 504; marketing of, 485, 486, 487; risks and management challenges for, 53; sales/leasing of, 485, 486, 487, 497; and shape of cities, 32. *See also* department stores

retail.com, 504

retirement housing, 428

return; and allocating savings to investors, 65; components of, 36; and construction lenders, 49; and debt financing, 82; and debt markets, 71; and financial theory, 81, 82, 88; for long-term equity investors, 50; and permanent lenders, 49; in public/private partnerships, 283–84; variability of, 89. *See also type of return or specific project*

return on equity (ROE), 63, 82, 88, 89

RFA (Regional Financial Associates), 51, 382, 383, 384, 388, 389, 390, 391

RFP. *See* request for proposals

RFQ. *See* request for qualifications